How to use your Connected Casebook

Step 1: Go to **www.CasebookConnect.com** and redeem your access code to get started.

Access Code:

Step 2: Go to your **BOOKSHELF** and select your Connected Casebook to start reading, highlighting, and taking notes in the margins of your e-book.

Step 3: Select the **STUDY** tab in your toolbar to access a variety of practice materials designed to help you master the course material. These materials may include explanations, videos, multiple-choice questions, flashcards, short answer, essays, and issue spotting.

Step 4: Select the **OUTLINE** tab in your toolbar to access chapter outlines that automatically incorporate your highlights and annotations from the e-book. Use the My Notes area for copying, pasting, and editing your book notes or creating new notes.

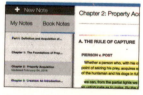

Step 5: If your professor has enrolled your class, you can select the **CLASS INSIGHTS** tab and compare your own study center results against the average of your classmates.

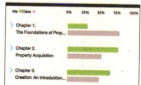

Is this a used casebook? Access code already scratched off?

You can purchase the Digital Version and still access all of the powerful tools listed above.
Please visit CasebookConnect.com and select Catalog to learn more.

PLEASE NOTE: Each access code can only be used once. This access code will expire one year after the discontinuation of the corresponding print title and must be redeemed before then. CCH reserves the right to discontinue this program at any time for any business reason. For further details, please see the Casebook Connect End User Agreement.

PIN: 9111149003

97278

PROPERTY
LAW

ASPEN CASEBOOK SERIES

PROPERTY LAW

D. BENJAMIN BARROS
Professor of Law
Widener University School of Law

ANNA P. HEMINGWAY
Associate Professor of Law
Widener University School of Law

Wolters Kluwer

Published by Wolters Kluwer in New York.

Wolters Kluwer serves customers worldwide with CCH, Aspen Publishers, and Kluwer Law International products. (www.wolterskluwerlb.com)

To contact Customer Service, e-mail customer.service@wolterskluwer.com, call 1-800-234-1660, fax 1-800-901-9075, or mail correspondence to:

Wolters Kluwer
Attn: Order Department
PO Box 990
Frederick, MD 21705

Printed in the United States of America.

2 3 4 5 6 7 8 9 0

ISBN 978-1-4548-3763-3

Library of Congress Cataloging-in-Publication Data
Barros, D. Benjamin, author.
Property law / D. Benjamin Barros, Professor of Law, Widener University School of Law;
Anna P. Hemingway, Associate Professor of Law, Widener University School of Law. pages cm. —
(Aspen casebook series)
Includes bibliographical references and index.
ISBN 978-1-4548-3763-3 (alk. paper)
1.Property—United States. 2. Possession (Law)—United States. I. Hemingway, Anna P., author. II. Title.
KF561.B37 2015
346.7304—dc23
2014048366

ABOUT WOLTERS KLUWER LAW & BUSINESS

Wolters Kluwer Law & Business is a leading global provider of intelligent information and digital solutions for legal and business professionals in key specialty areas, and respected educational resources for professors and law students. Wolters Kluwer Law & Business connects legal and business professionals as well as those in the education market with timely, specialized authoritative content and information-enabled solutions to support success through productivity, accuracy and mobility.

Serving customers worldwide, Wolters Kluwer Law & Business products include those under the Aspen Publishers, CCH, Kluwer Law International, Loislaw, ftwilliam.com and MediRegs family of products.

CCH products have been a trusted resource since 1913, and are highly regarded resources for legal, securities, antitrust and trade regulation, government contracting, banking, pension, payroll, employment and labor, and healthcare reimbursement and compliance professionals.

ASPEN PUBLISHERS products provide essential information to attorneys, business professionals and law students. Written by preeminent authorities, the product line offers analytical and practical information in a range of specialty practice areas from securities law and intellectual property to mergers and acquisitions and pension/benefits. Aspen's trusted legal education resources provide professors and students with high-quality, up-to-date and effective resources for successful instruction and study in all areas of the law.

KLUWER LAW INTERNATIONAL products provide the global business community with reliable international legal information in English. Legal practitioners, corporate counsel and business executives around the world rely on Kluwer Law journals, looseleafs, books, and electronic products for comprehensive information in many areas of international legal practice.

LOISLAW is a comprehensive online legal research product providing legal content to law firm practitioners of various specializations. Loislaw provides attorneys with the ability to quickly and efficiently find the necessary legal information they need, when and where they need it, by facilitating access to primary law as well as state-specific law, records, forms and treatises.

FTWILLIAM.COM offers employee benefits professionals the highest quality plan documents (retirement, welfare and non-qualified) and government forms (5500/PBGC, 1099 and IRS) software at highly competitive prices.

MEDIREGS products provide integrated health care compliance content and software solutions for professionals in healthcare, higher education and life sciences, including professionals in accounting, law and consulting.

Wolters Kluwer Law & Business, a division of Wolters Kluwer, is headquartered in New York. Wolters Kluwer is a market-leading global information services company focused on professionals.

To Jody, Griffin, and Brayden, with love.
—*D.B.B.*

To my husband Kevin
and my children Kevin and Patrick,
who make wherever we are together
a home.
—*A.P.H.*

SUMMARY OF CONTENTS

CONTENTS

PREFACE

This book is designed to introduce law students to the law of property. Property is a foundational part of the law school curriculum. Like other property textbooks, this book covers the basics of the law of ownership in the United States. A quick look at the table of contents of this book will reveal an outline of topics that is similar to that in other property textbooks, and that will be familiar to any experienced property professor.

This book, however, covers these topics in a fundamentally different way than the traditional law school casebook. The traditional approach starts from complexity and then attempts, often unsuccessfully, to move toward simplicity. We take the opposite approach, starting from simplicity and then moving toward complexity. The traditional approach begins each subject with a case and then expects students to derive legal principles from the case.

We clearly and concisely introduce the legal principles first, and then present cases as examples of application of those principles. We give the reader the basic concepts necessary to understand a case before we present the case itself. The traditional method of beginning with the case is intended in part to develop the student's case reading skills. These skills are vital to the practice of law, and we do not mean to minimize their importance. However, we have learned over the years that new law students do not have the background knowledge necessary to gain a full understanding of legal principles from cases alone. An entire industry of secondary sources has developed to help students understand the concepts that first-year casebooks unrealistically expect students to learn without introduction or explanation. We have written this book so that students should not need to use these secondary sources to fully understand the material.

Our ultimate goal is to give the reader a solid foundation in property law. Throughout the book, we use clear examples to illustrate the concepts that we are covering. We also use illustrations, charts, tables, and sidebars to present material clearly. We highlight recurring themes by noting them in the margin. Themes are indicated by markers like the one that accompanies this paragraph. In many places throughout the book, we include problems that allow students to apply the principles that we have covered. We include explanatory answers to these problems in the appendix at the end of the book.

THEME

We have not sacrificed sophistication in pursuit of clarity. We do not shy away from the hardest issue in property law, and we introduce issues of property theory at various points throughout the book. Property law is complex in part because it is the product of centuries of legal evolution. In some chapters in the book, we will study legal rules that have their origin in feudal England. In others, we will study rules that are thoroughly modern. In the remainder, we will study rules that are a mix of the old and the new.

Regardless of their historical origin, the rules that we will study have tremendous impacts on our daily lives. If you are renting an apartment, landlord-tenant law governs your rights and responsibilities regarding the place where you live. Throughout your life, you are likely to buy and sell several homes. These transactions will be some of the largest and most important that you will encounter in your personal life, and they are governed by the law that we will study in this book. Land use law shapes the lived environment of our communities. Even the simple process of dropping off a suit at the dry cleaner or leaving your car with a valet will implicate the law of bailments.

We hope that you enjoy using this book as much as we enjoyed writing it, and that you will find property law to be as fascinating as we do. Even if property does not turn out to be your favorite law school topic (for some unfathomable reason), we hope that you will find this book to be a clear and easy-to-use introduction to this vitally important subject.

D. Benjamin Barros
Anna P. Hemingway
December 2014

ACKNOWLEDGMENTS

The authors gratefully acknowledge permission to reprint excerpts or to reproduce images from the following:

Cohen, Charles E., *Eminent Domain After* Kelo v. City of New London: *An Argument for Banning Economic Development Takings,* Harvard Journal of Law and Public Policy Vol. 29 (2006): 491-510. Reprinted with permission.

Seller's Property Disclosure Statement (SPD), reprinted with the permission of the Pennsylvania Association of Realtors.

Strahilevitz, Lior Jacob, *Information Asymmetries and the Rights to Exclude*, 104 Mich. L. Rev. 1835 (2006). Reprinted with the permission of the author.

Tom the Dancing Bug © Ruben Bolling. Reprinted with permission of Universal Uclick. All rights reserved.

PROPERTY
LAW

CHAPTER 1

AN INTRODUCTION TO THE LAW OF OWNERSHIP

We begin our study of property law with an introduction to the law of ownership. What does it mean to own something? The U.S. legal tradition recognizes four classic "incidents" of ownership—possession, use, alienation, and exclusion. By "incidents" we mean rights that a property owner has in an object. In this context, "alienation" means the transfer (by sale or gift) of property. If I own a home I typically have the right to possess the home, use the home, alienate the home, and exclude others from the home.

Our first chapter focuses on the concept of possession. The chapter ends with a discussion of exclusion, and we will discuss alienation and use at points throughout the book. Possession is especially important in the law of personal property, which raises a preliminary issue: What is "personal property"?

- *Real property* is ownership of land and things, like buildings, that are physically attached to the land.
- *Personal property* is ownership of everything else.

The distinction between real property and personal property can be a bit blurry in some circumstances. If you are wondering whether your dishwasher is real property or personal property, wait until we get to the law of fixtures later in the course (hint—as the definition of real property suggests, the answer to this question will turn on whether the dishwasher is physically attached to your house). The definition of personal property is very broad and includes some intangible interests—like intellectual property and contract rights. We will discuss intangible property in a few discrete places, but our focus in this book largely is on the ownership of tangible objects.

Note that real property is defined as the *ownership* of land and things attached to the land and that personal property is defined as the *ownership* of everything else. In our everyday language, we might refer to our car or our house as our "property." We often do the same thing as lawyers, and we will do so sometimes in this book. At times, however, we will need to be more precise. We will often need to keep in mind that our focus is on the legal ownership rights in objects, not the objects themselves.

A. POSSESSION PART I—THE LAW OF PERSONAL PROPERTY

"Possession is very strong; rather more than nine points of the law."

—Lord Mansfield, *Corporation of Kingston-upon-Hull v. Horner*, 98 Eng. Rep. 807, 815 (1774)

Possession is one of the incidents of ownership, and as Lord Mansfield suggested, it can be very important for legal issues involving property. As we will soon see, however, possession can be a very slippery topic. We will have to explore the answers to two separate questions: (1) what, exactly, does "possession" mean?, and (2) what is the legal significance of having possession of an object?

Possession plays a central role in many legal rules relating to the ownership of personal property. The law of personal property therefore is a good place to start in our exploration of the concept of possession. For now, we will focus on the ownership of objects that are not real property—cars, computers, wedding rings, paintings, footballs, etc. For many objects like this, there are circumstances where possession is very clear. If I'm holding a football tightly in my hands, for example, we can say that I have possession of the football. As you have probably seen in watching a football game, though, there are far more ambiguous possession scenarios. If a receiver might have been juggling the ball while going out of bounds, the referee is likely to spend some time looking at instant replay trying to figure out whether the receiver had possession of the ball.

1. THE RULE OF CAPTURE

Our first case involves a question of possession of a different object—a fox. This classic case is at the beginning of most Property textbooks. On one level, the case has to do with the law of ownership of wild animals. On another, more important, level, the case has to do with possession. As you read the opinions in the case, keep our two primary questions in mind. What concept of possession does each judge use (even if they sometimes use words other than "possession")? And what legal significance does each judge place on a person being in possession of an object?

> Items of personal property are sometimes referred to as *chattels*. The word *chattel* derives from the Anglo-French word for cattle. This is not surprising, because cattle were very important items of personal property in the Middle Ages.

There is a lot going on in this case. The language is a bit antiquated, but work your way through it to identify the reasons that the judges give to support their opinions. What facts did they think were relevant? What did the different legal authorities that they cited have to say? What policies did they think were important in this context? To give you a sense of the level of detail that is necessary to have a good understanding of the case, here are two questions to answer as you work through the case: (a) What would the majority have to say about ownership of a wild animal that was caught in a trap? (b) What does the dissent have to say about the distinction between pursuit with large hounds compared to pursuit with beagles?

PIERSON V. POST

Supreme Court of New York, 1805
3. Cai. R. 175, 2 Am. Dec. 264

This was an action of trespass on the case commenced in a justice's court, by the present defendant against the now plaintiff.

The declaration stated that Post, being in possession of certain dogs and hounds under his command, did, "upon a certain wild and uninhabited, unpossessed and waste land, called the beach, find and start one of those noxious beasts called a fox," and whilst there hunting, chasing and pursuing the same with his dogs and hounds, and when in view thereof, Pierson, well knowing the fox was so hunted and pursued, did, in the sight of Post, to prevent his catching the same, kill and carry it off. A verdict having been rendered for the plaintiff below, the defendant there sued out a *certiorari*, and now assigned for error, that the declaration and the matters therein contained were not sufficient in law to maintain an action.

Tompkins, J. delivered the opinion of the court. This cause comes before us on a return to a *certiorari* directed to one of the justices of Queens county.

The question submitted by the counsel in this cause for our determination is, whether *Lodowick Post,* by the pursuit with his hounds in the manner alleged in his declaration, acquired such a right to, or property in, the fox, as will sustain an action against *Pierson* for killing and taking him away?

The cause was argued with much ability by the counsel on both sides, and presents for our decision a novel and nice question. It is admitted that a fox is an animal *feræ naturæ,* and that property in such animals is acquired by occupancy only. These admissions narrow the discussion to the simple question of what acts amount to occupancy, applied to acquiring right to wild animals?

If we have recourse to the ancient writers upon general principles of law, the judgment below is obviously erroneous. *Justinian's Institutes,* lib. 2. tit. 1. s. 13. and *Fleta,* lib. 3. c. 2. p. 175. adopt the principle, that pursuit alone vests no property or right in the huntsman; and that even pursuit, accompanied with wounding, is equally ineffectual for that purpose, unless the animal be actually taken. The same principle is recognised by *Bracton,* lib. 2. c. 1. p. 8.

PERSONAL PROPERTY CAUSES OF ACTION

You will see a variety of causes of action (i.e., legal claims brought by the plaintiff) in our personal property cases. Here is an overview of the most common personal property causes of action:

Conversion/Trover: An action for damages for the wrongful possession or destruction of personal property. If I take your watch and refuse to give it back, you can bring an action for conversion against me. Similarly, if I destroy your watch, you can sue me for conversion.

REMEDIES

The remedy for conversion is money damages. *Conversion* is the contemporary name for this claim; *trover* is a more antiquated name that you are more likely to see in older cases.

Replevin: An action for the return of property wrongfully possessed by the defendant. If I take your watch and refuse to give it back, you can sue me for replevin to force me to give it back. The remedy for replevin is a court order forcing the return of the property.

Trespass to Chattels: An action for damage to personal property. If I borrow your watch and damage it, you can sue me for trespass to chattels. The typical remedy for trespass to chattels is money damages.

Puffendorf, lib. 4. c. 6. s. 2. and 10. defines occupancy of beasts *feræ naturæ,* to be the actual corporal possession of them, and *Bynkershoek* is cited as coinciding in this definition. It is indeed with hesitation that *Puffendorf* affirms that a wild beast mortally wounded, or greatly maimed, cannot be fairly intercepted by another, whilst the pursuit of the person inflicting the wound continues. The foregoing authorities are decisive to show that mere pursuit gave *Post* no legal right to the fox, but that he became the property of *Pierson,* who intercepted and killed him.

It therefore only remains to inquire whether there are any contrary principles, or authorities, to be found in other books, which ought to induce a different decision. Most of the cases which have occurred in *England,* relating to property in wild animals, have either been discussed and decided upon the principles of their positive statute regulations, or have arisen between the huntsman and the owner of the land upon which beasts *feræ naturæ* have been apprehended; the former claiming them by title of occupancy, and the latter *ratione soli.* Little satisfactory aid can, therefore, be derived from the *English* reporters.

Barbeyrac, in his notes on *Puffendorf,* does not accede to the definition of occupancy by the latter, but, on the contrary, affirms, that actual bodily seizure is not, in all cases, necessary to constitute possession of wild animals. He does not, however, *describe* the acts which, according to his ideas, will amount to an appropriation of such animals to private use, so as to exclude the claims of all other persons, by title of occupancy, to the same animals; and he is far from averring that pursuit alone is sufficient for that purpose. To a certain extent, and as far as *Barbeyrac* appears to me to go, his objections to *Puffendorf's* definition of occupancy are reasonable and correct. That is to say, that actual bodily seizure is not indispensable to acquire right to, or possession of, wild beasts; but that, on the contrary, the mortal wounding of such beasts, by one not abandoning his pursuit, may, with the utmost propriety, be deemed possession of him; since, thereby, the pursuer manifests an unequivocal intention of appropriating the animal to his individual use, has deprived him of his natural liberty, and brought him within his certain control. So also, encompassing and securing such animals with nets and toils, or otherwise intercepting them in such a manner as to deprive them of their natural liberty, and render escape impossible, may justly be deemed to give possession of them to those persons who, by their industry and labour, have used such means of apprehending them. *Barbeyrac* seems to have adopted, and had in view in his notes, the more accurate opinion of *Grotius,* with respect to occupancy. . . . The case now under consideration is one of mere pursuit, and presents no circumstances or acts which can bring it within the definition of occupancy by *Puffendorf,* or *Grotius,* or the ideas of *Barbeyrac* upon that subject. . . .

We are the more readily inclined to confine possession or occupancy of beasts *feræ naturæ,* within the limits prescribed by the learned authors above cited, for the sake of certainty, and preserving peace and order in society. If the first seeing, starting, or pursuing such animals, without having so wounded, circumvented or ensnared them, so as to deprive them of their natural liberty, and subject them to the control of their pursuer, should afford the basis of actions against others for intercepting and killing them, it would prove a fertile source of quarrels and litigation.

However uncourteous or unkind the conduct of *Pierson* towards *Post,* in this instance, may have been, yet his act was productive of no injury or damage for which a legal remedy can be applied. We are of opinion the judgment below was erroneous, and ought to be reversed.

Livingston, J. My opinion differs from that of the court. Of six exceptions, taken to the proceedings below, all are abandoned except the third, which reduces the controversy to a single question.

Whether a person who, with his own hounds, starts and hunts a fox on waste and uninhabited ground, and is on the point of seizing his prey, acquires such an interest in the animal, as to have a right of action against another, who in view of the huntsman and his dogs in full pursuit, and with knowledge of the chase, shall kill and carry him away?

This is a knotty point, and should have been submitted to the arbitration of sportsmen, without poring over *Justinian, Fleta, Bracton, Puffendorf, Locke, Barbeyrac,* or *Blackstone,* all of whom have been cited; they would have had no difficulty in coming to a prompt and correct conclusion. In a court thus constituted, the skin and carcass of poor *reynard* would have been properly disposed of, and a precedent set, interfering with no usage or custom which the experience of ages has sanctioned, and which must be so well known to every votary of *Diana.* But the parties have referred the question to our judgment, and we must dispose of it as well as we can, from the partial lights we possess, leaving to a higher tribunal, the correction of any mistake which we may be so unfortunate as to make. By the pleadings it is admitted that a fox is a "wild and noxious beast." Both parties have regarded him, as the law of nations does a pirate, "*hostem humani generis,*" [an enemy of humanity] and although "*de mortuis nil nisi bonum,*" [do not speak ill of the dead] be a maxim of our profession, the memory of the deceased has not been spared. His depredations on farmers and on barn yards, have not been forgotten; and to put him to death wherever found, is allowed to be meritorious, and of public benefit. Hence it follows, that our decision should have in view the greatest possible encouragement to the destruction of an animal, so cunning and ruthless in his career. But who would keep a pack of hounds; or what gentleman, at the sound of the horn, and at peep of day, would mount his steed, and for hours together, "*sub jove frigido,*" [under the cold sky] or a vertical sun, pursue the windings of this wily quadruped, if, just as night came on, and his stratagems and strength were nearly exhausted, a saucy intruder, who had not shared in the honours or labours of the chase, were permitted to come in at the death, and bear away in triumph the object of pursuit? Whatever *Justinian* may have thought of the matter, it must be recollected that his code was compiled many hundred years ago, and it would be very hard indeed, at the distance of so many centuries, not to have a right to establish a rule for ourselves. In his day, we read of no order of men who made it a business, in the language of the declaration in this cause, "with hounds and dogs to find, start, pursue, hunt, and chase," these animals, and that, too, without any other motive than the preservation of *Roman* poultry; if this diversion had been then in fashion, the lawyers who composed his institutes, would have taken care not to pass it by, without suitable encouragement. If any thing, therefore, in the digests or pandects shall appear to militate against the defendant in error, who, on this occasion, was the foxhunter, we have only to say *tempora mutantur* [times have changed]; and if men themselves change with the times, why should not laws also undergo an alteration?

It may be expected, however, by the learned counsel, that more particular notice be taken of their authorities. I have examined them all, and feel great difficulty in determining, whether to acquire dominion over a thing, before in common, it be sufficient that we barely see it, or know where it is, or wish for it, or make a declaration of our will respecting it; or whether, in the case of wild beasts, setting a trap, or lying in wait, or starting, or pursuing, be enough; or if an actual wounding, or killing, or bodily tact and occupation be necessary. Writers on general law, who have favoured us with their speculations on these points, differ on them all; but, great as is the diversity of sentiment among them, some conclusion must be adopted on the question immediately before us. After mature deliberation, I embrace that of *Barbeyrac,* as the most rational, and least liable to objection. If at liberty, we might imitate the courtesy of a certain emperor, who, to avoid giving offence to the advocates of any of these different doctrines, adopted a middle course, and by ingenious distinctions, rendered it difficult to say (as often happens after a fierce and angry contest) to whom the palm of victory belonged. He ordained, that if a beast be followed with *large dogs and hounds,* he shall belong to the hunter, not to the chance occupant; and in like manner, if he be killed or wounded with a lance or sword; but if chased with *beagles only,* then he passed to the captor, not to the first pursuer. If slain with a dart, a sling, or a bow, he fell to the hunter, if still in chase, and not to him who might afterwards find and seize him.

Now, as we are without any municipal regulations of our own, and the pursuit here, for aught that appears on the case, being with dogs and hounds of *imperial stature,* we are at liberty to adopt one of the provisions just cited, which comports also with the learned conclusion of *Barbeyrac,* that property in animals *feræ naturæ* may be acquired without bodily touch or manucaption, provided the pursuer be within reach, or have a *reasonable* prospect (which certainly existed here) of taking, what he has *thus* discovered an intention of converting to his own use.

When we reflect also that the interest of our husbandmen, the most useful of men in any community, will be advanced by the destruction of a beast so pernicious and incorrigible, we cannot greatly err, in saying, that a pursuit like the present, through waste and unoccupied lands, and which must inevitably and speedily have terminated in corporal possession, or bodily *seisin,* confers such a right to the object of it, as to make any one a wrongdoer, who shall interfere and shoulder the spoil. The *justice's* judgment ought, therefore, in my opinion, to be affirmed.

Judgment of reversal.

THE TRAGEDY OF THE COMMONS

In this chapter, we will examine a number of theoretical justifications for the protection of private property. The capture of wild animals provides us with a good context to examine one theoretical justification: private property prevents the overconsumption of resources.

The rule of capture gives ownership of a previously unowned resource to the first person to gain possession of that resource. It is easy to see that this rule might lead to the overconsumption of a resource. For example, ocean fisheries tend to operate on a rule of capture basis. Today, large factory fishing vessels have become so efficient at capturing fish that many fishing stocks have collapsed. The overconsumption of ocean fish is an example of the *tragedy of the commons*, which takes its name from a famous article: Garrett Hardin, *The Tragedy of the Commons*, 162 Science 1243 (1968). "Commons" refers to resources that are unowned or subject to communal, as opposed to private, ownership. In a tragedy of the commons scenario, people acting in their rational self-interest will overconsume a resource that is unowned. If I am fishing in the ocean, I have an incentive to capture all the fish I can, even if I know that the rate of capture is unsustainable. I might want to leave some fish behind to protect the fish population, but if I refrain from capturing the fish, then you or someone else might come along and capture them. Because there is nothing preventing other people from capturing as many fish as possible, I have an incentive to capture as many as I can now.

A key problem with protecting ocean fisheries is that no one owns the sea or the fish. In other words, an absence of property rights is arguably the cause of the problem. For example, imagine that I own a large pond that contains fish. Because I own the pond, I can prevent you and anyone else from fishing there. I therefore don't have to worry about anyone else capturing the fish I leave behind. In these circumstances, it is in my interest to consume the fish on a sustainable basis. If I refrain from capturing some fish now, I will benefit later. Note the contrast with the ocean fisheries example, where if I refrain from capturing now, I likely will not benefit later because you or someone else will come along and capture the fish I leave behind. These examples illustrate that private property can help prevent the overconsumption of resources and solve the problem of the tragedy of the commons.

We do not mean to suggest here that private ownership is a solution to all overconsumption problems, or that common ownership structures inevitably collapse into tragedy of the commons scenarios. Rather, we are simply noting that solving tragedy of the commons problems is frequently used as a theoretical justification of private ownership of natural resources. There is a tremendous amount of scholarship on this issue, much of it centered on the work of Nobel Memorial Prize in Economic Sciences winner Elinor Ostrom. In some of her most important work, Ostrom argued that in certain circumstances common ownership of a resource will not lead to tragedy. *See, e.g.*, Elinor Ostrom, *Governing the Commons: The Evolution of Institutions for Collective Action* (1990).

NOTES AND QUESTIONS

1. *The Cited Authorities.* Because of a lack of case law on point, both the majority and dissenting opinions reference a series of treatises for authority. *Justinian's Institutes* was a famous Roman law treatise. Barbeyrac, Bynkershoek, Grotius, and Pufendorf were European civil law scholars. *Fleta* was an early treatise on English law. John Locke was an important English political philosopher; his work on Property is discussed later in this chapter. William Blackstone was the author of the tremendously influential *Commentaries on the Laws of England* (1765-1769).

2. *Possession of a Football.* We mentioned possession of a football in the text preceding *Pierson v. Post.* National Football League Rule 3, Section 2, Article 7 states that "A player is in possession when he is in firm grip and control of the ball inbounds." How does this definition compare to the court's definition of possession in *Pierson*?

3. *The Rule of Capture and First Possession.* The rule of capture states that a person gains ownership of a previously unowned wild animal by capturing or gaining possession of it. More broadly, the rule of capture applies (at least arguably) to other fugitive resources—that is, resources that move around on their own. The rule of capture gives us our first exposure to *first possession*, the idea that a person gains ownership of an unowned thing by gaining possession over that thing. Because very few objects in the modern world are unowned, first possession has more theoretical importance than practical importance in modern property law. A related concept, however, is of great practical importance, and runs throughout the course. This concept is *first in time, first in right*—the idea that if I had rights to an object before you, my rights are superior to yours. We will explore this theme in some depth as we progress through the course.

FIRST IN TIME

4. Ratione Soli, *Constructive Possession, and Landowner Rights.* The English common-law rule of *ratione soli* gave a landowner *constructive* possession of wild animals while they were located on the landowner's property. The landowner did not have *actual* possession, because wild animals move from place to place. If a deer is on my property right now, it might wander off onto neighboring property later today. By giving me constructive possession, *ratione soli* effectively gives me the exclusive right to capture wild animals on my land. The court in *Pierson* had to rely on treatise writers because most of the prior cases were disputes between landowners and hunters that turned on *ratione soli*. *Pierson* is unusual and interesting because the fox was captured on property that was treated as common (i.e., not privately owned) by members of the community.

We will see the word "constructive" many times in this course, and you will see it in many other legal contexts. "Constructive" is an all-purpose legal word that means "it isn't so, but we will pretend that it is." In the *ratione soli* context, we know that the landowner does not have actual possession, but we will pretend that the landowner does have possession.

Ratione soli was not widely adopted by U.S. courts. The default rule in most states is that the hunter gets ownership of a wild animal even if it is captured on private land. The landowner can avoid this result by posting the property "no hunting" or "no trespassing." Because this posting would make the capture of a wild animal on the property wrongful, the hunter gains no rights to the animal.

5. *Further Reading.* If beginning the course with *Pierson v. Post* wasn't enough to convince you that Property professors love the case, consider this recent scholarship: Angela Fernandez, *The Lost Record of* Pierson v. Post, *The Famous Fox Case*, 27 Law & Hist. Rev. 149 (2009); Angela Fernandez, Pierson v. Post: *A Great Debate, James Kent, and the Project of Building a Learned Law for New York State*, 34 Law & Soc. Inquiry 301 (2009); Andrea McDowell, *Legal Fictions in* Pierson v. Post, 105 Mich. L. Rev. 735 (2007); Bethany Berger, *It's Not About the Fox: The Untold Story of* Pierson v. Post, 55 Duke L.J. 1089 (2006).

2. BAILMENTS

A *bailment* is the rightful possession of goods by one who is not the true owner. The owner is called the *bailor*. The nonowner in rightful possession is called the *bailee*. For example, you take a suit and leave it at the dry cleaner. You are the bailor and the dry cleaner is the bailee. Bailments are often said to be based on an express or impled agreement by the bailee to return the property.

Bailments occur all the time in everyday life. If you check a coat at a restaurant, leave an item with the front desk at a hotel, or leave your car with a valet, you create a bailment. You also are involved in a bailment if you borrow a friend's car—when you have the car, you are in rightful possession of a good (the car), but you are not the true owner.

Bailments can be created with most types of tangible personal property. They cannot be created with goods that are fungible, such as cash or commodities like grain. As we will see, the major legal issues that arise with bailments involve the bailee's obligation to return the specific good. If you check your coat at a restaurant, the restaurant needs to give you your coat back and can't give you another coat as a substitute. With cash or other fungible goods, it doesn't matter whether the specific object is returned. If I'm holding a $20 bill for you, you shouldn't care if I give you the original bill or a different $20 bill back. (To be clear, we're talking about ordinary cash here, not something that has special value like a rare coin). Similarly, if I'm holding a bushel of commodity corn for you, you shouldn't care whether I give you that specific bushel of corn or a different bushel of the same quality back.

As we learned in *Pierson v. Post*, possession can be a slippery subject. But here is a good definition that we can use in most circumstances, including bailments:

$$Possession = Intent + Control$$

Most of the discussion in *Pierson* focused on control, but if you look closely you will see some discussion of the intent element as well.

Intent can be important in distinguishing between some bailment and non-bailment situations. If you slip your watch into my coat pocket without me knowing about it, I do not have possession of your watch even though I have control over it, because I had no intent to take possession. Similarly, we can distinguish a bailment from mere *custody*. If you are at a jewelry store and the jeweler hands you a watch to examine, there is no possession and thus no bailment, because the jeweler has manifested no intent to relinquish control, and you have manifested no intent to take control. You have custody of the watch, but not possession of it.

> ## ACCESSION
>
> Under the doctrine of *accession*, title to personal property might pass from the original owner to a person who innocently and in good faith adds significant value to the item. The classic case *Wetherbee v. Green*, 22 Mich. 311 (1871) provides a good example. Wetherbee took timber from the land owned by Green and two others. Wetherbee was under the good faith, but mistaken, impression that he had permission to take the timber. He later turned the timber into barrel hoops. The raw timber was worth $25, and the finished hoops were worth $700. Because of the great increase in value, the court held that ownership had passed to Wetherbee. Wetherbee was still liable to Green and his co-owners for damages for the value of the timber. Green et al., however, were not able to bring an action for replevin to reassert ownership and possession over the wood that was now in the form of finished barrel hoops.

Control also can be used to distinguish between some bailments and non-bailments. As noted above, if you leave your car with a valet, a bailment has been created for your car. On the other hand, if you park your car in a parking lot and keep your key (a type of parking known as "park-and-lock"), a bailment has not been created because by keeping the key you have maintained control of the car. Depending on the specific situation, park-and-lock creates either a lease or a license. We will cover both of these property interests later in the course. You probably have an intuitive idea of leases from renting an apartment. A license gives a person temporary and revocable permission to enter property.

It is worth pausing here to think a bit more about how we possess common items of personal property. As the parking examples suggest, keys are important to the possession of a car. If you are sitting in the driver's seat of a car, you have actual possession of it. If you are somewhere else but still have the keys, then you are in *constructive* possession of the car, because the keys give you control. You also have constructive possession of personal property in your home or some other area (e.g., an office) that you control. You don't have to be sitting on the couch in your living room to possess it.

The most common legal issues presented by bailments involve loss, destruction, or damage of the bailed property. The common-law rules on the bailee's liability turn on three categories, called *classifications*, of bailments. The classifications turn on who gets the benefit of the bailment. Under the common-law approach, the standard of care that will determine the bailee's liability turns on the classification of the bailment:

1. *Bailments solely for the benefit of the bailor.* Example: you find a handbag in the lobby of your office building. You bring it to your office for safekeeping. The owner of the handbag (the bailor) gets the benefit of the bailment. You (the bailee) get nothing out of it (other than the benefit of having done a good deed, which doesn't count in this context).

    With bailments solely for the benefit of the bailor, the bailee is liable for only *gross negligence* and is expected to exercise only *slight care* over the bailed good.

2. *Mutual benefit bailments.* Example: you leave your suit at the dry cleaners. You (the bailor) are getting something from the bailment—you are getting your suit cleaned. The dry cleaner (the bailee) is getting something from the bailment by getting paid as part of the transaction.

    Most bailments created as part of a commercial relationship are considered mutual benefit bailments, because both parties get something from the bailment. Sometimes the benefit can be more subtle than payment. Example: you leave your coat at a restaurant coat check. You (the bailor) get the benefit of having your coat taken care of. The restaurant (the bailee) gets the benefit of having you as a happy customer.

    With mutual benefit bailments, the bailee is liable for *ordinary negligence* and expected to exercise *ordinary care* over the bailed good.

3. *Bailments solely for the benefit of the bailee.* Example: an acquaintance lets you borrow her car. The owner of the car (the bailor) gets nothing out of the bailment (again, other than doing a good deed and being a good friend, which do not count in this context). You (the bailee) get the benefit of using the car.

    With bailments solely for the benefit of the bailee, the bailee is liable for even *slight negligence* and is expected to exercise *great care* over the bailed good.

The logic of the common-law classification system, such as it is, is that we should adjust the liability standard to the benefit that the bailee receives from the bailment. Even if this logic holds, the classification system is ambiguous and hard to apply. It has been roundly criticized by commentators. It has been rejected by the courts in many jurisdictions in favor of an approach that holds the bailee to a standard of exercising ordinary care under the circumstances. The classification system is still applicable in many jurisdictions, however, and it would be a mistake to treat it as an antiquated doctrine with no contemporary application.

To make things even more complicated, the law of bailments distinguishes between the rules for loss or damage to the good, on the one hand, and failure to return the good or delivery of the good to the wrong person, on the other. The common-law classification and modern ordinary care standards apply to loss or damage. Failure to return the good or delivery to the wrong person constitutes *misdelivery* of the good. Because the bailee has an obligation to return the bailed good, the bailee is *strictly liable* for misdelivery. If the bailee refuses or fails to deliver the good, the bailee has committed the tort of conversion, and conversion is a strict-liability tort. Like the common-law classification system, strict liability for misdelivery has been frequently criticized, and there seems to be no good reason why different standards should be applied to loss or destruction, on the one hand, and misdelivery, on the other. The misdelivery rule, however, remains in force in many jurisdictions.

> **EXAMPLE 1:** You leave your car with a valet. The valet manages to run into a dumpster with your car. The dumpster collapses onto the car, totaling it. Under our rules for loss, damage, or destruction, the valet is liable for ordinary negligence. Under the common-law classification system, this would be a mutual benefit bailment, and the standard for mutual benefit bailments is ordinary negligence. Under the modern approach, we apply ordinary negligence in all loss, damage, or destruction cases.

> **EXAMPLE 2:** You leave your car with a valet. The valet gives your car to another person, who drives off with it. The bailee is strictly liable for misdelivery.

This last example of misdelivery raises one last point to make about bailments. The bailee has superior rights to the bailed goods as compared to any third party. In the example, the valet was the bailee, and the stranger who drove off with the car is the third person. The valet could therefore sue the stranger to get the car back. Of course, you, as the actual owner of the car, have superior rights to both. This result is an illustration of what is often called *relativity of title*—the idea that a person (here, the valet) could have superior rights in an object as compared to one person (here, the stranger) but inferior rights in that object to another person (here, you). Relatively of title is a good example of our theme of first in time, first in right. You have superior rights to both the valet and the stranger because you were first in time as compared to both. The valet was first in time as compared to the stranger and so has superior rights to the stranger.

FIRST IN TIME

Our first bailments case is the famous *Peet v. Roth Hotel Co.* The case presents two major issues: (1) was there a bailment?, and (2) if so, what is the appropriate standard of care? On the first issue, pay close attention to the discussion of prior cases that held that no bailment existed. How were the facts of those cases different from the facts in *Peet*?

COMMON-LAW CLASSIFICATIONS AND STANDARDS OF CARE

Category	Standard of Care
Solely for Benefit of Bailor	Slight care; Bailee only liable for gross negligence
Mutual Benefit	Ordinary care; Bailee liable for ordinary negligence
Solely for Benefit of Bailee	Great care; Bailee liable even for slight negligence
Misdelivery	Strict liability

PEET V. ROTH HOTEL CO.

Supreme Court of Minnesota, 1934
253 N.W. 546

STONE, Justice. After an adverse verdict, defendant moved in the alternative for judgment notwithstanding or a new trial. That motion denied, defendant appeals.

The record is the story of a ring. Defendant operates the St. Paul Hotel in St. Paul. Mr. Ferdinand Hotz is a manufacturing jeweler. For twenty years or more he has visited St. Paul periodically on business making his local headquarters at the St. Paul Hotel. He has long been one of its regular patrons, personally known to the management. Plaintiff's engagement ring, a platinum piece set with a large cabochon sapphire surrounded by diamonds, was made to order by Mr. Hotz. One of its small diamonds lost, plaintiff had arranged with him to have it replaced and for that purpose was to leave it for him at the St. Paul Hotel. November 17, 1931, he was a guest there on one of his seasonal visits. About 4 p.m. of that day, plaintiff went to the cashier's desk of the hotel wearing the ring. The cashier on duty was a Miss Edwards. At this point, plaintiff may as well tell her own story, for upon it is based the jury's verdict. She thus testified:

"I had it [the ring] on my finger, and took it off my finger. The Cashier—I told the Cashier that it was for Mr. Ferdinand Hotz. She took out an envelope and wrote 'Ferdinand Hotz.' I remember spelling it to her, and then I left. . . . I handed the ring to the Cashier, and she wrote on the envelope. . . . The only instructions I remember are telling her that it was for Mr. Ferdinand Hotz who was stopping at the hotel."

Plaintiff's best recollection is that Miss Edwards told her that Mr. Hotz was registered but was not in at the moment. Miss Edwards frankly admitted, as a witness, that the ring had been delivered to her. It is conceded that it was immediately lost, doubtless stolen, probably by an outsider. Miss Edwards herself is beyond suspicion. But the ring, where she placed it upon its delivery to her by plaintiff was on her desk or counter and within easy reach of any one standing or passing just outside her cashier's window.

The loss was not then reported either to plaintiff or Mr. Hotz. About a month later, he was again in St. Paul, and then plaintiff was advised for the first time that her ring had never reached him. Upon inquiry at the hotel office, it was learned that it had been lost. The purpose of this action is to recover from defendant, as bailee of the ring, its reasonable value, fixed by the jury at $2,140.66. The reasonableness of that figure is not questioned.

> ## STATUTORY LIMITS ON BAILEE LIABILITY
>
> Many states have statutes that limit bailee liability in certain contexts. For example, a state might limit the liability of a hotel as a bailee for personal property it is holding for a guest. Or a state might limit the liability of a dry cleaner for damage to a customer's clothes. Generally speaking, bailees may not further limit their liability beyond the limit set by the statute. For example, if a statute limits a hotel's liability for goods that it is storing for guests to $1,000, the hotel will not be able to further reduce the limit of its liability (say, to $500) by agreement with its guests.

1. The jury took the case under a charge that there was a bailment as a matter of law. Error is assigned upon the supposition that there was at least a question of fact whether the evidence showed the mutual assent prerequisite to the contract of bailment which is the sine qua non of plaintiff's case. The supporting argument is put upon the cases holding that, where the presence or identity of the article claimed to have been bailed is concealed from the bailee, he has not assented to assume that position with its attendant obligation, and so there is no bailment. *Samples v. Geary* (Mo. App.) 292 S. W. 1066 (fur piece concealed in coat checked in parcel room); *U. S. v. Atlantic Coast Line R. Co.* (D.C.) 206 F. 190 (cut diamonds in mail package with nothing to indicate nature of contents); *Riggs v. Bank of Camas Prairie*, 34 Idaho, 176, 200 P. 118, 18 A.L.R. 83 (bailee of locked box supposed to contain only "papers and other valuables" not liable for money therein of which it had no knowledge).

The claim here is, not that plaintiff perpetrated fraud upon defendant, but that she failed to divulge the unusual value of her ring when she left it with Miss Edwards. The latter testified that, at the moment, she did not realize its value. Taking both facts and their implications as favorably as we may for defendant, the stubborn truth remains that plaintiff delivered and defendant accepted the ring with its identity and at least its outward character perfectly obvious.

The mutual assent necessary to a contract may be expressed as well by conduct as by words. Or it may be manifested by both. Restatement of Contracts, §21. The latter is the case here. The expression of mutual assent is found in what passed between plaintiff and Miss Edwards. The former delivered and the latter accepted the ring to be delivered to Mr. Hotz. Below that irreducible minimum, the case cannot be lowered. No decision has been cited and probably none can be found where the bailee of an article of jewelry, undeceived as to its identity, was relieved of liability because of his own erroneous underestimate of its value.

If there was mistake with legal effect worth while to defendant, it must have been of such character as to show no mutual assent and so no contract. There was no such error here. Identity of the property and all its attributes, except only its value, were as well known to defendant as to plaintiff. The case is identical in principle with *Wood v. Boynton*, 64 Wis. 265, 25 N. W. 42, 54 Am. Rep. 610. There the plaintiff had sold to defendant, for $1, a stone which she supposed was at best a topaz. It turned out to be an uncut diamond worth $700. Neither its true character nor value were known to either buyer or seller at the time of the sale. There being neither fraud nor mistake as to identity, the mutual mistake as to value was held no obstacle to completion of the contract. Plaintiff was denied recovery.

2. The jury was instructed also that defendant was a "nongratuitous" bailee. By that it is doubtless intended to say that the bailment was "reciprocally beneficial to both parties." *Dunnell*, §732. Clearly, that was a correct interpretation of the proof. The ring was accepted in the ordinary course of business by defendant in rendering a usual service for a guest, and so, plainly, it was for defendant's advantage, enough so, at least, to make the bailment as matter of law one for the benefit of both bailor and bailee.

3. The jury was charged also that, the bailment being for the reciprocal benefit of the parties, defendant, as bailee, was under duty of exercising, in respect to the subject-matter, ordinary care, that is the degree of care which an ordinarily prudent man would have exercised in the same or similar circumstances. The instruction was correct. *Dunnell*, §732. The former distinction between bailments for the sole benefit of the bailor; those for the mutual benefit of both bailor and bailee; and those for the sole benefit of the latter, in respect to the degree of care required of the bailee in order to protect him from liability for negligence, has long since been pretty much discarded here as elsewhere. "It is evident that the so-called distinctions between slight, ordinary, and gross negligence over which courts have perhaps somewhat quibbled for a hundred years can furnish no assistance." *Elon College v. Elon Banking & Trust Co.*, 182 N.C. 298, 109 S.E. 6, 8, 17 A.L.R. 1205.

Defendant's liability if any is for negligence. In that field generally, the legal norm is a care commensurate to the hazard, i.e., the amount and kind of care that would be exercised by an ordinarily prudent person in the same or similar circumstances. The character and amount of risk go far, either to decrease or increase the degree of care required. The value of the property, its attractiveness to lightfingered gentry, and the ease or difficulty of its theft, have much to say with triers of fact in determining whether there has been exercised a degree of care commensurate to the risk, whether the bailment be gratuitous or otherwise. However unsatisfactory it may be, until legal acumen has developed and formulated a more satisfactory criterion, that of ordinary care should be followed in every case without regard to former distinctions between slight, ordinary, and great care. Even the courts which adhere to the former distinctions will be found in most cases to be demanding no other degree of care than one commensurate to the risk and other relevant circumstances; e.g., in *Ridenour v. Woodard*, 132 Tenn. 620, 179 S. W. 148, 149, 4 A. L. R. 1192, it was held that a gratuitous bailee was answerable only for his gross negligence or bad faith. But, as the court proceeded to say, the care to be taken was "to be measured, however, with reference to the nature of the thing placed in his keeping." The defendant was relieved of liability because it was held as matter of law that he had "acted with a fairly commensurate discretion" in handling the bailed property. See annotation of that case, "Propriety of distinction between degrees of negligence." 4 A.L.R. 1201.

As long ago as 1887, this court speaking through Mr. Chief Justice Gilfillan, observed that "it is not easy, nor generally profitable, to define or point out the somewhat hazy distinction between these several degrees of diligence." *Cannon River Mfg'rs Ass'n v. First National Bank*, 37 Minn. 394, 34 N. W. 741, 742. "The doctrine that there are three degrees of negligence—slight, ordinary, and gross—does not prevail in this state." *Dunnell, Minn. Dig.* (2d Ed.) §6971.

4. The rule of our decision law (*Hoel v. Flour City F. & T. Co.*, 144 Minn. 280, 175 N.W. 300, following *Rustad v. G. N. R. Co.*, 122 Minn. 453, 142 N.W. 727) puts upon the bailee the burden of proving that the loss did not result from his negligence. This burden, in the language of the late Mr. Justice Dibell, is "not merely the burden of going forward with proofs, nor a shifting burden, but a burden of establishing before the jury that its negligence did not cause the loss." That proposition we adopted at "the practical working rule." We are not disposed to depart from it. . . .

Order affirmed.

The *Peet* opinion expresses deep skepticism about the common-law classification system and adopts the "modern" standard that the bailee is obligated to exercise ordinary care under the circumstances. We put "modern" in scare-quotes because our next case, of far more recent vintage than *Peet*, turns on the application of the classification system. As we noted above, the traditional classification system has been roundly criticized, but it still has a great amount of influence in some jurisdictions.

FIRST AMERICAN BANK, N.A. V. DISTRICT OF COLUMBIA

D.C. Court of Appeals, 1990
583 A.2d 993

BELSON, Associate Judge. This case arises from the unexplained disappearance of a bank dispatch bag from a vehicle owned by First American Bank after the vehicle had been towed to an impoundment lot because it was parked illegally in a rush hour zone. The main issue on appeal is whether the bank can recover from the District of Columbia and the towing company on a showing of failure to exercise ordinary care. We hold that it can.

The facts, as found by the trial court after trial without jury, are not in dispute. Appellant First American Bank employed Ronald Armstead as a courier whose duties included making deliveries between the bank's various branch offices and the main office. One afternoon, at approximately 4:20, Armstead parked the bank's station wagon near the entrance of Branch 13 on 7th Street, N.W., in violation of "No Parking Rush Hour Zone" signs, which were in clear view of Armstead. Four locked bank dispatch bags, marked as such, which Armstead had just picked up from four different branches, were in the rear luggage compartment of the station wagon and in plain view of anyone looking into the vehicle. The dispatch bags contained checks and other valuable documents.

Armstead had received tickets for illegal parking at this particular spot on at least five prior occasions and had been warned against future violations by traffic enforcement personnel. Traffic enforcement personnel had counseled Armstead to park across the street during rush hour to avoid being ticketed or towed. Armstead, who had received numerous parking tickets during his employment with the bank, would simply give the parking tickets to a supervisor for payment. The bank did not reprimand or discipline Armstead, nor did it dock his pay, for the parking tickets.

Within a short time after Armstead entered Branch 13, a parking control aide approached the bank's station wagon and began writing up a ticket for illegal parking. Almost immediately thereafter, a tow truck owned by Transportation Management, Inc. (TMI) arrived at the scene. While the parking control aide was completing the ticket and the tow truck operator was simultaneously preparing to tow the car, one of the employees at Branch 13 alerted Armstead that the bank's vehicle was being towed. Armstead, carrying a dispatch bag, ran out to the vehicle and told the tow truck operator that, as the driver of the vehicle, he was prepared to drive the vehicle away immediately. When the tow truck operator ignored his request to return the vehicle, Armstead asked that he be allowed at least to remove the dispatch bags from the vehicle. The tow truck operator, however, also ignored this latter request, and instead entered the truck and began to drive away with the bank's vehicle in tow. The crane form filled out by the tow truck operator indicated that the doors, trunk, and window of the bank's station wagon were locked when it was towed from 7th Street. When the tow truck operator arrived at the Brentwood impoundment lot at 4:45 p.m., the dispatch bags were still inside the luggage compartment of the vehicle. The tow truck operator observed the District's lot attendant test all the doors and the rear gate of the vehicle. The lot attendant found them all locked and so certified on the same crane form.

One and a half hours later, the bank's supervisor of mailroom couriers paid for the vehicle's release and retrieved it from the impoundment lot. The bank supervisor found the driver's door unlocked and one dispatch bag missing. There were no signs of forced entry, nor were there signs of the tape which is customarily affixed to car doors at the impoundment lot. The dispatch bag was never found, nor have the police identified or apprehended anyone who may have removed it from the vehicle. The value of the checks and other papers contained in the dispatch bag was determined to be $107,561. First American was able to recoup $57,616.71 of its loss,[1] but asserts that the cost of its recoupment effort was $10,555.[2] First American brought suit against the District of Columbia and TMI for breach of bailment and for conversion of its property.

The trial court ruled that the District and TMI were gratuitous bailees and therefore liable only for gross negligence. The trial court further ruled that First American did not meet its burden of proving that the District and TMI were grossly negligent, and that even if the defendants had been grossly negligent, First American was precluded from recovering because it was both contributorily negligent and assumed the risk. As for the claim of conversion, the trial court ruled that there was no conversion because the initial seizure of the vehicle was lawful. We affirm the disposition of the claim of conversion, but reverse on the bailment issue.

There is no dispute here that TMI and the District had sufficient possession and control of the bank's vehicle to establish a type of bailment. *See Bernstein v. Noble*, 487 A.2d 231, 234 (D.C.1985) (bailment is created when possession and control over an object

---

[1] First American was able to reduce its loss by such means as contacting customers who had presented checks contained in the bag and asking them to stop payment.

[2] This sum represents the time spent by existing staff on recoupment efforts.

pass from bailor to bailee).[3] The question we must resolve is whether the bailment was gratuitous or for hire. A bailee that takes possession of goods solely for the benefit of the owner is a gratuitous bailee and liable only for gross negligence, willful acts or fraud. *See Bernstein, supra*, 487 A.2d at 234; S. Williston, *Law of Contracts* §1038, at 900 (1967). In contrast, a bailee that receives compensation for its services is held to a standard of ordinary care:

> A person becomes a bailee for hire when he takes property into his care and custody for a compensation. The nature and amount of the compensation are immaterial. The law will not inquire into its sufficiency, or the certainty of its being realized by the bailee. The real question is, was the contract made for a consideration? If so, then it was a locatum, and not a depositum, and the defendant was liable for the want of ordinary care . . . . The law does not undertake to determine the adequacy of a consideration . . . . It is sufficient if the consideration be of some value, though slight, or of a nature which may inure to the benefit of the party making the promise.

Williston, *supra*, §1032, at 832 (quoting *Prince v. Alabama State Fair*, 106 Ala. 340, 17 So. 449 (1895)) (emphasis in original); *see also* 8 Am.Jur.2d *Bailments* §21 (1980).

A bailment for hire relationship may be created even in the absence of an explicit agreement. *See* 8 Am.Jur.2d *Bailments* §62. All that is required is the existence of a mutual benefit. . . .

While there was no explicit agreement here between the bank and the District for the safekeeping of the vehicle, the District's impoundment of the bank's vehicle involved a mutual benefit so as to create a quasi bailment for hire. The District and TMI actively took possession of the bank's vehicle with the expectation of deriving benefit therefrom. In addition to furthering its interest in insuring the smooth flow of traffic, the District tows and stores illegally-parked vehicles for compensation.[4] Likewise, TMI is under contract with the District for the purpose of towing illegally-parked vehicles to impoundment lots. Owners of vehicles, on the other hand, receive the direct benefit of having their vehicles safeguarded in the city's impoundment lot until they are ready to retrieve them. As users of the District's roads and highways, they also benefit indirectly from the District's practice of towing illegally parked vehicles that impede the flow of traffic.

---

[3] We find unpersuasive the District's argument that the bailment did not include the contents of the vehicle because First American failed to establish that the District's agents or employees had knowledge of the value of the dispatch bags. The bailment of a receptacle also entails liability for the contents if they are known to the bailee, regardless of their value. *See* S. Williston, *Law of Contracts* §1038A, at 906 (1967). Here, the District acknowledges that the dispatch bags were in plain view of anyone looking into the station wagon. In any event, Armstead's request that he be allowed to remove the dispatch bags gave the tow truck operator notice that the bags were of some value.

[4] 18 DCMR §2421.3 (1987) provides: The owner of the impounded vehicle, or other duly authorized person, shall be permitted to repossess the same upon the payment of a fifty dollar ($50.00) towing fee, plus a fee for storage, to the Bureau of Traffic Adjudication.

Holding the District and TMI liable as bailees for hire in this case is consistent with the long standing principle in this jurisdiction that a law enforcement officer who seizes goods under a writ of attachment is bound to exercise ordinary care to prevent their loss and destruction. *See Wilson v. Bittinger*, 104 U.S.App.D.C. 403, 406, 262 F.2d 714, 717 (1958); *Snyder v. Hart*, 64 App.D.C. 353, 355, 78 F.2d 237, 239 (1935); *Palmer v. Costello*, 41 App.D.C. 165, 168-69 (1913). In our view, absent any specific statutory provision to the contrary, the same standard of ordinary care applies whenever a marshal or like officer has custody of property under operation of law. *See Earl v. United States*, 262 A.2d 598, 599 (D.C.1970) ("A United States Marshal is responsible for any damage caused by his negligence to property he handles while carrying out his duties."); *accord, Kessman v. City & County of Denver*, 709 P.2d 975, 977 (Colo.Ct.App.1985) (sheriff who has custody of merchandise pursuant to an abatement of nuisance action is liable for ordinary negligence); *Simon v. City of New York*, 53 Misc.2d 622, 622-24, 279 N.Y.S.2d 223, 225 (1967) (city bound to exercise reasonable care in the towing of illegally parked motor vehicles). We hold, therefore, that the District and TMI are held to the standard of ordinary care when they tow and impound illegally-parked vehicles.

We reject appellees' argument that the illegal parking by the bank's driver constituted contributory negligence or assumption of the risk so as to bar recovery. . . . In view of the foregoing, we reverse and remand this case for a determination of whether the city and TMI exercised ordinary care in safeguarding the bank's vehicle and its contents.

So ordered.

FARRELL, Associate Judge, dissenting.

I respectfully dissent from the majority's conclusion that when the District of Columbia government tows and impounds cars, it acts in the role of a "bailee for hire" subject to an ordinary standard of negligence. Rather than equate the government in this respect with the owner of a commercial parking lot, I would hold that in exercising the police function of enforcing the motor vehicle laws, which may include impounding cars, the District acts in a manner akin to a "gratuitous bailee" and is liable only for gross negligence.

The District's obligation to tow, impound, and store vehicles derives from D.C.Code §40-812(a) (1990).[1] One purpose of this duty is to help abate the "parking nuisance" that "endangers the health, safety, and welfare of the general public." D.C.Code §40-802. I agree

---

[1] Section 40-812(a) provides in part: It shall be a violation of the District of Columbia Traffic Adjudication Act (D.C.Code, §40-601 et seq.), to park, store, or leave a vehicle of any kind, including an abandoned or junk vehicle, whether attended or not, or for the owner of any vehicle to allow the vehicle to be parked, stored, or left, whether attended or not, upon any public or private property in the District of Columbia, including a public highway, without the consent of the owner of the public or private property.

with the majority that if the District (as bailee) had a profit-making or benefit-seeking purpose in towing and impounding cars, then a mutual bailment would be formed. *See Prince v. Alabama State Fair*, 106 Ala. 340, 344-46, 17 So. 449, 450 (1895). But since it is the duty to abate the "parking nuisance" that motivates the District, any benefits derived from seizing and keeping cars temporarily flow to the general public, not to the government as a contracting party. The "compensation" the government receives in the form of towing charges or storage fees is completely incidental to this exclusive benefit to the public at large. Indeed, I am certain the government would willingly relinquish the "benefit" of storage fees if society did not require it to enforce the parking laws. . . .

I think, finally, that we must be concerned with the practical consequences of a rule that a person who parks illegally, and so endangers the public safety (certainly at rush hour), can reasonably require the District to insure against lapses from ordinary care in the impoundment process. It is true that reasonable care means care "under the circumstances" (which presumably would include rush hour and the like), but as between the rights of the owner who violates the law in parking, and the duty of the police to clear the streets and prevent accidents, I believe that a standard of ordinary negligence strikes too low a balance and acts as a disincentive to effective enforcement of the parking laws.

QUESTIONS

1. What do you think the worst fact in the record was for the District of Columbia?
2. Do you agree with the court's application of the common-law classification system? In other words, do you think that the court placed the bailment in the correct category?

PROBLEMS

Explain the standard of care that governs the bailee's liability, if any, in the following scenarios. Apply only the common law of bailments, and presume that there are no applicable statutory limits on liability. Explanatory answers can be found on page 1029.

1. Talia went to a restaurant for dinner. She left her car with the valet. The valet crashed her car into a telephone pole, causing substantial damage to it.
2. Bradley left his coat at the coat check at a restaurant. The clerk mistakenly gave the coat to a another person.
3. April borrowed an acquaintance's car and damaged it in an accident.
4. Lashuan went to dinner downtown and parked her car in a parking garage. She kept her keys. When she returned from dinner, she found that someone had hit her car, damaging it.

3. FINDING

Imagine that you are walking down the street and notice a valuable watch on the sidewalk. You pick it up. What rights do you have as the finder of the watch?

In a found property scenario, we have several potential characters. First, we have the *true owner* of the watch. Second, we have the *finder*. Third, we have a potential *subsequent possessor* of the found item. For example, after finding the watch you leave it with a jeweler to have it valued. The jeweler is a subsequent possessor compared to the finder. Fourth, we have the owner of the location—in this context, often called the *owner of the locus*—where the item was found. For example, if we change our scenario a bit, and you now find the watch on my front lawn, I might have some claim to the watch as the owner of the locus.

We will begin with a classic case that sheds light on the respective rights of the first three characters—the true owner, the finder, and a subsequent possessor. We will return shortly to the owner of the locus.

ARMORY V. DELAMIRIE

King's Bench, 1722
1 Strange 505

The plaintiff being a chimney sweeper's boy found a jewel and carried it to the defendant's shop (who was a goldsmith) to know what it was, and delivered it into the hands of the apprentice, who under the pretence of weighing it, took out the stones, and calling to the master to let him know it came to three halfpence, the master offered the boy the money, who refused to take it, and insisted to have the thing again; whereupon the apprentice delivered him back the socket without the stones. And now in trover against the master these points were ruled:

1. That the finder of a jewel, though he does not by such finding acquire an absolute property or ownership, yet he has such a property as will enable him to keep it against all but the rightful owner, and consequently may maintain trover.
2. That the action well lay against the master, who gives a credit to his apprentice, and is answerable for his neglect.
3. As to the value of the jewel several of the trade were examined to prove what a jewel of the finest water that would fit in the socket would be worth; and the Chief Justice (Pratt) directed the jury, that unless the defendant did produce the jewel, and shew it not to be of the finest water, they should presume the strongest against him, and make the value of the best jewels the measure of their damages, which they accordingly did.

NOTE

1. *Armory v. Delamirie* establishes two simple finding rules. First, the true owner always wins. This rule is ironclad and holds in all circumstances. "Finders keepers, losers weepers" might be the law on the playground, but nowhere else.

Second, the finder wins against everyone except the true owner. This rule applies broadly, but requires two caveats. First, as we will discuss further below, the finder might lose against the owner of the locus. Second, the finder might lose against a prior possessor who is not the true owner. Here is an example. Alice is the true owner of a necklace. She loses it, and Becky finds it. Becky then manages to lose the necklace herself, and Carol later finds it. As the true owner, Alice would win against either Becky or Carol. But say that Becky and Carol get into a dispute over ownership of the necklace. As a prior possessor, Becky will win against Carol. So we should modify our rule to state that a *finder wins against everyone except the true owner and any prior possessor*. (Again, we have left the owner of the locus out of the picture.)

Both of these rules are straightforward applications of the principle of first in time, first in right. The true owner is first in time as compared to any subsequent finder. Becky was first in time as compared to Carol, so Becky would win in a dispute between Becky and Carol. This is another example of the concept of relatively of title that we first encountered in our discussion of bailments—Becky may have superior rights as compared to one person (Carol) but inferior rights as compared to another (the true owner).

It is a good thing that the law of the playground is not the law of the courts.

So far, we have established that (a) true owners always win in finding cases, and (b) a finder wins against subsequent possessors of the property. In *Armory v. Delamirie*, however, one party was notably absent—the owner of the premises where the object was found. The owner of the premises has a strong intuitive claim to a found object—if a chimney sweep found a jewel in your house, you would probably feel that you had a good claim to it. Disputes between a finder and the owner of the premises turn on a number of factors, as discussed in our next two cases.

BENJAMIN V. LINDNER AVIATION, INC.

Supreme Court of Iowa, 1995
534 N.W.2d 400

TERNUS, Justice.

Appellant, Heath Benjamin, found over $18,000 in currency inside the wing of an airplane. At the time of this discovery, appellee, State Central Bank, owned the plane and it was being serviced by appellee, Lindner Aviation, Inc. All three parties claimed the money as against the true owner. After a bench trial, the district court held that the currency was mislaid property and belonged to the owner of the plane. The court awarded a finder's fee to Benjamin. Benjamin appealed and Lindner Aviation and State Central Bank cross-appealed. We reverse on the bank's cross-appeal and otherwise affirm the judgment of the district court.

[The following summary appears in the original opinion as Section IV; it is presented out of order to introduce concepts implicit in the early part of the opinion. —Ed.]

I. CLASSIFICATION OF FOUND PROPERTY

Under the common law, there are four categories of found property: (1) abandoned property, (2) lost property, (3) mislaid property, and (4) treasure trove. *Ritz*, 467 N.W.2d at 269. The rights of a finder of property depend on how the found property is classified. *Id.* at 268-69.

A. *Abandoned property*. Property is abandoned when the owner no longer wants to possess it. *Cf. Pearson v. City of Guttenberg*, 245 N.W.2d 519, 529 (Iowa 1976) (considering abandonment of real estate). Abandonment is shown by proof that the owner intends to abandon the property and has voluntarily relinquished all right, title and interest in the property. *Ritz*, 467 N.W.2d at 269; 1 Am.Jur.2d *Abandoned Property* §§11-14, at 15-20. Abandoned property belongs to the finder of the property against all others, including the former owner. *Ritz*, 467 N.W.2d at 269.

B. *Lost property.* "Property is lost when the owner unintentionally and involuntarily parts with its possession and does not know where it is." *Id.* (citing *Eldridge v. Herman*, 291 N.W.2d 319, 323 (Iowa 1980)); *accord* 1 Am.Jur.2d *Abandoned Property* §4, at 9-10. Stolen property found by someone who did not participate in the theft is lost property.

Flood, 218 Iowa at 905, 253 N.W. at 513; 1 Am.Jur.2d *Abandoned Property* §5, at 11. Under chapter 644, lost property becomes the property of the finder once the statutory procedures are followed and the owner makes no claim within twelve months. Iowa Code §644.11 (1991).

C. *Mislaid property*. Mislaid property is voluntarily put in a certain place by the owner who then overlooks or forgets where the property is. *Ritz*, 467 N.W.2d at 269. It differs from lost property in that the owner voluntarily and intentionally places mislaid property in the location where it is eventually found by another. 1 Am.Jur.2d *Abandoned Property* §10, at 14. In contrast, property is not considered lost unless the owner parts with it involuntarily. *Ritz*, 467 N.W.2d at 269; 1 Am.Jur.2d *Abandoned Property* §10, at 14; *see Hill v. Schrunk*, 207 Or. 71, 292 P.2d 141, 143 (1956) (carefully concealed currency was mislaid property, not lost property).

The finder of mislaid property acquires no rights to the property. 1 Am.Jur.2d *Abandoned Property* §24, at 30. The right of possession of mislaid property belongs to the owner of the premises upon which the property is found, as against all persons other than the true owner. *Ritz*, 467 N.W.2d at 269.

D. *Treasure trove*. Treasure trove consists of coins or currency concealed by the owner. *Id.* It includes an element of antiquity. *Id.* To be classified as treasure trove, the property must have been hidden or concealed for such a length of time that the owner is probably dead or undiscoverable. *Id.*; 1 Am.Jur.2d *Abandoned Property* §8, at 13. Treasure trove belongs to the finder as against all but the true owner. *Zornes*, 223 Iowa at 1145, 274 N.W. at 879.

II. BACKGROUND FACTS AND PROCEEDINGS

In April of 1992, State Central Bank became the owner of an airplane when the bank repossessed it from its prior owner who had defaulted on a loan. In August of that year, the bank took the plane to Lindner Aviation for a routine annual inspection. Benjamin worked for Lindner Aviation and did the inspection.

As part of the inspection, Benjamin removed panels from the underside of the wings. Although these panels were to be removed annually as part of the routine inspection, a couple of the screws holding the panel on the left wing were so rusty that Benjamin had to use a drill to remove them. Benjamin testified that the panel probably had not been removed for several years.

Inside the left wing Benjamin discovered two packets approximately four inches high and wrapped in aluminum foil. He removed the packets from the wing and took off the foil wrapping. Inside the foil was paper currency, tied in string and wrapped in handkerchiefs. The currency was predominately twenty-dollar bills with mint dates before the 1960s, primarily in the 1950s. The money smelled musty.

Benjamin took one packet to his jeep and then reported what he had found to his supervisor, offering to divide the money with him. However, the supervisor reported the discovery to the owner of Lindner Aviation, William Engle. Engle insisted that they contact the authorities and he called the Department of Criminal Investigation. The money was eventually turned over to the Keokuk police department.

Two days later, Benjamin filed an affidavit with the county auditor claiming that he was the finder of the currency under the provisions of Iowa Code chapter 644 (1991). Lindner Aviation and the bank also filed claims to the money. The notices required by chapter 644 were published and posted. *See* Iowa Code §644.8 (1991). No one came forward within twelve months claiming to be the true owner of the money. *See id.* §644.11 (if true owner does not claim property within twelve months, the right to the property vests in the finder).

[Chapter 644 was moved to Chapter 556F in a 1995 revision of the Iowa Code. The relevant provisions of the code are as follows:

§556F.7 (formerly §644.7)

If the owner is unknown, the finder shall, within five days after finding the property, take the money, bank notes, and a description of any other property to the county sheriff of the county or the chief of police of the city in which the property was found, and provide an affidavit describing the property, the time when and place where the property was found, and attesting that no alteration has been made in the appearance of the property since the finding. The sheriff or chief of police shall send a copy of the affidavit to the county auditor who shall enter a description of the property and the value of the property, as nearly as the auditor can determine it, in the auditor's lost property book, together with the copy of the affidavit of the finder.

§556F.8 (formerly §644.8)

The finder of the lost goods, money, bank notes, or other things shall give written notice of the finding of the property. The notice shall contain an accurate description of the property and a statement as to the time when and place where the same was found, and the post-office address of the finder. The notice shall:

1. Be posted at the door of the courthouse in the county in which the property was found or at the city hall or police station if found within a city and in one other of the most public places in the county; and

2. If the property found exceeds forty dollars in value, the notice shall be published once each week for three consecutive weeks in some newspaper published in and having general circulation in the county.

I.C.A. §556F.11 (formerly §644.11)

If no person appears to claim and prove ownership to said goods, money, bank notes, or other things within twelve months of the date when proof of said publication and posting is filed in the office of the county auditor, the right to such property shall irrevocably vest in said finder.

I.C.A. §556F.13 (formerly §644.13)

As a reward . . . for finding lost goods, money, bank notes, and other things, before restitution of the property or proceeds thereof shall be made, the finder shall be entitled to ten percent upon the value thereof . . . .]

Benjamin filed this declaratory judgment action against Lindner Aviation and the bank to establish his right to the property. The parties tried the case to the court. The district court held that chapter 644 applies only to "lost" property and the money here was mislaid property. The court awarded the money to the bank, holding that it was entitled to possession of the money to the exclusion of all but the true owner. The court also held that Benjamin was a "finder" within the meaning of chapter 644 and awarded him a ten percent finder's fee. *See id.* §644.13 (a finder of lost property is entitled to ten percent of the value of the lost property as a reward).

Benjamin appealed. He claims that chapter 644 governs the disposition of all found property and any common law distinctions between various types of found property are no longer valid. He asserts alternatively that even under the common law classes of found property, he is entitled to the money he discovered. He claims that the trial court should have found that the property was treasure trove or was lost or abandoned rather than mislaid, thereby entitling the finder to the property.

The bank and Lindner Aviation cross-appealed. Lindner Aviation claims that if the money is mislaid property, it is entitled to the money as the owner of the premises on which the money was found, the hangar where the plane was parked. It argues in the alternative that it is the finder, not Benjamin, because Benjamin discovered the money during his work for Lindner Aviation. The bank asserts in its cross-appeal that it owns the premises where the money was found—the airplane—and that no one is entitled to a finder's fee because chapter 644 does not apply to mislaid property.

III. STANDARD OF REVIEW

This case was tried as an ordinary proceeding at law. Therefore, the standard of review is for correction of errors at law. Iowa R.App.P. 4; *Kuehl v. Freeman Bros. Agency, Inc.*, 521 N.W.2d 714, 717 (Iowa 1994); *Eldridge v. Herman*, 291 N.W.2d 319, 321 (Iowa 1980).

Whether the money found by Benjamin was treasure trove or was mislaid, abandoned or lost property is a fact question. 1 Am.Jur.2d *Abandoned, Lost, and Unclaimed Property* §41, at 49 (2d ed. 1994) (hereinafter "1 Am.Jur.2d *Abandoned Property*"); *cf. Bennett v. Bowers*, 238 Iowa 702, 706, 28 N.W.2d 618, 620 (1947) (whether realty has been abandoned is a question of fact); *Roberson v. Ellis*, 58 Or. 219, 114 P. 100, 103 (1911) (whether money was hidden long enough to be classified as treasure trove was a fact question for the jury). Therefore, the trial court's finding that the money was mislaid is binding on us if supported by substantial evidence. Iowa R.App.P. 14(f)(1);

see Eldridge, 291 N.W.2d at 323 (affirming trial court's finding that property was lost property because supported by substantial evidence).

IV. DOES CHAPTER 644 SUPERSEDE THE COMMON LAW CLASSIFICATIONS OF FOUND PROPERTY?

Benjamin argues that chapter 644 governs the rights of finders of property and abrogates the common law distinctions between types of found property. As he points out, lost property statutes are intended "to encourage and facilitate the return of property to the true owner, and then to reward a finder for his honesty if the property remains unclaimed." *Paset v. Old Orchard Bank & Trust Co.*, 62 Ill.App.3d 534, 19 Ill.Dec. 389, 393, 378 N.E.2d 1264, 1268 (1978) (interpreting a statute similar to chapter 644); *accord Flood v. City Nat'l Bank*, 218 Iowa 898, 908, 253 N.W. 509, 514 (1934), *cert. denied*, 298 U.S. 666, 56 S.Ct. 749, 80 L.Ed. 1390 (1936) (public policy reflected in lost property statute is "to provide a reward to the finder of lost goods"); *Willsmore v. Township of Oceola*, 106 Mich.App. 671, 308 N.W.2d 796, 804 (1981) (lost goods act "provides protection to the finder, a reasonable method of uniting goods with their true owner, and a plan which benefits the people of the state through their local governments").[2] These goals, Benjamin argues, can best be achieved by applying such statutes to all types of found property.

The Michigan Court of Appeals had an additional reason in *Willsmore* to apply the Michigan statute to all classes of discovered property. The Michigan court noted that the common law distinctions between categories of found property were embraced in Michigan after the enactment of its lost property statute. *Willsmore*, 308 N.W.2d at 803. Based on this fact, the Michigan court concluded that the legislature could not have intended to reflect in the term "lost property" distinctions not then in existence. *Id.* However, the Michigan court did not address the fact that the common law distinctions were first developed in England, before the enactment of most states' lost property statutes. *See Goodard v. Winchell*, 86 Iowa 71, 52 N.W. 1124 (1892) (citing to English common law); *Hurley v. City of Niagara Falls*, 30 A.D.2d 89, 289 N.Y.S.2d 889, 891 (1968) (stating that common law principles relating to lost property were established as early as 1722).

Although a few courts have adopted an expansive view of lost property statutes, we think Iowa law is to the contrary. In 1937, we quoted and affirmed a trial court ruling that "the old law of treasure trove is not merged in the statutory law of chapter 515, 1935

---

[2] The Michigan statute had two provisions lacking in the Iowa lost property statute. The Michigan law provided for registration of a find in a central location so that the true owner could locate the goods with ease. *Willsmore*, 308 N.W.2d at 803. It also required notice to potential true owners. *Id.* Because Iowa's statute has no central registry and requires only posting and publication of notice, Iowa's law does not accomplish as well the goal of reuniting property with its true owner. Finally, under the Michigan statute, the local government obtains one half the value of the goods. *Id.* Iowa's law does not include this public benefit.

Code of Iowa." *Zornes v. Bowen*, 223 Iowa 1141, 1145, 274 N.W. 877, 879 (1937). Chapter 515 of the 1935 Iowa Code was eventually renumbered as chapter 644. The relevant sections of chapter 644 are unchanged since our 1937 decision. As recently as 1991, we stated that "[t]he rights of finders of property vary according to the characterization of the property found." *Ritz v. Selma United Methodist Church*, 467 N.W.2d 266, 268 (Iowa 1991). We went on to define and apply the common law classifications of found property in deciding the rights of the parties. *Id.* at 269. As our prior cases show, we have continued to use the common law distinctions between classes of found property despite the legislature's enactment of chapter 644 and its predecessors.

The legislature has had many opportunities since our decision in *Zornes* to amend the statute so that it clearly applies to all types of found property. However, it has not done so. When the legislature leaves a statute unchanged after the supreme court has interpreted it, we presume the legislature has acquiesced in our interpretation. *State v. Sheffey*, 234 N.W.2d 92, 97 (Iowa 1975). Therefore, we presume here that the legislature approves of our application of chapter 644 to lost property only. Consequently, we hold that chapter 644 does not abrogate the common law classifications of found property. We note this position is consistent with that taken by most jurisdictions. *See, e.g., Bishop v. Ellsworth*, 91 Ill.App.2d 386, 234 N.E.2d 49, 51 (1968) (holding lost property statute does not apply to abandoned or mislaid property); *Foster v. Fidelity Safe Deposit Co.*, 264 Mo. 89, 174 S.W. 376, 379 (1915) (refusing to apply lost property statute to property that would not be considered lost under the common law); *Sovern v. Yoran*, 16 Or. 269, 20 P. 100, 105 (1888) (same); *Zech v. Accola*, 253 Wis. 80, 33 N.W.2d 232, 235 (1948) (concluding that if legislature had intended to include treasure trove within lost property statute, it would have specifically mentioned treasure trove).

In summary, chapter 644 applies only if the property discovered can be categorized as "lost" property as that term is defined under the common law. Thus, the trial court correctly looked to the common law classifications of found property to decide who had the right to the money discovered here.

[Section IV of the opinion is reproduced above]

V. IS THERE SUBSTANTIAL EVIDENCE TO SUPPORT THE TRIAL COURT'S FINDING THAT THE MONEY FOUND BY BENJAMIN WAS MISLAID?

We think there was substantial evidence to find that the currency discovered by Benjamin was mislaid property. In the *Eldridge* case, we examined the location where the money was found as a factor in determining whether the money was lost property. *Eldridge*, 291 N.W.2d at 323; *accord* 1 Am.Jur.2d *Abandoned Property* §6, at 11-12 ("The place where money or property claimed as lost is found is an important factor in the determination of the question of whether it was lost or only mislaid."). Similarly, in *Ritz*, we considered the manner in which the money had been secreted in deciding that it had not been abandoned. *Ritz*, 467 N.W.2d at 269.

The place where Benjamin found the money and the manner in which it was hidden are also important here. The bills were carefully tied and wrapped and then concealed in a location that was accessible only by removing screws and a panel. These circumstances support an inference that the money was placed there intentionally. This inference supports the conclusion that the money was mislaid. *Jackson v. Steinberg*, 186 Or. 129, 200 P.2d 376, 378 (1948) (fact that $800 in currency was found concealed beneath the paper lining of a dresser indicates that money was intentionally concealed with intention of reclaiming it; therefore, property was mislaid, not lost); *Schley v. Couch*, 155 Tex. 195, 284 S.W.2d 333, 336 (1955) (holding that money found buried under garage floor was mislaid property as a matter of law because circumstances showed that money was placed there deliberately and court presumed that owner had either forgotten where he hid the money or had died before retrieving it).

The same facts that support the trial court's conclusion that the money was mislaid prevent us from ruling as a matter of law that the property was lost. Property is not considered lost unless considering the place where and the conditions under which the property is found, there is an inference that the property was left there unintentionally. 1 Am.Jur.2d *Abandoned Property* §6, at 12; *see Sovern*, 20 P. at 105 (holding that coins found in a jar under a wooden floor of a barn were not lost property because the circumstances showed that the money was hidden there intentionally); *see Farrare v. City of Pasco*, 68 Wash.App. 459, 843 P.2d 1082, 1084 (1993) (where currency was deliberately concealed, it cannot be characterized as lost property). Contrary to Benjamin's position the circumstances here do not support a conclusion that the money was placed in the wing of the airplane unintentionally. Additionally, as the trial court concluded, there was no evidence suggesting that the money was placed in the wing by someone other than the owner of the money and that its location was unknown to the owner. For these reasons, we reject Benjamin's argument that the trial court was obligated to find that the currency Benjamin discovered was lost property.

We also reject Benjamin's assertion that as a matter of law this money was abandoned property. Both logic and common sense suggest that it is unlikely someone would voluntarily part with over $18,000 with the intention of terminating his ownership. The location where this money was found is much more consistent with the conclusion that the owner of the property was placing the money there for safekeeping. *See Ritz*, 467 N.W.2d at 269 (property not abandoned where money was buried in jars and tin cans, indicating a desire by the owner to preserve it); *Jackson*, 200 P.2d at 378 (because currency was concealed intentionally and deliberately, the bills could not be regarded as abandoned property); 1 Am.Jur.2d *Abandoned Property* §13, at 17 (where property is concealed in such a way that the concealment appears intentional and deliberate, there can be no abandonment). We will not presume that an owner has abandoned his property when his conduct is consistent with a continued claim to the property. *Linscomb v. Goodyear Tire & Rubber Co.*, 199 F.2d 431, 435 (8th Cir.1952) (applying Missouri law); *Hoffman Management Corp. v. S.L.C. of N. Am., Inc.*, 800 S.W.2d 755, 762 (Mo.Ct.App.1990); *Foulke v. New York Consolidated R.R.*, 228 N.Y. 269, 127 N.E. 237, 238 (1920); 1 Am.Jur.2d *Abandoned Property* §§14, 42, at 20, 49; *cf. Bennett*, 238 Iowa at 706, 28 N.W.2d at 620 (stating that there is no presumption that real property is abandoned). Therefore, we cannot rule that the district court erred in failing to find that the currency discovered by Benjamin was abandoned property.

Finally, we also conclude that the trial court was not obligated to decide that this money was treasure trove. Based on the dates of the currency, the money was no older than thirty-five years. The mint dates, the musty odor and the rusty condition of a few of the panel screws indicate that the money may have been hidden for some time. However, there was no evidence of the age of the airplane or the date of its last inspection. These facts may have shown that the money was concealed for a much shorter period of time.

Moreover, it is also significant that the airplane had a well-documented ownership history. The record reveals that there were only two owners of the plane prior to the bank. One was the person from whom the bank repossessed the plane; the other was the original purchaser of the plane when it was manufactured. Nevertheless, there is no indication that Benjamin or any other party attempted to locate and notify the prior owners of the plane, which could very possibly have led to the identification of the true owner of the money. Under these circumstances, we cannot say as a matter of law that the money meets the antiquity requirement or that it is probable that the owner of the money is not discoverable.

We think the district court had substantial evidence to support its finding that the money found by Benjamin was mislaid. The circumstances of its concealment and the location where it was found support inferences that the owner intentionally placed the money there and intended to retain ownership. We are bound by this factual finding.

VI. IS THE AIRPLANE OR THE HANGAR THE "PREMISES" WHERE THE MONEY WAS DISCOVERED?

Because the money discovered by Benjamin was properly found to be mislaid property, it belongs to the owner of the premises where it was found. Mislaid property is entrusted to the owner of the premises where it is found rather than the finder of the property because it is assumed that the true owner may eventually recall where he has placed his property and return there to reclaim it. *Willsmore*, 308 N.W.2d at 802; *Foster*, 174 S.W. at 378; *Foulke*, 127 N.E. at 238-39.

We think that the premises where the money was found is the airplane, not Lindner Aviation's hangar where the airplane happened to be parked when the money was discovered. The policy behind giving ownership of mislaid property to the owner of the premises where the property was mislaid supports this conclusion. If the true owner of the money attempts to locate it, he would initially look for the plane; it is unlikely he would begin his search by contacting businesses where the airplane might have been inspected. Therefore, we affirm the trial court's judgment that the bank, as the owner of the plane, has the right to possession of the property as against all but the true owner.[4]

VII. IS BENJAMIN ENTITLED TO A FINDER'S FEE?

Benjamin claims that if he is not entitled to the money, he should be paid a ten percent finder's fee under section 644.13. The problem with this claim is that only the finder of "lost goods, money, bank notes, and other things" is rewarded with a finder's fee under chapter 644. Iowa Code §644.13 (1991). Because the property found by Benjamin was mislaid property, not lost property, section 644.13 does not apply here. The trial court erred in awarding Benjamin a finder's fee.

VIII. SUMMARY

We conclude that the district court's finding that the money discovered by Benjamin was mislaid property is supported by substantial evidence. Therefore, we affirm the district court's judgment that the bank has the right to the money as against all but the true owner. This decision makes it unnecessary to decide whether Benjamin or Lindner Aviation was the finder of the property. We reverse the court's decision awarding a finder's fee to Benjamin.

AFFIRMED IN PART; REVERSED IN PART.

All justices concur except HARRIS, SNELL, and ANDREASEN, JJ., who dissent.

SNELL, Justice (dissenting).

I respectfully dissent.

The life of the law is logic, it has been said. *See Davis v. Aiken*, 111 Ga.App. 505, 142 S.E.2d 112, 119 (1965) (quoting Sir Edward Coke). If so, it should be applied here.

The majority quotes with approval the general rule that whether money found is treasure trove, mislaid, abandoned, or lost property is a fact question. 1 Am.Jur.2d *Abandoned, Lost, and Unclaimed Property* §41, at 49 (2d ed. 1994). In deciding a fact question, we are to consider the facts as known and all reasonable inferences to be drawn from them. *Wright v. Thompson*, 254 Iowa 342, 347, 117 N.W.2d 520, 523 (1962). Thus does logic, reason, and common sense enter in.

After considering the four categories of found money, the majority decides that Benjamin found mislaid money. The result is that the bank gets all the money; Benjamin,

---

[4] Some jurisdictions require that one in possession of mislaid property use ordinary care to return the property to its owner. E.g., *Kimbrough v. Giant Food Inc.*, 26 Md.App. 640, 339 A.2d 688, 696 (1975); *see generally* 1 Am.Jur.2d *Abandoned Property* §24, at 31-32.

the finder, gets nothing. Apart from the obvious unfairness in result, I believe this conclusion fails to come from logical analysis.

Mislaid property is property voluntarily put in a certain place by the owner who then overlooks or forgets where the property is. *Ritz v. Selma United Methodist Church*, 467 N.W.2d 266, 268 (Iowa 1991). The property here consisted of two packets of paper currency totalling $18,910, three to four inches high, wrapped in aluminum foil. Inside the foil, the paper currency, predominantly twenty dollar bills, was tied with string and wrapped in handkerchiefs. Most of the mint dates were in the 1950s with one dated 1934. These packets were found in the left wing of the Mooney airplane after Benjamin removed a panel held in by rusty screws.

These facts satisfy the requirement that the property was voluntarily put in a certain place by the owner. But the second test for determining that property is mislaid is that the owner "overlooks or forgets where the property is." *See Ritz*, 467 N.W.2d at 269. I do not believe that the facts, logic, or common sense lead to a finding that this requirement is met. It is not likely or reasonable to suppose that a person would secrete $18,000 in an airplane wing and then forget where it was.

Cases cited by the majority contrasting "mislaid" property and "lost" property are appropriate for a comparison of these principles but do not foreclose other considerations. After finding the money, Benjamin proceeded to give written notice of finding the property as prescribed in Iowa Code chapter 644 (1993), "Lost Property." As set out in section 556F.8, notices were posted on the courthouse door and in three other public places in the county. In addition, notice was published once each week for three consecutive weeks in a newspaper of general circulation in the county. Also, affidavits of publication were filed with the county auditor who then had them published as part of the board of supervisors' proceedings. Iowa Code §556F.9. After twelve months, if no person appears to claim and prove ownership of the property, the right to the property rests irrevocably in the finder. Iowa Code §556F.11.

The purpose of this type of legal notice is to give people the opportunity to assert a claim if they have one. *See, e.g., Neeley v. Murchison*, 815 F.2d 345, 347 (5th Cir.1987). If no claim is made, the law presumes there is none or for whatever reason it is not asserted. Thus, a failure to make a claim after legal notice is given is a bar to a claim made thereafter. *See, e.g., Tulsa Professional Collection Servs., Inc. v. Pope*, 485 U.S. 478, 481, 108 S.Ct. 1340, 1343, 99 L.Ed.2d 565, 572-73 (1988).

Benjamin followed the law in giving legal notice of finding property. None of the parties dispute this. The suggestion that Benjamin should have initiated a further search for the true owner is not a requirement of the law, is therefore irrelevant, and in no way diminishes Benjamin's rights as finder.

The scenario unfolded in this case convinces me that the money found in the airplane wing was abandoned. Property is abandoned when the owner no longer wants to possess it. *See Ritz*, 467 N.W.2d at 269; *Pearson v. City of Guttenberg*, 245 N.W.2d 519,

529 (Iowa 1976). The money had been there for years, possibly thirty. No owner had claimed it in that time. No claim was made by the owner after legally prescribed notice was given that it had been found. Thereafter, logic and the law support a finding that the owner has voluntarily relinquished all right, title, and interest in the property. Whether the money was abandoned due to its connection to illegal drug trafficking or is otherwise contraband property is a matter for speculation. In any event, abandonment by the true owner has legally occurred and been established.

I would hold that Benjamin is legally entitled to the entire amount of money that he found in the airplane wing as the owner of abandoned property.

HARRIS and ANDREASEN, JJ., join this dissent.

QUESTIONS

1. Leaving aside the question of whether the state legislature acquiesced over time, do you agree with the Iowa Supreme Court's interpretation of the Iowa statute? Why/why not? What do you think was the purpose behind the statute? Is the Iowa Supreme Court's interpretation consistent with this purpose?

2. The dissent argues that the property at issue was abandoned. Do you agree?

NOTES

1. *Lost, Mislaid, Abandoned, and Treasure Trove.* The common-law categories described in *Benjamin v. Lindner Aviation* are still applied (unmodified by any statute) in many jurisdictions throughout the United States. The typical summary of the common-law rule is that, as between the finder and the owner of the locus, lost and abandoned property go to the finder, while mislaid property goes to the owner of the locus. Treasure trove also typically goes to the finder, though, as we will see in the next case, the law is not as uniform on this particular point.

> The distinctions between the lost, mislaid, and abandoned turn on possession. Unlike our prior possession-based issues, however, the distinctions turn on how the object left the true owner's possession, rather than how the object came into the true owner's possession.

The lost-mislaid distinction is best understood through examples. Imagine that you are walking down the street and your keys fall out of your pocket. Your keys are lost, because they left your possession involuntarily. Now imagine that you put your watch down on a table and later forget where it is. Your watch is mislaid, because you voluntarily placed it on the table, but later forgot where you put it. One justification for giving mislaid property to the owner of the locus is that the true owner is more likely to retrace her steps with mislaid property than with lost property. Giving ownership to the owner of the locus therefore makes it more likely that the true owner will be able to get her property back. Do you agree with this reasoning?

Note two things about the category of abandoned property. First, abandonment is a question of intent—for property to be abandoned, the true owner must intend to relinquish ownership. Second, as a result, the finder of abandoned property will win even against the true owner. Abandoned property is therefore an exception to our general rule that the true owner will always win.

The legal rules for lost, mislaid, and abandoned property are relatively clear in the abstract, but it can be hard to determine which category should be applied to a given found object. The majority and dissenting opinions in *Benjamin* provide a good example. It often is possible to come up with plausible stories about how the object got to the location where it was found that would allow us to fit the object into more than one category. One potential problem with legal rules that are this vague is that they provide little guidance to courts. Indeed, it is easy to imagine a court deciding which of the claimants (the finder and the owner of the locus) has a more sympathetic claim and then constructing an argument to justify placing the object into a category that will reach the court's desired result. Whether this kind of decisionmaking would be good or bad raises deep questions about legal theory. Generally speaking, however, we want our legal rules to be specific enough to lead to predictable outcomes.

2. *Contraband.* As suggested by the dissent, there is one other category of property that might have been relevant in *Benjamin*. *Contraband* is typically defined by statute to be property used in certain crimes, or the proceeds gained from crimes. Contraband is usually subject to seizure by the state. If the state cannot prove that the property is contraband, ownership of the property will turn on the finding rules that we have been discussing. *See State v. $281,420.00 in United States Currency*, 312 S.W.3d 547 (Tex. 2010).

CORLISS V. WENNER

Idaho Court of Appeals, 2001
34 P.3d 1100

Schwartzman, Chief Judge.

Gregory Corliss appeals from the district court's orders granting summary judgment in favor of Jann Wenner on the right to possess ninety-six gold coins unearthed by Anderson and Corliss on Wenner's property . . . . [Wenner is the co-founder and publisher of *Rolling Stone* magazine. —Ed.]. We affirm.

I. FACTUAL AND PROCEDURAL BACKGROUND

A. The Gold Coins

In the fall of 1996, Jann Wenner hired Anderson Asphalt Paving to construct a driveway on his ranch in Blaine County. Larry Anderson, the owner of Anderson Asphalt Paving, and his employee, Gregory Corliss, were excavating soil for the driveway when they unearthed a glass jar containing paper wrapped rolls of gold coins. Anderson and Corliss collected, cleaned, and inventoried the gold pieces dating from 1857 to 1914.[1] The coins themselves weighed about four pounds. Anderson and Corliss agreed to split the gold coins between themselves, with Anderson retaining possession of all the coins. At some point Anderson and Corliss argued over ownership of the coins and Anderson fired Corliss. Anderson later gave possession of the coins to Wenner in exchange for indemnification on any claim Corliss might have against him regarding the coins.

Corliss sued Anderson and Wenner for possession of some or all of the coins. Wenner, defending both himself and Anderson, filed a motion for summary judgment. The facts, except whether Corliss found all or just some of the gold coins without Anderson's help, are not in dispute. All parties agree that the coins were unearthed during excavation by Anderson and Corliss for a driveway on Wenner's ranch, that the coins had been protected in paper tube rolls and buried in a glass jar estimated to be about seventy years old. Following a hearing on Wenner's motion for summary judgment, the district court declined to grant the motion and allowed approximately five months for additional discovery. Six months later the court held a status conference at which counsel for Wenner and Anderson asked the court to rule on Wenner's motion and counsel for Corliss did not object. No new facts were offered.

The district court then entered a memorandum decision stating that the "finders keepers" rule of treasure trove had not been previously adopted in Idaho, that it was not a part of the common law of England incorporated into Idaho law at the time of statehood by statute, and that the coins, having been carefully concealed for safekeeping, fit within the legal classification of mislaid property, to which the right of possession goes to the land owner. Alternatively, the court ruled that the coins, like the topsoil being excavated, were a part of the property owned by Wenner and that Anderson and Corliss were merely Wenner's employees. Corliss appeals. . . .

---

[1] Of the ninety-six coins gathered up by Anderson and Corliss, there were thirty-six five-dollar gold pieces with mint dates ranging from 1857 to 1909, twenty-two ten-dollar gold pieces dating from 1882 to 1910, and thirty-eight twenty-dollar gold pieces dating from 1870 to 1914. Corliss claimed the value of the coins was in excess of $30,000 and at oral argument offered a value of between $500,000 and $1,000,000. Counsel for Wenner countered that the value of the coins was between $25,000 and $30,000. There is no independent appraisal of the coins in the record.

II. STANDARD OF REVIEW

Summary judgment is proper only when there is no genuine issue of material fact and the moving party is entitled to judgment as a matter of law. I.R.C.P. 56(c); *Dunham v. Hackney Airpark, Inc.*, 133 Idaho 613, 616, 990 P.2d 1224, 1227 (Ct. App.1999) (citing *Edwards v. Conchemco, Inc.*, 111 Idaho 851, 852, 727 P.2d 1279, 1280 (Ct.App.1986)). In order to determine whether judgment should be entered as a matter of law, the trial court must review the pleadings, depositions, affidavits, and admissions on file. I.R.C.P. 56(c).

In general, a party opposing summary judgment is entitled to favorable inferences from the underlying facts. *See Tolmie Farms v. J.R. Simplot Co., Inc.*, 124 Idaho 607, 609, 862 P.2d 299, 301 (1993). In this case, we note that none of the parties requested a jury trial, thus the court was to be the trier of fact. Furthermore, at a status conference, held after allowing the completion of discovery into the antiquity of the coins, counsel for Wenner and Anderson stated that the case was ready for summary judgment. Counsel for Corliss stated that he had nothing to add to the record. "When the evidentiary facts are not disputed and the judge rather than the jury will be the ultimate trier of fact, the judge may draw the inferences he or she deems most probable since the judge alone would be responsible for drawing such inferences from the same facts at trial." *Dunham*, 133 Idaho at 616, 990 P.2d at 1227. Therefore, the court in this case was entitled to draw all reasonable inferences from the facts presented.

III. LAW APPLICABLE TO DETERMINING THE RIGHTFUL POSSESSOR OF THE GOLD COINS

A. Standard Applicable to Review of the District Court's Choice of Law

This is a case of first impression in Idaho, the central issue being the proper rule to apply in characterizing the gold coins found by Corliss and Anderson on Wenner's property. The major distinctions between characterizations of found property turn on questions of fact, i.e., an analysis of the facts and circumstances in an effort to divine the intent of the true owner at the time he or she parted with the property. *See generally* 1 Am.Jur.2d *Abandoned, Lost and Unclaimed Property* §§1-14 (1994). The material facts and circumstances surrounding the discovery of the gold coins are not in dispute. However, the characterization of that property, in light of these facts, is a question of law over which we exercise free review. *Schley v. Couch*, 155 Tex. 195, 284 S.W.2d 333, 336 (1955) (While the character of property is determined from all the facts and circumstances in the particular case of the property found, the choice among categories of found property is a question of law.); *see also Batra v. Batra*, 135 Idaho 388, 392, 17 P.3d 889, 893 (Ct.App.2001) (The characterization of an asset as separate or community, in light of the facts found, is a question of law.). With these principles in mind we now discuss, in turn, the choice of categories applicable to the district court's characterization of the gold coins found by Anderson and Corliss, recognizing that the choice of characterization of found property determines its rightful possessor as between the finder and landowner.

B. Choice of Categories

At common law all found property is generally categorized in one of five ways. *See Benjamin v. Lindner Aviation, Inc.*, 534 N.W.2d 400 (Iowa 1995); *see also* 36A C.J.S. *Finding Lost Goods* §5 (1961); 1 Am.Jur.2d, *Abandoned, Lost, Etc.*, §10 (1994). Those categories are:

- Abandoned Property—that which the owner has discarded or voluntarily forsaken with the intention of terminating his ownership, but without vesting ownership in any other person. *Terry v. Lock*, 343 Ark. 452, 37 S.W.3d 202, 206 (2001);
- Lost Property—that property which the owner has involuntarily and unintentionally parted with through neglect, carelessness, or inadvertence and does not know the whereabouts. Id; *Ritz v. Selma United Methodist Church*, 467 N.W.2d 266 (Iowa 1991);
- Mislaid Property—that which the owner has intentionally set down in a place where he can again resort to it, and then forgets where he put it. *Terry*, 37 S.W.3d at 206;
- Treasure Trove—a category exclusively for gold or silver in coin, plate, bullion, and sometimes its paper money equivalents, found concealed in the earth or in a house or other private place. *Id.* Treasure trove carries with it the thought of antiquity, i.e., that the treasure has been concealed for so long as to indicate that the owner is probably dead or unknown. 1 Am.Jur.2d *Abandoned, Lost, Etc.*, §8 (1994);
- Embedded Property—that personal property which has become a part of the natural earth, such as pottery, the sunken wreck of a steamship, or a rotted-away sack of gold-bearing quartz rock buried or partially buried in the ground. *See Chance v. Certain Artifacts Found and Salvaged from the Nashville*, 606 F.Supp. 801 (S.D.Ga.1984); *Ferguson v. Ray*, 44 Or. 557, 77 P. 600 (1904).

Under these doctrines, the finder of lost or abandoned property and treasure trove acquires a right to possess the property against the entire world but the rightful owner regardless of the place of finding. *Terry*, 37 S.W.3d at 206. The finder of mislaid property is required to turn it over to the owner of the premises who has the duty to safeguard the property for the true owner. *Id.* Possession of embedded property goes to owner of the land on which the property was found. *Allred v. Biegel*, 240 Mo.App. 818, 219 S.W.2d 665 (1949) (citing *Elwes v. Brigg Gas Co.*, 33 Ch. D. 562 (Eng.1886)); 1 Am.Jur.2d *Abandoned, Lost, Etc.*, §29.

One of the major distinctions between these various categories is that only lost property necessarily involves an element of involuntariness. *Campbell v. Cochran*, 416 A.2d 211, 221 (Del.Super.Ct.1980). The four remaining categories involve voluntary and intentional acts by the true owner in placing the property where another eventually finds it. *Id.* However, treasure trove, despite not being lost or abandoned property, is treated as such in that the right to possession is recognized to be in the finder rather than the premises owner.

C. Discussion and Analysis

On appeal, Corliss argues that the district court should have interpreted the undisputed facts and circumstances surrounding the placement of the coins in the ground to indicate that the gold coins were either lost, abandoned, or treasure trove. Wenner argues that the property was properly categorized as either embedded or mislaid property.

As with most accidentally discovered buried treasure, the history of the original ownership of the coins is shrouded in mystery and obscured by time. The coins had been wrapped in paper, like coins from a bank, and buried in a glass jar, apparently for safekeeping. Based on these circumstances, the district court determined that the coins were not abandoned because the condition in which the coins were found evidenced an intent to keep them safe, not an intent to voluntarily relinquish all possessory interest in them. The district court also implicitly rejected the notion that the coins were lost, noting that the coins were secreted with care in a specific place to protect them from the elements and from other people until such time as the original owner might return for them. There is no indication that the coins came to be buried through neglect, carelessness, or inadvertence. Accordingly, the district court properly concluded, as a matter of law, that the coins were neither lost nor abandoned.

The district court then determined that the modern trend favored characterizing the coins as property either embedded in the earth or mislaid—under which the right of possession goes to the landowner—rather than treasure trove—under which the right of possession goes to the finder. Although accepted by a number of states prior to 1950, the modern trend since then, as illustrated by decisions of the state and federal courts, is decidedly against recognizing the "finders keepers" rule of treasure trove. *See, e.g., Klein v. Unidentified, Wrecked & Abandoned Sailing Vessel*, 758 F.2d 1511 (11th Cir.1985) (treasure and artifacts from a sunken sailing ship properly characterized as embedded property); *Ritz*, 467 N.W.2d 266 (silver coins and currency dated prior to 1910 and 1928 gold certificates buried in cans and jars under a garage floor classified as mislaid property); *Morgan v. Wiser*, 711 S.W.2d 220 (Tenn.Ct.App.1985) (gold coins found buried in an iron pot properly characterized as embedded property).

Corliss argues that the district court erred in deciding that the law of treasure trove should not apply in Idaho. However, the doctrine of treasure trove has never been adopted in this state. Idaho Code §73-116 provides: "[t]he common law of England, so far as it is not repugnant to, or inconsistent with, the constitution or laws of the United States, in all cases not provided for in these compiled laws, is the rule of decision in all courts of this state." Nevertheless, the history of the "finders keepers" rule was not a part of the common law of England at the time the colonies gained their independence. Rather, the doctrine of treasure trove was created to determine a rightful possessor of buried Roman treasures discovered in feudal times. *See* Leeanna Izuel, *Property Owner's Constructive Possession of Treasure Trove: Rethinking the Finders Keepers Rule*, 38 U.C.L.A. L.Rev. 1659, 1666-67 (1991). And while the common law initially awarded the treasure to the finder, the crown, as early as the year 1130, exercised its royal prerogative to take such property for itself. *Id.* Only after the American colonies gained their independence from England did some states grant possession of treasure trove to the finder. *Id.* Thus, it does not appear that the "finders keepers" rule of treasure trove was a part of the common law of England as defined by Idaho Code §73-116. We hold that the district court correctly determined that I.C. §73-116 does not require the treasure trove doctrine to be adopted in Idaho.

Additionally, we conclude that the rule of treasure trove is of dubious heritage and misunderstood application, inconsistent with our values and traditions. The danger of adopting the doctrine of treasure trove is laid out in *Morgan*, 711 S.W.2d at 222-23:

> [We] find the rule with respect to treasure-trove to be out of harmony with modern notions of fair play. The common-law rule of treasure-trove invites trespassers to roam at large over the property of others with their metal detecting devices and to dig wherever such devices tell them property might be found. If the discovery happens to fit the definition of treasure-trove, the trespasser may claim it as his own. To paraphrase another court: The mind refuses consent to the proposition that one may go upon the lands of another and dig up and take away anything he discovers there which does not belong to the owner of the land. [citation omitted]
>
> The invitation to trespassers inherent in the rule with respect to treasure-trove is repugnant to the common law rules dealing with trespassers in general. The common-law made a trespass an actionable wrong without the necessity of showing any damage therefrom. Because a trespass often involved a breach of the peace and because the law was designed to keep the peace, the common law dealt severely with trespassers.
>
> . . .
>
> Recognizing the validity of the idea that the discouragement of trespassers contributes to the preservation of the peace in the community, we think this state should not follow the common law rule with respect to treasure-trove. Rather, we adopt the rule suggested in the concurring opinion in *Schley v. Couch*, [. . .] which we restate as follows:

> Where property is found embedded in the soil under circumstances repelling the idea that it has been lost, the finder acquires no title thereto, for the presumption is that the possession of the article found is in the owner of the locus in quo.

Land ownership includes control over crops on the land, buildings and appurtenances, soils, and minerals buried under those soils. The average Idaho landowner would expect to have a possessory interest in any object uncovered on his or her property. And certainly the notion that a trespassing treasure hunter, or a hired handyman or employee, could or might have greater possessory rights than a landowner in objects uncovered on his or her property runs counter to the reasonable expectations of present-day land ownership.[2]

There is no reason for a special rule for gold and silver coins, bullion, or plate as opposed to other property. Insofar as personal property (money and the like) buried or secreted on privately owned realty is concerned, the distinctions between treasure trove, lost property, and mislaid property are anachronistic and of little value. The principle point of such distinctions is the intent of the true owner which, absent some written declaration indicating such, is obscured in the mists of time and subject to a great deal of speculation.[3]

By holding that property classed as treasure trove (gold or silver coins, bullion, plate) in other jurisdictions is classed in Idaho as personal property embedded in the soil, subject to the same limitations as mislaid property, possession will be awarded to the owner of the soil as a matter of law. Thus, we craft a simple and reasonable solution to the problem, discourage trespass, and avoid the risk of speculating about the true owner's intent when attempting to infer such from the manner and circumstances in which an object is found. Additionally, the true owner, if any, will have the opportunity to recover the property.

D. Conclusion

We hold that the owner of the land has constructive possession of all personal property secreted in, on or under his or her land. Accordingly, we adopt the district court's reasoning and conclusion melding the law of mislaid property with that of embedded property and conclude, as a matter of law, that the landowner is entitled to possession to the exclusion of all but the true owner, absence a contract between the landowner and finder. . . .

---

[2] We note that nothing would prevent a would-be treasure hunter or hired builder or excavator from contracting some type of arrangement where the right of possession is shared or purchased outright.

[3] As one commentator has wryly noted, "The old rule of treasure trove may make good theater, but it's poor law, and its death can come none to[sic] soon." Richard B. Cunningham, *The Slow Death of the Treasure Trove*, Archaeology (Feb. 7, 2000).

NOTES

1. *Treasure Trove vs. Embedded.* As the court explained in *Corliss*, there is a tension between the treasure trove and embedded categories. The two overlap to a significant degree, and reach opposite results—treasure trove goes to the finder, while embedded property goes to the owner of the locus. Based on the discussion in *Corliss*, what do you think is the right approach and why? Don't limit yourself to the two existing categories. If you were going to set up the rules on the ownership of buried treasure, what would you do?

2. *Other Relevant Factors.* In addition to the lost/mislaid/abandoned/treasure trove/ embedded classifications, disputes between the finder and the owner of the premises where the object was found might also turn, at least in part, on these other issues:

(a) Was the finder on the property in some kind of inferior legal position to the owner of the premises? Some of the court's reasoning in *Corliss* suggests that a finder who is a trespasser might have a harder time winning than a finder who was on the property as an invited guest. Similarly, a finder who is on the property as an employee or other agent of the owner of the premises might have a relatively weaker claim to found property. Indeed, the holding in *Corliss v. Wenner* could have been based on the alternative ground that Corliss and Anderson were working as Wenner's agents.

(b) Was the property found in a public or private part of the premises? The owner of a shop, for example, might have a stronger expectation that they would be entitled to property found in the private areas of the premises than to property found in the areas open to the public.

(c) Was the finder honest? Courts always like honesty. In the leading English case of *Hannah v. Peel*, [1945] K.B. 509, the court seemed impressed that the finder had been honest and turned the found property over to the police.

3. *The True Owner Always Wins.* Don't forget about the true owner, who will win against both the finder and the owner of the premises. In one recent case, a contractor named Bob Kitts found $182,000 in Depression-era currency hidden in a wall. Kitts and the owner of the house, Amanda Reece, couldn't agree on how to split the money, and the dispute between the two ended up in court. Press coverage of the lawsuit drew claims from the heirs of a former owner of the house, who purportedly was the true owner of the money. Some of the money disappeared, and no one ended up happy. *See* "Found: $182,000 and a Lot of Grief," *Washington Post* (Nov. 9, 2008), *http://www .washingtonpost.com/wp-dyn/content/article/2008/11/08/AR2008110802248.html.*

PROBLEMS

In each of the following fact patterns, apply the common-law categories described in *Benjamin* and *Corliss* and presume that the jurisdiction does not have any applicable statutes. Explanatory answers can be found on page 1029.

1. Cindy's Cinful Chocolates is a retail store owned by Cindy Wu. One day Paul Prescott was shopping in Cindy's store when he noticed a backpack on the floor by the door. Paul picked up the backpack and showed it to Cindy, asking if she knew whose it was. Cindy didn't know. Thinking he'd find some identification of the owner, Paul opened the backpack. It turned out that it was full of bundles of new $20 bills, $15,300 worth in all. The true owner was never identified, and Paul and Cindy soon ended up in a dispute over ownership of the money. Which one of them has a better claim? Would your answer change if the money had been found in a small envelope, rather than in a backpack? How about if the money was found in a small envelope, but the envelope was found on the counter, rather than the floor?

2. One day, Ryan Gual was walking in a small park. The park was located on land owned by Theresa Simmons, who allowed the public to access the park. Ryan was walking along a path when he noticed a small gully that appeared to have been created by a recent rainstorm. He saw a glint of metal and when looking closer noticed a gold ring set with diamonds sitting on the dirt in the gully. He picked it up and brought it to a jeweler. The jeweler cleaned the ring, which was very dirty, and said that it was more than a hundred years old. Theresa heard through the grapevine about Ryan's find, and now the two are in a dispute about ownership of the ring. Which one of them has a better claim?

4. FINDING REMEDIES AND THE RULE OF CAPTURE, AGAIN

All of the finder versus owner of the locus cases we have seen so far have led to all-or-nothing results—either the finder wins or the owner of the locus wins. There are other possible ways of resolving these disputes. One is suggested in *Benjamin v. Lindner Aviation*, where the Iowa statute provided that a finder would get a 10 percent reward before the property was returned to the true owner. A similar system could be made between finders and the owner of the locus. Having a rule where the finder gets something would, among other things, encourage finders to be honest.

The possibility of sharing the value of the found object raises a larger point about how we approach legal issues. In our adversary legal system, disputes are typically framed in terms of which of two (or more) parties should win on any given issue. Sometimes we might be better off if instead we ask a different question. Rather than ask "who should win, A or B?," we might ask "what is the best resolution of this dispute?" This more abstract question might lead us to think more about the best outcome and would give us more options than the binary choice between giving all or nothing to A and B. Our next case illustrates the potential strengths and weaknesses of this alternative approach. It also includes a sophisticated discussion of our primary topic, possession.

POPOV V. HAYASHI

California Superior Court, Dec. 18, 2002
2002 WL 31833731

McCarthy, J. In 1927, Babe Ruth hit sixty home runs. That record stood for thirty four years until Roger Maris broke it in 1961 with sixty one home runs. Mark McGwire hit seventy in 1998. On October 7, 2001, at PacBell Park in San Francisco, Barry Bonds hit number seventy three. That accomplishment set a record which, in all probability, will remain unbroken for years into the future.

The event was widely anticipated and received a great deal of attention.

The ball that found itself at the receiving end of Mr. Bond's bat garnered some of that attention. Baseball fans in general, and especially people at the game, understood the importance of the ball. It was worth a great deal of money[1] and whoever caught it would bask, for a brief period of time, in the reflected fame of Mr. Bonds.

With that in mind, many people who attended the game came prepared for the possibility that a record setting ball would be hit in their direction. Among this group were plaintiff Alex Popov and defendant Patrick Hayashi. They were unacquainted at the time. Both men brought baseball gloves, which they anticipated using if the ball came within their reach.

They, along with a number of others, positioned themselves in the arcade section of the ballpark. This is a standing room only area located near right field. It is in this general area that Barry Bonds hits the greatest number of home runs.[2] The area was crowded with people on October 7, 2001 and access was restricted to those who held tickets for that section.

Barry Bonds came to bat in the first inning. With nobody on base and a full count, Bonds swung at a slow knuckleball. He connected. The ball sailed over the right-field fence and into the arcade.

Josh Keppel, a cameraman who was positioned in the arcade, captured the event on videotape. Keppel filmed much of what occurred from the time Bonds hit the ball until the commotion in the arcade had subsided. He was standing very near the spot where the ball landed and he recorded a significant amount of information critical to the disposition of this case.

In addition to the Keppel tape, seventeen percipient witnesses testified as to what they saw after the ball came into the stands. The testimony of these witnesses varied on many important points. Some of the witnesses had a good vantage point and some did not. Some appeared disinterested in the outcome of the litigation and others had a clear

---

[1] It has been suggested that the ball might sell for something in excess of $1,000,000.

[2] The Giants' website contains a page which shows where each of Bonds' home runs landed in 2001. This page was introduced into evidence and is part of the record. It shows that most of the balls are clustered in the arcade area.

bias. Some remembered the events well and others did not. Some were encumbered by prior inconsistent statements which diminished their credibility.

The factual findings in this case are the result of an analysis of the testimony of all the witnesses as well as a detailed review of the Keppel tape. Those findings are as follows:

When the seventy-third home run ball went into the arcade, it landed in the upper portion of the webbing of a softball glove worn by Alex Popov. While the glove stopped the trajectory of the ball, it is not at all clear that the ball was secure. Popov had to reach for the ball and in doing so, may have lost his balance.

Even as the ball was going into his glove, a crowd of people began to engulf Mr. Popov.[3] He was tackled and thrown to the ground while still in the process of attempting to complete the catch. Some people intentionally descended on him for the purpose of taking the ball away, while others were involuntarily forced to the ground by the momentum of the crowd.

Eventually, Mr. Popov was buried face down on the ground under several layers of people. At one point he had trouble breathing. Mr. Popov was grabbed, hit and kicked. People reached underneath him in the area of his glove. Neither the tape nor the testimony is sufficient to establish which individual members of the crowd were responsible for the assaults on Mr. Popov.

The videotape clearly establishes that this was an out of control mob, engaged in violent, illegal behavior. Although some witnesses testified in a manner inconsistent with this finding, their testimony is specifically rejected as being false on a material point.[4]

Mr. Popov intended at all times to establish and maintain possession of the ball. At some point the ball left his glove and ended up on the ground. It is impossible to establish the exact point in time that this occurred or what caused it to occur.

Mr. Hayashi was standing near Mr. Popov when the ball came into the stands. He, like Mr. Popov, was involuntarily forced to the ground. He committed no wrongful act.[5] While on the ground he saw the loose ball. He picked it up, rose to his feet and put it in his pocket.

---

[3] Ted Kobayashi, a defense expert, testified that there was insufficient reaction time for the crowd to descend on Mr. Popov. This opinion is completely unconvincing. It is premised on the assumption that people did not begin to react until the ball hit Mr. Popov's glove. A number of witnesses testified that they began reacting while the ball was in the air. People rushed to the area where they thought the ball would land. If people were unable to anticipate where a ball will land while it is still in the air, no outfielder would ever catch a ball unless it was hit directly to him or her. Moreover, the tape itself shows people descending on Mr. Popov even as he was attempting to catch the ball.

[4] Because the probability of truth does not favor the testimony of any of these witnesses in other particulars, their entire testimony is rejected. BAJI 2.22. This finding does not apply to Mr. Hayashi.

[5] Plaintiff argues that the Keppel tape shows Mr. Hayashi biting the leg of Brian Shepard. The tape does not support such a conclusion. The testimony which suggests that a bite occurred is equally unconvincing. In addition, there is insufficient evidence that Mr. Hayashi assaulted or attempted to take the ball away from Mr. Popov.

Although the crowd was still on top of Mr. Popov, security guards had begun the process of physically pulling people off. Some people resisted those efforts. One person argued with an official and another had to be pulled off by his hair.

Mr. Hayashi kept the ball hidden. He asked Mr. Keppel to point the camera at him. At first, Mr. Keppel did not comply and Mr. Hayashi continued to hide the ball. Finally after someone else in the crowd asked Mr. Keppel to point the camera at Mr. Hayashi, Mr. Keppel complied. It was only at that point that Mr. Hayashi held the ball in the air for others to see. Someone made a motion for the ball and Mr. Hayashi put it back in his glove. It is clear that Mr. Hayashi was concerned that someone would take the ball away from him and that he was unwilling to show it until he was on videotape. Although he testified to the contrary, that portion of his testimony is unconvincing.

Mr. Popov eventually got up from the ground. He made several statements while he was on the ground and shortly after he got up which are consistent with his claim that he had achieved some level of control over the ball and that he intended to keep it. Those statements can be heard on the audio portion of the tape. When he saw that Mr. Hayashi had the ball he expressed relief and grabbed for it. Mr. Hayashi pulled the ball away.[6] Security guards then took Mr. Hayashi to a secure area of the stadium.[7]

It is important to point out what the evidence did not and could not show. Neither the camera nor the percipient witnesses were able to establish whether Mr. Popov retained control of the ball as he descended into the crowd. Mr. Popov's testimony on this question is inconsistent on several important points, ambiguous on others and, on the whole, unconvincing. We do not know when or how Mr. Popov lost the ball.

Perhaps the most critical factual finding of all is one that cannot be made. We will never know if Mr. Popov would have been able to retain control of the ball had the crowd not interfered with his efforts to do so. Resolution of that question is the work of a psychic, not a judge.

LEGAL ANALYSIS

Plaintiff has pled causes of actions for conversion, trespass to chattel, injunctive relief and constructive trust.

Conversion is the wrongful exercise of dominion over the personal property of another.[8] There must be actual interference with the plaintiff's dominion.[9] Wrongful

---

[6] Defense counsel has attempted to characterize this encounter as one in which Mr. Popov congratulates Mr. Hayashi for getting the ball and offers him a high five. This is an argument that only a true advocate could embrace.

[7] Testimony was also received about events which occurred after baseball officials escorted Mr. Hayashi to a secure area. This evidence was admitted to allow counsel to explore the possibility that Major League Baseball retained constructive possession of the ball after it landed in the stands and later gifted it to Mr. Hayashi. Defense counsel has properly abandoned this theory. There is no evidence to support it.

[8] See generally, Witkin, *Summary of California Law*, Ninth Edition, section 610. See also, *Fresno Air Service v. Wood* (1965) 232 Cal.App.2d 801, 806, 43 Cal.Rptr. 276.

[9] *Jordan v. Talbot* (1961) 55 Cal.2d 597, 610, 12 Cal.Rptr. 488, 361 P.2d 20.

withholding of property can constitute actual interference even where the defendant lawfully acquired the property. If a person entitled to possession of personal property demands its return, the unjustified refusal to give the property back is conversion.[10]

The act constituting conversion must be intentionally done. There is no requirement, however, that the defendant know that the property belongs to another or that the defendant intends to dispossess the true owner of its use and enjoyment. Wrongful purpose is not a component of conversion.[11]

The injured party may elect to seek either specific recovery of the property or monetary damages.[12]

Trespass to chattel, in contrast, exists where personal property has been damaged or where the defendant has interfered with the plaintiff's use of the property. Actual dispossession is not an element of the tort of trespass to chattel.[13]

In the case at bar, Mr. Popov is not claiming that Mr. Hayashi damaged the ball or that he interfered with Mr. Popov's use and enjoyment of the ball. He claims instead that Mr. Hayashi intentionally took it from him and refused to give it back. There is no trespass to chattel. If there was a wrong at all, it is conversion.

Conversion does not exist, however, unless the baseball rightfully belongs to Mr. Popov. One who has neither title nor possession, nor any right to possession, cannot sue for conversion.[14] The deciding question in this case then, is whether Mr. Popov achieved possession or the right to possession as he attempted to catch and hold on to the ball.

The parties have agreed to a starting point for the legal analysis. Prior to the time the ball was hit, it was possessed and owned by Major League Baseball. At the time it was hit it became intentionally abandoned property.[15] The first person who came in possession of the ball became its new owner.[16]

The parties fundamentally disagree about the definition of possession. In order to assist the court in resolving this disagreement, four distinguished law professors

---

[10] *Edwards v. Jenkins* (1932) 214 Cal. 713, 720, 7 P.2d 702, *Witkin, supra,* at section 622.

[11] *Henderson v. Security National Bank* (1977) 72 Cal.App.3d 764, 771, 140 Cal.Rptr. 388; *Witkin, supra,* at section 624.

[12] *Witkin, supra,* at section 611.

[13] *Zaslow v. Kroenert* (1946) 29 Cal.2d 541, 551, 176 P.2d 1.

[14] *Metropolitan Life Insurance Company v. San Francisco Bank* (1943) 58 Cal.App.2d 528, 534, 136 P.2d 853; *Witkin, supra,* at section 617.

[15] *See generally, Fugitive Baseballs and Abandoned Property: Who Owns the Home Run Ball?,* Cardozo Law Review, May 2002, Paul Finkelman, (Chapman Distinguished Professor of Law).

[16] *See generally, Past and Future: The Temporal Dimension in the Law of Property,* (1986) 64:667; Washington U.L. Quarterly, Professor Richard A. Epstein (James Parker Hall Professor of Law, University of Chicago; *Irwin v. Phillips* (1855) 5 Cal. 140; *Potter v. Knowles* (1855) 5 Cal. 87.

participated in a forum to discuss the legal definition of possession.[17] The professors also disagreed.

The disagreement is understandable. Although the term possession appears repeatedly throughout the law, its definition varies depending on the context in which it is used.[18] Various courts have condemned the term as vague and meaningless.[19]

This level of criticism is probably unwarranted.

While there is a degree of ambiguity built into the term possession, that ambiguity exists for a purpose. Courts are often called upon to resolve conflicting claims of possession in the context of commercial disputes. A stable economic environment requires rules of conduct which are understandable and consistent with the fundamental customs and practices of the industry they regulate. Without that, rules will be difficult to enforce and economic instability will result. Because each industry has different customs and practices, a single definition of possession cannot be applied to different industries without creating havoc.

This does not mean that there are no central principles governing the law of possession. It is possible to identify certain fundamental concepts that are common to every definition of possession.

Professor Roger Bernhardt[20] has recognized that "[p]ossession requires both physical control over the item and an intent to control it or exclude others from it. But these generalizations function more as guidelines than as direct determinants of possession issues. Possession is a blurred question of law and fact."[21]

Professor Brown argues that "[t]he orthodox view of possession regards it as a union of the two elements of the physical relation of the possessor to the thing, and of intent. This physical relation is the actual power over the thing in question, the ability to hold and make use of it. But a mere physical relation of the possessor to the thing in question is not enough. There must also be manifested an intent to control it."[22]

The task of this court is to use these principles as a starting point to craft a definition of possession that applies to the unique circumstances of this case.

---

[17] They are Professor Brian E. Gray, University of California, Hastings College of the Law; Professor Roger Bernhardt, Golden Gate University School of Law; Professor Paul Finkelman, The Chapman Distinguished Professor of Law, The University of Tulsa School of Law; and Professor Jan Stiglitz, California Western School of Law. The discussion was held during an official session of the court convened at The University of California, Hastings College of the Law. The session was attended by a number of students and professors including one first year property law class which used this case as vehicle to understand the law of possession.

[18] Brown, *The Law on Personal Property* (Callaghan and Company, 3rd Edition, 1975) section 2.6, page 19.

[19] *Kramer v. United States* 408 F.2d 837, 840 (C.A.8th.1969); *State v. Strutt* (1967) 4 Conn.Cir.Ct. 501, 236 A.2d 357, 359.

[20] Professor Bernhardt is the author of the textbook *Property, Cases and Statutes*, published by the West Group as well as the co-author of *Real Property in a Nutshell* with Professor Ann M. Burkhart.

[21] *Real Property in a Nutshell*, Roger Bernhardt and Ann M. Burkhart, chapter one, page 3.

[22] Brown, *The Law on Personal Property* (Callaghan and Company, 3rd Edition, 1975) section 2.6, page 21.

We start with the observation that possession is a process which culminates in an event. The event is the moment in time that possession is achieved. The process includes the acts and thoughts of the would be possessor which lead up to the moment of possession.

The focus of the analysis in this case is not on the thoughts or intent of the actor. Mr. Popov has clearly evidenced an intent to possess the baseball and has communicated that intent to the world.[23] The question is whether he did enough to reduce the ball to his exclusive dominion and control. Were his acts sufficient to create a legally cognizable interest in the ball?

Mr. Hayashi argues that possession does not occur until the fan has complete control of the ball. Professor Brian Gray, suggests the following definition "A person who catches a baseball that enters the stands is its owner. A ball is caught if the person has achieved complete control of the ball at the point in time that the momentum of the ball and the momentum of the fan while attempting to catch the ball ceases. A baseball, which is dislodged by incidental contact with an inanimate object or another person, before momentum has ceased, is not possessed. Incidental contact with another person is contact that is not intended by the other person. The first person to pick up a loose ball and secure it becomes its possessor."[24]

Mr. Popov argues that this definition requires that a person seeking to establish possession must show unequivocal dominion and control, a standard rejected by several leading cases.[25] Instead, he offers the perspectives of Professor Bernhardt and Professor Paul Finkelman[26] who suggest that possession occurs when an individual intends to take control of a ball and manifests that intent by stopping the forward momentum of the ball whether or not complete control is achieved.

Professors Finkelman and Bernhardt have correctly pointed out that some cases recognize possession even before absolute dominion and control is achieved. Those cases require the actor to be actively and ably engaged in efforts to establish complete control.[27]

---

[23] Literally.

[24] This definition is hereinafter referred to as Gray's Rule.

[25] *Pierson v. Post* 3 Caines R. (N.Y.1805); *Young v. Hitchens* 6 Q.B. 606 (1844); *State v. Shaw* (1902) 67 Ohio St. 157, 65 N.E. 875.

[26] Professor Finkelman is the author of the definitive law review article on the central issue in this case, *Fugitive Baseballs and Abandoned Property: Who Owns the Home Run Ball?*, Cardozo Law Review, May 2002, Paul Finkelman, (Chapman Distinguished Professor of Law).

[27] The degree of control necessary to establish possession varies from circumstance to circumstance. "The law . . . does not always require that one who discovers lost or abandoned property must actually have it in hand before he is vested with a legally protected interest. The law protects not only the title acquired by one who finds lost or abandoned property but also the right of the person who discovers such property, and is actively and ably engaged in reducing it to possession, to complete this process without interference from another. The courts have recognized that in order to acquire a legally cognizable interest in lost or abandoned property a finder need not always have manual possession of the thing. Rather, a finder may be protected by taking such constructive possession of the property as its nature and situation permit." *Treasure Salvors Inc. v. The Unidentified Wrecked and Abandoned Sailing Vessel* (1981) 640 F.2d 560, 571. (emphasis added)

Moreover, such efforts must be significant and they must be reasonably calculated to result in unequivocal dominion and control at some point in the near future.[28]

This rule is applied in cases involving the hunting or fishing of wild animals[29] or the salvage of sunken vessels.[30] The hunting and fishing cases recognize that a mortally wounded animal may run for a distance before falling. The hunter acquires possession upon the act of wounding the animal not the eventual capture. Similarly, whalers acquire possession by landing a harpoon, not by subduing the animal.[31]

In the salvage cases, an individual may take possession of a wreck by exerting as much control "as its nature and situation permit."[32] Inadequate efforts, however, will not support a claim of possession. Thus, a "sailor cannot assert a claim merely by boarding a vessel and publishing a notice, unless such acts are coupled with a then present intention of conducting salvage operations, and he immediately thereafter proceeds with activity in the form of constructive steps to aid the distressed party."[33]

These rules are contextual in nature. The[y] are crafted in response to the unique nature of the conduct they seek to regulate. Moreover, they are influenced by the custom and practice of each industry. The reason that absolute dominion and control is not required to establish possession in the cases cited by Mr. Popov is that such a rule would be unworkable and unreasonable. The "nature and situation" of the property at issue does not immediately lend itself to unequivocal dominion and control. It is impossible to wrap ones arms around a whale, a fleeing fox or a sunken ship.

The opposite is true of a baseball hit into the stands of a stadium. Not only is it physically possible for a person to acquire unequivocal dominion and control of an abandoned baseball, but fans generally expect a claimant to have accomplished as much. The custom and practice of the stands creates a reasonable expectation that a person will achieve full control of a ball before claiming possession. There is no reason for the legal rule to be inconsistent with that expectation. Therefore Gray's Rule is adopted as the definition of possession in this case.

The central tenant of Gray's Rule is that the actor must retain control of the ball after incidental contact with people and things. Mr. Popov has not established by a preponderance of the evidence that he would have retained control of the ball

---

[28] *Brady v. S.S. African Queen* 179 F.Supp. 321 (E.D.Va., 1960); *Eads v. Brazelton* (1861) 22 Ark. 499; *Treasure Salvors Inc. id.* at 571.

[29] *Liesner v. Wanie* (1914) 156 Wis. 16, 145 N.W. 374; *Ghen v. Rich* 8 F. 159 (D.Mass.1881); *Pierson v. Post* 3 Caines R. (N.Y.1805); *Young v. Hitchens* 6 Q.B. 606 (1844); *State v. Shaw* (1902) 67 Ohio St. 157, 65 N.E. 875. *See also* Herbert Hovenkamp and Sheldon Kurtz, *The Law of Property* (5th ed. West Group 2001) at page 2.

[30] *Indian River Recovery Company v. The China* 645 F.Supp. 141, 144 (D.Del.1986); *Treasure Salvors Inc. v. The Unidentified Wrecked and Abandoned Sailing Vessel* (1981) 640 F.2d 560; *Richard v. Pringle* 293 F.Supp. 981 (S.D.N.Y.1968).

[31] *Swift v. Gifford* 23 F. Cas. 558 (D.Mass.1872).

[32] See note 27.

[33] *Brady v. S.S. African Queen* 179 F.Supp. 321, 324 (E.D.Va., 1960).

after all momentum ceased and after any incidental contact with people or objects. Consequently, he did not achieve full possession.

That finding, however, does not resolve the case. The reason we do not know whether Mr. Popov would have retained control of the ball is not because of incidental contact. It is because he was attacked. His efforts to establish possession were interrupted by the collective assault of a band of wrongdoers.[34]

A decision which ignored that fact would endorse the actions of the crowd by not repudiating them. Judicial rulings, particularly in cases that receive media attention, affect the way people conduct themselves. This case demands vindication of an important principle. We are a nation governed by law, not by brute force.[35]

As a matter of fundamental fairness, Mr. Popov should have had the opportunity to try to complete his catch unimpeded by unlawful activity. To hold otherwise would be to allow the result in this case to be dictated by violence. That will not happen.

For these reasons, the analysis cannot stop with the valid observation that Mr. Popov has not proved full possession.[36]

The legal question presented at this point is whether an action for conversion can proceed where the plaintiff has failed to establish possession or title. It can. An action for conversion may be brought where the plaintiff has title, possession or the right to possession.[37]

Here Mr. Popov seeks, in effect, a declaratory judgment that he has either possession or the right to possession. In addition he seeks the remedies of injunctive relief and a constructive trust. These are all actions in equity. A court sitting in equity has the authority to fashion rules and remedies designed to achieve fundamental fairness.

LAW AND EQUITY

Consistent with this principle, the court adopts the following rule. Where an actor undertakes significant but incomplete steps to achieve possession of a piece of abandoned personal property and the effort is interrupted by the unlawful acts of others, the actor has a legally cognizable pre-possessory interest in the property. That pre-possessory interest constitutes a qualified right to possession that can support a cause of action for conversion.

---

[34] Professor Gray has suggested that the way to deal with this problem is to demand that Mr. Popov sue the people who assaulted him. This suggestion is unworkable for a number of reasons. First, it was an attack by a large group of people. It is impossible to separate out the people who were acting unlawfully from the people who were involuntarily pulled into the mix. Second, in order to prove damages related to the loss of the ball, Mr. Popov would have to prove that but for the actions of the crowd he would have achieved possession of the ball. As noted earlier, this is impossible.

[35] There are a number of ways courts can enforce the rule of law. Major League Baseball, as well as each individual team has a duty to provide security against foreseeable violence in the stands. The failure to provide that security, or worse, the tacit acceptance of some level of violence, will inevitable lead to lawsuits against the teams and the parent organization.

[36] The court is indebted to Professor Jan Stiglitz of California Western School of Law for his valuable insights and suggestions on this issue.

[37] See note 14.

Possession can be likened to a journey down a path. Mr. Popov began his journey unimpeded. He was fast approaching a fork in the road. A turn in one direction would lead to possession of the ball—he would complete the catch. A turn in the other direction would result in a failure to achieve possession—he would drop the ball. Our problem is that before Mr. Popov got to the point where the road forked, he was set upon by a gang of bandits, who dislodged the ball from his grasp.

Recognition of a legally protected pre-possessory interest, vests Mr. Popov with a qualified right to possession and enables him to advance a legitimate claim to the baseball based on a conversion theory. Moreover it addresses the harm done by the unlawful actions of the crowd.

It does not, however, address the interests of Mr. Hayashi. The court is required to balance the interests of all parties.

Mr. Hayashi was not a wrongdoer. He was a victim of the same bandits that attacked Mr. Popov. The difference is that he was able to extract himself from their assault and move to the side of the road. It was there that he discovered the loose ball. When he picked up and put it in his pocket he attained unequivocal dominion and control.

If Mr. Popov had achieved complete possession before Mr. Hayashi got the ball, those actions would not have divested Mr. Popov of any rights, nor would they have created any rights to which Mr. Hayashi could lay claim. Mr. Popov, however, was able to establish only a qualified pre-possessory interest in the ball. That interest does not establish a full right to possession that is protected from a subsequent legitimate claim.

On the other hand, while Mr. Hayashi appears on the surface to have done everything necessary to claim full possession of the ball, the ball itself is encumbered by the qualified pre-possessory interest of Mr. Popov. At the time Mr. Hayashi came into possession of the ball, it had, in effect, a cloud on its title.

An award of the ball to Mr. Popov would be unfair to Mr. Hayashi. It would be premised on the assumption that Mr. Popov would have caught the ball. That assumption is not supported by the facts. An award of the ball to Mr. Hayashi would unfairly penalize Mr. Popov. It would be based on the assumption that Mr. Popov would have dropped the ball. That conclusion is also unsupported by the facts.

Both men have a superior claim to the ball as against all the world. Each man has a claim of equal dignity as to the other. We are, therefore, left with something of a dilemma.

Thankfully, there is a middle ground.

The concept of equitable division was fully explored in a law review article authored by Professor R.H. Helmholz in the December 1983 edition of the Fordham Law Review.[38]

---

[38] *Equitable Division and the Law of Finders*, (1983) Fordham Law Review, Professor R.H. Helmholz, University of Chicago School of Law. This article built on a student comment published in 1939. *Lost, Mislaid and Abandoned Property* (1939) 8 Fordham Law Review 222.

Professor Helmholz addressed the problems associated with rules governing finders of lost and mislaid property. For a variety of reasons not directly relevant to the issues raised in this case, Helmholz suggested employing the equitable remedy of division to resolve competing claims between finders of lost or mislaid property and the owners of land on which the property was found.

There is no reason, however, that the same remedy cannot be applied in a case such as this, where issues of property, tort and equity intersect.

The concept of equitable division has its roots in ancient Roman law.[39] As Helmholz points out, it is useful in that it "provides an equitable way to resolve competing claims which are equally strong." Moreover, "[i]t comports with what one instinctively feels to be fair."[40]

Although there is no California case directly on point, *Arnold v. Producers Fruit Company* (1900) 128 Cal. 637, 61 P. 283 provides some insight. There, a number of different prune growers contracted with Producer's Fruit Company to dry and market their product. Producers did a bad job. They mixed fruit from many different growers together in a single bin and much of the fruit rotted because it was improperly treated.

When one of the plaintiffs offered proof that the fruit in general was rotten, Producers objected on the theory that the plaintiff could not prove that the prunes he contributed to the mix were the same prunes that rotted. The court concluded that it did not matter. After the mixing was done, each grower had an undivided interest in the whole, in proportion to the amount of fruit each had originally contributed.

The principle at work here is that where more than one party has a valid claim to a single piece of property, the court will recognize an undivided interest in the property in proportion to the strength of the claim.

Application of the principle of equitable division is illustrated in the case of *Keron v. Cashman* (1896) 33 A. 1055. In that case, five boys were walking home along a railroad track in the city of Elizabeth New Jersey. The youngest of the boys came upon an old sock that was tied shut and contained something heavy. He picked it up and swung it. The oldest boy took it away from him and beat the others with it. The sock passes from boy to boy. Each controlled it for a short time. At some point in the course of play, the sock broke open and out spilled $775 as well as some rags, cloths and ribbons.

The court noted that possession requires both physical control and the intent to reduce the property to one's possession. Control and intent must be concurrent. None of the boys intended to take possession until it became apparent that the sock contained money. Each boy had physical control of the sock at some point before that discovery was made.

Because none could present a superior claim of concurrent control and intent, the court held that each boy was entitled to an equal share of the money. Their legal claims

---

[39] Helmholz at fn. 14.

[40] *Id.* at 315.

to the property were of equal quality, therefore their entitlement to the property was also equal.

Here, the issue is not intent, or concurrence. Both men intended to possess the ball at the time they were in physical contact with it. The issue, instead, is the legal quality of the claim. With respect to that, neither can present a superior argument as against the other.

Mr. Hayashi's claim is compromised by Mr. Popov's pre-possessory interest. Mr. Popov cannot demonstrate full control. Albeit for different reasons, they stand before the court in exactly the same legal position as did the five boys. Their legal claims are of equal quality and they are equally entitled to the ball.

The court therefore declares that both plaintiff and defendant have an equal and undivided interest in the ball. Plaintiff's cause of action for conversion is sustained only as to his equal and undivided interest. In order to effectuate this ruling, the ball must be sold and the proceeds divided equally between the parties.

The parties are ordered to meet and confer forthwith before Judge Richard Kramer to come to an agreement as to how to implement this decision. If no decision is made by December 30, 2002, the parties are directed to appear before this court on that date at 9:00 a.m.

The court retains jurisdiction to issue orders consistent with this decision. The ball is to remain in the custody of the court until further order.

NOTES AND QUESTIONS

1. By this time, you have a pretty sophisticated understanding of the issue of possession. Put yourself in Judge McCarthy's position. How would you have ruled and why?

2. In discussing the concept of equitable division in the law of finding, Judge McCarthy refers to the 1896 case of *Keron v. Cashman*. How is *Keron* similar or different from *Popov v. Hayashi*? What do the two cases tell you about when equitable division should or should not be used?

3. Immediately after Barry Bonds set the single-season home-run record, the ball at issue in *Popov* was estimated to be worth $1.5 million. Perhaps because of the delay caused by the litigation, the ball ended up being sold at auction for $450,000. All of Alex Popov's share went to pay his attorney.

LAW AND EQUITY

REMEDIES

5. GIFTS OF PERSONAL PROPERTY

Our next topic is *inter vivos* gifts of personal property. We will discuss gifts of real property later, but for now you should know that real property typically can only be transferred (as a gift or otherwise) through a formal legal instrument.

"*Inter vivos*" means "during life," so we are talking about gifts made while the donor is alive. The law treats gifts made at death very differently. The law generally requires gifts made at death to be made through a written will. This requirement is intended to minimize the opportunity for fraud or dishonesty and to help avoid disputes about the disposition of property where it is impossible to ask the donor for clarification.

There are three elements of a valid *inter vivos* gift of personal property: (1) intent, (2) delivery, and (3) acceptance.

Intent: The intent element can be divided into two subparts. First, did the donor intend to make a gift?

> **EXAMPLE 1:** A hands a ring to B, saying "here, this is a gift for you." A had the intent to make a gift.

> **EXAMPLE 2:** A hands a ring to B, saying "here, could you hold this for me for a minute?" A did not have the intent to make a gift.

Second, did the donor intend to make a gift during life, or did the donor intend to give a gift at death? If the donor intended to make a gift during life, then the gift will be valid if the other elements are met. If the donor intended to make a gift at death, however, the gift will likely be invalid. Compare Example 1, where A had the intent to give a gift during life, with the following scenario:

> **EXAMPLE 3:** A hands a ring to B, saying "here, you can borrow this ring for a while, and it will be yours when I die."

In Example 3, *A* intended to transfer ownership of the ring at A's death. The transfer in Example 3 therefore would *not* constitute a valid *inter vivos* gift.

Delivery: There are three types of delivery: (1) actual, (2) constructive, and (3) symbolic.

Actual delivery involves an actual physical transfer of the object from the donor to the donee, such as the transfer of the ring in Example 1. The common law required actual delivery if it was possible to physically transfer the object. This rule is often stated as "if it can be handed over, it must be handed over."

Constructive delivery involves the transfer of some object, usually a key, that will give access to the property that is the subject of the gift.

> **EXAMPLE 4:** A hands a key to B, saying "This key opens my safe. I give you all of the safe's contents."

Delivery of the key is constructive delivery of the safe's contents. Note, though, that constructive delivery might not be enough to establish a valid gift. If it was possible to hand over either the safe or the contents, then a court strictly applying the common law "if it can be handed over, it must be handed over" rule might hold that the delivery element is not met. A court taking a less strict view might hold that the gift was valid. If it was not possible to hand over the safe or the contents (perhaps because they were too heavy), then delivery of the key would constitute constructive delivery of the safe and its contents even under the strict common-law approach.

Symbolic delivery involves the transfer of a written document that evidences intent to make a gift of personal property.

EXAMPLE 5: A hands B a note that reads "Dear B, I give you all of the furniture in my living room. Love, A."

Delivery of the note constitutes symbolic delivery of the furniture. As was the case with constructive delivery, symbolic delivery might not be enough to satisfy a court strictly applying the common-law approach to delivery. The furniture in Example 5 is likely large and bulky, so even a strict common-law court probably would be satisfied with symbolic delivery. If the item being transferred was a ring, however, a strict common-law court would likely not accept symbolic delivery.

There is something of a modern trend in allowing constructive and symbolic delivery, even if the object is capable of being handed over. Some courts, however, still follow the traditional common-law rule.

Acceptance: Acceptance of a gift is presumed so long as the object has some value. As a result, this element is rarely an issue in disputes over gifts.

Once all three elements are met, then a typical *inter vivos* gift becomes irrevocable. There is one type of gift that is an exception to this rule. A gift *causa mortis* is one that is made when the donor expects to die soon. If circumstances change, and the donor recovers, then the gift *causa mortis* is revocable. Gifts *causa mortis* are otherwise identical to other *inter vivos* gifts.

EXAMPLE 6: A is in the hospital suffering from severe pneumonia. A says to B: "I'm dying, B. Here, I want you to have my ring." A then hands the ring over to B. Because the gift was made in view of impending death, if A recovers then A can revoke the gift and reclaim the ring from B.

Note that in Example 6, A demonstrates the intent to give the ring to B at the moment of transfer. A therefore had the intent to transfer the ring during A's life, making this a valid *inter vivos* gift. If A instead had said "I'm dying, B. Here, hold this ring for me, I want you to have it when I die," then A would have intended to transfer the ring at death, and the transfer would not have been a valid *inter vivos* gift. Real life situations, of course, are often far less clear than these stylized examples, and it can be very hard to determine the donor's intent after the donor has died.

NOTE

1. *Possession and Intent.* We have already considered the relationship between control, possession, and intent in some other contexts. The gifts context is a little different from some of the others, because we are focused on the intent of the person giving up possession rather than the intent of the person gaining possession. (The acceptance element presumes the intent of the recipient of the gift.) With *inter vivos* gifts, we ask whether the donor has given up control with the intent of giving up possession and transferring ownership. Donor control can be a significant issue in some gift contexts. For example, if the donor gives the contents of a safe deposit box to the donee, but the donor maintains the right to access the box, then the donor's continued control may mean that the delivery requirement has not been met. Similarly, if the donor

gives the donee a check, the donor may be able to stop payment on the check up until the time the donee deposits it. This degree of control by the donor might mean that delivery is not complete until the donee deposits the check. This fact pattern comes up in our next case.

CARTER V. PERCY

Supreme Court of Nebraska, 2006
708 N.W.2d 645

GERRARD, J. After the death of Edward Lamplaugh, Deborah Carter deposited two checks written to her on Lamplaugh's account at Adams Bank & Trust (the Bank). Upon learning of Lamplaugh's death and contacting the pay-on-death beneficiary of Lamplaugh's account, the Bank reversed the transaction and placed a hold on Lamplaugh's account. Carter filed a claim against the estate of Lamplaugh for the amount of the checks, and the county court granted the claim in full. The successor personal representative of the estate appeals the judgment of the county court. For the reasons that follow, we affirm.

FACTUAL AND PROCEDURAL BACKGROUND

During the 10 years prior to Lamplaugh's death, Carter performed housekeeping and other household duties for him. Among other tasks, Carter paid Lamplaugh's bills, cleaned his home, dispensed his medicine, mowed his yard, did his laundry, took him on errands, and accompanied him to the doctor. On the morning of June 10, 2002, Carter arrived at Lamplaugh's home and discovered Lamplaugh on the floor, deceased. Carter notified the authorities and traveled to the hospital, where Lamplaugh was pronounced dead. When Carter left the hospital, she stopped at the Bank to deposit two checks written to her on Lamplaugh's account. One check, dated June 6, 2002, was in the amount of $50 for cleaning services Carter had performed the previous week. The other check, dated June 9, 2002, was in the amount of $80,000. According to Carter, Lamplaugh gave her the check to enable her to buy a liquor store located in North Platte that was for sale at the time of Lamplaugh's death.

When Carter returned to Lamplaugh's home after depositing the checks into her account, an employee of the Bank called the residence to speak with Lamplaugh. After learning of Lamplaugh's death and subsequently contacting Lamplaugh's sister, the pay-on-death beneficiary of the account, the Bank reversed the transaction, placed a hold on the account, and notified Carter accordingly. Carter was never able to gain access to the funds.

Lamplaugh's sister was appointed as personal representative of Lamplaugh's estate. After her health deteriorated, Charles Percy was appointed as successor personal representative (hereinafter personal representative).

Carter filed a petition for allowance of claim against the estate for $80,098, including the amount of the two checks and an additional $48 that Carter spent to change the locks at Lamplaugh's home on the day he died. The amended inventory of Lamplaugh's estate shows under schedule F (as personal property) the disputed $80,000 which is being held in the Bank and under schedule C (as cash) the remaining amount contained in Lamplaugh's checking account with Lamplaugh's sister as the pay-on-death beneficiary. A trial was held, and the county court granted Carter's claim. No fraud had been alleged by the estate, and the court found that Carter acted out of "genuine fondness or love" for Lamplaugh and found no evidence of fraudulent intent or action on Carter's part. The court concluded that the check showed sufficient indicia of donative intent to be a valid gift and rejected the personal representative's argument that Lamplaugh's death before redemption of the check nullified the gift. The court also granted payment of $50 for Carter's cleaning services and $48 expended in changing the locks at Lamplaugh's residence, and those findings are not at issue here.

The personal representative appealed the judgment of the county court.

ASSIGNMENTS OF ERROR

The personal representative assigns, summarized and restated, that the county court erred in (1) finding donative intent on the part of Lamplaugh in transferring the $80,000 check to Carter, (2) finding effective delivery of the purported gift, and (3) failing to find that the purported gift was revoked by Lamplaugh's death. . . .

ANALYSIS

The personal representative assigns that the county court erred in finding the $80,000 check to be a valid gift from Lamplaugh to Carter. To make a valid and effective gift inter vivos, there must be an intention to transfer title to the property, and a delivery by the donor and acceptance by the donee. *Guardian State Bank & Trust Co. v. Jacobson*, 220 Neb. 235, 369 N.W.2d 80 (1985). The personal representative first challenges the county court's finding of donative intent, arguing that the court was presented with conflicting evidence as to Lamplaugh's intent in giving the check to Carter and that, thus, Carter failed to prove the requisite donative intent. The personal representative also argues that Carter failed to prove that Lamplaugh effectively delivered the $80,000 to Carter. As a result, the personal representative asserts that the gift was incomplete and, consequently, revoked upon Lamplaugh's death.

Sufficient Evidence was Presented at Trial to Support County Court's Finding of Donative Intent

One of the essential elements of a gift is the intention to make it. *Masonic Temple Craft v. Stamm*, 152 Neb. 604, 42 N.W.2d 178 (1950). A clear and unmistakable intention on the part of the donor to make a gift of his or her property is an essential element of the gift, and this contention must be inconsistent with any other theory. *Id.*

The personal representative argues that Carter did not present clear evidence at trial to show that Lamplaugh intended to make a gift of $80,000 to Carter. Carter argues that the county court's finding of donative intent was supported by competent evidence, and based on the evidence offered at trial and the applicable standard of review, we agree.

At trial, Carter testified that on many occasions, Lamplaugh expressed a desire that Carter have all his money upon his death. Carter testified that Lamplaugh gave her money as gifts, paid her sick leave, paid for her "car tags," and expressed his desire to take care of her. Carter testified that she and Lamplaugh discussed the purchase of the liquor store on multiple occasions and that Lamplaugh offered to assist her with the investment.

Carter described the usual process in which she would assist Lamplaugh in paying his bills—filling out the checks according to his instructions for him to then review and sign, one at a time. Carter testified that the same process was used at the time Lamplaugh signed the $80,000 check at issue. She testified that after spending the day cleaning and doing laundry at Lamplaugh's residence on June 9, 2002, Lamplaugh told her that she "needed to slow down and take time and get that—that liquor store bought." Carter testified that Lamplaugh instructed her to write "to pay bills" on the "memo" line of the check, explaining that it was not his family's business how he spent his money. Further, Carter testified that Lamplaugh did not mention anything about repayment terms and that she understood the check to be a gift from him. At the end of the evening, Carter placed the check in her purse and went home, after making arrangements to stop at Lamplaugh's residence the following morning.

Debby Baker, Carter's close friend and former employer, also testified at trial. Baker testified that due to Carter's multiple jobs and hectic schedule, Baker served as an answering service for Carter and kept track of her whereabouts in case anyone needed to reach her. Baker testified that she spoke to Lamplaugh on the telephone on multiple occasions while Carter was working for him. Baker explained that on the day before Lamplaugh's death, she called Lamplaugh's residence to speak to Carter. Lamplaugh answered the telephone, explained that Carter was busy cleaning, and expressed to Baker his desire to give Carter a check for $80,000. Lamplaugh told Baker that he hoped owning her own business would allow Carter to spend more time assisting him. Baker testified that Lamplaugh had also expressed his intent to give Carter the check on a prior occasion.

Finally, the deposition of Janet Spencer, a former business development officer and personal banker at the Bank, was received into evidence at trial. Spencer testified that she first met Lamplaugh when he came to the Bank, along with Carter, to open a personal checking account. Spencer was already acquainted with Carter at that time, having served as her banker. In discussing with Lamplaugh the ways in which to title the new account, Spencer testified that Lamplaugh wanted Carter on the account. Spencer testified that when Carter discouraged the idea, Lamplaugh told Spencer that he wanted

Carter to have all of his money and that, although he kept asking her to marry him, she repeatedly declined. Carter acknowledged Lamplaugh's marriage proposals during her testimony but described Lamplaugh's substantial role in her life as more like a father-daughter relationship.

In her deposition, Spencer stated that, ultimately, Lamplaugh agreed to place his sister on the account. Spencer testified about other occasions in which Lamplaugh would visit the Bank. During such visits, Lamplaugh was very vocal about his appreciation for Carter and the assistance she provided to him and, on approximately six occasions, expressed his desire that Carter have his money upon his death.

The evidence offered by Carter is sufficient to support the county court's conclusion that Lamplaugh intended the check to be a gift to Carter, and the estate offered no contradictory evidence. When considering the evidence in the light most favorable to Carter, the county court's factual finding of donative intent on the part of Lamplaugh is neither arbitrary nor unreasonable and is supported by competent evidence. The personal representative's first assignment of error is without merit.

Delivery of Gift of $80,000 was Accomplished by Operation of Law at Time of Lamplaugh's Death

Once it is ascertained that it was the intention of the donor to make a gift inter vivos of an undivided interest in a chattel or chose in action, and all is done under the circumstances which is possible in the matter of delivery, the gift will be sustained. *Lewis v. Poduska*, 240 Neb. 312, 481 N.W.2d 898 (1992). Ordinarily, actual delivery is necessary where the subject of the gift is capable of manual delivery, but where actual manual delivery cannot be made, the donor may do that which, under the circumstances, will in reason be considered equivalent to actual delivery. *Guardian State Bank & Trust Co. v. Jacobson*, 220 Neb. 235, 369 N.W.2d 80 (1985).

In the present case, the personal representative asserts that delivery of the purported gift was not accomplished by Lamplaugh's transfer of the check to Carter, because a check is not itself a transfer of funds. Rather, the personal representative argues that delivery of the amount of the check is not effectuated until it is cashed or deposited, placing the funds beyond the dominion and control of the donor. Furthermore, the personal representative argues that Carter's failure to cash the $80,000 check prior to Lamplaugh's death rendered the gift incomplete and that as a result, the gift was automatically revoked upon Lamplaugh's death.

In support of his position, the personal representative cites *Matter of Estate of Bolton*, 444 N.W.2d 482 (Iowa 1989). In *Matter of Estate of Bolton*, 444 N.W.2d at 483, the Iowa Supreme Court discussed the general rule with respect to gifts by check, as recognized in Iowa:

> "[T]he donor's check, prior to acceptance or payment by the bank, is not the subject of a valid gift either inter vivos or causa mortis . . . . The difficulty with

respect to a gift of the donor's check . . . is that mere delivery of the check to the donee or to some other person for him does not place the gift beyond the donor's power of revocation, prior to payment or acceptance. Moreover, there is the further consideration . . . that the death of the drawer works a revocation of the check, so that where the check is intended as a gift causa mortis and the donor dies before payment or acceptance, the death revokes the gift. Thus, the death of the drawer effects a revocation of the alleged gift of a check not presented for payment until after such death. . . ."

(Quoting 38 Am.Jur.2d *Gifts* §65 (1968).) Based on these principles, the personal representative asserts that Lamplaugh's death revoked the purported gift to Carter.

In contrast, Carter argues that Lamplaugh's transfer of the check itself was sufficient to accomplish delivery of the gift prior to Lamplaugh's death. Carter asserts that delivery is accomplished when all that can be done to effectuate delivery under the circumstances is done; Carter argues that Lamplaugh's transfer of the check on the evening before his death was sufficient to complete delivery under that standard. Furthermore, Carter asserts that even jurisdictions that take the position urged by the personal representative recognize an exception in which the transfer of a check constitutes constructive delivery of the funds where (1) the donor's intent is clear, (2) creditors are not prejudiced, (3) no fraud or undue influence is at issue, and (4) the check is not cashed prior to the donor's death due to circumstances beyond the control of the donor and donee. *See, e.g., Sinclair v. Fleischman*, 54 Wash.App. 204, 773 P.2d 101 (1989). Such an exception, Carter argues, would apply in the present case.

But the parties fail to cite §30-2723(d), which states in part that

[t]he ownership right of a surviving party or beneficiary, or of the decedent's estate, in sums on deposit is subject to requests for payment made by a party before the party's death, whether paid by the financial institution before or after death, or unpaid. The surviving party or beneficiary, or the decedent's estate, is liable to the payee of an unpaid request for payment.

The comments accompanying article VI of the Uniform Probate Code, upon which §30-2723(d) is based, discuss the effect of amendments made to article VI, stating, in part, "[t]he changes include recognition of checks issued by an account owner before death and presented for payment after death . . . ." Prefatory Note, Unif. Probate Code, 8 U.L.A. 426 (1998). Such a rule is a departure from common-law rules pertaining to gift and agency law providing that a drawee bank must honor a check before the donor's death. *See* Ronald R. Volkmer, *Legislative Bill 250: The New Nonprobate Transfers Article of the Nebraska Probate Code*, 27 Creighton L.Rev. 239 (1993). *See, also,* William M. McGovern, Jr., *Nonprobate Transfers Under the Revised Uniform Probate Code*, 55 Alb. L.Rev. 1329 (1992).

The plain language of §30-2723(d) does not distinguish between checks intended as gifts, checks transferred in satisfaction of debts, or otherwise. Rather, the statute requires, without limitation, that unpaid checks written on a party's account before the party's death be paid by the beneficiary from the sums on deposit in the decedent's account.

Statutory language is to be given its plain and ordinary meaning, and an appellate court will not resort to interpretation to ascertain the meaning of statutory words which are plain, direct, and unambiguous. *Tyson Fresh Meats v. State*, 270 Neb. 535, 704 N.W.2d 788 (2005). Here, the Legislature made a clear policy decision to enact statutory language that supplants any common-law rules regarding presentment of checks after the death of the drafter. Thus, although the parties focus their arguments on the question whether delivery of a gift by check is complete at the time the check is transferred or, alternatively, at the time the check is cashed or deposited, we conclude that regardless of whatever common-law rule would have been applicable, the gift was completed by operation of law upon Lamplaugh's death pursuant to §30-2723(d).

Pursuant to §30-2723(d), the check given to Carter under the circumstances became irrevocable upon Lamplaugh's death, and the check remains payable by Lamplaugh's estate from the funds being held in the Bank. Such a result is consistent with the requirements for a valid gift—the donor's dominion and control of the funds represented by the check are surrendered upon the donor's death, and delivery is thereby completed.

We conclude that Lamplaugh's gift of $80,000 was complete upon his death and is payable pursuant to §30-2723(d). Although, upon our independent review on this question of law, our reasoning differs from that of the county court, the court did not err in finding the check was payable. Where the record adequately demonstrates that the decision of the trial court is correct, although such correctness is based on a ground or reason different from that assigned by the trial court, an appellate court will affirm. *Troshynski v. Nebraska State Bd. of Pub. Accountancy*, 270 Neb. 347, 701 N.W.2d 379 (2005).

CONCLUSION

Having reviewed the proceedings for error on the record, we conclude that sufficient evidence was presented at trial to support the county court's finding of donative intent on the part of Lamplaugh. In addition, delivery of the gift was accomplished, at the latest, at the time of Lamplaugh's death. Under §30-2723(d), Lamplaugh's estate is liable to Carter for the amount of the check. The county court's decision conforms to the law and is supported by competent evidence. The remainder of the claim against the estate is not at issue on appeal; we, therefore, affirm the judgment of the county court.

Affirmed.

QUESTIONS

1. What do you think is the best fact in the record for Carter? What do you think is the worst fact for her?

2. The court discusses two common-law approaches and one statutory approach to delivery of a check. What are they? Why, exactly, did the court conclude that the check was delivered?

Our next case involves the gift of a painting. To give you the background needed to fully understand the case, we need to introduce the concept of present and future interests in property. We will cover this topic in depth in the next chapter. For now, you need to know that we can split ownership of property over time, with one person owning the present interest and another person owning the future interest. (As we will see, there can be multiple owners of present and future interests; for now, we will focus on one present interest holder and one future interest holder.)

> ### ENGAGEMENT RINGS
>
> What happens to an engagement ring if the engagement is later broken off? Engagement rings are often viewed as a type of conditional gift—that is, a gift intended to be permanent on the happening of a condition, here, marriage. In some jurisdictions, the ring must be returned if the recipient was responsible for calling off the marriage, but need not be returned if the donor was responsible for breaking the engagement. Other states have adopted a no-fault rule, where the ring must be returned regardless of who was responsible. *See* Elaine Marie Tomko, *Rights in Respect of Engagement and Courtship Presents When Marriage Does Not Ensue*, 44 A.L.R.5th 1 (1996).

The owner of the present interest has all of the rights of possession, use, and exclusion that we typically associate with the ownership of property. The future interest holder will not have any of these rights until the present interest expires.

One type of present interest is a life estate. As its name implies, a life estate lasts for the present interest holder's life and expires at the present interest holder's death. The owner of property could convey the property "to Father for life, then to Son." In this conveyance, Father has a life estate, and Son has a type of future interest called a remainder. Father will be the present owner of the property during his life. He will have all of the rights to possess, use, and exclude that we typically associate with property ownership. (The right to alienate is a little bit more complicated—we will leave that discussion to our next chapter.) During Father's life, Son will have no present rights in the property. When Father dies, Son will then become the present owner of the property and will have the attendant rights of possession, use, and exclusion.

You might have a host of questions about how present and future interests work. Hold on to those questions until we get to our chapter on present and future interests. One thing that you need to know now is that future interests are property interests that exist at the time of creation. In our example above, Son's remainder interest existed from the time the conveyance was made. The remainder interest will become possessory, giving Son all of the basic rights of ownership, later when Father dies. But the future interest itself was created at the time of conveyance.

Understanding that future interests exist at the time of conveyance is crucial to understanding our next case. Like our example, the case involves a father and son. The father already owned the item that he gave to his son. The father wanted to keep possession of the item during his life, so his conveyance took this form: "to myself for life, then to my son." As we have been discussing, the son's future interest existed at the time the father made the gift. We already know that there is an important distinction between gifts made during life and gifts made at death. Because the future interest is created at the time of conveyance, when the father is alive, the gift of the future interest is an *inter vivos* gift. It may help you understand the case to remember that a valid *inter vivos* gift is irrevocable. If the father's conveyance of "to myself for life, then to my son" meets all of the elements of a valid *inter vivos* gift, then the father can't later change his mind and retract the gift.

GRUEN V. GRUEN

New York Court of Appeals, 1986
496 N.E.2d 869

SIMONS, Judge. Plaintiff commenced this action seeking a declaration that he is the rightful owner of a painting which he alleges his father, now deceased, gave to him. He concedes that he has never had possession of the painting but asserts that his father made a valid gift of the title in 1963 reserving a life estate for himself. His father retained possession of the painting until he died in 1980. Defendant, plaintiff's stepmother, has the painting now and has refused plaintiff's requests that she turn it over to him. She contends that the purported gift was testamentary in nature and invalid insofar as the formalities of a will were not met or, alternatively, that a donor may not make a valid inter vivos gift of a chattel and retain a life estate with a complete right of possession. Following a seven-day nonjury trial, Special Term found that plaintiff had failed to establish any of the elements of an inter vivos gift and that in any event an attempt by a donor to retain a present possessory life estate in a chattel invalidated a purported gift of it. The Appellate Division held that a valid gift may be made reserving a life estate and, finding the elements of a gift established in this case, it reversed and remitted the matter for a determination of value (104 A.D.2d 171, 488 N.Y.S.2d 401). That determination has now been made and defendant appeals directly to this court, pursuant to CPLR 5601(d), from the subsequent final judgment entered in Supreme Court awarding plaintiff $2,500,000 in damages representing the value of the painting, plus interest. We now affirm.

The subject of the dispute is a work entitled "Schloss Kammer am Attersee II" painted by a noted Austrian modernist, Gustav Klimt. It was purchased by plaintiff's father, Victor Gruen, in 1959 for $8,000. On April 1, 1963 the elder Gruen, a successful architect with offices and residences in both New York City and Los Angeles during most of the time involved in this action, wrote a letter to plaintiff, then an undergraduate student at Harvard, stating that he was giving him the Klimt painting for his birthday but that he wished to retain the possession of it for his lifetime. This letter is not in evidence, apparently because plaintiff destroyed it on instructions from his father. Two other letters were received, however, one dated May 22, 1963 and the other April 1, 1963. Both had been dictated by Victor Gruen and sent together to plaintiff on or about May 22, 1963. The letter dated May 22, 1963 reads as follows:

> Dear Michael:
>
> I wrote you at the time of your birthday about the gift of the painting by Klimt.
>
> Now my lawyer tells me that because of the existing tax laws, it was wrong to mention in that letter that I want to use the painting as long as I live. Though I still want to use it, this should not appear in the letter. I am enclosing, therefore, a new letter and I ask you to send the old one back to me so that it can be destroyed.
>
> I know this is all very silly, but the lawyer and our accountant insist that they must have in their possession copies of a letter which will serve the purpose of making it possible for you, once I die, to get this picture without having to pay inheritance taxes on it.
>
> Love,
> s/Victor

Enclosed with this letter was a substitute gift letter, dated April 1, 1963, which stated:

> Dear Michael:
>
> The 21st birthday, being an important event in life, should be celebrated accordingly. I therefore wish to give you as a present the oil painting by Gustav Klimt of Schloss Kammer which now hangs in the New York living room. You know that Lazette and I bought it some 5 or 6 years ago, and you always told us how much you liked it.
>
> Happy birthday again.
>
> Love,
> s/Victor

Plaintiff never took possession of the painting nor did he seek to do so. Except for a brief period between 1964 and 1965 when it was on loan to art exhibits and when restoration work was performed on it, the painting remained in his father's possession, moving with him from New York City to Beverly Hills and finally to Vienna, Austria, where Victor

Gruen died on February 14, 1980. Following Victor's death plaintiff requested possession of the Klimt painting and when defendant refused, he commenced this action.

The issues framed for appeal are whether a valid inter vivos gift of a chattel may be made where the donor has reserved a life estate in the chattel and the donee never has had physical possession of it before the donor's death and, if it may, which factual findings on the elements of a valid inter vivos gift more nearly comport with the weight of the evidence in this case, those of Special Term or those of the Appellate Division. The latter issue requires application of two general rules. First, to make a valid inter vivos gift there must exist the intent on the part of the donor to make a present transfer; delivery of the gift, either actual or constructive to the donee; and acceptance by the donee (*Matter of Szabo,* 10 N.Y.2d 94, 98, 217 N.Y.S.2d 593, 176 N.E.2d 395; *Matter of Kelly,* 285 N.Y. 139, 150, 33 N.E.2d 62 [dissenting in part opn]; *Matter of Van Alstyne,* 207 N.Y. 298, 306, 100 N.E. 802; *Beaver v. Beaver,* 117 N.Y. 421, 428, 22 N.E. 940). Second, the proponent of a gift has the burden of proving each of these elements by clear and convincing evidence (*Matter of Kelley, supra,* 285 N.Y. at p. 150, 33 N.E.2d 62; *Matter of Abramowitz,* 38 A.D.2d 387, 389-390, 329 N.Y.S.2d 932, *affd. on opn.* 32 N.Y.2d 654, 342 N.Y.S.2d 855, 295 N.E.2d 654).

DONATIVE INTENT

There is an important distinction between the intent with which an inter vivos gift is made and the intent to make a gift by will. An inter vivos gift requires that the donor intend to make an irrevocable present transfer of ownership; if the intention is to make a testamentary disposition effective only after death, the gift is invalid unless made by will (*see, McCarthy v. Pieret,* 281 N.Y. 407, 409, 24 N.E.2d 102; *Gannon v. McGuire,* 160 N.Y. 476, 481, 55 N.E. 7; *Martin v. Funk,* 75 N.Y. 134, 137-138).

Defendant contends that the trial court was correct in finding that Victor did not intend to transfer any present interest in the painting to plaintiff in 1963 but only expressed an intention that plaintiff was to get the painting upon his death. The evidence is all but conclusive, however, that Victor intended to transfer ownership of the painting to plaintiff in 1963 but to retain a life estate in it and that he did, therefore, effectively transfer a remainder interest in the painting to plaintiff at that time. Although the original letter was not in evidence, testimony of its contents was received along with the substitute gift letter and its covering letter dated May 22, 1963. The three letters should be considered together as a single instrument (*see, Matter of Brandreth,* 169 N.Y. 437, 440, 62 N.E. 563) and when they are they unambiguously establish that Victor Gruen intended to make a present gift of title to the painting at that time. But there was other evidence for after 1963 Victor made several statements orally and in writing indicating that he had previously given plaintiff the painting and that plaintiff owned it. Victor Gruen retained possession of the property, insured it, allowed others to exhibit it and made necessary repairs to it but those acts are not inconsistent with his retention of a life estate. Furthermore, whatever probative value could be attached to his statement that he had bequeathed the painting to his heirs, made 16 years later when he prepared an export license application so that he could take the painting out of Austria, is negated by the overwhelming evidence that he intended a present transfer of title in 1963. Victor's failure to file a gift tax return on the transaction was partially explained by allegedly erroneous legal advice he received, and while that omission sometimes may indicate that the donor had no intention of making a present gift, it does not necessarily do so and it is not dispositive in this case.

Defendant contends that even if a present gift was intended, Victor's reservation of a lifetime interest in the painting defeated it. She relies on a statement from *Young v. Young*, 80 N.Y. 422 that " '[a]ny gift of chattels which expressly reserves the use of the property to the donor for a certain period, or . . . as long as the donor shall live, is ineffectual' " (*id.*, at p. 436, quoting 2 Schouler, *Personal Property*, at 118). The statement was dictum, however, and the holding of the court was limited to a determination that an attempted gift of bonds in which the donor reserved the interest for life failed because there had been no delivery of the gift, either actual or constructive (*see, id.*, at p. 434; *see also, Speelman v. Pascal,* 10 N.Y.2d 313, 319-320, 222 N.Y.S.2d 324, 178 N.E.2d 723). The court expressly left undecided the question "whether a remainder in a chattel may be created and given by a donor by carving out a life estate for himself and transferring the remainder" (*Young v. Young, supra,* at p. 440). We answered part of that question in *Matter of Brandreth* (169 N.Y. 437, 441-442, 62 N.E. 563, *supra*) when we held that "[in] this state a life estate and remainder can be created in a chattel or a fund the same as in real property." The case did not require us to decide whether there could be a valid gift of the remainder.

Defendant recognizes that a valid inter vivos gift of a remainder interest can be made not only of real property but also of such intangibles as stocks and bonds. Indeed, several of the cases she cites so hold. That being so, it is difficult to perceive any legal basis for the distinction she urges which would permit gifts of remainder interests in those properties but not of remainder interests in chattels such as the Klimt painting here. The only reason suggested is that the gift of a chattel must include a present right to possession. The application of *Brandreth* to permit a gift of the remainder in this case, however, is consistent with the distinction, well recognized in the law of gifts as well as in real property law, between ownership and possession or enjoyment (*see, Speelman v. Pascal,* 10 N.Y.2d 313, 318, 222 N.Y.S.2d 324, 178 N.E.2d 723, *supra; McCarthy v. Pieret,* 281 N.Y. 407, 409-411, 24 N.E.2d 102, *supra; Matter of Brandreth,* 169 N.Y. 437, 442, 62 N.E. 563, *supra*). Insofar as some of our cases purport to require that the donor intend to transfer both title and possession immediately to have a valid inter vivos gift (*see, Gannon v. McGuire,* 160 N.Y. 476, 481, 55 N.E. 7, *supra; Young v. Young,* 80 N.Y. 422, 430, *supra*), they state the rule too broadly and confuse the effectiveness of a gift with the transfer of the possession of the subject of that gift. The correct test is " 'whether the maker intended the [gift] to have *no effect* until after the maker's death, or whether he intended it to transfer *some present interest*'" (*McCarthy v. Pieret,* 281 N.Y. 407, 409, 24 N.E.2d 102, *supra* [emphasis added]; *see also,* 25 N.Y.Jur., Gifts, §14, at 156-157). As long as the evidence establishes an intent to make a present and irrevocable transfer of title or the right of ownership, there is a present transfer of some interest and the gift is effective immediately (see, *Matter of Brady,* 228 App. Div. 56, 60, 239 N.Y.S. 5, *affd. no opn.* 254 N.Y. 590, 173 N.E. 879; *In re Sussman's Estate,* 125 N.Y.S.2d 584, 589-591, *affd. no opn.* 283 App. Div. 1051, 134 N.Y.S.2d 586, *Matter of Valentine,* 122 Misc. 486, 489, 204 N.Y.S. 284; Brown, *Personal Property* §48, at 133-136 [2d ed]; 25 N.Y.Jur., Gifts, §30, at 173-174; *see also, Farmers' Loan & Trust Co. v. Winthrop,* 238 N.Y. 477, 485-486, 144 N.E. 686). Thus, in *Speelman v. Pascal* (*supra*), we held valid a gift of a percentage of the future royalties to the play "My Fair Lady" before the play even existed. There, as in this case, the donee received title or the right of ownership to some property immediately upon the making of the gift but possession or enjoyment of the subject of the gift was postponed to some future time.

Defendant suggests that allowing a donor to make a present gift of a remainder with the reservation of a life estate will lead courts to effectuate otherwise invalid testamentary dispositions of property. The two have entirely different characteristics, however, which make them distinguishable. Once the gift is made it is irrevocable and the donor is limited to the rights of a life tenant not an owner. Moreover, with the gift of a remainder title vests immediately in the donee and any possession is postponed until the donor's death whereas under a will neither title nor possession vests immediately. Finally, the postponement of enjoyment of the gift is produced by the express terms of the gift not by the nature of the instrument as it is with a will (*see, Robb v. Washington & Jefferson Coll.,* 185 N.Y. 485, 493, 78 N.E. 359).

DELIVERY

In order to have a valid inter vivos gift, there must be a delivery of the gift, either by a physical delivery of the subject of the gift or a constructive or symbolic delivery such as by an instrument of gift, sufficient to divest the donor of dominion and control over the property (*see, Matter of Szabo,* 10 N.Y.2d 94, 98-99, 217 N.Y.S.2d 593, 176 N.E.2d 395, *supra; Speelman v. Pascal,* 10 N.Y.2d 313, 318-320, 222 N.Y.S.2d 324, 178 N.E.2d 723, *supra; Beaver v. Beaver,* 117 N.Y. 421, 428-429, 22 N.E. 940, *supra; Matter of Cohn,* 187 App. Div. 392, 395, 176 N.Y.S.2d 225). As the statement of the rule suggests, the requirement of delivery is not rigid or inflexible, but is to be applied in light of its purpose to avoid mistakes by donors and fraudulent claims by donees (*see, Matter of Van Alstyne,* 207 N.Y. 298, 308, 100 N.E. 802, *supra; Matter of Cohn, supra,* 187 App. Div. at pp. 395-396, 176 N.Y.S.2d 255; Mechem, *Requirement of Delivery in Gifts of Chattels and of Choses in Actions Evidenced by Commercial Instruments,* 21 Ill. L. Rev. 341, 348-349). Accordingly, what is sufficient to constitute delivery "must be tailored to suit the circumstances of the case" (*Matter of Szabo, supra,* 10 N.Y.2d at p. 98, 217 N.Y.S.2d 593, 176 N.E.2d 395). The rule requires that " '[t]he delivery necessary to consummate a gift must be as perfect as the nature of the property and the circumstances and surroundings of the parties will reasonably permit' " (*id.; Vincent v. Rix,* 248 N.Y. 76, 83, 161 N.E. 425; *Matter of Van Alstyne, supra,* 207 N.Y. at p. 309, 100 N.E. 802; *see, Beaver v. Beaver, supra,* 117 N.Y. at p. 428, 22 N.E. 940).

Defendant contends that when a tangible piece of personal property such as a painting is the subject of a gift, physical delivery of the painting itself is the best form of delivery and should be required. Here, of course, we have only delivery of Victor Gruen's letters which serve as instruments of gift. Defendant's statement of the rule as applied may be generally true, but it ignores the fact that what Victor Gruen gave plaintiff was not all rights to the Klimt painting, but only title to it with no right of possession until his death. Under these circumstances, it would be illogical for the law to require the donor to part with possession of the painting when that is exactly what he intends to retain.

Nor is there any reason to require a donor making a gift of a remainder interest in a chattel to physically deliver the chattel into the donee's hands only to have the donee redeliver it to the donor. As the facts of this case demonstrate, such a requirement could impose practical burdens on the parties to the gift while serving the delivery requirement poorly. Thus, in order to accomplish this type of delivery the parties would have been required to travel to New York for the symbolic transfer and redelivery of the Klimt painting which was hanging on the wall of Victor Gruen's Manhattan apartment. Defendant suggests that such a requirement would be stronger evidence of a completed gift, but in the absence of witnesses to the event or any written confirmation of the gift it would provide less protection against fraudulent claims than have the written instruments of gift delivered in this case.

ACCEPTANCE

Acceptance by the donee is essential to the validity of an inter vivos gift, but when a gift is of value to the donee, as it is here, the law will presume an acceptance on his part (*Matter of Kelsey,* 26 N.Y.2d 792, 309 N.Y.S.2d 219, 257 N.E.2d 663, *affg. on opn. at* 29 A.D.2d 450, 456, 289 N.Y.S.2d 314; *Beaver v. Beaver,* 117 N.Y. 421, 429, 22 N.E. 940, *supra*). Plaintiff did not rely on this presumption alone but also presented clear and convincing proof of his acceptance of a remainder interest in the Klimt painting by evidence that he had made several contemporaneous statements acknowledging the gift to his friends and associates, even showing some of them his father's gift letter, and that he had retained both letters for over 17 years to verify the gift after his father died. Defendant relied exclusively on affidavits filed by plaintiff in a matrimonial action with his former wife, in which plaintiff failed to list his interest in the painting as an asset. These affidavits were made over 10 years after acceptance was complete and they do not even approach the evidence in *Matter of Kelly* (285 N.Y. 139, 148-149, 33 N.E.2d 62 [dissenting in part opn.], *supra*) where the donee, immediately upon delivery of a diamond ring, rejected it as "too flashy." We agree with the Appellate Division that interpretation of the affidavit was too speculative to support a finding of rejection and overcome the substantial showing of acceptance by plaintiff.

Accordingly, the judgment appealed from and the order of the Appellate Division brought up for review should be affirmed, with costs.

NOTES AND QUESTIONS

1. Make sure that you understand the court's analysis of each of the elements of a valid *inter vivos* gift. In particular, be sure that you do not misunderstand the holding of the case. *Gruen does not* stand for the proposition that it is possible to make a valid *inter vivos* gift of a painting by giving the donee a written document stating that "I want you to have this painting when I die." Be sure that you understand why.

2. As you think about the court's discussion of the delivery element, keep two questions in mind. First, is there any practical way of making a delivery of a future interest other than symbolically? Second, if Victor had wanted to make an outright gift of the painting, rather than reserving a life estate for himself, could he have satisfied the delivery requirement symbolically? For this second question, you may want to review our discussion of the delivery element from the beginning of this section.

3. Make a note to come back and reread *Gruen* again after you have finished our chapter on present and future interests in property, especially if you are not completely confident in your understanding of the case now.

4. After the litigation was complete, Michael sold the painting at auction in 1987 for $5.3 million. It sold in the late 1990s for $23.5 million and is currently housed in the Galleria Nazionale d'Arte Moderna in Rome, Italy.

PROBLEMS

Consider whether a valid *inter vivos* gift was made in each of the following scenarios. Explanatory answers can be found on page 1031.

1. Maurice Eto was crossing Main Street one day last month when he was struck by a car. Maurice was very seriously injured, and as the ambulance was taking him away, Maurice said to Sally, one of the paramedics, "I think I'm dying—here, I want you to have this ring." With that, he slipped the ring off his finger and handed it to Sally. Maurice recovered a few months later and now wants his ring back. Sally refused to return it, so Maurice has brought an action for replevin against her.

2. Theresa Spencer had a pretty good life. She did very well for herself in business and owned a number of classic cars. Last March, Theresa decided to give her 1973 Jaguar XKE to her oldest daughter Holly for Holly's 25th birthday. Theresa gave Holly a card on her birthday that said in part "In honor of your 25th birthday, I hereby give you my 1973 Jag." Before Theresa could drive the car to Holly's house or give Holly the keys, Theresa

was killed when she wrapped her Bentley around a telephone poll. Theresa left all of her personal property to the Symphony, and her executor has refused to let Holly have the Jaguar. As a result, Holly has brought a suit against the executor for possession of the car. In your answer, use the common-law rules of gifts that we have been studying and presume that the jurisdiction does not require ownership of cars to be transferred by written title.

3. Nick Kasisa was very close to his granddaughter Katie. Nick knew that Katie was very attached to a Tiffany lamp that he had in his living room. One day, Nick said to Katie, "Here, take the lamp and use it for now. You will own it when I die." Katie took the lamp and kept it in her apartment. Nick died recently, and left all his property to his son Mark. Mark and Katie never got along, and they are now in a dispute about ownership of the lamp.

B. POSSESSION PART II—POSSESSION OF REAL PROPERTY

So far, we have talked about possession of personal property. Our next group of issues involves possession of real property. As we have seen, possession of personal property can be blurry, but at least we can hold a baseball or other similar object in our hands. How, exactly, do we possess real property? We know that possession involves intent and control, so we can reframe the question in this way: how, exactly, do we manifest the intent to possess land, and how do we control it?

One way we might possess real property is to occupy it. It is as intuitive to say that I possess the home I live in as it is to say that I possess a baseball that I am holding in my hand. But what if I own a large, undeveloped parcel of property that I never visit? How can I possess that land?

Recall that at the very first paragraph of this chapter we noted that possession is one of four classic incidents of ownership. The others are the rights to exclude, use, and alienate the property. Exercising the rights to exclude and use might help us as we think about possession of real property—we might demonstrate possession by excluding other people from it or by using it. Clear cases—the equivalent of holding a baseball in our hand—might involve installing a fence around the property or farming the property. By excluding others (by installing the fence) or by using the property (by farming it), we demonstrate both the intent and control needed to establish possession. It would be impractical, however, to always require this level of exclusion or use to establish possession. This unit will give us the opportunity to think about more borderline cases.

1. THE DOCTRINE OF DISCOVERY

Our next case, *Johnson v. M'Intosh*, is one of the most famous cases in the U.S. property canon. In a very real sense, it is the foundation of land title in the United States.

The case involved competing claims to land in Illinois. The plaintiffs had purchased the land from the Illinois and Piankeshaw Indians. The defendant had purchased the same land from the United States. The Supreme Court, in an opinion by Chief Justice Marshall, held that the defendant had superior claim to the land.

As you will see, the doctrine of discovery plays an important role in Chief Justice Marshall's analysis. This doctrine held that ownership of land went to the European colonial power whose subjects had discovered it. Hence the familiar scene in movies where a European explorer steps onto a beach and claims the land in the name of his King or Queen.

The doctrine of discovery has little, if any, application in modern law, but we present the case here for several reasons. First, the case is historically important, establishing the legal superiority of U.S. claims to land over Native American claims to land. It is just one in a long series of cases where Native American land claims did not fare well in the U.S. courts. Second, the doctrine of discovery is a first-in-time rule, though one that minimizes or ignores the claims of native peoples. Third, Chief Justice Marshall's analysis gives us an opportunity to think about the significance of possession of the land by Native American tribes. Pay close attention, in particular, to what Marshall has to say about Native American rights of possession and alienation.

FIRST IN TIME

JOHNSON V. M'INTOSH

Supreme Court of the United States, 1823
21 U.S. (8 Wheat.) 543

Error to the District Court of Illinois. This was an action of ejectment for lands in the State and District of Illinois, claimed by the plaintiffs under a purchase and conveyance from the Piankeshaw Indians, and by the defendant, under a grant from the United States. It came up on a case stated, upon which there was a judgment below for the defendant. . . .

Mr. Chief Justice MARSHALL delivered the opinion of the Court. The plaintiffs in this cause claim the land, in their declaration mentioned, under two grants, purporting to be made, the first in 1773, and the last in 1775, by the chiefs of certain Indian tribes, constituting the Illinois and the Piankeshaw nations; and the question is, whether this title can be recognised in the Courts of the United States?

The facts, as stated in the case agreed, show the authority of the chiefs who executed this conveyance, so far as it could be given by their own people; and likewise show, that the particular tribes for whom these chiefs acted were in rightful possession of the land they sold. The inquiry, therefore, is, in a great measure, confined to the power of Indians to give, and of private individuals to receive, a title which can be sustained in the Courts of this country.

As the right of society, to prescribe those rules by which property may be acquired and preserved is not, and cannot be drawn into question; as the title to lands, especially, is and must be admitted to depend entirely on the law of the nation in which they lie; it will be necessary, in pursuing this inquiry, to examine, not singly those principles of abstract justice, which the Creator of all things has impressed on the mind of his creature man, and which are admitted to regulate, in a great degree, the rights of civilized nations, whose perfect independence is acknowledged; but those principles also which our own government has adopted in the particular case, and given us as the rule for our decision.

On the discovery of this immense continent, the great nations of Europe were eager to appropriate to themselves so much of it as they could respectively acquire. Its vast extent offered an ample field to the ambition and enterprise of all; and the character and religion of its inhabitants afforded an apology for considering them as a people over whom the superior genius of Europe might claim an ascendency. The potentates of the old world found no difficulty in convincing themselves that they made ample compensation to the inhabitants of the new, by bestowing on them civilization and Christianity, in exchange for unlimited independence. But, as they were all in pursuit of nearly the same object, it was necessary, in order to avoid conflicting settlements, and consequent war with each other, to establish a principle, which all should acknowledge as the law by which the right of acquisition, which they all asserted, should be regulated as between themselves. This principle was, that discovery gave title to the government by whose subjects, or by whose authority, it was made, against all other European governments, which title might be consummated by possession.

The exclusion of all other Europeans, necessarily gave to the nation making the discovery the sole right of acquiring the soil from the natives, and establishing settlements upon it. It was a right with which no Europeans could interfere. It was a right which all asserted for themselves, and to the assertion of which, by others, all assented.

Those relations which were to exist between the discoverer and the natives, were to be regulated by themselves. The rights thus acquired being exclusive, no other power could interpose between them.

In the establishment of these relations, the rights of the original inhabitants were, in no instance, entirely disregarded; but were necessarily, to a considerable extent, impaired. They were admitted to be the rightful occupants of the soil, with a legal as well as just claim to retain possession of it, and to use it according to their own discretion; but their rights to complete sovereignty, as independent nations, were necessarily diminished, and their power to dispose of the soil at their own will, to whomsoever they pleased, was denied by the original fundamental principle, that discovery gave exclusive title to those who made it.

While the different nations of Europe respected the right of the natives, as occupants, they asserted the ultimate dominion to be in themselves; and claimed and exercised, as a consequence of this ultimate dominion, a power to grant the soil, while yet in possession of the natives. These grants have been understood by all, to convey a title to the grantees, subject only to the Indian right of occupancy.

The history of America, from its discovery to the present day, proves, we think, the universal recognition of these principles. [Chief Justice Marshall here summarizes claims to territory in the Americas by Spain, France, Portugal, and the Netherlands.]

No one of the powers of Europe gave its full assent to this principle, more unequivocally than England. The documents upon this subject are ample and complete. So early as the year 1496, her monarch granted a commission to the Cabots, to discover countries then unknown to Christian people, and to take possession of them in the name of the king of England. Two years afterwards, Cabot proceeded on this voyage, and discovered the continent of North America, along which he sailed as far south as Virginia. To this discovery the English trace their title.

In this first effort made by the English government to acquire territory on this continent, we perceive a complete recognition of the principle which has been mentioned. The right of discovery given by this commission, is confined to countries "then unknown to all Christian people;" and of these countries Cabot was empowered to take possession in the name of the king of England. Thus asserting a right to take possession, notwithstanding the occupancy of the natives, who were heathens, and, at the same time, admitting the prior title of any Christian people who may have made a previous discovery.

The same principle continued to be recognised. . . . [The Court proceeded to discuss successive charters to land in North America granted by the English crown. The earliest charters gave the recipient the right to discover and take possession of land that was not then "actually possessed by any Christian prince or people." Later charters were specific grants of large areas of land to specific people or companies.]

Thus has our whole country been granted by the crown while in the occupation of the Indians. These grants purport to convey the soil as well as the right of dominion to the grantees. In those governments which were denominated royal, where the right to the soil was not vested in individuals, but remained in the crown, or was vested in the colonial government, the king claimed and exercised the right of granting lands, and of dismembering the government at his will. The grants made out of the two original colonies, after the resumption of their charters by the crown, are examples of this. The governments of New-England, New-York, New-Jersey, Pennsylvania, Maryland, and a part of Carolina, were thus created. In all of them, the soil, at the time the grants were made, was occupied by the Indians. Yet almost every title within those governments is dependent on these grants. In some instances, the soil was conveyed by the crown unaccompanied by the powers of government, as in the case of the northern neck of Virginia. It has never been objected to this, or to any other similar grant, that the title as well as possession was in the Indians when it was made, and that it passed nothing on that account. . . .

Further proofs of the extent to which this principle has been recognised, will be found in the history of the wars, negotiations, and treaties, which the different nations, claiming territory in America, have carried on, and held with each other. [The Court proceeded to discuss the conflicts between European powers over North American territory.]

Thus, all the nations of Europe, who have acquired territory on this continent, have asserted in themselves, and have recognised in others, the exclusive right of the discoverer to appropriate the lands occupied by the Indians. Have the American States rejected or adopted this principle?

By the treaty which concluded the war of our revolution, Great Britain relinquished all claim, not only to the government, but to the "propriety and territorial rights of the United States," whose boundaries were fixed in the second article. By this treaty, the powers of government, and the right to soil, which had previously been in Great Britain, passed definitively to these States. We had before taken possession of them, by declaring independence; but neither the declaration of independence, nor the treaty confirming it, could give us more than that which we before possessed, or to which Great Britain was before entitled. It has never been doubted, that either the United States, or the several States, had a clear title to all the lands within the boundary lines described in the treaty, subject only to the Indian right of occupancy, and that the exclusive power to extinguish that right, was vested in that government which might constitutionally exercise it.

Virginia, particularly, within whose chartered limits the land in controversy lay, passed an act, in the year 1779, declaring her "exclusive right of pre-emption from the Indians, of all the lands within the limits of her own chartered territory, and that no person or persons whatsoever, have, or ever had, a right to purchase any lands within the same, from any Indian nation, except only persons duly authorized to make such purchase; formerly for the use and benefit of the colony, and lately for the Commonwealth." The act then proceeds to annul all deeds made by Indians to individuals, for the private use of the purchasers.

Without ascribing to this act the power of annulling vested rights, or admitting it to countervail the testimony furnished by the marginal note opposite to the title of the law, forbidding purchases from the Indians, in the revisals of the Virginia statutes, stating that law to be repealed, it may safely be considered as an unequivocal affirmance, on the part of Virginia, of the broad principle which had always been maintained, that the exclusive right to purchase from the Indians resided in the government.

In pursuance of the same idea, Virginia proceeded, at the same session, to open her land office, for the sale of that country which now constitutes Kentucky, a country, every acre of which was then claimed and possessed by Indians, who maintained their title with as much persevering courage as was ever manifested by any people.

The States, having within their chartered limits different portions of territory covered by Indians, ceded that territory, generally, to the United States, on conditions expressed in their deeds of cession, which demonstrate the opinion, that they ceded the soil as well as jurisdiction, and that in doing so, they granted a productive fund to the government of the Union. The lands in controversy lay within the chartered limits of Virginia, and were ceded with the whole country northwest of the river Ohio. This grant contained reservations and stipulations, which could only be made by the owners of the soil; and concluded with a stipulation, that "all the lands in the ceded territory, not reserved, should be considered as a common fund, for the use and benefit of such of the United States as have become, or shall become, members of the confederation," &c. "according to their usual respective proportions in the general charge and expenditure, and shall be faithfully and bona fide disposed of for that purpose, and for no other use or purpose whatsoever."

The ceded territory was occupied by numerous and warlike tribes of Indians; but the exclusive right of the United States to extinguish their title, and to grant the soil, has never, we believe, been doubted.

After these States became independent, a controversy subsisted between them and Spain respecting boundary. By the treaty of 1795, this controversy was adjusted, and Spain ceded to the United States the territory in question. This territory, though claimed by both nations, was chiefly in the actual occupation of Indians.

The magnificent purchase of Louisiana, was the purchase from France of a country almost entirely occupied by numerous tribes of Indians, who are in fact independent. Yet, any attempt of others to intrude into that country, would be considered as an aggression which would justify war.

Our late acquisitions from Spain are of the same character; and the negotiations which preceded those acquisitions, recognise and elucidate the principle which has been received as the foundation of all European title in America.

The United States, then, have unequivocally acceded to that great and broad rule by which its civilized inhabitants now hold this country. They hold, and assert in themselves, the title by which it was acquired. They maintain, as all others have maintained, that discovery gave an exclusive right to extinguish the Indian title of occupancy, either by purchase or by conquest; and gave also a right to such a degree of sovereignty, as the circumstances of the people would allow them to exercise.

The power now possessed by the government of the United States to grant lands, resided, while we were colonies, in the crown, or its grantees. The validity of the titles given by either has never been questioned in our Courts. It has been exercised uniformly over territory in possession of the Indians. The existence of this power must negative the existence of any right which may conflict with, and control it. An absolute title to lands cannot exist, at the same time, in different persons, or in different governments. An absolute, must be an exclusive title, or at least a title which excludes all others not compatible with it. All our institutions recognise the absolute title of the crown, subject only to the Indian right of occupancy, and recognise the absolute title of the crown to extinguish that right. This is incompatible with an absolute and complete title in the Indians.

We will not enter into the controversy, whether agriculturists, merchants, and manufacturers, have a right, on abstract principles, to expel hunters from the territory they possess, or to contract their limits. Conquest gives a title which the Courts of the conqueror cannot deny, whatever the private and speculative opinions of individuals may be, respecting the original justice of the claim which has been successfully asserted. The British government, which was then our government, and whose rights have passed to the United States, asserted title to all the lands occupied by Indians, within the chartered limits of the British colonies. It asserted also a limited sovereignty over them, and the exclusive right of extinguishing the title which occupancy gave to them. These claims have been maintained and established as far west as the river Mississippi, by the sword. The title to a vast portion of the lands we now hold, originates in them. It is not for the Courts of this country to question the validity of this title, or to sustain one which is incompatible with it.

Although we do not mean to engage in the defence of those principles which Europeans have applied to Indian title, they may, we think, find some excuse, if not justification, in the character and habits of the people whose rights have been wrested from them.

The title by conquest is acquired and maintained by force. The conqueror prescribes its limits. Humanity, however, acting on public opinion, has established, as a general rule, that the conquered shall not be wantonly oppressed, and that their condition shall remain as eligible as is compatible with the objects of the conquest. Most usually, they are incorporated with the victorious nation, and become subjects or citizens of the government with which they are connected. The new and old members of the society mingle with each other; the distinction between them is grandually lost, and they make one people. Where this incorporation is practicable, humanity demands, and a wise policy requires, that the rights of the conquered to property should remain unimpaired; that the new subjects should be governed as equitably as the old, and that confidence in their security should gradually banish the painful sense of being separated from their ancient connexions, and united by force to strangers.

When the conquest is complete, and the conquered inhabitants can be blended with the conquerors, or safely governed as a distinct people, public opinion, which not even the conqueror can disregard, imposes these restraints upon him; and he cannot neglect them without injury to his fame, and hazard to his power.

But the tribes of Indians inhabiting this country were fierce savages, whose occupation was war, and whose subsistence was drawn chiefly from the forest. To leave them in possession of their country, was to leave the country a wilderness; to govern them as a distinct people, was impossible, because they were as brave and as high spirited as they were fierce, and were ready to repel by arms every attempt on their independence.

What was the inevitable consequence of this state of things? The Europeans were under the necessity either of abandoning the country, and relinquishing their pompous claims to it, or of enforcing those claims by the sword, and by the adoption of principles adapted to the condition of a people with whom it was impossible to mix, and who could not be governed as a distinct society, or of remaining in their neighbourhood, and exposing themselves and their families to the perpetual hazard of being massacred.

Frequent and bloody wars, in which the whites were not always the aggressors, unavoidably ensued. European policy, numbers, and skill, prevailed. As the white population advanced, that of the Indians necessarily receded. The country in the immediate neighbourhood of agriculturists became unfit for them. The game fled into thicker and more unbroken forests, and the Indians followed. The soil, to which the crown originally claimed title, being no longer occupied by its ancient inhabitants, was parcelled out according to the will of the sovereign power, and taken possession of by persons who claimed immediately from the crown, or mediately, through its grantees or deputies.

That law which regulates, and ought to regulate in general, the relations between the conqueror and conquered, was incapable of application to a people under such circumstances. The resort to some new and different rule, better adapted to the actual state of things, was unavoidable. Every rule which can be suggested will be found to be attended with great difficulty.

However extravagant the pretension of converting the discovery of an inhabited country into conquest may appear; if the principle has been asserted in the first instance, and afterwards sustained; if a country has been acquired and held under it; if the property of the great mass of the community originates in it, it becomes the law of the land, and cannot be questioned. So, too, with respect to the concomitant principle, that the Indian inhabitants are to be considered merely as occupants, to be protected, indeed, while in peace, in the possession of their lands, but to be deemed incapable of transferring the absolute title to others. However this restriction may be opposed to natural right, and to the usages of civilized nations, yet, if it be indispensable to that system under which the country has been settled, and be adapted to the actual condition of the two people, it may, perhaps, be supported by reason, and certainly cannot be rejected by Courts of justice. . . .

It has never been contended, that the Indian title amounted to nothing. Their right of possession has never been questioned. The claim of government extends to the complete ultimate title, charged with this right of possession, and to the exclusive power of acquiring that right. . . .

After bestowing on this subject a degree of attention which was more required by the magnitude of the interest in litigation, and the able and elaborate arguments of the bar, than by its intrinsic difficulty, the Court is decidedly of opinion, that the plaintiffs do not exhibit a title which can be sustained in the Courts of the United States; and that there is no error in the judgment which was rendered against them in the District Court of Illinois.

Judgment affirmed, with costs.

LABOR AND UTILITY THEORIES OF PROPERTY

Chief Justice Marshall's opinion in *Johnson v. M'Intosh* is often associated with the labor theory of property developed by the English political philosopher John Locke. Locke was tremendously influential on early American thought, and Marshall and other educated people at the time would have been familiar with Locke's political philosophy. Locke's influence is still felt today, and if you studied political science or philosophy as an undergraduate, you probably are already familiar with him.

Locke's labor theory of property is a theory of initial ownership. Under this theory, a person becomes the owner of a previously unowned object by mixing her labor with that object. If, for example, I plow and farm a piece of unowned land, I become the owner of that land. Because I own my labor, I own the land with which I mixed my labor. My expending labor would, for Locke, justify my private ownership of the land.

FIRST IN TIME

Locke's focus on labor as a justification for ownership provided a theoretical basis for colonial powers to minimize Native American and other aboriginal claims to land. Colonial Europeans believed (often incorrectly) that aboriginal peoples did not farm the land. This belief led to the view that Europeans who mixed their labor with the land by farming had a superior claim to aboriginal peoples who hunted and gathered on the land. You can see some hints of this kind of reasoning in *Johnson v. M'Intosh*.

Labor also plays a role in a very different type of theoretical justification for private property. Utilitarian and economic theories of property justify private ownership through the benefits that a legal system of private property creates for society. Under these theories, private ownership benefits society by encouraging effort by private owners. By allowing people to preserve the fruits of their labor, the legal system of private property incentivizes effort and economic productivity. The influential utilitarian philosopher Jeremy Bentham put it this way in *The Theory of Legislation* (1789):

> Law does not say to man, *Labour, and I will reward you;* but it says: *Labour, and I will assure to you the enjoyment of the fruits of your labour—that natural and sufficient recompense which without me you cannot preserve; I will insure it by arresting the hand which may seek to ravish it from you.* If industry creates, it is law which preserves; if at the first moment we owe all to labour, at the second moment, and at every other, we are indebted for everything to law. (bk. II, pt. I, ch. VII)

Recall that Justice Livingston argued in his *Pierson v. Post* dissent that no hunter would get out of bed in the morning if at the end of the hunt "a saucy intruder" could come in and grab the pursued animal. As we discussed in the context of the rule of capture, Livingston might not have been correct in his assessment of which rule would incentivize the most labor. Livingston's argument, however, is a good example of the widespread influence and potential scope of labor-maximizing theories of property. Beyond providing a justification for systems of private ownership, these theories suggest that we should tailor our specific rules of property to best incentivize labor and economic productivity.

NOTES AND QUESTIONS

1. There are a lot of reasons why you might not like the holding of *Johnson v. M'Intosh*. Indeed, it is not clear that Chief Justice Marshall liked the holding—if you read the case closely, you will find places where he seems to indicate some embarrassment with his own analysis. Put yourself in Marshall's shoes. How would you have decided the case and why? What would have been the practical effect of deciding the case in favor of the plaintiffs, who had purchased the land from the Native American tribes?

2. An overarching theme of this chapter is the relationship between the rights of possession, use, alienation, and exclusion. What, exactly, does Chief Justice Marshall say about Native American rights to possess and alienate? How valuable or useful is one without the other?

2. ADVERSE POSSESSION

Imagine that you own property in a remote rural area. You have not visited the property in many years. One day you decide to drive out to see the property, and you discover that someone is living there. We will call this person the Adverse Possessor. After asking around, you find out that the Adverse Possessor has been on your property for the past 20 years. If the circumstances are right, the Adverse Possessor might have acquired title to your property by adverse possession. In other words, you might not own the property anymore.

Adverse possession is a product of the statute of limitations. When the Adverse Possessor first entered your property, you could have brought an action for trespass or ejectment to kick the person off. If enough time has passed, the statute of limitations might have run on your action against the Adverse Possessor. Because you cannot bring an action to get the Adverse Possessor off of your property, title passes from you to the Adverse Possessor.

Each state's statute of limitations will set the time for bringing an action for trespass or ejectment. In most states, this time period will be somewhere in the range of 10-21 years. Although adverse possession is rooted in the statute of limitations, the actual operation of the doctrine involves a number of elements that have been developed by the common-law courts. You will see the elements of adverse possession stated in various different ways, and each has its complexities. Here are the basics:

1. The adverse possessor must make an *actual entry giving exclusive possession*. The entry by the adverse possessor starts the statute of limitations clock running. We have talked a lot about the idea of possession already and know that it involves intent and control. So the adverse possessor must intend to possess the property and must exert some degree of control over it. As we suggested at the outset of this unit, thinking about adverse possession will give us an opportunity to think about how we demonstrate possession of real property.

2. The adverse possession must be *open and notorious*. The adverse possessor can't hide the possession. If the adverse possessor uses the property in the same way as a typical owner, then this element will typically be met. (Note here the connection between possession and use.) There are exceptions, though, as we will see in both the *Marengo Cave* and *Mannillo v. Gorski* cases.

3. The adverse possession must be *adverse and under a claim of right*. This element goes to the adverse possessor's state of mind. There are three possible approaches to this element: (a) The "objective standard" holds that the adverse possessor's state of mind is irrelevant. (b) The "good-faith" standard requires that the adverse possessor honestly believe that the adverse possessor owned the property. In other words, this standard requires the adverse possession to have been the result of an honest mistake. (c) The "bad faith" or "aggressive trespasser" standard requires that the adverse possessor know that the property was owned by someone else. In other words, this standard requires the adverse possession to have been motivated by a conscious desire to acquire someone else's property. *See* Margaret Jane Radin, *Time, Possession, and Alienation*, 64 Wash. U. L.Q. 739, 746-747 (1986). We will consider these alternatives in *Mannillo v. Gorski*.

4. The adverse possession must be *continuous for the statutory period*. This element requires that the statutory time period be met. This seemingly simple issue can be very complex, as we will see in *Howard v. Kunto*.

As we mentioned, these basic elements of adverse possession can be stated in different ways by different courts. We begin with the classic *Marengo Cave* case. As you will see, the court in *Marengo Cave* organizes the adverse possession elements slightly differently than we have, but we think it will be fairly easy for you to fit the court's analysis into our framework. This classic case involves a dispute about a claim of adverse possession of part of a cave. It is an excellent introduction to the concept of adverse possession, and because it involves a claim of adverse possession of something underground, it gives us a very good opportunity to think in detail about the open and notorious element.

THE *AD COLEUM* DOCTRINE

Under the *ad coleum* doctrine, the owner of the surface also owns the airspace above and the subsurface below. The doctrine takes its name from the Latin maxim *cuius est solum, eius est usque ad coelum et ad inferos*—whoever owns the soil owns all the way to heaven and to hell. Taken literally, the surface owner would own from the center of the earth to the edge of space. In practice, the scope of ownership is not so broad. Surface owners do own some airspace above their land, but upward ownership is limited to the extent that it would interfere with air travel. *See United States v. Causby*, 328 U.S. 256 (1946). Downward ownership of the subsurface might also be limited. *See* John G. Sprankling, *Owning the Center of the Earth*, 55 U.C.L.A. L. Rev. 979 (2008). This said, our default position is that the surface owner will own minerals and other natural resources located below the surface. The surface owner will also own caves below the surface. This is only our default position, however, because subsurface ownership can be separated from surface ownership. For example, the surface owner could transfer the right to extract subsurface minerals to a mining company. The process of separating mineral ownership from surface ownership is often called *severance*—a term you will see in the *Marengo Cave* case. Similarly, the surface owner can transfer some air rights. For example, in some circumstances, the right to build a tower above a particular piece of land can be transferred from the owner of the surface to a different person.

MARENGO CAVE CO. V. ROSS

Supreme Court of Indiana, 1937
212 Ind. 624, 10 N.E.2d 917

ROLL, Judge. Appellee and appellant were the owners of adjoining land in Crawford county, Ind. On appellant's land was located the opening to a subterranean cavity known as "Marengo Cave." This cave extended under a considerable portion of appellant's land, and the southeastern portion thereof extended under lands owned by appellee. This action arose out of a dispute as to the ownership of that part of the cave that extended under appellee's land. Appellant was claiming title to all the cave and davities, including that portion underlying appellee's land. Appellee instituted this action to quiet his title as by a general denial and filed a cross-complaint by a general denial and filed a crosscomplaint wherein he sought to quiet its title to all the cave, including that portion underlying appellee's land. There was a trial by jury which returned a verdict for the appellee. Appellant filed its motion for a new trial which was overruled by the court, and this the only error assigned on appeal. Appellant assigns as grounds for a new trial that the verdict of the jury is not sustained by sufficient evidence, and is contrary to law. These are the only grounds urged for a reversal of this cause.

The facts as shown by the record are substantially as follows: In 1883 one Stewart owned the real estate now owned by appellant, and in September of that year some young people who were upon that land discovered what afterwards proved to be the entrance to the cavern since known as Marengo Cave, this entrance being approximately 700 feet from the boundary line between the lands now owned by appellant and appellee, and the only entrance to said cave. Within a week after discovery of the cave, it was explored, and the fact of its existence received wide publicity through newspaper articles, and otherwise. Shortly thereafter the then owner of the real estate upon which the entrance was located took complete possession of the entire cave as now occupied by appellant and used for exhibition purposes, and began to charge an admission fee to those who desired to enter and view the cave, and to exclude therefrom those who were unwilling to pay for admission. This practice continued from 1883, except in some few instances when persons were permitted by the persons claiming to own said cave to enter same without payment of the usual required fee, and during the following years the successive owners of the land upon which the entrance to the cave was located, advertised the existence of said cave through newspapers, magazines, posters, and otherwise, in order to attract visitors thereto; also made improvements within the cave, including the building of concrete walks, and concrete steps where there was a difference in elevation of said cavern, widened and heightened portions of passageways; had available and furnished guides, all in order to make the cave more easily accessibly to visitors desiring to view the same; and continuously, during all this time, without asking or obtaining consent from any one, but claiming a right so to do, held and possessed said subterranean passages constituting said cave, excluding therefrom the "whole world," except such persons as entered after paying admission for the privilege of so doing, or by permission.

Appellee has lived in the vicinity of said cave since 1903, and purchased the real estate which he now owns in 1908. He first visited the cave in 1895, paying an admission fee for the privilege, and has visited said cave several times since. He has never, at any time, occupied or been in possession of any of the subterranean passages or cavities of which the cave consists, and the possession and use of the cave by those who have done so has never interfered with his use and enjoyment of the lands owned by him. For a period of approximately 25 years prior to the time appellee purchased his land, and for a period of 21 years afterwards, exclusive possession of the cave has been held by appellant, its immediate and remote grantors.

The cave, as such, has never been listed for taxation separately from the real estate wherein it is located, and the owners of the respective tracts of land have paid the taxes assessed against said tracts.

A part of said cave at the time of its discovery and exploration extended beneath real estate now owned by appellee, but this fact was not ascertained until the year 1932, when the boundary line between the respective tracts through the cave was established by means of a survey made by a civil engineer pursuant to an order of court entered in this cause. Previous to this survey neither of the parties to this appeal, nor any of their predecessors in title, knew that any part of the cave was in fact beneath the surface of a portion of the land now owned by appellee. Possession of the cave was taken and held by appellant's remote and immediate grantors, improvements made, and control exercised, with the belief on the part of such grantors that the entire cave as it was explored and held was under the surface of lands owned by them. There is no evidence of and dispute as to ownership of the cave, or any portion thereof, prior to the time when in 1929 appellee requested a survey, which was approximately 46 years after discovery of the cave and the exercise of complete dominion thereover by appellant and its predecessors in title.

It is appellant's contention that it has a fee-simple title to all of the cave; that it owns that part underlying appellee's land by adverse possession. Section 2-602, Burns' Ann. St.1933, section 61, Baldwin's Ind.St.1934, provides as follows: "The following actions shall be commenced within the periods herein prescribed after the cause of action has accrued, and not afterward: . . . Sixth. Upon contracts in writing other than those for the payment of money, on judgments of courts of record, and for the recovery of the possession of real estate, within twenty (20) years."

It will be noted that appellee nor his predecessors in title had never effected a severance of the cave from the surface estate. Therefore the title of the appellee extends from the surface to the center but actual possession is confined to the surface. Appellee and his immediate and remote grantors have been in possession of the land and estate here in question at all times, unless it can be said that the possession of the cave by appellant as shown by the evidence above set out has met all the requirements of the law relating to the acquisition of land by adverse possession. A record title may be defeated by adverse possession. All the authorities agree that, before the owner of the legal title can be deprived of his land by another's possession, through the operation of the statute of limitation, the possession must have been actual, visible, notorious, exclusive, under claim of ownership and hostile to the owner of the legal title and to the world at large (except only the government), and continuous for the full period prescribed by the statute. The rule is not always stated in exactly the same words in the many cases dealing with the subject of adverse possession, yet the rule is so thoroughly settled that there is no doubt as to what elements are essential to establish a title by adverse possession. *Craven v. Craven* (1913) 181 Ind. 553, 103 N.E. 333, 105 N.E. 41; *Rennert v. Shirk* (1904) 163 Ind. 542, 72 N.E. 546; *Vandalia R. Co. v. Wheeler* (1914) 181 Ind. 424, 103 N.E. 1069; *Tolley v. Thomas* (1910) 46 Ind.App. 559, 93 N.E. 181; *McBeth v. Wetnight* (1914) 57 Ind.App. 47, 106 N.E. 407. Let us examine the various elements that are essential to establish title by adverse possession and apply them to the facts that are established by the undisputed facts in this case.

(1) The possession must be actual. It must be conceded that appellant in the operation of the "Marengo Cave" used not only the cavern under its own land but also that part of the cavern that underlaid appellee's land, and assumed dominion over all of it. Yet it must also be conceded that during all of the time appellee was in constructive possession, as the only constructive possession known to the law is that which inheres in the legal title and with which the owner of that title is always endowed. *Morrison v. Kelly* (1859) 22 Ill. 609, 610, 74 Am.Dec. 169; *Cook v. Clinton* (1887) 64 Mich. 309, 31 N.W. 317, 8 Am.St.Rep. 816; *Ables v. Webb* (1905) 186 Mo. 233, 85 S.W. 383, 105 Am.St.Rep. 610; 1 R.C.L. 692; 2 C.J. 51 et seq. and authorities there cited. Whether the possession was actual under the peculiar facts in this case we need not decide.

(2) The possession must be visible. The owner of land who, having notice of the fact that it is occupied by another who is claiming dominion over it, nevertheless stands by during the entire statutory period and makes no effort to eject the claimant or otherwise protect his title, ought not to be permitted, for reasons of public policy, thereafter to maintain an action for the recovery of his land. But, the authorities assert, in order that the possession of the occupying claimant may constitute notice in law, it must be visible and open to the common observer so that the owner or his agent on visiting the premises might readily see that the owner's rights are being invaded. *Holcroft v. Hunter* (1832) 3 Blackf. 147; *Towle v. Quante* (1910) 246 Ill. 568, 92 N.E. 967; *Tinker v. Bessel* (1912) 213 Mass. 74, 99 N.E. 946; *Jasperson v. Scharnikow* (1907) 150 F. 571, 80 C.C.A. 373, 15 L.R.A. (N.S.) 1178 and note. What constitutes open and visible possession has been stated in general terms, thus; it is necessary and sufficient if its nature and character is such as is calculated to apprise the world that the land is occupied and who the occupant is;

Dempsey v. Burns (1917) 281 Ill. 644, 118 N.E. 193, and such an appropriation of the land by claimant as to apprise, or convey visible notice to the community or neighborhood in which it is situated that it is in his exclusive use and enjoyment. *Goodrich v. Mortimer* (1919) 44 Cal.App. 576, 186 P. 844. It has been declared that the disseisor "must unfurl his flag" on the land, and "keep it flying," so that the owner may see, if he will, that an enemy has invaded his domains, and planted the standard of conquest. *Robin v. Brown* (1932) 308 Pa. 123, 162 A. 161; *Willamette Real Estate Co. v. Hendrix* (1895) 28 Or. 485, 42 P. 514, 52 Am.St.Rep. 800; *People's Savings Bank v. Bufford* (1916) 90 Wash. 204, 155 P. 1068; 1 Amer.Juris. p. 865.

(3) The possession must be open and notorious. The mere possession of the land is not enough. It is knowledge, either actual or imputed, of the possession of his lands by another, claiming to own them bona fide and openly, that affects the legal owner thereof. Where there has been no actual notice, it is necessary to show that the possession of the disseisor was so open, notorious, and visible as to warrant the inference that the owner must or should have known of it. In *Philbin v. Carr* (1920) 75 Ind.App. 560, 129 N.E. 19, 29, 706, it was said: "However, in order that the possession of the occupying claimant may constitute notice in law, it must be visible and open to the common observer so that the owner or his agent on visiting the premises might readily see that the owner's rights are being invaded. In accordance with the general rule applicable to the subject of constructive notice, before possession can operate as such notice, it must be clear and unequivocal." *Holcroft v. Hunter* (1832) 3 Blackf. 147; *Towle v. Quante supra.*

And again, the possession must be notorious. It must be so conspicuous that it is generally known and talked of by the public. "It must be manifest to the community." Thus, the Appellate Court said in *Philbin v. Carr supra*, that: "Where the persons who have passed frequently over and along the premises have been unable to see any evidence of occupancy, evidently the possession has not been of the character required by the rule. The purpose of this requirement is to support the principle that a legal title will not be extinguished on flimsy and uncertain evidence. Hence, where there has been no actual notice, the possession must have been so notorious as to warrant the inference that the owner ought to have known that a stranger was asserting dominion over his land. Insidious, desultory, and fugitive acts will not serve that purpose. To have that effect the possession should be clear and satisfactory, not doubtful and equivocal." See cases there cited on page 585 of 75 Ind.App., 129 N.E. 19, 28, 706.

(4) The possession must be exclusive. It is evident that two or more persons cannot hold one tract of land adversely to each other at the same time. "It is essential that the possession of one who claims adversely must be of such an exclusive character that it will operate as an ouster of the owner of the legal title; because, in the absence of ouster the legal title draws to itself the constructive possession of the land. A possession which

does not amount to an ouster or disseisin is not sufficient." *Philbin v. Carr, supra.* See cases cited on page 585 of 75 Ind.App., 129 N.E. 19, 28, 706.

The facts as set out above show that appellee and his predecessors in title have been in actual and continuous possession of his real estate since the cave was discovered in 1883. At no time were they aware that any one was trespassing upon their land. No one was claiming to be in possession of appellee's land. It is true that appellant was asserting possession of the "Marengo Cave." There would seem to be quite a difference in making claim to the "Marengo Cave," and making claim to a portion of appellee's land, even though a portion of the cave extended under appellee's land, when this latter fact was unknown to any one. The evidence on both sides of this case is to the effect that the "Marengo Cave" was thought to be altogether under the land owned by appellant, and this erroneous supposition was not revealed until a survey was made at the request of appellee and ordered by the court in this case. It seems to us that the following excerpt from *Lewey v. H. C. Frick Coke Co.* (1895) 166 Pa. 536, 31 A. 261, 263, 28 L.R.A. 283, 45 Am.St.Rep. 684, is peculiarly applicable to the situation here presented, inasmuch as we are dealing with an underground cavity. It was stated in the above case:

> "The title of the plaintiff extends from the surface to the center, but actual possession is confined to the surface. Upon the surface he must be held to know all that the most careful observation by himself and his employés could reveal, unless his ignorance is induced by the fraudulent conduct of the wrongdoer. But in the coal veins, deep down in the earth, he cannot see. Neither in person nor by his servants nor employés can he explore their recesses in seach for an intruder. If an adjoining owner goes beyond his own boundaries in the course of his mining operations, the owner on whom he enters has no means of knowledge within his reach. Nothing short of an accurate survey of the interior of his neighbor's mines would enable him to ascertain the fact. This would require the services of a competent mining engineer and his assistants, inside the mines of another, which he would have no right to insist upon. To require an owner, under such circumstances, to take notice of a trespass upon his underlying coal at the time it takes place, is to require an impossibility; and to hold that the statute begins to run at the date of the trespass is in most cases to take away the remedy of the injured party before he can know that an injury has been done him. A result so absurd and so unjust ought not to be possible. . . .

> "The reason for the distinction exists in the nature of things. The owner of land may be present by himself or his servants on the surface of his possessions, no matter how extensive they may be. He is for this reason held to be constructively present wherever his title extends. He cannot be present in the interior of the earth. No amount of vigilance will enable him to detect the approach of a trespasser who may be working his way through the coal seams underlying adjoining lands. His senses cannot inform him of the encroachment by such trespasser upon the

coal that is hidden in the rocks under his feet. He cannot reasonably be held to be constructively present where his presence is, in the nature of things, impossible. He must learn of such a trespass by other means than such as are within his own control, and, until these come within his reach, he is necessarily ignorant of his loss. He cannot reasonably be required to act until knowledge that action is needed is possible to him."

We are not persuaded that this case falls within the rule of mistaken boundary as announced in *Rennert v. Shirk* (1904) 163 Ind. 542, 72 N.E. 546, 549, wherein this court said: "Appellant insists, however, that, if one takes and holds possession of real estate under a mistake as to where the true boundary line is, such possession cannot ripen into a title. In this state, when an owner of land, by mistake as to the boundary line of his land, takes actual, visible, and exclusive possession of another's land, and holds it as his own continuously for the statutory period of 20 years, he thereby acquires the title as against the real owner. The possession is regarded as adverse, without reference to the fact that it is based on mistake; it being prima facie sufficient that actual, visible, and exclusive possession is taken under a claim of right."

The reason for the above rule is obvious. Under such circumstances appellant was in possession of the necessary means of ascertaining the true boundary line, and to hold that a mere misapprehension on the part of appellant as to the true boundary line would nullify the well-established law on adverse possession. In that case appellee had actual, visible, notorious, and exclusive possession. The facts in the present case are far different. Here the possession of appellant was not visible. No one could see below the earth's surface and determine that appellant was trespassing upon appellee's lands. This fact could not be determined by going into the cave. Only by a survey could this fact be made known. The same undisputed facts clearly show that appellant's possession was not notorious. Not even appellant itself nor any of its remote grantors knew that any part of the "Marengo Cave" extended beyond its own boundaries, and they at no time even down to the time appellee instituted this action made any claim to appellee's lands. Appellee and his predecessors in title at all times have been in possession of the land which he is now claiming. No severance by deed or written instrument was ever made to the cave, from the surface. In the absence of a separate estate could appellant be in the exclusive possession of the cave that underlies appellee's land.

"If there is no severance, an entry upon the surface will extend downward, and draw to it a title to the underlying minerals; so that he who disseises another, and acquires title by the statute of limitations, will succeed to the estate of him upon whose possession he has entered." *Delaware & Hudson Canal Co. v. Hughes* (1897) 183 Pa. 66, 38 A. 568, 570, 38 L.R.A. 826, 63 Am.St.Rep. 743.

Even though it could be said that appellant's possession has been actual, exclusive, and continuous all these years, we would still be of the opinion that appellee has not lost his land. It has been the uniform rule in equity that the statute of limitation does not begin to run until the injured party discovers, or with reasonable diligence might have discovered, the facts constituting the injury and cause of action. Until then the owner cannot know that his possession has been invaded. Until he has knowledge, or ought to have such knowledge, he is not called upon to act, for he does not know that action in the premises is necessary and the law does not require absurd or impossible things of any one. *Lewey v. Frick Coke Co.* (1895) 166 Pa. 536, 31 A. 261, 28 L.R.A. 283, 45 Am.St. Rep. 684; *Delaware & Hudson Canal Co. v. Hughes, supra.*

In the case of *Bailey v. Glover* (1874) 21 Wall. (88 U.S.) 342, 348, 22 L.Ed. 636, the court said:

> "We also think that in suits in equity the decided weight of authority is in favor of the proposition that where the party injured by the fraud remains in ignorance of it without any fault or want of diligence or care on his part, the bar of the statute does not begin to run until the fraud is discovered, though there be no special circumstances or efforts on the part of the party committing the fraud to conceal it from the knowledge of the other party. . . .
>
> "To hold that by concealing a fraud, or by committing a fraud in a manner that it concealed itself until such time as the party committing the fraud could plead the statute of limitations to protect it, is to make the law which was designed to prevent fraud the means by which it is made successful and secure."

In *Livingston v. Rawyards* (1880) L.R. 5 App.Cas. 34, Lord Hatherly treats an underground trespass as a species of fraud. While there is no active fraud shown in this case, yet the facts come clearly within the case of *Lightner Mining Co. v. Lane* (1911) 161 Cal. 689, 120 P. 771, 776, and cases cited on page 776, Ann.Cas.1913C, 1093. The following excerpt from this opinion clearly sets forth our view:

> "In the English decisions the willful and secret taking of coal from a neighbor's mine is usually characterized as fraudulent. *Hilton v. Woods*, L.R. 4 Eq.Cas. 440; *Dean v. Thwaite*, 21 Beav. 623; *Ecclesiastical Coms. v. North E. Ry. Co.*, L.R. 4, Ch.Div. 860; *Trotter v. McLean*, L.R. 13, Ch.Div. 586. Such an act, so committed, has all the substantial elements of fraud. Where one by misrepresentation induces another knowingly to part with his property, because his mind is so beclouded by the falsehood that he is unaware of the wrong done him, it is called a fraud. It is a taking of another's property without his knowledge of the fact that it is really taken from him. The ignorance in that case is produced by artifice. Where one betrays a trust and appropriates trust property to his own use, it is called a fraud. The injured party allows the other to have the possession and the opportunity to convert the property secretly, because of faith and confidence in the wrongdoer. In the case of underground mining of a neighbor's ore, nature has supplied the situation which

gives the opportunity to the trespasser to take it secretly and causes the ignorance of the owner. Relying upon this ignorance, he takes an unfair advantage of his natural opportunities, and thereby clandestinely appropriates another's property while appearing to be making only a lawful use of his own. The act in its very nature constitutes the deceit which makes it a fraud."

So in the case at bar, appellant pretended to use the "Marengo Cave" as his property and all the time he was committing a trespass upon appellee's land. After 20 years of secret user, he now urges the statute of limitation, section 2-602, Burns' St.1933, section 61, Baldwin's Ind.St.1934, as a bar to appellee's action. Appellee did not know of the trespass of appellant, and had no reasonable means of discovering the fact. It is true that appellant took no active measures to prevent the discovery, except to deny appellee the right to enter the cave for the purpose of making a survey, and disclaiming any use of appellee's lands, but nature furnished the concealment, or where the wrong conceals itself. It amounts to the taking of another's property without his knowledge of the fact that it is really being taken from him. In most cases the ignorance is produced by artifice. But in this case nature has supplied the situation which gives the trespasser the opportunity to occupy the recesses on appellee's land and caused the ignorance of appellee which he now seeks to avail himself. We cannot assent to the doctrine that would enable one to trespass upon another's property through a subterranean passage and under such circumstances that the owner does not know, or by the exercise of reasonable care could not know, of such secret occupancy, for 20 years or more and by so doing obtained a fee-simple title as against the holder of the legal title. The fact that appellee had knowledge that appellant was claiming to be the owner of the "Marengo Cave," and advertised it to the general public, was no knowledge to him that it was in possession of appellee's land or any part of it. We are of the opinion that appellant's possession for 20 years or more of that part of "Marengo Cave" underlying appellee's land was not open, notorious, or exclusive, as required by the law applicable to obtaining title to land by adverse possession.

We cannot say that the evidence is not sufficient to support the verdict or that the verdict is contrary to law.

Judgment affirmed.

NOTES AND QUESTIONS

1. *Open and Notorious*: As we noted at the outset, the facts of *Marengo Cave* give us a good opportunity to think about the open and notorious element. To be sure that you have a good handle on the court's analysis of this element, answer the following questions. Why, exactly, was the possession by the Marengo Cave Company not open and notorious? What, if anything, could the company have done differently that would have changed the outcome? What is the court's view of the purpose of the open and

notorious element? The court treated visibility as a separate, but related, element. Modern courts would typically consider visibility as a subset of the open and notorious element. Do you think that considering visibility separately adds anything to the analysis?

2. *Adversity*. We will leave an in-depth discussion of the adversity element to our next case. Recall from our introductory materials that this element gets at the adverse possessor's state of mind. An adverse possessor can either have a good faith state of mind or a bad faith state of mind. Cases of good faith adverse possession involve an honest mistake—the adverse possessor thought she owned the property, but in fact did not. Cases of bad faith adverse possession involve a knowing and intentional effort to possess someone else's property. Which state of mind did the adverse possessor in *Marengo Cave* have? Do you think that it may have changed over time?

3. *The Discovery Rule and the Statute of Limitations*. Toward the end of the opinion, the court cites cases that equate underground trespass with fraud. Under the *discovery rule*, the statute of limitations period typically does not start to run in fraud cases until the victim discovers the fraud. The rule makes sense because victims cannot bring actions against the perpetrators of the fraud if they are not aware of the fraud. Can you see how an underground trespass case is similar to a fraud case, even if the underground trespasser had a good faith state of mind? More broadly, can you see how there is a similar logic behind both the discovery rule and the open and notorious element of adverse possession?

ADVERSE POSSESSION OF PERSONAL PROPERTY

Adverse possession of personal property operates in a similar way to adverse possession of real property. Over time, the statute of limitations on an action for replevin will expire, and the adverse possessor will own the personal property. The open and notorious element, however, presents a major hurdle to the adverse possessor of personal property. Imagine, for example, that you are the true owner of a painting. I currently possess the painting and have it hanging in my living room. Even though I am not doing anything to hide my possession, it is hard to see how my possession is open and notorious. It is possible, of course, to imagine the open and notorious possession of personal property. For example, if the painting was famous and was hanging in a museum open to the public, the possession of the painting might very well be open and notorious.

Perhaps the most famous case involving adverse possession of personal property is *O'Keeffe v. Snyder*, 416 A.2d 862 (N.J. 1980). *O'Keeffe* involved a dispute between Georgia O'Keeffe and a gallery owner about the ownership of three of her paintings. Using an analysis that you would find familiar from our discussion of underground trespass, the court applied the discovery rule and held that the statute of limitations clock does not run against the owner of personal property until she knows, or should have known, that the property was possessed by the putative adverse possessor.

CONSTRUCTIVE ADVERSE POSSESSION AND COLOR OF TITLE

Legal title to property gives the owner constructive possession of that property. If, for example, you own title to Blackacre, you constructively possess Blackacre, even if you are not in actual possession of Blackacre. The court referenced this rule in *Marengo Cave*, when it noted "that during all of the time appellee was in constructive possession, as the only constructive possession known to the law is that which inheres in the legal title and with which the owner of that title is always endowed." Actual possession, however, trumps constructive possession. As a result, constructive possession does not help the owner in the adverse possession context, because the adverse possessor's actual possession will win against the owner's constructive possession.

There is one context in which constructive possession may help the adverse possessor. Typically, a successful adverse possessor will obtain ownership only of the land that she actually possessed.

EXAMPLE 1: Imagine that Blackacre is a ten-acre parcel. If Adverse Possessor actually possesses one of the ten acres and meets all of the other elements of adverse possession, then she will own that one acre. Owner will still own the other nine acres of Blackacre that Adverse Possessor did not possess.

The exception to this general rule is when the adverse possessor takes possession under *color of title*. Color of title refers to a circumstance where the adverse possessor takes possession in reliance on some kind of written instrument that appears to give title to the property, but that is defective for some reason. The idea is that the adverse possessor has a written document—typically a deed or will—that appears to give title to the land, but the document is invalid. Perhaps the written document is a forged deed, or a will that was improperly executed. The defective document gives the adverse possessor color of title, even though it does not give actual title. The benefit of color of title is that it gives the adverse possessor constructive possession of all of the property described by the document. As a result, the adverse possessor may obtain title to all of the property described by the document, not just the property actually possessed by the adverse possessor. In jurisdictions that recognize constructive adverse possession, the adverse possessor's constructive possession under color of title will trump the owner's constructive possession as the actual title holder of the property.

EXAMPLE 2: As with Example 1, imagine that Blackacre is a ten-acre parcel, that Adverse Possessor only possessed one of the ten acres, and that Adverse Possessor otherwise met all of the elements of adverse possession. In this example, however, Adverse Possessor has taken possession under color of title under a defective deed that describes the entire ten acres. In these circumstances, Adverse Possessor will own all ten acres—one acre that she actually possessed and nine acres that she constructively possessed.

Recall that actual possession will always trump constructive possession. The owner of the property will therefore be able to defeat the adverse possessor's constructive possession under color of title for land that the owner actually possessed.

EXAMPLE 3: As with Examples 1 and 2, Blackacre is a ten-acre parcel, Adverse Possessor only possessed one of the ten acres, and Adverse Possessor met all of the other elements of adverse possession. As with Example 2, Adverse Possessor has take possession under color of title under a defective deed that describes all ten acres. Now, however, Owner actually possessed the other nine acres. In other words, of the ten acres, Adverse Possessor actually possessed one and Owner possessed nine. The Owner's actual possession of those nine acres will be superior to the Adverse Possessor's constructive possession of the under color of title. As a result, Adverse Possessor will only gain ownership of the one acre she actually possessed, and Owner will retain ownership of the other nine acres.

Recall that in our introduction to the elements of adverse possession, we noted that the "adverse and under a claim of right" element turned on the adverse possessor's state of mind. We also noted that there are three potential standards for this element:

a. The "objective standard" holds that the adverse possessor's state of mind is irrelevant.
b. The "good-faith" standard requires that the adverse possessor honestly believe that the adverse possessor owned the property. In other words, this standard requires the adverse possession to have been the result of an honest mistake.
c. The "bad faith" or "aggressive trespasser" standard requires that the adverse possessor know that the property was owned by someone else. In other words, this standard requires the adverse possession to have been motivated by a conscious desire to acquire someone else's property.

Our next case includes an in-depth discussion of this element. Think about how the standards discussed in the case map on to our three options. We will return to this issue in the notes after the case.

MANNILLO V. GORSKI

Supreme Court of New Jersey, 1969
255 A.2d 258

HANEMAN, J.

Plaintiffs filed a complaint in the Chancery Division seeking a mandatory and prohibitory injunction against an alleged trespass upon their lands. Defendant counterclaimed for a declaratory judgment which would adjudicate that she had gained title to the disputed premises by adverse possession under N.J.S. 2A:14-6, N.J.S.A., which provides:

> "Every person having any right or title of entry into real estate shall make such entry within 20 years next after the accrual of such right or title of entry, or be barred therefrom thereafter."

After plenary trial, judgment was entered for plaintiffs. *Mannillo v. Gorski*, 100 N.J. Super. 140, 241 A.2d 276 (Ch.Div.1968). Defendant appealed to the Appellate Division. Before argument there, this Court granted defendant's motion for certification. R.R. 1:10-1a.

The facts are as follows: In 1946, defendant and her husband entered into possession of premises in Keansburg known as Lot No. 1007 in Block 42, under an agreement to purchase. Upon compliance with the terms of said agreement, the seller conveyed said lands to them on April 16, 1952. Defendant's husband thereafter died. The property consisted of a rectangular lot with a frontage of 25 feet and a depth of 100 feet. Plaintiffs are the owners of the adjacent Lot 1008 in Block 42 of like dimensions, to which they acquired title in 1953.

In the summer of 1946 Chester Gorski, one of the defendant's sons, made certain additions and changes to the defendant's house. He extended two rooms at the rear of the structure, enclosed a screened porch on the front, and put a concrete platform with steps on the west side thereof for use in connection with a side door. These steps were built to replace existing wooden steps. In addition, a concrete walk was installed from the steps to the end of the house. In 1953, defendant raised the house. In order to compensate for the resulting added height from the ground, she modified the design of the steps by extending them toward both the front and the rear of the property. She did not change their width.

Defendant admits that the steps and concrete walk encroach upon plaintiffs' lands to the extent of 15 inches. She contends, however, that she has title to said land by adverse possession. N.J.S.A. 2A:14-6, quoted above. Plaintiffs assert contrawise that defendant did not obtain title by adverse possession as her possession was not of the requisite hostile nature. They argue that to establish title by adverse possession, the entry into and continuance of possession must be accompanied by an intention to invade the rights of another in the lands, I.e., a knowing wrongful taking. They assert that, as defendant's encroachment was not accompanied by an intention to invade plaintiffs' rights in the land, but rather by the mistaken belief that she owned the land, and that therefore an essential requisite to establish title by adverse possession, I.e., an intentional tortious taking, is lacking.

The trial court concluded that defendant had clearly and convincingly proved that her possession of the 15-inch encroachment had existed for more than 20 years before the institution of this suit and that such possession was "exclusive, continuous, uninterrupted, visible, notorious and against the right and interest of the true owner." There is ample evidence to sustain this finding except as to its visible and notorious nature, of which more hereafter. However, the judge felt impelled by existing New Jersey case law, holding as argued by plaintiffs above, to deny defendant's claim and entered judgment for plaintiffs. 100 N.J. Super, at 150, 241 A.2d 276. The first issue before this Court is, therefore, whether an entry and continuance of possession under the mistaken belief that the possessor has title to the lands involved, exhibits the requisite hostile possession to sustain the obtaining of title by adverse possession.

The first detailed statement and acceptance by our then highest court, of the principle that possession as an element of title by adverse possession cannot be bottomed on mistake, is found in *Folkman v. Myers*, 93 N.J. Eq. 208, 115 A. 615 (E. & A. 1921), which embraced and followed that thesis as expressed in *Myers v. Folkman*, 89 N.J.L. 390, 99 A. 97 (Sup.Ct.1916). . . . In so doing, the former Court of Errors and Appeals aligned this State with that branch of a dichotomy which traces its genesis to *Preble v. Maine Cent. R. Co.*, 85 Me. 260, 27 A. 149, 21 L.R.A. 829 (Sup.Jud.Ct.Me.1893) and has become known as the Maine doctrine. In *Preble*, the court said at 27 A. at p. 150:

> "There is every presumption that the occupancy is in subordination to the true title, and, if the possession is claimed to be adverse, the act of the wrongdoer must be strictly construed, and the character of the possession clearly shown. *Roberts v. Richards*, 84 Me. 1, 24 Atl.Rep. 425, and authorities cited. 'The intention of the possessor to claim adversely,' says Mellen, C.J., in *Ross v. Gould, supra* (5 Me. 204), 'is an essential ingredient in disseisin.' And in *Worcester v. Lord, supra* (56 Me. 266) the court says: 'To make a disseisin in fact, there must be an intention on the part of the party assuming possession to assert title in himself.' Indeed, the authorities all agree that this intention of the occupant to claim the ownership of land not embraced in his title is a necessary element of adverse possession; and in case of occupancy by mistake beyond a line capable of being ascertained this intention to claim title to the extent of the occupancy must appear to be absolute, and not conditional; otherwise the possession will not be deemed adverse to the true owner. It must be an intention to claim title to all land within a certain boundary on the face of the earth, whether it shall eventually be found to be the correct one or not. If, for instance, one in ignorance of his actual boundaries takes and holds possession by mistake up to a certain fence beyond his limits, upon the claim and in the belief that it is the true line, with the intention to claim title, and thus, if necessary, to acquire 'title by possession' up to that fence, such possession, having the requisite duration and continuity, will ripen into title. *Hitchings v. Morrison*, 72 Me. 331, is a pertinent illustration of this principle. *See, also, Abbott v. Abbott*, 51 Me. 575; *Ricker v. Hibbard*, 73 Me. 105.
>
> If, on the other hand, a party through ignorance, inadvertence, or mistake occupies up to a given fence beyond his actual boundary, because he believes it to be the true line, but has no intention to claim title to that extent if it should be ascertained that the fence was on his neighbor's land, an indispensable element of adverse possession is wanting. In such a case the intent to claim title exists only

upon the condition that the fence is on the true line. The intention is not absolute, but provisional, and the possession is not adverse."

This thesis, it is evident, rewards the possessor who entered with a premeditated and predesigned "hostility"—the intentional wrongdoer and disfavors an honest, mistaken entrant. 3 *American Law of Property* (Casner ed. 1952), §104, pp. 773, 785; Bordwell, "Desseisin and Adverse Possession," 33 Yale L.J. 1, 154 (1923); Darling, "Adverse Possession in Boundary Cases," 19 Ore.L.Rev. 117 (1940); Sternberg, "The Element of Hostility in Adverse Possession," 6 Temp.L.Q. 206 (1932); Annotation, "Adverse possession involving ignorance or mistake as to boundaries—modern views," 80 A.L.R.2d 1171 (1961).

The other branch of the dichotomy relies upon *French v. Pearce*, 8 Conn. 439 (Sup. Ct.Conn.1831). The court said in Pearce on the question of the subjective hostility of a possessor, at pp. 442, 445-446:

"Into the recesses of his (the adverse claimant's) mind, his motives or purposes, his guilt or innocence, no enquiry is made. . . .

The very nature of the act (entry and possession) is an assertion of his own title, and the denial of the title of all others. It matters not that the possessor was mistaken, and had he been better informed, would not have entered on the land."
8 Conn. at 442, 445-446.

The Maine doctrine has been the subject of much criticism in requiring a knowing wrongful taking. The criticism of the Maine and the justification of the Connecticut branch of the dichotomy is well stated in 6 Powell, *Real Property* (1969) 1015, pp. 725-28:

"Do the facts of his possession, and of his conduct as if he were the owner, make immaterial his mistake, or does such a mistake prevent the existence of the prerequisite claim of right. The leading case holding the mistake to be of no importance was *French v. Pearce*, decided in Connecticut in 1831. . . . This viewpoint has gained increasingly widespread acceptance. The more subjectively oriented view regards the 'mistake' as necessarily preventing the existence of the required claim of right. The leading case on this position is *Preble v. Maine Central R.R.*, decided in 1893. This position is still followed in a few states. It has been strongly criticized as unsound historically, inexpedient practically, and as resulting in better treatment for a ruthless wrongdoer than for the honest landowner. . . . On the whole the law is simplified, in the direction of real justice, by a following of the Connecticut leadership on this point."

Again, 4 Tiffany, *Real Property* (3d ed. 1939), §1159, pp. 474-475, criticizes the employment of mistake as negating hostility as follows:

". . . Adopting this view, it is only in so far as the courts, which assert the possible materiality of the mistake, recognize a contrary presumption, of an intention on the part of the wrongful possessor not to claim title if he is mistaken as to the boundary, that the assertion of the materiality of mistake as to boundary becomes of substantial importance. That the presumption is properly in favor of the adverse or hostile character of the possession rather than against it has been previously argued, but whatever presumption in this regard may be recognized, the introduction of the element of mistake in the discussion of the question of adverse possession is, it is submitted, unnecessary and undesirable. In no case except in that of a mistake as to boundary has the element of mistake been regarded as having any significance, and there is no reason for attributing greater weight thereto when the mistake is as to the proper location of a boundary than when it is a mistake as to the title to all the land wrongfully possessed. And to introduce the element of mistake, and then limit its significance by an inquiry as to the intention which the possessor may have as to his course of action in case there should be a mistake, an intention which has ordinarily no existence whatsoever, is calculated only to cause confusion without, it is conceived, any compensating advantage."

Our Appellate Division in *Predham v. Holfester*, 32 N.J.Super. 419, 108 A.2d 458 (App. Div.1954) although acknowledging that the Maine doctrine had been severely criticized felt obliged because of Stare decisis to adhere thereto. *See also Rullis v. Jacobi*, 79 N.J.Super. 525, 528, 192 A.2d 186 (Ch.Div.1963).

We are in accord with the criticism of the Maine doctrine and favor the Connecticut doctrine for the above quoted reasons. As far as can be seen, overruling the former rule will not result in undermining any of the values which Stare decisis is intended to foster. The theory of reliance, a cornerstone of Stare decisis, is not here apt, as the problem is which of two mistaken parties is entitled to land. Realistically, the true owner does not rely upon entry of the possessor by mistake as a reason for not seeking to recover possession. Whether or not the entry is caused by mistake or intent, the same result eventuates—the true owner is ousted from possession. In either event his neglect to seek recovery of possession, within the requisite time, is in all probability the result of a lack of knowledge that he is being deprived of possession of lands to which he has title.

Accordingly, we discard the requirement that the entry and continued possession must be accompanied by a knowing intentional hostility and hold that any entry and possession for the required time which is exclusive, continuous, uninterrupted, visible and notorious, even though under mistaken claim of title, is sufficient to support a claim of title by adverse possession.

However, this conclusion is not dispositive of the matter sub judice. Of equal importance under the present factual complex, is the question of whether defendant's acts meet the necessary standard of "open and notorious" possession. It must not be forgotten that the foundation of so-called "title by adverse possession" is the failure of the true owner to commence an action for the recovery of the land involved, within the period designated by the statute of limitations. The justifications for the doctrine are aptly stated in 4 Tiffany, *Real Property* (3d ed. 1939) §1134, p. 406 as follows:

"The desirability of fixing, by law, a definite period within which claims to land must be asserted has been generally recognized, among the practical considerations in favor of such a policy being the prevention of the making of illegal claims after the evidence necessary to defeat them has been lost, and the interest which the community as a whole has in the security, of title. The moral justification of the policy lies in the consideration that one who has reason to know that land belonging to him is in the possession of another, and neglects, for a considerable period of time, to assert his right thereto, may properly be penalized by his preclusion from thereafter asserting such right. It is, apparently, by reason of the demerit of the true owner, rather than any supposed merit in the person who has acquired wrongful possession of the land, that this possession, if continued for the statutory period, operates to debar the former owner of all right to recover the land."

See also 5 Thompson, *Real Property* (1957 Replacement), 497.

In order to afford the true owner the opportunity to learn of the adverse claim and to protect his rights by legal action within the time specified by the statute, the adverse possession must be visible and notorious. In 4 *Tiffany, Supra* (Supp.1969, at 291), the character of possession for that purpose, is stated to be as follows:

". . . it must be public and based on physical facts, including known and visible lines and boundaries. Acts of dominion over the land must be so open and notorious as to put an ordinarily prudent person on notice that the land is in actual possession of another. Hence, title may never be acquired by mere possession, however long continued, which is surreptitious or secret or which is not such as will give unmistakable notice of the nature of the occupant's claim."

See also 5 *Thompson, Supra*, §2546; 6 Powell, *Real Property*, 1013 (1969).

Generally, where possession of the land is clear and unequivocal and to such an extent as to be immediately visible, the owner may be presumed to have knowledge of the adverse occupancy. In *Foulke v. Bond*, 41 N.J.L. 527, 545 (E. & A. 1879), the court said:

"Notoriety of the adverse claim under which possession is held, is a necessary constituent of title by adverse possession, and therefore the occupation or possession must be of that nature that the real owner is Presumed to have known that there was a possession adverse to his title, under which it was intended to make title against him." (Emphasis supplied)

However, when the encroachment of an adjoining owner is of a small area and the fact of an intrusion is not clearly and self-evidently apparent to the naked eye but requires an on-site survey for certain disclosure as in urban sections where the division line is only infrequently delineated by any monuments, natural or artificial, such a presumption is fallacious and unjustified. See concurring opinion of Judge (now Justice) Francis in *Predham v. Holfester*, 32 N.J.Super. 419, 428-429, 108 A.2d 458 (App.Div.1954). The precise location of the dividing line is then ordinarily unknown to either adjacent owner and there is nothing on the land itself to show by visual observation that a hedge, fence, wall or other structure encroaches on the neighboring land to a minor extent. Therefore, to permit a presumption of notice to arise in the case of minor border encroachments not exceeding several feet would fly in the face of reality and require the true owner to be on constant alert for possible small encroachments. The only method of certain determination would be by obtaining a survey each time the adjacent owner undertook any improvement at or near the boundary, and this would place an undue and inequitable burden upon the true owner. Accordingly we hereby hold that no presumption of knowledge arises from a minor encroachment along a common boundary. In such a case, only where the true owner has actual knowledge thereof may it be said that the possession is open and notorious.

It is conceivable that the application of the foregoing rule may in some cases result in undue hardship to the adverse possessor who under an innocent and mistaken belief of title has undertaken an extensive improvement which to some extent encroaches on an adjoining property. In that event the situation falls within the category of those cases of which *Riggle v. Skill*, 9 N.J.Super. 372, 74 A.2d 424 (Ch.Div.1950), *affirmed* 7 N.J. 268, 81 A.2d 364 (1951) is typical and equity may furnish relief. Then, if the innocent trespasser of a small portion of land adjoining a boundary line cannot without great expense remove or eliminate the encroachment, or such removal or elimination is impractical or could be accomplished only with great hardship, the true owner may be forced to convey the land so occupied upon payment of the fair value thereof without regard to whether the true owner had notice of the encroachment at its inception. Of course, such a result should eventuate only under appropriate circumstances and where no serious damage would be done to the remaining land as, for instance, by rendering the balance of the parcel unusable or no longer capable of being built upon by reason of zoning or other restrictions.

We remand the case for trial of the issues (1) whether the true owner had actual knowledge of the encroachment, (2) if not, whether plaintiffs should be obliged to convey the disputed tract to defendant, and (3) if the answer to the latter question is in the affirmative, what consideration should be paid for the conveyance. The remand, of course, contemplates further discovery and a new pretrial.

Remanded for trial in accordance with the foregoing.

NOTES

1. *Bad Faith, Good Faith, and the State of Mind Requirement.* At the outset, we asked you to think about how the state of mind standards in *Mannillo* mapped on to our three options. The Maine Doctrine matches up well with the "bad faith" or "aggressive trespass" standard, requiring the adverse possessor to have taken possession with knowledge that the property was not hers and with an intention to acquire ownership of the property. The Connecticut Doctrine, as originally articulated by the Connecticut Supreme Court in *French v. Pearce* matches up well with the "objective standard," with

the court making no inquiry into the adverse possessor's state of mind. We should note, however, that a mistaken adverse possessor would win under the "good-faith" standard. Indeed, the "good-faith" standard requires the adverse possession to have been mistaken.

After having read *Mannillo*, do you have an opinion on which approach to state of mind is best? If you agree with the court's critique of the Maine/bad faith approach, which of the two remaining options—objective or good faith—would be best? A key difference between the two is that a bad faith adverse possessor would win under the objective standard but would lose under the good faith standard. We might find that the good faith standard is preferable because we do not want to reward bad faith. For example, the Colorado and New York legislatures both moved to a good faith standard after highly publicized cases involving bad faith adverse possession. *See* Jonathan Vecchi, *New York's Adverse Possession Law: An Abdication of Personal Responsibility*, 29 Touro L. Rev. 727 (2013); Geoffrey P. Anderson & David M. Pittinos, *Adverse Possession after House Bill 1148*, 37 The Colorado Lawyer 63 (Nov. 2008). On the other hand, we might prefer the objective standard because it is easier to administer. Do you see why? If not, think about how, exactly, you would prove that an adverse possessor had either good faith or bad faith.

2. *Are Minor Encroachments Open and Notorious?* The Gorskis' steps and walk encroached onto the Mannillos' land by 15 inches. Is this encroachment open and notorious? On the one hand, the steps and the walk were clearly visible to everyone. On the other hand, the fact that the steps and walk were encroaching onto the Mannillos' land was not obvious to the naked eye, and could only be established by a survey. We can call this kind of trespass, where the existence and the location of the improvement were clearly visible but the fact of encroachment onto the neighbor's property was not clearly visible, a *minor encroachment*. The court in *Mannillo* held that minor encroachments are not open and notorious unless the owner had actual knowledge that the improvements were encroaching onto her property. Most courts would probably go the other way and hold that a minor encroachment is open and notorious if the existence of the improvement is open and notorious. Which approach do you think is preferable? What does your answer say about the role and purpose of the open and notorious element and of adverse possession more generally? In this context, you should think about how the minor encroachment fact pattern is similar to, or different from, the fact pattern presented in *Marengo Cave*.

3. *Should the Adverse Possessor Pay Compensation to the Owner?* At several points throughout this book, we will ask whether the all-or-nothing way that our legal system frames issues leads to the best results. Adverse possession gives us a good context to think about this issue. When courts consider an adverse possession case, the issue is typically framed in terms of who should win, the adverse possessor or the property

owner. If the adverse possessor wins, the adverse possessor owns the property. If the property owner wins, the property owner owns the property. Perhaps it would be better to frame the issue in terms of the best result on the facts. *Mannillo* hints at an alternative to the all-or-nothing approach that courts often take by suggesting that in a minor encroachment case, the property owner might be forced to convey the encroached land to the adverse possessor in return for compensation. This raises a broader question—why don't we generally require adverse possessors to pay compensation to the true owner? If we did require compensation, would that change the way you think we should approach the elements of adverse possession in any way?

REMEDIES

Our next case, *Howard v. Kunto*, is another classic. Its peculiar facts give us the opportunity to think about both the open and notorious and continuous for the statutory period elements. The basic factual scenario of the case can be a bit confusing. Because of a surveying error, there was a mismatch between the deeds and the homes people were living in. In other words, people were living in one house, but had deeds to their next-door neighbors' house. We have illustrated the starting position as the state of affairs at Time 1. Later, to make this complicated situation even more confusing, two owners swapped deeds, leading to the state of affairs at Time 2.

Time 1:

House:		Kunto	Moyer	Howard
Deed:	Kunto	Moyer	Howard	

Time 2:

Deed:	Kunto	Howard	Moyer

Because of the surveying error, at Time 1, the Kuntos, Moyers, and Howards each had the deed to the wrong house. At Time 2, the Moyers and Howards swapped title. This gave the Moyers title to the house they were living in and gave the Howards the title to the house the Kuntos were living in. We've never found out (a) who owned the title to the Howards' house or (b) why the Howards thought that this transaction was a good idea. Whatever the Howards' motivation, the transaction led to a dispute between the Howards and the Kuntos over the house the Kuntos were living in. The Howards claimed to be owners of the house because they had the deed to the property. The Kuntos claimed to be owners of the house they were living in by adverse possession.

HOWARD V. KUNTO

Washington Court of Appeals, 1970
477 P.2d 210

PEARSON, Judge. Land surveying is an ancient art but not one free of the errors that often creep into the affairs of men. In this case, we are presented with the question of what happens when the descriptions in deeds do not fit the land the deed holders are occupying. Defendants appeal from a decree quieting title in the plaintiffs of a tract of land on the shore of Hood Canal in Mason County.

At least as long ago as 1932 the record tells us that one McCall resided in the house now occupied by the appellant-defendants, Kunto. McCall had a deed that described a 50-foot-wide parcel on the shore of Hood Canal. The error that brings this case before us is that 50 feet described in the deed is not the same 50 feet upon which McCall's house stood. Rather, the described land is an adjacent 50-foot lot directly west of that upon which the house stood. In other words, McCall's house stood on one lot and his deed described the adjacent lot. Several property owners to the west of defendants, not parties to this action, are similarly situated.

Over the years since 1946, several conveyances occurred, using the same legal description and accompanied by a transfer of possession to the succeeding occupants. The Kuntos' immediate predecessors in interest, Millers, desired to build a dock. To this end, they had a survey performed which indicated that the deed description and the physical occupation were in conformity. Several boundary stakes were placed as a result of this survey and the dock was constructed, as well as other improvements. The house as well as the others in the area continued to be used as summer recreational retreats.

The Kuntos then took possession of the disputed property under a deed from the Millers in 1959. In 1960 the respondent-plaintiffs, Howard, who held land east of that of the Kuntos, determined to convey an undivided one-half interest in their land to the Yearlys. To this end, they undertook to have a survey of the entire area made. After expending considerable effort, the surveyor retained by the Howards discovered that according to the government survey, the deed descriptions and the land occupancy of the parties did not coincide. Between the Howards and the Kuntos lay the Moyers' property. When the Howards' survey was completed, they discovered that they were the record owners of the land occupied by the Moyers and that the Moyers held record title to the land occupied by the Kuntos. Howard approached Moyer and in return for a conveyance of the land upon which the Moyers' house stood, Moyer conveyed to the Howards record title to the land upon which the Kunto house stood. Until plaintiffs Howard obtained the conveyance from Moyer in April, 1960, neither Moyer nor any of his predecessors ever asserted any right to ownership of the property actually being possessed by Kunto and his predecessors. This action was then instituted to quiet title in the Howards and Yearlys. The Kuntos appeal from a trial court decision granting this remedy.

At the time this action was commenced on August 19, 1960,[3] defendants had been in occupance of the disputed property less than a year. The trial court's reason for denying their claim of adverse possession is succinctly stated in its memorandum opinion: "In this instance, defendants have failed to prove, by a preponderance of the evidence, a continuity of possession or estate to permit tacking of the adverse possession of defendants to the possession of their predecessors."

Finding of fact 6,[4] which is challenged by defendants, incorporates the above concept and additionally finds defendant's possession not to have been "continuous" because it involved only "summer occupancy."

Two issues are presented by this appeal:

(1) Is a claim of adverse possession defeated because the physical use of the premises is restricted to summer occupancy?

(2) May a person who receives record title to tract A under the mistaken belief that the has title to tract B (immediately contiguous to tract A) and who subsequently occupies tract B, for the purpose of establishing title to tract B by adverse possession, use the periods of possession of tract B by his immediate predecessors who also had record title to tract A?

In approaching both of these questions, we point out that the evidence, largely undisputed in any material sense, established that defendant or his immediate predecessors did occupy the premises, which we have called tract B, as though it was their own for far more than the 10 years as prescribed in RCW 4.16.020.[5]

We also point out that findings of fact is not challenged for its factual determinations but for the conclusions contained therein to the effect that the continuity of possession

---

[3] The inordinate delay in bringing this matter to trial appears from the record to be largely inexcusable. However, neither counsel who tried the case was at fault in any way. We have intentionally declined to consider defendant's motion (probably well founded) to dismiss this case for want of prosecution (Rules of Pleading, Practice and Procedure 41.04W (1950)) for the reason that a new trial of the same issues would be inevitable and in light of our disposition of the case on the merits, defendants are not prejudiced by disregarding the technical grounds.

[4] 'In the instant case the defendants' building was not simply over the line, but instead was built wholly upon the wrong piece of property, not the property of defendants, described in Paragraph Four (4) of the complaint herein, but on the property of plaintiffs, described in Paragraph Three of the complaint and herein. That the last three deeds in the chain of title, covering and embracing defendants' property, including defendants' deed, were executed in other states, specifically, California and Oregon. And there is no evidence of pointing out to the grantees in said three deeds, aforesaid, including defendants' deed, of any specific property, other than the property of defendants, described in their deed, and in Paragraph Four (4) of the complaint, and herein; nor of any immediate act of the grantees, including defendants, in said Three (3) deeds, aforesaid, of taking possession of any property, other than described in said three (3) deeds, aforesaid; and the testimony of husband, defendant, was unequivocally that he had no intention of possessing or holding anything other than what the deed called for; and, that there is no showing of any continuous possession by defendants or their immediate predecessors in interest, since the evidence indicates the property was in the nature, for us, as a summer occupancy, and such occupancy and use was for rather limited periods of time during comparatively short portions of the year, and was far from continuous.'

[5] This statute provides:

"4.16.020 Actions to be commenced within ten years. The period prescribed in RCW 4.16.010 for the commencement of actions shall be as follows:

may not be established by summer occupancy, and that a predecessor's possession may not be tacked because a legal "claim of right" did not exist under the circumstances.

We start with the oft-quoted rule that:

> (T)o constitute adverse possession, there must be actual possession which is *Uninterrupted*, open and notorious, hostile and exclusive, and under a *Claim of right* made in good faith for the statutory period.

(Italics ours.) *Butler v. Anderson*, 71 Wash.2d 60, 64, 426 P.2d 467, 470 (1967). *Also see Fadden v. Purvis*, 77 Wash.Dec.2d 22, 459 P.2d 385 (1969) and cases cited therein.

We reject the conclusion that summer occupancy only of a summer beach home destroys the continuity of possession required by the statute. It has become firmly established that the requisite possession requires such possession and dominion "as ordinarily marks the conduct of owners in general in holding, managing, and caring for property of like nature and condition." *Whalen v. Smith*, 183 Iowa 949, 953, 167 N.W. 646, 647 (1918). *Also see Mesher v. Connolly*, 63 Wash.2d 552, 388 P.2d 144 (1964); *Skoog v. Seymour*, 29 Wash.2d 355, 187 P.2d 304 (1947); *Butler v. Anderson, Supra*; *Fadden v. Purvis, Supra*.

We hold that occupancy of tract B during the summer months for more than the 10-year period by defendant and his predecessors, together with the continued existence of the improvements on the land and beach area, constituted "uninterrupted" possession within this rule. To hold otherwise is to completely ignore the nature and condition of the property. *See Fadden v. Purvis, Supra*.

We find such rule fully consonant with the legal writers on the subject. In F. Clark, *Law of Surveying and Boundaries*, §561 (3d ed. 1959) at 565: "Continuity of possession may be established although the land is used regularly for only a certain period each year." Further, at 566:

> This rule (which permits tacking) is one of substance and not of absolute mathematical continuity, provided there is no break so as to sever two possessions. It is not necessary that the occupant should be actually upon the premises continually. If the land is occupied during the period of time during the year it is capable of use, there is sufficient continuity.

We now reach the question of tacking. The precise issue before us is novel in that none of the property occupied by defendant or his predecessors coincided with the property described in their deeds, but was contiguous.

In the typical case, which has been subject to much litigation, the party seeking to establish title by adverse possession claims more land than that described in the deed. In such cases it is clear that tacking is permitted.

"Within ten years:

"Actions for the recovery of real property, or for the recovery of the possession thereof; and no action shall be maintained for such recovery unless it appears that the plaintiff, his ancestor, predecessor or grantor was seized or possessed of the premises in question within ten years before the commencement of the action."

In *Buchanan v. Cassell*, 53 Wash.2d 611, 614, 335 P.2d 600, 602 (1959) the Supreme Court stated:

> This state follows the rule that a purchaser may tack the adverse use of its predecessor in interest to that of his own where the land was intended to be included in the deed between them, but was mistakenly omitted from the description.

El Cerrito, Inc. v. Ryndak, 60 Wash.2d 847, 376 P.2d 528 (1962).

The general statement which appears in many of the cases is that tacking of adverse possession is permitted if the successive occupants are in "privity." *See Faubion v. Elder*, 49 Wash.2d 300, 301 P.2d 153 (1956). The deed running between the parties purporting to transfer the land possessed traditionally furnishes the privity of estate which connects the possession of the successive occupants. Plaintiff contends, and the trial court ruled, that where the deed does not describe any of the land which was occupied, the actual transfer of possession is insufficient to establish privity.

To assess the cogency of this argument and ruling, we must turn to the historical reasons for requiring privity as a necessary prerequisite to tacking the possession of several occupants. Very few, if any, of the reasons appear in the cases, nor do the cases analyze the relationships that must exist between successive possessors for tacking to be allowed. *See* W. Stoebuck, *The Law of Adverse Possession In Washington* in 35 Wash.L.Rev. 53 (1960).

The requirement of privity had its roots in the notion that a succession of trespasses, even though there was no appreciable interval between them, should not, in equity, be allowed to defeat the record title. The "claim of right," "color of title" requirement of the statutes and cases was probably derived from the early American belief that the squatter should not be able to profit by his trespass.[6]

However, it appears to this court that there is a substantial difference between the squatter or trespasser and the property purchaser, who along with several of his neighbors, as a result of an inaccurate survey or subdivision, occupies and improves property exactly 50 feet to the east of that which a survey some 30 years later demonstrates that they in fact own. It seems to us that there is also a strong public policy favoring early certainty as to the location of land ownership which enters into a proper interpretation of privity.

On the irregular perimeters of Puget Sound exact determination of land locations and boundaries is difficult and expensive. This difficulty is convincingly demonstrated in this case by the problems plaintiff's engineer encountered in attempting to locate the corners. It cannot be expected that every purchaser will or should engage a surveyor to ascertain that the beach home he is purchasing lies within the boundaries described in

---

[6] The English common law does not require privity as a prerequisite for tacking. *See* F. Clark, *Law of Surveying and Boundaries*, §561 (3d ed. 1959) at 568.

his deed. Such a practice is neither reasonable nor customary. Of course, 50-foot errors in descriptions are devasting where a group of adjacent owners each hold 50 feet of waterfront property.

The technical requirement of "privity" should not, we think, be used to upset the long periods of occupancy of those who in good faith received an erroneous deed description. Their "claim of right" is no less persuasive than the purchaser who believes he is purchasing more land than his deed described.

In the final analysis, however, we believe the requirement of "privity" is no more than judicial recognition of the need for some reasonable connection between successive occupants of real property so as to raise their claim of right above the status of the wrongdoer or the trespasser. We think such reasonable connection exists in this case.

Where, as here, several successive purchasers received record title to tract A under the mistaken belief that they were acquiring tract B, immediately contiguous thereto, and where possession of tract B is transferred and occupied in a continuous manner for more than 10 years by successive occupants, we hold there is sufficient privity of estate to permit tacking and thus establish adverse possession as a matter of law.

We see no reason in law or in equity for differentiating this case from *Faubion v. Elder*, 49 Wash.2d 300, 301 P.2d 153 (1956) where the appellants were claiming more land than their deed described and where successive periods of occupation were allowed to be united to each other to make up the time of adverse holding. To the same effect see *Naher v. Farmer*, 60 Wash. 600, 111 P. 768 (1910), and cases cited therein; *Buchanan v. Cassell*, 53 Wash.2d 611, 335 P.2d 600 (1959) and cases cited therein; *El Cerrito, Inc. v. Ryndak*, 60 Wash.2d 847, 376 P.2d 528 (1962); *See* 17 A.L.R.2d 1128 (1951). This application of the privity requirement should particularly pertain where the holder of record title to tract B acquired the same with knowledge of the discrepancy.

Judgment is reversed with directions to dismiss plaintiffs' action and to enter a decree quieting defendants' title to the disputed tract of land in accordance with the prayer of their cross-complaint.

NOTES

1. *Summer Occupancy.* The Kuntos only occupied the house during the summer. The court held that summer occupancy satisfies the requirement that the adverse possession be continuous for the statutory period, reasoning that the continuity requirement is satisfied if the adverse possessor acts as a typical owner of that type of property. For a summer home in an area where summer use is typical, summer occupancy satisfies the requirement. Note that this standard—use of the property in the same way that a typical owner would use the property—is essentially the same standard as that used for the open and notorious element. Indeed, summer occupancy could have been discussed as an open and notorious issue rather than a continuity issue.

2. *Tacking.* The Kuntos themselves had not lived on the property long enough to meet the statutory period for adverse possession. The Kuntos nonetheless won, because they were permitted to tack (i.e., add) the prior possessors' time of possession onto theirs to meet the statutory period. Tacking generally is permitted if the prior possessors (here, the Millers) and the adverse possessor (here, the Kuntos) are in privity with each other. Privity is a slippery concept that we will encounter a few times during this course. For now, we can say that parties are in privity of estate with each other if they are on the opposite sides of a consensual real estate transaction. If I convey Blackacre to you, you and I are in privity of estate. The odd facts of *Howard* made the privity issue unusually complex, because the Millers never actually purported to conveyed title to the property being adversely possessed to the Kuntos. Rather, they purportedly conveyed title to the property next door. The appellate court in *Howard* reached the logical conclusion that in this context, the privity requirement could be met by a transfer of possession of the adversely possessed property. Tacking does not apply when the prior possessor and the adverse possessor are not in privity. Here is an example of a fact pattern where the privity requirement would not be met:

> **EXAMPLE:** O is the owner of Blackacre. The jurisdiction where Blackacre is located has a 21-year statute of limitations. A entered Blackacre in 1980 and adversely possessed it for 15 years. A then abandoned Blackacre. A year later, in 1996, B entered and adversely possessed Blackacre. In 2006, O brought an action for ejectment against B. O will win, because B has not satisfied the 21-year statutory period. B alone adversely possessed Blackacre for ten years. A adversely possessed Blackacre for 15 years. Adding the two periods together amounts to 25 years, which is more the statutory period. A and B, however, were not in privity, because A never transferred title or possession of Blackacre to B. Rather, A abandoned Blackacre, and B later entered Blackacre. B therefore cannot tack A's time of possession onto her own, and B fails to satisfy the statutory period.

3. *State of Mind, Again. Howard v. Kunto* has language suggesting that a good faith state of mind is necessary to a claim of adverse possession. The Supreme Court of Washington later clarified its rule on hostility and state of mind in *Chaplin v. Sanders*, 676 P.2d 431 (1984). We think that the court's analysis in *Chaplin* is worth quoting at length:

> In order to establish a claim of adverse possession, the possession must be: (1) exclusive, (2) actual and uninterrupted, (3) open and notorious and (4) hostile and under a claim of right made in good faith. *Peeples v. Port of Bellingham*, 93 Wash.2d 766, 613 P.2d 1128 (1980); *Skansi v. Novak*, 84 Wash. 39, 146 P. 160 (1915). The period throughout which these elements must concurrently exist is 10 years. RCW 4.16.020. Hostility, as defined by this court, "does not import enmity or ill-will, but rather imports that

the claimant is in possession as owner, in contradistinction to holding in recognition of or subordination to the true owner." *King v. Bassindale*, 127 Wash. 189, 192, 220 P. 777 (1923). We have traditionally treated the hostility and claim of right requirements as one and the same. *Bowden-Gazzam Co. v. Hogan*, 22 Wash.2d 27, 154 P.2d 285 (1944).

Although the definition of hostility has remained fairly constant throughout this last century, the import we have attributed to this definition has varied. For example, in *King v. Bassindale, supra*, we held that, because the claimant believed the land to be his own and treated it as such, his possession was hostile as to the rest of the world. In contrast, in *Bowden-Gazzam Co. v. Hogan, supra*, we held that an adverse user who appropriated land knowing it was not his own, but who used it as his own for over the statutory period, was entitled to title by adverse possession. Our reasoning was that the claimant's subjective belief as to who owned the land was irrelevant so long as he intended to claim the land as his own. Yet, in dicta, we affirmed the age-old requirement that the claimant neither recognize a superior interest nor claim in bad faith. Our interpretation of this definition was further muddied in *Brown v. Hubbard*, 42 Wash.2d 867, 259 P.2d 391 (1953) wherein the claimant had mistakenly included a portion of his neighbor's property when fencing his own land. Although he had openly claimed and used the land as his own for well over the statutory period, we held that he had never formed the requisite hostile intent because he would not have claimed the land as his own had he known it belonged to his neighbor.

Thus, in *Bassindale* we required the claimant to possess a good faith belief that the land possessed was his own, in *Hogan* we deemed the claimant's belief irrelevant and in Hubbard we required the claimant to possess the unrighteous intent to deprive the true owner of his land. Shortly after *Hubbard* we set forth a test for hostility which took much of the emphasis off of the claimant's subjective intent. *O'Brien v. Schultz*, 45 Wash.2d 769, 278 P.2d 322 (1954).

In *O'Brien*, we observed that "[c]ourts have had considerable difficulty in determining 'intention' in adverse possession cases, because intention may be evidenced (1) by the acts of a party, or (2) by his declarations." *O'Brien*, at 780, 278 P.2d 322. We noted that, in Washington,

> the acts of the user most frequently control. If his acts clearly evince an intention to claim land as its owner, a general declaration by the user that he did not intend to claim another's land will not prove lack of intention. But a specific declaration by a user that he knew a fence was not the boundary and that he agreed to consider it as a temporary barrier will prove lack of intention. And if his acts are equivocal or do

not clearly evince his intention to claim as owner, his declaration that he did not intend to take another's land, though not conclusive proof of lack of intention, may be considered in determining his intention while using the land.

(Citations omitted.) *O'Brien*, at 780, 278 P.2d 322.

O'Brien has not achieved the goal of setting forth a workable definition of hostile intent. Whenever acts are equivocal or declarations arguably specific the courts will be required to inquire into the claimant's subjective intentions, motives and beliefs regarding the land. *See, e.g., Peeples v. Port of Bellingham, supra.* The specific intent, motive and belief required is even less clear. In addition, because *O'Brien* attempted to reconcile, rather than overrule, disparate case law, many post-*O'Brien* cases exhibit a misunderstanding of the applicable rule. *See Fadden v. Purvis*, 77 Wash.2d 23, 459 P.2d 385 (1969); *Roy v. Goerz*, 26 Wash.App. 807, 614 P.2d 1308 (1980); *Hunt v. Matthews*, 8 Wash.App. 233, 505 P.2d 819 (1973). The resulting confusion necessitates our reexamination of this area of the law and mandates a new approach to the requirement of hostility. *See In re Marriage of Johnson*, 96 Wash.2d 255, 264, 634 P.2d 877 (1981).

The doctrine of adverse possession was formulated at law for the purpose of, among others, assuring maximum utilization of land, encouraging the rejection of stale claims and, most importantly, quieting titles. 7 R. Powell, *Real Property* ¶1012[3] (1982); C. Callahan, *Adverse Possession* 91-94 (1961). Because the doctrine was formulated at law and not at equity, it was originally intended to protect both those who knowingly appropriated the land of others and those who honestly entered and held possession in full belief that the land was their own. R. Powell, at ¶1013 [2]; C. Callahan, at 49-50; 3 Am.Jur.2d *Advancements* §104 (1962). Thus, when the original purpose of the adverse possession doctrine is considered, it becomes apparent that the claimant's motive in possessing the land is irrelevant and no inquiry should be made into his guilt or innocence. *Accord, Springer v. Durette*, 217 Or. 196, 342 P.2d 132 (1959); *Agers v. Reynolds*, 306 S.W.2d 506 (Mo.1957); *Fulton v. Rapp*, 59 Ohio Law Abs. 105, 98 N.E.2d 430 (1950); *see also* Stoebuck, *The Law of Adverse Possession in Washington*, 35 Wash.L.Rev. 53, 76-80 (1960).

Washington is not the only state which looks to the subjective belief and intent of the adverse claimant in determining hostility. *See, e.g., Ellis v. Jansing*, 620 S.W.2d 569 (Tex.1981); *Van Valkenburgh v. Lutz*, 304 N.Y. 95, 106 N.E.2d 28 (1952); *see generally* 3 *American Law of Property* §15.4 (A.J. Casner ed. 1952). However, the requirement has been regarded as unnecessarily confusing by many legal commentators, see Dockray, *Adverse Possession and Intention—I*, 1981-82 Conv. & Prop.Law. (n.s.) 256; C. Callahan, *supra*;

Stoebuck, 35 Wash.L.Rev. at 76-80; and A.J. Casner, *supra*, and has been abandoned by the apparent majority of states. 3 *American Law of Property* §15.5, at 785.

For these reasons, we are convinced that the dual requirement that the claimant take possession in "good faith" and not recognize another's superior interest does not serve the purpose of the adverse possession doctrine. *See Dunbar v. Heinrich*, 95 Wash.2d 20, 622 P.2d 812 (1980); and *Wickert v. Thompson*, 28 Wash.App. 516, 624 P.2d 747 (1981). The "hostility/claim of right" element of adverse possession requires only that the claimant treat the land as his own as against the world throughout the statutory period. The nature of his possession will be determined solely on the basis of the manner in which he treats the property. His subjective belief regarding his true interest in the land and his intent to dispossess or not dispossess another is irrelevant to this determination. *Cf.* RCW 7.28.070 and 7.28.080. Under this analysis, permission to occupy the land, given by the true title owner to the claimant or his predecessors in interest, will still operate to negate the element of hostility.

This analysis provides a strong defense of the objective standard for the state of mind element. Consider again the alternatives. Which do you think is best?

DISABILITIES AND THE ADVERSE POSSESSION CLOCK

In many states, the statute of limitations clock for adverse possession does not run against the owner of the property if the owner is a minor, is mentally incompetent, or is imprisoned. We typically call these categories *disabilities*, because a person falling into any of these categories would be disabled from asserting her legal rights in a timely fashion. The basic concept is fairly intuitive—we do not let the statute of limitations expire in some circumstances where it would be unfair. There are some technical complications, however, that can make it tricky to calculate the time of expiration of the statute of limitations in a disability case.

The exact rules on disabilities in any given jurisdiction will be governed by the text of the statute of limitations in that jurisdiction. Here is a hypothetical statute that contains elements that are common to many jurisdictions:

> An action to recover the title to or possession of real property shall be brought within 21 years after the cause thereof accrued. However, if a person entitled to bring such action, at the time the cause thereof accrues, is within the age of minority [the age of majority in this jurisdiction is 18], of unsound mind, or imprisoned, such person (or anyone claiming from, by, or under such person) may bring such action either (a) within the ordinary 21-year period or (b) within ten years after such disability is removed, whichever is longer.

Our hypothetical statute is a bit clearer than the typical statute and expressly states a number of concepts that are implicit in many state statutes. Here are the key concepts that you need to know to apply the statute:

1. The basic limitations period under this statute is 21 years. If the owner is disabled at the time the cause of action accrues (i.e., when the adverse possessor enters the property), then the owner will have 10 years after the disability is removed to bring an action to eject the adverse possessor. The exact number of years varies by jurisdiction, but our statute follows the typical structure by having a *base period* (here, 21 years) and a *disabilities period* (here, 10 years).

2. The ten-year disabilities period runs from the time the disability is removed. The basic idea is simple—it would be unfair to have the statute run against the owner while the owner is disabled, so we will give the owner extra time to bring a claim after the disability has been removed. The disability of being a minor is removed when the owner reaches the age of majority (here, 18). The disability of mental impairment is removed when the owner recovers mental competency. The disability of imprisonment is removed by release from prison. Further, any disability is removed by the owner's death. The language "or anyone claiming from, by, or under such person" makes it clear that if a disabled owner has died, the owner's executor or the person who inherits from the owner will get the benefit of the ten-year disabilities period.

3. The language "whichever is longer" at the end of the statute reminds us to be sure to only use the disabilities period if it benefits the owner. Put another way, be sure to only use the disabilities period if it is longer than the base period. Here is an example that illustrates this point:

   EXAMPLE 1: Adverse Possessor entered the property in 1980. At the time, Owner was 17. Owner reached 18, the age of majority, in 1981. Adding ten years to the time that the disability was lifted would have the disabilities period end in 1991. The base period of 21 years from entry, however, ends in 2001. Clearly, applying the base period is better for the Owner. If Owner brought an action for ejectment in 1999, Owner would win—we would not punish Owner by saying that time had expired when the disabilities period ended in 1991.

4. Note well the language "at the time the cause thereof accrues." If the owner is disabled when the adverse possessor enters, then the owner will get the benefit of the ten-year disabilities period. If the owner becomes disabled later, then the owner will *not* get the benefit of the disabilities period. Consider these examples:

   EXAMPLE 2: Owner became mentally impaired in 1980, and remained impaired when Adverse Possessor entered in 1981. Because Owner is disabled when Adverse Possessor enters, Owner will get the benefit of the ten-year disabilities period. That is, the statute of limitation will expire ten years after Owner's disability is removed.

EXAMPLE 3: Adverse Possessor entered in 1981. At the time, Owner was not disabled. In 1982, Owner became mentally impaired. Because Owner was not disabled at the time Adverse Possessor entered, Owner will not get the benefit of the ten-year disabilities period. That is, the statute of limitations will expire at the end of the 21-year base period. Owner's disability is irrelevant because it was not in place at the time of Adverse Possessor's entry.

The logic of this distinction, such as it is, is that in Example 3, Owner could have brought an action for ejectment in 1981 when Adverse Possessor entered. In many circumstances, the result will seem unfair. In both of our examples, Owner was disabled for at least 20 years of the statutory period, but in one Owner gets the benefit of the disabilities period while in the other Owner does not. Disabilities statutes, however, are typically applied mechanically. If the owner was not disabled at the time the adverse possessor entered, then the owner will not get the benefit of the disabilities period.

ADVERSE POSSESSION AND FUTURE INTERESTS

We introduced the concept of present and future interests in our section on gifts before *Gruen v. Gruen*. We will cover them in depth in our next chapter. Recall that *Gruen* involved a type of present interest called a life estate. A life estate ends at the holder's death. At that time, present possession of the property will transfer to the holder of a future interest.

What happens if an adverse possessor enters property that is divided between present and future interest holders and later satisfies all of the requirements of adverse possession? For example, imagine that A has a life estate in Blackacre, and B has a remainder. In other words, A has a present interest (the life estate), and B has a future interest (the remainder) that will become possessory on A's death. If Adverse Possessor enters Blackacre and satisfies all of the requirements of adverse possession, then Adverse Possessor will have adversely possessed A's life estate. That is, Adverse Possessor will have a present interest that ends when A dies. B still owns her future interest, however, because *the statute of limitations clock does not run against future interest holders*. In our example, the adverse possession clock will not start running against B until A dies and becomes the owner of a present interest in Blackacre.

This rule only applies if, as in our example, the adverse possessor enters after ownership has been divided into present and future interests. If the adverse possessor enters before the property is divided, then the adverse possession clock runs against both the present and future interest holder. For example, imagine that Blackacre is owned by O. Adverse Possessor enters. Later, O grants a life estate to A and a remainder to B. The clock started running against O when Adverse Possessor entered and continues to run against both A and B after the property is divided into present and future interests. In this sense, the rules on present and future interests resemble the rules on disabilities. Disabilities only matter if they were present when the adverse possessor entered. (See Disability Example 3.) Similarly, future interests only matter if they were in place when the adverse possessor entered.

5. In some circumstances, the owner will be disabled when the adverse possessor enters and then later become subject to a second disability. In these cases, we disregard the second disability that occurs after the adverse possessor has entered. Put another way, the owner cannot tack together two disabilities. Here is an example:

EXAMPLE 4: Adverse Possessor entered the property in 1980. At the time, Owner was three years old. In 1985, Owner became mentally impaired. Owner died in 2010. We disregard the second disability. Owner reaches the 18, the age of majority, in 1995. The ten-year disability period therefore expires in 2005 (ten years after Owner reached the age of majority), not 2020 (ten years after the mental impairment disability was removed by Owner's death). It is worth noting that the disability period benefits Owner, because the base 21-year period would have expired in 2001.

Combining this point with the prior one, we can see that disabilities that occur after the adverse possessor has entered never count. If the owner has more than one disability at the time the adverse possessor enters, then the owner gets the benefit of whichever disability lasts longer. The key distinction here is between disabilities that are in place when the adverse possessor enters (which count) and disabilities that are not in place when the adverse possessor enters (which do not count).

The same rule applies if the person who inherits from the owner is disabled at the time of inheritance. Because we ignore disabilities that were not in place at the time that the adverse possessor entered, we ignore the fact that the heir is disabled. Consider this example:

EXAMPLE 5: Owner became mentally impaired in 1980 and remained impaired when Adverse Possessor entered in 1981. Owner died in 1995, leaving all of her property to Granddaughter, who was five years old at the time. The statute of limitations period would expire in Adverse Possessor's favor in 2005. Owner was disabled when Adverse Possessor enters, so Owner gets the benefit of the disability period. The disability period expires in 2005, ten years after the disability was removed by Owner's death. We ignore the fact that Granddaughter was a minor when she became owner of the property, because her disability was not present when Adverse Possessor entered.

We note in conclusion that many of these rules lead to results that might seem unfair or inconsistent. It seems odd, for example, to respect the first disability but to ignore a second disability that occurs after the adverse possessor enters. We think it is best not to think too hard about whether or not these rules make sense. Just learn how to apply them.

The best way to master these rules is to apply them. Some of the questions in the following problem set raise disabilities issues. The remainder raise other adverse possession issues. Explanatory answers to the problem set can be found on page 1031.

ADVERSE POSSESSION PROBLEMS

For the following problems, us the statute of limitations with disabilities provisions that we provided above.

1. O bought Blackacre in 1970. In 1971, O died, leaving Blackacre to B for life, remainder to C. When B died in 1975, C was ten years old. In 1977, A took possession of Blackacre and used it continuously in the typical manner. Presuming that all of the other elements of adverse possession were met, in what year would A satisfy the statutory period and establish adverse possession of Blackacre?

2. O bought Blackacre in Widener in 1970. In 1971, O was imprisoned for assault. In 1972, A took possession of Blackacre and used it continuously in the typical manner. In 1985, O was killed in a prison brawl, leaving Blackacre to B, who at the time was four years old. Presuming that all of the elements of adverse possession were met other than the expiration of the statutory period, who would win if B brings an action for ejectment against A in (a) 1994, (b) 1996, and (c) 2006?

3. O bought Blackacre in 1970. In 1975, A took possession of Blackacre and used it continuously and in the typical manner until his death in 1990. A few months after A's death, B took possession of Blackacre and used it continuously and in the typical manner. In 1997, O brought an action to eject B from Blackacre. Presuming that all elements of adverse possession other than the expiration of the statutory period have been met, who wins and why?

4. O bought Blackacre in 1970. In 1975, A took possession of Blackacre and used it continuously in the typical manner until 1990, when he transferred possession to B, who subsequently used Blackacre continuously and in the typical manner. In 1997, O brought an action to eject B from Blackacre. Presuming that all elements of adverse possession other than the expiration of the statutory period have been met, who wins and why?

5. O bought Blackacre in 1970. In 1975, A bought the adjoining Whiteacre. A immediately took possession of Whiteacre and put up a fence. Although A intended to fence in just Whiteacre, her fence in fact includes an acre of Blackacre. A month later O was severely injured in a car accident and as a result was subsequently mentally incompetent. In 1997, O's guardian discovered that A had fenced off part of Blackacre and brought an action to eject A from Blackacre. Who wins and why?

6. O bought Blackacre in 1970. In 1971, O died, leaving Blackacre to B for life, remainder to C. In 1975, A took possession of Blackacre and used it continuously in the typical manner. In 1979, B died. Presuming that all elements of adverse possession other than the expiration of the statutory period have been met, who would win if C brought an action for ejectment in (a) 1997 and (b) 2002?

ADVERSE POSSESSION SUMMARY

Adverse possession is a product of the statute of limitations. If the limitations period on the owner's claim for trespass has expired, and the other elements have been met, the adverse possessor becomes the owner of the property by operation of law. Adverse possession has four elements:

- *Actual Entry Giving Exclusive Possession.* Entry by the adverse possessor starts the clock on the statute of limitations period. The entry must give the adverse possessor exclusive possession of the land.
- *Open and Notorious.* Generally speaking, an adverse possessor satisfies this element by using the property in the way a typical owner of that type of property would. *Marengo Cave*, *Mannillo*, and *Howard* all involved open and notorious issues. Watch out in particular for the minor encroachment issue raised by *Mannillo*.
- *Adverse and Under Claim of Right.* This element goes to the adverse possessor's state of mind. We discussed three approaches to this element: the *objective standard* (state of mind is irrelevant), the *good faith* standard (the adverse possessor must have a good faith state of mind—i.e., the adverse possession must have been the result of an honest mistake), and the *bad faith* or *aggressive trespasser* standard (the adverse possessor must have knowingly and intentionally trespassed onto another's property). It is important to remember how a case of mistaken adverse possession plays out under these standards. A mistaken adverse possessor wins under either the objective or good faith standards, but loses under the bad faith standard. This element was discussed in depth in *Mannillo* and in the notes after *Howard*.
- *Continuous for the Statutory Period.* Seemingly straightforward, this element can present some tricky issues. *Howard* presenting the *tacking* issue—if the adverse possessor is in privity with a prior adverse possessor, she can *tack* on the prior possessor's time of possession onto her own to satisfy the statutory period. The statute of limitations may not run against the owner if the owner is *disabled*.

POSSESSION'S ROLE IN PROPERTY LAW

We began this unit with Lord Mansfield's observation that "Possession is very strong; rather more than nine points of the law." You have now considered a series of legal issues involving possession, you now have a sophisticated understanding of the concept. We close our materials on the subject by suggesting that the idea of possession plays three important, but distinct, roles in property law and theory.[5]

First, possession is central to theories justifying individual ownership of objects that previously had been unowned. We briefly discussed John Locke's theory of property, under which people gain ownership of unowned objects by possessing those objects and mixing labor with them. Initial ownership theories rest on an idea of *first possession*, in which the first possessor becomes the first owner of an object. We saw this kind of thinking in action in *Pierson v. Post* and *Johnson v. M'Intosh*, but first possession has more of a role in property theory than it does in most aspects of property law.

Second, the idea of *prior possession* lies at the heart of many property law doctrines. Under the rule of prior possession, a prior possessor will generally have a superior claim to

FIRST IN TIME

an object as compared to a subsequent possessor. If formal ownership cannot be established between two claimants for the same object, the rule of prior possession states that the prior possessor will be given ownership of the object. We saw this rule applied in our materials on bailments and finding.

Third, possession plays an evidentiary role in disputes about ownership. Absent other evidence about ownership, *current possession* may create a presumption of ownership. This evidentiary role of possession is reflected in Lord Mansfield's observation about possession being more than nine points of the law. Despite its evidentiary significance, however, current possession is rarely going to allow a person to win ownership against a prior possessor. If person B has current possession, and person A can demonstrate prior possession, then the rules of property law will generally operate to vindicate A's ownership of the object. Adverse possession is an exception, because an adverse possessor's current possession can defeat the original owner's prior possession. Even here, however, the owner's prior possession will win against the adverse possessor's current possession if the owner brings an action for ejectment before the statute of limitations expires.

---

[5] These observations draw on D. Benjamin Barros, *The Biology of Possession*, 20 Widener L.J. 291 (2011).

C. EXCLUSION

As we noted at the beginning of this chapter, there are four classic incidents of property ownership: possession, use, alienation, and exclusion. We have just considered possession in depth and will discuss use and alienation at points throughout this book. In contemporary property law and theory, exclusion is often thought to lie at the heart of property ownership. After all, if you cannot exclude me from your land, it is hard to see how we can call that land your private property. We therefore end our first chapter with a brief discussion of the right to exclude. We begin with an excerpt from an article by Lior Jacob Strahilevitz that gives us an opportunity to think about how we achieve exclusion in practice. We then discuss two classic cases that allow us to consider the full scope of the right to exclude.

LIOR JACOB STRAHILEVITZ, *INFORMATION ASYMMETRIES AND THE RIGHTS TO EXCLUDE*

104 Mich. L. Rev. 1835 (2006)

THE RIGHTS TO EXCLUDE

This Part introduces the four distinct rights to exclude and elaborates on their uses, importance, and relative merits. . . .

A. The Hermit's Right

The traditional account of the property right to exclude emphasizes a solitary, isolated individual who excludes everyone from his land. This is the hermit's property right. Framed so narrowly, it seems to be a right of little value. Few people want to live permanently in total isolation. Rather, the prospect of hosting friends, neighbors, relatives, and service providers on one's property for visits of varying durations is a large part of what makes land ownership valuable. Although the assertion of a hermit's right is rather uncontroversial in the residential context, the law will not let any man truly become an island. Hence the hermit's land may be invaded by another who can raise a necessity defense to trespass, and public agents like firemen or police officers in hot pursuit may be privileged to enter the hermit's land.

The hermit's right, then, is perhaps only useful in a few real-property situations. Surely a true recluse will value his solitude. But beyond that, most uses of the hermit's right will be governmental. The state might establish a protected wilderness area for conservation or wildlife protection reasons, or it may create a minefield as a way to prevent invaders (or anyone else) from traversing a strategic space. Alternatively, the state may embrace paternalistic justifications for a rule that excludes everyone. For example, a government that owns a site where nuclear weapons have been tested may want to prevent anyone from setting foot on the property in question.

Intuitively, profit-making enterprises will have little use for a strict keep-out regime. It is difficult to make a profit off land if its owner will allow neither customers nor employees to set foot on it. We can expect to see firms utilizing their hermit's right only in those rare circumstances when permitting entry onto the land might expose them to substantial legal liability, as with a toxic waste dump that cannot be cleaned up in a cost-effective manner, or when utilizing the hermit's right arises out of a conflict between management and labor (i.e., a lockout).

In light of the very narrow circumstances in which private landowners seek to assert the hermit's right, it is appropriate to deem this right to exclude as practically trivial, except when legitimate, altruistic conservation interests arise. Permanent isolation is usually so unappealing that virtually no one in his right mind aspires to it. The proof for this assertion is in the pudding. It is almost impossible to locate a reported case involving a permanent invocation of the hermit's right with respect to land that has positive economic value but little environmental value. The closest case, *Brown v. Burdett*, involves a testator's wishes that her home be bricked and boarded up "with good long nails" for twenty years following the testator's death, a will provision that the court invalidated on public policy grounds. So although the hermit's right perhaps retains importance in philosophical discussions of real property rights, its practical import is sufficiently minimal so as to warrant little more discussion here.

B. The Bouncer's Right

Once we move away from extreme and economically unproductive exercises of the right to exclude, we arrive quickly at rights that take on enormous economic importance. As soon as an owner wishes to allow potential entrants onto his property at certain times of day, or admit some parties while refusing entry to others, or establish some criteria that will govern entry onto the land, he is exercising the sort of discretion that makes the right to exclude valuable. The greater power to exclude may include the lesser power, but it is the lesser power that takes on greater importance. Moreover, while one cannot exercise the hermit's right and the bouncer's right simultaneously, the latter three rights in the bundle are by no means mutually exclusive. Indeed, the bouncer's right, exclusionary vibes, and exclusionary amenities often will be used conjunctively by a resource owner.

The bouncer's right, then, is the landowner's right to discriminate among various parties, permitting some to enter or use the land while keeping others off the property entirely. Like the bouncer at a nightclub, the owner must exercise discretion as to who can utilize the resource, and the criteria for exclusion need not be transparent to those seeking admission. There are commercial and non-commercial variations on the bouncer's right, but they are analytically similar. A business owner will value the right to admit some customers and vendors but not others, whereas a homeowner will care about his right to invite friends and family into his home while excluding foes and strangers. . . .

C. Exclusionary Vibes

When I was an undergraduate at a large, state-subsidized university, I got the sense that there was a fair bit of homogeneity within each of the many fraternity and sorority houses on campus and attributed this homogeneity to the rush and pledge processes. But then I moved into cooperative student housing and noticed a similar level of homogeneity within particular houses, which was initially puzzling, since any student could move into a campus cooperative. The co-ops did not exercise the bouncer's right at all (except to exclude non-student residents), and yet each house seemed to have a distinct personality, not unlike the fraternities and sororities that I occasionally visited. Governance and socialization seemed like incomplete explanations for this homogeneity. If my impressions were correct, this homogeneity in the campus cooperatives raised interesting questions about what was substituting for the bouncer's right. . . .

An exclusionary vibes approach involves the landowner's communication to potential entrants about the character of the community's inhabitants. Such communication tells potential entrants that certain people may not feel welcome if they enter the community in question, because they will not share certain affinities with existing or future residents. Although the landowner invokes no legal right to exclude anyone from the property in question, an exclusionary vibe may still be effective at excluding a targeted population thanks to two mechanisms. First, a prospective entrant may view the exclusionary vibe as an effective tool for creating a focal point around which people can organize their affairs. A variation on this focal points effect arises if the prospective entrant assumes that the exclusionary vibe will create a community population that is likely to embrace bouncer's exclusion at a later date as a means of removing the entrant from the community. Second, the potential entrant may assume, incorrectly, that the exclusionary vibe is backed by a bouncer's right to exclude those who are not made to feel welcome by the exclusionary vibe. I will elaborate on both of these mechanisms in detail, using a hypothetical community.

Suppose that a condo developer sees a market niche for residential communities targeted toward extroverted individuals. To that end, the developer advertises his new condominium as "Social Butterfly Place." This advertising should suffice to make the condominium attractive to social butterflies and their families, and unattractive to more introverted individuals, even if the developer does not invest in any amenities that are designed to appeal to the extroverted.

How come? Here we see the dynamics working together. Extroverted individuals probably will value proximity to fellow extroverts, so that they can easily find outgoing partners for conversation and joint social activities. Introverts may feel left out or marginalized living in the building, and this marginalization may impose real social and psychological costs on them. Because they may anticipate incurring some of these costs if they move in to Social Butterfly Place, many introverts will opt for a residence in some other building, ceteris paribus. This phenomenon illustrates the possibility for exclusionary vibes to serve as focal points.

Savvier introverted prospective condominium purchasers may be deterred from moving into Social Butterfly Place as well. These potential entrants would understand that the developer could do nothing to stop them from purchasing a home in the building, but would recognize the effectiveness of the focal point strategy at establishing a homogeneous population of residents consisting largely of extroverts. Even if one of these introverts did not care whether he felt left out of his neighbor's social interactions, he would rightly worry about the prospects that his extroverted neighbors might in the future: a) decide to use the bouncer's right to expel introverts if they concluded that there were too many introverts in their midst; or b) adopt, by majority vote, governance rules that made life pleasant for extroverts and unpleasant for introverts, such as mandatory weekly condominium association meetings, or lax nighttime noise regulations for hallway conversations and parties within units.

Finally, some would-be condominium purchasers will see the sign "Social Butterfly Place" and erroneously assume that only extroverts are permitted to reside there. In other words, they may misread the exclusionary vibe as indicative of a developer's intent and authority to exercise a trespass-based right to exclude them. If they were to ask the developer whether introverts may reside in the tower, the developer would say that all are welcome, but many people are embarrassed to ask questions of that sort or ignorant of their legal rights. Hence an exclusionary vibe may act as an effective bluff that prevents some potential entrants who are targeted for exclusion from moving into a community. At some level, then, a fence and a "Beware of Dog" sign are fungible, even if there is no dog.

As these examples indicate, the simple act of naming a new development "Social Butterfly Place" could prove effective at excluding the introverted from residence in the development. Exclusionary vibes can function as a substitute for, or a complement to, the bouncer's right. Thus, what might superficially appear to be a developer's First Amendment commercial speech right actually takes on much greater significance as a property right, and it is appropriate to characterize the exclusionary vibe as a right to exclude. It should be equally clear that every exclusionary message is implicitly inclusionary with respect to those people who would prefer to live in a community that is devoid of those people who are targeted for exclusion.

In the real world, real estate developers sometimes do market their residences as paradise for extroverts. The exclusionary vibes strategy is prevalent where other groups or attributes are targeted for exclusion or inclusion as well. Condominium buildings adopt names like Cotton Hope Plantation and Sholom House. And individual cooperative houses near my old university campus described the character of their communities in great detail on the Internet. Indeed, entire campuses sometimes engage in heated debates over exclusionary vibes, as the recent controversy over the rebranding of "The University of the South" as "Sewanee" makes clear. We need not strain our minds too much in order to see the power of exclusionary vibes. Imagine, for example, the sales center for a mixed-income planned development in a large southern city. The sales center looks identical to any other sales center, with one difference: a large confederate battle flag flies on the flagpole out front. The mere presence of this flag would produce a first generation of homeowners who are overwhelmingly white. [In a passage that has been edited out, Strahilevitz next surveys the legal regulation of exclusionary vibes. We will touch on some of them later in the course, particularly in our discussion of the Fair Housing Act]. . . .

Exclusionary vibes . . . raise a host of new difficulties. For example, exclusionary vibes may be ineffective if too many people whom the landowner would prefer to exclude are oblivious to the signal, are poor at self-assessing, or have contrarian instincts. Alternatively, exclusionary vibes may be too controversial if they are noticed and denounced by third parties who object to the content of the exclusionary message, asserting that such a message implies second-class citizenship for the part of the community that is targeted for exclusion. In such instances, a landowner may seek an exclusion strategy that is both more effective and less in-your-face than an exclusionary vibe. Exclusionary amenity strategies present an attractive alternative.

D. Exclusionary Amenities

An exclusionary amenity is a common amenity that is embedded in a residential community at least in part because willingness to pay for the amenity functions as a proxy for some desired characteristic. An exclusionary amenity is a collective resource that provokes a polarizing response among people who are considering purchasing a home or renting an apartment in a particular community. Prospective purchasers (or renters) whom the developer (or landlord) would like to attract will regard the community as more attractive because of the presence of the amenity, and prospective purchasers whom the developer would not like to attract will regard the community as less attractive because of the amenity's presence. In another paper, I hypothesized that, during the 1990s, golf courses in residential developments functioned as exclusionary amenities because golf participation was a better proxy for race than wealth, income, or virtually any other characteristic. The paper provided circumstantial evidence to indicate that by purchasing homes in mandatory-membership golf communities, some non-golfing homeowners were essentially purchasing Caucasian residential homogeneity. The punch line of that paper was that the exclusionary amenities strategy might permit developers to circumvent laws that prohibit race discrimination in sales (the bouncer's right) and advertising (exclusionary vibes).

The residential golf course is not the only possible manifestation of the exclusionary amenities strategy. On the contrary, real estate developers seeking to create a "Catholic Gated Community" have noticed how placing a new, conservative Catholic school—Ave Maria University—at the center of their planned residential community can help promote the overwhelmingly Catholic character of their new development. Virginia real estate developers interested in minimizing the number of families with school-aged children in their condominium building invested heavily in an attractive bar and billiards room, but consciously avoided putting a playroom anywhere in the structure. And, by the same token, many communities forego investing in public transportation hubs or basketball courts that their residents would very much like to use, because of a fear that such inclusionary amenities might attract the wrong kinds of people to the community.

It is an expensive proposition, of course, to construct a golf course or religious university at the center of a residential development. So why would someone seeking to achieve residential homogeneity go to all that trouble? Precisely because an exclusionary amenities strategy may work better than exclusionary vibes alone. After all, an exclusionary amenity may be as effective in establishing a focal point as an exclusionary vibe, allowing people with similar preferences or attributes to find each other and live as neighbors. And the exclusionary amenity will provide added punch: a tax that falls most heavily on people who lack those similar preferences or attributes. So, let us assume that the Ave Maria Township residents subsidize the adjacent university by picking up the costs of its police protection, utilities, and land acquisition costs. As a result, homeowners in Ave Maria Township will face higher monthly assessments than homeowners in a neighboring homeowners association that is not affiliated with an institution of higher learning. A devout, traditionalist Catholic homeowner might be happy to pay this extra assessment, perhaps because he plans to make use of the theological books in the university's library and values proximity to it, or because he wants to live near the sorts of neighbors who would value proximity to such a library. But a non-Catholic Ave Maria homeowner who did not particularly want to live in an overwhelmingly Catholic neighborhood would get nothing of value in exchange for his higher monthly assessment: He would not use the library himself, and would not particularly care about whether his neighbors used the library or not. If there are otherwise similar neighborhoods surrounding Ave Maria, we should expect to see Ave Maria Township take on an overwhelmingly Catholic character and other neighborhoods take on a relatively non-Catholic character. The result will be religious residential segregation, achieved with no overt discrimination and an advertising campaign that need not include blatant exclusionary vibes. The differential tax on non-Catholic homeowners in Ave Maria will serve the same focal points purpose as the exclusionary vibe and will further exclude prospective entrants who might have been impervious or oblivious to exclusionary vibes. Furthermore, unlike a one-time advertising campaign, the presence of the university will directly affect the purchasing decisions of several generations of owners.

1. What do you think of Professor Strahilevitz's categories? Do exclusionary vibes and exclusionary amenities trouble you? If so, in what contexts? Can you think of ways of addressing the troubling aspects through legal rules?

JACQUE V. STEENBERG HOMES, INC.

Supreme Court of Wisconsin, 1997
563 N.W.2d 154

WILLIAM A. BABLITCH, Justice. Steenberg Homes had a mobile home to deliver. Unfortunately for Harvey and Lois Jacque (the Jacques), the easiest route of delivery was across their land. Despite adamant protests by the Jacques, Steenberg plowed a path through the Jacques' snow-covered field and via that path, delivered the mobile home. Consequently, the Jacques sued Steenberg Homes for intentional trespass. At trial, Steenberg Homes conceded the intentional trespass, but argued that no compensatory damages had been proved, and that punitive damages could not be awarded without compensatory damages. Although the jury awarded the Jacques $1 in nominal damages and $100,000 in punitive damages, the circuit court set aside the jury's award of $100,000. The court of appeals affirmed, reluctantly concluding that it could not reinstate the punitive damages because it was bound by precedent establishing that an award of nominal damages will not sustain a punitive damage award. We conclude that when nominal damages are awarded for an intentional trespass to land, punitive damages may, in the discretion of the jury, be awarded. We further conclude that the $100,000 awarded by the jury is not excessive. Accordingly, we reverse and remand for reinstatement of the punitive damage award.

The relevant facts follow. Plaintiffs, Lois and Harvey Jacques, are an elderly couple, now retired from farming, who own roughly 170 acres near Wilke's Lake in the town of Schleswig. The defendant, Steenberg Homes, Inc. (Steenberg), is in the business of selling mobile homes. In the fall of 1993, a neighbor of the Jacques purchased a mobile home from Steenberg. Delivery of the mobile home was included in the sales price.

Steenberg determined that the easiest route to deliver the mobile home was across the Jacques' land. Steenberg preferred transporting the home across the Jacques' land because the only alternative was a private road which was covered in up to seven feet of snow and contained a sharp curve which would require sets of "rollers" to be used when maneuvering the home around the curve. Steenberg asked the Jacques on several separate occasions whether it could move the home across the Jacques' farm field. The Jacques refused. The Jacques were sensitive about allowing others on their land because they had lost property valued at over $10,000 to other neighbors in an adverse possession action in the mid-1980s. Despite repeated refusals from the Jacques,

Steenberg decided to sell the mobile home, which was to be used as a summer cottage, and delivered it on February 15, 1994.

On the morning of delivery, Mr. Jacque observed the mobile home parked on the corner of the town road adjacent to his property. He decided to find out where the movers planned to take the home. The movers, who were Steenberg employees, showed Mr. Jacque the path they planned to take with the mobile home to reach the neighbor's lot. The path cut across the Jacques' land. Mr. Jacque informed the movers that it was the Jacques' land they were planning to cross and that Steenberg did not have permission to cross their land. He told them that Steenberg had been refused permission to cross the Jacques' land.

One of Steenberg's employees called the assistant manager, who then came out to the Jacques' home. In the meantime, the Jacques called and asked some of their neighbors and the town chairman to come over immediately. Once everyone was present, the Jacques showed the assistant manager an aerial map and plat book of the township to prove their ownership of the land, and reiterated their demand that the home not be moved across their land.

At that point, the assistant manager asked Mr. Jacque how much money it would take to get permission. Mr. Jacque responded that it was not a question of money; the Jacques just did not want Steenberg to cross their land. Mr. Jacque testified that he told Steenberg to "[F]ollow the road, that is what the road is for." Steenberg employees left the meeting without permission to cross the land.

At trial, one of Steenberg's employees testified that, upon coming out of the Jacques' home, the assistant manager stated: "I don't give a —— what [Mr. Jacque] said, just get the home in there any way you can." The other Steenberg employee confirmed this testimony and further testified that the assistant manager told him to park the company truck in such a way that no one could get down the town road to see the route the employees were taking with the home. The assistant manager denied giving these instructions, and Steenberg argued that the road was blocked for safety reasons.

The employees, after beginning down the private road, ultimately used a "bobcat" to cut a path through the Jacques' snow-covered field and hauled the home across the Jacques' land to the neighbor's lot. One employee testified that upon returning to the office and informing the assistant manager that they had gone across the field, the assistant manager reacted by giggling and laughing. The other employee confirmed this testimony. The assistant manager disputed this testimony.

When a neighbor informed the Jacques that Steenberg had, in fact, moved the mobile home across the Jacques' land, Mr. Jacque called the Manitowoc County Sheriff's Department. After interviewing the parties and observing the scene, an officer from the sheriff's department issued a $30 citation to Steenberg's assistant manager.

The Jacques commenced an intentional tort action in Manitowoc County Circuit Court, Judge Allan J. Deehr presiding, seeking compensatory and punitive damages from Steenberg. The case was tried before a jury on December 1, 1994. At the completion of the Jacques' case, Steenberg moved for a directed verdict under Wis. Stat. §805.14(3)(1993-94). For purposes of the motion, Steenberg admitted to an intentional trespass to land, but asked the circuit court to find that the Jacques were not entitled to compensatory damages or punitive damages based on insufficiency of the evidence. The circuit court denied Steenberg's motion and the questions of punitive and compensatory damages were submitted to the jury. The jury awarded the Jacques $1 nominal damages and $100,000 punitive damages. . . .

Steenberg argues that, as a matter of law, punitive damages could not be awarded by the jury because punitive damages must be supported by an award of compensatory damages and here the jury awarded only nominal and punitive damages. The Jacques contend that the rationale supporting the compensatory damage award requirement is inapposite when the wrongful act is an intentional trespass to land. We agree with the Jacques. . . .

We turn first to the individual landowner's interest in protecting his or her land from trespass. The United States Supreme Court has recognized that the private landowner's right to exclude others from his or her land is "one of the most essential sticks in the bundle of rights that are commonly characterized as property." *Dolan v. City of Tigard*, 512 U.S. 374, 384, 114 S.Ct. 2309, 2316, 129 L.Ed.2d 304 (1994); (quoting *Kaiser Aetna v. United States*, 444 U.S. 164, 176, 100 S.Ct. 383, 391, 62 L.Ed.2d 332 (1979)). *Accord Nollan v. California Coastal Comm'n*, 483 U.S. 825, 831, 107 S.Ct. 3141, 3145, 97 L.Ed.2d 677 (1987) (quoting *Loretto v. Teleprompter Manhattan CATV Corp.*, 458 U.S. 419, 433, 102 S.Ct. 3164, 3175, 73 L.Ed.2d 868 (1982)). This court has long recognized "[e]very person ['s] constitutional right to the exclusive enjoyment of his own property for any purpose which does not invade the rights of another person." *Diana Shooting Club v. Lamoreux*, 114 Wis. 44, 59, 89 N.W. 880 (1902) (holding that the victim of an intentional trespass should have been allowed to take judgment for nominal damages and costs). Thus, both this court and the Supreme Court recognize the individual's legal right to exclude others from private property.

Yet a right is hollow if the legal system provides insufficient means to protect it. Felix Cohen offers the following analysis summarizing the relationship between the individual and the state regarding property rights:

[T]hat is property to which the following label can be attached:

To the world:

Keep off X unless you have my permission, which I may grant or withhold.

Signed: Private Citizen

Endorsed: The state

Felix S. Cohen, *Dialogue on Private Property*, IX Rutgers Law Review 357, 374 (1954). Harvey and Lois Jacque have the right to tell Steenberg Homes and any other trespasser, "No, you cannot cross our land." But that right has no practical meaning unless protected by the State. And, as this court recognized as early as 1854, a "halfpenny" award does not constitute state protection. . . .

In sum, the individual has a strong interest in excluding trespassers from his or her land. Although only nominal damages were awarded to the Jacques, Steenberg's intentional trespass caused actual harm. We turn next to society's interest in protecting private property from the intentional trespasser.

Society has an interest in punishing and deterring intentional trespassers beyond that of protecting the interests of the individual landowner. Society has an interest in preserving the integrity of the legal system. Private landowners should feel confident that wrongdoers who trespass upon their land will be appropriately punished. When landowners have confidence in the legal system, they are less likely to resort to "self-help" remedies. In *McWilliams,* the court recognized the importance of " 'prevent[ing] the practice of dueling, [by permitting] juries [ ] to *punish* insult by exemplary damages.' " *McWilliams,* 3 Wis. at 428. Although dueling is rarely a modern form of self-help, one can easily imagine a frustrated landowner taking the law into his or her own hands when faced with a brazen trespasser, like Steenberg, who refuses to heed no trespass warnings. . . .

Reversed and remanded with directions.

STATE V. SHACK

Supreme Court of New Jersey, 1971
277 A.2d 369

WEINTRAUB, C.J. Defendants entered upon private property to aid migrant farmworkers employed and housed there. Having refused to depart upon the demand of the owner, defendants were charged with violating N.J.S.A. 2A:170-31 which provides that "(a)ny person who trespasses on any lands . . . after being forbidden so to trespass by the owner . . . is a disorderly person and shall be punished by a fine of not more than $50." Defendants were convicted in the Municipal Court of Deerfield Township and again on appeal in the County Court of Cumberland County on a trial De novo. R. 3:23-8(a). We certified their further appeal before argument in the Appellate Division.

Before us, no one seeks to sustain these convictions. The complaints were prosecuted in the Municipal Court and in the County Court by counsel engaged by the complaining landowner, Tedesco. However Tedesco did not respond to this appeal, and the county prosecutor, while defending abstractly the constitutionality of the trespass statute, expressly disclaimed any position as to whether the statute reached the activity of these defendants.

Complainant, Tedesco, a farmer, employs migrant workers for his seasonal needs. As part of their compensation, these workers are housed at a camp on his property.

Defendant Tejeras is a field worker for the Farm Workers Division of the Southwest Citizens Organization for Poverty Elimination, known by the acronym SCOPE, a nonprofit corporation funded by the Office of Economic Opportunity pursuant to an act of Congress, 42 U.S.C.A. §§2861-2864. The role of SCOPE includes providing for the "health services of the migrant farm worker."

Defendant Shack is a staff attorney with the Farm Workers Division of Camden Regional Legal Services, Inc., known as "CRLS," also a nonprofit corporation funded by the Office of Economic Opportunity pursuant to an act of Congress, 42 U.S.C.A. §2809(a)(3). The mission of CRLS includes legal advice and representation for these workers.

Differences had developed between Tedesco and these defendants prior to the events which led to the trespass charges now before us. Hence when defendant Tejeras wanted to go upon Tedesco's farm to find a migrant worker who needed medical aid for the removal of 28 sutures, he called upon defendant Shack for his help with respect to the legalities involved. Shack, too, had a mission to perform on Tedesco's farm; he wanted to discuss a legal problem with another migrant worker there employed and housed. Defendants arranged to go to the farm together. Shack carried literature to inform the migrant farmworkers of the assistance available to them under federal statutes, but no mention seems to have been made of that literature when Shack was later confronted by Tedesco.

Defendants entered upon Tedesco's property and as they neared the camp site where the farmworkers were housed, they were confronted by Tedesco who inquired of their purpose. Tejeras and Shack stated their missions. In response, Tedesco offered to find the injured worker, and as to the worker who needed legal advice, Tedesco also offered to locate the man but insisted that the consultation would have to take place in Tedesco's office and in his presence. Defendants declined, saying they had the right to see the men in the privacy of their living quarters and without Tedesco's supervsion. Tedesco thereupon summoned a State Trooper who, however, refused to remove defendants except upon Tedesco's written complaint. Tedesco then executed the formal complaints charging violations of the trespass statute.

The constitutionality of the trespass statute, as applied here, is challenged on several scores. . . . These constitutional claims are not established by any definitive holding. We think it unnecessary to explore their validity. The reason is that we are satisfied that under our State law the ownership of real property does not include the right a bar access to governmental services available to migrant workers and hence there was no trespass within the meaning of the penal statute. The policy considerations which underlie that conclusion may be much the same as those which would be weighed with respect to one or more of the constitutional challenges, but a decision in nonconstitutional terms is more satisfactory, because the interests of migrant workers are more expansively served in that way than they would be if they had no more freedom than these constitutional concepts could be found to mandate if indeed they apply at all.

Property rights serve human values. They are recognized to that end, and are limited by it. Title to real property cannot include dominion over the destiny of persons the owner permits to come upon the premises. Their well-being must remain the paramount concern of a system of law. Indeed the needs of the occupants may be so imperative and their strength so weak, that the law will deny the occupants the power to contract away what is deemed essential to their health, welfare, or dignity.

Here we are concerned with a highly disadvantaged segment of our society. We are told that every year farmworkers and their families numbering more than one million leave their home areas to fill the seasonal demand for farm labor in the United States. . . .

The migrant farmworkers are a community within but apart from the local scene. They are rootless and isolated. Although the need for their labors is evident, they are unorganized and without economic or political power. It is their plight alone that summoned government to their aid. In response, Congress provided under Title III-B of the Economic Opportunity Act of 1964 (42 U.S.C.A. §2701 et seq.) for "assistance for migrant and other seasonally employed farmworkers and their families." Section 2861 states "the purpose of this part is to assist migrant and seasonal farmworkers and their families to improve their living conditions and develop skills necessary for a productive and self-sufficient life in an increasingly complex and technological society." Section 2862(b)(1) provides for funding of programs "to meet the immediate needs of migrant and seasonal farmworkers and their families, such as day care for children, education, health services, improved housing and sanitation (including the provision and maintenance of emergency and temporary housing and sanitation facilities), legal advice and representation, and consumer training and couseling.' As we have said, SCOPE is engaged in a program funded under this section, and CRLS also pursues the objectives of this section although, we gather, it is funded under §2809(a)(3), which is not limited in its concern to the migrant and other seasonally employed farmworkers and seeks "to further the cause of justice among persons living in poverty by mobilizing the assistance of lawyers and legal institutions and by providing legal advice, legal representation, counseling, education, and other appropriate services."

These ends would not be gained if the intended beneficiaries could be insulated from efforts to reach them. It is in this framework that we must decide whether the camp operator's rights in his lands may stand between the migrant workers and those who would aid them. The key to that aid is communication. Since the migrant workers are outside the mainstream of the communities in which they are housed and are unaware of their rights and opportunities and of the services available to them, they can be reached only by positive efforts tailored to that end. The Report of the Governor's Task Force on Migrant Farm Labor (1968) noted that "One of the major problems related to seasonal farm labor is the lack of adequate direct information with regard to the availability of public services," and that "there is a dire need to provide the workers with basic educational and informational material in a language and style that can be readily understood by the migrant" (pp. 101-102). The report stressed the problem of access and deplored the notion that property rights may stand as a barrier, saying "In our judgment, 'no trespass' signs represent the last dying remnants of paternalistic behavior" (p. 63).

A man's right in his real property of course is not absolute. It was a maxim of the common law that one should so use his property as not to injure the rights of others.

Broom, *Legal Maxims* (10th ed. Kersley 1939), p. 238; 39 *Words and Phrases*, "Sic Utere Tuo ut Alienum Non Laedas," p. 335. Although hardly a precise solvent of actual controversies, the maxim does express the inevitable proposition that rights are relative and there must be an accommodation when they meet. Hence it has long been true that necessity, private or public, may justify entry upon the lands of another. For a catalogue of such situations, see Prosser, *Torts* (3d ed. 1964), §24, pp. 127-129; 6A *American Law of Property* (A. J. Casner ed. 1954) §28.10, p. 31; 52 Am.Jur., "Trespass," §§40-41, pp. 867-869. *See also* Restatement, Second, Torts (1965) §§197-211; *Krauth v. Geller*, 31 N.J. 270, 272-273, 157 A.2d 129 (1960).

The subject is not static. As pointed out in 5 Powell, *Real Property* (Rohan 1970) §745, pp. 493-494, while society will protect the owner in his permissible interests in land, yet

> ". . . (s)uch an owner must expect to find the absoluteness of his property rights curtailed by the organs of society, for the promotion of the best interests of others for whom these organs also operate as protective agencies. The necessity for such curtailments is greater in a modern industrialized and urbanized society than it was in the relatively simple American society of fifty, 100, or 200 years ago. The current balance between individualism and dominance of the social interest depends not only upon political and social ideologies, but also upon the physical and social facts of the time and place under discussion."

Professor Powell added in §746, pp. 494-496:

> "As one looks back along the historic road traversed by the law of land in England and in America, one sees a change from the viewpoint that he who owns may do as he pleases with what he owns, to a position which hesitatingly embodies an ingredient of stewardship; which grudgingly, but steadily, broadens the recognized scope of social interests in the utilization of things. . . .
>
> To one seeing history through the glasses of religion, these changes may seem to evidence increasing embodiments of the golden rule. To one thinking in terms of political and economic ideologies, they are likely to be labeled evidences of 'social enlightenment,' or of 'creeping socialism' or even of 'communistic infiltration,' according to the individual's assumed definitions and retained or acquired prejudices. With slight attention to words or labels, time marches on toward new adjustments between individualism and the social interests."

The process involves not only the accommodation between the right of the owner and the interests of the general public in his use of this property, but involves also an accommodation between the right of the owner and the right of individuals who are parties with him in consensual transactions relating to the use of the property. Accordingly substantial alterations have been made as between a landlord and his tenant. *See Reste Realty Corp. v. Cooper*, 53 N.J. 444, 451-453, 251 A.2d 268 (1969); *Marini v. Ireland*, 56 N.J. 130, 141-143, 265 A.2d 526 (1970). . . .

We see no profit in trying to decide upon a conventional category and then forcing the present subject into it. That approach would be artificial and distorting. The quest is for a fair adjustment of the competing needs of the parties, in the light of the realities of the relationship between the migrant worker and the operator of the housing facility.

Thus approaching the case, we find it unthinkable that the farmer-employer can assert a right to isolate the migrant worker in any respect significant for the worker's well-being. The farmer, of course, is entitled to pursue his farming activities without interference, and this defendants readily concede. But we see no legitimate need for a right in the farmer to deny the worker the opportunity for aid available from federal, State, or local services, or from recognized charitable groups seeking to assist him. Hence representatives of these agencies and organizations may enter upon the premises to seek out the worker at his living quarters. So, too, the migrant worker must be allowed to receive visitors there of his own choice, so long as there is no behavior hurtful to others, and members of the press may not be denied reasonable access to workers who do not object to seeing them.

It is not our purpose to open the employer's premises to the general public if in fact the employer himself has not done so. We do not say, for example, that solicitors or peddlers of all kinds may enter on their own; we may assume or the present that the employer may regulate their entry or bar them, at least if the employer's purpose is not to gain a commercial advantage for himself or if the regulation does not deprive the migrant worker of practical access to things he needs.

And we are mindful of the employer's interest in his own and in his employees' security. Hence he may reasonably require a visitor to identify himself, and also to state his general purpose if the migrant worker has not already informed him that the visitor is expected. But the employer may not deny the worker his privacy or interfere with his opportunity to live with dignity and to enjoy associations customary among our citizens. These rights are too fundamental to be denied on the basis of an interest in real property and too fragile to be left to the unequal bargaining strength of the parties. *See Henningsen v. Bloomfield Motors, Inc.*, 32 N.J. 358, 403-404, 161 A.2d 69 (1960); *Ellsworth Dobbs, Inc. v. Johnson*, 50 N.J. 528, 555, 236 A.2d 843 (1967).

It follows that defendants here invaded no possessory right of the farmer-employer. Their conduct was therefore beyond the reach of the trespass statute. The judgments are accordingly reversed and the matters remanded to the County Court with directions to enter judgments of acquittal.

NOTES AND QUESTIONS

1. *Jacque v. Steenberg Homes* suggests that the right to exclude is a critically important aspect of our property system. *State v. Shack* suggests that the right to exclude is subject to significant limitations. There is nothing inconsistent with these two positions—just because something is important does not mean that it is immune from limitation. Looking at the facts of the two cases, what do you think led to the different emphasis in the courts' opinions?

2. William Blackstone famously wrote that property is "that sole and despotic dominion which one man claims and exercises over the external things of the world, in total exclusion of the right of any other individual in the universe." As *Shack* illustrates, there are some limits to this dominion. What limits would you place on a property owner's right to exclude?

3. Imagine that you are walking down a beach. You come across a sign stating that part of the beach is closed to the public because it is part of a private nature preserve. A bit later, you come across a sign stating that part of the beach is private property and that access is reserved to beachfront homeowners. Are these signs trying to achieve the same thing? Is the right to exclude a good thing or a bad thing?

FREEDOM-BASED THEORIES OF PRIVATE PROPERTY

Private property is often justified because it protects and promotes individual freedom. Proponents of freedom-based theories make three distinct types of arguments about the relationship between property and freedom. First, property creates zones of individual autonomy and privacy. As Charles Reich put it, property "draw[s] a boundary between public and private power . . . maintaining independence, dignity and pluralism in society by creating zones within which the majority has to yield to the owner." Charles A. Reich, *The New Property*, 73 Yale L.J. 733, 771-772 (1964). Second, private property disperses power that otherwise would be held exclusively by the government. The economist Milton Friedman wrote that private-property-based capitalism "promotes personal freedom because it separates economic power from political power and in this way enables the one to offset the other." Milton Friedman, *Capitalism and Freedom*, 9 (1962). Third, private property gives people access to the resources that they need to make basic life decisions for themselves. As Reich observed, "[p]olitical rights presuppose that individuals and private groups have the will and the means to act independently." Reich, *supra*. People cannot have the will and the means to act independently if they are beholden to others for resources that they need to live their lives. Of course, one person's freedom can conflict with another person's freedom. If I am able to exclude you from my property, I gain a zone of individual autonomy and privacy at the expense of your freedom to access my property. The private property system therefore "is a distribution of freedom *and* unfreedom." G.A. Cohen, *Illusions About Private Property and Freedom*, in 4 *Issues in Marxist Philosophy* 226, 226-227 (1981). Do not make the mistake of associating freedom-based arguments for private property with any particular part of the political spectrum. Comparing Friedman and Reich is instructive. Friedman's arguments about property and freedom were made in the context of defending the institution of free market capitalism. Reich's arguments were made in the context of making an argument for the recognition of a property right to receive welfare payments and other types of government largess.

CHAPTER 2

PRESENT AND FUTURE INTERESTS

In this chapter, we will learn about the system of present and future interests that form the backbone of our system of property ownership. This system applies to both real and personal property, but we will focus on the ownership of land. Our system of ownership has its origins in feudal England, and some feudal concepts still crop up from time to time in this area of law. We will focus on the modern system of ownership and will note important historical events and concepts in places along the way.

To this point, we have generally focused on ownership of objects by one person. Our ownership system, however, includes various ways to divide ownership of the same object among multiple people. Division of ownership will be a theme that comes up in many contexts throughout the course.

DIVISION OF OWNERSHIP

The type of division of ownership allowed by the estates and future interests system is *division of ownership by time*. When we divide ownership in this way, one person might have the present right to possession of piece of land, and another person might have a future right of possession of that land. You are probably already intuitively familiar with this kind of division if you have ever rented an apartment. During the term of your lease, you have the right to possess the apartment. The landlord maintains the right to possess the apartment once the lease expires. We therefore have two people with rights to possession of the apartment—you (the tenant), with a present right of possession, and the landlord, with a future right of possession.

To divide ownership over time, our system of ownership distinguishes between present and future interests in property. *Present interests* give the owner a present right of possession (or in some cases use) of the land. *Future interests* give the owner a future right of possession (or use) of the land. Note that present and future interests are defined in terms of possession, not ownership. This is because *a future interest exists at the time it is created*. If I have a future interest in Blackacre, that means that I own that future interest now. It is my right of possession, not my ownership, that is delayed to the future. It is therefore misleading to speak of a future interest giving its holder future ownership of the land at issue. The future interest holder has present ownership of an interest that gives a future right of possession. We have already seen the importance of this point in *Gruen v. Gruen*. Victor's gift to Michael was valid because it was a present gift of a future interest, rather than a promise of a later gift at death.

In the text that follows, we will introduce the present and future interests. Pay very close attention to the terminology. It is often said that learning the present and future interests is like learning a foreign language. This subject is not actually that difficult, but you will need to keep the names and characteristics of the different interests straight in your mind. In this area of law, labels matter.

A. PRESENT INTERESTS: THE SYSTEM OF PRESENT ESTATES IN LAND

In our system of ownership, present interests in land are typically called *estates in land*. Consistent with our theme of dividing ownership over time, we begin with three types of interests that are defined, at least in part, by their duration: the fee simple absolute, the life estate, and the leasehold estates. These three types of estates form the core of our present interests system. We then examine some specialized estates that are defined by characteristics other than time.

1. THE FEE SIMPLE ABSOLUTE

The *fee simple absolute* is unlimited in duration and is the closest thing that the U.S. legal system has to absolute ownership of land. Ownership of land in fee simple absolute is ownership forever. Because the fee simple absolute is of unlimited duration, it is not accompanied by a future interest. In this sense, the fee simple absolute is unique. All other estates in land are of at least potentially limited duration and so are accompanied by a future interest.

Lawyers often leave off the "absolute," and refer to this estate simply as a "fee simple." In later chapters in this book, we will do the same thing. The word "absolute" is needed to distinguish this estate from some relatively uncommon estates that are discussed further below. "Fee simple," standing alone, is generally presumed to mean "fee simple absolute."

Ownership in fee simple absolute is common in the United States. If you buy a house, you will typically purchase the house in fee simple absolute. Note the phrasing we just used—we first described what was owned (the house), then said that you owned the house "in" fee simple absolute. We will often use the word "in" in this way to describe an owner's interest in property.

LANGUAGE OF CONVEYANCE

A critical point here is that interests in property are created by the use of specific words. We are looking for specific *language of conveyance*—this will be a recurring theme in our course. When we read a document that conveys property (typically a deed or a will), we look at the granting language to determine the interest in property created by the document. Perhaps the most important thing to learn at this stage is what language creates what interest.

In our examples of language of conveyance, we follow common convention and denote the grantor with the letter O, signifying that this person was the owner of the land before the conveyance. Grantees are typically denoted with letters A, B, C, and so on.

The language of conveyance required to create a fee simple absolute has changed over time. At traditional common law, a fee simple absolute was created by the language "to A and her heirs." The "to A" part of this phrase historically was called *words of purchase*—those words identified the recipient of the interest. The "and her heirs" part was called *words of limitation*—those words identified the interest being created. The "to A and her heirs" language still creates a fee simple absolute at modern law, but today we no longer need the words "and her heirs." Today, all states by statute or court decision recognize that a grant of property "to A" creates a fee simple absolute.

> **EXAMPLE 1:** O grants Blackacre "to A and her heirs." Under both modern and common law, A owns Blackacre in fee simple absolute.

> **EXAMPLE 2:** O grants Blackacre "to A." Under modern law, A owns Blackacre in fee simple absolute.

The use of "and her heirs" in the traditional common-law language of conveyance can be confusing. This language was required to make it clear that the conveyance was of an interest of unlimited duration. Under the old (and now obsolete) common-law rule, a grant of "to A" would create a life estate—a different interest that we discuss next. The *only* significance of the language "and her heirs" is to signify that the grant is in of fee simple absolute. *A's heirs get absolutely nothing in the conveyance.* (For more on "heirs," see the sidebar.)

> **EXAMPLE 3:** O grants Blackacre "to A and her heirs." A sells Blackacre to B. A few years later, A dies. A's heirs have no interest whatsoever in Blackacre.

Most of the conveyances in this chapter will transfer an interest in land to one person. Sometimes conveyances transfer interests in land to more than one person. Here are two examples:

> **EXAMPLE 4:** O grants Blackacre "to A and B." A and B own Blackacre in fee simple absolute in common.

> **EXAMPLE 5:** O grants Blackacre "to A's children who are now living." A has two children, B and C. B and C own Blackacre in common.

The phrase "in common" indicates that the holders have a concurrent interest in the land—that is, they both own the land at the same time. We will look at concurrent interests in depth in the next chapter.

As we noted at the outset, the system of present and future interests applies to both real and personal property. The personal property equivalent for the fee simple absolute is called *absolute ownership*. For all of the other interests we will study in this chapter, the name is the same for both real and personal property.

COMMON INHERITANCE TERMS AND RULES

Property conveyances often include terms that have specific legal meaning. Here are some of the most common terms:

Children are fairly self-explanatory. Under modern law, adopted children count as children in conveyances.

Issue are lineal descendants—children, grandchildren, great grandchildren, and so on.

Ancestors are parents, grandparents, and so on. In inheritance situations, it is rare for ancestors other than parents to be relevant.

Collaterals are blood relatives who are not descendants or ancestors—brothers, sisters, cousins, aunts, uncles, nephews, nieces.

Devisees are people who inherit from a person who dies testate. *Testate* means with a will. If a person dies testate, then the provisions of the person's will control the distribution of the person's property.

Heirs are people who inherit from a person who dies intestate. *Intestate* means without a will. Each state has rules of intestate succession. These rules define who qualifies as an heir and set priorities between categories of potential heirs. State law varies, but a fairly common approach is for surviving spouses and children to be in the first category of heirs. (The rules for surviving spouses can be complex and are discussed in Chapter 3). If a person dies without a surviving spouse or children, then issue inherit next. If there are no issue, then preference typically goes in order to parents then collaterals. Collaterals with a more direct relationship to the decedent typically inherit before collaterals with a more remote relationship—for example, siblings typically inherit before cousins.

Escheat: If a person dies intestate and without heirs (generally this means that they die without a will and without a surviving spouse or surviving blood relatives), then the person's property goes to the state. The legal term for this process is that the property *escheats* to the state.

Note that *a living person has no heirs or devisees*. A living person will have potential heirs or devisees, but actual heirs and devisees are determined at death. This point may help you understand the reason why the "and her heirs" language in a fee simple absolute conveyance does not give anything to the heirs. If O grants Blackacre "to A and her heirs" and A is a living person, A has no heirs at the time of conveyance.

Executor: The person appointed to administer a deceased person's estate. In some jurisdictions, the person fulfilling this role is known as a *personal representative*.

Note that you will often see the suffix –trix used to denote that the person being described is female, especially in older decisions. A testatrix is a female testator. An executrix is a female executor. The use of the –trix suffix is gradually falling out of favor, with the same term (testator, executor, etc.) being used for both men and women.

Per stirpes and *per capita by generation*: These terms refer to different approaches to the division of inherited property across generations. The underlying problem, and the difference between the two approaches, are best illustrated with an example:

Parent:		A	
Children:	B̶	C	D̶
Grandchildren:	B1 B2		D1

This diagram shows three generations of a family—A, the parent, had three children, B, C, and D. B had two children, B1 and B2. D had one child, D1. As indicated by the strikethroughs, B and D predeceased A.

The problem that we have is how to divide A's estate. To be clear on the facts, when A dies, A is survived by one child, C, and three grandchildren, B1, B2, and D1. A *per stirpes* distribution gives equal shares of A's estate to each branch of the family. In this example, there are three branches, one for each of A's three children. Each of these branches would get one-third of the estate. B's one-third would go in equal shares to B1 and B2, so each of these two children would get one-sixth of the estate. C would get one-third. D's one-third would go to D1. The end result is that under the *per stirpes* approach, B1 would get one-sixth, B2 would get one-sixth, C would get one-third, and D1 would get one-third:

Parent:		A	
Children:	B̶	C (1/3)	D̶
Grandchildren:	B1 (1/6) B2 (1/6)		D1 (1/3)

A per capita by generation distribution gives equal shares to each person at each generational level. C, as the only living child of A's three children, would get a one-third share. The three grandchildren, B1, B2, and D1 would share the remaining two-thirds equally among themselves. So B1, B2, and D1 would each get two-ninths of the estate.

Parent:		A	
Children:	B̶	C (1/3)	D̶
Grandchildren:	B1 (2/9) B2 (2/9)		D1 (2/9)

As you can see, the difference between the two approaches is reflected in the amounts inherited by the grandchildren. Under the *per stirpes* approach, where each branch of the family gets an equal share, B1 and B2 would share their branch's one-third, and would each get one-sixth—half as much as D1, who as an only child does not have to share D's branch's one-third. Under the per capita by generation approach, all three grandchildren get equal shares.

These two rules are often applied in intestacy situations. They are also often selected by a grantor in a conveyance—for example, "then to my issue *per stirpes*." In the United States, the *per stirpes* approach is more common, both as a default rule and as selected by grantors. The per capita by generation approach also has its adherents and is used in provisions of the Uniform Probate Code that have been adopted in 12 states.

2. THE LIFE ESTATE

A *life estate* is an interest that has a duration measured by a human life. It is created by the language "to A for life." Here are two examples:

EXAMPLE 6: O grants Blackacre "to A for life."

EXAMPLE 7: O grants Blackacre "to A for life, then to B."

In both of these examples, A owns a life estate in Blackacre. The owner of a life estate is commonly called a "life tenant." A's life estate will end at her death, and a life estate is of obviously limited duration. A life estate is always accompanied by a future interest. If the future interest is created in the grantor, it will be a reversion. In Example 6, O has a reversion. If the future interest is created in someone other than the grantor, it typically will be a remainder. In Example 7, B has a remainder. We will learn more about these future interests below.

Like other property interests, life estates can be sold. For example, A could sell her life estate to C. The life estate, however, would be continued to be measured by A's life. The traditional legal term for a life estate measured by another person's life is a life estate *pur autre vie.* By its nature, the life estate that C has bought from A will end when A dies.

As suggested by our initial definition, a life estate must be measured by a human life. A life estate cannot be measured by the life of a non-human animal or a non-human entity such as a corporation. Although we will generally use "to A for life," language that clearly creates an estate measured by a human life will suffice create a life estate. For example, grants "to A until A's death" or "to A for the duration of her life" will create a life estate.

3. THE TENANCIES

Our legal system recognizes three basic types of tenancies: the term of years, the periodic tenancy, and the tenancy at will. At traditional common law, these property interests were leasehold estates. The fee simple absolute and life estate, in contrast, were freehold estates. Traditionally, freehold estates were superior to leasehold estates (see the sidebar). Today, the freehold-leasehold distinction no longer has any significant legal impact.

SEISIN, THE FREEHOLD-LEASEHOLD DISTINCTION, AND FOUR IMPORTANT PROPERTY STATUTES

In feudal England, the crucial distinction between freehold and leasehold estates was that the owner of a freehold estate had *seisin* while the owner of a leasehold estate did not. Seisin gave the owner of a freehold estate certain privileges and obligations in the feudal system. It also had a number of important legal consequences. Here are two things that are useful to know about seisin. First, feudal law would not accept breaks in seisin of land—someone had to have seisin at all times. Second, in feudal England, a freehold estate could only be transferred by a ceremony called *feoffment with livery of seisin*. In this ceremony, the grantor and grantee met on the land with witnesses. The grantor made a physical indication of transferring possession of the land to the grantee, for example by handing the grantee a handful of soil, and said words to the effect that the grantor was transferring the land to the grantee. In Chapter 1, we discussed the possession of real property at some length. However antiquated it might be, the ritual of transfer of seisin is an example of a method of achieving a physical manifestation of a transfer of possession of real property.

The requirement of the ritual of transfer of seisin was eroded by the 1536 Statute of Uses, which allowed an alternative form of conveyance called a bargain and sale. It was eliminated by the 1677 Statute of Frauds. The original Statute of Frauds, and the successor versions that are still in force today, require that real property be transferred by a written document—today we typically use a written instrument called a deed to transfer title. We will study the Statute of Frauds in some depth in Chapter 5. For now, it is useful to briefly note the Statute of Uses and the Statute of Frauds are two of four statutes that had particularly significant impacts on property law:

Statute Quia Emptores (1290). This statute made important changes to the feudal rules on land ownership. For our purpose, *Quia Emptores* is important because it made the fee simple absolute freely alienable.

Statute of Uses (1536). The Statute of Uses undercut the requirement of the ritual transfer of seisin to convey a freehold interest in property. It also permitted executory interests, a type of future interest that we will study later in this chapter.

Statute of Wills (1540). This statute allowed the transfer of real property by will. It also created rules for the transfer of property at death. As we already saw in our material on gifts of personal property, courts are often hostile to attempts to circumvent the requirements of the Statute of Wills. We will see this hostility again when we study real estate transactions in Chapter 5.

Statute of Frauds (1677). This statute was intended to prevent fraud by requiring certain types of agreements and transactions to be made in writing. As we will see later in the course, documents that actually transfer title must be in writing. Contracts for the sale of real property must be in writing, or at least evidenced by a written memorandum that satisfies the Statute.

The *term of years* is created by language that establishes the duration of the tenancy by reference to a fixed period of time or to calendar dates for its beginning or ending time.

EXAMPLE 8: O grants Blackacre "to A for one year."

A owns a term of years in Blackacre. It is possible to convey a term of years with a duration of much more than one year—terms of 25 or 50 years are not unusual for commercial properties, and terms of 999 years are not unheard of. When a tenancy is created, O and A most often are referred to as the landlord and tenant, respectively. All of the tenancies are of limited duration and are accompanied by a future interest. In Example 8, O retains a reversion in fee simple absolute in Blackacre.

The *periodic tenancy* is created by language that is measured by a fixed period of time and automatically continues for successive periods of time until either the landlord or tenant gives notice of termination.

EXAMPLE 9: O grants Blackacre "to A from year to year."

A owns a periodic tenancy in Blackacre. O has a reversion in fee simple absolute.

The *tenancy at will* is created by language that sets no fixed period for the duration of the tenancy.

EXAMPLE 10: O grants Blackacre "to A so long we mutually agree to continue the tenancy."

A owns a tenancy at will in Blackacre. A tenancy at will terminates at the latest on the death of the landlord or tenant and therefore is of limited duration. O has a reversion in fee simple absolute.

We will return to the tenancies below in Chapter 4, when we cover the law of landlord-tenant in depth.

4. THE (LARGELY EXTINCT) FEE TAIL

The fee tail was a traditional common-law estate intended to keep land in a particular family. The estate was designed to pass to the grantee's lineal descendants generation after generation. If the grantee's line ever died out, the land would revert back to the grantor or the grantor's successors in interest. The fee tail therefore was of potentially limited duration. It was created by language in the form of "to A and the heirs of her body."

EXAMPLE 11: O grants Blackacre "to A and the heirs of her body." At traditional common law, A would own Blackacre in fee tail. Because A's line could eventually die out, O would have a reversion in fee simple absolute.

The fee tail has been abolished in most U.S. jurisdictions and is of largely historical interest. It only survives, in a modified form, in Delaware, Maine, Massachusetts, and Rhode Island. In a majority of states, the "to A and the heirs of her body" language today creates a fee simple absolute. Prior to 1290, the "to A and the heirs of her body" language created a similar estate called a *fee simple conditional.* Due to a historical quirk, a few U.S. states recognized the fee simple conditional, rather than the fee tail. Today, the fee simple conditional appears to survive in South Carolina and Iowa. For more on these subjects, see *Powell on Real Property* §§14.04-14.06.

5. DEFEASIBLE INTERESTS

Defeasible interests are interests that will terminate on the happening of an uncertain event. Here is an example:

> **EXAMPLE 12:** O grants Blackacre "to the School Board, so long as the land is used for school purposes."

The idea of the conveyance is clear from the language. The School Board will own the land as long it is used for school purposes. If the land is no longer used for school purposes, the School Board's interest will terminate. The happening of this event—the land no longer being used for school purposes—is uncertain. The School Board might use the land for school purposes forever. Or, it might stop using it for school purposes tomorrow. The School Board's interest is one that will terminate on the happening of an uncertain event, and under our definition this interest is defeasible.

Traditionally, only fee simple interests could be defeasible. The modern approach is to allow any interest—fee simple, life estate, or tenancy—to be defeasible. For simplicity, however, we will focus largely on defeasible fee simple interests.

There are three types of defeasible fee simple interests. Each is created by a conveyance that includes a condition that, if broken, will lead to the termination of the present possessory estate. All of them are of potentially unlimited duration—if the termination event never occurs, then the interest will never end. Because they can terminate, they are accompanied by a future interest.

The first type is called a *fee simple determinable.* A fee simple determinable is created if the conditional language is phrased in terms of duration, such as "so long as" or "until." The School Board's interest in Example 12 is a fee simple determinable because it used the words "so long as." The future interest that accompanies a fee simple determinable is called a *possibility of reverter.* The possibility of reverter does not arise in any other context—it only exists as the future interest that accompanies a determinable interest. In Example 12, O has a possibility of reverter in fee simple absolute.

The second type is called a *fee simple subject to condition subsequent.* This interest is created if the conditional language is phrased in terms of condition, such as "but if," "on the condition that," or "provided that." Here are two examples:

> **EXAMPLE 13:** O grants Blackacre "to the School Board, *but if* the property is not used for school purposes, then grantor may re-enter and retake the property."

EXAMPLE 14: O grants Blackacre "to the School Board *on the condition that* the property is used for school purposes, and if it is not, then grantor may re-enter and retake the property."

In each of these two examples, the School Board owns Blackacre in fee simple subject to condition subsequent. The future interest that accompanies a fee simple subject to condition subsequent is called a *right of entry*. This future interest goes by various other names, including *power of termination*. In Examples 13 and 14, O retains a right of entry in fee simple absolute.

The most important distinction between the fee simple determinable and fee simple subject to condition subsequent is in the way they terminate if the condition is broken. A fee simple determinable terminates automatically by operation of law once the termination event occurs. A fee simple subject to condition subsequent, in contrast, terminates only when the holder of the right of entry exercises her right to terminate the fee simple interest. This disparate treatment follows the language that creates the two interests. In Example 12, the School Board received the land "so long as" it was used for school purposes. By its terms, this interest should terminate automatically as soon as the land is no longer used for school purposes. In Example 13, conveyance granted the land "to the School Board, but if the property is not used for school purposes, then grantor may re-enter and retake the property." By its terms, this interest terminates only when the holder of the right of entry exercises her right to terminate the fee simple interest. Another way of putting this distinction is that a possibility of reverter operates automatically, while a right of entry must be affirmatively exercised by the future interest holder.

The difference in how these interests terminate can impact the rules for when the statute of limitations starts running on the future interest holder. Because the fee simple determinable terminates automatically, a case can be made that the fee simple determinable holder becomes an adverse possessor immediately upon the happening of the termination event and that the statute of limitations should start to run immediately against the holder of the possibility of reverter on the happening of that event. In contrast, the statute of limitations would not run immediately against the holder of a right of entry because the fee simple subject to condition subsequent did not terminate automatically. Until termination, the holder of the fee simple subject to condition subsequent has rightful possession of the land, and the holder arguably cannot be adverse to the right of entry holder. Some jurisdictions follow this distinction for the statute of limitations. Others by statute or judicial decision have made the statute of limitations start to run immediately for both the fee simple determinable and the fee simple subject to condition subsequent.

With both the fee simple determinable and fee simple subject to condition subsequent, the accompanying future interest is created in the grantor of the land. Our third type of defeasible fee simple, the *fee simple subject to executory limitation*, is created when the accompanying future interest is created in someone other than the original grantor.

> **EXAMPLE 15:** O grants Blackacre "to the School Board so long as it is used for school purposes, then to the State College."

> **EXAMPLE 16:** O grants Blackacre "to the School Board, but if the property is not used for school purposes, then the State College may enter and take the property."

These conveyances are identical to those in Examples 12 and 13, except that in each the future interest is held by a third party—the State College. This type of future interest, called an *executory interest*, is discussed further below. In Examples 15 and 16, the School Board has a fee simple subject to executory limitation. Note that in placing a label on the School Board's interest, no distinction is made between durational language ("so long as") and conditional language ("but if") if the future interest is created in someone other than the grantor. In both examples, the State College has an executory interest in fee simple absolute.

As we noted above, life estates and tenancies may be defeasible. One type of defeasible life estate warrants special mention. At one time it was not unusual for a man to leave to his widow a life estate that was defeasible if she remarried. The idea behind this kind of conveyance was that the widow would hold the life estate to support her so long as she remained unmarried, but that if she remarried her new husband would support her so she would no longer need the life estate in the devised property. Social and legal changes have made life estates defeasible on remarriage increasingly rare. In case you ever come across this kind of conveyances, you should be aware that the condition in a grant requiring defeasance on remarriage may be invalid as violating the common-law rule against restraints on marriage. Generally speaking, if the purpose of the condition was to inhibit remarriage courts would invalidate the provision, but if the purpose of the condition was to provide support until remarriage, courts would allow it.

SUMMARY TABLE: PRESENT INTERESTS

INTEREST	DURATION	CREATED BY	ACCOMPANYING FUTURE INTEREST
Fee Simple Absolute	Unlimited	"to A" "to A and A's heirs"	None
Life Estate	Limited	Conveyance indicating creation of interest measured by a human life. "to A for life	Remainder or reversion

THE TENACIES

INTEREST	DURATION	CREATED BY	ACCOMPANYING FUTURE INTEREST
Term of Years	Limited	Conveyance indicating creation of an interest measured by a fixed period of time or fixed calendar dates. "to A for one year" "to A from January 1, 2014 to June 30, 2015" "to A for 999 years"	Remainder or reversion
Periodic Tenancy	Limited	Conveyance indicating creation of an interest measured by successive periods of time. "to A from year to year" "to A from month to month"	Remainder or reversion
Tenancy at Will	Limited	Conveyance indicating creation of an interest that sets no fixed time. "to A for as long as we both desire"	Remainder or reversion

DEFEASIBLE INTERESTS

INTEREST	DURATION	CREATED BY	ACCOMPANYING FUTURE INTEREST
Fee Tail (largely extinct)	Potentially Unlimited	"to A and the heirs of A's body"	Typically a reversion
Fee Simple Determinable	Potentially Unlimited	Conveyance indicating potential defeasance condition expressed in terms of duration. "to A, so long as . . ." "to A, until . . ."	Possibility of Reverter

(continues)

INTEREST	DURATION	CREATED BY	ACCOMPANYING FUTURE INTEREST
Fee Simple Subject to Condition Subsequent	Potentially Unlimited	Conveyance indicating potential defeasance condition expressed in terms of condition. "to A, but if . . ." "to A, on the condition that . . ." "to A, provided that"	Right of Entry, a.k.a., Power of Termination
Fee Simple Subject to Executory Limitation	Potentially Unlimited	Conveyance that would create a fee simple determinable or fee simple subject to condition subsequent, but the future interest is held by a third person, rather than the grantor.	Executory Interest

B. FUTURE INTERESTS

The system of future interests is illustrated in the following chart:

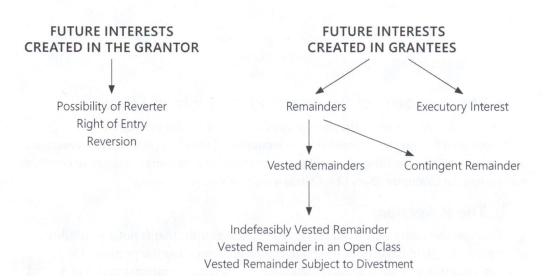

FUTURE INTERESTS CREATED IN THE GRANTOR

Possibility of Reverter
Right of Entry
Reversion

FUTURE INTERESTS CREATED IN GRANTEES

Remainders   Executory Interest

Vested Remainders   Contingent Remainder

Indefeasibly Vested Remainder
Vested Remainder in an Open Class
Vested Remainder Subject to Divestment

We will follow the structure of the chart, first covering the future interests created in the grantor and then moving on to future interests created in the grantee.

Before we get to the details of the future interests we should note three important points.

First, as we noted above, a future interest exists at the time it is created. It is the right of possession, not the existence of the interest itself, that is delayed to the future.

Second, under modern law future interests are transferrable. They can be sold or given away by their owner during her life. They can also pass by will or intestacy after their holder's death. Under traditional common law, some contingent interests were not transferrable. In the text and examples that follow, we follow the modern approach and presume that any future interest is freely transferrable during life and at death.

Third, future interests get their basic characteristics when they are created. As we will see, future interests created in grantors are categorized separately from future interests created in grantees. The words "created in" are important. A future interest created in a grantor that is later transferred to a grantee does not change into a future interest created in a grantee. Rather, it is a future interest created in a grantor that is not owned by a grantee. For example, if a reversion (an interest only created in grantors) is transferred to a grantee, it is still an interest created in a grantor and is still called a reversion. Similarly, if a remainder (an interest only created in a grantee) is transferred to a grantor, it is still an interest created in a grantee, and is still called a remainder.

1. FUTURE INTERESTS CREATED IN THE GRANTOR

FUTURE INTERESTS
CREATED IN THE GRANTOR

↓

Possibility of Reverter
Right of Entry
Reversion

a. The Possibility of Reverter and the Right of Entry

As we have already seen, the *possibility of reverter* is the future interest that accompanies a fee simple determinable. In Example 12, O held a possibility of reverter. The *right of entry* is the future interest that accompanies a fee simple subject to condition subsequent. In Examples 13 and 14, O held a right of entry.

b. The Reversion

The *reversion* is any future interest created in the grantor that is not a possibility of reverter or a right of entry. A reversion can be understood as the portion of the grantor's interest that the grantor retains after transferring an interest that is of limited or potentially limited duration. In Example 6, above, O transferred Blackacre to "A for life." O's reversion can be understood to be the portion of O's fee simple absolute that remained after O transferred the life estate to A. Sometimes, as in Example 6, O's reversion is certain to become possessory—when A dies, the land will revert back to O.

What, you might ask, happens if O has died before A dies? O's reversion will have passed to some other person at some point. O might have sold it during life, or it might have transferred by will or intestacy after O's death. The new owners of the reversion might have transferred the interest themselves. This is an illustration of the point we made above about future interests being transferrable. When A dies, someone will own the reversion. If O has died intestate without heirs, then the reversion will have escheated to the state. Even here, the reversion survives, and whoever owns the reversion at A's death will get present possession of Blackacre.

Sometimes a reversion will not be certain to be possessory. Here is an example:

> **EXAMPLE 17:** O grants Blackacre "to A for life, then to B if B survives A." A is still alive.

After this transfer, A has a life estate. B has a contingent remainder in fee simple absolute. We will explore contingent remainders below. For now, the important point is that B's interest might or might not become possessory. If A dies before B, then B will have possession of Blackacre on A's death. If B dies before A, however, B's contingent remainder fails. In this case, possession of Blackacre will revert back to O. Because of the contingency in B's future interest, O has a reversion in the conveyance in Example 17. Note that even though O's reversion is not certain to become possessory, we simply call it a reversion, not a contingent reversion. We will never use the term "contingent reversion."

As these two examples show, any time a grantor fails to transfer all of her interest *with certainty*, the grantor will have a reversion. If the grantor gives away all of her interest with certainty, then there will be no reversion. We will see many examples of each type of case as we discuss future interests created in grantees.

2. FUTURE INTERESTS CREATED IN GRANTEES

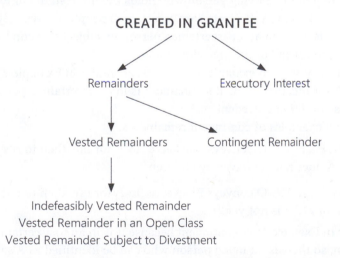

Following our chart, future interests created in grantees are divided into two categories: remainders and executory interests. The conceptual difference between the two is clear:

A *remainder* is a future interest created in a grantee that will become possessory, if at all, on the *natural end* of the preceding interest. Remainders are *polite*—they patiently wait around for the prior interest to end. We have already seen some remainders, including the one in Example 7. That conveyance was "to A for life, then to B." B has a remainder. This remainder will wait patiently until the end of A's life estate and will then become possessory.

An *executory interest* is a future interest created in a grantee that will *cut short or divest* the preceding interest. Executory interests are *rude*—they jump in and end the preceding interest. Executory interests can cut short a preceding present interest, giving the executory interest holder present possession of the land. We saw some executory interests like this in Examples 15 and 16, where they were laying in wait to rudely end the fee simple subject to executory limitation on the occurrence of a defeasance condition. Executory interests can also divest (i.e., take away) a future interest. We will see some examples of this kind of executory interest shortly.

a. The Remainders

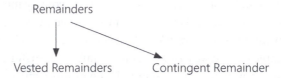

Our next key distinction is between contingent and vested remainders. A remainder is *vested* if it is *both* in an ascertained person *and* not subject to a condition precedent other than the natural end of the preceding estate. An interest is in an *ascertained person* if it is possible to point to a living person who holds the interest. In our examples, people denoted by letters (A, B, C, etc.) are ascertained people. Conversely, a remainder is *contingent* if it is *either* in an unascertained person *or* subject to a condition precedent other than the natural end of the preceding estate.

We have already seen an example of a vested remainder in Example 7, where O conveyed "to A for life, then to B." B's remainder is in an ascertained person, B, and is not subject to a condition precedent.

Here are two examples of contingent remainders:

> **EXAMPLE 18:** O conveys Blackacre "to A for life, then to A's first child." A does not yet have any children.

> **EXAMPLE 19:** O conveys Blackacre "to A for life, then to B if B reaches the age of 21." B is not yet 21.

The remainder in Example 18 is contingent because it is in an unascertained person—A has no children, so there is no living person who can be identified as A's first child. The remainder in Example 19 is in an ascertained person, B, but is contingent because it is subject to a condition precedent—B must reach the age of 21. In Examples 18 and 19, O also has a reversion that will become possessory if the contingent remainder fails.

We have already seen the classic example of a vested remainder in Example 7, where O granted "to A for life, then to B." B is an ascertained person, and there is no condition precedent, so B has a vested remainder. (As a reminder from our definition above, the natural end of the preceding estate—here, A's life estate—is not a condition precedent.) Here are two other examples of vested remainders:

> **EXAMPLE 20:** O conveys Blackacre "to A for life, then to A's first child." A has one child, C.

> **EXAMPLE 21:** O conveys Blackacre "to A for life, then to B if B reaches the age of 21." B is now 22.

These are the same conveyances as in Examples 18 and 19, but we have now changed some relevant facts. In Example 20, A has a child, C. C is A's first child, and so we now have an ascertained person holding the remainder in "A's first child." Because the remainder is in an ascertained person and is not subject to a condition precedent, C's remainder is vested. In Example 21, B is now 22 and has satisfied the condition of living to age 21. Because the condition is satisfied, B's interest is no longer subject to a condition precedent, and B's remainder is now vested. Because the remainders are vested, O's reversion disappears in both examples.

This set of examples illustrates an important characteristic of present and future interests—they can sometimes change over time as contingencies resolve themselves. We noted earlier in this section that future interests take their name when they are created and keep their basic name into the future. This is true—a remainder, for example, will never become a reversion. Contingent remainders, however, can become vested over time. Similarly, defeasible present interests can sometimes become non-defeasible if it becomes impossible for the uncertain defeasance event to occur. For example, in the conveyance "to A, but if A dies before reaching the age of 21, then B may enter and take the land," A will have a fee simple subject to executory limitation until A reaches the age of 21. If and when A lives to reach the age of 21, then it is impossible for the uncertain defeasance event to occur. A will own Blackacre in fee simple absolute, and B's executory interest will disappear. We will see more examples below.

i. The Vested Remainders

Vested Remainders

↓

Indefeasibly Vested Remainder
Vested Remainder in an Open Class
Vested Remainder Subject to Divestment

As we can see on our chart, there are three types of vested remainders: indefeasibly vested, vested in an open class, and vested subject to divestment. We will look at each in turn.

An *indefeasibly vested remainder* is one that is certain to become possessory in the future. Our prototypical vested remainder from Example 7 is an indefeasibly vested remainder. In that example, O granted "to A for life, then to B." B's remainder is an indefeasibly vested remainder in fee simple absolute. It is certain to become possessory upon A's death. (Remember that if B dies before A, B's vested remainder will have passed on to someone else and will still become possessory.)

A *vested remainder in an open class* is one that is held by an open class of people. Here is an example:

> **EXAMPLE 22:** O grants Blackacre "to A for life, then to my [O's] children." A and O are alive, and O has one child, B.

The remainder in this grant was made to a class of people—here, O's children—rather than an individual. Because O is alive, the class of O's children is open—that is, additional people can come into the class. In this and other contexts involving present and future interests, *we presume that any living person can have children.* We will discuss this presumption further below. For now it is sufficient for our purposes to know that the class of O's children is still open. Therefore in our example B has a vested remainder in an open class in fee simple absolute. If O later has another child, C, then B and C will both have vested remainders in an open class. If O then dies, the class will close and B and C will have indefeasibly vested remainders in fee simple absolute in common. If A then dies, then B and C would own Blackacre in fee simple absolute in common.

The vested remainder in an open class also is often called a *vested remainder subject to open* or a *vested remainder subject to partial divestment*. The subject to partial divestment label is descriptive of what happened to B in our example when C was born. When C joined the class of A's children, C took away part of B's interest. Prior to C's birth, B had a vested remainder in an unshared interest in Blackacre; after C's birth, B had a vested remainder in an interest in Blackacre in common with C. We prefer the name vested remainder in an open class because it is more descriptive of the nature of the interest.

A *vested remainder subject to divestment* is a vested remainder that may be divested by an executory interest before it becomes possessory. Here is an example:

> **EXAMPLE 23:** O grants Blackacre "to A for life, then to B, but if B ever becomes a lawyer, then to C."

Here, B has a vested remainder subject to divestment in fee simple absolute, and C has an executory interest in fee simple absolute. B's remainder is vested, but may be divested by C's executory interest if B violates the condition and becomes a lawyer. If A dies and B still has not become a lawyer, then B will have a possessory fee simple subject to executory limitation; C will still have an executory interest in fee simple absolute.

A vested remainder can be both in an open class and subject to divestment. Here is an example:

> **EXAMPLE 23A:** O grants Blackacre "to A for life, then to B's children, but if B ever becomes a lawyer, then to C. A and B are alive, and B has one child, D."

D has a vested remainder in an open class subject to divestment. D's remainder is in an open class because B could have more children. It is subject to divestment because it will be divested by C's executory interest if B ever becomes a lawyer.

ii. The Contingent Remainder

Our next category of future interests is the contingent remainder. As we discussed above, a remainder is contingent if it is *either* in an unascertained person *or* subject to a condition precedent. Example 18 involved a remainder that was contingent because it was in an unascertained person. The grant conveyed Blackacre "to A for life, then to A's first child," and at the time of conveyance A did not have any children. Because there was no living person who qualified as A's first child, the remainder was in an unascertained person and therefore was contingent. If A dies without children, the interest will fail. Example 19 involved a remainder that was contingent because it was subject to a condition precedent. The grant conveyed Blackacre "to A for life, then to B if B reaches the age of 21," and B was not yet 21. Because B was still subject to the condition precedent, B's remainder was contingent. Generally speaking, when a conveyance ends with a contingent remainder in fee simple absolute, O will have a reversion in fee simple absolute that will become possessory if the contingent remainder fails.

Sometimes conveyances create contingent remainders in open classes of people. Here is an example:

> **EXAMPLE 24:** O grants Blackacre "to A for life, then to A's children who survive A." A is alive and has one child, B.

In this conveyance, A has a life estate. B has a contingent remainder in fee simple absolute because of the condition precedent requiring the children to survive A. This contingent remainder also is in an open class—A could have more children who end up surviving A. We do not, however, use the term "contingent remainder in an open class." By convention, B's interest is simply called a contingent remainder. The conditionality created by the open class is captured by this label.

Some conveyances create what are called *alternative contingent remainders*. Here is an example:

COMMON MISTAKES

Here are some common mistakes in future-interests terminology that you should be sure to avoid:

- Possibility of reversion. There is no such thing. There is a possibility of reverter and a reversion. Be sure not to confuse "reverter" and "reversion."
- Contingent remainder in an open class. It is true that contingent remainders can be in an open class. By convention, however, we leave off the words "in an open class" to describe a contingent remainder.
- Contingent reversion. Not all reversions are certain to become possessory. By convention, however, we never use the term "contingent" when we are talking about a reversion.
- Fee simple defeasible. This term could be used to accurately describe the set of the fee simple determinable, the fee simple subject to condition subsequent, and the fee simple subject to executory limitation. If, however, you are talking about the specific estate of fee simple determinable, be sure to use "determinable," not "defeasible."

EXAMPLE 25: O grants Blackacre "to A for life, then to B if B survives A, and if B does not survive A, then to C." A, B, and C are alive.

The key thing to note here is that we have two contingent remainders and that they revolve around the same contingency—whether B survives A or not. If B survives A, then B's contingent remainder will become possessory. If B does not survive A, then C's contingent remainder will become possessory. You can think of these contingencies as flip sides of the same coin. Heads, A dies before B, and B's interest becomes possessory. Tails, B dies before A, and C's interest becomes possessory. Although both remainders are contingent, O has transferred her entire fee simple interest with certainty—right now, we are not sure whether B's or C's remainder will become possessory, but we are sure one will. For this reason, when there are alternative contingent remainders in fee simple absolute, as in Example 25, O does not have a reversion. This is an exception to our general rule that if the conveyance ends with a contingent remainder in fee simple absolute, then O has a reversion in fee simple absolute. Note that this only occurs if the remainders are truly alternative and together account for all possible scenarios because they both revolve around the same contingency. Consider this variant on Example 25:

EXAMPLE 25A: O grants Blackacre "to A for life, then to B if B survives A, and to C if B does not survive A and if C lives to the age of 21." A, B, and C are alive, and C is 18 years old.

This conveyance adds an extra contingency to C's interest. For C's interest to become possessory, (i) B must die before A, and (ii) C must live to age 21. The extra contingency creates the possibility that both contingent remainders will fail. Because O has not given away her entire interest with certainty, O has a reversion. Consider, for example, what happens if B and C die tomorrow. A is still alive. B's contingent remainder fails because B did not survive A. C's contingent remainder fails because C did not live to age 21. Because both remainders fail, Blackacre reverts back to O.

Here is another example of alternative contingent remainders:

> **EXAMPLE 26:** O grants Blackacre "to A and B for the life of the first of them to die, then to the survivor."

The life estate portion of the conveyance might look strange at first, but on reflection you will see that A and B have a life estate in common measured by the life of whichever of them dies first. A and B also have alternative contingent remainders in fee simple absolute. If A dies before B, B will get Blackacre in fee simple absolute. If B dies before A, then A will get Blackacre in fee simple absolute.

You might ask what would happen in Examples 25 and 26 if A and B die at the same time. For the answer to this question, see the sidebar on simultaneous death.

SIMULTANEOUS DEATH

At one time, the simultaneous death of two or more people who might take property under a conveyance was a highly unusual event. The increase in automobile and airplane travel in the twentieth century made simultaneous deaths less unusual. Faced with an increasing number of court cases involving simultaneous death, the Uniform Law Commission developed the Uniform Simultaneous Death Act. There have been two major version of this Act, and most U.S. jurisdictions have adopted at least one of them. For our purposes, the Act does two things.

First, when an interest is contingent on the holder surviving the death of another person, in a simultaneous death situation the holder will be treated as having predeceased the other person and the condition will fail. In Example 25, B's interest was contingent on B surviving A. If A and B died at the same time, B would be deemed to have predeceased A, and B's contingent remainder would fail. As a result, on A and B's simultaneous death, C would take Blackacre in fee simple absolute.

Second, if each of the people who died simultaneously would have been entitled to a property interest if they had survived the other, the Act divides the interest into equal portions shared between the people who died simultaneously. Example 26 raises the possibility of this scenario. There, A and B had a life estate in common measured by the life of whichever of them died first, and A and B each had alternative contingent remainders in fee simple absolute that turned on which of the two survived the other. If A and B died simultaneously, the Act first would presume that A predeceased B and then presume that B predeceased A. The result is an equal division of the interest—each of their estates would take an equal portion in common of Blackacre.

The original 1940 version of the Uniform Simultaneous Death Act (which is still in force in many U.S. jurisdictions) applies only if there is insufficient evidence to prove which person died first. Disputes would sometimes arise where litigants would try to prove that one person died before the other, often offering gruesome medical evidence in support of their position. The more recent 1993 version of the Act avoids this problem by treating people as having died simultaneously unless there is clear evidence that one has survived the other by 120 hours.

Distinguishing between conveyances that create two (often alternative) contingent remainders and conveyances that create a vested remainder subject to divestment and an executory interest can be challenging. Consider this example:

EXAMPLE 27: O grants Blackacre "to A for life, then to B, but if B does not survive A, then to C." A, B, and C are alive.

This conveyance appears to try to do the same thing as the conveyance in Example 25—give Blackacre to B if B survives A, but give Blackacre to C if B dies before A. This conveyance, however, creates a vested remainder subject to divestment followed by an executory interest, where the conveyance in Example 25 created two contingent remainders. We will explain how to correctly identify the interests in each conveyance below.

b. Executory Interests

As we noted above, executory interests are future interests in grantees that may cut short or divest the preceding interest. Unlike the polite remainders, which patiently wait around for the end of the preceding estate, executory interests are rude—they can cut short or take away another interest. If an interest created in a grantee is not a remainder, by definition it is an executory interest.

We have already seen examples of executory interests. Examples 15 and 16 involved fee simples subject to executory limitation accompanied by executory interests. On the occurrence of the uncertain defeasance condition, the executory interest would operate to cut short the fee simple subject to executory limitation, giving ownership and possession of Blackacre in fee simple absolute to the holder of the executory interest. Example 23 involved a vested remainder subject to divestment accompanied by an executory interest. On the occurrence of the uncertain event, the executory interest would operate to divest, or take away, the vested remainder and give it to the holder of the executory interest.

We have followed convention and used the term "subject to executory limitation" to describe a present interest that is subject to an executory interest and the term "subject to divestment" to describe a future interest that is subject to an executory interest. As a matter of substance, the two terms are equivalent—both mean that the described interest is subject to being taken away by an executory interest.

Executory interests are often divided further into two categories: springing and shifting. A *springing executory interest* divests the grantor. A *shifting executory interest* divests a grantee. All of the examples of executory interests we have seen so far are shifting executory interests—each would divest an interest held by a grantee. Here is an example of a springing executory interest:

EXAMPLE 28: O grants Blackacre: "to A on the occasion of her marriage." A is alive and presently unmarried. O owns Blackacre in fee simple subject to executory limitation. A has an executory interest in fee simple absolute that will become possessory if and when A gets married.

Beyond noting it here, we do not use the springing/shifting terminology in this book. There is no legal difference between shifting and springing executory interests in modern law, and the distinction has not mattered at least since the Statute of Uses was enacted in 1536.

C. CLASSIFYING PRESENT AND FUTURE INTERESTS

Our next step is to put our basic understanding of the present and future interests to work in interpreting the interests created by conveyances of land. This process is called *classification*—going through a conveyance interest by interest and identifying each in turn. The conveyances in this section will be clear, and there will be only one correct classification for each conveyance. We will address the problem of ambiguous conveyances later in this chapter.

Here are some easy examples to start with:

O grants Blackacre "to A."

A owns Blackacre in fee simple absolute.

O grants Blackacre "to A for life, then to B."

A has a life estate.

B has an indefeasibly vested remainder in fee simple absolute.

More complicated conveyances can be harder to classify. There are a few basic rules and tips that will help us.

Rule 1: Classify interests comma by comma. At each comma, stop. If the words you have so far create an interest, stop and classify the interest. If not, move on to the next comma and try to classify the interest. Then move on through the conveyance.

Moving comma to comma helps with the difficult classification task that we mentioned above—distinguishing between contingent remainders and executory interests. Let's look first at the conveyance from Example 25:

O grants Blackacre "to A for life, then to B if B survives A, and if B does not survive A, then to C." A, B, and C are alive.

Moving comma to comma, we have:

"to A for life"—A has a life estate.

"then to B if B survives A"—B has a contingent remainder in fee simple absolute.

"and if B does not survive A, then to C"—C has a contingent remainder in fee simple absolute. Because B's and C's contingent remainders revolve around the only two possible outcomes of the same contingency (whether

B survives A or not), the two contingent remainders are alternative. Because they are alternative, O does not have a reversion.

Let's now look at the conveyance in Example 27:

O grants Blackacre "to A for life, then to B, but if B does not survive A, then to C." A, B, and C are alive.

Moving comma to comma, we have:

"to A for life"—A has a life estate.

"then to B"—B has a vested remainder in fee simple absolute. We will find out more about this vested remainder as we proceed through the conveyance.

"but if B does not survive A, then to C"—this is an executory interest that will divest B's vested remainder if B dies before A. So C has an executory interest in fee simple absolute, and we now know that B has a vested remainder subject to divestment in fee simple absolute.

If we had not moved comma to comma, it would be easy to become confused and label B's interest a contingent remainder—looking at the conveyance as a whole, it is obvious that B's interest is subject to some contingency. When the conveyance is properly classified, this contingency is reflected in the fact that B's vested remainder is subject to divestment.

This outcome leads us to our next rule:

Rule 2: If the first future interest in fee simple absolute is a vested remainder, then the next future interest (if any) in fee simple absolute will be an executory interest. If the first future interest in fee simple absolute is a contingent remainder, then the next future interest (if any) in fee simple absolute will be a contingent remainder.

The two conveyances that we just classified are examples. You will never have a vested remainder in fee simple absolute followed by a contingent remainder in fee simple absolute, and you will never have a contingent remainder in fee simple absolute followed by an executory interest.

Our next rule and our first tip both have to do with reversions. We have already seen this rule in our discussion of future interests.

Rule 3: O will have a reversion any time O does not give away her entire interest with certainty.

Corollary 3.1: A reversion occurs any time a conveyance ends with a contingent remainder (except for alternative contingent remainders). This is a corollary of Rule 3 because a conveyance that ends with a nonalternative contingent remainder does not give away all of the grantor's interest *with certainty*.

Tip: Watch out for reversions! They can be tricky because they typically arise by implication, rather than the express language of the conveyance.

Here are classifications of two conveyances that include reversions:

O grants Blackacre "to A for life."

> A has a life estate.
>
> O has a reversion in fee simple absolute.

O grants Blackacre "to A for life, then to B if B reaches the age of 21." B is alive and is 18 years old.

> A has a life estate.
>
> B has a contingent remainder in fee simple absolute.
>
> O has a reversion in fee simple absolute. This is an example of Corollary 3.1 in action.

As we have seen before, interests can change over time as circumstances change. We will formalize this as a rule:

> **Rule 4:** Classification of interests can change over time as circumstances change. This most often occurs when (a) a future interest becomes possessory, (b) an interest transfers to another person, (c) a class closes, or (d) a contingency resolves itself. Remember, though, that an interest created in a grantor will never become an interest created in a grantee, and vice versa.

Let's look at a conveyance that can illustrate all four types of changes:

O grants Blackacre "to A for life, then to B's children." A and B are alive, and B has no children.

> A has a life estate.
>
> B's children have a contingent remainder in fee simple absolute, because this interest is in an unascertained person—there is no living person we could point to as being one of B's children.
>
> O has a reversion in fee simple absolute (Corollary 3.1).

Tip: Watch out for interests in unascertained persons!

Moving forward in time, A and B are alive, and B now has two children, C and D.

> A has a life estate.
>
> C and D have vested remainders in an open class in fee simple absolute. These remainders are no longer contingent because the interests are now in ascertained persons, and there is no condition precedent (*Contingency resolving itself*). Note that as a result, O's reversion disappears.

Moving further forward, A, B, and C are still alive, but D has died, leaving all of his property to his spouse E.

A has a life estate.

C and E have vested remainders in an open class in fee simple absolute. D's will has simply transferred D's interest to E. The same thing would have happened if D had sold his interest to someone else (*Interest being transferred to another person*).

Moving further forward again, A, C, and E are alive, but B has just died.

A has a life estate.

C and E have indefeasibly vested remainders in fee simple absolute in common, because B's death has closed the class of B's children (*Class closing*).

Finally, A has just died; C and E are alive.

C and E own Blackacre in fee simple absolute in common (*Future interest becoming possessory*).

Next, here is another example of a contingent interest that changes over time, using the conveyance from Example 19:

O grants Blackacre "to A for life, then to B if B reaches the age of 21." A is alive. B is alive and is age five.

A has a life estate.

B has a contingent remainder in fee simple absolute.

O has a reversion in fee simple absolute (Corollary 3.1 again!).

Moving forward in time, A is still alive and B is now 22.

A has a life estate.

B has an indefeasibly vested remainder in fee simple absolute.

Let's stay with this conveyance but move back in time and change our facts:

O grants Blackacre "to A for life, then to B if B reaches the age of 21." B is alive and is age five. A now dies.

The problem in classifying this interest should be clear—A's life estate has ended, but the contingency in B's interest has not resolved itself one way or the other. Under traditional common law, the *rule of destructibility of contingent remainders* would destroy B's contingent remainder. O's reversion would become possessory, and O would own Blackacre in fee simple absolute. We will discuss the historical rule of destructibility of contingent remainders further below.

The modern approach does not destroy B's future interest. Rather, it converts it into an executory interest that can divest O. So under the modern approach, this conveyance is classified as follows:

O has a fee simple subject to executory limitation.

B has an executory interest in fee simple absolute.

If B dies before reaching 21, B's executory interest will fail, and O will own Blackacre in fee simple absolute. If B survives to 21, B's executory interest will take away O's interest, and B will own Blackacre in fee simple absolute.

ESTATES AND FUTURE INTERESTS PROBLEM SET

All of the topics we have covered so far come together in the following problem set. The set is divided into two parts. Part 1 involves relatively straightforward conveyances. Part 2 involves some harder conveyances. We recommend that you complete Part 1 and review the answers before you move on to Part 2.

Part 1

For each of the following conveyances, classify the estates and future interests created by the grant. Unless the question states otherwise, presume that all people named in the conveyance are alive. Answers to this part of the problem set are on page 1032.

1. O grants Blackacre "to A for life."
2. O grants Blackacre "to the School Board so long as used for school purposes."
3. O grants Blackacre "to A for life, then to B." A year later, B conveys her interest to O.
4. O grants Blackacre "to A for 20 years."
5. O grants Blackacre "to A for life, then to B if B survives A."
6. O grants Blackacre "to A and A's heirs."
7. O grants Blackacre "to A and the heirs of A's body."
8. O grants Blackacre "to the School Board so long as used for school purposes, then to the State University."
9. O grants Blackacre "to A for life, then to A's children." A is alive and has no children.
10. Same conveyance as 9, but now A has one child, B.
11. O grants Blackacre "to A for life, then to B, but if B ever is convicted of drunk driving, then to C."
12. O grants Blackacre "to the School Board, but if the property is no longer used for school purposes, then O may re-enter and retake the property."
13. O grants Blackacre "to A for life, then to B if B survives A, and if B does not survive A, then to C."
14. O grants Blackacre "to A for life, then to B for life, then to A's children." A and B are alive, and A has no children.
15. Same conveyance as in 14, but now A has one child, C.

Part 2

For each of the following conveyances, classify the estates and future interests created by the grant. Unless the question states otherwise, presume that all people named in the conveyance are alive. Answers to this part of the problem set are on page 1033.

16. O grants Blackacre "to A for life, then to the School Board so long as used for school purposes."
17. Same conveyance as 16, but now A has died.
18. Same conveyance as 16, but now A has died and the School Board has stopped using the property for school purposes.
19. O grants Blackacre "to A for life, then to A's children who survive A and their heirs, but if A dies without being survived by children, then to B's children and their heirs." A and B are alive, and B has one child, C.
20. Same conveyance as 19, but now A has a child, D.
21. Same conveyance as 19, but now A dies, survived by B, C, and D.
22. O grants Blackacre "to A for life, then to B for life, then to C so long as C survives both A and B."
23. Same conveyance as 22, but B has died. A and C are both still alive.
24. Same conveyance as 22, but B has died and C has died. A is alive.
25. O conveys Blackacre "to A for life, then to A's children and their heirs who reach the age of 21, but if any of A's children are arrested for drug possession prior to the age of 21, then Blackacre shall go to B and her heirs." A's only child C, is 17 and is a fine, upstanding young man.
26. O conveys Blackacre "to A for life, then to A's children, but if C passes the Bar Exam, then to C." A is alive and has one child, B.
27. Same conveyance as 26, but now A has had another child, D, and A has just died. B and C are alive. C has not yet attended law school.
28. Same conveyance as 26, and same facts as 27, but C has just died never having attended law school.
29. O conveys Blackacre "to A for life, then to B for life if B survives A."
30. Same conveyance as 29, but now A has sold her life estate to C. A and B are alive.
31. O conveys Blackacre "to A for life so long as A is a member of the First Baptist Church, then at A's death to B."
32. O conveys Blackacre "to A for life, then to A's children and their heirs, but if A dies without surviving children, then to C." A is alive and has one child, B.
33. Same conveyance as 32, but now B has died, leaving all of his property to D. A is alive, but has no other children.
34. O conveys Blackacre "to A for life, then to A's children who survive A, and if A has no surviving children, then to C." A is alive and has one child, B.
35. O conveys Blackacre "to A for life, then to A's children who survive A, but if A dies without surviving issue, then to C." A is alive and has one child, B.

Now that you have a good handle on future interests, go back and review *Gruen v. Gruen* and our discussion of the rule that the adverse possession clock does not run against future interest holders. Both should be more intuitive now than they were the first time you encountered them.

D. RULES AGAINST RESTRAINTS ON ALIENABILITY

Recall that alienation is one of the four classic incidents of property ownership. Courts tend to be hostile to restraints on the alienation of property. Whether they will allow them or not depends in significant part on three factors. The *first factor* is the *type of interest* being restricted: is it a fee simple, life estate, tenancy, or other kind of property interest?

The *second factor* is which of three categories the restraint falls into:

Category 1: *disabling restraints*. A disabling restraint denies the grantee of the property the power to alienate the property:

EXAMPLE 29: O conveys Blackacre "to A, but A does not have the power to transfer the property to any other person."

EXAMPLE 30: O conveys Blackacre "to A, but any transfer of the property to any other person shall be null and void."

Category 2: *promissory restraints*. In a promissory restraint, the grantee promises not to alienate the property:

EXAMPLE 31: O conveys Blackacre "to A." In return, A promises "not to convey or otherwise transfer Blackacre to any other person."

Category 3: *forfeiture restraints*. In a forfeiture restraint, the grantee will forfeit the property if the grantee attempts to alienate the property:

EXAMPLE 32: O conveys Blackacre "to A, but if A attempts to transfer the property to another person, then the property shall return to the grantor."

The *third factor* is whether the restraint is *total*, on the one hand, or *partial* or *temporary* on the other. All of the examples we have used so far are total—they prevent the alienation of the property to any person at any time. Here are some examples of *partial* restraints on alienation:

EXAMPLE 33: O conveys Blackacre "to A, but any transfer by A to any member of his mother's family will be null and void."

EXAMPLE 34: O conveys Blackacre "to A, but A agrees not to transfer the property to B."

These restraints are partial because they do not completely prevent the alienation of property. Rather, they prevent alienation to a specific person or class of people. Restraints may also be *temporary*:

EXAMPLE 35: O conveys Blackacre "to A, but A agrees not to transfer the property for two years."

Restating these factors as questions, we have three things to consider when we are considering the validity of a restraint on alienation:

1. What type of interest is involved? Fee simple, life estate, tenancy, or something else?
2. What type of restraint is it? Disabling, promissory, or forfeiture?
3. Is the restraint total, or is it partial or temporary?

Courts historically have been especially hostile to restraints on the alienation of fee simple interests. As we noted above, the Statute *Quia Emptores*, enacted in 1290, made the fee simple absolute freely alienable. In part because of *Quia Emptores*, courts often say that restraints on alienation are contrary to the very nature of the fee simple interest. Total restraints on the alienability of fee simple interests are void and unenforceable, whether disabling, promissory, or forfeiture. Courts are also hostile to partial or temporary restraints on the alienability of fee simple interests, but these are sometimes held to be valid if a court finds them to be reasonable. The partial and temporary restraints on fee simple interest that are upheld tend to be modest in scope and duration.

You may have noticed that the conveyance in Example 32 created what appears to be a fee simple subject to condition subsequent. Because the total forfeiture restraint would be void, this language in fact conveys an unencumbered fee simple absolute. Many of the conveyances that we have seen, however, seem to create practical restraints on alienability. A conveyance "to the School Board so long as it is used for school purposes," for example, greatly restrains the ability of the School Board to sell the property. As long as the condition is framed in terms of a restriction on use, rather than on restraints on alienability, courts tend to allow the condition.

Courts are more tolerant of restraints on the alienation of life estates. Even in the context of life estates, total disabling restraints on alienation are void. Forfeiture and promissory restraints on life estates, however, typically are valid. A minority of courts will treat promissory and forfeiture restraints on life estates as void, as they would with total restraints on fee simple interests. Partial and temporary restraints on the alienability of a life estate are also more likely to be allowed than they would be if applied to a fee simple interest.

We will discuss restraints on the alienability of tenancies in Chapter 4, and the general topic will come up from time to time in some other contexts throughout the book. Generally speaking, the farther we move from a fee simple interest, the more likely courts will be to allow a reasonable restraint on alienation. Remember, however, that courts will still police these restraints on reasonableness grounds and that courts are generally suspicious of restraints on alienation of property.

You may have noticed that we used a lot of words and phrases like "generally," "tend to," and "more likely" in the preceding paragraphs. We also used the word "reasonable," which can be hard to pin down. The truth is that once we move away from the clear rule against total restraints on the alienation of a fee simple, the details of rules on restraints on alienation can be very fact dependent and become a bit blurry across jurisdictions. For more on these topics, see *Thomson on Real Property* (Thomas ed.) §29; Restatement (Second) of Property, Donative Transfers Ch. 4.

E. AMBIGUOUS CONVEYANCES AND NUMERUS CLAUSUS

You might not have believed it as you were going through the prior sections, but the conveyances we have seen so far have been clear. There are conveyances that are ambiguous even if you know the rules cold. Here is an example:

> **EXAMPLE 36:** O grants Blackacre "to the State College for so long as it is used for college purposes, but if the land is no longer used for college purposes, then O may re-enter and retake the land."

Does the State College have a fee simple determinable or a fee simple subject to condition subsequent? It is hard to tell. We learned that a fee simple determinable is created by language of duration, such as "so long as" or "until." We also learned that a fee simple subject to condition subsequent is created by language of condition, such as "but if." The problem with this conveyance is that it uses both kinds of language. Looking at the conveyance alone, it is not clear what interest was created.

We have some tools to deal with problems like this. The first thing we need to know is that we have to fit every interest created by a conveyance into one of our established categories of present and future interests. This follows from the *numerus clausus* principle. Under this principle, we have a fixed number of property interests—numerus clausus literally means "closed number." A grantor cannot intentionally or inadvertently create a new property interest by using creative language. When a conveyance is ambiguous, we need to fit the interests into our existing categories. If the best fit involves cramming a round peg into a square hole, we just need to hit the hammer harder and get it in there.

The law frequently deals with ambiguity in language by looking to *rules of construction*. These rules give us principles to use to help interpret ambiguous language. We will see these rules often throughout this course. Rules of construction are used in contexts other than grants of land: statutes and contracts, for example, often contain ambiguities that can be addressed by rules of construction. Here are some rules of construction that are commonly applied to interpret ambiguous property conveyances:

RULES OF CONSTRUCTION

1. *Conveyances should be interpreted to best achieve the intent of the grantor.* This rule is straightforward in principle, but can be difficult to apply in practice. The grantor's intent often is not clear from the language of the conveyance. Even if the intent is clear, the grantor's intent might run contrary to an important policy reflected in another rule of construction.

2. *Conveyances should be interpreted to favor a fee simple absolute.* This rule helps explain why the conveyance "to A" creates a fee simple absolute in all states. Because we have a rule of construction that that presumes that a grant, absent clear language to the contrary, creates a fee simple absolute, we do not need additional language to create the interest. This modern rule reverses the traditional common-law rule of construction that presumed ambiguous language conveyed a life estate.

3. *Conveyances in wills should be interpreted to avoid partial intestacy.* If a person dies with a will, then conveyances in the will should be interpreted to avoid partial intestacy—that is, a situation where the will gives away some, but not all, of the testator's assets. This rule can be seen as a corollary of the rule requiring an interpretation that honors the grantor's intent. If someone went through the trouble of leaving a will, it is reasonable to presume that the person intended the will to give away all of her assets.

4. *Conveyances should be interpreted to favor the free alienability of property.* As we saw in the prior section, the law disfavors restraints on alienability. Sometimes a court will void language in a conveyance restricting alienability and disregard this language entirely. Other times, a court will apply a more flexible rule interpreting an ambiguous conveyance in a way that best favors the free alienability of property.

5. *Conveyances should be interpreted to favor a fee simple subject to condition subsequent over a fee simple determinable.* This rule would help us resolve the problem presented in Example 36 and would favor an interpretation of that conveyance as creating a fee simple subject to condition subsequent. The justification for this rule is that the law generally disfavors the forfeiture of property. Because the right of entry that accompanies a fee simple subject to condition subsequent must be affirmatively exercised, it makes forfeiture of the present interest less likely than the self-actuating possibility of reverter that accompanies a fee simple determinable.

6. *Conveyances should be interpreted to favor vested interests and disfavor contingent interests.* Like the other rules of construction, this one can be overcome by clear language. It is possible to create contingent interests, but the grantor needs to use clear language to do so. Any ambiguity should be resolved in favor of vesting.

7. *Documents should be read as a whole. Provisions in a document should be read, if possible, to be consistent with one another, and one provision in a document should not be read in a way that renders another section of a document inoperative or a nullity.* These broadly applicable rules of construction are based on the reasonable idea that the authors of a document intended to be consistent throughout the document. Ambiguous provisions should therefore be read, if possible, in a way that is consistent with the rest of the document.

It is important to recognize that rules of construction do not turn the interpretation of ambiguous language into a science. They are designed to create presumptions and can be overcome by the language of the grant, or, in some circumstances, other evidence. Beyond this inherent limitation in scope, rules of construction sometimes conflict with each other. It is not unusual to see a majority opinion cite one rule of construction and a dissent cite another one. Other times, there is room for disagreement about how a given rule applies to a particular conveyance. Rules of construction therefore are useful, but imperfect, tools.

The following case is a classic and illustrates how hard the interpretation of some conveyances can be.

WHITE V. BROWN

Supreme Court of Tennessee, 1977
559 S.W.2d 938

Brock, Justice.

This is a suit for the construction of a will. The Chancellor held that the will passed a life estate, but not the remainder, in certain realty, leaving the remainder to pass by inheritance to the testatrix's heirs at law. The Court of Appeals affirmed.

Mrs. Jessie Lide died on February 15, 1973, leaving a holographic [i.e., handwritten] will which, in its entirety, reads as follows:

> April 19, 1972
>
> I, Jessie Lide, being in sound mind declare this to be my last will and testament. I appoint my niece Sandra White Perry to be the executrix of my estate. I wish Evelyn White to have my home to live in and *not* to be *sold*.
>
> I also leave my personal property to Sandra White Perry. My house is not to be sold.
>
> Jessie Lide
> (Italics by testatrix).

Mrs. Lide was a widow and had no children. Although she had nine brothers and sisters, only two sisters residing in Ohio survived her. These two sisters quitclaimed any interest they might have in the residence to Mrs. White. The nieces and nephews of the testatrix, her heirs at law, are defendants in this action.

Mrs. White, her husband, who was the testatrix's brother, and her daughter, Sandra White Perry, lived with Mrs. Lide as a family for some twenty-five years. After Sandra married in 1969 and Mrs. White's husband died in 1971, Evelyn White continued to live with Mrs. Lide until Mrs. Lide's death in 1973 at age 88.

Mrs. White, joined by her daughter as executrix, filed this action to obtain construction of the will, alleging that she is vested with a fee simple title to the home. The defendants contend that the will conveyed only a life estate to Mrs. White, leaving the remainder to go to them under our laws of intestate succession. The Chancellor held that the will unambiguously conveyed only a life interest in the home to Mrs. White and refused to consider extrinsic evidence concerning Mrs. Lide's relationship with her surviving relatives. Due to the debilitated condition of the property and in accordance with the desire of all parties, the Chancellor ordered the property sold with the proceeds distributed in designated shares among the beneficiaries.

I.

Our cases have repeatedly acknowledged that the intention of the testator is to be ascertained from the language of the entire instrument when read in the light of surrounding circumstances. *See, e.g., Harris v. Bittikofer*, 541 S.W.2d 372, 384 (Tenn.1976); *Martin v. Taylor*, 521 S.W.2d 581, 584 (Tenn.1975); *Hoggatt v. Clopton*, 142 Tenn. 184, 192, 217 S.W. 657, 659 (1919). But, the practical difficulty in this case, as in so many other cases involving wills drafted by lay persons, is that the words chosen by the testatrix are not specific enough to clearly state her intent. Thus, in our opinion, it is not clear whether Mrs. Lide intended to convey a life estate in the home to Mrs. White, leaving the remainder interest to descend by operation of law, or a fee interest with a restraint on alienation. Moreover, the will might even be read as conveying a fee interest subject to a condition subsequent (Mrs. White's failure to live in the home).

In such ambiguous cases it is obvious that rules of construction, always yielding to the cardinal rule of the testator's intent, must be employed as auxiliary aids in the courts' endeavor to ascertain the testator's intent.

In 1851 our General Assembly enacted two such statutes of construction, thereby creating a statutory presumption against partial intestacy.

RULES OF CONSTRUCTION

Chapter 33 of the Public Acts of 1851 (now codified as T.C.A. §§64-101 and 64-501) reversed the common law presumption that a life estate was intended unless the intent to pass a fee simple was clearly expressed in the instrument. T.C.A. §64-501 provides:

> Every grant or devise of real estate, or any interest therein, shall pass all the estate or interest of the grantor or devisor, unless the intent to pass a less estate or interest shall appear by express terms, or be necessarily implied in the terms of the instrument.

Chapter 180, Section 2 of the Public Acts of 1851 (now codified as T.C.A. §32-301) was specifically directed to the operation of a devise. In relevant part, T.C.A. §32-301 provides:

> A will . . . shall convey all the real estate belonging to (the testator) or in which he had any interest at his decease, unless a contrary intention appear by its words and context.

Thus, under our law, unless the "words and context" of Mrs. Lide's will clearly evidence her intention to convey only a life estate to Mrs. White, the will should be construed as passing the home to Mrs. White in fee. " 'If the expression in the will is doubtful, the doubt is resolved against the limitation and in favor of the absolute estate.' " *Meacham v. Graham*, 98 Tenn. 190, 206, 39 S.W. 12, 15 (1897) (quoting *Washbon v. Cope*, 144 N.Y. 287, 39 N.E. 388); *Weiss v. Broadway Nat'l Bank*, 204 Tenn. 563, 322 S.W.2d 427 (1959); *Cannon v. Cannon*, 182 Tenn. 1, 184 S.W.2d 35 (1945).

Several of our cases demonstrate the effect of these statutory presumptions against intestacy by construing language which might seem to convey an estate for life, without provision for a gift over after the termination of such life estate, as passing a fee simple instead. In *Green v. Young*, 163 Tenn. 16, 40 S.W.2d 793 (1931), the testatrix's disposition of all of her property to her husband "to be used by him for his support and comfort during his life" was held to pass a fee estate. Similarly, in *Williams v. Williams*, 167 Tenn. 26, 65 S.W.2d 561 (1933), the testator's devise of real property to his children "for and during their natural lives" without provision for a gift over was held to convey a fee. And, in *Webb v. Webb*, 53 Tenn.App. 609, 385 S.W.2d 295 (1964), a devise of personal property to the testator's wife "for her maintenance, support and comfort, for the full period of her natural life" with complete powers of alienation but without provision for the remainder passed absolute title to the widow.

II.

Thus, if the sole question for our determination were whether the will's conveyance of the home to Mrs. White "to live in" gave her a life interest or a fee in the home, a conclusion favoring the absolute estate would be clearly required. The question, however, is complicated somewhat by the caveat contained in the will that the home is "not to be sold" a restriction conflicting with the free alienation of property, one of the most significant incidents of fee ownership. We must determine, therefore, whether Mrs. Lide's will, when taken as a whole, clearly evidences her intent to convey only a life estate in her home to Mrs. White.

Under ordinary circumstances a person makes a will to dispose of his or her entire estate. If, therefore, a will is susceptible of two constructions, by one of which the testator disposes of the whole of his estate and by the other of which he disposes of only a part of his estate, dying intestate as to the remainder, this Court has always preferred that construction which disposes of the whole of the testator's estate if that construction is reasonable and consistent with the general scope and provisions of the will. *See Ledbetter v. Ledbetter*, 188 Tenn. 44, 216 S.W.2d 718 (1949); *Cannon v. Cannon, supra*; *Williams v. Williams, supra*; *Jarnagin v. Conway*, 21 Tenn. 50 (1840); 4 Page, *Wills* §30.14 (3d ed. 1961). A construction which results in partial intestacy will not be adopted unless such intention clearly appears. *Bedford v. Bedford*, 38 Tenn.App. 370, 274 S.W.2d 528 (1954); *Martin v. Hale*, 167 Tenn. 438, 71 S.W.2d 211 (1934). It has been said that the courts will prefer any reasonable construction or any construction which does not do violence to a testator's language, to a construction which results in partial intestacy. *Ledbetter, supra*.

The intent to create a fee simple or other absolute interest and, at the same time to impose a restraint upon its alienation can be clearly expressed. If the testator specifically declares that he devises land to A "in fee simple" or to A "and his heirs" but that A shall not have the power to alienate the land, there is but one tenable construction, viz., the testator's intent is to impose a restraint upon a fee simple. To construe such language to create a life estate would conflict with the express specification of a fee simple as well as with the presumption of intent to make a complete testamentary disposition of all of a testator's property. By extension, as noted by Professor Casner in his treatise on the law of real property:

Since it is now generally presumed that a conveyor intends to transfer his whole interest in the property, it may be reasonable to adopt the same construction, (conveyance of a fee simple) even in the absence of words of inheritance, if there is no language that can be construed to create a remainder. 6 *American Law of Property* §26.58 (A. J. Casner ed. 1952).

In our opinion, testatrix's apparent testamentary restraint on the alienation of the home devised to Mrs. White does not evidence such a clear intent to pass only a life estate as is sufficient to overcome the law's strong presumption that a fee simple interest was conveyed.

Accordingly, we conclude that Mrs. Lide's will passed a fee simple absolute in the home to Mrs. White. Her attempted restraint on alienation must be declared void as inconsistent with the incidents and nature of the estate devised and contrary to public policy. *Nashville C & S.L. Ry. v. Bell*, 162 Tenn. 661, 39 S.W.2d 1026 (1931).

The decrees of the Court of Appeals and the trial court are reversed and the cause is remanded to the chancery court for such further proceedings as may be necessary, consistent with this opinion. Costs are taxed against appellees.

HARBISON, J., dissenting. With deference to the views of the majority, and recognizing the principles of law contained in the majority opinion, I am unable to agree that the language of the will of Mrs. Lide did or was intended to convey a fee simple interest in her residence to her sister-in-law, Mrs. Evelyn White.

The testatrix expressed the wish that Mrs. White was "to have my home to live in and *not* to be *sold*." The emphasis is that of the testatrix, and her desire that Mrs. White was not to have an unlimited estate in the property was reiterated in the last sentence of the will, to wit: "My house is not to be sold."

The testatrix appointed her niece, Mrs. Perry, executrix and made an outright bequest to her of all personal property.

The will does not seem to me to be particularly ambiguous, and like the Chancellor and the Court of Appeals, I am of the opinion that the testatrix gave Mrs. White a life estate only, and that upon the death of Mrs. White the remainder will pass to the heirs at law of the testatrix.

The cases cited by petitioners in support of their contention that a fee simple was conveyed are not persuasive, in my opinion. Possibly the strongest case cited by the appellants is *Green v. Young*, 163 Tenn. 16, 40 S.W.2d 793 (1931), in which the testatrix bequeathed all of her real and personal property to her husband "to be used by him for his support and comfort during his life." The will expressly stated that it included all of the property, real and personal, which the testatrix owned at the time of her death. There was no limitation whatever upon the power of the husband to use, consume, or dispose of the property, and the Court concluded that a fee simple was intended.

In the case of *Williams v. Williams*, 167 Tenn. 26, 65 S.W.2d 561 (1933), a father devised property to his children "for and during their natural lives" but the will contained other provisions not mentioned in the majority opinion which seem to me to distinguish the case. Unlike the provisions of the present will, other clauses in the Williams will contained provisions that these same children were to have "all the residue of my estate personal or mixed of which I shall die possessed or seized, or to which I shall be entitled at the time of my decease, to have and to hold the same to them and their executors and administrators and assigns forever."

Further, following some specific gifts to grandchildren, there was another bequest of the remainder of the testator's money to these same three children. The language used by the testator in that case was held to convey the fee simple interest in real estate to the children, but its provisions hardly seem analogous to the language employed by the testatrix in the instant case.

In the case of *Webb v. Webb*, 53 Tenn.App. 609, 385 S.W.2d 295 (1964), the testator gave his wife all the residue of his property with a clear, unqualified and unrestricted power of use, sale or disposition. Thereafter he attempted to limit her interest to a life estate, with a gift over to his heirs of any unconsumed property. Again, under settled rules of construction and interpretation, the wife was found to have a fee simple estate, but, unlike the present case, there was no limitation whatever upon the power of use or disposition of the property by the beneficiary.

On the other hand, in the case of *Magevney v. Karsch*, 167 Tenn. 32, 65 S.W.2d 562 (1933), a gift of the residue of the large estate of the testator to his daughter, with power "at her demise (to) dispose of it as she pleases . . . ." was held to create only a life estate with a power of appointment, and not an absolute gift of the residue. In other portions of the will the testator had given another beneficiary a power to use and dispose of property, and the Court concluded that he appreciated the distinction between a life estate and an absolute estate, recognizing that a life tenant could not dispose of property and use the proceeds as she pleased. 167 Tenn. at 57, 65 S.W.2d at 569.

In the present case the testatrix knew how to make an outright gift, if desired. She left all of her personal property to her niece without restraint or limitation. As to her sister-in-law, however, she merely wished the latter have her house "to live in," and expressly withheld from her any power of sale.

The majority opinion holds that the testatrix violated a rule of law by attempting to restrict the power of the donee to dispose of the real estate. Only by thus striking a portion of the will, and holding it inoperative, is the conclusion reached that an unlimited estate resulted.

In my opinion, this interpretation conflicts more greatly with the apparent intention of the testatrix than did the conclusion of the courts below, limiting the gift to Mrs. White to a life estate. I have serious doubt that the testatrix intended to create any illegal restraint on alienation or to violate any other rules of law. It seems to me that she rather emphatically intended to provide that her sister-in-law was not to be able to sell the house during the lifetime of the latter a result which is both legal and consistent with the creation of a life estate.

In my opinion the judgment of the courts below was correct and I would affirm.

NOTES AND QUESTIONS

1. *What Did She Intend?* Look back at the language from Jessie Lide's will. Leaving all presumptions and rules of construction aside, what do you think she was trying to achieve?

2. *Rules of Construction.* What rules of construction were used by the court in this case? Did the majority and dissent disagree on the rules to use or on their application?

RULES OF CONSTRUCTION

3. *Restraints on Alienability.* How did the majority and dissent use the concept that restraints on alienability are repugnant to a fee simple interest?

F. FUTURE INTERESTS AND ALIENABILITY

Imagine that you want to buy Blackacre from me, and that I own Blackacre in fee simple absolute. This would be a simple transaction—you and I agree on the terms of the deal, and then I convey my fee simple absolute interest to you.

Now imagine that you want to buy Blackacre, but now the ownership is a little more complicated. A has a life estate in Blackacre, and B has an indefeasible vested remainder in fee simple absolute. If you want to buy Blackacre in fee simple absolute, you have to negotiate with both A and B. If you are able to buy all of the existing present and future interests in Blackacre, these interests will merge into a fee simple absolute (see the sidebar on merger). Negotiating with two people is obviously more complicated than negotiating with one. Problems might arise, for example, in valuing the present and future interests (see the sidebar on valuation).

MERGER OF INTERESTS

In our simple example, A has a life estate in Blackacre, and B has an indefeasibly vested remainder in fee simple absolute. If A transfers the life estate to B, then B will own both the life estate and the vested remainder. These two interests added together constitute a fee simple absolute. Once they are owned by one person (here, B), the life estate and vested remainder will *merge* into a fee simple absolute. B would therefore own Blackacre in fee simple absolute. B could convey a fee simple absolute to you, and there would be no need for B to separately convey to you the life estate and the vested remainder. The same thing would happen anytime all of the outstanding interests in an asset, that together would constitute a fee simple absolute, come into ownership by one person.

VALUATION OF FUTURE INTERESTS

In our example, A has a life estate in Blackacre and B has an indefeasibly vested remainder in fee simple absolute. Let's assume that Blackacre is worth $100,000. If Blackacre is sold, how would this be divided between A and B? In some contexts, A and B might be able to come to an agreement on how to divide the purchase price. In other contexts, however, we might need to come up with a valuation of the life estate and the remainder.

In this particular context, valuing the two interests is relatively straightforward. The first step is to look at actuarial life expectancy tables to determine the expected duration of the life estate. The Internal Revenue Service publishes life expectancy tables that are often used for this purpose, although they are relatively crude—they do not distinguish, for example, between the life expectancies of men and women. In any event, according to these tables, if a life tenant is 10 years old, the expected duration of her life, and therefore the life estate, is another 72.8 years. If the life tenant is 55, the expected duration is 29.6 years. If the life tenant is 90, the expected duration is 5.5 years. And so on.

If you know how to discount to present value, then you can fairly easily place values on the life estate and the remainder. We will not go through the discounting calculations here. It is sufficient for our purposes to know that at a 7 percent discount rate, if the life tenant is 10 years old, the life estate is worth $97,405 and the remainder is worth $2,595. Another way of putting this is that the right to own a $100,000 parcel of property 72.8 years from now (recall that the tables tell us that a 10-year old is expected to live another 72.8 years) is worth $2,595. If the life tenant is 90, the life estate is worth $24,253 and the remainder is worth $75,748.

The valuation process becomes more complex as the number and complexity of interests increases. Contingent interests are especially hard to value because of the lack of certainty about whether they will ever become possessory. In some circumstances, the likelihood of the contingent interest becoming possessory might be so remote that the interest will be considered valueless. *See Right of Owner of Contingent or Defeasible Future Interest to Maintain Action for Relief in Respect of Property*, 144 A.L.R. 769.

Despite these potential problems, negotiation with A and B might be manageable. To make it more complicated, now imagine that Blackacre was conveyed as follows:

> **EXAMPLE 37:** O granted Blackacre "to C for life, then to C's children for life, then to C's grandchildren who are alive at C's death." C is alive, and has two children, D and E, and two grandchildren, F and G.

First, let's classify the present and future interests:

> C has a life estate.
>
> D and E have vested remainders in an open class in life estate. The class is open because C is still alive.

F and G have contingent remainders in fee simple absolute. The remainders are contingent because there is a condition precedent—the grandchildren have to be alive at the time of C's death. For our purposes, it also is useful to note that the class of C's grandchildren is also open.

O has a reversion in fee simple absolute.

You are faced with a number of difficulties if you want to purchase a fee simple absolute interest in Blackacre. First, there are five living people with interests in Blackacre, and you would have to negotiate with each one. Second, there are interests held by open classes of people. How do you negotiate with the potential future members of the open class of people? Third, there is a contingent remainder, and the contingency will not resolve itself until A dies. That makes it impossible to know who will hold the future interest on A's death. It could be an individual grandchild, a combination of grandchildren, or O if none of A's grandchildren survive A. Even if you could identify the holders of the contingent interests, placing a value on them would be difficult, and it is hard to negotiate a selling price for hard-to-value assets.

The major point being made here is that future interests can substantially impair the alienability of property. The alienability problems associated with future interests increase when (a) the number of future interest holders increases, (b) some future interests are held in open classes, and (c) some future interests are contingent. As the conveyance in Example 37 shows, open classes and contingent interests can create particularly acute alienability problems.

In the remainder of this section, we cover two topics. First, we look at how the trust can cure the alienability problems created by future interests. Second, we look at a number of rules intended to further the alienability of property by destroying certain future interests.

1. HOW TRUSTS SOLVE ALIENABILITY PROBLEMS

The trust is one of the great inventions of the Anglo-American legal system. It arose in part due to a historical quirk in the English court system. There were two sets of courts in England. The first were the law courts. The second were the equity courts. The sidebar summarizes some of the relevant history and the key differences between law and equity. The distinction between law and equity plays an important role in property law and will be a recurring theme in this course.

LAW AND EQUITY

LAW AND EQUITY

The distinction between law and equity in the U.S. legal system is the product of the history of the English courts. The judgments of early English law courts could be appealed to the King, who could overturn or alter the courts' judgments as an exercise of mercy or conscience. This review function was often delegated to the Chancellor, a senior government official. Over time, the Chancellor's office developed into the Court of Chancery. As a result, the English legal system had two parallel court systems applying different rules. The law courts applied legal rules, and the Court of Chancery applied equitable rules.

It can be difficult to pin down the precise differences between law and equity. Generally speaking, law courts were concerned with the strict application of legal rules that had developed over time. Equity courts were more flexible and concerned with notions of fairness and justice. The equity courts were particularly concerned with the good faith of the parties and with preventing overreaching by parties exercising their legal rights.

In both England and a majority of U.S. jurisdictions, the law and equity courts have been merged. One court system applies both sets of rules. Some states still have separate courts of law and equity. Today, equitable rules resemble legal rules in some respects: you will research them in the same way and typically look to court precedent for authority. It is important to remember, however, that the sets of rules can operate differently in some important respects. A person, for example, can often act in bad faith and still enforce her legal rights, where bad faith is often a bar to the enforcement of equitable rights.

The distinction between law and equity remains especially important in our rules on remedies. Remedies are the redress that a court can award a party that wins a legal claim. The most common legal remedy is money damages. Equitable remedies include injunctions and specific performance. An injunction is a court order requiring a person to do or refrain from doing a particular act. Specific performance is a court order requiring a person to fulfill an obligation, typically one incurred by contract.

Trusts became possible because the law/equity division allowed the English legal system to separate legal and equitable ownership. In a trust, the *trustee* is the legal owner of the assets held in trust. The *beneficiaries* are the equitable owners of the assets. Equity is superior to law, so the beneficiaries' interest is superior to the trustee's interest. The trustee holds legal ownership for the benefit of the beneficiaries and owes fiduciary duties to them (see the sidebar).

FIDUCIARY DUTIES

Fiduciary relationships, and the fiduciary duties that accompany them, arise when one person acts for another in a relationship of special trust and confidence. Trustees are fiduciaries of the beneficiaries of a trust. Executors are fiduciaries of the devisees of a will or the heirs of a person who dies intestate. Lawyers are fiduciaries of their clients. Agents are fiduciaries of their principals.

You will study fiduciary duties in depth in courses in business organizations, wills, and trusts. For now, it is sufficient to know that there are two basic fiduciary duties, the *duty of loyalty* and the *duty of care*. In a trust, for example, duty of loyalty makes the interests of the beneficiary paramount. The trustee must place the beneficiary's interests above her own. The duty of loyalty prevents, among other things, self-dealing—the trustee, for example, cannot have the trust purchase an asset that she owns. The duty of care requires the trustee to act in a careful and professionally prudent manner. These duties are strictly enforced, and courts take breaches of fiduciary duties very seriously.

The person who creates a trust is called a *settlor*. We will identify the settlor as S and the trustee as T. Trusts often convey to beneficiaries successive interests in the income generated by the trust assets, with the assets being distributed to a different set of beneficiaries in the future. Here is an example:

> **EXAMPLE 38:** S conveys $100,000 "to T in trust, to pay the income to A for life, then to pay the income to B for life, then to pay the principal to B's issue then living *per stirpes*, and if B dies without living issue, then to pay the principal to the American Cancer Society." Note first that the trust assets are conveyed to T, as trustee. T is the legal owner of the assets. All of the other interests created by the conveyance are equitable. A has an equitable life estate in the income generated by the trust assets. B has an indefeasibly vested remainder in life estate in the income of the trust. B's issue have an alternative contingent remainder in the principal (i.e., the assets) of the trust. The American Cancer Society has an alternative contingent remainder in the principal of the trust.

During A's life, T will pay the trust income to A. After A dies, T will pay the income to B, if B is still alive. When B dies, T will pay the trust principal to B's issue then living *per stirpes*. If B has no living issue, T will pay the trust principal to the American Cancer Society. Once the principal is paid out, the trust will terminate. If T is an individual and dies or resigns at any time during this process, T will be replaced with another trustee. Banks and other institutions may be trustees, and the settlors of trusts of long expected durations often choose institutional trustees.

Note the terminology used in Example 38. The present and future interests created in this example are *equitable* interests. The conveyance in Example 38 creates an equitable life estate in A. The future interests likewise are equitable. In contrast, the interests in the other examples that we have seen are *legal* interests. In the conveyance "to A for life, then to B," for example, A has a legal life estate, and B has a legal indefeasibly vested remainder in fee simple absolute.

In Example 38, the trust asset was a sum of money. Trusts can be created with any sort of property. Most often, the trustee has the power to sell trust assets and reinvest the proceeds in other assets. Because of this power to alienate trust assets, conveyances that create equitable future interests in trust avoid many of the alienability problems that are created by conveyances that create legal future interests. If Blackacre is conveyed in trust to T, for the benefit of a set of equitable present and future interest holders, then T in most circumstances can sell Blackacre and reinvest the proceeds in another asset. If you wanted to purchase Blackacre, you only need to negotiate with T, rather than a host of present and future interest holders.

Because of alienability and other issues, *you should almost never advise clients to convey property in a way that creates legal future interests*. When future interests are involved, creating a trust should be your default rule, and you should deviate from this default rule only if you have a good reason to do so.

2. RULES FAVORING ALIENABILITY

As we saw above, future interests in open class and contingent interests can present substantial alienability problems. In this section, we consider four traditional rules that were designed to further the alienability of property by in some circumstances destroying these interests. The first three rules are largely archaic, and our consideration of them will be very brief. The fourth, the Rule Against Perpetuities, is still important in many U.S. jurisdictions, and we will cover it in some depth.

a. The Doctrine of Worthier Title

The operation of the Doctrine of Worthier Title is best illustrated through an example:

EXAMPLE 39: O conveys Blackacre "to A for life, then to O's heirs."

Classifying this conveyance, A has a life estate, O's heirs have a contingent remainder in fee simple absolute, and O has a reversion in fee simple absolute. Heirs are not identified until a person's death, so the remainder is contingent because it is in an unascertained person. The Doctrine of Worthier Title destroyed the contingent remainder in O's heirs, leaving O with a more straightforward reversion in fee simple absolute. The operation of the doctrine therefore rewrites the conveyance to read "to A for life." By destroying the contingent remainder, the Doctrine of Worthier Title promoted the alienability of property—if you want to buy Blackacre, you only need to negotiate with A and O, and don't have to wait around until A's death to identify O's heirs.

The Doctrine of Worthier Title originally applied to both transfers at death and transfers during life. The branch that applied to transfers at death is now defunct. Section 2-710 of the Uniform Probate Code (which, to be clear, has not been adopted by all states) abolishes the doctrine. The branch applying to transfers during life is out of favor and has been abolished in many jurisdictions. To the extent it survives, today it is more of a rule of construction than a rule of law—that is, it is used as an aid in interpreting the language of a conveyance, rather than a hard-and-fast rule that is always binding. The Doctrine gained its second life as a rule of construction in Judge Cardozo's opinion in *Doctor v. Hughes*, 122 N.E. 221 (N.Y. 1919). Whatever the abstract merits of Judge Cardozo's position, the use of the Doctrine as a rule of construction has been something of a fiasco in practice. One court remarked that the rule of construction approach has led "to a shower of strained decisions difficult to reconcile with one another and [has been] generative of considerable confusion in the law." *Hatch v. Riggs National Bank*, 361 F.2d 559, 563 (D.C. App. 1966). The Doctrine was abolished in England in 1833 and is sliding into oblivion here. It may, however, still have some life in some jurisdictions.

b. The Rule in Shelley's Case

The Rule in Shelley's Case, like the Doctrine of Worthier Title, promotes alienability by destroying a contingent remainder created in a person's heirs. The Rule applies to the following scenario:

EXAMPLE 40: O conveys Blackacre "to A for life, then to A's heirs."

Note that the contingent remainder in this example is in A's heirs, rather than O's heirs as was the case with the Doctrine of Worthier Title. The Rule operates to merge the remainder and the life estate, creating a fee simple absolute in A. As with the Doctrine of Worthier Title, the destruction of the contingent remainder in A's heirs by the Rule encourages the alienability of property. If you want to buy Blackacre, you do not have to worry about who might qualify as A's heirs at A's death.

The Rule in Shelley's Case has been abolished in most U.S. jurisdictions—it appears to thrive only in Arkansas and Delaware. The Rule was abolished in England in 1925.

c. Destructibility of Contingent Remainders

In our materials on contingent remainders, we looked at the conveyance "to A for life, then to B if B reaches the age of 21." What happens if A dies and B is 18 years old? Under the common-law rule of destructibility, B's interest was destroyed. The result under the traditional rule is that Blackacre would revert back to O in fee simple absolute. The destruction of the contingent remainder aids alienability by reducing the number of interests and eliminating the need to worry about the resolution of the contingency.

The destructibility rule has been widely abolished and appears to thrive only in Florida. In jurisdictions that have abolished the rule, on A's death O would have a fee simple subject to executory limitation and B would have an executory interest in fee simple absolute that would take away O's interest if and when B reaches the age of 21.

d. The Rule Against Perpetuities

The Rule Against Perpetuities is our most important rule favoring alienability. It is more broadly applicable than the other three rules and still survives in some form in most U.S. jurisdictions. It is also incredibly hard to apply. The California Supreme Court famously dismissed a malpractice action against an attorney who botched the Rule because of the Rule's complexity. *See Lucas v. Hamm*, 364 P.2d 685 (Cal. 1961).

Despite its complexity, we think that it is possible for everyone to achieve a good basic understanding of the Rule and its operation. We will take the Rule in a series of steps and will focus on examples of Rule in action. We will also explain how an attorney with even an imperfect understanding of the Rule can competently advise clients. We do not want you to find yourself in a position of having to rely on *Lucas v. Hamm*.

Before we go any further, you should be sure you have completed the present and future interest problem sets and know the classification of future interests cold. The application of the Rule turns on the identity of future interests, and if you are still confused about how to identify interests, you will be even more confused with this material.

The Rule applies to only a limited set of types of interests. It applies to:

    Contingent remainders

    Executory Interests

    Vested Remainders in an Open Class

    Option and similar contracts

It does *not* apply to:

    Future interests created in the grantor:

        Reversions

        Possibilities of Reverter

        Rights of Entry

    Vested interests not in an open class created in the grantee:

        Indefeasibly Vested Remainders

        Vested Remainders Subject to Divestment

We will focus on the Rule's application to future interests and will cover options and similar contracts towards the end of our discussion.

John Chipman Gray gave us the classic statement of the Rule, to which we have added two small insertions: "No interest [subject to the Rule] is good unless it must vest [in a closed class], if at all, no later than 21 years after some life in being at the creation of the interest." Let's take each part of this statement in turn:

> *"No interest [subject to the Rule] is good . . ."* As we noted above, three types of future interests are subject to the Rule: contingent remainders, executory interests, and vested remainders in an open class. *If they do not satisfy the*

Rule, they are void from the time of creation—it is as if they never existed. If an interest violates the Rule, we simply cross it out of the conveyance. We added the modification "[subject to the Rule]" to remind us that the Rule does not apply to all future interests.

"unless it must vest [in a closed class], if at all . . ." To satisfy the Rule, the interest in question must vest, or fail, within a certain period.

> For contingent remainders and executory interests, this means that the contingencies reflected in the interest must resolve themselves one way or the other within the period stated by the Rule. Note well that the Rule *does not* require the interests to vest within this period. Rather, it requires that they either vest *or* fail during the period. We just want to know how things turn out, one way or the other. Note also that we are concerned here about when the interests vest or fail, not about when they might become possessory.

> For vested remainders in an open class, this means that the *class must close* within the period set by the Rule. We added "[in a closed class]" to highlight the application of the Rule to vested remainders in an open class. For these interests, we care about the class closing, not vesting.

"no later than 21 years after some life in being at the creation of the interest." This part of the rule sets the period within which the interests subject to the Rule must vest in a closed class or fail. This period—which we will call the "perpetuities period"—is defined as 21 years after a life in being at the time of creation of the interest. We will need to be more precise in our definition of a "life in being," but for now, we can understand it as a person who was alive when the interest was created. The perpetuities period ends 21 years after the death of the last life in being. Interests subject to the Rule that do not vest in a closed class or fail within this time period are void.

Before we get further into the operation of the Rule, we should pause to see how it accomplishes its policy goals. As we have already noted, one goal of the Rule is to further the alienability of property. We have seen how contingent remainders, executory interests, and vested remainders in an open class can impede the alienability of property. The Rule aids alienability by limiting the amount of time for the contingencies in contingent remainders and executory interests to resolve themselves, and for the open classes in vested remainders in an open class to become closed. It also aids alienability by destroying interests that do not comply with the Rule.

The Rule has other policy justifications. One of these justifications is limiting the period of dead hand control of property. The dead hand issue is just what it sounds like—problems might arise when a person tries to control land or other assets after their death. Circumstances change, and what might have seemed like a good idea when the grantor made a decision might not seem like a good idea now. Because the grantor is dead, she cannot change her mind based on new circumstances. By limiting the time for future interests to vest or fail, the Rule places some limits on the practical duration of dead hand control. Another justification for the Rule is inhibiting the creation of permanent concentrations of wealth. By forcing land and other assets into certain ownership by the end of the perpetuities period, the Rule makes it easier for concentrations of wealth to be broken up or dissipate.

To apply the Rule, we first classify the future interests created by the grant without regard to their validity under the Rule. We then see if any of these interests are subject to the Rule. Next, we test those interests to see if they vest or fail in a closed class within the perpetuities period. If they do, they are valid. If they do not, they are void. Finally, if any of the interests are invalid under the Rule, we reclassify the valid interests created by the grant. Of these steps, the third—identifying lives in being—is by far the hardest.

There are two major ways to test whether an interest satisfies the Rule. The first is the *common-law approach*. The common-law approach looks forward from the time an interest is created and asks whether the interest is certain to vest or fail in a closed class within the perpetuities period. The common-law approach is often described as making the Rule a matter of mathematical or logical proof. We need to be able to prove, with certainty, that the interest will vest or fail in a closed class within 21 years of a life in being. An advantage of the common-law approach is that it allows us to know right away whether an interest is valid under the Rule. A disadvantage is that, as we will see, the common-law approach often voids interests because of the possibility of extremely unlikely events.

The second is the *wait-and-see approach*. Rather than looking forward from the date of creation of the interest, this approach waits to see how facts actually develop. It looks backward at the end of the perpetuities period and asks whether the interests in question have vested or failed in a closed class. Any interest that satisfies the common-law approach will also satisfy the wait-and-see approach: if we have proved with certainty that the interest will vest or fail in a closed class during the perpetuities period, we don't have to wait and see how things actually turn out. The wait-and-see approach will validate some interests that would be invalid under the common-law approach. This approach has the advantage of avoiding the often silly results that follow from the common-law approach. It has the disadvantage of leading to uncertainty about whether an interest is valid while the perpetuities period plays itself out.

As we apply the Rule to various conveyances, we will analyze each interest under both the common-law and wait-and-see approaches. Before we get to our first examples, we need establish two more important points:

> First, when we apply the common-law approach, we evaluate the interests at the time the conveyance is made. Transfers made by will occur *when the testator dies*, not when the will is written. Wills can be changed at any time up to the testator's death. We should note that conveyances made in trust

are evaluated when they become irrevocable. We will not present examples involving revocable trusts and note this rule simply to be thorough.

Second, not everyone alive at the time of conveyance qualifies as a life in being. Rather, only *people who in some way affect the vesting* (or class closing) of the interest count. Often potential lives in being are obvious from the language of the conveyance. Other times, potential lives in being are more subtle, as we will see from our examples below.

Let's look at some examples to see the Rule in operation.

EXAMPLE 41: O grants Blackacre "to A for life, then to B if B reaches the age of 50." At the time of the conveyance, B is alive and is two years old.

Classifying without the RAP: A has a life estate, B has a contingent remainder in fee simple absolute, and O has a reversion in fee simple absolute. B's contingent remainder is subject to the Rule.

Common-law approach: B's contingent remainder will vest or fail during B's life—either B will live to 50, or will not. B therefore provides the life in being for this interest, and it is valid under the common-law approach.

Wait-and-see approach: Any interest that is valid under the common-law approach will also be valid under the wait-and-see approach. We could wait around to see if B lives to age 50 or not, but we don't need to do so—we know that this contingency will resolve itself one way or the other during B's life.

EXAMPLE 42: O grants Blackacre "to A for life, then to A's children." At the time of conveyance, A has one child, B.

Classifying without the RAP: A has a life estate and B has a vested remainder in an open class. B's vested remainder in an open class is subject to the Rule.

Common-law approach: B's vested remainder will vest *in a closed class* on A's death. A is alive, and so provides the life in being to validate B's vested remainder in an open class.

Wait-and-see approach: Because B's vested remainder in an open class is valid under the common-law approach, it also is valid under the wait-and-see approach. We do not need to wait around for the class to actually close to determine whether B's interest is valid under the Rule.

EXAMPLE 43: O grants Blackacre "to A for life, then to A's first child to reach the age of 25." A is alive, and has one child, B, who is 22 years old.

Classifying without the RAP: A has a life estate. B has a contingent remainder in fee simple absolute. O has a reversion in fee simple absolute.

Common-law approach: The contingent remainder in fee simple absolute is void under the common-law approach. You might think that it is valid because B is alive and B will reach the age of 25, or not, during B's lifetime. Plus, B is only three years away from reaching the age of 25! There are scenarios, however, where the contingent remainder might vest or fail outside of the perpetuities period. Here is an example:

> 2000: Grant is made. A is alive, and has one child B, who is 22 years old.

> 2001: A has a second child, C.

> 2002: A and B die.

> 2026: C reaches the age of 25 more than 21 years after a life in being at the time of the creation of the grant.

Because of this possibility, the contingent remainder is void. Under the common-law approach, we would reclassify the interests in the grant: A has a life estate. O has a reversion in fee simple absolute. B has nothing whatsoever. Note that this is true even if B has reached the age of 25 by the time the dispute is adjudicated. *An interest that violates the Rule is void from the time of the grant—*we treat it as if it never existed in the first place.

In this example, C is an *afterborn child*—that is a child born after the grant was made. The possibility of afterborn children is a frequent source of problems under the Rule Against Perpetuities.

Watch out for afterborn children!

Wait-and-see approach: The contingent remainder in fee simple absolute might be void or it might be valid—we have to wait and see. If B or another of A's children reaches the age of 25 during the perpetuities period, the contingent remainder will vest and be valid. If an afterborn child scenario like the one set forth above occurs, then the contingent remainder will be void. Note that there is also a possibility that the contingent remainder will simply fail on its own terms—for example, if A and B die in 2001 and A has no other children.

EXAMPLE 44: O grants Blackacre "to A for life, then to A's first child to reach the age of 21." A is alive, and has one child, B.

Classifying without the RAP: A has a life estate. B has a contingent remainder in fee simple absolute. O has a reversion in fee simple absolute.

Common-law approach: The contingent remainder in fee simple absolute is valid. Even in an afterborn child scenario, the contingent remainder will vest or fail within the perpetuities period because any child of A will reach 21, or not, within 21 years of A's death. Here is an example:

2000: Grant is made. A is alive, and has one child B.

2001: B dies.

2022: A has another child, C.

2023: A dies.

2041: C reaches the age of 21.

Because the contingent remainder must vest or fail within 21 years of A's death, it is valid under the common-law approach.

Wait-and-see approach: Because the contingent remainder is valid under the common-law approach, it is valid under the wait-and-see approach.

You might think from the last two examples that conveyances that create contingencies requiring people to reach an age of greater than 21 are problematic under the Rule Against Perpetuities. This is an overgeneralization. An age restriction of more than 21 years should raise a red flag, but many such restrictions are valid. For instance, the conveyance in Example 41, created this contingent remainder: "then to B if B reaches the age of 50." Conveyances turning on the age of a specific named person will be valid because the contingency will resolve itself one way or the other during that person's lifetime. Note in this context the difference between "then to B if B reaches the age of 50" and "then to A's first child to reach the age of 50." The first is to a specific living person. The second is not.

Interests created in unspecified people with age restrictions of more than 21 years may also be valid in other context. Our next example introduces a new character to our cast: T. T stands for Testator. When we say that T granted Blackacre "to A," we mean that T died and left Blackacre to A in her will. The key thing to understand is that the conveyance is made at T's death. One important ramification of this fact is that T is dead and so cannot have any more children. Another is that some interests in the text of the conveyance might not become possessory because facts might have changed between the time the testator wrote her will and the time the testator died. Here are some examples of how T's death at the time of conveyance can affect the validity of conveyances under the Rule Against Perpetuities.

EXAMPLE 45: T grants Blackacre "to A for life, then to my first child to reach the age of 25." A is alive and T has one child, B, age one.

Classifying without the RAP: A has a life estate. B has a contingent remainder in fee simple absolute. T's estate has a reversion in fee simple absolute. This conveyance is similar to that in Example 43, but the contingent remainder is in T's first child to reach 25, not A's first child to reach 25.

Common-law approach: B's contingent remainder is valid under the common-law approach. This is because T is dead and therefore cannot have any more children. The afterborn child problem that was present in Example 43 therefore is absent here. B was alive at the time of conveyance and provides her own measuring life to validate her interest.

Wait-and-see approach: Because B's interest is valid under the common-law approach, it is valid under the wait-and-see approach.

EXAMPLE 46: T grants Blackacre "to A for life, then to A's first child to reach the age of 25." At the time of the conveyance (T's death), A has died and has one child, B, age 23.

Classifying without the RAP: Because A is dead at the time of conveyance, A's life estate never becomes possessory—it effectively disappears. Under the modern approach that does not follow the rule of destructibility of contingent remainders, B's contingent remainder is converted into an executory interest. To classify the grant, T's estate has a fee simple subject to executory limitation, and B has an executory interest in fee simple absolute. This executory interest is subject to the Rule.

Common-law approach: B's executory interest is valid under the Rule. B was alive at the time of conveyance, and provides the measuring life that validates her executory interest—B obviously will reach 25 or not within her own lifetime.

Note three things about this conveyance. First, we care about the facts at the time of conveyance. With testamentary conveyances, this is the time of death. The facts at the time the will was drafted are irrelevant. Second, because A was dead at the time of conveyance, there was no afterborn child problem. Third, the result is that the exact same language that was a problem in Example 43 was not a problem here.

Wait-and-see approach: Because B's interest is valid under the common-law approach, it is valid under the wait-and-see approach.

The differences between conveyances made during life and those made at death are further illustrated by the following examples involving class gifts.

EXAMPLE 47: O grants Blackacre "to my children for life, then to my grandchildren." O is 80 years old, and has one child, A, and one grandchild, B.

Classifying without the RAP: A has a life estate that may have to be shared if additional children are born. B has a vested remainder in an open class in fee simple absolute.

Common-law approach: B's vested remainder in an open class is void under the common-law approach because of the potential for afterborn children. Classifying the interests applying the common-law Rule, A has a life estate that may have to be shared if additional children are born; O has a reversion in fee simple absolute.

Here is an example of a scenario that would cause the remainder to vest in a closed class outside of the perpetuities period:

2000: Conveyance is made. O, A, and B are alive.

2001: O has another *child*, C.

2002: O, A, and B die.

2030: C has a child, D.

2080: C dies, closing the class of O's *grandchildren*.

As this scenario shows, the class of O's grandchildren could close well past the perpetuities period. You might intuitively rebel against the idea of O having another child after the age of 80. Remember, however, in this area *the law will act as if any living person can have additional children* (see the sidebar).

PRESUMPTIONS OF FERTILITY AND CHILDREN BORN AFTER DEATH

As this problem shows, the legal presumption that any living person can have a child can sometimes lead to absurd results. The presumption applies to people of any age, whether they are 2 years old or 80 years old. At least where older people are concerned, recent medical developments and the possibility of adoption both make this presumption possibility less unrealistic than it may once have been.

Advances in reproductive technology present another potential problem. Because human reproductive cells can be frozen (whether fertilized or not), there is now a very real possibility that a person might have a child many years after her death. The possibility that a child might be born after a parent's death has always existed—a father might conceive a child and die before the child was born. Children born in this particular circumstance are typically treated as being alive at the time of their parent's death for property law purposes. But what do we do with a child born 15 years after a parent's death? Do they, for example, fall into the class of a conveyance made to the parent's children? The answer is blurry. *See* Benjamin C. Carpenter, *A Chip Off the Old Iceblock: How Cryopreservation Has Changed Estate Law, Why Attempts to Address the Issue Have Fallen Short, and How to Fix It*, 21 Cornell J.L. & Pub. Pol'y 347 (2011). As to our topic at hand, the possibility of this type of children should not be relevant to the operation of the Rule Against Perpetuities, at least unless the grantor clearly contemplated including such children in the conveyance at issue. *See* Sharona Hoffman & Andrew P. Morriss, *Birth After Death: Perpetuities and the New Reproductive Technologies*, 38 Ga. L. Rev. 575 (2004).

There are three important lessons to take from this scenario. First, remember that for the Rule Against Perpetuities, any living person can have children. Second, conveyances in this general pattern are often called *fertile octogenarian problems*, for the obvious reason that they turn on the idea that an 80-year old can have children. Third, conveyances to *a living person's grandchildren* are often problematic under the common-law approach to the Rule Against Perpetuities.

Wait-and-see approach: B's vested remainder in an open class may or may not be valid. If O dies without having any further children, then the vested remainder in the open class of O's grandchildren will be valid—all of O's *children* are lives in being, and when the last child dies, the class of O's *grandchildren* will vest in a closed class. If O does have an afterborn child, the vested remainder might vest too late and be void under the Rule.

EXAMPLE 48: T grants Blackacre "to my children for life, then to my grandchildren." At her death, T is survived by one child, A, and one grandchild, B.

Classifying without the RAP: A has a life estate that may have to be shared if additional children are born. B has a vested remainder in an open class in fee simple absolute.

Common-law approach: B's vested remainder in an open class is valid. The key difference from Example 47 is that at the time of conveyance, T was dead. Because T has died, T cannot have afterborn children. The class of T's *children* is closed at the time of conveyance. T's children provide the measuring lives for the class of T's *grandchildren*, because the class of grandchildren will close on the death of the last child.

Wait-and-see approach: Because B's interest is valid under the common-law approach, it is valid under the wait-and-see approach.

The last two examples show us that a conveyance to a living person's grandchildren raises problems under the common-law Rule Against Perpetuities, but that a conveyance to a dead person's grandchildren avoids these problems. This is not to say that all conveyances to a dead person's grandchildren will be valid—a conveyance to "any of T's grandchildren to reach the age of 25" will raise problems. At this point, you should be able to work out why this conveyance is problematic for yourself. If you need some help, it is included in the exercises with explanatory answers below.

The fertile octogenarian is one of three classic Rule Against Perpetuities problems that you should be familiar with. Here are the other two:

EXAMPLE 49: O conveys Blackacre "to A for life, then to A's widow for life, then to A's children then living." A is alive and is married to B. A has one child, C.

Classifying without the RAP: A has a life estate. A's widow has a contingent remainder in life estate. Why is this remainder contingent? Because it is in an unascertained person—we do not know the identity of A's widow until A dies. C has a contingent remainder in fee simple absolute, and O has a reversion in fee simple absolute.

Common-law approach: Both of the contingent remainders are subject to the Rule. A's widow's contingent remainder is valid under the Rule, because it will vest or fail on A's death, and A is a life in being. C's contingent remainder, however, is void under the Rule. We therefore need to reclassify the interests as follows: A has a life estate, A's widow has a contingent remainder in life estate, and O has a reversion in fee simple absolute.

Here is a scenario that illustrates the invalidity of the contingent remainder in O's children who survive A and A's widow:

> 2000: Conveyance is made. A, B, and C are alive.
>
> 2001: D is born. D is unrelated to A, B, or C.
>
> 2002: B and C die.
>
> 2025: A marries D.
>
> 2026: A and D have a child, E.
>
> 2027: A dies. D is now A's widow.
>
> 2075: D dies. C's contingent remainder, if valid, would become possessory.

In this scenario, the contingent remainder in A's children vests or fails far outside of the perpetuities period. The problem is created because *both* (a) A's widow might be born after the conveyance, *and* (b) the contingent remainder will not vest or fail until A's widow's death. Unsurprisingly, the name of this problem is *the unborn widow*.

Do not make the mistake in thinking that all conveyances that create remainder in life estate in a widow raise perpetuities problems. For example, if the remainder at the end of this conveyance is rewritten to be "then to A's children," the remainder would be valid, because it would vest in a closed class on A's death.

Wait-and-see approach: The contingent remainder in A's children who survive A's widow may or may not be valid. So long as the person who becomes A's widow was alive at the time of conveyance, the remainder will vest or fail during the perpetuities period (at the end of the widow's life) and will be valid.

EXAMPLE 50: O conveys Blackacre "to A for life, then to B when A's will is probated."

Classifying without the RAP: A has a life estate. O has a reversion in fee simple subject to executory limitation. B has an executory interest. Why isn't B's interest a remainder? Because it will not become possessory, if at all, on the natural end of the preceding estate. When A dies, some period of time will pass before A's will is probated—probate is a legal process that takes some time.

Common-law approach: B's executory interest is void under the common-law approach. Reclassifying the interests taking the application of the Rule into account, A has a life estate and O has a reversion in fee simple absolute. Here is a scenario that illustrates why the executory interest is void.

2000: Conveyance is made. A and B are alive.

2001: A dies.

2002: B dies. If it was valid, the executory interest would now be held by B's devisees or heirs.

2025: A's will is finally probated. The contingency in the executory interest has resolved itself more than 21 years after the death of A and B, who are the only people in the conveyance who affect the vesting and could possibly be lives in being.

> Three classic problems: the fertile octogenarian (Example 47), the unborn widow (Example 49), and the slothful executor (Example 50).

The name of this problem is *the slothful executor*. Most wills are probated within a short time of the testator's death. There remains a possibility, however remote, that the executor will not successfully probate the will for more than 21 years after lives in being. As a result, the executory interest is void under the common-law approach.

Like the slothful executor, our next few examples involve executory interests.

EXAMPLE 51: O conveys Blackacre "to the School Board so long as it is used for school purposes."

Classifying without the RAP: The School Board has a fee simple determinable. O has a possibility of reverter in fee simple absolute. All interests created in the grantor (reversions, possibilities of reverter, and rights of entry) are exempt from the Rule Against Perpetuities, so the Rule does not apply here at all.

EXAMPLE 52: O conveys Blackacre "to the School Board so long as it is used for school purposes, then to A."

Classifying without the RAP: The School Board has a fee simple subject to executory limitation. A has an executory interest in fee simple absolute.

Common-law approach: The exectory interest violates the Rule Against Perpetuities. This one should be fairly intuitive—the School Board could stop using Blackacre 500 years from now. Therefore it is possibility for the executory interest to vest or fail well outside of the perpetuities period.

Reclassifying the interest to take the application of the Rule into account, the School Board has a fee simple determinable and O has a possibility of reverter in fee simple absolute.

Wait-and-see approach: The executory interest may or may not be valid. If the School Board stops using Blackacre for school purposes within the perpetuities period, then the executory interest will be valid. If not, it will be void.

EXAMPLE 53: O conveys Blackacre "to the School Board, but if the property is no longer used for school purposes then A may enter and take the property."

Classifying without the RAP: The School Board has a fee simple subject to executory limitation. A has an executory interest in fee simple absolute.

Common-law approach: The executory interest violates the Rule Against Perpetuities. The reason is the same as in the last example—the School Board could stop using Blackacre for school purposes 500 years from now.

Remember that if an interest violates the Rule, we simply cross it out of the conveyance. Note what happens when you cross the language creating the executory interest out of this conveyance—you are left with "to the School Board." The School Board owns Blackacre in fee simple absolute. It is best not to try to think of a good reason for the difference in result between this example and Example 52, where the elimination of the executory interest resulted in a fee simple determinable. The Rule Against Perpetuities is a mechanical rule, so apply it mechanically.

Wait-and-see approach: As in the previous example, the executory interest may or may not be valid. If the School Board stops using Blackacre for school purposes within the perpetuities period, then the executory interest will be valid. If not, it will be void.

EXAMPLE 54: O conveys Blackacre "to the School Board for so long as the property is used for school purposes, then to the State University."

Classifying without the RAP: The School Board has a fee simple subject to executory limitation. The State University has an executory interest in fee simple absolute.

Common-law approach: The State University's executory interest is valid under the Rule Against Perpetuities. This is due to the *charity-to-charity exception.* This exception states that if both interests—the interest subject to executory limitation or divestment, and the executory interest that might take it away—are held by charities, then the executory interest is exempt from the Rule Against Perpetuities.

Wait-and-see approach: Because the State University's executory interest is valid under the common-law approach, it is valid under the wait-and-see approach.

Finally, as we noted at the outset, the Rule Against Perpetuities has been held to apply to options and similar contracts. We will distinguish between two types of contracts—*options* and *rights of first refusal.* A purchase option gives the holder the right to purchase the property in question in accordance with the terms of the option agreement. A right of first refusal gives the holder the right to purchase the property in accordance with the terms of the agreement, but only if the owner offers to sell the property to someone else first. The crucial difference is that the holder of an option has the power to compel the sale of the subject property, where the holder of a right of first refusal does not have the power to compel the sale if the owner has not offered to sell to someone else. Before we get to the application of the Rule Against Perpetuities to these contracts, let's take a look at an example of each.

EXAMPLE 55: O grants A an option to purchase Blackacre "for $100,000 within one year of the date of this option agreement." O has an option to purchase Blackacre for $100,000 within one year. If O refuses to sell Blackacre to A, A can compel the sale.

EXAMPLE 56: O grants A a right of first refusal to purchase Blackacre "within one year of the date of this agreement." A has a one-year right of first refusal in Blackacre. If O offers to sell Blackacre to anyone else during the one-year period, A has the right to step in and purchase the property. If O does not offer to sell to anyone else, however, A cannot compel O to sell Blackacre.

The majority common-law view is that options are subject to the Rule Against Perpetuities. A less strong majority of jurisdictions also hold that rights of first refusal are subject to the Rule. In our examples that follow, we will follow this majority rule. We should note that the majority common-law rule applying the Rule to options has been altered in many states by statute. The Uniform Statutory Rule Against Perpetuities (USRAP), adopted in about half of U.S. jurisdictions and discussed further below, abolishes the application of the Rule to options and rights of first refusal.

An option satisfies the common-law Rule Against Perpetuities if it must be exercised, if at all, within the perpetuities period. The option in Example 55 easily satisfies the Rule—it must be exercised within one year of its creation. The following two options raise perpetuities problems:

EXAMPLE 57: O grants A an option to purchase Blackacre "for $100,000 at any time prior to 30 years from the date of this agreement."

Classifying without the RAP: O owns Blackacre in fee simple absolute. A has an option to purchase Blackacre.

Common-law approach: A's option is void. O and A could die tomorrow, and A's estate could try to exercise the option in 30 years—more than 21 years after the deaths of O and A, who are our potential lives in being.

Wait-and-see approach: A's option may or may not be valid. So long as either O or A survives for nine years, the option period will fall within the perpetuities period of lives in being plus 21 years, and the interest will be valid. Even if O and A die soon after the option was executed, the option will be valid if A exercises the option during the perpetuities period.

EXAMPLE 58: ABC Inc. grants XYZ LLC an option to purchase Blackacre "for $100,000 at any time prior to 30 years from the date of this agreement."

Classifying without the RAP: ABC Inc. owns Blackacre in fee simple absolute. XYZ LLC has an option to purchase Blackacre.

Common-law approach: XYZ LLC's option is void. This is the same basic conveyance as the previous example. Here, however, both the grantor and the grantee are legal entities, not natural people. As a result, neither can provide lives in being. The perpetuities period therefore ends up being 21 years. Because the option by its terms has a 30-year period, it is possible that the option will be exercised outside of the perpetuities period.

Wait-and-see approach: XYZ LLC's option may or may not be valid. Because both the grantor and the grantee are entities, the perpetuities period will be 21 years. If XYZ LLC exercises the option within 21 years, it will be valid. If not, it will be void.

G. RULE AGAINST PERPETUITIES PROBLEM SET

For each of the following conveyances, classify the interests (a) without application of the Rule Against Perpetuities, (b) with application of the common-law approach to the Rule Against Perpetuities, and (c) with application of the wait-and-see approach to the Rule Against Perpetuities. Explanatory answers to this set of exercises are provided on page 1034.

1. O grants Blackacre "to A for life, then to A's oldest child then living for life, then to A's grandchildren then living and their heirs."
2. T devises Blackacre "to A for life, then to B for life, then to B's children."
3. O grants Blackacre "to A for life, then to A's children, but if any of A's issue are ever convicted of a felony, then the interest in A's children will be divested and shall go to the Widener City School Board."
4. T devises Blackacre "to A for life, then to A's children for life, then to A's grandchildren for life, then to A's great-grandchildren and their heirs." At the time of T's death, A is alive and has two children, B and C, each of which have two children, B1 and B2, and C1 and C2.
5. Same as (4), but 25 years later, A, B, and C have died without having more children. B1 has had a child, B3. C2 has had two children, C3 and C4.
6. T devises "to my widow for life, then to my issue then living."
7. O sells A an option to purchase Blackacre "for $100,000 at any time prior to the date 30 years from the date of execution of this agreement."
8. T's will gives Blackacre "to A for life, then to A's children for their lives, then to B's children." When T dies, A is alive and has two children, A1 and A2. B has died and is survived by three children, B1, B2, and B3.
9. O gives Blackacre "to my children for life, then to my first grandchild to reach the age of 25."
10. O conveys Blackacre "to my children for life, then to my grandchildren who reach the age of 21."
11. T grants Blackacre to "to my children for life, then to their children for life, then to my surviving issue." T is survived by two children, A and B.
12. T dies, leaving a will that states in part: "my estate in North Widener City shall be sold and the proceeds divided equally amongst my surviving issue."
13. T grants Blackacre "to my child, A, for life, then to A's children, but if any of A's children fail to graduate from college by age 30, then that child's share shall go to A's other children." A is alive and has two children, B and C. B received her B.A. in 1999; C is a junior in high school.
14. T conveys Blackacre "to my children for life, then to my grandchildren who reach the age of 25." At T's death, T is survived by her children A and B, and one grandchild, C, who is 18 years old.

15. O conveys Blackacre "to A for life, then to A's children for life, then to A's issue born during the lifetime of any of the issue of President John F. Kennedy alive at the time of this conveyance."
16. T devises Blackacre "to A and her heirs, but if A dies childless, then to B's children then living."
17. T conveys Blackacre "to my sister, Maura, for life, then to Maura's husband Max for his life should he still be married to Maura at her death, then to Maura and Max's children then living."
18. O conveys Blackacre "to A until my first grandchild reaches the age of 21, then to that grandchild."
19. T grants Blackacre "to my son, David, for life, then to his children for their lives, then to his grandchildren and their heirs." At T's death, David is alive and has two children, Katie and Laura.
20. Same as 19, but now 15 years later, David has died, survived by Katie and Laura. Neither Katie nor Laura have children.

1. PERPETUITIES REFORM

As we discussed above, the Rule Against Perpetuities serves several important policy goals. It promotes the alienability of property, limits dead hand control, and places some limits on the development of concentrations of wealth across generations. As we have seen, however, the Rule imperfectly promotes these goals. It does not eliminate all problematic future interests, and it is possible to have a conveyance that satisfies the common-law rule that creates uncertain interests that might last for more than 100 years. It is very difficult to apply, even for people with a solid understanding of the Rule. The Rule therefore has presented a ripe target for reform.

The pure common-law rule only survives in a handful of jurisdictions. We will highlight four broad categories of reforms to the Rule:

1. *The Wait-and-See Approach.* As we have seen, the wait-and-see approach judges the validity of interests under the Rule based on facts as they actually occur, rather than speculating on what might happen. It has the advantage of validating some interests that would have been voided under the common-law approach because of the possible occurrence of highly unlikely events. It has the downside of leaving the validity of some interests uncertain while we wait and see how facts will develop. It also has the downside of being just as technically difficult to apply as the common-law Rule.

2. *USRAP.* The Uniform Statutory Rule Against Perpetuities (USRAP) was promulgated in 1986. It has been adopted, often with some modification, by about half of U.S. jurisdictions. Under USRAP, an interest is valid if it either (a) satisfies the common-law Rule or (b) vests or fails within 90 years. The 90-year provision is a modification of the wait-and-see approach—rather than wait and see whether the interest vests or fails within the traditional perpetuities period of lives in being plus 21 years, we wait and see whether it vests or fails within a flat 90 years. USRAP makes a number of other modifications to the common-law Rule. For example, as noted above, it abolishes the application of the Rule to options.

3. *Elimination of Application to Trusts.* A number of states have abolished the application of the Rule to property held in trust. Some states limit this exclusion to personal property held in trust; others apply it to both real and personal property held in trust. As we discussed above, many of the alienability problems created by contingent future interests disappear when the property is held in trust. These reforms to the Rule allow what are often called *dynasty trusts*—trusts that have the potential to last forever.

4. *Outright Abolition of the Rule.* An increasing number of states have abolished the Rule Against Perpetuities outright. These states include Alaska, Idaho, Kentucky, New Jersey, Pennsylvania, Rhode Island, and South Dakota.

In thinking about reform to the Rule Against Perpetuities, we should keep in mind that there are other potential ways to achieve the policy goals of the Rule. As we have already seen, alienability concerns can be addressed with the use of trusts. Concerns about accumulations of wealth over time can be addressed through tax policy. Courts also have the authority of doctrine of cy pres ("as near as is possible") to alter the language of the conveyance to achieve the presumed intent of the grantor. Combining these and other tools may allow us to achieve our policy goals without resort to the complex and unwieldy Rule Against Perpetuities.

2. AVOIDING PERPETUITIES PROBLEMS IN PRACTICE

At the outset of our discussion of the Rule Against Perpetuities, we noted that there are ways to avoid perpetuities problems even if you have an imperfect understanding of the technical operation of the Rule. Here are five tips for avoiding perpetuities problems in practice:

1. *Know the Rule in your jurisdiction.* This is an obvious lawyering basic, but the Rule Against Perpetuities has been substantially modified in most U.S. jurisdictions. You need to know the current state of the Rule in the jurisdiction where you are practicing.

2. *Use trusts whenever future interests are being created.* This is more of a general practice point than a perpetuities-specific point. As discussed above, trusts are incredibly useful devices, and they avoid many of the problems created by legal future interests. In some jurisdictions, use of a trust will protect future interests from the application of the Rule Against Perpetuities.

3. *Watch out for conveyances to grandchildren and age contingencies of more than 21 years.* As we saw in our examples, the potential for afterborn children can cause perpetuities problems with conveyances to grandchildren. Age contingencies of more than 21 years can also cause problems. Each can be valid in some circumstances, but be careful with them. Concerns about both are likely to be reduced in wait-and-see jurisdictions.

4. *Watch out for options and rights of first refusal.* Unless you are certain of its validity in your jurisdiction, you should not create an option or right of first refusal that can last more than 21 years.

5. *Use savings clauses.* A perpetuities savings clause is a clause in an instrument that prevents a Rule Against Perpetuities violation. These clauses can take various forms, but the most common approach is to have the clause terminate all interests created by the document at the end of the perpetuities period. Here is an example of a perpetuities savings clause from a trust:

> Notwithstanding any other provision of this instrument, any interest created by this instrument shall terminate, if it has not already terminated, 21 years after the death of the last surviving beneficiary who was alive at the time of the creation of this trust. Any remaining trust assets will be disbursed on that date in equal shares to the beneficiaries then living, and if none are then living, to the American Cancer Society.

This provision terminates all interests created by the trust, if they have not already terminated, on the last day of the perpetuities period. Because these interests have terminated within the perpetuities period, they cannot violate the Rule Against Perpetuities.

H. RELATIONS BETWEEN PRESENT AND FUTURE INTEREST HOLDERS—THE LAW OF WASTE

It is easy to see how conflicts could arise between present and future interest holders. Imagine that I hold the life estate in Blackacre and you have an indefeasible vested remainder in fee simple absolute. If I fail to maintain the house located on Blackacre, I have harmed not only my interest but yours as well. Similarly, I might harm your interest if I cut timber or extract mineral from the property.

As the present interest holder, I can generally use Blackacre as I see fit. As the future interest holder, you have no present right of possession or use, so you cannot tell me what to do with Blackacre. My ability to freely use Blackacre, however, is limited by an obligation not to harm your interest. I have an obligation to ensure that you receive the land in the same basic condition that it was in when I first took possession.

The obligation of the present interest holder to leave the land in an essentially unchanged condition is the subject of the law of waste. If a present interest holder breaches this obligation, the future interest holder may bring a claim for waste against the present interest holder. There are two basic categories of waste:

1. *Affirmative Waste.* Affirmative waste involves a voluntary act by the present interest holder that damages the property. The classic example of affirmative waste is the intentional destruction or alteration of a building or other valuable improvement to the land. Cutting timber or mining minerals could also be considered affirmative waste, although here the law is more flexible. Under what is often called the *good husbandry*

doctrine, the present interest holder may harvest timber to the extent that it is consistent with good management of the forest, but excessive timber harvesting is prohibited. Under the *open mines doctrine*, the present interest holder may continue to extract mineral resources if extraction was already being done when the present estate began. The present interest holder may not, however, begin new mineral extraction.

2. *Permissive Waste.* Permissive waste involves the failure of the present interest holder to exercise reasonable care to protect and maintain the property. It is a matter of negligence, rather than an affirmative intentional act. The classic examples of permissive waste are the failure to maintain a building and the failure to pay taxes. Failure to eject an adverse possessor may also constitute permissive waste.

There is a third, more controversial, category of waste:

3. *Ameliorative Waste.* Ameliorative waste involves a voluntary act by the present interest holder that *increases* the value of the property. Remember that the present interest holder is obligated to leave the property in a substantially unchanged condition. A valuable improvement would violate this obligation. A claim for ameliorative waste would probably be rejected in a majority of U.S. jurisdictions. A leading case rejecting a claim for ameliorative waste is *Melms v. Pabst Brewing Co.*, 79 N.W. 738 (Wis. 1899).

Litigated waste claims often arise in the context of life estates, but the theory of waste applies to other contexts where ownership is shared. For example, it applies to landlord-tenant contexts, where the tenant is obligated not to commit waste. It also applies in the mortgage context, where the borrower is obligated not to commit waste. Lease and mortgage documents, however, typically set out in detail the obligations of the party in possession to maintain the property. Disputes in these other contexts are therefore less likely to turn on the common law of waste. The instruments creating life estates often do not cover these issues, leaving their resolution to the law of waste. If an instrument does address these issues, the instrument will control. A grantor can even absolve the present interest holder from claims of waste in the document creating the interest.

Many U.S. jurisdictions allow claims for waste only by holders of vested future interests. Holders of contingent future interests can in some cases get some protection in equity against waste by the present interest holder. Generally speaking, the more speculative and remote the possibility that the contingent interest will become possessory, the less likely a court will be to step in on the future interest holder's behalf. Similarly, courts tend to give present interest holders more latitude to act when the duration of their interest is likely to be long.

The potential for conflict between present and future interest holders is yet another area where the use of a trust can avoid problems. The trustee is responsible for balancing between the interests of present and future beneficiaries. Striking this balance can be a challenge, but the problem of unilateral action (or inaction) by the present interest holder is less likely when a trust is used.

CHAPTER 3

CONCURRENT OWNERSHIP

In our last chapter, we saw how present and future interests can be used to divide ownership among multiple people over time. The conveyance of Blackacre "to A for life, then to B" creates a life estate in A and a vested remainder in fee simple absolute in B. A holds the present possessory interest, and B holds a future interest.

Our topic in this chapter is *concurrent ownership.* More than one person can own a property interest at the same time. Consider, for example, the conveyance of Blackacre "to A and B." A and B together own Blackacre in fee simple absolute. They both own a present interest and share ownership at the same time.

There are three concurrent interests in common use in the United States today: the *tenancy in common,* the *joint tenancy,* and the *tenancy by the entirety.* We will consider each of these in turn. We begin with the most basic interest, the tenancy in common, which gives us an opportunity to consider some of the issues and difficulties that can arise when multiple people own the same property at the same time. We will then move to joint tenancies, tenancies by the entirety, and marital property. Married couples, of course, commonly have concurrent ownership of property. The legal status of marriage adds a number of layers to concurrent ownership problems, and we consider those issues separately at the end of the chapter.

A. THE TENANCY IN COMMON

The tenancy in common is our default concurrent interest. As we will soon see, the joint tenancy and tenancy by the entirety both have certain requirements for creation. Joint tenancies, for example, require special language for creation. The tenancy in common does not require special language. Here are some examples of conveyances and other property transfers that create tenancies in common:

EXAMPLE 1: O grants Blackacre "to A and B." A and B own Blackacre as tenants in common. (More specifically, they own Blackacre in fee simple absolute as tenants in common. In this chapter, we will omit the nature of the present interest if it is a fee simple absolute.)

EXAMPLE 2: O grants Blackacre "to A, B, C, D, E, F, and G." A, B, C, D, E, F, and G own Blackacre as tenants in common. There is no limit to the number of people who can be tenants in common. As we will see, though, there are some complications that can arise as the number of tenants in common increases.

EXAMPLE 3: O grants Blackacre "to A for life, then to my children." A has now died. At the time of A's death, O is survived by three children: B, C, and D. B, C, and D own Blackacre as tenants in common. (Before A died, A's children had a vested remainder in an open class in fee simple absolute in common. As we saw in the last chapter, we often leave off the "in common" when we are talking about future interests. This convention is due in part to the fact that, as we will see, concurrent ownership problems arise most often among present interest holders.)

EXAMPLE 4: T dies, and in her will leaves Blackacre "to my grandchildren living at the time of my death." At the time of her death, T is survived by five grandchildren, A, B, C, D, and E. A, B, C, D, and E own Blackacre as tenants in common.

EXAMPLE 5: T, the owner of Blackacre, dies intestate. Under her state's laws of intestacy, Blackacre goes to her three children, A, B, and C. A, B, and C own Blackacre as tenants in common.

So far, in all of our examples, the tenants in common have equal shares of the property. In Example 1, the two tenants in common each have one-half interests. In Example 2, the seven tenants in common each have one-seventh interests. In Example 5, the three tenants in common each have one-third interests. Tenants in common, however, need not have equal shares. Here are two examples:

EXAMPLE 6: O grants Blackacre "to my son, A, who will take a one-half share, and my grandchildren, B and C, who each will take a one-quarter share." A, B, and C are tenants in common. A has a one-half share. B and C each have one-quarter shares.

EXAMPLE 7: T, the owner of Blackacre, dies intestate. T had three children, A, B, and C. C predeceased T. C was survived by two children, D and E. Under her state's laws of intestacy, on T's death, D and E inherit their deceased parent's share. A and B each have a one-third share. D and E split their parent C's one-third share, so each have a one-sixth share. As a result, on T's death, A, B, D, and E are tenants in common. A and B each have one-third shares, and D and E each have one-sixth shares.

Example 7 gives us an opportunity to preview one of the issues that we will consider in this chapter. Imagine that Blackacre has been in the same family for several generations. Initially, it was owned by a married couple. When the couple died, it first passed to their children. When the children died, it passed to their children, and so on. You can imagine how after just a few generations Blackacre could be owned by tens, or even hundreds, of people, with a range of different shares. Just repeat the scenario in Example 7 for three successive generations and you start to see the scope of the problem. When a parcel of property is owned by many people, each of whom owns a relatively small fraction of the whole, we call the ownership *highly fractionated*. We will look at some of the problems that can arise from highly fractionated ownership shortly.

Co-tenants each have an *undivided* share of the ownership of the whole property. This means that each co-tenant has the right to possess and use the entire property. If you and I are co-tenants, neither of us has the right to exclude the other from the property, and neither of us has the ability to prevent the other from using the property in a particular way. This is true regardless of the number of co-owners or of the proportionality of the shares. Even if you have a 1 percent interest and I have a 99 percent interest, I cannot exclude you from the property. It should be intuitive that the undivided nature of co-tenancy can lead to a host of potential problems. If you and I own a house as tenants in common, and we cannot agree on when each of us can use the house, we will be stuck at an impasse because neither of us can exclude the other. Similarly, if you want to build an office park on what had been our family's farm, I won't have the power to stop you so long as we remain in the co-tenancy relationship.

Although things easily can go wrong in a tenancy in common, the law makes it easy for co-tenants to get out of the relationship. At any time and for any reason, any tenant in common can petition a court for *partition* of the co-owned property. We consider partition in the next section. We will then consider the rights of co-tenants and the obligations that co-tenants owe to each other.

1. PARTITION

The partition process begins when one or more co-tenants bring an equitable action for partition in a court. Co-tenants have a right to partition, and in almost all circumstances the court will grant the request for partition. At the end of the partition process, the co-tenancy relationship will be terminated, and the property will be divided between the former co-tenants. There are two types of partition. *Partition in kind* involves a physical division of the property between the former co-tenants. *Partition by sale* involves a sale of the property at auction, with the proceeds divided among the co-tenants according to their shares. Here are two examples of each kind of partition:

REMEDIES

LAW AND EQUITY

> EXAMPLE 8: Imagine that you and I own a ten-acre parcel of land as tenants in common. Each of us has a one-half share. The ten acres are all identical to each other, and no part of the land is more valuable than any other. If the land was partitioned in kind, the land would be physically divided, and we would each receive a five-acre parcel. If the land was

partitioned by sale and sold for $100,000, then proceeds of sale would be divided between us, and each of us would receive $50,000.

EXAMPLE 9: Let's take the same ten-acre parcel as in the last example, but now there are three owners, A, B, and C. A has a one-half share. B and C each have one-quarter shares. If the land was partitioned in kind, then A would receive a five-acre parcel (half of the ten acres). B and C would receive two-and-a-half-acre parcels (each one-quarter of the ten acres). If the land was partitioned by sale and sold for $100,000, then A would receive $50,000. B and C would each receive $25,000.

> You may wonder why we start with partition and then move to the rights and obligations of co-tenants. After all, partition involves the end of a co-tenancy relationship, so it would make a degree of sense to end with partition, rather than start with it. We start with partition because the availability of the partition remedy helps explain why the rights and obligations of co-tenants are structured the way they are. When we are thinking about rights and obligations of co-tenants, it is important to understand that co-tenants can get out of the co-tenancy relationship at any time by seeking partition.

ARK LAND CO. V. HARPER

Supreme Court of West Virginia, 2004
599 S.E.2d 754

DAVIS, Justice. This is an appeal by Rhonda Gail Harper, Edward Caudill, Rose M. Thompson, Edith D. Kitchen, Therman R. Caudill, John A. Caudill, Jr., Tammy Willis, and Lucille M. Miller (hereinafter collectively identified as the "Caudill heirs"), appellants/defendants below, from an order of the Circuit Court of Lincoln County. The circuit court's order authorized a partition and sale of real property jointly owned by the Caudill heirs and Ark Land Company (hereinafter referred to as "Ark Land"), appellee/plaintiff below. Here, the Caudill heirs contend that the legal precedents of this Court warrant partitioning the property in kind, not a sale. After a careful review of the briefs and record in this case, we agree with the Caudill heirs and reverse the circuit court.

I. FACTUAL AND PROCEDURAL HISTORY

This is a dispute involving approximately 75 acres of land situate in Lincoln County, West Virginia. The record indicates that "[t]he Caudill family has owned the land for nearly 100 years." The property "consists of a farmhouse, constructed around 1920, several small barns, and a garden[.]" Prior to 2001, the property was owned exclusively by the Caudill family. However, in 2001 Ark Land acquired a 67.5% undivided interest in the land by purchasing the property interests of several Caudill family members. Ark Land attempted to purchase the remaining property interests held by the Caudill heirs, but they refused to sell. Ark Land sought to purchase all of the property for the express purpose of extracting coal by surface mining.

After the Caudill heirs refused to sell their interest in the land, Ark Land filed a complaint in the Circuit Court of Lincoln County in October of 2001. Ark Land filed the complaint seeking to have the land partitioned and sold. The circuit court appointed three commissioners, pursuant to W. Va.Code §37-4-3 (1957) (Repl. Vol. 1997), to conduct an evidentiary hearing. The commissioners subsequently filed a report on August 19, 2002, wherein they concluded that the property could not be conveniently partitioned in kind.

The Caudill heirs objected to the report filed by the commissioners. The circuit court held a *de novo* review that involved testimony from lay and expert witnesses. On October 30, 2002, the circuit court entered an order directing the partition and sale of the property. . . . From this ruling the Caudill heirs appealed. . . .

III. DISCUSSION

The dispositive issue is whether the evidence supported the circuit court's conclusion that the property could not be conveniently partitioned in kind, thus warranting a partition by sale. During the proceeding before the circuit court, the Caudill heirs presented expert testimony by Gary F. Acord, a mining engineer. Mr. Acord testified that the property could be partitioned in kind. Specifically, Mr. Acord testified that lands surrounding the family home did not have coal deposits and could therefore be partitioned from the remaining lands. On the other hand, Ark Land presented expert testimony which indicated that such a partition would entail several million dollars in additional costs in order to mine for coal.

We note at the outset that "[p]artition means the division of the land held in cotenancy into the cotenants' respective fractional shares. If the land cannot be fairly divided, then the entire estate may be sold and the proceeds appropriately divided." 7 Powell on Real Property, §50.07[1] (2004). It has been observed that, "[i]n the United States, partition was established by statute in each of the individual states. Unlike the partition in kind which existed under early common law, the forced judicial sale was an American innovation." Phyliss Craig-Taylor, *Through a Colored Looking Glass: A View of Judicial Partition, Family Land Loss, and Rule Setting*, 78 Wash. U.L.Q. 737, 752 (2000). This Court has recognized that, by virtue of W. Va.Code §37-4-1 *et seq.*, "[t]he common law right to compel partition has been expanded by [statute] to include partition by sale." Syl. pt. 2, in part, *Consolidated Gas Supply Corp. v. Riley*, 161 W.Va. 782, 247 S.E.2d 712 (1978).[5] . . .

Partition by sale, when it is not voluntary by all parties, can be a harsh result for the cotenant(s) who opposes the sale. This is because "'[a] particular piece of real estate cannot be replaced by any sum of money, however large; and one who wants a particular estate for a specific use, if deprived of his rights, cannot be said to receive an exact equivalent or complete indemnity by the payment of a sum of money.'" *Wight v. Ingram-Day Lumber Co.*, 195 Miss. 823, 17 So.2d 196, 198 (1944) (quoting *Lynch v. Union Inst. for Savings*, 159 Mass. 306, 34 N.E. 364, 364-365 (1893)). Consequently, "[p]artition in kind . . . is the preferred method of partition because it leaves cotenants holding the same estates as before and does not force a sale on unwilling cotenants." Powell, §50.07[4][a]. The laws in all jurisdictions "appear to reflect this longstanding principle by providing a presumption of severance of common ownership in real property by partition in-kind[.]" Craig-Taylor, 78 Wash. U.L.Q. at 753. "Thus, partitioning sale statutes should be construed narrowly and used sparingly because they interfere with property rights." John G. Casagrande, Jr., *Acquiring Property Through Forced Partitioning Sales: Abuses and Remedies*, 27 Boston C.L. Rev. 755, 775 (1986). *See also* Syllabus, in part, *Smith v. Greene*, 76 W.Va. 276, 85 S.E. 537 (1915) ("The right to a partition of real estate in kind, as required at the common law, cannot be denied, where demanded, unless it affirmatively appears upon the record that such partition cannot conveniently be made[.]").

In syllabus point 3 of *Consolidated Gas Supply Corp.*, this Court set out the following standard of proof that must be established to overcome the presumption of partition in kind:

> By virtue of W. Va. Code §37-4-3, a party desiring to compel partition through sale is required to demonstrate (1) that the property cannot be conveniently partitioned in

---

[5] All jurisdictions provide for partition in kind or by sale. *See* Ala.Code §35-6-57 (Law. Co-op. 1991); Alaska Stat. tit. 9, §09.45.290 (Lexis 2000); Ariz.Rev.Stat. Ann. §12-1218 (West 2003); Ark. Stat. Ann. §18-60-420 (Lexis 2003); Cal.Civ.Proc. Code §872.820 (West 1980); Colo.Rev.Stat. §38-28-107 (Bradford 2002); Conn. Gen.Stat. Ann. §52-500 (West 1991); Del.Code Ann. tit. 25, §729 (Michie 1989); D.C.Code Ann. §16-2901 (Lexis 2001); Fla. Stat. Ann. §64.071 (West 1997); Ga.Code Ann. §44-6-166.1 (Michie 1991); Haw.Rev.Stat. §668-7 (1993); Idaho Code §6-512 (Lexis 1998); 735 Ill. Comp. Stat. §5/17-101 (West 2003); Ind.Code Ann §32-17-4-12 (Lexis 2002); Iowa Code Ann. Rule 1.1201 (West 2002); Kan. Stat. Ann. §60-1003 (1994); Ky.Rev.Stat. Ann. §389A.030 (Lexis 1999); La. Stat. Ann. Civ.Code art. 1336 (West 2000); Me.Rev.Stat. Ann. tit. 18-A, §3-911 (West 1998); Md. Real Prop.Code Ann. §14-107 (Lexis 2003): Mass. Gen. Laws Ann. ch. 241, §31 (West 1988); Mich. Comp. Laws §600.3332 (West 2000): Minn.Stat. Ann. §558.14 (West 2000); Miss.Code Ann. §11-21-27 (West 1999); Mo. Ann. Stat. §528.340 (Vernon 1953); Mont.Code Ann. §70-29-202 (West 2003); Neb. Rev.Stat. §25-2181 (1995); Nev.Rev.Stat. §39.120 (2003); N.H.Rev.Stat. Ann. §547-C:25 (Michie 1997); N.J. Stat. Ann. §2A:56-2 (West 2000); N.M. Stat. Ann. §42-5-7 (Michie 1978); N.Y. Real Prop. Acts. Proc. Law §922 (West 1979); N.C. Gen.Stat. §46-22 (Lexis 2003); N.D. Cent.Code §32-16-12 (Michie 1996); Ohio Rev.Code Ann. §5307.09 (Anderson 1989); Okla. Stat. Ann. tit. 12, §1509 (West 1993); Or.Rev.Stat. §105.245 (2003); Pa. Cons.Stat. Ann., R. Civ. Pro. Rule 1558 (West 2002); R.I. Gen. laws §34-15-16 (Michie 1995); S.C.Code Ann. §15-61-50 (Law. Co-op. 1977); S.D. Codified Laws Ann. §21-45-28 (Michie 1987); Tenn.Code Ann. §29-27-201 (Lexis 2000); Tex.Code Ann. Property §23.001 (West 2000); Utah Code Ann. §78-39-12 (Lexis 2002); Vt. Stat. Ann. tit. 12, §5174 (Lexis 2002); Va.Code Ann. §8.01-83 (Lexis 2000); Wash. Rev.Code Ann. §7.52.080 (West 1992); Wis. Stat. Ann. §842.11 (West 1994); Wyo. Stat. §1-32-109 (Lexis 2003).

kind, (2) that the interests of one or more of the parties will be promoted by the sale, and (3) that the interests of the other parties will not be prejudiced by the sale.[6] (Footnote added). In its lengthy order requiring partition and sale, the circuit court addressed each of the three factors in *Consolidated Gas Supply Corp.* as follows:

(14) That upon the Court's review and consideration of the entire record, even after the [Caudill heirs'] expert witness testified, the Court has determined that it is clearly evident that the subject property's nature, character, and amount are such that it cannot be conveniently, (that is "practically or justly") partitioned, or divided by allotment among its owners. Moreover, it is just and necessary to conclude that such a proposal as has been made by the [Caudill heirs], that of allotting the manor house and the surrounding "bottom land" unto the [Caudill heirs], cannot be affected without undeniably prejudicing [Ark Land's] interests, in violation of the mandatory provisions of Code §37-4-3; and,

(15) That while its uniform topography superficially suggests a division-in-kind, as proposed by Mr. Acord, the access road, the bottom lands and the relatively flat home site is, in fact, integral to establishing the fair market value of the subject property in its entirety, as its highest and best use as mining property, as shown by the uncontroverted testimony of [Ark Land's] experts Mr. Morgan and Mr. Terry; and,

(16) That from a review of the Commissioners' Report, it indicates that sale of the subject property will promote the interests of [Ark Land], "but may prejudice the best interest of the [Caudill heirs]." Obviously, from the legal principles and the reviewing standards set out above, the "best interests" of either party is not the standard upon which the Court must determine these issues. In that respect, it is undisputed that the remaining heirs, that are [the Caudill heirs] herein, do not wish to sell, or have the Court sell, their interests in the subject property, solely due to their sincere sentiment for it as the family's "home place." Other family members, however, did not feel the same way. Given the equally undisputed testimony of [Ark Land's] experts, it is just and reasonable for the Court to conclude that the interests of all the subject property's owners will not be financially prejudiced, but will be financially promoted, by sale of the subject property and distribution among them of the proceeds, according to their respective interests. The subject property's value as coal mining property, its uncontroverted highest and best use, would be substantially impaired by severing the family's "home place" and allotting it to

---

[6] The relevant part of W. Va.Code §37-4-3 reads as follows:

When partition cannot be conveniently made, the entire subject may be allotted to any party or parties who will accept it, and pay therefor to the other party or parties such sum of money as his or their interest therein may entitle him or them to; *or in any case in which partition cannot be conveniently made, if the interests of one or more of those who are entitled to the subject, or its proceeds, will be promoted by a sale of the entire subject, or allotment of part and sale of the residue, and the interest of the other person or persons so entitled will not be prejudiced thereby,* the court . . . may order such sale[.]

(Emphasis added).

them separately. Again, the evidence is not only a preponderance, but unrebutted, that Mr. Acord's proposal would greatly diminish the value of the subject property. Accordingly, the Court does hereby conclude as a matter of law that the subject property should be sold as a whole in its entirety, and that it cannot be partitioned in kind by allotment of part and a sale of the residue.

We are troubled by the circuit court's conclusion that partition by sale was necessary because the economic value of the property would be less if partitioned in kind. We have long held that the economic value of property *may* be a factor to consider in determining whether to partition in kind or to force a sale.

> "Whether the aggregate value of the several parcels into which the whole premises must be divided will, when distributed among, and held in severalty by, the different parties, be materially less than the value of the same property if owned by one person, is a fair test by which to determine whether the interests of the parties will be promoted by a sale."

Syl. pt. 6, *Croston v. Male*, 56 W.Va. 205, 49 S.E. 136. However, our cases *do not* support the conclusion that economic value of property is the exclusive test for determining whether to partition in kind or to partition by sale. In fact, we explicitly stated in *Hale v. Thacker*, 122 W.Va. 648, 650, 12 S.E.2d 524, 526 (1940), "that many considerations, other than monetary, attach to the ownership of land, and courts should be, and always have been, slow to take away from owners of real estate their common-law right to have the same set aside to them in kind." *See also Wilkins v. Wilkins*, 175 W.Va. 787, 791, 338 S.E.2d 388, 392 (1985) (per curiam) ("Prejudice is not measured solely in monetary terms."(citing *Vincent v. Gustke*, 175 W.Va. 521, 336 S.E.2d 33 (1985); *Harris v. Crowder*, 174 W.Va. 83, 322 S.E.2d 854 (1984); and *Murredu v. Murredu*, 160 W.Va. 610, 236 S.E.2d 452 (1977)) (additional citation omitted)).

Other courts have also found that monetary consideration is not the only factor to contemplate when determining whether to partition property in kind or by sale. In the case of *Eli v. Eli*, 557 N.W.2d 405 (S.D.1997), the South Dakota Supreme Court addressed the issue of the impact of monetary considerations in deciding whether to partition property in kind or by sale. In that case over 100 acres of land were jointly owned by three members of the Eli family. The land had been owned by the Eli family for almost 100 years, and was used solely as farm land. Two of the co-owners sought to have the land partitioned and sold. A trial judge found that the land would be worth less if partitioned in kind, therefore the court ordered the land be sold at public auction. The co-owner who sought a partition in kind appealed the trial court's decision. The South Dakota Supreme Court found that the trial court erroneously relied upon the fact that the property would be worth less if partitioned in kind. In reversing the trial court's decision, the *Eli* court reasoned as follows:

> [M]onetary considerations, while admittedly significant, do not rise to the level of excluding all other appropriate considerations. . . . The sale of property "without

[the owner's] consent is an extreme exercise of power warranted only in clear cases." We believe this to be especially so when the land in question has descended from generation to generation. While it is true that the Eli brothers' expert testified that if partitioned, the separate parcels would sell for $50 to $100 less per acre, this fact alone is not dispositive. One's land possesses more than mere economic utility; it "means the full range of the benefit the parties may be expected to derive from their ownership of their respective shares." Such value must be weighed for its effect upon all parties involved, not just those advocating a sale.

557 N.W.2d at 409-410 (internal citations omitted). *See also Harris v. Harris,* 51 N.C.App. 103, 275 S.E.2d 273, 276 (1981) ("[M]any considerations, other than monetary, attach to the ownership of land."); *Schnell v. Schnell,* 346 N.W.2d 713, 721 (N.D.1984) (finding sentimental attachment to land by co-owner was sufficient to prevent forced sale by other co-owner); *Fike v. Sharer,* 280 Or. 577, 571 P.2d 1252, 1254 (1977) ("[S]entimental reasons, especially an owner's desire to preserve a home, may also be considered [in a partition suit].").

Similarly, in *Delfino v. Vealencis,* 181 Conn. 533, 436 A.2d 27 (1980), two plaintiffs owned a 20.5 acre tract of land with the defendant. The defendant used part of the property for her home and a garbage removal business. The plaintiffs filed an action to force a sale of the property so that they could use it to develop residential properties. The trial court concluded that a partition in kind could not be had without great prejudice to the parties, and that the highest and best use of the property was through development as residential property. The trial court therefore ordered that the property be sold at auction. The defendant appealed. The Connecticut Supreme Court reversed for the following reasons:

> The [trial] court's . . . observations relating to the effect of the defendant's business on the probable fair market value of the proposed residential lots . . . are not dispositive of the issue. *It is the interests of all of the tenants in common that the court must consider; and not merely the economic gain of one tenant, or a group of tenants.* The trial court failed to give due consideration to the fact . . . that the [defendant] has made her home on the property; and that she derives her livelihood from the operation of a business on this portion of the property, as her family before her has for many years. A partition by sale would force the defendant to surrender her home and, perhaps, would jeopardize her livelihood. It is under just such circumstances, which include the demonstrated practicability of a physical division of the property, that the wisdom of the law's preference for partition in kind is evident.

Delfino, 436 A.2d at 32-33 (emphasis added). *See also Leake v. Casati,* 234 Va. 646, 363 S.E.2d 924, 927 (1988) ("Even evidence that the property would be less valuable if divided [has been] held 'insufficient to deprive a co-owner of his "sacred right" to property.'" (quoting *Sensabaugh v. Sensabaugh,* 232 Va. 250, 349 S.E.2d 141, 146 (1986))).

PERSONAL VS. FUNGIBLE PROPERTY

The court's focus on emotional ties to property brings to mind Margaret Jane Radin's arguments in her classic article *Property and Personhood*, 34 Stan. L. Rev. 957 (1982). Radin observed that people become personally attached to certain types of property. Building on this observation, Radin divided property into two categories—personal and fungible. Personal property cannot be completely replaced by market value compensation; fungible property in contrast can be replaced by market value compensation.

Radin's classic example of the distinction used a wedding ring. To a jeweler, a wedding ring is fungible—the jeweler would be equally happy with one ring, another similar ring, or the monetary value of the ring. Once wedding rings are exchanged with a spouse, the rings take on personal meaning and cannot be fully replaced with their monetary value. Other examples include personal photographs, heirlooms, and homes. The family homestead at issue in *Ark Land* would qualify as personal in Radin's categories: the Caudill heirs were concerned about their personal connection to the property and would not be satisfied by market value compensation. Radin argued that ownership of personal property should be given more legal protection than ownership of fungible property. *Ark Land* can be seen as an example of this approach, with the court giving special protection to ownership in circumstances where the owner has a personal connection to the property.

In view of the prior decisions of this Court, as well as the decisions from other jurisdictions, we now make clear and hold that, in a partition proceeding in which a party opposes the sale of property, the economic value of the property is not the exclusive test for deciding whether to partition in kind or by sale. Evidence of longstanding ownership, coupled with sentimental or emotional interests in the property, may also be considered in deciding whether the interests of the party opposing the sale will be prejudiced by the property's sale. This latter factor should ordinarily control when it is shown that the property can be partitioned in kind, though it may entail some economic inconvenience to the party seeking a sale.

In the instant case, the Caudill heirs were not concerned with the monetary value of the property. Their exclusive interest was grounded in the longstanding family ownership of the property and their emotional desire to keep their ancestral family home within the family.[7] It is quite clear that this emotional interest would be prejudiced through a sale of the property.

---

[7] The circuit court's order suggests that, because some family members sold their interest in the property, no real interest in maintaining the family home existed. While it may be true that the family members who sold their interest in the property did not have any emotional attachment to the family home, this fact cannot be dispositively attributed to the Caudill heirs. The interest of the Caudill heirs cannot be nullified or tossed aside, simply because other family members do not share the same sentiments for the family home.

The expert for the Caudill heirs testified that the ancestral family home could be partitioned from the property in such a way as to not deprive Ark Land of any coal. The circuit court summarily and erroneously dismissed this uncontradicted fact because of the increased costs that Ark Land would incur as a result of a partition in kind. In view of our holding, the additional economic burden that would be imposed on Ark Land, as a result of partitioning in kind, is not determinative under the facts of this case.

We have held that "[t]he question of what promotes or prejudices a party's interest when a partition through sale is sought must necessarily turn on the particular facts of each case." *Consolidated Gas Supply Corp.,* 161 W.Va. at 788, 247 S.E.2d at 715. The facts in this case reveal that, prior to 2001, Ark Land had no ownership interest in the property. Conversely, for nearly 100 years the Caudill heirs and their ancestors owned the property and used it for residential purposes.[8] In 2001 Ark Land purchased ownership rights in the property from some Caudill family members. When the Caudill heirs refused to sell their ownership rights, Ark Land immediately sought to force a judicial sale of the property. In doing this, Ark Land established that its proposed use of the property, surface coal mining, gave greater value to the property. This showing is self-serving. In most instances, when a commercial entity purchases property because it believes it can make money from a specific use of the property, that property will increase in value based upon the expectations of the commercial entity. This self-created enhancement in the value of property cannot be the determinative factor in forcing a pre-existing co-owner to give up his/her rights in property. To have such a rule would permit commercial entities to always "evict" pre-existing co-owners, because a commercial entity's interest in property will invariably increase its value. *See Butte Creek Island Ranch v. Crim,* 136 Cal.App.3d 360, 368, 186 Cal.Rptr. 252 (1982) ("Plaintiff . . . sought a forced sale of the land in order to acquire defendant's interest which he did not desire to sell. This is nothing short of the private condemnation of private land for private purposes, a result which is abhorrent to the rights of defendant as a freeholder.").

We are very sensitive to the fact that Ark Land will incur greater costs in conducting its business on the property as a result of partitioning in kind. However, Ark Land voluntarily took an economical gamble that it would be able to get all of the Caudill family members to sell their interests in the property. Ark Land's gamble failed. The Caudill heirs refused to sell their interests. The fact that Ark Land miscalculated on its ability to acquire outright all interests in the property cannot form the basis for depriving the Caudill heirs of their emotional interests in maintaining their ancestral family home. The additional cost to Ark Land that will result from a partitioning in kind simply does not impose the type of injurious inconvenience that would justify stripping the Caudill heirs of the emotional interest they have in preserving their ancestral family

---

[8] No one lives permanently at the family home. However, the family home is used on weekends and for special family events by the Caudill heirs.

home. *See* Syl. pt. 4, in part, *Croston v. Male,* 56 W.Va. 205, 49 S.E. 136 ("Inconvenience of partition as one of the circumstances authorizing such sale, . . . is not satisfied by anything short of a real and substantial obstacle of some kind to division in kind, such as would make it injurious to the owners[.]"). . . .

IV. CONCLUSION

In view of the foregoing, we find that the circuit court erred in determining that the property could not be partitioned in kind. We, therefore, reverse the circuit court's order requiring sale of the property. This case is remanded with directions to the circuit court to enter an order requiring the property to be partitioned in kind, consistent with the report and testimony of the Caudill heirs' mining engineer expert, Gary F. Acord.

Reversed and Remanded.

MAYNARD, Chief Justice, concurring, in part, and dissenting, in part. I concur with the new law created by the majority in this case. That is to say, I agree that evidence of longstanding ownership along with sentimental or emotional attachment to property are factors that should be considered and, in some instances, control the decision of whether to partition in kind or sale jointly-owned property which is the subject of a partition proceeding.

I dissent in this case, however, because I do not believe that evidence to support the application of those factors was presented here. In that regard, the record shows that none of the appellants have resided at the subject property for years. At most, the property has been used for weekend retreats. While this may have been the family "homeplace," a majority of the family has already sold their interests in the property to the appellee. Only a minority of the family members, the appellants, have refused to do so. I believe that the sporadic use of the property by the appellants in this case does not outweigh the economic inconvenience that the appellee will suffer as a result of this property being partitioned in kind.

I am also troubled by the majority's decision that this property should be partitioned in kind instead of being sold because I don't believe that such would have been the case were this property going to be put to some use other than coal mining. For instance, I think the majority's decision would have been different if this property was going to be used in the construction of a four-lane highway. Under those circumstances, I believe the majority would have concluded that such economic activity takes precedence over any long-term use or sentimental attachment to the property on the part of the appellants. In my opinion, coal mining is an equally important economic activity. This decision destroys the value of this land as coal mining property because the appellee would incur several million dollars in additional costs to continue its mining operations. As a result of the majority's decision in this case, many innocent coal miners will be out of work.

Accordingly, for the reasons set forth above, I respectfully concur, in part, and dissent, in part, to the decision in this case.

NOTES

1. *Presumptions vs. Actual Outcomes.* As *Ark Land* illustrates, there is a strong legal presumption in favor of partition in kind. Although this presumption is widely recognized in U.S. case law, partition by sale is more common than partition in kind. The presumption in one direction and the common outcome in the other are not inconsistent with each other. Partition by sale is more common because there are many circumstances where partition in kind is impossible or impracticable. Consider, for example, the partition of a ten-acre parcel among 50 tenants in common. Or, the partition of a house on a one-acre parcel among five tenants in common. Or, the partition of a five-acre parcel among two tenants in common, where the local zoning regulations require all residential lots to be a minimum of five acres.

2. *Potential Worries About Partition by Sale.* Partition by sale is typically accomplished by the court-ordered auction of the property, with the proceeds divided among the co-tenants according to their share of the property. There are at least two potential worries presented by partition by sale. First, if one co-tenant has more resources than the others, that co-tenant typically will be able to buy the property at auction. For example, there is little doubt that Ark Land could have outbid the Caudill heirs for the property at auction. Second, courts and commentators often assume that a partition by sale process will lead to the sale of the property for its fair market value. Often, however, the property is sold at auction for a below-market price. Property sold at court-ordered auction typically is not widely marketed or advertized, and it often is harder to get mortgage financing to buy auctioned property than it is to buy property in a typical sale. These and other factors can combine to depress partition by sale auction prices. *See* Thomas W. Mitchell, Stephen Malpezzi & Richard K. Green, *Forced Sale Risk: Class, Race, and the "Double Discount,"* 37 Fla. St. U. L. Rev. 589 (2010).

HEIRS PROPERTY AND THE UNIFORM PARTITION OF HEIRS PROPERTY ACT

As we noted above, property that has been held in one family for generations often ends up being owned by a large number of relatives, each of whom has a relatively small interest. The eight Caudill heirs who objected to the partition by sale in *Ark Land*, for example, together owned 32.5 percent of the property, with the average share for each individual being around 4 percent. It is not unusual for family shares to be even more fractionated, especially when the land has passed by intestacy over several generations. Family property that passes by will, rather than intestacy, can also end up highly fractionated. With a will, however, the testator has to make a conscious choice about whether to divide the property further in the next generation. When property passes through intestacy, the property will typically be divided among members of the following generation or generations. For example, if a person dies intestate with four children, the person's interest in the property typically will be divided in equal shares among the four children. If this happens over several generations, the property will likely end up with highly fractionated ownership.

The term *heirs property* is often used to describe property that has been held in a family for multiple generations. The term is also often used to refer more specifically to property that has passed in African-American communities through multiple generations of intestacy. A number of scholars called attention to the problem of land loss in African-American communities that was the result of partition by sale scenarios similar to that in *Ark Land*, where an outsider bought some family members' shares and then used the partition by sale process to force the sale of the remainder of the property. *See, e.g.*, Phyliss Craig-Taylor, *Through a Colored Looking Glass: A View of Judicial Partition, Family Land Loss, and Rule Setting*, 78 Wash. U. L.Q. 737 (2000); Thomas W. Mitchell, *From Reconstruction to Deconstruction: Undermining Black Landownership, Political Independence, and Community Through Partition Sales of Tenancies in Common*, 95 N.W. U. L. Rev. 505 (2001); Faith Rivers, *Inequity in Equity: The Tragedy of Tenancy in Common for Heirs' Property Owners Facing Partition in Equity*, 17 Temp. Pol. & Civ. Rts. L. Rev. 1 (2007).

In response to the heirs property problem, the National Conference of Commissioners on Uniform State Laws approved the Uniform Partition of Heirs Property Act (UPHPA) in 2010. As of this writing, the UPHPA has been enacted in four states (Alabama, Georgia, Montana, and Nevada), and has been introduced in several others. The UPHPA takes a number of steps to make the partition process more fair and less subject to abuse. Among the law's more notable provisions, Section 6 of the UPHPA sets up an appraisal process to protect co-tenants from being bought out at a below-market price. Section 7 then sets up a co-tenant buyout process. If a co-tenant petitions for partition by sale, the other co-tenants have the option of buying that co-tenant out at a fair price based on the appraisal required by Section 6:

Uniform Partition of Heirs Property Act

Section 7. Cotenant Buyout

(a) If any cotenant requested partition by sale, after the determination of value under section 6 of this act, the court shall send notice to the parties that any cotenant except a cotenant that requested partition by sale may buy all the interests of the cotenants that requested partition by sale.

(b) Not later than forty-five days after the date on which the notice is sent under subsection (a) of this section, any cotenant except a cotenant that requested partition by sale may give notice to the court that it elects to buy all the interests of the cotenants that requested partition by sale.

(c) The purchase price for each of the interests of a cotenant that requested partition by sale is the value of the entire parcel determined under section 6 of this act, multiplied by the cotenant's fractional ownership of the entire parcel. . . .

PROBLEM

The Schulenburg family has owned an undeveloped 12-acre parcel of land, called the Schulenburg Farm, for years. The parcel currently is owned by siblings Zach, John, and Cathy Schulenburg as tenants in common. The three have been using the property for recreation since they were children. The zoning in the area where Schulenburg

Farm is located limits development of the Farm to residential use and requires a five-acre minimum lot size. That is, the only way to develop the property is by building houses, and each house must be placed on a lot that is at least five acres. John is starting a business and so wants to sell his share of the Farm. After failing to agree on a price to sell his share to his siblings, John has petitioned to partition the property and has requested partition by sale. Zach and Cathy have opposed this request and instead have asked the court to partition the property in kind. How should the court rule? Answer the question first under the common law of partition, then think about how the alternative approach suggested by the Uniform Partition of Heirs Property Act might help solve the problem. An explanatory answer can be found on page 1040.

2. RIGHTS AND OBLIGATIONS OF CO-TENANTS

In our next two cases, we will consider the financial obligations of co-tenants to each other. We want to highlight two types of issues at the outset. One type of issue involves co-tenant's liability to one another for the basic costs of ownership of the property. For example, if one co-tenant pays for necessary repairs or pays a tax bill, is she entitled to contribution from the other co-tenants for their share of the costs? Say that you and I are co-tenants in a beach house, with each of us having a one-half share. You spend $10,000 to pay the entire property tax bill. Am I liable to you for my proportional share of the taxes? The other type of issue involves the liability of a co-tenant who is in sole possession of the property for rent to the other co-tenants. Again, let's say that you and I are co-tenants in a beach house. You live in the beach house year round. I live in London and never go to the beach house. Are you liable to me for my proportional share of the rental value of the beach house?

We should note at the outset that co-tenants are generally free to resolve these issues by agreement. The cases and the notes that follow discuss the default rules that apply when, as is typically the case, there is no agreement between the parties.

> **WASTE**
>
> We discussed the law of waste at the end of the previous chapter. The rules of waste apply to concurrent interests, and a co-tenant who commits waste will be liable to the other co-tenants.

ESTEVES V. ESTEVES

Superior Court of New Jersey, Appellate Division, 2001
775 A.2d 163

LESEMANN, J.A.D. This appeal deals with the proper division of the proceeds from the sale of a one-family house held by a tenancy in common, with plaintiffs, the parents of defendant owning one-half of the house and defendant owning the other half.

The trial court held that plaintiffs, who had occupied the house by themselves for approximately eighteen years before it was sold, and had paid all of the expenses relating to the house during that period, were entitled to reimbursement from defendant for one-half of the sums they had paid, without any offset for the value of their occupancy. The net effect of that ruling amounted to a determination that plaintiffs were permitted to occupy the premises "rent free" for approximately eighteen years, while they paid one-half of the costs attributable to the house and defendant paid the other half. The trial court found that such a result was compelled by applicable law. We disagree, and conclude that when plaintiffs sought reimbursement from defendant for one-half of the costs of occupying and maintaining the premises, plaintiffs were required to allow defendant credit for the reasonable value of their occupancy of the house. Accordingly we reverse.

The case involves an unhappy family schism, but the facts, as found by the trial court and not disputed on appeal, are uncomplicated. In December 1980, plaintiffs Manuel and Flora Esteves, together with their son Joao Esteves, bought a house. They took title as tenants in common, with Manuel and Flora owning a one-half interest and Joao owning the other one-half. The purchase price was $34,500. Manuel and Flora paid $10,000 in cash as did Joao, and the parties took a mortgage loan for the remaining $14,500. They then moved into the house, and Joao undertook a considerable amount of work involving repairs and improvements while he lived there with his parents for somewhere between three months and eighteen months after closing. Joao then moved out and for approximately the next eighteen years, until the house was sold on February 26, 1998, Manuel and Flora lived there by themselves. At no time did they rent out any portion of the house.

Sale of the house produced net proceeds of $114,453.18. With the parties unable to agree on distribution of the proceeds, they agreed to each take $10,000 and deposit the remaining $94,453.18 in escrow. They then proceeded to trial, after which the trial court made the following findings and conclusions.

The court found that Manuel and Flora had paid out $17,336 in mortgage payments, including principal and interest; $14,353 for capital expenses; $21,599 for real estate taxes; $3,971 for sewer charges; and $4,633 for homeowners insurance. Those amounts totaled $61,892, and the court found that Joao was obligated to reimburse his parents for one-half that amount. However, the court also found that Joao had supplied labor with a value of $2,000 more than any labor expended by Manuel and Flora, and thus Joao was entitled to a credit for that amount. On the critical issue of credit for the value of plaintiffs' occupancy of the house, the court said this:

> I conclude there being no ouster of the defendant by the plaintiffs that there is
> no entitlement to the equivalent rent or rental value of the premises where the
> plaintiffs lived. The defendant could have continued to live there if he wanted to;
> he chose not to. And the law is clear that that being the case, he's not—there being

no ouster, he's not entitled to anything for the rental value or what the rental could have been to the plaintiffs.

Over the years, there have been varying statements by our courts as to the rights and obligations of tenants in common respecting payment for maintenance of the parties' property and their rights and obligations respecting occupancy thereof. *See, e.g., Baker v. Drabik*, 224 N.J.Super. 603, 541 A.2d 229 (App.Div.1988); *Asante v. Abban,* 237 N.J.Super. 495, 568 A.2d 146 (Law Div.1989); and the most frequently cited decision, *Mastbaum v. Mastbaum,* 126 N.J. Eq. 366, 9 A.2d 51 (Ch.1939). While those decisions may not always have been consistent, in *Baird v. Moore,* 50 N.J.Super. 156, 141 A.2d 324 (App.Div.1958), this court, in a comprehensive, scholarly opinion by Judge Conford set out what we conceive to be the most appropriate, fair and practical rules to resolve such disputes. Those principles can be summarized as follows.

First, as a general proposition, on a sale of commonly owned property, an owner who has paid less than his pro-rata share of operating and maintenance expenses of the property, must account to co-owner who has contributed more than his pro-rata share, and that is true even if the former had been out of possession and the latter in possession of the property.

Second, the fact that one tenant in common occupies the property and the other does not, imposes no obligation on the former to make any contribution to the latter. All tenants in common have a right to occupy all of the property and if one chooses not to do so, that does not give him the right to impose an "occupancy" charge on the other.

Third, notwithstanding those general rules, when on a final accounting following sale, the tenant who had been in sole possession of the property demands contribution toward operating and maintenance expenses from his co-owner, fairness and equity dictate that the one seeking that contribution allow a corresponding credit for the value of his sole occupancy of the premises. To reject such a credit and nonetheless require a contribution to operating and maintenance expenses from someone who (like the defendant here) had enjoyed none of the benefits of occupancy would be patently unfair.

Finally, this court held in *Baird,* that the party seeking the credit for the other's occupancy of the property has the burden of demonstrating the "actual rental value" of the property enjoyed by the occupying co-tenant (*id.* at 172, 141 A.2d 324).[2]

We believe the principles of *Baird* are sound and should be applied here. They support the trial court's conclusions as to defendant's obligation to contribute one-half

---

[2] The court in *Baird* also said that in any final accounting between the co-tenants, equitable considerations which would weigh against a simple mathematical balancing should be considered and could have an effect. Thus, *e.g.,* in *Baird,* where the co-tenants were brother and sister and the sister had expended extraordinary efforts to maintain the property for their mother and care for their mother in the property, those efforts were to be recognized in considering what if any occupancy credit should be imposed against the daughter. We *see* no such extraordinary equitable considerations here, but in the hearing which must follow the remand of this case, either party may submit evidence thereof for consideration by the trial court.

of the $61,892 expended by his parents respecting the house they all owned. However, against that obligation, the court should offset a credit for the reasonable value of the occupancy enjoyed by the parents over the approximately eighteen years while they, and not their son, occupied the property. The obligation to present evidence of that value, which would normally be represented by rental value of the property, rests on the defendant. Although no such proof was presented at the prior trial, the uncertainty of the law in this area satisfies us that it would be unreasonable to deprive the defendant of the opportunity to do so now. Accordingly, the matter is reversed and remanded to the trial court for further proceedings at which the defendant shall have an opportunity to present evidence related to the value of the plaintiffs' sole occupancy of the property. We do not retain jurisdiction.

SPILLER V. MACKERETH

Supreme Court of Alabama, 1976
334 So. 2d 859

JONES, Justice. This is an appeal from a suit based upon a complaint by John Robert Spiller seeking sale for division among tenants in common and a counterclaim by Hettie Mackereth and others seeking an accounting for Spiller's alleged "ouster" of his cotenants. By agreement of the parties, the trial Court entered a decree on the complaint ordering the sale of the property. A trial was then held . . . on the counterclaim.

At the conclusion of the trial, the Judge entered a finding that Spiller had ousted Mackereth . . . Based on these findings, the trial Judge awarded Mackereth $2,100 rental . . . Spiller appeals . . . We reverse. . . .

The pertinent facts are undisputed. In February, 1973, Spiller purchased an undivided one-half interest in a lot in downtown Tuscaloosa. Spiller's cotenants were Mackereth and the other appellees. At the time Spiller bought his interest, the lot was being rented by an automobile supply business called Auto-Rite. In May, 1973, Spiller offered to purchase Mackereth's interest in the property. Mackereth refused and made a counteroffer to purchase Spiller's interest which Spiller refused. Spiller then filed the complaint seeking sale for division on July 11, 1973.

In October, 1973, Auto-Rite vacated the building which it had been renting for $350 per month and Spiller begun to use the entire building as a warehouse. On November 15, 1973, Mackereth's attorney sent a letter to Spiller demanding that he either vacate one-half of the building or pay rent. Spiller did not respond to the letter, vacate the premises, or pay rent; therefore, Mackereth brought this counterclaim to collect the rental she claimed Spiller owed her.

Since there is no real dispute concerning the essential facts in this case, we will limit our review to the trial Judge's application of the law to the facts. On the question of

Spiller's liability for rent, we start with the general rule that in absence of an agreement to pay rent or an ouster of a cotenant, a cotenant in possession is not liable to his cotenants for the value of his use and occupation of the property. *Fundaburk v. Cody*, 261 Ala. 25, 72 So.2d 710, 48 A.L.R.2d 1295 (1954); *Turner v. Johnson*, 246 Ala. 114, 19 So.2d 397 (1944). Since there was no agreement to pay rent, there must be evidence which establishes an ouster before Spiller is required to pay rent to Mackereth. The difficulty in this determination lies in the definition of the word "ouster." Ouster is a conclusory word which is used loosely in cotenancy cases to describe two distinct fact situations. The two fact situations are (1) the beginning of the running of the statute of limitations for adverse possession and (2) the liability of an occupying cotenant for rent to other cotenants. Although the cases do not acknowledge a distinction between the two uses of "ouster," it is clear that the two fact situations require different elements of proof to support a conclusion of ouster.

The Alabama cases involving adverse possession require a finding that the possessing cotenant asserted complete ownership to the land to support a conclusion of ouster. The finding of assertion of ownership may be established in several ways. Some cases find an assertion of complete ownership from a composite of activities such as renting part of the land without accounting, hunting the land, cutting timber, assessing and paying taxes and generally treating the land as if it were owned in fee for the statutory period. *See Howard v. Harrell*, 275 Ala. 454, 156 So.2d 140 (1963). Other cases find the assertion of complete ownership from more overt activities such as a sale of the property under a deed purporting to convey the entire fee. *Elsheimer v. Parker Bank & Trust Co.*, 237 Ala. 24, 185 So. 385 (1938). But whatever factual elements are present, the essence of the finding of an ouster in the adverse possession cases is a claim of absolute ownership and a denial of the cotenancy relationship by the occupying cotenant.

In the Alabama cases which adjudicate the occupying cotenant's liability for rent, a claim of absolute ownership has not been an essential element. The normal fact situation which will render an occupying cotenant liable to out of possession cotenants is one in which the occupying cotenant refuses a demand of the other cotenants to be allowed into use and enjoyment of the land, regardless of a claim of absolute ownership. *Judd v. Dowdell*, 244 Ala. 230, 12 So.2d 858 (1943); *Newbold v. Smart*, 67 Ala. 326 (1880).

The instant case involves a cotenant's liability for rent. Indeed, the adverse possession rule is precluded in this case by Spiller's acknowledgment of the cotenancy relationship as evidenced by filing the bill for partition. We can affirm the trial Court if the record reveals some evidence that Mackereth actually sought to occupy the building but was prevented from moving in by Spiller. To prove ouster, Mackereth's attorney relies upon the letter of November 15, 1973, as a sufficient demand and refusal to establish Spiller's liability for rent. This letter, however, did not demand equal use and enjoyment of the premises; rather, it demanded only that Spiller either vacate half of the building or pay rent. The question of whether a demand to vacate or pay rent is sufficient to establish an occupying cotenant's liability for rent has not been addressed in Alabama; however, it has been addressed by courts in other jurisdictions. In jurisdictions which adhere to the majority and Alabama rule of nonliability for mere occupancy, several cases have held that the occupying cotenant is not liable for rent notwithstanding a demand to vacate or pay rent. *Grieder v. Marsh*, 247 S.W.2d 590 (Tex. Civ.App.1952); *Brown v. Havens*, 17 N.J.Super. 235, 85 A.2d 812 (1952).

There is a minority view which establishes liability for rents on a continued occupancy after a demand to vacate or pay rent. *Re Holt's Estate*, 14 Misc.2d 971, 177 N.Y.S.2d 192 (1958). We believe that the majority view on this question is consistent with Alabama's approach to the law of occupancy by cotenants. As one of the early Alabama cases on the subject explains:

> ". . . Each [co-tenant] has an equal right to occupy; and unless the one in actual possession denies to the other the right to enter, or agrees to pay rent, nothing can be claimed for such occupation." *Newbold v. Smart, supra.*

Thus, before an occupying cotenant can be liable for rent in Alabama, he must have denied his cotenants the right to enter. It is axiomatic that there can be no denial of the right to enter unless there is a demand or an attempt to enter. Simply requesting the occupying cotenant to vacate is not sufficient because the occupying cotenant holds title to the whole and may rightfully occupy the whole unless the other cotenants assert their possessory rights.

Besides the November 15 letter, Mackereth's only attempt to prove ouster is a showing that Spiller put locks on the building. However, there is no evidence that Spiller was attempting to do anything other than protect the merchandise he had stored in the building. Spiller testified that when Auto-Rite moved out they removed the locks from the building. Since Spiller began to store his merchandise in the building thereafter, he had to acquire new locks to secure it. There is no evidence that either Mackereth or any of the other cotenants ever requested keys to the locks or were ever prevented from entering the building because of the locks. There is no evidence that Spiller intended to exclude his cotenants by use of the locks. Again, we emphasize that as long as Spiller did not deny access to his cotenants, any activity of possession and occupancy of the building was consistent with his rights of ownership. Thus, the fact that Spiller placed locks on the building, without evidence that he intended to exclude the other cotenants, is insufficient to establish his liability to pay rent.

After reviewing all of the testimony and evidence presented at trial, we are unable to find any evidence which supports a legal conclusion of ouster. We are, therefore, compelled to reverse the trial Court's judgment awarding Mackereth $2,100 rental. . . .

NOTES

1. *Ouster.* As the court explained in *Spiller,* ouster is a conclusion. Most courts will find ouster only if (a) the co-tenant out of possession has demanded entry or shared possession of the co-owned property, and (b) the co-tenant in possession has refused. You should be sure that you understand why Spiller did not oust Mackereth even though Spiller put locks on the building. Ouster is important because the rules on the liability of co-tenants to each other for rent and contribution for expenses turn in part on whether there has been an ouster. Ouster is also important because if one co-tenant ousts the other, it starts the adverse possession clock running against the ousted tenant. If the ousted co-tenant does not bring an action to assert her interest within the statutory period, the ousting co-tenant may obtain her interest by adverse possession.

2. *Co-Tenant in Possession Liability for Rental Value. Esteves* and *Spiller* explain the basic rules on the liability of co-tenants to each other for the rental value of the property. Absent ouster, a co-tenant in possession is not liable to other co-tenants for rent. If there has been an ouster, the co-tenant in possession is liable to the others for their shares of the fair rental value of the property. Let's return to our example where you and I own a beach house as tenants in common. You live there full time, and I live in London. Absent ouster, you are not liable to me for rent. (As explained in *Esteves,* though, I might be able to make a claim for the rental value to set off against a claim by you for maintenance costs. It would be unfair to charge me for my share of the maintenance if you have sole possession and are not paying me rent.) If you did oust me, you would be liable to me for my share of the rental value of the property.

3. *Co-Tenant in Possession Liability for Rents and Profits Collected from Third Parties.* Say that in our beach house example you rent the house to a third party for the summer. In considering whether you are liable to me for rent, we need to distinguish between two scenarios. In the first, you only purport to lease your share, and the third party would need to share the house with me if I decided to show up. In this scenario, you would not be liable to me for rent, because I still retain all my rights to share in the possession and use of the house. In the second, you purport to lease the entire property, and the third party would not expect to share the property with me. In this scenario, you would need to account to me for the rent that you collected. If you rented the beach house to a third person for the summer with the understanding that they would have sole possession, and collected $8,000, you would have to account to me (i.e., pay me) $4,000, representing my 50 percent share of the rents that you collected. To add one more layer of complication, if you had ousted me, you would have to account to me for my share of the fair rental value of the property, rather than the amount you actually collected. Let's say that you collected $8,000 in rent from a third party, but that the fair rental value was actually $20,000. Absent ouster, you would need to pay me my share of the $8,000 actually collected, or $4,000. If you had ousted me, however, you would likely

need to pay me $10,000, representing my 50 percent share of the fair rental value of $20,000. This rule protects the ousted co-tenant from the possibility that the co-tenant in possession might collude with a third party to rent the property for less than it is worth. The same basic rules typically apply to other payments received by one co-tenant, such as payments for the sale of minerals, timber, and other natural resources. *See generally* W.W. Allen, *Accountability of Cotenants for Rents and Profits or Use and Occupation*, 51 A.L.R.2d 388.

4. *Co-Tenant Right to Contribution for Costs and Improvements.* One co-tenant who bears more than her share of the costs of necessary repairs to the property generally has the right to receive contribution from the other co-tenants. The same rule applies to taxes and mortgage payments—if one co-tenant pays more than her share, she is entitled to contribution from the other co-tenants. The rule is different for valuable, but non-necessary improvements. If one co-tenant pays for a voluntary improvement to the property, that co-tenant cannot make an independent claim for contribution from her co-tenants. If the property is later sold or partitioned, however, the co-tenant can obtain some credit for the improvement. *Esteves* illustrates many of these rules in action.

5. *Rental Value as Set-Off Against Charges for Maintenance.* In note 2, we discussed the rule that co-tenants out of possession generally are not entitled to rent from a co-tenant in possession absent ouster. *Esteves* illustrates an exception to this rule. If on the sale of the co-owned property the co-tenant in possession seeks an allowance for costs she incurred in maintaining the property (note 4), then the tenant out of possession can claim rental value from the tenant in possession as a set-off against these costs. The idea here is that the co-tenant in possession had the benefit of occupying the co-owned property. It would be unfair for the co-tenant in possession to get both this benefit and to charge the other co-tenants for a share of the costs of maintenance. With this set-off, the co-tenant in possession should not be liable for the entire fair rental value. Rather, the set-off amount should be the based on the co-tenants' proportional shares of the rental value. After all, the co-tenant in possession did have the right to possess the property to begin with. For example, if the co-tenant in possession had a one-third interest, and the co-tenants out of possession had the remaining two-thirds interest, the set-off should be limited to two-thirds of the fair rental value.

6. *Default Rules vs. Agreement.* As we noted at the beginning of this section, the rules that we are discussing here are all legal default rules. The co-tenants generally can agree on their own arrangements on any of these issues. A grantor creating a co-tenancy can also set rules governing these issues in the conveyance.

7. *Co-Tenants Generally Are Not Fiduciaries.* Recall that we discussed fiduciary duties in the previous chapter when we introduced the trust. Generally speaking, co-tenants do not owe fiduciary duties to each other. Some courts have made exceptions to this general rule and have held co-tenants to be fiduciaries if the co-tenants are siblings or other closely related members of the same family.

PROBLEM

Angela and Maya Wong are sisters. They own a warehouse as tenants in common, with each owning a one-half share. For years, the sisters were partners in a business that used the warehouse. Two years ago, they sold the business but kept ownership of the warehouse. Angela continued to occupy the warehouse. For the past two years, Angela alone made the mortgage payments and paid the cost of upkeep of the warehouse. These costs together amounted to $15,000 per year. For the first year, Angela used the warehouse for a new business that she started. For the second year, Angela vacated the warehouse and rented it to her friend Sidney Sloan for $500 per month. Sidney's understanding was that she was renting the entire warehouse and did not have to share it with Maya. The fair rental value of the warehouse during this time period was $1,000 per month. At the end of the second year, Angela and Maya sold the warehouse. They got in a dispute over the allocation of costs and rents between them, and Maya has now brought an action for an accounting. How should costs and rents be allocated between the parties? How would your answer change if Angela had ousted Maya from the warehouse? An explanatory answer can be found on page 1041.

B. THE JOINT TENANCY

Our second type of concurrent interest is the joint tenancy. Unlike the tenancy in common, the joint tenancy has a *right of survivorship*. This means that if A and B own Blackacre as joint tenants and A dies, A's share disappears, leaving B the sole owner of Blackacre. Lawyers often speak of A's share passing or transferring to B upon A's death. This way of speaking will rarely lead to practical problems. We think, however, that it is easier to understand the legal issues that come up with joint tenancies if you use the correct terminology. When one joint tenant dies, that joint tenant's interest in the property disappears into thin air. The proportional share of the other joint tenant (or joint tenants) increases, but there is no actual transfer of an interest from one party to another.

Let's look at two examples to see the difference between a tenancy in common and a joint tenancy when one co-owner dies:

> Joint tenancies are often used as a way to make a transfer at death that avoids probate. Joint tenancies are also often used as a substitute for a will by lay people. While joint tenancies may have their place in estate planning, lawyers should use them as a compliment to, rather than a substitute for, a will.

A and B are co-tenants:

A ———TIC——— B

A dies, leaving all of her property in her will to her spouse C. After A's death, B and C are tenants in common:

EXAMPLE 11:

A and B are joint tenants:

A ———JT——— B

A dies, leaving all of her property in her will to her spouse C. After A's death, B alone owns Blackacre:

B

The crucial thing to understand about the last example is that C gets *nothing*. The heirs and devisees do not receive anything when a joint tenant dies. A's interest disappeared, and B owns Blackacre.

The existence of the right of survivorship is the only practical difference between a tenancy in common and a joint tenancy. That's it. Joint tenancies are treated just like tenancies in common for the issues that we examined in the prior section. Joint tenancies can be partitioned like a tenancy in common, and the rights and obligations of joint tenants are the same as those of co-tenants.

Joint tenancies present two sets of issues. The first involves their creation. There are certain requirements for the creation of a joint tenancy. If a grantor intends to create a joint tenancy and fails to meet the requirements of creation, then a tenancy in common will result. The second involves the *severance* of the joint tenancy relationship. As we will see, a joint tenant can sever, or end, the joint tenancy relationship, converting it to a tenancy in common and ending the right of survivorship.

1. CREATION OF JOINT TENANCIES

RULES OF CONSTRUCTION

Joint tenancies require clear language of conveyance for creation. There is a rule of construction in favor of tenancies in common. As a result, ambiguous language will be read to create a tenancy in common. Unfortunately, the language needed to create a joint tenancy varies from jurisdiction to jurisdiction. Here are some examples of conveyances, some of which are more likely to create joint tenancies than the others:

EXAMPLE 12: O conveys "to A and B as joint tenants." This conveyance will create a joint tenancy in most jurisdictions. A relatively small number of jurisdictions require more specificity. In these jurisdictions, one of the conveyances in the next two examples is likely to work.

EXAMPLE 13: O conveys "to A and B as joint tenants with right of survivorship." This conveyance will create a joint tenancy in most jurisdictions. Some states expressly require this language to create a joint tenancy. In some jurisdictions, the requirement of clear language of survivorship is the result of statutes that abolish the joint tenancy unless the grant creates an express right of survivorship.[1] On the other hand, in a few jurisdictions, this conveyance would be interpreted as creating a joint life estate in A and B, with a contingent remainder in the survivor.[2]

EXAMPLE 14: O conveys "to A and B as joint tenants and not as tenants in common." The intent of the grantor to create a joint tenancy is clear in this conveyance. It should create a joint tenancy in all jurisdictions other than those that require the conveyance in the previous example.

EXAMPLE 15: O conveys "to A and B jointly." This conveyance will be interpreted as creating a joint tenancy in many jurisdictions, but using it is asking for trouble. A court could easily interpret this conveyance as reflecting an intent to create a concurrent interest, but not an intent to create a right of survivorship.

The practical lesson here is that you should be completely clear on the required language in your jurisdiction before you draft a conveyance intended to create a joint tenancy. For further discussion of this issue, see Stoebuck & Whitman, *The Law of Property* §5.3 (3d ed. 2000).

Joint tenancies also require certain "unities" for the creation of a joint tenancy. The common law required four. Modern courts tend to be more lenient. The original four common-law unities are as follows:

> *Time*: The joint tenants must acquire their interests at the same time.

EXAMPLE 16: A and B receive their interests in the property at the same time on the same day. The unity of time is met.

> The modern rule of construction in favor of tenancies in common is the opposite of the old common-law rule, which preferred joint tenancies to avoid the division of land that can result from tenancies in common.

---

[1] *See Hoover v. Smith*, 444 S.E.2d 546 (Va. 1994); *Zomisky v. Zamiska*, 449 A.2d 722 (Pa. 1972).

[2] *See Albro v. Allen*, 454 N.W.2d 85 (Mich. 1990); *Sanderson v. Saxon*, 834 S.W.2d 676 (Ky. 1992).

EXAMPLE 17: A receives her interest on Monday, while B receives his interest on Tuesday. The unity of time is not met.

Title: The joint tenants must acquire title from the same instrument.

EXAMPLE 18: A and B receive their interest in the same deed (or will). The unity of title is met.

EXAMPLE 19: A receives her interest in one deed, while B receives her interest in a different deed. The unity of title is not met.

Interest: The joint tenants must have equal shares in the property.

EXAMPLE 20: A and B each receive one-half shares of the property. The unity of interest is met.

EXAMPLE 21: A receives a two-thirds share of the property, while B receives a one-third share of the property. The unity of interest is not met.

Possession: The joint tenants must have equal rights of possession and use.

EXAMPLE 22: The conveyance imposes no restrictions on the possession or use of the property by either A or B. The unity of possession is met.

EXAMPLE 23: The conveyance does not restrict A's use or possession, but allows B to use the property only six months out of the year. The unity of possession is not met.

Here is a common scenario that creates unities problems:

> A owns Blackacre. A wants to create a joint tenancy in Blackacre between herself and her daughter, B.
>
> A grants Blackacre "to A and B as joint tenants with right of survivorship."

A may have created a tenancy in common between A and B, rather than a joint tenancy, because the unities of time and title have not been met. A already had her interest in Blackacre before the conveyance. Therefore A and B did not receive their interest in Blackacre at the same time from the same instrument. In many jurisdictions, the conveyance would not have created a joint tenancy. In those jurisdictions, how does A create a joint tenancy between herself and B?

The answer is to use a *straw person*. A straw person is a person—for example, a paralegal in A's lawyer's office—who holds title temporarily as a convenience to another party. Here is how a straw person can be used to solve our conveyance problem:

> A owns Blackacre. A wants to create a joint tenancy in Blackacre between herself and her daughter, B.
>
> A conveys Blackacre to Straw Person.

Straw Person conveys Blackacre "to A and B as joint tenants with right of survivorship."

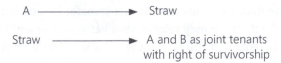

Now the conveyance meets the unities of time and title, because A and B both receive their interests in Blackacre at the same time from the same instrument. If it strikes you that this process is an artifice, you are correct. It would make more sense to allow A to create a joint tenancy with B without the use of a straw person, and some jurisdictions allow A to create a joint tenancy simply by conveying to herself and B. This approach makes sense, but many jurisdictions still require the use of a straw person to create a joint tenancy in these circumstances.

Many jurisdictions still follow the traditional common-law approach that a conveyance that does not meet the four unities creates a tenancy in common. Other jurisdictions have relaxed the unities requirements by statute or by judicial decision. The jurisdictions that allow the creation of a joint tenancy in our last scenario (A granting "to A and B as joint tenants with right of survivorship") without the use of a straw person, for example, have relaxed the requirement that the conveyance meet the unities of time and title. Jurisdictions that relax some or all of the unities requirements tend to focus their analysis on the grantor's intent and tend to find a joint tenancy if the grantor clearly intended to create a joint tenancy.

2. SEVERANCE OF JOINT TENANCIES

If a joint tenancy is severed, the joint tenancy relationship is terminated. Joint tenancies are easy to sever. Any joint tenant can unilaterally sever the joint tenancy by conveying her interest to a third party. Here is an example:

EXAMPLE 24:

A and B own Blackacre as joint tenants:

$$A \underline{\quad JT \quad} B$$

B conveys her interest to C. This conveyance severs the joint tenancy and creates a tenancy in common between A and C:

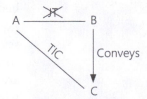

The conveyance from B to C severs the joint tenancy because it destroys the unities of time and title. A and C did not receive their interests in Blackacre at the same time or from the same instrument.

If there are more than two joint tenants, the transfer by one joint tenant of her interest will sever the joint tenancy relationship between her and the other joint tenants, but the other joint tenants will still be joint tenants with each other. For example:

EXAMPLE 25:

A, B, and C own Blackacre as joint tenants:

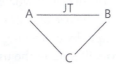

C conveys her interest to D. This conveyance severs the joint tenancy for C's interest. A and B are tenants in common with D, but remain joint tenants with each other:

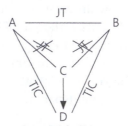

If A later dies, B and D would be tenants in common, with B owning a two-thirds share and D owning a one-third share:

B ——— TIC ——— D

2/3   1/3

The severance of a joint tenancy is a big deal because it destroys the right of survivorship. Disputes about the severance of a joint tenancy tend to arise after one joint tenant dies, and the surviving joint tenant is arguing about ownership with the deceased joint tenant's heirs or devisees. As we just explained, a joint tenancy is clearly severed when one joint tenant conveys title to a third party. There are a few circumstances, however, where severance of a joint tenancy can be ambiguous.

> Interests in tenancies in common are freely transferrable during life and devisable at death. Interests in joint tenancies are freely transferrable during life. Of course, interests in joint tenancies are not devisable at death, because of the right of survivorship.

The first circumstance where severance can be ambiguous involves a unilateral conveyance between a joint tenant and herself. Here is an example:

EXAMPLE 26:

A and B own Blackacre as joint tenants:

$$A \underline{\quad JT \quad} B$$

B then conveys her interest "to B." In other words, she conveys her interest to herself:

The issue is whether this conveyance severs the joint tenancy. Under the traditional common-law approach, this conveyance would not sever the joint tenancy. This is because the traditional common law would view a conveyance from one person to herself as not being an actual conveyance. If you think about it, you can see why a conveyance from B "to B" is something of a nullity. The traditional common-law approach is still the majority rule in the United States. Under the modern/minority rule, the unilateral conveyance from B to herself would sever the joint tenancy. The modern/minority approach is informed by the fact that B could unilaterally sever the joint tenancy even in a traditional/majority jurisdiction by using a straw person:

EXAMPLE 27:

A and B own Blackacre as joint tenants:

$$A \underline{\quad JT \quad} B$$

B then conveys her interest to Straw Person. Straw Person then conveys the interest back "to B":

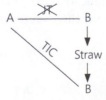

This approach will sever a joint tenancy in all jurisdictions. The modern/minority approach recognizes the fact that a transfer of an interest by a person to herself has its oddities, but takes the position that it would be silly to force a person to go through the trouble of using a straw person to sever a joint tenancy. *Riddle v. Harmon*, 162 Cal. Rptr. 530 (1980) is a case that applied the modern/minority approach. Francis and Jack Riddle, a married couple, owned property as joint tenants. Francis and Jack were estranged, and Francis did not want Jack to get her share of the property through the right of survivorship. Shortly before her death Francis conveyed her interest to herself in an attempt to sever the joint tenancy. The court held that her unilateral conveyance to herself severed the joint tenancy, and the opinion includes a well-reasoned defense of the modern/minority approach.

The second circumstance in which a severance can be ambiguous is if one joint tenant conveys something less than a fee simple interest to a third party. One common scenario that can raise this ambiguity involves on joint tenant leasing her share to a third person. Another common scenario involves one joint tenant mortgaging her share to a third person. We will cover mortgages in depth later. For now, you need to know that a mortgage is a security interest in property that a borrower gives a lender to secure an obligation. The mortgage is the property interest that allows the lender to foreclose if the borrower defaults on the obligation. The key point for our purposes is that if one joint tenant mortgages her share, she grants a property interest to the lender.

There are majority and minority rules for both the lease scenario and the mortgage scenario. A majority of jurisdictions hold that the conveyance of a lease by one joint tenant does not sever the joint tenancy. The split on mortgages is more even. We will take a closer look at the different approaches to the mortgage issue in our next case. Before we get there, let's take a look at an example that illustrates the consequences of severance in the mortgage context. The example would work just as well in the lease context.

EXAMPLE 28:

A and B own Blackacre as joint tenants:

$$A \underline{\quad JT \quad} B$$

B then grants a mortgage on her interest to Lender. On the left we have an illustration of the relationships between the parties if the mortgage severs the joint tenancy. On the right we have an illustration of the relationships if the mortgage does not sever the joint tenancy.

Mortgage Severs: Mortgage Does Not Sever:

Now B has died, leaving all of her property to C. On the left, the mortgage survives because the joint tenancy has been severed, ending the right of survivorship. C owns what had been B's share, as a tenant in common with A. C's share is still encumbered by the mortgage. On the right, however, B's interest has vanished into thin air on B's death. The mortgage therefore also disappears.

```
           TIC
A ─────────────── C                          A
                  │
                  │ Mortgage
                  │
                Lender
```

As this example shows, it is in Lender's interest for the mortgage to sever the joint tenancy if the mortgaging joint tenant (B in our example) dies. This is one context in which it is useful to have a good conceptual understanding of what happens to a joint tenant's interest at death. It disappears. The mortgage (or lease) on that interest therefore also disappears.

Let's look at another example, identical to the last one up to the stage where B grants the mortgage to Lender. In this example, A, rather than B, will die.

EXAMPLE 29:

As before, A and B owned Blackacre as joint tenants, and B granted a mortgage on her interest to Lender. On the left we have an illustration of the relationships between the parties if the mortgage severs the joint tenancy. On the right we have an illustration of the relationships if the mortgage does not sever the joint tenancy.

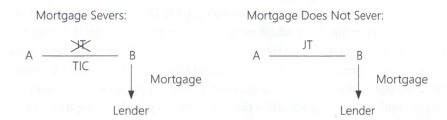

Now A has died, leaving all of her property to D. The illustration on the left is similar to the prior example. B owns Blackacre in a tenancy in common with D. Lender's mortgage on B's share survives. The illustration on the right is very different. B now owns Blackacre alone. D gets nothing because of the right of survivorship. Lender's mortgage survives. Rather than being only on B's half share, the mortgage is now on the entire interest in Blackacre.

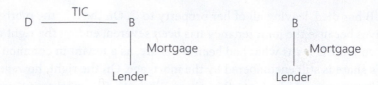

```
         TIC
D ——————————— B                    B
              |                     |
          Mortgage              Mortgage

          Lender                Lender
```

In this example, the Lender benefits when the joint tenancy is not severed because the mortgage is on the whole interest, not just the portion that was initially mortgaged. Even so, no commercial lender would take the risk of having the mortgage wiped out if the mortgaging joint tenant dies. This fact pattern tends to occur when an individual is the lender, or when a commercial lender makes a mistake.

Our next case involves a mortgage of one joint tenant's share. As you will see, the outcome turns in part on the jurisdiction's approach to mortgages. Some jurisdictions follow the *title theory* of mortgages, where the granting of a mortgage is viewed as a conveyance of title to the lender. Other jurisdictions follow the *lien theory* of mortgages, where the granting of a mortgage is viewed as the granting of a lien (i.e., a security interest) to the lender. Unsurprisingly, title theory states are more likely to view the granting of a mortgage by one joint tenant as severing the joint tenancy, because the title theory views a mortgage as a conveyance of the property, rather than the granting of a mere lien in the property.

HARMS V. SPRAGUE

Supreme Court of Illinois, 1984
473 N.E.2d 930

Thomas J. MORAN, Justice. Plaintiff, William H. Harms, filed a complaint to quiet title and for declaratory judgment in the circuit court of Greene County. Plaintiff had taken title to certain real estate with his brother John R. Harms, as a joint tenant, with full right of survivorship. The plaintiff named, as a defendant, Charles D. Sprague, the executor of the estate of John Harms and the devisee of all the real and personal property of John Harms. Also named as defendants were Carl T. and Mary E. Simmons, alleged mortgagees of the property in question. Defendant Sprague filed a counterclaim against plaintiff, challenging plaintiff's claim of ownership of the entire tract of property and asking the court to recognize his (Sprague's) interest as a tenant in common, subject to a mortgage lien. At issue was the effect the granting of a mortgage by John Harms had on the joint tenancy. Also at issue was whether the mortgage survived the death of John Harms as a lien against the property.

William and John Harms were joint tenants:

John unilaterally mortgaged his share to Carl and Mary Simmons:

Mortgage Severs:

William ——X—— John
         TIC
              │
              ↓ Mortgage

         Carl and
         Mary

Mortgage Does Not Sever:

William ——JT—— John
              │
              ↓ Mortgage

         Carl and
         Mary

John later died, leaving all his property to Charles Sprague. Whether Charles is entitled to John's share, and whether the mortgage survives, depends on whether the mortgage severed the joint tenancy:

William ——TIC—— Charles
                │
                │ Mortgage

            Carl and
            Mary

William

The trial court held that the mortgage given by John Harms to defendants Carl and Mary Simmons severed the joint tenancy. Further, the court found that the mortgage survived the death of John Harms as a lien against the undivided one-half interest in the property which passed to Sprague by and through the will of the deceased. The appellate court reversed, finding that the mortgage given by one joint tenant of his interest in the property does not sever the joint tenancy. Accordingly, the appellate court held that plaintiff, as the surviving joint tenant, owned the property in its entirety, unencumbered by the mortgage lien. (119 Ill.App.3d 503, 75 Ill.Dec. 155, 456 N.E.2d 976.) Defendant Sprague filed a petition for leave to appeal in this court. (87 Ill.2d R. 315.) . . . .

Two issues are raised on appeal: (1) Is a joint tenancy severed when less than all of the joint tenants mortgage their interest in the property? and (2) Does such a mortgage survive the death of the mortgagor as a lien on the property?

A review of the stipulation of facts reveals the following. Plaintiff, William Harms, and his brother John Harms, took title to real estate located in Roodhouse, on June 26, 1973, as joint tenants. The warranty deed memorializing this transaction was recorded on June 29, 1973, in the office of the Greene County recorder of deeds.

Carl and Mary Simmons owned a lot and home in Roodhouse. Charles Sprague entered into an agreement with the Simmons whereby Sprague was to purchase their property for $25,000. Sprague tendered $18,000 in cash and signed a promissory note for the balance of $7,000. Because Sprague had no security for the $7,000, he asked his friend, John Harms, to co-sign the note and give a mortgage on his interest in the joint tenancy property. Harms agreed, and on June 12, 1981, John Harms and Charles Sprague, jointly and severally, executed a promissory note for $7,000 payable to Carl and Mary Simmons. The note states that the principal sum of $7,000 was to be paid from the proceeds of the sale of John Harms' interest in the joint tenancy property, but in any event no later than six months from the date the note was signed. The note reflects that five monthly interest payments had been made, with the last payment recorded November 6, 1981. In addition, John Harms executed a mortgage, in favor of the Simmonses, on his undivided one-half interest in the joint tenancy property, to secure payment of the note. William Harms was unaware of the mortgage given by his brother.

John Harms moved from his joint tenancy property to the Simmons property which had been purchased by Charles Sprague. On December 10, 1981, John Harms died. By the terms of John Harms' will, Charles Sprague was the devisee of his entire estate. The mortgage given by John Harms to the Simmonses was recorded on December 29, 1981.

Prior to the appellate court decision in the instant case (119 Ill.App.3d 503, 75 Ill.Dec. 155, 456 N.E.2d 976) no court of this State had directly addressed the principal question we are confronted with herein—the effect of a mortgage, executed by less than all of the joint tenants, on the joint tenancy. Nevertheless, there are numerous cases which have considered the severance issue in relation to other circumstances surrounding a joint tenancy. All have necessarily focused on the four unities which are fundamental to both the creation and the perpetuation of the joint tenancy. These are the unities of interest, title, time, and possession. (*Jackson v. O'Connell* (1961), 23 Ill.2d 52, 55, 177 N.E.2d 194; *Tindall v. Yeats* (1946), 392 Ill. 502, 507, 64 N.E.2d 903.) The voluntary or involuntary destruction of any of the unities by one of the joint tenants will sever the joint tenancy. *Van Antwerp v. Horan* (1945), 390 Ill. 449, 451, 61 N.E.2d 358.

In a series of cases, this court has considered the effect that judgment liens upon the interest of one joint tenant have on the stability of the joint tenancy. In *Peoples Trust & Savings Bank v. Haas* (1927), 328 Ill. 468, 160 N.E. 85, the court found that a judgment lien secured against one joint tenant did not serve to extinguish the joint tenancy. As such, the surviving joint tenant "succeeded to the title in fee to the whole of the land by operation of law." 328 Ill. 468, 471, 160 N.E. 85. . . .

Clearly, this court adheres to the rule that a lien on a joint tenant's interest in property will not effectuate a severance of the joint tenancy, absent the conveyance by a deed following the expiration of a redemption period. (*See Johnson v. Muntz* (1936), 364 Ill. 482, 4 N.E.2d 826.) It follows, therefore, that if Illinois perceives a mortgage as merely a lien on the mortgagor's interest in property rather than a conveyance of title from mortgagor to mortgagee, the execution of a mortgage by a joint tenant, on his interest in the property, would not destroy the unity of title and sever the joint tenancy.

Early cases in Illinois, however, followed the title theory of mortgages. In 1900, this court recognized the common-law precept that a mortgage was a conveyance of a legal estate vesting title to the property in the mortgagee. (*Lightcap v. Bradley* (1900), 186 Ill. 510, 519, 58 N.E.2d 221.) Consistent with this title theory of mortgages, therefore, there are many cases which state, in *dicta,* that a joint tenancy is severed by one of the joint tenants mortgaging his interest to a stranger. (*Lawler v. Byrne* (1911), 252 Ill. 194, 196, 96 N.E. 892; *Hardin v. Wolf* (1925), 318 Ill. 48, 59, 148 N.E. 868; *Partridge v. Berliner* (1927), 325 Ill. 253, 258-59, 156 N.E. 352; *Van Antwerp v. Horan* (1945), 390 Ill. 449, 453, 61 N.E.2d 358; *Tindall v. Yeats* (1946), 392 Ill. 502, 511, 64 N.E.2d 903; *Illinois Public Aid Com. v. Stille* (1958), 14 Ill.2d 344, 353, 153 N.E.2d 59 (personal property).) Yet even the early case of *Lightcap v. Bradley,* cited above, recognized that the title held by the mortgagee was for the limited purpose of protecting his interests. The court went on to say that "the mortgagor is the owner for every other purpose and against every other person. The title of the mortgagee is anomalous, and exists only between him and the mortgagor . . . ." *Lightcap v. Bradley* (1900), 186 Ill. 510, 522-23, 58 N.E. 221.

Because our cases had early recognized the unique and narrow character of the title that passed to a mortgagee under the common-law title theory, it was not a drastic departure when this court expressly characterized the execution of a mortgage as a mere lien in *Kling v. Ghilarducci* (1954), 3 Ill.2d 455, 121 N.E.2d 752. In *Kling,* the court was confronted with the question of when a separation of title, necessary to create an easement by implication, had occurred. The court found that title to the property was not separated with the execution of a trust deed but rather only upon execution and delivery of a master's deed. The court stated:

> "In some jurisdictions the execution of a mortgage is a severance, in others, the execution of a mortgage is not a severance. In Illinois the giving of a mortgage is not a separation of title, for the holder of the mortgage takes only a lien thereunder. After foreclosure of a mortgage and until delivery of the master's deed under the foreclosure sale, purchaser acquires no title to the land either legal or equitable. Title to land sold under mortgage foreclosure remains in the mortgagor or his grantee until the expiration of the redemption period and conveyance by the master's deed." 3 Ill.2d 455, 460, 121 N.E.2d 752.

Kling and later cases rejecting the title theory (*Department of Transportation v. New Century Engineering & Development Corp.* (1983), 97 Ill.2d 343, 73 Ill.Dec. 538, 454 N.E.2d 635; *Kerrigan v. Unity Savings Association* (1974), 58 Ill.2d 20, 317 N.E.2d 39; *Mutual Life Insurance Co. of New York v. Chambers* (1980), 88 Ill.App.3d 952, 43 Ill.Dec. 829, 410 N.E.2d 962; *Commercial Mortgage & Finance Co. v. Woodcock Construction Co.* (1964), 51 Ill.App.2d 61, 200 N.E.2d 923) do not involve the severance of joint tenancies. As such, they have not expressly disavowed the *dicta* of joint tenancy cases which have stated that the act of mortgaging by one joint tenant results in the severance of the joint tenancy. We find, however, that implicit in *Kling* and our more recent cases which follow the lien theory of mortgages is the conclusion that a joint tenancy is not severed when one joint tenant executes a mortgage on his interest in the property, since the unity of title has been preserved. As the appellate court in the instant case correctly observed: "If giving a mortgage creates only a lien, then a mortgage should have the same effect on a joint tenancy as a lien created in other ways." (119 Ill.App.3d 503, 507, 75 Ill.Dec. 155, 456 N.E.2d 976.) Other jurisdictions following the lien theory of mortgages have reached the same result. *People v. Nogarr* (1958), 164 Cal.App.2d 591, 330 P.2d 858; *D.A.D., Inc. v. Moring* (Fla.App.1969), 218 So.2d 451; *American National Bank & Trust Co. v. McGinnis* (Okla.1977), 571 P.2d 1198; *Brant v. Hargrove* (Ariz. Ct.App.1981), 129 Ariz. 475, 632 P.2d 978.

A joint tenancy has been defined as "a present estate in all the joint tenants, each being seized of the whole . . . ." (*Partridge v. Berliner* (1927), 325 Ill. 253, 257, 156 N.E. 352.) An inherent feature of the estate of joint tenancy is the right of survivorship, which is the right of the last survivor to take the whole of the estate. (*In re Estate of Alpert* (1983), 95 Ill.2d 377, 381, 69 Ill.Dec. 361, 447 N.E.2d 796; *Bonczkowski v. Kucharski* (1958), 13 Ill.2d 443, 451, 150 N.E.2d 443.) Because we find that a mortgage given by one joint tenant of his interest in the property does not sever the joint tenancy, we hold that the plaintiff's right of survivorship became operative upon the death of his brother. As such plaintiff is now the sole owner of the estate, in its entirety.

Further, we find that the mortgage executed by John Harms does not survive as a lien on plaintiff's property. A surviving joint tenant succeeds to the share of the deceased joint tenant by virtue of the conveyance which created the joint tenancy, not as the successor of the deceased. (*In re Estate of Alpert* (1983), 95 Ill.2d 377, 381, 69 Ill.Dec. 361, 447 N.E.2d 796.) The property right of the mortgaging joint tenant is extinguished at the moment of his death. While John Harms was alive, the mortgage existed as a lien on his interest in the joint tenancy. Upon his death, his interest ceased to exist and along with it the lien of the mortgage. (*Merchants National Bank v. Olson* (1975), 27 Ill.App.3d 432, 434, 325 N.E.2d 633.) . . . .

For the reasons stated herein, the judgment of the appellate court is affirmed.

NOTE

More on Title Theory and Lien Theory. As explained in *Harms*, the mortgage by one joint tenant of her share of the property will sever the joint tenancy in a title theory state. The law in lien theory states is less uniform. Some lien theory jurisdictions follow the approach used in *Harms* and hold that the mortgage does not sever the joint tenancy. Other lien theory jurisdictions, typically motivated by the desire to protect the creditor's interest in the property, hold that the mortgage does sever the joint tenancy. Note well that these rules focus only on the effect of the joint tenant's grant of the mortgage to a third party. An actual sale of the joint tenant's interest in a foreclosure sale would be a conveyance of the property and would sever the joint tenancy in all jurisdictions.

PROBLEM

Toby Sinclair had three children, Cathy, John, and Louise. When he died, he left his vacation beach house to his three children "to hold as joint tenants with right of survivorship." In 1985, Louise sold her interest in the beach house to her cousin Ralph. A few years later, Cathy mortgaged her share of the beach house to her acquaintance, Bill.

Cathy died last April, leaving her property to her second husband, Jeremy. Bill just got a letter from Ralph and John stating that his mortgage on the Widener beach property was no longer valid. Ralph and John, in turn, are in a bit of a dispute. They agree that they want to partition the property, but John doesn't want the property to be sold in the partition process. Ralph and John also disagree on the respective shares they should get: Ralph claims he is entitled to one-half, while John claims that Ralph is entitled to one-third. Now Jeremy has shown up and said that he should get one-third of the property.

Explain the current state of ownership of the beach house. An explanatory answer can be found on page 1042.

C. THE TENANCY BY THE ENTIRETY AND MARITAL PROPERTY

In this section, we examine the tenancy by the entirety and marital property. The tenancy by the entirety is our third type of co-ownership. We place it in the section on marital property because a tenancy by the entirety can only be created between married couples.

1. TENANCY BY THE ENTIRETY

The tenancy by the entirety is a concurrent interest between spouses that in most respects resembles a joint tenancy. It typically will require the same unities as a joint tenancy, plus the additional requirement that the couple be married when they receive

> For a tenancy by the entirety to be created, the couple must be married at the time of conveyance. Problems will arise if a conveyance to an engaged, but not married, couple purports to convey a tenancy by the entirety. For example, O conveys "to A and B as tenants by the entirety," where A and B are not married. This conveyance will not create a tenancy by the entirety, because A and B are not married. In some jurisdictions, this conveyance will create a tenancy in common. In others, it will create a joint tenancy.

the interest. This interest is best created with a conveyance "to Spouse 1 and Spouse 2 as tenants by the entirety." There is a presumption in favor of a tenancy by the entirety, however, so a conveyance to a married couple that meets the unities requirement is likely to create a tenancy by the entirety even if the words "as tenants by the entirety" are omitted from the conveyance.

Like a joint tenancy, the tenancy by the entirety has a right of survivorship. Unlike a joint tenancy, the spouses cannot unilaterally convey their interests. An attempted conveyance by one spouse alone of a tenancy by the entirety interest will be ineffective. Consider this example:

EXAMPLE 30:

Spouse 1 and Spouse 2 are tenants by the entirety. Spouse 2 unilaterally conveys her interest to A:

```
                      TBE
Spouse 1 ───────────────── Spouse 2
                                 │
                                 │   Purports to convey
                                 ▼
                                 A
```

The purported conveyance from Spouse 2 to A will be ineffective. Spouse 1 and Spouse 2 still own the property as tenants by the entirety.

```
                      TBE
Spouse 1 ───────────────── Spouse 2
```

A tenancy by the entirety therefore cannot be severed unilaterally by one tenant in the way that a joint tenancy can be unilaterally severed. There are three basic ways that a tenancy by the entirety can end. First, the spouses may together transfer the property to another person. Second, one spouse may die, with the right of survivorship operating to give sole ownership to the surviving spouse. Third, the spouses may obtain a decree of divorce, which will sever the tenancy by the entirety by ending the marriage.

Fewer than half of U.S. jurisdictions recognize the tenancy by the entirety. In those jurisdictions that do recognize the interest, however, it can be very important. Recall that spouses may not unilaterally convey their interest in a tenancy by the entirety. One consequence of the spouses' inability to unilaterally convey is that the creditor of one spouse may not be able to reach property held by the entirety to satisfy the spouse's debt. Our next case provides a good illustration of why this can be a very big deal. It also provides a good explanation of the different approaches taken by U.S. jurisdictions to the ability of a creditor to reach property held by the entirety.

SAWADA V. ENDO

Supreme Court of Hawaii, 1977
561 P.2d 1291

MENOR, Justice.

This is a civil action brought by the plaintiffs-appellants, Masako Sawada and Helen Sawada, in aid of execution of money judgments in their favor, seeking to set aside a conveyance of real property from judgment debtor Kokichi Endo to Samuel H. Endo and Toru Endo, defendants-appellees herein, on the ground that the conveyance as to the Sawadas was fraudulent.

On November 30, 1968, the Sawadas were injured when struck by a motor vehicle operated by Kokichi Endo. On June 17, 1969, Helen Sawada filed her complaint for damages against Kokichi Endo. Masako Sawada filed her suit against him on August 13, 1969. The complaint and summons in each case was served on Kokichi Endo on October 29, 1969.

On the date of the accident, Kokichi Endo was the owner, as a tenant by the entirety with his wife, Ume Endo, of a parcel of real property situate at Wahiawa, Oahu, Hawaii. By deed, dated July 26, 1969, Kokichi Endo and his wife conveyed the property to their sons, Samuel H. Endo and Toru Endo. This document was recorded in the Bureau of Conveyances on December 17, 1969. No consideration was paid by the grantees for the conveyance. Both were aware at the time of the conveyance that their father had been involved in an accident, and that he carried no liability insurance. Kokichi Endo and Ume Endo, while reserving no life interests therein, continued to reside on the premises.

On January 19, 1971, after a consolidated trial on the merits, judgment was entered in favor of Helen Sawada and against Kokichi Endo in the sum of $8,846.46. At the same time, Masako Sawada was awarded judgment on her complaint in the amount of $16,199.28. Ume Endo, wife of Kokichi Endo, died on January 29, 1971. She was survived by her husband, Kokichi. Subsequently, after being frustrated in their attempts to obtain satisfaction of judgment from the personal property of Kokichi Endo, the Sawadas brought suit to set aside the conveyance which is the subject matter of this controversy. The trial court refused to set aside the conveyance, and the Sawadas appeal.

I

The determinative question in this case is, whether the interest of one spouse in real property, held in tenancy by the entireties, is subject to levy and execution by his or her individual creditors. This issue is one of first impression in this jurisdiction.

A brief review of the present state of the tenancy by the entirety might be helpful. Dean Phipps, writing in 1951,[1] pointed out that only nineteen states and the District of Columbia continued to recognize it as a valid and subsisting institution in the field of property law. Phipps divided these jurisdictions into four groups. He made no mention of Alaska and Hawaii, both of which were then territories of the United States.

In the Group I states (Massachusetts, Michigan, and North Carolina) the estate is essentially the common law tenancy by the entireties, unaffected by the Married Women's Property Acts. [Since *Sawada* was decided, all three of these states altered their rules for tenancy by the entirety by statute. As a result, no U.S. jurisdiction currently follows the Group I approach. —Ed.] As at common law, the possession and profits of the estate are subject to the husband's exclusive dominion and control. *Pineo v. White*, 320 Mass. 487, 70 N.E.2d 294 (1946); *Speier v. Opfer*, 73 Mich. 35, 40 N.W. 909 (1888); *Johnson v. Leavitt*, 188 N.C. 682, 125 S.E. 490 (1924). In all three states, as at common law, the husband may convey the entire estate subject only to the possibility that the wife may become entitled to the whole estate upon surviving him. *Phelps v. Simons*, 159 Mass. 415, 34 N.E. 657 (1893); *Arrand v. Graham*, 297 Mich. 559, 298 N.W. 281 (1911); *Hood v. Mercer*, 150 N.C. 699, 64 S.E. 897 (1909). As at common law, the obverse as to the wife does not hold true. Only in Massachusetts, however, is the estate in its entirety subject to levy by the husband's creditors. *Splaine v. Morrissey*, 282 Mass. 217, 184 N.E. 670 (1933). In both Michigan and North Carolina, the use and income from the estate is not subject to levy during the marriage for the separate debts of either spouse. *Dickey v. Converse*, 117 Mich. 449, 76 N.W. 80 (1898); *Nood v. Mercer, supra*.

> ## MARRIED WOMEN'S PROPERTY ACTS
>
> At traditional common law, married women had very little right to own property independent of their husband. The Married Women's Property Acts were laws passed in the 1800s that gave married women more rights to their property than they had at common law. The Acts gave married women, like single women, direct control over their property. We discuss the Married Women's Property Acts further below.

---

[1] Phipps, "Tenancy by Entireties," 25 Temple L.Q. 24 (1951).

In the Group II states (Alaska, Arkansas, New Jersey, New York, and Oregon) the interest of the debtor spouse in the estate may be sold or levied upon for his or her separate debts, subject to the other spouse's contingent right of survivorship. *Pope v. McBride*, 207 Ark. 940, 184 S.W.2d 259 (1945); *King v. Greene*, 30 N.J. 395, 153 A.2d 49 (1959); *Hiles v. Fisher*, 144 N.Y. 306, 39 N.E. 337 (1895); *Brownley v. Lincoln County*, 218 Or. 7, 343 P.2d 529 (1959). Alaska, which has been added to this group, has provided by statute that the interest of a debtor spouse in any type of estate, except a homestead as defined and held in tenancy by the entirety, shall be subject to his or her separate debts. *Pilip v. United States*, 186 F.Supp. 397 (D.Alaska, 1960).

In the Group III jurisdictions (Delaware, District of Columbia, Florida, Indiana, Maryland, Missouri, Pennsylvania, Rhode Island, Vermont, Virginia, and Wyoming) an attempted conveyance by either spouse is wholly void, and the estate may not be subjected to the separate debts of one spouse only. *Citizens Savings Bank Inc. v. Astrin*, 5 Terry 451, 44 Del. 451, 61 A.2d 419 (1948); *Golden v. Glens Falls Indemnity Co.*, 102 U.S.App.D.C. 106, 250 F.2d 769 (1957); *Hunt v. Covington*, 145 Fla. 706, 200 So. 76 (1941); *Sharp v. Baker*, 51 Ind.App. 547, 96 N.E. 627 (1911); *McCubbin v. Stanford*, 85 Md. 378, 37 A. 214 (1897); *Otto F. Stifel's Union Brewing Co. v. Saxy*, 273 Mo. 159, 201 S.W. 67 (1918); *O'Malley v. O'Malley*, 272 Pa. 528, 116 A. 500 (1922); *Bloomfield v. Brown*, 67 R.I. 452, 25 A.2d 354 (1942); *Citizens' Savings Bank & Trust Co. v. Jenkins*, 91 Vt. 13, 99 A. 250 (1916); *Vasilion v. Vasilion*, 192 Va. 735, 66 S.E.2d 599 (1951); *Ward Terry and Company v. Hensen*, 75 Wyo. 444, 297 P.2d 213 (1956).

In Group IV, the two states of Kentucky and Tennessee hold that the contingent right of survivorship appertaining to either spouse is separately alienable by him and attachable by his creditors during the marriage. *Hoffmann v. Newell*, 249 Ky. 270, 60 S.W.2d 607 (1933); *Covington v. Murray*, 220 Tenn. 265, 416 S.W.2d 761 (1967). The use and profits, however, may neither be alienated nor attached during coverture.

It appears, therefore, that Hawaii is the only jurisdiction still to be heard from on the question. Today we join that group of states and the District of Columbia which hold that under the Married Women's Property Acts the interest of a husband or a wife in an estate by the entireties is not subject to the claims of his or her individual creditors during the joint lives of the spouses. In so doing, we are placing our stamp of approval upon what is apparently the prevailing view of the lower courts of this jurisdiction.

Hawaii has long recognized and continues to recognize the tenancy in common, the joint tenancy, and the tenancy by the entirety, as separate and distinct estates. *See Paahana v. Bila*, 3 Haw. 725 (1876). That the Married Women's Property Act of 1888 was not intended to abolish the tenancy by the entirety was made clear by the language of Act 19 of the Session Laws of Hawaii, 1903 (now HRS §509-1). *See also* HRS §509-2. The tenancy by the entirety is predicated upon the legal unity of husband and wife, and the estate is held by them in single ownership. They do not take by moieties, but both and each are seized of the whole estate. *Lang v. Commissioner of Internal Revenue*, 289 U.S. 109, 53 S.Ct. 534, 77 L.Ed. 1066 (1933).

Neither husband nor wife has a separate divisible interest in the property held by the entirety that can be conveyed or reached by execution. *Fairclaw v. Forrest*, 76 U.S.App.D.C. 197, 130 F.2d 829 (1942). A joint tenancy may be destroyed by voluntary alienation, or by levy and execution, or by compulsory partition, but a tenancy by the entirety may not. The indivisibility of the estate, except by joint action of the spouses, is an indispensable feature of the tenancy by the entirety. *Ashbaugh v. Ashbaugh*, 273 Mo. 353, 201 S.W. 72 (1918). *Newman v. Equitable Life Assur. Soc.*, 119 Fla. 641, 160 So. 745 (1935); *Lang v. Commissioner of Internal Revenue, supra*. . . .

In *Hurd v. Hughes, supra*, the Delaware court, recognizing the peculiar nature of an estate by the entirety, in that the husband and wife are the owners, not merely of equal interests but of the whole estate, stated:

> "The estate (by the entireties) can be acquired or held only by a man and woman while married. Each spouse owns the whole while both live; neither can sell any interest except with the other's consent, and by their joint act; and at the death of either the other continues to own the whole, and does not acquire any new interest from the other. There can be no partition between them. From this is deduced the indivisibility and unseverability of the estate into two interests, and hence that the creditors of either spouse cannot during their joint lives reach by execution any interest which the debtor had in land so held. . . . One may have doubts as to whether the holding of land by entireties is advisable or in harmony with the spirit of the legislation in favor of married women; but when such an estate is created due effect must be given to its peculiar characteristics." 12 Del.Ch. at 190, 109 A. at 419. . . .

We are not persuaded by the argument that it would be unfair to the creditors of either spouse to hold that the estate by the entirety may not, without the consent of both spouses, be levied upon for the separate debts of either spouse. No unfairness to the creditor in involved here. We agree with the court in *Hurd v. Hughes, supra*:

"But creditors are not entitled to special consideration. If the debt arose prior to the creation of the estate, the property was not a basis of credit, and if the debt arose subsequently the creditor presumably had notice of the characteristics of the estate which limited his right to reach the property." 12 Del.Ch. at 193, 109 A. at 420.

We might also add that there is obviously nothing to prevent the creditor from insisting upon the subjection of property held in tenancy by the entirety as a condition precedent to the extension of credit. Further, the creation of a tenancy by the entirety may not be used as a device to defraud existing creditors. *In re Estate of Wall*, 142 U.S.App.D.C. 187, 440 F.2d 215 (1971).

Were we to view the matter strictly from the standpoint of public policy, we would still be constrained to hold as we have done here today. In *Fairclaw v. Forrest, supra*, the court makes this observation:

"The interest in family solidarity retains some influence upon the institution (of tenancy by the entirety). It is available only to husband and wife. It is a convenient mode of protecting a surviving spouse from inconvenient administration of the decedent's estate and from the other's improvident debts. It is in that protection the estate finds its peculiar and justifiable function." 130 F.2d at 833.

It is a matter of common knowledge that the demand for single-family residential lots has increased rapidly in recent years, and the magnitude of the problem is emphasized by the concentration of the bulk of fee simple land in the hands of a few. The shortage of single-family residential fee simple property is critical and government has seen fit to attempt to alleviate the problem through legislation. When a family can afford to own real property, it becomes their single most important asset. Encumbered as it usually is by a first mortgage, the fact remains that so long as it remains whole during the joint lives of the spouses, it is always available in its entirety for the benefit and use of the entire family. Loans for education and other emergency expenses, for example, may be obtained on the security of the marital estate. This would not be possible where a third party has become a tenant in common or a joint tenant with one of the spouses, or where the ownership of the contingent right of survivorship of one of the spouses in a third party has cast a cloud upon the title of the marital estate, making it virtually impossible to utilize the estate for these purposes.

If we were to select between a public policy favoring the creditors of one of the spouses and one favoring the interests of the family unit, we would not hesitate to choose the latter. But we need not make this choice for, as we pointed out earlier, by the very nature of the estate by the entirety as we view it, and as other courts of our sister jurisdictions have viewed it, "(a) unilaterally indestructible right of survivorship, an inability of one spouse to alienate his interest, and, importantly for this case, a broad immunity from claims of separate creditors remain among its vital incidents." *In re Estate of Wall, supra*, 440 F.2d at 218.

Having determined that an estate by the entirety is not subject to the claims of the creditors of one of the spouses during their joint lives, we now hold that the conveyance of the marital property by Kokichi Endo and Ume Endo, husband and wife, to their sons, Samuel H. Endo and Toru Endo, was not in fraud of Kokichi Endo's judgment creditors. *Cf. Jordan v. Reynolds, supra.*

Affirmed. [The dissenting opinion of Justice Kidwell is omitted.].

NOTES

1. *The Three Groups.* The *Sawada* court referenced four groups of jurisdictional approaches to the question of whether the creditor of one spouse can access property held by the entirety to satisfy the debt. The groups were established by Dean Phipps in 1951. As we noted in the text of the case, Group I no longer exists, because the three states that followed this approach have since changed their law by statute. This leaves us with three groups. For consistency's sake, we continue to refer to these as Group II, Group III, and Group IV.

When this issue arises, we typically have three people involved—two spouses and the Creditor. We will call the spouse who owes the debt to the Creditor the Debtor Spouse. We will call the other spouse the Innocent Spouse.

In Group II, the Creditor can access the Debtor Spouse's share of the property to satisfy the debt. This means that the Creditor and the Innocent Spouse are now in an odd co-ownership relationship that looks a little bit like a tenancy in common and a little bit like a joint tenancy. The Creditor and the Innocent Spouse have shared ownership of the property. Think back to all the issues that we discussed in the context of the tenancy in common, and consider how strange it would be to be in a co-ownership relationship with a creditor. As a practical matter, these problems might lead the parties to some kind of financial settlement to satisfy the Creditor. If no settlement is reached, however, the problems remain. The right of survivorship is still in place. If the Debtor Spouse dies first, then the Innocent Spouse will have ownership free and clear of the Creditor's interest (because the Creditor has stepped into the Debtor Spouse's shoes). If the Innocent Spouse dies first, then the Creditor will have complete ownership.

In Group III, the Creditor cannot access any part of the property held by the entirety to satisfy the debt. Period. As a result, tenancy by the entirety is a *very big deal* in Group III jurisdictions. The facts of *Sawada* illustrate why.

In Group IV, the Creditor can access the Debtor Spouse's right of survivorship, but cannot gain access to the property during the spouses' lives. This avoids the complications of having the Creditor and the Innocent Spouse sharing ownership during life that is present in Group II. The outcomes with the right of survivorship are the same as they are in Group II. If the Debtor Spouse dies first, the Innocent Spouse owns the property free and clear of the debt. If the Innocent Spouse dies first, then the Creditor owns the property.

2. *Contract Creditors vs. Tort Creditors.* The *Sawada* court made a serious reasoning error in its opinion when it failed to distinguish between two types of creditors. A *contract creditor* is a creditor who is owed a debt that arises from a consensual transaction. An example would be a bank that voluntarily lends money to the debtor. A *tort creditor* is a creditor who is owed a debt because the creditor was the victim of a tort. The Sawadas were tort creditors—they were owed a debt that arose because Kokichi Endo hit them with his car. In deciding to follow the Group III approach, the *Sawada* court claimed that "[n]o unfairness to the creditor" would result because "there is obviously nothing to prevent the creditor from insisting upon the subjection of property held in tenancy by the entirety as a condition precedent to the extension of credit." That clearly is true with a contract creditor, who can refuse to lend money unless both spouses agree that the property held by the entirety is subject to the debt. Mortgage lenders in Group III states, for example, make sure that both spouses execute the mortgage and related documents so that they can reach the property held by the entirety if the borrowers default on the loan. Tort creditors like the Sawadas, however, do not become creditors voluntarily and do not have the opportunity to bargain with the debtor before the tort is committed. The Sawadas could not have stopped Endo from hitting them with his car unless he and his wife agreed to give them access to the property held by the entirety to satisfy the debt. We are not suggesting here that the *Sawada* court reached the wrong result. Reasonable minds can disagree on the right rule, and the court articulated other justifications for the result it reached. Rather, we are suggesting that in part of its opinion, the court made an error by applying reasoning from the contract creditor context, where it works, to the tort creditor context, where it does not.

3. *Criminal Activity.* The fact that married spouses own property as tenants by the entirety may not protect an innocent spouse from forfeiture of that property on the criminal conviction of the other spouse. There is a split in authority in the U.S. Court of Appeals on this issue. In *United States v. Lee*, 232 F.3d 556 (7th Cir. 2000), the husband/defendant pleaded guilty to money laundering, and the U.S. government attempted to execute a forfeiture judgment against him by taking the home he owned as tenants in the entirety with his wife. The court ruled that "[p]roperty owned as a tenancy by the entiret[y] cannot be made available to answer for the judgment debts of one of the tenants individually." In *United States v. Fleet*, 498 F.3d. 1225 (11th Cir. 2007), the Eleventh Circuit disagreed with the *Lee* decision, holding that property held by spouses as tenants by the entirety is reachable by one spouse's creditors when that spouse commits a federal crime. In *Fleet*, like *Lee*, the defendant was convicted of the federal crime of money laundering. The court, however, allowed the government to reach the property, stating that "there is no innocent spouse defense to criminal forfeiture because the only property being forfeited is the interest that belongs to the defendant. The fact that the innocent spouse, even though she retains her property interest, may be adversely affected by the forfeiture of her guilty mate's interest is no bar to forfeiture of his interest."

PROBLEM

Julia Barzel and Larry Rose were married in August 1995 and bought a house together as tenants by the entirety in 1997. Julia is an entrepreneur and set up a software company in 1998. In 2000, Julia bought $150,000 in computer equipment from Perry Newman on credit, securing the debt by granting Perry a mortgage on her interest in her house (Julia and Larry own the house in equal shares). Julia's company failed last year, and Perry has now brought an action seeking to attach Julia's share in the house to satisfy the debt. Will Perry's action be successful? An explanatory answer can be found on page 1043.

2. MARITAL PROPERTY

a. The Evolution of Marital Property Law

In this section, we briefly discuss the history of marital property law. As we will see, marital property rules have mirrored societal views on gender roles, especially the economic roles of women. As views on the social roles of women changed, the law of property gradually changed with it.

i. The Eighteenth Century

Prior to the 1800s, married women had limited property rights based on the *unity* principle, the idea that husband and wife were recognized as one person upon marriage. The unity principle was explained by Sir William Blackstone, the preeminent English legal scholar of the time.

WILLIAM BLACKSTONE

1 Commentaries on the Laws of England 430 (1766)

By marriage, the husband and wife are one person in law: that is, the very being or legal existence of the woman is suspended during the marriage, or at least is incorporated and consolidated into that of the husband: under whose wing, protection, and *cover,* she performs every thing; and is therefore called in our law-french a *feme-covert, fœmina viro co-operta;* is said to be *covert-baron,* or under the protection and influence of her husband, her *baron,* or lord; and her condition during her marriage is called her *coverture.* . . . The husband is bound to provide his wife with necessaries by law, as much as himself; and, if she contracts debts for them, he is obliged to pay them; but for any thing besides necessaries he is not chargeable. . . . If the wife be indebted before marriage, the husband is bound afterwards to pay the debt; for he has adopted her and her circumstances together. If the wife be injured in her person or her property, she can bring no action for redress without her husband's concurrence, and in his name, as well as her own: neither can she be sued without making the husband a defendant. . . .

But though our law in general considers man and wife as one person, yet there are some instances in which she is separately considered; as inferior to him, and acting by his compulsion. And therefore all deeds executed, and acts done, by her, during her coverture, are void; except it be a fine, or the like matter of record, in which case she must be solely and secretly examined, to learn if her act be voluntary. She cannot by will devise lands to her husband, unless under special circumstances; for at the time of making it she is supposed to be under his coercion. . . .

The husband also, by the old law, might give his wife moderate correction. For, as he is to answer for her misbehaviour, the law thought it reasonable to intrust him with this power of restraining her, by domestic chastisement, in the same moderation that a man is allowed to correct his apprentices or children; for whom the master or parent is also liable in some cases to answer. . . .

These are the chief legal effects of marriage during the coverture; upon which we may observe, that even the disabilities which the wife lies under are for the most part intended for her protection and benefit: so great a favourite is the female sex of the laws of England.

NOTES AND QUESTIONS

1. *Unity in Marriage.* According to Blackstone, a wife's property relationship to her husband was defined under the doctrine of *coverture*, or dependency. She became a *femme covert*, that is, a dependent who would be supported for her entire life by her husband in exchange for providing domestic services to him. Although she retained title to the real property she owned entering marriage, her husband obtained an interest in the property at the time of the marriage and had the right to possess and control the property. This estate, named an *estate jure uxoris* (meaning "in the right of the wife") also allowed his creditors to reach the property. How does the creation of this estate impact what you think Blackstone meant by "the husband and wife are one person in law"?

2. *Relinquishment of Rights.* Consider Blackstone's statement that "all deeds executed, and acts done, by her, during her coverture, are void." Prior to marriage, a woman had the right to hold and manage property and to enter into contracts. Presumably in exchange for her husband's support, married women relinquished those rights. Although many women today would not consider this an equal exchange, consider how different the opportunities available to women were in the eighteenth, nineteenth, and even twentieth centuries.

ii. The Nineteenth Century

Common law in the mid-1800s provided some important property rights to women. A wife had the ability to regain control over her property if she divorced her husband or if he died. Upon divorce, property would be divided between the spouses in accordance with which spouse held title. Upon the husband's death, the wife was entitled to *dower*, a special life estate that usually amounted to one-third of her deceased husband's property. Dower was provided so that she could support herself and any children they had through marriage. Upon the wife's death, so long as the couple had a child during marriage, the husband was entitled to *curtesy consummate*, a life estate in all lands held by his wife in fee simple or fee tail. Before his death, the curtesy was referred to as *curtesy initiate*. The spouses' respective claims to dower and curtesy prevented both wife and husband from transferring title without the other's consent.

In the mid- to late-nineteenth century, states enacted *Married Women's Property Acts* abolishing the common-law rules of dower, curtesy, and coverture.

MARRIED WOMEN'S PROPERTY ACT

New York, 1848 (amended 1849)

An act for the more effectual protection of the property of married women:

§1. The real property of any female who may hereafter marry, and which she shall own at the time of marriage, and the rents, issues, and profits thereof, shall not be subject to the sole disposal of her husband, nor be liable for his debts, and shall continue her sole and separate property, as if she were a single female.

§2. The real and personal property, and the rents, issues, and profits thereof, of any female now married, shall not be subject to the disposal of her husband; but shall be her sole and separate property, as if she were a single female, except so far as the same may be liable for the debts of her husband heretofore contracted.

§3. Any married female may take by inheritance, or by gift, grant, devise, or bequest, from any person other than her husband, and hold to her sole and separate use, and convey and devise real and personal property, and any interest or estate therein, and the rents, issues, and profits thereof, in the same manner and with like effect as if she were unmarried, and the same shall not be subject to the disposal of her husband nor be liable for his debts.

NOTE AND QUESTIONS

1. *Statutory Reform.* As suggested by the Married Women's Property Acts, the common-law approach to marital property has been heavily impacted by statutory reform. The Acts allowed married women to retain the same property rights as single women. They allowed women to contract, litigate, hold property, and manage property. In theory, they provided the legal opportunity for both husband and wife to enjoy equal property ownership rights during marriage. The Acts gave women control over their earnings because the earnings were considered their separate property. Recall however, that women had different opportunities in the mid-1800s than they do today. Most earning opportunities arose only inside the home in the form of taking in laundry or sewing. Because most married women were not working outside the home they had

few, if any, earnings. How do earning opportunities of today compare to the nineteenth century? Do stay-at-home dads now encounter the same earning issues that women in the 1800s did?

iii. The Twentieth Century and Today

Two basic issues flow throughout both our historical and contemporary law of marital property: (1) how married couples own property and (2) whether a particular piece of property can be classified as marital property. To help illustrate these themes in contemporary times, consider the following example:

> James and Jillian were high school sweethearts who got married when they were 18 years old. After the wedding, Jillian decided to go college and then to law school, and James attended a community college and enrolled in a plumbing technology program. Jillian is now a successful real estate attorney. James advanced from apprentice plumber to journeyman plumber and is now a master plumber. Because his educational path took less time to complete, he supported Jillian through school and paid for her entire law school education. They own a house in the suburbs in New Jersey. One day, James decided to try his luck playing blackjack in Atlantic City. Unfortunately, he placed several bad bets and lost $75,000. He had to take an advance to cover the bet, and now his creditors are trying to collect his debt. The blackjack incident led to marital discord and James and Jillian are now divorcing.

Can the creditors go after James and Jillian's home for his $75,000 loss? Can they go after Jillian's assets? Can James claim a property interest in Jillian's law degree? What if James were to die before the divorce? Would the creditors then be able to go after James and Jillian's home for his $75,000 loss?

Answers to these questions depend on how James and Jillian owned their property (e.g., the house) and whether a piece of property (e.g., the law degree) was marital property. These two themes provide the basis for the remainder of this chapter and, as you can guess, can arise (a) during marriage, (b) when spouses divorce, and (c) when one spouse dies.

Today's marital property laws are not uniform throughout the United States. Rather, there are currently two different marital property systems: the *separate property system* and the *community property system.*

b. The Common-Law Marital Property Model, a.k.a. the Separate Property System

The *common-law property model* is also called the *separate property system* because it views property as being separately owned by the spouse who owned the property before marriage or obtained it during marriage. It also provides that each spouse is individually liable for separate debts. Under the separate property system, property obtained by one spouse is owned solely by that spouse. As a result, this system for the most part follows the basic rules of property acquisition and ownership that we study in other parts of this book.

i. During Marriage

Each spouse will continue to own property separately unless they take action to own it jointly. Applying this concept to James and Jillian during marriage, whatever property they owned individually when they entered into marriage, they would continue to own individually. Any property they individually earned or received by gift or by inheritance during marriage would be owned individually.

Creditors Generally

Creditors cannot touch a spouse's individual assets in a separate property system to satisfy the debt of the other spouse. Therefore, in a separate property state, Jillian's individual property could not be reached by James's creditors for his $75,000 gambling debt because she did not undertake that debt. It is his alone. The creditors, however, could reach the property the married couple owned jointly (unless, of course, they owned it jointly as tenants by the entirety in a Group III state). In most separate property states, James's creditor could reach one-half of the money in the joint account. For example, if James and Jillian own a joint bank account under a joint tenancy arrangement, the creditors could go after half of the money in that account to satisfy James's debt.

Necessaries

Married couples can chose to informally share property. For example, they could informally share the cost of maintaining the household or share their earnings with each other. Because spouses have a legal duty to support one another, a spouse who fails to share property earned during marriage in order to support the other spouse could face a court order for payment of necessaries. As the following case illustrates, the law on the payment of necessaries varies among states following the separate property system.

CONNOR V. SOUTHWEST FLORIDA REGIONAL MEDICAL CENTER, INC.

Supreme Court of Florida, 1996
668 So. 2d 175

GRIMES, Chief Justice.

Southwest Florida Regional Medical Center sued Kenneth Connor and his wife Barbara Connor in 1993 for payment of medical services the hospital had rendered to Kenneth. The trial court dismissed the hospital's complaint against Barbara Connor on the ground that she had not executed an agreement to pay for the services rendered to Kenneth Connor. In so doing, the trial court declined to expand the doctrine of necessaries to hold the wife responsible for her husband's medical bills. The district court of appeal reversed and remanded, thereby giving the hospital a cause of action against Barbara Connor.

This case involves what is known as the doctrine of necessaries. At common law, a married woman's legal identity merged with that of her husband, a condition known as coverture. She was unable to own property, enter into contracts, or receive credit. A married woman was therefore dependent upon her husband for maintenance and support, and he was under a corresponding legal duty to provide his wife with food, clothing, shelter, and medical services. The common law doctrine of necessaries mitigated the possible effects of coverture in the event a woman's husband failed to fulfill his support obligation. Under the doctrine, a husband was liable to a third party for any necessaries that the third party provided to his wife. Because the duty of support was uniquely the husband's obligation, and because coverture restricted the wife's access to the economic realm, the doctrine did not impose a similar liability upon married women.

This state recognized the doctrine of necessaries in *Phillips v. Sanchez,* 35 Fla. 187, 17 So. 363 (1895). However, the disability of coverture was later abrogated. Ch. 21977, Laws of Fla. (1943); *see* §708.08, Fla.Stat. (1993). Further, the responsibilities for alimony between husband and wife are now reciprocal. §61.08, Fla. Stat. (1993).

The first case to address the question of whether the obligations under the doctrine of necessaries should run both ways was *Manatee Convalescent Center, Inc. v. McDonald,* 392 So.2d 1356 (Fla. 2d DCA 1980). In holding a wife liable for the necessaries of her husband, the court stated:

> Changing times demand reexamination of seemingly unchangeable legal dogma. Equality under law and even handed treatment of the sexes in the modern market place must also carry the burden of responsibility which goes with the benefits.

Id. at 1358. *Accord Parkway Gen. Hosp., Inc. v. Stern,* 400 So.2d 166 (Fla. 3d DCA 1981). However, in *Shands Teaching Hospital & Clinics, Inc. v. Smith,* 497 So.2d 644 (Fla.1986), this Court declined to hold a wife liable for the husband's hospital bills and disapproved *Parkway General Hospital* and *Manatee Convalescent Center.* In reaching our decision, we first stated that it was an anachronism to hold the husband responsible for the necessaries of the wife without also holding the wife responsible for the necessaries of her husband. We also acknowledged that the respective arguments of both parties had merit. However, we concluded that because the issue had broad social implications and the judiciary was the branch of government least capable of resolving the question, it was best to leave to the legislature the decision of whether to modify the common law doctrine of necessaries. In a footnote we stated that the issue of whether it was a denial of equal protection to hold a husband liable for a wife's necessaries when a wife was not liable for a husband's necessaries was not before us.

Following our opinion in *Shands,* an equal protection issue was raised by a husband who suffered a judgment which required him to pay his wife's hospital bill. *Webb v. Hillsborough County Hosp. Auth.,* 521 So.2d 199 (Fla. 2d DCA 1988). The court ruled that the doctrine of necessaries remained viable so as to obligate a husband to pay for his wife's necessaries and went on to hold that the duty was reciprocal between spouses. In two subsequent decisions, the Fourth District Court of Appeal disagreed with *Webb* and held that a wife could not be held responsible for her husband's necessaries. *Faulk; Heinemann.* In the meantime, the Fifth District Court of Appeal held that a husband continues to be liable for his wife's necessaries.

The case before us today is in essentially the same posture as *Shands.* Yet, we are faced with a series of cases in which the parties agree that husbands and wives must be treated alike but disagree over whether the doctrine of necessaries should be applied to both spouses or simply abolished. Therefore, we have concluded that we must now address this issue in the context of equal protection considerations. Mrs. Connor contends that with the removal of coverture, the doctrine of necessaries is no longer justifiable because wives are now freely able to enter into contracts and obtain their own necessaries. Southwest posits that while the initial reason for the doctrine has disappeared, it now serves the important function of promoting the partnership theory of marriage and should be expanded so that both men and women are liable to third-party creditors who provide necessaries to their respective spouses.

The courts of other states have split on the proper remedy to adopt. Some have abrogated the doctrine entirely, preferring to defer to the legislature. . . . Others have extended the common law doctrine to apply to both sexes. . . .

Legislative action in this area has been just as diverse. Oklahoma and Kentucky have codified the doctrine in its original common law form, while the Georgia Legislature repealed the doctrine in 1979. Okla. Stat.tit. 43, §209 (1994); Ky. Rev. Stat. Ann. §404.040 (Baldwin 1994); 1979 Ga. Laws 466, 491. Somewhere in the middle of these two extremes are those jurisdictions that have retained the doctrine in a modified form. For example, North Dakota imposes joint and several liability for debts incurred by either spouse for the necessaries of food, clothing, fuel, and shelter, but excludes medical care. N.D. Cent. Code §14-07-08 (1993).

The fact that courts and other legislatures have treated this problem in different ways illustrates the lack of consensus regarding the doctrine's place in modern society and reinforces the position we took in *Shands.* Yet, our legislature has not chosen to address this issue, and we know of no circumstances occurring since our decision in *Shands* which would suggest that we were wrong in refusing to hold the wife liable for the husband's necessaries. Because constitutional considerations demand equality between the sexes, it follows that a husband can no longer be held liable for his wife's necessaries. We therefore abrogate the common law doctrine of necessaries, thereby leaving it to the legislature to determine the policy of the state in this area. We do not make a judgment as to which is the better policy for the state to adopt. We merely leave it to the appropriate branch to decide this question.

We quash the decision below. . . .

It is so ordered.

Overton, Justice, dissenting.

I dissent. The common law doctrine of necessaries was born of the need to provide a legal means to protect and enforce the moral terms of the marital obligation. I find that the doctrine is just as important today, under the partnership theory of marriage, as it was when the doctrine was created under the unity theory of marriage. In this day and age, we should not weaken the obligations of marriage by eliminating the spousal duty to care for one another. However, that is exactly what the majority opinion does, and, by doing so, it places this Court in the minority of state supreme courts that have addressed this issue.

I agree that the common law doctrine of necessaries in its present form violates the equal protection clause by imposing a duty of spousal support only on the husband. However, unlike the majority, I conclude that this Court, as a matter of policy, should extend the doctrine to apply to both spouses rather than abrogate it entirely. In doing so, I would make the spouse who incurred the debt primarily liable.

The majority's decision to abrogate the doctrine is premised on the theory that altering the doctrine would have broad social implications and, as such, is a task best left to the legislature. If the legislature disagreed with the policies behind the doctrine of necessaries, it has had ample opportunity during the last one hundred years to abolish the doctrine. Instead, the legislature has left the doctrine intact. This legislative inaction implies an agreement with the current, judicially-created policy regarding the doctrine of necessaries. The majority's abrogation of the doctrine of necessaries appears to shift the policy of this state by, in effect, requiring each spouse to take care of himself or herself. It also reduces the legal obligations of the marriage contract.

I believe that, because the doctrine's incorporation into Florida's common law was a matter of judicial policy when the doctrine was adopted in 1895, today's decision regarding whether to extend the doctrine to both spouses is a matter of judicial policy. This Court should decide this case on its merits rather than by abrogating the doctrine and unnecessarily placing the responsibility on the legislature to *reinstate* a long-standing policy of the state established by this Court.

The majority's determination that a lack of consensus exists among other states regarding the proper role of the doctrine of necessaries is, in my view, incorrect. A national survey of how state courts have resolved this issue reveals that this Court's decision to abrogate the doctrine places Florida in the minority of jurisdictions that have considered this issue. Approximately sixteen state courts have addressed the issue of whether the doctrine of necessaries should be modified or abrogated. The majority of those state courts have extended the doctrine to apply to both spouses. Only four have abrogated the doctrine and placed the responsibility on the legislature to reinstate the doctrine through codification. . . .

I would follow the majority of other jurisdictions by extending the doctrine of necessaries to both spouses, and I would make the spouse who incurred the obligation primarily liable. I reach this conclusion because, while Florida has moved from a unity theory of marriage to a partnership theory of marriage, the partnership theory of marriage is fully consistent with the underlying principles of the doctrine of necessaries. . . .

Under the partnership theory of marriage, each spouse is entitled to share in the fruits of the marital partnership. This concept is reflected by equitable distribution principles recognized by this State. *Canakaris v. Canakaris,* 382 So.2d 1197, 1203-04 (Fla.1980) (holding that spouses should be treated as partners when considering the equitable distribution of the marital assets upon divorce); *Thompson v. Thompson,* 576 So.2d 267, 268 (Fla.1991) (holding that professional goodwill obtained after the formation of the marriage partnership belongs to the marriage partnership). The majority's decision to abrogate the common law doctrine of necessaries departs from the partnership theory of marriage and eliminates a common law doctrine even though the policy and need for the doctrine continue to exist.

As we recognized in *Via v. Putnam,* 656 So.2d 460 (Fla.1995), " '[t]he institution of marriage has been a cornerstone of western civilization for thousands of years and is the most important type of contract ever formed.' " *Id.* at 465. Although the *Via* case does not discuss the doctrine of necessaries, the case illustrates this Court's commitment to spousal support. This Court should again reaffirm this long-standing commitment requiring spouses to care for one another by extending the doctrine of necessaries to apply to both spouses.

I believe that extending the doctrine of necessaries to apply to both spouses is the best, most logical, and least destructive method of altering the doctrine to comply with the equal protection clause. I would make the spouse who incurred the obligation primarily responsible. Extending the doctrine in this manner would further both a long-standing obligation of spousal support and the needs of our changing society. It would also advance a policy that acknowledges the partnership theory of marriage and the social value inherent in requiring marital partners to support one another.

NOTES AND QUESTIONS

1. *Doctrine of Necessaries.* Traditional law placed a legal obligation on the husband to provide necessaries for his wife and children. Wives did not have a reciprocal duty. Why did the Florida court abolish the doctrine of necessaries? Why have other states expanded it to cover both spouses? Do you think the doctrine should be abolished, or do you think it should be extended to cover both spouses? If you believe it should cover both spouses, what expenses should be covered?

2. *Legislative Action.* The courts that have abolished the doctrine of necessaries routinely call on the legislature to reinstate it through codification. Why would the courts send the issue to the legislature? Why would a legislature reinstate the doctrine after the courts have ruled on the issue?

3. *Aftermath from* Connor. Following *Connor*, Florida legislators introduced two bills aimed at reinstating the doctrine. Florida House Bill 1211 §1 (1996); and Florida Senate Bill 906 §1 (1996) stated: "The husband and wife are liable jointly and severally for any debts contracted by either, while living together, for necessary household supplies of food, clothing, and fuel, for medical care, and for shelter for themselves and family, and for the education of their minor children." Both bills failed.

ii. When Spouses Divorce

Upon divorce, separate property states generally provide for *equitable distribution* of the property owned by each of the spouses. *Equitable distribution* is limited to property acquired during marriage in almost all separate property states, although some will also include property acquired before the marriage.

As the term suggests, marital property is divided based on equitable principles. Factors the court considers in dividing the property include the length of the marriage, each spouse's income, each spouse's contribution during marriage, the lifestyle shared during marriage (status), and whether support will be needed to allow one spouse to obtain marketable skills so that support will not be needed in the future (rehabilitation). In general, the length of the marriage is directly correlated with the property distribution. Shorter marriages receive less property redistribution; longer marriages receive more property redistribution. Some states call for a presumption of equal distribution of marital property if the marriage lasted for at least ten years. Other states give considerable discretion to the courts hearing the divorce proceeding.

Courts can also consider age, debts, health, occupation, and contributions of one spouse to the other spouse's education. Although most courts have decided that contributions to the spouse's education do not result in an educational degree that constitutes marital property, they will allow for spouses who paid for the education to be reimbursed for the cost. Consider the following case.

MAHONEY V. MAHONEY

Supreme Court of New Jersey, 1982
453 A.2d 527

PASHMAN, J.

The question here is whether the defendant has the right to share the value of a professional business (M.B.A.) degree earned by her former husband during their marriage. The Court must decide whether the plaintiff's degree is "property" for purposes of *N.J.S.A.* 2A:34-23, which requires equitable distribution of "the property, both real and personal, which was legally and beneficially acquired . . . during the marriage." If the M.B.A. degree is not property, we must still decide whether the defendant can nonetheless recover the money she contributed to her husband's support while he pursued his professional education. For the reasons stated below, we hold that the plaintiff's professional degree is not property and therefore reject the defendant's claim that the degree is subject to equitable distribution. . . .

I

When the parties married in Indiana in 1971, plaintiff, Melvin Mahoney, had an engineering degree and defendant, June Lee Mahoney, had a bachelor of science degree. From that time until the parties separated in October 1978 they generally shared all household expenses. The sole exception was the period between September 1975 and January 1977, when the plaintiff attended the Wharton School of the University of Pennsylvania and received an M.B.A. degree.

During the 16-month period in which the plaintiff attended school, June Lee Mahoney contributed about $24,000 to the household. Her husband made no financial contribution while he was a student. Melvin's educational expenses of about $6,500 were paid for by a combination of veterans' benefits and a payment from the Air Force. After receiving his degree, the plaintiff went to work as a commercial lending officer for Chase Manhattan Bank.

Meanwhile, in 1976 the defendant began a part-time graduate program at Rutgers University, paid for by her employer, that led to a master's degree in microbiology one year after the parties had separated. June Lee worked full-time throughout the course of her graduate schooling.

In March 1979, Melvin Mahoney sued for divorce; his wife filed a counterclaim also seeking a divorce. In May 1980, the trial court granted dual judgments of divorce on the ground of 18 months continuous separation.

At the time of trial, plaintiff's annual income was $25,600 and defendant's income was $21,000. No claim for alimony was made. The parties owned no real property and divided the small amount of their personal property by agreement. . . .

II

. . . Regarding equitable distribution, this Court has frequently held that an "expansive interpretation [is] to be given to the word 'property,'" *Gauger v. Gauger,* 73 *N.J.* 538, 544, 376 *A.2d* 523 (1977). *Accord Kruger v. Kruger,* 73 *N.J.* 464, 468, 375 *A.2d* 659 (1977); *Painter v. Painter,* 65 *N.J.* 196, 217, 320 *A.2d* 484 (1974). New Jersey courts have subjected a broad range of assets and interests to equitable distribution . . . .

This Court, however, has never subjected to equitable distribution an asset whose future monetary value is as uncertain and unquantifiable as a professional degree or license. The Appellate Division discussed at some length the characteristics that distinguish professional licenses and degrees from other assets and interests, including intangible ones, that courts equitably distribute as marital property. Quoting from *In re Marriage of Graham*, 574 *P.*2d 75, 77 (1978), in which the Colorado Supreme Court held that an M.B.A. degree is not subject to equitable distribution, the court stated:

> An educational degree, such as an M.B.A., is simply not encompassed even by the broad views of the concept of "property." It does not have an exchange value or any objective transferable value on an open market. It is personal to the holder. It terminates on death of the holder and is not inheritable. It cannot be assigned, sold, transferred, conveyed, or pledged. An advanced degree is a cumulative product of many years of previous education, combined with diligence and hard work. It may not be acquired by the mere expenditure of money. It is simply an intellectual achievement that may potentially assist in the future acquisition of property. In our view, it has none of the attributes of property in the usual sense of that term.

A professional license or degree is a personal achievement of the holder. It cannot be sold and its value cannot readily be determined. A professional license or degree represents the opportunity to obtain an amount of money only upon the occurrence of highly uncertain future events. By contrast, the vested but unmatured pension at issue in *Kikkert, supra,* entitled the owner to a definite amount of money at a certain future date.

The value of a professional degree for purposes of property distribution is nothing more than the possibility of enhanced earnings that the particular academic credential will provide. In *Stern v. Stern*, 66 *N.J.* 340, 345, 331 *A.*2d 257 (1975), we held that a lawyer's

> "earning capacity, even where its development has been aided and enhanced by the other spouse . . . should not be recognized as a separate, particular item of property within the meaning of *N.J.S.A.* 2A:34-23. Potential earning capacity . . . should not be deemed property as such within the meaning of the statute."

Equitable distribution of a professional degree would similarly require distribution of "earning capacity"—income that the degree holder might never acquire. The amount of future earnings would be entirely speculative. Moreover, any assets resulting from income for professional services would be property acquired *after* the marriage; the statute restricts equitable distribution to property acquired *during* the marriage.

Valuing a professional degree in the hands of any particular individual at the start of his or her career would involve a gamut of calculations that reduces to little more than guesswork. As the Appellate Division noted, courts would be required to determine far more than what the degree holder could earn in the new career. The admittedly speculative dollar amount of

> earnings in the "enhanced" career [must] be reduced by the . . . income the spouse should be assumed to have been able to earn if otherwise employed. In our view . . . [this] is ordinarily nothing but speculation, particularly when it is fair to assume that a person with the ability and motivation to complete professional training

or higher education would probably utilize those attributes in concomitantly productive alternative endeavors.

Even if such estimates could be made, however, there would remain a world of unforeseen events that could affect the earning potential—not to mention the actual earnings—of any particular degree holder.

A person qualified by education for a given profession may choose not to practice it, may fail at it, or may practice in a specialty, location or manner which generates less than the average income enjoyed by fellow professionals. The potential worth of the education may never be realized for these or many other reasons. An award based upon the prediction of the degree holder's success at the chosen field may bear no relationship to the reality he or she faces after the divorce.

Moreover, the likelihood that an equitable distribution will prove to be unfair is increased in those cases where the court miscalculates the value of the license or degree.

The potential for inequity to the failed professional or one who changes careers is at once apparent; his or her spouse will have been awarded a share of something which never existed in any real sense.

The finality of property distribution precludes any remedy for such unfairness. "Unlike an award of alimony, which can be adjusted after divorce to reflect unanticipated changes in the parties' circumstances, a property division may not [be adjusted]."

Because of these problems, most courts that have faced the issue have declined to treat professional degrees and licenses as marital property subject to distribution upon divorce. Several courts, while not treating educational degrees as property, have awarded the supporting spouse an amount based on the cost to the supporting spouse of obtaining the degree. In effect, the supporting spouse was reimbursed for her financial contributions used by the supported spouse in obtaining a degree.

Even if it were marital property, valuing educational assets in terms of their cost would be an erroneous application of equitable distribution law. As the Appellate Division explained, the cost of a professional degree "has little to do with any real value of the degree and fails to consider at all the nonfinancial efforts made by the degree holder in completing his course of study." 182 *N.J. Super.* at 610, 442 *A.2d* 1062. *See also DeWitt, supra,* 296 *N.W.2d* at 767. Once a degree candidate has earned his or her degree, the amount that a spouse—or anyone else—paid towards its attainment has no bearing whatever on its value. The cost of a spouse's financial contributions has no logical connection to the value of that degree.

As the Appellate Division correctly noted, "the cost approach [to equitable distribution] is plainly not conceptually predicated on a property theory at all but rather represents a general notion of how to do equity in this one special situation." 182 *N.J. Super.* at 610, 442 *A.2d* 1062. Equitable distribution in these cases derives from the proposition that the supporting spouse should be reimbursed for contributions to the marital unit that, because of the divorce, did not bear its expected fruit for the supporting spouse.

The trial court recognized that the theoretical basis for the amount of its award was not equitable distribution, but rather reimbursement. It held that "the education and degree obtained by plaintiff, under the circumstances of this case, constitute a property right *subject to equitable offset* upon the dissolution of the marriage." 175 *N.J. Super.* at 447, 419 A.2d 1149 (emphasis added). The court allowed a "reasonable sum as a credit . . . on behalf of the maintenance of the household and the support of the plaintiff during the educational period." *Id.* Although the court found that the degree was distributable property, it actually reimbursed the defendant without attempting to give her part of the *value* of the degree.

This Court does not support reimbursement between former spouses in alimony proceedings as a general principle. Marriage is not a business arrangement in which the parties keep track of debits and credits, their accounts to be settled upon divorce. Rather, as we have said, "marriage is a shared enterprise, a joint undertaking . . . in many ways it is akin to a partnership." *Rothman v. Rothman*, 65 *N.J.* 219, 229, 320 A.2d 496 (1974). But every joint undertaking has its bounds of fairness. Where a partner to marriage takes the benefits of his spouse's support in obtaining a professional degree or license with the understanding that future benefits will accrue and inure to both of them, and the marriage is then terminated without the supported spouse giving anything in return, an unfairness has occurred that calls for a remedy.

In this case, the supporting spouse made financial contributions towards her husband's professional education with the expectation that both parties would enjoy material benefits flowing from the professional license or degree. It is therefore patently unfair that the supporting spouse be denied the mutually anticipated benefit while the supported spouse keeps not only the degree, but also all of the financial and material rewards flowing from it.

Furthermore, it is realistic to recognize that in this case, a supporting spouse has contributed more than mere earnings to her husband with the mutual expectation that both of them—she as well as he—will realize and enjoy material improvements in their marriage as a result of his increased earning capacity. Also, the wife has presumably made personal financial sacrifices, resulting in a reduced or lowered standard of living. Additionally, her husband, by pursuing preparations for a future career, has foregone gainful employment and financial contributions to the marriage that would have been forthcoming had he been employed. He thereby has further reduced the level of support his wife might otherwise have received, as well as the standard of living both of them would have otherwise enjoyed. In effect, through her contributions, the supporting spouse has consented to live at a lower material level while her husband has prepared for another career. She has postponed, as it were, present consumption and a higher standard of living, for the future prospect of greater support and material benefits. The supporting spouse's sacrifices would have been rewarded had the marriage endured and the mutual expectations of both of them been fulfilled. The unredressed sacrifices—loss of support and reduction of the standard of living—coupled with the unfairness attendant upon the defeat of the supporting spouse's shared expectation of future advantages, further justify a remedial reward. In this sense, an award that is referable to the spouse's monetary contributions to her partner's education significantly implicates basic considerations of marital support and standard of living—factors that are clearly relevant in the determination and award of conventional alimony. . . .

III

We stated in *Stern, supra,* that while earning potential should not be treated as a separate item of property,

> [p]otential earning capacity is doubtless a factor to be considered by a trial judge in determining what distribution will be "equitable" and it is even more obviously relevant upon the issue of alimony. [66 *N.J.* at 345, 331 *A.*2d 257]

We believe that *Stern* presents the best approach for achieving fairness when one spouse has acquired a professional degree or license during the marriage. Courts may not make any permanent distribution of the value of professional degrees and licenses, whether based upon estimated worth or cost. However, where a spouse has received from his or her partner financial contributions used in obtaining a professional degree or license with the expectation of deriving material benefits for both marriage partners, that spouse may be called upon to reimburse the supporting spouse for the amount of contributions received.

In the present case, the defendant's financial support helped her husband to obtain his M.B.A. degree, which assistance was undertaken with the expectation of deriving material benefits for both spouses. Although the trial court awarded the defendant a sum as "equitable offset" for her contributions, the trial court's approach was not consistent with the guidelines we have announced in this opinion. Therefore, we are remanding the case so the trial court can determine whether reimbursement alimony should be awarded in this case and, if so, what amount is appropriate.

The judgment of the Appellate Division is reversed and the cause remanded for further proceedings not inconsistent with this opinion.

NOTES

1. *Minority View.* Although New Jersey is in the majority, a few states recognize graduate degrees as property that is divisible upon divorce. For example, in *O'Brien v. O'Brien*, 489 N.E.2d 712 (1985), New York concluded that the husband's medical license constituted marital property under the New York Domestic Relations Law §236 (McKinney 1986). This rule has been reaffirmed repeatedly in New York. *See, e.g., Holterman v. Holterman*, 814 N.E.2d 765 (N.Y. 2004) (refusing to reduce child support payments because of equitable distribution payments made of the value of the husband's medical degree).

2. *Understanding the Court's Reasoning.* Review the court's reasoning in *Mahoney v. Mahoney* for concluding that a degree is not marital property. What reasoning do you think the courts recognizing graduate degrees as property employ?

3. *Goodwill.* Although enhanced earnings from a professional degree may not always be treated as a marital asset subject to equitable distribution, professional goodwill is often classified as a divisible marital asset. This issue also arises in celebrity divorce cases. In *Piscopo v. Piscopo*, 557 A.2d 1040 (NJ 2007), the court concluded that Joe Piscopo's celebrity goodwill was a marital asset and agreed with the lower court's valuation of it at $158,863. An accountant arrived at that value by "calculat[ing] plaintiff's celebrity goodwill by taking 25% of his average gross earnings over the three year period." *Id.* at 1041. The court declined to base the amount on possible future earnings, instead of probable future earnings. *Id.* at 1040. If New Jersey refuses to consider a professional degree a marital asset, why do you think the court recognized celebrity goodwill as an asset?

4. *Prenuptial Agreements.* Many issues involving the division of property at divorce can be somewhat avoided by prenuptial agreements. A prenuptial agreement is a written contract created by two people before they are married that (1) lists all of the property and debts each person owns and (2) specifies what each person's property rights will be after the marriage. Prenuptial agreements are generally enforceable, although courts will sometimes refuse to enforce certain types of provisions on policy grounds.

PROBLEMS

Explanatory answers to these problems can be found on page 1044.
1. Would Jillian's law degree be considered marital property in New Jersey?
2. Would Jillian's law degree be considered marital property in New York?

iii. When One Spouse Dies

Marital property rights are protected upon one spouse's death in separate property states by *elective share statutes.* Elective share statutes give the surviving spouse the right to claim a significant share of the decent spouse's estate regardless of the provisions of the decedent spouse's will. If, for example, the decedent spouse had completely written the surviving spouse out of the will, the surviving spouse can elect to disclaim the will and take the statutory share of the decedent spouse's estate. A surviving spouse thus usually has a choice to either take what was left to the surviving spouse in the decedent spouses' will or take an elective share of the decedent's estate. The elective share in most statutes is usually one-third or one-half of the decedent's estate. The decedent spouse typically cannot avoid the elective share by giving away property before death—most states will apply the elective share to gifts made before death if they were made intentionally to avoid the elective share. On the other hand, the elective share statutes typically apply only to interests that will pass through the decedent's estate. As a result, elective share statutes typically do not reach life insurance payments if the life insurance policy names a beneficiary other than the surviving spouse.

If the decedent spouse dies without a will, the surviving spouse's share is distributed according to the state's intestacy laws. Intestacy laws typically leave the entire estate to the surviving spouse or leave it to the surviving spouse and their children.

The pendency of a divorce action typically does not affect the surviving spouse's rights to inherit from the decedent spouse's estate. The spouses are legally married and continue to have the legal rights of marriage until the divorce is final.

c. The Community Property System

Nine states have statutorily created community property systems: Arizona, California, Idaho, Louisiana, Nevada, New Mexico, Texas, Washington, and Wisconsin.[3] There are vast differences among the community property states. This said, the community property system at its core treats earnings of each spouse during marriage as being owned equally in undivided shares by both spouses. Because the community property system views each spouse as contributing equally to the marriage, each spouse owns an equal share of property acquired during marriage. Property owned before marriage and property acquired during marriage by inheritance or by gift is treated as separate property.

Under the community property systems of most states, debt occurring before marriage is generally treated as separate debt. Debt incurred by one spouse before marriage cannot be satisfied by the other spouse's separate property. Community property, however, can be used to satisfy the debt to the extent the community property can be attributable to the earning efforts of the debtor.

i. During Marriage

Consider the following statutory provision defining separate property and community property in California (§770 & §760) and Texas (§3.001 & §3.002).

West's Ann. Cal. Fam. Code §770 (West 2014)

§770. Separate property of married person

(a) Separate property of a married person includes all of the following:

(1) All property owned by the person before marriage.

(2) All property acquired by the person after marriage by gift, bequest, devise, or descent.

(3) The rents, issues, and profits of the property described in this section.

(b) A married person may, without the consent of the person's spouse, convey the person's separate property.

---

[3] Ariz. Rev. Stat. §§25-211 to 25-217; Cal. Fam. Code §§750 to 1620; Idaho Code §§32-903 to 32-912; La. Civ. Code §§2325 to 2437; Nev. Rev. Stat. §§123.010 to 123.310; N.M. Stat. §§40-3-6 to 40-3-13; Tex. Fam. Code §§3.001 to 3.006; Wash. Rev. Code §§26.16.010 to 26.16.140; Wis. Stat. §§766.001 to 766.31.

V.T.C.A., Family Code §3.001 (West 2014)

§3.001. Separate Property

A spouse's separate property consists of:
(1) the property owned or claimed by the spouse before marriage;
(2) the property acquired by the spouse during marriage by gift, devise, or descent; and
(3) the recovery for personal injuries sustained by the spouse during marriage, except any recovery for loss of earning capacity during marriage.

West's Ann. Cal. Fam. Code §760 (West 2014)

§760. "Community property" defined

Except as otherwise provided by statute, all property, real or personal, wherever situated, acquired by a married person during the marriage while domiciled in this state is community property.

V.T.C.A. Family Code §3.002 (West 2014)

Community Property

Community property consists of the property, other than separate property, acquired by either spouse during marriage.

NOTES AND QUESTIONS

1. *Defining Community Property.* Similar to Texas, most statutes will define community property to include all earnings during marriage and the rents, profits, and fruits of those earnings. If James and Jillian lived in a community property state such as Texas, and James earned $2,000 on a major plumbing job, Jillian would have a community property right in one-half. If James were to take that $2,000 and purchase stock in his name only, one-half of that stock would belong to Jillian.

2. *Comparing Statutory Language.* Compare the California and Texas definitions of separate property. What commonalities do you see between the two statutes? What differences do you see between the two statutes? How would "[t]he rents, issues, and profits of the property" described in West's Ann. Cal. Fam. Code §770 be treated in California? In Texas? Why would the Texas legislature explicitly include "the recovery for personal injuries sustained by the spouse during marriage, except any recovery for loss of earning capacity during marriage" while not explicitly including other property?

3. *Out-of-State Real Property.* Under California Fam. Code §760, the definition of community property includes the language "wherever situated." This language suggests that all out-of-state real property will be treated as community property in California. Why would the California legislature explicitly include this property while Texas

§3.002 does not? Would the Texas statute require out-of-state property acquired by a married person during the marriage to be treated as community property? Compare the commonalities and distinctions of both community property definitions.

4. *Debt.* The treatment of one spouse's debt varies considerably between the community property states. Most community property states agree that the separate property of the other spouse cannot be reached to satisfy that debt. *See* Cal. Fam. Code §913 (West 1994); La. Civ. Code art. 2345 (West 1980); Ariz. Rev. Stat. §25-215A (West 1973). California, however, allows community property to be used to satisfy the debt of one spouse. *See* Cal. Fam. Code §910 (West 1994). Why would California allow the community property to be used to satisfy the debt of one spouse but not allow the individual separate property of the non-debtor spouse to be used to satisfy the debt?

PROBLEMS

Explanatory answers to these problems can be found on page 1044.

1. Suppose Jillian was injured and unable to work. If James earns $100,000 a year as a master plumber and they live in a community property state, who owns James's earnings?

2. Suppose Jillian and James live in Texas, and Jillian was injured and unable to work while James earned $100,000 a year as a master plumber. If James wants to surprise Jillian with the purchase of a modest lake home in Texas that he has titled in his name only, who would own the lake home?

3. Suppose Jillian and James are married and live in California. Jillian's uncle passes away and leaves her $50,000 while she is married to James. Who owns the $50,000?

4. Suppose Jillian and James live in Arizona. Before James incurs the $75,000 gambling debt, Jillian inherits $50,000 from her uncle. Could James' creditors reach Jillian's $50,000 inheritance to partially satisfy James debt? In California, could their jointly owned bank account be used to satisfy the debt?

SEPARATE PROPERTY VS. COMMUNITY PROPERTY

Determining when separate property becomes marital property is an important concept to grasp as a practicing attorney and as a student. Sometimes the best way to attack these types of questions is to set up a checklist of questions to be answered. For example, on an exam asking you a question involving when separate property became marital property, your initial two questions would be: (1) Was the property acquired before marriage? (2) If it was acquired before marriage, was the title to the property changed to include the spouse? What questions would follow? These questions can set up a checklist of all of the points you would cover with your client or on the exam.

The following illustrates how most states treat the management and control of community property during marriage.

Arizona Revised Statutes §25-214 (West 2014)

Management and Control

A. Each spouse has the sole management, control and disposition rights of each spouse's separate property.

B. The spouses have equal management, control and disposition rights over their community property and have equal power to bind the community.

C. Either spouse separately may acquire, manage, control or dispose of community property or bind the community, except that joinder of both spouses is required in any of the following cases:

1. Any transaction for the acquisition, disposition or encumbrance of an interest in real property other than an unpatented mining claim or a lease of less than one year.

2. Any transaction of guaranty, indemnity or suretyship.

3. To bind the community, irrespective of any person's intent with respect to that binder, after service of a petition for dissolution of marriage, legal separation or annulment if the petition results in a decree of dissolution of marriage, legal separation or annulment.

NOTES

1. *Equality.* Arizona, as most community property states, grants spouses equal rights to manage and control community property. Prior to the 1960s, most community property states named the husband as the manager of the property. In the late 1960s, the eight then-existing community property states[4] enacted statutes giving both spouses equal management roles. Under the Arizona statute, when can a spouse manage the community property by acting alone? When must both parties act together in the management of the community property?

2. *Fiduciary Obligations.* The manager of the community property acts as a fiduciary because the community property must be managed for the benefit of the community—presumably the spouses. This fiduciary role brings with it the duty to act in good faith when managing the property.

---

[4] Wisconsin did not become a community property state until the 1990s when it patterned its law on the Uniform Marital Property Act.

ii. When Spouses Divorce

Some community states also differ from separate property states on what happens with the community property upon divorce. In some states, the community property is divided equally on divorce. In other states, principles of equitable distribution similar to those used in separate property states are used.

West's Ann. Cal. Fam. Code §2550 (West 1994)

Manner of Division of Community Estate

Except upon the written agreement of the parties, or on oral stipulation of the parties in open court, or as otherwise provided in this division, in a proceeding for dissolution of marriage or for legal separation of the parties, the court shall, either in its judgment of dissolution of the marriage, in its judgment of legal separation of the parties, or at a later time if it expressly reserves jurisdiction to make such a property division, divide the community estate of the parties equally.

V.T.C.A. Family Code §7.001 (West 1997)

General Rule of Property Division

In a decree of divorce or annulment, the court shall order a division of the estate of the parties in a manner that the court deems just and right, having due regard for the rights of each party and any children of the marriage.

NOTE AND QUESTIONS

1. *Equitable Distribution in Community Property States.* When studying the separate property system you learned that separate property states use equitable distribution principles to divide marital property at divorce and that judges will consider a variety of factors in dividing the marital property. What factors do you believe a Texas court would consider according to §7.001? Do you believe the court would start with the presumption that an equitable division would be to give each spouse their separate property and one-half of the community property? Why or why not?

iii. When One Spouse Dies

In community property states, each spouse owns one-half of the community property. Therefore, each spouse may dispose of the separate property of that spouse and one-half of the community property by will. The spouse cannot dispose of the other half of the community property by will because it belongs to the surviving spouse. Because the surviving spouse already owns one-half of the community property, elective share statutes generally do not exist in community property states. If a spouse dies intestate, community property states either give the decedent's community property share to the surviving spouse or split the decedent's community property share between the surviving spouse and surviving children.

PROBLEM

An explanatory answer to this problem can be found on page 1044.

If James and Jillian own community property worth $1 million, and James leaves a will leaving $500,000 to his favorite charity, will Jillian be able to successfully contest James's will?

d. Migrating Couples

As you have just learned, marital property law can vary in significant ways between jurisdictions. The characterization of an asset for marital property purposes typically is governed by the law of the jurisdiction where the spouses were domiciled when the asset was first acquired. For example, if James and Jillian live in New Jersey and Jillian earns a $50,000 bonus and purchases a race car with it, New Jersey law would govern, and the race car would be separate property belonging to her alone. If she was living in Texas at the time of the purchase, the race car would be community property and would belong to both James and Jillian. The ownership of the property will not change even if James and Jillian move from New Jersey to Texas or vice versa. Once the property has been characterized as either separate property or community property, it will keep that characterization if the spouses move to another jurisdiction with different rules.

When a spouse dies, the law of that decedent's domicile at death governs disposition of personal property. The law where land is located will govern the disposition of land, regardless of the domicile of the decedent. These rules can sometimes lead to difficulties for migrating spouses. What would happen, for example, if a couple with a working spouse and a stay-at-home spouse migrated from a separate property state to a community property state and the working spouse died intestate while they were living in the community property state? Remember, most community property states do not provide for a forced share in the decedent's property. Would the nonworking spouse receive a larger estate in the separate property state or the community property state?

Quasi-community property laws have been adopted by some community property states to help alleviate this potential problem. Quasi-community property laws treat separate property earned in a separate property state as community property if the property would have been defined as community property had it been earned in the community property state where the death occurred.[5]

West's Ann. Cal. Prob. Code §66 (West 1991)

Quasi-Community Property

"Quasi-community property" means the following property, other than community property as defined in Section 28:

---

[5] Some states allow for quasi-community property classifications for divorce proceedings as well. Cal. Fam. Code. §912 (West 1994).

(a) All personal property wherever situated, and all real property situated in this state, heretofore or hereafter acquired by a decedent while domiciled elsewhere that would have been the community property of the decedent and the surviving spouse if the decedent had been domiciled in this state at the time of its acquisition.

(b) All personal property wherever situated, and all real property situated in this state, heretofore or hereafter acquired in exchange for real or personal property, wherever situated, that would have been the community property of the decedent and the surviving spouse if the decedent had been domiciled in this state at the time the property so exchanged was acquired.

PROBLEM

James and Jillian lived in New Jersey for 20 years where James accumulated personal property from his earnings worth $250,000. They moved to California where James suffered a major heart attack and died intestate. How would a court determine what was James' personal property, what was community property, and what was quasi-community property? An explanatory answer can be found on page 1045.

e. Unmarried Couples

Many unmarried couples live together in long-term relationships. Complicated legal issues can arise as the couple's financial and personal lives intertwine. As we have seen, our legal system has a host of rules that govern the property relationships of married couples. These rules are absent for unmarried couples.

Historically, many cases involving unmarried couples involved same-sex couples who were not permitted to marry. If you read *Harms v. Sprague* carefully, you will see that it likely involved a same-sex couple. Without access to the legal regime of marriage, same-sex couples often had to resort to imperfect legal solutions to govern their relationships.

As we are completing this book, the United States is undergoing a rapid shift in the law on same-sex marriage. A majority of states now permit same-sex couples to marry. We appear to be heading in a direction where, as Judge John Jones wrote, "[i]n future generations the label same-sex marriage will be abandoned, to be replaced simply by marriage." *Whitewood v. Wolf*, 992 F. Supp. 2d 410 (2014) (recognizing same-sex marriages in Pennsylvania).

Even as our marriage laws change, millions of unmarried same-sex and opposite-sex couples will continue to share their lives together. These couples may choose to enter into a legal agreement governing their relationship. In our next case, the court considers the enforcement of a long-term domestic partnership agreement.

POSIK V. LAYTON

District Court of Appeals of Florida, 1997
695 So. 2d 759

Harris, Judge.

Emma Posik and Nancy L.R. Layton were close friends and more. They entered into a support agreement much like a prenuptial agreement. The trial court found that the agreement was unenforceable because of waiver. We reverse.

Nancy Layton was a doctor practicing at the Halifax Hospital in Volusia County and Emma Posik was a nurse working at the same facility when Dr. Layton decided to remove her practice to Brevard County. In order to induce Ms. Posik to give up her job and sell her home in Volusia County, to accompany her to Brevard County, and to reside with her "for the remainder of Emma Posik's life to maintain and care for the home," Dr. Layton agreed that she would provide essentially all of the support for the two, would make a will leaving her entire estate to Ms. Posik, and would "maintain bank accounts and other investments which constitute non-probatable assets in Emma Posik's name to the extent of 100% of her entire non-probatable assets." Also, as part of the agreement, Ms. Posik agreed to loan Dr. Layton $20,000 which was evidenced by a note. The agreement provided that Ms. Posik could cease residing with Dr. Layton if Layton failed to provide adequate support, if she requested in writing that Ms. Posik leave for any reason, if she brought a third person into the home for a period greater than four weeks without Ms. Posik's consent, or if her abuse, harassment or abnormal behavior made Ms. Posik's continued residence intolerable. In any such event, Dr. Layton agreed to pay as liquidated damages the sum of $2,500 per month for the remainder of Ms. Posik's life.

It is apparent that Ms. Posik required this agreement as a condition of accompanying Dr. Layton to Brevard. The agreement was drawn by a lawyer and properly witnessed. Ms. Posik, fifty-five years old at the time of the agreement, testified that she required the agreement because she feared that Dr. Layton might become interested in a younger companion. Her fears were well founded. Some four years after the parties moved to Brevard County and without Ms. Posik's consent, Dr. Layton announced that she wished to move another woman into the house. When Ms. Posik expressed strong displeasure with this idea, Dr. Layton moved out and took up residence with the other woman.

Dr. Layton served a three-day eviction notice on Ms. Posik. Ms. Posik later moved from the home and sued to enforce the terms of the agreement and to collect on the note evidencing the loan made in conjunction with the agreement. Dr. Layton defended on the basis that Ms. Posik first breached the agreement. Dr. Layton counterclaimed for a declaratory judgment as to whether the liquidated damages portion of the agreement was enforceable.

The trial judge found that because Ms. Posik's economic losses were reasonably ascertainable as to her employment and relocation costs, the $2,500 a month payment upon breach amounted to a penalty and was therefore unenforceable. The court further found that although Dr. Layton had materially breached the contract within a year or so of its creation, Ms. Posik waived the breach by acquiescence. Finally, the court found that Ms. Posik breached the agreement by refusing to continue to perform the house work, yard work and cooking for the parties and by her hostile attitude which required Dr. Layton to move from the house. Although the trial court determined that Ms. Posik was entitled to quantum meruit, it also determined that those damages were off-set by the benefits Ms. Posik received by being permitted to live with Dr. Layton. The court did award Ms. Posik a judgment on the note executed by Dr. Layton.

Although neither party urged that this agreement was void as against public policy, Dr. Layton's counsel on more than one occasion reminded us that the parties had a sexual relationship. Certainly, even though the agreement was couched in terms of a personal services contract, it was intended to be much more. It was a nuptial agreement entered into by two parties that the state prohibits from marrying. But even though the state has prohibited same-sex marriages and same-sex adoptions, it has not prohibited this type of agreement. By prohibiting same-sex marriages, the state has merely denied homosexuals the rights granted to married partners that flow naturally from the marital relationship. In short, "the law of Florida creates no legal rights or duties between live-ins." *Lowry v. Lowry,* 512 So.2d 1142 (Fla. 5th DCA 1987). (Sharp, J., concurring specially). This lack of recognition of the rights which flow naturally from the break-up of a marital relationship applies to unmarried heterosexuals as well as homosexuals. But the State has not denied these individuals their right to either will their property as they see fit nor to privately commit by contract to spend their money as they choose. The State is not thusly condoning the lifestyles of homosexuals or unmarried live-ins; it is merely recognizing their constitutional private property and contract rights.

Even though no legal rights or obligations flow as a matter of law from a non-marital relationship, we see no impediment to the parties to such a relationship agreeing between themselves to provide certain rights and obligations. Other states have approved such individual agreements. In *Marvin v. Marvin,* 18 Cal.3d 660, 134 Cal. Rptr. 815, 557 P.2d 106 (1976), the California Supreme Court held:

> [W]e base our opinion on the principle that adults who voluntarily live together and engage in sexual relations are nonetheless as competent as any other persons to contract respecting their earnings and property rights. . . . So long as the agreement does not rest upon illicit meretricious consideration, the parties may order their economic affairs as they choose. . . .

In *Whorton v. Dillingham,* 202 Cal.App.3d 447, 248 Cal.Rptr. 405 (1988), the California Fourth District Court of Appeal extended this principle to same-sex partners. We also see no reason for a distinction. . . .

In a case involving unmarried heterosexuals, a Florida appellate court has passed on the legality of a non-marital support agreement. In *Crossen v. Feldman,* 673 So.2d 903 (Fla. 2d DCA 1996), the court held:

> Without attempting to define what may or may not be "palimony," this case simply involves whether these parties entered into a contract for support, which is something that they are legally capable of doing.

Addressing the invited issue, we find that an agreement for support between unmarried adults is valid unless the agreement is inseparably based upon illicit consideration of sexual services. Certainly prostitution, heterosexual or homosexual, cannot be condoned merely because it is performed within the confines of a written agreement. The parties, represented by counsel, were well aware of this prohibition and took pains to assure that sexual services were not even mentioned in the agreement. That factor would not be decisive, however, if it could be determined from the contract or from the conduct of the parties that the primary reason for the agreement was to deliver and be paid for sexual services. *See Bergen v. Wood,* 14 Cal.App.4th 854, 18 Cal.Rptr.2d 75 (1993). This contract and the parties' testimony show that such was not the case here. Because of the potential abuse in marital-type relationships, we find that such agreements must be in writing. The Statute of Frauds (section 725.01, Florida Statutes) requires that contracts made upon consideration of marriage must be in writing. This same requirement should apply to non-marital, nuptial-like agreements. In this case, there is (and can be) no dispute that the agreement exists.

The obligations imposed on Ms. Posik by the agreement include the obligation "to immediately commence residing with Nancy L.R. Layton at her said residence for the remainder of Emma Posik's life . . . ." This is very similar to a "until death do us part" commitment. And although the parties undoubtedly expected a sexual relationship, this record shows that they contemplated much more. They contracted for a permanent sharing of, and participating in, one another's lives. We find the contract enforceable.

We disagree with the trial court that waiver was proved in this case. Ms. Posik consistently urged Dr. Layton to make the will as required by the agreement and her failure to do so was sufficient grounds to declare default. And even more important to Ms. Posik was the implied agreement that her lifetime commitment would be reciprocated by a lifetime commitment by Dr. Layton—and that this mutual commitment would be monogamous. When Dr. Layton introduced a third person into the relationship, although it was not an express breach of the written agreement, it explains why Ms. Posik took that opportunity to hold Dr. Layton to her express obligations and to consider the agreement in default.

We also disagree with the trial court that Ms. Posik breached the agreement by refusing to perform housework, yard work, provisioning the house, and cooking for the parties. This conduct did not occur until after Dr. Layton had first breached the agreement. One need not continue to perform a contract when the other party has first breached. *City of Miami Beach v. Carner,* 579 So.2d 248 (Fla. 3d DCA 1991). Therefore, this conduct did not authorize Dr. Layton to send the three-day notice of eviction which constituted a separate default under the agreement.

We also disagree that the commitment to pay $2,500 per month upon termination of the agreement is unenforceable as a penalty. We agree with Ms. Posik that her damages, which would include more than mere lost wages and moving expenses, were not readily ascertainable at the time the contract was created. Further, the agreed sum is reasonable under the circumstances of this case. It is less than Ms. Posik was earning some four years earlier when she entered into this arrangement. It is also less than Ms. Posik would have received had the long-term provisions of the contract been performed. She is now in her sixties and her working opportunities are greatly reduced.

We recognize that this contract, insisted on by Ms. Posik before she would relocate with Dr. Layton, is extremely favorable to her. But there is no allegation of fraud or overreaching on Ms. Posik's part. This court faced an extremely generous agreement in *Carnell v. Carnell,* 398 So.2d 503 (Fla. 5th DCA 1981). In *Carnell,* a lawyer, in order to induce a woman to become his wife, agreed that upon divorce the wife would receive his home owned by him prior to marriage, one-half of his disposable income and one-half of his retirement as alimony until she remarried. Two years after the marriage, she tested his commitment. We held:

> The husband also contends that the agreement is so unfair and unreasonable that it must be set aside . . . "The freedom to contract includes the right to make a bad bargain." (Citation omitted). The controlling question here is whether there was *overreaching* and not whether the bargain was good or bad.

Contracts can be dangerous to one's well-being. That is why they are kept away from children. Perhaps warning labels should be attached. In any event, contracts should be taken seriously. Dr. Layton's comment that she considered the agreement a sham and never intended to be bound by it shows that she did not take it seriously. That is regrettable.

We affirm that portion of the judgment below which addresses the promissory note and attorney's fees and costs associated therewith. We reverse that portion of the judgment that fails to enforce the parties' agreement.

NOTE AND QUESTIONS

1. *Palimony.* The court referenced *Marvin v. Marvin,* a landmark California decision involving the actor Lee Marvin. In *Marvin,* the court held that a domestic partner could enforce property rights even without a written agreement. *See Marvin v. Marvin,* 557 P.2d 106 (Cal. 1976). Palimony, a play on the term "alimony," is compensation that is made to one member of an unmarried couple after the couple separates. Although the court in *Marvin* awarded palimony absent a written agreement, many courts hold

that an express contract is needed between the unmarried couple. Other courts refuse to recognize claims for palimony because agreements involving sexual relationships outside of marriage go against public policy. Do you agree? *See Potter v. Davie*, 713 N.Y.S.2d 627 (App. Div. 2000) ("an express oral agreement may create a 'domestic partnership' between unmarried cohabiting persons, provided that the agreement is not based or dependent upon illicit sexual relations for its consideration and does not have an unlawful or immoral objective."); *Kastil v. Carro*, 536 N.Y.S.2d 63 (App. Div. 1988) (refusing to enforce an alleged oral agreement between a lawyer and the law firm's bookkeeper to pay for past services, both sexual and otherwise.). Would you advise an unmarried couple to enter into a written cohabitation agreement? Would it make a difference whether you were advising a same-sex or opposite-sex couple?

CHAPTER 4

LEASING REAL PROPERTY— LANDLORD AND TENANT LAW

In this chapter, you will learn about property and contract principles governing the shared ownership of land that occurs when a landlord leases real property to a tenant. You will learn about landlord-tenant law by first becoming familiar with the new vocabulary and developing a context for the substantive law. You will then learn substantive landlord-tenant law by following a leasehold through its creation to its end. Specifically, you will learn about:

- Creating a leasehold
- Types of leaseholds
- Negotiating and entering a leasehold
- Tenant's rights and remedies in a leasehold
- Landlord's rights and the tenant's duties in a leasehold
- Transferring a leasehold
- Ending a leasehold

In Chapter 2, we briefly discussed the three types of leasehold estates—the term of years, the periodic tenancy, and the tenancy at will. We will discuss these types of leaseholds in more depth in our next section. For now, we want to reinforce the fact that *a lease is a conveyance of an interest in real property.* When a landlord leases real property to a tenant, the landlord is conveying a present interest in real property to the tenant. The landlord retains a reversion that becomes possessory when the leasehold interest expires.

A lease is also a contract. Part of a lease contains a conveyance of a property interest. The rest of the lease contains contractual terms that govern a host of issues in the landlord-tenant relationship. If you have ever rented an apartment, this contractual aspect of a lease should be familiar. In a lease, the landlord and tenant each make binding contractual promises to each other.

The term *landlord* comes from feudal England, where peasants worked land that belonged to their lord, and used the word "land 'lord'" to refer to the lessor.

The *hybrid property-contract nature of a lease* lies at the heart of an overarching theme of this chapter. Historically, the property aspect of the lease dominated. The

PROPERTY VS. CONTRACT

tenant was treated as the present owner of the property, with all the rights and responsibilities of ownership. The landlord-tenant relationship was seen as a relationship between future- and present-interest holders. Beginning in the 1960s and 1970s, the contractual aspect of the lease began to dominate. The landlord-tenant relationship came to be seen as a consumer transaction. In case after case, courts began to use tenant-friendly contract principles to reach results that were different from those reached under more landlord-friendly property principles. This shift toward contract principles, however, was not universal, and some jurisdictions still apply more traditional property-based principles for certain issues. Even in jurisdictions that take a strongly contractual view of the lease, the property aspect of the lease remains relevant in certain contexts. We will see many examples of the tension between property and contract principles throughout this chapter.

Another theme that we will see is that residential leases are often treated differently than commercial leases. Residential tenants have comparatively little

RESIDENTIAL VS. COMMERCIAL

bargaining power compared to commercial tenants. Courts and legislatures therefore are more willing to step in to protect residential tenants than they are commercial tenants.

A. CREATING A LEASEHOLD

In this section, we will examine the beginning of the landlord-tenant relationship. We will begin with a more in-depth examination of the three types of leasehold estates. We will then consider issues related to negotiation of the lease and key lease terms. We then examine the landlord's obligation to deliver possession to the tenant. We conclude the section with the Fair Housing Act and other anti-discrimination laws that apply to the landlord-tenant relationship.

1. TYPES OF LEASEHOLD ESTATES

As we discussed in Chapter 2, there are three types of leasehold estates: the term of year, the periodic tenancy, and the tenancy at will. We will discuss each in turn.

A rose by any other name . . . These terms are often used interchangeably:

- A *leasehold* can be called a *tenancy* or a *landlord-tenant estate.*
- A *landlord* can be called a *lessor.* In everyday language, the landlord is often referred to as the *owner* of the property. In property law language, we need to be more precise—during the duration of the lease, the landlord has a reversion. Typically, this reversion is in fee simple absolute, and it is fine to call the landlord the *fee simple owner.*
- A *tenant* can be called a *lessee* or the owner of the leasehold.

a. The Term of Years

The term of years is a leasehold that has a duration measured by a fixed period of time. A lease satisfies this requirement if the duration can be reduced to fixed calendar dates. The most common type of term of years lease is a one-year residential lease. The actual duration of term of years leases, however, can vary widely. Have you ever rented a beach house or mountain cabin for a week? Chances are you entered a term of years tenancy, even though it was just for a week. Commercial leases often last for 20 years. Leases of land for much longer periods of time are not unheard of. Consider *Monbar, Inc. v. Monaghan*, 18 Del. Ch. 395, 162 A. 50 Del. Ch. (1932) where, when considering a term of years leasehold estate, the court reasoned "[t]here being no statute in this state to the contrary, the law permitted the lease notwithstanding its length of two thousand years." Today, some states do limit the length of leasehold estates. *See* Alabama Code 1975 §35-4-6 (2013) (limiting leasehold estates to 99 years).

A term of years leasehold expires when the period establishing the leasehold ends. Unless the parties have agreed to the contrary, the tenant must vacate the premises and surrender possession to the landlord at the end of the lease term. The death of the landlord or the tenant does not affect a term of years leasehold unless the parties agree otherwise. If, for example, the tenant dies, the tenant's estate typically will continue to be responsible for the obligations under the lease until the lease ends.

b. The Periodic Tenancy

A periodic tenancy lasts for a fixed period of time and then automatically renews for successive time periods unless either party gives notice of termination. A periodic tenancy therefore has no specific ending date. The most common types of periodic tenancies are month-to-month and year-to-year. As the name implies, a month-to-month periodic tenancy lasts for a period of a month and automatically renews for the next month unless it is terminated by the parties. Similarly, a year-to-year periodic tenancy lasts for a year, then renews for the next year unless it is terminated.

While a periodic tenancy can be created expressly in a lease, it can also rise by implication in two ways. First, if a lease fails to include the duration of the lease but indicates how often rent is due, an implied periodic tenancy is created. For example, if a lease does not mention duration but states that rent is due on the first of each month, an implied month-to-month periodic tenancy is created. Ambiguities arise if the rental provision says something like "at a rent of $12,000 per year, payable in installments of $1,000 per month." In some jurisdictions, this language would create a year-to-year periodic tenancy. In others, it would create a month-to-month periodic tenancy. Second, paying rent on an oral agreement that violates the Statute of Frauds can create an implied periodic tenancy. The Statute of Frauds requires leases that are for more than three years to be in writing. For example, if two parties verbally agree to a five-year lease and set rent at $2,000 a month, the oral lease will not be enforceable because it violates the Statute of Frauds. When the tenant begins paying the $2,000 rent, however, an implied month-to-month periodic tenancy is created.

Termination is often a source of controversy between the landlord and tenant. If one party wants the lease to continue, it may try to contest the effectiveness of the other party's attempt to terminate. The lease will often but not always contain provisions that establish the procedure for termination. A termination provision in a lease typically will proscribe how much advance notice must be given, with a longer term usually increasing the period of time for giving notice of termination.

If there are no relevant provisions in the lease, notice periods are provided by the common law. Common-law notice periods are tied to the duration of the lease period. For a lease period of less than a year, notice equal to the length of the lease period must be given, not to exceed six months. A week-to-week periodic tenancy will require a week's notice. A month-to-month periodic tenancy will require a month's notice. A year-to-year periodic tenancy will require six months' notice.

What happens if a party gives notice to terminate too late? For example, a month-to-month periodic tenancy typically requires a month's notice to terminate. Say that the period on a month-to-month lease begins at the first of the month and that the tenant gives notice on January 15 that the lease will terminate on January 31. In other words, the tenant gives two weeks' notice, rather than the required one month's notice. What is the effect of the tenant's notice? There are two options. The first, and better, option is to treat the tenant's notice as being a valid notice of termination that will take effect at the end of the next full period. In our example, the tenant's notice on January 15 would not be effective to terminate the lease on January 31. It would, however, be effective to terminate the lease on February 28, at the end of the next period. The second approach treats the tenant's insufficient notice as a legal nullity. Under this approach, the lease will continue to renew for successive periods until the tenant gives proper notice. We think that this second approach is completely unsupportable. Nonetheless, it has been followed in some jurisdictions.

The death of the landlord or tenant will have no effect on a periodic tenancy. If the landlord dies, the landlord's estate will be bound by the lease. If the tenant dies, the tenant's estate will be bound by the lease. In some jurisdictions, a tenant's death will terminate a residential periodic tenancy. To be safe, however, the tenant's estate should affirmatively terminate the periodic tenancy if it wants to end the lease.

RENEWABLE TERM OF YEARS VS. PERIODIC TENANCY

A term of years tenancy can be made to act like a periodic tenancy by including an automatic renewal clause in the lease. For example, a lease made for a term "of one year" could include a clause that allowed for automatic renewal of the lease unless one of the parties provided notice of termination. Although this lease behaves like a year-to-year periodic tenancy, it is still a term of years tenancy. The year-to-year periodic tenancy renews because of the nature of the leasehold. The renewable term of years lease renews because of the renewal clause in the lease.

c. The Tenancy at Will

As the name implies, a *tenancy at will* is a tenancy that is "at the will" of the parties. The landlord and tenant agree that the tenant may retain possession for an unspecified amount of time. Either party can end the tenancy at any time. Many states have statutes that set minimum time periods for notice, often based on the time of rental payments. If a state does not set a minimum time, either party can terminate a tenancy at will without notice.

Tenancies at will can arise contrary to the parties' intent. If a tenancy does not qualify as a term of years or periodic tenancy, then it will be a tenancy at will. In other words, tenancy at will is our catchall category that we use for leases that do not fit into either of the two other categories. Consider, for example, a lease from the landlord to the tenant during World War II "for the duration of the war." This lease does not create a term of years because we cannot reduce the duration to fixed calendar dates—we don't know when the war will end. It also does not create a periodic tenancy. Therefore, it is a tenancy at will. As a result, it is terminable at the will of either party at any time. This result, which is clearly contrary to the parties' original intent, is a product of the *numerus clausus* principle that we studied in Chapter 2. We have to cram a conveyance into one of our existing categories. Because this conveyance did not fit into the other two categories of lease, it has to be a tenancy at will.

Unlike the term of years and periodic tenancy, a tenancy at will terminates automatically on the death of either the landlord or tenant. In some circumstances, this can lead to harsh results, as we will see in our next case. Before we get to that case, however, we have a set of Problems that highlight the differences between the three different types of leasehold interests.

PROBLEMS

For each of the following problems, presume that the lease contains no other relevant provisions and that the jurisdiction has no relevant statutes. Explanatory answers to this problem set can be found on page 1045.

1. On August 15, a landlord leased an apartment to a first-year law student "for one year, beginning August 15." (a) What type of leasehold was created? (b) If the law

student moved out in June of the following year without giving any notice, would the law student be liable for rent for the June-August time period? What if the student gave one month's notice before moving out? (c) Would the law student be liable for rent for the following year if the student moved out on August 14 without providing any notice?

2. Same questions as the prior problem, but now the landlord leased the apartment to the student "from year to year, beginning August 15."

3. Same questions as the first problem, but now the landlord leased the apartment to the student "for as long as you are a law student."

4. Your property professor decides to take a position as a visiting professor in Guam for a year and leases her home to a family. After being in Guam for a semester, she misses her school and students so much she decides to quit her visiting position and come back early. Under what circumstances could she move back into her home? (a) The agreement she made with the family was a term of years leasehold for a year. (b) The agreement with the family was a month-to-month periodic tenancy. (c) The agreement with the family was a tenancy at will.

5. What type of tenancy would be created if your professor leased her home for "$24,000 per year, to be paid in monthly installments of $2,000"?

6. What type of tenancy would be created if your professor leased her home for "$24,000 for the next year beginning August first, payable in monthly installments of $2,000"?

As we mentioned in the text before the problem set, a lease creates a tenancy at will if it does not fit into either of the other two categories. The fact that a tenancy at will can be terminated at any time can create real hardships. Our next case provides a good example.

EFFEL V. ROSBERG

Court of Appeals of Texas, 2012
360 S.W.3d 626

MORRIS, Justice. This is an appeal from the trial court's judgment awarding Robert G. Rosberg possession of property in a forcible detainer action. Appellant Lena Effel brings seventeen issues generally contending the trial court did not have jurisdiction to make the award and, in the alternative, that it erred in concluding Rosberg was entitled to possession of the property. After examining the record on appeal and reviewing the applicable law, we conclude appellant's arguments are without merit. We affirm the trial court's judgment.

I.

On March 1, 2006, Robert G. Rosberg filed suit against Henry Effel and Jack Effel in district court asserting various claims . . . . The parties settled the dispute and signed a settlement agreement and release of claims. As part of the settlement, Rosberg purchased residential property in Dallas county owned by Henry and Jack Effel. The settlement agreement stated that the current resident of the property, appellant, "shall continue to occupy the property for the remainder of her natural life, or until such time as she voluntarily chooses to vacate the premises." The settlement agreement further stated that a lease agreement incorporating the terms of the settlement agreement would be prepared before the closing date of the purchase. Appellant was neither a party nor a signatory to the settlement agreement.

The property in question was deeded to Rosberg with no reservation of a life estate. A lease for appellant was prepared by the Effels' attorney. The term of the lease was "for a term equal to the remainder of the Lessee's life, or until such time that she voluntarily vacates the premises." The lease also contained various covenants relating to payment of rent and charges for utilities as well as the use and maintenance of the grounds. The lease provided that if there was any default in the payment of rent or in the performance of any of the covenants, the lease could be terminated at the option of the lessor. The lease was signed by Rosberg as lessor and by Henry Effel on behalf of appellant under a power of attorney as lessee.

Three years later, on February 24, 2010, Rosberg, through his attorney, sent a letter to appellant both by regular mail and certified mail stating that he was terminating her lease effective immediately. The reason for the termination, according to the letter, was Rosberg's discovery that appellant had installed a wrought iron fence in the front yard of the property in violation of two covenants of the lease. The letter stated that appellant was required to leave and surrender the premises within ten days and, if she did not vacate the premises, Rosberg would commence eviction proceedings. Appellant did not vacate the property.

On April 29, 2010, Rosberg filed this forcible detainer action in the justice court. The justice court awarded possession of the property to Rosberg, and appellant appealed the decision to the county court at law. The county court held a trial de novo without a jury and, again, awarded the property to Rosberg. The court concluded the lease created a tenancy at will terminable at any time by either party. The court further concluded that Rosberg was authorized to terminate the lease, whether because it was terminable at will or because appellant violated the terms of the lease, and the lease was properly terminated on February 24, 2010. Appellant now appeals the county court's judgment.

> Forcible detainer is a cause of action that can be brought by a landlord to recover possession from a tenant.

II.

. . .

In appellant's remaining issues, she challenges the findings of fact and conclusions of law made by the county court. In her tenth issue, appellant challenges the county court's first conclusion of law in which it stated "[t]he lease, which purported to be for the rest of Lena Effel's life, created only a tenancy at will terminable at any time by either party." Appellant argues that the lease must be read together with the settlement agreement and the court must give effect to the intent of the parties. Appellant was not a party to the settlement agreement, however. Appellant was a party only to the lease. It is the lease, and not the settlement agreement, that forms the basis of this forcible detainer action. Accordingly, we look solely to the lease to determine appellant's rights in this matter.

The lease states that appellant was a lessee of the property "for a term equal to the remainder of Lessee's life, or until such time as she voluntarily vacates the premises." It is the long-standing rule in Texas that a lease must be for a certain period of time or it will be considered a tenancy at will. *See Holcombe v. Lorino,* 124 Tex. 446, 79 S.W.2d 307, 310 (1935). Courts that have applied this rule to leases that state they are for the term of the lessee's life have concluded that the uncertainty of the date of the lessee's death rendered the lease terminable at will by either party.

Appellant argues the current trend in court decisions is away from finding a lease such as hers to be terminable at will. Appellant relies on the 1982 decision of *Philpot v. Fields,* 633 S.W.2d 546 (Tex.App.-Texarkana 1982, no writ). In *Philpot,* the court stated that the trend in law was away from requiring a lease to be of a definite and certain duration. *Id.* at 538. In reviewing the law since *Philpot,* however, we discern no such trend. *See Kajo,* 2003 WL 1848555 at *5. The rule continues to be that a lease for an indefinite and uncertain length of time is an estate at will. *See Providence Land Servs., L.L.C. v. Jones,* 353 S.W.3d 538, 542 (Tex.App.-Eastland 2011, no pet. h.). In this case, not only was the term of the lease stated to be for the uncertain length of appellant's life, but her tenancy was also "until such time that she voluntarily vacates the premises." If a lease can be terminated at the will of the lessee, it may also be terminated at the will of the lessor. *See Holcombe,* 79 S.W.2d at 310. Because the lease at issue was terminable at will by either party, the trial court's first conclusion of law was correct. We resolve appellant's tenth issue against her. . . .

In her fourth issue, appellant contends the trial court erred in concluding that Rosberg sent her a proper notice to vacate the premises under section 24.005 of the Texas Property Code. Section 24.005 states that a landlord must give a tenant at will at least three days' written notice to vacate before filing a forcible detainer suit unless the parties contracted for a longer or shorter notice period in a written lease or agreement. TEX. PROP.CODE ANN. §24.005(b) (West Supp.2011). The section also states that the notice must be delivered either in person or by mail at the premises in question. *Id.* §24.005(f). If the notice is delivered by mail, it may be by regular mail, registered mail, or certified mail, return receipt requested, to the premises in question. *Id.*

The undisputed evidence in this case shows that Rosberg, through his attorney, sent appellant a written notice to vacate the premises by both regular mail and certified mail on February 24, 2010. The notice stated that appellant had ten days to surrender the premises. Nothing in the lease provided for a longer notice period. Henry Effel testified at trial that appellant received the notice and read it. Rosberg did not bring this forcible detainer action until April 29, 2010. The evidence conclusively shows, therefore, that Rosberg's notice to vacate the property complied with section 24.005. . . .

Because Rosberg had the right to terminate appellant's tenancy at any time and properly notified her of the termination under section 24.005 of the Texas Property Code, the trial court did not err in awarding the property at issue to Rosberg. Consequently, it is unnecessary for us to address the remainder of appellant's issues.

We affirm the trial court's judgment.

NOTE

For a case reaching a contrary result on somewhat similar facts to *Effel, see Garner v. Gerrish*, 473 N.E.2d 233 (N.Y. 1984).

2. THE LEASE: CONSIDERATIONS FOR LANDLORDS AND TENANTS NEGOTIATING AND ENTERING THE LEASEHOLD

a. Negotiating the Lease

In entering a lease, landlords and tenants sometimes rely on standard fill-in-the-blank forms. Even when the parties are using a standard form, the numerous blanks to be completed indicate the complexities of leases and lease negotiations. Consider for a moment what terms would be most important for the tenant and what terms would be the most important for the landlord in negotiating a lease.

While all attorneys need to learn effective negotiation skills, these skills are especially important for attorneys practicing in an area of property law. Attorneys who are effective negotiators have an understanding of negotiation theory and use a combination of approaches to achieve good results for their clients. Negotiation theory focuses primarily on two types of bargaining: positional bargaining and interest-based bargaining.

In positional bargaining, the parties approach negotiations as an adversarial process, where one party makes an extreme high or low opening offer and the other party makes a correspondingly extreme low or high offer. A series of concessions are then made until either (a) an agreement is not reached or (b) an agreement is reached somewhere in the middle of the opening positions. This is considered a zero-sum exercise because one party's gain is the other party's loss.

In interest-based bargaining, both parties collaborate to find a win-win solution. The negotiation is treated as a joint problem-solving effort to resolve each party's underlying issues and concerns. It focuses on the interests rather than the positions of the parties. What type of bargaining do you think would best serve a landlord negotiating the terms of a lease? Would the same type best serve the tenant? What variables might need to be considered in deciding which type of bargaining to use?

One lease term of special interest to both parties is the *security deposit*. A security deposit is money a tenant pays to the landlord that is kept separately in a fund for use if the tenant causes damage to the property or violates the terms of the lease. Most states do not regulate the maximum rent that a landlord may charge a tenant. Most states do have laws regulating the maximum amount of a security deposit, the amount of time a landlord has to return an unused security deposit, and how a security deposit must be held by the landlord. These statutes typically apply only to residential leases and typically do not apply to commercial leases. Here is an example:

Pennsylvania Consolidated Statutes Annotated
Title 68 §§250.511a to 250.512

Section 250.511a. Escrow funds limited

(a) No landlord may require a sum in excess of two months' rent to be deposited in escrow for the payment of damages to the leasehold premises and/or default in rent thereof during the first year of any lease.

(b) During the second and subsequent years of the lease or during any renewal of the original lease the amount required to be deposited may not exceed one month's rent . . .

(f) Any attempted waiver of this section by a tenant by a contract or otherwise shall be void and unenforceable.

Section 250.511b. Interest on escrow funds held more than two years

(a) Except as otherwise provided in this section, all funds over one hundred dollars ($100) deposited with a lessor to secure the execution of a rental agreement on residential property in accordance with section 511.1 and pursuant to any lease newly executed or reexecuted after the effective date of this act shall be deposited in an escrow account of an institution regulated by the Federal Reserve Board, the Federal Home Loan Bank Board, Comptroller of the Currency, or the Pennsylvania Department of Banking. When any funds are deposited in any escrow account, interest-bearing or noninterest-bearing, the lessor shall thereupon notify in writing each of the tenants making any such deposit, giving the name and address of the banking institution in which such deposits are held, and the amount of such deposits.

. . .

Section 250.512. Recovery of improperly held escrow funds

(a) Every landlord shall within thirty days of termination of a lease or upon surrender and acceptance of the leasehold premises, whichever first occurs, provide a tenant with a written list of any damages to the leasehold premises for which the landlord claims the tenant is liable. Delivery of the list shall be accompanied by payment of the difference between any sum deposited in escrow, including any unpaid interest thereon, for the payment of damages to the leasehold premises and the actual amount of damages to the leasehold premises caused by the tenant. Nothing in this section shall preclude the landlord from refusing to return the escrow fund, including any unpaid interest thereon, for nonpayment of rent or for the breach of any other condition in the lease by the tenant.

(b) Any landlord who fails to provide a written list within thirty days as required in subsection (a), above, shall forfeit all rights to withhold any portion of sums held in escrow, including any unpaid interest thereon, or to bring suit against the tenant for damages to the leasehold premises.

. . .

(d) Any attempted waiver of this section by a tenant by contract or otherwise shall be void and unenforceable.

(e) Failure of the tenant to provide the landlord with his new address in writing upon termination of the lease or upon surrender and acceptance of the leasehold premises shall relieve the landlord from any liability under this section.

(f) This section shall apply only to residential leaseholds and not to commercial leaseholds.

QUESTIONS

1. Why do states seem to regulate security deposits more strictly than rent? Why would Pennsylvania not allow the parties to waive these regulations?

b. The Lease Itself

Recall that the Statute of Frauds requires that a lease for a term of more than three years to be in writing. A written lease must at a minimum contain certain essential terms: the names of the parties, the identity of the property to be leased, the duration of the lease, the amount of rent, and the signatures of both parties. The landlord-tenant relationship is complex, and a well-drafted lease should anticipate and address foreseeable problems between the landlord and tenant. As a result, leases often end up being lengthy documents. Consider the following form residential lease:

BASIC RENTAL AGREEMENT OR RESIDENTIAL LEASE

This Rental Agreement or Residential Lease shall evidence the complete terms and conditions under which the parties whose signatures appear below have agreed. Landlord/Lessor/Agent, _____, shall be referred to as "OWNER" and Tenant(s)/Lessee, _____, shall be referred to as "RESIDENT." As consideration for this agreement, OWNER agrees to rent/lease to RESIDENT and RESIDENT agrees to rent/lease from OWNER for use solely as a private residence, the premises located at _____ _____in the city of _____.

1. TERMS: RESIDENT agrees to pay in advance $_____ per month on the ___ day of each month. This agreement shall commence on _____ and continue; (check one)

A.____ until _____, ___ as a leasehold. Thereafter it shall become a month-to-month tenancy. If RESIDENT should move from the premises prior to the expiration of this time period, he shall be liable for all rent due until such time that the Residence is occupied by an OWNER approved paying RESIDENT and/or expiration of said time period, whichever is shorter.

B.____ until _____, _____ on a month-to-month tenancy until either party shall terminate this agreement by giving a written notice of intention to terminate at least 30 days prior to the date of termination.

2. PAYMENTS: Rent and/or other charges are to be paid at such place or method designated by the owner as follows_____. All payments are to be made by check or money order and cash shall be acceptable. OWNER acknowledges receipt of the First Month's rent of $_____, and a Security Deposit of $_____, and additional charges/fees for _____, for a total payment of $_____. All payments are to be made payable to _____.

3. SECURITY DEPOSITS: The total of the above deposits shall secure compliance with the terms and conditions of this agreement and shall be refunded to RESIDENT within ____ days after the premises have been completely vacated less any amount necessary to pay OWNER; a) any unpaid rent, b) cleaning costs, c) key replacement costs, d) cost for repair of damages to premises and/or common areas above ordinary wear and tear, and e) any other amount legally allowable under the terms of this agreement. A written accounting of said charges shall be presented to RESIDENT within ____ days of move-out. If deposits do not cover such costs and damages, the RESIDENT shall immediately pay said additional costs for damages to OWNER.

4. LATE CHARGE: A late fee of $____, (not to exceed ___% of the monthly rent), shall be added and due for any payment of rent made after the _____ of the month. Any dishonored check shall be treated as unpaid rent, and subject to an additional fee of $_____.

5. UTILITIES: RESIDENT agrees to pay all utilities and/or services based upon occupancy of the premises except _____.

6. OCCUPANTS: Guest(s) staying over 15 days without the written consent of OWNER shall be considered a breach of this agreement. ONLY the following individuals and/or animals, AND NO OTHERS shall occupy the subject residence for more than 15 days unless the expressed written consent of OWNER obtained in advance_____.

7. PETS: No animal, fowl, fish, reptile, and/or pet of any kind shall be kept on or about the premises, for any amount of time, without obtaining the prior written consent and meeting the requirements of the OWNER. Such consent if granted, shall be revocable at OWNER'S option upon giving a 30 day written notice. In the event laws are passed or permission is granted to have a pet and/or animal of any kind, an additional deposit in the amount of $_____ shall be required along with additional monthly rent of $_____ along with the signing of OWNER'S Pet Agreement. RESIDENT also agrees to carry insurance deemed appropriate by OWNER to cover possible liability and damages that may be caused by such animals.

8. LIQUID FILLED FURNISHINGS: No liquid filled furniture, receptacle containing more than ten gallons of liquid is permitted without prior written consent and meeting the requirements of the OWNER. RESIDENT also agrees to carry insurance deemed appropriate by OWNER to cover possible losses that may be caused by such items.

9. PARKING: When and if RESIDENT is assigned a parking area/space on OWNER'S property, the parking area/space shall be used exclusively for parking of passenger automobiles and/or those approved vehicles listed on RESIDENT'S Application attached hereto. RESIDENT is hereby assigned or permitted to park only in

the following area or space _____. The parking fee for this space (if applicable) is $_____ monthly. Said space shall not be used for the washing, painting, or repair of vehicles. No other parking space shall be used by RESIDENT or RESIDENT'S guest(s). RESIDENT is responsible for oil leaks and other vehicle discharges for which RESIDENT shall be charged for cleaning if deemed necessary by OWNER.

10. NOISE: RESIDENT agrees not to cause or allow any noise or activity on the premises which might disturb the peace and quiet of another RESIDENT and/or neighbor. Said noise and/or activity shall be a breach of this agreement.

11. DESTRUCTION OF PREMISES: If the premises become totally or partially destroyed during the term of this Agreement so that RESIDENT'S use is seriously impaired, OWNER or RESIDENT may terminate this Agreement immediately upon three day written notice to the other.

12. CONDITION OF PREMISES: RESIDENT acknowledges that he has examined the premises and that said premises, all furnishings, fixtures, furniture, plumbing, heating, electrical facilities, all items listed on the attached property condition checklist, if any, and/or all other items provided by OWNER are all clean, and in good satisfactory condition except as may be indicated elsewhere in this Agreement. RESIDENT agrees to keep the premises and all items in good order and good condition and to immediately pay for costs to repair and/or replace any portion of the above damaged by RESIDENT, his guests and/or invitees, except as provided by law. At the termination of this Agreement, all of above items in this provision shall be returned to OWNER in clean and good condition except for reasonable wear and tear and the premises shall be free of all personal property and trash not belonging to OWNER. It is agreed that all dirt, holes, tears, burns, and stains of any size or amount in the carpets, drapes, walls, fixtures, and/or any other part of the premises, do not constitute reasonable wear and tear.

13. ALTERATIONS: RESIDENT shall not paint, wallpaper, alter or redecorate, change or install locks, install antenna or other equipment, screws, fastening devices, large nails, or adhesive materials, place signs, displays, or other exhibits, on or in any portion of the premises without the written consent of the OWNER except as may be provided by law.

14. PROPERTY MAINTENANCE: RESIDENT shall deposit all garbage and waste in a clean and sanitary manner into the proper receptacles and shall cooperate in keeping the garbage area neat and clean. RESIDENT shall be responsible for disposing of items of such size and nature as are not normally acceptable by the garbage hauler. RESIDENT shall be responsible for keeping the kitchen and bathroom drains free of things that may tend to cause clogging of the drains. RESIDENT shall pay for the cleaning out of any plumbing fixture that may need to be cleared of stoppage and for the expense or damage caused by stopping of waste pipes or overflow from bathtubs, wash basins, or sinks.

15. CHANGE OF TERMS: The terms and conditions of this agreement are subject to future change by OWNER after the expiration of the agreed lease period upon 30-day written notice setting forth such change and delivered to RESIDENT. Any changes are subject to laws in existence at the time of the Notice of Change of Terms.

16. TERMINATION: After expiration of the leasing period, this agreement is automatically renewed from month to month, but may be terminated by either party giving to the other a 30-day written notice of intention to terminate. Where laws require "just cause," such just cause shall be so stated on said notice. The premises shall be considered vacated only after all areas including storage areas are clear of all RESIDENT'S belongings, and keys and other property furnished for RESIDENT'S use are returned to OWNER. Should the RESIDENT hold over beyond the termination date or fail to vacate all possessions on or before the termination date, RESIDENT shall be liable for additional rent and damages which may include damages due to OWNER'S loss of prospective new renters.

17. POSSESSION: If OWNER is unable to deliver possession of the residence to RESIDENTS on the agreed date, because of the loss or destruction of the residence or because of the failure of the prior residents to vacate or for any other reason, the RESIDENT and/or OWNER may immediately cancel and terminate this agreement upon written notice to the other party at their last known address, whereupon neither party shall have liability to the other, and any sums paid under this Agreement shall be refunded in full. If neither party cancels, this Agreement shall be prorated and begin on the date of actual possession.

18. INSURANCE: RESIDENT acknowledges that OWNERS insurance does not cover personal property damage caused by fire, theft, rain, war, acts of God, acts of others, and/or any other causes, nor shall OWNER

be held liable for such losses. RESIDENT is hereby advised to obtain his own insurance policy to cover any personal losses.

19. RIGHT OF ENTRY AND INSPECTION: OWNER may enter, inspect, and/or repair the premises at any time in case of emergency or suspected abandonment. OWNER shall give 24 hours advance notice and may enter for the purpose of showing the premises during normal business hours to prospective renters, buyers, lenders, for smoke alarm inspections, and/or for normal inspections and repairs. OWNER is permitted to make all alterations, repairs and maintenance that in OWNER'S judgment is necessary to perform.

20. ASSIGNMENT: RESIDENT agrees not to transfer, assign or sublet the premises or any part thereof.

21. PARTIAL INVALIDITY: Nothing contained in this Agreement shall be construed as waiving any of the OWNER'S or RESIDENT'S rights under the law. If any part of this Agreement shall be in conflict with the law, that part shall be void to the extent that it is in conflict, but shall not invalidate this Agreement nor shall it affect the validity or enforceability of any other provision of this Agreement.

22. NO WAIVER: OWNER'S acceptance of rent with knowledge of any default by RESIDENT or waiver by OWNER of any breach of any term of this Agreement shall not constitute a waiver of subsequent breaches. Failure to require compliance or to exercise any right shall not be constituted as a waiver by OWNER of said term, condition, and/or right, and shall not affect the validity or enforceability of any provision of this Agreement.

23. ATTORNEY FEES: If any legal action or proceedings be brought by either party of this Agreement, the prevailing party shall be reimbursed for all reasonable attorney's fees and costs in addition to other damages awarded.

24. JOINTLY AND SEVERALLY: The undersigned RESIDENTS are jointly and severally responsible and liable for all obligations under this agreement.

25. REPORT TO CREDIT/TENANT AGENCIES: You are hereby notified that a nonpayment, late payment or breach of any of the terms of this rental agreement may be submitted/reported to a credit and/or tenant reporting agency, and may create a negative credit record on your credit report.

26. ADDITIONS AND/OR EXCEPTIONS

_____.

27. NOTICES: All notices to RESIDENT shall be served at RESIDENT'S premises and all notices to OWNER shall be served at _____.

28. INVENTORY: The premises contains the following items, that the RESIDENT may use.

_____.

29. KEYS AND ADDDENDUMS: RESIDENT acknowledges receipt of the following which shall be deemed part of this Agreement: (Please check)

___ Keys #of keys and purposes

___ House Rules

___ Pet Agreement

___ Other

30. ENTIRE AGREEMENT: This Agreement constitutes the entire Agreement between OWNER and RESIDENT. No oral agreements have been entered into, and all modifications or notices shall be in writing to be valid.

31. RECEIPT OF AGREEMENT: The undersigned RESIDENTS have read and understand this Agreement and hereby acknowledge receipt of a copy of this Rental Agreement.

RESIDENT'S Signature_____

Date_____

OWNER'S Signature _____

Date_____

http://www.dca.ga.gov/housing/specialneeds/programs/documents/C-2SampleLEASE.pdf.

Clearly, this form lease goes beyond the minimum requirements of the Statute of Frauds. What terms appear negotiable? Why would landlords want certain terms to not be negotiable? What information is not in this residential lease that a tenant might want to know before signing? What types of recurring problems in the landlord-tenant relationship are reflected in the terms of the lease?

3. DELIVERY OF POSSESSION

Consider paragraph 17 of our sample residential lease. It contemplates a scenario in which the landlord is unable to deliver physical possession of the premises to the tenant. Under the terms of the lease, the tenant is able to cancel the lease if the landlord is unable to deliver possession. Imagine that you have rented an apartment. When you arrive to move in, you find that the prior tenant is still in the apartment. Would your ability to cancel the lease be enough to satisfy you? Note that under paragraph 17 the *landlord* may immediately cancel the lease if the prior tenant remains in possession of the apartment. How would you feel if you showed up with your moving van and the landlord handed you notice that your lease was canceled because the prior tenant refused to move out? Under the terms of paragraph 17, "neither party shall have liability to the other" in the event of cancellation due to the landlord's inability to deliver possession. Having considered this issue, would you sign the sample lease as written? Would you advise a client to sign the sample lease as written?

If the lease does not expressly address the landlord's obligation to deliver possession to the tenant, the common-law rules on delivery of possession would apply. The majority rule requires landlords to deliver actual, physical possession to tenants. This majority rule, also known as the *English rule*, places the burden on the landlord to deliver physical possession. If the landlord is unable to deliver physical possession, in most jurisdictions the landlord would be in breach of the lease and the tenant would be suspended from the obligation to pay rent. The tenant would be entitled to damages. Note in this context that paragraph 17 of the residential lease limits the landlord's liability for failure to deliver possession, though it does obligate the landlord to refund any money that the tenant has already. Without that language, the landlord could be liable for the tenant's costs of moving to a different location, and the difference in cost between the new rent and the rent that would have been due under the original lease for the duration of the term.

The *American rule* is a competing, minority rule followed by some states. Under the American rule the landlord is only obligated to provide the tenant with the legal right of possession. Under this rule, the landlord has no obligation to deliver actual physical possession. The obligation to deliver the legal right of possession is satisfied if the landlord delivers a valid lease to the tenant. If the new tenant showed up and found that the prior tenant had wrongfully stayed past the end of the lease, the new tenant be would be responsible for evicting the old tenant. The new tenant also would be liable to the landlord for the rent under the lease, even though the old tenant remained in possession.

In our view, the English rule is much better suited to the modern landlord-tenant relationship. The landlord is in a much better position to know about a holdover

A tenant who wrongfully stays past the end of her lease is called a *holdover*. We will consider legal issues involving landlords and holdover tenants toward the end of the chapter in our materials on the end of the landlord-tenant relationship.

Under the English rule the burden of dealing with the holdover rests with the landlord. Under the American rule, the burden of dealing with the holdover rests with the tenant, unless there is an express provision in the lease to the contrary. Don't be confused by the names of the rules. The English rule is the majority rule in the United States.

tenant and is likely to be more knowledgeable than a typical tenant about the legal process involved in evicting a holdover. The American rule might have made sense in the nineteenth century, when tenants often were more interested in farming the land than in acquiring a place to live. We think that it makes little sense today. *See* Glenn Weissenberger, *The Landlord's Duty to Deliver Possession, The Overlooked Reform*, 46 U. Cin. L. Rev. 937 (1977) (arguing for the adoption of the English Rule).

The following case, *Adrian v. Rabinowitz*, provides an example of the reasoning used by states in determining whether to adopt the English rule or the American rule.

ADRIAN V. RABINOWITZ

Supreme Court of New Jersey, 1935
186 A. 29

HEHER, Justice. [Landlord leased premises to the tenant for use as a shoe store. The lease was to begin June 15, 1934. The prior tenant failed to vacate the premises. The landlord brought a suit to evict the prior tenant. This suit was successful, and the tenant took possession of the premises on July 7, 1934. The tenant sued for damages, and won in the lower court.]

It is apparent that the tenant in possession when the lease was executed wrongfully held over after the termination of the tenancy; and the primary question, raised by motions to nonsuit and direct a verdict in defendant's favor, is whether, expressly or by implication, the contract imposed upon the lessor the duty of putting the lessee in actual and exclusive possession of the demised premises at the beginning of the term. . . .

It remains to consider whether the lessor, in the absence of an express undertaking to that effect, is under a duty to put the lessee in actual as well as legal possession of the demised premises at the commencement of the term. We are of the view that he is. There seems to be no dissent from the doctrine that the lessor impliedly covenants that the lessee shall have the legal right of possession at the beginning of the term. But there is a contrariety of view as to whether this implied obligation extends as well to actual possession, especially where, as here, the prior tenant wrongfully holds over. See 70 A.L.R. 151 et seq.

In some of our American jurisdictions, the rule obtains that, while the lessee is entitled to have the legal right of possession, there is no implied covenant to protect the lessee against wrongful acts of strangers. *Gardner v. Keteltas*, 3 Hill (N.Y.) 330, 38 Am. Dec. 637; *Snider v. Deban*, 249 Mass. 59, 144 N.E. 69; *Hannan v. Dusch*, supra; *Gazzolo v. Chambers*, 73 Ill. 75. The English rule is that, where the term is to commence in futuro, there is an implied undertaking by the lessor that the premises shall be open to the lessee's entry, legally and actually, when the time for possession under the lease arrives . . . This rule has the support of respectable American authority. *King v. Reynolds*, supra; . . .

The English rule, so-called, is on principle much the better one. It has the virtue, ordinarily, of effectuating the common intention of the parties—to give actual and exclusive possession of the premises to the lessee on the fixed for the commencement of the term. This is what the lessee generally bargains for; and it is the thing the lessor undertakes to give. Such being the case, there is no warrant for placing upon the lessee, without express stipulation to that effect, the burden of ousting, at his own expense, the tenant wrongfully holding over, or the trespasser in possession of the premises without color of right at the commencement of the term; and thus to impose upon him who is not in possession of the evidence the burden of establishing the respective rights and duties of the lessor and the possessor of the lands inter se, as well as the consequences of the delay incident to the adjudication of the controversy, and the obligation to pay rent during that period. As was said by Baron Vaughan in *Coe v. Clay*, supra: "He who lets agrees to give possession, and not merely to give a chance of a law suit." This doctrine is grounded in reason and logic. The underlying theory is that the parties contemplated, as an essential term of their undertaking, without which the lease would not have been made, that the lessor should, at the beginning of the term, have the premises open to the entry and exclusive possession of the lessee. This is certainly the normal course of dealing, and, in the absence of stipulation to the contrary, is to be regarded as the parties' understanding of the lessor's covenant to deliver possession of the demised premises at the time prescribed for the commencement of the term. . . .

Therefore, the motions for a nonsuit and a direction of a verdict in defendant's favor on the ground that there was no evidence of a breach of defendant's undertaking to deliver possession of the demised premises at the stipulated time were rightly denied.

NOTES AND QUESTIONS

1. *Place Yourself in the Incoming Tenant's Shoes.* Suppose that you are a 1L who has signed a one-year lease to rent an apartment close to campus. You are set to move in to your new apartment on the first day of the rental period, which is also a week before

your law school classes start. When you arrive with your moving truck, you discover that the former tenant, a 3L who just graduated that May, has not yet moved out, even though his lease expired. When you consult your lease, assume that it is silent on the issue of the landlord's duty to deliver physical possession to you. What actions would you take under the English rule? The American rule?

2. *Legal Possession vs. Actual Possession.* The distinction between the American rule and the English rule turns on the landlord's obligation to deliver actual possession. Both rules presume that the landlord must give the tenant the legal right of possession. The landlord clearly cannot rent the premises to one person then turn around and rent the premises to another person for the same time period. What happens if the landlord delivers actual possession to the tenant, but the legal right of possession is questionable? For example, imagine that you entered into a one-year lease for a two-bedroom apartment when you started law school. After taking possession and paying rent for four months, you discover that, prior to creating a leasehold with you, the landlord entered into a lease with a student who never showed up to go to law school, for the same rental period and for the same rental property. You are in actual possession, but you have questions about your legal right to possession. Can you stop paying rent? At least one court has said no, reasoning that you would have no claim because you are in actual, undisturbed possession of the apartment. *See Campbell v. Hershey*, 50 S.W.2d 501 (Ky. 1970). Under this approach, the landlord's obligation to give you actual possession would be violated if the other student showed up and tried to kick you out of the apartment.

3. *Delivery of Possession and Lease Language.* At least in the commercial context, the parties may be able to use language in the lease to alter the landlord's obligation to deliver possession. Consider, for example, the facts of *Fox Paper, Ltd. v. Schwartzman*, 168 A.D.2d 604 (N.Y. 1990). Tenant entered a five-year lease for warehouse space at a fixed annual rent of $50,000, payable in monthly installments. The lease contained an addendum stating that the lease would not begin until certain work was completed by the landlord on the warehouse. The lease further contained an express provision that was contrary to the landlord's obligation to deliver possession. The provision stated that the landlord would not be liable for failing to give possession at the commencement of the lease, but that tenant would not be obligated to pay rent until the warehouse was ready for occupancy. Delivery of possession of the warehouse was initially delayed by two months as the needed work was completed. When the tenant received a notice of a further ten-day delay, the tenant advised the landlord that he was terminating the lease for failure to deliver actual possession. The tenant sued for a return of deposit money and damages. The landlord counterclaimed for rent due under the lease. The landlord prevailed under the express terms of the lease.

4. *Is the Tenant Obligated to Take Possession?* Under both rules, there is an implied covenant in the lease that the landlord has a duty to deliver the legal right of possession to the tenant. The tenant, however, does not have a reciprocal duty to actually take possession unless the lease expressly requires it. For example, let's suppose a corporation owns a failing strip mall but manages to lease out space to Chipotle, a popular chain

restaurant. Although the lease calls for the restaurant to pay $5,000 a month for a year, without an express requirement written into the lease, Chipotle has no duty to actually move in and operate the restaurant. To be clear, Chipotle would still have an obligation to pay rent. It will not, however, have to actually occupy the rented space, even though its absence will presumably hurt the economic well-being of the other stores in the strip mall and reduce the overall value of the property to the landlord.

Courts, however, will find a duty to occupy if a significant portion of the rent is computed as a percentage of the tenant's sale. For example, if the lease calls for the tenant to pay 10% of its gross sales as rent, without any fixed minimum, courts will typically find an implied covenant to operate the business. *See College Block v. Atlantic Richfield Co.*, 254 Cal. Rptr. 179 (Ct. App. 1988).

How will you handle a question on delivery of possession on a law school exam? Will you apply the majority rule? the minority rule? The answer is both.

On a law school exam, this question calls for a *branch point analysis*. The law requires a branch point analysis when there are competing interpretations of a law, or where jurisdictions apply different rules. In this situation, jurisdictions apply different rules and in order to provide the most complete answer, you will need to explain and apply both the English rule and the American rule. The term branch point analysis reflects the notion that the law branches off in different directions, much like a tree branch. After identifying the issue, you should provide a roadmap identifying the two rules, and then you should separately apply each rule to the facts. Organizationally, your answer would look like this:

Statement of overall issue
Roadmap explaining that there are two rules regarding physical possession
Issue applying English rule
Explanation of English rule
Application applying English rule
Conclusion applying English rule

Issue applying American rule
Explanation of American rule
Application applying American rule
Conclusion applying American rule
Overall Conclusion explaining that the result regarding physical possession depends on
    which rule the jurisdiction follows.

Note the importance of the roadmap because it signals to the professor that you understand that the ultimate conclusion depends on the court's choice of law (i.e., the branch the court chooses to follow). Because the conclusion depends on which law the court applies, you cannot make a prediction without explaining and running through the analysis for both rules. If you have a reason for concluding that the court would apply one rule over the other, you should make that reason clear in your overall conclusion.

PROBLEM

An explanatory answer to this problem can be found on page 1046.

Fiona is the owner of the Oak Arms, a 50-unit apartment building. One of Fiona's tenants, Edith, failed to move out when her lease expired in February. Fiona had rented the unit to Martha, and boy, was Martha upset when she showed up to move in and found Edith still there. Fiona told Martha that her lease was valid, and that it was Martha's problem to deal with Edith. Martha has sued Fiona, arguing that Fiona has breached her obligation to deliver actual possession to the apartment.

4. PROTECTION AGAINST DISCRIMINATION: CONSIDERATIONS FOR LANDLORDS SELECTING TENANTS

Generally speaking, landlords may select tenants as they see fit. You have probably seen advertisements for apartments stating "no smokers" or "no pets allowed." Landlords are within their rights to refuse to rent to smokers or pet owners (with an exception, as we will see, for service animals that help disabled people). They are also within their rights to refuse to rent to a tenant with bad credit or to a tenant who was rude on the phone.

Landlords may not, however, conduct themselves in a way that violates anti-discrimination statutes. We used "conduct themselves" rather than "refuse to rent" in the previous sentence because anti-discrimination statutes often are quite broad and go beyond the decision to rent to a given tenant. Anti-discrimination statutes tend to define protected classes of people and prohibit discrimination against people based on their membership in a protected class.

In the landlord-tenant context, the federal Fair Housing Act (FHA) is by far the most important anti-discrimination statute in the United States. The FHA was enacted in 1968 and has been amended many times. Similar to most statutes, it contains sections on policy, definitions, and exemptions. Also similar to many statutes, the material is organized in a manner that may be unexpected to some readers. For example, exceptions are found in the section titled "Effective Dates of Certain Prohibitions." These exceptions also numerically appear before the sections that establish the basic requirements.

We present an excerpt from the statute below in the order that it appears in the United States Code. We suggest that you read the statute in the following order and answer the questions that we pose for each section as you go.

1. Read §3601, the statement of policy. What is the FHA intended to achieve?

2. Read §3604(a). This provision makes it illegal to sell or rent to a person because that person falls within any of six protected classes. What, exactly, are those protected classes? The FHA was enacted in 1968, at a time in U.S. history when segregation was in the forefront of most lawmakers' thoughts. As societal concerns evolved, sex, and then familial status were later added to the FHA.

3. Read §3602(k). What, exactly, does "family status" mean? Hint—it doesn't mean what you probably thought it meant when you first read §3604(a).

4. Read §§3602(b)-(e). What, exactly, do these provisions prohibit? We hope that it is clear that a landlord can violate the FHA even if the landlord rents an apartment to a person. Put another way, the FHA goes far beyond refusal to rent.

5. Read §3603(b)(2). This is the so-called *Mrs. Murphy exception.* We are serious—everyone calls this provision the Mrs. Murphy exception. Apparently this exemption was named after an elderly widow who was forced by economic circumstance to rent out her home. Put bluntly, this exception is intended to allow landlords to discriminate when they are renting an apartment in the building where they live. What, exactly, are the requirements of the Mrs. Murphy exception?

6. Read §3603(b)(1). This is another exception. What, exactly, does it do?

7. Read the first line of §3603(b). It contains an exception to the two exceptions. Reread §3604(c) closely. What does the exception to the exceptions achieve? Why do you think that §3604(c) was treated differently than the other provisions of §3604?

8. Read §3604(f). What does it do? Note that §3604(f)(3)(B) requires landlords to make reasonable accommodations to handicapped persons. This type of requirement is common in statutes designed to help people with disabilities. Think about how this provision might affect a "no pets" policy in an apartment building. Read §3602(h). The note was added by Congress in 1988.

9. Read §3607(a). What does it achieve? Reread §3602(k), then read §3607(b). What does §3607(b) achieve?

10. Think about the FHA as a whole. Do you disagree with any of the provisions? What provisions would you add or remove if you could?

Excerpt from the Federal Fair Housing Act, 42 U.S.C. §§3601-3631

§3601. Declaration of Policy

It is the policy of the United States to provide, within constitutional limitations, for fair housing throughout the United States.

§3602. Definitions

As used in this subchapter . . .

(h) "Handicap" means, with respect to a person—

(1) a physical or mental impairment which substantially limits one or more of such person's major life activities,

(2) a record of having such an impairment, or

(3) being regarded as having such an impairment, but such term does not include current, illegal use of or addiction to a controlled substance (as defined in section 102 of the Controlled Substances Act (21 U.S.C. 802)).

Note: Neither the term "individual with handicaps" nor the term "handicap" shall apply to an individual solely because that individual is a transvestite.

(k) "Familial status" means one or more individuals (who have not attained the age of 18 years) being domiciled with—

(1) a parent or another person having legal custody of such individual or individuals; or

(2) the designee of such parent or other person having such custody, with the written permission of such parent or other person.

The protections afforded against discrimination on the basis of familial status shall apply to any person who is pregnant or is in the process of securing legal custody of any individual who has not attained the age of 18 years. . . .

§3603. Effective dates of certain prohibitions

(b) Nothing in section [3604] of this title (other than subsection (c)) shall apply to—

(1) any single-family house sold or rented by an owner: *Provided,* That such private individual owner does not own more than three such single-family houses at any one time: *Provided further,* That in the case of the sale of any such single-family house by a private individual owner not residing in such house at the time of such sale or who was not the most recent resident of such house prior to such sale, the exemption granted by this subsection shall apply only with respect to one such sale within any twenty-four month period: *Provided further,* That such bona fide private individual owner does not own any interest in, nor is there owned or reserved on his behalf, under any express or voluntary agreement, title to or any right to all or a portion of the proceeds from the sale or rental of, more than three such single-family houses at any one time: *Provided further,* That after December 31, 1969, the sale or rental of any such single-family house shall be excepted from the application of this subchapter only if such house is sold or rented (A) without the use in any manner of the sales or rental facilities or the sales or rental services of any real estate broker, agent, or salesman, or of such facilities or services of any person in the business of selling or renting dwellings, or of any employee or agent of any such broker, agent, salesman, or person and (B) without the publication, posting or mailing, after notice, of any advertisement or written notice in violation of section [3604(c)] of this title; but nothing in this proviso shall prohibit the use of attorneys, escrow agents, abstractors, title companies, and other such professional assistance as necessary to perfect or transfer the title, or

(2) rooms or units in dwellings containing living quarters occupied or intended to be occupied by no more than four families living independently of each other, if the owner actually maintains and occupies one of such living quarters as his residence.

§3604. Discrimination in sale or rental of housing and other prohibited practices

As made applicable by section [3603] of this title and except as exempted by sections [3603(b)] and [3607] of this title, it shall be unlawful—

(a) To refuse to sell or rent after the making of a bona fide offer, or to refuse to negotiate for the sale or rental of, or otherwise make unavailable or deny, a dwelling to any person because of race, color, religion, sex, familial status, or national origin.

(b) To discriminate against any person in the terms, conditions, or privileges of sale or rental of a dwelling, or in the provision of services or facilities in connection therewith, because of race, color, religion, sex, familial status, or national origin.

(c) To make, print, or publish, or cause to be made, printed, or published any notice, statement, or advertisement, with respect to the sale or rental of a dwelling that indicates any preference, limitation, or discrimination based on race, color, religion, sex, handicap, familial status, or national origin, or an intention to make any such preference, limitation, or discrimination.

(d) To represent to any person because of race, color, religion, sex, handicap, familial status, or national origin that any dwelling is not available for inspection, sale, or rental when such dwelling is in fact so available.

(e) For profit, to induce or attempt to induce any person to sell or rent any dwelling by representations regarding the entry or prospective entry into the neighborhood of a person or persons of a particular race, color, religion, sex, handicap, familial status, or national origin.

(f)

(1) To discriminate in the sale or rental, or to otherwise make unavailable or deny, a dwelling to any buyer or renter because of a handicap of—

(A) that buyer or renter,

(B) a person residing in or intending to reside in that dwelling after it is so sold, rented, or made available; or

(C) any person associated with that buyer or renter.

(2) To discriminate against any person in the terms, conditions, or privileges of sale or rental of a dwelling, or in the provision of services or facilities in connection with such dwelling, because of a handicap of—

(A) that person; or

(B) a person residing in or intending to reside in that dwelling after it is so sold, rented, or made available; or

(C) any person associated with that person.

(3) For purposes of this subsection, discrimination includes—

(A) a refusal to permit, at the expense of the handicapped person, reasonable modifications of existing premises occupied or to be occupied by such person if such modifications may be necessary to afford such person full enjoyment of the premises, except that, in the case of a rental, the landlord may where it is reasonable to do so condition permission for a modification on the renter agreeing to restore the interior of the premises to the condition that existed before the modification, reasonable wear and tear excepted.

(B) a refusal to make reasonable accommodations in rules, policies, practices, or services, when such accommodations may be necessary to afford such person equal opportunity to use and enjoy a dwelling; or

(C) in connection with the design and construction of covered multifamily dwellings for first occupancy after the date that is 30 months after the date of enactment of the Fair Housing Amendments Act of 1988, a failure to design and construct those dwelling in such a manner that—

    (i) the public use and common use portions of such dwellings are readily accessible to and usable by handicapped persons;

    (ii) all the doors designed to allow passage into and within all premises within such dwellings are sufficiently wide to allow passage by handicapped persons in wheelchairs; and

    (iii) all premises within such dwellings contain the following features of adaptive design:

        (I) an accessible route into and through the dwelling;

        (II) light switches, electrical outlets, thermostats, and other environmental controls in accessible locations;

        (III) reinforcements in bathroom walls to allow later installation of grab bars; and

        (IV) usable kitchens and bathrooms such that an individual in a wheelchair can maneuver about the space. . . .

(7) As used in this subsection, the term "covered multifamily dwellings" means—

    (A) buildings consisting of 4 or more units if such buildings have one or more elevators; and

    (B) ground floor units in other buildings consisting of 4 or more units.

§3607. Religious organization or private club exemption

(a) Nothing in this subchapter shall prohibit a religious organization, association, or society, or any nonprofit institution or organization operated, supervised or controlled by or in conjunction with a religious organization, association, or society, from limiting the sale, rental or occupancy of dwellings which it owns or operates for other than a commercial purpose to persons of the same religion, or from giving preference to such persons, unless membership in such religion is restricted on account of race, color, or national origin. Nor shall anything in this subchapter prohibit a private club not in fact open to the public, which as an incident to its primary purpose or purposes provides lodgings which it owns or operates for other than a commercial purpose, from limiting the rental or occupancy of such lodgings to its members or from giving preference to its members.

  (b)

    (1) Nothing in this title limits the applicability of any reasonable local, State, or Federal restrictions regarding the maximum number of occupants permitted to occupy a dwelling. Nor does any provision in this title regarding familial status apply with respect to housing for older persons.

(2) As used in this section "housing for older persons" means housing—

(A) provided under any State or Federal program that the Secretary determines is specifically designed and operated to assist elderly persons (as defined in the State or Federal program); or

(B) intended for, and solely occupied by, persons 62 years of age or older; or

(C) intended and operated for occupancy by persons 55 years of age or older, and—

(i) at least 80 percent of the occupied units are occupied by at least one person who is 55 years of age or older; . . .

NOTES

1. *The Civil Rights Act of 1866.* The FHA is not the only federal law providing protection against discrimination in housing. The Civil Rights Act of 1866 (CRA) states that "All citizens of the United States shall have the same right, in every State and Territory, as is enjoyed by white citizens thereof to inherit, purchase, lease, hold, and convey real and personal property." The CRA had little impact on housing practices until the Supreme Court clarified its scope in *Jones v. Alfred H. Mayer Co.*, 392 U.S. 409 (1968). There are at least three crucial differences between the CRA and the FHA. First, the CRA only applies to race. In 1866, it was common to refer to, say, German people as members of the German race. As a result, the CRA has been interpreted to apply to what we would now call national origin. The CRA, however, does not cover the other protected classes covered by the FHA. Second, the CRA does not have an analogue to the FHA's prohibition in discriminatory advertising in §3604(c). Third, there are no exceptions in the CRA similar to those in §3603(b) or §3607. Therefore, discrimination based on race that would be legal under the FHA because it fell within the Mrs. Murphy exception would be illegal under the CRA.

2. *Exclusionary Vibes and Exclusionary Amenities.* Now that you have read the FHA, reconsider Lior Jacob Strahilevitz's observations on exclusionary vibes and exclusionary amenities from our materials in Chapter 1 on exclusion. Does the FHA cover discrimination achieved through exclusionary vibes or exclusionary amenities? If not, should the FHA be amended to get at these issues? Is it desirable or practical to try to address exclusionary vibes and exclusionary amenities in statutes like the FHA?

3. *Burden Shifting and Non-Discriminatory Justifications.* Courts typically use a process of burden shifting to resolve discrimination claims. In the FHA context, the plaintiff has the initial burden to make a *prima facie* case that (a) the plaintiff is a member of a protected class and (b) the plaintiff was denied housing or otherwise treated in a manner that falls within the scope of the FHA. If the plaintiff does so, the landlord then has the burden of showing that there was a non-discriminatory business justification for the landlord's actions. If the landlord meets this requirement, the burden shifts back to the plaintiff to show that the asserted non-discriminatory justification was a mere pretext. We will see this type of burden shifting in action in our next case.

As a practical matter, it can be hard to prove discrimination. One method that can be effective in this context is the use of testers. Each tester is similar in all material respects (e.g., credit history and salary) to the others, but the testers in the group differ in whether they fall into a protected class. The testers then try to rent apartments. If testers are treated differently because of whether they are or are not in a protected class helps to establish that the landlord is acting in a discriminatory manner.

4. *More on Discriminatory Advertising.* Take another look at §3604(c). By its terms, it applies regardless of the speaker's intent. Courts have interpreted the provision as requiring only a discriminatory effect recognizable to the "ordinary listener" or "ordinary reader." Consider the characteristics of an ordinary listener or reader. Would they be particularly sensitive to these issues? Would they need to belong to a protected class? How would you describe the ordinary listener or reader?

The plain language of §3604(c) indicates that it applies to both the individual who drafted the advertisement and the media source that published the advertisement, and courts have in fact applied liability to the source of publication. *See United States v. Hunter*, 459 F.2d 205, 221 (4th Cir. 1972). Most newspapers and magazines are familiar with the FHA and screen out discriminatory advertisements, but in many instances, the Internet does not have a similar screening function. What happens when someone posts a discriminatory advertisement on Craigslist? The Federal Communications Decency Act of 1996 provides immunity from liability for website operators such as Roomates.com and Craigslist. What arguments can you make for and against this immunity? *See* Rigel Oliveri, *Discriminatory Housing Advertisements On-line: Lessons from Craigslist*, 43 Ind. L. Rev. 1125, 1146 (2010) (noting ad on Craigslist for roommate stating "No bible thumpers, no bigots, no strung out meth addicts, no former presidents, no one over eight feet tall, no white-collar criminals").

5. *A Bit More on the Mrs. Murphy Exception.* The Mrs. Murphy exception in §3603(b)(1) is probably the most important exception in the FHA. Be sure that you understand the exact scope of the exception. Having considered the overall structure of the FHA, and the roommate issue from the preceding note, what do you think is the policy behind the Mrs. Murphy exception? What is the policy of having an exception for the exception for discriminatory advertising?

6. *Discrimination Based on Occupation or Profession.* Generally speaking, landlords can discriminate against prospective tenants on the basis of their occupation or profession. A landlord might not want to rent to lawyers, for example, because they have a tendency to assert their rights. This type of discrimination is allowed unless it violates a specific state or local ordinance. New York City, for example, makes it illegal to discriminate based on profession.

7. *Sexual Orientation and Gender Identity.* The FHA does not prohibit discrimination based on sexual orientation or gender identity. Some state and local laws do prohibit this type of discrimination. We will turn to this subject after an exercise and a set of problems.

EXERCISE

The plain language of the FHA appears to prohibit an advertisement that specifies the desired sex of a roommate (e.g., "female roommate wanted"). The FHA prohibits discrimination based on sex, and advertisements are not protected by the Mrs. Murphy exemption. Courts have interpreted the FHA to avoid this problem. *See Fair Housing Council of San Fernando Valley v. Roommates.com, LLC,* 666 F.3d. 1216 (2012) (holding that because the FHA "doesn't apply to the sharing of living units, it follows that it's not unlawful to discriminate in selecting a roommate"). As an exercise, imagine the courts went the other way and prohibited the identification of a preference based on sex in an advertisement for a roommate. Draft an amendment to the FHA that allows advertisements that state a roommate sex preference but that still prohibits discriminatory advertisements in other contexts.

PROBLEMS

Explanatory answers to these problems can be found on page 1046.

1. Analyze each hypothetical and determine whether the advertisement or action would violate either the FHA, the Civil Rights Act of 1866, or both. If the advertisement or action violates the FHA, identify the relevant section or sections.

a. Advertisement to rent an apartment in an owner-occupied two-bedroom townhome in local newspaper stating "Only Muslims should apply."

b. A landlord refuses to rent a room in an owner-occupied two-apartment townhome to a non-Muslim, stating "I only rent to Muslims." The landlord lives in the other apartment.

c. A landlord refuses to rent a room in an owner-occupied two-apartment townhome to an African-American woman, stating "I only rent to white people." The landlord lives in the other apartment.

d. A landlord refuses to rent to a nonmarried couple, saying "I only rent to married couples."

e. A landlord refuses to rent to a single mom of three elementary-school-aged children because "I don't like kids."

f. A landlord rents to a family with two small children but only on the condition that they pay double the security deposit "because kids tend to cause a lot of damage."

g. A landlord refuses to rent to a black male law student stating that "law students are trouble because they like to sue."

h. A landlord rents to an Asian family but demands double the usual security deposit, saying "I've had trouble with you people before."

i. A landlord has a "no pets" policy and refuses to rent to a woman who is diagnosed with severe anxiety and depressive disorder and who has a psychiatric therapy dog.

2. Mary lives at 800 Pennock Street, a two-family home that she owns. Mary lives in the upstairs portion of the house, and rents out the downstairs portion of the house. After her long-time tenant moved out, she placed the following advertisement in a weekly

newspaper: "Downstairs portion of two family home for rent. Located on Pennock Street in Roseville. Two bedrooms, full bath, kitchen, living room. Married white couple preferred. No kids or pets." A local fair-housing group, the Roseville Residential Fairness Association (RRFA), complained to Mary about the advertisement. Mary told the RRFA that it is her house, and she can rent to whomever she wants. RRFA sued Mary in the U.S. District Court seeking a declaratory judgment that the advertisement is illegal.

The FHA does not protect against discrimination based on sexual orientation. Twenty-one states, however, have laws protecting against sexual orientation, and 16 states have laws protecting against discrimination based on gender identity. *See http://www.nationalfairhousing.org/portals/33/2013_fair_housing_trends_report.pdf.* Discrimination based on sexual orientation or gender identity may also be prohibited by municipalities.

Our next case involves a claim of discrimination by a gay man who was HIV positive. The case gives us the opportunity to consider discrimination on the basis of both sexual orientation and handicap, though the court's analysis focuses on the handicap issue. As you read the case, note the burden shifting approach that the court uses. As we discussed above, this type of burden shifting is common in cases under anti-discrimination statutes.

NEITHAMER V. BRENNEMAN PROPERTY SERVICES, INC.

United States District Court for the District of Columbia, 1999
81 F. Supp. 2d 1

KESSLER, District Judge. Plaintiff William Neithamer, who is gay and HIV positive, brings this action against Brenneman Property Services, Inc. and several of its agents under the Fair Housing Act ("FHA"), 42 U.S.C. §3601 *et seq.,* and the D.C. Human Rights Act ("DCHRA"), D.C.Code §1-2515. Plaintiff alleges that Defendants discriminated against him when he applied for housing because of his sexual orientation and his medical disability. This matter comes before the Court on Defendants' Motion for Summary Judgment and Plaintiff's Motion to Strike. Upon consideration of the pleadings and the entire record herein, for the reasons stated below, Defendants' Motion for Summary Judgment is **denied,** and Plaintiff's Motion to Strike is **denied** . . .

BACKGROUND

In September 1997, in his search for new rental housing, Plaintiff contacted Defendant Brenneman Property Services, Inc. ("Brenneman Property") in response to an advertisement for a townhouse on the Northwest side of the District of Columbia. Plaintiff viewed the property, and upon finding it to his liking, filed an application with Brenneman Property for rental of the property.

Plaintiff provided Defendant Padraig A. Wholihan, the agent of Brenneman Property who handled the transaction, with bank statements and credit references in addition to the application. He also informed Wholihan that his credit report would show that he failed to make payments to some of his creditors a few years earlier. He explained that the reason for this was that several years ago, he had devoted his financial resources to paying the medical bills of his lover, who died in 1994 of AIDS. Plaintiff assured Wholihan that since 1994, he had maintained good credit, and that the bank statements and credit references would confirm this.

After Wholihan presented Plaintiff's application to Alida Stephens, the owner of the property, Stephens rejected Plaintiff's application. Upon being informed of this, Plaintiff offered to pay a second month's rent as additional security to rent the property. Wholihan informed Plaintiff that Stephens had rejected this offer too. Plaintiff was then able to obtain a co-signor for the lease, Reverend Louise Lusignan, who completed a co-signor form on Plaintiff's behalf. Wholihan, however, did not run a credit report on Reverend Lusignan's application. Stephens also rejected Plaintiff's offer of a co-signor. At that point, Plaintiff made his final offer to pre-pay one year's rent. Wholihan informed Plaintiff that Mrs. Stephens had rejected this offer as well.

Upon learning of the rejection of his final offer, Plaintiff called Brenneman Property to inquire why his offer was rejected, and spoke with Defendant George Brenneman, the owner of Brenneman Property, as well as Wholihan. When Plaintiff stated he felt he was a victim of discrimination, Plaintiff alleges that Brenneman became angry and shouted, "if you try to sue me, I have a pack of bloodsucking lawyers who will place countersuits against you for libel and drive you into the ground." Wholihan's recollection of the conversation was that Brenneman did say he had a "bulldog of an attorney," and that he may countersue. . . .

Defendants bring their Motion for Summary Judgment, arguing that there is no basis in fact for either of Plaintiff's claims: discrimination under the FHA and the DCHRA, and intimidation and coercion under those same statutes. Plaintiff brings his Motion to Strike, arguing that Defendants' Motion should be struck as untimely and premature . . .

DISCRIMINATION IN VIOLATION OF FHA AND DCHRA

Although the D.C. Circuit Court of Appeals has not yet addressed the issue, a number of other Circuit Courts have already ruled that when a plaintiff offers no direct evidence of discrimination, his claim of discrimination under the FHA is to be examined under the burden-shifting framework of *McDonnell Douglas Corp. v. Green,* 411 U.S. 792, 802-05, 93 S.Ct. 1817, 36 L.Ed.2d 668 (1973), established in Title VII cases. *Gamble v. City of Escondido,* 104 F.3d 300, 305 (9th Cir. 1997); . . . Given the agreement between the Circuits, this Court adopts their reasoning here.

Under this framework, Plaintiff must establish a prima facie case of discrimination by showing: (1) that he is a member of a protected class and Defendants knew or suspected that he was; (2) that he applied for and was qualified to rent the property in question; (3) that Defendants rejected his application; and (4) that the property remained available thereafter. *Blackwell,* 908 F.2d at 870. Plaintiff must provide sufficient evidence to show that he was "rejected under circumstances which give rise to an inference of unlawful discrimination." *Texas Dep't of Community Affairs v. Burdine,* 450 U.S. 248, 253, 101 S.Ct. 1089, 67 L.Ed.2d 207 (1981); *Hayman v. National Academy of Sciences,* 23 F.3d 535, 537 (D.C.Cir.1994). Once Plaintiff establishes a prima facie case, the burden shifts to Defendants to articulate some legitimate, nondiscriminatory reason for their rejection of Plaintiff's application. *Id.* If Defendants satisfy this burden, Plaintiff must show either that Defendants' reasons are pretext, *id.,* or that material facts are disputed, precluding summary judgment. *Aka v. Washington Hosp. Ctr.,* 156 F.3d 1284, 1290 (D.C. Cir. 1998).

Of the four elements of a prima facie case, the last two are undisputed in this case (that Defendants rejected Plaintiff's application, and that the property remained available thereafter). Whether Plaintiff has established the first two elements, however, is very much in dispute.

As to the first element, it is clear that Plaintiff has established a prima facie case as to his sexual orientation. Plaintiff is gay, and Defendants knew or suspected that he was. Although the DCHRA prohibits discrimination based on sexual orientation, the FHA does not. Thus, in order to make a prima facie case under the FHA, Plaintiff must also establish that he is disabled, as that word is used in the FHA, and that Defendants knew or suspected he was.

It is undisputed that Plaintiff is HIV positive, and that being HIV positive constitutes a handicap under the FHA. *See, e.g., Hogar Agua y Vida en el Desierto, Inc. v. Suarez-Medina,* 36 F.3d 177, 179 (1st Cir. 1994). Plaintiff alleges that he is handicapped within the meaning of §3602(h)(3) of the FHA, that is, Defendants regarded or perceived him as being handicapped, while Defendants deny that they ever knew or suspected that Plaintiff was HIV positive. The question is whether Plaintiff has provided enough evidence to give rise to an inference that Defendants perceived he was HIV positive.

Plaintiff provides the following evidence in support of this inference. Plaintiff told Wholihan that his lover had died of AIDS; because of the pernicious stereotyping surrounding those infected with AIDS, Defendants likely suspected that Plaintiff had had sexual relations with his lover, and thus became exposed to the AIDS virus; there is no other explanation for the way that Plaintiff was treated by Defendants, especially given their failure to make exceptions to their rules for him, which they had done for others, and their failure to relay to the owner of the property all of Plaintiff's counteroffers. Plaintiff argues that these facts are sufficient to state a prima facie case that Defendants suspected he had AIDS. Plaintiff also argues that Defendants' denial of any such suspicions makes this issue a question for the jury, because it involves critical questions of credibility, and cannot be decided as a matter of law.

There are no cases which address the question of the plaintiff's burden of proving a prima facie case of perceived disability in a housing discrimination case. There are, however, two cases which address the question of whether the plaintiff can establish a prima facie case when the defendant denies knowledge of the plaintiff's protected-class status. In both *Sanders v. Dorris,* 873 F.2d 938, 942 (6th Cir.1989), and *Bullen v. Thanasouras,* 1994 WL 6868, *3-*4 (N.D.Ill.1994), the defendants denied knowing that the plaintiffs were black, and thus argued that plaintiffs had failed to establish a prima facie case of racial discrimination. Both cases found, however, considering all the facts in the light most favorable to the plaintiffs, that the defendants must have suspected that plaintiffs were black, because the defendants were presented with sufficient "clues" to have supported such suspicions, especially in light of their subsequent behavior towards the plaintiffs.

That reasoning is especially compelling here. First, HIV status is not easily identifiable as race usually is. Second, dismissing a case at the summary judgment stage because a plaintiff cannot prove a defendant's suspicions would subject HIV-positive individuals to the very discrimination that Congress sought to prevent, by denying them a remedy even when such discrimination existed. The very fact that this case is brought under the *perceived* disability section of the FHA informs how the question of the plaintiff's burden of proof at the prima facie stage must be approached. Given the difficulty of identifying a person's HIV status, rarely will another's perceptions of that status be obvious. Even if someone had suspicions of another's HIV status, such perceptions could easily be denied. Therefore, requiring a plaintiff to show definitive proof of a defendant's perceptions at the summary judgment stage creates an impossible burden of proof, one that is inappropriate at the prima facie stage. It is sufficient for a plaintiff to demonstrate that there is a material dispute as to the defendant's perception of him as an individual with HIV or AIDS. Defendant's credibility regarding denials of such perceptions is for the jury to decide.

Considering all the facts in this case most favorably to the Plaintiff, the non-moving party, there are enough "clues" to allow a reasonable jury to conclude that Defendants suspected that Plaintiff was infected with HIV or AIDS: Plaintiff immediately informed Defendants that his lover had died of AIDS. It is no leap of logic to assume that he had had sexual relations with this lover, and was probably exposed to the AIDS virus. Whether Defendants actually made assumptions and had suspicions based on these clues is, however, a material disputed fact, which Plaintiff will have to prove at trial by a preponderance of the evidence.

The second element of a prima facie case, that Plaintiff applied for and was qualified for the property in question, is hotly disputed. Defendants argue that Plaintiff's dismal credit record clearly shows that he was not qualified to rent the property.

It is undisputed that at the time he applied for the apartment in question, Plaintiff's credit report was, indeed, dismal. If his credit report were the only factor Defendants had to evaluate, it would be simple to conclude that Plaintiff was unqualified for the rental. That is not, however, all the information Defendants had at their disposal regarding his application. Specifically, Defendants also knew that Plaintiff's bad credit history was due to a one-time medical catastrophe; that he had significant assets in his bank accounts; that he had credit references and a co-signor; and that he offered to prepay one year's rent on the property. Looking at the record as a whole, Plaintiff has established that he was qualified to rent the property, and thus he has established a prima facie case of discrimination.

Defendants have proffered the following nondiscriminatory reasons for rejecting Plaintiff's application: (1) Plaintiff's credit was so extremely poor that any reasonable real estate agent examining his application would have likewise rejected it; and (2) the decisions to reject Plaintiff's application and subsequent offers were all made by Stephens, for whom Defendants were merely acting as agents.

Plaintiff has provided more than sufficient evidence to call into question Defendants' proffered reasons. Plaintiff has provided evidence indicating that Defendants did not consistently follow their own policy regarding rejecting applicants with poor credit. Additionally, Plaintiff has provided evidence that Defendants did not present Stephens with all of Plaintiff's offers, or all the relevant information about those offers. It is true that when an agent is acting in good faith on behalf of a principal, he is not held liable for the consequences of those actions. *Henderson v. Phillips*, 195 A.2d 400, 402 (D.C. 1963). However, Plaintiff has presented evidence that would lead to an inference of discrimination on the part of Defendants; that evidence would also lead to an inference that Defendants were not acting in good faith as agents.

Plaintiff has advanced evidence suggesting that Defendants' proffered reasons are pretext, and has also established that material disputed facts exist which cannot be resolved on summary judgment. Consequently, Defendants' motion shall be denied as to the discrimination claims . . .

NOTE

1. *Sexual Orientation and the DCHRA.* Because of the procedural posture of the case, the court did not discuss the District of Columbia's prohibition on discrimination based on sexual orientation other than to note that it exists. The relevant provisions of the District of Columbia Human Rights Act prohibit discrimination based on "race, color, religion, national origin, sex, age, marital status, personal appearance, sexual orientation, gender identity or expression, familial status, family responsibilities, disability, matriculation, political affiliation, source of income, status as a victim of an intrafamily offence, or place of residence or business of any individual." §2-1402.21. Compare the protected classes in this provision to the protected classes in the FHA. Which of the classes included in the DCHRA would you add to the FHA if you could?

B. THE TENANT'S RIGHTS AND REMEDIES

1. THE COVENANT OF QUIET ENJOYMENT AND CONSTRUCTIVE EVICTION

In both residential and commercial leases, the tenant has a right to quiet use and enjoyment of the property. Many leases include an express covenant of quiet enjoyment. If the lease is silent on this issue, courts will read an *implied covenant of quiet enjoyment* into the lease. A tenant has quiet use and enjoyment of the property if the tenant is able to use the property without interference and if no other person is asserting a right to be able to use or possess the property. If a landlord breaches the covenant of quiet enjoyment to the degree that the tenant is forced to move out of the property, then the landlord may be deemed to have *constructively evicted* the tenant.

At common law, the covenant of quiet enjoyment and the tenant's obligation to pay rent were originally seen as independent obligations. If obligations are independent, breach of one covenant by one party does not justify breach of the other obligation by the other party. Therefore, under the traditional approach, the landlord's breach of the covenant of quiet enjoyment would not excuse the tenant from continuing to fulfill the obligations of the lease, including the obligation to pay rent. Even under the traditional common law, however, actual eviction by the landlord ended the tenant's obligations to comply with the lease. Constructive eviction first developed out of the concept of actual eviction. When a landlord substantially interferes with the tenant's right to quiet enjoyment of the property to the point that the tenant is forced to move out, the landlord's conduct justifies relieving the tenant of the obligations of the lease just as if the tenant was actually evicted. Therefore, if a tenant could prove constructive eviction, the tenant would be relieved of the obligation to pay rent.

Historically, the scope of constructive eviction was fairly narrow and focused on direct actions by the landlord to interfere with the tenant's use or possession of the premises. More recently, the scope of the doctrine has expanded. Our next case provides an example.

FIDELITY MUTUAL LIFE INSURANCE V. KAMINSKY

Court of Appeals of Texas, Houston (14th Dist.), 1989
768 S.W.2d 818

MURPHY, Justice. The issue in this landlord-tenant case is whether sufficient evidence supports the jury's findings that the landlord and appellant, Fidelity Mutual Life Insurance Company ["Fidelity"], constructively evicted the tenant, Robert P. Kaminsky,

M.D., P.A. ["Dr. Kaminsky"] by breaching the express covenant of quiet enjoyment contained in the parties' lease. We affirm.

Dr. Kaminsky is a gynecologist whose practice includes performing elective abortions. In May 1983, he executed a lease contract for the rental of approximately 2,861 square feet in the Red Oak Atrium Building for a two year term which began on June 1, 1983. The terms of the lease required Dr. Kaminsky to use the rented space solely as "an office for the practice of medicine." Fidelity owns the building and hires local companies to manage it. At some time during the lease term, Shelter Commercial Properties ["Shelter"] replaced the Horne Company as managing agents. Fidelity has not disputed either management company's capacity to act as its agent.

The parties agree that: (1) they executed a valid lease agreement; (2) Paragraph 35 of the lease contains an express covenant of quiet enjoyment conditioned on Dr. Kaminsky's paying rent when due, as he did through November 1984; Dr. Kaminsky abandoned the leased premises on or about December 3, 1984 and refused to pay additional rent; anti-abortion protestors began picketing at the building in June of 1984 and repeated and increased their demonstrations outside and inside the building until Dr. Kaminsky abandoned the premises.

When Fidelity sued for the balance due under the lease contract following Dr. Kaminsky's abandonment of the premises, he claimed that Fidelity constructively evicted him by breaching Paragraph 35 of the lease. Fidelity apparently conceded during trial that sufficient proof of the constructive eviction of Dr. Kaminsky would relieve him of his contractual liability for any remaining rent payments. Accordingly, he assumed the burden of proof and the sole issue submitted to the jury was whether Fidelity breached Paragraph 35 of the lease, which reads as follows:

Quiet Enjoyment.

Lessee, on paying the said Rent, and any Additional Rental, shall and may peaceably and quietly have, hold and enjoy the Leased Premises for the said term.

A constructive eviction occurs when the tenant leaves the leased premises due to conduct by the landlord which materially interferes with the tenant's beneficial use of the premises. *See Downtown Realty, Inc. v. 509 Tremont Bldg.,* 748 S.W.2d 309, 313 (Tex. App.-Houston [14th Dist.] 1988, n.w.h.); *McNabb v. Taylor Oil Field Rental Co.,* 428 S.W.2d 714, 716 (Tex.Civ.App.-San Antonio 1968, writ ref'd n.r.e.). Texas law relieves the tenant of contractual liability for any remaining rentals due under the lease if he can establish a constructive eviction by the landlord . . . .

In order to prevail on his claim that Fidelity constructively evicted him and thereby relieved him of his rent obligation, Dr. Kaminsky had to show the following: 1) Fidelity intended that he no longer enjoy the premises, which intent the trier of fact could infer from the circumstances; 2) Fidelity, or those acting for Fidelity or with its permission, committed a material act or omission which substantially interfered with use and enjoyment of the premises for their leased purpose, here an office for the practice of medicine; 3) Fidelity's act or omission permanently deprived Dr. Kaminsky of the use and enjoyment of the premises; and 4) Dr. Kaminsky abandoned the premises within a reasonable period of time after the act or omission. *E.g., Downtown Realty, Inc.,* 748 S.W.2d at 311; . . .

During oral submission of this case, Fidelity conceded it did not object to an instruction or the four special issues which tracked the foregoing elements. By answering each special issue affirmatively, the jury found that Dr. Kaminsky had established each element of his constructive eviction defense. The trial court entered judgment that Fidelity take nothing on its suit for delinquent rent.

Fidelity raises four points of error . . .

Fidelity's first point of error relies on *Angelo v. Deutser,* 30 S.W.2d 707 (Tex.Civ.App. Beaumont 1930, no writ), *Thomas v. Brin,* 38 Tex.Civ.App. 180, 85 S.W. 842 (1905, no writ) and *Sedberry v. Verplanck,* 31 S.W. 242 (Tex.Civ.App. 1895, no writ). These cases all state the general proposition that a tenant cannot complain that the landlord constructively evicted him and breached a covenant of quiet enjoyment, express or implied, when the eviction results from the actions of third parties acting without the landlord's authority or permission. Fidelity insists the evidence conclusively establishes: a) that it did nothing to encourage or sponsor the protestors and; b) that the protestors, rather than Fidelity or its agents, caused Dr. Kaminsky to abandon the premises. Fidelity concludes that reversible error resulted because the trial court refused to set aside the jury's answers to the special issues and enter judgment in Fidelity's favor and because the trial court denied its motion for a new trial. We disagree.

Although this point of error appears to challenge both the legal and factual sufficiency of the evidence, we have construed it as raising only a "no evidence" or legal sufficiency challenge for two reasons. First, Fidelity relies on record references to "undisputed" evidence and bases its arguments on "established" rules of law. After reviewing Fidelity's oral and written arguments and its references to the record, we conclude that Fidelity essentially disputes the legal sufficiency of the evidence to show that *its own* conduct constructively evicted Dr. Kaminsky. This involves only a question of law in the instant case and thereby fails to raise a factual sufficiency challenge . . .

The protests took place chiefly on Saturdays, the day Dr. Kaminsky generally scheduled abortions. During the protests, the singing and chanting demonstrators picketed in the building's parking lot and inner lobby and atrium area. They approached patients to speak to them, distributed literature, discouraged patients from entering the building and often accused Dr. Kaminsky of "killing babies." As the protests increased, the demonstrators often occupied the stairs leading to Dr. Kaminsky's office and prevented patients from entering the office by blocking the doorway. Occasionally they succeeded in gaining access to the office waiting room area.

Dr. Kaminsky complained to Fidelity through its managing agents and asked for help in keeping the protestors away, but became increasingly frustrated by a lack of response to his requests. The record shows that no security personnel were present on

Saturdays to exclude protestors from the building, although the lease required Fidelity to provide security service on Saturdays. The record also shows that Fidelity's attorneys prepared a written statement to be handed to the protestors soon after Fidelity hired Shelter as its managing agent. The statement tracked Tex. PENAL CODE ANN. §30.05 (Vernon Supp. 1989) and generally served to inform trespassers that they risked criminal prosecution by failing to leave if asked to do so. Fidelity's attorneys instructed Shelter's representative to "have several of these letters printed up and be ready to distribute them and verbally demand that these people move on and off the property." The same representative conceded at trial that she did not distribute these notices. Yet when Dr. Kaminsky enlisted the aid of the Sheriff's office, officers refused to ask the protestors to leave without a directive from Fidelity or its agent. Indeed, an attorney had instructed the protestors to remain *unless* the landlord or its representative ordered them to leave. It appears that Fidelity's only response to the demonstrators was to state, through its agents, that it was aware of Dr. Kaminsky's problems.

Both action and lack of action can constitute "conduct" by the landlord which amounts to a constructive eviction. In *Steinberg v. Medical Equip. Rental Serv., Inc.*, 505 S.W.2d 692 (Tex.Civ.App.-Dallas 1974, no writ) accordingly, the court upheld a jury's determination that the landlord's failure to act amounted to a constructive eviction and breach of the covenant of quiet enjoyment. 5 05 S.W.2d at 697. Like Dr. Kaminsky, the tenant in *Steinberg* abandoned the leased premises and refused to pay additional rent after repeatedly complaining to the landlord. The *Steinberg* tenant complained that Steinberg placed trash bins near the entrance to the business and allowed trucks to park and block customer's access to the tenant's medical equipment rental business. The tenant's repeated complaints to Steinberg yielded only a request "to be patient." *Id.* Fidelity responded to Dr. Kaminsky's complaints in a similar manner: although it acknowledged his problems with the protestors, Fidelity, like Steinberg, effectively did nothing to prevent the problems.

This case shows ample instances of Fidelity's failure to act in the face of repeated requests for assistance despite its having expressly covenanted Dr. Kaminsky's quiet enjoyment of the premises. These instances provided a legally sufficient basis for the jury to conclude that Dr. Kaminsky abandoned the leased premises, not because of the trespassing protestors, but because of Fidelity's lack of response to his complaints about the protestors. Under the circumstances, while it is undisputed that Fidelity did not "encourage" the demonstrators, its conduct essentially allowed them to continue to trespass. The general rule of the *Angelo, Thomas* and *Sedberry* cases, that a landlord is not responsible for the actions of third parties, applies only when the landlord does not permit the third party to act. We see no distinction between Fidelity's lack of action here, which the record shows resulted in preventing patients' access to Dr. Kaminsky's medical office, and the Steinberg case where the landlord's inaction resulted in trucks' blocking customer access to the tenant's business. We overrule the first point of error . . .

Fidelity's third point of error disputes the factual sufficiency of the evidence to show that it committed a material act which substantially interfered with Dr. Kaminsky's use and enjoyment of the premises. Here Fidelity essentially raises the same contention we disposed of in its first point of error: that the record unequivocally establishes that Fidelity committed no act which would give rise to a constructive eviction because the protestors committed the acts which caused Dr. Kaminsky to leave. As we have already indicated, the landlord's acts *or omissions* can form the basis of a constructive eviction. *E.g., Steinberg,* 505 S.W.2d at 697. Special Issue Number Two, to which Fidelity offered no objection, asked whether Fidelity "committed a material act *or omission* if any, that substantially interfered with" Dr. Kaminsky's use and enjoyment of the premises. Having reviewed all the evidence, both supporting and contrary to the jury's affirmative answer to Special Issue Number Two, we find no basis for Fidelity's argument that the finding was so against the great weight and preponderance of the evidence as to be manifestly unjust. *Cain,* 709 S.W.2d at 176; *In re King's Estate,* 150 Tex. at 666, 244 S.W.2d at 662. We overrule the third point of error.

In its fourth point of error, Fidelity maintains the evidence is factually insufficient to support the jury's finding that its conduct permanently deprived Dr. Kaminsky of use and enjoyment of the premises. Fidelity essentially questions the permanency of Dr. Kaminsky's being deprived of the use and enjoyment of the leased premises. To support its contentions, Fidelity points to testimony by Dr. Kaminsky in which he concedes that none of his patients were ever harmed and that protests and demonstrations continued despite his leaving the Red Oak Atrium building. Fidelity also disputes whether Dr. Kaminsky actually lost patients due to the protests.

The evidence shows that the protestors, whose entry into the building Fidelity failed to prohibit, often succeeded in blocking Dr. Kaminsky's patients' access to his medical office. Under the reasoning of the *Steinberg* case, omissions by a landlord which result in patients' lack of access to the office of a practicing physician would suffice to establish a permanent deprivation of the use and enjoyment of the premises for their leased purpose, here "an office for the *practice* of medicine." *Steinberg,* 505 S.W.2d at 697; *accord, Downtown Realty, Inc.,* 748 S.W.2d at 312 (noting jury's finding that a constructive eviction resulted from the commercial landlord's failure to repair a heating and air conditioning system in a rooming house).

Texas law has long recited the requirement, first stated in *Stillman,* 266 S.W.2d at 916, that the landlord commit a "material and permanent" act or omission in order for his tenant to claim a constructive eviction. However, as the *Steinberg* and *Downtown Realty, Inc.* cases illustrate, the extent to which a landlord's acts or omissions permanently and materially deprive a tenant of the use and enjoyment of the premises often involves a question of degree. Having reviewed all the evidence before the jury in this case, we cannot say that its finding that Fidelity's conduct permanently deprived Dr. Kaminsky of the use and enjoyment of his medical office space was so against the great weight and preponderance of the evidence as to be manifestly unjust. *Cain,* 709 S.W.2d at 176; *In re King's Estate,* 150 Tex. at 666, 244 S.W.2d at 662. We overrule the fourth point of error.

We affirm the judgment of the trial court.

NOTES AND QUESTIONS

1. *Public vs. Private Space.* Would *Kaminsky* have come out differently if the protestors had been outside on a public sidewalk rather than in the building?

2. *Constructive Eviction vs. Damages.* In *Kaminsky*, the court identifies that "A constructive eviction occurs when the tenant leaves the leased premises due to conduct by the landlord which materially interferes with the tenant's beneficial use of the premises." Use this statement as a starting point to identify the elements of constructive eviction.

To bring a claim for constructive eviction, the tenant typically has to move out of the premises—after all, the tenant is claiming to be in the same effective position as if the landlord actually evicted the tenant. The tenant may stay on the premises and bring a claim for damages for breach of the covenant of quiet enjoyment. Recall, however, that constructive eviction is what relieves the tenant of the obligation to pay rent. Thus, a tenant who wants to bring a quiet enjoyment claim has two choices. First, the tenant can move out of the premises and claim constructive eviction. The tenant can stop paying rent, though the tenant will be liable for back rent if she loses on the constructive eviction claim. Second, the tenant can stay on the premises and sue for damages. The tenant is still obligated to pay rent, though if the tenant wins, the amount of damages might exceed the amount of rent due for the relevant period.

3. *Landlord Liability for Third Party Conduct.* At common law, a landlord is generally not liable for the conduct of others. In *Kaminsky*, however, the landlord was not a protestor, and the court affirmed the lower court's finding of constructive eviction. The court in *Kaminsky* indicated that the wrongful conduct of the landlord can be an act or an omission. What was Fidelity's act or omission?

4. *Common Areas and Criminal Activity.* The landlord has a duty to control the common areas of the property. Landlords are not liable for all criminal activity but might be liable if they fail to take reasonable precautions "arising from the covenant of quiet enjoyment." *See Sciascia v. Riverpark Apartments*, 44 N.E. 2d 40 (1981).

5. *Landlord Renting to Disruptive Tenants.* Consider *Kaminsky* in light of *Hannan v. Harper*, 208 N.W. 255 (1926), where the court concluded that a family was constructively evicted when the landlord rented the floor above them to a fraternity regardless of whether the "members of the fraternity are undesirable citizens, or that they behave in a boisterous and unseemly manner, or that the fraternity itself constitutes a nuisance . . . [The tenant] is entitled to relief if it appears that the occupancy of the upper flat by this fraternity as its headquarters and club renders the lower flat unfit or undesirable as a place of family residence." If renting a premise to a noisy fraternity can constitute constructive eviction, could renting a premise to a large family be grounds for constructive eviction? Could renting space to a doctor who provides elective abortions constitute constructive eviction of the other tenants in the building? If so, could the other tenants raise a constructive eviction claim even if the protestors had stayed on the public sidewalk outside of the building?

2. THE IMPLIED WARRANTY OF HABITABILITY

Imagine that a residential tenant lives in a disaster of an apartment. The heat doesn't work, the apartment is infested with vermin, and the plumbing frequently backs up. Does the tenant have a claim against the landlord because the premises are not habitable?

Traditionally, the answer to this question was "no." You may have heard the expression *caveat emptor*—"let the buyer beware." Until the 1960s, courts applied the doctrine of caveat emptor to conclude that either (1) tenants had the ability to negotiate for and contract for express warranties of habitability or (2) they could have inspected the premises prior to leasing to ensure the premises were habitable.

In the 1960s courts began rejecting the caveat emptor approach to leases and instead drew on contract principles to give relief to tenants. Courts began to recognize an *implied warranty of habitability*, drawing on the contract principle that goods being sold must be suitable for the purpose for which they are being sold. Courts also started to allow tenants to stop paying rent while remaining in the premises. In doing so, courts relieved the tenant from having to make the choice of staying and paying rent, on the one hand, and moving out and not paying rent, on the other. In this way, the implied warranty of habitability was far more tenant friendly than the older rules governing the covenant of quiet enjoyment and constructive eviction. The implied warranty of habitability is an important example of courts shifting from landlord-friendly property principles to more tenant-friendly contract principles.

PROPERTY VS. CONTRACT

The tenant's right to a habitable premise only extends to residential, not commercial, leases. Today, most states agree that the *implied warranty of habitability* is non-waivable, even by an express provision in the lease. As we will soon see, violations of state or housing codes played a major role in the evolution of the implied warranty of habitability. Today, breaches of the implied warranty of habitability tend to focus on (a) violations of housing codes and (b) conditions harmful to the health of the tenant. Some implied warranty of habitability cases involve gruesome facts. For example, in *Smithline v. Monica*, 1987 WL 14296, N.Y. City Ct. 1987, the court held that the implied warranty of habitability was breached after hearing testimony that cockroaches infested the tenants' food and had to be medically removed from a child's ear. Others involve less dramatic but still important threats to the tenant's health. For example, in *Poyck v. Bryant*, 13 Misc.3d 699, 820 N.Y.S.2d 774 (Civ. Ct. 2006), the court reasoned that secondhand smoke posed a significant health risk to the tenant and breached the warranty of implied habitability.

Our next case, *Javins v. First National Realty v. Corp*, 428 F.2d 1071 (D.C. Cir. 1970) is a landmark opinion in landlord-tenant law because it was one of the first cases to recognize the tenant's right to a habitable premise. As you are reading it, pay special attention to the court's reasoning. What justifications does the court provide for explaining why the common law should recognize the implied warranty of habitability? What reasons does the court suggest for making the warranty non-waivable?

Another case excerpt, *Hilder v. St. Peter*, immediately follows the *Javins* excerpt. *Hilder* allows us to see the modern implied warranty of habitability in action and provides an excellent statement of the rules that apply when a tenant makes an implied warranty of habitability claim against a landlord.

JAVINS V. FIRST NATIONAL REALTY CORPORATION

United States Court of Appeals, District of Columbia Circuit, 1970
428 F.2d 1071

WRIGHT, Circuit Judge. These cases present the question whether housing code violations which arise during the term of a lease have any effect upon the tenant's obligation to pay rent. The Landlord and Tenant Branch of the District of Columbia Court of General Sessions ruled proof of such violations inadmissible when proffered as a defense to an eviction action for nonpayment of rent. The District of Columbia Court of Appeals upheld this ruling. *Saunders v. First National Realty Corp.*, 245 A.2d 836 (1968).

Because of the importance of the question presented, we granted appellants' petitions for leave to appeal. We now reverse and hold that a warranty of habitability, measured by the standards set out in the Housing Regulations for the District of Columbia, is implied by operation of law into leases of urban dwelling units covered by those Regulations and that breach of this warranty gives rise to the usual remedies for breach of contract.

I

The facts revealed by the record are simple. By separate written leases, . . . each of the appellants rented an apartment in a three-building apartment complex in Northwest Washington known as Clifton Terrace. The landlord, First National Realty Corporation, filed separate actions in the Landlord and Tenant Branch of the Court of General Sessions on April 8, 1966, seeking possession on the ground that each of the appellants had defaulted in the payment of rent due for the month of April. The tenants, appellants here, admitted that they had not paid the landlord any rent for April. However, they alleged numerous violations of the Housing Regulations as "an equitable defense or (a) claim by way of recoupment or set-off in an amount equal to the rent claim," as provided in the rules of the Court of General Sessions . . . They offered to prove

> "that there are approximately 1500 violations of the Housing Regulations of the District of Columbia in the building at Clifton Terrace, where Defendant resides some affecting the premises of this Defendant directly, others indirectly, and all tending to establish a course of conduct of violation of the Housing Regulations to the damage of Defendants . . ."

Settled Statement of Proceedings and Evidence, p. 2 (1966). Appellants conceded at trial, however, that this offer of proof reached only violations which had arisen since the term of the lease had commenced. The Court of General Sessions refused appellants' offer of proof . . . and entered judgment for the landlord. The District of Columbia Court of Appeals affirmed, rejecting the argument made by appellants that the landlord was under a contractual duty to maintain the premises in compliance with the Housing Regulations. *Saunders v. First National Realty Corp., supra,* 245 A.2d at 838 . . .

II

Since, in traditional analysis, a lease was the conveyance of an interest in land, courts have usually utilized the special rules governing real property transactions to resolve controversies involving leases. However, as the Supreme Court has noted in another context, "the body of private property law . . ., more than almost any other branch of law, has been shaped by distinctions whose validity is largely historical." . . . . Courts have a duty to reappraise old doctrines in the light of the facts and values of contemporary life—particularly old common law doctrines which the courts themselves created and developed . . . As we have said before, "The continued vitality of the common law . . . depends upon its ability to reflect contemporary community values and ethics." . . .

The assumption of landlord-tenant law, derived from feudal property law, that a lease primarily conveyed to the tenant an interest in land may have been reasonable in a rural, agrarian society; it may continue to be reasonable in some leases involving farming or commercial land. In these cases, the value of the lease to the tenant is the land itself. But in the case of the modern apartment dweller, the value of the lease is that it gives him a place to live. The city dweller who seeks to lease an apartment on the third floor of a tenement has little interest in the land 30 or 40 feet below, or even in the bare right to possession within the four walls of his apartment. When American city dwellers, both rich and poor, seek "shelter" today, they seek a well known package of goods and services—a package which includes not merely walls and ceilings, but also adequate heat, light and ventilation, serviceable plumbing facilities, secure windows and doors, proper sanitation, and proper maintenance.

Professor Powell summarizes the present state of the law:

"The complexities of city life, and the proliferated problems of modern society in general, have created new problems for lessors and lessees and these have been commonly handled by specific clauses inserted in leases. This growth in the number and detail of specific lease covenants has reintroduced into the law of estates for years a predominantly contractual ingredient. In practice, the law today concerning estates for years consists chiefly of rules determining the construction and effect of lease covenants." . . .

Ironically, however, the rules governing the construction and interpretation of "predominantly contractual" obligations in leases have too often remained rooted in old property law.

Some courts have realized that certain of the old rules of property law governing leases are inappropriate for today's transactions. In order to reach results more in accord with the legitimate expectations of the parties and the standards of the community, courts have been gradually introducing more modern precepts of contract law in interpreting leases . . . Proceeding piecemeal has, however, led to confusion where "decisions are frequently conflicting, not because of a healthy disagreement on social policy, but because of the lingering impact of rules whose policies are long since dead." . . .

PROPERTY VS. CONTRACT

In our judgment the trend toward treating leases as contracts is wise and well considered. Our holding in this case reflects a belief that leases of urban dwelling units should be interpreted and construed like any other contract.[13]

III

Modern contract law has recognized that the buyer of goods and services in an industrialized society must rely upon the skill and honesty of the supplier to assure that goods and services purchased are of adequate quality. In interpreting most contracts, courts have sought to protect the legitimate expectations of the buyer and have steadily widened the seller's responsibility for the quality of goods and services through implied warranties of fitness and merchantability. Thus without any special agreement a merchant will be held to warrant that his goods are fit for the ordinary purposes for which such goods are used and that they are at least of reasonably average quality. Moreover, if the supplier has been notified that goods are required for a specific purpose, he will be held to warrant that any goods sold are fit for that purpose. These implied warranties have become widely accepted and well established features of the common law, supported by the overwhelming body of case law. Today most states as well as the District of Columbia have codified and enacted these warranties into statute, as to the sale of goods, in the Uniform Commercial Code.

Implied warranties of quality have not been limited to cases involving sales. The consumer renting a chattel, paying for services, or buying a combination of goods and services must rely upon the skill and honesty of the supplier to at least the same extent

---

[13] This approach does not deny the possible importance of the fact that land is involved in a transaction. The interpretation and construction of contracts between private parties has always required courts to be sensitive and responsive to myriad different factors. We believe contract doctrines allow courts to be properly sensitive to all relevant factors in interpreting lease obligations. We also intend no alteration of statutory or case law definitions of the term "real property" for purposes of statutes or decisions on recordation, descent, conveyancing, creditors' rights, etc. We contemplate only that contract law is to determine the rights and obligations of the parties to the lease agreement, as between themselves. The civil law has always viewed the lease as a contract, and in our judgment that perspective has proved superior to that of the common law. *See* 2 M. Planiol, Treatise on the Civil Law §1663 *et seq.* (1959); 11 La.Stat.Ann., Civil Code, Art. 2669 (1952).

as a purchaser of goods. Courts have not hesitated to find implied warranties of fitness and merchantability in such situations. In most areas product liability law has moved far beyond "mere" implied warranties running between two parties in privity with each other.

The rigid doctrines of real property law have tended to inhibit the application of implied warranties to transactions involving real estate. Now, however, courts have begun to hold sellers and developers of real property responsible for the quality of their product. For example, builders of new homes have recently been held liable to purchasers for improper construction on the ground that the builders had breached an implied warranty of fitness. In other cases courts have held builders of new homes liable for breach of an implied warranty that all local building regulations had been complied with. And following the developments in other areas, very recent decisions and commentary suggest the possible extension of liability to parties other than the immediate seller for improper construction of residential real estate.

Despite this trend in the sale of real estate, many courts have been unwilling to imply warranties of quality, specifically a warranty of habitability, into leases of apartments. Recent decisions have offered no convincing explanation for their refusal; . . . rather they have relied without discussion upon the old common law rule that the lessor is not obligated to repair unless he covenants to do so in the written lease contract . . . However, the Supreme Courts of at least two states, in recent and well reasoned opinions, have held landlords to implied warranties of quality in housing leases. *Lemle v. Breeden*, S.Ct. Hawaii, 462 P.2d 470 (1969); *Reste Realty Corp. v. Cooper*, 53 N.J. 444, 251 A.2d 268 (1969). *See also Pines v. Perssion*, 14 Wis.2d 590, 111 N.W.2d 409 (1961). In our judgment, the old no-repair rule cannot coexist with the obligations imposed on the landlord by a typical modern housing code, and must be abandoned in favor of an implied warranty of habitability.[29] In the District of Columbia, the standards of this warranty are set out in the Housing Regulations.

IV

A.

In our judgment the common law itself must recognize the landlord's obligation to keep his premises in a habitable condition. This conclusion is compelled by three separate considerations. First, we believe that the old rule was based on certain factual assumptions which are no longer true; on its own terms, it can no longer be justified. Second, we believe that the consumer protection cases discussed above require that the old rule be abandoned in order to bring residential landlord-tenant law into harmony

---

[29] Although the present cases involve written leases, we think there is no particular significance in this fact. The landlord's warranty is implied in oral and written leases for all types of tenancies.

with the principles on which those cases rest. Third, we think that the nature of today's urban housing market also dictates abandonment of the old rule.

The common law rule absolving the lessor of all obligation to repair originated in the early Middle Ages.[30] Such a rule was perhaps well suited to an agrarian economy; the land was more important[31] than whatever small living structure was included in the leasehold, and the tenant farmer was fully capable of making repairs himself.[32] These historical facts were the basis on which the common law constructed its rule; they also provided the necessary prerequisites for its application . . .

Court decisions in the late 1800's began to recognize that the factual assumptions of the common law were no longer accurate in some cases. For example, the common law, since it assumed that the land was the most important part of the leasehold, required a tenant to pay rent even if any building on the land was destroyed . . . Faced with such a rule and the ludicrous results it produced, in 1863 the New York Court of Appeals declined to hold that an upper story tenant was obliged to continue paying rent after his apartment building burned down . . . The court simply pointed out that the urban tenant had no interest in the land, only in the attached building.

Another line of cases created an exception to the no-repair rule for short term leases of furnished dwellings . . . The Massachusetts Supreme Judicial Court, a court not known for its willingness to depart from the common law, supported this exception, pointing out:

> "(A) different rule should apply to one who hires a furnished room, or a furnished house, for a few days, or a few weeks or months. Its fitness for immediate use of a particular kind, as indicated by its appointments, is a far more important element entering into the contract than when there is a mere lease of real estate. One who lets for a short term a house provided with all furnishings and appointments for immediate residence may be supposed to contract in reference to a well-understood purpose of the hirer to use it as a habitation . . . It would be unreasonable to hold, under such circumstances, that the landlord does not impliedly agree that what he is letting is a house suitable for occupation in its condition at the time . . ."

---

[30] The rule was "settled" by 1485. 3 W. Holdsworth, A History of English Law 122-123 (6th ed. 1934). The common law rule discussed in text originated in the even older rule prohibiting the tenant from committing waste. The writ of waste expanded as the tenant's right to possession grew stronger. Eventually, in order to protect the landowner's reversionary interest, the tenant became obligated to make repairs and liable to eviction and damages if he failed to do so.

[31] The land was so central to the original common law conception of a leasehold that rent was viewed as "issuing" from the land: "The governing idea is that the land is bound to pay the rent . . . We may almost go to the length of saying that the land pays it through (the tenant's) hand." 2 F. Pollock & F. Maitland, The History of English Law 131 (2d ed. 1923).

[32] Many later judicial opinions have added another justification of the old common law rule. They have invoked the timeworn cry of caveat emptor and argued that a lessee has the opportunity to inspect the premises. On the basis of his inspection, the tenant must then take the premises "as is," according to this reasoning. As an historical matter, the opportunity to inspect was not thought important when the rule was first devised.

These as well as other similar cases . . . demonstrate that some courts began some time ago to question the common law's assumptions that the land was the most important feature of a leasehold and that the tenant could feasibly make any necessary repairs himself. Where those assumptions no longer reflect contemporary housing patterns, the courts have created exceptions to the general rule that landlords have no duty to keep their premises in repair.

It is overdue for courts to admit that these assumptions are no longer true with regard to all urban housing. Today's urban tenants, the vast majority of whom live in multiple dwelling houses, are interested, not in the land, but solely in "a house suitable for occupation." Furthermore, today's city dweller usually has a single, specialized skill unrelated to maintenance work; he is unable to make repairs like the "jack-of-all-trades" farmer who was the common law's model of the lessee . . . Further, unlike his agrarian predecessor who often remained on one piece of land for his entire life, urban tenants today are more mobile than ever before. A tenant's tenure in a specific apartment will often not be sufficient to justify efforts at repairs. In addition, the increasing complexity of today's dwellings renders them much more difficult to repair than the structures of earlier times. In a multiple dwelling repair may require access to equipment and areas in the control of the landlord. Low and middle income tenants, even if they were interested in making repairs, would be unable to obtain any financing for major repairs since they have no long-term interest in the property.

Our approach to the common law of landlord and tenant ought to be aided by principles derived from the consumer protection cases referred to above . . . In a lease contract, a tenant seeks to purchase from his landlord shelter for a specified period of time. The landlord sells housing as a commercial businessman and has much greater opportunity, incentive and capacity to inspect and maintain the condition of his building. Moreover, the tenant must rely upon the skill and bona fides of his landlord at least as much as a car buyer must rely upon the car manufacturer. In dealing with major problems, such as heating, plumbing, electrical or structural defects, the tenant's position corresponds precisely with "the ordinary consumer who cannot be expected to have the knowledge or capacity or even the opportunity to make adequate inspection of mechanical instrumentalities, like automobiles, and to decide for himself whether they are reasonably fit for the designed purpose." *Henningsen v. Bloomfield Motors, Inc.*, 32 N.J. 358, 375, 161 A.2d 69, 78 (1960).[42]

Since a lease contract specifies a particular period of time during which the tenant has a right to use his apartment for shelter, he may legitimately expect that the apartment will be fit for habitation for the time period for which it is rented. We point

---

[42] Nor should the average tenant be thought capable of "inspecting" plaster, floorboards, roofing, kitchen appliances, etc. To the extent, however, that some defects are obvious, the law must take note of the present housing shortage. Tenants may have no real alternative but to accept such housing with the expectation that the landlord will make necessary repairs. Where this is so, caveat emptor must of necessity be rejected.

out that in the present cases there is no allegation that appellants' apartments were in poor condition or in violation of the housing code at the commencement of the leases. Since the lessees continue to pay the same rent, they were entitled to expect that the landlord would continue to keep the premises in their beginning condition during the lease term. It is precisely such expectations that the law now recognizes as deserving of formal, legal protection.

Even beyond the rationale of traditional products liability law, the relationship of landlord and tenant suggests further compelling reasons for the law's protection of the tenants' legitimate expectations of quality. The inequality in bargaining power between landlord and tenant has been well documented . . . Tenants have very little leverage to enforce demands for better housing. Various impediments to competition in the rental housing market, such as racial and class discrimination . . . and standardized form leases, . . . mean that landlords place tenants in a take it or leave it situation. The increasingly severe shortage . . . of adequate housing further increases the landlord's bargaining power and escalates the need for maintaining and improving the existing stock. Finally, the findings by various studies of the social impact of bad housing has led to the realization that poor housing is detrimental to the whole society, not merely to the unlucky ones who must suffer the daily indignity of living in a slum . . .

Thus we are led by our inspection of the relevant legal principles and precedents to the conclusion that the old common law rule imposing an obligation upon the lessee to repair during the lease term was really never intended to apply to residential urban leaseholds. Contract principles established in other areas of the law provide a more rational framework for the apportionment of landlord-tenant responsibilities; they strongly suggest that a warranty of habitability be implied into all contracts for urban dwellings.

PROPERTY VS. CONTRACT

B.

We believe, in any event, that the District's housing code requires that a warranty of habitability be implied in the leases of all housing that it covers. The housing code—formally designated the Housing Regulations of the District of Columbia—was established and authorized by the Commissioners of the District of Columbia on August 11, 1955 . . . Since that time, the code has been updated by numerous orders of the Commissioners. The 75 pages of the Regulations provide a comprehensive regulatory scheme setting forth in some detail: (a) the standards which housing in the District of Columbia must meet; . . . (b) which party, the lessor or the lessee, must meet each standard; and (c) a system of inspections, notifications and criminal penalties. The Regulations themselves are silent on the question of private remedies.

Two previous decisions of this court, however, have held that the Housing Regulations create legal rights and duties enforceable in tort by private parties. In *Whetzel v. Jess Fisher Management Co.*, 108 U.S. App. D.C. 385, 282 F.2d 943 (1960), we followed the leading case of *Altz v. Leiberson*, 233 N.Y. 16, 134 N.E. 703 (1922), in holding (1) that the housing code altered the common law rule and imposed a duty to repair upon the landlord, and (2) that a right of action accrued to a tenant injured by the landlord's breach of this duty. As Judge Cardozo wrote in Leiberson:

> "We may be sure that the framers of this statute, when regulating tenement life, had uppermost in thought the care of those who are unable to care for themselves. The Legislature must have known that unless repairs in the rooms of the poor were made by the landlord, they would not be made by any one. The duty imposed became commensurate with the need. The right to seek redress is not limited to the city or its officers. The right extends to all whom there was a purpose to protect . . ."

Recently, in *Kanelos v. Kettler*, 132 U.S. App. D.C. 133, 135, 406 F.2d 951, 953 (1968), we reaffirmed our position in *Whetzel*, holding that "the Housing Regulations did impose maintenance obligations upon appellee (landlord) which he was not free to ignore."

The District of Columbia Court of Appeals gave further effect to the Housing Regulations in *Brown v. Southall Realty Co.*, 237 A.2d 834 (1968). There the landlord knew at the time the lease was signed that housing code violations existed which rendered the apartment "unsafe and unsanitary." Viewing the lease as a contract, the District of Columbia Court of Appeals held that the premises were let in violation of Sections 2304[53] and 2501 . . . of the Regulations and that the lease, therefore, was void as an illegal contract. In the light of Brown, it is clear not only that the housing code creates privately enforceable duties as held in *Whetzel*, but that the basic validity of every housing contract depends upon substantial compliance with the housing code at the beginning of the lease term. The *Brown* court relied particularly upon Section 2501 of the Regulations which provides:

> "Every premises accommodating one or more habitations shall be maintained and kept in repair so as to provide decent living accommodations for the occupants. This part of this Code contemplates more than mere basic repairs and maintenance to keep out the elements; its purpose is to include repairs and maintenance designed to make a premises or neighborhood healthy and safe."

By its terms, this section applies to maintenance and repair during the lease term. Under the Brown holding, serious failure to comply with this section before the lease term begins renders the contract void. We think it untenable to find that this section has no effect on the contract after it has been signed. To the contrary, by signing the lease the landlord has undertaken a continuing obligation to the tenant to maintain the premises in accordance with all applicable law.

This principle of implied warranty is well established. Courts often imply relevant law into contracts to provide a remedy for any damage caused by one party's illegal

---

[53] "No person shall rent or offer to rent any habitation, or the furnishings thereof, unless such habitation and its furnishings are in a clean, safe and sanitary condition, in repair, and free from rodents or vermin."

conduct . . . In a case closely analogous to the present ones, the Illinois Supreme Court held that a builder who constructed a house in violation of the Chicago building code had breached his contract with the buyer:

> "The law existing at the time and place of the making of the contract is deemed a part of the contract, as though expressly referred to or incorporated in it . . .
>
> "The rationale for this rule is that the parties to the contract would have expressed that which the law implies 'had they not supposed that it was unnecessary to speak of it because the law provided for it.' . . .

Consequently, the courts, in construing the existing law as part of the express contract, are not reading into the contract provisions different from those expressed and intended by the parties, as defendants contend, but are merely construing the contract in accordance with the intent of the parties."[56]

We follow the Illinois court in holding that the housing code must be read into housing contracts—a holding also required by the purposes and the structure of the code itself.[57] . . . The duties imposed by the Housing Regulations may not be waived or shifted by agreement if the Regulations specifically place the duty upon the lessor.[58] . . . Criminal penalties are provided if these duties are ignored. This regulatory structure was established by the Commissioners because, in their judgment, the grave conditions in the housing market required serious action. Yet official enforcement of the housing code has been far from uniformly effective . . . Innumerable studies have documented the desperate condition of rental housing in the District of Columbia and in the nation. In view of these circumstances, we think the conclusion reached by the Supreme Court of Wisconsin as to the effect of a housing code on the old common law rule cannot be avoided:

---

[56] *Schiro v. W. E. Gould & Co.*, 18 Ill.2d at 544, 165 N.E.2d at 290. As a general proposition, it is undoubtedly true that parties to a contract intend that applicable law will be complied with by both sides. We recognize, however, that reading statutory provisions into private contracts may have little factual support in the intentions of the particular parties now before us. But, for reasons of public policy, warranties are often implied into contracts by operation of law in order to meet generally prevailing standards of honesty and fair dealing. When the public policy has been enacted into law like the housing code, that policy will usually have deep roots in the expectations and intentions of most people. *See* Costigan, Implied-in-Fact Contracts and Mutual Assent, 33 Harv.L.Rev. 376, 383-385 (1920).

[57] "The housing and sanitary codes, especially in light of Congress' explicit direction for their enactment, indicate a strong and pervasive congressional concern to secure for the city's slum dwellers decent, or at least safe and sanitary, places to live." *Edwards v. Habib*, 130 U.S. App. D.C. at 139, 397 F.2d at 700.

[58] Any private agreement to shift the duties would be illegal and unenforceable. The precedents dealing with industrial safety statutes are directly in point: "The only question remaining is whether the courts will enforce or recognize as against a servant an agreement express or implied on his part to waive the performance of a statutory duty of the master imposed for the protection of the servant, and in the interest of the public, and enforceable by criminal prosecution. We do not think they will. To do so would be to nullify the object of the statute." *Narramore v. Cleveland, C., C. & St. L.Ry. Co.*, 6 Cir., 96 F. 298, 302 (1899). *See* W. Prosser, Torts §67 at 468-469 (3d ed. 1964) and cases cited therein.

"The legislature has made a policy judgment—that it is socially (and politically) desirable to impose these duties on a property owner—which has rendered the old common law rule obsolete. To follow the old rule of no implied warranty of habitability in leases would, in our opinion, be inconsistent with the current legislative policy concerning housing standards . . ."

We therefore hold that the Housing Regulations imply a warranty of habitability, measured by the standards which they set out, into leases of all housing that they cover.

V

In the present cases, the landlord sued for possession for nonpayment of rent. Under contract principles,[61] . . . however, the tenant's obligation to pay rent is dependent upon the landlord's performance of his obligations, including his warranty to maintain the premises in habitable condition. In order to determine whether any rent is owed to the landlord, the tenants must be given an opportunity to prove the housing code violations alleged as breach of the landlord's warranty.[62]

At trial, the finder of fact must make two findings: (1) whether the alleged violations[63] . . . existed during the period for which past due rent is claimed, and (2) what portion, if any or all, of the tenant's obligation to pay rent was suspended by the landlord's breach. If no part of the tenant's rental obligation is found to have been suspended, then a judgment for possession may issue forthwith. On the other hand, if the jury determines that the entire rental obligation has been extinguished by the landlord's total breach, then the action for possession on the ground of nonpayment must fail.[64] . . .

The jury may find that part of the tenant's rental obligation has been suspended but that part of the unpaid back rent is indeed owed to the landlord . . . In these circumstances, no judgment for possession should issue if the tenant agrees to pay the partial rent found to be due . . . If the tenant refuses to pay the partial amount, a judgment for possession may then be entered.

---

[61] In extending all contract remedies for breach to the parties to a lease, we include an action for specific performance of the landlord's implied warranty of habitability.

[62] To be relevant, of course, the violations must affect the tenant's apartment or common areas which the tenant uses. Moreover, the contract principle that no one may benefit from his own wrong will allow the landlord to defend by proving the damage was caused by the tenant's wrongful action. However, violations resulting from inadequate repairs or materials which disintegrate under normal use would not be assignable to the tenant. Also we agree with the District of Columbia Court of Appeals that the tenant's private rights do not depend on official inspection or official finding of violation by the city government. *Diamond Housing Corp. v. Robinson*, 257 A.2d 492, 494 (1969).

[63] The jury should be instructed that one or two minor violations standing alone which do not affect habitability are de minimis and would not entitle the tenant to a reduction in rent.

[64] As soon as the landlord made the necessary repairs rent would again become due. Our holding, of course, affects only eviction for nonpayment of rent. The landlord is free to seek eviction at the termination of the lease or on any other legal ground.

The judgment of the District of Columbia Court of Appeals is reversed and the cases are remanded for further proceedings consistent with this opinion . . .

So ordered.

HILDER V. ST. PETER

Supreme Court of Vermont, 1984
478 A.2d 202

BILLINGS, Chief Justice. Defendants appeal from a judgment rendered by the Rutland Superior Court. The court ordered defendants to pay plaintiff damages in the amount of $4,945.00, which represented "reimbursement of all rent paid and additional compensatory damages" for the rental of a residential apartment over a fourteen month period in defendants' Rutland apartment building. Defendants filed a motion for reconsideration on the issue of the amount of damages awarded to the plaintiff, and plaintiff filed a cross-motion for reconsideration of the court's denial of an award of punitive damages. The court denied both motions. On appeal, defendants raise three issues for our consideration: first, whether the court correctly calculated the amount of damages awarded the plaintiff; secondly, whether the court's award to plaintiff of the entire amount of rent paid to defendants was proper since the plaintiff remained in possession of the apartment for the entire fourteen month period; and finally, whether the court's finding that defendant Stuart St. Peter acted on his own behalf and with the apparent authority of defendant Patricia St. Peter was error.

The facts are uncontested. In October, 1974, plaintiff began occupying an apartment at defendants' 10-12 Church Street apartment building in Rutland with her three children and new-born grandson.[1] Plaintiff orally agreed to pay defendant Stuart St. Peter $140 a month and a damage deposit of $50; plaintiff paid defendant the first month's rent and the damage deposit prior to moving in. Plaintiff has paid all rent due under her tenancy. Because the previous tenants had left behind garbage and items of personal belongings, defendant offered to refund plaintiff's damage deposit if she would clean the apartment herself prior to taking possession. Plaintiff did clean the apartment, but never received her deposit back because the defendant denied ever receiving it. Upon moving into the apartment, plaintiff discovered a broken kitchen window. Defendant promised to repair it, but after waiting a week and fearing that her two year old child might cut herself on the shards of glass, plaintiff repaired the window at her own expense. Although defendant promised to provide a front door key, he never did. For a period of time, whenever plaintiff left the apartment, a member of her family would remain behind for security reasons. Eventually, plaintiff purchased and

---

[1] Between October, 1974, and December, 1976, plaintiff rented apartment number 1 for $140.00 monthly for 18 months, and apartment number 50 for $125.00 monthly for 7 months.

installed a padlock, again at her own expense. After moving in, plaintiff discovered that the bathroom toilet was clogged with paper and feces and would flush only by dumping pails of water into it. Although plaintiff repeatedly complained about the toilet, and defendant promised to have it repaired, the toilet remained clogged and mechanically inoperable throughout the period of plaintiff's tenancy. In addition, the bathroom light and wall outlet were inoperable. Again, the defendant agreed to repair the fixtures, but never did. In order to have light in the bathroom, plaintiff attached a fixture to the wall and connected it to an extension cord that was plugged into an adjoining room. Plaintiff also discovered that water leaked from the water pipes of the upstairs apartment down the ceilings and walls of both her kitchen and back bedroom. Again, defendant promised to fix the leakage, but never did. As a result of this leakage, a large section of plaster fell from the back bedroom ceiling onto her bed and her grandson's crib. Other sections of plaster remained dangling from the ceiling. This condition was brought to the attention of the defendant, but he never corrected it. Fearing that the remaining plaster might fall when the room was occupied, plaintiff moved her and her grandson's bedroom furniture into the living room and ceased using the back bedroom. During the summer months an odor of raw sewage permeated plaintiff's apartment. The odor was so strong that the plaintiff was ashamed to have company in her apartment. Responding to plaintiff's complaints, Rutland City workers unearthed a broken sewage pipe in the basement of defendants' building. Raw sewage littered the floor of the basement, but defendant failed to clean it up. Plaintiff also discovered that the electric service for her furnace was attached to her breaker box, although defendant had agreed, at the commencement of plaintiff's tenancy, to furnish heat.

In its conclusions of law, the court held that the state of disrepair of plaintiff's apartment, which was known to the defendants, substantially reduced the value of the leasehold from the agreed rental value, thus constituting a breach of the implied warranty of habitability. The court based its award of damages on the breach of this warranty and on breach of an express contract. Defendant argues that the court misapplied the law of Vermont relating to habitability because the plaintiff never abandoned the demised premises and, therefore, it was error to award her the full amount of rent paid. Plaintiff counters that, while never expressly recognized by this Court, the trial court was correct in applying an implied warranty of habitability and that under this warranty, abandonment of the premises is not required. Plaintiff urges this Court to affirmatively adopt the implied warranty of habitability.

Historically, relations between landlords and tenants have been defined by the law of property. Under these traditional common law property concepts, a lease was viewed as a conveyance of real property. See Note, *Judicial Expansion of Tenants' Private Law Rights: Implied Warranties of Habitability and Safety in Residential Urban Leases,* 56 Cornell L.Q. 489, 489-90 (1971) (hereinafter cited as *Expansion of Tenants' Rights*). The relationship between landlord and tenant was controlled by the doctrine of caveat lessee;

that is, the tenant took possession of the demised premises irrespective of their state of disrepair. Love, *Landlord's Liability for Defective Premises: Caveat Lessee, Negligence, or Strict Liability?*, 1975 Wis.L.Rev. 19, 27-28. The landlord's only covenant was to deliver possession to the tenant. The tenant's obligation to pay rent existed independently of the landlord's duty to deliver possession, so that as long as possession remained in the tenant, the tenant remained liable for payment of rent. The landlord was under no duty to render the premises habitable unless there was an express covenant to repair in the written lease. *Expansion of Tenants' Rights, supra,* at 490. The land, not the dwelling, was regarded as the essence of the conveyance.

An exception to the rule of caveat lessee was the doctrine of constructive eviction. *Lemle v. Breeden,* 51 Haw. 426, 430, 462 P.2d 470, 473 (1969). Here, if the landlord wrongfully interfered with the tenant's enjoyment of the demised premises, or failed to render a duty to the tenant as expressly required under the terms of the lease, the tenant could abandon the premises and cease paying rent. *Legier v. Deveneau,* 98 Vt. 188, 190, 126 A. 392, 393 (1924).

Beginning in the 1960's, American courts began recognizing that this approach to landlord and tenant relations, which had originated during the Middle Ages, had become an anachronism in twentieth century, urban society. Today's tenant enters into lease agreements, not to obtain arable land, but to obtain safe, sanitary and comfortable housing.

> [T]hey seek a well known package of goods and services—a package which includes not merely walls and ceilings, but also adequate heat, light and ventilation, serviceable plumbing facilities, secure windows and doors, proper sanitation, and proper maintenance.

Javins v. First National Realty Corp., 428 F.2d 1071, 1074 (D.C.Cir.), *cert. denied,* 400 U.S. 925, 91 S.Ct. 186, 27 L.Ed.2d 185 (1970).

Not only has the subject matter of today's lease changed, but the characteristics of today's tenant have similarly evolved. The tenant of the Middle Ages was a farmer, capable of making whatever repairs were necessary to his primitive dwelling. *Green v. Superior Court,* 10 Cal.3d 616, 622, 517 P.2d 1168, 1172, 111 Cal.Rptr. 704, 708 (1974). Additionally, "the common law courts assumed that an equal bargaining position existed between landlord and tenant . . . ." Note, *The Implied Warranty of Habitability: A Dream Deferred,* 48 UMKC L.Rev. 237, 238 (1980) (hereinafter cited as *A Dream Deferred*).

In sharp contrast, today's residential tenant, most commonly a city dweller, is not experienced in performing maintenance work on urban, complex living units. *Green v. Superior Court, supra,* 10 Cal.3d at 624, 517 P.2d at 1173, 111 Cal.Rptr. at 707-08. The landlord is more familiar with the dwelling unit and mechanical equipment attached to that unit, and is more financially able to "discover and cure" any faults and break-downs. *Id.* at 624, 517 P.2d at 1173, 111 Cal.Rptr. at 708. Confronted with a recognized shortage of safe, decent housing, see 24 V.S.A. §4001(1), today's tenant is in an inferior bargaining position compared to that of the landlord. *Park West Management Corp. v. Mitchell,* 47 N.Y.2d 316, 324-25, 391 N.E.2d 1288, 1292, 418 N.Y.S.2d 310, 314, *cert. denied,* 444 U.S. 992, 100 S.Ct. 523, 62 L.Ed.2d 421 (1979). Tenants vying for this limited housing are "virtually powerless to compel the performance of essential services." *Id.* at 325, 391 N.E.2d at 1292, 418 N.Y.S.2d at 314.

In light of these changes in the relationship between tenants and landlords, it would be wrong for the law to continue to impose the doctrine of caveat lessee on residential leases.

> The modern view favors a new approach which recognizes that a lease is essentially a contract between the landlord and the tenant wherein the landlord promises to deliver and maintain the demised premises in habitable condition and the tenant promises to pay rent for such habitable premises. These promises constitute interdependent and mutual considerations. Thus, the tenant's obligation to pay rent is predicated on the landlord's obligation to deliver and maintain the premises in habitable condition.

PROPERTY VS. CONTRACT

Boston Housing Authority v. Hemingway, 363 Mass. 184, 198, 293 N.E.2d 831, 842 (1973).

Recognition of residential leases as contracts embodying the mutual covenants of habitability and payment of rent does not represent an abrupt change in Vermont law. Our case law has previously recognized that contract remedies are available for breaches of lease agreements. *Clarendon Mobile Home Sales, Inc. v. Fitzgerald,* 135 Vt. 594, 596, 381 A.2d 1063, 1065 (1977); *Keene v. Willis,* 128 Vt. 187, 188, 191-92, 260 A.2d 371, 371-72, 374 (1969); *Breese v. McCann,* 52 Vt. 498, 501 (1879). More significantly, our legislature, in establishing local housing authorities, 24 V.S.A. §4003, has officially recognized the need for assuring the existence of adequate housing.

> [S]ubstandard and decadent areas exist in certain portions of the state of Vermont and . . . there is not . . . an adequate supply of decent, safe and sanitary housing for persons of low income and/or elderly persons of low income, available for rents which such persons can afford to pay . . . this situation tends to cause an increase and spread of communicable and chronic disease . . . [and] constitutes a menace to the health, safety, welfare and comfort of the inhabitants of the state and is detrimental to property values in the localities in which it exists . . . .

24 V.S.A. §4001(4). In addition, this Court has assumed the existence of an implied warranty of habitability in residential leases. *Birkenhead v. Coombs,* 143 Vt. 167, 172, 465 A.2d 244, 246 (1983).

Therefore, we now hold expressly that in the rental of any residential dwelling unit an implied warranty exists in the lease, whether oral or written, that the landlord will deliver over and maintain, throughout the period of the tenancy, premises that are safe, clean and fit for human habitation. This warranty of habitability is implied in tenancies for a specific period or at will. *Boston Housing Authority v. Hemingway, supra,* 363 Mass.

at 199, 293 N.E.2d at 843. Additionally, the implied warranty of habitability covers all latent and patent defects in the essential facilities of the residential unit.[2] *Id.* Essential facilities are "facilities vital to the use of the premises for residential purposes. . . ." *Kline v. Burns,* 111 N.H. 87, 92, 276 A.2d 248, 252 (1971). This means that a tenant who enters into a lease agreement with knowledge of any defect in the essential facilities cannot be said to have assumed the risk, thereby losing the protection of the warranty. Nor can this implied warranty of habitability be waived by any written provision in the lease or by oral agreement.

In determining whether there has been a breach of the implied warranty of habitability, the courts may first look to any relevant local or municipal housing code; they may also make reference to the minimum housing code standards enunciated in 24 V.S.A. §5003(c)(1)-5003(c)(5). A substantial violation of an applicable housing code shall constitute prima facie evidence that there has been a breach of the warranty of habitability. "[O]ne or two minor violations standing alone which do not affect" the health or safety of the tenant, shall be considered de minimus and not a breach of the warranty. *Javins v. First National Realty Corp., supra,* 428 F.2d at 1082 n. 63; *Mease v. Fox,* 200 N.W.2d 791, 796 (Iowa 1972); *King v. Moorehead, supra,* 495 S.W.2d at 76. In addition, the landlord will not be liable for defects caused by the tenant. *Javins v. First National Realty Corp., supra,* 428 F.2d at 1082 n. 62.

However, these codes and standards merely provide a starting point in determining whether there has been a breach. Not all towns and municipalities have housing codes; where there are codes, the particular problem complained of may not be addressed. *Park West Management Corp. v. Mitchell, supra,* 47 N.Y.2d at 328, 391 N.E.2d at 1294, 418 N.Y.S.2d at 316. In determining whether there has been a breach of the implied warranty of habitability, courts should inquire whether the claimed defect has an impact on the safety or health of the tenant. *Id.*

In order to bring a cause of action for breach of the implied warranty of habitability, the tenant must first show that he or she notified the landlord "of the deficiency or defect not known to the landlord and [allowed] a reasonable time for its correction." *King v. Moorehead, supra,* 495 S.W.2d at 76.

Because we hold that the lease of a residential dwelling creates a contractual relationship between the landlord and tenant, the standard contract remedies of rescission, reformation and damages are available to the tenant when suing for breach of the implied warranty of habitability. *Lemle v. Breeden, supra,* 51 Haw. at 436, 462 P.2d at 475. The measure of damages shall be the difference between the value of the dwelling as warranted and the value of the dwelling as it exists in its defective condition. *Birkenhead v. Coombs, supra,* 143 Vt. at 172,

---

[2] The warranty also covers those facilities located in the common areas of an apartment building or duplex that may affect the health or safety of a tenant, such as common stairways, or porches. *Javins v. First National Realty Corp., supra,* 428 F.2d at 1082 n. 62; *King v. Moorehead,* 495 S.W.2d 65, 76 (Mo.App.1973).

465 A.2d at 246. In determining the fair rental value of the dwelling as warranted, the court may look to the agreed upon rent as evidence on this issue. *Id.* "[I]n residential lease disputes involving a breach of the implied warranty of habitability, public policy militates against requiring expert testimony" concerning the value of the defect. *Id.* at 173, 465 A.2d at 247. The tenant will be liable only for "the reasonable rental value [if any] of the property in its imperfect condition during his period of occupancy." *Berzito v. Gambino,* 63 N.J. 460, 469, 308 A.2d 17, 22 (1973).

We also find persuasive the reasoning of some commentators that damages should be allowed for a tenant's discomfort and annoyance arising from the landlord's breach of the implied warranty of habitability. See Moskovitz, *The Implied Warranty of Habitability: A New Doctrine Raising New Issues,* 62 Calif.L.Rev. 1444, 1470-73 (1974) (hereinafter cited as *A New Doctrine*); *A Dream Deferred, supra,* at 250-51. Damages for annoyance and discomfort are reasonable in light of the fact that

> the residential tenant who has suffered a breach of the warranty . . . cannot bathe as frequently as he would like or at all if there is inadequate hot water; he must worry about rodents harassing his children or spreading disease if the premises are infested; or he must avoid certain rooms or worry about catching a cold if there is inadequate weather protection or heat. Thus, discomfort and annoyance are the common injuries caused by each breach and hence the true nature of the general damages the tenant is claiming.

Moskovitz, *A New Doctrine, supra,* at 1470-71. Damages for discomfort and annoyance may be difficult to compute; however, "[t]he trier [of fact] is not to be deterred from this duty by the fact that the damages are not susceptible of reduction to an exact money standard." *Vermont Electric Supply Co. v. Andrus,* 132 Vt. 195, 200, 315 A.2d 456, 459 (1974).

Another remedy available to the tenant when there has been a breach of the implied warranty of habitability is to withhold the payment of future rent.[3] *King v. Moorehead, supra,* 495 S.W.2d at 77. The burden and expense of bringing suit will then be on the landlord who can better afford to bring the action. In an action for ejectment for nonpayment of rent, 12 V.S.A. §4773. "[t]he trier of fact, upon evaluating the seriousness of the breach and the ramification of the defect upon the health and safety of the tenant, will abate the rent at the landlord's expense in accordance with its findings." *A Dream Deferred, supra,* at 248. The tenant must show that: (1) the landlord had notice of the

---

[3] Because we hold that the tenant's obligation to pay rent is contingent on the landlord's duty to provide and maintain a habitable dwelling, it is no longer necessary for the tenant to first abandon the premises, *Northern Terminals, Inc. v. Smith Grocery & Variety, Inc.,* 138 Vt. 389, 396-97, 418 A.2d 22, 26-27 (1980); *Legier v. Deveneau, supra,* 98 Vt. at 190, 126 A. at 393; thus, the doctrine of constructive eviction is no longer a viable or needed defense in an action by the landlord for unpaid rent. *Lemle v. Breeden, supra,* 51 Haw. at 435-36, 462 P.2d at 475; *Boston Housing Authority v. Hemingway, supra,* 363 Mass. at 199-200, 293 N.E.2d at 843; *see also Expansion of Tenants' Rights, supra,* at 491 (constructive eviction "[w]ith its absolute requirement of abandonment . . . is utterly unsatisfactory for a tenant faced with today's urban housing shortage").

previously unknown defect and failed, within a reasonable time, to repair it; and (2) the defect, affecting habitability, existed during the time for which rent was withheld. See *A Dream Deferred, supra*, at 248-50. Whether a portion, all or none of the rent will be awarded to the landlord will depend on the findings relative to the extent and duration of the breach.[4] *Javins v. First National Realty Corp., supra*, 428 F.2d at 1082-83. Of course, once the landlord corrects the defect, the tenant's obligation to pay rent becomes due again. *Id.* at 1083 n. 64.

Additionally, we hold that when the landlord is notified of the defect but fails to repair it within a reasonable amount of time, and the tenant subsequently repairs the defect, the tenant may deduct the expense of the repair from future rent. 11 Williston on Contracts §1404 (3d ed. W. Jaeger 1968); *Marini v. Ireland*, 56 N.J. 130, 146, 265 A.2d 526, 535 (1970).

In addition to general damages, we hold that punitive damages may be available to a tenant in the appropriate case. Although punitive damages are generally not recoverable in actions for breach of contract, there are cases in which the breach is of such a willful and wanton or fraudulent nature as to make appropriate the award of exemplary damages. *Clarendon Mobile Home Sales, Inc. v. Fitzgerald, supra*, 135 Vt. at 596, 381 A.2d at 1065. A willful and wanton or fraudulent breach may be shown "by conduct manifesting personal ill will, or carried out under circumstances of insult or oppression, or even by conduct manifesting . . . a reckless or wanton disregard of [one's] rights. . . ." *Sparrow v. Vermont Savings Bank*, 95 Vt. 29, 33, 112 A. 205, 207 (1921). When a landlord, after receiving notice of a defect, fails to repair the facility that is essential to the health and safety of his or her tenant, an award of punitive damages is proper. *111 East 88th Partners v. Simon*, 106 Misc.2d 693, 434 N.Y.S.2d 886, 889 (N.Y.Civ.Ct.1980).

> The purpose of punitive damages . . . is to punish conduct which is morally culpable. . . . Such an award serves to deter a wrongdoer . . . from repetitions of the same or similar actions. And it tends to encourage prosecution of a claim by a victim who might not otherwise incur the expense or inconvenience of private action. . . . The public benefit and a display of ethical indignation are among the ends of the policy to grant punitive damages.

Davis v. Williams, 92 Misc.2d 1051, 402 N.Y.S.2d 92, 94 (N.Y.Civ.Ct.1977).

In the instant case, the trial court's award of damages, based in part on a breach of the implied warranty of habitability, was not a misapplication of the law relative to habitability. Because of our holding in this case, the doctrine of constructive eviction, wherein the tenant must abandon in order to escape liability for rent, is no longer

---

[4] Some courts suggest that, during the period rent is withheld, the tenant should pay the rent, as it becomes due, into legal custody. See, e.g., *Javins v. First National Realty Corp., supra*, 428 F.2d at 1083 n. 67; *see also King v. Moorehead, supra*, 495 S.W.2d at 77 (*King* requires the deposit of the rent into legal custody pending the litigation). Such a procedure assures the availability of that portion, if any, of the rent which the court determines is due to the landlord. *King v. Moorehead, supra*, 495 S.W.2d at 77; *see A Dream Deferred, supra*, at 248-50.

viable. When, as in the instant case, the tenant seeks, not to escape rent liability, but to receive compensatory damages in the amount of rent already paid, abandonment is similarly unnecessary. *Northern Terminals, Inc. v. Smith Grocery & Variety, Inc., supra,* 138 Vt. at 396-97, 418 A.2d at 26-27. Under our holding, when a landlord breaches the implied warranty of habitability, the tenant may withhold future rent, and may also seek damages in the amount of rent previously paid. . . .

[T]he [trial] court denied an award to plaintiff of punitive damages on the ground that the evidence failed to support a finding of willful and wanton or fraudulent conduct. See *Clarendon Mobile Home Sales, Inc. v. Fitzgerald, supra,* 135 Vt. at 596, 381 A.2d at 1065. The facts in this case, which defendants do not contest, evince a pattern of intentional conduct on the part of defendants for which the term "slumlord" surely was coined. Defendants' conduct was culpable and demeaning to plaintiff and clearly expressive of a wanton disregard of plaintiff's rights. The trial court found that defendants were aware of defects in the essential facilities of plaintiff's apartment, promised plaintiff that repairs would be made, but never fulfilled those promises. The court also found that plaintiff continued, throughout her tenancy, to pay her rent, often in the face of verbal threats made by defendant Stuart St. Peter. These findings point to the "bad spirit and wrong intention" of the defendants, *Glidden v. Skinner,* 142 Vt. 644, 648, 458 A.2d 1142, 1144 (1983), and would support a finding of willful and wanton or fraudulent conduct, contrary to the conclusions of law and judgment of the trial judge. However, the plaintiff did not appeal the court's denial of punitive damages, and issues not appealed and briefed are waived. *R. Brown & Sons, Inc. v. International Harvester Corp.,* 142 Vt. 140, 142, 453 A.2d 83, 84 (1982).

We find that defendants' third claimed error, that the court erred in finding that both defendant Stuart St. Peter and defendant Patricia St. Peter were liable to plaintiff for the breach of the implied warranty of habitability, is meritless. . . .

Affirmed in part; reversed in part and remanded for hearing on additional compensable damages, consistent with the views herein.

NOTES AND QUESTIONS

1. *Property vs. Contract. Javins* is an important example of a court using contract principles to depart from old rules based on property concepts in the landlord-tenant context. Be careful, however, not to overread *Javins.* In places, Judge Wright's opinion reads as if it is holding that property concepts are no longer relevant to residential leases. Such a reading would go too far. *Javins* and similar cases certainly apply contracts principles to residential leases. There are other contexts, however, where the property aspects of a lease may be important. There are also contexts where some courts in some jurisdictions continue to apply property concepts to residential leases.

2. *Mechanics of the Implied Warranty of Habitability. Hilder v. St. Peter* presents an excellent summary of the contemporary rules governing the implied warranty

of habitability. Note that *Hilder* goes beyond housing code violations to focus on conditions that are a threat to the tenant's health and safety. Housing code violations are still important but are not the exclusive basis for implied warranty of habitability claims. Read the *Hilder* opinion closely. What does it have to say about the basis of an implied warranty of habitability claim? Does the resident have to give the landlord an opportunity to fix the problem? Can the tenant withhold rent without moving out? In this context, we note that while most courts today agree that the landlord has a duty to provide a habitable dwelling and that the tenant has a duty to notify the landlord of a problem, the courts do not uniformly agree on when a breach of the duty occurs. Most courts hold that a violation occurs when the landlord has had a reasonable amount of time to remedy a problem and has not; others find a violation at the occurrence of the problem; and still others at the time the landlord is notified of the problem. The timing of the occurrence of the violation can impact the amount of damages received when the tenant is seeking a rent reduction for the time the violation existed.

REMEDIES FOR BREACH OF THE IMPLIED WARRANTY OF HABITABILITY

Tenants have legal, equitable, and administrative remedies available to them for breach of the implied warranty of habitability.

REMEDIES

Money damages: The tenant may sue the landlord for damages in the amount of past rent that was paid while the violation existed. If the tenant is injured or suffers damage to her personal property, the tenant can seek damages for those injuries. If the tenant needs to temporarily move out while repairs are being made, damages might include moving costs and the cost of the temporary housing. As the court in *Hilder* explained, punitive damages may be awarded in truly egregious situations. Extreme violations and landlord misconduct may also support a claim for the tort of intentional infliction of emotional distress. *See Haddad v. Gonzales*, 410 Mass. 855 (1991). In *Haddad*, the warranty was breached by the landlord's failure to fix broken windows, eliminate insect and rodent infestations, and provide adequate heat. The landlord's conduct was particularly outrageous because the landlord harassed the tenant with threats to "come over at night and give her heat" and sent drunk repairmen to "fix" the problems, one of whom vomited in the tenant's kitchen sink. *Id.* at 857-58.

Rescission, reformation, and repudiation of the contract: The court in *Hilder* noted that the contract remedies of rescission and reformation are available to a tenant for a breach of the implied warranty of habitability. Consider the following language from the Uniform Residential Landlord and Tenant Act, which has been enacted in 21 states:

§4.101. [Noncompliance by the Landlord—In General]

(a) Except as provided in this Act, if there is a material noncompliance by the landlord with the rental agreement or a noncompliance with Section 2.104

materially affecting health and safety, the tenant may deliver a written notice to the landlord specifying the acts and omissions constituting the breach and that the rental agreement will terminate upon a date not less than [30] days after receipt of the notice if the breach is not remedied in [14] days, and the rental agreement shall terminate as provided in the notice subject to the following:

(1) If the breach is remedial by repairs, the payment of damages or otherwise and the landlord adequately remedies the breach before the date specified in the notice, the rental agreement shall not terminate by reason of the breach.

(2) If substantially the same act or omission which constituted a prior noncompliance of which notice was given recurs within [6] months, the tenant may terminate the rental agreement upon at least [14 days'] written notice specifying the breach and the date of termination of the rental agreement.

(3) The tenant may not terminate for a condition caused by the deliberate or negligent act or omission of the tenant, a member of his family, or other person on the premises with his consent.

Withholding rent: The tenant may withhold all rent until the landlord fixes the breach, even for a partial breach. The tenant may also withhold rent and use the withheld money to repair the defects. Some states have statutes requiring the tenant to pay the rent into an escrow account under judicial control. If the landlord attempts to evict the tenant for nonpayment of rent, the tenant may assert breach of the implied warranty of habitability as a defense and will not be required to vacate the premises or pay back rent. Because the landlord is not collecting rent and the tenant has a defense to an eviction action, rent withholding provides the landlord with a strong incentive to remedy the breach.

Equitable remedies: The tenant may file an action in equity for an injunction or for specific performance to have the landlord remedy the breach.

Administrative remedy: The tenant may contact the local housing inspector and request to have the premises looked over. If the inspector finds a housing code violation, she may go to court and request a court order for the landlord to remedy the situation or pay a civil or criminal fine.

3. *How Far Should the Implied Warranty of Habitability Go?* How large should a problem be to violate the implied warranty of habitability? Put another way, what does a residential property need to be habitable? Would a leaky roof violate the implied warranty? A broken window? A broken air conditioner? Recurring roach problems? In this context, it is notable that a New York court held that a serious bedbug infestation violated the implied warranty of habitability. *See* Sewell Chan, *Everything You Need to Know About Bedbugs but Were Afraid to Ask*, New York Times (Oct. 15, 2006).

THE IMPLIED WARRANTY OF HABITABILITY VS. THE COVENANT OF QUIET ENJOYMENT

RESIDENTIAL VS. COMMERCIAL

A given set of facts might support claims by a tenant under both the implied warranty of habitability and the covenant of quiet enjoyment. It therefore is important to know the similarities and differences between the two. Here is a comparison:

Implied Warranty of Habitability	Covenant of Quiet Enjoyment
Applies only to residential leases.	Applies to both residential and commercial leases.
Breaches are based on problems that threaten health or safety of tenant. Violations of housing codes often play a major role.	Breaches are based on interference with tenant's ability to use or possess the premises.

PROBLEM

An explanatory answer to this problem can be found on page 1047.

Nancy lived in apartment 2C in a building owned by Kurt. Things weren't going well for Nancy. There appeared to be a problem with the venting from the kitchen of the seafood restaurant on the first floor, and serious odors would leak into 2C. The smell was so bad that Nancy often became ill, and she repeatedly complained to Kurt. Kurt tried to fix the problem a few times but failed to stop the smells. During an inspection of the restaurant, the building was cited for having a ventilation system that was not up to the local building code. Not wanting to give up her apartment, Nancy started wearing a clothespin on her nose and stopped paying rent. Kurt was furious, saying that Nancy was ungrateful for the efforts he had put in trying to fix the problem, and that Nancy should keep paying the rent. Discuss the respective rights of the parties.

C. THE LANDLORD'S RIGHTS AND THE TENANT'S DUTIES

In most jurisdictions, the tenant's duties include: (1) the duty to pay rent, (2) the duty to not use the premises for illegal purposes, and (3) the duty to not commit waste.

1. THE TENANT'S DUTY TO PAY RENT

A tenant's duty to pay rent usually arises from an express covenant in the lease. If a tenant fails to pay rent, the landlord typically has two options: (1) continue with the relationship and sue for back rent or (2) end the relationship and sue to evict the tenant and recover possession of the premises. All states allow landlords to recover possession if the tenant fails to pay rent. In most jurisdictions, the landlord cannot use self-help to forcibly evict the tenant or remove any of the tenant's possession. Rather, in most jurisdictions, the landlord must bring a legal proceeding to evict the tenant. We will consider eviction further below.

2. THE TENANT'S DUTY TO NOT USE THE PREMISES FOR ILLEGAL PURPOSES

An implied covenant not to use the property for an illegal purpose exists in both commercial and residential leases. If the landlord and tenant both contemplated that the premises would be used for illegal purposes, the lease will be void and unenforceable by either party. If the tenant alone intended to use the property for an illegal purpose, the lease is enforceable against the tenant, and the landlord is entitled for rent and may sue for damages for breach of the implied covenant. In some jurisdictions, a landlord may be held liable for criminal acts committed by the tenant if the landlord knew or should have known that the tenant was engaged in illegal activities. *See Rosales v. Stewart*, 113 Cal. App. 3d 130 (1980) (reasoning that the landlord/tenant relationship is a special relationship imposing a duty on the landlord to control the conduct of others or to warn others and holding the landlord liable for the gunshot death of a neighbor by the tenant known by the landlord to be dangerous).

3. THE TENANT'S DUTY TO NOT COMMIT WASTE

Recall that the doctrine of waste applies in circumstances where ownership of property is divided over time and prevents the present interest holder from acting in a way that harms the interests of the future interest holder. The same waste principles that we discussed in the context of life estates apply in the context of a lease. Most leases include express prohibitions on waste, so a waste dispute between a landlord and a tenant typically will turn more on the language of the lease than on the common law of waste. Nonetheless, the same basic principles apply. The tenant will be liable to the landlord for committing affirmative or permissive waste. One common type of waste in the landlord-tenant context occurs when a tenant removes a fixture from the premises. The landlord can use the security deposit to cover the cost of the damage and can also sue to recover for damages exceeding the security deposit. Landlords also use security deposits to cover tenants' acts of permissive waste. Recall that permissive waste occurs when the tenant fails to take reasonable action to maintain the property. Tenants have an implied duty to make minor repairs and will be liable if they fail to take reasonable steps to keep the property from falling into disrepair.

D. TRANSFERRING THE LEASE

1. ASSIGNMENTS AND SUBLEASES: WHEN TENANTS TRANSFER INTERESTS

In many circumstances, a tenant in a lease may transfer their rights under the lease to another tenant. There are two types of transfers: *assignments* and *subleases*. We will focus on commercial leases for now because they tend to be more freely transferrable than residential leases. The differences between the two types of transfer may vary by jurisdiction, but the basic idea is that in an assignment, the original tenant transfers all of her rights under the lease to the new tenant. In a sublease, the original tenant transfers something less than all of her rights to the new tenant. For simplicity's sake, we will focus on the duration of the lease. Consider these two examples:

> **EXAMPLE 1:** L leases to T for a term of five years, ending December 31, 2013. T transfers all of her rights under the lease to T_1 for a term ending on December 31, 2013. That is, T transfers the lease to T_1 for the entire remaining term of the original lease between L and T. The transfer from T to T_1 is an assignment because T transferred the entire remaining duration of the least to T_1.

> **EXAMPLE 2:** L leases to T for a term of five years, ending December 31, 2013. T transfers her rights under the lease to T_1 for a term ending on December 31, 2011. That is, T transfers some of the lease duration to T_1 but retains two years for herself (i.e., the period between January 1, 2012 and December 31, 2013). The transfer from T to T_1 is a sublease because T transferred something less than the remainder of the lease duration to T_1.

Courts generally look at the substance of the transfer, rather than what the parties call it, in deciding whether it is an assignment or sublease. Under this approach, the transfer in Example 1 would be an assignment even if the parties labeled it a sublease. Similarly, the transfer in Example 2 would be a sublease even if the parties called it an assignment. Some courts might take a different approach and look at the label given by the parties in an attempt to discern the parties' intent. To keep things simple, we will follow the general approach and look at the substance of the transfer rather than the label.

What if the leased property is two acres and the original tenant transfers all of her interests to one of the acres to another tenant? That is, the original tenant has transferred all of her interests (measured by duration or otherwise) to only a portion of the leased property. Is this an assignment of part of the property because the tenant has transferred all of her rights, or a sublease because the transfer is only part of the property? Most courts would see this as a partial assignment—that is, a full transfer of part of the property.

Whether a transfer is an assignment or a sublease can impact the privity relationships between the parties. We discussed the idea of privity before in the context of tacking in adverse possession, and the concept will pop up periodically throughout the course. Generally speaking, two people are in privity if they are parties to a certain type of transaction. Parties are in *privity of contract* if they are on opposite sides of a contract.

Parties are in *privity of estate* if they are on opposite sides of a real estate transaction. A lease is both a contract and a real estate transaction, so the parties to a lease are in both privity of estate and privity of contract.

Privity relationships may be illustrated using diagrams. The illustration below shows the privity relationships between a landlord and a tenant. The arrow on the left marked **K** shows that the landlord and tenant are in privity of contract. The arrow on the right marked **E** shows that the landlord and tenant are in privity of estate.

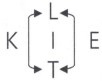

Assignments and subleases have different consequences for the privity relationships between the parties. Here are the privity relationships in an assignment:

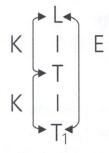

L and T are in privity of contract from the original lease, and T and T_1 are in privity of contract from the assignment agreement. The privity of estate arrow drops down to T_1 because in an assignment T has transferred her entire interest to T_1. So now L and T_1 are in privity of estate.

Here is a picture of the privity relationships in a sublease:

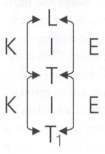

L and T are in privity of contract from the original lease, and T and T_1 are in privity of contract from the sublease agreement. Because T has retained a portion of her interest in the original lease, the privity of estate arrow does not drop down as it did in the assignment scenario. L remains in privity of estate with T, and T is in privity of estate with T_1.

KEY POINT

The most important thing to note about the differences between the assignment and sublease privity relationships is that in the sublease, L and T_1 are not in privity of estate or contract with each other. In the assignment, L and T_1 are in privity of estate with each other.

Why do we care about this difference? If two parties are in privity with each other, then they can interact directly with each other on various legal issues. If they are not in privity with each other, then they will not be able to interact directly with each other.

For our purposes, there is no practical difference between privity of estate and privity of contract. As long as the parties are in either kind of privity relationship, then they can interact directly with each other.

Here are two practical illustrations of how privity works and why the difference between an assignment and sublease matters so much.

EXAMPLE 3: Imagine that T_1 stops paying rent. In an assignment, L and T_1 are in privity of estate, so L can sue T_1 directly for the back rent. In a sublease, however, L and T_1 are not in privity of estate or contract. L therefore cannot sue T_1 directly for the back rent. Rather, L must sue T (who remains obligated to L under the original lease), and T must sue T_1.

EXAMPLE 4: Imagine that T_1 wants to exercise a renewal clause in the master lease that allows the lease to be extended for an additional term. In an assignment, T_1 may directly exercise this renewal clause because L and T_1

are in privity of estate. In a sublease, T_1 may not directly exercise the renewal clause and instead has to get T to exercise the renewal clause.

In each of these cases, the lack of privity relationships in a sublease makes the exercise of legal interest much harder. Indeed, if T is nowhere to be found or if T is an entity that has dissolved, it might be impossible for a party to exercise the legal interest at all.

Commercial properties are often assigned or subleased many times in succession. You can easily modify the diagrams to accommodate larger chains of assignments and subleases. If L leased to T, who then subleased to T_1, who then assigned to T_2, then the diagram would look like this:

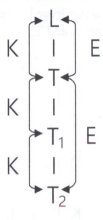

This diagram is created by starting with the original sublease diagram, then adding the assignment diagram below it. Note that in the assignment, the privity of estate arrow runs between T and T_2—it does not go all the way back up to L. Any time you have an assignment, you just drop the privity of estate arrow down one party.

If L leased to T, who then assigned to T_1, who then assigned to T_2, then the diagram would look like this:

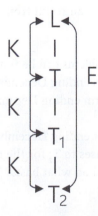

Chapter 4 **Leasing Real Property—Landlord and Tenant Law** • 335

You will have noticed that privity of contract, unlike privity of estate, does not drop down in assignments. There will always be privity of contract relationships between the parties next to each other in the chain of subleases and assignments. Once privity of contract relationships exist, they do not disappear unless the parties voluntarily relinquish their rights through a release or novation. Unless you see these specific words, keep all of the privity of contract arrows in your diagram.

One final privity of contract issue: a party further down the chain can create a privity of contract relationship with a party further up the chain by agreeing to be bound by an earlier agreement. One common way of expressing this action is to say that the party "assumed all of the covenants" of the prior agreement. In our last diagram, L leased to T, who then assigned to T_1, who then assigned to T_2. Say that T_2 agreed to "assume all of the covenants of the master lease between L and T." This would create a privity of contract relationship between L and T_2:

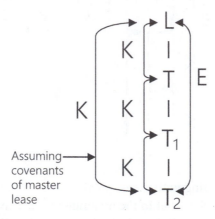

As a reminder: for our purposes, it does not matter whether a party is in privity of contract, privity of estate, or both. As long as there is a privity relationship, the parties can directly exercise legal interests with each other. If there is no privity relationship between the parties, then they cannot directly exercise legal interests. Our next case illustrates the potential problems that can result from a lack of privity relationships.

PROBLEMS

Explanatory answers to these problems can be found on page 1048.

1. L leases to T for a term of years ending December 31, 2006. T "subleases, assigns, and transfers" the lease to T_1 for a term ending December 31, 2005. Describe the privity relationship between the parties.

2. L leases to T for a term of years ending December 31, 2006. T then assigns her entire interest to T_1. T_1 in turn subleases to T_2 for the term ending December 31, 2005. T_2 stops paying rent. Who can L sue and on what basis? What are the privity relationship between the parties?

3. L leases to T for a term of years ending December 31, 2006. T subleases to T_1 for the term ending December 31, 2005. T_1 then assigns all of her interest to T_2. T_2 stops paying rent. Who can L sue and on what basis? What are the privity relationship between the parties?

4. L leases to T for a term of years ending December 31, 2006. T assigns all of his interest to T_1. T_1 then assigns all of her interest to T_2. T_2 then subleases to T_3 for the term ending December 31, 2005. In the sublease agreement, T_3 assumes all of the covenants in the master lease between L and T. A few months later, T_3 stops paying rent. Who can L sue and on what basis? What are the privity relationship between the parties?

5. L leases to T for a term of years ending December 31, 2006. T subleases to T_1 for a term ending December 31, 2005. In the sublease agreement, T_1 assumes all of the covenants in the master lease between L and T. T_1 then assigns all of her interest to T_2. A few months later, T_2 stops paying rent. Who can L sue and on what basis? What are the privity relationship between the parties?

The following case considers whether, absent a written agreement, a sublessee obtains a sublessor's right to renew a lease.

NEAL V. CRAIG BROWN, INC.

Court of Appeals of North Carolina, 1987
356 S.E.2d 912

MARTIN, Judge. In this civil action, plaintiff alleges that he is in possession of premises located at 6315 South Boulevard in Charlotte pursuant to certain fixed-term lease agreements which include, inter alia, options to renew the lease for two additional five year periods. He alleges that he gave proper notice of his intent to exercise his option to renew for the first additional five year term, but that defendants have refused to recognize his rights pursuant to the option and have notified him to vacate the premises. He seeks specific performance of the alleged lease or, in the alternative, damages for its breach.

In their answer, defendants deny the existence of any written lease agreement with plaintiff and allege that he has occupied the premises as a month-to-month tenant under an oral agreement. By counterclaim, defendants seek an order requiring plaintiff to vacate the premises and damages allegedly occasioned by his refusal to do so.

Defendants moved, pursuant to G.S. 1A-1, Rule 56, for summary judgment dismissing plaintiff's action. Plaintiff moved for partial summary judgment establishing his status as a "long term tenant" under the alleged lease agreements. The trial court granted defendants' motion, denied plaintiff's motion, and dismissed plaintiff's action. Plaintiff appeals.

MARTIN, Judge. Plaintiff assigns error to the entry of summary judgment dismissing his claims against defendants. He contends that genuine issues of material fact exist with respect to the nature of his tenancy in defendants' property. We affirm the judgment of the trial court. . . .

The record filed in this Court reflects that the evidentiary materials presented to the trial court at the summary judgment hearing consisted of the pleadings and attachments thereto as well as affidavits. These materials establish that, in 1967, Craig T. Brown, Sr. and his wife Gaynell H. Brown owned real property located at 6315 South Boulevard in Charlotte. On 25 October 1967, they entered into a written lease agreement leasing the property to 60 Minute Systems, Inc. (60 Minutes), a Florida corporation engaged in a national dry-cleaning franchise business. The term of the lease was for fifteen years, beginning upon completion of a building which the lessors were obligated to erect as a part of the lease. According to the lease, the building was to be completed no later than 15 April 1968. The lease provided for monthly rental payments of $585.00 and contained options to extend for two successive five year periods upon written notice of intent to exercise the option given at least 90 days prior to the expiration of the preceding term.

On 30 November 1967, 60 Minutes entered into a sublease agreement with William J. Hutchison. The sublease was to commence 1 March 1968 and run through 28 February 1983 at a monthly rental of $592.00. The sublease provided for options to renew at increased rentals for two additional five-year periods commencing 1 March 1983 and 1 March 1988. Hutchison opened a retail dry-cleaning and laundry business on the premises in the spring of 1968.

Sometime during 1970, 60 Minutes filed a petition for bankruptcy with the United States Bankruptcy Court, Middle Division of Florida. 60 Minutes was subsequently adjudicated bankrupt and a trustee in bankruptcy was appointed. The record properly before us contains no further information concerning the bankruptcy proceeding.

On 7 December 1970, Hutchison assigned "all of his right, title and interest" in the sublease to plaintiff, who began operating a laundry and dry-cleaning business on the premises. Plaintiff was thereafter directed by the bankruptcy trustee for 60 Minutes to pay rent "directly to the owners of the premises." In his affidavit, plaintiff stated that he paid monthly rent of $592.00 directly to Craig Brown, Sr. and that he and Craig Brown, Sr. considered the sublease from 60 Minutes to Hutchison to be the contract governing his use of the premises.

Upon the death of Craig T. Brown, Sr. in 1974, plaintiff paid the monthly rental payments to Gaynell H. Brown. In 1975, Gaynell Brown conveyed the subject property to defendant Craig Brown, Jr., who conveyed it to defendant Craig Brown, Inc. Since 1975, plaintiff has made all monthly rental payments to defendants.

Plaintiff offered evidence tending to show that on 20 December 1982 he gave written notice to defendants that he intended to exercise the option to extend the lease for five years and that, since that time, he has paid an increased monthly rental. He also made improvements to the property, including installation of a new boiler in 1983 at a cost of approximately $6,100.00. Defendants were aware of these improvements and never intimated to plaintiff that he was anything "other than a long-term tenant" under the terms and provisions of the Hutchison lease agreement.

By affidavit, Craig Brown, Jr. stated that he has never received a notice of renewal from plaintiff, has never discussed an extension of any term with plaintiff, and has always considered plaintiff to be a tenant at will. According to the affidavit, the increase in rent from $592.00 to $630.00 per month came about as a result of negotiations with plaintiff, during which the existence of a lease was not mentioned.

On 19 August 1985, defendants notified plaintiff to vacate the premises by 1 October 1985. Plaintiff remains in possession of the premises . . .

At oral argument, plaintiff contended that we should find that he is defendants' tenant under the terms of the original lease from Craig Brown, Sr. to 60 Minutes. The basis for this argument is plaintiff's contention that, although labeled a sublease, the instrument by which Hutchison acquired the property from 60 Minutes was, in fact, an assignment of 60 Minutes' original lease. We disagree.

> An "assignment" is a conveyance of the lessee's entire interest in the demised premises, without retaining any reversionary interest in the term in himself. A "sublease" . . . is a conveyance of only a part of the term of the lessee, the lessee retaining a reversion of some portion of the term.

Hetrick, Webster's Real Estate Law in North Carolina, §241 at 251 (Rev. ed. 1981). In the instrument by which 60 Minutes conveyed to Hutchison an interest in the premises, 60 Minutes retained a reversion of a brief portion of the lease term—from 28 February 1983 until the expiration of 60 Minutes' lease—and a right to reenter the premises upon default. Thus, the conveyance between 60 Minutes and Hutchison was a sublease. Hutchison, on the other hand, conveyed to plaintiff "all of his right, title and interest" in the sublease, without retaining any reversionary interest in the term or in the premises. As Hutchison's assignee, plaintiff succeeded only to those rights which Hutchison, as sublessee, held pursuant to the sublease from 60 Minutes.

> In general:
> "[P]rivity of estate" is not established between the original landlord and the sublessee and the landlord has no direct action with respect to the covenants in the original lease as against the sublessee; there is neither privity of estate nor privity of contract as between the original landlord and a sublessee, and the sublessee can sue only his immediate lessor . . . with respect to the lease.

Hetrick, supra, at 252. As a result, a sublessee may not exercise an option to renew granted to his sublessor in the original lease or demand such a renewal from the original landlord. 50 Am.Jur.2d, Landlord and Tenant, §1195 (1970).

In the present case, the original lease agreement provided for a lease term of fifteen years, beginning no later than 15 April 1968, and granted to 60 Minutes options to extend for two additional five year periods upon 90 days written notice. Hutchison's sublease agreement expired 28 February 1983 and included options to renew on 1 March 1983 and 1 March 1988. 60 Minutes never exercised its option to renew the original lease at any time prior to the expiration of its fifteen-year lease term. As a general rule, the rights of a sublessee are measured by the rights of his sublessor, *Nybor Corp. v. Ray's Restaurants, Inc.*, 29 N.C.App. 642, 225 S.E.2d 609, *disc. rev. denied*, 290 N.C. 662, 228 S.E.2d 453 (1976), and termination of the original lease terminates any dependent sublease. 51C C.J.S., *Landlord & Tenant*, §48(1)(a) (1968). This is true notwithstanding the fact that the sublease agreement contains options to renew. 50 Am.Jur.2d, *Landlord and Tenant*, §1195 (1970). As sublessee, plaintiff could neither exercise the option to extend contained in 60 Minutes' lease nor demand from defendants performance of the renewal option contained in the sublease.

In light of the foregoing discussion, the conflicting evidence with respect to whether or not plaintiff gave notice of his intent to extend the term of the lease for an additional five years is immaterial to our decision in this case and, thus, does not defeat summary judgment. *Kessing v. National Mortgage Corp., supra; Little v. National Service Industries, Inc.*, 79 N.C.App. 688, 340 S.E.2d 510 (1986). . .

The entry of summary judgment for defendants is affirmed.

HEDRICK, C.J., and GREENE, J., concur.

EXERCISE

Draw a chart of the privity relationships that were present in the *Neal* case. Draw a chart of the privity relationships that would have been present had the 60 Minutes-Hutchison transaction been an assignment.

2. RESTRICTING THE TENANT'S RIGHT TO TRANSFER

Assigning commercial leases from one tenant to another is common. Imagine that you have leased office space. You ask your landlord to allow you to assign your lease, and the landlord responds "no." Can a landlord do that? The answer will depend in part on whether the lease addresses the issue of assignability and, if so, what exactly the lease has to say. Recall from our chapter on Present and Future Interests that the law generally favors the free alienability of property. Subleases and assignments are the mechanism that tenants use to transfer their rights under a lease. A restriction on subleases and assignments, therefore, represents a restriction on the alienability of a property interest.

If the lease is silent on the issue, leases are freely assignable and transferrable. A lease might also expressly permit the free assignment and sublease of the premises. Restrictions on transferability in the lease typically will come in one of two forms. First, the lease might contain an outright prohibition: "No assignments or subleases." Second, the lease might require the landlord's permission: "No assignments or subleases without the landlord's permission."

The distinction between these two types of lease provisions is a key issue in our next case. The case involves the lease of a hangar at an airport. The facts of the case include several assignments and subleases. Creating a timeline as you read this case will help you better follow what happened.

KENDALL V. ERNEST PESTANA, INC.

Supreme Court of California, 1985
40 Cal. 3d 488, 709 P.2d 837

BROUSSARD, Justice. This case concerns the effect of a provision in a commercial lease[1] that the lessee may not assign the lease or sublet the premises without the lessor's prior written consent. The question we address is whether, in the absence of a provision that such consent will not be unreasonably withheld, a lessor may unreasonably and arbitrarily withhold his or her consent to an assignment.[2] This is a question of first impression in this court.

I.

. . . The lease at issue is for 14,400 square feet of hangar space at the San Jose Municipal Airport. The City of San Jose, as owner of the property, leased it to Irving and Janice Perlitch, who in turn assigned their interest to respondent Ernest Pestana, Inc. Prior to assigning their interest to respondent, the Perlitches entered into a 25-year sublease with one Robert Bixler commencing on January 1, 1970. The sublease covered an original five-year term plus four 5-year options to renew. The rental rate was to be increased every 10 years in the same proportion as rents increased on the master lease from the City of San Jose. The premises were to be used by Bixler for the purpose of conducting an airplane maintenance business.

Bixler conducted such a business under the name "Flight Services" until, in 1981, he agreed to sell the business to appellants Jack Kendall, Grady O'Hara and Vicki O'Hara. The proposed sale included the business and the equipment, inventory and improvements on the property, together with the existing lease. The proposed assignees had a stronger financial statement and greater net worth than the current lessee, Bixler, and they were willing to be bound by the terms of the lease.

---

[1] We are presented only with a commercial lease and therefore do not address the question whether residential leases are controlled by the principles articulated in this opinion.

[2] Since the present case involves an assignment rather than a sublease, we will speak primarily in terms of assignments. However, our holding applies equally to subleases. The difference between an assignment and a sublease is that an assignment transfers the lessee's entire interest in the property whereas a sublease transfers only a portion of that interest, with the original lessee retaining a right of reentry at some point during the unexpired term of the lease. (See *Hartman Ranch Co. v. Associated Oil Co.* (1937) 10 Cal.2d 232, 242-243, 73 P.2d 1163; *Gilman v. Nemetz* (1962) 203 Cal.App.2d 81, 86, 21 Cal.Rptr. 317.)

The lease provided that written consent of the lessor was required before the lessee could assign his interest, and that failure to obtain such consent rendered the lease voidable at the option of the lessor. Accordingly, Bixler requested consent from the Perlitches' successor-in-interest, respondent Ernest Pestana, Inc. Respondent refused to consent to the assignment and maintained that it had an absolute right arbitrarily to refuse any such request. The complaint recites that respondent demanded "increased rent and other more onerous terms" as a condition of consenting to Bixler's transfer of interest.

The proposed assignees brought suit for declaratory and injunctive relief and damages seeking, inter alia, a declaration "that the refusal of ERNEST PESTANA, INC. to consent to the assignment of the lease is unreasonable and is an unlawful restraint on the freedom of alienation. . . ." The trial court sustained a demurrer to the complaint without leave to amend and this appeal followed.

II.

The law generally favors free alienability of property, and California follows the common law rule that a leasehold interest is freely alienable. Contractual restrictions on the alienability of leasehold interests are, however, permitted. "Such restrictions are justified as reasonable protection of the interests of the lessor as to who shall possess and manage property in which he has a reversionary interest and from which he is deriving income."

The common law's hostility toward restraints on alienation has caused such restraints on leasehold interests to be strictly construed against the lessor. Thus, in *Chapman v. Great Western Gypsum Co.* (1932) 216 Cal. 420, 14 P.2d 758, where the lease contained a covenant against assignment without the consent of the lessor, this court stated: "It hardly needs citation of authority to the principle that covenants limiting the free alienation of property such as covenants against assignment are barely tolerated and must be strictly construed." *Id.*, at p. 426, 14 P.2d 758. This is particularly true where the restraint in question is a "forfeiture restraint," under which the lessor has the option to terminate the lease if an assignment is made without his or her consent . . .

Nevertheless, a majority of jurisdictions have long adhered to the rule that where a lease contains an approval clause (a clause stating that the lease cannot be assigned without the prior consent of the lessor), the lessor may arbitrarily refuse to approve a proposed assignee no matter how suitable the assignee appears to be and no matter how unreasonable the lessor's objection. The harsh consequences of this rule have often been avoided through application of the doctrines of waiver and estoppel, under which the lessor may be found to have waived (or be estopped from asserting) the right to refuse consent to assignment.

The traditional majority rule has come under steady attack in recent years. A growing minority of jurisdictions now hold that where a lease provides for assignment only with the prior consent of the lessor, such consent may be withheld *only where the lessor has a commercially reasonable objection to the assignment,* even in the absence of a provision in the lease stating that consent to assignment will not be unreasonably withheld.

For the reasons discussed below, we conclude that the minority rule is the preferable position . . .

III.

The impetus for change in the majority rule has come from two directions, reflecting the dual nature of a lease as a conveyance of a leasehold interest and a contract. The policy against restraints on alienation pertains to leases in their nature as *conveyances.* Numerous courts and commentators have recognized that "[i]n recent times the necessity of permitting reasonable alienation of commercial space has become paramount in our increasingly urban society." (*Schweiso v. Williams, supra,* 150 Cal. App.3d at p. 887, 198 Cal.Rptr. 238. See also *Homa-Goff Interiors, Inc. v. Cowden, supra,* 350 So.2d at 1037; . . .)

Civil Code section 711 provides: "Conditions restraining alienation, when repugnant to the interest created, are void." It is well settled that this rule is not absolute in its application, but forbids only *unreasonable* restraints on alienation. Reasonableness is determined by comparing the justification for a particular restraint on alienation with the quantum of restraint actually imposed by it. "[T]he greater the quantum of restraint that results from enforcement of a given clause, the greater must be the justification for that enforcement." (*Wellenkamp v. Bank of America, supra,* 21 Cal.3d at p. 949, 148 Cal. Rptr. 379, 582 P.2d 970.) In *Cohen v. Ratinoff,* the court examined the reasonableness of the restraint created by an approval clause in a lease: "Because the lessor has an interest in the character of the proposed commercial assignee, we cannot say that an assignment provision requiring the lessor's consent to an assignment is inherently repugnant to the leasehold interest created. We do conclude, however, that *if such an assignment provision is implemented in such a manner that its underlying purpose is perverted by the arbitrary or unreasonable withholding of consent, an unreasonable restraint on alienation is established.*" (*Id.,* 147 Cal.App.3d at p. 329, 195 Cal.Rptr. 84, italics added.)

One commentator explains as follows: "The common-law hostility to restraints on alienation had a large exception with respect to estates for years. A lessor could prohibit the lessee from transferring the estate for years to whatever extent he might desire. It was believed that the objectives served by allowing such restraints outweighed the social evils implicit in the restraints, in that they gave to the lessor a needed control over the person entrusted with the lessor's property and to whom he must look for the performance of the covenants contained in the lease. Whether this reasoning retains full validity can well be doubted. Relationships between lessor and lessee have tended to become more and more impersonal. Courts have considerably lessened the effectiveness of restraint clauses by strict construction and liberal applications of the doctrine of waiver. With the shortage of housing and, in many places, of commercial space as well, the allowance of lease clauses forbidding assignments and subleases is beginning to be curtailed by statutes." (2 Powell, *supra*, ¶246[1], at pp. 372.97-372.98, fns. omitted.)

The Restatement Second of Property adopts the minority rule on the validity of approval clauses in leases: "A restraint on alienation without the consent of the landlord of a tenant's interest in leased property is valid, *but the landlord's consent to an alienation by the tenant cannot be withheld unreasonably,* unless a freely negotiated provision in the lease gives the landlord an absolute right to withhold consent." (Rest.2d Property, §15.2(2) (1977), italics added.)[14] A comment to the section explains:

> "The landlord may have an understandable concern about certain personal qualities of a tenant, particularly his reputation for meeting his financial obligations. The preservation of the values that go into the personal selection of the tenant justifies upholding a provision in the lease that curtails the right of the tenant to put anyone else in his place by transferring his interest, but this justification does not go to the point of allowing the landlord arbitrarily and without reason to refuse to allow the tenant to transfer an interest in leased property." (*Id.,* com. a.)

Under the Restatement rule, the lessor's interest in the character of his or her tenant is protected by the lessor's right to object to a proposed assignee on reasonable commercial grounds. (See *id.,* reporter's note 7 at pp. 112-113.) The lessor's interests are also protected by the fact that the original lessee remains liable to the lessor as a surety even if the lessor consents to the assignment and the assignee expressly assumes the obligations of the lease.

The second impetus for change in the majority rule comes from the nature of a lease as a *contract.* As the Court of Appeal observed in *Cohen v. Ratinoff, supra,* "[s]ince *Richard v. Degan & Brody, Inc.* [espousing the majority rule] was decided, . . . there has been an increased recognition of and emphasis on the duty of good faith and fair dealing inherent in every contract." *Id.* 147 Cal.App.3d at p. 329, 195 Cal. Rptr. 84. Thus, "[i]n every contract there is an implied covenant that neither party shall do anything which will have the effect of destroying or injuring the right of the other party to receive the fruits of the contract . . . ." *Universal Sales Corp. v. California Press Mfg. Co.* (1942) 20 Cal.2d 751, 771, 128 P.2d 665. "[W]here a contract confers on one party a discretionary power affecting the rights of the other, a duty is imposed to exercise that discretion in good faith and in accordance with fair dealing." *Cal. Lettuce Growers v. Union Sugar Co.* (1955) 45 Cal.2d 474, 484, 289 P.2d 785. Here the lessor retains the discretionary power to approve or disapprove an assignee proposed by the other party to

---

[14] This case does not present the question of the validity of a clause absolutely prohibiting assignment, or granting absolute discretion over assignment to the lessor. We note that under the Restatement rule such a provision would be valid if freely negotiated.

the contract; this discretionary power should therefore be exercised in accordance with commercially reasonable standards. "Where a lessee is entitled to sublet under common law, but has agreed to limit that right by first acquiring the consent of the landlord, we believe the lessee has a right to expect that consent will not be unreasonably withheld." *Fernandez v. Vazquez, supra,* 397 So.2d at p. 1174 . . .

Under the minority rule, the determination whether a lessor's refusal to consent was reasonable is a question of fact. Some of the factors that the trier of fact may properly consider in applying the standards of good faith and commercial reasonableness are: financial responsibility of the proposed assignee; suitability of the use for the particular property; legality of the proposed use; need for alteration of the premises; and nature of the occupancy, i.e., office, factory, clinic, etc.

Denying consent solely on the basis of personal taste, convenience or sensibility is not commercially reasonable. Nor is it reasonable to deny consent "in order that the landlord may charge a higher rent than originally contracted for." *Schweiso v. Williams, supra,* 150 Cal.App.3d at p. 886, This is because the lessor's desire for a better bargain than contracted for has nothing to do with the permissible purposes of the restraint on alienation—to protect the lessor's interest in the preservation of the property and the performance of the lease covenants. " '[T]he clause is for the protection of the landlord *in its ownership and operation of the particular property*—not for its general economic protection.' " *Ringwood Associates v. Jack's of Route 23, Inc., supra,* 379 A.2d at p. 512, In contrast to the policy reasons advanced in favor of the minority rule, the majority rule has traditionally been justified on three grounds. Respondent raises a fourth argument in its favor as well. None of these do we find compelling.

First, it is said that a lease is a conveyance of an interest in real property, and that the lessor, having exercised a personal choice in the selection of a tenant and provided that no substitute shall be acceptable without prior consent, is under no obligation to look to anyone but the lessee for the rent. This argument is based on traditional rules of conveyancing and on concepts of freedom of ownership and control over one's property. *Funk v. Funk, supra,* 633 P.2d at p. 591 (Bakes, C.J., dis.).

A lessor's freedom at common law to look to no one but the lessee for the rent has, however, been undermined by the adoption in California of a rule that lessors—like all other contracting parties—have a duty to mitigate damages upon the lessee's abandonment of the property by seeking a substitute lessee. See Civ.Code, §1951.2. Furthermore, the values that go into the personal selection of a lessee are preserved under the minority rule in the lessor's right to refuse consent to assignment on any commercially reasonable grounds. Such grounds include not only the obvious objections to an assignee's financial stability or proposed use of the premises, but a variety of other commercially reasonable objections as well . . . The lessor's interests are further protected by the fact that the original lessee remains a guarantor of the performance of the assignee. See *ante,* p. 825 of 220 Cal.Rptr., p. 844 of 709 P.2d.

The second justification advanced in support of the majority rule is that an approval clause is an unambiguous reservation of absolute discretion in the lessor over assignments of the lease. The lessee could have bargained for the addition of a reasonableness clause to the lease (i.e., "consent to assignment will not be unreasonably withheld"). The lessee having failed to do so, the law should not rewrite the parties' contract for them.

Numerous authorities have taken a different view of the meaning and effect of an approval clause in a lease, indicating that the clause is not "clear and unambiguous," as respondent suggests. As early as 1940, the court in *Granite Trust Bldg. Corp. v. Great Atlantic & Pacific Tea Co., supra*, 36 F. Supp. 77, examined a standard approval clause and stated: "It would seem to be the better law that when a lease restricts a lessee's rights by requiring consent before these rights can be exercised, *it must have been in the contemplation of the parties that the lessor be required to give some reason for withholding consent." Id.* at p. 78, italics added. The same view was expressed by commentators in the 1950's. See Note, *Landlord and Tenant—Right of Lessor to Refuse Any Settlement When Lease Prohibits Transfer Without Consent* (1957) 41 Minn.L.Rev. 355, 358-359; Note, *Real Property—Landlord and Tenant—Lessor's Arbitrary Withholding of Consent to Sublease* (1957) 55 Mich.L.Rev. 1029, 1031; 2 Powell, *supra*, §229, n. 79 (1950).

In light of the interpretations given to approval clauses in the cases cited above, and in light of the increasing number of jurisdictions that have adopted the minority rule in the last 15 years, the assertion that an approval clause "clearly and unambiguously" grants the lessor absolute discretion over assignments is untenable. It is not a rewriting of a contract, as respondent suggests, to recognize the obligations imposed by the duty of good faith and fair dealing, which duty is implied by law in every contract.

The third justification advanced in support of the majority rule is essentially based on the doctrine of stare decisis. It is argued that the courts should not depart from the common law majority rule because "many leases now in effect covering a substantial amount of real property and creating valuable property rights were carefully prepared by competent counsel in reliance upon the majority viewpoint." . . . As pointed out above, however, the majority viewpoint has been far from universally held and has never been adopted by this court. Moreover, the trend in favor of the minority rule should come as no surprise to observers of the changing state of real property law in the 20th century. The minority rule is part of an increasing recognition of the contractual nature of leases and the implications in terms of contractual duties that flow there from. We would be remiss in our duty if we declined to question a view held by the majority of jurisdictions simply because it is held by a majority. As we stated in *Rodriguez v. Bethlehem Steel Corp.* (1974) 12 Cal.3d 382, 115 Cal.Rptr. 765, 525 P.2d 669, the "vitality [of the common law] can flourish only so long as the courts remain alert to their obligation and opportunity to change the common law when reason and equity demand it."

A final argument in favor of the majority rule is advanced by respondent and stated as follows: "Both tradition and sound public policy dictate that the lessor has a right, under circumstances such as these, to realize the increased value of his property." Respondent essentially argues that any increase in the market value of real property during the term of a lease properly belongs to the lessor, not the lessee. We reject this assertion. One California commentator has written: "[W]hen the lessee executed the lease he acquired the contractual right for the exclusive use of the premises, and all of the benefits and detriment attendant to possession, for the term of the contract. He took the downside risk that he would be paying too much rent if there should be a depression in the rental market. . . . Why should he be deprived of the contractual benefits of the lease because of the fortuitous inflation in the marketplace[?] By reaping the benefits he does not deprive the landlord of anything to which the landlord was otherwise entitled. The landlord agreed to dispose of possession for the limited term and he could not reasonably anticipate any more than what was given to him by the terms of the lease. His reversionary estate will benefit from the increased value from the inflation in any event, at least upon the expiration of the lease." (Miller & Starr, Current Law of Cal. Real Estate (1977) 1984 Supp., §27:92 at p. 321.)

Respondent here is trying to get *more* than it bargained for in the lease. A lessor is free to build periodic rent increases into a lease, as the lessor did here. (See *ante,* p. 821 of 220 Cal.Rptr., p. 840 of 709 P.2d.) Any increased value of the property beyond this "belongs" to the lessor only in the sense, as explained above, that the lessor's reversionary estate will benefit from it upon the expiration of the lease. We must therefore reject respondent's argument in this regard.[17] . . .

IV.

In conclusion, both the policy against restraints on alienation and the implied contractual duty of good faith and fair dealing militate in favor of adoption of the rule that where a commercial lease provides for assignment only with the prior consent of the lessor, such consent may be withheld only where the lessor has a commercially reasonable objection to the assignee or the proposed use. Under this rule, appellants have stated a cause of action against respondent Ernest Pestana, Inc. . . .

---

[17] Amicus Pillsbury, Madison & Sutro request that we make clear that, "whatever principle governs in the absence of express lease provisions, nothing bars the parties to commercial lease transactions from making their own arrangements respecting the allocation of appreciated rentals if there is a transfer of the leasehold." This principle we affirm; we merely hold that the clause in the instant lease established no such arrangement.

NOTES AND QUESTIONS

1. *Reading Reasonableness into the Lease.* The minority/*Kendall* rule reads a reasonableness requirement into the provision of the lease. "No assignments or subleases without landlord's permission" becomes "no assignments or subleases without landlord's permission, *and such permission shall not be unreasonably withheld.*" Do you think that courts do the right thing by reading this additional language into the agreement between the parties? Note well the comment in footnote 14 of the *Kendall* opinion, where the court suggests that a provision in the lease that reads "no assignment or sublease" will be enforceable as written. Of course, a landlord could waive that provision, but if the lease reads "no assignment or subleases," the landlord can refuse to waive it for arbitrary reasons. Why do you think the courts read in reasonableness for one type of provision but not for the other?

The minority/*Kendall* rule has been gaining popularity and was codified into statutory law by the California legislature. California Civil Code §1995.260. While the landlord's consent may not be unreasonably withheld under the *Kendall* approach, the law puts the burden of proving unreasonableness on the tenant. Jurisdictions following the majority/traditional rule allow the landlord to arbitrarily refuse permission sublease or assign. Proponents of this approach would point out that it enforces the clause as written rather than writing in a reasonableness clause. Although the *Kendall* rule is sometimes called a modern rule, some courts have recently rejected it. *See, e.g., Merchants Row Corp. v. Merchants Row Inc.,* 587 N.E.2d 788 (Mass. 1992); *First Federal Savings Bank v. Key Markets, Inc.,* 559 N.E.2d 600 (Ind. 1990).

2. *Commercial Reasonableness. Kendall* holds that the landlord must have a *commercially* reasonable reason to refuse permission to sublease or assign. It further holds that a desire to increase the rent is not a commercially reasonable reason to refuse permission. Do you agree with the court's analysis on this point? Commercially reasonable reasons typically do not include personal preferences or values. As the court in *Kendall* put it, "[d]enying consent solely on the basis of personal taste, convenience or sensibility is not commercially reasonable." Denying permission because the new tenant had a poor credit history typically will be commercially reasonable. Similarly, denying permission because of a business conflict between an existing tenant and the proposed new tenant should be commercially reasonable. For example, imagine that an existing tenant is operating a shoe store in a shopping mall. The existing tenant wants to sublease the space to a new tenant who wants to open a pharmacy. There already is a pharmacy a few stores down. It would be commercially reasonable for the landlord to refuse permission to sublease because of the business conflict between the proposed new tenant and the existing tenant.

3. *Assignments and Subleases of Residential Leases. Courts have not applied the Kendall* rule to the assignment or sublease of residential leases. Leasing to a residential tenant is more of a personal decision for a landlord than leasing to a commercial tenant. As a result, landlords can arbitrarily refuse permission to assign or sublease a residential lease.

RESIDENTIAL VS.
COMMERCIAL

4. *Transfers of Landlord's Reversion.* So far, we have talked about tenants assigning their rights under a lease. Recall that when a landlord grants a leasehold to a tenant, the landlord retains a reversion. Generally speaking, the landlord's reversion is freely transferable. The benefits of the lease transfer to the new owner of the reversion (i.e., the new landlord). Indeed, the benefit of the leases (especially, of course, the right to receive rent) account for a large portion of the value of a typical commercial property. The new landlord will not be able to terminate a lease before it expires by its terms. For a term of year lease, the landlord will have to wait until the term expires. For a periodic tenancy, the landlord will have to follow the notice procedure that we discussed above. For a tenancy at will, of course, either the landlord or the tenant can terminate at any time.

PROBLEMS

Explanatory answers to these problems can be found on page 1050.

1. Stuart owns a commercial strip mall on East Street. Isabella leased one of the store sites in the mall for a 20-year term that began on March 1, 2007. The lease includes the following provision: "No assignments or subleases without landlord's permission." Isabella wants to assign the remainder of the lease term to Richard. Richard is willing to pay Isabella $500/month more than Isabella pays Stuart under the lease. Richard has a very good track record in business and has a better credit rating than Isabella. Last week, Isabella asked Stuart to grant permission for the assignment. Stuart said that he would only grant permission if Isabella agreed to increase her rental payments to Stuart. Isabella said that Stuart had no right to demand an increase in rent. The two have now reached an impasse. How might this dispute turn out if the parties end up in court? Why?

2. You have entered into a lease for 12 years to rent space in a strip mall for your business selling jelly, jam, and other preserved fruit products. You decide to go to law school because you are tired of paying attorneys' fees. You want to assign your lease to the space in the strip mall. Suppose the following situations arise in California and you have a clause in the lease that reads "no assignments or subleases without landlord's permission." Would the landlord be able to refuse consent in the following situations?

a. The proposed new tenant wants to open a clinic that provides reproductive counseling for women. Options included in the counseling would include elective abortions. The landlord refuses to consent to the assignment because she morally objects to abortion.

b. The proposed new tenant wants to open a bookstore. The landlord objects because she thinks that book are an obsolete technology and that a bookstore would likely fail financially.

c. The proposed new tenant wants to open a Chinese restaurant. The landlord objects because there is another tenant who operates a Chinese restaurant in the strip mall and landlord believes the proposed assignment will negatively affect the other tenant.

E. ENDING THE LEASEHOLD

In this section, we consider three issues that happen at the end of the landlord-tenant relationship. First, we discuss the rights of the parties if a tenant moves out before the end of the lease. Second, we discuss the opposite problem—what happens when the tenant holds over and fails to move out after the lease expires. Finally, we discuss the landlord's ability to evict the tenant.

1. ABANDONMENT AND THE DUTY TO MITIGATE

When a lease expires according to its terms, the rights of the landlord and tenant are clear—the tenant needs to move out, and the landlord has the right to re-lease the premises. What happens, however, when the tenant wants to move out before the lease has expired? The tenant and landlord, of course, can mutually agree to end the leasehold. If the tenant offers to surrender the premises, and the landlord accepts the offer, the lease is terminated. What happens, however, if the tenant wants to move out, and the landlord seeks to hold the tenant liable for rent for the remainder of the lease? Consider the following case involving a tenant who offered to surrender an apartment and a landlord who refused the offer.

SOMMER V. KRIDEL

Supreme Court of New Jersey, 1977
378 A.2d 767

PASHMAN, J. We granted certification in these cases to consider whether a landlord seeking damages from a defaulting tenant is under a duty to mitigate damages by making reasonable efforts to re-let an apartment wrongfully vacated by the tenant. Separate parts of the Appellate Division held that, in accordance with their respective leases, the landlords in both cases could recover rents due under the leases regardless of whether they had attempted to re-let the vacated apartments. Although they were of different minds as to the fairness of this result, both parts agreed that it was dictated by *Joyce v. Bauman*, 113 N.J.L. 438 (E. & A. 1934), a decision by the former Court of Errors and Appeals. We now reverse and hold that a landlord does have an obligation to make a reasonable effort to mitigate damages in such a situation. We therefore overrule *Joyce v. Bauman* to the extent that it is inconsistent with our decision today.

I

A.

This case was tried on stipulated facts. On March 10, 1972 the defendant, James Kridel, entered into a lease with the plaintiff, Abraham Sommer, owner of the "Pierre Apartments" in Hackensack, to rent apartment 6-L in that building.[1] The term of the lease was from May 1, 1972 until April 30, 1974, with a rent concession for the first six weeks, so that the first month's rent was not due until June 15, 1972.

One week after signing the agreement, Kridel paid Sommer $690. Half of that sum was used to satisfy the first month's rent. The remainder was paid under the lease provision requiring a security deposit of $345. Although defendant had expected to begin occupancy around May 1, his plans were changed. He wrote to Sommer on May 19, 1972, explaining

> I was to be married on June 3, 1972. Unhappily the engagement was broken and the wedding plans cancelled. Both parents were to assume responsibility for the rent after our marriage. I was discharged from the U.S. Army in October 1971 and am now a student. I have no funds of my own, and am supported by my stepfather.
>
> In view of the above, I cannot take possession of the apartment and am surrendering all rights to it. Never having received a key, I cannot return same to you.
>
> I beg your understanding and compassion in releasing me from the lease, and will of course, in consideration thereof, forfeit the 2 month's rent already paid.
>
> Please notify me at your earliest convenience.

Plaintiff did not answer the letter.

Subsequently, a third party went to the apartment house and inquired about renting apartment 6-L. Although the parties agreed that she was ready, willing and able to rent the apartment, the person in charge told her that the apartment was not being shown since it was already rented to Kridel. In fact, the landlord did not re-enter the apartment or exhibit it to anyone until August 1, 1973. At that time it was rented to a new tenant for a term beginning on September 1, 1973. The new rental was for $345 per month with a six week concession similar to that granted Kridel.

Prior to re-letting the new premises, plaintiff sued Kridel in August 1972, demanding $7,590, the total amount due for the full two-year term of the lease. Following a mistrial, plaintiff filed an amended complaint asking for $5,865, the amount due between May 1, 1972 and September 1, 1973. The amended complaint included no reduction in the claim to reflect the six week concession provided for in the lease or the $690 payment made to plaintiff after signing the agreement. Defendant filed an amended answer to the complaint, alleging that plaintiff breached the contract, failed to mitigate damages and accepted defendant's surrender of the premises. He also counterclaimed to demand repayment of the $345 paid as a security deposit.

The trial judge ruled in favor of defendant. Despite his conclusion that the lease had been drawn to reflect "the 'settled law' of this state," he found that "justice and

---

[1] Among other provisions, the lease prohibited the tenant from assigning or transferring the lease without the consent of the landlord. If the tenant defaulted, the lease gave the landlord the option of re-entering or re-letting, but stipulated that failure to re-let or to recover the full rental would not discharge the tenant's liability for rent.

fair dealing" imposed upon the landlord the duty to attempt to re-let the premises and thereby mitigate damages. He also held that plaintiff's failure to make any response to defendant's unequivocal offer of surrender was tantamount to an acceptance, thereby terminating the tenancy and any obligation to pay rent. As a result, he dismissed both the complaint and the counterclaim. The Appellate Division reversed in a *per curiam* opinion, 153 *N.J. Super.* 1 (1976), and we granted certification. 69 *N.J.* 395 (1976). . . .

II

As the lower courts in both appeals found, the weight of authority in this State supports the rule that a landlord is under no duty to mitigate damages caused by a defaulting tenant. *See Joyce v. Bauman, supra;* . . . This rule has been followed in a majority of states, Annot. 21 *A.L.R.*3d 534, §2[a] at 541 (1968), and has been tentatively adopted in the American Law Institute's Restatement of Property. *Restatement (Second) of Property,* §11.1(3) (Tent. Draft No. 3, 1975).

Nevertheless, while there is still a split of authority over this question, the trend among recent cases appears to be in favor of a mitigation requirement. . . .

The majority rule is based on principles of property law which equate a lease with a transfer of a property interest in the owner's estate. Under this rationale the lease conveys to a tenant an interest in the property which forecloses any control by the landlord; thus, it would be anomalous to require the landlord to concern himself with the tenant's abandonment of his own property. *Wright v. Baumann,* 239 *Or.* 410, 398 *P.*2d 119, 120-21, 21 *A.L.R.*3d 527 (1965).

For instance, in *Muller v. Beck, supra,* where essentially the same issue was posed, the court clearly treated the lease as governed by property, as opposed to contract, precepts.[3] The court there observed that the "tenant had an estate for years, but it was an estate qualified by this right of the landlord to prevent its transfer," 94 *N.J.L.* at 313, and that "the tenant has an estate with which the landlord may not interfere." *Id.* at 314. Similarly, in *Heckel v. Griese, supra,* the court noted the absolute nature of the tenant's interest in the property while the lease was in effect, stating that "when the tenant vacated, . . . no one, in the circumstances, had any right to interfere with the defendant's possession of the premises." 12 *N.J. Misc.* at 213. Other cases simply cite the rule announced in *Muller v. Beck, supra,* without discussing the underlying rationale. *See Joyce v. Bauman, supra,* . . .

Yet the distinction between a lease for ordinary residential purposes and an ordinary contract can no longer be considered viable. As Professor Powell observed, evolving "social factors have exerted increasing influence on the law of estates for years." 2 *Powell on Real Property* (1977 ed.), §221[1] at 180-81. The result has been that

PROPERTY VS.
CONTRACT

---

[3] It is well settled that a party claiming damages for a breach of contract has a duty to mitigate his loss. . . .

[t]he complexities of city life, and the proliferated problems of modern society in general, have created new problems for lessors and lessees and these have been commonly handled by specific clauses in leases. This growth in the number and detail of specific lease covenants has reintroduced into the law of estates for years a predominantly contractual ingredient.

(*Id.* at 181). Thus, in 6 *Williston on Contracts* (3 ed. 1962), §890A at 592, it is stated:

There is a clearly discernible tendency on the part of courts to cast aside technicalities in the interpretation of leases and to concentrate their attention, as in the case of other contracts, on the intention of the parties, ...

This Court has taken the lead in requiring that landlords provide housing services to tenants in accordance with implied duties which are hardly consistent with the property notions expressed in *Muller v. Beck, supra,* and *Heckel v. Griese, supra. See Braitman v. Overlook Terrace Corp.,* 68 *N.J.* 368, 346 *A.*2d 76 (1975) (liability for failure to repair defective apartment door lock); *Berzito v. Gambino,* 63 *N.J.* 460, 308 *A.*2d 17 (1973) (construing implied warranty of habitability and covenant to pay rent as mutually dependent); *Marini v. Ireland,* 56 *N.J.* 130, 265 *A.*2d 526 (1970) (implied covenant to repair); *Reste Realty Corp. v. Cooper,* 53 *N.J.* 444, 251 *A.*2d 268 (1969) (implied warranty of fitness of premises for leased purpose). In fact, in *Reste Realty Corp. v. Cooper, supra,* we specifically noted that the rule which we announced there did not comport with the historical notion of a lease as an estate for years. 53 *N.J.* at 451-52, 251 *A.*2d 268. And in *Marini v. Ireland, supra,* we found that the "guidelines employed to construe contracts have been modernly applied to the construction of leases." 56 *N.J.* at 141, 265 *A.*2d at 532.

Application of the contract rule requiring mitigation of damages to a residential lease may be justified as a matter of basic fairness.[4] Professor McCormick first commented upon the inequity under the majority rule when he predicted in 1925 that eventually

the logic, inescapable according to the standards of a `jurisprudence of conceptions' which permits the landlord to stand idly by the vacant, abandoned premises and treat them as the property of the tenant and recover full rent, will yield to the more realistic notions of social advantage which in other fields of the law have forbidden a recovery for damages which the plaintiff by reasonable efforts could have avoided.

[McCormick, "The Rights of the Landlord Upon Abandonment of the Premises by the Tenant," 23 *Mich. L. Rev.* 211, 221-22 (1925)]. Various courts have adopted this position.

The pre-existing rule cannot be predicated upon the possibility that a landlord may lose the opportunity to rent another empty apartment because he must first rent the apartment vacated by the defaulting tenant. Even where the breach occurs in a

---

[4] We *see* no distinction between the leases involved in the instant appeals and those which might arise in other types of residential housing. However, we reserve for another day the question of whether a landlord must mitigate damages in a commercial setting. . . .

multi-dwelling building, each apartment may have unique qualities which make it attractive to certain individuals. Significantly, in *Sommer v. Kridel,* there was a specific request to rent the apartment vacated by the defendant; there is no reason to believe that absent this vacancy the landlord could have succeeded in renting a different apartment to this individual.

We therefore hold that antiquated real property concepts which served as the basis for the pre-existing rule, shall no longer be controlling where there is a claim for damages under a residential lease. Such claims must be governed by more modern notions of fairness and equity. A landlord has a duty to mitigate damages where he seeks to recover rents due from a defaulting tenant.

If the landlord has other vacant apartments besides the one which the tenant has abandoned, the landlord's duty to mitigate consists of making reasonable efforts to re-let the apartment. In such cases he must treat the apartment in question as if it was one of his vacant stock.

As part of his cause of action, the landlord shall be required to carry the burden of proving that he used reasonable diligence in attempting to re-let the premises. We note that there has been a divergence of opinion concerning the allocation of the burden of proof on this issue. See Annot., *supra,* §12 at 577. While generally in contract actions the breaching party has the burden of proving that damages are capable of mitigation, here the landlord will be in a better position to demonstrate whether he exercised reasonable diligence in attempting to re-let the premises.

III

The *Sommer v. Kridel* case presents a classic example of the unfairness which occurs when a landlord has no responsibility to minimize damages. Sommer waited 15 months and allowed $4658.50 in damages to accrue before attempting to re-let the apartment. Despite the availability of a tenant who was ready, willing and able to rent the apartment, the landlord needlessly increased the damages by turning her away. While a tenant will not necessarily be excused from his obligations under a lease simply by finding another person who is willing to rent the vacated premises, here there has been no showing that the new tenant would not have been suitable. We therefore find that plaintiff could have avoided the damages which eventually accrued, and that the defendant was relieved of his duty to continue paying rent. Ordinarily we would require the tenant to bear the cost of any reasonable expenses incurred by a landlord in attempting to re-let the premises, but no such expenses were incurred in this case . . .

In assessing whether the landlord has satisfactorily carried his burden, the trial court shall consider, among other factors, whether the landlord, either personally or through an agency, offered or showed the apartment to any prospective tenants, or advertised it in local newspapers. Additionally, the tenant may attempt to rebut such evidence by showing that he proffered suitable tenants who were rejected. However, there is no standard formula for measuring whether the landlord has utilized satisfactory efforts in attempting to mitigate damages, and each case must be judged upon its own facts. *Compare Hershorin v. La Vista, Inc.,* 110 *Ga.App.* 435, 138 *S.E.*2d 703 (App.1964) ("reasonable effort" of landlord by showing the apartment to all prospective tenants); *Carpenter v. Wisniewski,* 139 *Ind.App.* 325, 215 *N.E.*2d 882 (App.1966) (duty satisfied where landlord advertised the premises through a newspaper, placed a sign in the window, and employed a realtor); *Re Garment Center Capitol, Inc.,* 93 *F.*2d 667, 115 *A.L.R.* 202 (2 Cir. 1938) (landlord's duty not breached where higher rental was asked since it was known that this was merely a basis for negotiations); *Foggia v. Dix,* 265 *Or.* 315, 509 *P.*2d 412, 414 (1973) (in mitigating damages, landlord need not accept less than fair market value or "substantially alter his obligations as established in the pre-existing lease"); *with Anderson v. Andy Darling Pontiac, Inc.,* 257 *Wis.* 371, 43 *N.W.*2d 362 (1950) (reasonable diligence not established where newspaper advertisement placed in one issue of local paper by a broker); *Scheinfeld v. Muntz T. V., Inc.,* 67 *Ill.App.*2d 8, 214 *N.E.*2d 506 (Ill.App.1966) (duty breached where landlord refused to accept suitable subtenant); *Consolidated Sun Ray, Inc. v. Oppenstein,* 335 *F.*2d 801, 811 (8 Cir. 1964) (dictum) (demand for rent which is "far greater than the provisions of the lease called for" negates landlord's assertion that he acted in good faith in seeking a new tenant).

IV

The judgment in *Sommer v. Kridel* is reversed. . . .

NOTES AND QUESTIONS

1. *Landlord's Options Before and After* Sommer. Before *Sommer v. Kridel*, if a tenant abandoned the leased property, the landlord could choose to (1) end the lease and treat the abandonment as an offer by the tenant to end the lease, (2) keep the premises vacant and sue the tenant for rent, or (3) mitigate damages by renting to another tenant and suing the original tenant for any shortfalls. After *Sommer v. Kridel*, what options are available to landlords in New Jersey?

The duty to mitigate reflected in *Sommer* is now the majority rule. The Restatement (Second) of Property, Landlord and Tenant §12.1(3) rejects this majority rule. The drafters of the Restatement (Second) were concerned with (a) discouraging abandonment, (b) avoiding a scenario where the tenant could create duties for the landlord by breaching the tenant's own duties, and (3) undercutting the amount of rent the landlord could charge by imposing a duty to re-let the abandoned premises.

Do you agree with the changes in the law made by *Sommer*? Or do you agree with the Restatement approach?

2. *Satisfying the Duty to Mitigate*. Under *Sommer*, what does the landlord need to do to mitigate? What steps must the landlord take to mitigate? Would placing an "apartment for rent" sign on the front door of the building be enough? Would a

landlord's refusal of an offer for less rent than the original tenant paid be considered a failure to mitigate damages? In this context, what do you think was the worst fact for the landlord in *Sommer*?

3. *The Tenant's Personal Property*. What happens if the tenant leaves behind personal property? Can the landlord sell it or keep it? In California, the landlord has a duty to store the property and mail a notice to the tenant's last known address that describes the property. The tenant may be charged a reasonable storage fee but must be given at least 18 days to claim the personal property. If the property is not claimed, the value of the property determines whether the landlord may retain the property or auction it. *See* California Civil Code §1984. In Virginia, the landlord is obligated to follow certain notice procedures, then may "dispose of the property so abandoned as the landlord sees fit or appropriate." Virginia Code 55-248.38:1. What do you think the landlord should be able to do with personal property left behind by a tenant?

4. *Property vs. Contract*. As the court in *Sommer* suggests, tenant-surrender cases bring the distinction between property and contract principles into sharp relief. From a property perspective, the tenant is the owner of a present interest in the leased premises.

PROPERTY VS. CONTRACT If the tenant doesn't want to use the property interest the tenant owns, that is the tenant's problem, not the landlord's problem. From a contract perspective, the non-breaching party has a clear duty to mitigate damages.

Sommer is another excellent example of a contemporary court applying contract principles to craft more tenant-friendly rules. Remember, though, that not all jurisdictions follow the contract approach and impose a duty on the landlord to mitigate. Whether the landlord's duty to mitigate is good for the class of tenants as a whole is also not entirely clear. Do you see why that might be? In this context, think about who ultimately bears the costs of the landlord's efforts to mitigate damages. Will landlords simply absorb those costs, or will they pass them along to the tenants in their buildings in the form of higher rent?

PROBLEMS

Explanatory answers to these problems can be found on page 1051.

1. Gordon rented an apartment to Cylie. Two months into the one-year lease, Cylie surrendered the apartment to Gordon, explaining that she had to go home to Japan to take care of her ailing grandmother. Gordon never made any attempt to re-rent the apartment. Further, when a person approached Gordon and asked whether the apartment was available, Gordon said that it was not available because it was rented to Cylie. Gordon sent Cylie a bill for ten months of unpaid rent. Cylie argues that she doesn't owe Gordon anything for these ten months because Gordon failed to mitigate damages.

2. Steve rented an apartment to Mary. Two months into the one-year lease, Mary surrendered the apartment to Steve, explaining that she had to go home to Japan to take care of her ailing grandmother. Steve placed advertisements for the apartment in a local

The word "sufferance" can mean to endure pain, but in the property law context, "sufferance" means "passive permission resulting from lack of interference." *See http://dictionary.reference.com/ browse/Sufferance.*

newspaper and on websites like Craigslist. He showed the apartment to several potential tenants, but none of them were interested. Steve sent Mary a bill for ten months of unpaid rent. Mary argues that she doesn't owe Steve anything for these ten months because Steve failed to mitigate damages.

2. HOLDOVERS AND THE TENANCY AT SUFFERANCE

A tenant who stays in possession of the leased premises after the lease has expired is a *holdover*. When a tenant holds over, the landlord has two options. First, the landlord can treat the holdover as a trespasser and bring an action for eviction. Second, the landlord can elect to hold the tenant over for a new lease term. This second option is often called a *tenancy at sufferance*—the tenant has a new lease term at the sufferance of the landlord. Sometimes you will see the tenancy at sufferance listed as a type of tenancy alongside the term of years, periodic tenancy, and tenancy at will. We think it is best to see the tenancy at sufferance as a remedy that is available to the landlord if the tenant holds over after the expiration of the lease.

Our next case provides a good overview of the landlord's options when faced with a holdover tenant.

CRECHALE & POLLES, INC. V. SMITH

Supreme Court of Mississippi, 1974
295 So. 2d 275

RODGERS, Presiding Justice. This action originated in the Chancery Court of the First Judicial District of Hinds County, Mississippi, pursuant to a bill for specific performance of a lease contract filed by Crechale and Polles, Inc., appellant herein. The court awarded the complainants one thousand seven hundred and fifty dollars ($1,750.00) in back rent payment, and seven hundred sixty dollars ($760.00) for damages to the leasehold premises, as well as costs incurred in the proceeding. From this judgment appellant files this appeal and appellees cross-appeal.

The testimony shows that on February 5, 1964, the appellant, Crechale and Polles, Inc., a Mississippi corporation, entered into a lease agreement with appellees, John D. Smith, Jr. and Mrs. Gloria Smith, with appellant as lessor and appellees as lessees. The lease was for a term of five (5) years commencing February 7, 1964, and expiring February 6, 1969, with rental in the amount of one thousand two hundred fifty dollars ($1,250.00) per month.

Smith was informed near the end of his lease that the new building which he planned to occupy would not be complete until a month or two after his present lease expired. With this in mind, he arranged a meeting with his landlord, Crechale, in late December, 1968, or early January, 1969, for the purpose of negotiating an extension of the lease on a month-to-month basis. The outcome of this meeting is one of the focal points of this appeal and the parties' stories sharply conflict. Crechale maintains that he told Smith that since he was trying to sell the property, he did not want to get involved in any month-to-month rental. Smith asserts that Crechale informed him that he was trying to sell the building, but that he could stay in it until it was sold or Smith's new building was ready. Smith's attorney drafted a thirty (30) day extension, but Crechale refused to sign it, saying, "Oh, go ahead. It's all right." Crechale denies that he was ever given the document to sign.

The following is a chronological explanation of the events which led to the subsequent litigation:

February 4, 1969—Smith sent a letter to Crechale confirming their oral agreement to extend the lease on a monthly basis.

February 6, 1969—Crechale wrote Smith denying the existence of any oral agreement concerning extension of the lease and requesting that Smith quit and vacate the premises upon expiration of the term at midnight, February 6, 1969. The letter also advised Smith that he was subject to payment of double rent for any holdover.

March 3, 1969—Smith paid rent for the period of February to March. The check was accepted and cashed by Crechale.

April 6, 1969—Smith paid rent for the period of March to April, but the check was not accepted by Chechale, because it was for 'final payment.'

April 7, 1969—Smith sent a telegram to Crechale stating that he was tendering the premises for purposes of lessor's inventory. The telegram confirmed a telephone conversation earlier that day in which Crechale refused to inventory the building.

April 19, 1969—Approximately three and one-half (3 1/2) months after the expiration of the lease, Crechale's attorney wrote Smith stating that since the lessee had held over beyond the normal term, the lessor was treating this as a renewal of the lease for a new term expiring February 6, 1974.

April 24, 1969—Smith again tendered the check for the final month's occupancy and it was rejected by Crechale.

April 29, 1969—Crechale's attorney wrote Smith again stating the lessor's intention to consider the lessees' holdover as a renewal of the terms of the lease.

There was no further communication between the parties until a letter dated May 15, 1970, from Crechale to Smith requesting that Smith pay the past-due rent or vacate the premises.

May 27, 1970—Smith's attorney tendered the keys to the premises to Crechale.

Subsequently, this lawsuit was filed by Crechale to recover back rent and damages beyond ordinary wear and tear to the leasehold premises. From the chancellor's decision, appellant files the following assignments of error:

(1) The lower court erred in holding that the appellees were not liable as holdover tenants for an additional term of one (1) year.

(2) The lower court's award of damages to the appellant was so inadequate in its amount as to be contrary to the overwhelming evidence.

The cross-appellants, John D. Smith, Jr. and Mrs. Gloria Smith, assign the following as error:

(1) That the chancellor erred in overruling cross-appellants' general demurrer to the original bill for specific performance.

(2) That the lower court erred in assessing damages against the cross-appellants.

The appellant, Crechale and Polles, Inc., contends that the appellees became holdover tenants for a new term under the contract at the election of the landlord appellant, and that appellees owe appellant the rent due each month up to the filing of suit, less the rent paid; and, in addition thereto, it is entitled to specific performance of the holdover contract. This argument is based upon the general rule expressed in 3 Thompson on Real Property §1024, at 65-66 (1959), wherein it is said:

> "As a general rule, a tenancy from year to year is created by the tenant's holding over after the expiration of a term for years and the continued payment of the yearly rent reserved. . . . By remaining in possession of leased premises after the expiration of his lease, a tenant gives the landlord the option of treating him as a trespasser or as a tenant for another year, . . ."

In support of this rule the appellant cites *Tonkel, et al. v. Riteman*, 163 Miss. 216, 141 So. 344 (1932) wherein it is said:

> "It is firmly established that where, without a new contract, a tenant continues to occupy the property which he has held under an annual lease, he becomes liable as tenant for another year at the same rate and under the same terms. *Love v. Law*, 57 Miss. 596; *Usher v. Moss*, 50 Miss. 208. It is the duty of a tenant when his period of tenancy has expired to surrender the premises to his landlord or else to have procured a new contract, and, if he fails to do either, the landlord may treat him as a trespasser or as a tenant under the previous terms, according to the option of the landlord." 163 Miss. at 219, 141 So. at 344.

An examination of the testimony in this case has convinced us that the appellant is not entitled to specific performance so as to require the appellees to pay rent for a new term of the rental contract as a holdover tenant for the following reasons.

After receiving a letter from one of the appellees in which appellee Smith confirmed an alleged agreement to extend the lease on a month-to-month basis, Crechale immediately wrote Smith and denied that there was such an agreement, and demanded that Smith quit and vacate the premises at the end of the lease.

In addition to the rule expressed in 3 Thompson on Real Property §1024, above cited, another rule is tersely expressed in American Law of Property §3.33, at 237 (1952) as follows: "When a tenant continues in possession after the termination of his lease, the landlord has an election either to evict him, treat him as a trespasser it is said, or to hold him as a tenant."

The letter from the appellant dated February 6, 1969, was an effective election on the part of appellant to terminate the lease and to treat the appellees as trespassers.

After having elected not to accept the appellees as tenants, the appellant could not at a later date, after failing to pursue his remedy to evict the tenants, change the election so as to hold the appellees as tenants for a new term.

It is pointed out by the text writer in 49 Am.Jur.2d under the title of Landlord and Tenant that:

> "After the landlord has once exercised his election not to hold the tenant for another term, his right to hold him is lost. On the other hand, if he has signified his election to hold the tenant for another term he cannot thereafter rescind such election and treat the tenant as a trespasser, since his election when once exercised is binding upon the landlord as well as the tenant." (Emphasis added) 49 Am.Jur.2d Landlord and Tenant §1116, at 1070 (1970).

Although the landlord, appellant, expressly refused to extend the lease on a month-to-month basis, nevertheless, the appellant accepted and cashed the rent check for the month of February. The normal effect of such action by the landlord is tantamount to extension of the lease for the period of time for which the check was accepted, unless, of course, the landlord had elected to treat the tenant as a holdover tenant.

The following excerpt from Annot., 45 A.L.R.2d 827, 831 (1956) points out this rule: "It is the rule that, absent evidence to show a contrary intent on the part of the landlord, a landlord who accepts rent from his holding-over tenant will be held to have consented to a renewal or extension of the leasing."

Although there is authority to the contrary [see Annot., 45 A.L.R.2d at 842] the overwhelming weight of authority has adopted the rule above expressed.

On April 6, 1969, the tenants mailed a check for rent for the month of March accompanied by a letter stating that the enclosed check represented the final payment of rent. The next day the tenants tendered the lease premises to the landlord and requested an inventory of certain personal property described in the lease. The landlord refused to accept the tender and rejected the check as a final payment. On April 19, 1969 (three and one-half (3 1/2) months after the expiration of the lease) the landlord attempted to change its position. It then notified the tenants that it had elected to treat them as holdover tenants so as to extend the lease for another term.

We are of the opinion that once a landlord elects to treat a tenant as a trespasser and refuses to extend the lease on a month-to-month basis, but fails to pursue his remedy of ejecting the tenant, and accepts monthly checks for rent due, he in effect agrees to an extension of the lease on a month-to-month basis. See *Lally v. The New Voice*, 128 Ill. App. 455 (1906); *Stillo v. Pellettieri*, 173 Ill.App. 104 (1912).

There is authority to the contrary, but we believe this rule to be based on the best reasoned authority. . . .

We hold, therefore, that the decree of the trial court should be and is hereby affirmed.

Affirmed.

NOTE AND QUESTIONS

1. According to *Crechale*, what remedies are available to a landlord if a tenant continues in possession of the leasehold property after the termination of the lease? In *Crechale*, the tenants did not want to vacate the property because the new building they were moving to was not yet ready. Are there situations where the facts may warrant a court waiving the remedies and penalties typically imposed on holdover tenants? In one old case, the tenants were unable to move their elderly mother from the premises because she was under doctor's orders to not be moved because of her grave illness. The court held that "The holding over was unavoidable and in no manner the fault of the tenant. It could not be avoided, and for it defendants are not liable as hold-over tenants for another year. . . ." *Herter v. Mullen*, 44 L.R.A. 703 (N.Y. 1899). Do you think that this was the right result? Is this a context where we may want to have different rules for commercial and residential leases? Would your perspective change if there was a new tenant who needed to move into the premises? More broadly, does your perspective on holdovers change when there is a new tenant who is planning to use the space?

PROBLEM

An explanatory answer to this question can be found on page 1051.

Linda owned a commercial property. She leased it to Margo for one year. The lease expired January 1. On January 2, however, Margo was still occupying the premises. How would you advise Linda on how to deal with Margo's holdover?

3. EVICTION

Eviction is a process landlords use to remove tenants and recover possession of their leased property. Perhaps the most common reason why landlords evict tenants is failure to pay rent. Landlords might also evict tenants because of other violations of a lease or because the lease has expired.

a. Legal Process vs. Self-Help

Most states have a legal procedure that landlords may use to evict tenants. These procedures are often designed to be relatively fast but in reality are often slow. Typically, we want a landlord to be able to evict a tenant relatively quickly if eviction is justified, but we don't want to deny the tenant due process and a chance to show that the eviction is not justified. We might be especially concerned with due process in residential leases, when a tenant is being evicted from her home.

Faced with a lengthy legal procedure to evict a tenant, a landlord might be tempted to use *self-help* to evict the tenant, for example, by changing the locks and removing the tenant's belongings. Self-help evictions were permitted at common law so long as they were peaceable. Today, most states prohibit self-help evictions and require landlords to use legal process to evict a tenant. In these states, a landlord who uses self-help has engaged in a *wrongful eviction*. In our next case, the landlord changed the locks and barred the commercial tenant from the rental while the tenant was remodeling. As you are reading the case, consider why the court embraced the modern trend of requiring landlords to follow eviction procedures instead of continuing with the common-law practice of permitting self-help.

BERG V. WILEY

Supreme Court of Minnesota, 1978
264 N.W.2d 145

ROGOSHESKE, Justice. Defendant landlord, Wiley Enterprises, Inc., and defendant Rodney A. Wiley (hereafter collectively referred to as Wiley) appeal from a judgment upon a jury verdict awarding plaintiff tenant, A Family Affair Restaurant, Inc., damages for wrongful eviction from its leased premises. The issues for review are whether the evidence was sufficient to support the jury's finding that the tenant did not abandon or surrender the premises and whether the trial court erred in finding Wiley's reentry forcible and wrongful as a matter of law. We hold that the jury's verdict is supported by sufficient evidence and that the trial court's determination of unlawful entry was correct as a matter of law, and affirm the judgment.

On November 11, 1970, Wiley, as lessor and tenant's predecessor in interest as lessee, executed a written lease agreement letting land and a building in Osseo, Minnesota, for use as a restaurant. The lease provided a 5-year term beginning December 1, 1970, and specified that the tenant agreed to bear all costs of repairs and remodeling, to "make no changes in the building structure" without prior written authorization from Wiley, and to "operate the restaurant in a lawful and prudent manner." Wiley also reserved the right "at (his) option (to) retake possession" of the premises "(s)hould the Lessee fail to meet the conditions of this Lease."[1] In early 1971, plaintiff Kathleen Berg took assignment of the lease from the prior lessee, and on May 1, 1971, she opened "A Family Affair Restaurant" on the premises. In January 1973, Berg incorporated the restaurant and assigned her interest in the lease to "A Family Affair Restaurant, Inc." As sole shareholder of the corporation, she alone continued to act for the tenant.

The present dispute has arisen out of Wiley's objection to Berg's continued remodeling of the restaurant without procuring written permission and her consequent operation of the restaurant in a state of disrepair with alleged health code violations. Strained relations between the parties came to a head in June and July 1973. In a letter dated June 29, 1973, Wiley's attorney charged Berg with having breached lease items 5 and 6 by making changes in the building structure without written authorization and by operating an unclean kitchen in violation of health regulations. The letter demanded that a list of eight remodeling items be completed within 2 weeks from the date of the letter, by Friday, July 13, 1973, or Wiley would retake possession of the premises under lease item 7. Also, a June 13 inspection of the restaurant by the Minnesota Department of Health had produced an order that certain listed changes be completed within specified time limits in order to comply with the health code. The major items on the inspector's list, similar to those listed by Wiley's attorney, were to be completed by July 15, 1973.

During the 2-week deadline set by both Wiley and the health department, Berg continued to operate the restaurant without closing to complete the required items of remodeling. The evidence is in dispute as to whether she intended to permanently close the restaurant and vacate the premises at the end of the 2 weeks or simply close for about 1 month in order to remodel to comply with the health code. At the close of business on Friday, July 13, 1973, the last day of the 2-week period, Berg dismissed her employees, closed the restaurant, and placed a sign in the window saying "Closed for Remodeling." Earlier that day, Berg testified, Wiley came to the premises in her absence and attempted to change the locks. When she returned and asserted her right to continue in possession, he complied with her request to leave the locks unchanged. Berg also testified that at about 9:30 p. m. that evening, while she and four of her friends were in the restaurant, she observed Wiley hanging from the awning peering into the window. Shortly thereafter, she heard Wiley pounding on the back door demanding admittance. Berg called the county sheriff to come and preserve order. Wiley testified that he observed Berg and a group of her friends in the restaurant removing paneling

---

[1] The provisions of the lease pertinent to this case provide: "Item # 5 The Lessee will make no changes to the building structure without first receiving written authorization from the Lessor. The Lessor will promptly reply in writing to each request and will cooperate with the Lessee on any reasonable request.

"Item # 6 The Lessee agrees to operate the restaurant in a lawful and prudent manner during the lease period.

"Item # 7 Should the Lessee fail to meet the conditions of this Lease the Lessor may at their option retake possession of said premises. In any such event such act will not relieve Lessee from liability for payment the rental herein provided or from the conditions or obligations of this lease."

from a wall. Allegedly fearing destruction of his property, Wiley called the city police, who, with the sheriff, mediated an agreement between the parties to preserve the status quo until each could consult with legal counsel on Monday, July 16, 1973.

Wiley testified that his then attorney advised him to take possession of the premises and lock the tenant out. Accompanied by a police officer and a locksmith, Wiley entered the premises in Berg's absence and without her knowledge on Monday, July 16, 1973, and changed the locks. Later in the day, Berg found herself locked out. The lease term was not due to expire until December 1, 1975. The premises were re-let to another tenant on or about August 1, 1973. Berg brought this damage action against Wiley and three other named defendants, including the new tenant, on July 27, 1973. A second amended complaint sought damages for lost profits, damage to chattels, intentional infliction of emotional distress, and other tort damages based upon claims in wrongful eviction, contract, and tort. Wiley answered with an affirmative defense of abandonment and surrender and counterclaimed for damage to the premises and indemnification on mechanics lien liability incurred because of Berg's remodeling. At the close of Berg's case, all defendants other than Rodney A. Wiley and Wiley Enterprises, Inc., were dismissed from the action. Only Berg's action for wrongful eviction and intentional infliction of emotional distress and Wiley's affirmative defense of abandonment and his counterclaim for damage to the premises were submitted by special verdict to the jury. With respect to the wrongful eviction claim, the trial court found as a matter of law that Wiley did in fact lock the tenant out, and that the lockout was wrongful.

The jury, by answers to the questions submitted, found no liability on Berg's claim for intentional infliction of emotional distress and no liability on Wiley's counterclaim for damages to the premises, but awarded Berg $31,000 for lost profits and $3,540 for loss of chattels resulting from the wrongful lockout. The jury also specifically found that Berg neither abandoned nor surrendered the premises. The trial court granted Wiley's post-trial motion for an order decreeing that Berg indemnify Wiley for any mechanics lien liability incurred due to Berg's remodeling by way of set-off from Berg's judgment and ordered the judgment accordingly amended.

On this appeal, Wiley seeks an outright reversal of the damages award for wrongful eviction, claiming insufficient evidence to support the jury's finding of no abandonment or surrender and claiming error in the trial court's finding of wrongful eviction as a matter of law.

The first issue before us concerns the sufficiency of evidence to support the jury's finding that Berg had not abandoned or surrendered the leasehold before being locked out by Wiley. Viewing the evidence to support the jury's special verdict in the light most favorable to Berg, as we must, we hold it amply supports the jury's finding of no abandonment or surrender of the premises. While the evidence bearing upon Berg's intent was strongly contradictory, the jury could reasonably have concluded, based on Berg's testimony and supporting circumstantial evidence, that she intended to retain possession, closing temporarily to remodel. Thus, the lockout cannot be excused on ground that Berg abandoned or surrendered the leasehold.

The second and more difficult issue is whether Wiley's self-help repossession of the premises by locking out Berg was correctly held wrongful as a matter of law.

Minnesota has historically followed the common-law rule that a landlord may rightfully use self-help to retake leased premises from a tenant in possession without incurring liability for wrongful eviction provided two conditions are met: (1) The landlord is legally entitled to possession, such as where a tenant holds over after the lease term or where a tenant breaches a lease containing a reentry clause; and (2) the landlord's means of reentry are peaceable. *Mercil v. Broulette,* 66 Minn. 416, 69 N.W. 218 (1896). Under the common-law rule, a tenant who is evicted by his landlord may recover damages for wrongful eviction where the landlord either had no right to possession or where the means used to remove the tenant were forcible, or both. . . .

Wiley contends that Berg had breached the provisions of the lease, thereby entitling Wiley, under the terms of the lease, to retake possession, and that his repossession by changing the locks in Berg's absence was accomplished in a peaceful manner. In a memorandum accompanying the post-trial order, the trial court stated two grounds for finding the lockout wrongful as a matter of law: (1) It was not accomplished in a peaceable manner and therefore could not be justified under the common-law rule, and (2) any self-help reentry against a tenant in possession is wrongful under the growing modern doctrine that a landlord must always resort to the judicial process to enforce his statutory remedy against a tenant wrongfully in possession. Whether Berg had in fact breached the lease and whether Wiley was hence entitled to possession was not judicially determined. That issue became irrelevant upon the trial court's finding that Wiley's reentry was forcible as a matter of law because even if Berg had breached the lease, this could not excuse Wiley's nonpeaceable reentry. The finding that Wiley's reentry was forcible as a matter of law provided a sufficient ground for damages, and the issue of breach was not submitted to the jury.

In each of our previous cases upholding an award of damages for wrongful eviction, the landlord had in fact been found to have no legal right to possession. In applying the common-law rule, we have not before had occasion to decide what means of self-help used to dispossess a tenant in his absence will constitute a nonpeaceable entry, giving a right to damages without regard to who holds the legal right to possession. Wiley argues that only actual or threatened violence used against a tenant should give rise to damages where the landlord had the right to possession. We cannot agree.

It has long been the policy of our law to discourage landlords from taking the law into their own hands, and our decisions and statutory law have looked with disfavor upon any use of self-help to dispossess a tenant in circumstances which are likely to result in breaches of the peace. We gave early recognition to this policy in *Lobdell v. Keene,* 85 Minn. 90, 101, 88 N.W. 426, 430 (1901), where we said:

"The object and purpose of the legislature in the enactment of the forcible entry and unlawful detainer statute was to prevent those claiming a right of entry or possession of lands from redressing their own wrongs by entering into possession in a violent and forcible manner. All such acts tend to a breach of the peace, and encourage high-handed oppression. The law does not permit the owner of land, be his title ever so good, to be the judge of his own rights with respect to a possession adversely held, but puts him to his remedy under the statutes."

To facilitate a resort to judicial process, the legislature has provided a summary procedure in Minn.St. 566.02 to 566.17 whereby a landlord may recover possession of leased premises upon proper notice and showing in court in as little as 3 to 10 days. As we recognized in *Mutual Trust Life Ins. Co. v. Berg*, 187 Minn. 503, 505, 246 N.W. 9, 10 (1932), "(t)he forcible entry and unlawful detainer statutes were intended to prevent parties from taking the law into their own hands when going into possession of lands and tenements . . . ." To further discourage self-help, our legislature has provided treble damages for forcible evictions, §§557.08 and 557.09, and has provided additional criminal penalties for intentional and unlawful exclusion of a tenant. §504.25. In *Sweeney v. Meyers, supra,* we allowed a business tenant not only damages for lost profits but also punitive damages against a landlord who, like Wiley, entered in the tenant's absence and locked the tenant out.

In the present case, as in *Sweeney,* the tenant was in possession, claiming a right to continue in possession adverse to the landlord's claim of breach of the lease, and had neither abandoned nor surrendered the premises. Wiley, well aware that Berg was asserting her right to possession, retook possession in her absence by picking the locks and locking her out. The record shows a history of vigorous dispute and keen animosity between the parties. Upon this record, we can only conclude that the singular reason why actual violence did not erupt at the moment of Wiley's changing of the locks was Berg's absence and her subsequent self-restraint and resort to judicial process. Upon these facts, we cannot find Wiley's means of reentry peaceable under the common-law rule. Our long-standing policy to discourage self-help which tends to cause a breach of the peace compels us to disapprove the means used to dispossess Berg. To approve this lockout, as urged by Wiley, merely because in Berg's absence no actual violence erupted while the locks were being changed, would be to encourage all future tenants, in order to protect their possession, to be vigilant and thereby set the stage for the very kind of public disturbance which it must be our policy to discourage.

Consistent with our conclusion that we cannot find Wiley's means of reentry peaceable under the common-law rule is *Gulf Oil Corp. v. Smithey*, 426 S.W.2d 262 (Tex. Civ.App.1968). In that case the Texas court, without departing from the common-law rule, held that a landlord's reentry in the tenant's absence by picking the locks and locking the tenant out, although accomplished without actual violence, was forcible as a matter of law. The Texas courts, by continuing to embrace the common-law rule, have apparently left open the possibility that self-help may be available in that state to dispossess a tenant in some undefined circumstances which may be found peaceable.

We recognize that the growing modern trend departs completely from the common-law rule to hold that self-help is never available to dispossess a tenant who is in possession and has not abandoned or voluntarily surrendered the premises. This growing rule is founded on the recognition that the potential for violent breach of peace inheres in any situation where a landlord attempts by his own means to remove a tenant who is claiming possession adversely to the landlord. Courts adopting the rule reason that there is no cause to sanction such potentially disruptive self-help where adequate and speedy means are provided for removing a tenant peacefully through judicial process. At least 16 states have adopted this modern rule, holding that judicial proceedings, including the summary procedures provided in those states' unlawful detainer statutes, are the exclusive remedy by which a landlord may remove a tenant claiming possession. . . .

While we would be compelled to disapprove the lockout of Berg in her absence under the common-law rule as stated, we approve the trial court's reasoning and adopt as preferable the modern view represented by the cited cases. To make clear our departure from the common-law rule for the benefit of future landlords and tenants, we hold that, subsequent to our decision in this case, the only lawful means to dispossess a tenant who has not abandoned nor voluntarily surrendered but who claims possession adversely to a landlord's claim of breach of a written lease is by resort to judicial process. We find that Minn.St. 566.02 to 566.17 provide the landlord with an adequate remedy for regaining possession in every such case. Where speedier action than provided in §§566.02 to 566.17 seems necessary because of threatened destruction of the property or other exigent circumstances, a temporary restraining order under Rule 65, Rules of Civil Procedure, and law enforcement protection are available to the landlord. Considered together, these statutory and judicial remedies provide a complete answer to the landlord. In our modern society, with the availability of prompt and sufficient legal remedies as described, there is no place and no need for self-help against a tenant in claimed lawful possession of leased premises.

Applying our holding to the facts of this case, we conclude, as did the trial court, that because Wiley failed to resort to judicial remedies against Berg's holding possession adversely to Wiley's claim of breach of the lease, his lockout of Berg was wrongful as a matter of law. The rule we adopt in this decision is fairly applied against Wiley, for it is clear that, applying the older common-law rule to the facts and circumstances peculiar to this case, we would be compelled to find the lockout nonpeaceable for the reasons previously stated. The jury found that the lockout caused Berg damage and, as between Berg and Wiley, equity dictates that Wiley, who himself performed the act causing the damage, must bear the loss.

Affirmed.

NOTES AND QUESTIONS

1. *Real vs. Personal Property.* The ban on self-help eviction in the real estate context presents an interesting contrast with the repossession of personal property. The UCC allows creditors to use self-help to retake personal property. For example, if you fall behind on your car payments, the lender can have the car repossessed. Does it make sense to allow self-help repossession of a car but not of an apartment? *See* Adam Badawi, *Self-Help and the Rules of Engagement*, 29 Yale J. on Reg. 1 (2012).

2. *Why Not Just Use Legal Process?* If legal proceedings are readily available, why would a landlord be frustrated by the eviction process and prefer one of these self-help methods instead? We mentioned the problem of delay when we introduced *Berg*. Although the court stated that "adequate and speedy means are provided for removing a tenant peacefully," the eviction proceedings called for in most state statutes continue to be time consuming and, as a result, expensive. Most states employ summary proceedings, which are designed to promote quick action but often require notice to the tenant ranging from 20 days to 90 days. *See* California Civil Code §1954.535. If eviction is being sought for nonpayment of rent, the landlord will most likely never recover the loss of rent for that period of time.

3. *What Would Constitute Peaceable Self-Help? Berg* represents the majority rule that prohibits self-help repossession. Some states, however, allow peaceful self-help if there is a lease provision that specifically contemplates the landlord's use of self-help to take possession of the premises. *See Rucker v. Wynn*, 441 S.E.2d 417 (1994) and *94th Aero Squadron of Memphis v. Memphis Shelby Cnty. Airport Auth.*, 169 S.W.3d 627 (2004). When dealing with self-help eviction provisions courts are strict about what constitutes reasonable and permissible force. How would you define reasonable and permissible force? Consider in this context the landlord's use of self-help in *Berg*. Is there anything more the landlord could have done to make the self-help eviction more peaceable?

PROBLEM

Keith owns an apartment building near downtown. Trisha's lease for apartment 4G ran out last month, but she won't move out. Keith elected to treat her like a trespasser, decided to take matters into his own hands, and had a locksmith change the locks when Trisha was at work. Trisha is now suing Keith, arguing that his lockout was wrongful. What is the likely result? An explanatory answer can be found on page 1051.

b. Eviction for Acts of Third Parties

Many leases contain clauses prohibiting illegal activities in the premises. Congress solidified a landlord's ability to remove a tenant from public housing with the Anti-Drug Abuse Act of 1988. The Act imposes an almost strict liability on public housing tenants who are directly or even indirectly involved in drug crimes.

DEPARTMENT OF HOUSING AND URBAN DEVELOPMENT V. RUCKER

Supreme Court of the United States, 2002
535 U.S. 125

REHNQUIST, Chief Justice. With drug dealers "increasingly imposing a reign of terror on public and other federally assisted low-income housing tenants," Congress passed the Anti-Drug Abuse Act of 1988. §5122, 102 Stat. 4301, 42 U.S.C. §11901(3) (1994 ed.). The Act, as later amended, provides that each "public housing agency shall utilize leases which . . . provide that any criminal activity that threatens the health, safety, or right to peaceful enjoyment of the premises by other tenants or any drug-related criminal activity on or off such premises, engaged in by a public housing tenant, any member of the tenant's household, or any guest or other person under the tenant's control, shall be cause for termination of tenancy." 42 U.S.C. §1437d(*l*)(6) (1994 ed., Supp. V). Petitioners say that this statute requires lease terms that allow a local public housing authority to evict a tenant when a member of the tenant's household or a guest engages in drug-related criminal activity, regardless of whether the tenant knew, or had reason to know, of that activity. Respondents say it does not. We agree with petitioners.

Respondents are four public housing tenants of the Oakland Housing Authority (OHA). Paragraph 9(m) of respondents' leases, tracking the language of §1437d(*l*)(6), obligates the tenants to "assure that the tenant, any member of the household, a guest, or another person under the tenant's control, shall not engage in . . . [a]ny drug-related criminal activity on or near the premise[s]." Respondents also signed an agreement stating that the tenant "understand[s] that if I or any member of my household or guests should violate this lease provision, my tenancy may be terminated and I may be evicted." *Id.* at 69.

In late 1997 and early 1998, OHA instituted eviction proceedings in state court against respondents, alleging violations of this lease provision. The complaint alleged: (1) that the respective grandsons of respondents William Lee and Barbara Hill, both of whom were listed as residents on the leases, were caught in the apartment complex parking lot smoking marijuana; (2) that the daughter of respondent Pearlie Rucker, who resides with her and is listed on the lease as a resident, was found with cocaine and a crack cocaine pipe three blocks from Rucker's apartment; and (3) that on three instances within a 2-month period, respondent Herman Walker's caregiver and two others were found with cocaine in Walker's apartment. OHA had issued Walker notices of a lease violation on the first two occasions, before initiating the eviction action after the third violation.

United States Department of Housing and Urban Development (HUD) regulations administering §1437d(*l*)(6) require lease terms authorizing evictions in these circumstances. The HUD regulations closely track the statutory language, and provide that "[i]n deciding to evict for criminal activity, the [public housing authority] shall have discretion to consider all of the circumstances of the case. . . ." 24 CFR §966.4(*l*)(5) (i) (2001). The agency made clear that local public housing authorities' discretion to evict for drug-related activity includes those situations in which "[the] tenant did not know, could not foresee, or could not control behavior by other occupants of the unit." 56 Fed. Reg. 51560, 51567 (1991).

After OHA initiated the eviction proceedings in state court, respondents commenced actions against HUD, OHA, and OHA's director in United States District Court. They challenged HUD's interpretation of the statute under the Administrative Procedure Act, 5 U.S.C. §706(2)(A), arguing that 42 U.S.C. §1437d(*l*)(6) does not require lease terms authorizing the eviction of so-called "innocent" tenants, and, in the alternative, that if it does, then the statute is unconstitutional. The District Court issued a preliminary injunction, enjoining OHA from "terminating the leases of tenants pursuant to paragraph 9(m) of the 'Tenant Lease' for drug-related criminal activity that does not occur within the tenant's apartment unit when the tenant did not know of and had no reason to know of, the drug-related criminal activity." App. to Pet. for Cert. in No. 00-1770, pp. 165a-166a.

A panel of the Court of Appeals reversed, holding that §1437d(*l*)(6) unambiguously permits the eviction of tenants who violate the lease provision, regardless of whether the tenant was personally aware of the drug activity, and that the statute is constitutional. See *Rucker v. Davis,* 203 F.3d 627 (C.A.9 2000). An en banc panel of the Court of Appeals reversed and affirmed the District Court's grant of the preliminary injunction. That court held that HUD's interpretation permitting the eviction of so-called "innocent" tenants "is inconsistent with Congressional intent and must be rejected" under the first step of *Chevron U.S.A. Inc. v. Natural Resources Defense Council, Inc.,* 467 U.S. 837, 842-843, 104 S.Ct. 2778, 81 L.Ed.2d 694 (1984).

We granted certiorari, and now reverse, holding that 42 U.S.C. §1437d(*l*)(6) unambiguously requires lease terms that vest local public housing authorities with the discretion to evict tenants for the drug-related activity of household members and guests whether or not the tenant knew, or should have known, about the activity.

That this is so seems evident from the plain language of the statute. It provides that "[e]ach public housing agency shall utilize leases which . . . provide that . . . any drug-related criminal activity on or off such premises, engaged in by a public housing tenant, any member of the tenant's household, or any guest or other person under the tenant's control, shall be cause for termination of tenancy." 42 U.S.C. §1437d(*l*)(6) (1994 ed., Supp. V). The en banc Court of Appeals thought the statute did not address "the level of personal knowledge or fault that is required for eviction." 237 F.3d, at 1120. Yet Congress' decision not to impose any qualification in the statute, combined with its use of the term "any" to modify "drug-related criminal activity," precludes any knowledge requirement. As we have explained, "the word 'any' has an expansive meaning, that is, 'one or some indiscriminately of whatever kind.' " *United States v. Gonzales,* 520 U.S. 1, 5, 117 S.Ct. 1032, 137 L.Ed.2d 132 (1997). Thus, *any* drug-related activity engaged in by the specified persons is grounds for termination, not just drug-related activity that the tenant knew, or should have known, about.

The en banc Court of Appeals also thought it possible that "under the tenant's control" modifies not just "other person," but also "member of the tenant's household" and "guest." 237 F.3d, at 1120. The court ultimately adopted this reading, concluding that the statute prohibits eviction where the tenant, "for a lack of knowledge or other reason, could not realistically exercise control over the conduct of a household member or guest." *Id.* at 1126. But this interpretation runs counter to basic rules of grammar. The disjunctive "or" means that the qualification applies only to "other person." Indeed, the view that "under the tenant's control" modifies everything coming before it in the sentence would result in the nonsensical reading that the statute applies to "a public housing tenant . . . under the tenant's control." HUD offers a convincing explanation for the grammatical imperative that "under the tenant's control" modifies only "other person": "by 'control,' the statute means control in the sense that the tenant has permitted access to the premises." 66 Fed. Reg. 28781 (2001). Implicit in the terms "household member" or "guest" is that access to the premises has been granted by the tenant. Thus, the plain language of §1437d(*l*)(6) requires leases that grant public housing authorities the discretion to terminate tenancy without regard to the tenant's knowledge of the drug-related criminal activity.

Comparing §1437d(*l*)(6) to a related statutory provision reinforces the unambiguous text. The civil forfeiture statute that makes all leasehold interests subject to forfeiture when used to commit drug-related criminal activities expressly exempts tenants who had no knowledge of the activity: "[N]o property shall be forfeited under this paragraph . . . by reason of any act or omission established by that owner to have been committed or omitted without the knowledge or consent of that owner." 21 U.S.C. §881(a)(7) (1994 ed.). Because this forfeiture provision was amended in the same Anti-Drug Abuse Act of 1988 that created 42 U.S.C. §1437d(*l*)(6), the en banc Court of Appeals thought Congress "meant them to be read consistently" so that the knowledge requirement should be read into the eviction provision. 237 F.3d at 1121-1122. But the two sections deal with distinctly different matters. The "innocent owner" defense for drug forfeiture cases was already in existence prior to 1988 as part of 21 U.S.C. §881(a)(7). All that Congress did in the 1988 Act was to add leasehold interests to the property interests that might be forfeited under the drug statute. And if such a forfeiture action were to be brought against a leasehold interest, it would be subject to the pre-existing "innocent owner" defense. But 42 U.S.C. §1437(d)(*l*)(6), with which we deal here, is a quite different measure. It is entirely reasonable to think that the Government, when seeking to transfer private property to itself in a forfeiture proceeding, should be subject to an "innocent owner defense," while it should not be when acting as a landlord in a public housing project. The forfeiture provision shows that Congress knew exactly how to provide an "innocent owner" defense. It did not provide one in §1437d(*l*)(6).

The en banc Court of Appeals next resorted to legislative history. The Court of Appeals correctly recognized that reference to legislative history is inappropriate when the text of the statute is unambiguous. 237 F.3d, at 1123. Given that the en banc Court of Appeals' finding of textual ambiguity is wrong, see *supra*, at 1233-1234, there is no need to consult legislative history.

Nor was the en banc Court of Appeals correct in concluding that this plain reading of the statute leads to absurd results. The statute does not *require* the eviction of any tenant who violated the lease provision. Instead, it entrusts that decision to the local public housing authorities, who are in the best position to take account of, among other things, the degree to which the housing project suffers from "rampant drug-related or violent crime," 42 U.S.C. §11901(2) (1994 ed. and Supp. V), "the seriousness of the offending action," 66 Fed.Reg., at 28803, and "the extent to which the leaseholder has . . . taken all reasonable steps to prevent or mitigate the offending action." It is not "absurd" that a local housing authority may sometimes evict a tenant who had no knowledge of the drug-related activity. Such "no-fault" eviction is a common "incident of tenant responsibility under normal landlord-tenant law and practice." 56 Fed. Reg., at 51567. Strict liability maximizes deterrence and eases enforcement difficulties.

And, of course, there is an obvious reason why Congress would have permitted local public housing authorities to conduct no-fault evictions: Regardless of knowledge, a tenant who "cannot control drug crime, or other criminal activities by a household member which threaten health or safety of other residents, is a threat to other residents and the project." 56 Fed.Reg., at 51567. With drugs leading to "murders, muggings, and other forms of violence against tenants," and to the "deterioration of the physical environment that requires substantial government expenditures," 42 U.S.C. §11901(4) (1994 ed., Supp. V), it was reasonable for Congress to permit no-fault evictions in order to "provide public and other federally assisted low-income housing that is decent, safe, and free from illegal drugs," §11901(1) (1994 ed.).

In another effort to avoid the plain meaning of the statute, the en banc Court of Appeals invoked the canon of constitutional avoidance. But that canon "has no application in the absence of statutory ambiguity." *United States v. Oakland Cannabis Buyers' Cooperative,* 532 U.S. 483, 494 (2001). "Any other conclusion, while purporting to be an exercise in judicial restraint, would trench upon the legislative powers vested in Congress by Art. I, §1, of the Constitution." *United States v. Albertini,* 472 U.S. 675, 680, 105 S.Ct. 2897, 86 L.Ed.2d 536 (1985). There are, moreover, no "serious constitutional doubts" about Congress' affording local public housing authorities the discretion to conduct no-fault evictions for drug-related crime. *Reno v. Flores,* 507 U.S. 292, 314, n. 9 (1993) (emphasis deleted).

The en banc Court of Appeals held that HUD's interpretation "raise[s] serious questions under the Due Process Clause of the Fourteenth Amendment," because it permits "tenants to be deprived of their property interest without any relationship to individual wrongdoing." 237 F.3d, at 1124-1125. But both of these cases deal with the acts of government as sovereign. In *Scales,* the United States criminally charged the defendant with knowing membership in an organization that advocated the overthrow of the United States Government. In *Danaher,* an Arkansas statute forbade discrimination among customers of a telephone company. The situation in the present cases is entirely different. The government is not attempting to criminally punish or civilly regulate respondents as members of the general populace. It is instead acting as a landlord of property that it owns, invoking a clause in a lease to which respondents have agreed and which Congress has expressly required. *Scales* and *Danaher* cast no constitutional doubt on such actions.

The Court of Appeals sought to bolster its discussion of constitutional doubt by pointing to the fact that respondents have a property interest in their leasehold interest, citing *Greene v. Lindsey,* 456 U.S. 444 (1982). This is undoubtedly true, and *Greene* held that an effort to deprive a tenant of such a right without proper notice violated the Due Process Clause of the Fourteenth Amendment. But, in the present cases, such deprivation will occur in the state court where OHA brought the unlawful detainer action against respondents. There is no indication that notice has not been given by OHA in the past, or that it will not be given in the future. Any individual factual disputes about whether the lease provision was actually violated can, of course, be resolved in these proceedings.

We hold that "Congress has directly spoken to the precise question at issue." *Chevron U.S.A. Inc. v. Natural Resources Defense Council, Inc.,* 467 U.S., at 842. Section 1437d(*l*)(6) requires lease terms that give local public housing authorities the discretion to terminate the lease of a tenant when a member of the household or a guest engages in drug-related activity, regardless of whether the tenant knew, or should have known, of the drug-related activity.

Accordingly, the judgment of the Court of Appeals is reversed, and the cases are remanded for further proceedings consistent with this opinion.

NOTES AND QUESTIONS

1. *Congress Has Spoken.* The Court used classic statutory interpretation to hold that the statute passed by Congress was clear. Do you agree with the Court's analysis? The decision in *Rucker* has lead to many heart-wrenching outcomes where an innocent old lady gets evicted through no fault of her own. Imagine that you are a member of Congress considering an amendment to the statutory provision at issue in *Rucker.* Would you want to amend the statute? If so, how? What policy justifications support amending the statute? What policy justifications support the current version of the statute as applied in *Rucker?*

2. *"Compassion and Common Sense."* Tenants and poverty law experts understandably were alarmed by the *Rucker* decision. The Department of Housing and Urban Development tried to temper their concerns by urging public housing authorities to use "compassion and common sense" when dealing with drug cases. *See* Letter from Mel Martinez, U.S. Sec'y for Hous. & Urban Dev., to Public Housing Directors (Apr. 16, 2002), available at *http://www.hud.gov/offices/pih/regs/rucker6jun2002.pdf*. Would you find that comforting as a public-housing tenant?

3. *Nuisance Property Ordinances and the Victim's Dilemma.* Some municipalities have ordinances that force a landlord to evict tenants from households that generate numerous 911 calls and police visits. The intent of these ordinances is to protect the community from disruptive, or "nuisance," households. One unforeseen consequence of these statutes is that tenants might not call 911 to avoid being evicted from their homes. Consider the quandary facing Lakisha Briggs:

> The police had warned Lakisha Briggs: one more altercation at her rented row house here, one more call to 911, and they would force her landlord to evict her.
>
> They could do so under the town's "nuisance property" ordinance, a law intended to protect neighborhoods from seriously disruptive households. Officials can invoke the measure and pressure landlords to act if the police have been called to a rental home three times within four months.
>
> So she faced a fearful dilemma, Ms. Briggs recalled, when her volatile boyfriend showed up last summer, fresh out of a jail stint for their previous fight, and demanded to move in.
>
> "I had no choice but to let him stay," said Ms. Briggs, 34, a certified nursing assistant, even though, she said in an interview, she worried about the safety of her 3-year-old daughter as well as her own.
>
> "If I called the police to get him out of my house, I'd get evicted," she said. "If I physically tried to remove him, somebody would call 911 and I'd be evicted."

Erik Eckholm, *Victim's Dilemma: 911 Calls Can Bring Eviction*, New York Times (Aug. 16, 2013).

c. Retaliatory Eviction

When landlords file for eviction, tenants may be able to raise a defense of *retaliatory eviction*. Retaliatory eviction applies when tenants are evicted in retaliation for raising a legitimate legal issue such as a violation of a housing code. Consider the following case of Yvonne Edwards, who was evicted from her apartment after she reported housing code violations to the proper government officials. The court's opinion is by J. Skelly Wright, the author of *Javins*. As you read the case, think about the relationship between housing codes, the implied warranty of habitability, and retaliatory eviction.

EDWARDS V. HABIB

United States Court of Appeals District of Columbia Circuit, 1968
397 F.2d 687

J. SKELLY WRIGHT, Circuit Judge. In March 1965 the appellant, Mrs. Yvonne Edwards, rented housing property from the appellee, Nathan Habib, on a month-to-month basis. Shortly thereafter she complained to the Department of Licenses and Inspections of sanitary code violations which her landlord had failed to remedy. In the course of the ensuing inspection, more than 40 such violations were discovered which the Department ordered the landlord to correct. Habib then gave Mrs. Edwards a 30-day statutory notice to vacate and obtained a default judgment for possession of the premises. Mrs. Edwards promptly moved to reopen this judgment, alleging excusable neglect for the default and also alleging as a defense that the notice to quit was given in retaliation for her complaints to the housing authorities. Judge Greene, sitting on motions in the Court of General Sessions, set aside the default judgment and, in a very thoughtful opinion, concluded that a retaliatory motive, if proved, would constitute a defense to the action for possession. At the trial itself, however, a different judge apparently deemed evidence of retaliatory motive irrelevant and directed a verdict for the landlord.

Mrs. Edwards then appealed to this court for a stay pending her appeal to the District of Columbia Court of Appeals, and on December 3, 1965, we granted the stay, provided only that Mrs. Edwards continue to pay her rent. *Edwards v. Habib,* 125 U.S.App.D.C. 49, 366 F.2d 628 (1965). She then appealed to the DCCA, which affirmed the judgment of the trial court. 227 A.2d 388 (1967). In reaching its decision the DCCA relied on a series of its earlier decisions holding that a private landlord was not required, under the District of Columbia Code, to give a reason for evicting a month-to-month tenant and was free to do so for any reason or for no reason at all. The court acknowledged that the landlord's right to terminate a tenancy is not absolute, but felt that any limitation on his prerogative had to be based on specific statutes or very special circumstances. Here, the court concluded, the tenant's right to report violations of law and to petition for redress of grievances was not protected by specific legislation and that any change in the relative rights of tenants and landlords should be undertaken by the legislature, not the courts. We granted appellant leave to appeal that decision to this court. We hold that the promulgation of the housing code by the District of Columbia Commissioners at the direction of Congress impliedly effected just such a change in the relative rights of landlords and tenants and that proof of a retaliatory motive does constitute a defense to an action of eviction. Accordingly, we reverse the decision of the DCCA with directions that it remand to the Court of General Sessions for a new trial where Mrs. Edwards will be permitted to try to prove to a jury that her landlord who seeks to evict her harbors a retaliatory intent. . . .

We need not . . . decide whether 45 D.C. CODE §910 could validly compel the court to assist the plaintiff in penalizing the defendant for exercising her constitutional right to inform the government of violations of the law; for we are confident that Congress did not intend it to entail such a result.

45 D.C. CODE §910, in pertinent part, provides:

> "Whenever . . . any tenancy shall be terminated by notice as aforesaid, and the tenant shall fail or refuse to surrender possession of the leased premises, . . . the landlord may bring an action to recover possession before the District of Columbia Court of General Sessions, as provided in sections 11-701 to 11-749."

And 16 D.C. CODE §1501, in pertinent part, provides:

> "When a person detains possession of real property . . . after his right to possession has ceased, the District of Columbia Court of General Sessions . . . may issue a summons to the party complained of to appear and show cause why judgment should not be given against him for restitution of possession."

These provisions are simply procedural. They neither say nor imply anything about whether evidence of retaliation or other improper motive should be unavailable as a defense to a possessory action brought under them. It is true that in making his affirmative case for possession the landlord need only show that his tenant has been given the 30-day statutory notice, and he need not assign any reason for evicting a tenant who does not occupy the premises under a lease. But while the landlord may evict for any legal reason or for no reason at all, he is not, we hold, free to evict in retaliation for his tenant's report of housing code violations to the authorities. As a matter of statutory construction and for reasons of public policy, such an eviction cannot be permitted.

The housing and sanitary codes, especially in light of Congress' explicit direction for their enactment, indicate a strong and pervasive congressional concern to secure for the city's slum dwellers decent, or at least safe and sanitary, places to live. Effective implementation and enforcement of the codes obviously depend in part on private initiative in the reporting of violations. Though there is no official procedure for the filing of such complaints, the bureaucratic structure of the Department of Licenses and Inspections establishes such a procedure, and for fiscal year 1966 nearly a third of the cases handled by the Department arose from private complaints. To permit retaliatory evictions, then, would clearly frustrate the effectiveness of the housing code as a means of upgrading the quality of housing in Washington.

As judges, "we cannot shut our eyes to matters of public notoriety and general cognizance. When we take our seats on the bench we are not struck with blindness, and forbidden to know as judges what we see as men." *Ho Ah Kow v. Nunan*, C.C.D.Cal., 12 Fed.Cas. 252, 255 (No. 6546) (1879). In trying to effect the will of Congress and as a court of equity we have the responsibility to consider the social context in which our decisions will have operational effect. In light of the appalling condition and shortage of housing in Washington, the expense of moving, the inequality of bargaining power between tenant and landlord, and the social and economic importance of assuring at least minimum standards in housing conditions,[47] we do not hesitate to declare that retaliatory eviction cannot be tolerated. There can be no doubt that the slum dweller, even though his home be marred by housing code violations, will pause long before he complains of them if he fears eviction as a consequence. Hence an eviction under the circumstances of this case would not only punish appellant for making a complaint which she had a constitutional right to make, a result which we would not impute to the will of Congress simply on the basis of an essentially procedural enactment, but also would stand as a warning to others that they dare not be so bold, a result which, from the authorization of the housing code, we think Congress affirmatively sought to avoid.

The notion that the effectiveness of remedial legislation will be inhibited if those reporting violations of it can legally be intimidated is so fundamental that a presumption against the legality of such intimidation can be inferred as inherent in the legislation even if it is not expressed in the statute itself. Such an inference was recently drawn by the Supreme Court from the federal labor statutes to strike down under the supremacy clause a Florida statute denying unemployment insurance to workers discharged in retaliation for filing complaints of federally defined unfair labor practices. While we are not confronted with a possible conflict between federal policy and state law, we do have the task of reconciling and harmonizing two federal statutes so as to best effectuate the purposes of each. The proper balance can only be struck by interpreting 45 D.C. CODE §§902 and 910 as inapplicable where the court's aid is invoked to effect an eviction in retaliation for reporting housing code violations.

> Both the majority and dissent mention *Berman v. Parker*, a case involving the use of eminent domain to clear wide areas of Washington D.C. as part of an urban renewal project. We include an excerpt from *Berman* in our chapter on Takings.

---

[47] "Miserable and disreputable housing conditions may do more than spread disease and crime and immorality. They may also suffocate the spirit by reducing the people who live there to the status of cattle. They may indeed make living an almost insufferable burden. They may also be an ugly sore, a blight on the community which robs it of charm, which makes it a place from which men turn. The misery of housing may despoil a community as an open sewer may ruin a river." *Berman v. Parker*, 348 U.S. 26, 32-33, 75 S.Ct. 98, 102, 99 L.Ed. 27 (1954). *See also Frank v. State of Maryland*, 359 U.S. 360, 371, 79 S.Ct. 804, 811, 3 L.Ed.2d 877 (1959): "The need to maintain basic, minimal standards of housing, to prevent the spread of disease and of that pervasive breakdown in the fiber of a people which is produced by slums and the absence of the barest essentials of civilized living, has mounted to a major concern of American government."

According to the *Report of the Planning Commission, supra* Note 45, at pp. 5-6, "more than 100,000 children are growing up in Washington now under one or more housing conditions which create psychological, social, and medical impairments, and make satisfactory home life difficult or a practical impossibility."

This is not, of course, to say that even if the tenant can prove a retaliatory purpose she is entitled to remain in possession in perpetuity. If this illegal purpose is dissipated, the landlord can, in the absence of legislation or a binding contract, evict his tenants or raise their rents for economic or other legitimate reasons, or even for no reason at all.[53] The question of permissible or impermissible purpose is one of fact for the court or jury, and while such a determination is not easy, it is not significantly different from problems with which the courts must deal in a host of other contexts, such as when they must decide whether the employer who discharges a worker has committed an unfair labor practice because he has done so on account of the employee's union activities. As Judge Greene said, "There is no reason why similar factual judgments cannot be made by courts and juries in the context of economic retaliation [against tenants by landlords] for providing information to the government."

Reversed and remanded. . . .

DANAHER, Circuit Judge (dissenting):

Basically at issue between my colleagues and me is a question as to the extent to which the power of the court may here be exercised where by their edict the landlord's right to his property is being denied. They concede as they must

> "that in making his affirmative case for possession the landlord need only show that
> his tenant has been given the 30-day statutory notice, and he need not assign any
> reason for evicting a tenant who does not occupy the premises under a lease."

That fundamental rule of our law of property must give way, it now develops. My colleagues so rule despite the absence of a statutory prescription of discernible standards as to what may constitute "violations," or of provision for compensating the landlord for the deprivation of his property. They say that the court will not "frustrate the effectiveness of the housing code as a means of upgrading the quality of housing in Washington." Since they recognize that there is an "appalling condition and shortage of housing in Washington,"[3] they say the court must take account of the "social and economic importance of assuring at least minimum standards in housing conditions."

---

[53] Of course, because of his prior taint the landlord may not be able to disprove an illicit motive unless he can show a legitimate affirmative reason for eviction.

[3] It is common knowledge that following *Berman v. Parker*, the housing structures in one entire quadrant of the City of Washington were razed, driving thousands of tenants to seek whatever "appalling" accommodations they could find. In place of the destroyed housing, beautiful apartment buildings have been built, to be sure, with "co-ops" in some costing up to $100,000 per apartment, with rentals in others priced far beyond the capacity to pay of thousands of those who had been displaced. And even the affluent tenants having chosen to do so, must be presumed, at least until now, to have taken the premises in the condition in which they found them, cockroaches and all.

The Washington Post on April 1, 1968 editorialized upon the need for a renewal project after "the wholesale bulldozing of slums and massive uprooting of families with them which characterized the Southwest development."

So to meet such needs, the burden would now be met, not pursuant to a congressionally prescribed policy, with adequate provision for construction or acquisition costs, or for compensation to property owners, but by private landlords who will be saddled with what should have been a public charge.

Note how my colleagues achieve that result as they rule:

> "But while the landlord may evict for any legal reason or for no reason at all, he is not, we hold, free to evict in retaliation for his tenant's report of housing code violations to the authorities. As a matter of statutory construction and for reasons of public policy, such an eviction cannot be permitted."

Just as do my colleagues, I deplore the effort of any landlord for a base reason to secure possession of his own property, but if his right so to recover in accordance with our law is to be denied, Congress should provide the basis. . . .

I am not alone in my position, I dare say, as I read the Congressional Record for March 13, 1968, page H 1883. In President Johnson's message to the Congress he said:

> "One of the most abhorrent injustices committed by some landlords in the District is to evict—or threaten to evict—tenants who report building code violations to the Department of Licenses and Inspections.

> "This is intimidation, pure and simple. It is an affront to the dignity of the tenant. It often makes the man who lives in a cold and leaking tenement afraid to report those conditions.

> "Certainly the tenant deserves the protection of the law when he lodges a good faith complaint.

> *"I recommend legislation to prevent retaliatory evictions by landlords in the District."* (Emphasis added.)

He seems to think as do I that congressional action is required. . . .

That my colleagues ultimately upon reflection began to doubt the sufficiency of their position seems clear enough, for they observe:

> "This is not, of course, to say that *even if the tenant can prove a retaliatory purpose* she is entitled to remain in possession in perpetuity." (Emphasis added.)

"Of course" *not,* I say; *not at all* as the law has read, until now, I may add. My colleagues continue:

> "If this illegal purpose is dissipated, the landlord can, in the absence of legislation or a binding contract, evict his tenants or raise their rents for economic or other legitimate reasons, or even for no reason at all."

And so, it may be seen according to the majority, we need never mind the Congress, the aid of which the *President* would invoke. We may disregard, even reject, our law of such long standing. We will simply leave it to a jury to say when a landlord may regain possession of his own property, although "the determination is not easy," my colleagues concede.

I leave my colleagues where they have placed themselves.

NOTES AND QUESTIONS

1. *Policies Behind Prohibitions on Retaliatory Evictions.* What policies did the *Edwards* court identify as being important in reaching its decision to bar retaliatory evictions? Did the majority and dissent disagree on these policies or on something else?

2. *Retaliatory Eviction Statutes.* The District of Columbia now has a statute that bars retaliatory eviction.

Retaliatory Action

(a) No housing provider shall take any retaliatory action against any tenant who exercises any right conferred upon the tenant by this chapter, by any rule or order issued pursuant to this chapter, or by any other provision of law. Retaliatory action may include any action or proceeding not otherwise permitted by law which seeks to recover possession of a rental unit, action which would unlawfully increase rent, decrease services, increase the obligation of a tenant, or constitute undue or unavoidable inconvenience, violate the privacy of the tenant, harass, reduce the quality or quantity of service, any refusal to honor a lease or rental agreement or any provision of a lease or rental agreement, refusal to renew a lease or rental agreement, termination of a tenancy without cause, or any other form of threat or coercion.

(b) In determining whether an action taken by a housing provider against a tenant is retaliatory action, the trier of fact shall presume retaliatory action has been taken, and shall enter judgment in the tenant's favor unless the housing provider comes forward with clear and convincing evidence to rebut this presumption, if within the 6 months preceding the housing provider's action, the tenant:

(1) Has made a witnessed oral or written request to the housing provider to make repairs which are necessary to bring the housing accommodation or the rental unit into compliance with the housing regulations;

(2) Contacted appropriate officials of the District government, either orally in the presence of a witness or in writing, concerning existing violations of the housing regulations in the rental unit the tenant occupies or pertaining to the housing accommodation in which the rental unit is located, or reported to the officials suspected violations which, if confirmed, would render the rental unit or housing accommodation in noncompliance with the housing regulations;

(3) Legally withheld all or part of the tenant's rent after having given a reasonable notice to the housing provider, either orally in the presence of a witness or in writing, of a violation of the housing regulations;

(4) Organized, been a member of, or been involved in any lawful activities pertaining to a tenant organization;

(5) Made an effort to secure or enforce any of the tenant's rights under the tenant's lease or contract with the housing provider; or

(6) Brought legal action against the housing provider.

D.C. Official Code §42-3505.02 (1985).

Presuming that there is a retaliatory motive, would a landlord violate this statute by (a) increasing the tenant's rent? (b) decreasing services by draining a pool? (c) locking the laundry room? (d) canceling security services? (e) making noisy repairs to common areas during early morning hours or after midnight?

3. *Tenant Bill of Rights.* The landlord-tenant law in any given jurisdiction may be a complicated mix of statutes, regulations, and case law. Several states and the District of Columbia have tenant advocacy offices that prepare and promulgate documents that seek to explain tenant's rights and obligations in plain language. These documents are often titled "Tenant Bill of Rights." The District of Columbia Tenant Bill of Rights is available at: *http://ota.dc.gov/sites/default/files/dc/sites/ota/publication/attachments/2009_10_27_OTA_DC_Tenant_Bill_of_Rights_FOR_SH_COMMENT.pdf.*

CHAPTER 5

REAL ESTATE TRANSACTIONS

In this chapter, we explore some of the legal and nonlegal issues surrounding real estate transactions. As we explore these issues, we will frequently use this diagram:

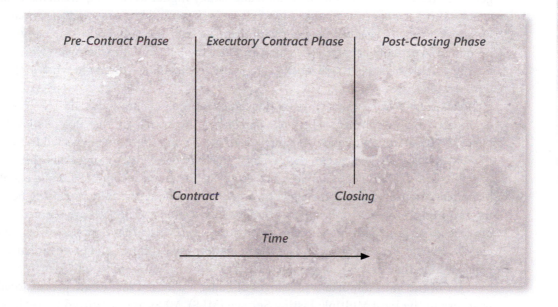

This diagram divides the real estate transaction into three phases, with the vertical lines indicated by the *two major events* in the transaction. The first event is the *signing of the purchase and sale contract*, where the seller agrees to sell, and the buyer agrees to buy the subject real estate. The second event is the *closing*, where, among other things, the seller delivers title to the buyer, and the buyer delivers the purchase price to the seller. The phase before the contract is signed is called the pre-contract phase. The middle phase is the time when the parties' contract is executory—in other words, when the parties have signed the contract but not yet performed the obligations they have undertaken in the contract. The post-closing phase is the time after the seller and the buyer have performed their core obligations under the contract: for the seller, to deliver title and possession of the property to the buyer, and for the buyer to deliver the purchase price to the seller.

A. BROKERS, AGENTS, AND THE LAW OF REAL ESTATE PROFESSIONALS

Before any real estate transaction can occur, a willing seller must be matched up with a willing buyer. The matching of buyers and sellers in the residential real estate market is typically facilitated by real estate professionals—agents and brokers. We will therefore begin with a brief overview of some of the issues that can arise in the relationships between real estate professionals and their clients.

If you want to buy or sell a home, a logical first step is to consult with a real estate professional. Precise terminology can vary from state to state, but we can make some generalizations about real estate agents and brokers. First, both agents and brokers are typically licensed real estate professionals. They typically have to meet certain educational and testing requirements to obtain their licenses. Second, brokers generally have to receive more education and satisfy higher testing requirements than agents. Third, agents typically have to work for brokers, and brokers are responsible for supervising the agents who work with them. Fourth, only brokers are typically permitted to actually list properties for sale. Fifth, the person with whom you work in buying a home most often will be an agent, though sometimes you might work directly with a broker.

Real estate brokers and agents are fiduciaries for their clients. Fiduciary relationships are created in circumstances where one person is representing another in a relationship of special trust and confidence. As fiduciaries, brokers and agents are expected to fulfill the duties of loyalty and care to their clients. The duty of loyalty, among other things, prohibits self-dealing. For example, a real estate agent cannot recommend that a client buy a piece of property that the agent owns, at least without first fully disclosing her interest in the property to the client. More broadly, agents and brokers are required to disclose all material information about a property transaction that they possess to their clients. The duty of care requires agents and brokers to be diligent and professionally competent in their representation of clients.

One of the most important privileges of being a licensed real estate professional is access to the local Multiple Listing Service (MLS). MLSs are organized by region. Generally speaking, only brokers can list a property with the MLS. All other brokers who are members of a particular MLS and the agents who work for them can see the listing. MLS rules prohibit the dissemination of information from MLS listings to nonmembers. Sellers have a strong interest in hiring an MLS broker because the MLS listing greatly increases the number of potential buyers who will see the listing for the property. Buyers similarly have a strong interest in working with a broker or agent who has access to the MLS to get access to the broadest range of properties to buy.

In many real estate transactions, both the seller and the buyer will work with real estate agents or brokers. Let's see how this would play out in a hypothetical transaction. The sellers in our transaction are James Lin and Alice Stevens, a married couple. They own a house on a one-third-acre plot at 12 Oak Street in a small suburban subdivision. The buyer is Laura Williams, a young lawyer who is moving to town to take a job with a local firm. Although some property owners try to sell their property on their own, most list their property with a real estate professional. James and Alice followed the more common approach and chose to retain Eric Aspen, a licensed real estate agent who worked at Colonial Park Real Estate LLC, to list their home. Eric has agreed to act as a seller's agent, and the broker who supervises Eric will list the 12 Oak Street property on the local MLS for James and Alice.

At around the same time, Laura decided to relocate and started looking for a home in the area. On the recommendation of a friend, Laura approached Cindy Gans for help in finding a house to purchase. Cindy is a licensed real estate agent who works for Progress Real Estate LLC. Laura met with Cindy, and Cindy provided Laura with information on various homes that met Laura's basic criteria. Cindy obtained this information from the MLS. One of the homes in Cindy's list was the 12 Oak Street property owned by James and Alice. Cindy showed the 12 Oak Street property to Laura, and Laura decided to make an offer on the home to James and Alice.

To recap, the sellers, James and Alice, are working with Eric from Colonial Park Real Estate. The buyer, Laura, is working with Cindy from Progress Real Estate.

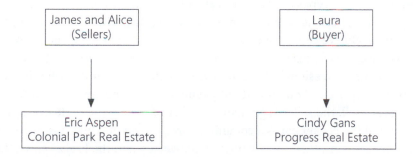

1. THE SELLER-LISTING AGENT RELATIONSHIP

Let's first look at the relationship between James and Alice, as sellers, and Eric, who they have hired to help them sell their house. Eric has two primary responsibilities. First, Eric will help James and Alice find a buyer for their home. Through his broker, Eric will list the home for sale, posting the listing on the local MLS and otherwise advertising the listing. Because of their role in listing the property for sale, the person in Eric's position is often called the *listing agent*. Eric will also facilitate the showing of the home to prospective buyers. Second, Eric will assist James and Alice in negotiating with potential buyers and in completing the transaction once a buyer is found. Listing agents often help the seller complete the contract of sale and assist the seller at the closing.

In return for their services, listing agents are typically paid commissions. To be more precise, the commission is typically paid to the listing broker, and the broker pays the bulk of the commission to the agent. There are three basic types of listing agreements, differing from one another in their provisions on the broker's right to a commission. These are:

1. *Open listing.* In an open listing, the broker earns her commission by securing a ready, willing, and able buyer. The seller can list the property with other brokers, and if someone else secures the buyer, the broker in the open listing will not get paid anything.

2. *Exclusive agency.* In an exclusive agency, the seller agrees that the broker will be the only real estate professional allowed to sell the property. If another broker finds a buyer, the broker in an exclusive agency agreement will still get paid a commission. If, however, the seller finds a buyer on her own, the broker in an exclusive agency agreement will not get paid a commission.

3. *Exclusive right to sell.* In an exclusive right to sell, the broker is the only person allowed to sell the property. The broker earns a commission regardless of who finds a buyer. The key difference between exclusive agency and exclusive right to sell is what happens if the seller finds a buyer on her own. In an exclusive agency, the broker *does not* get a commission in this circumstance. In an exclusive right to sell, the broker *does* get a commission in this circumstance.

The names of the three types of listing agreement capture the differences between them. With an open listing, the right to a commission is open to multiple brokers: no one broker has any exclusive right to a commission. With an exclusive agency agreement, the broker is the exclusive agent—that is, the seller is giving the broker the right to be the only real estate professional who can earn a commission, but the seller is retaining a right to find a buyer on her own without paying the broker a commission. With an exclusive right to sell, the seller is giving the broker just that—the exclusive right to sell the property, and the broker earns a commission regardless of who finds the buyer.

In most transactions, there is a distinction between when the broker earns the commission and when the broker gets paid the commission. Typically, a broker earns a commission when the broker locates a buyer who is *ready, willing, and able* to buy the property. As a matter of contract or custom, the broker is typically paid at a later point when the closing occurs and the transaction is complete. The seller and the broker may alter these general rules in their contract. It is important to understand that under the typical approach, the seller will still owe the broker a commission if a transaction falls apart after a broker has found a ready, willing, and able buyer. As you might imagine, what constitutes a ready, willing, and able buyer can be a bit blurry in some circumstances. Two factors are often especially important in deciding this issue. First, has the potential expressed a willingness to enter into a binding contract for the purchase of the property? Second, does the buyer have the financial wherewithal to pay the purchase price (either in cash or with borrowed money)? If the answers to these two questions are "yes," then the broker will have gone a long way toward establishing that the buyer was ready, willing, and able.

Listing agreements typically have a provision, often referred to as a *tail*, that entitles the broker to a commission if the property is sold within a certain time after the listing agreement terminates. A tail provision would look something like this:

> Broker is entitled to a commission under this agreement if a sale of the property occurs within six months of the ending date of this agreement.

Brokers worry that they will put a great deal of effort into selling the property and that the seller will somehow interfere with their ability to collect a commission. The seller, for example, could exercise a contractual right to terminate the contract before the broker becomes formally entitled to a commission. Alternatively, the seller could drag her feet and allow the contract to expire according to its terms before the broker formally earns a commission. A tail protects the broker by requiring the payment of a commission if the property is sold within the tail period. The seller can avoid paying the commission by waiting out the tail period but will have to pay the price of delaying the sale of the property. Tails serve the legitimate purpose of protecting a broker against seller misbehavior but do so in a manner that places the seller at risk of misbehavior by the broker. Where brokers are worried about sellers who try to cut them out of commissions, sellers are worried about brokers who do little or nothing to sell the property. Imagine, for example, that you are a seller who has hired a broker to sell your home. You soon become disenchanted with the broker, who does not appear to be doing a whole lot to sell your home. If you fire the broker and terminate your agreement, you still may be subject to the tail provision. The specific terms of the agreement will determine where the balance is struck between the broker's and the seller's interests.

2. THE BUYER-AGENT RELATIONSHIP

Imagine that you walked into a real estate agency and talked to an agent about helping you find a house. You explain to the agent what you are looking for and how much you want to spend. The agent shows you listings and takes you to see houses that seem to match your interests. You would reasonably believe that the agent was representing you and therefore owed fiduciary duties to you. In many jurisdictions, however, the law of agency will hold that the agent you were working with actually represents the seller, and not you, the buyer. This is *an absolutely shocking result*, and if you were not disturbed by reading the last few sentences then you should go back and read them again. As we will see, this default rule can be easily altered by contract. Before we get to how to fix the result, however, we should take a closer look at how it comes about. Let's return to our diagram of the agents involved in the 12 Oak Street transaction, where the arrows show who is working with whom, not the legal relationships between them:

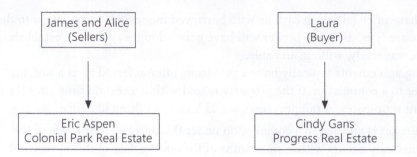

Following the default rule, the law of agency in many jurisdictions would hold that Cindy is working for the sellers, James and Alice, rather than Laura. This logic of this result is based on the role of the MLS listing. In the first step of our transaction, James and Alice agreed to work with Eric to list the property. Eric's supervising broker listed the property on MLS. Under the traditional approach, this listing is viewed as an *invitation to subagency*. That is, the listing is seen as an invitation by the listing broker to other brokers and agents to cooperate in the sale of the listed property. By accessing the listing and showing the home to potential buyers, other professionals in the MLS system accept this invitation to subagency. Under this approach, when Cindy accessed the listing and showed the 12 Oak Street property to Laura, Cindy was accepting the seller's broker's invitation to cooperate in the sale of the property as a subagent. When this approach is followed, the person in Cindy's position is called a *cooperating* or *selling* broker or agent, even though they primarily work with the buyer. Here is how our diagram would look under the traditional approach:

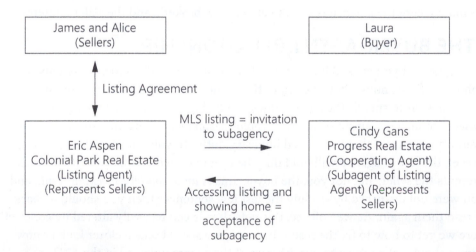

Our next case provides a good overview of this traditional approach and illustrates some of the consequences that that result from it.

STORTROEN V. BENEFICIAL FINANCE CO. OF COLORADO

Supreme Court of Colorado, 1987
736 P.2d 391

QUINN, Chief Justice. We granted certiorari under C.A.R. 50 to review a decision of the District Court of Jefferson County, which entered a summary judgment in favor of the defendant-respondent, Beneficial Finance Company, the owner of a home that was offered for sale through a real estate broker who listed the property with a multiple listing service, and against the plaintiffs, Odell R. and Kathy E. Stortroen, who were the putative purchasers of the home. The district court held that a principal-agent relationship existed between the purchasers and the selling (or "cooperating") broker in connection with the sale and that the purchasers' act of notifying the selling broker's associate of the acceptance of the seller's counteroffer did not constitute notice to the sellers of the acceptance. We hold that in a multiple listing real estate transaction involving residential property the selling broker or salesperson, in the absence of a written agreement creating a different agency relationship, is an agent of the listing broker and, as such, is within a chain of agency to the seller. We accordingly reverse the summary judgment and remand the case to the district court for further proceedings.

I.

The Stortroens and Beneficial Finance Company (Beneficial) stipulated to the following chronology of events. The Stortroens wished to sell their home at 4270 Stuart Street in Denver and to purchase a larger residence. To accomplish these goals the Stortroens sought the assistance of Mary Panio, a broker-associate with Foremost Realty, which had sold the Stortroens their current home. The Stortroens listed their home for sale with Foremost on November 4, 1983, and relied on Panio to show them a suitable property to buy. In order to find the Stortroens a home Panio consulted a compilation of listings published by Metrolist, Inc., a multiple listing service operated by several boards of realtors in the Denver metropolitan area. Panio learned through the listing book issued by Metrolist that Beneficial had listed for sale with Paul Olthoff, doing business as Olthoff Realty Company, a house at 6927 Quay Court in Arvada. The listing agreement between Beneficial and Olthoff was captioned "Exclusive Right To Sell Listing Contract (Residential)" and provided, in pertinent part, as follows:

> In consideration of the services of the hereinafter named real estate broker, I
> hereby list with said broker, from Oct. 26, 1983, to March 26, 1983 [sic], inclusive,

the property described below and I hereby grant said broker the exclusive and irrevocable right to sell the same within said time at the price and on the terms herein stated, or at such other price and terms which may be accepted by me, and to accept deposits thereon and retain same until the closing of, or defeat of, the transaction. I further authorize said broker to list the property with any multiple listing service in which he is a participant, at the broker's expense, and to accept the assistance and cooperation of other brokers. I hereby agree to pay said broker 6% of the selling price for his services (1) in case of any sale or exchange of same within said listing period by the undersigned owner, the said broker, or by any person, or (2) upon the said broker finding a purchaser who is ready, willing and able to complete the purchase as proposed by the owner, or (3) in case of any such sale or exchange of said property withing [sic] 120 days subsequent to the expiration of this agreement to any party with whom the said broker negotiated and whose name was disclosed to the owner by the broker during the listing period. . . .

Additional provisions: If Paul Olthoff, personally procures a purchaser for subject property then brokerage fee shall be 4% of purchase price.

If Beneficial Finance procures a purchaser for subject property then the brokerage fee shall be 2% of purchase price.

In January 1984, Panio showed the Stortroens the Quay Court property and assisted them in preparing a written offer to purchase the property for $105,000, of which $1,000 was paid as earnest money. The Stortroens' offer was on a document entitled "Residential Contract to Buy and Sell Real Estate" and designated a closing date of March 26, 1984. The contract was contingent upon the sale and closing of the Stortroens' current home, although it provided that the Quay Court property "may remain on the market and in the event of a successful offer to seller, the purchaser has 72 hours to remove contingency on the sale of their home." Donald Reh, an officer of Beneficial, reviewed the offer with Olthoff and rejected it. Reh drafted a counterproposal offering the property for $110,000. The counterproposal stated: "If this counterproposal is accepted by Purchaser, as evidenced by Purchaser's signature hereon, and if Seller receives notice of such acceptance on or before 9 P.M. 2-3-84, 1984, the said proposed contract, as amended hereby, shall become a contract between the parties." Beneficial submitted the counterproposal through Olthoff to Panio on February 1, 1984.

In the meantime, Carol Ann and Eugene Carelli, who were defendants and third-party plaintiffs in the district court, were shown the Quay Court property by a licensed real estate salesperson employed by another broker. The Carellis prepared an offer of $112,000 for the property and submitted it to Paul Olthoff, the listing broker, on the afternoon of Friday, February 3, 1984. Olthoff informed Reh, the officer of Beneficial who was dealing with the property, of the higher offer and then instructed Carol Carelli and the real estate salesperson to take the offer directly to Reh's office because of the outstanding counteroffer to the Stortroens. When Reh received the Carelli offer, he phoned Olthoff to tell him that he wanted to accept the higher offer and directed him to withdraw the counteroffer to the Stortroens. At approximately 4:30 p.m. on the afternoon of February 3, Olthoff left telephone messages at Panio's office and residence to the effect that Beneficial had withdrawn the counteroffer. After Olthoff informed Reh that he had left these messages, Reh accepted the Carelli offer in writing.

Panio, who was unaware of the Carelli negotiations with Beneficial, took Beneficial's counteroffer to the Stortroens at their home where the Stortroens signed their acceptance at approximately 4:10 p.m. Panio then brought the signed copy back to her office and discovered the withdrawal message from Olthoff.

At a meeting of the real estate brokers and salespersons at Olthoff's office the following Monday, Panio delivered to Olthoff the counteroffer signed by the Stortroens on February 3, 1984, and a document withdrawing the contingency clause, prepared on February 4, 1984. Although the respective positions of Beneficial, the Stortroens, and the Carellis were discussed, no agreement was reached. The Stortroens subsequently recorded the contract and its modifications with the Jefferson County Clerk and Recorder. The Carellis refused to close the transaction when the title examination revealed a cloud on the title caused by the Stortroens' recordation, and they moved into the property under a month-to-month lease.

On April 26, 1984, the Stortroens filed a complaint in the District Court of Jefferson County against Beneficial and the Carellis, alleging breach of a real estate sales contract and seeking a specific performance decree against Beneficial, money damages at the rate of $45 per day from the designated date of closing, which was March 26, 1984, and an order requiring the Carellis to vacate the Quay Court property. The Carellis cross-claimed against Beneficial and added a third-party complaint against Olthoff.

The Stortroens and Beneficial executed a written stipulation of facts, and each filed motions for summary judgment. The district court concluded that Panio was the agent of the Stortroens and that the Stortroens' delivery of the written acceptance of Beneficial's counterproposal to Panio did not constitute notice of acceptance to Beneficial. As a consequence, the court granted the motion for summary judgment on behalf of Beneficial, and denied the Stortroens' motion for summary judgment. The parties then filed a joint motion with this court, requesting that we grant certiorari under C.A.R. 50 and consider whether under the circumstances of this case the selling broker, Mary Panio, was acting as an agent of the purchasers, the Stortroens, or as an agent of the seller, Beneficial.

II.

Where, as here, the issue is whether a real estate broker or salesperson is an agent of the seller or the purchaser in connection with the sale of a home, we must turn to basic principles of agency and contract law for necessary guidance.

A.

"Agency is the fiduciary relation which results from the manifestation of consent by one person to another that the other shall act on his behalf and subject to his control, and consent by the other so to act." Restatement (Second) of Agency §1(1) (1957). The one for whom the action is to be taken is the principal, and the one who is to act is the agent. *Id.* §1(2) and (3). Agency is thus a legal relation having its source in the mutual consent of the parties. The consensual arrangement may but need not amount to a contract. *Id.* §1 comment b. Furthermore, an agency relation may exist even though the parties do not call it an agency and do not subjectively intend that legal consequences flow from their relation. *Id.* What is critical is that the parties materially agree to enter into a particular relation to which the law attaches the legal consequences of agency, even though those consequences might not have been within the contemplation of the parties at the time of their agreement. *Id.* The existence of an agency relationship is ordinarily a question of fact, e.g., *Marron v. Helmecke*, 100 Colo. 364, 67 P.2d 1034 (1937); *Eckhardt v. Greeley Nat'l Bank*, 79 Colo. 337, 245 P. 710 (1926); *Schoelkopf v. Leonard*, 8 Colo. 159, 6 P. 209 (1884), but the court may properly decide the question as one of law when the facts are not in dispute, *Marron*, 100 Colo. 364, 67 P.2d 1034; *Smith v. Davis*, 67 Colo. 128, 186 P. 519 (1920).

Agents may be classified into two general types. A general agent is "an agent authorized to conduct a series of transactions involving a continuity of service," Restatement (Second) of Agency §3(1), such as one "who is an integral part of a business organization and does not require fresh authorization for each transaction." *Id.* §3 comment a. A special agent is defined as "an agent authorized to conduct a single transaction or series of transactions not involving continuity of service." *Id.* §3(2). Under some circumstances, authority can be further delegated to subagents. A subagent is "a person appointed by an agent empowered to do so, to perform functions undertaken by the agent for the principal, but for whose conduct the agent agrees with the principal to be primarily responsible." *Id.* §5(1). A subagent is the agent of both the appointing agent and the principal. *Id.* §5 comment d. Notice to an agent given in the course of a transaction which is within the scope of the agency is notice to the principal. *Gray v. Blake*, 131 Colo. 560, 564, 283 P.2d 1078, 1080 (1955); *Denver, S.P. & Pac. R.R. v. Conway*, 8 Colo. 1, 9, 5 P. 142, 147 (1884). So too, notice to a subagent who is under a duty to communicate the notice to the agent is effective to the same extent as if notice had been given to the agent. Restatement (Second) of Agency §283(a) and comment b.

B.

In the context of residential real estate transactions, it is a widely accepted rule of agency law that a real estate broker operating under an exclusive listing contract with the seller of the property stands in an agency relationship to the seller. E.g., *Marcotte Realty & Auction, Inc. v. Schumacher*, 229 Kan. 252, 624 P.2d 420 (1981); *Vogt v. Town &*

Country Realty, 194 Neb. 308, 231 N.W.2d 496 (1975); *Bartsas Realty, Inc. v. Leverton*, 82 Nev. 6, 409 P.2d 627 (1966); *Mersky v. Multiple Listing Bureau*, 73 Wash. 2d 225, 437 P.2d 897 (1968); *Myer v. Miller*, 631 P.2d 441 (Wyo.1981). This rule has been recognized, albeit implicitly, and applied in several Colorado decisions. *See Circle T. Corp. v. Deerfield*, 166 Colo. 238, 444 P.2d 404 (1968); *Shriver v. Carter*, 651 P.2d 436 (Colo.App.1982); *Hickam v. Colorado Real Estate Comm'n*, 36 Colo.App. 76, 534 P.2d 1220 (1975). The seller-broker relationship is a special agency created and defined by the listing agreement between the parties. This agreement describes the property or interest to be sold, the price or range of prices acceptable to the seller, the broker's commission, and the length of time the agreement is binding, and authorizes the broker to find a ready, willing, and able purchaser for the listed property on terms acceptable to the seller. D. Burke, Jr., *Law of Real Estate Brokers* §2.3 (1982); *Colo. Real Estate Comm'n, Real Estate Manual*, ch. VIII, at 1 (1985). Because it is customary for a real estate broker to employ salespersons to deal with prospective purchasers of the listed property, the authority given to the broker by the listing agreement will generally include the implied authority to appoint these salespersons as subagents to perform the tasks assigned to the broker by the listing agreement. *Rosenthal v. Art Metal, Inc.*, 95 N.J. Super. 8, 229 A.2d 676 (1967); Restatement (Second) of Agency §80.

The listing agreement may authorize the broker to list the property with a multiple listing service. A multiple listing service is basically an arrangement for brokers in a given locality to pool their listings and split their commissions. *See Frisell v. Newman*, 71 Wash. 2d 520, 429 P.2d 864, 868 (1967). Brokers who are members of the multiple listing service submit their listings to a central bureau which then publishes and distributes a catalog of available properties. Under traditional agency principles, a listing contract which authorizes the listing broker to list the property with a multiple listing service permits the listing broker to create a subagency with other members of the multiple listing service.[2] As we stated in *People v. Colorado Springs Board of Realtors*, 692 P.2d 1055, 1059 (Colo.1984), the listing broker's act of listing the property with the multiple listing service "constitutes an offer of subagency by the listing broker to other [multiple listing service] members to procure a buyer in exchange for a percentage of the sale commission."[3]

---

[2] Our analysis of the multiple listing service is consistent with the understanding of the real estate profession. Colo. Real Estate Comm'n, *Real Estate Manual*, ch. VIII, at 3, states that "[g]enerally [a multiple listing] is an exclusive right to sell listing, with the additional feature that other participating brokers may also sell the property as sub-agents of the listing broker." Since we deal in this case with an exclusive listing agreement that expressly authorized the listing broker to list the property with a multiple listing service, it is unnecessary to address whether an exclusive listing agreement that is silent on multiple listing authorization might nonetheless result in an agency relationship between the seller and selling ("cooperating") broker or salesperson when the listing broker lists the property with a multiple listing service.

[3] In some situations we have found that a selling broker has acted as agent of a purchaser. In *Hiller v. Real Estate Comm'n*, 627 P.2d 769 (Colo.1981), for example, we reversed an order suspending the license of Hiller, a real estate broker, for unworthy, incompetent, and dishonest conduct in violation of section 12-61-113(1)(n) and (1)(t), 5 C.R.S.

We acknowledge that some courts have rejected the characterization of the relationship between the seller of a home and a broker-member of a multiple listing service as one of subagency, primarily on the basis that some aspects of the relationship do not fit the classic description of a consensual fiduciary relation involving one person acting on behalf of and subject to another's control. E.g., *Wise v. Dawson*, 353 A.2d 207 (Del.Super.1975);[4] *Pumphrey v. Quillen*, 102 Ohio App. 173, 141 N.E.2d 675 (1955). Indeed, one commentator has not only rejected the proposition that there is an agency relationship between the seller and a broker-member of a multiple listing service, but has also advanced the notion that a cooperative sale by a broker-member of a multiple listing service establishes an agency relationship between the purchaser and the selling broker. *Comment, A Reexamination of the Real Estate Broker-Buyer-Seller Relationship*, 18 Wayne L. Rev. 1344, 1353 (1972);[5] *see also* Gulitz, *Broker's Responsibilities in Co-op Sales: Whose Agent is He?*, 10 Real Estate L.J. 126, 129-31 (1981). The reasoning here is that agency law should reflect the expectations of the parties and that a purchaser of real estate reasonably believes that a selling broker or salesperson is acting on behalf of and in the interest of the purchaser. While this view undoubtedly has some merit, we believe there are cogent reasons to support the traditional rule that a principal-agent relationship flows from the seller to the selling ("cooperating") broker in a multiple listing transaction.

The selling broker's role is to use his expertise and judgment in promoting the interests of the seller by finding a buyer for the property, and, to this end, the selling broker makes use of information furnished by the seller in the listing arrangement. Upon

---

(1973). Hiller was the listing broker for the sale of his wife's home. Both Hiller and his wife intended to purchase a home listed by another broker and to sell Hiller's condominium prior to the purchase. We determined that Hiller's conduct in connection with the prospective purchase of a home and the broker's act in signing the purchase agreement as "agent" clearly indicated that the broker was acting as agent for his wife in the transaction and not as agent of the seller. Again, in *Lester v. Marshall*, 143 Colo. 189, 352 P.2d 786 (1960), the court determined that the selling and listing broker was liable in tort to the purchasers of a home on the basis of the selling broker's failure "to carry out an express undertaking which the [purchasers] had relied on them to carry out" and "as a result of which the [purchasers] suffered a loss." These decisions were fact-specific, and we did not in either case adopt a general rule of agency between a purchaser and a selling broker or salesperson.

[4] In concluding that the relationship between a seller and a broker-member of a multiple listing service was not one of subagency, the Delaware Court in *Wise v. Dawson*, 353 A.2d 207 (Del.Super.1975), emphasized that the service arrangement has as its purpose the exchange of information rather than the establishment of an agency, that a split commission was not an indication of agency since it can occur between independent contractors, that the listing broker had no control over the selling broker, and that the widespread acceptance of the multiple listing service was indicative of the absence of any agency relationship between brokers.

[5] The Wayne Law Review article states:

Reliance on agency doctrine in this situation results in a great inequity to the buyer, especially where a buyer specifically requests the broker's representation and aid in securing a home free of defects or where he specifically requests disclosure of the defects in each house shown to him. In the absence of a listing agreement between the broker and the seller, the broker should be deemed the agent of the buyer and not the subagent of the listing broker. There is no compelling reason for a court to invariably adhere to the agency doctrine that this selling broker is a subagent of the listing broker.

18. Wayne L.Rev. at 1353.

finding a purchaser for the property, the selling broker becomes entitled to collect the commission from the seller. The basic structure of this business relationship derives from the listing contract between the seller and the listing broker and the agreement between the listing broker and other members of the multiple listing service. There is no such similarly structured relationship between the selling broker and the buyer in the typical residential real estate transaction. The buyer, for example, has no duty to the selling broker to complete his contract with the seller so as to enable the broker to collect his commission. *Note,* Ellsworth Dobbs, Inc. v. Johnson: *A Reexamination of the Broker-Buyer-Seller Relationship in New Jersey,* 23 Rutgers L. Rev. 83, 99-100 (1968). Furthermore, in the event the seller defaults on a real estate sales contract, the selling broker is under obligation to return to the buyer the full amount of the deposit or down payment received from the buyer. *Perino v. Jarvis,* 135 Colo. 393, 312 P.2d 108 (1957); *Victor M. Cox & Co. v. Borstadt,* 49 Colo. 83, 111 P. 64 (1910).

Also, although some of the ostensible indicia of an agency relationship may be present in situations where a real estate broker or salesperson maintains close contact with a prospective purchaser of a home, we believe that finding an agency relationship in such circumstances would lead inevitably to the creation of a dual agency between the seller and the prospective purchaser as principals and the real estate broker or salesperson as agent. Such dual agency holds out the potential for serious conflicts of interest in the typical residential real estate transaction. Under Colorado law, a real estate broker or salesperson is prohibited from representing both the seller and the buyer in the same real estate transaction unless the parties know of and consent to the arrangement. *Finnerty v. Fritz,* 5 Colo. 174, 175-76 (1879).[6] This same principle is codified in Colorado statutes and rules governing the real estate profession. §12-61-113(1)(d), 5 C.R.S. (1985) (real estate broker or salesperson subject to license suspension or revocation for "[a]cting for more than one party in a transaction without the knowledge

---

[6] Over 100 years ago the *Finnerty* court observed as follows:

> [I]t is a well settled rule that the same person cannot be both agent of the owner to sell, and agent of the purchaser to buy, for the reason that the interests of buyer and seller necessarily conflict, and the same agent cannot serve both employers with efficiency and fidelity. The interest of the agent conflicts with his duty in such case. His duty to the vendor to sell for the highest price is wholly incompatible with his duty to the purchaser to buy for the lowest price, and these inconsistent relations, if assumed, would expose him to the temptation to sacrifice the interests of one party or the other, in order to secure his double commissions. Wherefore, it is the established policy of the law to remove all such temptations, and to this end, every contract whereby an agent is placed under a direct inducement to violate the confidence reposed in him by his principal, is declared to be opposed to public policy, and not capable of being enforced as against any person who has a right to object. The effect of the rule is, that if an agent act for both parties in the same transaction, he cannot recover compensation from either, unless the parties knew and assented to his acting for both. The rule cannot be avoided by proof that no injury has resulted from his double dealing, for the policy of the law is not remedial of actual wrong, but preventive of its possibility.

5. Colo. at 175-76; *see* also H. Fusilier, *The Law of Real Estate Practice* §8.3, at 238 (1970).

of all parties thereto"); Real Estate Comm'n Rule E-32, 4 C.C.R. 725-1, at 7.05b (licensee representing purchaser pursuant to agency contract prohibited from simultaneously representing owner or acting as subagent of licensed broker representing owner unless written disclosure is made and express written consent given by all parties; written disclosure must state that licensee is acting as agent for both purchaser and seller and must identify source and nature of compensation to be paid licensee).

Finally, the legal recognition of an agency relationship between the prospective purchaser and selling broker or salesperson, solely on the basis of the selling broker's or salesperson's contacts with the purchaser and efforts expended to find the purchaser a home, would not necessarily inure to the benefit of the purchaser. As one commentator has observed:

> With the seller-selling agent relationship established, the seller may become liable to the buyer in tort for any misrepresentations of his agent through the ratification doctrine. *See* Restatement (Second) of Agency §§82, 92-93, 98-100, 218 (1957). Such liability allows the remedy of rescission against the seller. If there is no agency relationship between the seller and the selling broker, but the agency relationship is between the buyer and the selling broker, this remedy of rescission is no longer available to the buyer because the ratification doctrine would not be applicable, and the buyer's only recourse may be a suit against the broker for damages. In such a situation, the finding of agency between buyer and selling broker may be more harmful to the buyer than beneficial, because the buyer would lose his action for rescission and restitution against the seller. *See* Restatement (Second) of Agency §§82, 92-93, 98-100, 218 (1957). Furthermore, if the agent breaches his fiduciary duty to his principal, one of the remedies available to the principal is a return of compensation paid. If the selling broker is the agent of the buyer, it could be argued that the buyer did not pay any compensation to the agent, because the agent was paid by the seller through the listing broker. Again, the finding of an agency relationship between the selling broker and the buyer may not enhance the buyer's legal position.

Romero, *Theories of Real Estate Broker Liability: Arizona's Emerging Malpractice Doctrine*, 20 Ariz.L.Rev. 767, 773 n. 33 (1978).

The well-defined relationship that can be traced from the seller to the listing broker and then to the selling broker or salesperson leads us to conclude that in a typical multiple listing real estate transaction the selling ("cooperating") broker or salesperson functions as an agent of the listing broker and, consequently, stands in a subagency relationship to the seller. This conclusion is not only in harmony with our characterization of the relationship in *People v. Colorado Springs Board of Realtors*, 692 P.2d at 1059, where we noted that a "[multiple listing service] listing constitutes an offer of subagency by the listing broker to other [multiple listing service] members to procure a buyer in exchange for the percentage of the sale commission," but is also in substantial accord with the majority of jurisdictions which have specifically addressed the agency relationship created through a multiple listing service in a residential real estate transaction. *See, e.g., Fennell v. Ross*, 289 Ark. 374, 711 S.W.2d 793 (1986); *Vanderschoot v. Christiana*, 10 A.D.2d 188, 198 N.Y.S.2d 768 (1960); *Jackson v. Williams*, 510 S.W.2d 645 (Tex.Civ.App.1974); *Frisell v. Newman*, 71 Wash. 2d 520, 429 P.2d 864 (1967); *First Church of the Open Bible v. Cline J. Dunton Realty, Inc.*, 19 Wash.App. 275, 574 P.2d 1211 (1978); *cf. Kruse v. Miller*, 143 Cal.App.2d 656, 300 P.2d 855 (1956) (subagency between selling broker and seller found on basis of permission of listing broker rather than multiple listing agreement).

The listing broker's offer of subagency to other multiple listing service members is an offer for a unilateral contract—that is, an offer requesting return performance rather than a promise to perform. It is, of course, a fundamental principle of contract law that offers to enter into a contract may not be revoked after acceptance without liability for breach. 1 S. Williston, *A Treatise on the Law of Contracts* §55 (3d ed. 1957); 1 *Corbin on Contracts* §38 (1963). A unilateral offer is accepted when substantial performance has been rendered by the offeree. 1 *Corbin on Contracts* §49. In the context of the multiple listing arrangement, therefore, a broker accepts the unilateral offer by making a demonstrable effort to obtain a purchaser for the property. There can be no question that the actual production of a ready, willing, and able purchaser will constitute acceptance of the subagency offer. Short of this, such acts as contacting potential purchasers about the listed property and showing the property by appointment, especially when considered in combination, can well evince the level of effort required for substantial performance. Of course, the fact that a broker accepts the offer of subagency does not preclude the same broker from acting as agent with respect to the sale of other property, including the property of a prospective purchaser. *Hale v. Wolfsen*, 276 Cal.App.2d 285, 291, 81 Cal. Rptr. 23, 27 (1969).

Once created, the subagency relationship continues until terminated by the expiration of time, the expiration of the listing agreement, the sale of the listed property, the withdrawal of consent by either the listing broker or the seller, or other circumstances which indicate that the principal no longer wishes the subagent to act in accordance with the initial authorization. *See generally* Restatement (Second) of Agency §§105-07, 117-19. A principal's revocation of agency authority terminates only upon notice to the agent. *Lowell v. Hessey*, 46 Colo. 517, 105 P. 870 (1909); *see also* Restatement (Second) of Agency §118.

C.

Our determination that the selling broker or salesperson acts as a subagent of the seller is not intended to preclude a real estate broker and a prospective purchaser from entering into a written agreement designating the broker as the purchaser's agent for the purpose of locating and purchasing property. However, while general agency principles permit the establishment of an agency relationship through the conduct of the principal and agent, *Guy Martin Buick, Inc. v. Colorado Springs Nat'l Bank*, 184 Colo. 166, 519 P.2d 354 (1974); *Rhodes v. Industrial Comm'n*, 99 Colo. 271, 61 P.2d 1035 (1936), such an agency relationship cannot arise by implication between a purchaser and a real estate broker or salesperson in the inherently ambiguous circumstances of a residential sale. The prevailing perception of the broker as an agent of the seller is too firmly imbedded in the real estate business to permit such a finding on the basis of conduct alone. Furthermore, as previously noted, Colorado law prohibits a real estate broker or salesperson from simultaneously representing both the seller and the purchaser in the same transaction unless written disclosure of such dual representation is given to the seller and purchaser and they consent in writing to the dual agency arrangement. §12-61-113(1)(d), 5 C.R.S. (1985); Real Estate Comm'n Rule E-32, 4 C.C.R. 725-1, at 7.05b; Colo. Real Estate Comm'n, *Real Estate Manual*, ch. VIII, at 4.

Since the multiple listing service is a fact of life in modern real estate practice, and since a real estate broker or salesperson operating within a multiple listing service is clearly in a chain of agency to the seller and is prohibited from representing both parties to a real estate sale unless there is a written disclosure of a dual agency and written consent of the parties, we conclude that a real estate broker or salesperson who wishes to act as the agent of a prospective purchaser in connection with the purchase of a home must establish that agency by a written agreement with the purchaser. Written documentation of the agency relationship under these circumstances not only will serve to obviate any uncertainty on the part of the prospective purchaser regarding the authority of the broker or salesperson to act on the purchaser's behalf in connection with the details of a contemplated purchase but should also remove all doubt on the part of the broker or salesperson as to their fiduciary obligation to act with loyalty and candor in their relationship with the purchaser. In the absence of any such written agreement we will consider a selling broker or salesperson only as an agent of the listing broker and subagent of the seller. When there is a written agency agreement between the broker or salesperson and the prospective purchaser, then obviously the terms of the agreement, rather than the multiple listing arrangement, determine the rights and duties of the parties with respect to the agency relationship.

The absence of an agency relationship between the purchaser and the selling broker does not leave the purchaser unprotected in his dealings with the selling broker or salesperson. A selling broker or salesperson may be held liable for wrongful acts causing damage to a third person. This principle is recognized in both the statutory and decisional law of this state. In order to protect the public from unscrupulous brokers, the legislature has extensively regulated the real estate profession, §§12-61-101 to -407, 5 C.R.S. (1985 & 1986 Supp.), and licensed brokers and salespersons are subject to sanctions for various forms of unethical and unprofessional conduct, §12-61-113, 5 C.R.S. (1985 & 1986 Supp.).[7] Moreover, Colorado courts have consistently held a licensed broker or salesperson accountable where the licensee failed to deal fairly and honestly with the purchaser, *see, e.g., Lear v. Bawden*, 75 Colo. 385, 225 P. 831 (1924); *Fitzgerald v. Edelen*, 623 P.2d 418 (Colo.App.1980), as have the courts of other states. *See, e.g., Bevins v. Ballard*, 655 P.2d 757 (Alaska 1982) (a duty to purchaser can arise when broker becomes aware of suspicious facts regarding his representation or when a purchaser makes an affirmative inquiry and broker fails to check the accuracy of his representation); *Hagar v. Mobley*, 638 P.2d 127 (Wyo.1981) (broker liable to purchasers for misrepresenting material terms of lease in connection with sale of leasehold interest); *see generally Note, A Real Estate Broker's Duty to His Purchaser: Washington State's Position and Some Projections For the Future*, 17 Gonzaga L.Rev. 79 (1981). These obligations exist and are accordingly enforceable notwithstanding the absence of an agency relationship between the purchaser and the selling broker or salesperson.

III.

The remaining aspect of this case concerns the application of the aforementioned guidelines to the undisputed facts. We are dealing here with a summary judgment based on a written stipulation of fact and several documents relating to the purported purchase of the Quay Court property by the Stortroens. No one is claiming that a trier of fact, notwithstanding the undisputed facts, might nonetheless draw conflicting factual inferences on critical elements of a claim or defense. On the contrary, what the parties are contesting here are the legal principles that should be applied to the uncontroverted evidence. Under these circumstances we may appropriately apply those principles to the facts and enter the requisite legal conclusions in resolving this controversy. *See, e.g., Jones v. Dressel*, 623 P.2d 370 (Colo.1981); *Stagecoach Property Owners Ass'n v. Young's Ranch*, 658 P.2d 1378 (Colo.App.1982).

The stipulated facts demonstrate that the Stortroens, who wished to sell their home and to purchase a new home in the Denver metropolitan area, sought the assistance of Mary Panio, a broker-associate at Foremost Realty, who had previously assisted them in locating their current home. Panio consulted the multiple listing service published by Metrolist and discovered in the multiple listing Beneficial's Quay Court property which was listed under Olthoff Realty Company's listing contract with Beneficial.

---

[7] The license of a broker or salesperson may be temporarily suspended or permanently revoked for such acts as making substantial or repeated misrepresentations or false promises, acting as a dual agent without the knowledge and consent of the parties, or failing to account for or remit monies which belong to others. §12-61-113, 5 C.R.S. (1985 & 1986 Supp.). A person who obtains a final judgment against a licensed broker or salesperson on the grounds of negligence, fraud, willful misrepresentation, deceit, or conversion of funds, arising from a real estate transaction, may apply to the real estate recovery fund, which is financed by license fees and operated by the Real Estate Commission, for payment of the unpaid actual and direct loss in the transaction, including court costs and reasonable attorney fees. *See* §§12-61-301 to -305, 5 C.R.S. (1985 & 1986 Supp.).

By consulting the multiple listing service, Panio thus became aware of Olthoff Realty Company's unilateral offer of subagency to all members of the multiple listing service, including Panio, to produce a buyer of the Beneficial property in exchange for a percentage of the sale commission. This offer of subagency was expressly authorized by the terms of Beneficial's exclusive listing contract with Olthoff Realty Company. Panio's efforts in showing the home to the Stortroens, assisting them in preparing an offer, and facilitating communication between the Stortroens and Beneficial clearly rose to the level of substantial performance sufficient to constitute Panio's acceptance of the subagency offer extended by Olthoff Realty Company.

The agency relationship flowing to Olthoff Realty Company and through the company to Beneficial is not affected by the fact that the Stortroens had listed their current home in Denver for sale with Foremost Realty on November 4, 1983. The listing agreement executed by the Stortroens and Foremost Realty created a special agency for a single transaction, the sale of their home. *See* Restatement (Second) of Agency §3. There is no legal impediment to a listing broker's simultaneous entry into special agency relationships with more than one seller. Since the scope of the listing broker's agency is limited by the listing contract, a selling broker's authority would likewise be limited to matters affecting the sale of the real property described in the listing agreement. Thus, although Panio may have been a special agent to the Stortroens for the sale of their

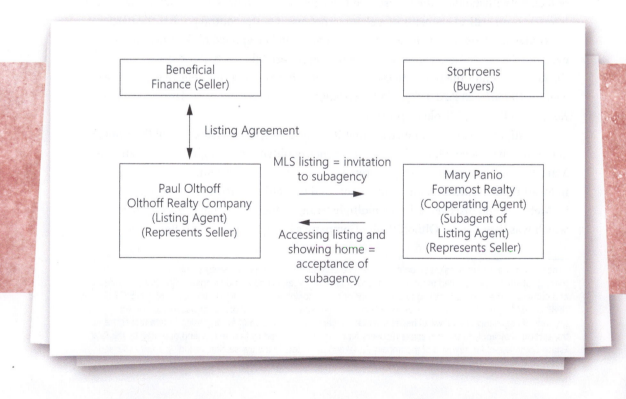

home, she was also a special agent to Olthoff Realty Company by virtue of the multiple listing service and was a subagent to Beneficial for the sale of the Quay Court property.[8]

Beneficial's counterproposal delivered to Panio for submission to the Stortroens expressly stated that acceptance should be by signature on the face of the instrument and that the counterproposal would become a binding contract if notice of the acceptance was received by the seller on or before 9 P.M. on February 3, 1984. Panio, in accordance with the instructions from her principal, made arrangements with the Stortroens to discuss the counterproposal at their home. Although Olthoff Realty Company attempted to terminate the agency relationship before Panio kept that appointment, the revocation was not effective, since a principal's revocation of agency authority terminates only upon notice to the agent. E.g., *Lowell v. Hessey*, 46 Colo. at 521, 105 P. at 871. When Panio received notice of the Stortroens' signed acceptance of Beneficial's counterproposal, therefore, she was acting as an agent of the listing broker, Olthoff Realty Company, and a subagent of the seller, Beneficial. The notice given to Panio of the Stortroens' acceptance must be imputed to the listing broker and the seller. E.g., *Gray v. Blake*, 131 Colo. at 564, 283 P.2d at 1080; Restatement (Second) of Agency §283(a) and comment b.

The Stortroens' acceptance of Beneficial's counterproposal clearly took place before Beneficial's attempted revocation of that counteroffer. Just as the Olthoff Realty Company's attempted revocation of Panio's agency authority was ineffective due to the lack of notice to Panio, Beneficial's revocation of the counteroffer was not effective because it was never communicated to the Stortroens before their acceptance. *See* 1 *Corbin on Contracts* §39. When the Stortroens presented Panio with the signed and accepted counterproposal, therefore, a binding contract was formed between the Stortroens and Beneficial for the purchase of the Quay Court property.

The district court incorrectly entered summary judgment in favor of Beneficial, and erred in not granting the Stortroens' motion for summary judgment. Because the court erroneously entered summary judgment in favor of Beneficial, it never considered the propriety of a specific performance decree in favor of the Stortroens and the other relief requested by them in their complaint. These matters should be addressed by the district court upon remand of the case.

The judgment is reversed and the cause is remanded for further proceedings not inconsistent with the views herein expressed.

[The concurring opinion of Justice Erickson is omitted.]

---

[8] While homeowners who wish their listing broker to represent them for the purpose of acquiring property may enter into an agency agreement to that effect, there is nothing in the record to indicate that the Stortroens entered into such an agreement with Foremost Realty or Panio. The agency relationship between the Stortroens and Foremost Realty, including its broker-associate Panio, was solely with respect to the sale of the Stortroens' current home.

Stortroen is a slightly unusual case, because the application of the traditional approach worked to the buyers' benefit. In many other circumstances, the traditional rule of treating the cooperating agent as a subagent of the listing agent works to the buyer's detriment, and it often is contrary to the buyer's expectations. Under the traditional rule applied by the court, Mary Panio, the broker nominally working with the Stortroens, owed fiduciary duties to the seller, Beneficial. Fiduciaries have a duty to disclose all material information in their possession to their clients. Panio therefore had a duty to disclose all material information, including information she received from the Stortroens, to Beneficial. This duty to disclose would include information about how much the Stortroens' were willing to pay for the house.

At the time *Stortroen* was decided, the traditional rule was firmly entrenched in both law and in market custom. Since the 1980s, however, there has been a pronounced and widespread change in real estate practice. Increasingly, buyers enter into written agreements to hire *buyers' brokers*. As their name implies, buyers' brokers explicitly work for the buyer. Even in a jurisdiction that follows the traditional rule exemplified by *Stortroen*, an explicit agreement between a buyer and a broker will establish this broker as an agent for the buyer and will defeat the presumption that the broker is working for the seller as a subagent of the listing broker. The *Stortroen* court explicitly stated that its holding was "not intended to preclude a real estate broker and a prospective purchaser from entering into a written agreement designating the broker as the purchaser's agent for the purpose of locating and purchasing property."

The recent trend towards buyers' brokers has coincided with an increase in state legislation requiring disclosure to the consumer of the details of a brokerage relationship. Forms promulgated by the National Association of Realtors and state associations of realty professionals help ensure that clients are aware of the nature of their relationship with their broker or agent.

From the buyer's perspective, then, there are two key things to know. First, under the traditional approach, the real estate professional who shows properties to the buyer will typically be representing the seller, not the buyer. Second, the result of this traditional rule is easy to change contractually—if the buyer and the real estate professional enter an agreement that explicitly states that the professional is working for the buyer, then the professional will owe duties to the buyer and not the seller.

Let's return to the 12 Oak Street transaction. Just before *Stortroen*, we illustrated how the relationships in that transaction would look following the traditional approach. This diagram shows how the relationships would look if Laura entered into a buyer's broker agreement with Cindy and Progress Real Estate:

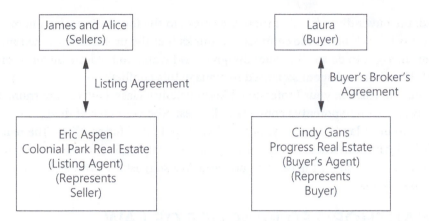

Like seller's brokers, buyer's brokers are typically paid a commission. In most areas, as a matter of custom, the seller's broker and the buyer's broker split the commission paid by the seller. A very common commission rate for residential real estate is 6 percent. The seller typically pays this commission from the sale price. If the buyer is represented by a broker, the seller's broker and the buyer's broker typically split this commission, with each getting 3 percent of the sale price. For example, if the sale price for the home was $100,000, the seller would pay a commission of $6,000. The seller's broker and the buyer's broker would split this amount, with each getting $3,000.

For further reading on the subject of buyer's brokers, *see* Alex M. Johnson, *Understanding Modern Real Estate Transactions*, 34-35 (Matthew Bender, 3d ed. 2012); Ronald Benton Brown, Joseph M. Grohman & Manuel R. Valcarcel, *Real Estate Brokerage: Recent Changes in Relationships and a Proposed Cure*, 29 Creighton L. Rev. 25 (1995).

3. DUAL AGENCY

Many states allow one broker to represent both the seller and the buyer in a transaction. This relationship is called *dual agency*. The seller and the buyer typically have conflicting interests in the transaction. Dual agency is supposed to avoid these conflicts by having the broker handle the logistics of the transaction without getting involved in any contentious issues. The classic transaction that is supposed to be suitable for dual agency is one where the seller and the buyer agree on the price and other essential terms of the transaction and only want the broker to help them with the ministerial tasks involved in completing the transaction.

Members of the legal profession tend to hate the idea of dual agency, and we are no exception. As we will see later in this chapter, real estate transactions have a lot of complexities, and there are a lot of issues where the parties can have conflicting interests even if they have already agreed on the basic terms. Parties can change their minds, and facts can develop in unforeseen ways. Imagine, for example, that after the contract is signed, the buyer discovers that there are cracks in the foundation of the home. The buyer wants to back out of the contract and thinks that the problem with the foundation gives her the right to do so. The seller disagrees and wants to hold the buyer to the contract. How is a dual agent supposed to manage this conflict?

As you will learn in your Professional Responsibility class, lawyers are trained to be acutely sensitive to potential conflicts of interest. The very idea of dual agency is disturbing to most lawyers because of the obvious potential for conflicts. The real estate broker's lobby has convinced many state legislatures to permit dual agency in the real estate context. That doesn't make it a good idea. We suggest that you and your clients avoid it like the plague.

4. UNAUTHORIZED PRACTICE OF LAW

Every state regulates the practice of law. In almost every circumstance, a person has to be admitted to the bar of a state to be allowed to practice law in that state. If a person not admitted to the bar practices law, then that person has committed the unauthorized practice of law. Sanctions for unauthorized practice can be severe.

The boundaries of the practice of law can be blurry at the edges. Everyone would agree that representing a client in court constitutes the practice of law. But what about helping a client negotiate a contract to purchase a parcel of real estate? As we will see later in this chapter, real estate contracts present a host of complicated legal issues, and advising clients on these issues falls within the boundaries of the practice of law. On the other hand, real estate contracts also present nonlegal business issues that fall within a broker's area of expertise.

In part because of this uncertain boundary, lawyers and real estate brokers have frequently come into conflict over their respective roles in real estate transactions. These conflicts have sometimes played out in the context of unauthorized practice of law complaints brought by lawyers against real estate brokers. The New Jersey Supreme Court addressed this type of complaint in *In re Opinion No. 26 of the Committee on the Unauthorized Practice of Law*, 139 N.J. 323, 654 A.2d 1344 (1995). Real estate practice, including the respective roles of lawyers and brokers, varies widely throughout the United States. This variance is highlighted by the difference between what the court described as the North Jersey practice, where lawyers were involved in most real estate transactions, and the South Jersey practice, where lawyers typically had no role in real estate transactions. In the *Opinion No. 26* case, the court was considering an unauthorized practice of law complaint against the South Jersey practice brought by the New Jersey State Bar Association. The court held that the South Jersey practice involved the practice of law by non-lawyers. The court, however, allowed the South Jersey practice to continue on policy grounds, so long as the parties to the transaction signed a written form that demonstrated that they understood the risks of proceeding without a lawyer:

[T]he sale of real estate, especially real estate with a home on it, . . . cannot be handled competently except by those trained in the law. The most important parts of it, without which it could not be accomplished, are quintessentially the practice of law. The contract of sale, the obligations of the contract, the ordering of a title search, the analysis of the search, the significance of the title search, the quality of title, the risks that surround both the contract and the title, the extent of those risks, the probability of damage, the obligation to close or not to close, the closing itself, the settlement, the documents there exchanged, each and every one of these, to be properly understood must be explained by an attorney. And the documents themselves to be properly drafted, must be drafted by an attorney. Mixed in with these activities are many others that clearly do not require an attorney's knowledge, such as the ordering of inspection and other reports, and the price negotiation. But after that, even though arguably much can be accomplished by others, practically all else, to be done with full understanding, requires the advice of counsel. . . .

In this case, the record clearly shows that the South Jersey practice has been conducted without any demonstrable harm to sellers or buyers, that it apparently saves money, and that those who participate in it do so of their own free will presumably with some knowledge of the risk; as Judge Miller found, the record fails to demonstrate that brokers are discouraging the parties from retaining counsel, or that the conflict of interest that pervades the practice has caused material damage to the sellers and buyers who participate in it. Given that record, and subject to the conditions mentioned hereafter, we find that the public interest will not be compromised by allowing the practice to continue. We note again that our prior decisions and those of the Committee on this issue did not have the benefit of such a record and were premised on the irrefutable finding that the activities of the non-lawyers in the South Jersey practice constituted the practice of law. That they do, but with the benefit of the record before us it is equally clear that the practice does not disserve the public interest.

Of decisive weight in our determination is the value we place on the right of parties to a transaction to decide whether or not they will retain counsel. We should not force them to do so absent persuasive reasons. Given the importance in our decision of the assumption that the parties have chosen not to retain counsel, and without coercion have made that decision, we have attached a condition to the conclusion that the South Jersey practice does not constitute the unauthorized practice of law. [The condition, published later in the opinion, required that "both buyer and seller be made aware of the conflicting interests of brokers and title companies in these matters and of the general risks involved in not being represented by counsel." The court published form of notice as an appendix to its opinion, and tasked a committee with developing a final version of the form.] The condition is designed to assure that the decision is an informed one. If that condition is not met, the brokers (and title officers, if aware of the fact) are engaged in the unauthorized practice of law, and attorneys with knowledge of that fact who participate are guilty of ethical misconduct.

As you progress through this chapter and learn more about the legal complexities in residential real estate transactions that were identified in this opinion, think about whether the court reached the correct decision in the *Opinion No. 26* case. On the one hand, the risks of proceeding without a lawyer may be high. On the other hand, lawyers are expensive, and the court may have been correct not to force unwanted legal representation on the public. For further discussion of these issues, including the different approaches taken by various U.S. jurisdictions, *see* Joyce Palomar, *The War Between Attorneys and Lay Conveyancers—Empirical Evidence Says "Cease Fire!,"* 31 Conn. L. Rev. 423 (1999).

One other professional responsibility issue involving attorneys and brokers warrants a brief mention. As we noted above, states typically have certain requirements that a person has to meet to become a real estate broker. Many of the statutes that set these requirements contain exemptions for attorneys. New Jersey's licensing requirement, for example, states that "No person shall engage either directly or indirectly in the business of a real estate broker, broker-salesperson, salesperson or referral agent, . . . without being licensed so to do as hereinafter provided." N.J.S.A. 45:15-1. The exemption states that the provisions of the licensing requirement "shall not apply to or be construed to include attorneys . . . ." N.J.S.A. 45:15-4. On its face, then, the statute appears to suggest that attorneys might be able to act as brokers without meeting the broker licensing agreement. The New Jersey Supreme Court, however, read the exemption very narrowly and held that attorneys could only engage in limited brokerage activity ancillary to their legal practice. Under this narrow reading, the exemption did not give attorneys the right to act generally as real estate brokers or to collect brokerage commissions. *See In re Roth*, 120 N.J. 665, 577 A.2d 490 (1990). The crucial lesson to take from this case is that you should not rely on this type of exemption as an attorney unless you are very certain of its scope in the jurisdiction where you practice. For a summary of the range of approaches taken in U.S. jurisdictions, *see* J.P. Sawyer, *When Does an Attorney Need a Real Estate License?*, 17 J. Legal Prof. 329 (1992).

B. MAJOR RISKS IN A REAL ESTATE TRANSACTION

One of the themes in this chapter is the role that risk plays in transactional law and practice. Transactional lawyers spend a great deal of time thinking about the allocation of risk between the parties to a transaction. There are three basic layers to the allocation of any given risk.

The first layer is the *default allocation of risk*. The law in any jurisdiction tends to establish default rules for the allocation of any given risk. These default rules may be established by the common law or by statute. As we will see below, for example, most U.S. jurisdictions place risk of physical defects in commercial transactions on the buyer (the rule for residential transactions is more buyer friendly). If you buy a shopping mall, and it turns out that the roof leaks, then under this default rule the leaky roof is your problem, not the seller's problem.

The second layer is the *contractual allocation of risk*. Contracts, deeds, and other legal documents can change the default allocations of risk, and *one of the most important functions of contracts and other transactional documents is to allocate risk between the parties.* As we just saw, in a commercial transaction the default physical condition risk typically is on the buyer. The buyer and seller, however, can change this risk allocation by contract. If you buy a shopping mall, the default risk of a leaky roof is on you, not the seller. You and the seller, however, can agree to contractually shift this risk back to the seller.

The third layer is embodied by the problem of *counterparty risk*. What we are labeling as counterparty risk is also often called *credit risk*. A counterparty is a person on the other side of a transaction or contract from you. If you are the seller, the buyer is the counterparty. If you are a borrower, the lender is the counterparty. Broadly speaking, counterparty risk is the risk that the counterparty will default on an obligation and will be unable to satisfy a court judgment of damages for that default. For example, imagine that you have a contractual agreement from me that I will pay you $100,000 on January 1 of this year. My contractual obligation is ironclad, and any court in any U.S. jurisdiction would award you an enforceable judgment against me if I fail to pay. Now imagine that I am broke, bankrupt, and living in Bali. As a practical matter, your ironclad contractual obligation from me is worthless. This is an extreme example, but counterparty risk is present in almost any transaction. The key point is that you cannot just focus on the legal obligations created by a transaction. You need to also think about what might happen if the other party defaults. Simply allocating a particular risk to your counterparty may not fully protect your client.

As we move through the material in this chapter, try to identify risks and think about the three layers of risk allocation. What is the default allocation of this risk? How can the parties contractually allocate the risk? How does the problem of counterparty risk play into the allocation of a given risk between the parties? As we will see, the allocation of risks often changes as we move through the three phases of a transaction illustrated in the diagram at the beginning of the chapter.

It is important to note at the outset that it is *not* the job of a transactional lawyer to advise the client avoid all risks. Rather, it is the job of the transactional lawyer to advise the client about the risks presented by a transaction and about steps that can be taken to mitigate those risks. It is often in a client's interests to take certain risks, and a client might be willing to enter into a risky transaction if the price is right. Some clients specialize in taking certain risks. For example, a client who is in the business of renovating dilapidated homes would be better suited to taking the risk of a leaky roof than the typical homebuyer. This client would likely be willing to accept the risk of the leaky roof as a buyer in return for a discount in the purchase price from the seller. At the end of the day, it is the lawyer's job to advise the client about risks and risk mitigation, and it is the client's job to decide whether or not to accept any given risk.

Real estate transactions present two major risks. The first is *title risk.* A real estate transaction involves a transfer of title (i.e., legal ownership of the property) from the seller to the buyer. This transfer occurs when the seller delivers a deed to the property to the buyer at closing. The buyer in a real estate transaction is faced with the risk that there will be problems with the title delivered by the seller. There are three common types of title problems.

1. There might be core problems with the *ownership* of the property. In the most extreme example, the seller might not have any interest in the property at all. In less extreme examples, the seller might own less than she is purporting to convey to the buyer. The seller, for instance, might own only a life estate when the buyer is expecting to purchase a fee simple. Or, the seller might own only four of the ten acres she is purporting to convey.

2. There may be one or more *encumbrances* on the property. Liens, mortgages, easements, and covenants all encumber the title to property. (See the sidebar on common encumbrances.) Some encumbrances are more problematic than others. At one extreme, a lien or mortgage might lead to the buyer losing the property through foreclosure. At the other, a covenant might place a relatively trivial restriction on the use of property. No matter where they fall on this spectrum, encumbrances need to be accounted for and addressed in real estate transactions.

3. There may be an *encroachment* on the property. An encroachment is a physical intrusion onto the property, typically by a neighboring property owner. A neighbor, for instance, might have built a fence or a part of a building that crossed over the property boundary.

COMMON ENCUMBRANCES—EASEMENTS, COVENANTS, AND LIENS

Three common types of encumbrances are easements, covenants, and liens. *Easements* are property interests that give a party the right to physically enter and use the property of another. For example, I might have an easement that gives me the right to use a driveway across your property. The easement is an encumbrance on your property, because it restricts your right to exclude me from the property. *Covenants that run with the land* are promises that bind the present and future owners of property. For example, a covenant might require that any house built on your property be at least two floors and 2,500 square feet. The covenant is an encumbrance because it restricts your use of the property. In some contexts, covenants are often referred to as deed restrictions. We will cover both easements and covenants in depth later in our chapter on servitudes.

Liens are security interests in property that provide security for a debt or other obligation. If the owner of the property defaults on the obligation secured by the lien, the holder of the lien can force the sale of the property through foreclosure and use the proceeds to satisfy the obligation. The most common type of lien is a *mortgage*. A mortgage is a security interest that the borrower grants to the lender to secure a loan. For example, if you borrow money from a bank to buy a home, you give the bank a mortgage. If you fail to repay the bank, the bank can foreclose on the mortgage and use the proceeds to repay the debt. We will cover mortgages in depth later in this chapter.

Liens can be divided into two major categories. *Consensual liens* are created by a voluntary transaction. Mortgages are a common example. If you grant a mortgage to a bank, you do so in return for the bank loaning you money as part of a voluntary transaction. *Involuntary liens* are created by operation of law and do not arise out of a voluntary transaction. Some involuntary liens arise out of common law. Others arise out by statute and, not surprisingly, are called *statutory liens*. Here are some examples of some common (and uncommon) liens:

- *Tax Liens*. Tax liens are created when the property owner fails to pay taxes to the state, local, or federal government. Tax liens typically are statutory liens.
- *Mechanic's Liens*. Mechanic's liens secure payment for contractors and other people making improvements to property. For example, if you have a contractor remodel your kitchen, a mechanic's lien will secure your obligation to pay the contractor for the work. Mechanic's liens have common-law origins, but today they are typically statutory liens.
- *Judgment Liens*. Judgment liens secure the payment of a court judgment. Imagine that you win a court judgment against me for $100,000. I refuse to pay the judgment voluntarily. You can get a judgment lien on property that I own. If I still fail to pay the judgment, you can foreclose on the property. In other words, judgment liens provide a legal mechanism that

allows the winner of a judgment for money damages to access the judgment debtor's property to satisfy the judgment.

- *Agister's Liens.* Agister's liens secure the payment of money owed for the care and feeding of an animal. For example, if I care for your dog for six months, an agister's lien secures your payment to me for the cost of caring for and feeding the dog. Compared to the other liens we list here, agister's liens are not particularly common. We include them here to illustrate the flexibility and breadth of the concept of a lien. We also include them because we think they are pretty cool.

This list is far from exhaustive. Liens are used in a wide variety of contexts to secure a wide variety of obligations.

The second major risk in a real estate transaction is *physical condition risk*. The buyer in a real estate transaction is faced with the possibility that there will be problems with the physical condition of the property being purchased. The most common physical condition problems arise from defects in buildings and other improvements on the land. If you are buying a home, for example, you would be concerned with the risk that the roof might leak. You would also be concerned with the potential presence of problems like foundation cracks, termites, and lead paint. There may also be problems with the physical condition of the land itself that might render it unsuitable for building.

Real estate transactions present other risks, but title risk and physical condition risk are probably the two most prominent. In the next two sections, we will examine these two risks and how they are addressed at various points in a transaction, in depth.

C. TITLE ISSUES

As we noted in the previous section, there are three types of title problems. First, the seller might not own what the seller is purporting to convey. Second, there might be one or more encumbrances on the property. Third, there might be one or more encroachments on the property. Title risk is the risk that one or more of these types of problems might be present in a real estate transaction.

In most circumstances, title risk is of much greater concern to buyers than to sellers—the buyer, after all, will be the owner of the property if the transaction is completed. Title risk changes for the buyer as we move through the three phases of the transaction. In the pre-contract and executory contract phases, the buyer will seek to gather information about the title to the property. The buyer will also seek to be able to walk away from the transaction without penalty if a title problem is discovered. After closing, the buyer is the owner of the property. It is incredibly hard to unwind a real estate transaction once it is completed—that is, it is very difficult for a buyer to try to void the transaction and force a transfer of title back to the seller. After closing, therefore, the property is the buyer's, and the buyer will have to deal with any title problems. As we will see below, there are several steps that the buyer can take to protect against post-closing title risk.

In this section, we discuss different methods of addressing title risk, covering a number of related topics along the way. We begin with an in-depth look at the recording system. This system is an important source of information about title to real property. The recording system also provides protection to buyers against certain title problems. We then discuss the allocation of title risk in real estate contracts and deeds. In this context, we also discuss the crucially important doctrine of merger. We next discuss title insurance and some of the common issues that arise with title insurance policies. Finally, we briefly discuss the role of surveys and physical inspection of the property in title protection.

1. THE RECORDING SYSTEM AND RECORDING ACTS

The state Recording Acts do three major things. First, they create a system of public land records. These records are typically arranged by county. Documents relating to land ownership (deeds, mortgages, easements, etc.) can be filed with the county land records office. The land records are open to the public and provide an important source of information on land ownership. If you want to buy Blackacre, you can search the land records to find information about the current and past ownership of Blackacre.

Second, the Recording Acts establish consequences for the failure to record a document. *Recording has no effect on the validity of a legal document as between the parties to that document.* For example, if A conveys Blackacre to B by deed, the failure to record the deed has no effect on its validity as a transfer of ownership from A to B. The failure to record the deed, however, will often render it *invalid and unenforceable* against *other people* who might assert ownership claims to Blackacre. Combining these first two points, people who perform diligent title searches can feel reasonably comfortable about title risk because (a) they will be aware of recorded documents, and (b) unrecorded documents typically will be unenforceable against them.

Third, the Recording Acts establish *priority* between competing claims relating to the property. Often these competing claims will be between creditors who are looking to the property as security for a debt. We will discuss the concept of senior and junior creditors and will explain how the recording system establishes the priority between creditors below. We will also briefly examine how parties can alter the priority established by the recording system.

a. The Indexes and Title Searching

As we noted above, the state Recording Acts create a system of public land records. Documents filed with the recorder of deeds can be accessed by any member of the public. You would find the documents you are looking for by using the recording office's index. There are two types of indexes in wide use in the United States, *name indexes* and *tract indexes*. Name indexes are common in the Eastern states, where the title systems were developed in colonial times. Tract indexes are more common in the Western states, where the title system developed later.

Title searching using a tract index is relatively simple. Each piece of land is given a *parcel identifying number*. Using this number, a person can easily obtain the records for a parcel of property.

Title searching using a name index is more complex. Documents are indexed by the names of the parties. There are two basic steps to a title search using a name index. First, the title searcher goes backwards in time to determine who owned the property at what time. This establishes the *chain of title* for the property. Second, the title searcher then goes forward in time to find documents recorded during each person's time of ownership. How this works is best illustrated by example.

Let's say that you are doing a title search for Jane Smull, who has agreed to buy Blackacre from Lydia Myers. Your first step is to go backwards in time to find out when and from whom Lydia acquired the property. Using the name index, you use Lydia's name and look for a deed granting Blackacre property to her. Doing this, you find a deed granting the property from Richard Scott to Lydia Myers dated June 21, 2002. Now you want to find the deed that granted the property to Richard. So you start looking in the name index under Richard's name, going back in time from June 21, 2002. You discover a deed from Martha Black to Richard Scott dated December 2, 1980. You repeat the process, now using Martha's name. Continuing back in time, you come up with this chain of title for Blackacre. You discover that Martha acquired the property from Henry Smith on March 17, 1962 and that Henry acquired the property from Elizabeth Whitman on February 2, 1940. This tells you who owned Blackacre when:

June 21, 2002-present:	Lydia Myers
December 2, 1980-June 21, 2002:	Richard Scott
March 17, 1962-December 2, 1980:	Martha Black
February 2, 1940-March 17, 1962:	Henry Smith

In many circumstances, you might want to go back farther in time, but this chain of title is sufficient for us to illustrate the basics of title searching. (Local practice in many areas is to go back 50 or 75 years.) So far, you have established who owned Blackacre when going back to 1940. You would need to verify from the terms of each deed that each grant was of a fee simple absolute interest. If a deed transferred a lesser interest, then you would need to separately track the ownership of the future interests, which you could do using the same searching process.

In many jurisdictions, the local practice is to include information in a deed about the prior deed in the chain of title in a deed by date, grantor, grantee, and indexing information. For example, the deed from Martha Black to Richard Scott would include information about the prior deed, from Henry Smith to Martha Black. This practice makes title searching a lot easier and is a good one to follow yourself.

Having established the times of ownership, you would now go forward in time to look for recorded documents other than the fee simple deeds regarding the property. You would do this by searching in the name index by the name of the owner during the period of their ownership. So for the period February 2, 1940-March 17, 1962, you would search using Henry Smith's name. For the period March 17, 1962-December 2, 1980, you would search using Martha Black's name. For the period December 2, 1980-June 21, 2002, you would search using Richard Scott's name. And for the period June 21, 2002-present, you would search using Lydia Myers' name.

By doing the search in this way, you should be able to find all of the recorded documents for the property. If, for example, Henry Smith granted an easement across the property to a neighbor on April 3, 1958 and that easement was recorded, then that easement should be indexed under Henry's name during his period of ownership. To be safe, you might search for a few months after each owner's period of ownership to account for delays in indexing.

This is a simple overview, and title searching in any given jurisdiction might have additional complexities. Some documents relating to title, for example, might be recorded somewhere other than the main recorder of deeds' office. Transfers of property by will, for example, might be recorded at a courthouse. Judgment liens and mechanic's liens are also recorded at a courthouse in some jurisdictions.

The best way to get a good understanding of the recording system is to do a title search yourself. Try searching the records for the house you grew up in or the land where your law school is located. Many counties now have online access to title records, so you might not even have to make a trip down to the recorder of deeds' office. If you do go to the recorder's office, you are likely to find that the staff are very helpful and can help show you how to navigate the indexes and the records.

b. Protecting Subsequent Interest Holders: Race, Notice, and Race-Notice Statutes

As we noted above, the Recording Acts establish the consequences of failing to record an interest in property. In many circumstances, an unrecorded document will be invalid against a subsequent owner of the property. The precise rules governing the validity or invalidity of the unrecorded document will depend on the type of Recording Act in place in the jurisdiction where the property is located.

There are three major types of Recording Acts in the United States. We will illustrate the operation of the three types of Acts with a simple fact pattern:

O conveys Blackacre to A; A does not record the deed.

O then conveys Blackacre to B.

A's deed is a *prior unrecorded interest*—that is, it is an interest in the property that is prior in time of creation to B's interest but is unrecorded. B's interest is a *subsequent interest*—that is, B's interest was created after A's interest.

You may intuitively rebel against the idea of a person conveying a fee simple interest the same property twice, but it does happen on occasion. More importantly, people frequently grant mortgages to the same property more than once; this happens thousands of times every day. The same basic principles that apply in our conveyance example will apply to establishing the priority between successive creditors secured by the property. People also frequently convey interests of less than a fee simple in property. For example, O might convey an easement over Blackacre to A and then later convey a fee simple interest in Blackacre to B. If A does not record the easement, the basic recording principles we will learn will govern whether the easement is enforceable against B as the subsequent owner of Blackacre.

Before we get to the details of each type of Act, we first need to discuss the categories of people protected by the Acts. As our basic example shows, most recording problems involve a conflict between two persons. The first is the holder of the prior unrecorded interest (A in our example). The second is the holder of a subsequent interest

Many students have a fundamental problem with our basic fact pattern. How can O convey Blackacre to B when O has previously conveyed Blackacre to A? Because O has already conveyed Blackacre to A, O doesn't seem to own anything when O later conveys Blackacre to B. How can O convey something that O doesn't own anymore? One way to think about it is that the Recording Acts often operate to make the original O to A conveyance invalid. If that original conveyance was invalid, then O indeed had an interest to later convey to B. Another way to think about it is that the Recording Acts don't really care about whether O had any interest to convey and often make the subsequent conveyance to B valid without regard to your logical questions or contrary intuitions on the subject.

(B in our example). Recording Acts typically protect *subsequent purchasers for value*. That is, they protect the person in B's position if that person purchased her interest for money or other valuable consideration. The Recording Acts also typically protect *subsequent creditors for value*—people who lend money secured by an interest in the property. The Recording Acts typically *do not* protect subsequent donees. That is, if the person in B's position received her interest in Blackacre as a gift, she likely will *not* be protected by the Recording Acts against A's prior unrecorded interest. Note that donees should still record their interests—this will protect them against subsequent interest holders later in the chain of ownership. When we say that donees are not protected by the Recording Acts, we mean that they are not protected against *prior* unrecorded interests. Another way of putting it is that subsequent donees (i.e., donees in the subsequent position) are typically not protected by the Recording Acts, but prior donees (i.e., donees in the prior position) are typically protected by the Recording Acts.

Race Statutes. In a race statute jurisdiction, the first person to record wins. These statutes take their name from the proverbial race to the courthouse to record a document—the person who wins the race, and records first, typically wins. For example:

> O conveys Blackacre to A. A does not record.
>
> O conveys Blackacre to B.
>
> A records.
>
> B records.

Under a race statute, A would have superior rights to B because A recorded first. Let's change the facts so that B records first:

> O conveys Blackacre to A. A does not record.
>
> O conveys Blackacre to B.
>
> B records.
>
> A records.

Now B would have superior rights to A because B recorded first. Only North Carolina and Louisiana have race statutes that are applicable to all property interests. Arkansas, Ohio, and Pennsylvania have race statutes that apply to the priority between mortgage lenders. Although race statutes are relatively rare in the real property context, understanding how they work is important for two reasons. First, the race concept is incorporated into another type of statute that we will see shortly. Second, the recording provisions of Article 9 of the UCC—which governs secured finance involving personal property—operate on race statute principles. *See* U.C.C. §§9-317, 9-322.

Here is North Carolina's race statute, N.C. Gen. Stat. §47-18(a):

> No (i) conveyance of land, or (ii) contract to convey, or (iii) option to convey, or (iv) lease of land for more than three years shall be valid to pass any property interest as against lien creditors or purchasers for a valuable consideration from the donor, bargainor or lessor but from the time of registration thereof in the county where the land lies, or if the land is located in more than one county, then in each county where any portion of the land lies to be effective as to the land in that county. Unless otherwise stated either on the registered instrument or on a separate registered instrument duly executed by the party whose priority interest is adversely affected, (i) instruments registered in the office of the register of deeds shall have priority based on the order of registration as determined by the time of registration, and (ii) if instruments are registered simultaneously, then the instruments shall be presumed to have priority as determined by: (1) The earliest document number set forth on the registered instrument. (2) The sequential book and page number set forth on the registered instrument if no document number is set forth on the registered instrument. . . .

Make sure you understand (a) the interests subject to this statute, (b) the types of subsequent interests protected by the statute, and (c) how the statute establishes time of recording as the criterion for establishing validity and priority between prior and subsequent interests.

Notice Statutes. With a notice statute, subsequent purchasers or lenders will win so long as they had no notice of a prior unrecorded interest at the time they acquired their interest. For example:

> O conveys Blackacre to A. A does not record.

> O conveys Blackacre to B, who has no notice of A's interest, for value.

Under a notice statute, B would have superior rights to A because (a) A failed to record, and (b) B had no notice of A's prior unrecorded interest.

Note that under a notice statute, the order of recording after B has obtained her interest does not matter. Consider this example:

> O conveys Blackacre to A. A does not record.

> O conveys Blackacre to B, who has no notice of A's interest, for value.

> A records.

> B records.

Under a notice statute, B would still win against A even though B recorded after A. Under a notice statute, all that matters is the state of affairs at the time B obtained her subsequent interest. If B had no notice of A's interest, B will win. Period.

In the recording context, "good faith" (or the Latin "*bone fide*") is often a synonym for lack of notice. If a person obtains a subsequent interest with no notice of the prior interest, that person took that interest in good faith. In contrast, if a person obtains a subsequent interest with notice of the prior interest, that person acted in bad faith. Here is Iowa's notice provision, Iowa Code §558.41:

> An instrument affecting real estate is of no validity against subsequent purchasers for a valuable consideration, without notice, or against the state or any of its political subdivisions during and after condemnation proceedings against the real estate, unless the instrument is filed and recorded in the county in which the real estate is located, as provided in this chapter.

Race-Notice Statutes. As their name implies, race-notice statutes combine both race and notice elements. To win under a race-notice statute, a subsequent interest holder must *both* (a) take the subsequent interest without notice of the prior interest *and* (b) record first. Let's return to the example we just used for the notice statute:

> O conveys Blackacre to A. A does not record.
>
> O conveys Blackacre to B, who has no notice of A's interest, for value.
>
> A records.
>
> B records.

In this scenario, B had no notice of the prior interest, but would lose to A under a race-notice statute because A recorded first. Now let's change the order of recording:

> O conveys Blackacre to A. A does not record.
>
> O conveys Blackacre to B, who has no notice of A's interest, for value.
>
> B records.
>
> A records.

Here, B had no notice of the prior interest and recorded first. Because B satisfies both elements, B would win against A in a race-notice jurisdiction.

Here is Michigan's race-notice provision, Mich. Comp. L. §565.29:

> Every conveyance of real estate within the state hereafter made, which shall not be recorded as provided in this chapter, shall be void as against any subsequent purchaser in good faith and for a valuable consideration, of the same real estate or any portion thereof, whose conveyance shall be first duly recorded. . . .

COMMON MISTAKE: MISREADING NOTICE STATUTE AS RACE-NOTICE STATUTE

Go back and read the Iowa notice provision reproduced above. The wording of notice statutes often makes them easy to confuse with race-notice statutes. This confusion typically arises because notice statutes talk about the need to record a document—the Iowa statute contains the words "unless the instrument is filed and recorded in the county in which the real estate is located." This language refers to the need for the *prior* interest holder, not the subsequent interest holder, to record. It does not impose a requirement that the *subsequent* interest holder record to win against the prior interest holder.

FIRST IN TIME AND RECORDING

First in time is a theme that has run throughout our course. Before the Recording Acts were enacted, disputes over competing interests in property were resolved on a pure first-in-time basis—the first interest created won against subsequent interests. The Recording Acts change this basic first-in-time rule in different ways. Race statutes operate on a first-in-time basis, but replace first-in-time of conveyance with first-in-time of recording. Notice statutes create an exception to basic first-in-time principles for subsequent good faith purchasers and creditors for value. Race-notice statutes combine the two, favoring the person who is first in time to record, but also imposing a good faith requirement for subsequent purchasers.

FIRST IN TIME

i. The Shelter Rule

The Shelter Rule is best illustrated by an example. Consider this scenario:

O conveys Blackacre to A. A does not record.

O conveys Blackacre to B, who has no notice of A's interest, for value.

B records.

A records.

B conveys Blackacre to C. *C has notice of A's interest.*

C records.

Up until the B to C conveyance, this is the same as our last example. B would win against A in both a notice and a race-notice jurisdiction. But what of C? C has notice of A's interest. Shouldn't C lose against A on notice grounds? Similarly, B would win against A in a race jurisdiction. But A recorded before C. Shouldn't C lose against A in a race jurisdiction because A recorded first?

The short answer is that C will win against A in any type of jurisdiction under the Shelter Rule. There are various ways to define the Shelter Rule. Here is our definition:

> Under the *Shelter Rule*, if a person who would win under the applicable Recording Act conveys the property to another person, that other person (the conveyee) would also win under the Recording Act.

In our example, C is *sheltered* by B's superior interest in the property. Because B would win against A under any applicable Recording Act, C would also win against A.

The purpose of the Shelter Rule is to allow the winner under a Recording Act (B in our example) to convey the property. A prior unrecorded interest holder (A in our example) should not be able to undercut the winner's ability to convey by, for example, providing actual notice of a prior unrecorded interest to a potential conveyee (C in our example). Note that the conveyee (C in our example) does not have to pay value for the property. The purpose of the Shelter Rule is to protect the winner's ability to convey as she sees fit, whether by purchase or by gift.

The best way to be sure that you have a good handle on the three types of Recording Acts and the Shelter Rule is to work through the following problem set.

Basic Recording Problems. When analyzing a recording problem, it is often helpful to translate the fact pattern into a timeline. We do so in the explanatory answers to these problems, which are found on page 1052.

In each of the following problems, who would win under (a) a race statute, (b) a notice statute, and (c) a race-notice statute? Why?

1. In 2000, O conveyed Blackacre to A by deed. A did not record the deed. In 2001, O sold Blackacre for value to B. B did not have notice A's deed. B immediately recorded her deed. In 2002, A finally got around to recording his deed. A and B are now in a dispute about ownership of Blackacre.

2. Same facts as 1, but when B bought Blackacre from O, B had notice of A's deed at the time B acquired Blackacre from O.

3. In 2000, O conveyed Blackacre to A by deed. A did not record the deed. In January 2001, O sold Blackacre for value to B; B did not have notice of A's deed. B did not immediately record the deed. In February 2001, A recorded his deed. In March 2001, B recorded her deed. A and B are now in a dispute about ownership of Blackacre.

4. In 2000, O conveyed Blackacre to A by deed. A did not record the deed. In 2001, O sold Blackacre for value to B. B did not have notice of A's deed. B immediately recorded her deed. In 2002, A recorded his deed. In 2003, B conveyed Blackacre to C. At the time of this conveyance, C had notice of A's deed. C immediately recorded the deed. A and C are now in a dispute about ownership of Blackacre.

c. Three Types of Notice

As we have already seen, notice plays an important role in recording law. Notice also is important in a wide range of other legal issues. There are three types of notice that commonly arise in recording scenarios and in other contexts: (1) actual notice, (2) record notice, and (3) inquiry notice.

Actual notice is exactly what it sounds like—a person has actual notice of a fact if the person has been given notice of the fact.

Record notice and inquiry notice are both species of constructive notice. Both will impute notice, in certain circumstances, to a person who does not have actual notice.

Record notice is notice that a person would obtain by performing a diligent record search. A person is on record notice of all documents that have been properly recorded and that as a result would have been found in a title search. A person is on record notice of all recorded documents even if that person does not perform a title search.

Inquiry notice is notice of facts that would have been found if (a) a reasonable person under the circumstances would have inquired further into the facts, and (b) a person had performed a diligent inquiry into these circumstances. Inquiry notice is triggered by facts that would cause a reasonable person to ask further questions or otherwise investigate the facts. If the person at issue does not perform this further investigation, she will be charged with inquiry notice of the facts that the further investigation would have discovered.

Inquiry notice is based on a duty to make a reasonable inquiry into the circumstances. If a person makes such a reasonable inquiry, that person will not be imputed with inquiry notice of undiscovered facts. The duty of reasonable inquiry requires reasonable effort. It does not require a person to engage in heroic efforts to discover all possible facts.

There are two inquiry notice scenarios that frequently arise in the property context. In the first, a person has actual or record notice of Document A. Document A makes reference to Document B. In many circumstances, the person will be held to have inquiry notice of the contents of Document B, because a reasonably diligent person would have inquired about Document B. In the second, one person's physical occupancy of the property will provide inquiry notice that the person has an interest in the property. If, for example, a potential buyer of a property sees another person occupying the property, the potential buyer has a duty to inquire into why the person is there.

So far, we have assumed that the person who is being held to inquiry notice actually knew about the facts that triggered the duty to inquire. In the physical occupancy example, the potential buyer actually saw another person occupying the property. Inquiry notice, however, often occurs *even if the person is not actually aware of the facts that give rise to the duty to inquire.* The entire concept of inquiry notice is based on an expectation that people will act in a reasonably diligent manner. If a reasonably diligent person would have become aware of the facts that warrant investigation, then inquiry notice will be imputed. A person cannot avoid inquiry notice of another person's physical occupancy of the property, for example, by buying the property sight unseen. A reasonably diligent buyer would at least look at the property before buying it, and would therefore have been aware of the physical occupancy.

Our two cases provide examples of each of the two classic inquiry notice fact patterns—one document referencing another and physical occupancy of the land.

HARPER V. PARADISE

Supreme Court of Georgia, 1974
210 S.E.2d 710

INGRAM, Justice. This appeal involves title to land. It is from a judgment and directed verdict granted to the appellees and denied to the appellants in the Superior Court of Oglethorpe County.

Appellants claim title as remaindermen under a deed to a life tenant with the remainder interest to the named children of the life tenant. This deed was delivered to the life tenant but was lost or misplaced for a number of years and was not recorded until 35 years later.

Appellees claim title as uninterrupted successors in title to an intervening mortgagee who purchased the property at a sheriff's sale following the foreclosure of a security deed given by the life tenant to secure a loan which became in default. Prior to the execution of the security deed by the life tenant, she obtained a quitclaim deed from all but one of the then living heirs of the original grantor who died earlier. Appellees also claim prescriptive title as a result of the peaceful, continuous, open and adverse possession of the property by them and their record predecessors in title for more than 21 years.

The life tenant died in 1972 and her children and representatives of deceased children, who were named as the remaindermen, then brought the present action to recover the land. The trial court determined that appellees held superior title to the land and it is this judgment, adverse to the remaindermen, that produced the present appeal to this court.

The above condensation of the title contentions of the parties can be understood best by reciting in detail the sequential occurrence of the facts which produced these conflicting claims of title.

On February 1, 1922, Mrs. Susan Harper conveyed by warranty deed a 106.65-acre farm in Oglethorpe County to her daughter-in-law, Maude Harper, for life with remainder in fee simple to Maude Harper's named children. The deed, which recited that it was given for Five Dollars and "natural love and affection," was lost, or misplaced, until 1957 when it was found by Clyde Harper, one of the named remaindermen, in an old trunk belonging to Maude Harper. The deed was recorded in July, 1957.

Susan Harper died sometime during the period 1925-1927 and was survived by her legal heirs, Price Harper, Prudie Harper Jackson, Mildred Chambers and John W. Harper, Maude Harper's husband. In 1928, all of Susan Harper's then living heirs, except John W. Harper, joined in executing an instrument to Maude Harper, recorded March 19, 1928 which contained the following language:

> "Deed, Heirs of Mrs. Susan Harper, to Mrs. Maude Harper. Whereas Mrs. Susan Harper did on or about the . . . day of March, 1927, make and deliver a deed of gift to the land hereinafter more fully described to Mrs. Maude Harper the wife of John W. Harper, which said deed was delivered to the said Mrs. Maude Harper and was not recorded; and Whereas said deed has been lost or destroyed and cannot be found; and Whereas the said Mrs. Susan Harper has since died and leaves as her heirs at law the grantors herein; Now therefore for and in consideration of the sum of $1.00, in hand paid, the receipt of which is hereby acknowledged, the undersigned Mrs. Prudence Harper Jackson, Price Harper and Ben Grant as guardian of Mildred Chambers, do hereby remise, release and forever quit claim to the said Mrs. Maude Harper, her heirs and assigns, all of their right, title, interest, claim or demand that they and each of them have or may have had in and to the (described property). To have and to hold the said property to the said Mrs. Maude Harper, her heirs and assigns, so that neither the said grantors nor their heirs nor any person or persons claiming under them shall at any time hereafter by any way or means, have, claim or demand any right, title or interest in and to the aforesaid property or its appurtenances or any part thereof. This deed is made and delivered to the said Mrs. Maude Harper to take the place of the deed made and executed and delivered by Mrs. Susan Harper during her lifetime as each of the parties hereto know that the said property was conveyed to the said Mrs. Maude Harper by the said Mrs. Susan Harper during her lifetime and that the said Mrs. Maude Harper was on said property and in possession thereof."

On February 27, 1933, Maude Harper executed a security deed, recorded the same day, which purported to convey the entire fee simple to Ella Thornton to secure a fifty dollar loan. The loan being in default, Ella Thornton foreclosed on the property, receiving a sheriff's deed executed and recorded in 1936. There is an unbroken chain of record title out of Ella Thornton to the appellees, Lincoln and William Paradise, who claim the property as grantees under a warranty deed executed and recorded in 1955. The appellees also assert title by way of peaceful, continuous, open and adverse possession by them and their predecessors in title beginning in 1940.

The appellees trace their title back through Susan Harper, but they do not rely on the 1922 deed from Susan Harper to Maude Harper as a link in their record chain of title. If appellees relied on the 1922 deed, then clearly the only interest they would have obtained would have been Maude Harper's life estate which terminated upon her death in 1972. "No forfeiture shall result from a tenant for life selling the entire estate in lands;

the purchaser shall acquire only his interest." Code §85-609. *See Mathis v. Solomon*, 188 Ga. 311, 4 S.E.2d 24; *Satterfield v. Tate*, 132 Ga. 256, 64 S.E. 60; *New South Building & Loan Assn. v. Gann*, 101 Ga. 678(3), 29 S.E. 15; *McDougal v. Sanders*, 75 Ga. 140.

Appellees contend that the 1928 instrument executed by three of Susan Harper's then living heirs must be treated under Code §67-2502 as having been executed by the heirs as agents or representatives of Susan Harper, thereby making both the 1922 and 1928 deeds derivative of the same source. That Code section provides:

> "All innocent persons, firms or corporations acting in good faith and without actual notice, who purchase for value, or obtain contractual liens, from distributees, devisees, legatees, or heirs at law, holding or apparently holding land or personal property by will or inheritance from a deceased person, shall be protected in the purchase of said property or in acquiring such a lien thereon as against unrecorded liens or conveyances created or executed by said deceased person upon or to said property in like manner and to the same extent as if the property had been purchased of or the lien acquired from the deceased person."

Appellees argue that since both deeds must be treated as having emanated from the same source, the 1928 deed has priority under Code §29-401 because it was recorded first. Code §29-401 provides:

> "Every deed conveying lands shall be recorded in the office of the clerk of the superior court of the county where the land lies. The record may be made at any time, but such deed loses its priority over a subsequent recorded deed from the same vendor, taken without notice of the existence of the first." . . .

In the present case, the remaindermen in the deed to the life tenant were not the heirs of the grantor. They were named children of the life tenant grantee. Therefore, after the death of the original grantor, Susan Harper, her heirs could have joined in a deed to an innocent person acting in good faith and without actual notice of the earlier deed. If such a deed had been made, conveying a fee simple interest without making any reference to a prior unrecorded lost or misplaced deed, Code §67-2502 might well apply to place that deed from the heirs within the protection of Code §29-401.

However, the 1928 deed relied upon by appellees was to the same person, Maude Harper, who was the life tenant in the 1922 deed. The 1928 deed recited that it was given in lieu of the earlier lost or misplaced deed from Susan Harper to Maude Harper and that Maude Harper was in possession of the property. Thus Maude Harper is bound to have taken the 1928 deed with knowledge of the 1922 deed. *See King v. McDuffie*, 144 Ga. 318, 320, 87 S.E. 22. The recitals of the 1928 deed negate any contention that the grantors in that deed were holding or apparently holding the property by will or inheritance from Susan Harper. Indeed, the recitals of the 1928 deed actually serve as a disclaimer by the heirs that they were so holding or apparently holding the land.

Therefore, Code §67-2502 is not applicable under the facts of this case and cannot be used to give the 1928 deed priority over the 1922 deed under the provisions of Code

§29-401. The recitals contained in the 1928 deed clearly put any subsequent purchaser on notice of the existence of the earlier misplaced or lost deed, and, in terms of Code §29-401, the 1928 deed, though recorded first, would not be entitled to priority. *See King v. McDuffie*, 144 Ga. 318(2), 87 S.E. 22, *supra*; *Hitchcock v. Hines*, 143 Ga. 377, 85 S.E. 119; *Stubbs v. Glass*, 143 Ga. 56, 84 S.E. 126; *Holder v. Scarborough*, 119 Ga. 256, 46 S.E. 93; *Zorn v. Thompson*, 108 Ga. 78, 34 S.E. 303.

We conclude that it was incumbent upon the appellees to ascertain through diligent inquiry the contents of the earlier deed and the interests conveyed therein. *See Henson v. Bridges*, 218 Ga. 6(2), 126 S.E.2d 226. *Cf. Talmadge Bros. & Co. v. Interstate Building & Loan Ass'n*, 105 Ga. 550, 553, 31 S.E. 618, holding that "a deed in the chain of title, discovered by the investigator, is constructive notice of all other deeds which were referred to in the deed discovered," including an unrecorded plat included in the deed discovered. Although the appellees at trial denied having received any information as to the existence of the interests claimed by the appellants, the transcript fails to indicate any effort on the part of the appellees to inquire as to the interests conveyed by the lost or misplaced deed when they purchased the property in 1955. "A thorough review of the record evinces no inquiry whatsoever by the defendants, or attempt to explain why such inquiry would have been futile. Thus it will be presumed that due inquiry would have disclosed the existent facts." *Henson v. Bridges, supra*, p. 10, of 218 Ga., p. 228 of 126 S.E.2d.

The appellees also contend that they have established prescriptive title by way of peaceful, continuous, open and adverse possession by them and their predecessors in title beginning in 1940. However, the remaindermen named in the 1922 deed had no right of possession until the life's tenant's death in 1972. "Prescription does not begin to run in favor of a grantee under a deed from a life tenant, against a remainderman who does not join in the deed, until the falling in of the life-estate by the death of the life tenant." *Mathis v. Solomon, supra*, p. 312, of 188 Ga., p. 25 of 4 S.E.2d. *See also Ham v. Watkins*, 227 Ga. 454(3), 181 S.E.2d 490; *Biggers v. Gladin*, 204 Ga. 481(6), 50 S.E.2d 585; *Seaboard Air-Line R. Co. v. Holliday*, 165 Ga. 200(2), 140 S.E. 507; *Brinkley v. Bell*, 131 Ga. 226(5), 62 S.E. 67. . . .

The trial court erred in granting appellees' motion for directed verdict and in overruling the appellants' motion for directed verdict. Therefore, the judgment of the trial court is reversed with direction that judgment be entered in favor of the appellants.

Judgment reversed with direction. All the Justices concur, except JORDAN, J., who dissents.

A NOTE ON PRIORITY

So far, we have focused on whether the prior or subsequent interest holder will "win" against the other under the applicable Recording Act. Our examples so far have typically involved a subsequent purchaser for value contesting the validity of a prior unrecorded interest. In these examples, the prior interest is *invalid* if the subsequent interest holder wins under the Recording Act.

In other contexts, the impact of winning or losing under the Recording Act will not be whether an interest is valid, but whether an interest has *priority* over another interest. Priority is just what it sounds like—an interest that has priority over another interest is superior to that interest. Priority issues are commonly raised by mortgages and other liens.

In the real estate context, priority is typically a matter of recording. If one interest would win against another interest under the applicable Recording Act, that mortgage has priority over the other. You have probably heard people talk about *first mortgages* and *second mortgages*. The first mortgage on a property has priority over the second mortgage. In most circumstances, the first mortgage has that status because the first mortgage would win against the second mortgage under the applicable Recording Act. An interest that has higher priority is often called *senior*, and an interest that has lower priority is often called *junior*. So a first mortgage would be senior to a second mortgage. The second mortgage would be junior to the first mortgage. Priority is relative, and it is possible for an interest to be senior to one interest and junior to another.

There are two important consequences of one mortgage having priority over another in the foreclosure context. First, the holder of the mortgage with priority gets paid first out of the foreclosure proceeds. Second, mortgages and other interests with lower priority may get wiped out in the foreclosure process. Interests with higher priority than the mortgage will survive the foreclosure.

We will discuss both of these consequences further below in our section on mortgage foreclosure. We introduce the concept of priority here, however, because our next case, *Clare House*, involves a dispute over priority. One set of parties in *Clare House* loaned money to the owners of the property secured by deeds of trust. (As we will explain further below, a deed of trust is a close cousin of a mortgage.) The other set of parties held leases to homes the property. The underlying issue in the case is whether the deeds of trust or the leases had priority. If the deeds of trust have priority, then the leases will be wiped out in foreclosure. If the leases have priority, then they will survive foreclosure. Which interest will have priority turns on which will win under the applicable Recording Act. As you will see, who wins under the Recording Act turns on the issue of inquiry notice.

IN RE CLARE HOUSE BUNGALOW HOMES, L.L.C.

United States Bankruptcy Court for the Eastern District of Washington, 2011
447 B.R. 617

PATRICIA C. WILLIAMS, Presiding Judge. [Clare House Bungalow Homes, L.L.C. ("Clare House") filed for bankruptcy. As part of the bankruptcy proceedings, a dispute arose between the residents of Clare House and creditors who had recorded Deeds of Trust against the Clare House property]. The creditors allege that their rights under the Deeds of Trust are superior to the rights of the residents to occupy the premises. The residents argue that their rights to occupancy are superior to the creditors and should the creditors foreclose, they would take title subject to the rights of occupancy by the residents.

Clare House is best described as a senior living facility. Residents must be 55 years old or older to occupy the individual units. Each unit or bungalow is the subject of a Resident Agreement. The terms of the individual Resident Agreement generally provide that upon occupancy, the resident pays a lump sum for the right to occupy the premises and use the common areas until death or until physically unable to care for themselves. At that time, the bungalow is marketed to another and some percentage of the lump sum paid by the prior resident, typically eighty percent (80%), is returned to that resident's estate. The initial lump sum paid by the resident and the percentage amount of that sum ultimately distributed to the resident's estate varies from unit-to-unit and some of the terms within the agreement, which terms are not material to resolution of this issue, also vary.

The plaintiff is an association composed of 24 residents of the 28 bungalows owned and managed by Clare House. The Deeds of Trust at issue burden the large parcel of real property upon which is located all of the bungalows as well as a community center, pool and other all-common areas. Two of the members of the association recorded their Resident Agreements with the Spokane County Auditor in the real property records prior to the existence of any of the loan transactions which are secured by the Deeds of Trust. By prior summary judgment motion, the rights of those two residents to occupy have been determined to be superior to the rights of the defendant Deed of Trust holders. . . . The summary judgment process did not determine the superiority of the right to occupy of the residents who did not record the Resident Agreements as disputed issues of fact existed.

The first position lienholder is the "Caudill Group." . . . The Caudill Group loaned $400,000 to Clare House and recorded a Deed of Trust to secure the loan on November 24, 2004. That Deed of Trust was re-recorded on December 22, 2004 to correct the beneficiary. An additional sum of $265,000 was loaned by the Caudill Group on April 11, 2005, with a Deed of Trust recorded on the same date.

Kevin Blanchat loaned Clare House $50,000 on January 5, 2008 and another $50,000 on February 21, 2008 and those Deeds of Trust were both recorded on July 25, 2008 (hereinafter "Blanchat liens").

Peter J. Noe loaned Clare House $50,000 on March 8, 2008 and the Deed of Trust was recorded on July 28, 2008 (hereinafter "Noe lien").

Lloyd Ross and Bonnie Guthrie-Ross loaned Clare House $200,000 on March 13, 2008 and the Deed of Trust was recorded on July 28, 2008 (hereinafter "Ross lien").

Thus, the first lien is held by the Caudill Group, the second and third position liens are held by Blanchat, the fourth position lien is held by Noe, and the fifth and last position lien is held by Ross.

THE CAUDILL GROUP LOAN

Mr. John Caudill testified he was the "point man" for the Caudill Group and passed whatever information he had about the loan to the individual members of the group. He is a retired business man who has, on behalf of the Caudill Living Trust, made what he characterized as "hard money" loans to borrowers who typically could not or did not wish to obtain loans from traditional lenders. Those loans were generally made in combination with others. He testified that the primary goal of such loans was repayment and in most situations that occurred, but he had been involved in foreclosure proceedings when necessary. His usual method of operating was to loan not more than fifty percent (50%) of the fair market value of the property and to rely upon the value of the collateral should payment not occur.

He was contacted by a loan broker, Mr. Webster, regarding this transaction and other prior transactions but, until this loan, had never consummated a transactions through Mr. Webster. He met with Mr. Webster, who has since died, on a couple of occasions regarding this transaction. He clearly recalled visiting the Clare House property with Mr. Green, the representative of Clare House. They toured the property, including one of the bungalows. Mr. Caudill testified that he knew this was a living facility for the elderly and that some of the units were occupied. The fact that the bungalows were residential units and that some were occupied would be apparent to any visitor to the property.

Initially, Mr. Caudill testified that he never asked for nor received any documents and had asked no questions regarding the loan transaction. He encouraged other members of the Caudill Group to visit the property. His answers to interrogatories, however, stated that he had received and reviewed financial information and other relevant documents regarding this transaction and that he did visit the property with at least some of the members of the group. The conclusion from his testimony was that by the time of trial, his recollection of the transaction or any discussions about it were faint. The conclusion from his testimony is that at the time of the transaction he did not, in any meaningful way, review documentation nor conduct an analysis of creditworthiness of the borrower nor review other factors commonly reviewed by a typical "hard money" lender. He principally relied upon his opinion of the value of the large parcel of property. No other member of the Caudill Group testified.

The exhibits at trial indicated that two members of the Caudill Group, "drove by" the property, two members never saw the property, and one member, prior to the loan transaction, not only visited the property but talked with an unidentified "sales associate" and toured one of the vacant bungalows. None of the Caudill Group indicated they had reviewed any title information.[1]

---

[1] The evidence leads to the conclusion that the Caudill Group had formed a joint venture and it was conceded at trial that there was no dispute that information provided to one member of the joint venture should be imputed to the other members.

The closing attorney had closed other loans for groups of lenders formed by Mr. Caudill. The attorney testified that his role was to place whatever loan terms had been negotiated into proper form, record appropriately, and disburse funds. He did no investigation of the loan desirability or property, but did obtain a title report which revealed the prior recorded Resident Agreements. This witness communicated mostly with Mr. Webster and, from those communications, understood that the collateral was rental property.

Mr. Green, the representative of Clare House, also testified regarding the meeting at the property with Mr. Caudill. Mr. Green's testimony was generally consistent with that of Mr. Caudill regarding that visit, although Mr. Caudill remembered that Mr. Green referenced "rent" being received from the bungalow. Mr. Green was unable to recount the conversation, but denied making a reference to "rent." He stated he had never considered the income from the bungalows as rent nor ever used that word describing it and would not have done so on that single occasion. His testimony on this question was credible. He also testified that he had no clear recollection of what materials he provided the loan broker, Mr. Webster, but had never made any approach to a loan broker or financial institution without preparing a loan package. The packages he prepared included information about the real property, including a description of the arrangements for occupancy and repurchase of the bungalows, income and expense information, plans for related developments, and his personal financial information. He had no specific recollection of providing a sample copy of the Resident Agreement to Mr. Webster, but believed he had done so and certainly would have provided a copy if asked.

BLANCHAT LOANS

Mr. Blanchat presented testimony by way of a declaration in which he stated that Mr. Green had provided a general description of the property and explained that it was a retirement community and was then at full capacity. There was no discussion of the existence of the Resident Agreements, but cash flow and other financial information was provided. Mr. Blanchat did not visit the property nor receive a title report. Mr. Green testified that he recalled no specific conversations regarding the Resident Agreements, although he assumes it would have been discussed during the process. He testified that he would have given a sample agreement if asked.

NOE AND ROSS LOANS

Mr. Robertson acted on behalf of both of these individuals and is now the personal representative of the Noe estate. Mr. Robertson did not testify, but his interrogatory answers indicate that he based his decision to lend upon the opinion of various appraisers as to the fair market value of the property, including the listing by T.J. Meenoch and that Mr. Robertson assumed that one of the appraisers had obtained a title report. There is a copy of an e-mail prior to these loans from Mr. Green to Mr. Robertson attaching information from Mr. Meenoch. That information describes the property as a retirement community and lists each bungalow with a market value and references a "resident equity" of eighty percent (80%) per unit and an assumption that each unit is resold every eight years. It also contains pictures of a row of bungalows and other amenities.

LEGAL ISSUE

The legal issue is whether, under the circumstances which existed at the time the liens attached to the real property, the lienholders had a duty to inquire as to the interest held by the residents. If so, did the lienholders fulfill that duty?

LEGAL ANALYSIS

Washington has adopted a statutory scheme to determine the priority and validity of various interests in real property. More than 100 years have passed since Washington adopted the cornerstone of that system, which requires the recording of documents effecting real property in the office of the auditor in which county the real property is located. Rem.Rev.Stat. §1439 (1897). Since that time, the applicable statute has provided that any unrecorded conveyance is void against a later bona fide purchaser.

The 1897 statute was repealed by 1927 Wash. Laws Ch. 278 §2, and replaced by Rem. Rev.Stat. §10596-2 (1927). The 1927 statute contained language identical to the current statute. RCW 65.08.070 states:

> A conveyance of real property, when acknowledged by the person executing the same (the acknowledgment being certified as required by law), may be recorded in the office of the recording officer of the county where the property is situated. Every such conveyance not so recorded is void as against any subsequent purchaser or mortgagee in good faith and for a valuable consideration from the same vendor, his heirs or devisees, of the same real property or any portion thereof whose conveyance is first duly recorded. An instrument is deemed recorded the minute it is filed for record.

With the exception of residents Raun and Hoffman whose interests were determined by prior summary judgment ruling, none of the Resident Agreements between Clare House and the plaintiff residents were recorded. Nine of the plaintiffs entered into a Resident Agreement prior to the Caudill Group Deed of Trust. Six of the residents entered into a Resident Agreement after the Caudill Group Deed of Trust, but before the Blanchat and the Noe and Ross Deeds of Trust. The right to occupy by seven other residents have since ended, thus seven bungalows are currently vacant. As the Resident Agreements were never recorded, the defendant lienholders argue that based upon the plain language in RCW 65.08.070, the rights of the residents to occupy the property is void and not enforceable as to the defendant lienholders. The plaintiff residents counter by arguing that the longstanding common law principle that a person who acquires an interest in real property with actual or constructive notice of the rights of another takes subject to the other's rights. The evidence presented by the plaintiffs demonstrated actual or, at a minimum, constructive notice of the resident's rights of occupancy to the lienholders. Constructive notice then imposes a duty upon the recipient of that constructive notice to inquire as to the circumstances of the other person's interest in the property.

By no means is this present controversy between an occupant of real property and a person who later acquires an interest in the property unique. *Oliver v. McEachran*, 149 Wash. 433, 271 P. 93 (1928), involved the occupancy of a strip of land subject to an unrecorded easement. At pages 439 and 95 respectively, the court held:

> But it seems to us that the law is well established that, where a party is in possession of land, even where the public records show the title to be in someone else, the purchaser cannot rely entirely upon the record testimony, but he must take notice also of the rights of those who are in possession. . . .

Together with the statutory scheme requiring recording of interests in property, it has been recognized in Washington law for 100 years that actual possession of real estate is sufficient notice to any other person acquiring an interest in that real property to impose a duty to make further inquiry regarding the specifics of occupancy. In *Field v. Copping, Agnew & Scales*, 65 Wash. 359, 118 P. 329 (1911) at pages 362 and 330, respectively, the court stated:

> The actual possession of the property by the appellants at the time the respondent acquired the title was notice to him of whatsoever rights a prudent and reasonable inquiry would have revealed. The actual possession of real property is notice to intending purchasers of the rights of those in possession, and the purchaser in such cases takes title subject to every right in the occupant that a reasonable inquiry would have disclosed. *Dennis v. Northern Pacific Ry. Co.*, 20 Wash. 320, 55 P. 210.

See also Karlsten v. Hamel, 123 Wash. 333, 212 P. 153 (1923), which involved real property used as a hotel. The court held that the actual possession of another at the time of the title transfer was notice to the purchaser of whatever rights a prudent or reasonable inquiry would have revealed.

In cases construing the 1897 and 1927 predecessors of RCW 65.08.070, Washington courts have determined that, as the right to occupy is a property right, the open apparent occupancy of a person places a duty on the person acquiring title to inquire as to the extent and nature of the occupant's interest. This conclusion is neither inconsistent with nor in conflict with the statutory language. *Nichols v. De Britz*, 178 Wash. 375, 35 P.2d 29 (1934).

In modern times, the longstanding common law rule that occupancy by a non-owner is actual notice of the right to occupy has been refined. The occupancy of the real property by a person not the owner is currently not sufficient to impose a duty to inquire as to the title to the real property. *Scott v. Woolard*, 12 Wash.App. 109, 529 P.2d 30 (1974). It is sufficient, however, to impose a duty to inquire as to the right to occupy, and a failure to inquire results in the new title holder taking title subject to whatever rights of occupancy existed.

In *Peoples Nat'l Bank of Washington v. Birney's Enterprises, Inc.*, 54 Wash.App. 668, 775 P.2d 466 (1989), the plaintiff made loans over the course of years to the individual owner of the real property and to the defendant corporation which occupied the premises. The plaintiff then made a loan just to the individual owner who was also the sole owner of the corporation. The plaintiff obtained title reports prior to making the loan, but such report did not disclose the unrecorded lease between the individual owner and the corporation. After citing RCW 65.08.070, the court concluded that the plaintiff could foreclose the Deed of Trust granted by the owner, but was subject to the continued right of occupancy of the corporation under the terms of the unrecorded lease. Noting that the corporation "was quite visibly in possession of the property" and that the owner would have provided a copy of the unrecorded lease if requested, the court held that the plaintiff's failure to inquire into the nature of the occupancy was neither reasonable nor prudent. After noting "we have found no case excusing inquiry where possession is viable and evident," the court held that the corporation's right of occupancy under the unrecorded lease was superior to the plaintiff's right to occupy after foreclosure of the Deed of Trust.

In this particular situation, the evidence indicated that it would have been apparent to the most casual observer that the real property consisted in part of several single family residential units. The business model of Clare House was to construct and sell bungalows and, upon the death of the resident, to pay the resident some lump sum and then resell the bungalow. It is difficult to believe that lenders who received financial and other information from Clare House would not have been aware of the basic business model of the borrower. Whether or not a sample Resident Agreement was provided, the bungalows were obviously occupied by individuals other than the owner of the property which imposed a duty to inquire as to the rights of those residents.

The Caudill Group obtained a title report on the property, which revealed the two recorded Resident Agreements, but the evidence at trial did not reveal that any inquiry was made regarding the existence of other Resident Agreements or even the terms of the recorded Resident Agreements. Mr. Green, at all times, was willing to provide a sample copy of a Resident Agreement and believed that he had done so to Mr. Webster. The representative of the lenders of the Noe and Ross liens received information from Mr. Meenoch regarding the individual units and Clare House's business model of selling and reselling bungalows. The evidence at trial did not reveal that any inquiry was made regarding the occupancy of the bungalows. Mr. Blanchat knew the real property constituted a retirement community which was at "full capacity." The evidence at trial did not reveal that any further inquiry was made.

Each lienholder had actual notice of the occupancy of the bungalows by residents. Each lienholder had a duty to make reasonable and prudent inquiry as to the terms of that occupancy if the lienholder desired to obtain rights greater than the occupants. By failing to make any inquiry, each of the defendant lienholders are subject to the terms of the Resident Agreement to the extent the Resident Agreement grants rights in the real property.

CONCLUSION

The court finds that the holders of the Resident Agreements have a right to occupy, which is superior to the rights of the lienholders. The lienholders have all remedies available under state law regarding the enforcement of the Deeds of Trust, but cannot enforce them in such a way as to interfere with the residents' superior right of occupancy. Due to the failure to make reasonable inquiry as to the rights of those occupying the property, the rights of the lienholders are subject to the right of occupancy granted by the Resident Agreements.

d. Further Recording Issues

i. Mechanics' Liens

Mechanics' liens protect contractors and other people who do work improving property from nonpayment. If you hire a contractor to build a house on your property, and you fail to pay the contractor for work actually completed, then the contractor will be entitled to a mechanics' lien on the property. Although mechanics' liens existed at common law, today they are primarily the product of state statute. Because mechanics'

MORTGAGE SATISFACTIONS

Imagine that a property owner pays off the loan that was secured by a mortgage. When this occurs, we often say that the mortgage has been *satisfied*, because the underlying obligation secured by the mortgage has been performed. Even if the loan has been satisfied, however, a recorded mortgage still creates a title problem. If you were thinking about buying the property and did a title search, you would see the mortgage and have questions about the state of title of the property. Recording systems typically do not have a way of removing documents, so the mortgage will stay in the land records forever. To avoid having the mortgage create title problems in perpetuity, we use a document called a *mortgage satisfaction*. This simple document states that the mortgage has been satisfied. It is recorded and clears the cloud on title created by the mortgage. A person doing a title search will typically make sure that there is a satisfaction recorded for each mortgage on record. A present owner's outstanding mortgage, of course, will not have a recorded satisfaction. Typically a buyer will be sure that satisfactions are recorded for any outstanding mortgages as part of the closing process. Most states have statutes that impose penalties on a lender who fails to execute or record a mortgage satisfaction when the mortgage has in fact been satisfied and have procedures that allow borrowers to obtain mortgage satisfactions if the lender is unwilling or unable to provide them. We provide an example of a mortgage satisfaction on the next page.

SATISFACTION PIECE

Made this day of: **02/12/2014**

Name of Mortgagor: MARTIN SMITH AND AMY SMITH

Name of Mortgagee: **First National Bank, Inc.**

Name of Last Assignee: First National Bank, Inc.

Date of Mortgage: **05/04/2009**

Original Mortgage Debt: **250000**

Mortgage Recorded on **07/01/2009**

In the Office of the Recorder of Deeds of **Dauphin** County, **Pennsylvania**, in Mortgage Book: **N/A**, Page: **N/A**, Instrument Number: **2009007921X**

Premises situated in ALL THAT CERTAIN PROPERTY SITUATED IN THE TOWNSHIP OF DERRY, COUNTY OF DAUPHIN, AND STATE OF PENNSYLVANIA BEING MORE PARTICULARLY DESCRIBED IN A DEED RECORDED IN DOCUMENT NO. 2007008821X AMONG THE LAND RECORDS OF THE COUNTY SET FORTH ABOVE.

The undersigned acknowledges that the debt secured by the above-mentioned Mortgage has been fully paid or otherwise discharged and that upon the recording hereof said Mortgage shall be and is hereby fully and forever satisfied and discharged.

> These three lines constitute the most important part of this document.

The undersigned hereby authorizes and empowers the recorder of said county to enter this satisfaction piece and to cause said Mortgage to be satisfied of record.

Witness the due execution hereof with the intent to be legally bound.

First National Bank, Inc.

By:

Cindy Schwab, Assistant Vice President

STATE OF ARIZONA
COUNTY OF Maricopa } S.S.

On **02/12/2014**, before me, **Mary Liu**, Notary Public, personally appeared **Cindy Schwab, Assistant Vice President** of **First National Bank, Inc.**, whose identity was proven to me on the basis of satisfactory evidence to be the person who he or she claims to be and whose name is subscribed to the within instrument and acknowledged to me that he/she executed the same in his/her authorized capacity, and that by his/her signature on the instrument the person, or entity upon behalf of which the person acted, executed the instrument.

IN WITNESS WHEREOF, I have hereunto set my hand and affixed my notarial seal the day and year last written.

MARY LIU
Notary Public-Arizona
My Commission Expires
December 9, 2015

Mary Liu
_____
Notary Public: Mary Liu

> Mechanics' liens present unique title problems because they often take priority as of the date of visible construction, not the date of recording, under the doctrine of relation back.

liens are statutory liens, they arise by operation of law. They do not require the consent or the agreement of the property owner to come into existence.

The statutes that create mechanics' liens typically require that the liens become *perfected* before they become effective. Perfection typically requires some form of notice to the property owner and recording within a certain time period after the work is completed. The recording might be in a court clerk's office rather than the land records, but the basic recording process is consistent with our discussion of the recording of other interests.

For most liens and other property interests, the key date for priority is the date of recording. In notice or race-notice jurisdictions, we might need to take notice issues into consideration. Leaving notice issues aside, in a conflict between two recorded property interests, the first to be recorded will have priority over the other.

Mechanics' liens present unique title problems because they often take priority not from the date of recording, but from the date visible construction began on the project. This outcome is the result of the doctrine of *relation back*, which has been incorporated into state mechanics' lien statutes. Under this doctrine, the mechanics' lien becomes effective as of, or relates back to, the date of visible construction.

Relation back has at least two important consequences. First, a mechanics' lien may get priority over another lien even though the other lien is recorded first. For example, consider this timeline:

January 15:   Visible construction begins
March 1:   Judgment lien is recorded on the property
July 30:   Mechanics lien is perfected

Under the doctrine of relation back, the mechanic's lien would get priority from the date of visible construction—January 15—and not the date of perfection—July 30. As a result, the mechanics' lien would have priority over the judgment lien even though the judgment lien was recorded first.

Second, a mechanics' lien may be effective against a subsequent purchaser even though the subsequent purchaser could not have found the lien through a diligent records search. Let's consider a slight modification of our last example, involving the purchase of the property by Buyer:

January 15:   Visible construction begins
February 15:   Buyer performs diligent records search
March 1:   Buyer purchases Blackacre and immediately records the deed
July 30:   Mechanics lien is perfected

You should always be concerned about mechanics' liens when construction has recently been done on a property. There are various ways to mitigate mechanics' lien risk. One way is to seek assurances from the contractor that the property owner has paid the contractor in full. Another way is to be sure that your title insurance policy covers mechanics' liens. Some policies exclude mechanics' liens, but even if this is the case, mechanics' liens coverage can typically be purchased as an add-on to the basic coverage.

When Buyer performed a records search on February 15, the mechanics' lien would not have turned up because it had not yet been recorded. Under the doctrine of relation back, however, the mechanics' lien would be effective against Buyer because the mechanics' lien takes priority as of the date of visible construction.

Because of scenarios like these, mechanics' liens are often called *secret liens*. They are secret in a sense, because they often cannot be discovered through a diligent records search. Relation back to the date of visible construction, however, is broadly consistent with the concept of inquiry notice. Visible construction puts a potential purchaser or creditor on notice that work is being done on the property and that a mechanics' lien might result.

ii. Wild Deeds

Recall that in a name-index recording system, the first step in doing a title search is establishing a chain of title. We begin with the current owner of the property and then move back in time owner by owner. If Jason is the current owner of Blackacre, we look for the deed that transferred ownership to Jason. If that turns out to be a deed from Allison, we then look for the deed that transferred ownership to Allison. We then repeat the process until we have a chain of title.

In a name-index system, some deeds might fall outside of the chain of title *even though they are properly recorded*. These deeds are called *wild deeds*. Wild deeds are best illustrated with an example:

> 1995—O sells Blackacre to Abbie; Abbie records.
>
> 2000—Abbie sells Blackacre to Beth; Beth does not record.
>
> 2005—Beth sells Blackacre to Carlos; Carlos records.
>
> 2010—Abbie sells Blackacre to Donna; Donna records; Donna has no notice of the Abbie-Beth deed or the Beth-Carlos deed.

Imagine that you are doing a title search for Donna before she buys Blackacre. You want to verify that Abbie has good title to Blackacre. Treating Abbie as the owner, you look backwards and find the O to Abbie deed from 1995. That deed establishes that Abbie received title in 1995. Because the Abbie-Beth deed was not recorded, it will not show up in your record search. Even though the Beth-Carlos deed was recorded, you will not find it, either, because you are searching by name, and you have no reason to search for Beth or Carlos as owners of Blackacre. In other words, the Beth-Carlos deed is outside of the chain of title for Blackacre. A diligent title searcher will not find the Beth-Carlos deed, even though it is recorded. The Beth-Carlos deed is a wild deed. (Wild deeds are deeds that are recorded and are outside of the chain of title. The Abbie-Beth deed is not a wild deed—it is simply an unrecorded deed.)

Even though they are recorded, wild deeds are not given protection against subsequent purchasers of the property. More broadly, they do not provide record notice of their existence even though they are recorded. As a result, in our example Donna would win against Carlos under the recording acts, even though Carlos's deed is a prior recorded interest.

To see why the law favors Donna over Carlos in this circumstance, we should focus on how, exactly, the wild deed problem could have been avoided. As an initial point, it should be clear that Donna would win against Beth—the Abbie-Beth deed was *unrecorded*, and under these facts, Donna would win against Beth under any of the three varieties of recording act. Why, however, should Donna win against Carlos? After all, the Beth-Carlos deed was properly recorded.

With Carlos and Donna, we have two relatively innocent parties. Both properly recorded their deeds. As between two innocent parties, the law often places the loss on the person who is in the best position to avoid the problem in the first place. Here, Carlos is in the best position to avoid the problem. Recall that the problem arises because the Abbie-Beth deed was not recorded. Carlos could have, and should have, insisted that the Abbie-Beth deed be recorded before he took title to Blackacre. If the Abbie-Beth deed had been recorded, then the Beth-Carlos deed would have been in Blackacre's chain of title, and Carlos would clearly win against Donna. Because Carlos could have, but did not, take this step, the law will favor Donna over Carlos.

Wild deeds are a product of name-indexing systems. The wild deed problem should not occur in a tract-index system, because the title searcher should be able to find all documents related to the property by looking up the parcel's identification number. Even in some name-index jurisdictions, modern computer searches might allow a searcher to find a deed outside of the chain of title. If the indexing system allows a searcher to find the deed, generally speaking, it will not be treated as a wild deed. Regardless of the type of indexing system used in a given jurisdiction, as a matter of prudence a buyer of property should always make sure that prior deeds in the chain of title are properly recorded.

iii. Misspellings

Grantor-Grantee indexes are organized by name. As common sense would tell you, misspellings can cause problems in the recording context. Take, for example, the case of *Orr v. Byers*, 244 Cal. Rptr. 13 (1988). William Elliott owned property. James Orr obtained a judgment for $50,000 against Elliott. In an effort to enforce this judgment, Orr's attorney filed a judgment lien against Elliott's property. The attorney, however, misspelled Elliott's name, recording the judgment lien under the names Elliot and Eliot. Elliott later sold the property to Rick Byers. Byers performed a title search, but did not locate the judgment lien because of the misspellings.

In the subsequent litigation, Orr argued that the misspellings were sufficient to provide Byers with record notice of the judgment lien. Orr relied on the doctrine of *idem sonans*. As the court explained,

> The doctrine of *idem sonans* is that though a person's name has been inaccurately written, the identity of such person will be presumed from the similarity of sounds between the correct pronunciation and the pronunciation as written. Therefore, absolute accuracy in spelling names is not required in legal proceedings, and if the pronunciations are practically alike, the rule of *idem sonans* is applicable. The rule is inapplicable, however, under circumstances where the written name is material. To be material, a variance must be such as has misled the opposite party to his prejudice.

244 Cal. Rptr. at 14 (internal quotations and citations omitted). The court rejected the applicability of *idem sonans* in the recording context, holding that spelling is material to the indexing system. There are many legal contexts where the correct spelling of a name is not essential. Recording is not one of them.

As *Orr* illustrates, attorneys must be precise with names when working with recorded documents. Name changes present a source of potential recording problems. People frequently change their last names, often after getting married. If a person purchases a parcel of property with the last name Smith and sells the property after changing the last name to Jones, care will have to be exercised to allow the indexing system to function property. One way of addressing this problem is to record a notice of name change. Another way is to note the name change in the later deed and to be sure that the deed is indexed under both the old name and the new name.

iv. Technical Defects

Recording statutes often establish technical requirements for the recording of a document. Perhaps the most common technical requirement is that the document being recorded be notarized. *Failure to follow these technical requirements may result in the document as being deemed not recorded.* For example, in *Messersmith v. Smith*, 60 N.W.2d 276 (N.D. 1953), the court held that a document that was not properly notarized was not properly recorded, and that recording did not provide record notice to subsequent purchasers. As a result, the prior interest holder lost against the subsequent interest holder.

v. The Common Grantor Problem

Developers often subdivide large pieces of land into smaller parcels. In the process, the developers often impose covenants restricting the use of each parcel. (We will study these covenants in depth in a later chapter.) For example, a developer might impose a covenant restricting the use of each parcel to single-family residential use—that is, each parcel owner may only build a single-family home on the property.

The common grantor problem arises when such a covenant is imposed on most of the parcels in a development, but through an administrative error is not imposed on one (or perhaps more) of the parcels. For example, consider parcel X in a development where all of the parcels are supposed to be subject to a single-family residential use covenant. By its terms, the covenant applies to all parcels in the development, and the covenant was in fact included in the deed to all of the other parcels. Though an error it was not imposed on parcel X. Jordan Davis bought parcel X and performed a thorough title search. Because the covenant was never imposed on parcel X, the covenant did not turn up in the title search. If Jordan had searched the title records for any of the other parcels in the development, he would have found the covenant and would have known that it applied to parcel X because the covenant by its terms applied to all parcels in the development. Under these circumstances, is Jordan bound by the covenant? Put another way, can Jordan build a gas station on the parcel?

This scenario is called the common grantor problem because parcel X and all of the other parcels in the neighborhood were all conveyed by the same grantor—here, the developer of the neighborhood. Courts are equally split on the answer to our question. About half of U.S. jurisdictions would say that the covenant does not apply to Jordan and that he could build a gas station on parcel X. The other half of jurisdictions hold that Jordan is bound by the covenant. As you think about the advantages and disadvantages of each approach, think about (a) how the common scheme of covenants would be undercut by allowing Jordan to build a gas station on the parcel and (b) how the contrary rule would impact the practicalities of title searching, when the only way that Jordan could have discovered the covenant would have been to search the title for neighboring parcels as well as his own. The cases in this area can be fact specific and can turn in part on the nuances of the recording system in a particular jurisdiction. For more on this subject, *see* Stoebuck & Whitman, *The Law of Property*, §11.11 (3d ed. 2000).

Some of the common grantor cases may have a stated or unstated inquiry notice layer to them, if the facts and circumstances might have led a reasonable person in Jordan's situation to inquire further about the existence of a covenant. If, for example, all of the other parcels had single-family homes on them, and parcel X was the only remaining vacant lot in the development, a reasonable person might inquire into whether there was some kind of restriction in place on the parcels in the development.

Advanced Recording Problems. These problems present some of the issues that we have covered since our basic set of recording problems. Explanatory answers to these problems can be found on page 1053.

1. Presume that the following fact pattern occurs in a race-notice jurisdiction. Yvette Rawls recently bought a house from Tom Clarke. In doing a record search, Yvette discovered that the house had been in Clarke's family for years. Yvette found a 1970 deed conveying the property from Tom's father, Richard Clarke, to Tom. The 1970 deed also mentioned a

1930 deed conveying the property from Richard's father Henry to Richard. This 1930 deed was not recorded. Yvette asked Tom about the 1930 deed. Tom said that it had been lost. Yvette decided that under the circumstances she was comfortable with the title. Once Yvette bought the house, she promptly recorded her deed. Yvette has had two problems arise since closing. First, she received a letter from Tom's cousin Rosie Clarke-Higgins. The letter attached a copy of the 1930 deed, which in fact conveyed the house to Tom Clarke for life, remainder to Avery Clarke. Rosie is Avery's heir and successor-in-interest to the remainder interest. Rosie therefore claims that she owns the house. Second, Yvette noticed a neighbor, Gail Aspen, using an unpaved driveway to reach the street. This driveway is clearly located on the property that Yvette had bought from Tom. It turned out that way back when Henry Clarke owned the property, he had granted a driveway easement to the then-owner of the neighboring property. This easement was never recorded. Yvette is unhappy with Gail's use of the driveway and wants to try to stop her from using it. Focusing only on recording and related issues, discuss the likely outcomes of Yvette's disputes with Rosie and Gail.

2. Uphill Downs is a suburban subdivision that was developed by Yerger Homes, LLC. Yerger Homes bought a 70-acre parcel and divided it into 42 smaller lots. The community is governed by a set of recorded covenants that limit the use of the lots to single-family residences. In other words, lot owners can build traditional single-family houses on the lots, but cannot use the lots for multifamily residential buildings (e.g., duplexes or apartment buildings) or commercial uses (e.g., shops or gas stations). Thirty of the 42 lots already have single-family houses on them. One of the remaining vacant lots was purchased two years ago by Beth de Soto. Due to a clerical error, the covenants governing the community were not mentioned in the deed from Yerger Homes to Beth and were not otherwise recorded for Beth's lot. Last week, Beth sold her lot to Brian Kim. Brian had no actual knowledge of the covenants. He now wants to build a gas station on the lot. Focusing only on the recording issues, can he build the gas station?

3. Rick Brophy bought Blackacre from Nate Boone in 2013. Blackacre is located in a jurisdiction that uses a name-indexing system. Before buying Blackacre, Rick did a title search and discovered a deed that transferred Blackacre from Owen Arias to Nate in 2000. Rick had no actual knowledge of any other interests in Blackacre that were created after the Owen-Nate transaction. Right after Rick closed on the purchase, Camille Frantz asserted that she was the rightful owner of Blackacre and brought a quiet title action against Rick. It turns out that Camille had bought Blackacre from Talia Nixon in 2009. After purchasing Blackacre, Camille promptly recorded her deed. Talia, in turn, had purchased Blackacre from Nate in 2004. Talia, however, did not record her deed. On these facts, who should win the quiet title action?

e. Summary: The Recording System and Title Risk

Returning to our diagram of the phases of a real estate transaction, we see that the recording system plays different roles in protecting against title risk at different times. During the executory contract phase (and sometimes earlier during the pre-contract phase), a diligent title search will give the buyer information about the title to the property. Post-closing, the buyer will be protected against prior unrecorded interests so long as the buyer satisfies the requirements of the relevant recording act. Prompt recording of the deed also protects the buyer against subsequent interests in the property.

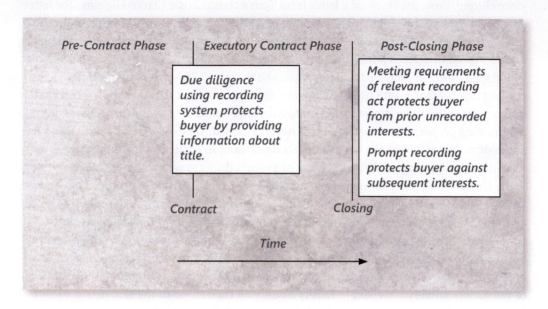

2. ALLOCATING TITLE RISK IN CONTRACTS AND DEEDS

The two key documents in a real estate transaction—the contract and the deed—both can address the allocation of title risk between the buyer and the seller. During the executory contract period of the transaction, when the contract controls, the concept of marketable title may give the buyer the ability to back out of the transaction without penalty if there is a title problem. After closing, warranties of title in the deed may give the buyer the ability to sue the seller to recover compensation for damages that result from title problems.

In this section, we discuss marketable title and deed warranties in turn. Along the way, we discuss the important concept of merger, under which the deed supplants the contract after closing.

a. Marketable Title

The seller of real property is obligated to provide the buyer with marketable title. Most real estate contracts contain an express marketable title provision. The obligation to convey marketable title is implied even if the contract is silent on the issue. The seller can only avoid this obligation if the contract expressly states that the seller is not obligated to convey marketable title.

Due diligence is a broad term that is often used to describe the investigation that the parties will do as part of a transaction. In the real estate context, the buyer's due diligence typically focuses on the state of title and physical condition of the property.

Marketable title is typically defined as title that would not create reasonable doubts in a reasonable person. It is often stated in terms of litigation risk: title is unmarketable if it exposes the buyer to the hazards of litigation. In some contracts, marketable title is stated in terms of insurability: title is marketable if the buyer can obtain title insurance for the property at standard rates. The presence of any of the three types of title problems—ownership, encumbrance, or encroachment—can render title unmarketable.

If title is unmarketable, the buyer can typically back out of the contract without penalty. The executory contract phase of the transaction allows the buyer to perform due diligence on the property. One component of the buyer's due diligence is an investigation into the property's title. If the buyer finds a title problem during the executory contract phase that would make title unmarketable, then the buyer can walk away from the deal. It is important to note, however, that the seller's obligation is to deliver marketable title at closing. If the buyer discovers a title problem, and the seller can cure that problem before closing, then the buyer will be required to complete the transaction.

Encumbrances are the most common source of marketable title issues, because almost all properties are encumbered in some way. Remember that encumbrances include not only mortgages and liens but also easements and covenants. Most homes in contemporary suburban developments are subject to restrictive covenants. Most recently built homes therefore have at least one encumbrance on title.

The *mere existence* of any kind of encumbrance makes title unmarketable. This raises a practical question: if many homes have title encumbrances, and the mere existence of an encumbrance makes title unmarketable, how do we ever create binding contracts for the purchase and sale of real estate? If many homes have unmarketable title, wouldn't the buyer have the ability to back out of most contracts on marketability of title grounds?

We solve this problem by having the buyer waive objections to certain title problems. The seller, for example, could disclose the existence of a set of covenants on the property, and the buyer could waive any marketable title objection to the covenants. Many real estate contracts limit the scope of the seller's obligation to convey marketable title by having the buyer waive any objection to all certain types of interests (e.g., all easements) or interests that could be easily discoverable by the buyer (e.g., recorded interests). The buyer needs to pay close attention to these carve-outs from the marketable title provision. If the marketable title provision excludes recorded interests, for example, the buyer should perform a title search before signing the agreement so that the buyer understands the impact of the exclusion.

As we noted above, the mere existence of the covenant on the property constitutes an encumbrance that makes title unmarketable. Consider a contract that excludes recorded covenants. There is a covenant on record that requires any house built on the property to be at least 2,500 square feet. The mere existence of this covenant would not be a problem under this contract, because the contract excludes recorded covenants from the scope of marketable title. Now say that the house on the property is only 2,000 square feet, constituting a violation of the covenant. This violation creates a *separate and independent marketable title issue*. Unless the buyer has expressly waived the violation, then title is unmarketable.

Many properties are subject to municipal land use ordinances. We will discuss this type of ordinance in some depth in a later chapter. For now, it is sufficient to know that these ordinances exist and that they often impose restrictions similar to those that can be imposed by a covenant. In contrast to covenants, the general rule is that the mere existence of a land use ordinance *does not* render title unmarketable. Violations of land use or other municipal ordinances, however, do render title unmarketable. Why is there a distinction between covenants and municipal ordinances? Unlike a covenant, the mere existence of an ordinance does not have any direct impact on the title of the property. A violation of an ordinance, however, typically can lead to the imposition of a lien by the local government, which would impact title.

Here is the marketable title provision from Pennsylvania's form residential purchase and sale contract:

> The Property will be conveyed with good and marketable title that is insurable by a reputable title insurance company at the regular rates, free and clear of all liens, encumbrances, and easements, *excepting however* the following: existing deed restrictions; historic preservation restrictions or ordinances; building restrictions; ordinances; easements of roads; easements visible upon the ground; easements of record; and privileges or rights of public service companies, if any.

Take a close look at what it covers. Note, for example, that it excludes "existing deed restrictions." Think about the difference between the word "existing" and the word "recorded" in this context. Restrictive covenants are sometimes stated in deeds and are sometimes stated in a separate document. How would this document handle covenants that are in a separate document?

Our next case involves marketable title issues raised by covenants and municipal ordinances. The court uses "merchantable title," a slightly antiquated synonym for "marketable title." As you read the case, note carefully what the contract has to say about marketable title.

LOHMEYER V. BOWER

Supreme Court of Kansas, 1951
227 P.2d 102

PARKER, Justice. [Plaintiff Kenneth L. Lohmeyer agreed to buy a home owned by defendants Carl A. Bower, Jr. and Anne S. Bower. Lohmeyer brought this action to rescind the contract on marketable title grounds. The Bowers denied that title was unmarketable, and counterclaimed seeking specific performance of the contract.

Lohmeyer raised two marketable title issues. First, a local ordinance required houses to be at least three feet from the property boundary. This house was located 18 inches from a boundary line, creating a violation of the ordinance. Second, a covenant (referred to in some places by the court as a "dedication restriction" or a "declaration restriction") required houses built in the subdivision to have two stories. The house on the property only had one story, creating a violation of the covenant. The contract between the parties stated in part that they Bowers agreed:

> "to convey the above described real estate to the second party by Warranty Deed with an abstract of title, certified to date showing good merchantable title or an Owners Policy of Title Insurance in the amount of the sale price, guaranteeing said title to party of the second part, free and clear of all encumbrances except special taxes subject, however, to all restrictions and easements of record applying to this property, it being understood that the first party shall have sufficient time to bring said abstract to date or obtain Report for Title Insurance and to correct any imperfections in the title if there be such imperfections."]

Conceding he purchased the property, subject to all restrictions of record [Lohmeyer] makes no complaint of the restrictions contained in the declaration forming a part of the dedication of Berkley Hills Addition nor of the ordinance restricting the building location on the lot but bases his right to rescission of the contract solely upon presently existing violations thereof. This, we may add, limited to restrictions imposed by terms of the ordinance, relating to the use of land or the location and character of buildings that may be located thereon, even in the absence of provisions in the contract excepting them, must necessarily be his position for we are convinced, although it must be conceded there are some decisions to the contrary, the rule supported by the better reasoned decisions, indeed if not by the great weight of authority, is that municipal restrictions of such character, existing at the time of the execution of a contract for the sale of real estate, are not such encumbrances or burdens on title as may be availed of by a vendee to avoid his agreement to purchase on the ground they render his title unmerchantable. . . .

On the other hand there can be no question the rule respecting restrictions upon the use of land or the location and type of buildings that may be erected thereon fixed by covenants or other private restrictive agreements, including those contained in the declaration forming a part of the dedication of Berkley Hills Addition, is directly contrary to the one to which we have just referred. Such restrictions, under all the authorities, constitute encumbrances rendering the title to land unmerchantable. . . .

There can be no doubt regarding what constitutes a marketable or merchantable title in this jurisdiction. This court has been called on to pass upon that question on numerous occasions. See our recent decision in *Peatling v. Baird*, 168 Kan. 528, 213 P.2d 1015, 1016, and cases there cited, wherein we held:

> "A marketable title to real estate is one which is free from reasonable doubt, and a title is doubtful and unmarketable if it exposes the party holding it to the hazard of litigation.
>
> 'To render the title to real estate unmarketable, the defect of which the purchaser complains must be of a substantial character and one from which he may suffer injury. Mere immaterial defects which do not diminish in quantity, quality or value the property contracted for, constitute no ground upon which the purchaser may reject the title. Facts must be known at the time which fairly raise a reasonable doubt as to the title; a mere possibility or conjecture that such a state of facts may be developed at some future time is not sufficient."

Under the rule just stated, and in the face of facts such as are here involved, we have little difficulty in concluding that the violation of section 5-224 of the ordinances of the city of Emporia as well as the violation of the restrictions imposed by the dedication declaration so encumber the title to Lot 37 as to expose the party holding it to the hazard of litigation and make such title doubtful and unmarketable. It follows, since, as we have indicated, the appellees had contracted to convey such real estate to appellant by warranty deed with an abstract of title showing good merchantable title, free and clear of all encumbrances, that they cannot convey the title contracted for and that the trial court should have rendered judgment rescinding the contract. This, we may add is so, notwithstanding the contract provides the conveyance was to be made subject to all restrictions and easements of record, for, as we have seen, it is the violation of the restrictions imposed by both the ordinance and the dedication declaration, not the existence of those restrictions, that renders the title unmarketable. . . .

To the same effect is 66 C.J. 912 §592, where the following statement appears: "Existing violations of building restrictions imposed by law warrant rejection of title by a purchaser contracting for a conveyance free of encumbrances. The fact that the premises to be conveyed violate tenement house regulations is ground for rejection of title where the contract of sale expressly provided against the existence of such violations, . . ." *See, also, Moran v. Borrello*, 132 A. 510, 4 N.J.Misc. 344.

With respect to covenants and restrictions similar to those involved in the dedication declaration, notwithstanding the agreement—as here—excepted restrictions of record, see *Chesebro v. Moers*, 233 N.Y. 75, 134 N.E. 842, 21 A.L.R. 1270, holding that the violation by a property owner of covenants restricting the distance from front and rear lines within which buildings may be placed renders the title to such property unmarketable.

See, also, *Hebb v. Severson*, 32 Wash.2d 159, 201 P.2d 156, which holds, that where a contract provided that building and use restrictions general to the district should not be deemed restrictions, the purchaser's knowledge of such restrictions did not estop him from rescinding the contract of purchase on subsequent discovery that the position of the house on the lot involved violated such restrictions. At page 172 of 32 Wash.2d, at page 162 of 201 P.2d it is said:

> "Finally, the fact that the contract contains a provision that protective restrictions shall not be deemed encumbrances cannot aid the respondents. It is not the existence of protective restrictions, as shown by the record, that constitutes the encumbrances alleged by the appellants; but, rather, it is the presently existing violation of one of these restrictions that constitutes such encumbrance, in and of itself. The authorities so hold, on the rationale, to which we subscribe, that to force a vendee to accept property which in its present state violates a building restriction without a showing that the restriction is unenforcible, would in effect compel the vendee to buy a lawsuit. 66 C.J. 911, *Vendor and Purchaser*, §590; *Dichter v. Issacson*, 4. N.J.Misc. 297; 132 A. 481, [Affirmed, 104 N.J.L. 167], 138 A. 920; *Chesebro v. Moers*, 233 N.Y. 75, 134 N.E. 842, 21 A.L.R. 1270."

Finally appellees point to the contract which, it must be conceded, provides they shall have time to correct imperfections in the title and contend that even if it be held the restrictions and the ordinance have been violated they are entitled to time in which to correct those imperfections. Assuming, without deciding, they might remedy the violation of the ordinance by buying additional ground the short and simple answer to their contention with respect to the violation of the restrictions imposed by the dedication declaration is that any changes in the house would compel the purchaser to take something that he did not contract to buy.

Conclusions heretofore announced require reversal of the judgment with directions to the trial court to cancel and set aside the contract and render such judgment as may be equitable and proper under the issues raised by the pleadings.

It is so ordered.

PROBLEM

Maurice Zephyr owned a house located at 47 Oak Drive in West Easton. Last month, Maurice entered into a contract to sell the house to Linda Ellickson. The contract states that the property is subject to written covenants and that the buyer waives any objection to these covenants. One of these covenants requires that all buildings be located at least 15 feet from the property boundaries on all sides. Right now, the house is located at least 17 feet from each boundary line. Linda, however, bought the house with the intention of putting an addition on the back. In consultation with her architect, Linda has just discovered that the 15-foot requirement will not allow her to build the addition that she wanted.

a. On these facts, could Linda refuse to close because the covenants render the title unmarketable?

b. What would happen on the same basic facts if the contract had not noted the existence of the written covenants and Maurice had not otherwise disclosed the existence of the covenants to Linda?

c. What would happen on the same basic facts if it turned out that the house was presently located only 12 feet from one of the property boundaries?

d. What would happen on the same basic facts if the setback requirements were established by the local zoning ordinance, and the existence of the ordinance was not addressed in the contract?

e. What would happen on the same basic facts if the setback requirements were established by the local zoning ordinance, and it turned out that the house presently was only 12 feet from one of the property boundaries?

An explanatory answer to this problem can be found on page 1054.

b. Merger

The merger doctrine is based on the idea that the deed is the final expression of the agreement between the buyer and seller. As a result, when the deed is delivered at closing, the contract between the buyer and seller is deemed to have merged into the deed. In plainer terms, this means that at closing, *the contract disappears, and the terms of the deed control.* This is, as they say, a *big deal.* If the parties made a promise in the contract, and this promise is not made in the deed, then the promise may not be enforceable after closing.

There are ways to easily avoid the merger of contract provisions. Before we discuss ways around the merger doctrine, however, it is worth pausing to consider further what the doctrine achieves at its core. Before closing, the buyer and seller typically have a written contract that covers a host of issues. It is not unusual for a contract for a simple residential real estate transaction to be 30 pages long. At closing, the seller delivers a deed to the buyer. Deeds are often only one or two pages long. Merger therefore replaces a long document with a short one. The reduction in length, in and of itself, is not that surprising. Many of the provisions of the contract concern issues that will be resolved before or at closing. Other provisions of the contract, however, concern issues that will continue to be relevant after closing. For example, if the seller promises in the contract that there are no easements on the property, and it turns out that there is in fact an easement on the property, then the buyer will be as concerned about this promise after closing as before closing. The merger doctrine, however, will prevent the buyer from enforcing this promise after closing. If the buyer wants to hold the seller accountable for the easement post-closing, the buyer will have to look to promises that the seller made, if any, in the deed.

The merger doctrine has a number of exceptions. Generally speaking, the less a promise has to do with title, the more likely it is to survive merger. *See* Lawrence Berger, *Merger by Deed—What Provisions of a Contract for the Sale of Land Survive the Closing?*, 21 Real Estate L.J. 22 (1992). Promises about the quality or physical condition of the property, for example, are often deemed to fall outside of the scope of merger. Courts, however, tend to be a bit erratic in their application of merger, and it is risky to assume in advance that a particular provision will be exempt from the doctrine.

Fortunately, it is simple to avoid the merger of a contract term by including specific language in the contract. Including the language "this provision will not merge into the deed and will survive closing" will protect a contract provision from merger. Because it is easy to use contract language to avoid merger, your assumption going into a transaction should always be that all provisions in the contract, no matter how unrelated they are to title, that do not contain protective language will merge. If you want a provision unrelated to title to survive, include explicit language to make sure that it does. If you want a provision related to title to survive, it is best to include it directly in the deed.

c. Deeds and Deed Warranties

After closing, the merger doctrine requires the buyer to look to deed warranties, not provisions in the contract, to hold a seller accountable for title defects. There are three types of deeds currently in use in the United States, and the salient difference between them is the title warranties that they contain. These are:

> 1. *General warranty deeds.* In a general warranty deed, the seller provides a series of warranties to the buyer against all defects in title. We will examine these warranties in more detail below. For now, the important thing to know is that the warranties in a general warranty deed provide protection against *all defects in title, regardless of when they arose, that existed at the time the deed was delivered.* Of the three types of deeds, the general warranty deed provides the most protection to the buyer.

2. *Special warranty deeds.* In a special warranty deed, the seller provides a series of warranties that are similar to those in a general warranty deed. The scope of the warranties, however is limited. In a general warranty deed, the seller warrants against all title defects existing at the time of deed delivery, regardless of when those defects first arose. In a special warranty deed, in contrast, the seller only warrants against *defects that arose during the seller's ownership of the property.* Here are two examples that illustrate the difference:

EXAMPLE 1: O purchased Blackacre in 2010. It turns out that the prior owner placed a mortgage on Blackacre in 2008. O sold Blackacre to A on June 1, 2012. The mortgage had never been satisfied and therefore was an encumbrance on title at the time of the O-A transaction. If O gave A a general warranty deed, O would be liable to A for the defect in title resulting from the mortgage. If O gave A a special warranty deed, however, O would *not* be liable to A for the mortgage, because the mortgage arose prior to O's ownership of Blackacre.

EXAMPLE 2: Same facts as the previous example, but now the mortgage arose on May 1, 2011, during O's ownership of Blackacre. O would be liable to A for the defect in title caused by the mortgage under a special warranty deed, because the defect arose during O's ownership of the property. Of course, O would also be liable for the defect under a general warranty deed as well.

3. *Quitclaim deeds.* A quitclaim deed contains *no warranties of title whatsoever.* If O delivers a quitclaim deed to A, and it turns out that there is a title problem, A has no recourse against O. Even if it turns out that O doesn't even own an interest in Blackacre, a cannot recover against O. A quitclaim deed simply transfers the grantor's interest in the property, if any, to the recipient of the deed.

We will return to the substance of deed warranties shortly. We want to pause here to make a crucial point about how the seller's title obligations change over time. During the executory contract phase, the seller's obligation to provide marketable title gives the buyer the ability to walk away from the transaction without penalty on the discovery of undisclosed title defects. At closing, the contract merges into the deed, and any promises in the contract about the state of title are no longer enforceable by the buyer. Post-closing the buyer therefore will need to look to deed warranties, if any, to obtain recourse from the seller for title defects.

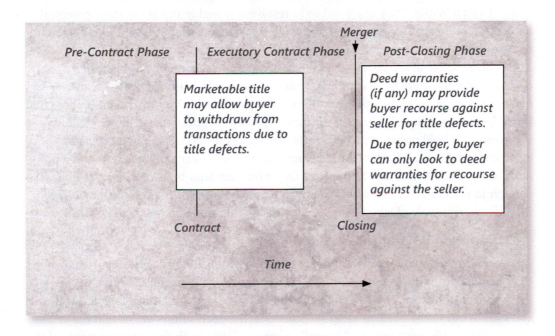

i. More on Quitclaims

Most people's initial reaction to a quitclaim deed is to ask, "Why would anyone ever accept one?" The short answer is that while a quitclaim deed may cause some worries in a typical residential transaction, they are remarkably useful in certain contexts. One context is gifts—sometimes the donor of a gift of property will not want to take on liability for title risk through deed warranties. Another context is the settlement of disputes over the ownership of property. Say that Amy and Bob are engaged in litigation over the ownership of Blackacre. They agree to settle their dispute, with Amy agreeing that Bob will have ownership of Blackacre in return for a payment of money from Bob. As part of the settlement, Amy can quitclaim her interest in Blackacre to Bob. It does not matter in this context whether Amy in fact had an interest in Blackacre.

By delivering a quitclaim to Bob, Amy is simply conveying whatever interest, if any, she has in Blackacre to Bob. After receiving the quitclaim from Amy, Bob has clear title to Blackacre.

We have seen this type of use of quitclaims before. In *Harper v. Paradise*, one of our inquiry notice cases from earlier in this chapter, Susan Harper's heirs quitclaimed the property to Maude Harper in an attempt to replace the lost deed. The heirs were not claiming to own the property; rather, they were releasing any claim that they might have had to try to give Maude clear title. A quitclaim was used in a similar manner in *White v. Brown*, the case in the chapter on Present and Future Interests involving the construction of Jessie Lide's conveyance to "Evelyn White to have my home to live in and *not* to be *sold*." Jessie Lide was survived by two sisters. Even though the sisters likely had no claim to the property, they quitclaimed any interest they might have had to Evelyn White. They likely did so to resolve any ambiguity about their potential ownership interest. They may also have wanted to express support for White's claim of ownership by granting a quitclaim to her.

Quitclaims are also frequently used in the commercial context. Sophisticated commercial parties are often comfortable accepting a quitclaim and using the other means of protection against title risk outlined in this section. It is worth noting here that the frequent use of special purpose entities (typically corporations or limited liability companies) to hold commercial real estate also makes it difficult to pursue a claim against a grantor for breach of a deed warranty. You will likely appreciate this last point more after you take a course in Business Organizations later in law school. For now, it is enough to understand that you are likely going to be more willing to accept a quitclaim deed if a warranty deed is not going to do you a lot of good as a practical matter.

ii. More on Warranty Deeds

As their name implies, warranty deeds include promises (typically labeled *warranties* or *covenants*) from the grantor to the grantee about the state of title. The exact scope of these warranties can vary between jurisdictions. In some jurisdictions, the warranties are written out in the deed. In other jurisdictions, the deed simply states that the grantor "generally warrants" or "specially warrants" title, with the actual contents of the warranties being established by statute or case law.

Despite these jurisdictional variations, warranty deeds typically contain six warranties. The substance of the warranties in general warranty deeds and special warranty deeds tends to be the same, even though the scope of the warranties is different. General warranty deeds warrant against all defects in title, regardless of when they arose. Special warranty deeds warrant only against defects in title that arose during the grantor's ownership of the property.

Warranty deeds generally contain the following six promises. We will divide them into two sets of three, the *present covenants* and the *future covenants*. We begin with the present covenants:

1. *The covenant of seisin.* The grantor promises that she owns the interest that she is conveying. This promise is breached, for example, if the grantor does not have any interest in the property, if the grantor only owns a life estate but is purporting to convey a fee simple, or if the grantor only owns eight of the ten acres described in the deed.

2. *The covenant of right to convey.* The grantor promises that she has the right to convey the interest. In most circumstances, this will duplicate the covenant of seisin—if a person owns the interest, then she generally has the right to convey it. There are some circumstances where a person might own property but not have a right to convey. For example, a trustee might be the legal owner of property but the trust's governing document might restrict the trustee's right to convey the property.

3. *The covenant against encumbrances.* The grantor promises that there are no encumbrances on the property. This covenant is violated by the presence of any encumbrance on title. Liens and mortgages violate the covenant against encumbrances. So do easements and covenants. If the parties' expectation is that the property will be conveyed with an encumbrance present, then that encumbrance is *excepted* from the coverage of the covenant. (See sidebar.)

EXCEPTIONS AND DEED WARRANTIES

As we saw in our discussion of marketable title, buyers are often willing to accept encumbrances on the property that create formal title problems. Covenants and easements, in particular, are frequently present on properties and often do not raise real title concerns for the buyer. The mere presence of covenants and easements raise technical marketable title concerns, but these concerns are typically addressed through disclosure and waiver by the buyer of any objections to the disclosed encumbrances. Recall, for example, that in *Lohmeyer* that the seller's obligation to convey marketable title was limited by this language: "subject, however, to all restrictions and easements of record applying to this property." The same basic approach is taken with deed warranties, where encumbrances may be excepted from the conveyance. The language of the conveyance would read something like "Grantor grants Blackacre to Grantee, excepting, however, an easement granted to [Neighbor] on December 7, 1981, recorded in the County Recorder of Deeds office at [Index Number]." This language carves the easement out of the property conveyed to the grantee and out of the coverage of the covenant against encumbrances. You will often see conveyances described as being made "by general warranty deed with no exceptions." This means just what is sounds like—that the grantor did not make any exceptions from the conveyance. When there are no exceptions, any encumbrance on the property will violate the covenant against encumbrances.

The remaining three are the future covenants:

> 4. *The covenant of general warranty (or, in the case of a special warranty deed, the covenant of special warranty).* The grantor promises to defend the grantee against *lawful* claims of title by another person and to compensate the grantee for any losses that result for such a claim. The word "lawful" is critical here—the covenant is only breached if the other person asserting title wins. This limitation makes sense because if the other person loses, then the grantee has good title to the property and therefore has exactly what the grantor promised to convey. The scope of this covenant is broad enough to cover any type of title problem, and it is not just limited to competing claims of outright ownership.

> 5. *The covenant of quiet enjoyment.* The grantor promises that the grantee will have quiet enjoyment in their possession and ownership of the property. As a practical matter, this covenant is a duplicate of the covenant of general warranty.

> 6. *The covenant of further assurances.* The grantor promises to execute any document, or take any similar steps, necessary to fix any title problems that later arise.

The first three covenants are called present covenants because they are promises about the state of title at the time of conveyance. They are stated in the present tense and are breached, if at all, at the time of conveyances. The second three covenants are called future covenants because they are promises about contingent future events. They are stated in the future tense and are breached, if at all, at some point in the future if and when the contingent event takes place. The distinction is important because the *statute of limitations* operates differently for present and future covenants. The statute of limitations starts to run on present covenants from the time of the conveyance, because present covenants are breached (if at all) at the time of conveyance. The statute of limitations starts to run on future covenants only if and when they are breached in the future. As a practical matter, the statute of limitations will often bar claims under present covenants but will rarely bar claims under future covenants.

Let's take a look at some examples of how deed covenants work. The statute of limitations for claims under deed covenants in the jurisdiction is ten years.

> EXAMPLE 1: Alice conveyed Blackacre to Bruce by general warranty deed on July 8, 1991. A few months after the conveyance, Bruce learns that Alice actually owned only eight of the ten acres described by the deed. The remaining two acres are owned by Cindy. Cindy asserts both ownership and possession of the two acres. Bruce immediately asserts a claim against Alice for breach of the deed warranties. Bruce has valid claims against Alice for breaches of the present covenants of seisin and right to convey. Alice did not own the two acres, and these two present

covenants were breached at the time of conveyance. Bruce also has a valid claim against Alice for breaches of the future covenants of general warranty and quiet enjoyment, because Cindy is presently asserting lawful ownership and possession of the two acres. (Cindy's claim is lawful because the facts state that she owns the two acres.)

EXAMPLE 2: Same facts as Example 1, but now presume that as of the date of conveyance Alice had acquired title to the two acres by adverse possession. A few months after the conveyance, Cindy brings a claim against Bruce to quiet title to the two acres. Bruce successfully defends this suit. (Bruce would win because the facts state that Alice had already met all of the requirements of adverse possession.) He then brings suit against Alice for breach of the deed warranties. Bruce would lose on the present covenants, because Alice did in fact own all of the ten acres at the time of conveyance. Bruce would also lose on the future covenants, because Cindy's claim of ownership was not *lawful*.

EXAMPLE 3: Same facts as Example 1, but now Bruce discovers the fact that Alice did not own the two acres on August 12, 2012—more than ten years after the date of conveyance. Cindy is asserting ownership and possession of the two acres. Immediately after discovering the problem, Bruce brought a claim against Alice for breach of the deed warranties. Bruce does not have good claims against Alice for breach of the present covenants of seisin and right to convey—they were breached, as in Example 1, but the statute of limitations has run on these claims. Bruce does have good claims against Alice for breach of the future covenants of general warranty and quiet enjoyment, because Cindy is asserting lawful ownership and possession of the two acres. The statute of limitations only starts running against the future covenants when Alice refuses to defend Bruce against Cindy's claim to the two acres and to compensate Bruce for the damages he has suffered by not owning the two acres. This fact pattern illustrates how the statute of limitations is frequently a problem for present covenant claims but is rarely a problem for future covenant claims. The only way the statute of limitations can run on a future covenant claim is for the grantee (here, Bruce) to make a demand against the grantor (here, Alice), and then to fail to make a claim against the grantor for the entire statutory period.

EXAMPLE 4: Darcy conveyed Whiteacre to Eleanor by general warranty deed with no exceptions on April 14, 1995. Shortly after the transaction closed, Eleanor learned that at the time of the conveyance, there was a recorded, but unsatisfied, mortgage on the property held by First National Bank. First National Bank has not taken any action to foreclose on Whiteacre. Eleanor promptly brought an action against

Darcy for breach of the deed warranties. Eleanor has a good claim against Darcy for breach of the present covenant against encumbrances, which was breached at the time of conveyance because of the presence of the mortgage. Eleanor does not yet have a claim against Darcy for breach of the future covenants of general warranty and quiet enjoyment, however, because First National Bank has not yet taken any steps to foreclose and assert ownership and possession of the property. If and when First National Bank did foreclose, then Eleanor would have a good future covenants claim against Darcy. As illustrated in the prior example, the statute of limitations won't start running on Eleanor's future covenant claims until the Bank actually forecloses and Darcy refuses to take any action to fix the problem.

EXAMPLE 5: Same facts as Example 4, but now Eleanor did not discover the mortgage until May 4, 2006—more than 11 years after the transaction. As before, First National Bank has not brought a foreclosure action on the mortgage. At this point, Eleanor does not have an actionable claim against Darcy for breach of deed warranties. The present covenant against encumbrances was violated, but the statute of limitations has run on this claim. Because First National Bank has not yet foreclosed, Eleanor does not have presently actionable future covenants claim against Darcy. If and when First National Bank forecloses, then Eleanor could bring a future covenants claim against Darcy. To be sure, Eleanor's interest in Whiteacre is harmed by the presence of the mortgage, which impairs her title. The present covenants cover this kind of injury, but the statute of limitations has run on them. The future covenants protect basic ownership and possession, and those have not been impaired yet. For a case presenting this basic scenario—the statute of limitations has run on the present covenants but there is no assertion of title and possession to make a claim on the future covenants actionable—see *Brown v. Lober*, 389 N.E.2d 1188 (Ill. 1979).

We have one more layer to add to our analysis of claims for breach of deed warranties. Consider the following chain of conveyances: Andre conveys Blackacre by general warranty deed to Beth in 2002. Beth then conveys Blackacre by general warranty deed to Carlos in 2013. We can illustrate these conveyances like this:

As it happens, a municipal tax lien was on Blackacre in 2002 when Andre sold the property to Beth. This lien was still on the property when Beth sold the property

We hope that you noticed that Carlos's inability to enforce deed warranties against Beth is a great example of counterparty risk. The warranties in a general warranty deed are only as good, as a practical matter, as the credit of the grantor.

to Carlos in 2013. The municipality is now foreclosing on the tax lien. Carlos, understandably enough, is upset. We know from our prior examples that Carlos has good claims for breach of deed warranties against Beth. The present covenant against encumbrances was violated by the presence of the lien, and the foreclosure action violates the future covenants of general warranty and quiet enjoyment. Let's say, however, that Beth is bankrupt and living on a beach in Bali. As a practical matter, Beth is judgment proof, and Carlos will not be able to get redress against her.

Carlos will, however, be able to sue Andre for breach of at least some of the warranties in the 2002 deed from Andre to Beth. Carlos can sue Andre because the future covenants in a general warranty deed *run with the land* to subsequent owners. Interests that run with the land automatically transfer to subsequent owners of the land. Because future covenants in a general warranty deed run with the land, the future covenants in the Andre-Beth deed run to Carlos as the subsequent owner of Blackacre. The statute of limitations will not be a problem for Carlos because the future covenants cannot be breached (and the statute clock started) until after a lawful claim of title is asserted against the present owner.

Future covenants always run with the land to subsequent owners. Present covenants are a bit more complicated. It is technically incorrect to speak of present covenants running with the land because present covenants are breached, if at all, at the time of conveyance. If anything transfers to a subsequent owner of the property, it is the claim under the present covenant rather than the promise in the covenant itself. It is therefore more accurate to speak of the present covenants being *implicitly assigned* to subsequent owners. Using our example, the idea is that Beth had a claim against Andre under the present covenant against encumbrances. When Beth in turn sold Blackacre to Carlos, this claim against Andre may have been implicitly assigned to Carlos.

There is a split in authority about whether present covenants are implicitly assigned to subsequent owners. The *majority* rule is that present covenants *are not* implicitly assigned. The *minority* rule is that present covenants *are* implicitly assigned. Even in a jurisdiction where present covenants are implicitly assigned, the statute of limitations will often bar a claim by a subsequent owner. Remember that the statute of limitations on present covenant claims starts running from the time of conveyance of the general warranty deed at issue. In our example, the relevant deed for a claim by Carlos against Andre is the deed conveyed in 2002 from Andre to Beth. (Carlos, of course, can't make any claims against *Andre* based on the 2013 deed from Beth to Carlos—Andre didn't make any promises in this later deed.) Using our hypothetical jurisdiction's ten-year statute, any present covenant claim by Carlos against Andre based on the 2002 deed would be time barred. In another scenario, however, where the time period between conveyances was shorter, the statute of limitations might not have run against the person in Carlos's position.

Let's change our example slightly, so that the Beth—Carlos conveyance is a quitclaim deed. Our picture will now look like this:

Obviously, Carlos cannot bring a claim against Beth even if she was not broke and in Bali, because a quitclaim deed has no warranties of title. Can Carlos still sue Andre? The answer is yes—the intervening quitclaim deed has no impact on how the covenants in the Andre-Beth general warranty deed run with the land.

If we can add more links to the chain of title, the covenants behave in the same way. The future covenants in a general warranty deed will run with the land to subsequent owners forever, no matter how many intervening deeds there are in the chain of title. There are, of course, some practical limitations on how far deed warranty liability will extend into the future. First, the title problem must have existed at the time the general warranty deed was conveyed. The grantor of a general warranty deed is promising that there are no title problems at the time the deed is delivered and is making no promises about what title will look like in the future. Second, as time goes by, it will be harder to find and bring a claim against the grantor. The grantor might, for example, have moved away or died. Third, damages for a claim on a deed warranty are limited to the purchase price for that conveyance. As property prices go up over time, the relative value of a claim against a grantor of an old general warranty deed goes down.

SPECIAL WARRANTY DEEDS

We have focused on general warranty deeds in our discussion of deed warranties. Generally speaking, the warranties in a special warranty deed behave in the same way. The scope of the warranties, however, is different, with the grantor only giving warranties against title defects that arose during the grantor's ownership of the property.

The following problem brings all of these issues together. It is helpful to break this and other warranty deed problems into three discrete questions: (1) were any of the covenants violated?; (2) has the statute of limitations run?; and (3) if applicable, did the covenants run with the land (or, in the case of present covenants, were the claims implicitly assigned)? Because issues (2) and (3) will be different for present and future covenants, it makes sense to address each set of covenants separately.

PROBLEM

In 1990, Beatrice bought Wildacre, a ten-acre parcel, from Angela, who conveyed the property by quitclaim deed. In 1996, Beatrice conveyed Wildacre to Cathy by general warranty deed. In 1997, Cathy conveyed Wildacre to Dorothy by general warranty deed. In 2009, Dorothy discovered that there are some problems with Wildacre. Angela had mortgaged Wildacre in 1975. That mortgage was recorded and has never been satisfied. Angela also apparently didn't own two of the ten acres described in her deed to Beatrice. Eleanor, the true owner, brought a suit in 2009 to eject Dorothy from those two acres. Cathy appears to be bankrupt and living in Mongolia, so Dorothy brought suit in 2009 against Beatrice, who is rich and lives down the street. Is Dorothy likely to win against Beatrice? If so, why? If not, why not? *Presume in your answer* that Dorothy would lose an adverse possession claim against Eleanor. The statute of limitations for deed warranty claims in this jurisdiction is 15 years.

An explanatory answer to this problem can be found on page 1055. This exercise has some of the characteristics of a law school exam question. Think about it in those terms. The explanatory answer has some general exam-taking tips.

3. TITLE INSURANCE

Title insurance is just what it sounds like. Insurance companies will issue policies that cover the insured against title risk. Policy holders typically pay a one-time premium at the time of closing. In return, the insurance company agrees to pay litigation costs and cover losses that result from title problems.

Title insurance has several advantages over other methods of title assurance. One advantage is ease of making a claim. Making a claim on an insurance policy is much easier than, say, trying to recover against the grantor of the property under a general warranty deed. Another related advantage is that title insurance has relatively low counterparty risk compared to other methods of title assurance. As we saw in our discussion of deed warranties, general warranty deeds have high counterparty risk because they are only as good as the credit of the grantor. If the grantor is bankrupt and living in Bali, then the deed warranties are worthless. In contrast, title insurance has the credit of the insurance company behind it. To be sure, insurance companies occasionally become insolvent, but this is a rare event and state departments of insurance often will step in to protect the policyholders of an insolvent insurer. In most circumstances, a property owner should be able to quickly and easily make a claim on a title insurance policy.

In part because of these advantages, title insurance has become the most important and widely used method of title assurance in the United States over the last few decades. The ubiquity of title insurance has been aided by the mortgage lending industry, which typically requires title insurance as a condition for issuing a loan. Both the lender and the owner might have their own title insurance policies. Unsurprisingly, a policy insuring a lender is commonly called a *loan policy* or a *lender policy*, while a policy insuring an owner is called an *owner policy*.

Many insurers issue policies that are based on forms from the American Land Title Association (ALTA). These forms are available on ALTA's website: *http://www.alta.org/forms/*. If you take a quick look at the form policies, you will see that they begin with a section called Covered Risks. The following section is called Exclusions From Coverage. Many types of insurance policies are organized this way.

You need to be very careful with any insurance policy to be sure that the coverage that you want is (a) listed in the Covered Risks section and (b) is not later taken back in the Exclusions From Coverage section. Title insurance policies are only helpful if the policy actually covers the title problem that arises.

The exclusions from coverage in title insurance policies can vary widely. Two types of exclusions deserve special mention. The first is that basic title insurance policies often exclude coverage for mechanics' liens. As we explained above, mechanics' liens present special title risks. If mechanics' lien coverage is excluded from the basic policy, the insurer will typically offer separate mechanics' lien coverage at additional cost. Whether it is in the basic policy or offered separately, it is important to be sure that mechanics' liens are covered by the buyer's title insurance if construction or renovation work has recently been done on the property.

The second is that basic title insurance policies often exclude coverage for title risks that would be discoverable from a survey of the property. If the policy contains this exclusion, then the buyer will be out of luck if it turns out that, for example, a neighbor's garage is encroaching onto the property.

One risk that typically is covered by title insurance is *gap risk*. Imagine that you are buying Blackacre. Before closing, you do a diligent title search. You get the deed at closing. Some amount of time will pass before you can get down to the recorder's office to record your deed. This period of time is the "gap." Gap risk is the risk that someone will record an interest in the property during the gap. If that person does not have notice of your interest, then the other interest will probably win against your deed under the applicable Recording Act. You should be sure that this risk is covered by title insurance. The following language from the ATLA form owner's policy establishes coverage for gap risk:

> [The policy insures] against loss or damage, not exceeding the Amount of Insurance, sustained or incurred by the Insured by reason of: . . . Any defect in or lien or encumbrance on the Title or other matter included in [the other provisions establishing coverage] that has been created or attached

or has been filed or recorded in the Public Records subsequent to Date of Policy [the date of the policy is typically the date of closing] and prior to the recording of the deed or other instrument of transfer in the Public Records . . . .

Title insurance policies typically come into force at closing. Returning to our diagram of the phases of a real estate transaction, title insurance provides the buyer with post-closing protection against title defects.

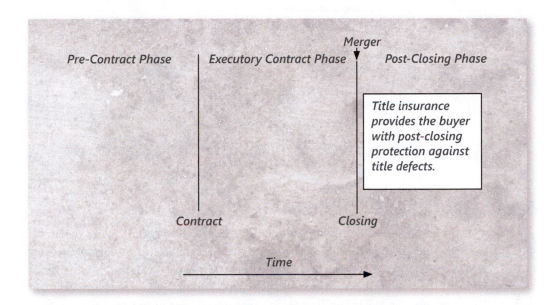

4. SURVEYS AND PHYSICAL INSPECTIONS

Surveys and physical inspections of the property can each play a role in the mitigation of title risk. Surveys can identify encroachment and boundary issues and can indentify discrepancies between the parties' understanding of the property being conveyed and the legal description of the property in the deed. A survey might be especially important if the title insurance policy being used for the transaction excludes coverage for title defects that would have been revealed by a survey.

Less formal physical inspections can also identify potential title issues. For example, a walk around the boundaries of the property (or a look at the property on Google Maps) might reveal an unpaved driveway that is being used by a neighbor pursuant to an unrecorded easement. It also might reveal the physical occupancy of all or part of the property by a tenant pursuant to an unrecorded lease. Recall that physical occupancy can lead to the creation of inquiry notice. A diligent buyer of property will take a look at the property and will take reasonable steps to inquire into potential issues raised by the physical inspection.

Surveys and physical inspections are part of the due diligence process and generally occur during the executory contract phase of a real estate transaction:

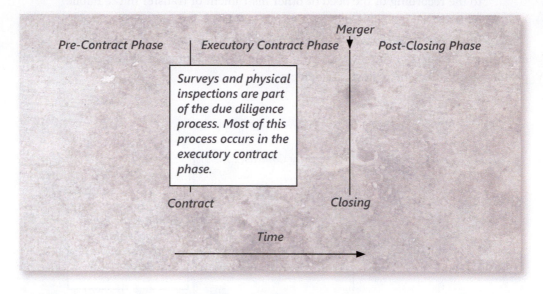

5. SELLER DISCLOSURE LAWS

Many states have enacted laws that require sellers to disclose certain types of defects to buyers. These statutes are typically limited to residential transactions. Because most of the defects covered by the statutes are physical defects, we focus on them in the next section. Some of these laws, however, contain provisions that require disclosure of title defects. The Pennsylvania Seller Disclosure Law that we excerpt in the next section, for example, requires the use of a seller disclosure form that covers "Legal issues affecting title or that would interfere with use and enjoyment of the property." Seller disclosure laws typically require the delivery of the disclosure statement before the parties enter into a purchase and sale contract. In some jurisdictions, then, these laws create a pre-contract method of title assurance. The statutes typically provide an action for money damages as a remedy and do not give the buyer the option to rescind the contract and avoid closing. This remedy is created by statute and as a result is not affected by merger. A buyer therefore can bring a lawsuit for nondisclosure either pre- or post-closing (subject, of course, to the applicable statute of limitations).

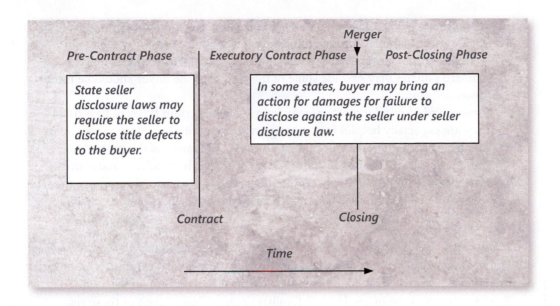

6. SUMMARY: TITLE ASSURANCE

As we have seen, buyers have several methods of protecting themselves against title risk.

- The *recording system* provides the backbone of our system of title assurance. A *diligent title search* should reveal all recorded documents affecting title. The seller's obligation to deliver *marketable title* typically allows the buyer to back out of the transaction if an undisclosed title defect is discovered. So long as the requirements of the applicable *Recording Act* are met, the buyer should be protected against prior unrecorded interests. The recording system and Recording Acts, however, do not provide perfect title protection. Buyers on inquiry notice of a prior interest, for example, will not be protected by a notice or race-notice statute. The recording acts also do not protect against certain types of title defects—for example, encroachments.
- *Deed warranties* may allow the buyer to seek recourse against the seller for title defects. Because of the *merger doctrine*, deed warranties are typically the buyer's only avenue to obtain recourse against the seller post-closing. Perhaps the biggest weakness of a warranty deed as a method of title assurance is counterparty risk. A general warranty deed from an insolvent or absent grantor isn't going to be of much use to the grantee.

- *Title insurance* is increasingly the most important method of obtaining post-closing title assurance. It has significantly lower counterparty risk than a warranty deed. The biggest potential downside of title insurance is that the standard policies may exclude some of the risks that the buyer should be most concerned about.
- *Surveys and physical inspections* may help mitigate certain types of title risks. They are especially helpful in revealing encroachments, boundary issues, and unrecorded interests reflected by physical occupancy of the property. These problems might not be addressed by other methods of title assurance.
- *State seller disclosure laws* may require the seller to disclose title issues to the buyer and may provide the buyer with an action for money damages against the seller for failure to comply.

None of these methods of title assurance is perfect. A diligent buyer will typically use all of them in combination. Taken together, they provide a diligent buyer with a high degree of protection against title risk. (See sidebar on layers of risk mitigation.)

The following version of our by now familiar diagram places each of these risk mitigation strategies into the three phases of a real estate transaction.

LAYERS OF RISK MITIGATION

Risk mitigation methods are rarely perfect, and each method to mitigate a given risk will tend to have its own strengths and weaknesses. As a result, a person will often want to take several steps to mitigate a particular risk. Taken together, the strengths of each step will cancel out some of the weaknesses of the others, leaving the person well protected against the risk. A common metaphor for this approach to risk mitigation involves slices of Swiss cheese. (Don't believe us that the metaphor is common? Look up "Swiss Cheese Model" on Wikipedia.) Imagine that you cut ten slices off of a block of Swiss cheese. Each slice of cheese has small holes in it. Now imagine that you made a stack of the slices, but rather than stacking them neatly, you just tossed them into a loose pile. Because of the loose stacking, and the nonuniform occurrence of holes within the cheese, it is likely that there will not be a hole that goes all the way through your stack of ten slices. In other words, it is unlikely that you could look down through your stack of cheese and see all the way to the counter. Each slice of cheese in this metaphor represents a layer of mitigating a risk. None of the layers is perfect, and each has holes in it. Each layer of mitigation, however, has different holes, typically located in different locations. Taken together, the imperfect layers add up to strong mitigation of the risk. If, by the way, you find this metaphor kind of cheesy, sorry—that just can't be helped.

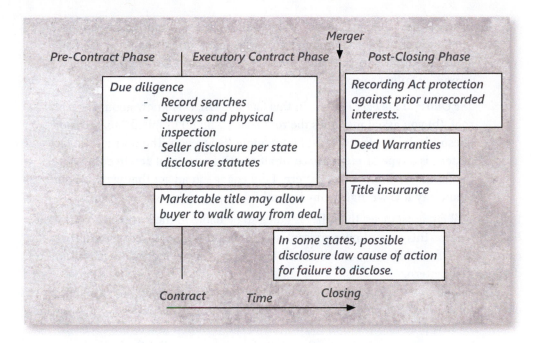

D. PHYSICAL CONDITION ISSUES

Our second major risk in a real estate transaction is physical condition risk. Physical defects (foundation cracks, termites, lead paint, leaky roofs, etc.) are the most common manifestation of physical condition risk. In this section, we will focus on the legal issues surrounding physical defects. We will then briefly consider a few other issues relating to the physical condition of the property.

1. DUTY TO DISCLOSE PHYSICAL DEFECTS—FROM CAVEAT EMPTOR TO STATE DISCLOSURE STATUTES

Say that you buy a house from me. After closing, you discover that the roof leaks. Can you sue me and recover the cost of repairing the roof?

The answer depends in significant part on whether I had a *duty to disclose* the leaky roof to you. Generally speaking, I don't have any obligation to convey the house to you in perfect physical condition, so the mere fact that the roof leaks typically won't give you a claim against me. If, however, I knew about the problem, failed to disclose it to you and had a duty to disclose the problem to you, then you will likely have a claim against me.

At the outset, we need to distinguish between two basic fact patterns:

The Failure to Disclose Fact Pattern. In this fact pattern, (a) I knew about the leaky roof, (b) you didn't ask me about it, and (c) I didn't tell you about it. Failure to disclose is a type of *nonfeasance*, or failure to act. I did not engage in any affirmative act that we could point to and say "that was wrongful." My failure to act does not, however, mean that I am off the hook. If I had a duty to disclose to you, and I failed to do so, then I have committed a wrong by failing to act.

The Outright Lie Fact Pattern. In this fact pattern, (a) I knew about the leaky roof, (b) you asked me "does the roof leak?," and (c) I replied "no, the roof doesn't leak." In other words, I knowingly lied to you. The outright lie fact pattern is a type of *misfeasance*, or affirmative wrongful act. In contrast to the failure to disclose fact pattern, I did engage in an act that we can point to and say it is wrongful—my untruthful response to your question.

In almost all circumstances, the seller is going to be liable to the buyer in an outright lie fact pattern. This type of misrepresentation typically supports a cause of action for common-law fraud. The rest of our discussion focuses on the more difficult failure to disclose fact pattern.

The obligation of a seller of residential real property to disclose physical defects has changed over time. We can divide this evolution into three phases:

1. The first phase lasted from the origins of the common law to the 1960s. In this phase, the common-law doctrine of *caveat emptor* (let the buyer beware) prevailed in the real property context. Under this doctrine, sellers had no duty to disclose physical defects.

2. The second phase began in the 1960s when courts began to change the law to require sellers to disclose material defects in residential transactions. In this phase, the common-law doctrine of *caveat emptor* began to erode in the residential context.

3. The third phase began in the mid-1980s, when states began to enact statutes that require mandatory disclosure of physical defects. Although these statutes did not displace the common-law rules on disclosure, they are now the most important source of disclosure obligations in most states.

For a detailed analysis of these developments, see George Lefcoe, *Property Condition Disclosure Forms: How the Real Estate Industry Eased the Transition From Caveat Emptor to "Seller Tell All,"* 39 Real Prop. Prob. & Tr. J. 193 (2004).

Because *caveat emptor* no longer applies in most jurisdictions in the residential context, we will not take a close look at it here. It is enough for you to know two things. First, that historically there was no obligation to disclose physical defects in real estate transactions. Second, that *caveat emptor is still widely applied in the commercial context.* If you are buying a shopping mall, you should assume that the seller has no duty to disclose physical defects. You will need to perform your own due diligence about the physical condition of the property. This due diligence can involve asking questions of the seller. Remember the distinction between the failure to disclose and the outright lie fact patterns. Even where *caveat emptor* applies, the seller cannot affirmatively lie about the physical condition of the property.

In our next case, the Supreme Court of Florida rejected *caveat emptor* in the residential context. It is a good example of the court-driven changes that happened during the second phase of the evolution of the duty to disclose.

JOHNSON V. DAVIS

Supreme Court of Florida, 1985
480 So. 2d 625

ADKINS, Justice. In May of 1982, the Davises entered into a contract to buy for $310,000 the Johnsons' home, which at the time was three years old. The contract required a $5,000 deposit payment, an additional $26,000 deposit payment within five days and a closing by June 21, 1982. The crucial provision of the contract, for the purposes of the case at bar, is Paragraph F which provided:

> F. Roof Inspection: Prior to closing at Buyer's expense, Buyer shall have the right to obtain a written report from a licensed roofer stating that the roof is in a watertight condition. In the event repairs are required either to correct leaks or to replace damage to facia or soffit, seller shall pay for said repairs which shall be performed by a licensed roofing contractor.

The contract further provided for payment to the "prevailing party" of all costs and reasonable fees in any contract litigation.

Before the Davises made the additional $26,000 deposit payment, Mrs. Davis noticed some buckling and peeling plaster around the corner of a window frame in the family room and stains on the ceilings in the family room and kitchen of the home. Upon inquiring, Mrs. Davis was told by Mr. Johnson that the window had had a minor problem that had long since been corrected and that the stains were wallpaper glue and the result of ceiling beams being moved. There is disagreement among the parties as to whether Mr. Johnson also told Mrs. Davis at this time that there had never been any problems with the roof or ceilings. The Davises thereafter paid the remainder of their deposit and the Johnsons vacated the home. Several days later, following a heavy rain, Mrs. Davis entered the home and discovered water "gushing" in from around the window frame, the ceiling of the family room, the light fixtures, the glass doors, and the stove in the kitchen.

Two roofers hired by the Johnsons' broker concluded that for under $1,000 they could "fix" certain leaks in the roof and by doing so make the roof "watertight." Three roofers hired by the Davises found that the roof was inherently defective, that any repairs would be temporary because the roof was "slipping," and that only a new $15,000 roof could be "watertight."

The Davises filed a complaint alleging breach of contract, fraud and misrepresentation, and sought recission of the contract and return of their deposit. The Johnsons counterclaimed seeking the deposit as liquidated damages.

The trial court entered its final judgment on May 27, 1983. The court made no findings of fact, but awarded the Davises $26,000 plus interest and awarded the Johnsons $5,000 plus interest. Each party was to bear their own attorneys' fees.

The Johnsons appealed and the Davises cross-appealed from the final judgment. The Third District found for the Davises affirming the trial court's return of the majority of the deposit to the Davises ($26,000), and reversing the award of $5,000 to the Johnsons as well as the court's failure to award the Davises costs and fees. Accordingly, the court remanded with directions to return to the Davises the balance of their deposit and to award them costs and fees.

The trial court included no findings of fact in its order. However, the district court inferred from the record that the trial court refused to accept the Davises' characterization of the roof inspection provision of the contract. The district court noted that if there was a breach, the trial court would have ordered the return of the Davises' entire deposit because there is no way to distinguish the two deposit payments under a breach of contract theory. We agree with this interpretation and further find no error by the trial court in this respect.

The contract contemplated the possibility that the roof may not be watertight at the time of inspection and provided a remedy if it was not in such a condition. The roof inspection provision of the contract did not impose any obligation beyond the seller correcting the leaks and replacing damage to the facia or soffit. The record is devoid of any evidence that the seller refused to make needed repairs to the roof. In fact, the record reflects that the Davises' never even demanded that the areas of leakage be repaired either by way of repair or replacement. Yet the Davises insist that the Johnsons breached the contract justifying recission. We find this contention to be without merit.

We also agree with the district court's conclusions under a theory of fraud and find that the Johnsons' statements to the Davises regarding the condition of the roof constituted a fraudulent misrepresentation entitling respondents to the return of their $26,000 deposit payment. In the state of Florida, relief for a fraudulent misrepresentation may be granted only when the following elements are present: (1) a false statement concerning a material fact; (2) the representor's knowledge that the representation is false; (3) an intention that the representation induce another to act on it; and, (4) consequent injury by the party acting in reliance on the representation. *See Huffstetler v. Our Home Life Ins. Co.*, 67 Fla. 324, 65 So. 1 (1914).

The evidence adduced at trial shows that after the buyer and the seller signed the purchase and sales agreement and after receiving the $5,000 initial deposit payment the Johnsons affirmatively repeated to the Davises that there were no problems with the roof. The Johnsons subsequently received the additional $26,000 deposit payment from the Davises. The record reflects that the statement made by the Johnsons was a false representation of material fact, made with knowledge of its falsity, upon which the Davises relied to their detriment as evidenced by the $26,000 paid to the Johnsons.

The doctrine of caveat emptor does not exempt a seller from responsibility for the statements and representations which he makes to induce the buyer to act, when under the circumstances these amount to fraud in the legal sense. To be grounds for relief, the false representations need not have been made at the time of the signing of the purchase and sales agreement in order for the element of reliance to be present. The fact that the false statements as to the quality of the roof were made after the signing of the purchase and sales agreement does not excuse the seller from liability when the misrepresentations were made prior to the execution of the contract by conveyance of the property. It would be contrary to all notions of fairness and justice for this Court to place its stamp of approval on an affirmative misrepresentation by a wrongdoer just because it was made after the signing of the executory contract when all of the necessary elements for actionable fraud are present. Furthermore, the Davises' reliance on the truth of the Johnsons' representation was justified and is supported by this Court's decision in *Besett v. Basnett*, 389 So.2d 995 (1980), where we held "that a recipient may rely on the truth of a representation, even though its falsity could have been ascertained had he made an investigation, unless he knows the representation to be false or its falsity is obvious to him." *Id.* at 998.

In determining whether a seller of a home has a duty to disclose latent material defects to a buyer, the established tort law distinction between misfeasance and nonfeasance, action and inaction must carefully be analyzed. The highly individualistic philosophy of the earlier common law consistently imposed liability upon the commission of affirmative acts of harm, but shrank from converting the courts into an institution for forcing men to help one another. This distinction is deeply rooted in our case law. Liability for nonfeasance has therefore been slow to receive recognition in the evolution of tort law.

In theory, the difference between misfeasance and nonfeasance, action and inaction is quite simple and obvious; however, in practice it is not always easy to draw the line and determine whether conduct is active or passive. That is, where failure to disclose a material fact is calculated to induce a false belief, the distinction between concealment and affirmative representations is tenuous. Both proceed from the same motives and are attended with the same consequences; both are violative of the principles of fair dealing and good faith; both are calculated to produce the same result; and, in fact, both essentially have the same effect.

Still there exists in much of our case law the old tort notion that there can be no liability for nonfeasance. The courts in some jurisdictions, including Florida, hold that where the parties are dealing at arms's length and the facts lie equally open to both parties, with equal opportunity of examination, mere nondisclosure does not constitute a fraudulent concealment. *See Ramel v. Chasebrook Construction Co.*, 135 So.2d 876 (Fla. 2d DCA 1961). The Fourth District affirmed that rule of law in *Banks v. Salina*, 413 So.2d 851 (Fla. 4th DCA 1982), and found that although the sellers had sold a home without disclosing the presence of a defective roof and swimming pool of which the sellers had knowledge, "[i]n Florida, there is no duty to disclose when parties are dealing at arms length." *Id.* at 852.

These unappetizing cases are not in tune with the times and do not conform with current notions of justice, equity and fair dealing. One should not be able to stand behind the impervious shield of caveat emptor and take advantage of another's ignorance. Our courts have taken great strides since the days when the judicial emphasis was on rigid rules and ancient precedents. Modern concepts of justice and fair dealing have given our courts the opportunity and latitude to change legal precepts in order to conform to society's needs. Thus, the tendency of the more recent cases has been to restrict rather than extend the doctrine of caveat emptor. The law appears to be working toward the ultimate conclusion that full disclosure of all material facts must be made whenever elementary fair conduct demands it.

The harness placed on the doctrine of caveat emptor in a number of other jurisdictions has resulted in the seller of a home being liable for failing to disclose material defects of which he is aware. This philosophy was succinctly expressed in *Lingsch v. Savage*, 213 Cal.App.2d 729, 29 Cal.Rptr. 201 (1963):

> It is now settled in California that where the seller knows of facts materially affecting the value or desirability of the property which are known or accessible only to him and also knows that such facts are not known to or within the reach of the diligent attention and observation of the buyer, the seller is under a duty to disclose them to the buyer.

In *Posner v. Davis*, 76 Ill.App.3d 638, 32 Ill.Dec. 186, 395 N.E.2d 133 (1979), buyers brought an action alleging that the sellers of a home fraudulently concealed certain defects in the home which included a leaking roof and basement flooding. Relying on Lingsch, the court concluded that the sellers knew of and failed to disclose latent material defects and thus were liable for fraudulent concealment. *Id.* 32 Ill.Dec. at 190, 395 N.E.2d at 137. Numerous other jurisdictions have followed this view in formulating law involving the sale of homes. *See Flakus v. Schug*, 213 Neb. 491, 329 N.W.2d 859 (1983) (basement flooding); *Thacker v. Tyree*, 297 S.E.2d 885 (W.Va.1982) (cracked walls and foundation problems); *Maguire v. Masino*, 325 So.2d 844 (La.Ct.App.1975) (termite infestation); *Weintraub v. Krobatsch*, 64 N.J. 445, 317 A.2d 68 (1974) (roach infestation); *Cohen v. Vivian*, 141 Colo. 443, 349 P.2d 366 (1960) (soil defect).

We are of the opinion, in view of the reasoning and results in Lingsch, Posner and the aforementioned cases decided in other jurisdictions, that the same philosophy regarding the sale of homes should also be the law in the state of Florida. Accordingly, we hold that where the seller of a home knows of facts materially affecting the value of the property which are not readily observable and are not known to the buyer, the seller is under a duty to disclose them to the buyer. This duty is equally applicable to all forms of real property, new and used.

In the case at bar, the evidence shows that the Johnsons knew of and failed to disclose that there had been problems with the roof of the house. Mr. Johnson admitted during his testimony that the Johnsons were aware of roof problems prior to entering into the contract of sale and receiving the $5,000 deposit payment. Thus, we agree with the district court and find that the Johnsons' fraudulent concealment also entitles the Davises to the return of the $5,000 deposit payment plus interest. We further find that the Davises should be awarded costs and fees.

The decision of the Third District Court of Appeal is hereby approved.

It is so ordered.

[The dissenting opinion of Chief Justice Boyd is omitted].

NOTES

1. *Contract vs. Tort.* Note that the Davises made two types of claims. First, the Davises made a contract claim seeking rescission based on the roof inspection provision of the contract. Under this provision, the Johnsons were obligated to pay for repair the roof if the Davises requested it. The court rejected this claim because it concluded that the Davises had never requested that the Johnsons comply with this provision of the contract and that the Johnsons therefore could not have been in breach. Second, the Davises made tort claims of fraud and misrepresentation. The facts supported a judgment against the Johnsons for misfeasance because Mr. Johnson appeared to lie about the existing problems with the roof. The court went out of its way to hold that the Johnsons also had a duty to disclose the water problems and therefore would have been liable even for nonfeasance. Under this holding, both misfeasance and nonfeasance would support a misrepresentation claim.

The distinction between these two types of claims raises two points about remedies. First, while there are some circumstances where nondisclosure will support rescission of the contract, damages are a more typical remedy for failure to disclose a material defect. As we will see below, state disclosure statutes typically limit the remedy for nondisclosure to money damages. Second, because misrepresentation claims (of both the misfeasance and nonfeasance varieties) are tort claims, they are not subject to merger. A buyer can make a misrepresentation claim for damages after closing.

REMEDIES

2. *Knowledge, Materiality, and Latency.* In jurisdictions that adopted a common-law duty to disclose, the seller was obligated to disclose defects that were *known, material,* and *latent.* It stands to reason that a seller would only be obligated to disclose known defects—as a practical matter, a seller cannot disclose defects that she does not know about. Materiality is a concept that you will see in many areas of the law. The materiality requirement is intended to relieve the seller of the obligation to disclose minor defects. Depending on the jurisdiction, material might be established through an objective standard (the defect would be important to any reasonable buyer of the property)

or a subjective standard (the defect would be material to the specific buyer in the transaction). The latency requirement is intended to relieve the seller of the obligation to disclose obvious defects. Latent defects are those that could not be discovered through reasonable investigation. Patent defects are those that could be discovered through reasonable investigation. As you might imagine, any of these three issues—whether the seller knew of the defect, whether the defect was material, and whether the defect was latent—might be hard to pin down in litigation.

In the mid-1980s, states began to enact mandatory disclosure laws. These state disclosure laws represent the third phase of the evolution of the duty to disclose in residential real estate transactions. The effort to pass these laws was led by the National Association of Realtors. The Realtors were motivated to push for these laws in significant part because of a series of cases where courts held that both the sellers *and their brokers* could be held liable for failure to disclose material defects. The disclosure laws typically have provisions protecting brokers and agents from this kind of liability.

Despite the Realtors' self-interest in getting the seller disclosure laws passed, the laws themselves represent a positive development in residential real estate law and practice. The laws typically require a seller to disclose material defects. They also typically mandate the creation of a *seller disclosure form*. These forms are not limited to defects and provide for the disclosure of a wide range of fact relating to the physical condition of the property. Seller disclosure forms are increasingly used even in jurisdictions that do not have seller disclosure laws. The disclosure forms are typically given to potential buyers before the parties enter into a purchase and sale contract. Through these forms, buyers in residential real estate transactions today typically receive a wealth of information about the property at a very early stage in the transaction.

Pennsylvania's Real Estate Seller Disclosure Law is typical of the laws passed as part of the Realtors' efforts. Excerpts from this law, annotated by our comments, follow:

68 Pa.C.S.A. §7102

Definitions

Subject to additional definitions contained in subsequent provisions of this part which are applicable to specific provisions of this part, the following words and phrases when used in this part shall have the meanings given to them in this section unless the context clearly indicates otherwise:

"Agent." Any broker, associate broker or salesperson, as defined in the act of February 19, 1980 (P.L. 15, No. 9), [63 P.S. §455.101 et seq.] known as the Real Estate Licensing and Registration Act. . . .

"Material defect." A problem with a residential real property or any portion of it that would have a significant adverse impact on the value of the property or that involves an unreasonable risk to people on the property. The fact that a structural element, system or subsystem is near, at or beyond the end of the normal useful life of such a structural element, system or subsystem is not by itself a material defect. . . .

68 Pa.C.S.A. §7301

Short title of chapter. This chapter shall be known and may be cited as the Real Estate Seller Disclosure Law.

68 Pa.C.S.A. §7302

Application of chapter

(a) General rule.—This chapter shall apply to all residential real estate transfers except the following:

(1) Transfers by a fiduciary in the course of the administration of a decedent's estate, guardianship, conservatorship or trust.

(2) Transfers of new residential construction that has not been previously occupied when:

(i) the buyer has received a one-year or longer written warranty covering such construction;

(ii) the dwelling has been inspected for compliance with the applicable building code or, if there is no applicable code, for compliance with a nationally recognized model building code; and

(iii) a certificate of occupancy or a certificate of code compliance has been issued for the dwelling. . . .

68 Pa.C.S.A. §7303

Disclosure of material defects

Any seller who intends to transfer any interest in real property shall disclose to the buyer any material defects with the property known to the seller by completing all applicable items in a property disclosure statement which satisfies the requirements of section 7304 (relating to disclosure form). A signed and dated copy of the property disclosure statement shall be delivered to the buyer in accordance with section 7305 (relating to delivery of disclosure form) prior to the signing of an agreement of transfer by the seller and buyer with respect to the property.

> The definition of *material defect* is one of the most important provisions of this law. Note that it is phrased objectively and focuses on significant negative impact on value and risk to people on the property (implicitly to their physical safety).

> This law, like other seller disclosure laws enacted throughout the country, applies only to residential real estate transactions.

> This section creates an obligation in the seller to disclose material defects and to deliver a disclosure statement to the buyer. Note the language "known to the seller"— the seller cannot be expected to disclose something that the seller does not know about.

68 Pa.C.S.A. §7304

Disclosure form

(a) General rule.—A form of property disclosure statement that satisfies the requirements of this chapter shall be promulgated by the State Real Estate Commission. Nothing in this chapter shall preclude a seller from using a form of property disclosure statement that contains additional provisions that require greater specificity or that call for the disclosure of the condition or existence of other features of the property.

(b) Contents of property disclosure statement.—The form of property disclosure statement promulgated by the State Real Estate Commission shall call for disclosures with respect to all of the following subjects:

(1) Seller's expertise in contracting, engineering, architecture or other areas related to the construction and conditions of the property and its improvements.

(2) When the property was last occupied by the seller.

> This list provides a good overview of the most common and important areas of physical condition issues in residential real estate transactions. Note that subparagraphs (15) and (16) go beyond physical condition. Subparagraph (15) requires disclosure if the residence is governed by a condominium or other homeowners association. Subparagraph (16) requires disclosure of *title issues*. Seller disclosure laws therefore have a role in our system of title assurance. We discuss this further in the notes following our excerpts from the statute.

(3) Roof.

(4) Basements and crawl spaces.

(5) Termites/wood destroying insects, dry rot and pests.

(6) Structural problems.

(7) Additions, remodeling and structural changes to the property.

(8) Water and sewage systems or service.

(9) Plumbing system.

(10) Heating and air conditioning.

(11) Electrical system.

(12) Other equipment and appliances included in the sale.

(13) Soils, drainage and boundaries.

(14) Presence of hazardous substances.

(15) Condominiums and other homeowners associations.

(16) Legal Issues affecting title or that would interfere with use and enjoyment of the property. . . .

68 Pa.C.S.A. §7305

Delivery of disclosure form

(a) Method of delivery.—The seller shall deliver the property disclosure statement to the buyer by personal delivery; first class mail; certified mail, return receipt requested; or facsimile transmission to the buyer or the buyer's agent.

(b) Parties to whom delivered.—For purposes of this chapter, delivery to one prospective buyer or buyer's agent is deemed delivery to all persons intending to take title as co-tenants, joint tenants or as a tenant by the entireties with the buyer. Receipt may be acknowledged on the statement, in an agreement of transfer for the residential real property or shown in any other verifiable manner.

68 Pa.C.S.A. §7306

Information unavailable to seller

If at the time the disclosures are required to be made, an item of information required to be disclosed is unknown or not available to the seller, the seller may make a disclosure based on the best information available to the seller.

68 Pa.C.S.A. §7307

Information subsequently rendered inaccurate

If information disclosed in accordance with this chapter is subsequently rendered inaccurate prior to final settlement as a result of any act, occurrence or agreement subsequent to the delivery of the required disclosures, the seller shall notify the buyer of the inaccuracy.

68 Pa.C.S.A. §7308

Affirmative duty of seller

The seller is not obligated by this chapter to make any specific investigation or inquiry in an effort to complete the property disclosure statement. In completing the property disclosure statement, the seller shall not make any representations that the seller or the agent for the seller knows or has reason to know are false, deceptive or misleading and shall not fail to disclose a known material defect.

68 Pa.C.S.A. §7309

Nonliability of seller

(a) General rule.—A seller shall not be liable for any error, inaccuracy or omission of any information delivered pursuant to this chapter if:

(1) the seller had no knowledge of the error, inaccuracy or omission;
(2) the error, inaccuracy or omission was based on a reasonable belief that a material defect or other matter not disclosed had been corrected; or
(3) the error, inaccuracy or omission was based on information provided by a public agency, home inspector, contractor or person registered or licensed under [applicable law] about matters within the scope of the agency's jurisdiction or such other person's occupation and the seller had no knowledge of the error, inaccuracy or omission. . . .

68 Pa.C.S.A. §7310

Nonliability of agent

An agent of a seller or a buyer shall not be liable for any violation of this chapter unless the agent had actual knowledge of a material defect that was not disclosed to the buyer or of a misrepresentation relating to a material defect.

68 Pa.C.S.A. §7311

Failure to comply

(a) General rule.—A residential real estate transfer subject to this chapter shall not be invalidated solely because of the failure of any person to comply with any provision of this chapter. However, any person who willfully or negligently violates or fails to perform any duty prescribed by any provision of this chapter shall be liable in the amount of actual damages suffered by the buyer as a result of a violation of this chapter. This subsection shall not be construed so as to restrict or expand the authority of a court to impose punitive damages or apply other remedies applicable under any other provision of law.

(b) Statute of limitations.—An action for damages as a result of a violation of this chapter must be commenced within two years after the date of final settlement [i.e., closing]. . . .

This type of limitation on agent liability was the motivation for the National Association of Realtors to lead the effort to get seller disclosure laws passed throughout the country.

This provision creates the remedy for failure to comply with the statutory disclosure obligations. The first sentence prevents the buyer from using the seller's failure to disclose to invalidate the transaction, either pre- or post-closing. The second sentence gives the buyer a claim against the seller for actual money damages that the buyer suffers from the undisclosed material defect.

In addition to establishing a statute of limitations, this provision makes it clear that the buyer may sue the seller for failure to disclose after closing. As a statutory remedy, the buyer's claim against the seller is not affected by merger.

68 Pa.C.S.A. §7313

Specification of items for disclosure no limitation on other disclosure obligations

(a) General rule.—The specification of items for disclosure in this chapter or in any form of property disclosure statement promulgated by the State Real Estate Commission does not limit or abridge any obligation for disclosure created by any other provision of law or that may exist in order to avoid fraud, misrepresentation or deceit in the transaction. . . .

68 Pa.C.S.A. §7314

Cause of action

A buyer shall not have a cause of action under this chapter against the seller or the agent for either or both of the seller or the buyer for:

(1) material defects to the property disclosed to the buyer prior to the signing of an agreement of transfer by the seller and buyer;

(2) material defects that develop after the signing of the agreement of transfer by the seller and buyer; or

(3) material defects that occur after final settlement [i.e., closing].

This paragraph makes it clear that the Seller Disclosure Law does not undercut other disclosure obligations created by statutory or common law. Among other things, this means that the existing common-law obligations to disclose still apply. In most circumstances, however, a seller who complies with the Seller Disclosure Law will also comply with common-law disclosure obligations.

This section establishes three clear areas on nonliability for the seller. The first and third are intuitive. The whole point of the law is to obligate the seller to disclose material defects, so it makes sense that the seller would not be liable for defects that were actually disclosed. It also makes sense that the seller would not be liable for defects that arise after closing, when the seller is no longer the owner of the property. The second might not make as much intuitive sense. Why should the seller be off the hook for a defect that arises after the contract is signed but before closing? You should also consider how the obligation to correct disclosures in §7307 might apply to a defect that arises during the executory contract period. Keep in mind as well that seller disclosure laws provide a baseline of protection for the buyer. As we will see shortly, the buyer can negotiate for additional protection in the purchase and sale contract.

NOTES

1. *Nonphysical Problems.* We already touched on this, but it bears repeating that the Seller Disclosure Law is not limited to physical defects, with §7304(b)(16) requiring the inclusion of title issues in the scope of the seller disclosure statement promulgated under the law.

2. *Knowledge, Materiality, and Latency Revisited.* In our discussion of the common-law duty to disclose, above, we noted that the seller had an obligation to disclose defects that were known, material, and latent. The Pennsylvania Seller Disclosure Law maintains the knowledge and materiality requirements (§§7102, 7303). It does not, however, include any explicit latency requirement. To the contrary, the approach taken in the seller disclosure statement promulgated under the law is to encourage the disclosure of any defect, latent or patent.

The seller disclosure laws do two distinct things. First, they create liability for the seller for nondisclosure of material defects. Second, they mandate the creation and use of *seller disclosure forms.* These forms are now in wide use even in jurisdictions that do not have seller disclosure laws. The forms are very broad and go beyond the disclosure of material defects by requiring the seller to answer a series of questions about the property.

The Pennsylvania form is a good example. Take a look at the form at *http://www. parealtor.org/clientuploads/StandardForms/Sample_Forms/SPD.pdf.* This form gives the buyer a tremendous amount of information about the property before the parties enter into a purchase and sale contract.

It is worth pausing to consider how the law on the seller's duty to disclose has radically transformed over a relatively short period of time. Prior to the 1960s, *caveat emptor* was the rule in real estate transactions, and the seller had no duty to disclose at all. Beginning in the 1960s, *caveat emptor* began to erode, and state courts started to impose a duty on sellers in residential transactions to disclose material defects. This erosion of *caveat emptor* was not universal, and the doctrine still survives in the common law of some states. Beginning in the 1980s, state seller disclosure laws and the increasing use of seller disclosure statements led, as a matter of both law and practice, to a broad obligation on residential sellers to disclose a wide range of facts about the property to the buyer. This trend, we should note, is not universal. Massachusetts, for example, does not have a seller disclosure law and still adheres to the common law of *caveat emptor.* Throughout most of the United States, however, comprehensive seller disclosure has become the norm in residential real estate transactions.

PERCOLATION TESTS AND THE QUALITY OF THE LAND

So far, we have focused on the physical condition of buildings and other improvements on the property. There may be issues with the physical condition of the land, as well. It would be very hard, if not impossible, for example, to build on land that is located on a cliff. One common issue related to the quality of land deserves special mention. A percolation test, or perc test for short, is used to determine whether the land is suitable for an on-site septic system. Every building needs to address the disposal of sewage. If the building cannot be connected to municipal sewage systems, then the building typically will need to have an on-site septic system. Most of the wastewater from the septic system will drain into the soil. Municipalities typically allow septic systems only where the water will drain within a certain range of rates—not too slow and not too fast. A perc test is performed by digging or drilling holes in the soil, filling these holes with water, and then timing how long it takes for the water to drain (or percolate) into the soil. Especially in rural areas, the ability of land to pass a perc test is a big deal—it often determines whether or not the owner can build on the property.

2. INSPECTION CONTINGENCIES

Both *Johnson v. Davis* and the Pennsylvania Seller Disclosure law contemplate money damages, rather than rescission of the contract, as a remedy for nondisclosure of a physical defect. The buyer, however, can negotiate for the ability to back out of the transaction without penalty. One method of achieving this result is through an *inspection contingency*. Contingencies are contract provisions that allow one party to withdraw from the contract if certain conditions are met. Inspection contingencies allow the buyer to perform one or more types of inspection of the property and to withdraw from the contract if the results of the inspection are not satisfactory. The contract typically places a tight time limit (often ten days) on the exercise of the contingency. This time limit protects the seller by forcing the buyer to complete the inspection, and to decide whether to withdraw from the contract if any problems are found, quickly.

Form purchase and sale contracts often contain multiple inspection contingencies. Pennsylvania's form contract, for example, has a provision contemplating a general inspection into the physical condition of the home and potential presence of environmental hazards, then has specific provisions for inspections related to wood infestation, radon, water service, on-lot sewage, property boundaries, land use restrictions, and lead paint. The contract gives the buyer three options once the inspections are complete: (a) accept the property, (b) terminate the agreement and have all deposit monies returned, or (c) request a corrective proposal from the seller.

Inspection contingencies present two practical issues that are important to bear in mind. First, inspection contingencies are often so broad that they can serve as buyer's remorse clauses, giving the buyer the ability to construct a reason to back out of a contract that they are having second thoughts about. Even if the buyer's asserted reason for withdrawing is questionable at best, the seller typically isn't going to want to litigate the issue. The breadth of inspection contingencies highlights the importance of placing short time limits on their exercise. Having a ten-day period for the buyer to back out is one thing; having a two-month period is another. Second, the results of home inspections are often used by buyers as a tool to seek a reduction in the purchase price of the property. If the buyer requests a reduction in price, then the seller has to decide whether to agree or to refuse and risk the buyer walking away from the deal.

MORTGAGE CONTINGENCIES

Another type of contingency common in real estate transactions is a mortgage contingency. As its name implies, this contingency allows the buyer to back out of the deal if she is not able to obtain mortgage financing on particular terms for the purchase of the property.

REPRESENTATIONS, WARRANTIES, COVENANTS, AND INDEMNITIES

Real estate contracts contain a variety of types of promises. These promises are often labeled representations, warranties, covenants, or indemnities. Although usage can vary from contract to contract, here is a brief explanation of what these labels mean:

In brief, a *representation* is a statement of current fact, such as, "The Seller represents that there are no tenants currently occupying any portion of the property." A *warranty* is a statement or promise of a future fact, such as, "The Seller warrants that there will be no tenants occupying any portion of the property on the closing date," although the terms "representation" and "warranty" often are used interchangeably. A *covenant* is a promise of future action, such as, "The Seller covenants that it will remove all tenants currently occupying any portion of the property by the closing date." An *indemnity* is a promise to make the other party whole in the event that a representation or warranty proves to be untrue or a covenant is not performed. For example, the contract might state, "The Seller agrees to indemnify the Buyer and hold the Buyer harmless against any expenses that it incurs, including reasonable attorneys' fees and costs, if any of the Seller's representations or warranties are untrue."

Gregory Stein, Morton P. Fisher, Jr. & Marjorie P. Fisher, *A Practical Guide to Commercial Real Estate Transactions* 29 (2008).

"AS IS" CLAUSES

Real estate contracts often have a clause stating that the buyer is accepting the property "as is" and in its current condition. These clauses protect sellers against certain types of claims but not others. One type of claim that a buyer could make is based on an express or implied warranty regarding the condition of the property. That is, the buyer could make a claim arguing that the seller expressly or impliedly promised that the property would be in a certain condition. "As is" clauses generally are effective in barring this kind of claim against the seller. A second type of claim is based on affirmative misrepresentation or failure to disclose. These are the type of claim that we have been discussing in this section. "As is" clauses generally *will not* protect the seller against a misrepresentation or nondisclosure claim. *See generally* Frank J. Wozniak, *Construction and Effect of Provision in Contract for Sale of Realty by Which Purchaser Agrees to Take Property "As Is" or in its Existing Condition*, 8 A.L.R.5th 312.

3. THE STIGMA ISSUE

So far, we have focused on tangible defects in the property. Should sellers have a duty to disclose "defects" that might be better characterized as reputational or psychological? Buyers have sued sellers for failing to disclose, for example, the fact that a murder-suicide had recently occurred in the house. The commitment of a heinous crime on the property might attach a psychological or social stigma to the property because of the reluctance (rational or not) of people to want to live in the home. In one prominent case, a California appellate court held that a buyer could sue the seller and the seller's agent for failure to disclose the fact that the home had been the site of a multiple murder. *Reed v. King*, 193 Cal. Rptr. 130 (Cal. App. 1983).

In the late 1980s and early 1990s, some states began to enact what are often referred to as *stigma statutes*. These statutes protect sellers who fail to disclose psychological defects to buyers. At the time these stigma statutes were enacted, legislatures tended to focus on two specific issues. The first was the disclosure of crimes, as legislatures reacted to the recently decided *Reed* case. The second was the fear of disease, especially the HIV/AIDS epidemic that was then at its peak. Oklahoma's law is a good example of the stigma statutes that were enacted in that era.

Okla. St. Title 59 §858-513

A. The fact or suspicion that real estate might be or is psychologically impacted, such impact being the result of facts or suspicions, including but not limited to:

1. That an occupant of the real estate is, or was at any time suspected to be infected, or has been infected, with Human Immunodeficiency Virus or diagnosed with Acquired Immune Deficiency Syndrome, or other disease which has been

determined by medical evidence to be highly unlikely to be transmitted through the occupancy of a dwelling place; or

    2. That the real estate was, or was at any time suspected to have been the site of a suicide, homicide or other felony, is not a material fact that must be disclosed in a real estate transaction.

    B. No cause of action shall arise against an owner of real estate or any licensee [i.e., a licensed real estate broker or agent] assisting the owner for the failure to disclose to the purchaser or lessee of such real estate or any licensee assisting the purchaser or lessee that such real estate was psychologically impacted as provided for in subsection A of this section.

    C. Notwithstanding the fact that this information is not a material defect or fact, in the event that a purchaser or lessee, who is in the process of making a bona fide offer, advises the licensee assisting the owner, in writing, that knowledge of such factor is important to the person's decision to purchase or lease the property, the licensee shall make inquiry of the owner and report any findings to the purchaser or lessee with the consent of the owner and subject to and consistent with applicable laws of privacy; provided further, if the owner refuses to disclose, the licensee assisting the owner shall so advise the purchaser or lessee.

Fewer than half of U.S. states have enacted stigma statutes. In the rest of the country, the obligation to disclose stigma-creating facts is often unsettled. *Reed* remains a leading case in support of a duty to disclose. The Pennsylvania Superior Court recently reached the opposite conclusion, holding that there was no duty to disclose a murder-suicide in the home under either common law or Pennsylvania's Seller Disclosure Law. *Milliken v. Jacono*, 60 A.3d 133 (Pa. Super. 2012).

Do you think that these kinds of facts should be disclosed? Putting the question another way, are stigma statutes a good idea? In considering these issues, you might want to distinguish between different types of crimes and the concerns that they might raise in potential buyers. A murder-suicide involving only the residents of the house might raise only stigma concerns. A crime committed by strangers, however, might raise fears about neighborhood crime rates in addition to stigma concerns. *See Van Camp v. Bradford*, 623 N.E.2d 731 (Ohio Com. Pl. 1993) (holding that buyer could sue seller for failure to disclose fact that prior resident had been raped by attacker who broke into home; other rapes had also occurred in the neighborhood). If you think that at least some types of crimes should be disclosed, where would you draw the line on the duty to disclose? What types of crimes should be disclosed? And how far into the past would you go? Would you treat a murder that occurred 20 years ago the same as one that occurred 6 months ago?

If there is a duty to disclose crimes on the property, should it extend to crimes in the neighborhood? Should a seller have to disclose the fact that there is a convicted murderer or sex offender living in the neighborhood? Related to this last point, the Megan's Law registries enacted by many states allow potential buyers to look up registered sex offenders who live nearby, but these registries do not cover other types of convicted criminals. On these topics generally, *see* Shelley Ross Saxer, *"Am I My Brother's Keeper?": Requiring Landowner Disclosure of the Presence of Sex Offenders and Other Criminal Activity*, 80 Neb. L. Rev. 522 (2001).

What about ghosts? A famous New York case allowed a buyer to bring a nondisclosure case against a seller based on a claim that the house was haunted. *Stambovsky v. Ackley*, 572 N.Y.S.2d 672 (App. Div. 1991). In *Stambovsky*, however, the seller had reported ghost sightings to the local and national press. On these facts, the court held that the seller was estopped from denying that the house was haunted and allowed the buyer's claim to proceed. Even on these specific facts, the holding in *Stambovksy* is questionable at best. The better view is that there is no obligation to disclose ghosts in the house under any circumstances because ghosts don't exist.

4. THE IMPLIED WARRANTY OF QUALITY

Purchasers of newly constructed homes will typically be able to make a claim against the builder for physical defects. Even if there are no express warranties in the agreement between the buyer and the seller, the buyer will typically be able to assert a claim against the builder under the *implied warranty of quality*. This warranty is only implied against sellers who are *merchants of housing*. Merchants of housing are individuals or entities who are in the business of building or selling new properties—contractors, developers, and the like. The implied warranty promises that the construction will be completed in a competent and skillful manner consistent with professional standards. It is breached by material physical defects in the construction. Most states imply the warranty in residential construction. It is more rare, but not unheard of, for courts to imply the warranty in the commercial context. *See, e.g., Chin v. Hodgson*, 403 A.2d 942 (N.J. Super. Ct. 1979) (implying warranty to commercial property that included stores and apartments, where buyers were small business persons).

You might wonder why the doctrine of merger does not bar implied warranty of quality claims. After all, the warranty was implied into a contract between the seller and buyer, and the claim is being brought by the buyer after closing. The short answer is that promises about the quality or physical condition will typically be deemed to be unrelated to the seller's obligation to deliver title and so will likely fall outside of the scope of merger. In many implied quality cases, the construction obligations might be in an entirely separate agreement from the purchase and sale contract.

If the initial homebuyer can bring an implied warranty claim, can a subsequent purchaser also bring a claim? For example, consider a home built by Ace Construction, LLC and sold to Anthony. Anthony in turn sells the house to Beth.

Ace Construction → Anthony → Beth

Beth discovers a physical defect that was result of poor work done by Ace Construction. Can Beth sue Ace? The traditional answer was no, because the warranty was implied into the contract between Ace and Anthony, and there is no privity of contract between Ace Construction and Beth. This traditional rule first began to erode when courts allowed remote grantees (here, Beth) to make claims against the contractor (here, Ace) for physical injuries that resulted from breaches of the implied warranty. These cases distinguished between physical injury (suit by Beth against Ace allowed) and mere pecuniary loss (suit by Beth against Ace not allowed). Under this approach, Beth could sue Ace if a construction problem resulted in a ceiling collapsing on her head, injuring her. She could not sue Ace if the ceiling collapse did not physically injure anyone and instead resulted in only pecuniary loss.

Courts are now increasingly rejecting this distinction between physical injury and pecuniary loss and are allowing claims by remote grantees against the contractor for both kinds of claims. For a thorough and thoughtful analysis of these issues, *see Lempke v. Dagenais*, 547 A.2d 290 (N.H. 1988). In *Lempke*, the New Hampshire Supreme Court allowed a remote grantee to sue the contractor for pecuniary loss, reversing a decision to the contrary that the court had issued just two years earlier. The court limited its extension of remote liability to claims for latent defects and required those claims to be brought within a reasonable time from the completion of construction.

QUANTITY OF LAND

Imagine that you are purchasing a large parcel of vacant land. You and the seller both think that it is 50 acres. You agree to a price and sign a contract. Shortly thereafter you discover that the property is in fact only 40 acres. Can you get a discount on the purchase price? It depends on whether the price in the contract was *in gross* or *per acre*. Property is sold in gross if the price is set for the property without regard to its specific size. Property is sold per acre if it the price is specifically tied to the size of the property. If the contract stated the purchase price as $500,000, the pricing was in gross. If the contract stated the purchase price as 50 acres at $10,000 per acre, then the pricing was per acre. If the pricing is in gross, the price will not be adjusted to account for the actual size of the property. If the price was per acre, then the price will be adjusted to account for the actual size of the property. Note, by the way, that while the discrepancy in our example favored the seller, the facts could easily been set so that the discrepancy favored the buyer. For example, the buyer (you in our example) and the seller could have thought that the property was 50 acres when in fact it was 60 acres. For a discussion of the in gross-per acre distinction and some of the issues that a court might face in deciding which category applies to a particular fact pattern, *see Perfect v. McAndrew*, 798 N.E.2d 470 (Ind. Ct. App. 2003).

FIXTURES

Fixtures are objects of personal property that have become attached (or affixed) to the land. If there is ambiguity about whether an object is affixed to the property, courts often ask whether the object can be easily removed without damage to the surrounding physical structure. Under this test, if it can be removed without damage, it is not a fixture. If removing it would cause damage, it is a fixture.

The distinction between fixtures and non-fixtures matters because fixtures become part of the real property, and ownership of fixtures therefore transfers with the ownership of the land. Most parts of a building are clearly fixtures. The foundation, walls, ceiling, windows, electrical wiring, and so forth are all physically attached to the land and cannot be removed without damage. Other items of personal property, such as most items of furniture, clearly are not attached to the property and are not fixtures. Disputes often arise, however, on more ambiguous items such as kitchen appliances and chandeliers. Many of these (especially refrigerators) typically are not considered fixtures. This can lead to problems if the buyer expected a particular item (e.g., an expensive refrigerator or chandelier) to remain with the house, but the seller expected to take the item with her before transferring the property.

The crucial point about these ambiguous items is that the parties should address what stays with the property and what the seller will remove before closing in their contract. If the matter came to litigation, an ambiguous item may or may not be considered a fixture, depending on the specific facts of its attachment to the property and the specific case law in that jurisdiction. It is best to avoid that problem up front so that the parties have consistent expectations about what will happen. Most form purchase and sale contracts have a section that lists appliances and similar objects and allows the parties to agree on whether these objects transfer with the real property.

The general rule is that fixtures transfer with the real property. *Trade fixtures*, however, do not follow this general rule. Trade fixtures are fixtures that are used in a business, and unless the parties agree otherwise, the seller can remove them before closing. In other words, ownership of trade fixtures is presumed to stay with the seller and to *not* transfer with the real property. Pieces of restaurant or manufacturing equipment that are physically attached to the property are examples of trade fixtures. Another example is a bar (i.e., the drink-serving kind) that is attached to the property in a restaurant. These objects all can be very valuable, and it is important for potential buyers to know that they do not transfer with the real property.

In the landlord-tenant context, an object that is a fixture remains with the property when the tenant leaves. This rule applies even if the tenant installed the fixture. If, for example, you install a built-in bookshelf in your rented apartment, that bookshelf will be a fixture and will be owned by the landlord. Trade fixtures, in contrast, may be removed by the tenant at the end of the lease. This presumes, of course, that the tenant installed the trade fixture. If it was there before the lease began, it was owned by the landlord from the beginning, and the landlord owns it at the end of the lease. If the tenant owned the object when it was unattached personal property, and it is installed as a trade fixture during the lease term, the tenant will be able to remove the trade fixture at the end of the lease. If, for example, you are a tenant operating a tavern, and you install an expensive bar during your lease term, you will be able to remove the bar and take it with you at the end of the lease.

E. OTHER MAJOR CONTRACTING ISSUES

1. THE STATUTE OF FRAUDS

The original Statute of Frauds was enacted in England in 1677, and versions of the Statute have been enacted by the states. The Statute of Frauds is a rare context where the actual language of the statute takes secondary importance to judicial decisions as a source of authority. Over time, the courts have taken the general principles of the Statute and constructed a set of rules that govern the transfer of real property. As interpreted by the courts, the Statute does two important things in the real estate context. First, it requires transfers of interests in real property (other than leases of less than three years) to be created or transferred by written instrument. In most voluntary transfers, this written document is a deed. We will return to deeds later in this chapter.

Second, the Statute of Frauds requires contracts for the purchase and sale of real property to be in writing, or evidenced by a written memorandum. Note well that the contract itself does not have to be in writing to satisfy the Statute. Rather, a written memorandum that sets out the essential terms of the contract can satisfy the Statute. In the real estate context, a memorandum generally must at a minimum:

(a) be signed by the party to be bound;

(b) describe the real estate; and

(c) state the price.

Let's take a closer look at each of these elements. First, the memorandum must be signed by the party to be bound. In any fact pattern that raises the Statute of Frauds and a purported agreement to purchase and sell real estate, one of the parties to the transaction is trying to back out of the deal, while the other party is trying to enforce the agreement. *The party that is trying to back out is the party to be bound. The memorandum must be signed by this person.* Depending on the circumstances, the party to be bound could be either the seller or the buyer.

Second, the memorandum must describe the real estate. Courts vary on the specificity that they require for the description of the property. A very strict court might

People often say that the Statute of Frauds requires a contract for the purchase and sale of real estate to be in writing. Make sure that you understand why this statement is wrong. The Statute of Frauds can be satisfied by a written memorandum that contains only a few key terms.

require a full legal description establishing the precise legal boundaries of the property. A very liberal court might be satisfied with a street address. A good general rule to keep in mind is that the description of the property in the memorandum should be specific enough that it is sufficient to allow a reader to *uniquely identify the property and distinguish it from all of the other parcels of real property in the world.*

Third, the purchase price is an essential term of the property and must be stated in the memorandum. Beyond a specific price, this requirement can be met with *a formula that would allow the reader to calculate the purchase price.* A memorandum that states that the price will be $5,000 per acre, for example, will satisfy this requirement. Some courts in some jurisdictions might hold that this requirement is met if the memorandum states that the property will be purchased for fair market value.

You have probably noticed that we use a lot of wishy-washy language in our description of the requirements for a memorandum that satisfies the Statute of Frauds. The truth is that the case law on the Statute of Frauds can be very blurry, even within a given jurisdiction. This lack of consistency is likely due to two factors. First, the rules for what constitutes a memorandum satisfying the Statute of Frauds are the product of centuries of judicial decisions, and the messy nature of common-law decision making has resulted in ambiguity that creates the opportunity for divergent outcomes. Second, some judges like the Statute of Frauds while others hate it. More precisely, some judges think that the Statute of Frauds serves an important purpose by requiring transactions to be evidenced by a written instrument. Other judges think that the Statute of Frauds is often used by parties to get out of obligations that they had agreed to. Combining vague rules with differing policy views leads to an area of law that often is messy.

To complicate things further, there are two major exceptions to the Statute of Frauds that apply to the real estate context:

> *Estoppel:* If you haven't already, you will see estoppel in various contexts throughout law school. In the real estate context, estoppel provides an exception to the Statute of Frauds to a person who *reasonably and detrimentally relies* on an oral agreement to purchase or sell real estate. Estoppel is an equitable concept. The core idea of the estoppel exception is that it would be unfair to let a party who has orally agreed to do something back out after the other party has relied on that oral agreement. The requirement of reasonable detrimental reliance is often met by a party changing her legal position. If a seller, for example, reasonably relies on an oral promise to purchase her home and enters into a binding contract to buy another home, she has met this requirement. Similarly, if a buyer relies on an oral promise to buy a home and enters into a binding contract to sell her existing home, then she has met this requirement. As suggested by these two examples, the estoppel exception can easily apply to both buyers and sellers.

LAW AND EQUITY

Part performance: The part performance exception to the Statute of Frauds has *three factors/elements:* (1) delivery and assumption of actual and exclusive possession of the land to the buyer; (2) payment or tender of the consideration, whether in money, other property, or services to the seller; and (3) the making of permanent, substantial, and valuable improvements by the buyer referable to the contract. The core idea of the part performance exception is that the buyer has engaged in a series of actions, and the seller has acquiesced to those actions, which are only explainable if there had been an agreement between the parties. The key thing to look for in the part performance exception is actions by the buyer. In the most common scenario, the buyer is seeking to enforce an oral agreement against the seller. The parties have orally agreed to purchase and sell the property but have not closed the transaction (i.e., the buyer has not received a deed to the property from the seller). The buyer, however, has moved in, paid some consideration to the seller, and made improvements to the property. The seller then tries to back out of the obligation to close the transaction and deliver a deed to the buyer. If the three elements are met, the part performance exception will apply, and the seller will be forced to deliver the deed. Although part performance is typically asserted by the buyer, it is possible to imagine a seller trying to enforce an oral agreement on part performance grounds in a troubled real estate market.

Of the two exceptions, estoppel is broader and applicable to a wider range of fact patterns. It is possible for a fact pattern to support both exceptions. In particular, there is a good chance that a buyer who satisfies the part performance requirements will also be able to satisfy the estoppel requirements.

Our next case is a classic example of the estoppel exception to the Statute of Frauds. One interesting aspect of the case is that it involves two different deposit checks. Depending on what is written on them, deposit checks might alone satisfy the Statute of Frauds. Consider, for example, a check signed by the buyer that has "Deposit for purchase of home located at 123 Main Street, Hillsville, from [Seller], purchase price = $100,000" written in the memo line. This check might constitute a memorandum that satisfies the Statute of Frauds if the buyer tries to back out because it is signed by the buyer (on these facts the party to be bound), describes the real estate (at least for a court that does not require a precise legal description of the property), and states the purchase price. If the seller endorses the check (i.e., signs on the back of the check), then the check might constitute a memorandum binding against the seller. In the case that follows, pay close attention to the two checks, whether they satisfy the Statute of Frauds, and what role they play in the court's analysis.

HICKEY V. GREEN

Appeals Court of Massachusetts, 1982
442 N.E.2d 37

CUTTER, Justice. This case is before us on a stipulation of facts (with various attached documents). A Superior Court judge has adopted the agreed facts as "findings." We are in the same position as was the trial judge (who received no evidence and saw and heard no witnesses).

Mrs. Gladys Green owns a lot (Lot S) in the Manomet section of Plymouth. In July, 1980, she advertised it for sale. On July 11 and 12, Hickey and his wife discussed with Mrs. Green purchasing Lot S and "orally agreed to a sale" for $15,000. Mrs. Green on July 12 accepted a deposit check of $500, marked by Hickey on the back, "Deposit on Lot . . . Massasoit Ave. Manomet . . . Subject to Variance from Town of Plymouth." Mrs. Green's brother and agent "was under the impression that a zoning variance was needed and [had] advised . . . Hickey to write" the quoted language on the deposit check. It turned out, however, by July 16 that no variance would be required. Hickey had left the payee line of the deposit check blank, because of uncertainty whether Mrs. Green or her brother was to receive the check and asked "Mrs. Green to fill in the appropriate name." Mrs. Green held the check, did not fill in the payee's name, and neither cashed nor endorsed it. Hickey "stated to Mrs. Green that his intention was to sell his home and build on Mrs. Green's lot."

"Relying upon the arrangements . . . with Mrs. Green," the Hickeys advertised their house on Sachem Road in newspapers on three days in July, 1980, and agreed with a purchaser for its sale and took from him a deposit check for $500 which they deposited in their own account.[1] On July 24, Mrs. Green told Hickey that she "no longer intended to sell her property to him" but had decided to sell to another for $16,000. Hickey told Mrs. Green that he had already sold his house and offered her $16,000 for Lot S. Mrs. Green refused this offer.

The Hickeys filed this complaint seeking specific performance. Mrs. Green asserts that relief is barred by the Statute of Frauds contained in G.L. c. 259, §1. The trial judge granted specific performance. Mrs. Green has appealed.

The present rule applicable in most jurisdictions in the United States is succinctly set forth in Restatement (Second) of Contracts, §129 (1981). The section reads, "A contract for the transfer of an interest in land may be specifically enforced notwithstanding failure to comply with the Statute of Frauds if it is established that the party seeking enforcement, in reasonable reliance on the contract and on the continuing assent of the party against whom enforcement is sought, has so changed his position that

---

[1] On the back of the check was noted above the Hickeys' signatures endorsing the check "Deposit on Purchase of property at Sachem Rd. and First St., Manomet, Ma. Sale price, $44,000."

injustice can be avoided only by specific enforcement" (emphasis supplied). The earlier Massachusetts decisions laid down somewhat strict requirements for an estoppel precluding the assertion of the Statute of Frauds. . . . Frequently there has been an actual change of possession and improvement of the transferred property, as well as full payment of the full purchase price, or one or more of these elements.

It is stated in Park, Real Estate Law, §883, at 334, that the "more recent decisions . . . indicate a trend on the part of the [Supreme Judicial C]ourt to find that the circumstances warrant specific performance." This appears to be a correct perception. . . .

The present facts reveal a simple case of a proposed purchase of a residential vacant lot, where the vendor, Mrs. Green, knew that the Hickeys were planning to sell their former home (possibly to obtain funds to pay her) and build on Lot S. The Hickeys, relying on Mrs. Green's oral promise, moved rapidly to make their sale without obtaining any adequate memorandum of the terms of what appears to have been intended to be a quick cash sale of Lot S. So rapid was action by the Hickeys that, by July 21, less than ten days after giving their deposit to Mrs. Green, they had accepted a deposit check for the sale of their house, endorsed the check, and placed it in their bank account. Above their signatures endorsing the check was a memorandum probably sufficient to satisfy the Statute of Frauds under *A.B.C. Auto Parts, Inc. v. Moran*, 359 Mass. 327, 329-331, 268 N.E.2d 844 (1971). *Cf. Guarino v. Zyfers*, 9 Mass.App. 874, 401 N.E.2d 857 (1980). At the very least, the Hickeys had bound themselves in a manner in which, to avoid a transfer of their own house, they might have had to engage in expensive litigation. No attorney has been shown to have been used either in the transaction between Mrs. Green and the Hickeys or in that between the Hickeys and their purchaser.

There is no denial by Mrs. Green of the oral contract between her and the Hickeys. This, under §129 of the Restatement, is of some significance. There can be no doubt (a) that Mrs. Green made the promise on which the Hickeys so promptly relied, and also (b) she, nearly as promptly, but not promptly enough, repudiated it because she had a better opportunity. The stipulated facts require the conclusion that in equity Mrs. Green's conduct cannot be condoned. This is not a case where either party is shown to have contemplated the negotiation of a purchase and sale agreement. If a written agreement had been expected, even by only one party, or would have been natural (because of the participation by lawyers or otherwise), a different situation might have existed. It is a permissible inference from the agreed facts that the rapid sale of the Hickeys' house was both appropriate and expected. These are not circumstances where negotiations fairly can be seen as inchoate. *Compare Tull v. Mister Donut Development Corp.*, 7 Mass.App. 626, 630-632, 389 N.E.2d 447 (1979). . . .

Over two years have passed since July, 1980, and over a year since the trial judge's findings were filed on July 6, 1981. At that time, the principal agreed facts of record bearing upon the extent of the injury to the Hickeys (because of their reliance on

Mrs. Green's promise to convey Lot S) were those based on the Hickeys' new obligation to convey their house to a purchaser. Performance of that agreement had been extended to May 1, 1981. If that agreement has been abrogated or modified since the trial, the case may take on a different posture. If enforcement of that agreement still will be sought, or if that agreement has been carried out, the conveyance of Lot S by Mrs. Green should be required now.

The case, in any event, must be remanded to the trial judge for the purpose of amending the judgment to require conveyance of Lot S by Mrs. Green only upon payment to her in cash within a stated period of the balance of the agreed price of $15,000. The trial judge, however, in her discretion and upon proper offers of proof by counsel, may reopen the record to receive, in addition to the presently stipulated facts, a stipulation or evidence concerning the present status of the Hickeys' apparent obligation to sell their house. If the circumstances have changed, it will be open to the trial judge to require of Mrs. Green, instead of specific performance, only full restitution to the Hickeys of all costs reasonably caused to them in respect of these transactions (including advertising costs, deposits, and their reasonable costs for this litigation) with interest.

The case is remanded to the Superior Court Department for further action consistent with this opinion. The Hickeys are to have costs of this appeal. So ordered.

PROBLEM

An explanatory answer to this problem can be found on page 1056.

Linda Davidson lives at 19 Boulder Lane in Eagle Falls. A few months ago, Linda was talking with Celia Canales at a cocktail party. Linda was musing about being tired of small-town life and wanting to sell her house and move to Boston. Celia, who was living in a one-bedroom condominium that she owned and who wanted to buy a house, said that she was interested in buying Linda's. Linda and Celia drove over to Linda's house, and Linda showed Celia around. Celia liked what she saw, and the two orally agreed that Linda would sell Celia the house for $250,000. Celia gave Linda a check for $1,000 and wrote on the memo line "down payment for 19 Boulder Lane in Eagle Falls; purchase price = $250,000." A few days later, Linda decided that she didn't want to move to the big city, and she called Celia to tell her that she wouldn't sell the house to her. Linda, who had never endorsed or deposited the check, returned it to Celia. Celia was quite upset and is now trying to force Linda to complete the sale of the property. If Celia sues Linda for specific performance, who is likely to win, and why? How would things change, if at all, if we change the facts slightly and now Celia entered into a binding contract to sell her condominium in reliance on Linda's promise to sell the 19 Boulder Lane house to her?

a. Electronic Contracting and the Statute of Frauds

The Statute of Frauds requires a contract for the purchase and sale of real estate to be evidenced by a written memorandum. Does e-mail count? How about a series of messages on Facebook? On the one hand, written electronic communication is a form of writing. On the other hand, you might wonder how to meet the "signed by the party to be bound" requirement might be met electronically. Electronic communication also is often informal, and you might worry about parties unwittingly agreeing to a binding agreement through a casual e-mail exchange.

Federal and state legislation addresses some of these issues. The federal Electronic Signatures in Global and National Commerce Act, enacted in 2000 and generally known as E-sign, provides that "a signature, contract, or other record . . . may not be denied legal effect, validity, or enforceability solely because it is in electronic form." 15 U.S.C.A. §7001(a)(1). What constitutes an electronic signature? The statute provides the answer. An electronic signature is "an electronic sound, symbol, or process, attached to or logically associated with a contract or other record and executed or adopted by a person with the intent to sign the record." 15 U.S.C.A. §7006(5). Most states have adopted the Uniform Electronic Transactions Act (UETA),[2] which takes a similar approach to E-sign:

UNIFORM ELECTRONIC TRANSACTIONS ACT

Section 7. Legal Recognition of Electronic Records, Electronic Signatures, and Electronic Contracts.

(a) A record or signature may not be denied legal effect or enforceability solely because it is in electronic form.

(b) A contract may not be denied legal effect or enforceability solely because an electronic record was used in its formation.

(c) If a law requires a record to be in writing, an electronic record satisfies the law.

(d) If a law requires a signature, an electronic signature satisfies the law.

Our next case involves a dispute about an agreement to purchase and sell real property that purportedly resulted from an e-mail exchange between the parties.

---

[2] Forty-seven states have adopted UETA. The three other states, New York, Illinois, and Washington, have their own legislation on electronic contracting. *See http://www.ncsl.org/issues-research/telecom/uniform-electronic-transactions-acts.aspx.*

BRANTLEY V. WILSON

United States District Court, W.D. Ark., Feb. 22, 2006
2006 WL 436121, 2006 U.S. Dist. LEXIS 17722

HENDREN, J.

1. Plaintiffs contend that they negotiated the sale of real estate owned by defendants via telephone and e-mail, in February, 2005, and that a contract was formed on the basis of provisions in the Arkansas Uniform Electronic Transactions Act, A.C.A. §25-32-101 et seq. Plaintiffs further allege that they prepared to perform, by obtaining a loan commitment, paying earnest money, and providing the title company information for closing. Then, they allege that the defendants refused to sell because they decided the price was not high enough. . . .

Defendants now move for summary judgment, arguing that the parties did not intend to form a contract through their e-mails; that any agreement that was reached was too uncertain to be enforced as a contract; and that it would, in any event, violate the Statute of Frauds. . . .

2. Summary judgment should be granted when the record, viewed in the light most favorable to the nonmoving party, and giving that party the benefit of all reasonable inferences, shows that there is no genuine issue of material fact and the movant is entitled to judgment as a matter of law. *Walsh v. United States*, 31 F.3d 696 (8th Cir. 1994). . . . .

3. Pursuant to Local Rule 56.1, the parties have filed statements of facts which they contend are not in dispute. From those statements, the following significant undisputed facts are made to appear:

- Scarlett Wilson and her daughter, Lara Rosenblum, own the parcel of real property at issue in this case (the "Property"). It is approximately 37 acres in size, and is located in Benton County, Arkansas.
- In late 2004 or early 2005, Larry Brantley contacted Scarlett Wilson by telephone to determine whether the Property was for sale, and if so, at what price. Wilson informed Brantley that the Property was for sale, and was priced at $10,000 per acre, or $370,000 for the parcel.
- After this telephone conversation, Larry Brantley and Scarlett Wilson began communicating about the Property, exclusively by e-mail, beginning on February 7, 2005. Copies of those e-mail communications are attached to defendants' Brief In Support, and their authenticity is not disputed.
- Neither plaintiffs nor defendants were represented by a real estate agent during their communications about the Property.
- On February 18, 2005, plaintiffs signed a real estate contract prepared by their attorney, and forwarded it to Wilson. None of the defendants signed this contract.

- A specific closing date for sale of the Property was not identified by the parties.
- The parties did not discuss a deposit of earnest money in connection with the sale of the Property.
- The parties did not discuss whether the Brantleys would be taking title to the Property in fee simple absolute, or whether the defendants would retain the mineral interests.
- On February 20, 2005, Wilson notified Brantley that she was not willing to sell the Property for $10,000 per acre.
- After consulting an attorney, the Brantleys filed suit for specific performance and placed a lis pendens against the Property on May 4, 2005.

4. Defendants first argue that the parties never entered into a contract, because certain elements essential to the formation of a contract are missing from their e-mails. . . .

Defendants break their argument down into three segments: they contend there was no offer by Wilson; that the parties did not intend their e-mails to form a contract; and that several essential terms were neither reasonably certain nor agreed upon between the parties.

Plaintiffs rely on the content of the e-mails as evidence that there is a genuine dispute about what the parties intended. They point out that the memoranda required to satisfy the Statute of Frauds do not need to be all in one document, citing *Moore v. Exelby*, 170 Ark. 908, 281 S.W. 671 (1926), wherein it was said that

a complete contract for the sale of lands, binding under the statute of frauds, may be gathered from letters between the parties relating to the subject-matter of the contract, and so connected with each other that they may be fairly said to constitute one paper relating to the contract. In order to be sufficient, the letters relied upon must by reference to each other disclose every material part of a valid contract, and must be signed by the party sought to be charged. In other words, the letters must set out the parties, the subject-matter, the price, the description, and terms, and leave nothing to rest in parol.

Plaintiffs contend that the e-mails, taken as a whole, are objective evidence of an intent to form a contract and a meeting of the mind on all essential terms thereof.

A review of the e-mails reflects the following:

- In her first e-mail to Brantley dated February 7, 2005, Wilson stated that she "prefer[red] to sell the land for the stated price and not carry a loan/interest, etc.," and that Brantley should contact her if he wanted to buy it.
- In his response on February 8, Brantley stated that he wanted to make a formal offer, which will be "$370,000 as you stated, entire amount due at time of closing, buyer and seller splitting closing costs 50/50 and a fair amount of time allowed for me to arrange financing. Ernest money will be included with the offer." He subsequently inquired about the legal description of the land and obtained that information.

- On February 10, 2005, Wilson e-mailed Brantley and suggested, as to the 50/50 split of closing costs, that "it would be a good idea if you listed those with your bid, so there are no surprises."
- That same day, Brantley responded with estimated figures on these costs, and stated that he had "contacted my bank and discussed the purchase. They have given us a list of information they will require and a list of steps we will need to go thru [sic] to arrange financing. There is not [sic] doubt in our minds we will be able to arrange the financing. Rhonda and I are not going to go to the work of securing financing until we have a signed offer and acceptance in hand." He noted that he was mailing an offer and acceptance with the estimated closing costs to Wilson that day.
- On February 11, Wilson noted the acreage and price, and stated her expectation that taxes would be pro-rated, and that a survey, if required, would be at the Brantleys' expense. She suggested that the Brantleys might need to adjust their offer if it did not address these two items.
- On February 14, Brantley e-mailed Wilson, stating that "Rhonda and I agree to your terms," contingent on "our obtaining financing from our local bank." He noted that his attorney was preparing an offer and acceptance.
- On February 15, Brantley updated Wilson on the preparation of the offer and acceptance, noting that he had instructed the attorney "to draw it up exactly as you stated," to which Wilson responded on February 16, "I shall be watching for the materials to arrive."
- On February 20, Wilson e-mailed Brantley that she had "decided not to sell my 37 acres on the Old Wire Road at this time for $10,000.00 per acre. Early Saturday morning I was in contact with a longtime neighbor and he advised me not to sell at that price as other owners/locations in the immediate vicinity had sold and have been offered significantly higher prices." After reciting other information about the value of the land, Wilson concluded, "[a]t this time it does not seem appropriate for me to sell at $10,000.00 per acre."

The Court believes reasonable jurors could find this group of e-mails "so connected with each other that they may be fairly said to constitute one paper relating to the contract." They might also deduce therefrom that Wilson offered to sell—and Brantley agreed to buy—specific land for $370,000, cash price in full at closing, with closing costs to be split. They might also deduce, from Wilson's February 20 e-mail, that she later changed her mind about a previous decision to enter into a contract to sell, because she had been told she could get more money. Thus the Court concludes that there is a genuine issue of material fact as to whether objective indicators showed a meeting of the minds of Wilson and Brantley as to the sale of the Property.

5. Defendants next argue that, even if a contract was formed, it is unenforceable as a matter of law under the Arkansas Statute of Frauds, A.C.A. §4-59-101(a)(4), which provides that

[u]nless the agreement, promise, or contract, or some memorandum or note thereof, upon which an action is brought is made in writing and signed by the party to be charged therewith . . . no action shall be brought to charge any . . . [p]erson upon any contract for the sale of lands, tenements, or hereditaments, or any interest in or concerning them.

Defendants argue that Wilson's typed name on her e-mails does not constitute a signature, citing an unreported Massachusetts Land Court case, *Singer v. Adamson*, 2003 WL 23641985 (2003). The Court sees no need to rely on this case, which has no precedential value and was not decided on the Statute of Frauds issue, because the State of Arkansas has adopted specific legislation dealing with the matter, the Uniform Electronic Transactions Act, which contains the following relevant provisions:

- "Agreement" means the bargain of the parties in fact, as found in their language or inferred from other circumstances. A.C.A. §25-32-101(1);

- "Contract" means the total legal obligation resulting from the parties' agreement as affected by this chapter and other applicable law. A.C.A. §25-32-101(4);

- "Electronic signature" means an electronic sound, symbol, or process attached to or logically associated with a record and executed or adopted by a person with the intent to sign the record. A.C.A. §25-32-101(8);

- The Act applies only to transactions between parties who have agreed to conduct transactions by electronic means, and whether they have so agreed is determined from the context and surrounding circumstances, including their conduct. A.C.A. §25-32-105(b);

- A signature may not be denied legal effect solely because it is in electronic form. A.C.A. §25-32-107(a);

- A contract may not be denied legal effect solely because an electronic record was used in its formation. A.C.A. §25-32-107(b);

- If a law requires a record to be in writing, an electronic record satisfies the law. A.C.A. §25-32-107(c); and

- If a law requires a signature, an electronic signature satisfies the law. A.C.A. §25-32-107(d).

Viewing the various documents submitted by the parties in light of these statutory provisions, the Court finds that genuine issues of material fact are in dispute with regard to the Statute of Frauds, i.e., whether Wilson agreed to conduct a land sale transaction involving the Property by electronic means, and whether she intended her typed name on her e-mails to be her signature.

6. Finally, defendants contend that certain terms, deemed by them essential to the formation of a contract for the sale of the Property, were not spelled out with sufficient certainty in the e-mails to be enforced as a contract. They refer to the length of time that plaintiffs would have to obtain financing; whether and how much earnest money would be paid; whether mineral interests would be transferred; what type of title insurance

would be provided; the identity of the title company to issue such insurance and handle the closing; and when payment would be made. They rely on *Wyatt v. Yingling*, 213 Ark. 160, 210 S.W.2d 122 (1948), wherein the Arkansas Supreme Court quoted 49 Am.Jur.Sec. 354, to the effect that

> [i]t is not sufficient that the note or memorandum express the terms of a contract; it is essential that it completely evidence the contract which the parties made by giving all of the essential terms. The writing must be such that all of the contract can be collected therefrom; resort cannot be had to the terms of the oral contract to supply deficiencies in the memorandum. . . . A contract in writing which leaves some essential term thereof to be shown by parol is only a parol contract, and is, therefore, not enforceable under the statute of frauds.

Defendants also cite *Jonesboro Investment Corp. v. Cherry*, 239 Ark. 1035, 396 S.W.2d 284 (1965), wherein the Statute of Frauds was successfully invoked because, while the purchase price of the land was in writing, none of the terms and conditions of the sale, nor the time for payment, were set forth.

Plaintiffs respond that the essential terms are not in question, and that those terms which are undecided are not such as would prevent the formation of a contract. As noted by defendants, the time for payment is the most important of the challenged terms, and the fact that Wilson had specified she did not want to carry a note is argued by plaintiffs in support of their position that the agreement was for full payment in cash at closing.

The matter of the contingency for obtaining financing, they assert, obligated them to use their best efforts to obtain financing and tender adequate and timely performance.

As for the failure to specify the time of closing, plaintiffs argue that a reasonable time is implied where there is no "time is of the essence" term, citing *Taylor v. George*, 212 S.W.3d 17, 2005 WL 2160161 (2005) ("where there is no provision as to the time of the performance of the contract, the law implies that it must be performed within a reasonable time").

As for whether mineral interests were to be conveyed, plaintiffs argue that it was incumbent on the sellers to so state if they intended to exclude mineral interests, and, not having done so, the whole estate was to be conveyed.

Finally, they point out that the other challenged terms, such as the identity of the title agent, the type of title insurance, whether earnest money will be paid and, if so, how much—are not required under any of the cases cited by defendants.

The Court is not persuaded by defendants' argument that the foregoing terms are so essential to performance that, not having been spelled out, they prevent a contract from coming into existence. Reasonable jurors could well agree that the payment term was cash in full at closing, and that it was implied that plaintiffs would use their best efforts to promptly obtain financing, which, if not obtained within a reasonable time, would relieve defendants of the obligation to sell. Although Taylor did not involve the Statute of Frauds, the Court finds it applicable. Every party to a contract has "an implied obligation not to do anything that would prevent, hinder, or delay performance," *Cantrell-Waind & Associates, Inc. v. Guiallaume Motorsports, Inc.*, 62 Ark.App. 66, 968 S.W.2d 72 (1998). Thus plaintiffs were under an obligation to promptly seek financing, and could escape their obligation to purchase on this score only by showing that they had been turned down. This is not such a term as would leave it to the plaintiffs to seek financing if and when they got around to it, meanwhile tying up any alternative sale of the Property.

As to the interest to be conveyed, it was said anciently, but in a case which is still good law, that

> where a party agrees to convey land, and there is nothing said as to the nature and extent of the title to be conveyed, nor anything connected with the transaction going to indicate the particular species of conveyance intended, the law implies a deed in fee simple with covenants of general warranty.

Witter v. Biscoe, 13 Ark. 422 (1853).

The Court also agrees with plaintiffs that the other challenged terms are not such as are considered "essential terms." Thus the failure to spell them out is not fatal to plaintiffs' theory of recovery.

For all the foregoing reasons, the Court concludes that defendants' Motion For Summary Judgment should be denied. . . .

IT IS SO ORDERED.

NOTES AND QUESTIONS

1. *Multiple Documents.* As the court noted in *Brantley*, a memorandum satisfying the Statute of Frauds can be stitched together from a group of related documents.

2. *Negotiating a Contract by E-mail.* Based on your personal experience, do you think that the result in *Brantley* is a good one? Do you worry about allowing the formation of a real estate contract by e-mail? Does the court's finding "that genuine issues of material fact are in dispute with regard to the Statute of Frauds, i.e., whether Wilson agreed to conduct a land sale transaction involving the Property by electronic means, and whether she intended her typed name on her e-mails to be her signature" worry you? Do you think about whether you are legally signing an e-mail when you type your name or attach your signature block to it?

3. *Contemplating a Formal Contract.* Should the fact that Brantley's attorney "was preparing an offer and acceptance" (presumably a formal written purchase and sale agreement) matter in this context?

4. *Procedural Posture.* Note that the court did not conclude that a contract had been formed. Rather, the court concluded that there were open issues of material fact making the case inappropriate for summary judgment. This holding is very important, however, because parties rarely want to risk the time, expense, and uncertainty of trial. The Statute of Frauds often provides a solid basis for summary judgment. Holding that it did not here is a big deal.

2. EQUITABLE CONVERSION AND RISK OF LOSS

One of the biggest issues in real estate law is risk of loss during the executory contract phase of a transaction. By risk of loss, we mean the risk of physical damage to the property. What happens if, say, the house burns down? Before a contract is signed, the original owner clearly bears the risk of loss to the property. After closing, the buyer takes on the risk of loss. But what happens in the time between the contract signing and closing? Under the doctrine of *equitable conversion*, the buyer becomes the equitable owner of the property once the contract is signed. As a result, the *buyer* bears the risk of loss unless the parties agree otherwise in the contract. In other words, the buyer will have to close on the property and pay the full contract purchase price even though the house has been destroyed. This outcome is counterintuitive and contrary to most people's expectations. The seller likely has homeowner's insurance and is in a better position than the buyer to keep the property insured during the executory period. Nonetheless, the rule is the rule, and the buyer bears the risk of loss during the executory period.

Understanding this rule is critical because risk of loss is relevant to every real estate transaction. Contracts for the purchase and sale of real estate should *always* address the risk of loss and should generally transfer the risk back to the seller, who is in the best position to insure against the loss. The buyer might not be out of luck if they fail to do so, because the buyer will likely be able to get access to the proceeds from the seller's insurance policy under a constructive trust theory. (Recall that a constructive trust is an equitable remedy designed to protect against unjust enrichment. The seller would be unjustly enriched if she was able to keep both the purchase price and the insurance proceeds.) This said, the risk of loss during the executory contract period is almost always best placed with the seller, and the parties should address this issue in their contract.

UNIFORM LAWS ON RISK OF LOSS

The Uniform Vendor and Purchaser Risk Act (UVPRA) reverses the traditional equitable conversion rule and places the risk of loss on the seller during the executory contract period. As of this writing, the UVPRA has been adopted in 13 states: California, Hawaii, Illinois, Michigan, Nevada, New Mexico, New York, North Carolina, Oklahoma, Oregon, South Dakota, Texas, and Wisconsin. The Uniform Land Transactions Act (ULTA) does the same thing, but this law has not been adopted in any jurisdiction. The ULTA was part of a failed effort to remake U.S. land transactions law in the mold of the Uniform Commercial Code. Whatever its merits on an academic level, the ULTA was a failure on a practical level.

Beyond risk of loss, equitable conversion is relevant to a fairly unusual inheritance problem. Here is the fact pattern: O signs a contract to sell Blackacre to Z. Before closing, O dies, leaving her real property to A and her personal property to B. Under the doctrine of equitable conversion, O's interest in Blackacre is treated as personal property. Because equitable ownership has passed to the buyer, Z, O no longer has a real property interest in Blackacre. Instead, O has a personal property interest in the purchase price under the contract. As a result, B will be entitled to the value of Blackacre. Unlike risk of loss, this fact pattern is extremely rare in the real world. Both the risk of loss and inheritance fact patterns, however, are popular with the bar examiners.

LAW AND EQUITY

3. REMEDIES FOR BREACH OF CONTRACT

If one party wrongfully breaches a real estate purchase and sale contract, and the other party sues and wins, the winning party may have access to two types of remedies. First, the winning party may be entitled to the equitable remedy of *specific performance*, which requires the losing party to perform its obligations under the contract. Second, the winning party may be entitled to the legal remedy of *money damages*. In the real estate context, money damages are often tied to forfeiture (if the seller wins) or return (if the buyer wins) of the buyer's deposit.

Generally speaking, a party can only obtain an equitable remedy if it can show that an award of the legal remedy of money damages is inadequate. As a result, awards of specific performance are very rare in most legal contexts. In most circumstances, an award of money damages will be sufficient to make the wronged party whole. In the real estate context, however, *awards of specific performance are common remedies for breaches of contract by sellers*. Because each piece of real property is unique, courts have held that wronged buyers cannot be made whole by an award of money damages. If you sign a contract to buy a specific house, you want that house, not another one down the street or in another town. You could imagine some circumstances where houses are fairly interchangeable—for example, homes in a cookie-cutter suburban development. In most circumstances, however, real property truly is unique. Most successful specific performance claims are by wronged buyers. A wronged seller is likely to be satisfied with money damages. A wronged seller, after all, can turn around and try to sell the property to someone else. Perhaps the new buyer will offer less money, but that possibility should be covered by an award of money damages.

LAW AND EQUITY

REMEDIES

The legal remedy of money damages will always be available to a wronged party who has suffered a monetary loss. Some complicated issues arise, however, with the relationship between the wronged party's actual damages and the amount of buyer's deposit. A simple example will illustrate the problem. Buyer and Seller enter into a contract where Buyer agrees to purchase Seller's home for $100,000. Buyer puts down a $10,000 deposit. Buyer breaches. Seller is later able to sell the property for $96,000. To keep the numbers simple, we will put Seller's actual damages at $4,000, representing the

ELECTION OF REMEDIES

If the winning party to a lawsuit satisfies the requirements of multiple remedies, that party can choose which remedy to receive. For example, a wronged buyer who wins a lawsuit for breach of contract against the seller might meet the requirements of both specific performance and money damages. The buyer can elect which of the two remedies to receive. In many procedural circumstances, the losing party can force the winning party to make this choice and elect a remedy.

difference between the contract price ($100,000) and the eventual sale price to another party ($96,000) and will ignore other factors such as interest. So we have:

Contract Price:	$100,000
Sale Price:	$96,000
Seller's Damages:	$4,000
Buyer's Deposit:	$10,000

These facts raise an issue: can Seller keep all of the Buyer's deposit ($10,000), or does Seller have to refund the $6,000 difference between the deposit ($10,000) and Seller's actual damages ($4,000)? (We will focus on this particular fact pattern, but it is easy to imagine a situation where the difference between the deposit and seller's actual damages went the other way, and the seller's damages exceeded the amount of the deposit.)

The answer to this question will depend on at least two things: (a) whether the parties addressed this issue in their contract and (b) the law in the jurisdiction where the property is located. Parties often agree in advance to damages for breach of contract. The provision in the contract that contains this agreement is often called a *liquidated damages clause.* Liquidated damages are the amount that the parties agree to at the time of contracting will satisfy the wronged party. If Buyer and Seller agreed that on Buyer's breach, Seller's damages would be set at the amount of Buyer's deposit, then the parties would have agreed on liquidated damages of $10,000 (the amount of the deposit) for any breach by the Buyer. If enforced by the courts, Seller would be able to keep the entire $10,000 even if Seller's actual damages were only $4,000. Of course, if the clause was enforced and Seller's actual damages were greater than the amount of the deposit, then Seller would be limited to the amount of the deposit. In many circumstances, courts are hostile to liquidated damages clauses and will often limit them if they result in what the court considers to be excessive damages. In the real estate context, courts are a bit inconsistent but will often allow the seller to keep the entire deposit if the seller did suffer some actual damages by later selling the property for less than the contract price. Courts are less likely to enforce the clause if the seller turns around and sells the property to another person at more than the contract price. *See* James O. Pearson, Jr.,

Modern Status of Defaulting Vendee's Right to Recover Contractual Payments Withheld by Vendor as Forfeited, 4 A.L.R.4th 993.

What happens if the contract is silent on the seller's right to keep the deposit? In most U.S. jurisdictions, the seller will be allowed to keep the deposit, at least if it does not exceed 10 percent of the purchase price in the contract. (Ten percent is a customary deposit amount that has traditionally been presumed reasonable by most courts.) Under this rule, in our example, Seller would be allowed to keep the entire $10,000 deposit. A minority of jurisdictions will require the seller to refund the difference between the actual damages and the amount of the deposit. Under this rule, in our example, Seller would have to refund the $6,000 difference between the deposit ($10,000) and Seller's actual damages ($4,000). *See* Pearson, *supra*, 4 A.L.R.4th 993.

SUMMARY OF DAMAGES FOR BREACH OF CONTRACT

Seller's Breach:

- In most cases where a seller breaches a real estate contract, the buyer will seek specific performance. The buyer, after all, wanted the property, and it is the seller who is backing out. Courts tend to allow specific performance in the real estate context. Because each parcel of real property is unique, the aggrieved buyer cannot be made whole by money damages.

Buyer's Breach:

- In most cases where a buyer breaches a real estate contract, the seller will seek money damages.
- Often the seller will seek to keep the buyer's deposit.
    - If the contract included a liquidated damages clause contemplating forfeiture of the deposit, courts will tend to enforce the contract, at least if the seller later sold the property to another person at a loss.
        - The seller will be able to keep the deposit even if the actual damages were less than the deposit amount.
        - On the flip side, the seller will be limited by the liquidated damages clause to the deposit amount even if the actual damages were more.
    - If the contract was silent on liquidated damages:
        - A majority of jurisdictions allow the seller to keep the deposit as damages even if the deposit amount is greater than the seller's actual damages. The seller might have a harder time keeping a deposit that is more than 10 percent of the purchase price.
        - A minority of jurisdictions will require the seller to refund the difference between actual damages and the deposit amount to the buyer.

F. THE CLOSING AND DEED DELIVERY

1. THE CLOSING PROCESS

As we mentioned above, the closing is where the parties actually perform their core obligations under the purchase and sale contract. The seller delivers the deed to the buyer, and the buyer delivers the purchase price to the seller. A lot of other things also typically happen at a closing. If the buyer is borrowing part of the purchase price, the buyer and the buyer's lender complete a mortgage transaction at the closing, and the buyer's lender provides a substantial portion of the purchase price that is delivered to the seller. If the seller had a mortgage loan on the property, that loan is satisfied (i.e., paid off) as part of the closing. All of this, of course, is more complicated if the buyer or the seller has multiple mortgage loans to deal with. The buyer's title insurance policy is also often put into place at the closing.

A lot of things, therefore, need to happen at once at a closing. The seller does not want to deliver the deed until the buyer delivers the purchase price, but the buyer does not want to deliver the purchase price until the seller delivers the deed. Similarly, the buyer's lender does not want to deliver the loan amount until the seller delivers the deed, because if the buyer does not own the property the buyer's grant of a mortgage to the lender would not be valid. The purchase price also needs to be divided up and distributed to the appropriate parties. Most of the purchase price will go to the seller and/or the seller's mortgage lender, but a substantial amount of the price will go to pay closing costs and the broker's fee. Closing costs can include real estate transfer taxes, recording fees, and the like.

Real estate practice tends to be very local, and the approach taken to closings varies throughout the country. This said, there are two basic approaches to solving the problem of having a bunch of things happen at once:

> The approach first is what is often called a *conventional closing*. In a conventional closing, everything happens at once. All of the parties gather at the same place and same time, and execute the documents all at once. All of the money goes into the account of the person holding the closing (typically a lawyer or a title company), and this money is disbursed by the end of the closing. Of course, not everything literally happens at once, but everything happens in quick sequence as part of the same process, with all of the parties present.

> The second is what is often called an *escrow closing*. In an escrow closing, the parties appoint an *escrow agent* to conduct the closing. The escrow agent holds the relevant documents and money and then disburses them to the appropriate party. Escrow relationships should always be created by written agreement. The agreement should give specific instructions to the escrow agent and should make it clear that the escrow

agent is serving to facilitate the transaction and is not acting as the agent of one or other of the parties. The escrow relationship allows the steps of the closing to take place at different times. The seller, for example, could deliver the deed to the escrow agent. The escrow agreement would instruct the escrow agent not to deliver the deed to the buyer until the buyer has delivered the purchase price to the escrow agent. Because the seller is confident that the escrow agent will hold the deed in escrow until the buyer delivers the purchase price, the seller will be comfortable delivering the deed to the escrow agent without worrying whether the buyer will deliver the purchase price to the escrow agent at the same time, or at some point in the future.

2. DEEDS AND DEED DELIVERY

We have already discussed the three common types of deeds—general warranty, special warranty, and quitclaim—in our material on title assurance. We will now focus on the essential nature of the deed itself: what does a deed achieve, and what elements does it need to be valid?

A deed is a legal instrument for the transfer of real property. Recall from our earlier chapter on Present and Future Interests that the early common-law method of the transfer of real property was the ritual of seisin. In this ritual, the grantor and the grantee would meet on the land with witnesses, the grantor would hand a physical part

TIME IS OF THE ESSENCE CLAUSES

In most real estate transactions, the time of closing will be important to both parties. Imagine, for example, that you are selling one home and buying another. You may need to close on the sale of your existing home by a certain date to allow you to use the purchase price to buy your new home. It is therefore important to set the closing date with precision in the purchase and sale contract. It is also important to include a *time is of the essence* clause in the contract. A time is of the essence clause (often a provision that simply states that "time is of the essence") establishes that dates in the contract are important and should prevent a court from giving the other party an extension for the time to perform. Absent a time is of the essence clause, a court might not strictly enforce the dates in the contract and instead give the parties a reasonable time to perform.

of the property (e.g., a handful of soil) to the grantee, and the grantor would state that the grantor was transferring the property to the grantee. The Statute of Frauds, enacted in 1677, required that the transfer of real property be done through a written instrument. In most circumstances, that instrument is a deed.

To be valid, a deed must (1) satisfy the Statute of Frauds and (2) be delivered to and accepted by the grantee. To satisfy the Statute of Frauds, a deed must:

(a) Be in writing
(b) State the essential terms of the conveyance
    (i) The identity of the grantor and the grantee
    (ii) The legal description of the property
    (iii) Contain words of conveyance indicating a transfer of the interest from the grantor to the grantee
(c) Be signed by the grantor

Deeds often contain more than these bare essentials. Some of these additional terms are empty formalities that are repeated out of habit rather than need. Others might be legally significant. Language in a deed, for example, might create a restrictive covenant that places limits on the use of the property. The basic elements, however, are all that is needed to create a valid deed that satisfies the Statute of Frauds.

On the next two pages, we provide a simple sample general warranty deed, with our annotations, for the 12 Oak Street transaction that we saw in our materials on real estate brokers. It omits much of the extra verbiage that you might see in many deeds.

There is no requirement that the consideration be stated in the deed. Indeed, property can be transferred by deed for no consideration as a gift. Local practice on whether to state the consideration varies.

This is the crucial language of conveyance. This language conveys a fee simple absolute—it is what we often shorted as "to A" in our Chapter on Present and Future Interests. If this deed was conveying a life estate, it would read "grant and convey to the Grantee for life." Many deeds have a lot of unnecessary language in the conveyance. One deed we recently saw, for example, had this for its granting clause: Grantors "have granted, bargained, sold, aliened, released, conveyed and confirmed, and by these presents to grant, bargain, sell, alien, release, convey and confirm, unto the said Grantees, their heirs and assigns forever."

This type of legal description is common for parcels in a subdivision that has a recorded set of plans that lay out the location of each unit. This recorded document would include the metes and bounds description of the land. We state the metes and bounds description in the next paragraph, but the description in this paragraph using this set of plans would be a valid legal description standing alone.

This is a very simple metes and bounds description. Following the directions in the description, you should be able to draw a rectangular lot, 200 feet by 100 feet, located between Unit 72 to the West and Unit 74 to the East. Few properties have boundaries that are so regular and that follow the cardinal points of the compass. Although the metes and bounds description of most properties would be more complex, the basic principles would be the same—you start at a fixed point, and then describe the boundaries of the parcel using directions and distances until you get back to the starting point.

This reference to the street address does not constitute a legal description and is technically unnecessary. Including the street address, however, gives the reader an ordinary-language description of the property conveyed in the deed.

Deeds often contain a clause beginning "To have and to hold." This clause is called the *habendum* clause (from the Latin for to have and to hold). These clauses are feudal relics, and are unnecessary is modern deeds. You will often see them, however, and should be careful with them. Although they are unnecessary, the language in a *habendum* clause way be read to place limits on the granted interest.

This reference to the prior deed is technically unnecessary, but is incredibly helpful to people doing title searches in the future. If each deed references the immediately prior deed, then it is easy to quickly create the chain of title for the property.

In some jurisdictions, the six warranties in the generally warranty deed will be spelled out here.

Note that the Deed is signed by the grantors, but not the grantee. Grantees do not need to sign a deed.

Deeds do not need to be notarized to be valid. Why, then, are most deeds are notarized, or at least witnessed? One reason is that a notary or witness provides a source of third party testimony if a dispute later arises about the execution of the deed. Another, probably more important, reason is that many jurisdictions require instruments to be notarized or witnessed as a requirement of recording.

General Warranty Deed

Made the 2nd day of December, 2013,

BETWEEN

James Lin and Alice Stevens, a married couple, ("Grantors")

AND

Laura Williams, ("Grantee")

WITNESSETH

That the Grantors, in consideration of FOUR HUNDRED THOUSAND DOLLARS ($400,000.00), paid by the Grantee to the Grantors, the receipt whereof is hereby acknowledged, do hereby grant and convey to the Grantee:

ALL THAT CERTAIN lot of land, together with all the buildings, improvements, and other interests attaching thereto, being Unit No. 73 (the "Unit") of Winter Oaks, A Planned Community Located in the Town of Winterville, Prince County, Pennsylvania, which Unit is designated in the Declaration of Covenants and Restrictions for Winter Oaks, A Planned Community (the "Declaration") and Declaration Plats and Plans recorded as an exhibit thereto in the Office of the Prince County Recorder of Deeds as Instrument No. 20040003287, together with any and all amendments thereto said lot being more particularly bounded and described as follows:

Beginning at a point on the southern line of Oak Street, said point being the northwest corner of the herein described lot and a corner of Unit 72 of the aforementioned Declaration, thence along Unit 72, South 200 feet to a point, a corner of Unit 72, then East 100 feet to a point, a corner of Unit 74, then North 200 feet to a point on the eastern line of Oak Street, said point being a corner of Unit 74, then West 100 feet along the southern line of Oak Street, the point of the beginning

Containing also a dwelling with a street address of 12 Oak Street, Winterville, Pennsylvania

TO HAVE AND TO HOLD the said premises, with all the privileges and appurtenances thereto, forever.

BEING THE SAME PREMISES conveyed by Marjorie Smith to James Lin and Alice Stevens, a married couple, by Deed dated April 2, 2001, and recorded April 7, 2001, in the Office of the Prince County Recorder of Deeds as Instrument No. 20010004531.

The Grantor shall and will GENERALLY WARRANT the property hereby conveyed.

IN WITNESS WHEREOF, the Grantor has caused this Deed to be executed as of the day and year first written above.

_____
James Lin

_____
Alice Stevens

COMMONWEALTH OF PENNSYLVANIA   :

COUNTY OF PRINCE   :

On this, the 2nd Day of December 2013, before me, a Notary Public, the undersigned officer, personally appeared James Lin and Alice Stevens, known to me (or satisfactorily proven) to be the persons whose names are subscribed to the within instrument, and acknowledged that they executed the same for the purposes therein contained.

IN WITNESS WHEREOF, I have hereunto set my hand and notarial seal.

_____
Notary Public

Remember that deeds do not need to be recorded to be a valid conveyance from the grantor to the grantee. Deeds, of course, should be recorded to protect the grantee against subsequent interest holders.

Even if a deed satisfies the Statute of Frauds, it also must be delivered to be effective. Deed delivery is almost never a problem in sales of real property, because the buyer is unlikely to give the purchase price to the seller unless the deed is delivered. Lack of delivery, however, can be an issue in gifts of real property, especially if the grantor is trying to use the deed as a will substitute. Imagine, for example, that Father owns Blackacre. Father wants Daughter to have Blackacre after he dies, so he executes a deed conveying Blackacre to Daughter. Father does not deliver the deed to Daughter, and instead leaves it in his desk drawer with instructions that the daughter take the deed when he dies. The deed would be ineffective for lack of delivery.

ESTOPPEL BY DEED

The doctrine of estoppel by deed applies in the rare circumstance where (a) the grantor delivers a deed to a grantee at a time when the grantor does not have actual ownership of the property, but (b) at some time after deed delivery, the grantor gets ownership of the property. Consider this example:

A delivers a deed to Blackacre to B. At the time, A does not own Blackacre. Rather, at the time, Blackacre is owned by O.

At a later time, O delivers a deed to Blackacre to A.

Under the doctrine of estoppel by deed, title automatically transfers by operation of law to B when A receives the deed from O. There is no need for A to deliver another deed to B, or for B to have to bring an action to quiet title to establish clear title to Blackacre. This said, B may want to take steps to establish a clear chain of title, as discussed in our materials on wild deeds, above. Estoppel by deed typically only applies when the deed contains some kind of assertion about the quality of title. As a result, it typically applies to warranty deeds, but not to quitclaim deeds. If you are having a hard time imagining a real world scenario where estoppel by deed comes into play, consider two examples. First, imagine that A is a wheeler-dealer business person who plays fast and loose with the details of transactions. A is expecting to get a deed to Blackacre from O shortly, but does not wait to actually get the deed before conveying Blackacre to B. O later conveys Blackacre to A as expected. Second, imagine that A expects to inherit Blackacre from O. Before O dies, A conveys Blackacre to B. O later dies and in fact leaves Blackacre to A. In either case, estoppel by deed will operate to convey good title to B as soon as O conveys title to A.

Gifts of real property present some of the same issues that we saw in our discussion of gifts of personal property. Delivery must be made with the present intent to transfer the interest then and there. Courts are going to be hostile to gifts that are intended to take effect at the death of the grantor, even if delivery is made, because this kind of gift undercuts the Statute of Wills. On the other hand, courts are lenient on the physical act of delivery if the intent to presently transfer the interest is clear. Indeed, it is often said that the *delivery of a deed does not require the deed to be physically handed over.* As the great English jurist Sir Edward Coke put it, "As a deed may be delivered to the party without words, so may a deed be delivered by words without any act of delivery." 1 Co. Litt. 36A. If Father stands up at a party and says "through this deed I am giving Blackacre to Daughter," that will likely constitute delivery even if the deed is not physically handed over. The key point is that the grantor must clearly intend to make a present transfer of the interest in the deed.

As we will see in our next case, physically handing the deed over might not be enough to constitute delivery if there are worries about the grantor's intent.

ROSENGRANT V. ROSENGRANT

Court of Appeals of Oklahoma, 1981
629 P.2d 800

BOYDSTON, Judge. This is an appeal by J.W. (Jay) Rosengrant from the trial court's decision to cancel and set aside a warranty deed which attempted to vest title in him to certain property owned by his aunt and uncle, Mildred and Harold Rosengrant. The trial court held the deed was invalid for want of legal delivery. We affirm that decision.

Harold and Mildred were a retired couple living on a farm southeast of Tecumseh, Oklahoma. They had no children of their own but had six nieces and nephews through Harold's deceased brother. One of these nephews was Jay Rosengrant. He and his wife lived a short distance from Harold and Mildred and helped the elderly couple from time to time with their chores.

In 1971, it was discovered that Mildred had cancer. In July, 1972 Mildred and Harold went to Mexico to obtain laetrile treatments accompanied by Jay's wife. Jay remained behind to care for the farm.

Shortly before this trip, on June 23, 1972, Mildred had called Jay and asked him to meet her and Harold at Farmers and Merchants Bank in Tecumseh. Upon arriving at the bank, Harold introduced Jay to his banker J.E. Vanlandengham who presented Harold and Mildred with a deed to their farm which he had prepared according to their instructions. Both Harold and Mildred signed the deed and informed Jay that they were going to give him "the place," but that they wanted Jay to leave the deed at the bank with Mr. Vanlandengham and when "something happened" to them, he was to take it to Shawnee and record it and "it" would be theirs. Harold personally handed the deed to Jay to "make this legal." Jay accepted the deed and then handed it back to the banker who told him he would put it in an envelope and keep it in the vault until he called for it.

In July, 1974, when Mildred's death was imminent, Jay and Harold conferred with an attorney concerning the legality of the transaction. The attorney advised them it should be sufficient but if Harold anticipated problems he should draw up a will.

In 1976, Harold discovered he had lung cancer. In August and December 1977, Harold put $10,000 into two certificates of deposit in joint tenancy with Jay.

Harold died January 28, 1978. On February 2, Jay and his wife went to the bank to inventory the contents of the safety deposit box. They also requested the envelope containing the deed which was retrieved from the collection file of the bank.

Jay went to Shawnee the next day and recorded the deed.

The petition to cancel and set aside the deed was filed February 22, 1978, alleging that the deed was void in that it was never legally delivered and alternatively that since it was to be operative only upon recordation after the death of the grantors it was a testamentary instrument and was void for failure to comply with the Statute of Wills.

The trial court found the deed was null and void for failure of legal delivery. The dispositive issue raised on appeal is whether the trial court erred in so ruling. We hold it did not and affirm the judgment.

The facts surrounding the transaction which took place at the bank were uncontroverted. It is the interpretation of the meaning and legal result of the transaction which is the issue to be determined by this court on appeal.

In cases involving attempted transfers such as this, it is the grantor's intent at the time the deed is delivered which is of primary and controlling importance. It is the function of this court to weigh the evidence presented at trial as to grantor's intent and unless the trial court's decision is clearly against the weight of the evidence, to uphold that finding.

The grantor and banker were both dead at the time of trial. Consequently, the only testimony regarding the transaction was supplied by the grantee, Jay. The pertinent part of his testimony is as follows:

A. (A)nd was going to hand it back to Mr. Vanlandingham [sic], and he wouldn't take it.

Q. What did Mr. Vanlandingham [sic] say?

A. Well, he laughed then and said that "We got to make this legal," or something like that. And said, "You'll have to give it to Jay and let Jay give it back to me."

Q. And what did Harold do with the document?

A. He gave it to me.

Q. Did you hold it?

A. Yes.

Q. Then what did you do with it?

A. Mr. Vanlandingham [sic], I believe, told me I ought to look at it.

Q. And you looked at it?

A. Yes.

Q. And then what did you do with it?

A. I handed it to Mr. Vanlandingham [*sic*].

Q. And what did he do with the document?

A. He had it in his hand, I believe, when we left.

Q. Do you recall seeing the envelope at any time during this transaction?

A. I never saw the envelope. But Mr. Vanlandingham [*sic*] told me when I handed it to him, said, "Jay, I'll put this in an envelope and keep it in a vault for you until you call for it."

A. Well, Harold told me while Mildred was signing the deed that they were going to deed me the farm, but they wanted me to leave the deed at the bank with Van, and that when something happened to them that I would go to the bank and pick it up and take it to Shawnee to the court house and record it, and it would be mine.

When the deed was retrieved, it was contained in an envelope on which was typed: "J.W. Rosengrant- or Harold H. Rosengrant."

The import of the writing on the envelope is clear. It creates an inescapable conclusion that the deed was, in fact, retrievable at any time by Harold before his death. The bank teller's testimony as to the custom and usage of the bank leaves no other conclusion but that at any time Harold was free to retrieve the deed. There was, if not an expressed, an implied agreement between the banker and Harold that the grant was not to take effect until two conditions occurred—the death of both grantors and the recordation of the deed.

In support of this conclusion conduct relative to the property is significant and was correctly considered by the court. Evidence was presented to show that after the deed was filed Harold continued to farm, use and control the property. Further, he continued to pay taxes on it until his death and claimed it as his homestead.

Grantee confuses the issues involved herein by relying upon grantors' goodwill toward him and his wife as if it were a controlling factor. From a fair review of the record it is apparent Jay and his wife were very attentive, kind and helpful to this elderly couple. The donative intent on the part of grantors is undeniable. We believe they fully intended to reward Jay and his wife for their kindness. Nevertheless, where a grantor delivers a deed under which he reserves a right of retrieval and attaches to that delivery the condition that the deed is to become operative only after the death of grantors and further continues to use the property as if no transfer had occurred grantor's actions are nothing more than an attempt to employ the deed as if it were a will. Under Oklahoma law this cannot be done. The ritualistic "delivery of the deed" to the grantee and his redelivery of it to the third party for safe keeping created under these circumstances only a symbolic delivery. It amounted to a pro forma attempt to comply with the legal aspects of delivery. Based on all the facts and circumstances the true intent of the parties is expressed by the notation on the envelope and by the later conduct of the parties in relation to the land. Legal delivery is not just a symbolic gesture. It necessarily carries all the force and consequence of absolute, outright ownership at the time of delivery or it is no delivery at all.

The trial court interpreted the envelope literally. The clear implication is that grantor intended to continue to exercise control and that the grant was not to take effect until such time as both he and his wife had died and the deed had been recorded. From a complete review of the record and weighing of the evidence we find the trial court's judgment is not clearly against the weight of the evidence. Costs of appeal are taxed to appellant.

BACON, P.J., concurs.

BRIGHTMIRE, Judge, concurring specially. In a dispute of this kind dealing with the issue of whether an unrecorded deed placed in the custody of a third party is a valid conveyance to the named grantee at that time or is deposited for some other reason, such as in trust or for a testamentary purpose, the fact finder often has a particularly tough job trying to determine what the true facts are.

The law, on the other hand, is relatively clear. A valid in praesenti conveyance requires two things: (1) actual or constructive delivery of the deed to the grantee or to a third party; and (2) an intention by the grantor to divest himself of the conveyed interest. Here the trial judge found there was no delivery despite the testimony of Jay Rosengrant to the contrary that one of the grantors handed the deed to him at the suggestion of banker J.E. Vanlandengham.

So the question is, was the trial court bound to find the fact to be as Rosengrant stated? In my opinion he was not for several reasons. Of the four persons present at the bank meeting in question only Rosengrant survives which, when coupled with the self-serving nature of the nephew's statements, served to cast a suspicious cloud over his testimony. And this, when considered along with other circumstances detailed in the majority opinion, would have justified the fact finder in disbelieving it. I personally have trouble with the delivery testimony in spite of the apparent "corroboration" of the lawyer, Jeff Diamond. The only reason I can see for Vanlandengham suggesting such a physical delivery would be to assure the accomplishment of a valid conveyance of the property at that time. But if the grantors intended that then why did they simply give it to the named grantee and tell him to record it? Why did they go through the delivery motion in the presence of Vanlandengham and then give the deed to the banker? Why did the banker write on the envelope containing the deed that it was to be given to either the grantee "or" a grantor? The fact that the grantors continued to occupy the land, paid taxes on it, offered to sell it once and otherwise treated it as their own justifies an inference that they did not make an actual delivery of the deed to the named grantee. Or, if they did, they directed that it be left in the custody of the banker with the intent of reserving a de facto life estate or of retaining a power of revocation by instructing the banker to return it to them if they requested it during their lifetimes or to give it to the named grantee upon their deaths. In either case, the deed failed as a valid conveyance.

I therefore join in affirming the trial court's judgment.

NOTES AND QUESTIONS

1. *Donative Intent.* The court indicated that "The donative intent on the part of grantors is undeniable." Why, then, did Jay lose? Do you think the court came to the right result on these facts?

2. *The Correct Solution.* We hope it is obvious that the Rosengrants' attorney should have advised Harold to execute a will or create a trust to make it clear that Jay would get the property. If they wanted to keep possession during their lifetimes, Harold and Mildred (or Harold alone after Mildred's death) could have conveyed the property to Jay while retaining a life estate in themselves. As we discussed in the Present and Future Interests chapter, this kind of transfer is best achieved using a trust.

3. *Matters of Proof.* Do you think that the case would have turned out differently if Mr. Vanlandengham had lived long enough to testify at trial? Compare, in this regard, *Carter v. Percy*, our case from Chapter 1 involving a gift made by check. In that case, a bank official gave testimony in favor of the done. The donee won on circumstances where evidence of donative intent was weaker (in our opinion, at least) than in *Rosengrant*.

CONDITIONAL DELIVERY AND DELIVERY TO A THIRD PARTY

What happens if a grantor tries to put a condition on the delivery of a deed? Conditions tied to the grantor's death almost always render the deed invalid because of Statute of Wills concerns. The outcome for other types of conditions is less clear. As an example, consider a conveyance where the Arthur, the grantor, conditions a conveyance to Brenda, the grantee, on the condition that Brenda survive Arthur. To be clear, Arthur is not conveying a contingent future interest to Brenda. Rather, the deed itself conveys a fee simple absolute, and Arthur is attempting to place a condition on the delivery of the deed and to make delivery effective only if the condition is met. The authorities are split on the effect of conditions other than the death of the grantor. The *majority* view is that the condition is unenforceable and the delivery is valid. Under this approach, the conveyance from Arthur to Brenda would be valid, whether or not Brenda survived Arthur. The *minority* view is that the condition is enforceable and the delivery is valid only if the condition is met. Under this approach, the conveyance from Arthur to Brenda would be valid only if Brenda survives Arthur. There may be something of a modern trend towards the minority approach.

What happens if the grantor delivers a deed to a third person, with an instruction to deliver the deed to the grantee if a condition is met? In this circumstance, the condition will be valid and the delivery effective *so long as the grantor does not maintain a degree of control over the deed by reserving the right to take back the deed*. (This issue of control was important in *Rosengrant*.) This is true even if the *condition is the grantor's death*. The involvement of the third party gives us an unbiased source of confirmation of the grantor's intent that is absent if the third party was not involved, mitigating some of the concerns that we might have about a transfer at death without a will.

If a third party is involved, delivery to the grantee is effective as soon as delivery is made to the third party, so long as the grantor has given up control of the deed and has not retained the power to get it back. In this context, delivery is often said to *relate back* to the date of delivery to the third party, even if it is delivered to the grantee at a significantly later time.

A deed must be accepted by the grantee to be effective. As we saw with gifts of personal property, acceptance is presumed if the property is valuable, and acceptance is rarely contested. The acceptance requirement does allow an unwilling grantee to avoid taking ownership of an undesirable property. For example, if I attempted to give you a deed to my toxic waste dump, you could refuse to accept the deed. Although acceptance is rarely contested, it does have an important legal consequence. By accepting the deed, *the grantee is bound by any conditions or obligations in the deed, even though the grantee did not sign the deed.*

A deed signed by only the grantor is sometimes called a *deed poll*. A deed signed by both parties is sometimes called an *indenture*, although you will often see the word indenture used in modern deeds signed by only the grantor. Both terms are archaic. An indenture was a deed executed by both parties in duplicate on a single piece of parchment and cut in half along a ragged line. Each party would retain one of the halves, and the ability to match the two halves into one piece would provide some evidence of the authenticity of the document. "Poll" was a term for an instrument that was cut on a straight, rather than ragged, edge.

FORGERY AND FRAUD

Sometimes deeds are forged. Sometimes they are procured by fraud. The law treats forged deeds and deeds procured by fraud differently. Forged deeds are void and do not pass good title to any person in the subsequent chain of title. Deeds procured by fraud, in contrast, are voidable but do convey good title to subsequent good faith purchasers. To illustrate these rules, and to explain the rationale for the differences between them, let's consider two examples. In each case, we have three characters: Owner is the owner of Blackacre. Crook is our forger/fraudster. Buyer is a subsequent good faith purchaser who buys from Crook, but who has no notice that there is anything amiss with the transaction.

EXAMPLE 1: Owner owned Blackacre. Crook forged a deed to Blackacre. The deed made it appear that Owner granted Blackacre to Crook. Crook then conveyed to Buyer. Buyer purchased in good faith, with no notice of the forgery. The forged Owner-Crook deed is void. It did not convey any title to Crook. More importantly, it did not convey any interest to Buyer, or any person further down the chain of title. In other words, Owner will win a quiet title action to Blackacre against Crook, Buyer and anyone who later buys from Buyer. (At some point, the Statute of Limitations might run against Owner, under the adverse possession rules that we covered in Chapter 1. Recall our discussion of color of title and constructive adverse possession, which would apply to a forged deed.)

EXAMPLE 2: Owner owned Blackacre. Crook procured a deed to Blackacre by fraud by tricking Owner into signing the deed when she thought she was signing something else. This deed, which had Owner's actual signature, conveyed Blackacre from Owner to Crook. At this point, this deed is voidable as between Owner and Crook. That is, in a lawsuit by Owner against Crook, Owner will win and will be able to a court to void the deed procured by fraud. Later, Crook conveyed Blackacre to Buyer, who purchased in good faith, with no notice of the fraud. Buyer will win a quiet tile action against Owner. Where a deed has been procured by fraud, subsequent good faith purchasers will win against the original owner of the property.

Why do these rules treat forged deeds and deeds procured by fraud differently when they are conveyed to subsequent good faith purchasers? In each scenario, we have two innocent parties—Owner and Buyer. In the forged deed scenario, there is nothing that Owner could have done to avoid the problem. In the scenario where the deed was procured by fraud, however, if Owner had been more attentive and careful, she might have noticed the fraud and have been able to prevent it. In the deed procured by fraud scenario, then, we can place at least some blame on the Owner, and it makes sense that Owner will lose against the innocent Buyer.

G. REAL ESTATE FINANCE

1. INTRODUCTION: SECURED FINANCE, MORTGAGES, AND DEEDS OF TRUST

Real estate tends to be expensive, and very few people can pay cash for a home or other real estate purchase. As a result, most real estate transactions are paid for largely with borrowed money. In this section we will discuss the fundamentals of the real estate finance process.

We have already seen mortgages at a few points, and you already probably have some intuitive idea of how a mortgage transaction works. The traditional mortgage loan, however, is only one of many ways to structure a real estate finance transaction. Before we get into the details of different transactional structures, we will first start at a more basic level and examine the interests of the parties involved.

Let's imagine that I am borrowing $400,000 from you to purchase a home. As the borrower, my interests are fairly straightforward—I want access to your money on the most favorable terms possible. We will discuss some important mortgage terms below, but probably the most important single term for the borrower is the interest rate—the lower the better for the borrower. We will likely set things up so that I make monthly payments to you that, over time, will pay you both the principal of the loan (i.e., the $400,000 that I borrowed from you) and the interest that you are charging me in return for making the loan. As the lender, your single biggest worry is that I will not repay the money that I owe you. You don't want to risk lending me that amount of money with only my promise as assurance of my repayment. To protect yourself from my failure to pay, you will insist that I provide the house as *collateral* to secure my repayment of the loan. That is, you will seek to set up our transaction so that if I fail to pay you back, you will be able to use the value of the home to repay the loan.

In sum, the lender in a real estate transaction will typically want two primary things: (1) a series of payments of money representing the principal and interest on the loan and (2) a way to access the property as collateral if the borrower fails to pay the loan back. There are several ways to structure a real estate finance transaction, but all of them allow the lender to achieve these two goals.

The most common forms of residential real estate finance are loans secured by the traditional mortgage and its cousin the deed of trust. In its modern form, the *mortgage loan* has two basic components. In return for the loan of money, the borrower delivers to the lender (a) a promissory note and (b) a mortgage. The promissory note, or *note* for short, is the borrower's promise to repay the loan.

The *mortgage* itself is a grant of a security interest in the property from the borrower to the lender. This security interest allows the lender to foreclose on the property in the event the borrower fails to honor the promissory note. The note and the mortgage are linked by a statement in the note that it is secured by the mortgage. We will cover foreclosure in more depth shortly, but for now it is enough to know that the foreclosure process allows the lender to force a sale of the property and use the proceeds as repayment of the loan.

A mortgage must secure an obligation. The obligation typically is embodied in a note, but it may be embodied in another type of document. If there is no obligation, then the mortgage is a nullity. There is no requirement, however, that there be consideration for a mortgage. A mortgage securing a gratuitous obligation, or a mortgage securing a pre-existing obligation, generally will be valid. *See* Restatement (Third) of Property, Mortgages §§1.1-1.2. (We presume here that you have studied consideration in your Contracts class; a detailed discussion of the concept of consideration is beyond the scope of this course.)

HISTORICAL MORTGAGE FORMS AND THE TITLE THEORY AND LIEN THEORY OF MORTGAGES

In historical England, a lender's collateral for a loan secured by real property was structured as a grant of a defeasible interest from the borrower to the lender. The borrower would grant title to the lender, on the condition subsequent that if the borrower repaid the loan the borrower could exercise a right of entry and retake title to the property. Consistent with our discussion of defeasibile interests in our chapter on Present and Future Interests, the grant of this interest would be in a form like this: "Borrower grants Blackacre to Lender, but if Borrower repays the loan amount on the amount due, Borrower may re-enter and retake ownership of Blackacre." In a transaction like this, the lender was the present interest holder of the property. As the present interest holder, the lender had the present right of possession of the property, although the parties might agree that the borrower could continue to occupy the property during the loan term.

In contemporary U.S. property law, there are two common theories of mortgages, the title theory and the lien theory. We briefly introduced these theories in our material on the severance of joint tenancies. Broadly speaking, the *title theory* of mortgages views a mortgage as a conveyance of title to the lender/mortgagee. The *lien theory*, in contrast, views a mortgage as the conveyance of lien to the lender/mortgagee.

Over time, the differences between these two approaches have eroded. Title theory jurisdictions now treat the grant of title in a mortgage as a grant of a security interest, rather than a grant of a defeasible fee interest. A lien, of course, is a security interest, and with this change in approach title theory jurisdictions have evolved to take similar approaches on most issues to lien theory jurisdictions.

This said, two significant differences remain between title theory and lien theory jurisdictions. First, as we discussed in the chapter on Concurrent Ownership, title theory jurisdictions often treat the unilateral mortgage of the property by one joint tenant as a conveyance that severs the joint tenancy. Lien theory jurisdictions are much less likely to treat a unilateral mortgage as a severance of a joint tenancy. Second, title theory jurisdictions tend to retain the view that the lender/mortgagee has certain possessory rights during the mortgage. The right to receive rents generated by the property, for example, typically goes with the possession of the property. In a title theory jurisdiction, the lender/mortgagee will often have the right to receive rents during the term of the mortgage. In a lien theory jurisdiction, the borrower/mortgagor would have clear possession of the property and would be entitled to the rents. Even this distinction, however, increasingly has little significance because possessory issues like the entitlement to rents typically are addressed by the parties in the mortgage. In most circumstances, courts will respect the language of the mortgage on these issues.

With these basic components, the basic mortgage transaction looks like this:

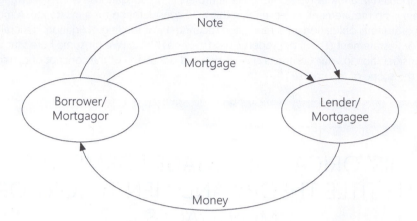

The lender gives the borrower money. In return, the borrower delivers the note and the mortgage to the lender. Note well that *the borrower grants the mortgage to the lender*, not the other way around. As a result, *the borrower is the mortgagor, and the lender is the mortgagee*. We often speak colloquially about a person getting a mortgage from a bank. What we actually mean when we say this is that the person is getting a loan from the bank that is secured by a mortgage. The mortgage itself is the security interest granted by the borrower to the lender, not the underlying loan.

The entire purpose of the mortgage is to allow the lender to foreclose on the property in the event that the borrower defaults on the obligations in the note. As we noted above, the foreclosure process involves the sale of the property. In the United States today, there are two common types of foreclosure, and jurisdictions typically follow one approach or the other. The first is *judicial foreclosure*. In a judicial foreclosure jurisdiction, foreclosure occurs through a judicial proceeding and the foreclosure sale is subject to judicial supervision. The second is *power of sale foreclosure*. In a power of sale jurisdiction, foreclosure is a private process. The lender or other private party is given the power to sell the property on default by the borrower. There is no direct judicial supervision of the foreclosure sale.

We will discuss the pros and cons of judicial and power of sale foreclosures further below. In jurisdictions that allow power of sale foreclosure, an alternative to a mortgage called a *deed of trust* is commonly used in real estate finance. In a mortgage, there are two parties to the transaction—the borrower and the lender. In a deed of trust, there are three parties to the transaction—the borrower, the lender, and the trustee. The borrower conveys title to the property to the trustee through an instrument called a deed of trust. The trustee is given the power to sell the property if the borrower defaults on the note.

Here is what a deed of trust transaction looks like:

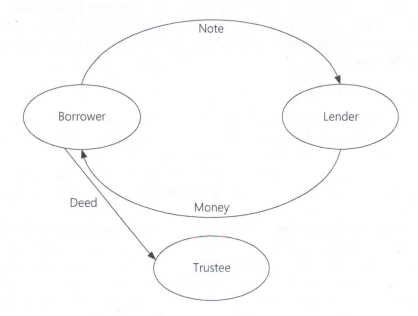

The deed of trust structure is used to make a power of sale foreclosure clean and easy. Despite the differences in formal structure, the deed of trust generally behaves like a mortgage in the power of sale jurisdictions that allow them. You should be aware of the formal differences between the two, but in most legal contexts, deeds of trust are treated identically to mortgages. Indeed, the mortgage and deed of trust forms promulgated by the Federal Home Loan Mortgage Corporation (widely known as Freddie Mac) are identical in most respects. The granting clauses of the two forms, however, are different. Remember that a mortgage is an interest in property. A document creating a mortgage or deed of trust, just like a deed, will have a granting clause that conveys the property interest to the grantee. Here are the granting clauses from the forms:

> *Granting Clause from a Mortgage*: This Security Instrument secures to Lender: (i) the repayment of the Loan, and all renewals, extensions and modifications of the Note; and (ii) the performance of Borrower's covenants and agreements under this Security Instrument and the Note. For this purpose, Borrower *does hereby mortgage, grant and convey to Lender the following described property* . . .

> *Granting Clause from a Deed of Trust*: This Security Instrument secures to Lender: (i) the repayment of the Loan, and all renewals, extensions and modifications of the Note; and (ii) the performance of Borrower's covenants and agreements under this Security Instrument and the Note. For this purpose, Borrower *irrevocably grants and conveys to Trustee, in trust, with power of sale, the following described property* . . . .

Later in this section, we will briefly discuss other ways to structure a real estate financing. For now, we will focus on mortgages and deeds of trust transactions. Because mortgages and deeds of trust are often functionally identical, we will generally talk about mortgages, with the understanding that in most circumstances deeds of trust operate in the same way.

2. FORECLOSURES

The entire point of a mortgage is to give the lender access to the value of the property in the event that the borrower defaults on the obligation in the note to repay the loan. In contemporary legal practice, this purpose is achieved by a foreclosure sale. By foreclosing on the property, the lender/mortgagee forces a sale of the property and uses the proceeds from the sale to satisfy the obligation that the borrower/mortgagor has defaulted upon.

Before we get to the foreclosure sale process, we need to take a step back and look at some history. At early common law, the borrower would typically be obligated to repay the entire debt on a particular day, rather than make monthly payments as we typically do today. If the borrower failed to make the payment even a day late, the borrower would typically lose the land to the lender. To protect borrowers from overreaching lenders, the equity courts began to allow borrowers to retain ownership of the property by paying off the loan even if the borrower missed the formal due date. This right became known as the *equity of redemption*. The development of the equity of redemption solved one problem—abusive conduct by lenders—but created another one. If no time limit was set on the borrower's exercise of the equity of redemption, then the lender could never get clear ownership of the property to satisfy the obligation that the borrower had defaulted upon. The equity courts therefore set a time limit for the defaulting borrower's exercise of the equity of redemption. After the expiration of this time period, the borrower's equity of redemption

LAW AND EQUITY

CLOGGING AND THE EQUITY OF REDEMPTION

Having created it, courts have consistently and strongly protected the equity of redemption. As a result, a term in a mortgage or note that purports to waive or otherwise interfere with the borrower's right to redeem the property will typically be invalid. Courts often describe such terms as impermissibly "clogging" the equity of redemption.

POST-FORECLOSURE STATUTORY RIGHTS OF REDEMPTION

About half of U.S. jurisdictions have statutes that allow the borrower/mortgagor to redeem the property even *after* the property is foreclosed. These statutes, many of which date from the Depression era, typically apply only to homes and farms. The borrower/mortgagor typically has a set period of time (often one year) after the date of foreclosure to redeem the property. The borrower/mortgagor often retains possession during the statutory redemption period. As a result, the buyer from the foreclosure sale may have to wait a full year (a) to find out whether the borrower/mortgagor will redeem and (b) to take possession of the property. Post-foreclosure redemption statutes are intended to help defaulting borrower/mortgagors by giving them more time to come up with the money to pay off the debt and redeem the property. These statutes, however, make bidding on a property in a foreclosure sale less desirable for potential buyers by creating uncertainty and delay before the winning bidder can take ownership and possession of the property. By making purchase of a property in a foreclosure sale less desirable, statutory post-foreclosure rights of redemption arguably harm the very people (borrower/mortgagors facing foreclosure) that they are intended to protect.

would be terminated, or *foreclosed*. Once the equity of redemption was foreclosed, the lender became the fee simple owner of the property. This process, where the foreclosure ends with the lender getting fee simple ownership, is called *strict foreclosure*. Over time, strict foreclosure gave way to our current process of foreclosure sales. The termination of the borrower's equity of redemption remains a crucial component of the foreclosure process.

a. The Foreclosure Process—Judicial Foreclosure and Power of Sale Foreclosure

As we noted above, there are two common methods of foreclosure being used in the United States today—judicial foreclosure and power of sale foreclosure. Both methods result in a public sale of the foreclosed property. In a judicial foreclosure, the foreclosure process is initiated as a judicial proceeding and the foreclosure sale process is supervised by the court. In a power of sale foreclosure, the sale process is conducted by the lender. Deeds of trust are often popular in power of sale jurisdictions. If the obligation was secured by a deed of trust, the trustee, rather than the lender, holds the power of sale and conducts the foreclosure sale. In most U.S. jurisdictions, one process or the other dominates foreclosure practice. Power of sale foreclosure typically is not available in judicial foreclosure jurisdictions. Judicial foreclosure is available in power of sale jurisdictions, but will rarely be used if the local practice is to use power of sale foreclosures.

ACCELERATION

Most notes and mortgages today contain *acceleration clauses*. Acceleration typically is a preliminary step to foreclosure. Under these clauses, the full amount of the loan accelerates and becomes immediately due on the borrower's default. Consider, for example, a transaction where Borrower borrows $200,000 from the Lender and gives Lender a note agreeing to repay the loan with 5 percent interest by making monthly payments of $1,061 per month for 30 years. A few years later, Borrower stops making the monthly payments, defaulting on the note. At the time, Borrower still owes $175,000 in principal on the loan. On Borrower's default, the entire amount outstanding accelerates and becomes immediately due. This process is called *acceleration* because the parties originally agreed that the principal would be repaid in a series of payments made over 30 years. On default, the obligation to repay accelerates and the entire outstanding amount of debt becomes immediately due.

The main advantage of the judicial foreclosure process is that it provides due process protection and court supervision for property owners facing foreclosure. Its main disadvantage is that, like any judicial process, it can be slow and expensive. The main advantage of power of sale foreclosure is that it is relatively quick and inexpensive. The main disadvantage is that it lacks the process and fairness protections that are provided by judicial foreclosure.

b. Deficiency Judgments and the Recourse—Non-Recourse Distinction

A foreclosure typically ends with a sale of the property, with the proceeds of the sale going to satisfy the debt that had been secured by the mortgage. A *surplus* occurs if the sale brings in more than enough money to pay off the lender and cover the expenses of foreclosure. If there is a surplus, then it goes to the owner/mortgagor. For example, if you lose your home through foreclosure, and the foreclosure sale nets more than you owed to the lender, you will be entitled to the surplus.

A *deficiency* occurs if the foreclosure sale does not bring in enough money to pay off the lender/mortgagee. The deficiency is the difference between the amount owed and the foreclosure sale proceeds. Here is an example:

Outstanding debt:	$100,000
Foreclosure sale proceeds:	$90,000
Deficiency:	$10,000

In many jurisdictions, the lender/mortgagee can obtain a *deficiency judgment* against the borrower/mortgagor for the amount of the deficiency. A deficiency judgment is a court judgment against the borrower/mortgagor individually. The borrower/mortgagor, after all, signed a note promising to repay the amount of the loan. By defaulting, the borrower/mortgagor has breached this promise, and the lender/mortgagee can make a legal claim against the borrower/mortgagor for failure to repay. In a jurisdiction that permits deficiency judgments, the lender/mortgagee would be able to get a deficiency judgment of $10,000 against the borrower/mortgagor on the facts of the example above. This judgment, of course, might be of little or no actual value to the lender/mortgagee—people who default on their mortgage loans typically do not have other assets that can be used to satisfy the judgment. Recall in this context our discussion of counterparty risk—an ironclad court judgment against a person who is broke might not be worth the paper it is written on.

THE MIRACLE, AND CURSE, OF LEVERAGE

In the finance world, *leverage* is a synonym for debt. If a person owns an asset that is encumbered by a large amount of debt, that person's ownership is often called *highly leveraged*.

Leverage magnifies both the potential upside and potential downside of an investment. Say, for example, that you purchase an asset for $100,000 in cash. A year later, you sell that asset for $110,000. You have made $10,000 on your investment of $100,000 for a 10% profit. Now say that you purchased that same asset for $100,000, using $10,000 of your own money and borrowing the remaining $90,000 of the purchase price. A year later, you again sell the property for $110,000. You pay off the $90,000 that you borrowed, leaving you with $20,000. (We are ignoring interest and other expenses to keep the numbers simple.). In one year, you have doubled your initial investment of $10,000 for a 100% profit. Using borrowed money to purchase the asset has dramatically magnified the return on your investment.

Let's change the example to illustrate the potential downside of leverage. As before, you purchase an asset for $100,000. In one scenario, you pay $100,000 in cash for the asset. In the other, you pay $10,000 of your own money, and borrow the remaining $90,000. Now, however, the value of the property declines. A year after you bought it, you sell the property for $90,000. In the scenario where you paid $100,000 in cash, you have lost $10,000, or 10% of your investment. In the scenario where you used $10,000 of your own money and borrowed the remaining $90,000, you have again lost $10,000, but now that $10,000 represents a 100% loss of your investment.

Most people's homes are highly leveraged, because they borrow the majority of the purchase price of the home. As our examples showed, if a person borrowed a high percentage of the purchase price, a relatively small increase in value of the home can lead to a large return on investment but a relatively small decline in value can entirely wipe out the person's investment.

Some jurisdictions have *anti-deficiency statutes*. As their name implies, these statutes prohibit the lender/mortgagee from obtaining a deficiency judgment against the borrower/mortgagor. Anti-deficiency statutes typically apply only to residential mortgage transactions. In a jurisdiction with an anti-deficiency statute, the lender/mortgagee would not be able to obtain a deficiency judgment against the borrower/mortgagor in the above example. The borrower/mortgagor would walk away from the foreclosure with no personal liability. Anti-deficiency statutes have their detractors and defenders. On the one hand, they allow borrower/mortgagors to walk away from obligations that they had agreed to undertake. On the other hand, they force lenders, who often are far more sophisticated than borrowers, to be more careful in the loans that they make.

Recall that the core point of secured finance is to allow the lender to reach the collateral to satisfy the debt if the borrower defaults. The transaction could be set up so that if the collateral is not sufficient, the lender can obtain a judgment against the borrower for the remainder of the debt. If the transaction is set up in this way, it is called a *recourse* transaction, because the lender has recourse (i.e., can obtain a judgment) against the borrower individually. In a jurisdiction that allows deficiency judgments, mortgage transactions typically are recourse transactions.

The transaction, however, could also be set up so that the lender is limited to the amount of collateral. In this type of transaction, the lender cannot obtain a judgment against the borrower for the remainder of the debt. If the transaction is set up in this way, it is called a *non-recourse* transaction, because the lender does not have recourse against the borrower individually. In jurisdictions with anti-deficiency statutes, residential mortgage transactions are non-recourse as a matter of law.

Anti-deficiency statutes, however, are not the only way for a transaction to be non-recourse. Transactions, for example, may be made non-recourse by contract or by corporate structure, and there are many areas of secured finance where non-recourse transactions are very common. We will not go into depth about these other mechanisms for making transactions non-recourse. You should understand the basic recourse versus non-recourse distinction, however, because these terms and concepts are frequently used in a wide range of legal transactions.

"UNDERWATER" PROPERTIES AND SHORT SALES

When a mortgage loan is made, the value of the property is almost always higher than the amount of the loan. Property values can decline, however, leading to situations where the value of the property is less than the outstanding amount of the loan. When the current value of a property is less than the amount owed on the mortgage loan, we often say that the property is "underwater" or "upside-down."

The owner of a property that is underwater might want to sell, but potential buyers will be unwilling to purchase the property unless the existing mortgage is satisfied. Owners in this situation often ask the lender to agree to what is called a *short sale*. In a short sale, the lender/mortgagee agrees to release the mortgage on the property in return for less than full payment of the amount outstanding on the loan. In some cases, the lender will agree to release the borrower/mortgagor from liability for the additional amount due on the loan. In other cases, the borrower/mortgagor will remain liable for the remaining deficiency. The crucial point for the sale going forward is that the lender/mortgage will agree to release the mortgage, allowing the buyer to take the property with clear title.

For example, consider a home owned by Linda. Linda owes First National Bank $325,000 on a loan secured by a mortgage on the home. Linda wants to sell the property, and Mark is willing to buy it. The sale to Mark, however, will only bring in $300,000 after expenses are paid. This amount will not be enough to pay off First National Bank in full, and Mark will not buy the property unless First National Bank releases the mortgage. If First National Bank agrees to a short sale, it will accept the $300,000 and will release the mortgage. Mark will take title free and clear of the mortgage. Depending on the specifics of the transaction, Linda may or may not be liable to First National Bank for the $25,000 difference between the amount owed ($325,000) and the net proceeds from the sale ($300,000).

c. Adequacy of Foreclosure Sale Price

It is not unusual for properties to sell at foreclosure for less than their fair market value. There are a host of potential reasons for depressed foreclosure sale prices. The rules governing foreclosure sales often require notice of the sale that falls far short of the advertising efforts that would be made by a real estate broker in a typical transaction, leading to a relatively small pool of potential buyers. Those potential buyers who do bid might be worried about potential title issues that might arise from problems with the foreclosure process. Potential buyers might also be worried about physical condition issues—homes that are subject to foreclosure often are not well maintained, and the owner of the foreclosed home might not be cooperative in allowing inspection by potential buyers.

Courts will often be willing to overturn a foreclosure sale for procedural defects. If the foreclosure sale was conducted in a procedurally appropriate manner, however, courts will rarely interfere with a foreclosure sale on the grounds that the foreclosure sale price was inadequate. Generally speaking, a court will only invalidate a foreclosure sale on price grounds if the sale price was *grossly inadequate*. The grossly inadequate standard is a demanding one. According to the Restatement, "a court is warranted in invalidating a sale where the price is less than 20 percent of fair market value and, absent other foreclosure defects, is usually not warranted in invalidating a sale that yields in excess of that amount." Restatement (Third) of Property, Mortgages §8.3 cmt. b. Thus, a foreclosure sale for $100,000 of a home with a fair market value of $400,000 would be adequate and upheld under the Restatement test, because the sale price was 25 percent of the fair market value.

The courts in some jurisdictions are more protective of the foreclosed property owner and may require the people conducting the foreclosure sale to take affirmative steps to get the best sale price possible. *See, e.g., Murphy v. Fin. Dev. Corp.*, 495 A.2d 1245 (1985). The Restatement argues for legislative reform of the foreclosure system to address price issues:

> [P]rice inadequacy must be addressed in the context of a fundamental legislative reform of the entire foreclosure process so that it yields a price more closely approximating "fair market value." In order to ameliorate the price-suppressing tendency of the "forced sale" system, such legislative reform could incorporate many of the sale and advertising techniques found in the normal real estate market place. These could include, for example, the use of real estate brokers and commonly used print and pictorial media advertising. While such a major restructuring of the foreclosure process is desirable, it is more appropriate subject for legislative action than for the Restatement process.

Restatement (Third) of Property, Mortgages §8.3 cmt. a. While this type of reform may, indeed, be desirable, only a small minority of jurisdictions provide meaningful price-based protections for property owners facing foreclosure. The strong *majority rule* remains that courts will only interfere with a procedurally correct foreclosure sale if the sale price is grossly inadequate.

Because foreclosure sales often lead to reduced prices, the best option for a person facing foreclosure is often to try to voluntarily sell the property on the open market. People facing the loss of their homes understandably often want to resist foreclosure and to try to find a way to keep their property. If default and the loss of the home become inevitable, however, listing the property for sale will often be a good idea. Even if the price is a bit below market value, there is a strong likelihood that a voluntary sale will be better than a foreclosure sale for the owner.

d. The Assumption—Subject-To Distinction

In most real estate transactions, the existing mortgage loan will be paid off and the mortgage satisfied as part of the closing process. Sometimes, however, the parties will leave the loan and the mortgage in place. Sometimes this is the result of an error by the parties. Other times, the loan and the mortgage will be left in place intentionally. There are circumstances where it can be financially beneficial to do so. For example, if interest rates have increased dramatically, the buyer of the property might be better off taking on the seller's lower-rate note and the mortgage that secures it. As another example, some jurisdictions have mortgage-registration taxes that must be paid when a mortgage is recorded. New York State and New York City both have mortgage registration taxes that together add up to almost 2 percent of the loan value. To avoid paying taxes on recording a new mortgage, it may make sense for the buyer to try to step into the shoes of the seller and take on the obligations of the seller's mortgage loan.

Let's use an example to illustrate the consequences of leaving the loan and mortgage in place. Blackacre is owned by Original Borrower/Mortgagor, who borrowed money from Lender/Mortgagee secured by a recorded mortgage on Blackacre. Original Borrower/Mortgagor then sells Blackacre to New Owner. The money owed to Lender/Mortgagee is not paid off, and the mortgage is not satisfied as part of the closing.

At a minimum, New Owner is *subject to* the mortgage. This means that if Original Borrower/Mortgagor defaults on the note, Lender/Mortgagee can foreclose on the mortgage on Blackacre. As a prior recorded interest, the mortgage will be valid against New Owner. New Owner could pay off the note to Lender/Mortgagee to avoid foreclosure, but if New Owner fails to do so then the property will be sold at foreclosure. This is not a happy circumstance for New Owner, especially if the mortgage was left in place due to an error. As bad as it is, however, New Owner's worst-case scenario is losing the property through foreclosure. If New Owner is merely subject to Lender/Mortgagee's mortgage, New Owner will not be personally liable for any deficiency that arises from the foreclosure sale.

In some circumstances, New Owner will *assume* Original Borrower/Mortgagor's obligations under the note and mortgage. Assumption is achieved through an affirmative agreement by New Owner to take on these obligations. In an assumption, New Owner is not only subject to the mortgage, but is also personally liable for the note and mortgage obligations. As a result, if there is a default, New Owner not only faces loss of the property through foreclosure, but also will be responsible for any deficiency that arises out of the foreclosure sale.

The crucial difference between a subject to transaction and an assumption is in New Owner's personal liability and exposure to a deficiency judgment. With a subject to transaction, New Owner is not personally liable and will not face a deficiency judgment. With an assumption, New Owner is personally liable and will face a deficiency judgment.

Here is a fact pattern where the distinction matters. Say that Borrower/Mortgagor sells the property to New Owner, then defaults on the note and mortgage. The Lender/Mortgagee forecloses on the property. The outstanding debt is $200,000. After expenses, the foreclosure sale bring in $150,000. In other words, there is a deficiency—the

WASTE AND THE OBLIGATION OF BORROWER/MORTGAGOR TO MAINTAIN THE PROPERTY

Most notes and mortgages contain language requiring the Borrower/Mortgagor to maintain the property in good condition. Even if the transactional documents were silent on this issue, however, the Borrower/Mortgagor would still have an obligation to maintain the property under the common-law doctrine of waste. We saw this doctrine in our materials on present and future interests. The rules of waste apply in the mortgagor/mortgagee context just as much as they do in the life estate/future interest context. Courts rarely have to reach the common-law doctrine of waste in the mortgage context, however, because in most circumstances the governing documents have expressly addressed the issue.

foreclosure does not bring in enough money to pay off the debt. Unless we are in a jurisdiction that prevents deficiency judgments, Borrower/Mortgagor is still liable for the $50,000 difference. Say that Borrower/Mortgagor, however, is bankrupt and living in Bali. Can Lender/Mortgagee recover the $50,000 deficiency from New Buyer? The answer is "yes" if New Buyer assumed the obligations under the note and mortgage. The answer is "no" if New Buyer merely took title subject to the mortgage.

Language in the note and/or mortgage often gives the Lender/Mortgagee the ability to require the New Owner to assume the obligations in the note and mortgage. Many notes, for example, contain a *due on sale* clause. As its name implies, a due on sale clause makes the entire amount of debt due immediately on the sale of the property. Unless this clause is waived by the Lender/Mortgagee, the note and mortgage cannot survive the sale of the property. If there is a due on sale clause or other similar provision in the note or mortgage, the Lender/Mortgagee has the power to force the new owner to assume the obligations in the note and mortgage as a condition for waiving the due on sale clause.

Regardless of whether the New Owner has assumed the obligations or is merely subject to the mortgage, the Original Borrower/Mortgagor will remain liable on the underlying obligations unless released from these obligations by the Lender/Mortgagee.

e. Foreclosure and Priority

As we discussed above, interests have priority relative to each other that is based largely on the Recording Acts. If interest A would win against interest B under the applicable Recording Act, then interest A will have priority over interest B. The parties can change their priorities through a process known as *subordination*. We discuss subordination in a sidebar.

SUBORDINATION

Parties can agree to contractually alter their relative priority. This alternation is often achieved through a *subordination agreement*, where the senior interest agrees to *subordinate*, or become junior to, the junior interest. You might wonder why a senior interest holder would ever agree to subordinate her interest. One counterintuitive reason is that the senior interest holder might be put in a better position by agreeing to subordinate. Consider, for example, this scenario:

EXAMPLE 1: Owner owns Blackacre, an undeveloped parcel of land. Owner has borrowed money from Blue Bank secured by a recorded mortgage on the land. Owner wants to borrow money from Green Bank to build a home on the property. Green Bank is willing to lend Owner the money, but will only do so if its mortgage has first priority. As things stand now, Green Bank's mortgage would have second priority because Blue Bank's mortgage is recorded. Blue Bank, however, will likely be willing to enter into a subordination agreement that will give Green Bank first priority. Why? Because having a second mortgage on a property with a home on it likely will be better than having a first mortgage on undeveloped property. Properties with homes on them are typically easier to sell than undeveloped lots, and the increase in value to the property from the home being built will likely be more than the amount of the loan from Green Bank. Blue Bank therefore is likely to be in a better position by agreeing to subordinate its mortgage to Green Bank's mortgage.

In other circumstances, the senior interest holder might be contractually obligated to subordinate her interest. Commercial leases, for example, often have clauses that require the tenant to subordinate the lease to later-recorded mortgages. These clauses typically include additional terms that protect the tenant's interests while allowing the mortgage to have superior priority.

Priority has two important consequences in the foreclosure context. First, as we explained above, if there are multiple interests secured by the property, *the interest with the highest priority will get paid first from the proceeds from the foreclosure sale.* Here is a simple example of why priority matters:

EXAMPLE 2: Blackacre is owned by Owner. Owner borrowed money from Green Bank and Blue Bank. Each loan is secured by a mortgage on Blackacre. Green Bank is owed $100,000, and Blue Bank is owed $100,000. Owner defaults on both loans, and both Green Bank and Blue Bank foreclose on the property. The foreclosure sale brings in $150,000 after expenses. We have an obvious problem—Green Bank and Blue Bank together are owed $200,000. The foreclosure sale did not bring in enough money to pay both loans in full. Whichever of the two banks has priority will receive $100,000 and will be paid in full. The other bank will receive only partial payment of $50,000. If the foreclosure sale had brought in only $100,000 (or less), the bank with lower priority would receive nothing.

Second, *interests that are junior to the interest that is being foreclosed upon are destroyed by the foreclosure process.* Foreclosure destroys two distinct sets of interests in the foreclosed property. First, as we discussed above, it terminates the borrower/mortgagor's equity of redemption, ending that person's ownership of the property. Second, it terminates any interests in the property that are junior in priority to the mortgage being foreclosed. In other words, the purchaser in the foreclosure sale takes the property free and clear of the junior interests that have been terminated in the foreclosure process. Junior interests are not limited to mortgages and liens. Easements, covenants, and leases may all be terminated by foreclosure if they are junior in priority. Here are two examples:

> **EXAMPLE 3:** Blackacre is owned by Owner. Owner borrowed money from Red Bank and Orange Bank secured by mortgages in Blackacre. Red Bank's mortgage has priority over Orange Bank's mortgage. Owner defaults on the loan to Red Bank, and Red Bank forecloses. Orange Bank's junior mortgage will be wiped out as part of the foreclosure process. Depending on the amount raised by the foreclosure sale, Orange Bank may or may not be entitled to some money. Regardless of the amount of money, if any, that Orange Bank receives, its mortgage in Blackacre will be destroyed, and the purchaser in the foreclosure sale will take the property free and clear of the Orange Bank mortgage.

> **EXAMPLE 4:** Blackacre is owned by Owner. Owner borrowed money from Blue Bank, which immediately recorded a mortgage securing the loan. Later, Owner granted an easement across Blackacre to Neighbor. Also later, Owner granted a lease on Blackacre to Tenant. As a prior recorded instrument, Blue Bank's mortgage has priority over both the easement and the lease. Owner defaults on the loan to Blue Bank, and Blue Bank forecloses. The easement and the lease will both be terminated by the foreclosure, and the purchaser from the foreclosure sale will take the property free and clear of the easement and the lease.

Note well the difference between this last example and the scenario presented in *Clare House*. There, the leases were first in time but had not been recorded. In other words, they were prior unrecorded interests. Whether the leases or the deeds of trust had priority therefore turned on the issue of inquiry notice. Here, the mortgage was first in time and was promptly recorded. As a prior recorded interest, the mortgage will have priority over subsequent interests, whether those interests are recorded or not.

PURCHASE MONEY MORTGAGES AND SUPERPRIORITY

A *purchase money mortgage* is a mortgage that secures a loan used to acquire title to the property. Hence the name—a purchase money mortgage secures the loan used by the buyer to finance the purchase of the property. Purchase money mortgages often are given special beneficial priority treatment, though this treatment applies only in limited circumstances.

Purchase money mortgages generally get priority over all other mortgages and liens against the property that arise (a) against the property before the property is purchased using money secured by the purchase money mortgage and (b) out the *obligations of the borrower/mortgagor*. This rule is important but narrow—the borrower/mortgagor in a purchase money mortgage transaction is the *buyer* of the property. How can the buyer have an obligation that encumbers the property even before the buyer even acquires the property? Perhaps the two most common scenarios involve judgment liens and after-acquired property clauses. A judgment lien is a lien imposed by a court to enforce a judgment. An *after-acquired property clause* is a clause in a mortgage that states that the mortgage will apply not only to the initial property, but also to any property that the borrower/ mortgagor later acquires. The following examples, derived from Illustrations 3 and 5 to §7.2 of the Restatement (Third) of Property, Mortgages, illustrate each of these scenarios.

EXAMPLE 5: On February 1, Victor obtains a judgment lien from a court against Buyer for $15,000. On March 1, Buyer agrees to buy Blackacre from Seller for $50,000. Buyer borrows $40,000 of the purchase price from Green Bank. At closing on April 1, Buyer delivers a note and mortgage on Blackacre to Green Bank. At the time, Green Bank has actual knowledge of Victor's judgment lien. Bank never records its mortgage. Green Bank's purchase money mortgage has priority over Victor's judgment lien.

EXAMPLE 6: On February 1, Buyer grants Blue Bank a mortgage on Whiteacre to secure a loan. This mortgage contains an after-acquired property clause that states that "The lien of this mortgage is effective against any real estate, wherever situated, hereafter acquired by Buyer so long as the obligation secured hereby remains unsatisfied." As in the previous example, on March 1, Buyer agrees to buy Blackacre from Seller for $50,000. Buyer borrows $40,000 of the purchase price from Green Bank. At closing on April 1, Buyer delivers a note and mortgage on Blackacre to Green Bank. At the time, Green Bank has actual knowledge of Blue Bank's mortgage on Whiteacre and the fact that the mortgage contains an after-acquired property clause. Green Bank's mortgage is never recorded. Green Bank's purchase money mortgage has priority over Blue Bank's lien on Blackacre arising from the after-acquired property clause in the Whiteacre mortgage.

Note that in each case, Green Bank's purchase money mortgage has priority over the competing interest even though (a) Green Bank had notice of the other interest, and (b) Green Bank never recorded its purchase money mortgage. *Do not* take from these examples the idea that purchase money mortgages do not need to be recorded. Like any other property interest, purchase money mortgages should always be recorded. Recording, however, is not relevant to the special priority treatment that purchase money mortgages are given against interests that arise from prior obligations of the buyer/borrower/mortgagor.

Beyond this specific rule, purchase money mortgages may be given other special treatment in other related contexts. A state may, for example, give purchase money mortgages priority over mechanics' liens.

One other special rule involving purchase money mortgages is worth noting. The seller of real property sometimes takes a note and a mortgage for part of the purchase price from the buyer, rather than requiring the seller to pay the full purchase price. Say, for example, Seller is selling Blackacre to Buyer for $100,000. Seller might accept $40,000 in cash from Buyer and take a note and mortgage for the remaining $60,000 of the purchase price. We can call this kind of mortgage loan a *vendor's purchase money mortgage*, because it is held by the vendor of the property. Sometimes the buyer will get a third party purchase money mortgage for part of the purchase price and will get a vendor's purchase money mortgage for another part of the purchase price. Returning to our example where Seller is selling Blackacre to Buyer for $100,000, Buyer might put together the purchase price by paying $10,000 in cash, getting a $70,000 third party purchase money mortgage loan from a bank, and getting a $20,000 vendor's purchase money mortgage loan from Seller. Our special rule involves this last scenario. As between the vendor's purchase money mortgage and the third-party purchase money mortgage, the vendor's purchase money mortgage will have priority unless the parties agree otherwise or the jurisdiction's recording act would lead to a different result. (Unlike our first rule involving superpriority, the recording acts can alter this rule.) *See* Restatement (Third) of Property, Mortgages, §7.2(c).

The term *superpriority* is often used to describe instances where an interest is given better priority than it would have been given under general priority rules. The special treatment given to purchase money mortgages is one example of superpriority. Other types of liens are often given superpriority by statute. Tax liens, for example, are often given superpriority treatment—the government, after all, can write the rules to favor itself. As another example, some state statutes give superpriority to liens for the nonpayment of homeowners' association fees.

As you can see, foreclosure is a big deal for junior interest holders. The protection that junior interest holders get in the foreclosure process varies from jurisdiction to jurisdiction. In a majority of judicial foreclosure jurisdictions, junior interest holders are viewed as *necessary parties* to the lawsuit that initiates the judicial foreclosure proceeding. If a junior interest holder is not given notice of the foreclosure proceeding and joined as a party to the proceeding, then the junior interest holder's interest will survive foreclosure. In power of sale jurisdictions, junior interest holders may receive less protection. Many of power of sale jurisdictions have statutes that require that notice of foreclosure be given to junior interest holders. In some power of sale jurisdictions, however, junior interest holders do not have any right to receive notice of foreclosure unless they have acquired that right by contract.

Our next case provides an illustration of what happens when a foreclosing creditor fails to join a junior interest holder as a party to the foreclosure action. The case also provides a good discussion of the majority and minority approaches to the issue of the impact of foreclosure on a non-joined junior interest holder. Note well that the court is discussing the impact of foreclosure on *junior* lessees. Senior lessees would not be affected by foreclosure of a junior mortgage.

CITIZENS BANK & TRUST V. BROTHERS CONSTRUCTION & MANUFACTURING, INC.

Court of Appeals of Kansas, 1993
859 P.2d 394

Lewis, Presiding Judge. Citizens Bank & Trust (Bank) appeals from the trial court's decision in favor of Brothers Construction & Manufacturing, Inc. (Brothers). We affirm the decision of the trial court.

The Bank was the owner and holder of the first and second mortgages on the real estate involved in this action. These mortgages were executed and delivered to the Bank in the years of 1986 and 1989 and were placed of record in a timely manner.

In December 1990, Brothers entered into a written lease agreement, leasing the property in question. The lease was for three years and will expire on January 1, 1994. Brothers occupies the property under the terms of the lease described. Brothers has not recorded its lease, and there is nothing of record indicating it has a leasehold interest in the property.

In 1991, a mechanic's lien foreclosure action was filed against the property and its owners by a third party. The Bank was made a party to this action and filed a cross-claim and third-party petition to foreclose the first and second mortgages. The Bank did not join Brothers as a party to its action to foreclose the two mortgages.

The mortgage foreclosure action proceeded to judgment in favor of the Bank. The Bank's mortgages were foreclosed, and a sheriff's sale was ordered of the premises. The Bank purchased the property at the sheriff's sale and ultimately received a sheriff's deed to the property.

It is agreed that, prior to judgment being entered in the foreclosure action, the Bank had actual knowledge that Brothers was in possession of and occupying the property in question. Despite this knowledge, the Bank took no action to include Brothers as a party to its foreclosure lawsuit.

After receiving a sheriff's deed to the premises, the Bank made demand upon Brothers to quit and vacate the premises. Brothers refused to do so, and the Bank filed the instant action of forcible detainer.

The Bank contended that Brothers' interest in the property as a lessee was foreclosed and determined by the mortgage foreclosure action even though Brothers was not a party to that action. Brothers filed a motion for summary judgment, claiming that its interest in the property was not affected by the foreclosure action to which it was not made a party. The trial court granted summary judgment in favor of Brothers, and the Bank appeals.

PURCHASE BY LENDER IN THE FORECLOSURE SALE

In *Citizens Bank*, the foreclosing lender purchased the property from the foreclosure sale. This is a very common occurrence, in part because foreclosing lenders have a built-in advantage in the bidding process. In a foreclosure sale, the foreclosing lender may bid the amount outstanding on the loan without coming up with any new cash as part of its bid. For example, if the foreclosing lender is owed $200,000, it may bid that $200,000 at the sale. Any other bidder at the sale will have to exceed this bid to purchase the property. If the lender ends up purchasing the property from foreclosure, it typically will try to sell the property through a traditional listing arrangement. You may have heard of listed property being "bank owned," a term often used to describe property purchased out of foreclosure by the foreclosing lender.

The deed of trust structure, by the way, was developed in part to allow foreclosing banks to easily bid on the property. In a power of sale jurisdiction, the foreclosing lender often runs the foreclosure sale. It looks a little bit unseemly for the lender to purchase the property from a sale the lender is running. Having the sale run by a trustee avoids this problem.

There is only one issue on appeal. Was Brothers' leasehold interest in the property foreclosed by a mortgage foreclosure action to which it was not made a party where the Bank had actual knowledge that Brothers was occupying the property in question? We hold that question is properly answered in the negative, and we affirm the entry of summary judgment in favor of Brothers.

There is a distinct split of authority on this issue among several states. In 51C C.J.S., Landlord & Tenant §93(5), that split of authority is discussed:

> "Although there is some authority to the contrary, it has generally been held that a lease is terminated by the foreclosure of a prior mortgage *if, and only if, the tenants are made parties to the foreclosure proceedings*, although it would seem that the institution of a foreclosure suit without making the tenant a party will not bar a reforeclosure against the tenant. It has been held that a lease is not terminated by the mere institution of foreclosure proceedings, or the appointment of a receiver to collect rents, or the entry of judgment of foreclosure, but continues as valid and subsisting until the foreclosure sale, except where the title theory of mortgages is followed and the mortgagee is regarded as possessing an unqualified right to possession of the mortgaged premises on condition broken." (Emphasis added.)

Kansas is a lien theory state, not a title theory state:

> "Kansas is a 'lien theory' jurisdiction, not a 'title theory' jurisdiction. In a 'title theory' jurisdiction, the mortgage is viewed as a form of title to property. Randolph,

The Mortgagee's Interest in Rents: Some Policy Considerations and Proposals, 29 Kan. L. Rev. 1, 9 (1980). In lien theory states, a mortgagee is not entitled to immediate possession of the property upon default because the mortgage is merely a lien and not a form of title. *Mid-Continent Supply Co. v. Hauser*, 176 Kan. 9, 15, 269 P.2d 453 (1954)." *Missouri Valley Investment Co. v. Curtis*, 12 Kan. App.2d 386, 388, 745 P.2d 683 (1987).

In 55 Am. Jur. 2d, *Mortgages* §574, the following appears:

"In general, if a mortgage is duly foreclosed and the time for redemption has passed, this cuts off all the interest of the mortgagor in the lands and, consequently, bars one holding a leasehold estate which was subject to the mortgage. *Ordinarily, however, the foreclosure of a mortgage affects the rights and interests of only such persons as are made parties; and one in possession of real estate under claim of right from a mortgagor is a necessary party to a foreclosure of the mortgage, and a decree of foreclosure is not effective as to him unless he is joined.* Accordingly, whether a foreclosure action and sale terminate a lease of real estate previously mortgaged is held by the majority of the decisions to depend on the joinder of the lessee as a party to the foreclosure action; these courts hold that such a lease is thus terminated in case, and only in case, the lessee is made a party to the foreclosure suit. However, the authorities are not unanimous in holding that a lessee of mortgaged premises should be made a party to foreclose proceedings; it has been held that leasehold rights acquired subsequently to a mortgage are extinguished by such proceedings although the lessee is not a party thereto. Furthermore, in other decisions, the position has been taken broadly that leasehold rights acquired after the execution of a mortgage on the premises leased were extinguished by the foreclosure of the mortgage, the question of making the lessee a party not being considered." (Emphasis added.)

See Annot., 14 A.L.R. 664.

Kansas has long been recognized as following the majority rule on the issue in question. In this state, a mortgage foreclosure action will only terminate a lessee's interest in the real estate if the lessee is made a party to the action. *See* Randolph, *The Mortgagee's Interest in Rents: Some Policy Considerations and Proposals*, 29 Kan. L. Rev. 1, 27 (1980).

Kansas has followed the majority rule since 1896. In that year, the original Court of Appeals of this state decided *Wheat v. Brown*, 3 Kan. App. 431, 43 P. 807 (1896). *Wheat v. Brown* was a replevin action in which the plaintiff sought to recover possession of 35 head of cattle which were in the possession of the defendant. Wheat had foreclosed a mortgage covering real estate on which Brown had an oral lease. Wheat did not join Brown as a party to that action. After Wheat received the sheriff's deed, he rounded up Brown's cattle, which were on the real estate pursuant to the oral lease, and held them for damages. Brown sued to replevin the cattle. The court held in favor of Brown. . . .

Wheat v. Brown has been the law in this state for 97 years. During that time, neither the legislature nor the Supreme Court has made any effort to set aside, nullify, or temper the language of that decision or the legal precedent it established. We are not inclined to do so either, and we hold that *Wheat v. Brown* controls and supports the decision of the trial court.

There are decisions in other jurisdictions in accord with the Kansas rule. *See, e.g., Farm Credit Bank of St. Paul v. Martinson*, 478 N.W.2d 810 (N.D. 1991); *Kleven v. Brunner*, 229 Neb. 883, 429 N.W.2d 384 (1988); *Kerr v. McCreary*, 84 Neb. 315, 120 N.W. 1117 (1909).

As pointed out earlier, there are states which take a contrary position. *Treetop Apartments Gen. Part. v. Oyster*, 800 S.W.2d 628, 630 (Tex. App. 1990) ("A foreclosure sale voids all junior leases."). *See Reilly v. Firestone Tire and Rubber Co.*, 764 F.2d 167, 171 (3d Cir. 1985); *Dover Mobile Estates v. Fiber Form Prod.*, 220 Cal. App.3d 1494, 1498, 270 Cal. Rptr. 183 (1990); *United General Ins. v. American Nat. Ins.*, 740 S.W.2d 885, 887 (Tex. App. 1987); *City Bank & Trust Co. of Moberly v. Thomas*, 735 S.W.2d 121 (Mo. App. 1987).

In *Prudential Ins. Co., etc. v. Bull Market, Inc.*, 66 Ohio Misc. 9, 420 N.E.2d 140 (1979), the Ohio Court of Common Pleas held that Ohio law did not require the tenant to be joined. However, the court explained this was a minority view and stated:

> "[T]here exists a more basic split of authority concerning the effect of foreclosure on lessees of the mortgagor, irrespective of whether tenants' rights or obligations are being asserted. The majority position . . . is that foreclosure has no effect on lessee rights if the lessee is not joined in the foreclosure proceeding. The minority position . . . is that the lease terminates with foreclosure of the mortgagor's interest, whether or not the lessee was joined in the foreclosure proceeding because the lessee is not in privity with the final owner." 66 Ohio Misc. at 11, 420 N.E.2d 140.

We are not impressed by the privity argument and conclude that it has little relevance to the question at hand. We think that the Kansas approach to this issue is the best reasoned. The mere fact that a leasehold interest is junior in time to a first mortgage does not automatically make it subject to that mortgage. There are facts and circumstances which might result in the lease being given a priority over an earlier recorded mortgage. The rule which we follow in Kansas provides an orderly method for adjudication of competing claims to the real estate and prioritization of those claims. Our procedure is activated by joining all known competing interests in and claims to the real estate as parties to the action. There is no logic and no order to a theory which binds a tenant and automatically terminates his or her interest in real estate by a court decision to which he or she was not a party. Indeed, our sense of due process is offended by a rule which forecloses an interest in real estate where the holder of that interest is not given an opportunity to be heard on the issue. The Kansas rule is designed to ensure that a tenant may not have his or her leasehold interest in property automatically forfeited without the due process right of a day in court. We reject the argument that expediency and the complexities of modern society require that we abandon our present process for one which would adjudicate the property interests of non-parties to an action and bind them without their having an opportunity to present their claims in court. . . .

There is another factor in this action which we consider to be of great importance. It is clear, and the parties agree, the Bank had notice that Brothers was occupying the property involved in its foreclosure action. It had this notice prior to judgment in that action and had ample time to join Brothers as a necessary party or at least as a "contingently necessary" party under K.S.A. 60-219(a). The Bank failed to do so. We think that, under the circumstances shown, the failure of the Bank to join Brothers was inexcusable and is fatal to the position the Bank seeks to assert. Title examiners in this state have long cautioned mortgage lenders and purchasers of real estate to be cognizant of the rights of persons in possession of real estate. The validity of such advice becomes readily apparent when the provisions of K.S.A. 1992 Supp. 58-3404 are considered. That statute makes a marketable record title in this state subject to "all interests preserved by the filing of proper notice or by possession by the same owner continuously for a period of 25 years or more." (Emphasis added.) K.S.A. 1992 Supp. 58-3404(b). The Bank is in no position to seek relief from its own failure to join Brothers as a party to its foreclosure action when it had ample opportunity to do so. Under the circumstances, it would be a miscarriage of justice to conclude that the Bank can foreclose Brothers' interest in the lease on the real estate without having joined Brothers to its foreclosure action.

The Kansas Bankers Association has filed an amicus curiae brief in support of the position argued by the Bank. The Association suggests that the rule of *Wheat v. Brown* is outdated and is not functional in a modern commercial setting. It suggests that the rule of *Wheat v. Brown* is burdensome and too cumbersome to place on commercial institutions in this age of urban enlightenment. We do not agree.

Our holding in this case does nothing more than reiterate that the law in Kansas is as it has been for 97 years. We do not place an unimaginable burden on commercial lending institutions. Our decision requires only that a bank join as parties to a foreclosure action all parties which it knows or should know are making some claim to the property in question. In this case, the Bank was only required to join Brothers, who it knew was occupying and claiming some interest in the real estate. In other factual settings, a lender would be required to know who was in possession of the real estate and what rights they claim to the property in question. If a Bank seeks to foreclose a mortgage, joinder of other parties claiming an interest in the real estate is good law practice and not an overwhelming burden. We think it not outrageous to require that a party be joined before a foreclosure action can be held to foreclose his or her rights to real estate. We might suggest that a commercial lending institution make some use of interrogatories, depositions, or other discovery methods to determine the existence of unrecorded leases, easements, mechanics' liens, etc. Through such methods, all parties claiming an interest in that real estate will be known and can be joined in the foreclosure action. We believe that such procedure will support the principles of due process and justice on which our legal system was founded.

We hold that *Wheat v. Brown* controls this action. The interest of Brothers as a lessee in the real estate in question was not terminated by the foreclosure action to which it was not made a party.

Affirmed.

Even if she is given notice of the foreclosure proceeding, a junior interest holder will typically have limited options. Presuming that the senior interest holder is in fact entitled to foreclose and that the senior interest is in fact senior to the junior interest, the foreclosure process is designed to protect the senior interest holder. Priority matters, and having a junior interest in a property subject to foreclosure is not a comfortable situation to be in. In some narrow circumstances, however, the doctrine of *marshalling of assets* will help protect junior interests in foreclosure. The doctrine applies when a senior creditor is secured by liens on more than one source of collateral. Marshalling requires a senior creditor seeking to satisfy the debt to first go after sources of collateral that are not also subject to junior interests. Consider this example:

> **EXAMPLE 7:** Borrower owes a debt to Senior Lender. Senior Lender's debt is secured by mortgages on Blackacre and Whiteacre, both parcels of real property owned by Borrower. Senior Lender's mortgage is the only lien on Blackacre. Borrower also owes a debt to Junior Lender. Junior Lender's debt is secured by a second mortgage on Whiteacre.

> | Blackacre | Whiteacre |
> |---|---|
> | Senior Lender mortgage only | Senior Lender mortgage and Junior Lender mortgage |

> If Borrower defaults on the debt owed to Senior Lender, Senior Lender can foreclose on the mortgages on either or both Blackacre and Whiteacre. The marshalling of assets doctrine, however, would require Senior Lender to first look to foreclosure on Blackacre to satisfy the debt. If the debt was completely satisfied by foreclosure on Blackacre, then Senior Lender could not foreclose on Whiteacre. If the debt was not completely satisfied by Blackacre, Senior Lender could then foreclose on Whiteacre. Junior Lender is protected, at least to a degree, by the marshalling requirement

that Senior Lender look first to collateral that is not security for a junior creditor. Even if Senior Lender is not fully satisfied by the foreclosure on Blackacre and later forecloses on Whiteacre, Junior Lender may be helped because the earlier foreclosure on Blackacre makes it more likely that there will be money left over for Junior Lender in the Whiteacre foreclosure sale.

Marshalling of assets is a fairly broad concept and often applies when some of the collateral is personal, rather than real, property. For example, imagine that Senior Lender was secured by both a mortgage on the real property and by an Article 9 security interest in personal property (say, restaurant equipment). (Recall that secured finance in personal property is governed by Article 9 of the Uniform Commercial Code.) If there is a junior interest in the personal property but not the real property, then marshalling would require Senior Lender to look first to the real property. If, conversely, there was a junior interest in the real property but not in the personal property, marshalling would require Senior Lender to look first to the personal property.

FORECLOSURE BY JUNIOR INTEREST ALONE

What happens if a junior lender forecloses but the senior lender does not? Foreclosure by a junior interest has no effect on the senior interest. In other words, the senior interest survives the foreclosure. The junior interest may foreclose, but the person buying the property in the foreclosure sale will still be subject to the senior mortgage. Here is an example:

EXAMPLE 8: Blackacre is owned by Borrower. Borrower borrowed money from Red Bank and Orange Bank secured by recorded mortgages in Blackacre. Red Bank's mortgage has priority over Orange Bank's mortgage. Borrower defaults on the loan to Orange Bank, and Orange Bank (the junior lender) forecloses. The foreclosure has no effect whatsoever on Red Bank's mortgage. New Owner buys Blackacre from the foreclosure sale. New Owner will own Blackacre subject to Red Bank's mortgage. If Borrower defaults on the loan to Red Bank, Red Bank can still foreclose on Blackacre. Red Bank's mortgage, after all, is a prior recorded interest when New Owner buys Blackacre. Obviously, this possibility greatly reduces the desirability of owning Blackacre. The price that New Owner was willing to pay for Blackacre at the foreclosure sale presumably reflected the continued presence of Red Bank's mortgage on the property.

3. INSTALLMENT LAND CONTRACTS

At the outset of our discussion of mortgages and deeds of trust, we noted that the lender in a real estate transaction will typically want two primary things: (1) a series of payments of money representing the principal and interest on the loan and (2) a way to access the property as collateral if the borrower fails to pay the loan back. Mortgage and deeds of trust transactions give the lender these two things by obligating the borrower to make payments through the note and by giving the lender the ability to foreclose on default through the mortgage or deed of trust. There are, however, other ways of structuring a transaction that meet the lender's two primary goals. One alternative method is the installment land contract.

An installment land contract is rent-to-own for real property. The seller effectively acts as the lender in the transaction. The buyer agrees to make regular payments to the seller over a period of time. In return, the seller agrees to convey title to the buyer once the final payment has been made. In the intervening time, the buyer has the right to possess the property as a tenant. The payments are structured so that they include both the purchase price of the property and interest. In this way, the payments are roughly equivalent of payments made on a mortgage loan, which include both principal and interest components.

If the buyer defaults on the payments, then the seller can simply evict the buyer. There is no need to foreclose, because the seller remains the fee simple owner of the property until the final payment is made. Indeed, as the fee simple owner during the term of the contract, the seller has the best possible access to the value of the land to secure the buyer's obligations. If the buyer defaults, the seller simply evicts the tenant and remains the owner of the property.

Installment land contracts have their advantages and disadvantages for both the seller and the buyer. The seller obtains a buyer for the property and receives payments that include an interest payment over time. As the fee simple owner, the seller has excellent collateral securing the buyer's obligations. The installment land contract, however, forces the seller into the role as the lender. As a result, the seller has to wait to receive the full purchase price of the property until the end of the contract term. In a typical transaction financed by a loan from a third party lender, in contrast, the seller would get the full purchase price as soon as the transaction closes.

For the buyer, the installment land contract has the advantage of often allowing the purchase of the property with little or no down payment. Installment land contracts are also often used to sell property to people who might not qualify for a traditional mortgage loan. The major disadvantage of an installment land contract is that the buyer does not build up equity in the property as she makes payments over time to the seller. Even if the buyer has made payments on the property for many years, in many jurisdictions, the buyer will have no interest in the property if she defaults.

As an extreme example, compare a 15-year mortgage and a 15-year installment land contract for the same $100,000 in property. For simplicity's sake, we will assume that the buyer put no money down, borrowing the entire $100,000 (plus interest) in the mortgage transaction and committing to pay the entire $100,000 (plus interest) over time in the installment transaction. This is an unrealistic assumption for the mortgage transaction, because lenders typically require a down payment from the borrower, but a realistic assumption for the installment transaction, because installment transactions are often made with little or no money down. After 14 years, the buyer has paid off approximately $90,000 of the money owed, plus interest over time. The buyer then defaults. In the mortgage transaction, if the lender forecloses, there is a good chance that they buyer will recover some money from the foreclosure sale. If the foreclosure sale nets more than $10,000 (the amount still outstanding on the loan), the balance will go to the buyer. In contrast, in the installment land contract, the buyer will receive nothing on default, because the buyer has no ownership interest in the property until the final payment is made. Nor will the buyer, in many jurisdictions, have an equity of redemption allowing the buyer to redeem the property for the outstanding amount due on the contract.

There is something of a modern trend of courts stepping in and exercising their equitable powers to protect defaulting buyers by treating installment land contracts as mortgages. The recent Restatement supports this approach. *See* Restatement (Third) of Property, Mortgages §3.4(b). The courts in many jurisdictions, however, still enforce installment land contracts as written and allow the seller to forfeit the buyer's interest in the contract on default.

CHAPTER 6

SERVITUDES

In our discussion of title issues, we briefly introduced easements and covenants. Easements and covenants both belong to a category of non-possessory interests in property called *servitudes*. In this chapter, we will cover the servitudes in depth. We will start with some basic and slightly oversimplified definitions:

An *easement* gives a party the right to physically enter and use the property of another.

> **EXAMPLE:** A has the right to use a driveway across B's land to get to the nearest road. A has an easement across B's land.

A *license* gives a party the *revocable* right to physically enter the property of another.

> **EXAMPLE:** B gives A permission to cross B's land to get access to the nearest road. This permission is revocable. A has a license to cross B's land.

A *profit* gives a party the right to physically enter the property of another and remove certain resources. A profit can be understood as an easement plus the right to remove resources.

> **EXAMPLE:** A has the right to enter B's land and harvest and remove a certain amount of timber from B's land. A has a profit over B's land.

A *covenant that runs with the land* is a promise that is binding on both the present and subsequent owners of the property. Covenants that run with the land can be enforced in law as *real covenants* or in equity as *equitable servitudes*.

> **EXAMPLE:** A promises that neither she nor any future owner of her property will paint the house on the property any color other than white. Presuming that certain requirements are met, A's property is subject to a covenant that runs with the land.

We will first cover easements (and the related licenses and profits), and will then cover covenants that run with the land. Before we get to the substance of these interests in property, we first will go over some basic concepts. As with estates and future interests, servitudes involve some complicated terminology. *Mastering this terminology is a necessary first step to mastering the material that follows.*

A. FUNDAMENTAL CONCEPTS

Grants vs. Reservations. The diagram below shows two parcels of property, A and B:

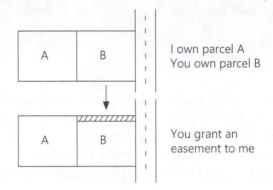

Say that I own parcel A and you own parcel B. You and I agree that you will sell me an easement to cross your property to reach the road. You will *grant* the easement to me. Like other property interests, easements are typically conveyed by deed. In this example, you will expressly convey the easement to me by deed.

Now consider the following diagram:

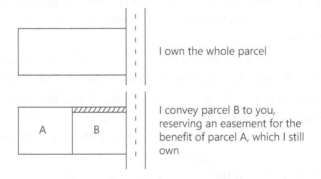

I own the entirety of the property. I agree to sell you the portion of the property nearest to the road. After our transaction, we will be in the same position as shown in our first diagram: I will own parcel A, and you will own parcel B next to the road. As before, I need an easement across parcel B to reach the road. When I convey parcel B to you in fee simple, I can *reserve* an easement in myself. Put another way, I will convey to you all of my fee simple interest in parcel B except for the easement, which I will keep for myself.

In a reservation, the conveying property owner holds back a property interest from the conveyance. Reservations can be used with all sorts of property interests.

RESERVATIONS AND EXCEPTIONS DISTINGUISHED

You will sometimes see what looks like a reservation called an *exception*. Although the terminology is sometimes used loosely, an exception typically excludes from a conveyance a pre-existing interest, while a reservation creates a new one.

For example, I could convey Blackacre to you while reserving a life estate in myself. Or I could reserve the mineral interests in myself. We focus on grants and reservations in this section of the book because, as you will see, the distinction can be very important in the creation of easements.

Running with the Land. We have seen the concept of running with the land before, for example, when we studied general warranty deeds. It is especially important in the law of servitudes. An interest in property *runs with the land* if it automatically transfers to subsequent owners of the land.

Dominant vs. Servient; Benefit vs. Burden. Let's return to our diagram of parcels A and B, where parcel A has an easement over parcel B to reach the road.

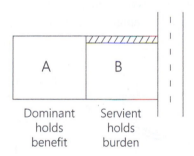

In this example, parcel A is the *dominant* estate, and parcel B is the *servient* estate. Put another way, parcel A has the *benefit* of the easement, while parcel B has the *burden* of the easement. In servitudes law, the property that has the benefit of the servitude is often called the dominant estate, while the property that has the burden is often called the servient estate. Sometimes the word "tenement" is used rather than estate: dominant tenement and servient tenement. The dominant/servient terminology is most often used with easements, while the benefit/burden terminology is most often used with covenants than run with the land.

Appurtenant vs. In Gross. The benefit of a servitude is *appurtenant* if it is tied up with a parcel of property. The benefit is *in gross* if it is not tied up with a parcel of property. The same terminology may also be used with the burden of a servitude, but the distinction is most often used when we are talking about the benefit.

The easiest way to understand this distinction is with some examples. Let's start with the example we just used of the driveway easement across parcel B for the benefit of parcel A.

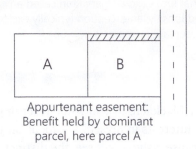

Appurtenant easement:
Benefit held by dominant
parcel, here parcel A

This is an *appurtenant* easement because the benefit is tied up with a parcel of property. If I am the owner of parcel A, I hold the benefit of the easement by virtue of my ownership of parcel A. If I later sell parcel A to another person, that person will then hold the benefit of the easement as the owner of the parcel. One way of conceptualizing this point is to view the appurtenant easement as being owned by the parcel of property, rather than an individual. If an individual owns the property, that person also owns the easement.

The classic example of an *in gross* easement is a power-line easement. Imagine that the Power Company has an easement that allows it to place power lines across Blackacre.

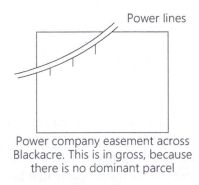

Power lines

Power company easement across
Blackacre. This is in gross, because
there is no dominant parcel

Looking at the diagram, you can see that the benefit of the easement is not tied up with a parcel of property—there isn't a neighboring parcel of property that holds the benefit of the easement. Rather, the Power Company holds the easement in gross. With an in gross easement, *there is no dominant estate.*

We will discuss the appurtenant/in gross distinction further below in our materials on easements.

Affirmative vs. Negative. An *affirmative* servitude entitles the holder of the benefit to engage in a positive use of the burdened property. For example, with a driveway easement, the owner of the benefit has the privilege of crossing the burdened property. A *negative* servitude prohibits the owner of the burdened property from using the burdened property in a particular way. For example, a covenant running with the land might prohibit the owner of the burdened property from painting the house pink. Due to a historical quirk, in the United States, *easements are almost always affirmative.* If we want to prohibit a property owner from engaging in a particular use of the land, we will use a covenant that runs with the land.

B. EASEMENTS

At the beginning of the chapter, we distinguished between easements, licenses, and profits. From this point forward, we will focus on easements, although licenses and profits will crop up from time to time.

Like other property interests, easements can be of limited duration. For example, I could grant you an easement that lasts for your life. Or I could grant you an easement that lasts 20 years. If an instrument is ambiguous as to the duration of an easement, the duration is presumed to be unlimited. *See* Restatement (Third) of Property, Servitudes §4.3(5). We will focus almost exclusively on easements of unlimited duration.

1. EXPRESS EASEMENTS

Most easements are created expressly in a deed or other legal instrument. Express easements can be created by grant or reservation. As interests in property, easements typically must be created by written instrument to satisfy the Statute of Frauds. As we will soon see, there are a number of ways that an easement can be created without an express writing between the parties. We will consider these non-express easements in the next section.

a. The Rule Against Reservations in Third Persons

We mentioned above that the distinction between grants and reservations can be very important in the easements context. The single most important consequence of this distinction comes from a quirky common-law rule. This rule states that an easement may not be reserved in a third person. Alternatively, the rule is sometimes articulated as a prohibition against reserving easements in a "stranger to the deed."

In a typical reservation, the grantor reserves an easement in herself. So, in our example above, I owned an entire parcel, then sold the half nearest the road to you.

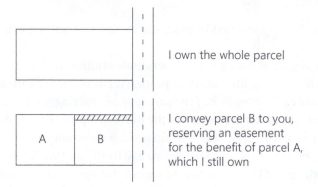

In my conveyance of parcel B to you, I reserved an easement across parcel B in myself for the benefit of parcel A so that I could reach the road. There are no problems whatsoever with this kind of reservation at common law.

To illustrate the rule against reservations in third persons, we need to change our example. Alice owns a large parcel of land. She conveys this property to Beatrice. In the conveyance to Beatrice, Alice reserves a driveway easement in Carlos, who owns a nearby parcel of undeveloped land.

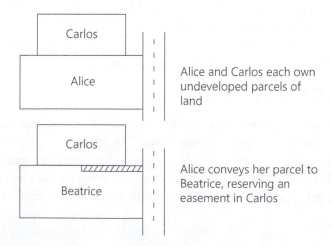

Here, a new interest (the easement) is being held back from the conveyance between Alice and Beatrice. Unlike the typical reservation, however, the grantor (Alice) is not trying to reserve the interest in herself; rather, she is trying to hold back the interest from her conveyance to Beatrice and simultaneously transfer it to Carlos. The two parties (i.e., the grantor and the grantee) to the conveyance are Alice and Beatrice. Carlos is a third party, or, in the alternative phrasing of the rule, a stranger to the deed.

Under the common-law rule, the attempted reservation of an easement in Carlos would be invalid. Commentators have universally condemned the rule. It has its roots in archaic feudal concepts that should have little or no impact today. Further, it lays a trap for the unwary because it is easy to achieve the same result by using two separate transactions. In the example above, Alice could have first granted an easement to Carlos and then conveyed the property to Beatrice. It doesn't make much sense to have the easement be invalid if it was created by reservation when the same easement would have been valid if it had been created by grant.

These criticisms aside, *the traditional common-law rule remains the majority rule.* A minority of courts have abandoned the common-law rule and allow easements to be created by reservations in a third person. The cases that follow illustrate each approach. As you read them, note in particular each court's view of its role in reforming property law.

TRIPP V. HUFF

Supreme Judicial Court of Maine, 1992
606 A.2d 792

COLLINS, Justice. Plaintiff David Lloyd Tripp appeals the judgment of the Superior Court (York County, Fritzsche, J.) entered in favor of defendants A. Kenneth Huff, Alfred Barlow and Joane Ouellette Barlow, in Tripp's action for a declaratory judgment to establish the existence of a right of way over defendants' property and for injunctive relief. Finding no merit in Tripp's arguments that he is entitled to such a right of way, we affirm.

Tripp is the owner of a 20-acre piece of property in Saco, which is set back about 3,000 feet from the Jenkins Road. His property is one half of a 40-acre parcel that was conveyed to Nicholas and Jeremiah Hearne by Captain Ichabod Jordan in March 1833, and on November 2, 1863 was divided so that Jeremiah Hearne got sole ownership of the northerly half of the 40-acre property, the land now owned by Tripp, and Nicholas Hearne got sole ownership of the southerly half of the property.

Huff and Barlow own parcels of land that are situated between Tripp's parcel and the Jenkins Road. They derive title to their property from a conveyance on November 4, 1863 from Nicholas Hearne to James and William Andrews. That conveyance transferred one half of the 40-acre parcel Nicholas formerly owned with Jeremiah, together with property that was conveyed to Nicholas as sole owner by Captain Jordan in 1830.

Tripp commenced the present action claiming a right of way over the southwest portion of Huff and Barlow's property. Tripp contends that he is entitled to that right of way by virtue of an express easement . . . . He sought a declaration as to the extent of that right of way and an injunction preventing defendants from interfering with his claimed way. Following a jury waived trial, the Superior Court entered judgment for Huff and Barlow. Tripp appealed.

Dealing first with the express right of way, Tripp claims that the deed of November 4, 1863 from Nicholas Hearne to James and William Andrews establishes an intention by Nicholas Hearne to provide Jeremiah Hearne, a predecessor in title, with a means of access to an otherwise landlocked parcel. The language in the deed to the Andrews, on which Tripp relies, is as follows: "saving and accepting a way for Jeremiah Hearne and assigns to his lot lying back of and adjoining the above." Tripp acknowledges that the reservation of a right of way in favor of Jeremiah is an easement in favor of a stranger and that under our existing case law such an easement conveyed no property rights to Tripp's predecessor in title. *See Fitanides v. Holman,* 310 A.2d 65, 67 (Me.1973). He argues, however, that our rule on reservations to a stranger in title is archaic and should now be abandoned by this court. We are unpersuaded that there is any compelling reason to depart from this well settled rule and thus decline to do so. As we have said on a prior occasion:

> Stare decisis must operate with plenary force in the law of real property to maintain the certainty and predictability which Courts, traditionally have made the benchmark of this area of jurisprudence and upon which, accordingly, the public has been induced to place strong reliance. We depart, therefore, from a real property policy long avowed by us, and still followed by the great majority of other Courts, only when the most compelling of reasons demand change.

Brown v. Heirs of Maria Fuller, 347 A.2d 127, 130 (Me.1975) (citation omitted). . . .

Judgment affirmed.

WILLARD V. FIRST CHURCH OF CHRIST, SCIENTIST

Supreme Court of California, 1972
7 Cal. 3d 473, 498 P.2d 987, 102 Cal. Rptr. 739

PETERS, Associate Justice. In this case we are called upon to decide whether a grantor may, in deeding real property to one person, effectively reserve an interest in the property to another. We hold that in this case such a reservation vests the interest in the third party.

Plaintiffs Donald E. and Jennie C. Willard filed an action to quiet title to a lot in Pacifica against the First Church of Christ, Scientist (the church). After a trial judgment was entered quieting the Willards' title. The church has appealed.

Genevieve McGuigan owned two abutting lots in Pacifica known as lots 19 and 20. There was a building on lot 19, and lot 20 was vacant. McGuigan was a member of the church, which was located across the street from her lots, and she permitted it to use lot 20 for parking during services. She sold lot 19 to one Petersen, who used the building as an office. He wanted to resell the lot, so he listed it with Willard, who is a realtor. Willard expressed an interest in purchasing both lots 19 and 20, and he and Petersen signed a deposit receipt for the sale of the two lots. Soon thereafter they entered into an escrow, into which Petersen delivered a deed for both lots in fee simple.

At the time he agreed to sell lot 20 to Willard, Petersen did not own it, so he approached McGuigan with an offer to purchase it. She was willing to sell the lot provided the church could continue to use it for parking. She therefore referred the matter to the church's attorney, who drew up a provision for the deed that stated the conveyance was "subject to an easement for automobile parking during church hours for the benefit of the church on the property at the southwest corner of the intersection of Hilton Way and Francisco Boulevard . . . such easement to run with the land only so long as the property for whose benefit the easement is given is used for church purposes." Once this clause was inserted in the deed, McGuigan sold the property to Petersen, and he recorded the deed.

Willard paid the agreed purchase price into the escrow and received Petersen's deed 10 days later. He then recorded this deed, which did not mention an easement for parking by the church. While Petersen did mention to Willard that the church would want to use lot 20 for parking, it does not appear that he told him of the easement clause contained in the deed he received from McGuigan.

Willard became aware of the easement clause several months after purchasing the property. He then commenced this action to quiet title against the church. At the trial, which was without a jury, McGuigan testified that she had bought lot 20 to provide parking for the church, and would not have sold it unless she was assured the church could thereafter continue to use it for parking. The court found that McGuigan and Petersen intended to convey an easement to the church, but that the clause they employed was ineffective for that purpose because it was invalidated by the common law rule that one cannot "reserve" an interest in property to a stranger to the title.

The rule derives from the common law notions of reservations from a grant and was based on feudal considerations. A reservation allows a grantor's whole interest in the property to pass to the grantee, but revests a newly created interest in the grantor. (4 Tiffany, The Law of Real Property (3d ed. 1939) §972.) While a reservation could theoretically vest an interest in a third party, the early common law courts vigorously rejected this possibility, apparently because they mistrusted and wished to limit conveyance by deed as a substitute for livery by seisin. (See Harris Reservations in Favor of strangers of the Title (1953) 6 Okla.L.Rev. 127, 132-133.) Insofar as this mistrust was the foundation of the rule, it is clearly an inapposite feudal shackle today. Consequently, several commentators have attacked the rule as groundless and have called for its abolition. . . .

California early adhered to this common law rule. (*Eldridge v. See Yup Company* (1860) 17 Cal. 44.) In considering our continued adherence to it, we must realize that our courts no longer feel constricted by feudal forms of conveyancing. Rather, our primary objective in construing a conveyance is to try to give effect to the intent of the grantor. In general, therefore, grants are to be interested in the same way as other contracts and not according to rigid feudal standards. The common law rule conflicts with the modern approach to construing deeds because it can frustrate the grantor's intent. Moreover, it produces an inequitable result because the original grantee has presumably paid a reduced price for title to the encumbered property. In this case, for example, McGuigan testified that she had discounted the price she charged Petersen by about one-third because of the easement. . . .

The highest courts of two states have already eliminated the rule altogether, rather than repealing it piecemeal by evasion. In *Townsend v. Cable* (Ky.1964) 378 S.W.2d 806, the Court of Appeals of Kentucky abandoned the rule. It said: "We have no hesitancy in abandoning this archaic and technical rule. It is entirely inconsistent with the basic principle followed in the construction of deeds, which is to determine the intention of grantor as gathered from the four corners of the instrument." (*Id.* at 808.) Relying on Townsend, the Supreme Court of Oregon, in *Garza v. Grayson* (1970) 255 Or. 413, 467 P.2d 960, rejected the rule because it was "derived from a narrow and highly technical interpretation of the meaning of the terms 'reservation' and 'exception' when employed in a deed" (*id.* at 961), and did not sufficiently justify frustrating the grantor's intention. Since the rule may frustrate the grantor's intention in some cases even though it is riddled with exceptions, we follow the lead of Kentucky and Oregon and abandon it entirely.

Willard contends that the old rule should nevertheless be applied in this case to invalidate the church's easement because grantees and title insurers have relied upon it. He has not, however, presented any evidence to support this contention, and it is clear that the facts of this case do not demonstrate reliance on the old rule. There is no evidence that a policy of title insurance was issued, and therefore no showing of reliance by a title insurance company. Willard himself could not have relied upon the common law rule to assure him of an absolute fee because he did not even read the deed containing the reservation. This is not a case of an ancient deed where the reservation has not been asserted for many years. The church used lot 20 for parking throughout the period when Willard was purchasing the property and after he acquired title to it, and he may not claim that he was prejudiced by lack of use for an extended period of time.

The determination whether the old common law rule should be applied to grants made prior to our decision involves a balancing of equitable and policy considerations. We must balance the injustice which would result from refusing to give effect to the grantor's intent against the injustice, if any, which might result by failing to give effect to reliance on the old rule and the policy against disturbing settled titles. The record before us does not disclose any reliance upon the old common law rule, and there is no problem of an ancient title. Although in other cases the balancing of the competing interests may warrant application of the common law rule to presently existing deeds, in the instant case the balance falls in favor of the grantor's intent, and the old common law rule may not be applied to defeat her intent. . . .

The judgment is reversed.

NOTES

1. *Effect of Invalidity.* Under the majority common-law rule, what happens if an easement reserved in a third person is declared invalid? U.S. jurisdictions follow one of two approaches. Under the first approach, the attempted reservation is treated as a nullity. The grantee therefore owns the granted property free and clear of the interest in question. Under the second option, the attempted reservation is unsuccessful in transferring the easement to the third party but results in the reservation of the easement in the grantor. The grantee therefore owns the granted property subject to the easement, and the grantor (or her successors) in interest holds the benefit of the easement. *See* James W. Ely, Jr. & Jon W. Bruce, *The Law of Easements and Licenses in Land* §3.9.

2. *Scope of the Rule.* The rule against reservations in a third person applies to interests other than easements. For example, it has been applied to invalidate the attempted reservation of mineral rights in a third person. *See, e.g., Nicoletti v. County of Allegheny,* 719 A.2d 1, 3-4 (P.A. Com. Ct. 1998).

3. Further reading: James W. Ely, Jr. & Jon W. Bruce, *The Law of Easements and Licenses in Land* §3.9; 2 *American Law of Property* §8.29; 4 *Powell on Real Property* §34.04[5]; W.W. Allen, *Reservation or Exception in Deed in Favor of Stranger,* 88 A.L.R.2d 1199.

PROBLEMS

Explanatory answers to these problems can be found on page 1057.

1. Amy has a problem with an easement. She bought her home from Steve two years ago. The parcel (Blackacre) has the benefit of an appurtenant recorded driveway easement across the neighboring property (Whiteacre) owned by Ashley. Amy and Ashley got into the predictable argument, and Ashley has now instituted a lawsuit arguing that the easement is invalid. Apparently, Ashley's property was at one time owned by Eduardo. The deed conveying Whiteacre from Eduardo to Ashley has the following provision: "Reserving in Steve, as owner of Blackacre, an appurtenant driveway easement to cross Whiteacre to reach State Route 23." The dispute between Amy and Ashley is limited to this express easement.

2. Stella is a loyal alumna of Hillside College. Stella owned two lots that are side by side. One lot contains her house; the other lot was vacant. Many Hillside students crossed the vacant lot on their way to class. A few months ago, Stella sold the vacant lot to Jake. As part of the transfer to Jake, Stella reserved an easement in Hillside College for Hillside students to cross one side of the vacant lot. Jake recently started building on the lot and has erected a fence that prevents students from crossing the lot. As a result, a dispute has developed between Jake and Hillside College about the student's right to cross the lot.

b. Interpreting Express Easements

Recall that an easement gives the holder of the benefit the privilege of entering and using the burdened property. It should be clear from this definition that the burden of an easement will always be appurtenant. The benefit may be either appurtenant or in gross. When we speak of an "appurtenant easement," we mean one where the benefit is tied to a parcel of property. When we speak of an "easement in gross," we mean one where the benefit is not tied to a parcel of property.

How can we tell whether an easement is appurtenant or in gross? The granting clause may be clear. For example, if a grant of an easement expressly mentions the dominant estate, then the easement typically will be appurtenant. Or a grant might specifically say whether the easement is appurtenant or in gross.

RULES OF CONSTRUCTION Many grants, however, are ambiguous. In cases of ambiguity, the benefit of an easement is *presumed to be appurtenant*. This presumption, however, can be rebutted by the facts surrounding the grant.

One common source of ambiguity occurs when an easement is granted to an individual, and the granting clause makes no mention of a parcel of property as the dominant estate. For example, a deed might grant an easement "to Joan Smith." If the

RECORDING AND SERVITUDES

Easements, covenants, and other servitudes are subject to the Recording Acts. When we say in this chapter that a servitude runs with the land and binds subsequent owners of the property, we are presuming that the servitude has been recorded. As we saw in our materials on the Recording Acts, an unrecorded servitude may be void and unenforceable against subsequent purchasers. Note in this context that use of an easement, or the presence of a driveway or other physical manifestation of an easement, might provide inquiry notice to a subsequent purchaser of the existence of an unrecorded easement.

easement is intended to be appurtenant, then the individual grantee typically will be the owner of a parcel intended to be the dominant estate. If the easement is intended to be in gross, then the individual grantee typically will not be the owner of a parcel intended to be the dominant estate. Looking at the granting clause "to Joan Smith" alone does not give us all of the information we need to determine whether the easement is appurtenant or in gross.

The benefit of an appurtenant easement runs with the land with the dominant estate. (The previous sentence is a good example of why it is important to master the servitudes terminology. If you understand the lingo, the sentence makes perfect sense. If you don't, it is a muddled mess.). The benefit of an in gross easement does not run with the land—because there is no dominant estate, there is no land for the benefit to run with. The benefit of an in gross easement may be transferred, although these transfers may present some complications that we will explore further below.

The burden of either type of easement runs with the land with the servient parcel. Any time we have an easement, we have a servient parcel that is subject to use and access by the holder of the benefit of the easement. If the servient parcel is sold, the burden remains. If I am the owner of a servient parcel burdened by an easement, and I sell the property to you, the property still will be burdened by the easement.

Here is an example of the granting clause and other relevant language from an appurtenant easement:

Everything to this point is background information, identifying the parties, the property, and the purpose of the transaction. The descriptions of the dominant and servient parcels make it clear that this is an appurtenant easement.

There is no need for consideration to make the grant valid—an easement may be created by deed as part of a gratuitous transaction.

This granting clause is unnecessarily wordy. "Grant" alone would suffice.

This language makes it clear that the easement covers both access and utilities.

A well-drafted easement will always locate the easement with specificity.

This statement of purpose elaborates on the permissible uses of the easement by the owner of the dominant parcel.

Note that there is no parcel of property associated with the Grantee, because this is an in gross easement. In the appurtenant easement above, there was a parcel of property associated with the Grantee. Remember that with an in gross easement, there is dominant parcel.

Note that the placement of the easement is relatively vague. It probably would have been better to identify the exact location of the easement to avoid potential disputes between the parties.

This provision gives the Electric Company a great deal of flexibility in what it builds in the easement. The laundry list of options should give the owner of the burdened land a good idea about the potential scope of what the utility might build on the land.

EASEMENT AGREEMENT made this 12th day of November, 2011 between DUTCH MILLS, LLC, a Pennsylvania company, with a mailing address of [address], hereinafter called "Grantor," and DAVID N. KNOX, of [address], hereinafter called "Grantee"

WHEREAS, Grantor owns that certain parcel of real property located in Middle Paxton Township, Dauphin County, Pennsylvania, known as [tax parcel number and legal description], (the "Grantor Property"), and

WHEREAS, Grantee owns that certain parcel of real property located adjacent to the Grantor Property in Middle Paxton Township, Dauphin County, Pennsylvania known as [tax parcel number and legal description], ("the Grantee Property"), and

NOW THEREFORE, in consideration of the sum of ($1.00) ONE DOLLAR, and other good and valuable consideration, the receipt and sufficiency of which is hereby acknowledged and intending to be legally bound hereby, the parties covenant and agree as follows:

1. GRANT OF ACCESS AND UTILITY EASEMENT. Grantor does hereby grant, bargain, sell, release, convey, and confirm unto the Grantee, his heirs, successors, and assigns, a perpetual, nonexclusive twenty foot (20') wide access and utility easement in, over, under, along, and through [the easement area shown on attached survey]. The purpose of this access and utility easement hereby granted is for ingress, egress, and regress at any time over, under, along, and through the Grantor Property to the Grantee Property, as well as for the construction, installation, operation, repair and maintenance solely within the Easement Area of electric, gas, sewer, telephone, television cable, and water lines by the Grantee.

Here is an example of the granting clause and other relevant language from an in gross easement:

The undersigned, GARY RADIN, of [address], (the "Grantor") is the owner of lands located in the Township of Conewago, County of Dauphin, Commonwealth of Pennsylvania, bounded and/or described as follows: [legal description of the land]. Grantor, for valuable consideration, the receipt of which is hereby acknowledged, and intending to be legally bound, hereby grants and conveys to the Pennsylvania Electric Company, a Pennsylvania corporation, (the "Grantee"), a permanent easement and uninterrupted right, from time to time, to construct, reconstruct, operate, inspect, renew, replace, improve, maintain, redesign, alter, relocate, extend, and remove overhead and underground facilities described below (the "Facilities") as may be deemed necessary or convenient by Grantee for electric purposes on, over, under and across the northerly portion of the land.

The Facilities may include, without limitation, poles (with or without crossarms), guywires, guy stubs, anchors, street lights and standards, transformers, transformer pads, switching compartments, conduits, conductors, ducts, wires, cables, fibers, terminal boxes, manholes, and other related equipment and apparatus from time to time deemed necessary or convenient by Grantee to accomplish the above purpose.

EASEMENTS IN EVERYDAY LIFE

As you are going about daily life, see if you can spot easements. Any time you see a power line, for example, there likely is an easement. Once you start paying attention, you will see easements all over the place.

As we have seen before, written conveyances can contain ambiguities. One potential ambiguity in an easement, as we discussed above, is whether it is appurtenant or in gross. Another potential ambiguity that might arise in the easements context is whether the instrument granted an easement or whether it granted ownership in fee simple. For example, say that the Railroad Company approaches Mary requesting permission to build a railroad track across her property. Depending on the circumstances, Mary might agree to sell the Railroad Company a strip of land in fee simple, or Mary might retain fee simple ownership of the property and convey an easement to the Railroad Company.

Whichever option the parties agree on, the conveyance might not be drafted as clearly as we might like it to be. The parties might, for example, use the term "right of way." This term could be interpreted to mean an easement or could be interpreted to mean a fee simple used as a right of way. Ambiguities like this one have led to hundreds of reported cases on the fee simple versus easement issue in the railroad context alone.

Interpreting an ambiguous conveyance can be a highly fact-specific inquiry, and courts often reach different conclusions on similar conveyances. Consider, for example, two cases decided by California intermediate appellate courts. The first case is *Johnson v. Ocean Shore R.R. Co.*, 94 Cal. Rptr. 68 (Ct. App. 1st Dist. Div. 4, 1971). In *Johnson*, the court interpreted a conveyance that included the following granting clause:

> That the said party of the first part, for and in consideration of the sum of Ten Dollars ($10.00) gold coin of the United States of America, to it in hand paid by the said party of the second part, the receipt whereof is hereby acknowledged, has granted, bargained and sold, conveyed and confirmed, and by these presents does grant, bargain and sell, convey and confirm, unto the said party of the second part, and to its successors and assigns forever, for railroad purposes only, all that certain lot, piece or parcel of land, situate, lying and being in the County of San Mateo, State of California, and particularly described as follows, to-wit: A strip of ground sixty (60) feet in width through property of Burlington Beach Land Company (a description by metes and bounds follows).

The court held that this language conveyed an easement, not a fee simple. There is a lot in the *Johnson* opinion that we do not have the space to examine here, but there are two key points that we want to highlight. First, the court applied a number of rules of construction, including the following: "In construing a deed for a railroad right of way, the deed is usually construed as giving a mere right of way, although the terms of the deed would be otherwise apt to convey a fee." Second, the court was influenced by the words "for railroad purposes only" in the grant. The second case is *Machado v. Southern Pacific Trans. Co.*, 284 Cal. Rptr. 560 (Ct. App. 2d Dist. Div. 5, 1991). The conveyance in this case included the following:

> [Grantor] has granted, bargained and sold and conveyed, and by these presents does grant, bargain, sell and convey unto the said party of the second part, its successors and assigns forever, that certain strip or parcel of land for a right of way for a standard gauge railroad, its main track, side tracks, switches, branches, turnouts, and all other uses necessary and incident to railway construction . . . [b]eing a strip of land 60 feet in width, 30 feet thereof being on each side of and parallel to the center line of location of the Southern California railway over and across the land of the grantor: [legal description follows].

The court held that this language conveyed a fee simple, not an easement. As with *Johnson*, there is a lot in *Machado* that we will not discuss here. The opinion in *Machado* included the following four points. First, the court applied rules of construction that "fee simple title is presumed to be intended to pass by a grant of real property, unless it appears from the grant that a lesser estate was intended" and that "a grant is to be interpreted in favor of the grantee." Second, the court held that *Johnson* was wrong as a matter of California law to apply a rule of construction in favor of an easement in a conveyance to a railroad. Third, the court "conclude[d] that the term 'for a right of way for a standard gauge railroad' merely constitutes a description of the intended purpose of the land rather than a limitation on its grant." Fourth, the court noted that "the deed recites that the land which is the subject of the grant runs 'over and across the land of the grantor.' This description seems to suggest, but does not require, construction as an easement, rather than a fee."

NOTES AND QUESTIONS

1. *Rules of Construction.* The general rules of construction in favor of a fee simple and against the grantor are often applied in easement cases. The rule of construction applied in *Johnson*, that an easement will be presumed in the railroad context, goes against both these general rules. This railroad-specific rule of construction has been applied by a wide number of courts. Whether or not it is a good rule of California law appears to be an open question. *See City of Manhattan Beach v. Superior Court*, 914 P.2d 160, 165-66 & n.7 (Cal. 1996). Can you think of any reasons why it would be a good idea to depart from the usual rules in favor of fee simple and against the grantor when a railroad is the grantee? What policies might be advanced by doing so?

RULES OF CONSTRUCTION

ELECTRICAL, TELEPHONE, CABLE, AND FIBER-OPTIC CABLES

Another commonly litigated ambiguity is whether an easement for electrical or telephone lines, often granted sometime in the early 1900s, allows the utility to use the easement for cable or fiber-optic lines. Like the railroad context we just examined, courts often reach divergent results. Some of the disparity is due to different legal approaches taken by the courts (as in *Johnson* and *Machado*), and some is due to variance in the language used in the conveyances. *Compare Henley v. Continental Cablevision of St. Louis County, Inc.*, 692 S.W.2d 825 (Mo. Ct. App. 1985) (cable lines appropriate use of easement for telephone and electric light) *with Marcus Cable Associates, L.P. v. Krohn*, 90 S.W.3d 697 (Tex. 2002) (cable lines not appropriate use of easement for distribution of electricity).

2. *The Conveyances.* Read the conveyances in *Johnson* and *Machado* closely. Both conveyances are very wordy—you might find it helpful to lightly cross out in pencil language that you don't think is relevant to the easement versus fee simple issue. Based on the language alone, what do you think they conveyed? What would your answer to each conveyance be applying the different rules of construction applied by the two courts? Put another way, would the selection of a rule of construction be dispositive?

3. *Advising Clients. Johnson* clearly and strongly stated a rule of construction in favor of an easement when the grantee was a railroad. If you were advising the successors-in-interest to the grantor in *Machado*, based on *Johnson* alone, you would have been on solid ground to tell your client that this rule of construction existed in California law. The outcome to the contrary in *Machado*, however, highlights the need to caveat this type of advice to clients. Because *Johnson* was issued by an intermediate appellate court, it was not binding precedent on another intermediate appellate court of the same level, and it would not have been binding had the case gone to the California Supreme Court. Caveats would have been in order even if *Johnson* had been issued by the California Supreme Court. As you have seen before, and as you will see many times again in the future, courts sometimes overrule prior precedent and change the law. Your clients should know that this could happen to them.

4. *Further Reading.* A.E. Korpela, *Deed to Railroad Company as Conveying Fee or Easement*, 6 A.L.R.3d 973; A.M. Swarthout, *Deed as Conveying Fee or Easement*, 136 A.L.R. 379.

Ambiguity problems can also arise in the interpretation of an express easement's scope. Let's go back to one of our prior examples, where I own parcel A and you own parcel B. You expressly grant me an appurtenant easement to cross parcel B to get to the road. Say that the grant says that you "grant to the present and future owners of parcel

TRANSFER OF EASEMENTS

In most circumstances, the transfer of an easement is straightforward. The benefit of an appurtenant easement is presumed to run with the land of the dominant parcel. Put another way, the benefit of an appurtenant easement will run with the land unless there is express language to the contrary in the transaction. If you buy a parcel of land that has the benefit of an easement, the benefit is presumed to run with the land to you, the new owner. Similarly, the burden of an easement runs with the land of the servient parcel. If you buy a parcel of property that is burdened by the easement, that parcel will still be burdened with the easement after you take ownership of it.

Occasionally, the owner of the benefit of an appurtenant easement tries to transfer the easement separately from the dominant parcel. In other words, the owner of the dominant parcel might try to transfer the benefit of the easement to a third party. This would go against the very nature of an appurtenant easement and would convert the appurtenant easement to an in gross easement. This type of attempted transfer is ineffective. The easement remains tied to the dominant parcel, and the attempted transfer to a third party does nothing. *See* Restatement (Third) of Property, Servitudes §5.6.

The transfer of in gross easements can be more complicated. The burden of an in gross easement runs with the land of the servient parcel, as it would with an appurtenant easement. The benefit of an in gross easement cannot run with the land, of course because there is no land for it to run with. The modern view is that the benefit of an in gross easement is presumed to be assignable. *See* Restatement (Third) of Property, Servitudes §4.6. So, for example, First Electric Company is presumed to be able to assign the benefit of an in gross power-line easement to Second Electric Company. Recall in this context our discussion above about whether an electric or telephone easement can be used for cable or fiber-optic lines. The Electric Company presumptively can assign an easement to the Cable Company, but this assignment would not permit the Cable Company to use the easement for purposes beyond its scope.

Transfers of in gross easements may present problems if the recipient of the transfer expands the use of the easement. Imagine, for example, that my small youth group has an in gross easement to use your beach for swimming. If I transfer this in gross easement to another association that is ten times the size, the burden of the easement on you will dramatically increase. Courts may limit the transferability of easements in contexts like these as exceeding the intended scope of the easement. Similar problems may arise with the transfer of an appurtenant easement, but the problem is particularly acute with in gross easements because they are not tied to the use of a parcel of property.

A an easement to cross parcel B to reach State Road 101." There are a host of issues that the grant leaves unanswered. Where, exactly, is the easement located? How wide is it? If I am using the easement for a driveway that is presently unpaved, can I pave it?

If the instrument has clear language, of course, that language will control. As they usually do in cases of ambiguity, courts will try to give effect to the intention of the parties. As Professor Korngold has noted, courts resolving ambiguity issues will often look at "the circumstances under which the deed was executed; the parties' practices since the execution of the easement; direct evidence of intention [e.g., affidavit testimony from one of the parties]; prior cases [i.e., how have prior cases interpreted similar language]; and a general rule of reason."[1]

When an instrument is silent or ambiguous as to an easement's location and dimensions, the easement is sometimes referred to as a "floating" easement. The most commonly applied rule for driveway easements is that if the location and dimensions are not stated, "the dominant estate is ordinarily entitled to a way of such width, length and location as is sufficient to afford necessary or reasonable ingress and egress." *Aladdin Petroleum Corp. v. Gold Crown Properties, Inc.*, 561 P.2d 818, 822 (Kan. 1977). A minority of jurisdictions apply a harsher rule that inadequate description of an easement's location and dimensions will render the easement void. *See* Jon W. Bruce & James W. Ely, Jr., *The Law of Easements and Licenses in Land*, §7:6 (2001).

2. NON-EXPRESS EASEMENTS

So far, we have discussed the classic express easements created by grant or reservation. They are created in what a property lawyer might describe as the correct way—expressly by means of a written instrument. If you ever want to create an easement, you should do it expressly.

As we've seen many times in this course already, however, people don't always do things the way we wish they would. Often, situations arise where it would make sense to have an easement, but the people involved failed to expressly create one.

Facing these situations, courts have recognized four types of non-express easements: (1) easements by prescription, (2) easements by estoppel, (3) easement implied by existing use, and (4) easement implied by necessity. We will consider each in turn.

a. Easements by Prescription

Acquisition of an easement by prescription is similar to acquisition of title to property by adverse possession. If I cross your land without your permission, then I commit a trespass. If I do so repeatedly, and you do nothing to stop me, then the statute of limitations might run on your ability to bring a trespass action against me. If the statute of limitations does expire, and the other elements of prescription are met, then I will have acquired a prescriptive easement across your property.

The elements of prescription are similar to those of adverse possession. The person claiming the prescriptive easement must use the other person's property in a manner that is (a) visible (or, open and notorious), (b) non-permissive (or, hostile), and (c) continuous for the statutory period. In some jurisdictions, the elements of prescription are easier to satisfy than the corresponding elements of adverse possession.

---

[1] Gerald Korngold, *Private Land Use Arrangements: Easements, Real Covenants and Equitable Servitudes* §4.02(a) (2d ed. 2004).

The statutory period for prescription may also be shorter than the statutory period for adverse possession. The end result is also different—the successful prescription claimant will obtain an easement, whereas the successful adverse possession claimant will obtain fee simple title. Our next case provides a good discussion of each of these elements and illustrates how an easement may be acquired by prescription.

McDONALD V. HARRIS

Supreme Court of Alaska, 1999
978 P.2d 81

FABE, Justice.

I. INTRODUCTION

When Denise McDonald discovered that Sylvia Harris's driveway encroached on McDonald's property, McDonald blocked Harris's use of the driveway. As a result, Harris sought a prescriptive easement, and the superior court found that Harris met the three requirements of a prescriptive easement—continuity, hostility, and notoriety—for the required period of ten years. On appeal, McDonald argues that the trial court used the wrong dates for determining the required period of continuity and that both McDonald's and Harris's lack of knowledge of the encroachment negated the hostility and notoriety elements. Because we conclude that the superior court correctly determined that Harris satisfied the requirements for a prescriptive easement, we affirm.

II. FACTS AND PROCEEDINGS

Sylvia Harris and Denise McDonald own adjacent lots of real property in Mountain Glacier Estates about fifteen miles east of Homer. David Truss previously owned a larger parcel that included both the Harris and McDonald lots, as well as a gravel pit. Truss sold the lot now owned by McDonald to a predecessor in title in 1978.

The Harrises bought their lot from Truss in November 1982. The bill of sale, recorded in February 1983, did not reserve an easement to Truss; it only provided that the Harrises would pay the $30,000 purchase price by performing construction work for the gravel pit on Truss's property. The Harrises then selected the exact site for their log home on the lot in late 1982 or early 1983.

Although Donald Harris did not complete construction of the log home until October 1985, he built a driveway to the property in the spring of 1983. Donald then erected a barbed wire fence on the side of the driveway that was thought to abut the lot later purchased by Denise McDonald. The Harrises have maintained and used the driveway year-round from 1983 to the present. In addition to posting "no trespassing" and "private drive" signs, Donald put logs across the access road behind the house in approximately 1986 to block public traffic.

While Donald and his workers occasionally used the driveway as a way to access the gravel pit when doing construction work for Truss, the public did not generally use the driveway. For the three months out of the year that the gravel pit was in use, alternative routes existed to access the pit. In fact, Donald had supervised the construction of Mossberry Avenue in 1985, which was intended to provide alternate access to the gravel pit.

When Denise McDonald bought her property in April 1986, she did not have a survey performed; instead, she relied on a rough sketch of the property that did not correctly identify its boundaries. When, approximately nine and a half years later, she commissioned a formal site survey, she discovered that the Harris driveway encroached on her property. She then blocked the driveway.

Because of the disputed driveway, Harris sought a prescriptive easement. After a bench trial on the matter, Superior Court Judge Harold Brown awarded the prescriptive easement to Harris. McDonald appeals.

III. DISCUSSION

Harris claims a prescriptive easement for the portion of the driveway that encroaches onto the McDonald property. The elements of a prescriptive easement are essentially the same as the elements of adverse possession, except that adverse possession focuses on possession rather than use. To be entitled to a prescriptive easement, a party must prove (1) *continuity*—that the use of the easement was continuous and uninterrupted; (2) *hostility*—that the user acted as the owner and not merely one with the permission of the owner; and (3) *notoriety*—that the use was reasonably visible to the record owner. A claimant must prove each element by clear and convincing evidence. Finally, a claimant must have engaged in the adverse use for at least ten years.

A. Standard of Review

The question of whether a claimant has satisfied the elements of a prescriptive easement is factual in nature. We will overturn such factual findings "only if they are clearly erroneous and there exists a definite and firm conviction that a mistake has been made."

B. Harris Has Proved the Elements of a Prescriptive Easement

1. Continuity

To meet the requirement of continuity, Harris must show continuous and uninterrupted use for at least ten years prior to December 1995, when McDonald interrupted the adverse use of the encroachment. We explained this concept, in the context of adverse possession, in *Alaska National Bank v. Linck:*

> The nature of [possession or use] sufficient to meet this requirement depends on the character of the property. One test is whether the adverse possessor has used and enjoyed the land as "an average owner of similar property would use and enjoy it." An interruption of possession caused by the record owner or third parties, or abandonment by the possessor, tolls the running of the statute of limitations.

We have applied this test in determining the existence of prescriptive easements as well. To establish interruption of use, the record owner or third party must usually do more than merely post signs against trespassing; the owner or party ordinarily needs to physically block access to the easement.

The superior court found that the commencement date for the required period of adverse use was in early or mid 1983, when Donald Harris built the driveway to the building site of his new home. But because Truss and others used this driveway as an access to Truss's gravel pit, McDonald argues that the Harrises' use was not exclusive and thus cannot be characterized as continuous and uninterrupted from the time of the driveway's construction. McDonald maintains that the Harrises' easement rights did not begin to accrue until Donald physically blocked Truss's access to the gravel pit in 1986.

While McDonald acknowledges our holding in *McGill v. Wahl* that "[e]xclusivity of use is not generally a requirement for a prescriptive easement," she relies on *McGill* for her argument that exclusivity of use should be considered as "a factor in determining whether a use was under a claim of right." In that case, the claimant and other adjacent lot owners had continuously used a roadway through the record owner's adjacent property as an access to their lots. The roadway existed before the owner of the adjacent property had come to the property, and it was the sole automobile access to the claimant's house. The other adjacent lot owners eventually used a newly constructed highway to access their properties, but the claimant continued to use the disputed road. We rejected the suggestion that nonexclusive use of the road precluded a prescriptive easement.

Here, both Harris and Truss used the driveway as an access to their properties. Like the roadway in *McGill*, the disputed driveway existed before McDonald purchased her property. While the other lot owners in *McGill* had ceased their use of the roadway, Truss may have continued to use the driveway as access to the gravel pit. Still, as long as the Harrises were the "primary and only consistent users of the [driveway]," a third party's occasional use of the driveway will not defeat the Harrises' claim for easement rights based on their use of the driveway as private access.

In accordance with this view, the trial court found that the Harrises maintained and continuously used the driveway throughout each year beginning in early or mid 1983 to the present. The Harrises built the driveway in its present location soon after they began living on the property. The Harrises continued to use the driveway as private access to their homesite, and later their completed home, until McDonald blocked that access in 1995. The trial court's finding that the requisite ten years of continuous use had elapsed before McDonald interrupted the adverse use was thus not clearly erroneous.

2. Hostility

McDonald contends that the element of hostility requires that the claimant of an easement have some knowledge that her use is in derogation of another's rights. The hostility requirement, however, is "determined by application of an *objective* test which simply asks whether the possessor acted toward the land as if he owned it, without the permission of one with legal authority to give possession."

Still, we will presume that the use of land by an alleged easement holder was permissive unless a claimant proves "a distinct and positive assertion of a right hostile to the owner." But this presumption does not arise if "a roadway was not established by the owner of the servient estate for its own use but was for many years the only means of passage to the dominant estate."

Here, the general presumption of permission does not arise. McDonald did not construct the driveway nor did she use it; the driveway existed when she first bought the property and there is no indication that her predecessors in title built or used the driveway. Moreover, the driveway was the only viable means of passage to the actual site of the Harris home. Thus, this case qualifies as an exception to the general presumption.

Even if the presumption did arise, Harris's actions objectively asserted a right hostile to McDonald's. A claimant's use is adverse or hostile "if the true owners merely acquiesce, and do not intend to permit a use." The key difference between acquiescence and permission is that "a permissive use requires the acknowledgment by the possessor that he holds in subordination to the owner's title."

As McDonald admits, neither she nor Harris had any knowledge of the encroachment of the driveway. Therefore, McDonald could not have intended to permit the Harrises to use that portion of the driveway. Moreover, because the Harrises had no knowledge of the encroachment, they could not have acknowledged that McDonald was the rightful owner of that portion. In fact, the Harrises used and maintained the driveway as if it were their own. Thus, the superior court correctly found that the Harrises met the requirement of hostility.

3. Notoriety

Finally, McDonald argues that although the disputed driveway was visible, the lack of actual knowledge by any party of the encroachment defeats the prerequisite of notoriety. But this claim is not supported by our case law. To the contrary, the adverse user need not demonstrate that the record owner had actual knowledge of the adverse party's presence. The adverse user must show only that a duly alert owner would have known of the adverse presence. In particular, "a landowner is responsible for knowing the physical encumbrances on and the boundaries of the owner's land." Harris thus only needs to show that her continued use of the driveway was open, not that the use was open and known by McDonald to be on her land.

The superior court found that McDonald, as a duly alert and reasonably diligent owner, should have known that a portion of the Harrises' driveway encroached on her property. McDonald observed the driveway when she bought her property and knew that the Harrises and their invitees used it. At the time of her purchase, McDonald had walked the corners of the property and saw no visible stakes. Instead of ordering an actual survey of the property, however, "she relied on a drawing that was undated, unsigned and failed to identify which way is north as assurance that the driveway did not encumber her property." Because McDonald bore the responsibility of knowing the boundaries of her property, we uphold the superior court's finding on the element of notoriety.

IV. CONCLUSION

Because the superior court's findings are not clearly erroneous, we AFFIRM its decision to grant Harris a prescriptive easement.

b. Easements by Estoppel

Imagine that you and I own adjacent parcels of land. You need to cross my land to get to a road. Right now, your land is vacant, and you want to build a house on it. You ask me if your contractor can cross my land to build the house. I say yes. So far, I've arguably only granted you a license. Remember that a license gives a *revocable* right to enter property. I raise no problems while the contractor builds the house. Shortly after the house is completed, however, you and I get into an argument. I forbid you to cross my property and put up a chain across the dirt driveway that provides you with access to the road.

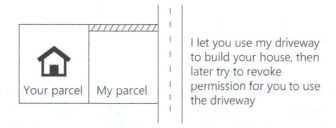

Your parcel | My parcel

I let you use my driveway to build your house, then later try to revoke permission for you to use the driveway

If I can revoke the license that I gave you, you will not have any way to access your property. Under these circumstances, however, you may have an *easement by estoppel* across my property. I may be prevented (or, in the lingo, *estopped*) from revoking the license. If you think about it a little bit, you should see that an irrevocable license is functionally the same thing as an easement. Revocability, after all, is the key difference between a license and an easement.

We have already seen the equitable concept of estoppel at work in our material on real estate transactions. Remember that, generally speaking, estoppel has two components: (a) conduct by one party and (b) a detrimental change in position by a second party made in reasonable reliance on the first party's conduct. Remember not to read "detrimental" as requiring some kind of truly negative harm. This requirement can be met, for example, by taking on a new legal obligation in reliance on the other party's conduct.

Easements by estoppel fit this general pattern. (1) We start with conduct by the owner of the putative servient estate. This conduct typically includes the express or implied grant of a

LAW AND EQUITY

license to cross or otherwise access the servient estate. (2) We then have a detrimental change in position by another party. Although it is possible to imagine an easement by estoppel in gross, this other party is typically the owner of the putative dominant tenement. This detrimental change in position must be made in reasonable reliance on the conduct in (1). If these requirements are met, the owner of the servient estate will be estopped from revoking the license, and the dominant estate will obtain an easement by estoppel over the servient estate.

In our example, I engaged in conduct by giving you permission to have your contractor cross my land. I also engaged in conduct, albeit in a passive way, when I sat by and let your contractor repeatedly cross my land during construction. In the estoppel context, conduct might be action or inaction. You detrimentally changed your position when you spent money to have the house built. We might argue about whether you reasonably relied on my conduct, but if you did, you will likely have a good claim for an easement by estoppel over my property.

The following case explores easements by estoppel further. The opinion discusses a number of prior estoppel cases in some detail. Pay close attention to the facts of those earlier cases as well as the facts of the case under review.

HOLBROOK V. TAYLOR

Supreme Court of Kentucky, 1976
532 S.W.2d 763

STERNBERG, Justice.

This is an action to establish a right to the use of a roadway, which is 10 to 12 feet wide and about 250 feet long, over the unenclosed, hilly woodlands of another. The claimed right to the use of the roadway is twofold: by prescription and by estoppel. Both issues are heatedly contested. The evidence is in conflict as to the nature and type of use that had been made of the roadway. The lower court determined that a right to the use of the roadway by prescription had not been established, but that it had been established by estoppel. The landowners, feeling themselves aggrieved, appeal. We will consider the two issues separately.

In *Grinestaff v. Grinestaff*, Ky., 318 S.W.2d 881 (1958), we said that an easement may be created by express written grant, by implication, by prescription, or by estoppel. It has long been the law of this commonwealth that "(a)n easement, such as a right of way, is created when the owner of a tenement to which the right is claimed to be appurtenant, or those under whom he claims title, have openly, peaceably, continuously, and under a claim of right adverse to the owner of the soil, and with his knowledge and acquiescence, used a way over the lands of another for as much as 15 years." *Flener v. Lawrence*, 187 Ky. 384, 220 S.W. 1041 (1920); *Rominger v. City Realty Company*, Ky., 324 S.W.2d 806 (1959).

In 1942 appellants purchased the subject property. In 1944 they gave permission for a haul road to be cut for the purpose of moving coal from a newly opened mine.

The roadway was so used until 1949, when the mine closed. During that time the appellants were paid a royalty for the use of the road. In 1957 appellants built a tenant house on their property and the roadway was used by them and their tenant. The tenant house burned in 1961 and was not replaced. In 1964 the appellees bought their three-acre building site, which adjoins appellants, and the following year built their residence thereon. At all times prior to 1965, the use of the haul road was by permission of appellants. There is no evidence of any probative value which would indicate that the use of the haul road during that period of time was either adverse, continuous, or uninterrupted. The trial court was fully justified, therefore, in finding that the right to the use of this easement was not established by prescription.

As to the issue on estoppel, we have long recognized that a right to the use of a roadway over the lands of another may be established by estoppel. In *Lashley Telephone Co. v. Durbin,* 190 Ky. 792, 228 S.W. 423 (1921), we said:

> "Though many courts hold that a licensee is conclusively presumed as a matter of law to know that a license is revocable at the pleasure of the licensor, and if he expend money in connection with his entry upon the land of the latter, he does so at his peril . . . , yet it is the established rule in this state that where a license is not a bare, naked right of entry, but includes the right to erect structures and acquire an interest in the land in the nature of an easement by the construction of improvements thereon, the licensor may not revoke the license and restore his premises to their former condition after the licensee has exercised the privilege given by the license and erected the improvements at considerable expense; . . . ."

In *Gibbs v. Anderson,* 288 Ky. 488, 156 S.W.2d 876 (1941), Gibbs claimed the right, by estoppel, to the use of a roadway over the lands of Anderson. The lower court denied the claim. We reversed. Anderson's immediate predecessor in title admitted that he had discussed the passway with Gibbs before it was constructed and had agreed that it might be built through his land. He stood by and saw Gibbs expend considerable money in this construction. We applied the rule announced in *Lashley Telephone Co. v. Durbin,* supra, and reversed with directions that a judgment be entered granting Gibbs the right to the use of the passway.

In *McCoy v. Hoffman,* Ky., 295 S.W.2d 560 (1956), the facts are that Hoffman had acquired the verbal consent of the landowner to build a passway over the lands of the owner to the state highway. Subsequently, the owner of the servient estate sold the property to McCoy, who at the time of the purchase was fully aware of the existence of the roadway and the use to which it was being put. McCoy challenged Hoffman's right to use the road. The lower court found that a right had been gained by prescription. In this court's consideration of the case, we affirmed, not on the theory of prescriptive right but on the basis that the owner of the servient estate was estopped. After announcing the rule for establishing a right by prescription, we went on to say:

> "On the other hand, the right of revocation of the license is subject to the qualification that where the licensee has exercised the privilege given him and

erected improvements or made substantial expenditures on the faith or strength of the license, it becomes irrevocable and continues for so long a time as the nature of the license calls for. In effect, under this condition the license becomes in reality a grant through estoppel. . . ."

In *Akers v. Moore,* Ky., 309 S.W.2d 758 (1958), this court again considered the right to the use of a passway by estoppel. Akers and others had used the Moore branch as a public way of ingress and egress from their property. They sued Moore and others who owned property along the branch seeking to have the court recognize their right to the use of the roadway and to order the removal of obstructions which had been placed in the roadway. The trial court found that Akers and others had acquired a prescriptive right to the use of the portion of the road lying on the left side of the creek bed, but had not acquired the right to the use of so much of the road as lay on the right side of the creek bed. Consequently, an appeal and a cross-appeal were filed. Considering the right to the use of the strip of land between the right side of the creek bed and the highway, this court found that the evidence portrayed it very rough and apparently never improved, that it ran alongside the house in which one of the protestors lived, and that by acquiescence or by express consent of at least one of the protestors the right side of the roadway was opened up so as to change the roadway from its close proximity to the Moore residence. The relocated portion of the highway had only been used as a passway for about six years before the suit was filed. The trial court found that this section of the road had not been established as a public way by estoppel. We reversed. In doing so, we stated:

"We consider the fact that the appellees, Artie Moore, et al, had stood by and acquiesced in (if in fact they had not affirmatively consented) the change being made and permitted the appellants to spend money in fixing it up to make it passable and use it for six years without objecting. Of course, the element of time was not sufficient for the acquisition of the right of way by adverse possession. But the law recognizes that one may acquire a license to use a passway or roadway where, with the knowledge of the licensor, he has in the exercise of the privilege spent money in improving the way or for other purposes connected with its use on the faith or strength of the license. Under such conditions the license becomes irrevocable and continues for so long a time as its nature calls for. This, in effect, becomes a grant through estoppel. *Gibbs v. Anderson,* 288 Ky. 488, 156 S.W.2d 876; *McCoy v. Hoffman,* Ky., 295 S.W.2d 560. It would be unconscionable to permit the owners of this strip of land of trivial value to revoke the license by obstructing and preventing its use."

In the present case the roadway had been used since 1944 by permission of the owners of the servient estate. The evidence is conflicting as to whether the use of the road subsequent to 1965 was by permission or by claim of right. Appellees contend that it had been used by them and others without the permission of appellants; on the other hand, it is contended by appellants that the use of the roadway at all times was by their permission. The evidence discloses that during the period of preparation for the construction of appellees' home and during the time the house was being built, appellees were permitted to use the roadway as ingress and egress for workmen, for hauling machinery and material to the building site, for construction of the dwelling, and for making improvements generally to the premises. Further, the evidence reflects that after construction of the residence, which cost $25,000, was completed, appellees continued to regularly use the roadway as they had been doing. Appellant J. S. Holbrook testified that in order for appellees to get up to their house he gave them permission to use and repair the roadway. They widened it, put in a culvert, and graveled part of it with "red dog," also known as cinders, at a cost of approximately $100. There is no other location over which a roadway could reasonably be built to provide an outlet for appellees.

No dispute had arisen between the parties at any time over the use of the roadway until the fall of 1970. Appellant J. S. Holbrook contends that he wanted to secure a writing from the appellees in order to relieve him from any responsibility for any damage that might happen to anyone on the subject road. On the other hand, Mrs. Holbrook testified that the writing was desired to avoid any claim which may be made by appellees of a right to the use of the roadway. Appellees testified that the writing was an effort to force them to purchase a small strip of land over which the roadway traversed, for the sum of $500. The dispute was not resolved and appellants erected a steel cable across the roadway to prevent its use and also constructed "notrespassing" signs. Shortly thereafter, the suit was filed to require the removal of the obstruction and to declare the right of appellees to the use of the roadway without interference.

The use of the roadway by appellees to get to their home from the public highway, the use of the roadway to take in heavy equipment and material and supplies for construction of the residence, the general improvement of the premises, the maintenance of the roadway, and the construction by appellees of a $25,000 residence, all with the actual consent of appellants or at least with their tacit approval, clearly demonstrates the rule laid down in *Lashley Telephone Co. v. Durbin,* supra, that the license to use the subject roadway may not be revoked.

The evidence justifies the finding of the lower court that the right to the use of the roadway had been established by estoppel.

The judgment is affirmed.

NOTES AND QUESTIONS

1. *Prescription.* Why, exactly, did the court find that there was no easement by prescription on these facts?

2. *Duration of an Easement by Estoppel.* Courts differ on how long an easement by estoppel lasts. Some say that easements by estoppel are of unlimited duration like a typical easement. Others say that the easement lasts for so long as it takes for the person in the servient position to recoup their investment. Still others say that it lasts for the life of the structure built in reliance on the license.

3. *Not All Jurisdictions Allow Easements by Estoppel.* Some courts refuse to recognize easements by estoppel on the grounds that they undercut the Statute of Frauds. For example, in *Henry v. Dalton*, 151 A.2d 362 (R.I. 1959), the court rejected an invitation to recognize easements by estoppel:

> This is plainly the rule of the statute [of frauds]. It is also, we believe, the rule required by public policy. It prevents the burdening of lands with restrictions founded upon oral agreements, easily misunderstood. It gives security and certainty to titles, which are most important to be preserved against defects and qualifications not founded upon solemn instruments. The jurisdiction of courts to enforce oral contracts for the sale of land is clearly defined and well understood, and is indisputable; but to change what commenced in a license into an irrevocable right, on the ground of equitable estoppel, is another and quite different matter. It is far better, we think, that the law requiring interests in land to be evidenced by deed, should be observed . . . .

c. Easements by Implication Part One: Easements Implied by Existing Use

I own Blackacre, a 50-acre parcel that on one side fronts on State Route 101. My house is in the back corner of the property, and I reach the road using a long driveway.

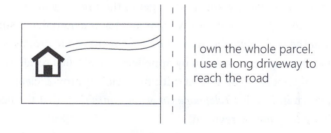

I own the whole parcel. I use a long driveway to reach the road

I agree to sell the 25 acres nearest the road to you, dividing the parcel in half. We'll call my half of Blackacre parcel A, and your half, parcel B.

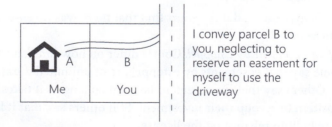

I convey parcel B to you, neglecting to reserve an easement for myself to use the driveway

As you can see, the driveway that I use to get to the road crosses the part of Blackacre that you will own after we complete the transaction. Clearly, the best thing for me to do would be to reserve a driveway easement for myself when I transfer parcel B to you. If I do not reserve an express easement in myself, however, I may still have an *easement implied by existing use* across parcel B.

As its name suggests, this type of easement is implied because of a use of the property that exists at the time of the division of the property. In our example, it is the driveway that I use to get to the road. Looking at the diagram, it seems pretty obvious that I should have an easement across your portion of Blackacre. Sure, we should have done it expressly, but if we don't, the law might imply an easement for my benefit.

In cases, the existing use is often called a *quasi-easement*. Look at the diagram dividing Blackacre into parcels A and B. Let's go back in time before I sold parcel B to you. Even though I own both parcels, I can be seen as using a driveway across one part of the property (what will become parcel B) for the benefit of the other part (what will become parcel A). If we pretend that the parcels are separately owned, we also might pretend that parcel A has an easement across parcel B. This pretend easement, of course, is not a real easement, and courts resorted to calling this type of use a "quasi-easement."

There are four elements of an easement implied by existing use:

1. There must have been a *unity of ownership* of the two parcels. In other words, at one time the two parcels were owned by one person.

2. When the parcels were separated, one of the parcels *visibly or apparently* made some *use* of the other parcel. This is the existing use or quasi-easement that we have been discussing. The requirement that the use be visible or apparent is important to the implication of the easement—if the use was visible or apparent, then both parties should have known about it.

3. The use must have been *continuous* at the time the parcels were separated. The requirement of continuity again goes to the grounds for implying the easement. If the use was continuous, then the parties should have expected it to continue.

4. Continued use of the quasi-easement must be *reasonably necessary* to the owner of the parcel claiming the benefit of the easement. Reasonable necessity is a relatively easy standard to meet. For example, in our driveway example, if it would be expensive for me (the owner of the parcel claiming the benefit) to reach a road a different way, the reasonable necessity standard would be met. But if there was another, low-cost, way for me to reach a road (e.g., if another road ran right by my house), then the reasonable necessity standard would not be met.

There is some authority, including that cited in our next case, that reasonable necessity applies to an implied grant of an easement but that *strict necessity* applies to an implied reservation of an easement. Strict necessity is a much higher standard and is only met in cases of impossibility or near impossibility. If it was very expensive for me to reach the road another way, we would say that my use of the contested driveway was reasonably necessary but not strictly necessary.

Our driveway example involved an implied reservation. I initially owned the entire parcel and sold you the land nearest the road. If I had had my act together, I would have reserved an easement to reach the road when I sold that land to you. An implied grant would involve a different scenario, where the person claiming the benefit of the implied easement was not the owner of the entire parcel and rather is a person who acquired the benefited parcel of land. In this scenario, the implied easement would be an implied grant.

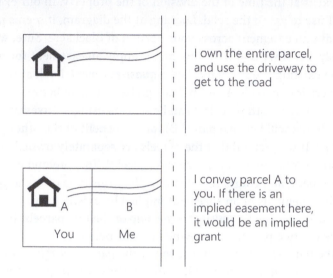

The logic of the distinction between implied reservations and implied grants, such as it is, is that the person claiming the easement is more at fault for causing the problem in a case of an implied reservation because that person was the owner of the entire parcel of land before it was severed.

Today, a majority of jurisdictions do not make a distinction between implied grants and implied reservations and apply a standard of reasonable necessity in both contexts. This distinction between implied grants and reservations, however, is still applied in some jurisdictions, as we will see in our next case.

HOUSTON BELLAIRE, LTD. V. TCP LB PORTFOLIO I, L.P.

Court of Appeals of Texas, 1998
981 S.W.2d 916

HEDGES, Justice.

Appellee, TCP LB Portfolio I, L.P., sued appellant, Houston Bellaire, Ltd., seeking a declaration that it was entitled to an easement by estoppel, implication, prescription, and necessity through property owned by Houston Bellaire, and for Houston Bellaire's tortious interference with existing and prospective business relationships. Prior to trial, TCP obtained a temporary injunction enjoining Houston Bellaire's construction of a fence that blocked the alleged easement. . . .

The remaining issues were tried to the court. The trial court rendered judgment granting TCP an easement by implication and permanently enjoining the building of a fence between the properties. TCP was awarded costs and attorney fees; all other relief was denied.

In four points of error, Houston Bellaire contends that the trial court erred: (1) in its holding that unity of ownership existed at the time the dominant and servient estates were severed; (2) in its holding that there existed an apparent use between the properties at the time the dominant and servient estates were severed; (3) in applying the standard of reasonable necessity instead of strict necessity; and (4) in awarding attorney fees to TCP and not to Houston Bellaire. . . . We affirm.

STATEMENT OF FACTS

This dispute involves a 7.1414 acre tract of property originally owned by Lincoln Property Co. No. 38. On September 15, 1977, Harvin Moore, as trustee, purchased the northern 2.7264 acres of the tract and obtained an option to purchase the southern 4.4150 acres. On that same day, through a series of transactions, the north tract was conveyed to Corporate Plaza Company, a Texas joint venture owned by Harvin C. Moore, Jr., Tyler D. Todd, the Ben H. Powell Trust, and the Marian Powell Trust. Each partner owned 25% of the joint venture. In 1977, this joint venture built Corporate Plaza 1, a two-story, 50,000 square foot office building.

On December 20, 1977, Lincoln conveyed the south tract to Harvin C. Moore, Trustee. On October 4, 1980, the south tract was conveyed to Corporate Plaza 2 Company, a Texas joint venture owned by Harvin C. Moore, Jr., Tyler D. Todd, and the Marian Powell Trust. Moore and Todd each owned 25% of this joint venture, and the Marian Powell Trust owned the remaining 50%.

In 1980, Corporate Plaza 2 Company developed the south tract and constructed a three-story, 100,000 square foot office building known as Corporate Plaza 2. A parking garage was built on the south side of the building because parking along the north side had been allocated to the Corporate Plaza 1 building. The main visitor entrance to Corporate Plaza 2 was situated near the entrance developed in connection with the construction of Corporate Plaza 1. When Corporate Plaza 2 was built, Corporate Plaza Company still owned Corporate Plaza 1.

Although the two tracts were owned by technically different entities, the properties were developed as part of a common plan and project. The buildings were viewed and intended as one economic unit, consisting of two phases and two buildings totaling 150,000 square feet, situated on approximately seven acres. Instead of constructing an additional drive along the north side of Corporate Plaza 2, the developers decided to widen Corporate Plaza 1's driveway, which was located between the two buildings on Corporate Plaza 1 property. The driveways to the east and west of both buildings were left open and unobstructed so that visitors to either building could reach each of the buildings from any entrance to the 7.1414 acre tract. Upon completion of Corporate Plaza 2 in 1980, use of the driveways by tenants and visitors of each building began immediately. The dual use of the driveway assisted the leasing of Corporate Plaza 2's office space.

On March 4, 1986, The Travelers Insurance Company purchased Corporate Plaza 2 out of foreclosure. Some time later, Hammerly Corporation purchased Corporate Plaza 2. Great-West Life Assurance purchased Corporate Plaza 1 out of foreclosure on March 7, 1989. Houston Bellaire purchased Corporate Plaza 1 on November 11, 1989.

In October 1996, TCP began negotiations with the Hammerly Corporation to purchase Corporate Plaza 2. Hammerly asked Houston Bellaire to execute a cross-easement between the north and south properties allowing the use of the curbcuts, parking lots, and driveways on the north property by tenants and visitors to the south property. Houston Bellaire declined and indicated that it had plans to build a wall between the properties. TCP purchased Corporate Plaza 2 on March 5, 1997.

Discussions continued between the parties. Houston Bellaire was unwilling to execute an easement agreement but offered a lease to TCP. The terms of the lease were discussed but no agreement could be reached. The dual use of the driveways, curbcuts, and parking lots continued until the time Houston Bellaire began building a fence in 1997. When Houston Bellaire started to build the fence between the properties, TCP brought this suit.

EASEMENT BY IMPLICATION

The trial court rendered judgment granting TCP an easement by implication across the north tract owned by Houston Bellaire. Elements of an easement by implied grant are: (1) there was unity of ownership between the dominant and servient estate when the two were severed; (2) at the time the dominant estate was granted, there was apparent use of the easement; (3) use of the easement before the severance was continuous, indicating an intent by the owners to pass the easement by grant with the dominant estate; and (4) the easement must be reasonably necessary to the use and enjoyment of the dominant estate. *Holden v. Weidenfeller*, 929 S.W.2d 124, 128-29 (Tex. App.-San Antonio 1996, writ denied). In its first three points of error, Houston Bellaire contends the trial court erred in its holding that an easement by implication existed between the two tracts of land. . . .

UNITY OF OWNERSHIP

In points of error one and two, Houston Bellaire argues that unity of ownership did not exist at the time users of the south tract began to use the driveways, cutouts, and parking lots on the north tract. It contends that the last time unity of ownership existed over the two tracts was when the property was owned by Lincoln. When Lincoln severed the lots, the tracts were raw land, such that there was no apparent use of the easement at the time the dominant estate was created.

The trial court found that unity of ownership existed during the ownership of the north and south tracts by Corporate Plaza Company and Corporate Plaza 2 Company. During this period, the apparent use of the easement began, and it continued through the time the dominant and servient estates were severed. The trial court held that unity of ownership between the north and south tracts was severed when the south property was foreclosed upon and title passed to an entity other than the Corporate Plaza 2 Company.

Houston Bellaire argues the trial court's conclusion is wrong because the tracts were owned by two different entities: Corporate Plaza Company and Corporate Plaza 2 Company. It contends that because the ownership of the tracts was technically different, as TCP admits, unity of ownership could not exist.

The trial court found although the ownership was technically different, there was sufficient unity of ownership to support easement by implication. Houston Bellaire argues that because Texas courts have called for strict adherence to the requirements for the establishment of an easement by implication, mere similarity of ownership is not enough, citing *Ortiz v. Spann*, 671 S.W.2d 909, 911 (Tex.App.-Corpus Christi, 1984, writ ref'd n.r.e.), and *Exxon Corp. v. Schutzmaier*, 537 S.W.2d 282, 284 (Tex.Civ.App.-Beaumont 1976, no writ).

We disagree with Houston Bellaire that these two cases demand strict and literal compliance with each of the four elements of easement by implication. Strict adherence in this context means that all elements necessary for a finding of an implied easement are essential, and absent all the necessary elements, an implied easement cannot exist. *Holden*, 929 S.W.2d at 129. This interpretation is supported by the *Exxon* court's disavowal of a contrary inquiry, one based primarily on the parties' intention and the circumstances surrounding the transaction. *Exxon*, 537 S.W.2d at 284 n. 2.

While Texas cases discuss the necessity of unity of ownership at the time of the severance of the estates and at the time the use is created, none discuss the requirement in the context of closely related or affiliated entities, or entities having identical majority ownership and control. TCP directs this Court to decisions from other jurisdictions that discuss unity of ownership in this context.

In *Cosmopolitan National Bank v. Chicago Title & Trust Co.*, 7 Ill.2d 471, 131 N.E.2d 4 (Ill.1955), the Illinois Supreme Court found that an easement by implication existed in a paved area between two tracts of land. Both tracts were originally owned by Joseph Trinz as one piece of property. *Id.*, 131 N.E.2d at 6. Trinz conveyed an undivided one-half interest to Harry Lubliner. *Id.* Trinz and Lubliner then executed two deeds dividing the property into two tracts, the apartment tract and the store tract. *Id.* Trinz and Lubliner then organized two separate corporations. *Id.* Trinz, Lubliner, and Lubliner's wife were the incorporators, subscribers, stockholders, and directors of both corporations. *Id.* By two separate deeds, Trinz and Lubliner conveyed the apartment tract to one corporation and conveyed the store tract to the other corporation. *Id.* Improvements were then made to each property, and the disputed area was paved. *Id.* at 7. Title to the properties remained the same for five years, at which time the apartment tract was conveyed to James Brown. *Id.* The Illinois Supreme Court held that unity of ownership existed even though the two tracts of land were owned by two separate corporations. *Id.*

While the court acknowledged that the ownership of the two lots was technically different, it held, "[t]here was, in effect, common ownership of both properties sufficient to indicate the ability to arrange and adapt the property in a manner sufficient to satisfy rules of property in the establishment of easement by implication." *Id.* The court determined that the individual shareholders remained the real parties in interest with the power to arrange and adapt the properties, and in fact did arrange matters by constructing the paved area for the use and benefit of both properties. *Id.*

This decision was followed in *United States v. O'Connell,* 496 F.2d 1329 (2d Cir.1974). In *O'Connell,* the court held that sufficient unity of interest existed "among various pieces of land owned by different corporations if the corporations are owned and controlled by one or two shareholders in such a manner that they can do with all of the pieces of land as they please and if the pieces of land are not treated as being separately owned." *Id.* at 1335. Clearly, the underpinning of the unity of ownership requirement is the concept of *authority:* the ability to impress or reserve an encumbrance on property without which an easement cannot be created.

The reasoning of *Cosmopolitan* and *O'Connell* support the trial court's holding that unity of ownership existed at the time the two tracts were owned by Corporate Plaza Company and Corporate Plaza 2 Company. The ownership of the two joint ventures was sufficiently similar, the two properties were developed as part of a common plan and project, and they were intended as one economic unit consisting of two phases and two buildings situated on 7.1414 acres.

Each joint venture had similar partners. Both Moore and Todd owned 25% of each joint venture. The Ben Powell Trust owned 25% of the Corporate Plaza Company, and the Marian Powell trust owned the remaining 25% percent of that joint venture and 50% of the Corporate Plaza 2 Company. The trustees and the beneficiaries of the two trusts were identical. Moore and Todd were the managing venturers of both joint ventures. The joint ventures, acting together, made the decision to provide access to the south property through the north property. The evidence supports the holding that unity of ownership existed during the ownership of the tracts by Corporate Plaza Company and Corporate Plaza 2 Company.

We overrule point of error one.

Houston Bellaire's second point of error is based on its contention that unity of ownership did not exist after 1977, a time when the property was raw land. Houston Bellaire argues that an easement by implication could not be found because there was no apparent use of an easement at the time the dominant estate was granted, nor was there any use that was continuous so that the parties intended its use to pass by grant with the dominant estate. Houston Bellaire has examined the wrong time frame.

As discussed in our disposition of point of error one, unity of ownership existed at the time the tracts were owned by Corporate Plaza Company and Corporate Plaza 2 Company. Unity of ownership ceased to exist at the time the south tract was purchased from foreclosure. It is that moment at which we must determine if the easement existed because it was then that the time the dominant and servient estates were severed. *Holden*, 929 S.W.2d at 128-29. Houston Bellaire does not contest the trial court's findings that there was an apparent use of the north property by the south property at the time the south tract was purchased from foreclosure and that the use of the north property was continuous at the time the estates were severed.

We overrule point of error two.

STANDARD OF NECESSITY

In its third point of error, Houston Bellaire argues that the trial court erred in using a standard of reasonable necessity instead of strict necessity. The requirement of strict necessity applies when an easement is reserved, and the requirement of reasonable necessity applies when an easement is granted. *See Mitchell v. Castellaw,* 151 Tex. 56, 246 S.W.2d 163, 168 (Tex.1952) (discussing easement by reservation); *Howell v. Estes,* 71 Tex. 690, 12 S.W. 62, 63 (Tex.1888) (discussing easement by grant). We are confronted with an easement as yet unaddressed in Texas: the creation of implied reciprocal easements.[1]

Houston Bellaire contends that a strict necessity standard should apply to reciprocal easements, that is, when both properties benefit from an easement across both tracts at the time of severance, citing *Ward v. Slavecek,* 466 S.W.2d 91, 92 (Tex.Civ.App.-Waco 1971, no writ). TCP Argues that the standard should be that of reasonable necessity. *See James v. Gray,* 281 S.W.2d 114, 116-17 (Tex.Civ.App.-Dallas 1955, writ ref'd n.r.e.)

In *Ward,* the original owner of two adjacent lots built a common driveway approximately on the division line between the two properties. *Ward,* 466 S.W.2d at 92. Ward's predecessor in title purchased the property from the common owner. *Id.* The successor in title to the remaining lot, Slavecek, subsequently built a fence that made it impossible for Ward to use the driveway. *Id.* Ward sought to establish an easement by implication on the part of the driveway on Slavecek's lot. *Id.* The court held that in order

---

[1] Although neither party specifically requested reciprocal easements, the judgment of the trial court granted implied reciprocal easements across both tracts. Therefore, we must determine what standard of necessity should apply to an implied reciprocal easement. Houston Bellaire does not complain of the reciprocal nature of the easement, if there is to be an easement.

for Ward to establish her easement by implication, she had to meet the strict necessity standard, which she failed to do. *Id.* (citing *Mitchell,* 246 S.W.2d at 168).

Houston Bellaire maintains that the holding in *Ward* supports its contention that a reciprocal easement must be supported by a finding of strict necessity. This analysis is wrong for two reasons. First, *Ward* does not in any way suggest that either party asserted a claim for a reciprocal easement. In fact, Slavecek's predecessors in title built a garage and began using the common driveway after Ward's predecessor in title purchased her lot. *Id.* Further, it cannot be said that Slavecek sought a reciprocal easement because Slavecek built the fence on the driveway indicating she had no need of an easement on Ward's property.

Second, we believe the court applied the wrong standard in *Ward.* Ward's lot was the dominant estate and her claim of an easement, if an easement arose at all, was a grant of an implied easement across the driveway given to her predecessor in title. Therefore, all Ward had to show was reasonable necessity. *Howell,* 12 S.W. at 63; *see also James,* 281 S.W.2d at 116-17 (using reasonable necessity standard in fact situation involving common driveway later obstructed by fence, citing *Howell*). *Ward'*s citation to *Mitchell* is erroneous.

Although no Texas case specifically addresses what standard should apply to reciprocal easements, the comments to section 476 of the Restatement of Property provide guidance. Comment h states:

> That the conveyor and the conveyee receive reciprocal benefits from the implication of an easement in favor of each contributes to the implication. The fact that both receive benefits and neither alone suffers from the creation of the easement makes it more probable that they intended its creation. Hence, even in cases where the necessity alone would not have been sufficient to justify the implication of an easement in favor of the conveyor, the fact that the circumstances are sufficient to warrant the implication in favor of the conveyee, and that like benefits would accrue to both the conveyee and the conveyor, may justify the inference that an easement in favor of each was intended.

Restatement of Property §476 cmt. h (1944). This comment clearly relies on the benefits received by both parties in the case of a reciprocal easement. Even though each party can be seen as reserving an easement, the fact that like benefits accrue to both pieces of property favor a finding of an implied easement even without a finding of strict necessity. Because both parties receive mutual benefit, a party only need show reasonable necessity when, as here, there is an implied reciprocal easement. Houston Bellaire does not contest the trial court's finding of reasonable necessity.

We overrule point of error three. . . .

CONCLUSION

We affirm the judgment of the trial court.

NOTE

1. *Implied Underground Easements.* Special problems can arise when an easement implied by existing use is claimed based on a use that is underground because it can be hard to establish that an underground use is visible or apparent. One leading case, for example, involved an easement implied by existing use for an underground sewer line. *See Van Sandt v. Royster,* 83 P.2d 698 (Kan. 1938). Courts typically will allow easements implied by existing use for underground utilities such as sewer, water, and electricity. *See* Joel Eichengrun, *The Problem of Hidden Easements and the Subsequent Purchaser Without Notice,* 40 Okla. L. Rev. 3 (1987); Restatement (Third) of Property, Servitudes, §2.12(4).

d. Easements by Implication Part Two: Easements Implied by Necessity

Say that I own a 50-acre parcel of land. A public road runs along one side of the parcel. I divide the land into two smaller 25-acre parcels. I keep parcel B, which runs along the road. I sell parcel A to you. Parcel A has no access to that road or any other road. We call a parcel of land that has no access to a road *landlocked.*

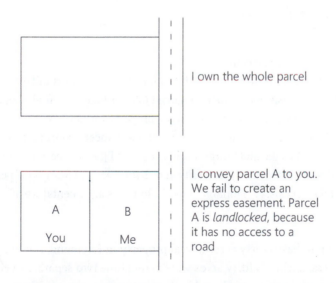

I own the whole parcel

I convey parcel A to you. We fail to create an express easement. Parcel A is *landlocked,* because it has no access to a road

Unlike the easement implied by existing use fact pattern, here there was no existing use, or quasi-easement, prior to the division of the parcels. Even without the prior use, however, it is reasonable under these circumstances to presume that I did not intend to create a landlocked parcel when I divided the land. We therefore might imply an easement for the benefit of parcel A across parcel B because the easement is necessary for parcel A to reach the road. Easements implied in these circumstances are called *easements implied by necessity* or simply *easements by necessity.*

There are three elements to the creation of an easement by necessity.

First, there must be *unity of ownership* of the land that later become the dominant and servient parcels. Easements by necessity are implied only over land once owned by the common grantor, not over land that was owned by a third party.

Second, the owner of this land must transfer a part of the larger piece of land in a way that creates a *landlocked parcel.*

Third, the easement must be *necessary* for the landlocked parcel to reach a road. Courts typically hold that this necessity must have *existed at the time* the property was divided from its initial common ownership. Courts also typically apply a standard of *strict necessity.* Recall from our discussion of easement implied by existing use that strict necessity means impossibility or near impossibility, not mere inconvenience.

Our next two cases involve claims of easements by necessity. In the first case, the person claiming the easement by necessity wins. In the second case, the person claiming the easement by necessity loses because the court is very strict in its interpretation of the strict necessity requirement.

FIKE V. SHELTON

Court of Appeals of Mississippi, 2003
860 So. 2d 1227

CHANDLER, J., for the court.

James B. Shelton, III filed a complaint in the Chancery Court of Hinds County for establishment of an easement. Shelton named John D. Fike, the Hinds County Board of Supervisors and any parties interested in the property formerly owned by Levi Sturgis, Sr. as defendants in the action. Shelton petitioned the chancery court to decree an easement by necessity across the Fike and Sturgis properties. . . . [T]he chancery court held that Shelton was entitled to an easement by necessity across the Fike and Sturgis properties. . . . Feeling aggrieved, Fike appeals. . . . Finding no merit [to Fike's arguments] we affirm.

FACTS

Shelton purchased forty acres of real property in Raymond, Mississippi that has no road access. Shelton's forty acres were at one time two separate twenty acre tracts of land, although Shelton purchased both twenty acre tracts together as one and on the same date. This appeal centers around which twenty acre tract of the forty acres provides Shelton with an easement by necessity through adjoining property.

Shelton asserted that he was entitled to an easement by necessity through Fike's property because twenty acres of Shelton's forty acre parcel were at one time part of a commonly-owned tract of land with the Fike property prior to its partitioning in 1932. Shelton's twenty acre tract that was in common ownership with the Fike property is hereinafter called parcel one. Shelton's twenty acre tract that was not in common ownership with the Fike property is hereinafter called parcel two.

Fike owns a sixty acre tract of land located to the southwest of Shelton's property and it connects with parcel one. The Fike property adjoins Lebanon-Pine Grove Road, a public road, along the southwest corner of the property. North of the Fike property and west of the Shelton property (parcel one) is a twenty acre tract of land owned by Levi Sturgis, Jr.

The Shelton, Fike and Sturgis properties were at one time part of a hundred acre tract of land owned by Christiana Sturgis. The land was partitioned among the three heirs of Christiana Sturgis in 1932, as follows: Fike's sixty acre tract was conveyed to Calvin Sturgis; the Levi Sturgis, Jr. property, which is north of Fike's property and consists of twenty acres, was conveyed to Levi Sturgis, Sr.; and the twenty acres owned by Shelton (parcel one), which is east of the Levi Sturgis property, was conveyed to Minnie Sturgis Washington. Shelton investigated the land records and discovered that road access for Christian Sturgis' property before partitioning had been through the Fike property because Lebanon-Pine Grove Road was in existence in 1932 and adjoined the Fike property prior to its partitioning.

Fike argues that Shelton had access to his property because other adjoining landowners had granted Shelton verbal permission to cross their property. Parcel one adjoins the Sturgis property and the Robinson property abuts the Sturgis property to the west. Parcel two is surrounded by the Berry property to the north and east. Shelton says he was given permission by Robinson to walk across his land to reach his property but was not given permission for motorized travel. Fike asserts that Shelton was given unrestricted access to Berry's land for entry to his property. Shelton contended that use of the Berry property was in the form of a license that was revocable at will.

Lebanon-Pine Grove Road and Dry Grove Road, are the only public roads that would provide access to Shelton's forty acres. Access from Dry Grove Road would require an easement through Berry's property that would intersect with Shelton's tract (parcel two) that was not in common ownership with the Christiana Sturgis property. Access from Lebanon-Pine Grove Road would require an easement through the Fike and Sturgis properties that would connect to Shelton's twenty acre tract (parcel one) that at one time had been in common ownership with the Christiana Sturgis property. . . .

There are two types of implication easements: easements essential to the enjoyment of the land and easements by necessity. *Bonelli v. Blakemore,* 66 Miss. 136, 143, 5 So. 228, 230-31 (1888). Necessity easements arise from "the implication that someone who owned a large tract of land would not intend to create inaccessible smaller parcels." *Cox v. Trustmark Bank,* 733 So.2d 353, 356 (¶11) (Miss.Ct.App.1999).

A claimant seeking an easement by necessity has the burden of proof and must establish that he is entitled to a right of way across another's land. *Broadhead v. Terpening,* 611 So.2d 949, 954 (Miss.1992). An easement by necessity arises by operation of law when part of a commonly-owned tract of land is severed in a way that renders either portion of the property inaccessible except by passing over the other portion or by trespassing on the lands of another. *Id. See also Rogers v. Marlin*, 754 So.2d 1267, 1272(¶11) (Miss.Ct.App.1999). The party asserting the right to an easement must demonstrate strict necessity and is required to prove there is no other means of access. *Id.* An easement by necessity has a "right of access that is appurtenant to the dominant parcel and travels with the land, so long as the necessity exists. By acquiring the dominant estate, one has already paid for and procured the legal right of access to and from that parcel." *Id.* The easement or right-of-way will last as long as the necessity exists and will terminate after other access to the landlocked parcel becomes available. *Pitts v. Foster*, 743 So.2d 1066, 1068-69 (¶8) (Miss.Ct.App.1999).

Fike argues the chancery court erred in encumbering his property with an easement because Shelton was given permission from adjoining landowners to access his property defeating the strict necessity prerequisite. Fike claims there was no right to an easement by necessity because Shelton had "unrestricted access" to his property. The access that Fike refers to is Shelton's permission to gain access from the Robinson property to the west and the Berry property to the north.

Shelton purchased the property in order to build a weekend home. Access from the Shelton property to the Robinson property was limited to foot travel and no permission for motorized travel was given. Access from the Berry property was by oral permission and was in the form of a license which is revocable at will. The limited scope of permission granted to Shelton by Robinson and Berry is not sufficient to extinguish his right to an easement by necessity. It does not rise to the level of unrestricted access.

Shelton has the burden to prove he is entitled to an easement by necessity. During the chancery court proceedings, Shelton's expert witness testified that parcel one was in common ownership with the Fike and Levi Sturgis properties, prior to its partitioning by Christiana Sturgis in 1932. Evidence at trial showed the Lebanon-Pine Grove Road was in existence in 1932. Fike submitted no evidence that parcel two was in common ownership with the Berry property at any time. Shelton, therefore, never possessed a legal right to an easement through the Berry and Robinson properties without their consent and compensation.

Based on the evidence at trial an easement by necessity arose by operation of law at the moment the property was severed in 1932. The "right of access to the property is appurtenant to the dominant parcel and travels with the land, so long as the necessity exists." *Broadhead*, 611 So.2d at 953.

The fact that Shelton purchased the property with knowledge that it was landlocked has no effect on the disposition of this case. Nor does it matter that prior property owners of the Shelton tracts (parcel one and two) had never asserted their right to an easement through the Fike or Sturgis properties. Accordingly, the chancellor properly applied the legal standard in granting Shelton an easement by necessity. . . .

Affirmed.

SCHWAB V. TIMMONS

Supreme Court of Wisconsin, 1999
589 N.W.2d 1

JON P. WILCOX, J.

The petitioners, James and Katherine Schwab and Dorice McCormick (petitioners), seek review of a decision affirming the circuit court's dismissal of their declaratory judgment action requesting an easement by necessity or by implication for both ingress and egress and utilities over the properties owned by the respondents in order to gain access to their landlocked parcels located in Door County. The circuit court, as affirmed by the court of appeals, concluded that the historical circumstances in this case do not fit the typical situation from which ways of necessity are implied and that even if they did, the easement would not have survived because it was not recorded.

On appeal, the petitioners claim they are entitled to an easement by necessity or by implication over the respondents' properties; or in the alternative, they seek an expansion of the common law in this state to recognize an easement by necessity where property is landlocked due to geographical barriers and due to the actions of the common owner and grantor, in this case the United States. We conclude that the petitioners have failed to establish entitlement to an easement by implication or by necessity either because of actions by the federal government or by geographical barriers. Not only were the parcels at issue not landlocked at the time of conveyance, but the petitioners themselves created their landlocked parcels when they conveyed away their highway access. We refuse to turn 100-plus years of Wisconsin common law on its head to accommodate such actions. Accordingly, we affirm the court of appeals.

The facts are not in dispute. The petitioners and the respondents all own property that is located on Green Bay in the Village of Ephraim in Door County. The properties are situated between the waters of Green Bay on the west and a bluff ranging in height from 37 to 60 feet on the east. The following is a diagram of the properties (lots and parcels) involved [see page 584].

This diagram can be found in the record and is designated as Exhibit A attached to the petitioners' original complaint with additions and deletions for illustrative purposes. . . .

Prior to 1854, the property involved was owned by the United States and was divided into three lots: Lot 2, the northernmost lot; Lot 3; and Lot 4, the southernmost lot. In 1854, the United States granted by patent Lot 4 to Ingebret Torgerson, but retained Lots 2 and 3. At the time that Lot 4 was severed from Lots 2 and 3, the United States did not retain a right-of-way through Lot 4 to get to Lots 2 and 3. At oral argument, it was explained that at the time of this conveyance by the United States, the eastern boundary of the lots extended to the east to what is now a public roadway. The lots were

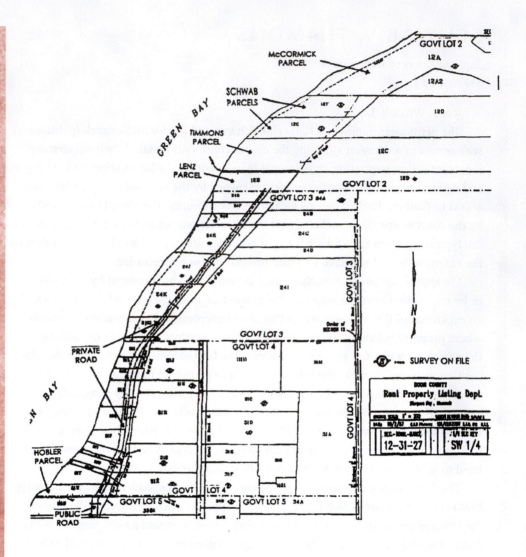

comprised of property both above and below the bluff with access to a public roadway from above. In 1882, the United States granted Lots 2 and 3 to Halvor Anderson.

At some point after the United States granted the lots, they were further subdivided into parcels.[1] After 1854, Lots 2, 3, and 4 were never fully owned by one person or entity, except that some unspecified parcels within Lots 2, 3, and 4 were owned by Malcolm and Margaret Vail during the years 1950 to 1963.

The petitioners' parcels are located in Lot 2, the northernmost lot. McCormick owns the northernmost parcel and the Schwabs own two adjacent parcels directly south

---

[1] Throughout this decision, our use of "lots" pertains to Lots 2, 3, and 4 which were originally conveyed by the United States to Torgerson and Anderson. We shall designate the subdivided land from Lots 2, 3, and 4, which is now owned by McCormick, the Schwabs, and the respondents, as "parcels."

of McCormick. Together the properties comprise over 1200 feet of frontage and over nine acres of property. Directly south of the Schwabs' parcels is a parcel owned by the Timmons within Lot 2, followed to the south by a parcel owned by the Lenzes, also in Lot 2; all of the remaining respondents' parcels follow sequentially to the south, located in Lots 3 and 4, with the parcel owned by Hobler being the southernmost parcel located at the southern boundary of Lot 4.

It was indicated at oral argument that the current eastern boundary line, the bluff line—which produced parcels above and below the bluff—was created at various unknown times.[2] The Schwabs' parcels were originally purchased by James' parents in the 1940s and were later gifted to James in 1965 and 1974. At purchase, the Schwabs' parcels extended east from the waters of Green Bay to property above the bluff where there was access to a public roadway and a house. Some time after the 1974 inheritance, the Schwabs conveyed the property above the bluff to James' relatives and retained the parcel below. McCormick also inherited her parcel which originally included land above and below the bluff with highway access from above, and she conveyed the property above the bluff to a third party, retaining the parcel below.

As they currently stand, both of the petitioners' parcels are bordered by water on the east and the bluff on the west. Because their properties are between the lake and the bluff, the petitioners claim their only access is over the land to the south, owned by the respondents, for which they do not have a right-of-way.

A private road runs north from Hobler's parcel across all of the respondents' properties terminating on the Lenz parcel. Timmons also has the right to use the private road. This is the road that the petitioners are seeking to extend for their use. Negotiations for an agreement to extend the road have failed.

In 1988, the petitioners petitioned the Village of Ephraim, pursuant to Wis. Stat. §80.13 (1985-86), to extend a public road—North Shore Drive—to the private road beginning at the Hobler property northward over all of the respondents' properties to McCormick's property. Section 80.13 allows a landowner to request the local government, in its discretion, to construct a public roadway at the petitioning landowners' expense. *Id.* The Village of Ephraim board, however, declined the request finding that extending the road was not in the public's interest.

Consequently, the petitioners brought this declaratory judgment action seeking an easement by necessity or by implication to gain access to their land. The easement would include the perpetual right to travel, including the right for ingress, egress and for public utilities, over the now private road, which stretches over 15 of the respondents' parcels to the Lenz property, as well as the right to build a road over the Lenz and Timmons

---

[2] According to the survey map contained in the record, it is apparent that some landowners, including at least one respondent, have retained property both above and below the bluff line.

properties up to the McCormick property. The respondents filed motions to dismiss the amended complaint.

The circuit court granted the motions to dismiss, concluding that the historical circumstances in this case do not fit the typical situation from which easements of necessity are implied. The court further stated that even if it found an implied retention of an easement over Lot 4 by the United States as of 1854, the respondents did not have actual or constructive notice of the existence of an easement and therefore, they took title to the land relieved of the burden or charge of the easement. The court of appeals summarily affirmed the circuit court's grant of the respondents' motions to dismiss. . . .

The petitioners claim an easement by implication or by necessity over the respondents' properties. An easement is a "liberty, privilege, or advantage in lands, without profit, and existing distinct from the ownership of the land." *Stoesser v. Shore Drive Partnership,* 172 Wis.2d 660, 667, 494 N.W.2d 204 (1993). With an easement, there are two distinct property interests—the dominant estate, which enjoys the privileges granted by an easement and the servient estate, which permits the exercise of those privileges. *Krepel v. Darnell,* 165 Wis.2d 235, 244, 477 N.W.2d 333 (Ct.App.1991). An easement can be used only in connection with the real estate to which it belongs. *S.S. Kresge Co. v. Winkelman Realty Co.,* 260 Wis. 372, 376, 50 N.W.2d 920 (1952).

Easements by implication and by necessity are similar, but legally distinguishable concepts. Since the early 1900s, the public policy in Wisconsin has strongly opposed the implication of covenants of conveyance, i.e., easements. . . .

An easement by implication arises when there has been a "separation of title, a use before separation took place which continued so long and was so obvious or manifest as to show that it was meant to be permanent, and it must appear that the easement is necessary to the beneficial enjoyment of the land granted or retained." *Bullis v. Schmidt,* 5 Wis.2d 457, 460-61, 93 N.W.2d 476 (1958) (quoting 1 thompson, Real Property §390 at 630 (perm. ed.)).[4] Implied easements may only be created when the necessity for the easement is "so clear and absolute that without the easement the grantee cannot enjoy the use of the property granted to him for the purposes to which similar property is customarily devoted." *Bullis,* 5 Wis.2d at 462, 93 N.W.2d 476 (quoting *Miller,* 126 Wis. at 270, 105 N.W. 790).

---

[4] The traditional elements of an implied easement are:

(1) common ownership followed by conveyance separating the unified ownership;

(2) before severance, the common owner used part of the property for the benefit of the other part, a use that was apparent, obvious, continuous and apparent;

(3) and the claimed easement is necessary and beneficial to the enjoyment of the parcel previously benefitted.

7. Thompson, Real Property §60.03(b)(4)(i) at 426 (Thompson ed.1994). Wisconsin courts have not specifically adopted these elements as the law of this state and we do not do so here.

The petitioners have failed to establish a claim for an easement by implication. While a landlocked parcel may satisfy the necessity element, it is apparent from the amended complaint that the private road the petitioners seek to extend does not and has never extended to the petitioners' properties. They have failed to allege that any use by the United States was so obvious, manifest or continuous as to show that it was meant to be permanent.

Instead, the petitioners claim their parcels are landlocked and the use and enjoyment of their property is permanently and substantially impaired without having access to their property. This claim is more akin to an easement by necessity.

An easement of necessity "arises where an owner severs a landlocked portion of his [or her] property by conveying such parcel to another." *Ludke v. Egan,* 87 Wis.2d 221, 229-30, 274 N.W.2d 641 (1979). To establish an easement by necessity, a party must show common ownership of the two parcels prior to severance of the landlocked parcel, *Ruchti v. Monroe,* 83 Wis.2d 551, 556, 266 N.W.2d 309 (1978), and that the owner of the now landlocked parcel cannot access a public roadway from his or her own property, *Ludke,* 87 Wis.2d at 230, 274 N.W.2d 641. If this can be demonstrated, an easement by necessity will be implied over the land retained by the grantor. *Id.*

The petitioners argue that the United States ownership of all three lots prior to 1854 satisfies the common ownership requirement—a question never before addressed by this court. We conclude that we need not reach that issue because even if the United States' possession of the three lots could constitute common ownership, the petitioners have conceded that neither Lot 2, nor Lot 3 were landlocked when the United States conveyed Lot 4. Rather, at the time of conveyance, the eastern boundary of the lots was above and east of the bluff (the current boundary line). Access to a public roadway was possible above the bluff. A party may only avail himself or herself of an easement by necessity when the common owner severs *a landlocked portion* of the property and the owner of the landlocked portion cannot access a public roadway. *Id.* at 229-30, 274 N.W.2d 641. Because the United States never severed a landlocked portion of its property that was inaccessible from a public roadway, the petitioners have failed to establish the elements for an easement by necessity.

Nevertheless, petitioners insist that the property was effectively landlocked because of the geographical barriers inhibiting access. As the petitioners see it, their land was landlocked because the land to the south was owned by an individual, the land to the east and north was bordered by a cliff and rocky terrain, and the land to the west was bordered by the waters of Green Bay. They cite to *Sorenson v. Czinger,* 70 Wash.App. 270, 852 P.2d 1124 (Wash.Ct.App.1993) and *Teich v. Haby,* 408 S.W.2d 562 (Tex.Civ.Ct.App. 1966), in support of their position.

Wisconsin courts have never before recognized geographical barriers alone as circumstances warranting an easement by necessity.[5] In fact, case law suggests otherwise. This court stated in *Backhausen* that a way of necessity is not merely one of convenience, and "the law will not imply such a way where it has provided another method for obtaining the same at a reasonable expense to the landowner." *Backhausen*, 204 Wis. at 289, 234 N.W. 904.

While the petitioners have provided evidence that the cost of building a road over the bluff would cost approximately $700,000—an unreasonable expense, it is apparent that they consider other methods of access—a stairway, an elevator—unacceptable. Petitioners narrowly focus on vehicular access to the lake itself as the only possible way to enjoy this property. Certainly it may be more convenient for the petitioners to seek an extension of the private road to their parcels rather than travel across the property above the bluff and navigate the bluff, but that in itself does not create the right to an easement by necessity. A grantor is not landlocked when he or she has difficulty getting from his or her land to a public road as long as he or she can get from his or her land to a public road. *See Ludke*, 87 Wis.2d at 230, 274 N.W.2d 641. *See also Sicchio v. Alvey*, 10 Wis.2d 528, 538, 103 N.W.2d 544 (1960) (Access to building at front, even though rear entry was used, does not allow for right-of-way by necessity to rear entry of store).

In this case, the petitioners had access to a public road, albeit not ideal or the most convenient access, which they sold off. Thus, the petitioners' current ownership of landlocked property resulted not from a grant of property to them but by their own acts in conveying away their highway access. They were not unwitting purchasers of landlocked property (stemming from the United States 1854 sale).

An easement by necessity only exists where an owner sells a *landlocked* parcel to another, in which case the law will recognize a way of necessity in the *grantee* over the land retained by the *grantor*. *Rock Lake Estates Unit Owners Ass'n v. Township of Lake Mills*, 195 Wis.2d 348, 372, 536 N.W.2d 415 (Ct.App.1995) (citing *Ludke*, 87 Wis.2d at 229-30, 274 N.W.2d 641). The petitioners in this case are the grantors, not the grantees, and as in *Rock Lake Estates*, the conveyances which resulted in their landlocked property were made by the petitioners when they sold off the property above the bluff. We conclude

---

[5] The cases cited by the petitioners are distinguishable. In *Sorenson v. Czinger*, 70 Wash.App. 270, 852 P.2d 1124, 1127 (Wash.Ct.App.1993), the easement was authorized under a state statute which allowed for private condemnation of land for a right of way for the construction of roads. Wisconsin does not provide for private condemnation and easements are viewed with disfavor. *Backhausen v. Mayer*, 204 Wis. 286, 288, 234 N.W. 904 (1931).

The question in *Teich v. Haby*, 408 S.W.2d 562, 564 (Tex.Civ.Ct.App.1966), was whether the owner of the servient parcel had notice that the owner of the dominant parcel used an existing private roadway to access a public roadway. Teich involved the continued use of a private roadway, not the creation of an easement for use of a private roadway.

that it would be contrary to this state's policy against encumbrances for this court to award an easement to the petitioners over parcels of unrelated third parties under these circumstances. . . .

The decision of the court of appeals is affirmed.

NOTES AND QUESTIONS

1. *Should Strict Necessity Be So Strict? Schwab* provides a good example of a court strictly construing the strict necessity requirement. A minority of courts would only require reasonable necessity for easements by necessity. Further, even some courts applying a strict necessity standards might hold that a $700,000 cost to reach a road constitutes strict necessity. Most courts, however, take seriously the idea that strict necessity means necessity, not convenience. *See, e.g., Thompson v. Whinnery,* 895 P.2d 537 (Colo. 1995) (holding that strict necessity is not met when landowner could obtain access to property on horseback and on foot). Should the strict necessity requirement be so strict? Perhaps one landowner or another should have been more careful, but is leaving a property landlocked the right result?

2. *Duration.* Easements by necessity end when the necessity ends. In other words, if the otherwise landlocked parcel somehow gets another way to access a road (e.g., by a new road being constructed on the other side of the parcel), the easement by necessity will end.

3. *Paying for the Easement—Private Road Acts.* At several points we have already seen situations where the all-or-nothing nature of our legal system sometimes leads to nonideal results. Wouldn't the best way to resolve the problem of landlocked parcels be to allow an implied easement over neighboring land but to require the owner of the landlocked parcel to pay compensation to the owner of the servient land?

Some states reach this result through *Private Road Acts,* which allow the owner of landlocked parcels to obtain an easement over neighboring land in return for fair market compensation. Private Road Acts often are described as involving a private use of eminent domain. A handful of courts have restricted their use as part of the backlash against the private use of eminent domain that followed the U.S. Supreme Court's decision in *Kelo v. New London. See, e.g., In re O'Reilly,* 5 A.3d 246 (Pa. 2010). (We will consider *Kelo* and related issues in depth in our chapter on Takings.). Leaving the eminent domain issue aside, what do you think of the Private Road Acts' solution to the problem of landlocked parcels? Is it preferable to the common-law easement by necessity?

i. Scope of Easements by Necessity

Say that a property owner is entitled to an easement by necessity. What should the scope of that easement be? For example, how wide should it be? Our next case explores that issue.

STROLLO V. IANNANTUONI

Appellate Court of Connecticut, 1999
53 Conn. App. 658, 734 A.2d 144

EDWARD Y. O'CONNELL, C. J.

The plaintiffs appeal from the trial court's judgment granting them an easement by necessity across the defendants' property. The plaintiffs claim that the trial court improperly limited the scope of the easement to twenty feet in width, and restricted the use of the easement to benefit only farming and recreational activities. We affirm the judgment of the trial court.

In their complaint, the plaintiffs allege that they "do not have an unobstructed, open or reliable means of ingress or egress to their property except over the defendants' property which fronts on Marion Road, and without such access their property is effectively landlocked." On appeal, the parties do not dispute the existence of a legal foundation for the imposition of an easement by necessity over the defendants' property. The sole issue, is whether the easement should have been fifty feet, not twenty feet, in width and whether the easement should not have been limited to benefit farming and recreational activities on the plaintiffs' property.[1] . . .

The record discloses that the plaintiffs' land historically had been used solely for agricultural pursuits and that the plaintiffs never alleged any claim to change the use of their property. The trial court found, however, that the plaintiffs were considering a major alteration in their property's use. In the memorandum of decision, the trial court stated in relevant part: "Roger Strollo testified that he would like to put a subdivision on his property and requires a fifty foot wide easement to do so. The court does not agree, however, that it is reasonably essential to the plaintiffs' use of their property to impose an easement of necessity that is fifty feet wide on the defendants' property simply to accommodate the plaintiffs' desire to profit from a potential subdivision. Moreover, the creation of such a right-of-way would work a serious inequity on the defendants."

The trial court continued that "[i]n considering of the surrounding circumstances, the nature of the land and the conduct of the parties, and in balancing the equities present in this case, the court concludes there is a reasonable necessity for a right-of-way over the defendants' land to accommodate the farming and recreational activities

---

[1] The trial court's order stated: "There shall be an easement by necessity located on the northerly border of defendants' property, which is shown as parcel 1 in exhibits I and S, and directly adjacent to the southerly border of Bird Lane, 20' in width and extending westerly 400' feet from Marion Road to the easterly border of the plaintiffs' property, which is shown as Parcel 10 in exhibits I and S. The plaintiffs shall bear the burden of creating and maintaining this right-of-way. The purpose of this easement is to provide beneficial use of the land for farming and recreational activities, as permitted by the zoning laws of the Town of Cheshire. It is subject to the common law regarding continuing necessity."

for which this land seems eminently suited. The court will order an easement by necessity in accordance with this conclusion."

The "use of an easement must be reasonable and as little burdensome to the servient estate as the nature of the easement and the purpose will permit." (Internal quotation marks omitted.) *Kuras v. Kope*, 205 Conn. 332, 341, 533 A.2d 1202 (1987). "The decision as to what would constitute a reasonable use of a right-of-way is for the trier of fact whose decision may not be overturned unless it is clearly erroneous." *Gioielli v. Mallard Cove Condominium Assn., Inc.*, supra, 37 Conn.App. at 833, 658 A.2d 134. The trial court found that a twenty foot wide right-of-way was sufficient to allow a reasonable and beneficial use of land and that the property has always been used in accordance with the zoning regulations that permit farming and recreational use. We hold that the trial court's conclusion was not clearly erroneous.

The judgment is affirmed.

NOTE AND QUESTION

1. *Reasonable Enjoyment vs. Most Profitable Use.* The court in *Strollo* affirmed the lower court's award of an easement that allowed the benefited parcel to be used for agricultural purposes, but that was not wide enough to allow the benefited parcel to be used for a residential development. Do you think that this was the right result?

PROBLEMS

Presume that these problems take place in a jurisdiction where the statutory period for an easement by prescription is ten years. Explanatory answers to these problems can be found on page 1058.

1. Shirley lives on a 20-acre parcel that she bought from Hal four years ago. Hal originally owned 100 acres, but he sold the 20 acres closest to Route 74 to Shirley and retained the remaining 80 acres for himself. Hal has always used an unpaved driveway to get from his home to Route 74. Part of this driveway crosses the land that he sold to Shirley. Hal and Shirley got into the predicable tiff, and now Shirley is trying to prevent

NON-EXPRESS EASEMENTS AND THE STATUTE OF FRAUDS

Recall that express easements must be created by written instrument to satisfy the Statute of Frauds. How can we square that requirement with the legal recognition of four types of non-express easements? For easements by estoppel, easements implied by existing use, and easements by necessity, circumstances may justify an inference of intent to create an easement. This inference is hard to make, however, for easements by prescription. In any event, doesn't the recognition of four types of non-express easements deeply undercut the Statute of Frauds?

Hal from using the driveway. Hal could build a new driveway on the other side of his property to get to Slate Hill Road but because of the topography of his land it would be very expensive to do so—one contractor estimated that it would cost Hal almost $200,000 to construct the new driveway. Hal thinks that under these circumstances, he should be able to keep using the original driveway to access Route 74.

2. Three years ago, Nestor bought an undeveloped parcel near Owl Road. To get to his property, Nestor used an unpaved driveway that crossed Greg's property. As far as Nestor knew, the driveway had always been there. Greg orally assured Nestor that he could use the driveway, and Nestor used it to build a house on his land. A few months ago, Nestor and Greg got into an argument, and Greg revoked his permission for Nestor to use the driveway. A lawsuit has ensued. After doing some research, Nestor discovered that both his parcel and Greg's parcel were once owned by Chuck. Nestor's parcel had no access to a road at the time Chuck divided the parcels, and today there is no way for Nestor to reach a road other than to cross Greg's parcel.

3. In 1970, Jim inherited a ten-acre parcel. The parcel is a peninsula, surrounded on three sides by an oxbow of the Mason River. The fourth side has frontage on County Route 12. Jim built a house overlooking the river on the end of the property opposite the road, using a long driveway to reach the house. High cliffs on the shoreline make it impossible for Jim to reach his land by boat, and the driveway is his means of access to his house. In 1999, Jim sold the half of the property nearest to Route 12 to Marc. Until last week, Jim continued to use the driveway to get in and out of his property. Marc recently put a chain up over the driveway, however, because of a disagreement with Jim over access to a boat ramp on the river. Jim has sued Marc, claiming that he has the right to use the driveway.

3. MISUSE OF EASEMENTS

We examined the scope of easements above. If the owner of the benefit uses an easement in a manner that is beyond the scope of the easement, then the owner of the benefit has *misused* the easement. The owner of the servient parcel can bring an action for misuse against the owner of the benefit. Traditionally, the remedy for misuse was an injunction. In our next case, the court awarded damages, rather than an injunction, for misuse. As you read the case, pay close attention to the court's analysis of both why a misuse occurred and why it held that damages were the appropriate remedy.

REMEDIES

LAW AND EQUITY

BROWN V. VOSS

Supreme Court of Washington, 1986
715 P.2d 514

BRACHTENBACH, Justice. The question posed is to what extent, if any, the holder of a private road easement can traverse the servient estate to reach not only the original dominant estate, but a subsequently acquired parcel when those two combined parcels are used in such a way that there is no increase in the burden on the servient estate. The trial court denied the injunction sought by the owners of the servient estate. The Court of Appeals reversed. *Brown v. Voss,* 38 Wash.App. 777, 689 P.2d 1111 (1984). We reverse the Court of Appeals and reinstate the judgment of the trial court.

A portion of an exhibit depicts the involved parcels.

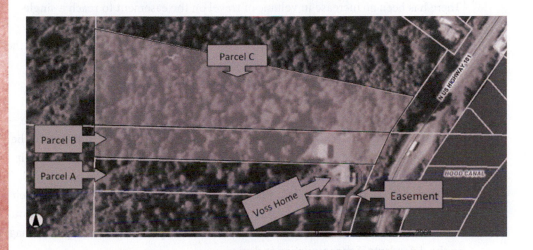

In 1952 the predecessors in title of parcel A granted to the predecessor owners of parcel B a private road easement across parcel A for "ingress to and egress from" parcel B. Defendants acquired parcel A in 1973. Plaintiffs bought parcel B on April 1, 1977 and parcel C on July 31, 1977, but from two different owners. Apparently the previous owners of parcel C were not parties to the easement grant.

When plaintiffs acquired parcel B a single family dwelling was situated thereon. They intended to remove that residence and replace it with a single family dwelling which would straddle the boundary line common to parcels B and C.

Plaintiffs began clearing both parcels B and C and moving fill materials in November 1977. Defendants first sought to bar plaintiff's use of the easement in April 1979 by which time plaintiffs had spent more than $11,000 in developing their property for building.

Defendants placed logs, a concrete sump and a chain link fence within the easement. Plaintiffs sued for removal of the obstructions, an injunction against defendant's interference with their use of the easement and damages. Defendants counterclaimed for damages and an injunction against plaintiffs using the easement other than for parcel B.

The trial court awarded each party $1 in damages. The award against the plaintiffs was for a slight inadvertent trespass outside the easement.

The trial court made the following findings of fact:

VI. The plaintiffs have made no unreasonable use of the easement in the development of their property. There have been no complaints of unreasonable use of the roadway to the south of the properties of the parties by other neighbors who grant easements to the parties to this action to cross their properties to gain access to the property of the plaintiffs. Other than the trespass there is no evidence of any damage to the defendants as a result of the use of the easement by the plaintiffs. There has been no increase in volume of travel on the easement to reach a single family dwelling whether built on tract B or on Tacts [sic] B and C. There is no evidence of any increase in the burden on the subservient estate from the use of the easement by the plaintiffs for access to parcel C.

VIII. If an injunction were granted to bar plaintiffs access to tract C across the easement to a single family residence, Parcel C would become landlocked; plaintiffs would not be able to make use of their property; they would not be able to build their single family residence in a manner to properly enjoy the view of the Hood Canal and the surrounding area as originally anticipated at the time of their purchase and even if the single family residence were constructed on parcel B, if the injunction were granted, plaintiffs would not be able to use the balance of their property in parcel C as a yard or for any other use of their property in conjunction with their home. Conversely, there is and will be no appreciable hardship or damage to the defendants if the injunction is denied.

IX. If an injunction were to be granted to bar the plaintiffs access to tract C, the framing and enforcing of such an order would be impractical. Any violation of the order would result in the parties back in court at great cost but with little or no damages being involved.

X. Plaintiffs have acted reasonable in the development of their property. Their trespass over a "little" corner of the defendants' property was inadvertent, and *de minimis.* The fact that the defendants counter claim seeking an injunction to bar plaintiffs access to parcel C was filed as leverage against the original plaintiffs' claim for an interruption of their easement rights, may be considered in determining whether equitable relief by way of an injunction should be granted.

Relying upon these findings of fact, the court denied defendant's request for an injunction and granted the plaintiffs the right to use the easement for access to parcels B & C "as long as plaintiffs [sic] properties (B and C) are developed and used solely for the purpose of a single family residence." Clerk's Papers, at 10.

The Court of Appeals reversed, holding:

> In sum, we hold that, in denying the Vosses' request for an injunction, the trial court's decision was based upon untenable grounds. We reverse and remand for entry of an order enjoining the use of the easement across parcel A to gain access to a residence any part of which is located on parcel C, or to further the construction of any residence on parcels B or C if the construction activities would require entry onto parcel C. *Washington Fed'n of State Employees v. State,* [99 Wash.2d 878, 887, 665 P.2d 1337 (1983)].

Brown v. Voss, supra at 784-85, 689 P.2d 1111.

The easement in this case was created by express grant. Accordingly, the extent of the right acquired is to be determined from the terms of the grant properly construed to give effect to the intention of the parties. *See Zobrist v. Culp,* 95 Wash.2d 556, 561, 627 P.2d 1308 (1981); *Seattle v. Nazarenus,* 60 Wash.2d 657, 665, 374 P.2d 1014 (1962). By the express terms of the 1952 grant, the predecessor owners of parcel B acquired a private road easement across parcel A and the right to use the easement for ingress to and egress from parcel B. Both plaintiffs and defendants agree that the 1952 grant created an easement appurtenant to parcel B as the dominant estate. Thus, plaintiffs, as owners of the dominant estate, acquired rights in the use of the easement for ingress to and egress from parcel B.

However, plaintiffs have no such easement rights in connection with their ownership of parcel C, which was not a part of the original dominant estate under the terms of the 1952 grant. As a general rule, an easement appurtenant to one parcel of land may not be extended by the owner of the dominant estate to other parcels owned by him, whether adjoining or distinct tracts, to which the easement is not appurtenant. *E.g., Heritage Standard Bank & Trust Co. v. Trustees of Schs.,* 84 Ill.App.3d 653, 40 Ill.Dec. 104, 405 N.E.2d 1196 (1980); *Kanefsky v. Dratch Constr. Co.,* 376 Pa. 188, 101 A.2d 923 (1954); *S.S. Kresge Co. of Mich. v. Winkelman Realty Co.,* 260 Wis. 372, 50 N.W.2d 920 (1952); 28 C.J.S. Easements §92, at 772-73 (1941).

Plaintiffs, nonetheless, contend that extension of the use of the easement for the benefit of nondominant property does not constitute a misuse of the easement, where as here, there is no evidence of an increase in the burden on the servient estate. We do not agree. If an easement is appurtenant to a particular parcel of land, any extension thereof to other parcels is a misuse of the easement. *Wetmore v. Ladies of Loretto, Wheaton,* 73 Ill.App.2d 454, 220 N.E.2d 491 (1966). *See also, e.g., Robertson v. Robertson,* 214 Va. 76, 197 S.E.2d 183 (1973); *Penn Bowling Rec. Ctr., Inc. v. Hot Shoppes, Inc.,* 179 F.2d 64 (D.C.Cir.1949). As noted by one court in a factually similar case, "[I]n this context this classic rule of property law is directed to the rights of the respective parties rather than the actual burden on the servitude." *National Lead Co. v. Kanawha Block Co.,* 288 F.Supp. 357, 364 (S.D.W.Va.1968), *aff'd,* 409 F.2d 1309 (4th Cir.1969). Under the express language of the 1952 grant, plaintiffs only have rights in the use of the easement for the benefit of parcel B. Although, as plaintiffs contend, their planned use of the easement to gain access to a single family residence located partially on parcel B and partially on parcel C is perhaps no more than technical misuse of the easement, we conclude that it is misuse nonetheless.

However, it does not follow from this conclusion alone that defendants are entitled to injunctive relief. Since the awards of $1 in damages were not appealed, only the denial of an injunction to defendants is in issue. Some fundamental principles applicable to a request for an injunction must be considered. (1) The proceeding is equitable and addressed to the sound discretion of the trial court. (2) The trial court is vested with a broad discretionary power to shape and fashion injunctive relief to fit the *particular facts, circumstances, and equities of the case before it.* Appellate courts give great weight to the trial court's exercise of that discretion. (3) One of the essential criteria for injunctive relief is actual and substantial injury sustained by the person seeking the injunction. *Washington Fed'n of State Employees v. State,* 99 Wash.2d 878, 665 P.2d 1337 (1983); *Port of Seattle v. International Longshoremen's Union,* 52 Wash.2d 317, 324 P.2d 1099 (1958).

LAW AND EQUITY

REMEDIES

The trial court found as facts, upon substantial evidence, that plaintiffs have acted reasonably in the development of their property, that there is and was no damage to the defendants from plaintiffs' use of the easement, that there was no increase in the volume of travel on the easement, that there was no increase in the burden on the servient estate, that defendants sat by for more than a year while plaintiffs expended more than $11,000 on their project, and that defendants' counterclaim was an effort to gain "leverage" against plaintiffs' claim. In addition, the court found from the evidence that plaintiffs would suffer considerable hardship if the injunction were granted whereas no appreciable hardship or damages would flow to defendants from its denial. Finally, the court limited plaintiffs' use of the combined parcels solely to the same purpose for which the original parcel was used—*i.e.,* for a single family residence.

Neither this court nor the Court of Appeals may substitute its effort to make findings of fact for those supported findings of the trial court. *State v. Marchand,* 62 Wash.2d 767, 770, 384 P.2d 865 (1963); *Thorndike v. Hesperian Orchards, Inc.,* 54 Wash.2d 570, 575, 343 P.2d 183 (1959). Therefore, the only valid issue is whether, under these established facts, as a matter of law, the trial court abused its discretion in denying defendants' request for injunctive relief. Based upon the equities of the case, as found by the trial court, we are persuaded that the trial court acted within its discretion. The Court of Appeals is reversed and the trial court is affirmed.

DORE, Justice (dissenting). The majority correctly finds that an extension of this easement to nondominant property is a misuse of the easement. The majority, nonetheless, holds that the owners of the servient estate are not entitled to injunctive relief. I dissent.

The comments and illustrations found in the Restatement of Property §478 (1944) address the precise issue before this court. Comment *e* provides in pertinent part that "if one who has an easement of way over Whiteacre appurtenant to Blackacre uses the way with the purpose of going to Greenacre, the use is improper even though he eventually goes to Blackacre rather than to Greenacre." Illustration 6 provides:

> 6. By prescription, A has acquired, as the owner and possessor of Blackacre, an easement of way over an alley leading from Blackacre to the street. He buys Whiteacre, an adjacent lot, to which the way is not appurtenant, and builds a public garage one-fourth of which is located on Blackacre and three-fourths of which is located on Whiteacre. A wishes to use the alley as a means of ingress and egress to and from the garage. He has no privilege to use the alley to go to that part of the garage which is built on Whiteacre, and he may not use the alley until that part of the garage built on Blackacre is so separated from the part built on Whiteacre that uses for the benefit of Blackacre are distinguishable from those which benefit Whiteacre.

The majority grants the privilege to extend the agreement to nondominant property on the basis that the trial court found no appreciable hardship or damage to the servient owners. However, as conceded by the majority, any extension of the use of an easement to benefit a nondominant estate constitutes a misuse of the easement. Misuse of an easement is a trespass. *Raven Red Ash Coal Co. v. Ball,* 185 Va. 534, 39 S.E.2d 231 (1946); *Selvia v. Reitmeyer,* 156 Ind.App. 203, 295 N.E.2d 869 (1973). The Brown's use of the easement to benefit parcel C, especially if they build their home as planned, would involve a continuing trespass for which damages would be difficult to measure. Injunctive relief is the appropriate remedy under these circumstances. *Selvia,* at 212, 295 N.E.2d 869; *Gregory v. Sanders,* 635 P.2d 795, 801 (Wyo.1981). In *Penn Bowling Rec. Ctr., Inc. v. Hot Shoppes, Inc.,* 179 F.2d 64, 66 (D.C.Cir.1949) the court states:

> It is contended by appellant that since the area of the dominant and nondominant land served by the easement is less than the original area of the dominant tenement, the use made by appellant of the right of way to serve the building located on the lesser area is not materially increased or excessive. It is true that where the nature and extent of the use of an easement is, by its terms, unrestricted, the use by the dominant tenement may be increased or enlarged. *McCullough et al. v. Broad Exchange Company et al.,* 101 App.Div. 566, 92 N.Y.S. 533 [(1905)]. But the owner of the dominant tenement may not subject the servient tenement to use or servitude in connection with other premises to which the easement is not appurtenant. *See Williams v. James,* Eng.Law.Rep. (1867), 2 C.P. 577. And when an easement is being used in such a manner, an injunction will be issued to prevent such use. *Cleve et al. v. Nairin,* 204 Ky. 342, 264 S.W. 741 [(1924)]; *Diocese of Trenton v. Toman et al.,* 74 N.J.Eq. 702, 70 A. 606 [(1908)]; *Shock v. Holt Lumber Co. et al.,* 107 W.Va. 259, 148 S.E. 73 [(1929)]. Appellant, therefore, may not use the easement to serve both the

dominant and nondominant property, even though the area thereof is less than the original area of the dominant tenement.

See also Kanefsky v. Dratch Constr. Co., 376 Pa. 188, 101 A.2d 923 (1954). Thus, the fact that an extension of the easement to nondominant property would not increase the burden on the servient estate does not warrant a denial of injunctive relief.

The Browns are responsible for the hardship of creating a landlocked parcel. They knew or should have known from the public records that the easement was not appurtenant to parcel C. *See Seattle v. Nazarenus,* 60 Wash.2d 657, 670, 374 P.2d 1014 (1962). In encroachment cases this factor is significant. As stated by the court in *Bach v. Sarich,* 74 Wash.2d 575, 582, 445 P.2d 648 (1968): "The benefit of the doctrine of balancing the equities, or relative hardship, is reserved for the innocent defendant who proceeds without knowledge or warning that his structure encroaches upon another's property or property rights."

In addition, an injunction would not interfere with the Brown's right to use the easement as expressly granted, *i.e.,* for access to parcel B. An injunction would merely require the Browns to acquire access to parcel C if they want to build a home that straddles parcels B and C. One possibility would be to condemn a private way of necessity over their existing easement in an action under RCW 8.24.010. *See Brown v. McAnally,* 97 Wash.2d 360, 644 P.2d 1153 (1982).

I would affirm the Court of Appeals decision as a correct application of the law of easements. If the Browns desire access to their landlocked parcel they have the benefit of the statutory procedure for condemnation of a private way of necessity.

NOTE AND QUESTIONS

1. *Misuse and Remedies.* It is often said that there is no right without a remedy. Do you think that the remedy awarded by the court to the Vosses is sufficient to protect them from misuse of the easement by the Browns? If you think that the damages remedy was appropriate under the facts of the case, can you imagine misuse situations where an injunction would be more appropriate? How would you distinguish situations where one remedy or the other is appropriate? On the topic of the appropriate remedy for easement misuse, see Lee Strang, *Damages and the Appropriate Remedy for "Abuse" of an Easement: Moving Toward Consistency, Efficiency, and Fairness in Property Law,* 15 Geo. Mason L. Rev. 933 (2008).

REMEDIES

PROBLEMS

Explanatory answers to these problems can be found on page 1060.

1. Mario is having some problems with a property he owns. He bought one property, Hilton Ranch, that has the benefit of an appurtenant driveway easement running over a neighboring property owned by Will. Mario recently bought an additional five acres of land on the other side of Hilton Ranch from Will's property. Mario plans to build a new

house on this new five-acre parcel and to continue to use the driveway across Will's property. Mario, however, recently said some mean things about Will's friend Stacy at a party, and, rather than resolve things in a neighborly fashion, Will has sued Mario to enjoin him from using the easement for the benefit of the new five-acre parcel.

2. Sarah and Eric have been neighbors for almost 20 years. Eric's property is subject to a recorded driveway easement that benefits Sarah's parcel and allows Sarah to reach Mill Creek Road. Last year, Sarah bough an adjoining parcel of property and built a new house on the new parcel. Though the new parcel borders Queen's Church Road on its far side, Sarah wanted to build her new house near her old house. As Sarah's house was being built, construction vehicles used the driveway over Eric's parcel to reach Sarah's land. After Sarah's house was complete, Eric and Sarah had a falling out, and Eric has now sued Sarah, seeking to prevent her from using the driveway easement to reach her new house.

TERMINATION OF EASEMENTS

Easements can terminate in a number of different ways:

Express Terms. Most easements are permanent. Some easements, however, have a limited duration. Sometimes this duration is stated in terms of a fixed period of time. In this case, the easement terminates with the end of the fixed period, just like a term of years interest in property terminates when the term ends. Sometimes this duration is stated in terms of the happening of an uncertain event. For example, a driveway easement might end by its terms if the holder of the dominant parcel obtains another way of accessing a road. If this conditional event occurs, then the easement will end, just like a defeasable present interest ends on the happening of the defeasance condition.

Release. An easement will be terminated if the holder of the dominant estate executes a written *release* of the easement. Like the creation of an easement, the Statute of Frauds requires a release ending an easement to be in writing. As we will see, however, there are a number of non-express ways that easements may be terminated. The termination of easements thus parallels the creation of easements, where the Statute of Frauds formally requires a writing, but the law will allow termination without a writing in a number of different circumstances.

Merger. An easement will be terminated if at any point in time the dominant and servient parcels are owned by the same person. We have seen merger before in our chapter on Present and Future Interests. If one person owns both the present and future interests in a parcel of property, those present and future interests merger into a fee simple absolute. Similarly, if one person owns the dominant and servient estates, the interests merger into fee simple ownership of the land unencumbered by the easement.

Destruction of an easement by merger can present a real problem if the owner later again divides the parcels but fails to re-create an express easement. For example, consider parcels A and B, where parcel A is the dominant estate that has the benefit of an express easement over parcel B. Parcel A is owed by Sally, and parcel B is owned by Matt:

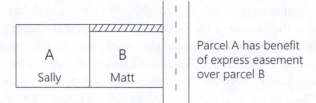

Parcel A has benefit of express easement over parcel B

At some point later, Sally later purchases parcel B from Matt. As a result, the dominant and servient parcels are owned by one person. The express easement therefore is destroyed by merger:

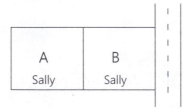

Sally now owns both dominant and servient parcels. Easement is destroyed by the merger

Merger destroys the easement. Therefore, if Sally later conveys one of the parcels to another person, Sally will need to re-create the express easement. If she does not, the owner of the supposedly dominant parcel will not have the benefit of an express easement. For example, if Sally conveys parcel B to Richard and fails to reserve an easement across parcel B for herself, she will find herself owning parcel A without an express easement across parcel B:

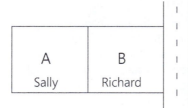

Sally conveys parcel B to Richard, failing to reserve an easement in herself. Parcel A does not have an express easement across parcel B because the original easement was destroyed by the merger

In these circumstances, Sally may have an easement implied by existing use or an easement implied by necessity. She does not, however, have an express easement. Sally probably assumed that she still would have the benefit of the old express easement. Indeed, that easement likely was recorded. Even though the document creating the easement can still be found in the land records, that easement has been destroyed by merger. Merger therefore creates a trap for the unwary because the person in Sally's position might not re-create the express easement on the assumption that the old easement still remains in force.

Abandonment. An easement is terminated if it is abandoned by the owner of the benefit. Recall that abandonment is an issue of intent—the owner of the benefit must intend to abandon the easement. Typically, *mere non-use* of the easement, standing alone, will not constitute abandonment of an easement. Put another way, we typically will need more evidence of abandonment than the mere fact that the owner of the benefit is no longer using the easements. In some states, an easement by prescription will terminate through abandonment if the owner of the benefit of that easement fails to use it for the statutory period required for the creation of a prescriptive easement.

Prescription. Just as an easement can be created by prescription, an easement can be terminated by prescription. Imagine, for example, that you have the benefit of an express driveway easement to cross my land. I am the owner of the servient parcel, and you are the owner of the dominant parcel. If I place a chain across the driveway, and you fail to do anything to enforce your rights for the prescriptive period, I may have terminated your express easement through prescription.

Estoppel. Easements may be terminated by estoppel. As we have seen before, estoppel typically involves the acts (or, sometimes, the failure to act) by one party and a detrimental change in position in reasonable reliance on those acts by another party. Let's return to the example where you have the benefit of a driveway easement over my land. If you act in a way that indicates that you are terminating the easement, and I reasonably rely on your acts to change my position, then you may be estopped from using the easement, effectively terminating the easement. For example, if you give me oral permission to build a structure on the location of your easement, and I reasonably rely on your permission, you may be estopped from relying on the easement to remove the structure.

Eminent Domain. Easements, like other property interests, may be taken by government use of the power of eminent domain. If the government takes the servient parcel by eminent domain, the government may also take the easement. If an easement is terminated by eminent domain, the owner of the benefit of the easement is entitled to just compensation. We will consider eminent domain in more depth in our chapter on Takings.

Recording Acts. The recording acts may terminate an *unrecorded* easement on the sale of the servient parcel to a good faith purchaser.

Foreclosure. Foreclosure on a mortgage (or other lien) may terminate an easement that is *junior in priority* to the mortgage.

Implied Easements. Recall that easements implied by necessity end when the necessity ends.

Changed Conditions. Section 7.18(2) of the Restatement (Third) of Property, Servitudes lists changed conditions as grounds to terminate easements. This position is a controversial change in easements law. Traditionally, covenants that run with the land, but *not* easements, could be terminated because of changed conditions. We discuss changed circumstances in the covenants context below. In any event, even in the covenants context, the changed circumstances doctrine is very strict and only applies when it is no longer possible to fulfill the original purpose of the covenant. Our next case, *AKG Real Estate, LLC v. Kosterman*, discusses these issues in depth.

PROBLEMS

Explanatory answers to these problems can be found on page 1061.

1. Rick and Wanda were neighbors. Rick owned Blackacre and Wanda owned Whiteacre. Blackacre held the benefit of a recorded appurtenant driveway easement across Whiteacre. Rick used the driveway to reach his house. About a year ago, Rick bought Whiteacre from Wanda. Six months ago, Rick sold Whiteacre to Marshall. The deed in the Rick-Marshall transaction says nothing about the easement. Last week, Rick and Marshall got into a tiff, and Marshall is now arguing that Rick cannot use the driveway to reach the road. If he cannot use the driveway, Rick could reach a road by going out the other side of his property, though it would be inconvenient for him to do so. Can Rick continue to use the driveway?

2. Max and Erma are neighbors. Max owns Blackacre. Erma owns Whiteacre. Blackacre has the benefit of an easement by necessity to reach the nearest road. At the time Blackacre and Whiteacre were divided, Blackacre was truly landlocked. The county recently built a new road on the far end of Blackacre. Max could now build a driveway to that new road, though it would cost him several thousand dollars to do so. Can Erma now prevent Max from using the easement by necessity across Whiteacre?

3. The Great Eastern Railroad Co. used to operate a rail line over property owned by Starla. Great Eastern used the line pursuant to a recorded easement across Starla's land. Great Eastern hasn't used the line for 20 years. The tracks are now rusted and in disrepair. Starla is now arguing that Great Eastern's easement has terminated. Is she right?

4. CHANGED CIRCUMSTANCES AND RELOCATION OF EASEMENTS

Our next case gives us an opportunity to consider two distinct issues that may in some cases overlap. The first issue is whether an easement may be modified or terminated because of changed circumstances. The second issue is whether the servient owner of property may unilaterally relocate the easement. These issues overlap in our case because the location of the existing easement presented problems for the servient parcel owner's development plans. The servient owner did not want to deny the dominant parcel owners ingress and egress to a public road but wanted to relocate the easement. The dominant owners refused to consent to relocation of the easement, and in the subsequent litigation the servient owner argued that the easement should be terminated or modified based on changed circumstances. The servient owner also made an independent argument that it was entitled to reasonably relocate the easement regardless of changed circumstances.

AKG REAL ESTATE, LLC V. KOSTERMAN

Supreme Court of Wisconsin, 2006
717 N.W.2d 835

DAVID T. PROSSER, J. This case presents the question whether an express easement may be relocated or terminated without the consent of the dominant estate. In a published decision, the court of appeals held that a servient estate could unilaterally terminate an express right-of-way easement once the servient estate provided an alternate route of ingress and egress to the dominant estate. We reverse the court of appeals because we conclude that the owner of a servient estate cannot unilaterally relocate or terminate an express easement.

I

We begin this case about easements by reviewing several key terms. An easement (or servitude) is an interest that encumbers the land of another. *McCormick v. Schubring*, 2003 WI 149, ¶8, 267 Wis. 2d 141, 672 N.W.2d 63 (citing *Ludke v. Egan*, 87 Wis. 2d 221, 227, 274 N.W.2d 641 (1979)). It is a liberty, privilege, or advantage in lands, without profit, and existing distinct from the ownership of the land. *Id.*; *Schwab v. Timmons*, 224 Wis. 2d 27, 35-36, 589 N.W.2d 1 (1999); *Stoesser v. Shore Drive P'ship*, 172 Wis. 2d 660, 667, 494 N.W.2d 204 (1993).

An easement creates two distinct property interests—the dominant estate, which enjoys the privileges as to other land granted by an easement, and the servient estate, which permits the exercise of those privileges. *Schwab*, 224 Wis. 2d at 36.

In the spring of 2000, Patrick and Susan Kosterman (the Kostermans) purchased a house on a four-acre lot from Edward and Audrey Chvilicek (the Chviliceks). The Kostermans' property (the Dominant Estate) lacked access to a public road except by means of three recorded, physically overlapping easements across part of an 80-acre parcel of land (the Servient Estate), which partially surrounded their property.

Nearly 50 years ago the Dominant Estate and the Servient Estate were under common ownership. Some time prior to 1960, Louis and Angeline Chvilicek bought approximately 84 acres of vacant land along Highway 31 in Racine County. In August of 1960 Louis and Angeline deeded the four-acre Dominant Estate to their son and daughter-in-law, the Chviliceks, and granted the Dominant Estate a 30-foot-wide easement over the 80-acre Servient Estate, because the Dominant Estate lacked access to a public road.

In 1961 Louis and Angeline granted the Chviliceks a second right-of-way easement along the same course as the 1960 easement. This second easement was 66 feet wide. By increasing the width of the easement, Louis and Angeline made it possible for the easement to be converted into a public road.

When Louis Chvilicek died, Angeline conveyed to the Chviliceks, as tenants-in-common, a 50 percent interest in the Servient Estate. Angeline conveyed the other 50 percent interest in the property to her daughter and son-in-law, Joyce and Vincent White. When Joyce and Vincent died, their interest in the Servient Estate transferred into the Vincent J. White Trust (the Trust).

In 1997 AKG Real Estate, LLC (AKG) offered to purchase the Servient Estate from the Chviliceks and the Trust, with the intention of developing a subdivision. AKG purchased the entire Servient Estate from the Chviliceks and the Trust in January 1998 by warranty deed and trustee's deed. The 1998 deeds expressly recognized a 30-foot-wide private road easement on the same location as the 1960 and 1961 easements:

> Reserving therefrom a private road easement for the benefit of Edward T. Chvilicek and Audrey M. Chvilicek, husband and wife, their heirs and assigns, or subsequent owners . . . until such time as public road access is made available for said real estate upon the following described easement of right of way. . . .

In addition, the two deeds reserved to the grantors (including the Chviliceks) all "recorded and/or existing easements and right of way reservations[.]"

While AKG was planning to develop the land, the Chviliceks sold the Dominant Estate to the Kostermans in 2000. Initially, AKG's development plan depicted two public roads connecting with Highway 31 from the planned subdivision. The first was along the path of the Kostermans' easements and the second, to the north, was at what is presently Cobblestone Drive. After meeting with Racine County officials, however, AKG realized that the Wisconsin Department of Transportation (DOT) was unlikely to approve a public road along the Kostermans' easements because Wis. Admin. Code §Trans 233.06 (Jan., 2004) requires a minimum distance of 1000 feet between roads that connect to state highways. If a public road affording access to Highway 31 were constructed over the Kostermans' easements, the road would have been within 600 feet of Valley Road to the south, and within 300 feet of Cobblestone Drive to the north.

After determining DOT would not consent to a public road located along the Kostermans' easements, AKG altered its subdivision plans and proposed to give the Kostermans access to Highway 31 via a cul-de-sac, which would connect with Cobblestone Drive, which in turn would connect with Highway 31. Under this plan, AKG would develop about seven lots over the Kostermans' easements and the Kostermans would be required to reconfigure their driveway so that it connected with AKG's proposed cul-de-sac. Before AKG could get the necessary governmental approval for its subdivision plat, however, the Kostermans needed to release their easement rights to AKG, or agree to move the location of the easements. To date, the Kostermans have refused to modify their right-of-way easements to accommodate AKG's development plans.

The Kostermans objected to relocating the easements for several reasons in addition to requiring them to reconfigure their driveway. AKG's development plan would put the Kostermans' house in an odd position relative to the cul-de-sac and the neighboring houses, require them to change their street address, and replace their direct access to Highway 31 with a circuitous route. Consequently, AKG again modified its plans to develop the subdivision. The modified plan calls for development to occur in two phases, the second of which awaits the denouement of this litigation.

In response to the Kostermans' unwillingness to relocate or terminate their easements, AKG sought a declaratory judgment that the easements terminated once AKG provided alternate public road access to the Dominant Estate. The Kostermans counterclaimed for a declaratory judgment that the 1960 and 1961 easements would remain in effect even if AKG provided an alternate means of ingress and egress to the Dominant Estate. The Kostermans moved for summary judgment. On summary judgment, the Racine County Circuit Court, Charles H. Constantine, Judge, ruled that the 1998 easement would terminate once AKG provided public road access, regardless of the location, but the 1961 easement of 66 feet would remain in effect even after AKG provided the Dominant Estate with alternate public road access. Both parties appealed.

The court of appeals affirmed the circuit court's holding that the 1998 easement terminated once AKG provided public road access, but it reversed the circuit court's holding that the 1961 easement would continue. *Kosterman*, 277 Wis. 2d 509, ¶55. First, the court of appeals concluded the 1998 easement was unambiguous and that it terminated once AKG afforded the Dominant Estate public road access regardless of the location. *Kosterman*, 277 Wis. 2d 509, ¶¶37-39. Second, the court of appeals held that both the 1961 and the 1998 easements should be modified under the doctrine of changed conditions to avoid a "grossly inefficient allocation of resources." *Id.*, ¶¶40, 53. Central to the court of appeals conclusion was its assessment that "the miniscule benefits the Kostermans derive impose aggregate costs far in excess of the sum total of benefits to all concerned parties." *Id.*, ¶52. Accordingly, the court of appeals modified the easement created by the 1960 deed as well as the 1961 easement so that both easements would terminate once the Dominant Estate received alternate public road access. *Id.*, ¶53. The Kostermans petitioned for review.

II

This case comes to us on summary judgment. We review a circuit court's grant or denial of summary judgment independently of the circuit court or court of appeals, applying the same methodology as the circuit court. *O'Neill v. Reemer*, 2003 WI 13, ¶8, 259 Wis. 2d 544, 657 N.W.2d 403. Summary judgment is appropriate if there are no genuine issues of material fact and the moving party is entitled to judgment as a matter of law. Wis. Stat. §802.08(2). Resolution of this case requires interpretation of the documents creating the 1961 and 1998 easements. Here, both the circuit court and the court of appeals decided the 1961 and 1998 easements were unambiguous. *See Kosterman*, 277 Wis. 2d 509, ¶¶36, 43. Whether a deed or other instrument is ambiguous is a question of law we review independently. *See Gojmerac v. Mahn*, 2002 WI App 22, ¶24, 250 Wis. 2d 1, 640 N.W.2d 178 (Ct. App. 2001). If the language of a deed is unambiguous, its construction is also a question of law. *Rikkers v. Ryan*, 76 Wis. 2d 185, 188, 251 N.W.2d 25 (1977).

III

Two easements are at issue in this case: (1) the 30-foot easement reserved in 1998; and (2) the 66-foot easement created in 1961. Both easements are express easements (easements by written grant or reservation). As the court of appeals recognized, if the 1961 easement remains in effect, it is unnecessary to consider under what conditions the 1998 easement terminates. Because we conclude that the 1961 easement is unambiguous and that it survived the 1998 deeds, we begin and end with the terms of the 1961 easement.

The 1961 conveyance to the Chviliceks created an express easement of right of way. The instrument states Louis and Angeline Chvilicek "[d]o give, grant and convey unto [Edward and Audrey Chvilicek], and to their heirs and assigns forever, an ease of rt of way for purposes of ingress and egress upon the fol desc real est," after which follows a metes and bounds description of the easement.

In attacking the continued vitality of the 1961 easement, AKG makes two distinct arguments. First, AKG argues that changed circumstances frustrate the purpose of the 1961 easement, requiring that the court modify the easement so that it will terminate once AKG provides the Kostermans with alternate access to a public road. Second, AKG argues that when it purchased the Servient Estate in 1998, the 1998 deeds released the 1960 and 1961 easements. We address each argument.

A. Should the 1961 Easement Be Terminated under the Doctrine of Changed Conditions?

AKG urges the court to adopt the changed conditions doctrine set forth in the *Restatement (Third) of Property: Servitudes* §7.10 (2000). Section 7.10 of the *Restatement* states:

> (1) When a change has taken place since the creation of a servitude that makes it impossible as a practical matter to accomplish the purpose for which the servitude was created, a court may modify the servitude to permit the purpose to be accomplished. If modification is not practicable, or would not be effective, a court may terminate the servitude. Compensation for resulting harm to the beneficiaries may be awarded as a condition of modifying or terminating the servitude.
>
> (2) If the purpose of a servitude can be accomplished, but because of changed conditions the servient estate is no longer suitable for uses permitted by the servitude, a court may modify the servitude to permit other uses under conditions designed to preserve the benefits of the original servitude.

Subsection (1) reflects the common law rule that an easement for a particular purpose terminates when it becomes impossible to use the easement for the purpose intended in the granting instrument. *Restatement (Third) of Property: Servitudes* §7.10, at 399 (Reporter's Note) (noting that traditionally courts terminate easements when the purpose becomes impossible to accomplish rather than by resort to the changed conditions doctrine); 25 Am. Jur. 2d *Easements and Licenses* §96 (2004) ("An easement granted for a particular purpose normally terminates as soon as such purpose . . . is rendered impossible of accomplishment.").

In contrast, prior to the *Restatement (Third) of Property: Servitudes*, the rule set forth in subsection (2) was traditionally not used to terminate easements. *Restatement (Third) of Property: Servitudes* §7.10 cmt. a; Susan F. French, *Toward a Modern Law of Servitudes: Reweaving the Ancient Strands*, 55 S. Cal. L. Rev. 1261, 1269, 1301 (1982) (noting there is nothing comparable to the changed conditions doctrine of equitable covenants in easement law); *see also Cortese v. United States*, 782 F.2d 845, 851 (9th Cir. 1986) (implying that covenants, but not easements, are subject to the doctrine of changed conditions). Subsection (2) permits an easement to be terminated—where changed conditions exist— because the easement has become unreasonably burdensome upon the servient estate, obsolete, or economically wasteful. *See* French, *supra* at 1316.

AKG appears to argue that the 1961 easement should be terminated or modified under both standards, impossibility of purpose and changed circumstances, suggesting that the latter leads to the former. We conclude that the easements should not be modified or terminated under *Restatement (Third) of Property: Servitudes* §7.10(1) or (2).

1. Should the 1961 Easement Be Terminated Because It Is Impossible to Fulfill Its Purpose?

AKG contends that the purpose of the 1961 easement was to provide ingress and egress until public road access was provided but that subsequent developments have rendered the easement useless for this purpose because DOT regulations make it impossible to construct a public road along the course of the easement. AKG emphasizes two changed conditions. First, in 1995 the Chviliceks deeded a portion of the 66-foot-wide easement to the State of Wisconsin and agreed that a public road could not be placed where the 1961 easement intersected with Highway 31. Second, as of 1999 the DOT assumed increased oversight of compliance with Wis. Admin. Code §Trans 233.06. According to AKG, these two facts make it impossible for the easement to become a public road, defeating the purpose of the easement. Therefore, given the Kostermans' refusal to bargain over relocating the easements, AKG contends it is appropriate for a court to modify the easements.

We disagree with AKG's characterization of the easements. The first step in analyzing impossibility of purpose is to determine the purpose of the easement. Jon W. Bruce & James W. Ely, Jr., *The Law of Easements and Licenses in Land* §10:8, at 10-15 (2001). Contrary to AKG's assertion, the primary purpose of the 1961 easement is not to become a public road. Rather, the primary purpose of this easement is to provide ingress and egress to the Dominant Estate over a specifically described course. The plain text of the 1961 instrument creates "an ease[ment of right of way] *for purposes of ingress and egress. . . .*" (Emphasis added.) That valid purpose has not been extinguished, frustrated, or otherwise rendered impossible to fulfill.

The court of appeals erred by concluding that the purpose of the easement was to authorize a public road. True, the 1961 easement made it possible to convert the private road into a public road. But, the 1961 easement did not change the overriding purpose of the easement from providing ingress and egress to providing a public road.

Next, AKG appears to shift ground, arguing that the 1961 easement should be terminated once its purpose—to provide ingress and egress to the Dominant Estate—can be accomplished by an alternative course; that is, once the easement becomes unnecessary it should terminate. AKG's position, however, is contrary to longstanding Wisconsin easement law, which holds that an express easement does *not* terminate even when the necessity or purpose of the easement ceases. *Niedfeldt v. Evans*, 272 Wis. 362, 364, 75 N.W.2d 307 (1956).

In *Niedfeldt* the defendant owned a prescriptive right of way across the plaintiff's land. *Id.* at 363. Once public road access was provided to the defendant's property, the plaintiff constructed a fence across the easement and brought suit for trespass against the defendant, claiming the prescriptive easement terminated once alternate public road access became available. *Id.* at 364. The court rejected the plaintiff's contention that a prescriptive easement terminates when the necessity for the easement ceases. *Id.* at 365.

Central to *Niedfeldt* were the distinctions among easements of necessity, easements for a particular purpose, prescriptive easements, and express easements. *See id.* at 364- 65. The circumstances under which an easement can be modified or terminated depend upon the type of easement. "Thus, if an easement is granted for a particular purpose only, the right continues while the dominant tenement is used for that purpose, but ceases when the specified use ceases." *Id.* at 364 (quoting 17 Am. Jur., *Easements* §137, at 1023). "Moreover, a way of *necessity* is a temporary right in the sense that it continues only so long as the necessity exists." *Id.* (emphasis added).

In contrast, neither a prescriptive easement nor an express easement can be modified or terminated solely because the necessity for the easement ceases. *Id.* at 365. Thus, "[t]he rule that the right ceases with necessity has no application to ways acquired by express grant or by prescription; *a right to a way so created cannot be defeated by showing that the owners have another convenient and accessible way of going to and from their premises.*" *Id.* (quoting 28 C.J.S. *Easements* §54, at 718) (emphasis added); *Millen v. Thomas*, 201 Wis. 2d 675, 679, 550 N.W.2d 134 (Ct. App. 1996). Thus, even if AKG did provide alternate public road access to the Kostermans, the 1961 easement would remain in force, because an express easement continues regardless of whether the dominant estate needs the easement.

The *Niedfeldt* court acknowledged the rule that an easement can terminate with the cessation of the particular purpose for which the easement is granted, *Niedfeldt*, 262 Wis. 2d at 364, but that is not the case here. In the 40-plus years since the easement was granted, the owners of the Dominant Estate have used the easement for ingress and egress. No circumstances have changed to frustrate this purpose or render it impossible. The Kostermans continue to use the driveway created by the 1960 and 1961 easements, and they are not required to give up this use even if a reasonable alternative becomes available. Another rule, that the right ceases with the necessity, has no application when the right was created not by "necessity" but by express grant. *Id.* at 365. As the court put it, "any offer to prove that the defendant [now] had another road to his farm would not defeat his easement and hence was immaterial." *Id.*

2. Should the Court Modify the Easement Because Changed Conditions Make It Unduly Burdensome upon the Servient Estate?

AKG also requests that, regardless the language of the 1961 instrument, the court adopt *Restatement (Third) of Property: Servitudes* §7.10(2), and thereby modify the easement because it inhibits the free and unrestricted use of property and unreasonably burdens its property. Alternatively, but in a closely related argument, AKG urges the court to modify the 1961 easement pursuant to *Restatement (Third) of Property: Servitudes* §4.8(3).

[§4.8(3) of the Restatement (Third) reads as follows:

(3) Unless expressly denied by the terms of an easement as defined in §1.2, the owner of the servient estate is entitled to make reasonable changes in the location or dimensions of an easement, at the servient owner's expense, to permit normal use or development of the servient estate, but only if the changes do not:

(a) significantly lessen the utility of the easement,

(b) increase the burdens on the owner of the easement in its use and enjoyment, or

(c) frustrate the purpose for which the easement was created. —Eds.]

We decline to apply either *Restatement (Third) of Property: Servitudes* §§7.10(2) or 4.8(3) to the facts of this case. Even at the risk of sanctioning unneighborly and economically unproductive behavior, this court must safeguard property rights. *See Schwab*, 224 Wis. 2d at 41; *Jacque v. Steenberg Homes, Inc.*, 209 Wis. 2d 605, 631, 563 N.W.2d 154 (1997); *Guse v. Flohr*, 195 Wis. 139, 147, 217 N.W. 730 (1928). Thus, in *Schwab* we refused to impose a right-of-way easement of necessity across land adjoining the petitioners even though doing so effectively rendered the petitioners' land useless because the cost of providing alternative vehicular access was prohibitive. *Schwab*, 224 Wis. 2d at 39-41. In *Jacque* we upheld a $100,000 punitive-damages verdict despite nominal damages of $1 in order to protect property rights, where the defendant intentionally trespassed across the plaintiff's land to avoid the high cost of the alternative route. *Jacque*, 209 Wis. 2d at 631.

Similarly, in *Guse* we concluded that the dominant estate could not unilaterally modify a right-of-way easement even though doing so would have been economically beneficial to both the dominant estate and the servient estate. *Guse*, 195 Wis. at 147 ("[T]he refusal of the plaintiff to permit the removal of the fence to a point one rod farther south . . . is unneighborly, spiteful, and unreasonable. However that may be, the legal rights of the plaintiff remain the same. . . . There can be no balancing of equities in this case."). Nothing in the host of cases AKG cites convinces us that we should sacrifice property rights in this case in favor of economic efficiency. As such, the court of appeals erred in placing overriding significance upon the need to prevent economic waste. *Kosterman*, 277 Wis. 2d 509, ¶1.

In support of its position, AKG relies upon *M.P.M. Builders, LLC v. Dwyer*, 809 N.E.2d 1053 (Mass. 2004), which concluded that four other jurisdictions had adopted or approved of *Restatement (Third) of Property: Servitudes* §4.8(3), while only two jurisdictions had expressly rejected it. Examination of *Dwyer* and the cases cited therein demonstrates that only in *Dwyer* did a court relocate an express easement with a specifically defined location.

The cases *Dwyer* cites as adopting *Restatement (Third) of Property: Servitudes* §4.8(3) evince a reluctance to relocate easements with a specifically agreed upon location. *See Burkhart v. Lillehaug*, 664 N.W.2d 41, 44 (S.D. 2003) (noting the course of the right-of-way easement was not "surveyed, platted with specificity, or otherwise clearly established"); *Roaring Fork Club, L.P. v. St. Jude's Co.*, 36 P.3d 1229, 1236 (Colo. 2001) ("under the Restatement, a burdened estate owner may unilaterally move an easement (*unless it is specified in deeds or otherwise to have a location certain*), subject both to a reasonableness test and to the constraints delimited in [§4.8(3)].") (emphasis added); *Lewis v. Young*, 705 N.E.2d 649, 658, 662 (N.Y. 1998) (noting that if the parties intended the location of the easement to be fixed and not subject to unilateral relocation they should have described it by metes and bounds rather than as a driveway "running in a generally southwesterly direction"); *Goodwin v. Johnson*, 591 S.E.2d 34, 37 (S.C. Ct. App. 2003) (relocating an easement of necessity while suggesting that express easements require mutual consent to be relocated).

Dwyer, therefore, appears to stand alone. We decline to follow *Dwyer* because it would mean altering the longstanding default rule in Wisconsin that a servient estate cannot unilaterally relocate or terminate an express easement. Notably, even under the *Restatement (Third) of Property: Servitudes* §4.8(3), parties can still prevent unilateral relocation by incorporating mutual consent requirements in their agreement. *See Restatement (Third) of Property: Servitudes* §4.8(3) & cmt. a (noting the section merely supplies terms when omitted by the parties); *see also Dwyer*, 809 N.E.2d at 1058. The ability to contract around unilateral modification, as authorized by §4.8(3), makes less convincing the argument that the interest in increased development of property should overcome the durability of easement rights. Accordingly, we conclude that parties need not include a provision in an express easement to prevent unilateral modification or relocation. Absent any mention of modification or relocation in the instrument creating an easement, the rule is that the owner of the servient estate cannot unilaterally modify an express easement. *See Lehner v. Kozlowski*, 245 Wis. 262, 266, 13 N.W.2d 910 (1944); *Guse*, 195 Wis. at 147-48.

We agree with the Kostermans and the courts that have rejected the *Restatement (Third) of Property: Servitudes* §§4.8(3) and 7.10(2) in favor of preventing the owners of servient estates from unilaterally relocating or terminating express easements. *See e.g., Herrin v. Pettengill*, 538 S.E.2d 735, 736 (Ga. 2000); *MacMeekin v. Low Income Hous. Inst., Inc.*, 45 P.3d 570, 579 (Wash. Ct. App. 2002); *see also Davis v. Bruk*, 411 A.2d 660, 665 (Me. 1980). These courts have rejected the position advanced by the *Restatement* as a threat to the certainty of property rights and real estate transactions, as a catalyst for increased litigation, and as a means for purchasers of servient estates to reap a windfall at the expense of owners of dominant estates. We agree that these reasons for rejecting the *Restatement*'s position are more compelling than the economic inefficiencies that might result from bilateral monopolies and holdout easement owners.

Thus, although a handful of courts have adopted *Restatement (Third) of Property: Servitudes* §4.8(3), these jurisdictions remain distinctly in the minority. Jon W. Bruce & James W. Ely, Jr., *The Law of Easements and Licenses in Land* §7:16 at 7-31 to 7-33 (2001); *see Restatement (Third) of Property: Servitudes*, Introductory Note to ch. 4, at 496 (noting §4.8(3) departs from the "common-law rule to adopt the civil-law rule on relocation of easements."); *id.*, Introductory Note to ch. 7, at 336 (noting §7.10 "provides for an expanded use of modification to permit more flexibility in adapting servitude arrangements to retain their utility over time.").

Moreover, the position articulated in *Restatement (Third) of Property: Servitudes* §§4.8(3) and 7.10(2) is inconsistent with longstanding precedent that Wisconsin courts do not balance the equities of adverse property owners when determining whether to grant or modify an easement. *See Schwab*, 224 Wis. 2d at 41-43; *Guse*, 195 Wis. 2d at 147. We decline to abandon this precedent.

Finally, vigorous academic debate persists over whether wise public policy warrants the extension of the changed conditions doctrine to easements. On one hand, proponents of the *Restatement* position argue that judicial intervention is necessary to rectify the problem of holdouts, who could otherwise single-handedly impede economic development. *See e.g.*, Uriel Reichman, *Toward a Unified Concept of Servitudes*, 55 S. Cal. L. Rev. 1177, 1233 (1982); Susan F. French, *Toward a Modern Law of Servitudes: Reweaving the Ancient Strands*, 55 S. Cal. L. Rev. 1261, 1265, 1300 (1982); Note, *Balancing the Equities: Is Missouri Adopting a Progressive Rule for Relocation of Easements?*, 61 Mo. L. Rev. 1039, 1057-61 (1996). Conversely, opponents of the *Restatement* position contend that the uncertainty caused by judicial modification of easements does more to hamper economic development than does current law because the *Restatement* discourages investment by rendering property rights uncertain. *See, e.g.*, Richard A. Epstein, *Covenants and Constitutions*, 73 Cornell L. Rev. 906, 914 (1987); Carol M. Rose, *Servitudes, Security, and Assent: Some Comments on Professors French and Reichman*, 55 S. Cal. L. Rev. 1403, 1412-13 (1982); Note, *The Right of Owners of Servient Estates to Relocate Easements Unilaterally*, 109 Harv. L. Rev. 1693, 1694-97 (1996).

Given the lack of consensus and lack of evidence that the changed-conditions doctrine produces superior economic and legal consequences, we reject the *Restatement*'s departure from the general rule that express easements cannot be unilaterally modified. We are not persuaded that the policy arguments are sufficiently compelling to justify overturning more than a century of precedent and upsetting the settled expectations of thousands of easement holders.

B. Did the 1998 Deeds Extinguish the 1961 Easement?

Alternatively, AKG contends the 1998 deeds extinguished the 1960 and 1961 easements. AKG's argument depends upon evidence extrinsic to the 1998 deeds, including the offer and counteroffer that preceded the completed transaction between the Chviliceks, the Trust, and AKG, the deposition testimony of Edward Chvilicek, the deposition testimony of members of AKG, and the 2000 deed in which the Kostermans purchased the Dominant Estate from the Chviliceks.

There are two major flaws with AKG's argument. The first is that before extrinsic evidence of the parties' intent can be considered, the 1998 deeds between AKG and the Chviliceks, and between AKG and the Trust must be ambiguous with respect to the 1960 and 1961 easements. *See Rikkers*, 76 Wis. 2d at 188 ("where a deed is susceptible to only one interpretation, extrinsic evidence may not be referred to in order to show the intent of the parties"). We find it telling that AKG points to no such ambiguity. Moreover, upon inspection, the 1998 deeds demonstrate no ambiguity with respect to the preexisting easements. The 1998 deeds contain three references to right-of-way easements: (1) Both the warranty deed and the trustee deed conveyed the fee title to AKG except for "recorded and/or existing easements and right of way reservations. . . ." (2) In an exhibit to the 1998 deeds, the Chviliceks and the Trust reserved the 30-foot-wide public road easement, which overlapped the 1960 and 1961 easements. (3) In the same exhibit, the Chviliceks and the Trust reserved another right-of-way easement for ingress and egress via Cobblestone Drive.

Nothing in the language of the easements created by the 1998 deeds suggests that the 1960 and 1961 easements are being released. Nothing in the language of the easements created by the 1998 deeds makes reference to any preexisting easements. Moreover, the 1998 deeds explicitly except from the title conveyed to AKG all recorded easements. Since the 1960 and 1961 easements are recorded, the only reasonable interpretation of the 1998 deed is that the property AKG purchased was encumbered by the 1960 and 1961 easements, along with all other recorded easements.

If there is any doubt that the 1960 and 1961 easements survived, AKG's commitment for title insurance confirms that the property was encumbered by these earlier easements. Both easements are clearly listed as exceptions to the title conveyed. Absent ambiguity, we decline to consider the negotiations leading up to the 1998 deeds or the deposition testimony AKG offered for purposes of establishing intent. To do otherwise would jeopardize the certainty and authoritative status of recorded titles and land records. *Cf. Kordecki v. Rizzo*, 106 Wis. 2d 713, 718-19, 317 N.W.2d 479 (1982).

The second flaw in AKG's position is that even if the 1998 deeds were silent with respect to the 1960 and 1961 easements, silence does not terminate an express easement. *See Union Falls Power Co. v. Marinette County*, 238 Wis. 134, 141, 298 N.W. 598 (1941). The long-established rule is that an express easement "passes by a subsequent conveyance of the dominant estate without express mention in the conveyance." *Id.; Barkhausen v. Chicago, Milwaukee & St. Paul Ry. Co.*, 142 Wis. 292, 298, 124 N.W. 649 (1910); *Gojmerac*, 250 Wis. 2d 1, ¶25; *Krepel v. Darnell*, 165 Wis. 2d 235, 245, 477 N.W.2d 333 (Ct. App. 1991). Conversely, a servient estate remains burdened by a recorded express easement even when the easement is not expressly mentioned in the conveyance, since the purchaser has constructive notice of the easement. Jon W. Bruce & James W. Ely, Jr., *The Law of Easements and Licenses in Land* §10:32, at 10-77 (2001). Thus, when AKG acquired title to the Servient Estate, the 1960 and 1961 easements burdened the property. Likewise, when the Kostermans acquired the Dominant Estate, the chain of title confirmed that the 1960 and 1961 easements remained appurtenant to the property. Accordingly, we reject AKG's argument that the 1998 deeds extinguished the 1960 and 1961 easements.

Although AKG couches its attack upon the easements burdening its land in terms of changed conditions, frustration of purpose, and subsequent easements extinguishing prior easements, we think AKG is really asking this court to relieve it of the duties placed upon every other buyer of real property. A buyer of real property is expected to determine the rights to the land he is about to purchase by consulting (1) the records in the office of the register of deeds; (2) other public records to discover rights which usually are not recorded in the office of the register of deeds, such as judgments and liens; and (3) the land itself. *Kordecki*, 106 Wis. 2d at 719 n.5. The testimony of all AKG members deposed reveals a failure to inspect the chain of title to determine whether their development plans were consistent with the rights conveyed by the title to the Servient Estate. While not necessary to our holding, evidence of this omission by AKG bolsters our conclusion that the court of appeals should not have modified the 1961 easement to relieve AKG of the burden upon the Servient Estate.

IV

Accordingly, we reverse the court of appeals. The 1961 easement will remain in effect even if AKG provides the Kostermans an alternative means of access to a public road, because the owner of a servient estate cannot unilaterally modify or terminate an express easement.

The decision of the court of appeals is reversed.

SHIRLEY S. ABRAHAMSON, C.J., concurring. I agree with the majority opinion that AKG Real Estate cannot get court approval to relocate or terminate the express easement without the consent of the Kostermans, the owners of the dominant estate.

The majority opinion, however, states its holding and applicable rule of law too broadly. The majority opinion declares its holding that "the owner of a servient estate cannot unilaterally relocate or terminate an express agreement," period. Not true! The majority opinion, also overstates the applicable rule as "even if AKG did provide alternate public road access to the [dominant estate], the 1961 easement would remain in force, because an express easement continues *regardless of whether the dominant estate needs the easement.*" (emphasis added). . . .

The majority opinion correctly explains that an express easement can terminate with the cessation of the particular purpose for which the easement was granted. *Niedfeldt v. Evans*, 272 Wis. 362, 364, 75 N.W.2d 307 (1956), clearly states this rule of law.

The court need not and should not decide whether to adopt Restatement (Third) of Property: Servitudes, §4.8(3) or §7.10(2). Neither provision applies in the instant case. Under §4.8(3) the owner cannot make reasonable changes in the location of an easement if the change increases the burdens on the owner of the easement in its use and enjoyment. Here the servient owner proposes extinguishing, not modifying, the easement. In any event, the owners of the dominant estate would be burdened.

Under §7.10(2) of the Restatement a court may modify the servitude (easement) to permit other uses because of "changed conditions." "Changed conditions" is a stringent standard, including the concept that the servitude no longer serves its intended purpose. Comment *a.* to §7.10 explains that the doctrine is used sparingly:

> Because servitudes create property interests that are generally valuable, courts apply the changed-conditions doctrine with caution. Of the many changed-conditions cases that have produced appellate decisions, few result in modification or termination of a servitude. The test is stringent: relief is granted only if the purpose of the servitude can no longer be accomplished. When servitudes are terminated under this rule, it is ordinarily clear that the continuance of the servitude would serve no useful purpose and would create unnecessary harm to the owner of the servient estate.

Indeed, the owners of the dominant estate are persuasive in arguing that there were no changed conditions.

Section 7.10(2) of the 1998 Restatement (Third) of Property: Servitudes is not as broad as the description of modifications of servitudes is in Professor French's 1982 law review article, entitled *Toward a Modern Law of Servitudes: Reweaving the Ancient Strands*, in 55 S. Cal. L. Rev. 1261 (often discussing injunctive relief), upon which the majority opinion relies.

For the reasons set forth, I write separately. I join the concurring opinion of Justice Ann Walsh Bradley.

Ann Walsh Bradley, J., concurring. I write separately because I think some basics have been lost in the shuffle.

The 1961 easement is the pivotal easement in this case. That easement is an express easement granted "for purposes of ingress and egress." It still can be, and is, used for these purposes. Therefore, this case does not involve the concepts of impossibility or cessation of purpose.

Whether the Kostermans' use of the 1961 easement for its expressly-granted purpose remains "necessary" is irrelevant. *See Niedfeldt v. Evans*, 272 Wis. 362, 365, 75 N.W.2d 307 (1956) ("The rule that the right ceases with necessity has no application to ways acquired by express grant . . . ; a right to a way so created cannot be defeated by showing that the owners have another convenient and accessible way of going to and from their premises." (quoting 28 C.J.S., Easements, §54, p. 718)); *accord Millen v. Thomas*, 201 Wis. 2d 675, 679, 550 N.W.2d 134 (Ct. App. 1996).

In addition, this case does not involve consent, abandonment, unity of ownership, or any other precept of Wisconsin's common law that could operate to extinguish or relocate an express easement. Thus, unless this court were to modify current Wisconsin law, the 1961 easement must continue under the facts of this case.

In a future case, when impossibility is an issue, this court may well consider whether an express easement could be terminated when the purpose becomes impossible to accomplish. Impossibility is a high standard when properly defined. Such a standard, nevertheless, would address the argument that a servient estate should not be bound in perpetuity when the purpose of the easement is impossible to achieve. The impossibility standard may provide an appropriate balance between the respective rights and interests of the dominant and servient estates.

For the reasons stated, I respectfully concur.

NOTES AND QUESTIONS

1. *Property Law Reform and the Restatement (Third).* The first two Restatements of Property did little more than restate the existing law of property. The Restatement (Third) is much more reformist. It is too soon to tell whether the more aggressive reforms in the Restatement (Third) will be adopted by courts. As we have already seen, courts can be especially hesitant to change the law in the property context. *AKG Real Estate* is a good example. It is especially hard to convince courts to change property law when there is active debate about whether the changes are desirable. As the court noted, there is debate among property academics about the provisions of the Restatement (Third) at issue in *AKG Real Estate*. What do you think about the approaches taken by the Restatement (Third)? Do you think that the Restatement (Third)'s rule for relocation of easements makes sense?

2. *Changed Circumstances.* As the court noted in *AKG Real Estate*, the idea that easements may be terminated based on changed conditions is one of the more aggressive reforms proposed by the Restatement (Third). We will discuss changed circumstances in some depth below in our materials on covenants that run with the land. Regardless of the merits of the Restatement (Third) position, it is clear that the requirements of the changed circumstances test were not met in *AKG Real Estate*. As the concurring justices noted, the changed circumstances test is stringent and requires that the changed circumstances undercut the initial purpose of the servitude. AKG Real Estate tried to get some traction on this point by arguing that the purpose of the easement was to allow a public road to reach the dominant parcel, but the court (correctly in our view) rejected that position and held that the purpose of the easement was ingress and egress from the dominant parcel. On this view of the easement, there were no changed circumstances at all.

3. *Economic Efficiency.* The intermediate appellate court in *AKG Real Estate* allowed the easement to be terminated so long as the dominant parcel was provided access to a public road. Its analysis was influenced by the fact that the servient parcel owner's development plans would be impeded by the easement in its current location and that maintaining the current easement would lead to an economically inefficient result. The Wisconsin Supreme Court was much less impressed by arguments based on economic efficiency. What do you think of the economic arguments raised by AKG Real Estate? Would a better result have been to allow AKG Real Estate to relocate the easements but to force them to pay compensation to the Kostermans?

5. BEACH ACCESS AND THE PUBLIC TRUST

Public beach access is a controversial issue in many states bordering oceans or large bodies of water. Beachfront property owners typically own at least part of the beach and often want to exclude the public from the privately owned portion of the beach. The public, in contrast, wants to be able to access and use the beach.

In all states, beaches involve a boundary between public and private property. Oceans and other large bodies of water are owned by the public. A boundary between public and private property will occur at some point between the ocean and privately held beachfront property. The exact location of this boundary varies widely between states. Two points on the beach tend to be important boundary markers. The first is the mean high tide line—that is, the point that the average high tide reaches on the beach. The second is the vegetation line—that is, the point where vegetation grows on the beach.

The exact boundary between public and private property can be a controversial issue. The public's right to access the publicly owned portion of the beach can be another. Just because the public owns a part of the beach does not mean that the public can easily get to the beach where private homes create a barrier between the street and the beach. Beach access cases therefore often talk about both *horizontal* and *vertical* access to the beach. To understand these orientations, imagine that you are on a street facing the beach and the ocean. Vertical access concerns your ability to get to the beach. Horizontal access concerns your ability to move along the beach once you are there.

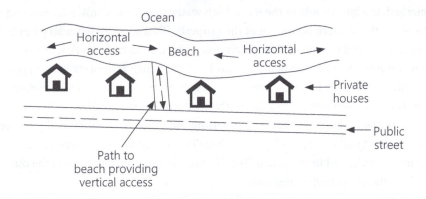

In a series of important and controversial cases, the New Jersey Supreme Court used the *public trust doctrine* to hold that public had an easement over privately owned property to reach and enjoy the publicly owned portion of the beach. Our next case is part of that series.

RALEIGH AVENUE BEACH ASSN. V. ATLANTIS BEACH CLUB

Supreme Court of New Jersey, 2005
879 A.2d 112

Chief Justice PORITZ delivered the opinion of the Court.

This case raises a question about the right of the public to use a 480-foot wide stretch of upland sand beach in Lower Township, Cape May County, owned by respondent Atlantis Beach Club, Inc., and operated as a private club. We hold today that, in the circumstances presented here, and on application of the factors set forth in *Matthews v. Bay Head Improvement Ass'n*, 95 *N.J.* 306, 326, 471 *A.*2d 355, *cert. denied, Bay Head Improvement Ass'n v. Matthews*, 469 *U.S.* 821, 105 *S.Ct.* 93, 83 *L.Ed.*2d 39 (1984), the public trust doctrine requires the Atlantis property to be open to the general public at a reasonable fee for services provided by the owner and approved by the Department of Environmental Protection.

I.

Atlantis Beach Club, Inc. (Atlantis or Beach Club) is the successor in title to a Riparian Grant, dated January 17, 1907, from the State of New Jersey to the Cape May

Real Estate Company. The grant encompassed a large area not relevant to this litigation except for certain submerged land that, in 1907, was located within the bed of Turtle Gut Inlet, a body of water that connected to the Atlantic Ocean. Today, the land is described on the Lower Township Municipal Tax Map as Block 730.02, Lot 1.02. No longer submerged, the lot extends to the mean high water line from a bulkhead running north/south along the western boundary of the property. That western boundary lies to the east of an unpaved section of Raleigh Avenue (which runs east/west), whereas the mean high water line serves as the boundary for Lot 1.03, which is entirely submerged beneath the ocean at high tide; Lot 1.02, however, consists of dry sand beach and protected dunes. The distance from the bulkhead (the western boundary of Lot 1.02) to the mean high water line is about 342 feet. Persons using the beach for recreational purposes cross over the bulkhead by walking on a boardwalk pathway that traverses the dunes and curves southward to the beach. The dry sand beach area lies beyond the dunes and extends to the mean high water line.

A pathway runs east/west along the unpaved section of Raleigh Avenue to the approximate midpoint of the bulkhead and then, as described, across the bulkhead and through the dunes. The pathway was approved by the New Jersey Department of Environmental Protection (DEP or Department) in a 1986 permit issued pursuant to the Coastal Area Facility Review Act (CAFRA), *N.J.S.A.* 13:19-1 to -21. The CAFRA permit related to the construction of the La Vida del Mar Condominiums (La Vida), a four-story, twenty-four-unit condominium structure along Raleigh Avenue, and required as a condition of condominium construction public access "down the center of Raleigh Avenue, . . . and [by means of] a timber walkway over the bulkhead to the beach." The permit also required Department-approved signs marking public access to be "conspicuously located at the end of [the] Raleigh Avenue pavement" and maintained by the condominium homeowners' association for the life of the condominium project.

As noted, the La Vida building stands immediately to the west of the bulkhead along the western boundary of the Atlantis property. Another four-story multiple unit condominium complex called the La Quinta del Mar sits to the south of La Vida and the path that runs from the end of the pavement on Raleigh Avenue and over the bulkhead. To the west of La Quinta del Mar are the Villa House and La Quinta Towers, both of which contain residential units. Seapointe Village (Seapointe) is located to the north of La Vida and consists of several structures, including a six-story, one-hundred-room hotel, and more than five hundred residential units. Seapointe occupies 63.4 acres, including the beach property to the north of the Atlantis beach.

When the Seapointe property was developed, the DEP, as a condition of its 1987 CAFRA permit, required the beach in front of Seapointe to be open to the public. Under the terms of the permit, Seapointe is allowed to sell daily, weekly, and seasonal beach passes at rates approved by the DEP, although residents can access the area beyond the mean high water line free-of-charge. Public access through Seapointe's beach along the water's edge is also free-of-charge, and beach usage fees, regulations, and operations are subject to continued periodic review and approval by the DEP. Seapointe provides lifeguards on its beach, as well as public restrooms, outdoor showers, and parking facilities. In August 2002 when this litigation began, the rates for use of the Seapointe beach were, per person, $2.50 a day, $10 a week, and $40 a season; however, Seapointe had submitted an application for a fee increase that was pending at that time.

The United States Coast Guard owns the property to the south of the Atlantis beach. That property is closed to the public from April 1 through August 15 to protect the piping plover, an endangered species, during breeding season. Although the Coast Guard beach is unavailable for most of the summer season, the property is open to the public the rest of the year.

Atlantis is located in the Diamond Beach neighborhood, a residential area of approximately three blocks by nine blocks that contains the only beach in Lower Township facing the Atlantic Ocean. In addition to the beach access point on the Atlantis property at the end of Raleigh Avenue, there are two other access points in Diamond Beach north of Atlantis: one at the eastern end of Dune Drive and the other at the eastern end of Memphis Avenue. Access is blocked by condominium buildings located at the terminus of the other streets in the area. According to certifications filed by residents of La Quinta Towers in support of plaintiff Raleigh Avenue Beach Association (Association), the closest free entry to the beach is Dune Drive, a nine-block walk from Raleigh Avenue and a distance of approximately one-half mile. The beach access problem in Lower Township is further compounded by the limited number of parking spaces available in the Diamond Beach neighborhood.

Until 1996, the beach on the Atlantis property was open to the public free-of-charge. In the summer of 1996, however, Atlantis established a private beach club known at the time as Club Atlantis Enterprises. The club limited public access to its beach by charging a fee of $300 for six seasonal beach tags. As of July 2003, a sign posted on the gate at the entrance to the Atlantis beach read: "FREE PUBLIC ACCESS ENDS HERE/MEMBERSHIP AVAILABLE AT GATE." Atlantis's 2003 Rules and Regulations, also posted, provided the following warning:

> ANYONE ATTEMPTING TO USE, ENTER UPON OR CROSS OVER CLUB PROPERTY FOR ANY REASON WITHOUT CLUB PERMISSION OR WHO IS NOT IN POSSESSION OF A VALID TAG AND AUTHORIZED TO USE SUCH TAG WILL BE SUBJECT TO PROSECUTION, CIVIL AND OR CRIMINAL, TO THE FULLEST EXTENT PERMITTED BY LAW[,] INCLUDING ALL COSTS AND LEGAL FEES INCURRED BY THE CLUB.

Prior to the commencement of this litigation, the membership fee for new members and members who had joined the beach club in 2002 was set at $700 for the 2003 summer season. Members were entitled to eight beach tags per household. Atlantis also sold "Access Easements" at $10,000 each, paid in cash. Easement holders were required to pay an annual membership fee determined by dividing the actual costs associated with operating the beach club by the total number of members (both easement holders and yearly members) to arrive at the holder's proportionate share. According to a March 14, 2003 letter to members, the payment of membership fees or the purchase of an easement entitled them "to use and enjoy the [club] facilities," which included uniformed private security personnel on club grounds, as well as lifeguards on duty from June 21 through September 1, 2003, seven days a week, between the hours of 10:00 a.m. and 5:00 p.m.

II.

On June 22, 2002, Tony Labrosciano, a member of the Association, was issued a summons for trespassing when he attempted to leave the wet sand area and walk across the Atlantis property to the eastern terminus of Raleigh Avenue in order to take the most direct route back to his home. On July 26, 2002, Atlantis filed an Order to Show Cause and Verified Complaint against Labrosciano, other unnamed persons, Lower Township, and the State of New Jersey, seeking, among other things, to enjoin Labrosciano and members of his class from "trespassing, entering onto and accessing" the Atlantis property, and declaring that Atlantis is not required to provide the public with access to or use of any portion of its property or the adjacent ocean.

The Association, which consists of individuals who reside on Raleigh Avenue in the Diamond Beach neighborhood, filed a complaint on August 14, 2002 against Atlantis, the Lower Township Police Department, Seapointe Village Association, and the State of New Jersey.[5] The Association claimed that Atlantis was in violation of the public trust doctrine and sought free public access through the Atlantis property to the beach, and to a sufficient amount of dry sand above the mean high water line to permit the public to enjoy the beach and beach-related activities. That Association action was subsequently consolidated with the Atlantis action. . . .

On September 19, 2003, the trial court issued a ruling from the bench, followed by both a Memorandum of Decision, dated September 22, 2003, and an Order of Final Judgment, dated November 3, 2003. The court considered and disposed of issues relating to both horizontal and vertical access to the Atlantis beach under the public trust doctrine. More specifically, the court held that the public was entitled to a right of horizontal access to the ocean by means of "a three-foot wide strip of dry sand, immediately landward of the mean high water line and extending from the northern to the southern boundaries of [the Atlantis] [p]roperty, which may be utilized by the public, at no charge, for the purpose of entering into and exiting from" the area located below the mean high water line. The trial court also held that the public was entitled to limited vertical access to the ocean, consisting of a path from the bulkhead through the dunes on the property. . . .

---

[5] Seapointe Village Association and the Lower Township Police Department are no longer parties to this litigation. The DEP is the state entity with regulatory responsibility in this matter.

Atlantis was prohibited from charging a fee or otherwise restricting the right of the public to horizontal or vertical ocean access. The court determined, however, that the provision of such services as lifeguards, equipment, or other facilities by Atlantis would entitle the Beach Club, on application to and with the DEP's approval, to charge a commercially reasonable fee to members of the public who use the horizontal access to swim in the ocean. The court denied without prejudice the Atlantis application to amend its pleadings so as to assert a regulatory takings claim.

The State and the Association appealed. . . . On June 3, 2004, the Appellate Division issued its opinion. *Raleigh Ave. Beach Ass'n v. Atlantis Beach Club, Inc.,* 370 *N.J. Super.* 171, 851 *A.*2d 19 (2004). The court reaffirmed the central premise of its Order that "Atlantis cannot limit vertical or horizontal public access to its dry sand beach area nor interfere with the public's right to free use of the dry sand for intermittent recreational purposes connected with the ocean and wet sand." *Id.* at 176, 851 *A.*2d 19. As permitted under the Order, Atlantis could charge a fee to members of the public who remain on and use its beach for an extended period of time, as long as Atlantis cleans the beach, picks up trash regularly, and provides shower facilities. *Ibid.* The panel ruled further that Atlantis was required to provide customary lifeguard services for members of the public who use the ocean areas up to the mean high water line, regardless of whether those individuals remain on the Atlantis beach area or merely pass through. *Ibid.* Reasonable and comparable fees, approved by the DEP, would be allowed in an amount sufficient to cover operating costs, including an amount related to management services. *Ibid.* The court remanded to the DEP the issue of the appropriate fee to be charged for beach use, ordering the Department to approve a fee schedule by June 10, 2004, so as not to unduly interfere with the beach season beginning June 15, 2004. *Id.* at 194, 851 *A.*2d 19. . . .

At oral argument before us, counsel for Atlantis conceded vertical access to the ocean by the public from the boardwalk pathway at the terminus of Raleigh Avenue, over the bulkhead and the dunes and across the dry sand area to the ocean. Atlantis maintained its position that persons who are not members of the Beach Club may only walk along the three feet of dry sand that lie landward of the mean high water line, as so held by the trial court, and may not use the dry sand beach beyond that horizontal three-foot strip of sand.

III.

The law we are asked to interpret in this case—the public trust doctrine—derives from the English common law principle that all of the land covered by tidal waters belongs to the sovereign held in trust for the people to use. *Borough of Neptune City v. Borough of Avon-by-the-Sea,* 61 *N.J.* 296, 303, 294 *A.*2d 47 (1972). That common law principle, in turn, has roots

in Roman jurisprudence, which held that "[b]y the law of nature[,] . . . the air, running water, the sea, and consequently the shores of the sea," were "common to mankind." . . . No one was forbidden access to the sea, and everyone could use the seashore "to dry his nets there, and haul them from the sea . . . ." The seashore was not private property, but "subject to the same law as the sea itself, and the sand or ground beneath it."

[*Matthews, supra,* 95 *N.J.* at 316-17, 471 *A.*2d 355 (citations and footnote omitted).]

In *Arnold v. Mundy,* 6 *N.J.L.* 1, 53 (*E. & A.* 1821), the first case to affirm and reformulate the public trust doctrine in New Jersey, the Court explained that upon the Colonies' victory in the Revolutionary War, the English sovereign's rights to the tidal waters "became vested in the people of New Jersey as the sovereign of the country, and are now in their hands." *Arnold, supra,* addressed the plaintiff's claim to an oyster bed in the Raritan River adjacent to his farm in Perth Amboy. *Id.* at 45. Chief Justice Kirkpatrick found that the land on which water ebbs and flows, including the land between the high and low water, belongs not to the owners of the lands adjacent to the water, but to the State, "to be held, protected, and regulated for the common use and benefit." *Id.* at 49, 71.

Early understanding of the scope of the public trust doctrine focused on the preservation of the "natural water resources" of New Jersey "for navigation and commerce . . . and fishing, an important source of food." *Neptune City, supra,* 61 *N.J.* at 304, 294 *A.*2d 47. In *Neptune City, supra,* the Court extended public rights in tidal lands "to recreational uses, including bathing, swimming and other shore activities." *Id.* at 309, 294 *A.*2d 47. We invalidated a municipal ordinance that required non-residents of Avon-by-the-Sea to pay a higher fee than the residents of Avon were required to pay to access and use the town's beaches. *Id.* at 310, 294 *A.*2d 47. The Court held:

[A]t least where the upland sand area is owned by a municipality . . . and dedicated to public beach purposes, a modern court must take the view that the public trust doctrine dictates that the beach and the ocean waters must be open to all on equal terms and without preference and that any contrary state or municipal action is impermissible.

[*Id.* at 308-09, 294 *A.*2d 47.]

Later, in *Matthews, supra,* we considered "the extent of the public's interest in privately-owned dry sand beaches," which, we noted, "may [include both] a right to cross [such] privately owned . . . beaches in order to gain access to the foreshore . . . [and a] right to sunbathe and generally enjoy recreational activities" on the dry sands. 95 *N.J.* at 322-23, 471 *A.*2d 355. We observed that New Jersey's beaches constitute a "unique" and "irreplaceable" resource, subject to increased pressure from population growth throughout the region and improved transportation to the shore. *Id.* at 323, 471 *A.*2d 355. Concerned about the great demand and the limited number of beaches open to the public, we repeated:

Exercise of the public's right to swim and bathe below the mean high water mark may depend upon a right to pass across the upland beach. Without some means of access the public right to use the foreshore would be meaningless. To say that the public trust doctrine entitles the public to swim in the ocean and to use the foreshore in connection therewith without assuring the public of a feasible access route would seriously impinge on, if not effectively eliminate, the rights of the public trust doctrine.

[*Id.* at 323-24, 471 *A.*2d 355.]

Matthews clearly articulates the concept already implicit in our case law that reasonable access to the sea is integral to the public trust doctrine. Indeed, as *Matthews, supra,* points out, without access the doctrine has no meaning. *Id.* at 323, 471 *A.*2d 355.

That leaves the question raised in this case: whether use of the dry sand ancillary to use of the ocean for recreation purposes is also implicit in the rights that belong to the public under the doctrine. *Matthews, supra,* states unequivocally that a "bather's right in the upland sands is not limited to passage . . . [and that] [r]easonable enjoyment of the foreshore and the sea cannot be realized unless some enjoyment of the dry sand area is also allowed." *Id.* at 325, 471 *A.*2d 355. Because the activity of swimming "must be accompanied by intermittent periods of rest and relaxation beyond the water's edge," the lack of an area available to the public for that purpose "would seriously curtail and in many situations eliminate the right to the recreational use of the ocean." *Ibid.* Although the *Matthews* Court did not compare that use of the dry sand to use associated with ancient fishing rights, it did point out that under Roman law, "everyone could use the seashore 'to dry his nets there, and haul them from the sea . . . .' " *Id.* at 317, 471 *A.*2d 355 (quoting Justinian *Institutes* 2.1.1) (T. Sandars trans. 1st Am. ed. 1876) (footnote omitted). It follows, then, that use of the dry sand has long been a correlate to use of the ocean and is a component part of the rights associated with the public trust doctrine.

The factual context in which *Matthews* was decided was critical to the Court's holding. *Neptune City, supra,* had held that the general public must be allowed to use a municipally-owned dry sand beach on equal terms with residents of the municipality. 61 *N.J.* at 310, 294 *A.*2d 47; *see Van Ness v. Borough of Deal,* 78 *N.J.* 174, 179-80, 393 *A.*2d 571 (1978) (holding that a municipality could not limit public use of municipal beach to fifty-foot strip along high water line when Deal residents and property owners were permitted to use entire beach area). *Matthews, supra,* involved a private non-profit entity, the Bay Head Improvement Association (Improvement Association), that owned/leased and operated certain upland sand areas in the Borough of Bay Head for the recreational use of Bay Head residents only. 95 *N.J.* at 314-15, 471 *A.*2d 355. The Improvement Association was closely connected with the municipality, which provided at various points in time, office space, liability insurance, and funding, among other things. *Id.* at 330, 471 *A.*2d 355. That symbiotic relationship, as well as the public nature of the activities conducted by the Improvement Association, led the Court to conclude that the Improvement Association was in reality a "quasi-public body" bound by the *Neptune City* holding. *Id.* at 328, 329, 471 *A.*2d 355.

Although decided on narrow grounds, *Matthews* established the framework for application of the public trust doctrine to privately-owned upland sand beaches. The *Matthews* approach begins with the general principle that public use of the upland sands is "subject to an accommodation of the interests of the owner," and proceeds by setting forth criteria for a case-by-case consideration in respect of the appropriate level of accommodation. *Id.* at 325-26, 471 *A.*2d 355. The Court's formulation bears repeating here:

> Archaic judicial responses are not an answer to a modern social problem. Rather, we perceive the public trust doctrine not to be "fixed or static," but one to "be molded and extended to meet changing conditions and needs of the public it was created to benefit." . . . .
>
> Precisely what privately-owned upland sand area will be available and required to satisfy the public's rights under the public trust doctrine will depend on the circumstances. Location of the dry sand area in relation to the foreshore, extent and availability of publicly-owned upland sand area, nature and extent of the public demand, and usage of the upland sand land by the owner are all factors to be weighed and considered in fixing the contours of the usage of the upper sand.
>
> Today, recognizing the increasing demand for our State's beaches and the dynamic nature of the public trust doctrine, we find that the public must be given both access to and use of privately-owned dry sand areas as reasonably necessary. While the public's rights in private beaches are not coextensive with the rights enjoyed in municipal beaches, private landowners may not in all instances prevent the public from exercising its rights under the public trust doctrine. The public must be afforded reasonable access to the foreshore as well as a suitable area for recreation on the dry sand.

[*Id.* at 326, 471 *A.*2d 355 (citations omitted).]

IV.

We turn now to an application of the *Matthews* factors to the circumstances of this case in order to determine "what privately-owned upland sand area will be available and required to satisfy the public's rights under the public trust doctrine." *Ibid.*

"Location of the Dry Sand Area in Relation to the Foreshore"

The dry sand beach at the center of this controversy extends horizontally 480 feet from the Coast Guard property south of Atlantis to the Seapointe property north of Atlantis, and vertically, from three feet landward of the mean high water line about 339 feet to the dunes adjacent to the bulkhead and the Raleigh Avenue extension. It is easily reached by pedestrians using the path bisecting the Raleigh Avenue extension from the end of the paved roadway to the bulkhead.

"[E]xtent and Availability of Publicly-Owned Upland Sand Area":

There is no publicly-owned beach area in Lower Township, although it was represented to us at oral argument that there are public beaches in the "Wildwoods" north of Lower Township. The Borough of Wildwood Crest, immediately north of Lower Township, owns dry sand beach that is used by the public. Seapointe, a private entity, as required by its 1987 CAFRA permit, has made its upland sands available to the public for a "reasonable" fee, approved by the DEP at a level comparable to fees charged by nearby town beaches (in 1987, Cape May City, Avalon, and Stone Harbor beaches). The Coast Guard beach to the south of Atlantis is closed to the public for the better part of the summer season (April 1 through August 15) to protect the endangered piping plover.

"[N]ature and Extent of the Public Demand":

The Diamond Beach section of Lower Township is not large (three blocks by nine blocks), and parking is limited but available along the area streets. Local residents whose homes are within easy walking distance of Atlantis are members of the plaintiff Association, through which they have expressed their individual concerns about access and use. That there is enormous public interest in the New Jersey shore is well-known; tourism associated with New Jersey's beaches is a $16 billion annual industry.

"[U]sage of the Upland Sand Land by the Owner":

The more or less rectangular area of dry sand that constitutes the Atlantis beach has been closed to non-members of Atlantis from the summer of 1996 to May 4, 2004. On May 4, the Appellate Division required open access and use by the public to the entirety of the beach area and permitted reasonable and comparable fees to be approved by the DEP on application by Atlantis. As for the period prior to 1996, the general public used the beach without limitation or fee during the ten years between 1986 and 1996 and, it appears, enjoyed the same open access and use prior to 1986 (although the record is sparse on the issue of prior use). The La Vida condominiums, situated directly to the west of Atlantis, were constructed in 1986. By the La Vida CAFRA permit, the developer/owner accepted as binding a condition on development making the homeowner's association responsible for public access "to the beach," with adequate signage, for the life of the condominium project. The permit describes the relationship between the La Vida site and the beach as follows:

> The site is adjacent, and provides access points for residents *and the public to the ocean beach,* which is about 220′ in width at the site. The proposed development will have minimal impact on the beach, but as required under the policy on Dunes (7:7E-3.21), the remaining dunes must be reconstructed, replanted, and maintained. Provided an acceptable plan is submitted and implemented for dune enhancement and management, and provided walkovers to the beach are provided as discussed under the policies on Dunes (3.21) and Public Access to the Waterfront (8.11), and as required by conditions of this permit, this policy is met.

[Emphasis added.]

Although the permit language is not without ambiguity, and the record is not clear in respect of the relationship between the developer/owner of La Vida and the owner of Atlantis, *see supra* at 43 n. 1, 879 *A*.2d at 114 n. 1, it may be inferred from this section of the permit that open access and use was ceded to the public by La Vida. Most telling, the permit describes access to a 220-foot strip of upland sand beach, not the foreshore. It is difficult to imagine that the DEP (or La Vida) anticipated anything other than public use of that area. That argument has not been made by any party, however; we, therefore, will not here consider the permit dispositive on the issue of public use. Suffice it to say that the Atlantis beach was used by the public for many years and that public access and, arguably, public use of 220 feet of ocean beach had been required as a condition of a CAFRA development permit.

From the summer of 1996 to May 4, 2004, Atlantis charged unregulated membership fees in varying amounts for access to and use of its beach. During the 2003 season, new members (and members who joined in 2002) paid $700 and received eight beach tags per household. In violation of the La Vida CAFRA permit, in the summer of 2003 Atlantis removed the public beach access sign at the western end of the Raleigh Avenue pathway extension and replaced it with a sign that read "FREE ACCESS TO GATE ONLY." The gate was located at the end of the pathway at the bulkhead. Later that summer, contradictory signs at the gate read "PUBLIC BEACH ACCESS" and "PUBLIC ACCESS ENDS HERE/MEMBERSHIP AVAILABLE AT GATE." The La Vida permit, however, required

> a landscaped public access pathway from the project site entrance down the center of Raleigh Avenue, and, according to the EIS and original site plan, a timber walkway over the bulkhead to the beach.

The permit stated:

> Although this accessway is minimal, it is considered adequate due to the small scale of this project. Public parking has not been lost at this site . . . and on-street parking is available to the public on surrounding roads. The proposed pathway and walkover will provide reasonable access to the beach, provided public access signs (available from the [DEP]) are conspicuously located at the end of Raleigh Avenue pavement. Therefore, as a condition of this permit, within 30 days of issuance, submit for review and approval a site plan specifically showing the proposed location and detail of the public walkover structure, and the proposed location of public access signage (a 1′ x 2′ metal sign available from the [DEP] on a standard metal signpost supplied by applicant), and construct the accessway improvements in accordance with the approved plan prior to occupancy of the structure. Maintenance and/ or reconstruction of this walkway shall be the responsibility of the Homeowner's Association for the life of this project.

On the one hand, guards hired by Atlantis have asked non-members to leave the beach, and violators have been prosecuted by Atlantis in municipal court. On the other hand, the DEP has issued notices of violation both to La Vida and to Atlantis because of the signage infractions, because a section of the dunes was destroyed by the Beach Club, and because structures were erected on the beach without CAFRA approval.

The private beach property held by Atlantis is an area of undeveloped upland sand and dunes at the end of a street in a town that does not have public beaches. The owner, after years of public access and use, and despite a condition in the La Vida permit providing for access and, arguably use, decided in 1996 to engage in a commercial enterprise—a private beach club—that kept the public from the beach. Atlantis recognizes that as a "place of public accommodation," *N.J.S.A.* 10:5-5l, under the Law Against Discrimination, *N.J.S.A.* 10:5-1 to -42, it must provide membership opportunities to the general public without regard to race, creed, or color, *Clover Hill Swimming Club v. Goldsboro,* 47 *N.J.* 25, 33-35, 219 *A.*2d 161 (1966). *See N.J.A.C.* 7:7E-8:11(b)(5) (requiring "establishments . . . [that] control access to tidal waters [to] comply with the Law Against Discrimination"). The Beach Club nonetheless asserts that it will lose one of the "sticks" in its bundle of property rights if it cannot charge whatever the market will bear, and, in setting fees for membership, decide who can come onto its property and use its beach and other services (lifeguards, trash removal, organized activities, etc.). But exclusivity of use, in the context here, has long been subject to the strictures of the public trust doctrine.

In sum, based on the circumstances in this case and on application of the *Matthews* factors, we hold that the Atlantis upland sands must be available for use by the general public under the public trust doctrine. In so holding we highlight the longstanding public access to and use of the beach, the La Vida CAFRA permit condition, the documented public demand, the lack of publicly-owned beaches in Lower Township, and the type of use by the current owner as a business enterprise. We also adopt the construct put forward by the Appellate Division in connection with an appropriate fee structure for use of the beach by the public. That issue, however, requires further discussion.

V. . . .

VI.

For the reasons expressed in this opinion, the decision of the Appellate Division is affirmed.

Justice WALLACE, JR., dissenting.

I would reverse and reinstate the judgment of the trial court granting access to the ocean and an easement across the private sand area owned by the Atlantic Beach Club to access the beach at Seapointe. However, because a three-foot-wide strip would not easily allow for an adult and child to walk within that limited area, I would expand the horizontal access across defendant's property to a ten-foot-wide strip above the high water mark.

I.

As the majority opinion makes clear, this Court has not previously defined the rights that the public has to privately-owned beaches. Because "it has been long established that the individual States have the authority to define the limits of the lands held in public trust and to recognize private rights in such lands as they see fit[,]" *Phillips Petroleum Co. v. Mississippi,* 484 *U.S.* 469, 475, 108 *S.Ct.* 791, 794-95, 98 *L.Ed.*2d 877 (1988), the lands subject to the public trust doctrine are to be determined by each State.

> New Jersey was the first state to recognize and apply the public trust doctrine:
> The public trust doctrine is the legal principle that the submerged lands and waters below mean highwater mark are owned by the state government in trust for public uses such as transportation and fishing. In 1821 the New Jersey Supreme Court was the first in the United States to verify its application in the New World, in *Arnold v. Mundy* [, 6 *N.J.L.* 1 (1821)]; in 1842 the U.S. Supreme Court reaffirmed that court's ruling in *Martin v. Waddell*[*'s Lessee,* 41 *U.S.* 367, 16 *Pet.* 367, 10 *L.Ed.* 997 (1842)]. Both came about because of conflicts over rights to oyster grounds in the Raritan River and Bay. . . . The outcome was recognition of the state's ownership as trustee for the people of the state. Subsequently, the doctrine has played important roles in waterfront development, uses and management of . . . wetlands, and public access to riverfronts and beaches.

[*Encyclopedia of New Jersey* 665-66 (Maxine N. Lurie & Marc Mappen eds., 2004).] . . . .

This case requires us to apply the *Matthews* test in evaluating the competing interests of the public to reasonable access and use of the ocean and dry beach against the interests of the private landowner to use and enjoy its land. The first factor of the *Matthews* test, the location of the dry sand area in relation to the foreshore, weighs in favor of plaintiff. The dry sand area of the Beach Club is directly adjacent to the wet sand and ocean and there are no barriers or structures creating any division between the two areas. Further, there is no direct access to the water except over the Beach Club property. In fact, defendant concedes that access to the ocean may be over its privately-owned property, and that the public has the right to use its property "at and below the mean high water line."

The second factor, the extent and availability of publicly-owned upland sand area, weighs in favor of defendant. The evidence shows that Seapointe is adjacent to the Beach Club and that Seapointe allows the public access and use of its beach. Thus, there is a beach in close proximity to the Beach Club that will permit the public to enjoy the beach without interfering with the rights of a private beach owner.

The third factor, the nature and extent of public demand, weighs in favor of plaintiff, at least with regard to access. There are a large number of multi-story condominium buildings in the Diamond Beach neighborhood adjacent to the Beach Club property that were constructed on land sold to the developers by one of defendant's principals. The numerous residents of those buildings seek to use the ocean. Thus, there is a public demand for reasonable access across the Beach Club's private property.

The final factor is the usage of the upland sand by the owner. Defendant uses its beach as a private-for-profit beach club, and offers two types of memberships, an annual membership and a lifetime easement. In 2003, the annual membership fee was $700 and the lifetime easement fee was $10,000. Defendant provides its members with security, beach maintenance, lifeguards, and some recreational activities. The only improvement on the land is the boardwalk. Therefore, I find that this factor weighs in favor of defendant. . . .

In balancing the above factors, it is obvious that the greater weight favors access to the ocean and the use of the water below the mean high water mark. Defendant recognizes and concedes that plaintiff has a right of access over its land and the use of the ocean. However, because there is an adjacent beach to defendant's private property that is available to the public, I find no need to apply the public trust doctrine beyond access to the ocean and access to a reasonable area across defendant's property to the adjacent Seapointe. In my view, that strikes a proper balance between the public trust doctrine, which requires reasonable access and use of the ocean and beaches, and a private owner's right to use its private property as it deems fit. The record here amply supports the conclusion that access to the water and to Seapointe over defendant's privately-owned beachfront will reasonably satisfy the public need at this time. I see no justification to exceed that minor intrusion.

II.

I agree with the position of the State before the trial court that the three-foot access across defendant's land to Seapointe was insufficient and that the public was entitled to unrestricted use of a reasonable area of dry sand, "which [the State] considers to be an area at least 10 feet wide above the mean high water line." In my view, ten feet is a reasonable area for a family to safely traverse defendant's property to reach Seapointe without excessively impinging on defendant's property rights. Moreover, for those members of the public who elect to use the beach and ocean at that location, the ten-foot area will also give them limited use of the beach. Under the circumstances of this case, that is the only reasonable accommodation that we should require to enforce the public trust doctrine.

NOTES

1. *Constitutional Issues.* If the legislature enacted a law that gave the public an easement over previously private property without compensating the property owners, that law would be a clear violation of the Fifth Amendment's Just Compensation Clause. If the judiciary does the same thing, the constitutional issues are far murkier. We will consider these issues in depth in our chapter on Takings.

2. *Further Reading.* For further information on the New Jersey beachfront cases, *see* Timothy M. Mulvaney & Brian Weeks, *"Waterlocked": Public Access to New Jersey's Coastline,* 34 Ecology L.Q. 579 (2007); Marc R. Poirier, *Modified Private Property: New Jersey's Public Trust Doctrine, Private Development and Exclusion, and Shared Public Uses of Natural Resources,* 15 Southeastern Envtl. L.J. 71 (2006). For further information on the history and modern scope of the public trust doctrine, *see* Alexandra B. Klass, *Modern Public Trust Principles: Recognizing Rights and Integrating Standards,* 82 Notre Dame L. Rev. 699 (2006); Carol Necole Brown, *Drinking from a Deep Well: The Public Trust Doctrine and Western Water Law,* 34 Fla. St. U. L. Rev. 1 (2006); Joseph D. Kearney & Thomas W. Merrill, *The Origins of the Public Trust Doctrine: What Really Happened in Illinois Central,* 71 U. Chi. L. Rev. 799 (2004).

6. NEGATIVE EASEMENTS

All of the easements that we have discussed so far are positive easements—they allow the owner of the dominant parcel to do something on the servient parcel. A negative easement would allow the owner of the dominant parcel to prohibit the owner of the servient parcel from doing something.

Negative easements are rare in our legal system because of an accident of history. With four small exceptions, English common law did not allow negative easements. The four exceptions were for easements that prevented a neighboring landowner from (a) blocking windows in a building, (b) blocking well-defined flows of air, (c) interfering with water flow in canals and other human-made channels, and (d) removing lateral support for a wall or foundation. As a result, when we want to impose a negative restriction on property in our legal system, we typically use a covenant that runs with the land. We discuss these covenants in the next section.

There is one category of negative easement that is common in our legal system. A *conservation easement* is an easement that places restrictions on the development of the servient parcel. As their name implies, conservation easements are designed to conserve land by prohibiting or restricting the development of that land. The benefit of a conservation easement typically is held by a land trust or other non-for-profit conservation entity. A close cousin of a conservation easement is an *agricultural easement,* which restricts the use of the servient parcel to agricultural uses. Because of the common-law prohibition on negative easements, conservation easements are the product of statutes. Many states have enacted the Uniform Conservation Easements Act promulgated by the Uniform Law Commission.

Conservation easements have presented a number of problems and controversies. First, although conservation of a parcel of property might be a good thing in the abstract, it might create some problems in practice. The decision to impose a conservation easement on a parcel of land tends to be a private decision made by an individual. Because there is little coordination or oversight, imposing a conservation easement on a parcel of property might or might not fit into the larger community's conservation needs. Indeed, placing a conservation easement on an unremarkable piece of land might put higher development pressure on other land that would be better to preserve.

Second, conservation easements typically are perpetual. To see why this is a problem, imagine someone in colonial America making land use decisions that would bind us 200 years later. Think about how much the world has changed in the past 200 years. The world may change even more radically in the next 200 years. In this context, does it make sense to allow private landowners to make decisions about conserving land that will be binding in perpetuity? On the other hand, our conception of conservation tends to include an idea of permanence. This issue has generated a tremendous amount of scholarly discussion in recent years. *See, e.g.*, Jessica Owley, *Changing Property in a Changing World: A Call for the End of Perpetual Conservation Easements*, 30 Stan. Envtl. L.J. 121 (2011); Sarah Harding, *Perpetual Property*, 61 Fla. L. Rev. 285 (2009); Nancy A. McLaughlin, *Conservation Easements: Perpetuity and Beyond*, 34 Ecology L.Q. 673 (2007); Gerald Korngold, *Solving the Contentious Issues of Conservation Easements: Promoting for the Future and Engaging in the Public Land Use Process*, 2007 Utah L. Rev. 1039; Susan French, *Perpetual Trusts, Conservation Servitudes, and the Problem of the Future*, 27 Cardozo L. Rev. 2523 (2006); Julia D. Mahoney, *The Illusion of Perpetuity and the Preservation of Privately Owned Lands*, 44 Nat. Resources J. 573 (2004); Barton H. Thompson, *The Trouble with Time: Influencing the Conservation Choices of Future Generations*, 44 Nat. Resources J. 601 (2004).

Third, a person who creates a conservation easement in property typically is entitled to a federal income tax deduction. As with many types of tax deductions, the deduction for conservation easements is ripe for abuse. For example, the person creating the conservation easement might overstate the easement's value. Or a person might create a conservation easement on land not worth preserving in order to gain the tax deduction. *See* Timothy Lindstrom, *Income Tax Aspects of Conservation Easements*, 5 Wyoming L. Rev. 1 (2005).

C. COVENANTS THAT RUN WITH THE LAND

As we mentioned in the introduction to this chapter, covenants that run with the land are promises that bind both present and future owners of the property. Say that you and I are neighbors, and we want to agree that each of us will paint our houses red and no other color. If we want to bind each other, we only need the law of contracts—we can make a contract that we will paint our houses red and no other color. If we want to bind subsequent owners of our property, though, we need the law of property. If we create covenants that run with the land that apply to both of our houses, subsequent owners will be bound by the promise to keep the houses painted red.

Covenants that run with the land can be enforced in law as real covenants and in equity as equitable servitudes. Real covenants and equitable servitudes are interests in property. We often speak in terms of a property owner having the benefit of a real covenant or an equitable servitude in the same way that we would speak in terms of a property owner having the benefit of an easement.

We think that it is easiest to learn about covenants that run with the land if we conceptualize them as promises intended to run with the land that property owners make to each other that may be enforceable in law as a real covenant or in equity as an equitable servitude. The same promise may be (and, indeed, often is) enforceable against subsequent owners as both a real covenant and as an equitable servitude.

As we will see, real covenants and equitable servitudes have slightly different elements for their creation. Once they are created, the only difference between the two is the remedy that the holder of the benefit can get from the holder of the burden for breach. Recall that real covenants are promises that run with the land at law.

LAW AND EQUITY

REMEDIES

If the covenant is enforceable as a real covenant, the holder of the benefit can get the legal remedy of money damages. Equitable servitudes are promises that run with the land in equity. If the covenant is enforceable as an equitable servitude, then the holder of the benefit can get equitable remedies, including an injunction, for breach. Returning to our red house example, if I paint my house bright yellow, I will be in breach of our covenant. If you want to sue me for money damages for breach, you need to show that our covenant met all the requirements of a real covenant. If you want to get an injunction against me, you need to show that our covenant met all of the requirements of an equitable servitude.

Recall that you and I could bind ourselves to the red house promise simply by using the law of contracts. If we want to bind subsequent owners, we need the promise to run with the land. Consider this diagram:

Owner of parcel A   Owner of parcel B
(Promisor)   Promise   (Promisee)
(Burden)   ⟶   (Benefit)

The owner of parcel A promises the owner of parcel B that she, and all subsequent owners of parcel A, will never paint the house on parcel A any color other than red. Parcel A has the burden of this promise. Parcel B has the benefit of this promise. Often, as in our example, the owners of the parcels will make reciprocal promises. If the owner of parcel B makes the reciprocal promise intended to run with the land that the house on parcel B will never be painted any color other than red, we would simply substitute parcels A and B in the diagram—parcel B would have the burden, and parcel A would have the benefit. For now, however, we will focus only on the promise made by the owner of parcel A. Parcel A has the burden, and parcel B has the benefit.

Let's move forward a few years. Both parcel A and parcel B have been sold to new owners. Say that the subsequent owner of parcel A paints the house blue, violating the covenant. If the subsequent owner of parcel B wants to enforce the promise against the subsequent owner of parcel A, two things need to have happened. First, the burden of the promise must have run with the land to the subsequent owner of parcel A. Second, the benefit of the promise must have run with the land to the subsequent owner of parcel B.

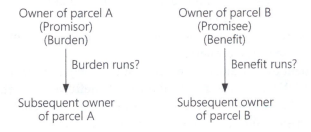

As we will see, the requirements for the benefit to run with the land are a bit more relaxed than the requirements for the burden to run with the land. This difference might make some intuitive sense—we might worry a lot about burdening subsequent owners of a parcel but not worry so much about giving subsequent owners the benefit of the covenant. As a practical matter, however, the distinction between the benefit and the burden running would only matter if the parcel with the burden remained with the original promisor and only the parcel with the benefit had been transferred to a subsequent owner. If both parcels have been transferred, the more stringent requirements for the burden running with the land will control the enforceability of the covenant. Put another way, if the burdened property has transferred to a subsequent owner, it doesn't matter much if the benefit has run with the land if the burden has not also run with the land.

Most of the elements of real covenants and equitable servitudes are the same:

1. The promise must be in *writing* and satisfy the Statute of Frauds to be enforced as both a real covenant and an equitable servitude. There is only one exception, which we have already seen. An equitable servitude may sometimes be implied in the context of the common grantor problem that we discussed in the last chapter in our materials on recording. As we previously discussed, that problem arises when a common grantor neglects to include a covenant in a parcel that is part of a larger planned development where all the parcels were supposed to have the covenant put in place. In this circumstance, a court might enforce an equitable servitude. Beyond this exception, a promise must be in writing to be enforced as a covenant that runs with the land in either law or equity.

2. The parties must *intend the promise to run with the land*. In other words, the parties must intend subsequent owners of the burdened parcel to be bound by the burden, and subsequent owner of the benefited parcel to be able to enforce the benefit. The intent to run with the land should be reflected in language written in the covenant that makes it clear that it is intended to bind future owners of the burdened parcel and to be enforced by future owners of the benefited parcel.

3. The promise must *touch and concern* the land. We will have more to say about this element below. For now, it is enough to know that this element clearly is met if the promise has to do with the occupancy, use, or enjoyment of the property. Our red house promise would meet this requirement because it concerns our use of the property.

4. The subsequent owner must have *notice* of the covenant for the burden to run with the land. Notice is not required for the benefit to run with the land. The notice distinction between the burden running and the benefit running makes perfect sense—if you buy a home burdened by an enforceable covenant, then you are bound to follow that covenant, where if you buy a home with the benefit of a covenant, that covenant will not bind your actions and you can choose whether or not to exercise the benefit and enforce the covenant. The notice requirement has common-law origins. Today, in most circumstances, notice will be a recording issue. Covenants should always be recorded, and, if they are recorded, the notice requirement will be met for the reasons we discussed in the previous chapter. Further, an unrecorded covenant might be unenforceable against a subsequent owner without notice on recording principles.

So far, the elements of enforcing a promise as a real covenant and an equitable servitude are essentially the same. The only exception is that covenants sometimes may be implied in equity and enforced as equitable servitudes in the common grantor scenario. Covenants will not be implied in law and enforced as real covenants in that scenario.

The four elements that we have discussed so far—writing, intent to run with the land, touch and concern, and notice—are the only required elements of enforcing a covenant as an equitable servitude. Real covenants have a fifth element:

Fifth, there must be *privity* for a promise to be enforced in law as a real covenant. There are two different types of privity—*vertical privity and horizontal privity*. Most, if not all, jurisdictions require vertical privity. Far fewer jurisdictions require horizontal privity.

To understand the difference between horizontal privity and vertical privity, let's return to our diagram:

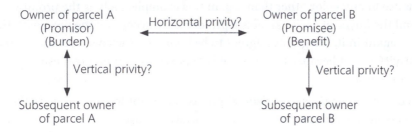

The names "horizontal privity" and "vertical privity" come from this diagram. Let's start with vertical privity, which is the easier of the two and makes the most sense. In this context, we are talking about privity of estate. Two people are in privity of estate if they are on opposite sides of a real estate transaction. Look at the transfer of parcel A from the original promisor to the subsequent owner of parcel A. In any voluntary real estate transaction (whether a sale or a gift), the original promisor and the subsequent owner will be in privity of estate because they are on opposite sides of a real estate transaction. We call this vertical privity because it relates to the vertical (i.e., up and down) axis of our diagram. Vertical privity will be met in almost all scenarios. It may not be met in an adverse possession scenario, where there is not a voluntary transfer of ownership and possession between the original owner and the subsequent owner.

Horizontal privity is much less intuitive. Horizontal privity relates to the horizontal axis of the diagram. In jurisdictions that impose the horizontal privity requirement, the original promisor and the original promisee must be in privity at the time they made the promise. The promisor and the promisee are in privity of contract because they are on opposite sides of a contract. In this context, however, we are concerned with privity of estate because we are considering whether the promise runs with the land to subsequent owners of the property as a matter of property law. Hence, for the horizontal privity requirement to be met, *the promisor and the promisee must be in privity of estate when the promise is made.* In other words, the promisor and the promisee must make the promise as part of a real estate transaction that is separate and independent of the effort to create a covenant that runs with the land. Consider these two examples:

> **EXAMPLE:** The owner of parcel A makes a promise to the owner of parcel B that is intended to run with the land that neither she nor any subsequent owner of parcel A will paint the house on parcel A any color other than red. The owners of parcel A and parcel B make this promise independent of any real estate transaction. The horizontal privity requirement is not met.

EXAMPLE: Sally owns a piece of land. She divides the land into multiple parcels. The deed to each parcel includes a covenant is intended to run with the land that states that each owner of each parcel will not paint their house in any color other than red. In this example, Sally is the promisee, and the buyer of each parcel is a promisor. By accepting the deed with the covenant in it, the grantee agrees to be bound by the covenant. Horizontal privity is met because the promise is imposed as part of a real estate transaction.

As the second example shows, horizontal privity tends not to be an issue in the subdivision context because covenants are typically imposed when the land is divided into smaller parcels. In most other scenarios, though, horizontal privity is likely to be a problem. If you and I are neighbors, and we already own our homes, then any promise between us intended to run with the land is unlikely to be made as part of a real estate transaction.

> The promises enforced as covenants that run with the land can be both positive (a promise to do an act) and negative (a promise not to do an act).

The horizontal privity requirement is an unfortunate relic of the Restatement (First) of Property and makes very little sense. Some U.S. jurisdictions require horizontal privity for a covenant to run with the land at law. Others do not. The law on this point can be confused even within a given jurisdiction.

Recall that the key difference between enforcing a promise as a real covenant and as an equitable servitude is the remedy. If the promise can be enforced as a real covenant, the remedy is money damages. If the promise can be enforced as an equitable servitude, equitable remedies including an injunction are available.

The table on page 637 shows a summary of the elements of real covenants and equitable servitudes. Note that the biggest differences between real covenants and equitable servitudes are (a) the available remedies and (b) the lack of a privity requirement (both horizontal and vertical) for equitable servitudes.

The best way to learn these requirements is to apply them. We provide a problem set below. Before we get to the problems, however, we need to say a bit more about the touch and concern requirement.

As we noted above, the promises in covenants that run with the land must touch and concern the land. Broadly speaking, the touch and concern element clearly will be met if the promise has to do with the occupancy, use, or enjoyment of the property. Here are some examples of promises that clearly touch and concern the land:

- A promise to only paint a house red.
- A promise not to paint a house red.
- A promise to only build a brick house.

	REAL COVENANT	EQUITABLE SERVITUDE
Writing	Required	Required. Possible exception: Common Grantor Scenario
Intent to Run With Land	Required	Required
Touch and Concern	Required	Required
Notice	Required for Burden to Run. Not required for Benefit to Run.	Required for Burden to Run. Not required for Benefit to Run.
Horizontal Privity	Required in some U.S. jurisdictions. Not required in other U.S. jurisdictions.	Not Required
Vertical Privity	Required	Not Required
Remedy	Legal remedy—Money Damages	Equitable remedies, including injunction

- A promise to build a two-story house.
- A promise that the house will be set back 50 feet from the street.
- A promise not to have a garden shed on the property.
- A promise not to have a satellite dish on the property.
- A promise to use the property only for single-family residential use.
- A promise to use the property only for a commercial use.
- A promise not to allow the grass on the lawn to get taller than six inches.
- A promise not to fly a flag outside of the house.
- A promise to fly a flag outside of the house.

Today, many people live in subdivisions that are governed by a homeowners' association consistent with a set of recorded covenants. We will discuss this type of community, called a *common interest community*, further below. For now, it is important to know that many homeowners' associations are funded by dues paid by homeowners and that the obligation to pay these dues is included in the covenants.

For some years, courts struggled with the question of whether an obligation to pay money to a homeowners' association touched and concerned the land. In the homeowners' association context, the law is now clear that these covenants do meet the touch and concern requirement and are enforceable.

Outside of the homeowners' association context, however, courts may still have touch and concern problems with a promise to pay money or another type of economic promise that does not have to do with the occupancy, use, and enjoyment of the land.

If a promise does not touch and concern the land, it is deemed a personal promise and does not run with the land. In our next case, the court considers whether a promise not to make a monetary claim for contribution for environmental cleanup from the prior owner touches and concerns the land.

EL PASO REFINERY, LP V. TRMI HOLDINGS, INC.

United States Court of Appeals for the Fifth Circuit, 2002
302 F.3d 343

EMILIO M. GARZA, Circuit Judge:

This appeal arises out of an attempt to allocate the contractual liability for environmental contamination among the past and present owners of an oil refinery in El Paso, Texas (the "Refinery"). The Appellee, Refinery Holding Company, L.P. ("RHC") is the current owner of the Refinery. The Appellants are former owners of the Refinery and include Andrew B. Krafsur, in his capacity as Chapter 7 Trustee (the "Trustee") for the bankruptcy estate of El Paso Refinery, L.P. (the "Estate"), Texaco Inc. ("Texaco"), and TRMI Holdings Inc. ("TRMI"). RHC originally sought declaratory relief in bankruptcy court, seeking a judgment defining the responsibilities of the parties in relation to the environmental contamination at the Refinery. After the bankruptcy court issued its final judgment, the parties separately appealed to the district court. The district court consolidated the appeals, and affirmed in part and reversed in part the bankruptcy court's judgment. The Trustee, Texaco, and TRMI then filed a joint appeal to this court. . . .

Texaco built the Refinery in 1929 in El Paso, Texas and operated it until 1984, when it spun off most of its refineries, including the El Paso Refinery, to a wholly-owned subsidiary. The subsidiary taking ownership was named Texaco Refining and Marketing, Inc., but later changed its name to TRMI Holdings, Inc. ("TRMI"). As part of the spin-off transaction, TRMI agreed to assume all responsibility for environmental contamination at the Refinery. Shortly thereafter, in 1986, TRMI sold the Refinery to El Paso Refinery, L.P. (the "Debtor"). The Debtor took ownership of the Refinery through a series of conveyances between corporate entities associated with the Debtor. First, TRMI signed a Purchase Agreement (the "Purchase Agreement") with El Paso Refinery, Inc. ("Old Inc."), and then conveyed the Refinery by special warranty deed (the "TRMI Deed") to El Paso Refining Co., Ltd. ("El Paso Ltd."). El Paso Ltd. then conveyed the Refinery to Old Inc., who in turn conveyed the Refinery to El Paso Refining, Inc., ("New Inc."), who finally transferred the Refinery to the Debtor. The documents accompanying this transfer are vitally important in this appeal, because both the Purchase Agreement and the TRMI Deed include warranties, representations, and indemnification provisions regarding environmental contamination at the Refinery. In particular, both documents include covenants preventing any subsequent owner from seeking contribution from TRMI, or from compelling TRMI to take any remedial action. . . .

[W]e must determine whether the covenants executed by the Debtor during its purchase of the Refinery from TRMI are binding on RHC. When TRMI sold the Refinery to the Debtor, it included covenants in the TRMI Deed preventing future owners from seeking contribution from TRMI or from compelling TRMI to take any remedial action at the Refinery. In regard to environmental liabilities, the TRMI Deed provides:

> Grantee [El Paso Ltd.] covenants and agrees that it shall never, directly or indirectly, attempt to compel Grantor [TRMI] to clean up, remove or take remedial action or any other response with respect to any of the buried sludge sites, the waste pile site, the Active Hazardous Waste Storage Sites, the underground liquid petroleum and petroleum vapors (including, without limitation, any leaching therefrom or contamination of the air, ground or the ground water thereunder or any effects related thereto), or any and all waste water treatment ponds or treatment systems on or in the vicinity of said premises or seek damages therefor. This covenant shall run with the land and shall bind Grantee's successors, assigns and all other subsequent owners of the property.

Appellants argue that this provision prevents RHC from seeking contribution or indemnity from TRMI for any environmental clean-up costs. The Appellants raise two arguments to support their position. First, they contend that the deed's language creates a real covenant that runs with the land. Alternatively, they argue that the restriction is enforceable as an equitable servitude.

We must first determine whether the TRMI Deed contains a real covenant enforceable at law. . . . [Because the other requirements are met], we must determine only whether the covenant "touches and concerns" the land.

The parties disagree as to the correct test to apply in order to determine if a covenant touches and concerns the land. In general, a covenant touches and concerns when it affects the "nature, quality or value of the thing demised, independently of collateral circumstances, or if it affect[s] the mode of enjoying it." *Westland Oil Dev. Corp. v. Gulf Oil Corp.*, 637 S.W.2d 903, 911 (Tex.1982); 3 Herbert T. Tiffany & Basil Jones, Tiffany, Real Property §854 (3d ed. 2001) (stating that the "touch and concern" requirement is met when a covenant "closely relates to the land or estate granted or its use, occupation or enjoyment"). A personal covenant, in contrast, does not touch and concern the land, because such a covenant affects the grantor personally and is unrelated to the use of the land. *Westland Oil*, 637 S.W.2d at 910.

Traditional Texas cases have employed a benefit/burden analysis when determining whether a covenant touches and concerns the land. In reliance on these cases, RHC argues that the TRMI Deed does not touch and concern the land because it conveys no benefit to the Refinery, even though it may impose a burden upon its owner.

See Davis v. Skipper, 125 Tex. 364, 371, 83 S.W.2d 318, 321-22 (Tex.Com.App.1935) ("In the absence of proof that a restriction was imposed for the benefit of other land, it is construed as a personal covenant merely with the grantor."); *McCart v. Cain*, 416 S.W.2d 463, 465 (Tex.Civ.App.-Fort Worth 1967, writ ref'd n.r.e.) (reiterating that party seeking to enforce restrictive covenant must establish benefit to land). In response, the Appellants have identified more recent Texas cases in which courts have dispensed with the benefit requirement, and have enforced restrictive covenants upon a burden-only showing. *See Westland Oil*, 637 S.W.2d at 911 (concluding that covenant touches and concerns land because it burdens the promisor's estate and renders it less valuable); *Wimberly v. Lone Star Gas Co.*, 818 S.W.2d 868, 871 (Tex.App.-Fort Worth 1991, writ denied) (rejecting requirement that covenant must benefit land in order to fulfill touch and concern requirement).

Although the caselaw is somewhat unclear, it is at least arguable that the benefit requirement has been abandoned by the Texas courts. Nevertheless, we still do not believe that the covenant in the TRMI Deed "touches and concerns" the land. Any burden or benefit created by the TRMI Deed affects only TRMI personally and has no direct impact upon the land itself. The Refinery's owner may, in accordance with the deed's provisions, take remedial action or not take remedial action, pollute or not pollute, as long as contribution is not sought from TRMI. The covenant does not compel nor preclude the promisor or any subsequent owner from doing anything on the land itself. The covenant is not predicated upon an agreement to refrain from taking any action on the land, as in the case of a negative covenant. *See Mobil Oil Corp. v. Brennan*, 385 F.2d 951, 953 (5th Cir.1967) (describing covenant preventing mineral estate owner from interfering with surface grazing and from placing pipelines above certain depth). Nor does it permit TRMI, the promisee, to enter or utilize the land for any purpose. *See, e.g. Wimberly*, 818 S.W.2d at 870-71 (holding that contract permitting gas company to purchase water from wells on owner's land was real binding covenant). Rather, it is a continuing and non-contingent contractual agreement under which the Debtor agrees to refrain from seeking environmental remediation or damages from TRMI. A personal contractual arrangement does not qualify as a covenant. *See Martindale v. Gulf Oil Corp.*, 345 S.W.2d 810, 813 (Tex.Civ.App.-Beaumont 1961, writ ref'd n.r.e.) (holding agreement between gas station owner and oil company, whereby owner agrees to purchase all petroleum requirements from company, was merely personal contract and not a covenant).

The deed's restrictive language does little more than shield TRMI from the possibility of a contribution suit by a future owner. In this respect, the covenant operates as a cost-shifting mechanism, by pushing all costs of remedial action forward onto the Debtor and any subsequent purchaser. We believe such a provision is more analogous to an obligation to assume an encumbrance, in this case the encumbrance being the responsibility to pay for all environmental clean-up costs. Under Texas law, a covenant to pay an encumbrance does not run with the land. *Talley v. Howsley,* 170 S.W.2d 240, 243 (Tex.Civ.App.-Eastland 1943), *aff'd,* 142 Tex. 81, 176 S.W.2d 158 (1943); *cf. Cunningham v. Buel,* 287 S.W. 683, 686 (Tex.Civ.App.-San Antonio 1926, n.w.h.) (enforcing covenant in deed holding *buyer* harmless from outstanding liability, taxes, and water charges).

The Appellants rely heavily on the Texas Supreme Court's decision in *Westland Oil* to argue that a covenant affecting the *value* of the land is enough. We disagree. First, the court's decision in *Westland Oil* is distinguishable because the party's obligations under the covenant were triggered by an action affecting the land itself. In that case, the covenant obligating the third-party to assign part of its interest in the oil and gas leases was predicated on the drilling of a test well on the land. *Westland Oil,* 637 S.W.2d at 907. Moreover, even when a covenant impacts the value of land, it must still affect the owner's interest in the property or its use in order to be a real covenant. *See* 16 Tex. Jur.3d *Covenants, Conditions, and Restrictions* §10 (2002) (stating that a covenant that does not "relate to, or concern, the property or its use or enjoyment" is purely personal and does not bind subsequent owners); *Inwood,* 736 S.W.2d at 635 (discussing real covenant requiring homeowners to pay maintenance assessments for purpose of repairing and improving common and recreational areas); *Davis,* 83 S.W.2d at 321-22 (discussing covenant restricting use of land to "church purposes").

The Appellants alternatively argue that the covenant in the TRMI Deed is enforceable as an equitable servitude. They argue that this type of contractual restriction is binding when a party purchases land with notice of a restriction, regardless of whether it is a real covenant running with the land. The Appellants' argument lacks merit. An equitable servitude is enforceable when the contracting parties are in privity of estate at the time of the conveyance, and the subsequent party purchases the land with notice of the restriction. *Tarrant Appraisal Dist. v. Colonial Country Club,* 767 S.W.2d 230, 235 (Tex.App.-Forth Worth 1989, writ denied). However, the restriction sought to be enforced must still "concern the land or its use or enjoyment" in the case of an equitable servitude. *Montgomery v. Creager,* 22 S.W.2d 463, 466 (Tex.Civ.App.-Eastland 1929, no writ); *see also Tarrant,* 767 S.W.2d at 235 (discussing deed restriction limiting land to recreational, park, or scenic use). Therefore, because we have already concluded that the covenant in the TRMI Deed does not "concern the land or its use," it is likewise not enforceable as an equitable servitude. *Tarrant,* 767 S.W.2d at 235.

In sum, we hold that the covenant in the TRMI Deed is a personal covenant that is not binding upon RHC, either as a real covenant or as an equitable servitude.

NOTE

1. *Equitable Servitudes and Touch and Concern.* At the end of this excerpt, the *El Paso* court held that a promise must touch and concern the land to be enforceable as an equitable servitude. Don't be confused by the slightly oblique way the court gets to this holding. Generally speaking, the touch and concern requirement applies to both real covenants and equitable servitudes.

The touch and concern requirement is often criticized for its vagueness. In part because exact scope of the requirement can be hard to pin down, courts have sometimes used touch and concern as grounds to refuse to enforce covenants on various policy grounds. The Restatement (Third) calls for the abolition of the touch and concern requirement, and advocates for replacing the requirement with more transparent policy-based grounds for non-enforcement of a covenant. *See* Restatement (Third) of Property, Servitudes §3.2.

The common law of servitudes includes a prohibition on the creation of a covenant that runs with the land where the benefit is held in gross. This rule is typically placed under the umbrella of touch and concern. In all of the examples we have seen so far, the benefit of the covenant is held by the owner of a parcel of land (i.e., the benefit is appurtenant, though you rarely see the term appurtenant used in the covenants context). Indeed, our diagram involving parcel A and parcel B is structured on the presumption that the benefit is held by parcel B.

The prohibition against covenants where the benefit is in gross has ancient historical roots. It can be justified on a policy related to encouraging the free alienability of property. Imagine that there is a recorded covenant on Blackacre, a vacant lot. The covenant requires that any house on Blackacre must be built by ABC Construction Co. In other words, the benefit of the house-building covenant is held in gross by ABC Construction. You decide that you want to buy Blackacre and build a house on it. It turns out that ABC Construction has gone bankrupt, and you cannot easily find its successor-in-interest. Where does that leave you? If you could find the holder of the benefit, then you might be able to negotiate a release of the covenant. If you can't find the holder of the benefit, you can't negotiate, and you are faced with uncertainty. Because of this uncertainty, you probably wouldn't buy Blackacre, and the covenant with the benefit held in gross impairs the alienability of the land. If the benefit of the covenant is tied to a parcel of property, in contrast, locating the owner of the benefit should be easier. You might still have some problems if the owner of the land is an entity and is bankrupt, but at least you have a fixed location to start your search and can look in the land records for the current record owner.

The prohibition against benefits in gross has been criticized, and you would not be alone if you did not find this policy argument to be compelling. *See* Restatement (Third) of Property, Servitudes §2.6. Nonetheless, there is a good amount of case law supporting the rule. Our next case is an example.

CAULLETT V. STANLEY STILWELL & SONS, INC.

Superior Court of New Jersey, Appellate Division, 1961
170 A.2d 52

FREUND, J.A.D.

This is an action in the nature of a bill to quiet title to a parcel of land in the Township of Holmdel. Defendant appeals from the entry of summary judgment in favor of plaintiffs.

Defendant, a developer, by warranty deed conveyed the subject property, consisting of a lot approximately one acre in size, to the plaintiffs for a consideration of $4,000. The deed was delivered on January 13, 1959. Following the collapse of negotiations directed towards agreement on the construction by defendant of a dwelling on the transferred premises, the present suit was instituted.

The focal point of the action is a recital in the deed, inserted under the heading of "covenants, agreements and restrictions," to the effect that:

"(i) The grantors reserve the right to build or construct the original dwelling or building on said premises."

The item is one of those designated in the instrument as "covenants running with the land . . . (which) shall bind the purchasers, their heirs, executors, administrators and assigns."

In support of their motion for summary judgment, plaintiffs set forth that no contract exists or ever did exist between the parties for the construction of a dwelling or building on the premises. The principal officer of the defendant corporation, in a countering affidavit, stated that one of the foremost considerations in fixing the price of the lot, and one of the primary conditions of the sale as it was effected, was the understanding that when the purchasers declared themselves ready and able to build, defendant would act as general contractor.

The trial judge held that the provision in question was unenforceable and should properly be stricken from the deed. He granted plaintiffs the relief demanded in their complaint, namely, an adjudication that: (1) defendant has no claim, right or interest in and to the lands by virtue of the clause in question; (2) defendant has no interest, right or cause of action against plaintiffs by virtue of the covenant; and (3) the clause in question is stricken from the deed and declared null, void and of no further force and effect.

The central issue argued on the appeal is whether the recital constitutes an enforceable covenant restricting the use of plaintiffs' land. Defendant urges that it comprises an ordinary property restriction, entered into for the benefit of the grantor and his retained lands. Plaintiff maintains that the clause is too vague to be capable of enforcement and that, in any event, it amounts to no more than a personal covenant which in no way affects or burdens the realty and has no place in an instrument establishing and delimiting the title to same.

While restrictive covenants are to be construed realistically in the light of the circumstances under which they were created, *Javna v. D. J. Fredericks, Inc.,* 41 *N.J. Super.* 353, 358, 125 *A.*2d 227 (*App. Div.* 1956), counter considerations, favoring the free transferability of land, have produced the rule that incursions on the use of property will not be enforced unless their meaning is clear and free from doubt, *Hammett v. Rosensohn,* 46 *N.J. Super.* 527, 535-536, 135 *A.*2d 6 (*App. Div.* 1957), affirmed 26 *N.J.* 415, 140 *A.*2d 377 (1958); *Bruno v. Hanna,* 63 *N.J. Super.* 282, 285, 164 *A.*2d 647 (*App. Div.* 1960); *Griscom v. Barcelonne,* 90 *N.J. Eq.* 369, 107 *A.* 587 (*Ch.* 1919); *Grossman v. Abate,* 19 *N.J. Super.* 516, 88 *A.*2d 658 (*Ch. Div.* 1952). Thus, if the covenants or restrictions are vague or ambiguous, they should not be construed to impair the alienability of the subject property. For a concise and cogent discussion of the unenforceability of restrictive covenants because of vagueness, see *Sutcliffe v. Eisele,* 62 *N.J. Eq.* 222, 50 *A.* 69 (*Ch.* 1901). Also see *Fortesque v. Carroll,* 76 *N.J. Eq.* 583, 75 *A.* 923 (*E. & A.* 1910); *Newbery v. Barkalow,* 75 *N.J. Eq.* 128, 133, 71 *A.* 752 (*Ch.* 1909); *Wilson v. Ocean Terrace Garden Apartments, Inc.,* 139 *N.J. Eq.* 376, 380, 51 *A.*2d 549 (*Ch.* 1947).

Approached from a direction compatible with the constructional principles set forth above, it is clear that the deed item in question is incapable of enforcement and is therefore not restrictive of plaintiffs' title. The clause is descriptive of neither the type of structure to be built, the cost thereof, or the duration of the grantees' obligation. While it might conceivably have been intended to grant to defendant a right of first refusal on construction bids on the property, this is by no means its palpable design. What, for example, would be its effect were plaintiffs to erect a structure by their own hands?

It must be remembered that a restrictive covenant is in its inception a mere contract, subject to the interpretative doctrines of contract law which focus on the parties' mutual purpose. See 3 *Williston, Contracts* (rev. ed. 1936), §620, pp. 1787-88, nn. 5 and 6. A purported contract so obscure that no one can be sure of its meaning is incapable of remedy at law or equity for its alleged breach, *cf. Bethlehem Engineering Export Co. v. Christie,* 105 *F.*2d 933, 125 *A.L.R.* 1441 (2 Cir. 1939), and therefore cannot constitute a valid impediment to title.

Moreover, assuming *arguendo* that the clause is sufficiently definite to give defendant a primary option to build whenever plaintiffs should decide to construct a dwelling or building on the premises, it still cannot operate either as a covenant running with the land at law, or as an equitable servitude enforceable against the original grantee and all successors, having notice, to his interest.

In the first place, it is clear to us that the item in question does not satisfy the primary requirement of covenants directly restrictive of title to land—that they "touch and concern" the subject property. To constitute a real rather than a personal covenant, the promise must exercise direct influence on the occupation, use or enjoyment of the premises. It must be a promise "respecting the use of the land," that is, "a use of identified land which is not merely casual and which is not merely an incident in the performance of the promise." 5 *Restatement, Property,* Scope Note to Part III, pp. 3147-48 (1944). Furthermore, in the language of the *Restatement*:

> "Even when the promise identifies a specific tract of land as the sphere of action contemplated by it, the use of the land may be so incidental in the performance of the promise, or the promised action may be of such a casual and temporary character, as to prevent the promise from being a 'promise respecting the use of land'. . . . The use of land involved must be a primary consideration of the undertaking of which the promise is a part and the promise must contemplate a degree of permanency in the particular use. . . . (T)he use of land involved is too casual to bring the promise of either party within the scope of promises respecting the use of land . . . (in the case of) a promise to permit the draining through the land of the promisor upon a single occasion of a pond upon the land of the promisee." (*Ibid.,* at pp. 3150-51).

In substantial accord with the *Restatement* analysis are *Dunn v. Ryan,* 82 *N.J. Eq.* 356, 88 *A.* 1025, 49 *L.R.A., N.S.,* 1015 (*E. & A.* 1913), and *Butterhof v. Butterhof,* 84 *N.J.L.* 285, 86 *A.* 394 (*E. & A.* 1913), holding that the breach of deed provisions, to the effect that the grantee would provide support and maintenance for the grantor during the latter's natural life, does not affect the fee conveyed but at most gives rise to an action for damages for failure to perform a collateral covenant.

Thus, to qualify as a covenant properly affecting the subject property, the deed provision must define in some measurable and reasonably permanent fashion the proscriptions of and limitations upon the uses to which the premises may be put. Typical provisions, some of them included in the deed of the parties herein, limit the property to residential purposes, provide minimum setback and acreage requirements, proscribe certain architectural forms, and limit the number of set the minimum cost of future dwellings to be constructed on the land.

The provision here in issue is not of the variety described above. It pertains to the use of plaintiffs' land only in the very incidental fashion that refusal to allow defendant to build the original structure would seemingly preclude plaintiffs from constructing at all. This is at best a personal arrangement between the two parties, designed to insure defendant a profit on the erection of a dwelling in return, allegedly, for a comparatively low sales price on the land. While there is nothing in our law precluding such an arrangement, as a contract Inter partes, this form of contract, contemplating a single personal service upon the property, does not affect the title. And the stipulation between the parties in their instrument to the effect that this was a covenant running with the land cannot override the inherently personal nature of their arrangement under established legal principles.

We note, in addition, that even if the deed clause were to be construed as directly restricting plaintiffs' use of their land, i.e., prohibiting erection of a structure until such time as the owner shall permit such construction to be performed by the grantor, the clause would nonetheless comprise neither a legal restriction nor an equitable servitude upon the estate. This is so because whatever the effect of the burden of the covenant, its benefit is clearly personal to the grantor, securing to him a mere commercial advantage in the operation of his business and not enhancing or otherwise affecting the use or value of any retained lands.

Generally prerequisite to a conclusion that a covenant runs with the land at law is a finding that both burdened and benefited properties exist and were intended to be so affected by the contracting parties. Where, however, the Benefit attaches to the property of one of the parties, the fact that the Burden is in gross, i.e., personal, does not preclude the covenant from running with the land conveyed. *National Union Bank at Dover v. Segur,* 39 *N.J.L.* 173 (*Sup. Ct.* 1877). There is no public policy opposed to the running of a benefit, since a continuing benefit is presumed to help rather than hinder the alienability of the property to which it is attached. 5 *Powell, Real Property,* §675, p. 173; 5 *Restatement, Property, supra,* §543, *comment* (c), pp. 3255-56. When, however, as here, the Burden is placed upon the land, and the Benefit is personal to one of the parties and does not extend to his or other lands, the burden is generally held not to run with the land at law. The policy is strong against hindering the alienability of one property where no corresponding enhancement accrues to surrounding lands. See 5 *Restatement, Property, supra,* §537, pp. 3218-24; 2 *American Law of Property,* §9.13, pp. 373-76 (1952).

Nor can the covenant be enforced as an equitable servitude where the benefit is in gross and neither affects retained land of the grantor nor is part of a neighborhood scheme of similar restrictions. Purporting to follow the case of *Tulk v. Moxhay,* 2 *Phil.* 774, 41 *Eng. Rep.* 1143 (*Ch.* 1848), our courts have consistently enforced the covenantal rights of an owner of benefited property against a successor, with notice, to the burdened land, even though the covenant did not run with the land at law. *De Gray v. Monnmouth Beach Club House Co.,* 50 *N.J. Eq.* 329, 24 *A.* 388 (*Ch.* 1892), *affirmed,* 67 *N.J. Eq.* 731, 63 *A.* 1118 (*E. & A.* 1894); *Cotton v. Cresse,* 80 *N.J. Eq.* 540, 85 *A.* 600, 49 *L.R.A., N.S.,* 357 (*E. & A.* 1912); *Coudert v. Sayre,* 46 *N.J. Eq.* 386, 395, 19 *A.* 190 (*Ch.* 1890). However, the right to urge enforcement of a servitude against the burdened land "depends primarily on the covenant's having been made for the benefit" of other land, either retained by the grantor or part of a perceptible neighborhood scheme. *Hayes v. Waverly & Passaic R.R. Co.,* 51 *N.J. Eq.* 345, 348, 27 *A.* 648 (*Ch.* 1893); *Cornish v. Wiessman,* 56 *N.J. Eq.* 610, 611-612, 35 *A.* 408 (*Ch.* 1896); *Roberts v. Scull,* 58 *N.J. Eq.* 396, 401, 43 *A.* 583 (*Ch.* 1899); *Morrow v. Hasselman,* 69 *N.J. Eq.* 612, 614, 61 *A.* 369 (*Ch.* 1905); *Lignot v. Jaekle,* 72 *N.J. Eq.* 233, 241, 65 *A.* 221 (*Ch.* 1906); *Lister v. Vogel,* 110 *N.J. Eq.* 35, 40, 158 *A.* 534 (*E. & A.* 1932). Where the benefit is purely personal to the grantor, and has not been directed towards the improvement of neighboring properties, it cannot pass as an incident to any of his retained land and therefore is not considered to burden the conveyed premises but only, at best, to obligate the grantee personally. See 2 *Tiffany, Real Property,* §399, pp. 1441-42 (1920).

The latter doctrine has recently come under considerable criticism, see 2 *American Law of Property, supra,* §9.32, pp. 428-30, and has even been rejected in some jurisdictions, thus permitting attachment of an equitable servitude even though the benefit is in gross. See, *e.g., Pratte v. Balatsos,* 99 *N.H.* 430, 113 *A.2d* 492 (*Sup. Ct.* 1955). But the law in this jurisdiction, as last authoritatively declared, is that "from the very nature of the equitable restriction arising from a restrictive covenant," the "existence of the dominant estate is . . . essential to the validity of the servitude granted. . . ." *Welitoff v. Kohl,* 105 *N.J. Eq.* 181, 189, 147 *A.* 390, 393, 66 *A.L.R.* 1317 (*E. & A.* 1929).

We therefore conclude that the clause in question, even were we to assume both its clarity and its direct operation upon the use of plaintiffs' land, cannot comprise an impairment of plaintiffs' title, because of the indisputably personal nature of the benefit conferred thereby. An intention to dispense broader land use benefits, in the form of a neighborhood scheme, cannot here be found, as in effect conceded by defendant and as expressly stipulated in the parties' deed.

Defendant raises the defense of "unclean hands," claiming that plaintiffs' alleged refusal to go through with their asserted promise, respecting the construction of a dwelling on the property by defendant, constitutes inequitable conduct barring their effort to obtain relief in equity upon the same transaction. This argument is without merit. Because of the vagueness and uncertainty of the alleged agreement, adverted to hereinabove, it is impossible to determine whether plaintiffs acted in good or in bad faith in not permitting defendant to erect a dwelling. In short, the very obscurity of the obligation asserted by defendant precludes definition of a standard by which to measure plaintiffs' conduct. We note, moreover, that according to the affidavit of defendant's principal officer, the parties attempted over a period of several months to negotiate a mutually satisfactory agreement. Thus, this is not a case in which the plaintiff merely turned his back on a provision whose insertion in the instrument he had previously approved. Furthermore, the social interest in promoting alienability of property might well be a factor militating in favor of striking this covenant, even against a provable assertion of "unclean hands." But we have no occasion to decide such a question here in view of the foregoing.

The right of plaintiffs to bring an action to quiet title, where the alleged restriction is in reality unenforceable, is questioned. But it is clear that such actions, *N.J.S.* 2A:62-1, *N.J.S.A.,* may be instituted to clear the title instrument of excess verbiage having the practical effect of inhibiting the transferability of the estate. Courts will not be blind to the understandable reluctance of title companies to insure in the face of a questionable and somewhat anomalous deed provision, and to the even greater unwillingness of prospective purchasers to accept an uninsurable title. The action was a proper one under the statute.

Defendant asserts that this action is basically one for rescission of the contract and that plaintiffs should restore defendant to *status quo* by reconveying the property in return for the consideration paid therefor. But we do not analyze the action as one for rescission. It purports to be, and is, in the nature of a bill to quiet title. Nor can we entertain defendant's alternative request for leave to amend its answer to seek rescission. No such request was made below and there is no proper basis for permitting it at this stage of the litigation.

The judgment of the trial court is affirmed.

NOTES AND QUESTIONS

1. *Benefits Held in Gross by Homeowners' Associations.* The rule against benefits being held in gross does not apply when the benefit is held by homeowners' associations. Does this exception to the general rule make sense to you? More broadly, what do you think of the rule against benefits held in gross?

2. *Touch and Concern.* Leaving aside the benefit in gross issue, did you agree or disagree with the court's analysis of whether the covenant touched and concerned the land? Do you think that this kind of covenant should be enforceable against subsequent owners?

3. *Vagueness.* As the court suggests, covenants will be unenforceable if they are too vague. Do you think that this covenant was too vague to be enforced?

4. *Law of Contracts vs. Law of Property.* The parties to this case were the original parties to the covenant. Why do you think that this dispute was framed in terms of the law of property, and whether the promise met the requirements of a covenant that runs with the land, rather than framed as a simple contract dispute between the parties?

PROBLEMS

Explanatory answers to these problems can be found on page 1061.

1. Larry lived at 15 Green Street. Alex was Larry's next-door neighbor, and lived at 17 Green Street. One day, Larry and Alex entered into a written covenant, intended to run with the land, that neither would ever put a satellite dish up on their house. They both promptly recorded the covenants with the local county records office. A few months later, Alex sold 17 Green Street to Rose. Within a few months, Rose had a satellite dish on her roof. Larry has now sued Rose, seeking both money damages for his annoyance at having to look at the dish and an injunction forcing Rose to take it down.

2. Mountain View Estates is a common interest community that is governed by a set of recorded covenants that were intended to run with the land. These covenants were put into place when the land was subdivided into individual parcels. One of the covenants requires all houses in the community to be painted white or gray. Daphna recently bought a house in Mountain View Estates from the house's original owner and promptly painted her house red. The homeowners' association has now brought an action against Daphna seeking an injunction requiring her to follow the covenant and

paint her house white or gray and money damages for the damages to property values caused by her unsightly home.

3. Max is a developer who works on a small scale. Rather than putting together 100-home developments, Max tends to buy smaller parcels of land and put a few houses on them. He often constructs the houses himself through his construction company, MW Homes LLC. Max himself lives on a five-acre parcel on Owl Road. He bought the five acres next door about ten years ago. About three years ago, he sold the neighboring parcel to Lee Anne. As part of that transaction, he imposed the following written covenant: "Any home built on the property [i.e., Lee Anne's parcel] will be constructed by MW Homes LLC. This covenant is intended to run with the land." Max promptly recorded the covenant. A few months later, Max and Lee Anne were chatting about a really ugly pink house that someone had built nearby. They agreed that they would never want to live next to a pink house. As a result, they got together and agreed to a written covenant, intended to run with the land and binding present and future owners of both parcels, that no structure on either parcel would ever be painted pink. Both Max and Lee Anne properly recorded this covenant. Six months ago, Lee Anne sold her property to Peggy. Max just found out that Peggy has just contracted with Wilson Construction Co. to build a house on the property— and (go figure), Peggy plans to paint her house pink. Max has sued Peggy on both covenants and is seeking an injunction *and* money damages for Peggy's putative violations of both.

THE RESTATEMENT (THIRD) AND COVENANTS THAT RUN WITH THE LAND

As we saw above in the *AKG Real Estate* case, the Restatement (Third) includes some major reforms of the law of servitudes. Section 1.4 of the Restatement (Third) abolishes the distinctions between real covenants and equitable servitudes and imposes the same requirements for a covenant to run with the land at law and in equity. Section 2.4 abolishes the horizontal privity requirement. Section 3.2 replaces the touch and concern requirement with more explicit policy-based restrictions on servitude enforcement. It remains to be seen how broadly these major reforms will be adopted by courts. We think that the abolition of the distinction between real covenants and equitable servitudes makes sense and should be widely followed. There should not be distinct requirements to enforce a covenant that runs with the land at law and in equity. We also agree with the abolition of the horizontal privity requirement and hope that change in particular is widely adopted by the courts.

1. CHANGED CIRCUMSTANCES

Promises that are enforceable as real covenants and/or equitable servitudes may lose their enforceability if circumstances have changed so much that it is no longer possible to achieve the original purpose of the covenant. "The test is stringent: relief is granted only if the purpose of the servitude can no longer be accomplished." Restatement (Third) of Property, Servitudes §7.10 cmt. a. As the Restatement (Third) suggests, the changed circumstances test is strict, and most challenges to covenants based on changed circumstances fail.

In our next two cases, covenants that run with the land were challenged on changed circumstances grounds. In the first case, the changed circumstances challenge fails. In the second, it succeeds. As you read the cases, think about the differences between them and about why they came to different results.

WESTERN LAND CO. V. TRUSKOLASKI

Supreme Court of Nevada, 1972
495 P.2d 624

Batjer, Justice:

The respondents, homeowners in the Southland Heights subdivision in southwest Reno, Nevada, brought an action in the district court to enjoin the appellant from constructing a shopping center on a 3.5-acre parcel of land located within the subdivision at the northeast corner of Plumas and West Plumb Lane. In 1941 the appellant subdivided the 40-acre development, and at that time it subjected the lots to certain restrictive covenants which specifically restricted the entire 40 acres of the subdivision to single family dwellings and further prohibited any stores, butcher shops, grocery or mercantile business of any kind.[1] The district court held these restrictive covenants to be enforceable, and enjoined the appellant from constructing a supermarket or using the 3.5 acres in any manner other than that permitted by the

---

[1] The agreement as to building restrictions for the Southland Heights Subdivision, signed and filed for record by the Western Land Co., Ltd., provides in pertinent part as follows:

"WHEREAS, the said Western Land Co. Ltd. desires to subject said lots to the conditions and restrictions hereinafter set forth for the benefit of said lots and of the present and subsequent owners thereof.

"NOW, THEREFORE, the Western Land Co. Ltd., for the benefits and considerations herein set forth accrued and accruing to it, does covenant and agree that said lots, pieces, and parcels of land shall be held or conveyed subject to the following conditions and restrictions, to wit:

"1. No structures shall be erected, altered, placed or permitted to remain on any of said lots or parcels of ground other than one single family dwelling . . .

". . . .

"4. No store, butcher shop, grocery or mercantile business of any kind shall be maintained, carried on, or conducted upon any of said lots or parcels . . .

". . . .

covenants. The appellant contends that the district court erred in enforcing these covenants because the subdivision had so radically changed in recent years as to nullify their purpose. We agree with the holding of the district court that the restrictive covenants remain of substantial value to the homeowners in the subdivision, and that the changes that have occurred since 1941 are not so great as to make it inequitable or oppressive to restrict the property to single-family residential use.

In 1941 the Southland Heights subdivision was outside of the Reno city limits. The property surrounding the subdivision was primarily used for residential and agricultural purposes, with very little commercial development of any type in the immediate area. At that time Plumb Lane extended only as far east as Arlington Avenue.

By the time the respondents sought equitable relief in an effort to enforce the restrictive covenants, the area had markedly changed. In 1941 the city of Reno had a population of slightly more than 20,000; that figure had jumped to approximately 95,100 by 1969. One of the significant changes, as the appellant aptly illustrates, is the increase in traffic in the surrounding area. Plumb Lane had been extended to Virginia Street, and in 1961 the city of Reno condemned 1.04 acres of land on the edge of the subdivision to allow for the widening of Plumb Lane into a fourlane arterial boulevard. A city planner, testifying for the appellant, stated that Plumb Lane was designed to be and now is the major east-west artery through the southern portion of the city. A person who owns property across Plumas from the subdivision testified that the corner of Plumb Lane and Plumas is "terribly noisy from 5:00 p.m. until midnight." One of the findings of the trial court was that traffic on Plumb Lane had greatly increased in recent years.

Another significant change that had occurred since 1941 was the increase in commercial development in the vicinity of the subdivision. On the east side of Lakeside Drive, across from the subdivision property, is a restaurant and the Lakeside Plaza Shopping Center. A supermarket, hardware store, drug store, flower shop, beauty shop and a dress shop are located in this shopping center. Still further east of the subdivision, on Virginia Street, is the Continental Lodge, and across Virginia Street is the Park Lane Shopping Center.

Even though traffic has increased and commercial development has occurred in the vicinity of the subdivision, the owners of land within Southland Heights testified to the

---

"10. These covenants are to run with the land and shall be binding upon all the parties and all persons claiming under them until January 1st, 1966, at which time said covenants shall be automatically extended for successive periods of ten years unless by a vote of the majority of the then owners of the lots it is agreed to change the said covenants in whole or in part; . . . and whether or not it be so expressed in the deeds or other conveyances of said lots, the same shall be absolutely subject to the covenants, conditions, and restrictions which run with and are appurtenant to said lots or every part thereof as herein expressed as fully as if expressly contained in proper and obligatory covenants and conditions in each and every deed, contract, and conveyance of or concerning any part of the said land or the improvements to be made thereon."

desirability of the subdivision for residential purposes. The traffic density within the subdivision is low, resulting in a safe environment for the children who live and play in the area. Homes in Southland Heights are well cared for and attractively landscaped.

The trial court found that substantial changes in traffic patterns and commercial activity had occurred since 1941 in the vicinity of the subdivision. Although it was shown that commercial activity outside of the subdivision had increased considerably since 1941, the appellant failed to show that the area in question is now unsuitable for residential purposes.

Even though nearby avenues may become heavily traveled thoroughfares, restrictive covenants are still enforceable if the single-family residential character of the neighborhood has not been adversely affected, and the purpose of the restrictions has not been thwarted. *Burden v. Lobdell*, 93 Ill.App.2d 476, 235 N.E.2d 660 (1968); *Gonzales v. Gackle Drilling Company*, 67 N.M. 130, 353 P.2d 353 (1960); *Continental Oil Co. v. Fennemore*, 38 Ariz. 277, 299 P. 132 (1931). Although commercialization has increased in the vicinity of the subdivision, such activity has not rendered the restrictive covenants unenforceable because they are still of real and substantial value to those homeowners living within the subdivision. *West Alameda Heights H. Ass'n v. Board of Co. Com'rs,* 169 Colo. 491, 458 P.2d 253 (1969); *Burden v. Lobdell, supra; Hogue v. Dreeszen,* 161 Neb. 268, 73 N.W.2d 159 (1955).

The appellant asks this court to reverse the judgment of the district court and declare as a matter of law that the objects and purposes for which the restrictive covenants were originally imposed have been thwarted, and that it is now inequitable to enforce such restrictions against the entity that originally created them. This we will not do. The record will not permit us to find as a matter of law that there has been such a change in the subdivision or for that matter in the area to relieve the appellant's property of the burden placed upon it by the covenants. There is sufficient evidence to sustain the findings of the trial court that the objects and purposes of the restrictions have not been thwarted, and that they remain of substantial value to the homeowners in the subdivision.

The case of *Hirsch v. Hancock,* 173 Cal.App.2d 745, 343 P.2d 959 (1959) as well as the other authorities relied upon by the appellant (*Key v. McCabe,* 54 Cal.2d 736, 8 Cal. Rptr. 425, 356 P.2d 169 (1960); *Strong v. Hancock,* 201 Cal. 530, 258 P. 60 (1927); *Downs v. Kroeger,* 200 Cal. 743, 254 P. 1101 (1927)) are inapposite for in those cases the trial court found many changes within as well as outside the subdivision and concluded from the evidence that the properties were entirely unsuitable and undersirable for residential use and that they had no suitable economic use except for business or commercial purposes, and the appellate courts in reviewing those cases held that the evidence supported the findings and sustained the judgments of the trial courts.

On the other hand, in the case of *West Alameda Heights, H. Ass'n v. Board of Co. Com'm, supra,* upon facts similar to those found in this case, the trial court decided that the changed conditions in the neighborhood were such as to render the restrictive covenants void and unenforceable. The appellate court reversed and held that the trial court misconceived and misapplied the rule as to change of conditions and said, 169 Colo. at 498, 458 P.2d at 256: "As long as the original purpose of the covenants can still be accomplished and substantial benefit will inure to the restricted area by their enforcement, the covenants stand even though the subject property has a greater value if used for other purposes." *See also Rombauer v. Compton Heights Christian Church*, 328 Mo. 1, 40 S.W.2d 545 (1931); *Porter v. Johnson*, 232 Mo.App. 1150, 115 S.W.2d 529 (1938); *Finley v. Batsel*, 67 N.M. 125, 353 P.2d 350 (1960); *Southwest Petroleum Co. v. Logan*, 180 Okl. 477, 71 P.2d 759 (1937); *Burden v. Lobdell, supra*.

There is substantial evidence in the record to support the trial court's findings of fact and conclusions of law that the covenants were of real and substantial value to the residents of the subdivision. Where the evidence is conflicting and the credibility of the witnesses is in issue, the judgment will not be disturbed on appeal if the evidence is substantially in support of the judgment of the lower court. *Bangston v. Brown,* 86 Nev. 653, 473 P.2d 829 (1970); *Brandon v. Travitsky,* 86 Nev. 613, 472 P.2d 353 (1970); *Havas v. Alger,* 85 Nev. 627, 461 P.2d 857 (1969). Here the appellant has not carried its burden of showing that the subdivision is not now suitable for residential purposes because of changed conditions.

In another attempt to show that the restrictive covenants have outlived their usefulness, the appellant points to actions of the Reno city council. On August 1, 1968, the council adopted a Resolution of Intent to reclassify this 3.5-acre parcel from R-1 (residential) to C-1(b) (commercial). The council never did change the zoning, but the appellant contends that since the counsel did indicate its willingness to rezone, it was of the opinion that the property was more suitable for commercial than residential use. This argument of the appellant is not persuasive. A zoning ordinance cannot override privately-placed restrictions, and a trial court cannot be compelled to invalidate restrictive covenants merely because of a zoning change. *Rice v. Heggy,* 158 Cal.App.2d 89, 322 P.2d 53 (1958).

Another of the appellant's arguments regarding changed conditions involves the value of the property for residential as compared to commercial purposes. A professional planning consultant, testifying for the appellant, stated that the land in question is no longer suitable for use as a single-family residential area. From this testimony the appellant concludes that the highest and best use for the land is non-residential. Even if this property is more valuable for commercial than residential purposes, this fact does not entitle the appellant to be relieved of the restrictions it created, since substantial benefit inures to the restricted area by their enforcement. *West Alameda Heights H. Ass'n v. Board of Co. Com'rs, supra; Cawthon v. Anderson,* 211 Ga. 77, 84 S.E.2d 66 (1954).

In addition to the alleged changed circumstances, the appellant contends that the restrictive covenants are no longer enforceable because they have been abandoned or waived due to violations by homeowners in the area. Paragraph 3 of the restrictive agreement provides that no residential structure shall be placed on a lot comprising less than 6,000 square feet. Both lot 24 and lot 25 of block E contain less than 6,000 square feet and each has a house located on it. This could hardly be deemed a violation of the restrictions imposed by the appellant inasmuch as it was the appellant that subdivided the land and caused these lots to be smaller than 6,000 feet. Paragraph 7 of the agreement provides that a committee shall approve any structure which is moved onto the subdivision, or if there is no committee, that the structure shall conform to and be in harmony with existing structures. The appellant did show that two houses were moved on to lots within the subdivision, but the appellant failed to show whether a committee existed and if so approved or disapproved, or whether the houses failed to conform or were out of harmony with the existing structures. Finally, in an effort to prove abandonment and waiver, the appellant showed that one house within the subdivision was used as a painting contractor's office for several years in the late 1940's, and that more recently the same house had been used as a nursery for a baby sitting business. However, the same witnesses testified that at the time of the hearing this house was being used as a single-family residence.

Even if the alleged occurrences and irregularities could be construed to be violations of the restrictive covenants they were too distant and sporadic to constitute general consent by the property owners in the subdivision and they were not sufficient to constitute an abandonment or waiver. In order for community violations to constitute an abandonment, they must be so general as to frustrate the original purpose of the agreement. *Thodos v. Shirk*, 248 Iowa 172, 79 N.W.2d 733 (1956).

Affirmed.

EL DI, INC. V. TOWN OF BETHANY BEACH

Supreme Court of Delaware, 1984
477 A.2d 1066

HERRMANN, Chief Justice for the majority:

This is an appeal from a permanent injunction granted by the Court of Chancery upon the petition of the plaintiffs, The Town of Bethany Beach, et al., prohibiting the defendant, El Di, Inc. ("El Di") from selling alcoholic beverages at Holiday House, a restaurant in Bethany Beach owned and operated by El Di.

I.

The pertinent facts are as follows:

El Di purchased the Holiday House in 1969. In December 1981, El Di filed an application with the State Alcoholic Beverage Control Commission (the "Commission") for a license to sell alcoholic beverages at the Holiday House. On April 15, 1982, finding "public need and convenience," the Commission granted the Holiday House an on-premises license. The sale of alcoholic beverages at Holiday House began within 10 days of the Commission's approval. Plaintiffs subsequently filed suit to permanently enjoin the sale of alcoholic beverages under the license.

On appeal it is undisputed that the chain of title for the Holiday House lot included restrictive covenants prohibiting both the sale of alcoholic beverages on the property and nonresidential construction.* The same restriction was placed on property in Bethany Beach as early as 1900 and 1901 when the area was first under development.

As originally conceived, Bethany Beach was to be a quiet beach community. The site was selected at the end of the nineteenth-century by the Christian Missionary Society of Washington, D.C. In 1900, the Bethany Beach Improvement Company ("BBIC") was formed. The BBIC purchased lands, laid out a development and began selling lots. To insure the quiet character of the community, the BBIC placed restrictive covenants on many plots, prohibiting the sale of alcohol and restricting construction to residential cottages. Of the original 180 acre development, however, approximately 1/3 was unrestricted.

The Town of Bethany Beach was officially incorporated in 1909. The municipal limits consisted of 750 acres including the original BBIC land (hereafter the original or "old-Town"), but expanded far beyond the 180 acre BBIC development. The expanded acreage of the newly incorporated Town, combined with the unrestricted plots in the original Town, left only 15 percent of the new Town subject to the restrictive covenants.

Despite the restriction prohibiting commercial building ("no other than a dwelling or cottage shall be erected . . . "), commercial development began in the 1920's on property subject to the covenants. This development included numerous inns, restaurants, drug stores, a bank, motels, a town hall, shops selling various items including food, clothing, gifts and novelties and other commercial businesses. Of the 34 commercial buildings presently within the Town limits, 29 are located in the old-Town originally developed by BBIC. Today, Bethany Beach has a permanent population of some 330 residents. In the summer months the population increases to approximately 10,000 people within the corporate limits and to some 48,000 people within a 4 mile radius. In 1952, the Town

---

* The restrictive covenant stated:

"This covenant is made expressly subject to and upon the following conditions: viz; That no intoxicating liquors shall ever be sold on the said lot, that no other than dwelling or cottage shall be erected thereon and but one to each lot, which must be of full size according to the said plan, excepting, however, suitable and necessary out or back building, which may be erected on the rear of said lot, and no building or buildings shall be erected thereon within ten feet of the front building line of said lot and, if said lot be a corner lot within ten feet of the building line of the side street on which it abuts, and that all buildings erected or to be erected on said lot shall be kept neatly painted; a breach of which said conditions, or any of them, shall cause said lot to revert to and become again the property of the grantor, his heirs and assigns; and upon such breach of said conditions or restrictions, the same may be restrained or enjoined in equity by the grantor, his heirs or assigns, or by any co-lot owner in said plan or other party injured by such breach."

enacted a zoning ordinance which established a central commercial district designated C-1 located in the old-Town section. Holiday House is located in this district.

Since El Di purchased Holiday House in 1969, patrons have been permitted to carry their own alcoholic beverages with them into the restaurant to consume with their meals. This "brown-bagging" practice occurred at Holiday House prior to El Di's ownership and at other restaurants in the Town. El Di applied for a license to sell liquor at Holiday House in response to the increased number of customers who were engaging in "brown-bagging" and in the belief that the license would permit restaurant management to control excessive use of alcohol and use by minors. Prior to the time El Di sought a license, alcoholic beverages had been and continue to be readily available for sale at nearby licensed establishments including: one restaurant ½ mile outside the Town limits, 3 restaurants within a 4 mile radius of the Town, and a package store some 200-300 yards from the Holiday House.

The Trial Court granted a stay pending the outcome of this appeal.

II.

In granting plaintiffs' motion for a permanent injunction, the Court of Chancery rejected defendant's argument that changed conditions in Bethany Beach rendered the restrictive covenants unreasonable and therefore unenforceable, citing *Restatement of Property,* §564; *Welshire, Inc. v. Harbison,* Del.Supr., 91 A.2d 404 (1952); and *Cruciano v. Ceccarone,* Del.Ch., 133 A.2d 911 (1957). The Chancery Court found that although the evidence showed a considerable growth since 1900 in both population and the number of buildings in Bethany Beach, "the basic nature of Bethany Beach as a quiet, family oriented resort has not changed." The Court also found that there had been development of commercial activity since 1900, but that this "activity is limited to a small area of Bethany Beach and consists mainly of activities for the convenience and patronage of the residents of Bethany Beach."

The Trial Court also rejected defendant's contention that plaintiffs' acquiescence and abandonment rendered the covenants unenforceable. In this connection, the Court concluded that the practice of "brown-bagging" was not a sale of alcoholic beverages and that, therefore, any failure to enforce the restriction as against the practice did not constitute abandonment or waiver of the restriction.

III.

We find that the Trial Court erred in holding that the change of conditions was insufficient to negate the restrictive covenant.

A court will not enforce a restrictive covenant where a fundamental change has occurred in the intended character of the neighborhood that renders the benefits underlying imposition of the restrictions incapable of enjoyment. *Welshire v. Harbison,* Del.Supr., 91 A.2d 404 (1952); *1.77 Acres of Land v. State,* Del.Supr., 241 A.2d 513 (1968);

Williams v. Tsiarkezos, Del.Ch., 272 A.2d 722 (1970). Review of all the facts and circumstances convinces us that the change, since 1901, in the character of that area of the old-Town section now zoned C-1 is so substantial as to justify modification of the deed restriction. We need not determine a change in character of the entire restricted area in order to assess the continued applicability of the covenant to a portion thereof. *See Noyes v. McDonnell,* Okl.Supr., 398 P.2d 838 (1965); *Palmer v. Circle Amusement Co.,* Ct.App.N.J., 130 N.J.Eq. 356, 22 A.2d 241 (1941).

It is uncontradicted that one of the purposes underlying the covenant prohibiting the sale of intoxicating liquors was to maintain a quiet, residential atmosphere in the restricted area. Each of the additional covenants reinforces this objective, including the covenant restricting construction to residential dwellings. The covenants read as a whole evince an intention on the part of the grantor to maintain the residential, seaside character of the community.

But time has not left Bethany Beach the same community its grantors envisioned in 1901. The Town has changed from a church-affiliated residential community to a summer resort visited annually by thousands of tourists. Nowhere is the resultant change in character more evident than in the C-1 section of the old-Town. Plaintiffs argue that this is a relative change only and that there is sufficient evidence to support the Trial Court's findings that the residential character of the community has been maintained and that the covenants continue to benefit the other lot owners. We cannot agree.

In 1909, the 180 acre restricted old-Town section became part of a 750 acre incorporated municipality. Even prior to the Town's incorporation, the BBIC deeded out lots free of the restrictive covenants. After incorporation and partly due to the unrestricted lots deeded out by the BBIC, 85 percent of the land area within the Town was not subject to the restrictions. Significantly, nonresidential uses quickly appeared in the restricted area and today the old-Town section contains almost all of the commercial businesses within the entire Town. Contrast *Whitaker v. Holmes,* Ariz.Supr., 74 Ariz. 30, 243 P.2d 462 (1952) (original grantors specifically provided for continued vitality of the covenants in the event a Town was later established). Moreover, these commercial uses have gone unchallenged for 82 years. Contrast *Humphreys v. Ibach,* N.J.Supr., 110 N.J.Eq. 647, 160 A. 531 (1932).

The change in conditions is also reflected in the Town's decision in 1952 to zone restricted property, including the lot on which the Holiday House is located, specifically for commercial use. Although a change in zoning is not dispositive as against a private covenant, it is additional evidence of changed community conditions. *Bard v. Rose,* Cal. Dist.Ct.App., 203 Cal.App.2d 232, 21 Cal.Rptr. 382, 384 (1962). *See Owens v. Camfield,* Ark. Ct.App., 1 Ark.App. 295, 614 S.W.2d 698 (1981).

Time has relaxed not only the strictly residential character of the area, but the pattern of alcohol use and consumption as well. The practice of "brown-bagging" has continued unchallenged for at least twenty years at commercial establishments located on restricted property in the Town. On appeal, plaintiffs rely on the Trial Court finding that the "brown-bagging," practice is irrelevant as evidence of waiver inasmuch as the practice does not involve the sale of intoxicating liquors prohibited by the covenant. We find the "brown-bagging" practice evidence of a significant change in conditions in the community since its inception at the turn of the century. Such consumption of alcohol in public places is now generally tolerated by owners of similarly restricted lots. The license issued to the Holiday House establishment permits the El Di management to better control the availability and consumption of intoxicating liquors on its premises. In view of both the ready availability of alcoholic beverages in the area surrounding the Holiday House and the long-tolerated and increasing use of "brown-bagging" enforcement of the restrictive covenant at this time would only serve to subvert the public interest in the control of the availability and consumption of alcoholic liquors.

Plaintiffs contend that the covenant prohibiting the sale of intoxicating liquors is separate from the other covenants. In the plaintiffs' view, the alcohol sale restriction serves a purpose distinct from the prohibition of nonresidential uses. Plaintiffs argue, therefore, that despite evidence of commercial uses, the alcohol sale restriction provides a substantial benefit to the other lot owners. We find the cases on which plaintiff relies distinguishable:

In *Jameson v. Brown,* 109 F.2d 830 (D.C.Cir.1939), all of the lots were similarly restricted and there was no evidence of waiver or abandonment of the covenant prohibiting the sale of spiritous liquors. The court found evidence of one isolated violation—in contrast to the long-tolerated practice of "brown-bagging" in Bethany Beach. Compare *Alamogordo Improvement Co. v. Prendergast,* N.M.Supr., 45 N.M. 40, 109 P.2d 254 (1940). In *Brookside Community, Inc. v. Williams,* Del.Ch., 290 A.2d 678, *aff'd,* 306 A.2d 711 (1972), the general rule in Delaware is stated as to the effect of a waiver of a separable covenant. The case is distinguishable because here we consider waiver in conjunction with our assessment of the change of conditions in the community. No such change was alleged or addressed in *Williams.* In *Benner v. Tacony Athletic Ass'n,* Pa.Supr., 328 Pa. 577, 196 A. 390 (1938), it was found that commercial encroachments were few and that residential properties still closely surrounded the commercial lots. In Bethany Beach commercial uses have not simply crept in, but have been given official sanction through the 1952 Zoning Ordinance.

It is further argued that the commercial uses are restricted to a small area within the old-Town section. But significantly, the section in which Holiday House is located is entirely commercial. The business uses, the availability of alcohol in close proximity to this section, and the repeated use of "brown-bagging" in the C-1 district render the originally intended benefits of the covenants unattainable in what has become an area detached in character from the strictly residential surroundings to the west.

In view of the change in conditions in the C-1 district of Bethany Beach, we find it unreasonable and inequitable now to enforce the restrictive covenant. To permit unlimited "brown-bagging" but to prohibit licensed sales of alcoholic liquor, under the circumstances of this case, is inconsistent with any reasonable application of the restriction and contrary to public policy.

We emphasize that our judgment is confined to the area of the old-Town section zoned C-1. The restrictions in the neighboring residential area are unaffected by the conclusion we reach herein.

Reversed.

CHRISTIE, Justice, with whom MOORE, Justice, joins, dissenting:

I respectfully disagree with the majority.

I think the evidence supports the conclusion of the Chancellor, as finder of fact, that the basic nature of the community of Bethany Beach has not changed in such a way as to invalidate those restrictions which have continued to protect this community through the years as it has grown. Although some of the restrictions have been ignored and a portion of the community is now used for limited commercial purposes, the evidence shows that Bethany Beach remains a quiet, family-oriented resort where no liquor is sold. I think the conditions of the community are still consistent with the enforcement of a restrictive covenant forbidding the sale of intoxicating beverages.

In my opinion, the toleration of the practice of "brown bagging" does not constitute the abandonment of a longstanding restriction against the sale of alcoholic beverages. The restriction against sales has, in fact, remained intact for more than eighty years and any violations thereof have been short-lived. The fact that alcoholic beverages may be purchased right outside the town is not inconsistent with my view that the quiet-town atmosphere in this small area has not broken down, and that it can and should be preserved. Those who choose to buy land subject to the restrictions should be required to continue to abide by the restrictions.

I think the only real beneficiaries of the failure of the courts to enforce the restrictions would be those who plan to benefit commercially.

I also question the propriety of the issuance of a liquor license for the sale of liquor on property which is subject to a specific restrictive covenant against such sales.

I think that restrictive covenants play a vital part in the preservation of neighborhood schemes all over the State, and that a much more complete breakdown of the neighborhood scheme should be required before a court declares that a restriction has become unenforceable.

I would affirm the Chancellor.

NOTE AND QUESTIONS

1. *Comparing* Western Land *and* El Di. *Western Land* rejected, and *El Di* accepted, a challenge to a covenant on changed circumstances grounds. Do both cases apply the same standard for changed circumstances? Compare the subject matter and scope of

the covenants in *Western Land* and *El Di*. Do you think that the subject matter in the *El Di* covenant made it more likely that circumstances would actually change than the covenant in *Western Land*? Put another way, can you imagine a scenario where circumstances had changed so much that the *Western Land* covenant would not be enforced?

PROBLEM

Sarah owns an undeveloped lot in Fox Run, a common interest community. Fox Run is governed by a set of Covenants, Conditions, and Restrictions (CC&Rs) that include a covenant limiting each lot to single-family residential use. Sarah's lot is in a corner at the edge of the development. When she first bought her lot, the surrounding area was undeveloped fields. Now the surrounding area has been developed commercially. Right next to her lot to one side is a convenience store. On the other side of her lot are two houses that are part of the Fox Run development. The owners of the convenience store have offered to buy Sarah's lot so that they can expand their operations so long as Sarah can free the lot from the restrictions in the CC&Rs. Sarah has brought a declaratory action seeking to terminate the single-family use covenant on changed circumstances grounds. Sarah has noted that the area surrounding her lot has fundamentally changed and that her lot would be more valuable without the covenant. The neighboring homeowners have opposed Sarah's declaratory action. How should the court rule and why? An explanatory answer can be found on page 1064.

> ### TERMINATION OF COVENANTS
>
> Generally speaking, covenants that run with the land may be terminated in the same way as easements. As we discussed in both the easements and covenants context, changed circumstances is more clearly a grounds for terminating covenants than for terminating easements, though in either circumstance the changed circumstances test will be strict. We will see below that covenants may become unenforceable based on abandonment but that abandonment means something slightly different in the covenants context than it does in the easements context.

2. COMMON INTEREST COMMUNITIES

Common interest communities are communities that are governed by a set of recorded covenants that run with the land. These sets of covenants, CC&Rs, can be quite lengthy. The CC&Rs typically create a governing board that has a duty to manage the community and enforce the covenants. Common interest communities are very common in the United States, and the number of people living in them increases every year.

There are several types of common interest communities. We have already seen communities of homes governed by *homeowners' associations* at several points. In a common interest community governed by a homeowners' association, each resident owns their home in fee simple. The association or a related entity owns the common areas. *Condominiums* are similar in ownership and governance structure to homeowners' associations. Apartment buildings and other multifamily housing structures are often organized as condominiums. Each resident has fee simple ownership of her apartment, while the condominium association has ownership of the common areas. The resident's ownership typically extends to the inside of the interior walls of the apartment. The rest of the building is part of the condominium's common areas.

Common interest communities may also be organized as *cooperatives*, or co-ops. Co-ops are relatively rare in most areas but are relatively common in some others. They are particularly common and important in New York City. In a co-op, the cooperative association retains fee simple ownership of the entire structure, including the individual apartments. Each resident owns shares of the co-op entity, and the co-op entity gives the resident the right to occupy her apartment. Co-op residents therefore own shares of an entity rather than real property. This allows co-op residents to avoid New York City's high mortgage registration tax. Co-ops tend to be very selective about admitting new residents (and courts often permit this selectivity) because the residents of a co-op are co-owners of a shared enterprise rather than fee simple owners of individual apartments. If the co-op association has financial difficulty or goes bankrupt, the co-op owners could lose everything because all they own is their share of the entity. If a condominium association has similar difficulty, the condominium owners will still own their apartments in fee simple.

The CC&Rs typically provide covenants that require residents to pay dues and that allow the governing board to assess additional financial contributions. As we noted above, these covenants tend to be immune from touch and concern and benefit in gross issues in the common interest community context. Because the CC&Rs typically are imposed as part of the subdivision process or creation of the condominium, horizontal privity (if it is required) tends not to be an issue for common interest communities.

The governing board has an obligation to enforce the CC&Rs. Common interest communities often include use restrictions. The CC&Rs, for example, might require that homes meet minimum or maximum square footage requirements. Or they might ban satellite dishes or pets.

These requirements present numerous opportunities for conflicts between the board and individual property owners. An individual property owner might argue that it is unreasonable to enforce the covenant in that owner's particular context. For example, if I have a satellite dish in my backyard, and because of the unique features of my yard the dish is not visible to any of my neighbors, I might argue that it is unreasonable to enforce a no-satellite-dish covenant against me.

As we will see in our next case, common interest community covenants will not be enforced if enforcement would be unreasonable. The satellite dish example sets up a critical issue in the case. Unsurprisingly, that issue involves the precise meaning of reasonableness. Cases involving common interest community covenants tend to frame reasonableness in one of two ways. The first approach would ask whether it is reasonable to enforce the covenant against a particular resident in light of that resident's specific circumstances. In the satellite dish example, this approach would ask whether it is reasonable to enforce the covenant against me in my specific circumstances where none of the neighbors can see the dish. The second approach would ask whether it is reasonable to enforce the covenant in light of the overall circumstances of the community. In the satellite dish example, this approach would ask whether it is reasonable for a community to have a ban on satellite dishes. The fact that no one can see my particular dish would not be relevant.

Our next case turns in large part on the distinction between these two approaches to reasonableness.

NAHRSTEDT V. LAKESIDE VILLAGE CONDOMINIUM ASSOCIATION, INC.

Supreme Court of California, 1994
878 P.2d 1275

KENNARD, Justice.

A homeowner in a 530-unit condominium complex sued to prevent the homeowners association from enforcing a restriction against keeping cats, dogs, and other animals in the condominium development. The owner asserted that the restriction, which was contained in the project's declaration[1] recorded by the condominium project's developer, was "unreasonable" as applied to her because she kept her three cats indoors and because her cats were "noiseless" and "created no nuisance." Agreeing with the premise underlying the owner's complaint, the Court of Appeal concluded that the homeowners association could enforce the restriction only upon proof that plaintiff's cats would be likely to interfere with the right of other homeowners "to the peaceful and quiet enjoyment of their property."

Those of us who have cats or dogs can attest to their wonderful companionship and affection. Not surprisingly, studies have confirmed this effect. (See, e.g., Waltham Symposium 20, Pets, Benefits and Practice (BVA Publications 1990); Melson, *The Benefits*

---

[1] The declaration is the operative document for a common interest development, setting forth, among other things, the restrictions on the use or enjoyment of any portion of the development. (Civ.Code, §§1351, 1353.) In some states, the declaration is also referred to as the "master deed." (See *Dulaney Towers Maintenance v. O'Brey* (1980) 46 Md.App. 464, 418 A.2d 1233, 1235.)

of Animals to Our Lives (Fall 1990) People, Animals, Environment, at pp. 15-17.) But the issue before us is not whether in the abstract pets can have a beneficial effect on humans. Rather, the narrow issue here is whether a pet restriction that is contained in the recorded declaration of a condominium complex is enforceable against the challenge of a homeowner. As we shall explain, the Legislature, in Civil Code section 1354, has required that courts enforce the covenants, conditions and restrictions contained in the recorded declaration of a common interest development "unless unreasonable."

Because a stable and predictable living environment is crucial to the success of condominiums and other common interest residential developments, and because recorded use restrictions are a primary means of ensuring this stability and predictability, the Legislature in section 1354 has afforded such restrictions a presumption of validity and has required of challengers that they demonstrate the restriction's "unreasonableness" by the deferential standard applicable to equitable servitudes. Under this standard established by the Legislature, enforcement of a restriction does not depend upon the conduct of a particular condominium owner. Rather, the restriction must be uniformly enforced in the condominium development to which it was intended to apply unless the plaintiff owner can show that the burdens it imposes on affected properties so substantially outweigh the benefits of the restriction that it should not be enforced against any owner. Here, the Court of Appeal did not apply this standard in deciding that plaintiff had stated a claim for declaratory relief. Accordingly, we reverse the judgment of the Court of Appeal and remand for further proceedings consistent with the views expressed in this opinion.

I

Lakeside Village is a large condominium development in Culver City, Los Angeles County. It consists of 530 units spread throughout 12 separate 3-story buildings. The residents share common lobbies and hallways, in addition to laundry and trash facilities.

The Lakeside Village project is subject to certain covenants, conditions and restrictions (hereafter CC & R's) that were included in the developer's declaration recorded with the Los Angeles County Recorder on April 17, 1978, at the inception of the development project. Ownership of a unit includes membership in the project's homeowners association, the Lakeside Village Condominium Association (hereafter Association), the body that enforces the project's CC & R's, including the pet restriction, which provides in relevant part: "No animals (which shall mean dogs and cats), livestock, reptiles or poultry shall be kept in any unit."[3]

In January 1988, plaintiff Natore Nahrstedt purchased a Lakeside Village condominium and moved in with her three cats. When the Association learned of the

---

[3] The CC & R's permit residents to keep "domestic fish and birds."

cats' presence, it demanded their removal and assessed fines against Nahrstedt for each successive month that she remained in violation of the condominium project's pet restriction.

Nahrstedt then brought this lawsuit against the Association, its officers, and two of its employees, asking the trial court to invalidate the assessments, to enjoin future assessments, to award damages for violation of her privacy when the Association "peered" into her condominium unit, to award damages for infliction of emotional distress, and to declare the pet restriction "unreasonable" as applied to indoor cats (such as hers) that are not allowed free run of the project's common areas. Nahrstedt also alleged she did not know of the pet restriction when she bought her condominium. The complaint incorporated by reference the grant deed, the declaration of CC & R's, and the condominium plan for the Lakeside Village condominium project.

The Association demurred to the complaint. In its supporting points and authorities, the Association argued that the pet restriction furthers the collective "health, happiness and peace of mind" of persons living in close proximity within the Lakeside Village condominium development, and therefore is reasonable as a matter of law. The trial court sustained the demurrer as to each cause of action and dismissed Nahrstedt's complaint. Nahrstedt appealed.

A divided Court of Appeal reversed the trial court's judgment of dismissal. In the majority's view, the complaint stated a claim for declaratory relief based on its allegations that Nahrstedt's three cats are kept inside her condominium unit and do not bother her neighbors. According to the majority, whether a condominium use restriction is "unreasonable," as that term is used in section 1354, hinges on the facts of a particular homeowner's case. Thus, the majority reasoned, Nahrstedt would be entitled to declaratory relief if application of the pet restriction in her case would not be reasonable. The Court of Appeal also revived Nahrstedt's causes of action for invasion of privacy, invalidation of the assessments, and injunctive relief, as well as her action for emotional distress based on a theory of negligence.

The dissenting justice took the view that enforcement of the Lakeside Village pet restriction against Nahrstedt should not depend on the "reasonableness" of the restriction as applied to Nahrstedt. To evaluate on a case-by-case basis the reasonableness of a recorded use restriction included in the declaration of a condominium project, the dissent said, would be at odds with the Legislature's intent that such restrictions be regarded as presumptively reasonable and subject to enforcement under the rules governing equitable servitudes. Application of those rules, the dissenting justice concluded, would render a recorded use restriction valid unless "there are constitutional principles at stake, enforcement is arbitrary, or the association fails to follow its own procedures."

On the Association's petition, we granted review to decide when a condominium owner can prevent enforcement of a use restriction that the project's developer has included in the recorded declaration of CC & R's.

To facilitate the reader's understanding of the function served by use restrictions in condominium developments and related real property ownership arrangements, we begin with a broad overview of the general principles governing common interest forms of real property ownership.

II

Today, condominiums, cooperatives, and planned-unit developments with homeowners associations have become a widely accepted form of real property ownership. These ownership arrangements are known as "common interest" developments. (4B Powell, Real Property (1993) Condominiums, Cooperatives and Homeowners Association Developments, §631, pp. 54-7 to 54-8; 15A Am.Jur.2d, Condominium and Co-operative Apartments, §1, p. 827.) The owner not only enjoys many of the traditional advantages associated with individual ownership of real property, but also acquires an interest in common with others in the amenities and facilities included in the project. It is this hybrid nature of property rights that largely accounts for the popularity of these new and innovative forms of ownership in the 20th century. (4B Powell, Real Property, *supra,* §631, pp. 54-7 to 54-8.)

The term "condominium," which is used to describe a system of ownership as well as an individually owned unit in a multi-unit development, is Latin in origin and means joint dominion or co-ownership. (4B Powell, Real Property, *supra,* §632.1[4], p. 54-18.) . . .

To divide a plot of land into interests severable by blocks or planes, the attorney for the land developer must prepare a declaration that must be recorded prior to the sale of any unit in the county where the land is located. (Natelson, *Consent, Coercion, and "Reasonableness" in Private Law: The Special Case of the Property Owners Association* (1990) 51 Ohio State L.J. 41, 47 [hereafter Natelson, *Consent, Coercion, and "Reasonableness"*].) The declaration, which is the operative document for the creation of any common interest development, is a collection of covenants, conditions and servitudes that govern the project. (*Ibid.;* see also 4B Powell, Real Property, *supra,* §632.4[1] & [2], pp. 54-84, 54-92; 15A Am.Jur.2d, *supra,* §14, p. 843.) Typically, the declaration describes the real property and any structures on the property, delineates the common areas within the project as well as the individually held lots or units, and sets forth restrictions pertaining to the use of the property. (15A Am.Jur.2d, *supra,* §14, p. 843.)

Use restrictions are an inherent part of any common interest development and are crucial to the stable, planned environment of any shared ownership arrangement. (Note, *Community Association Use Restrictions: Applying the Business Judgment Doctrine* (1988) 64 Chi.Kent L.Rev. 653, 673 [hereafter Note, *Business Judgment*]; see also Natelson, *Consent, Coercion and "Reasonableness," supra,* 51 Ohio State L.J. at p. 47.) The viability of shared ownership of improved real property rests on the existence of extensive reciprocal servitudes, together with the ability of each co-owner to prevent the property's partition. . . .

The restrictions on the use of property in any common interest development may limit activities conducted in the common areas as well as in the confines of the home itself. (Reichman, *Residential Private Governments* (1976) 43 U.Chi.L.Rev. 253, 270; 15A Am.Jur.2d, *supra,* §16, pp. 845-846.) Commonly, use restrictions preclude alteration of building exteriors, limit the number of persons that can occupy each unit, and place limitations on—or prohibit altogether—the keeping of pets. (4B Powell, Real Property, *supra,* §632.5 [11], p. 54-221; Reichman, *Residential Private Governments, supra,* at p. 270; Natelson, *Consent, Coercion, and "Reasonableness," supra,* 51 Ohio St.L.J. at p. 48, fn. 28 [as of 1986, 58 percent of highrise developments and 39 percent of townhouse projects had some kind of pet restriction]; see also *Noble v. Murphy* (1993) 34 Mass.App.Ct. 452, 612 N.E.2d 266 [enforcing condominium ban on pets]; *Dulaney Towers Maintenance Corp. v. O'Brey, supra,* 418 A.2d 1233 [upholding pet restriction]; *Wilshire Condominium Ass'n, Inc. v. Kohlbrand* (Fla.Dist.Ct.App.1979) 368 So.2d 629 [same].)[5]

Restrictions on property use are not the only characteristic of common interest ownership. Ordinarily, such ownership also entails mandatory membership in an owners association, which, through an elected board of directors, is empowered to enforce any use restrictions contained in the project's declaration or master deed and to enact new rules governing the use and occupancy of property within the project. (Cal Condominium and Planned Development Practice (Cont.Ed.Bar 1984) §1.7, p. 13; Note, *Business Judgment, supra,* 64 Chi.Kent L.Rev. at p. 65; Natelson, Law of Property Owners Associations, *supra,* §3.2.2, p. 71 et seq.) Because of its considerable power in managing and regulating a common interest development, the governing board of an owners association must guard against the potential for the abuse of that power. As Professor Natelson observes, owners associations "can be a powerful force for good or for ill" in their members' lives. (Natelson, *Consent, Coercion, and "Reasonableness" supra,* 51 Ohio State L.J. at p. 43.) Therefore, anyone who buys a unit in a common interest development with knowledge of its owners association's discretionary power accepts "the risk that the power may be used in a way that benefits the commonality but harms the individual." (*Id.* at p. 67.) Generally, courts will uphold decisions made by the governing board of an owners association so long as they represent good faith efforts to further the purposes of the common interest development, are consistent with the development's governing documents, and comply with public policy. (*Id.* at p. 43.)

Thus, subordination of individual property rights to the collective judgment of the owners association together with restrictions on the use of real property comprise the chief attributes of owning property in a common interest development. As the Florida District Court of Appeal observed in *Hidden Harbour Estates, Inc. v. Norman* (Fla.Dist.

---

[5] Even the dissent recognizes that pet restrictions have a long pedigree. (See dis. opn., *post,* p. 82, fn. 5 of 33 Cal. Rptr.2d, p. 1294, fn. 5 of 878 P.2d, citing Crimmins, The Quotable Cat (1992) p. 58 [English nuns living in a nunnery prohibited in 1205 from keeping any pet except a cat].)

Ct.App.1975) 309 So.2d 180, a decision frequently cited in condominium cases: "[I] nherent in the condominium concept is the principle that to promote the health, happiness, and peace of mind of the majority of the unit owners since they are living in such close proximity and using facilities in common, each unit owner must give up a certain degree of freedom of choice which he [or she] might otherwise enjoy in separate, privately owned property. Condominium unit owners comprise a little democratic sub-society of necessity more restrictive as it pertains to use of condominium property than may be existent outside the condominium organization." (*Id.* at pp. 181-182; see also Leyser, *The Ownership of Flats—A Comparative Study, supra,* 7 Int'l & Comp.L.Q. at p. 38 [explaining the French system's recognition that "flat ownership" has limitations that considerably exceed those of "normal" real property ownership, "limitations arising out of the rights of the other flat owners."].)

Notwithstanding the limitations on personal autonomy that are inherent in the concept of shared ownership of residential property, common interest developments have increased in popularity in recent years, in part because they generally provide a more affordable alternative to ownership of a single-family home. (See *Frances T. v. Village Green Owners Assn.* (1986) 42 Cal.3d 490, 500, fn. 9, 229 Cal.Rptr. 456, 723 P.2d 573 [noting that common interest developments at that time accounted for as much as 70 percent of the new housing market in Los Angeles and San Diego Counties]; *Laguna Royale Owners Assn. v. Darger* (1981) 119 Cal.App.3d 670, 681, 174 Cal.Rptr. 136; Natelson, *Consent, Coercion and "Reasonableness," supra,* 51 Ohio St.L.J. at pp. 42- 43 [as of 1988, more than 30 million Americans lived in housing governed by owners associations]; see also McKenzie, *Welcome Home. Do as We Say.,* N.Y. Times (Aug. 18, 1994) p. 23A, col. 1 [stating that 32 million Americans are members of some 150,000 homeowners associations and predicting that between 25 to 30 percent of Americans will live in community association housing by the year 2000.])

One significant factor in the continued popularity of the common interest form of property ownership is the ability of homeowners to enforce restrictive CC & R's against other owners (including future purchasers) of project units. (Natelson, Law of Property Owners Associations, *supra,* §1.3.2.1, p. 19; Note, *Business Judgment, supra,* 64 Chi.Kent L.Rev. at p. 673.) Generally, however, such enforcement is possible only if the restriction that is sought to be enforced meets the requirements of equitable servitudes or of covenants running with the land. (Cal.Condominium and Planned Development Practice, *supra,* §§8.42-8.44, pp. 666-668; Note, *Covenants and Equitable Servitudes in California* (1978) 29 Hastings L.J. 545, 553-573.)

Restrictive covenants will run with the land, and thus bind successive owners, if the deed or other instrument containing the restrictive covenant particularly describes the lands to be benefited and burdened by the restriction and expressly provides that successors in interest of the covenantor's land will be bound for the benefit of the covenantee's land. Moreover, restrictions must relate to use, repair, maintenance, or improvement of the property, or to payment of taxes or assessments, and the instrument containing the restrictions must be recorded. (See §1468; Advising Cal.Condominium and Homeowners Associations (Cont.Ed.Bar 1991) §7.33, p. 342.)

Restrictions that do not meet the requirements of covenants running with the land may be enforceable as equitable servitudes provided the person bound by the restrictions had notice of their existence. (*Riley v. Bear Creek Planning Committee* (1976) 17 Cal.3d 500, 507, 131 Cal.Rptr. 381, 551 P.2d 1213; Cal.Condominium and Planned Development Practice, *supra*, §8.44, pp. 667-668.)

When restrictions limiting the use of property within a common interest development satisfy the requirements of covenants running with the land or of equitable servitudes, what standard or test governs their enforceability? In California, as we explained at the outset, our Legislature has made common interest development use restrictions contained in a project's recorded declaration "enforceable . . . *unless unreasonable.*" (§1354, subd. (a), italics added.)

In states lacking such legislative guidance, some courts have adopted a standard under which a common interest development's recorded use restrictions will be enforced so long as they are "reasonable." (See *Riley v. Stoves* (1974) 22 Ariz.App. 223, 228, 526 P.2d 747, 752 [asking whether the challenged restriction provided "a reasonable means to accomplish the private objective"]; *Hidden Harbour Estates, Inc. v. Norman, supra,* 309 So.2d at p. 182 [to justify regulation, conduct need not be "so offensive as to constitute a nuisance"]; 15A Am.Jur.2d, *supra,* §31, p. 861.) Although no one definition of the term "reasonable" has gained universal acceptance, most courts have applied what one commentator calls "equitable reasonableness," upholding only those restrictions that provide a reasonable means to further the collective "health, happiness and enjoyment of life" of owners of a common interest development. (Note, *Business Judgment, supra,* 64 Chi.Kent L.Rev. at p. 655.) Others would limit the "reasonableness" standard only to those restrictions adopted by majority vote of the homeowners or enacted under the rulemaking power of an association's governing board, and would not apply this test to restrictions included in a planned development project's recorded declaration or master deed. Because such restrictions are presumptively valid, these authorities would enforce them regardless of reasonableness. The first court to articulate this view was the Florida Fourth District Court of Appeal.

In *Hidden Harbour Estates v. Basso* (Fla.Dist.Ct.App.1981) 393 So.2d 637, the Florida court distinguished two categories of use restrictions: use restrictions set forth in the declaration or master deed of the condominium project itself, and rules promulgated by the governing board of the condominium owners association or the board's interpretation of a rule. (*Id.* at p. 639.) The latter category of use restrictions, the court said, should be subject to a "reasonableness" test, so as to "somewhat fetter the discretion of the board of directors." (*Id.* at p. 640.) Such a standard, the court explained, best assures that governing boards will "enact rules and make decisions that are reasonably related to the promotion of the health, happiness and peace of mind" of the project owners, considered collectively. (*Ibid.*)

By contrast, restrictions contained in the declaration or master deed of the condominium complex, the Florida court concluded, should not be evaluated under a "reasonableness" standard. (*Hidden Harbour Estates v. Basso, supra*, 393 So.2d at pp. 639-640.) Rather, such use restrictions are "clothed with a very strong presumption of validity" and should be upheld even if they exhibit some degree of unreasonableness. (*Id.* at pp. 639, 640.) Nonenforcement would be proper only if such restrictions were arbitrary or in violation of public policy or some fundamental constitutional right. (*Id.* at pp. 639-640.) The Florida court's decision was cited with approval recently by a Massachusetts appellate court in *Noble v. Murphy, supra*, 612 N.E.2d 266.

In *Noble,* managers of a condominium development sought to enforce against the owners of one unit a pet restriction contained in the project's master deed. The Massachusetts court upheld the validity of the restriction. The court stated that "[a] condominium use restriction appearing in originating documents which predate the purchase of individual units" was entitled to greater judicial deference than restrictions "promulgated after units have been individually acquired." (*Noble v. Murphy, supra,* 612 N.E.2d at p. 270.) The court reasoned that "properly-enacted and evenly-enforced use restrictions contained in a master deed or original bylaws of a condominium" should be insulated against attack "except on constitutional or public policy grounds." (*Id.* at p. 271.) This standard, the court explained, best "serves the interest of the majority of owners [within a project] who may be presumed to have chosen not to alter or rescind such restrictions," and it spares overcrowded courts "the burden and expense of highly particularized and lengthy litigation." (*Ibid.*)

Indeed, giving deference to use restrictions contained in a condominium project's originating documents protects the general expectations of condominium owners "that restrictions in place at the time they purchase their units will be enforceable." (Note, *Judicial Review of Condominium Rulemaking, supra,* 94 Harv.L.Rev. 647, 653; Ellickson, *Cities and Homeowners' Associations* (1982) 130 U.Pa.L.Rev. 1519, 1526-1527 [stating that association members "unanimously consent to the provisions in the association's original documents" and courts therefore should not scrutinize such documents for "reasonableness."].) This in turn encourages the development of shared ownership housing—generally a less costly alternative to single-dwelling ownership—by attracting buyers who prefer a stable, planned environment. It also protects buyers who have paid a premium for condominium units in reliance on a particular restrictive scheme.

To what extent are these general principles reflected in California's statutory scheme governing condominiums and other common interest developments? We shall explore that in the next section.

III

In California, common interest developments are subject to the provisions of the Davis-Stirling Common Interest Development Act (hereafter Davis-Stirling Act or Act). (§1350 et seq.) The Act, passed into law in 1985, consolidated in one part of the Civil Code certain definitions and other substantive provisions pertaining to condominiums and other types of common interest developments. (Stats.1985, ch. 874, §14, p. 2774.)

The Act enumerates the specific shared ownership arrangements that fall under the rubric "common interest development." (§1351, subd. (c)(1)-(4).) It also sets out the requirements for establishing a common interest development (§1352), reserves to each homeowner in such a development limited authority to modify an individual unit (§1360), grants to the owners association of the development those powers necessary to the development's long-term operation (§§1363, 1364, 1365.5, 1366), and recognizes the right of homeowners collectively to alter or amend existing use restrictions, or to add new ones (§1356). . . .

Pertinent here is the Act's provision for the enforcement of use restrictions contained in the project's recorded declaration. That provision, subdivision (a) of section 1354, states in relevant part: "The covenants and restrictions in the declaration shall be enforceable equitable servitudes, *unless unreasonable,* and shall inure to the benefit of and bind all owners of separate interests in the development." (Italics added.) To determine when a restrictive covenant included in the declaration of a common interest development cannot be enforced, we must construe section 1354. In doing so, our primary task is to ascertain legislative intent, giving the words of the statute their ordinary meaning. . . . The words, however, must be read in context, considering the nature and purpose of the statutory enactment. . . .

In choosing equitable servitude law as the standard for enforcing CC & R's in common interest developments, the Legislature has manifested a preference in favor of their enforcement. This preference is underscored by the use of the word "shall" in the first phrase of section 1354: "The covenants and restrictions shall be enforceable equitable servitudes. . . ."

The Legislature did, however, set a condition for the mandatory enforcement of a declaration's CC & R's: a covenant, condition or restriction is "enforceable . . . *unless unreasonable.*" (§1354, subd. (a), italics added.) The Legislature's use of the phrase "unless unreasonable" in section 1354 was a marked change from the prior version of that statutory provision, which stated that "restrictions shall be enforceable equitable servitudes *where reasonable.*" (Former §1355, italics added; see fn. 10, *ante.*) Under settled principles of statutory construction, such a material alteration of a statute's phrasing signals the Legislature's intent to give an enactment a new meaning. (*McDonough Power Equipment Co. v. Superior Court* (1972) 8 Cal.3d 527, 534, fn. 5, 105 Cal.Rptr. 330, 503 P.2d 1338.) Here, the change in statutory language, from "where reasonable" to "unless unreasonable," cloaked use restrictions contained in a condominium development's recorded declaration with a presumption of reasonableness by shifting the burden of proving otherwise to the party challenging the use restriction. (Cal.Condominium and Planned Development Practice, *supra,* §1.9, p. 18 [stating that the change in statutory language "switches the burden to the person challenging the restriction to establish that it is unreasonable"]; Advising Cal.Condominium and Homeowners Associations, *supra,* §7.34, p. 344 [same].)

How is that burden satisfied? To answer this question, we must examine the principles governing enforcement of equitable servitudes. . . .

[W]hen enforcing equitable servitudes, courts are generally disinclined to question the wisdom of agreed-to restrictions. (Note, *Covenants and Equitable Servitudes in California, supra,* 29 Hastings L.J. at p. 577, citing *Walker v. Haslett* (1919) 44 Cal.App. 394, 397-398, 186 P. 622.) This rule does not apply, however, when the restriction does not comport with public policy. (*Ibid.*) Equity will not enforce any restrictive covenant that violates public policy. (See *Shelley v. Kraemer* (1948) 334 U.S. 1, 68 S.Ct. 836, 92 L.Ed. 1161 [racial restriction unenforceable]; §53, subd. (b) [voiding property use restrictions based on "sex, race, color, religion, ancestry, national origin, or disability"].) Nor will courts enforce as equitable servitudes those restrictions that are arbitrary, that is, bearing no rational relationship to the protection, preservation, operation or purpose of the affected land. (See *Laguna Royale Owners Assn. v. Darger, supra,* 119 Cal.App.3d 670, 684, 174 Cal. Rptr. 136.)

These limitations on the equitable enforcement of restrictive servitudes that are either arbitrary or violate fundamental public policy are specific applications of the general rule that courts will not enforce a restrictive covenant when "the harm caused by the restriction is so disproportionate to the benefit produced" by its enforcement that the restriction "ought not to be enforced." (Rest., Property, §539, com. *f,* pp. 3229-3230; see also 4 Witkin, Summary of Cal.Law (9th ed. 1987) Real Property, §494, pp. 671-672; Note, *Covenants and Equitable Servitudes in California, supra,* 29 Hastings L.J. at pp. 575-576.) When a use restriction bears no relationship to the land it burdens, or violates a fundamental policy inuring to the public at large, the resulting harm will always be disproportionate to any benefit. . . .

An equitable servitude will be enforced unless it violates public policy; it bears no rational relationship to the protection, preservation, operation or purpose of the affected land; or it otherwise imposes burdens on the affected land that are so disproportionate to the restriction's beneficial effects that the restriction should not be enforced.

With these principles of equitable servitude law to guide us, we now turn to section 1354. As mentioned earlier, under subdivision (a) of section 1354 the use restrictions for a common interest development that are set forth in the recorded declaration are "enforceable equitable servitudes, unless unreasonable." In other words, such restrictions should be enforced unless they are wholly arbitrary, violate a fundamental public policy, or impose a burden on the use of affected land that far outweighs any benefit.

This interpretation of section 1354 is consistent with the views of legal commentators as well as judicial decisions in other jurisdictions that have applied a presumption of validity to the recorded land use restrictions of a common interest development. (*Noble v. Murphy, supra,* 612 N.E.2d 266, 270; *Hidden Harbour Estates v. Basso, supra,* 393 So.2d 637, 639-640; Note, *Judicial Review of Condominium Rulemaking, supra,* 94 Harv.L.Rev. 647, 653.) As these authorities point out, and as we discussed previously, recorded CC & R's are the primary means of achieving the stability and predictability so essential to the success of a shared ownership housing development. In general, then, enforcement of a common interest development's recorded CC & R's will both encourage the development of land and ensure that promises are kept, thereby fulfilling both of the policies identified by the Restatement. (See Rest., Property, §539, com. *f,* p. 3230.)

When courts accord a presumption of validity to all such recorded use restrictions and measure them against deferential standards of equitable servitude law, it discourages lawsuits by owners of individual units seeking personal exemptions from the restrictions. This also promotes stability and predictability in two ways. It provides substantial assurance to prospective condominium purchasers that they may rely with confidence on the promises embodied in the project's recorded CC & R's. And it protects all owners in the planned development from unanticipated increases in association fees to fund the defense of legal challenges to recorded restrictions.

How courts enforce recorded use restrictions affects not only those who have made their homes in planned developments, but also the owners associations charged with the fiduciary obligation to enforce those restrictions. (See *Posey v. Leavitt* (1991) 229 Cal.App.3d 1236, 1247, 280 Cal.Rptr. 568; Advising Cal.Condominium and Homeowner Associations, *supra,* §6.11, pp. 259-261.) When courts treat recorded use restrictions as presumptively valid, and place on the challenger the burden of proving the restriction "unreasonable" under the deferential standards applicable to equitable servitudes, associations can proceed to enforce reasonable restrictive covenants without fear that their actions will embroil them in costly and prolonged legal proceedings. Of course, when an association determines that a unit owner has violated a use restriction, the association must do so in good faith, not in an arbitrary or capricious manner, and its enforcement procedures must be fair and applied uniformly. (See *Ironwood Owners Assn. IX v. Solomon* (1986) 178 Cal.App.3d 766, 772, 224 Cal.Rptr. 18; *Cohen v. Kite Hill Community Assn.* (1983) 142 Cal.App.3d 642, 650, 191 Cal.Rptr. 209.)

There is an additional beneficiary of legal rules that are protective of recorded use restrictions: the judicial system. Fewer lawsuits challenging such restrictions will be brought, and those that are filed may be disposed of more expeditiously, if the rules courts use in evaluating such restrictions are clear, simple, and not subject to exceptions based on the peculiar circumstances or hardships of individual residents in condominiums and other shared-ownership developments.

Contrary to the dissent's accusations that the majority's decision "fray[s]" the "social fabric" (dis.opn., *post,* p. 81 of 33 Cal.Rptr.2d, p. 1293 of 878 P.2d), we are of the view that our social fabric is best preserved if courts uphold and enforce solemn written instruments that embody the expectations of the parties rather than treat them as "worthless paper" as the dissent would (dis.opn., *post,* p. 84 of 33 Cal.Rptr.2d, p. 1296 of 878 P.2d). Our social fabric is founded on the stability of expectation and obligation that arises from the consistent enforcement of the terms of deeds, contracts, wills, statutes, and other writings. To allow one person to escape obligations under a written instrument upsets the expectations of all the other parties governed by that instrument (here, the owners of the other 529 units) that the instrument will be uniformly and predictably enforced.

The salutary effect of enforcing written instruments and the statutes that apply to them is particularly true in the case of the declaration of a common interest development. As we have discussed, common interest developments are a more intensive and efficient form of land use that greatly benefits society and expands opportunities for home ownership. In turn, however, a common interest development creates a community of property owners living in close proximity to each other, typically much closer than if each owned his or her separate plot of land. This proximity is feasible, and units in a common interest development are marketable, largely because the recorded declaration of CC & R's assures owners of a stable and predictable environment.

Refusing to enforce the CC & R's contained in a recorded declaration, or enforcing them only after protracted litigation that would require justification of their application on a case-by-case basis, would impose great strain on the social fabric of the common interest development. It would frustrate owners who had purchased their units in reliance on the CC & R's. It would put the owners and the homeowners association in the difficult and divisive position of deciding whether particular CC & R's should be applied to a particular owner. Here, for example, deciding whether a particular animal is "confined to an owner's unit and create[s] no noise, odor, or nuisance" (dis. opn., *post,* p. 83 of 33 Cal.Rptr.2d, p. 1295 of 878 P.2d) is a fact-intensive determination that can only be made by examining in detail the behavior of the particular animal and the behavior of the particular owner. Homeowners associations are ill-equipped to make such investigations, and any decision they might make in a particular case could be divisive or subject to claims of partiality.

Enforcing the CC & R's contained in a recorded declaration only after protracted case-by-case litigation would impose substantial litigation costs on the owners through their homeowners association, which would have to defend not only against owners contesting the application of the CC & R's to them, but also against owners contesting any case-by-case exceptions the homeowners association might make. In short, it is difficult to imagine what could more disrupt the harmony of a common interest development than the course proposed by the dissent.

IV

Here, the Court of Appeal failed to consider the rules governing equitable servitudes in holding that Nahrstedt's complaint challenging the Lakeside Village restriction against the keeping of cats in condominium units stated a cause of action for declaratory relief. Instead, the court concluded that factual allegations by Nahrstedt that her cats are kept inside her condominium unit and do not bother her neighbors were sufficient to have the trial court decide whether enforcement of the restriction against Nahrstedt would be reasonable. For this conclusion, the court relied on two Court of Appeal decisions, *Bernardo Villas Management Corp. v. Black* (1987) 190 Cal.App.3d 153, 235 Cal. Rptr. 509 and *Portola Hills Community Assn. v. James* (1992) 4 Cal.App.4th 289, 5 Cal. Rptr.2d 580, both of which had invalidated recorded restrictions covered by section 1354.

In *Bernardo Villas,* the manager of a condominium project sued two condominium residents to enforce a restriction that prohibited them from keeping any "truck, camper, trailer, boat . . . or other form of recreational vehicle" in the carports. (190 Cal. App.3d at p. 154, 235 Cal.Rptr. 509.) In holding that the restriction was unreasonable as applied to the clean new pickup truck with camper shell that the defendants used for personal transportation, the Court of Appeal observed that parking the truck in the development's carport would "not interfere with other owners' use or enjoyment of their property." (*Id.* at p. 155, 235 Cal.Rptr. 509.)

Thereafter, a different division of the same district Court of Appeal used a similar analysis in *Portola Hills.* There, the court refused to enforce a planned community's landscape restriction banning satellite dishes against a homeowner who had installed a satellite dish in his backyard. After expressing the view that "[a] homeowner is allowed to prove a particular restriction is unreasonable as applied to his property," the court observed that the defendant's satellite dish was not visible to other project residents or the public, leading the court to conclude that the ban promoted no legitimate goal of the homeowners association. (4 Cal.App.4th at p. 293, 5 Cal.Rptr.2d 580.)

At issue in both *Bernardo Villas Management Corp. v. Black, supra,* 190 Cal.App.3d 153, 235 Cal.Rptr. 509, and *Portola Hills Community Assn. v. James, supra,* 4 Cal.App.4th 289, 5 Cal.Rptr.2d 580, were recorded use restrictions contained in a common interest development's declaration that had been recorded with the county recorder. Accordingly, the use restrictions involved in these two cases were covered by section 1354, rendering them presumptively reasonable and enforceable under the rules governing equitable servitudes. As we have explained, courts will enforce an equitable servitude unless it violates a fundamental public policy, it bears no rational relationship to the protection, preservation, operation or purpose of the affected land, or its harmful effects on land use are otherwise so disproportionate to its benefits to affected homeowners that it should not be enforced. In determining whether a restriction is "unreasonable" under section 1354, and thus not enforceable, the focus is on the restriction's effect on the project as a whole, not on the individual homeowner. Although purporting to evaluate the use restrictions in accord with section 1354, both *Bernardo Villas* and *Portola Hills* failed to apply the deferential standards of equitable servitude law just mentioned. Accordingly, to the extent they differ from the views expressed in this opinion, we disapprove *Bernardo Villas* and *Portola Hills.*

V

Under the holding we adopt today, the reasonableness or unreasonableness of a condominium use restriction that the Legislature has made subject to section 1354 is to be determined *not* by reference to facts that are specific to the objecting homeowner, but by reference to the common interest development as a whole. As we have explained, when, as here, a restriction is contained in the declaration of the common interest development and is recorded with the county recorder, the restriction is presumed to be reasonable and will be enforced uniformly against all residents of the common interest development *unless* the restriction is arbitrary, imposes burdens on the use of lands it affects that substantially outweigh the restriction's benefits to the development's residents, or violates a fundamental public policy.

Accordingly, here Nahrstedt could prevent enforcement of the Lakeside Village pet restriction by proving that the restriction is arbitrary, that it is substantially more burdensome than beneficial to the affected properties, or that it violates a fundamental public policy. For the reasons set forth below, Nahrstedt's complaint fails to adequately allege any of these three grounds of unreasonableness.

We conclude, as a matter of law, that the recorded pet restriction of the Lakeside Village condominium development prohibiting cats or dogs but allowing some other pets is not arbitrary, but is rationally related to health, sanitation and noise concerns legitimately held by residents of a high-density condominium project such as Lakeside Village, which includes 530 units in 12 separate 3-story buildings.

Nahrstedt's complaint alleges no facts that could possibly support a finding that the burden of the restriction on the affected property is so disproportionate to its benefit that the restriction is unreasonable and should not be enforced. Also, the complaint's allegations center on Nahrstedt and her cats (that she keeps them inside her condominium unit and that they do not bother her neighbors), without any reference to the effect on the condominium development as a whole, thus rendering the allegations legally insufficient to overcome section 1354's presumption of the restriction's validity. . . .

CONCLUSION

In section 1354, the Legislature has specifically addressed the subject of the enforcement of use restrictions that, like the one in this case prohibiting the keeping of certain animals, are recorded in the declaration of a condominium or other common interest development. The Legislature has mandated judicial enforcement of those restrictions unless they are shown to be unreasonable when applied to the development as a whole.

Section 1354 requires courts determining the validity of a condominium use restriction in a recorded declaration to apply the deferential standards of equitable servitude law. These standards grant courts no unbridled license to question the wisdom of the restriction. Rather, courts must enforce the restriction unless the challenger can show that the restriction is unreasonable because it is arbitrary, violates a fundamental public policy, or imposes burdens on the use of the affected property that substantially outweigh the restriction's benefits.

By providing condominium homeowners with substantial assurance that their development's recorded use restrictions can be enforced, section 1354 promotes the stability and predictability so essential to the success of any common interest development. Persons who purchase homes in such a development typically submit to a variety of restrictions on the use of their property. In exchange, they obtain the security of knowing that all other homeowners in the development will be required to abide by those same restrictions. Section 1354 also protects the general expectations of condominium homeowners that they not be burdened with the litigation expense in defending case-by-case legal challenges to presumptively valid recorded use restrictions.

In this case, the pet restriction was contained in the project's declaration or governing document, which was recorded with the county recorder before any of the 530 units was sold. For many owners, the pet restriction may have been an important inducement to purchase into the development. Because the homeowners collectively have the power to repeal the pet restriction, its continued existence reflects their desire to retain it.

Plaintiff's allegations, even if true, are insufficient to show that the pet restriction's harmful effects substantially outweigh its benefits to the condominium development as a whole, that it bears no rational relationship to the purpose or function of the development, or that it violates public policy. We reverse the judgment of the Court of Appeal, and remand for further proceedings consistent with the views expressed in this opinion.

Lucas, C.J., and Mosk, Baxter, George and Werdegar, JJ., concur.

Arabian, Justice, dissenting.

"There are two means of refuge from the misery of life: music and cats."[1]

I respectfully dissent. While technical merit may commend the majority's analysis, its application to the facts presented reflects a narrow, indeed chary, view of the law that eschews the human spirit in favor of arbitrary efficiency. In my view, the resolution of this case well illustrates the conventional wisdom, and fundamental truth, of the Spanish proverb, "It is better to be a mouse in a cat's mouth than a man in a lawyer's hands."

As explained below, I find the provision known as the "pet restriction" contained in the covenants, conditions, and restrictions (CC & R's) governing the Lakeside Village project patently arbitrary and unreasonable within the meaning of Civil Code section 1354. Beyond dispute, human beings have long enjoyed an abiding and cherished association with their household animals. Given the substantial benefits derived from pet ownership, the undue burden on the use of property imposed on condominium owners who can maintain pets within the confines of their units without creating a nuisance or disturbing the quiet enjoyment of others substantially outweighs whatever meager utility the restriction may serve in the abstract. It certainly does not promote "health, happiness [or] peace of mind" commensurate with its tariff on the quality of life for those who value the companionship of animals. Worse, it contributes to the fraying of our social fabric. . . .

Pets that remain within the four corners of their owners' condominium space can have no deleterious or offensive effect on the project's common areas or any neighboring unit. Certainly, if other owners and residents are totally *unaware* of their presence, prohibiting pets does not in any respect foster the "health, happiness [or] peace of mind" of anyone except the homeowners association's board of directors, who are thereby able to promote a form of sophisticated bigotry. . . .

The proffered justification is all the more spurious when measured against the terms of the pet restriction itself, which contains an exception for domestic fish and birds. A squawking bird can readily create the very kind of disturbance supposedly prevented by banning other types of pets. At the same time, many animals prohibited by the restriction, such as hamsters and the like, turtles, and small reptiles, make no sound whatsoever. Disposal of bird droppings in common trash areas poses as much of a health concern as cat litter or rabbit pellets, which likewise can be handled in a manner that avoids potential problems. Birds are also known to carry disease and provoke allergies. . . . Defendants and the majority purport such solicitude for the "health, sanitation and noise concerns" of other unit owners, but fail to explain how the possession of pets, such as plaintiff's cats, under the circumstances alleged in her complaint, jeopardizes that goal any more than the fish and birds expressly allowed by the pet restriction. This inconsistency underscores its unreasonableness and discriminatory impact.

From the statement of the facts through the conclusion, the majority's analysis gives scant acknowledgment to any of the foregoing considerations but simply takes refuge

---

[1] Albert Schweitzer.

behind the "presumption of validity" now accorded *all* CC & R's irrespective of subject matter. . . .

Our true task in this turmoil is to strike a balance between the governing rights accorded a condominium association and the individual freedom of its members. To fulfill that function, a reviewing court must view with a skeptic's eye restrictions driven by fear, anxiety, or intolerance. In any community, we do not exist *in vacuo*. There are many annoyances which we tolerate because not to do so would be repressive and place the freedom of others at risk.

In contravention, the majority's failure to consider the real burden imposed by the pet restriction unfortunately belittles and trivializes the interest at stake here. Pet ownership substantially enhances the quality of life for those who desire it. When others are not only undisturbed by, but *completely unaware of,* the presence of pets being enjoyed by their neighbors, the balance of benefit and burden is rendered disproportionate and unreasonable, rebutting any presumption of validity. Their view, shorn of grace and guiding philosophy, is devoid of the humanity that must temper the interpretation and application of all laws, for in a civilized society that is the source of their authority. As judicial architects of the rules of life, we better serve when we construct halls of harmony rather than walls of wrath.

I would affirm the judgment of the Court of Appeal.

NOTE AND QUESTIONS

1. *Reasonableness.* Having read *Nahrstedt*, which approach to reasonableness do you think is better? Why? A majority of U.S. jurisdictions appear to follow the approach taken by the California Supreme Court in *Nahrstedt*, where the question is whether the covenant is reasonable in the context of the entire community. A minority of jurisdictions appear to take the approach taken by the intermediate appellate court in *Nahrstedt* that reasonableness should be determined in the context of each individual resident. Do you think that the California Supreme Court reached the right result in *Nahrstedt*?

2. *Reasonableness vs. Business Judgment.* Beyond disagreements about the definition of reasonableness, there is a lack of clarity among U.S. jurisdictions about the applicable standard to use to review common interest communities covenants and decisions by common interest community boards. Some courts in some contexts have applied the business judgment rule, rather than the reasonableness test. The business judgment rule is a highly deferential rule imported into the common interest community context from corporate law. In corporate law, management of a corporation generally is left to the discretion of the officers and directors, and courts rarely, if ever, question a decision made by officers or directors if the business judgment rule applies. In the common interest community context, it seems most appropriate to apply the business judgment rule (if at all) to the board's decisions related to the basic day-to-day management of the community and not to the enforcement of the recorded covenants in the CC&Rs. The law in this area is still developing. Two types of factual distinctions may have an impact on the choice of test

applied by a particular court in a particular context. The first, as we just mentioned, is the distinction between day-to-day management decisions made by the board and the enforcement of covenants in the CC&Rs. It may make sense to be more deferential in the context of basic board management decisions than in the context of covenant enforcement. The second involves the distinction between the covenants in the original CC&Rs and later covenants adopted by amendment. The CC&Rs typically provide that they can be amended by a supermajority of community residents. It makes sense for a court to be more deferential to the original covenants than to amended covenants because all residents came into the community with at least record notice of the original CC&Rs. Residents therefore should have come into the community with the expectation of being bound by the original CC&Rs. An amendment, in contrast, may apply to a resident who opposed it and who entered the community without the expectation of being bound by it.

THE PEOPLE SPEAK

After *Nahrstedt* was decided, the California legislature enacted the following law:

California Civil Code §4715 (enacted 2000)

(a) No governing documents shall prohibit the owner of a separate interest within a common interest development from keeping at least one pet within the common interest development, subject to reasonable rules and regulations of the association. This section may not be construed to affect any other rights provided by law to an owner of a separate interest to keep a pet within the development.

(b) For purposes of this section, "pet" means any domesticated bird, cat, dog, aquatic animal kept within an aquarium, or other animal as agreed to between the association and the homeowner.

(c) If the association implements a rule or regulation restricting the number of pets an owner may keep, the new rule or regulation shall not apply to prohibit an owner from continuing to keep any pet that the owner currently keeps in the owner's separate interest if the pet otherwise conforms with the previous rules or regulations relating to pets.

(d) For the purposes of this section, "governing documents" shall include, but are not limited to, the conditions, covenants, and restrictions of the common interest development, and the bylaws, rules, and regulations of the association.

(e) This section shall become operative on January 1, 2001, and shall only apply to governing documents entered into, amended, or otherwise modified on or after that date.

PROBLEM

Jane owns the house at 15 Watership Way in the Uphill Downs common interest community. She bought the house from Will Wilson, who in turn bought it from the original developer. Jane is in a dispute with the Uphill Downs homeowners' association because Jane wants to give yoga classes in her home. One of the Uphill Downs covenants prohibits commercial activity of any type. Jane argues that (a) the covenant shouldn't apply to her because she was not a party to the transaction where the covenants were imposed and (b) that it would be unreasonable to apply the covenant to her because she would only see a few clients each day and that her business would not have any negative impact on the community. An explanatory answer can be found on page 1064.

a. Abandonment of a Covenant

As we noted above, the board governing the homeowners' association has an obligation to enforce the CC&Rs. If the board fails to enforce the covenant, the covenant may become unenforceable. Typically, courts speak in terms of the covenant being *abandoned*. You may also see this is issue raised in terms of waiver. In either case, the issue is whether a pattern of non-enforcement makes a covenant unenforceable. Our next case provides an example.

FINK V. MILLER

Court of Appeals of Utah, 1995
896 P.2d 649

Orme, Presiding Judge:
Plaintiff appeals the trial court's order declaring a subdivision's restrictive covenant requiring wood shingle roofing to be unenforceable. . . . [W]e affirm.

FACTS

Plaintiff C.W. Fink and defendant Shannon Miller purchased lots in Maple Hills Subdivision No. 3, Plat D, located in the east bench area of Bountiful, Utah. Both parties received copies of the Agreement for Protective Covenants, recorded in Davis County by the developer of Maple Hills in 1978.[1] One of the covenants recites that "[w]ood shingles . . . shall be required on the exterior roofs of all structures." Also, prospective home builders, as well as owners intending to improve or alter existing structures, must

---

[1] The Agreement includes the following provisions, with our emphasis:

[I]t is the desire of said owner and intent thereof that the said property shall be conveyed hereafter subject to the restrictive covenants set forth below in order to enhance a more uniform development of the lots therein, maintain to the extent possible the natural environment in which they are located, and to maintain the value thereof.

. . . .

submit all plans and specifications, including proposed exterior colors and materials, to the Community Development Committee for its approval before commencing construction.

Sometime prior to 1985, Committee members received a copy of the Agreement with a handwritten addition to the roofing materials provision, so that the restriction read "wood shingles or bar tile." Consequently, prior to 1985 the Committee approved plans calling for tile roofs. In 1985 it learned that the covenant had not, in fact, been thus amended. Meanwhile, six homes were built with fiberglass/asphalt shingle roofs without Committee approval. By the end of 1985, twenty-nine homes had been completed in Maple Hills. Eight homes had wood shingle roofs, while twenty-one homes had either tile or fiberglass/asphalt shingle roofs.

Nevertheless, subsequent to 1985, the Committee has sought to enforce the covenant restricting roofing materials to wood shingles and has refused to approve plans that included tile or fiberglass/asphalt shingle roofs. In 1990, the Committee approved plans submitted by defendants Shannon Miller and her husband, Jim Miller, which called for a wood shingle roof. One year later, the Millers requested approval to change the originally specified roofing material from wood shingles to fiberglass shingles. After the Committee denied the change, the Millers nonetheless commenced installation of fiberglass shingles.

In November 1991, Fink commenced this action and filed an *ex parte* motion seeking injunctive relief to prevent the installation of fiberglass shingles on the Millers' home.

---

2. ARCHITECTURAL CONTROL

No building or structure shall be erected, placed, or altered on any lot in Maple Hills Subdivision No. 3 until the construction plans thereof, specifications and the plot plan showing the locations of such structures have been approved in writing by the Community Development Committee. Such approval will concern itself with the acceptability and harmony of external design of the proposed structure to the locale and as to the location of the proposed structure with respect to topography and grade, quality of materials, size, height, color, etc. No structure shall be built upon any lot with a height exceeding two stories above the existing ground elevations unless approved by the Community Development Committee. Buildings shall be designed to preserve the natural beauty of the area. Only those exterior materials which will blend harmoniously into the natural environment, with special emphasis on earth-toned colors, shall be permitted. *Wood shingles*, with fire retard[a]nt underlayment, *shall be required on the exterior roofs of all structures.* Masonry (brick and stone) exterior [is] strongly encouraged. Exterior television antennae [are] prohibited. Exposed metal flues, vents, ventilators or other metallic rooftop protuberances shall be coated or painted with a neutral color which will blend harmoniously with the wood shingles. The Community Development Committee shall have final control for approval of color and material plans.

. . . .

10. ECOLOGICAL CONSIDERATIONS

Only such foliage shall be removed from each lot as is necessary for clearing the driveway, excavation for the foundation, and for law[n]s and patio areas. In general, the lawn and patio area shall not exceed in area the square foot area of the main level of the house erected on the lot. Deviations from this standard will be allowed by the Community Development Committee after appropriate review. Owners are encouraged to plant tree [s] and shrubs to enhance the natural beauty, provide windbreaks and improve erosion control.

In response to his motion, the trial court issued a temporary restraining order and soon held a hearing regarding a preliminary injunction. Late in 1991, the court granted a preliminary injunction enjoining the Millers from installing any roofing material other than wood shingles. The court concluded there had "been no general waiver or abandonment of the Covenants."

Fink filed a motion for summary judgment and permanent injunction in July 1993, and the Millers filed their own motion for summary judgment in August 1993. After a hearing in September, the trial court considered the parties' written submissions, personally observed the subdivision, and then issued a minute entry on October 7, 1993. The court held that the covenant restricting roofing materials to only wood shingles is unenforceable. However, it continued the preliminary injunction in effect pending the parties' submission of memoranda on the issue of "irreparable harm."

Another hearing was held November 8, 1993. On February 2, 1994, the trial court issued its final order, quashing all prior injunctive relief and denying a permanent injunction. The court, noting in its factual findings that as of July 1993 the subdivision's eighty-one completed homes included fifty-eight homes with wood shingle roofs and twenty-three homes with non-wood roofs, concluded that the covenants still validly restricted the color and quality of materials, but could not restrict roofing materials by type. The court opined that the Committee must approve any roofing materials of adequate quality that blend "harmoniously with the current neighborhood." Fink now appeals from this order. . . .

As a general proposition, property owners who have purchased land in a subdivision, subject to a recorded set of restrictive covenants and conditions, have the right to enforce such restrictions through equitable relief against property owners who do not comply with the stated restrictions. *See Crimmins v. Simonds,* 636 P.2d 478, 480 (Utah 1981) (noting property owners' protectable interest in enforceability of covenants). *See generally* Roger A. Cunningham et al., *The Law of Property* §§8.32, 8.33 (1984). However, as explained below, property owners may lose this right if the specific covenant they seek to enforce has been abandoned, thereby rendering the covenant unenforceable.

1. Applicable Law

In the instant case, the trial court, as well as the parties, relied upon *Crimmins v. Simonds,* 636 P.2d 478 (Utah 1981), in analyzing the enforceability of the covenant restricting roofing materials. In *Crimmins,* the Utah Supreme Court examined a restriction forbidding the operation of a trade or business within a subdivision and held that a restrictive covenant is unenforceable if a change in circumstances in the neighborhood is "so great that it clearly neutralizes the benefits of the restriction to the point of defeating its purpose, or . . . renders the covenant valueless." *Id.* at 479.

This analysis is useful in the context of restrictions that are closely related to the use of the affected property, such as a covenant that forbids commercial operations or limits land use to agricultural activities. Repeated violations of such covenants may directly affect the nature and character of a particular area or neighborhood, thereby producing a discernible change in circumstances. The Court in *Crimmins* determined that most of the property owners operating existing businesses in the subdivision did so out of their homes, i.e., they were residents whose business activities were secondary to their residential activities. *Id.* at 480. Accordingly, the predominantly residential character of the neighborhood had not changed so dramatically as to render the prohibition on commercial activities valueless. *Id.*

However, unlike the covenant at issue in *Crimmins,* the covenant in the instant case restricts not the use of the property itself, but merely the selection of certain building materials for aesthetic purposes. Violations of this sort of covenant would not produce obvious changes in the fundamental nature of the Maple Hills subdivision—its upscale residential character remains unchanged. Instead, a more appropriate test to determine abandonment of such a covenant requires the party opposing enforcement to prove that existing "violations are so great as to lead the mind of the average [person] to reasonably conclude that the restriction in question has been abandoned." *Tanglewood Homes Ass'n v. Henke,* 728 S.W.2d 39, 43 (Tex.App.1987). In simplest terms, this test is met when the average person, upon inspection of a subdivision and knowing of a certain restriction, will readily observe sufficient violations so that he or she will logically infer that the property owners neither adhere to nor enforce the restriction.

In applying this test, courts consider the "'number, nature, and severity of the then existing violation[s], any prior acts of enforcement of the restriction, and whether it is still possible to realize to a substantial degree the benefits intended through the covenant.'" *Id.* at 43-44 (quoting *New Jerusalem Baptist Church, Inc. v. City of Houston,* 598 S.W.2d 666, 669 (Tex.App.1980)). *See also Lakeshore Property Owners Ass'n v. Delatte,* 579 So.2d 1039, 1043 (La.App.) ("abandonment of a restriction depends upon the character, materiality and number of violations and their proximity to the objecting residents"), *cert. denied,* 586 So.2d 560 (La.1991); *Tompkins v. Buttrum Constr. Co.,* 99 Nev. 142, 659 P.2d 865, 867 (1983) (abandonment of restriction will be found if "general and substantial violations" existed).

To maximize the benefits of the essentially objective quality of this test, courts applying it should first analyze violations as to their number, nature, and severity. If these elements alone are sufficient to lead the average person to believe the covenant has been abandoned, it is not necessary to go further. However, if abandonment is still in doubt, courts should then consider the other two factors—namely, prior enforcement efforts and possible realization of benefits—to resolve the abandonment question.

2. Analysis

We now consider whether, employing the above test, the existing violations of the Maple Hills roofing covenant demonstrate that it has been abandoned.

A. Number, Nature, and Severity of Violation

We may readily ascertain the actual "number, nature, and severity" of violations of the roofing materials covenant by merely looking at the undisputed facts. Twenty-three out of eighty-one houses in Maple Hills have roofs which do not conform to the wood shingle restriction. A plain reading of the covenant shows that permitted exterior roofing materials are limited to wood shingles only. *See Gosnay v. Big Sky Owners Ass'n*, 205 Mont. 221, 666 P.2d 1247, 1250 (1983) (interpreting covenants according to plain language contained therein). Fink incorrectly attempts to characterize the houses with tile roofs that were erroneously approved by the Committee as somehow less in violation of the covenant than the houses with fiberglass/asphalt shingles that were not approved by the Committee. The circumstances under which property owners obtained approval for tile roofing materials cannot mask the simple fact that there are twenty-three houses, a substantial number of the total houses in the subdivision, *not conforming* with the restrictive covenant.[5]

Accordingly, violations of the wood shingle restrictive covenant are sufficiently widespread that it must be concluded, as a matter of law, that the restriction has been abandoned and is unenforceable.

B. Other Factors: Enforcement and Benefits

Because objective analysis of the number and nature of the violations demonstrates the covenant has been abandoned, we need not extend our inquiry to the remaining factors discussed above. We briefly touch upon them only to aid future judicial application of the test adopted in this opinion.

First, the property owners' overall record of enforcement of the covenant is problematic. While there has been a fairly consistent pattern of enforcement since 1985, there was little or no enforcement between 1978 and 1985. Indeed, by 1985 only eight of the twenty-nine existing houses conformed with the wood shingle requirement. Fink attempts to minimize this fact by claiming the Committee inadvertently used a copy of the Agreement that appeared to allow houses with tile roofs. As we see it, however, the Committee's unquestioning reliance on a handwritten note of unknown origin only

---

[5] Because the covenant mandates use of a specific roofing material, wood shingles, we need not address the severity of each individual violation—a structure either has the required type of roof or it does not. Other restrictions may not be so clear-cut. For example, in the case of a covenant that mandates certain set back distances, a de minimis violation of a few inches may be accorded less significance than a flagrant violation of ten feet. *See Tanglewood Homes Ass'n v. Henke*, 728 S.W.2d 39, 43 (Tex.App.1987).

underscores the laxity of the Committee's enforcement approach during the 1978-85 period.

Next, we consider whether, notwithstanding the existing violations, it is possible to realize the benefits intended by the covenant. In so doing, we read the entire Agreement as a whole, and do not read a single covenant in isolation, in order to determine the intent of the restriction at issue. *Gosnay,* 666 P.2d at 1250. The Agreement plainly states its purposes: to maintain the natural environment; to promote uniform development; and to maintain property values. *See supra* note 1. Given the significant number of houses with nonconforming roofing materials in Maple Hills, uniformity of development—at least with respect to that particular design element—cannot be accomplished by belated enforcement of the covenant. However, property owners can still enforce other restrictions related to architectural design, such as the provision requiring approval of color and quality of materials, with colors limited to earth tones. Abandonment of one covenant does not suggest abandonment of other, albeit similar, covenants in the agreement. *See Tompkins v. Buttrum Constr. Co.,* 99 Nev. 142, 659 P.2d 865, 867 (1983) (violations of other covenants have no effect on covenant at issue).

CONCLUSION

We affirm the trial court's order denying permanent injunctive relief to Fink and granting summary judgment to the Millers.

NOTE AND QUESTIONS

1. *The Legal Standard and Its Application.* The court in *Fink* applied a test for abandonment that asked about the "number, nature, and severity of the then existing violation[s], any prior acts of enforcement of the restriction, and whether it is still possible to realize to a substantial degree the benefits intended through the covenant." Do these factors make sense in general? As applied in *Fink*? Where should we draw the line in interpreting these factors? For example, what exactly constitutes a sufficient number of violations to warrant a finding of abandonment? Or does it not make sense to talk about exact numbers and percentages given the nature of the overall test?

As we saw in *Fink*, a covenant may be deemed to have been abandoned by the governing body of a common interest community. Can a homeowner avoid enforcement of a covenant by abandoning the property? Our next case presents that issue. As we explained in the last chapter, land needs to pass a perc test to allow the owner to install an on-site septic system. In our case, the owners of a lot that failed a perc test tried to abandon the lot. The lot was located in a common interest community, and one of the covenants in the CC&Rs obligated the owners to pay dues to the homeowners' association. The owners therefore were in a quandary—because the lot failed a perc test, they couldn't build on it, but as the owners of the lot, they were still obligated to pay the homeowners' association dues.

POCONO SPRINGS CIVIC ASSOCIATION, INC. V. MACKENZIE

Superior Court of Pennsylvania, 1995
667 A.2d 233

ROWLEY, President Judge.

The issue in this appeal is whether real property owned by appellants Joseph W. MacKenzie and Doris C. MacKenzie has been abandoned, as they claim. In an order entered January 5, 1995, the trial court granted summary judgment, in the amount of $1,739.82, in favor of appellee Pocono Springs Civic Association, Inc., which argued successfully to the trial court that appellants had not abandoned their property located in appellee's development, and, therefore appellants were still obligated to pay association fees.[1]

The parties filed a stipulation of the facts "for disposition of this case," and the facts are in no manner disputed. Our determination, therefore, is simply whether the trial court erred as a matter of law in finding that appellee's right to summary judgment is clear and free from doubt.

We briefly outline the facts and procedural background of the case as follows: Appellants purchased a vacant lot at Pocono Springs Development, located in Wayne County, on October 14, 1969. In 1987, appellants decided to sell their still-vacant lot. A subsequent offer for the purchase of appellants' lot was conditioned upon the property being suitable for an on-lot sewage system. Upon inspection, the lot was determined to have inadequate soil for proper percolation, and appellants' sale was lost. Believing their investment to be worthless, appellants attempted to abandon their lot at Pocono Springs Development. Appellants claimed that because they successfully abandoned their lot, they are relieved from any duty to pay the association fees sought by appellee. The trial court held, however, that the appellant's abandonment defense is "not a valid defense." We agree with the trial court, and affirm. . . .

Appellants' argument, that they successfully abandoned their lot at Pocono Springs Development, is based upon several actions that they believe disassociate them from the land. First, appellants, after learning that the lot would not meet township sewage requirements, attempted to turn the lot over to appellee. Appellee declined to accept the property. Second, appellants tried to persuade appellee to accept the lot as a gift,

---

[1] The covenant upon which appellee relies reads as follows:

> An association of all property owners is to be formed by the Grantor and designated by such name as may be deemed appropriate, and when formed, the buyer covenants and agrees that he, his executors, heirs and assigns, shall be bound by the by-laws, rules and regulations as may be duly formulated and adopted by such association and that they shall be subject to the payment of annual dues and assessments of the same.

Deed, Covenant Number 11.

to be used as a park-like area for the community. Appellee again declined. Third, in 1986 appellants ceased paying real estate taxes on their lot, and in 1988 the Wayne County Tax Claim Bureau offered the property for sale, due to delinquent tax payments. There were no purchasers. Fourth, in 1990, the lot was again offered for sale by the Tax Claim Bureau. The property again was not sold. The Bureau then placed the lot on its "repository" list. Fifth, appellants signed a notarized statement, mailed to "all interested parties," Brief for Appellants at 9, which expressed their desire to abandon the lot. Sixth, appellants do not accept mail regarding the property. These occurrences, together with appellants having neither visited the lot nor utilized the development's services since 1986, cause appellants to "assert that they do not have 'perfect' title to Lot # 20, in Pocono Springs [Development,] [thus] they can and have abandoned said property back to the sovereign." *Id.* at 11. On the basis of the above, appellants argue that their conduct manifests an intent to abandon, and that their intent to abandon should be a question of fact which precludes summary judgment.

The law of abandonment in Pennsylvania does not support appellants' argument. This Court has held that abandoned property is that:

> . . . to which an owner has voluntarily relinquished all right, title, claim and possession with the intention of terminating his ownership, but without vesting it in any other person and with the intention of not reclaiming further possession or resuming ownership, possession or enjoyment.

Commonwealth v. Wetmore, 301 Pa.Super. 370, 373, 447 A.2d 1012, 1014 (1982) (citations omitted). However, in the instant case, appellants have *not* relinquished their rights, title, claim and possession of their lots. They remain owners of real property in fee simple, with a recorded deed and 'perfect' title. Absent proof to the contrary, possession is presumed to be in the party who has record title. *Overly v. Hixson,* 169 Pa.Super. 187, 82 A.2d 573 (1951). As appellants themselves concede, with commendable candor, *see* Brief for Appellants at 15, no authority exists in Pennsylvania that allows for the abandonment of real property when owned in fee simple with perfect title.[3] Additionally, appellants properly admit that neither refusal to pay taxes nor non use of real property constitutes abandonment. Brief for Appellants at 16; *see also Petition of Indiana County,* 360 Pa. 244, 248-49, 62 A.2d 3, 5 (1948) ("It has frequently been held that abandonment of title is not to be presumed from a mere failure to possess the land or from neglect to pay the taxes thereon; inchoate rights may be abandoned but abandonment is not predictable

---

[3] Most commonly, abandonment involves personal property or railway lines not owned in fee simple. *See Quarry Office Park Associates v. Philadelphia Electric Company,* 394 Pa.Super. 426, 576 A.2d 358 (1990) (Court reversed order granting summary judgment and remanded the case, holding that whether Conrail abandoned a rail line was a question for the factfinder, because Conrail owned a right of way, rather than a fee simple interest); *Commonwealth v. Wetmore,* 301 Pa.Super. 370, 447 A.2d 1012 (1982) (Court affirmed order of trial court that arrested judgment following a jury trial; Court held that abandonment of shotgun occurred when father told chief of police to keep and dispose of weapon); *In re Pearlman's Estate,* 348 Pa. 488, 35 A.2d 418 (1944) (fiduciary abandoned interest in life insurance policies).

of perfect titles[.]"). Yet, appellants nonetheless maintain that *their* non use, refusal to pay taxes, and offers to sell create an abandonment, because of a displayed intent to abandon.

But appellants simply do not accept that the record shows that they have retained 'perfect' title to their lot. Neither title nor deed has been sold or transferred. Indeed, appellants *admit* that they are the owners of the lots in question. *See* Stipulation of Facts, Number 1 ("[Appellants] own Lot # 20, Edgehill Road, in the real estate subdivision development generally known as Pocono Springs Estates, by virtue of deed attached . . . as Exhibit 'A,' which is incorporated herein by reference."). Perfect title, under Pennsylvania law, cannot be abandoned. *O'Dwyer v. Ream,* 390 Pa. 474, 136 A.2d 90 (1957). In *O'Dwyer,* our Supreme Court held that once it is determined that good title exists, then the abandonment theory cannot succeed. *See also A.D. Graham & Company, Inc. v. Pennsylvania Turnpike Commission,* 347 Pa. 622, 33 A.2d 22, 29 (1943) (which held that the doctrine of abandonment does not apply to perfect titles, only to imperfect titles). Appellants do not cite, and our own research has not discovered, any more recent cases that would cause us to question the authority of the cited decisions. Absent authority to support their argument, therefore, the appeal cannot be successful for appellants. In short, as the trial court held, "[appellant's] 'Abandonment Authorization' [is] not a valid defense." Trial Court Opinion (Conway, P.J.), 1/5/95, at 6.

Appellants further claim that the trial court erred in granting summary judgment because whether they abandoned their lots should be a question of intent, for a jury to determine. In an attempt to support this argument, appellants cite *Wetmore, supra,* and *O'Dwyer, supra.* Neither case, however, nor any other that appellants could have cited, stands for the proposition that summary judgment may not be granted when no genuine issue of material fact exists and the moving party is entitled to judgment as a matter of law. Intent is an element in the doctrine of abandonment only if the claim survives a motion for summary judgment, and, heretofore, only in cases involving personal property. In the instant case, appellants' intent is irrelevant. What is controlling is our law, which states that real property cannot be abandoned. The law, therefore, leaves nothing for a jury to decide on this claim, which amounts to a legal impossibility.

Having carefully read the entire deed, we cannot find language that would offset appellants' duty under covenant number 11, *supra* at footnote 1, nor any language that would serve as a guide to what appellee's remedies are via the covenant for failure to pay. Thus, appellants, retaining perfect title, albeit reluctantly, and having entered into an agreement with appellee to be subject to certain required payments, have not proven a genuine issue of material fact that would mandate reversal of the trial court's entry of summary judgment for appellee. Therefore, we are constrained to find that appellee is entitled to judgment as a matter of law.

Order affirmed.

NOTES

1. *Abandonment of Real Property.* As the *Pocono Springs* court holds, it generally is not possible to abandon ownership of real property. Why do you think that we would treat real property and personal property differently in this context?

2. *Property with Negative Value.* The lot in *Pocono Springs* is a good example of property that has negative value. The lot was essentially worthless because it was unbuildable, and it brought with it the obligation to pay dues and taxes. The MacKenzies were creative in their attempts to get out of ownership of the lot. Can you think of anything else that they could do in that situation? Is there any change in the law that you would suggest that might help people in the MacKenzies' situation?

b. Covenants and the Fair Housing Act

We studied the Fair Housing Act in some depth in the landlord-tenant context. The FHA applies to covenants that run with the land. A distressingly large number of parcels of land in the United States have racially restrictive covenants in their chains of title. These covenants clearly are illegal and unenforceable under the FHA.

The Fair Housing Act's prohibitions on discrimination based on handicap also apply in the covenants context. They are especially relevant in the group-home context, where people with disabilities live together in a small group. Many residential lots in the United States have covenants that run with the land that limit use of the lot to single-family residential use. Can a home on a lot with such a restriction be used as a group home? Put another way, can neighbors use such a covenant to prevent the home from being as a group home?

HILL V. COMMUNITY OF DAMIEN OF MOLOKAI

Supreme Court of New Mexico, 1996
911 P.2d 861

Frost, Justice.

Defendant-Appellant Community of Damien of Molokai (Community) appeals from the district court's ruling in favor of Plaintiffs-Appellees, enjoining the further use of the property at 716 Rio Arriba, S.E., Albuquerque, as a group home for individuals with AIDS. Plaintiffs-Appellees argue that the group home violates a restrictive covenant. The Community contends that the group home is a permitted use under the covenant and, alternatively, that enforcing the restrictive covenant against the group home would violate the Federal Fair Housing Act, 42 U.S.C. §§3601-3631 (1988) [hereinafter FHA]. We note jurisdiction under SCRA 1986, 12-102(A)(1) (Repl.Pamp.1992), and reverse.

I. FACTS

The underlying facts of this case are not in dispute. The Community is a private, nonprofit corporation which provides homes to people with AIDS as well as other terminal illnesses. In December 1992 the Community leased the residence at 716 Rio Arriba, S.E., Albuquerque, located in a planned subdivision called Four Hills Village, for use as a group home for four individuals with AIDS. The four residents who subsequently moved into the Community's group home were unrelated, and each required some degree of in-home nursing care.

Plaintiffs-Appellees, William Hill, III, Derek Head, Charlene Leamons, and Bernard Dueto (hereinafter Neighbors) live in Four Hills Village on the same dead-end street as the group home. Shortly after the group home opened, the Neighbors noticed an increase in traffic on Rio Arriba street, going to and from the group home. The Neighbors believed that the Community's use of its house as a group home for people with AIDS violated one of the restrictive covenants applicable to all the homes in the sixteenth installment of Four Hills Village. Installment sixteen encompasses the Community's group home and the Neighbors' houses. The applicable covenant provides in relevant part:

> 2. USE OF LAND
>
> No lot shall ever be used for any purpose other than *single family residence purposes.* No dwelling house located thereon shall ever be used for other than *single family residence purposes,* nor shall any outbuildings or structure located thereon be used in a manner other than incidental to such *family residence purposes.* The erection or maintenance or use of any building, or the use of any lot for other purposes, including, but not restricted to such examples as stores, shops, flats, duplex houses, apartment houses, rooming houses, tourist courts, schools, churches, hospitals, and filling stations is hereby expressly prohibited.

Reservations, Covenants and Restrictions, Four Hills Village (Sixteenth Installment) (filed in the Bernalillo County Clerk's Office, Apr. 5, 1973) (emphasis added). The Neighbors specifically argue that the term "single family residence" does not include group homes in which unrelated people live together.

On August 12, 1993, the Neighbors filed for an injunction to enforce the covenant and to prevent further use of the Community's house as a group home. The Community defended on the grounds that the covenant did not prohibit the group home and, in the alternative, that enforcement of the covenant would violate the FHA. The Community also counterclaimed to permanently enjoin enforcement of the covenant and to recover attorney's fees. After hearing evidence at two separate hearings, the trial court held that the restrictive covenant prevented the use of the Community's house as a group home for people with AIDS and issued a permanent injunction against the Community. The trial court entered specific findings that the Community's use of the home generated a significant number of vehicle trips up and down the street and that the increased traffic had detrimentally altered the character of the neighborhood.

The Community appealed the trial court's order, and we granted a stay of the permanent injunction pending this appeal. We now review, first, the Community's claims regarding the proper interpretation of the restrictive covenant, and second, the applicability of the FHA.

II. FOUR HILLS RESTRICTIVE COVENANTS

The first issue before us is the applicability of the Four Hills restrictive covenant to the Community's group home. As this Court noted in *Cain v. Powers,* 100 N.M. 184, 186, 668 P.2d 300, 302 (1983), in determining whether to enforce a restrictive covenant, we are guided by certain general rules of construction. First, if the language is unclear or ambiguous, we will resolve the restrictive covenant in favor of the free enjoyment of the property and against restrictions. Second, we will not read restrictions on the use and enjoyment of the land into the covenant by implication. Third, we must interpret the covenant reasonably, but strictly, so as not to create an illogical, unnatural, or strained construction. Fourth, we must give words in the restrictive covenant their ordinary and intended meaning. *Id.; see also Wilcox v. Timberon Protective Ass'n,* 111 N.M. 478, 483, 806 P.2d 1068, 1073 (Ct.App.1990) (applying four-part test to restrictive covenant prohibiting mobile homes), *cert. denied,* 111 N.M. 529, 807 P.2d 227 (1991).

A. Operating a Group Home Constitutes Residential Use

At issue here is the proper interpretation of the restriction, "No lot shall ever be used for any purpose other than single family residence purposes." The trial court held that the Community's use of property as a group home for four, unrelated individuals with AIDS violated this restriction. In reaching its conclusion that the group home violated the residential use restriction, the trial court made two specific findings regarding the nature of the current use of the home. The court found that the "Community uses the house . . . as a non profit hostel for providing services to handicapped individuals" and that the "Community uses of the residence are much closer to the uses commonly associated with health care facilities, apartment houses, and rooming houses than uses which are commonly associated with single family residences." Thus the trial court apparently concluded that the property was being used for commercial purposes rather than residential purposes. However, we find that the trial court's conclusions are incorrect as a matter of law.

It is undisputed that the group home is designed to provide the four individuals who live in the house with a traditional family structure, setting, and atmosphere, and that the individuals who reside there use the home much as would any family with a disabled family member. The four residents share communal meals. They provide support for each other socially, emotionally, and financially. They also receive spiritual guidance together from religious leaders who visit them on Tuesday evenings.

To provide for their health care needs, the residents contract with a private nursing service for health-care workers. These health-care workers do not reside at the home, and they are not affiliated with the Community in any way. The number of hours of service provided by the health-care workers is determined by a case-management group assigned by the state pursuant to a state program. The in-home health services that the residents receive from the health-care workers are precisely the same services to which any disabled individual would be entitled regardless of whether he or she lived in a group home or alone in a private residence. The health-care workers do most of the cooking and cleaning. The residents do their own shopping unless they are physically unable to leave the home.

The Community's role in the group home is to provide oversight and administrative assistance. It organizes the health-care workers' schedules to ensure that a nurse is present twenty-four hours per day, and it provides oversight to ensure that the workers are doing their jobs properly. It also receives donations of food and furniture on behalf of the residents. The Community provides additional assistance for the residents at times when they are unable to perform tasks themselves. A Community worker remains at the house during the afternoon and evening but does not reside at the home. The Community, in turn, collects rent from the residents based on the amount of social security income the residents receive, and it enforces a policy of no drinking or drug use in the home.

The Community's activities in providing the group home for the residents do not render the home a nonresidential operation such as a hospice or boarding house. As the South Carolina Supreme Court noted when faced with a similar situation involving a group home for mentally impaired individuals:

> This Court finds persuasive the reasoning of other jurisdictions which have held that the incident necessities of operating a group home such as maintaining records, filing accounting reports, managing, supervising, and providing care for individuals in exchange for monetary compensation are collateral to the prime purpose and function of a family housekeeping unit. Hence, these activities do not, in and of themselves, change the character of a residence from private to commercial.

Rhodes v. Palmetto Pathway Homes, Inc., 303 S.C. 308, 400 S.E.2d 484, 485-86 (1991). In *Jackson v. Williams*, 714 P.2d 1017, 1022 (Okla.1985), the Oklahoma Supreme Court similarly concluded:

> The essential purpose of the group home is to create a normal family atmosphere dissimilar from that found in traditional institutional care for the mentally handicapped. The operation of a group home is thus distinguishable from a use that is commercial—i.e., a boarding house that provides food and lodging only—or is institutional in character.

See also Gregory v. State Dep't of Mental Health, Retardation & Hosps., 495 A.2d 997, 1001-02 (R.I.1985) (finding the group home to be residential and not commercial in nature, and listing cases from other jurisdictions reaching the same conclusion); *Blevins v. Barry-Lawrence County Ass'n for Retarded Citizens,* 707 S.W.2d 407, 408-09 (Mo.1986) (en banc) (same, listing jurisdictions). *But see Omega Corp. of Chesterfield v. Malloy,* 228 Va. 12, 319 S.E.2d 728, 732 (1984) (finding group home for mentally disabled constituted a "facility" instead of a family residence in violation of covenant), *cert. denied,* 469 U.S. 1192, 105 S.Ct. 967, 83 L.Ed.2d 971 (1985). We agree with the conclusions reached by the South Carolina Supreme Court and other jurisdictions that the purpose of the group home is to provide the residents with a traditional family structure and atmosphere. Accordingly, we conclude as a matter of law that, given the undisputed facts regarding how the Community operates the group home and regarding the nature of the family life in the home, the home is used for residential purposes in compliance with the restrictive covenant.

B. Residents of Group Home Meet Single Family Requirement

The Neighbors also argue on appeal that the four, unrelated residents of the group home do not constitute a "single family" as required by the restrictive covenant. The Neighbors contend that the restrictive covenant should be interpreted such that the term "family" encompasses only individuals related by blood or by law. We disagree.

The word "family" is not defined in the restrictive covenant and nothing in the covenant suggests that it was the intent of the framers to limit the term to a discrete family unit comprised only of individuals related by blood or by law. Accordingly, the use of the term "family" in the covenant is ambiguous. As we noted above, we must resolve any ambiguity in the restrictive covenant in favor of the free enjoyment of the property. *Cain,* 100 N.M. at 186, 668 P.2d at 302. This rule of construction therefore militates in favor of a conclusion that the term "family" encompasses a broader group than just related individuals and against restricting the use of the property solely to a traditional nuclear family.

In addition, there are several other factors that lead us to define the term "family" as including unrelated individuals. First, the Albuquerque municipal zoning ordinance provides a definition of family that is at odds with the restrictive definition suggested by the Neighbors. The Albuquerque zoning ordinance includes within the definition of the term "family," "[a]ny group of not more than five [unrelated] persons living together in a dwelling." Albuquerque, N.M., Rev. Ordinances, art. XIV, §7-14-5(B)(41) (1974 & Supp.1991).

The Neighbors argue that the zoning code definition is irrelevant to the scope of the covenant. They point to *Singleterry v. City of Albuquerque,* 96 N.M. 468, 470, 632 P.2d 345, 347 (1981), in which this Court stated, "It is well established that zoning ordinances cannot relieve private property from valid restrictive covenants if the ordinances are less restrictive." However, we agree with the Colorado Court of Appeals which noted, "While [the zoning] statute has no direct applicability to private covenants, it is some indication of the type of groups that might logically, as a matter of public policy, be included within the concept of a single family." *Turner v. United Cerebral Palsy Ass'n,* 772 P.2d 628, 630 (Colo.Ct.App.1988) (construing term "family" in covenant to include unrelated group home residents), *cert. denied,* (Apr. 24, 1989); *see also Gregory,* 495 A.2d at 1002 n. 3 (referring to zoning ordinances when construing the term "family," as used in covenant). In the present case, we are not using the zoning ordinances to relieve the Community of its obligations under the restrictive covenant. We are instead looking to the definition of family within the zoning ordinance as persuasive evidence for a proper interpretation of the ambiguous term in the covenant. The Albuquerque zoning ordinance would include the residents of the group home within its definition of family.

Second, there is a strong public policy in favor of including small group homes within the definition of the term "family." The federal government has expressed a clear policy in favor of removing barriers preventing individuals with physical and mental disabilities from living in group homes in residential settings and against restrictive definitions of "families" that serve to exclude congregate living arrangements for the disabled. The FHA squarely sets out this important public policy. As the court in *United States v. Scott,* 788 F.Supp. 1555, 1561 n. 5 (D.Kan.1992), stated, "The legislative history of the amended Fair Housing Act reflects the national policy of deinstitutionalizing disabled individuals and integrating them into the mainstream of society." The *Scott* court further noted that the Act "is intended to prohibit special restrictive covenants or other terms or conditions, or denials of service because of an individual's handicap and which . . . exclud[e], for example, congregate living arrangements for persons with handicaps." *Id.* at 1561 (alterations in original) (quoting H.R.Rep. No. 711, 100th Cong., 2d Sess. 23-24 (1988), *reprinted in* 1988 U.S.C.C.A.N. 2173, 2184-85). It "protects against efforts to 'restrict the ability of individuals with handicaps to live in communities.'" *Id.* This policy is applicable to the present case because the FHA's protections for handicapped people extend to individuals with AIDS. *See Support Ministries for Persons with AIDS, Inc. v. Village of Waterford,* 808 F.Supp. 120, 129 (N.D.N.Y.1992) ("The legislative history of the 1988 amendments to the FHA reveals that Congress intended to include among 'handicapped' persons those who are HIV-positive . . . ."). The Developmental Disabilities Assistance and Bill of Rights Act, 42 U.S.C. §6000 (1988 & Supp. II 1990), and the Rehabilitation Act of 1973, 29 U.S.C. §701 (1988 & Supp. IV 1992), also identify a national policy favoring persons with disabilities living independently in normal communities and opposing barriers to this goal. *See Scott,* 788 F.Supp. at 1561 n. 5.

In New Mexico, the Developmental Disabilities Act, NMSA 1978, §28-16A-2 (Cum. Supp.1995), expresses a clear state policy in favor of integrating disabled individuals into communities. The Act provides in relevant part:

It is the purpose of the legislature in enacting the Developmental Disabilities Act . . . to promote opportunities for all persons with developmental disabilities to live, work and participate with their peers in New Mexico communities. Priority shall be given

> to the development and implementation of support and services for persons with developmental disabilities that will enable and encourage them to . . . achieve their greatest potential for independent and productive living by participating in inclusive community activities; and . . . live in their own homes and apartments or in facilities located within their own communities and in contact with other persons living in their communities.

Section 28-16A-2(A). Although this act is directed at assisting individuals with developmental disabilities, such as autism or mental retardation, we find that this important state policy applies with equal force to individuals with any form of disability or handicap.

Furthermore, the state grant of zoning authority to municipalities, NMSA 1978, §3-21-1(C) (Repl.Pamp.1995), expressly provides:

> All state-licensed or state-operated community residences for the mentally ill or developmentally disabled serving ten or fewer persons may be considered a residential use of property for purposes of zoning and may be permitted use in all districts in which residential uses are permitted generally, including particularly residential zones for single-family dwellings.

Although this section may not necessarily require that municipalities include community residences within single-family residential zones, it clearly indicates a preference for municipalities adopting this inclusionary approach.

Both the federal and state governments have expressed a strong policy encouraging locating group homes in single-family residential areas and treating them as if they constituted traditional families. This overwhelming public policy is extremely persuasive in directing us toward an expansive interpretation of the term "family." *See Crane Neck Ass'n v. New York City,* 61 N.Y.2d 154, 472 N.Y.S.2d 901, 904, 460 N.E.2d 1336, 1339 (refusing to enforce restrictive covenant that contravened long-standing public policy favoring the establishment of group homes for the mentally disabled), *cert. denied,* 469 U.S. 804, 105 S.Ct. 60, 83 L.Ed.2d 11 (1984); *Craig v. Bossenbery,* 134 Mich.App. 543, 351 N.W.2d 596, 599 (1984) (noting that strong public policy favoring group homes overrides enforcement even of unambiguous restrictive covenant), *appeal denied,* (Jan. 28, 1986); *cf. Jackson v. Fort Stanton Hosp. & Training Sch.,* 757 F.Supp. 1243, 1312-13 (D.N.M.1990) (noting importance of community placement for the mentally impaired and identifying shortages of adequate community-based group housing in New Mexico), *rev'd in part on other grounds,* 964 F.2d 980 (10th Cir.1992).

Third, other jurisdictions have consistently held that restrictive covenants mandating single-family residences do not bar group homes in which the occupants live as a family unit. For example the *Williams* court noted, "When . . . the restrictive covenant under consideration prohibits occupancy of more than one family unit but does not address itself to the composition of the family, a court is loathe to restrict a family unit to that composed of persons who are related, one to another, by consanguinity or affinity." *Williams,* 714 P.2d at 1023; *see also Welsch v. Goswick,* 130 Cal.App.3d 398, 181 Cal.Rptr. 703, 709-10 (1982) (noting that policy considerations mandate that covenant be interpreted to allow residential care facilities of six or fewer people); *Maull v. Community Living for the Handicapped, Inc.,* 813 S.W.2d 90, 92 (Mo.Ct.App.1991) ("[G]roup homes where the residents function in a family setting, interdependent on one another in carrying out the daily operation and routine of the residence meet the single family requirement of the covenant."), *transfer denied,* (Aug. 8, 1991); *Montana ex rel. Region II Child & Family Servs., Inc. v. District Court,* 187 Mont. 126, 609 P.2d 245, 248 (1980) (holding group home constituted family as required by covenant). *But see Adult Group Properties, Ltd. v. Imler,* 505 N.E.2d 459, 465-67 (Ind.Ct.App.1987) (questionable conclusion that the undefined term "family" in the covenant included only "father, mother and children, immediate blood relatives"), *transfer denied,* (Oct. 15, 1987).

Accordingly, we reject the Neighbors' claim that the term "family" in the restrictive covenants should be read to include only individuals related by blood or by law. We agree with the court in *Open Door Alcoholism Program, Inc. v. Board of Adjustment,* 200 N.J.Super. 191, 491 A.2d 17, 21 (App.Div.1985), which noted, "The controlling factor in considering whether a group of unrelated individuals living together as a single housekeeping unit constitutes a family . . . is whether the residents bear the generic character of a relatively permanent functioning family unit." As we already discussed above, the individuals living in the Community's group home do operate as a family unit. Much of the activities of the residents are communal in nature. More importantly, the residents provide moral support and guidance for each other and together create an environment that assists them in living with the disease that has afflicted them. We find that the Community's group home "exhibit[s] [the] kind of stability, permanency and functional lifestyle which is equivalent to that of the traditional family unit." *Id.,* 491 A.2d at 22. We therefore conclude that the Community's use of the property as a group home does not violate the Four Hills restrictive covenant.

C. Findings Regarding Increased Traffic

The Neighbors strenuously argue that the covenant should be interpreted to exclude the group home because the group home's operation has an adverse impact on the neighborhood. In support of this claim, the Neighbors point to the trial court's findings that "[t]he amount of vehicular traffic generated by [the] Community's use of the house . . . greatly exceeds what is expected in an average residential area" and that, as a result, "the character of [the] residential neighborhood relative to traffic and to parked vehicles has been significantly altered to the detriment of this residential neighborhood and is [*sic*] residents." The Neighbors contend that these facts are uncontradicted and point out that this Court is bound by the factual findings of the trial court unless the findings are not supported by substantial evidence. *Segal v. Goodman,* 115 N.M. 349, 353, 851 P.2d 471, 474 (1993).

However, the Neighbors fail to appreciate that the amount of traffic generated by the group home simply is not relevant to determining whether the use of the house as a group home violated the covenant in this case. A review of all the provisions in the covenant reveals that the restrictive covenants for the Four Hills Village, sixteenth installment, are not directed at controlling either traffic or on-street parking. The various covenants and restrictions that attach to the neighborhood homes merely regulate the structural appearance and use of the homes. For example, the covenants regulate building architecture, views, frontage, setback, visible fences and walls, signs and billboards, trash and weeds, trailers and campers parked in yards, maintaining livestock, and of course nonresidential uses of homes. However, not one of the fifteen provisions and numerous paragraphs of the covenants attempts to control the number of automobiles that a resident may accommodate on or off the property nor the amount of traffic a resident may generate.

The Neighbors do not contend that the amount of traffic and parking generated by the Community's home violates any covenant in and of itself, nor could they. They also do not argue that the covenants would prevent a traditional nuclear family, related by marriage or consanguinity, from generating a similar volume of traffic. The Neighbors do suggest, however, that the volume of traffic demonstrates that the group home is not functionally equivalent to a traditional single-family residence, as required by the covenants. However, the question whether the group home is equivalent to a traditional family residence must be evaluated in relation to the requirements of the covenants, which in this case are directed to maintaining the structural appearance of the house and restricting nonresidential uses. *Cf. Turner,* 772 P.2d at 630 (looking to other provisions of covenant to define nature of "family" restriction). There is no evidence that the volume of traffic generated by the group home interferes with the structural appearance of the house in violation of the covenants. Nor does the amount of traffic or parked vehicles alter the residential nature of the group home or modify the familial relationship of the residents.

We note that if we had concluded that the group home did violate the restrictive covenant, the amount of traffic generated by the nonconforming use might then become relevant in evaluating the harm suffered by the other landowners and in determining the appropriate remedy. However, the amount of traffic generated by the group home simply does not affect the threshold question whether Community's use of the property as a group home violates the restrictive covenant requirement that the property not be used for any purpose other than single-family residence purposes. Accordingly, because the covenants do not regulate traffic or off-street parking, and because the amount of traffic generated by the group home is irrelevant to whether the home is used for single family residential purposes, we conclude that the Neighbors' argument is without merit.

III. FAIR HOUSING ACT

The Community's second contention is that the trial court erred in concluding that the FHA did not apply in the present case. Although we have already agreed with the Community on its first argument that it did not violate the restrictive covenants, given the importance of the issues raised, we review the Community's second claim in order to correct the trial court's erroneous ruling on the legal effect of the FHA. *Whitehurst v. Rainbo Baking Co.,* 70 N.M. 468, 470, 374 P.2d 849, 850 (1962) ("Conclusions of Law are reviewable by the supreme court, and where the facts are not in dispute this court is not bound by the conclusions of the trial court but may independently draw its own legal conclusions."); *C.R. Anthony Co. v. Loretto Mall Partners,* 112 N.M. 504, 510, 817 P.2d 238, 244 (1991) ("[A]n appellate court need not defer to the trial court's conclusions of law and, upon analysis of the record as established below, may reach a conclusion different from that of the trial court."). We find that, even if we were to adopt the Neighbors' proposed definition that the term "family" only included individuals related by blood or by law, we would still find for the Community because such a restriction would violate the FHA. *See, e.g., Deep E. Tex. Regional Mental Health & Mental Retardation Servs. v. Kinnear,* 877 S.W.2d 550, 554-58 (Tex.Ct.App.1994) (finding group home did not violate restrictive covenants and further concluding enforcement of restrictive covenant violated FHA). We discuss the FHA below.

In the present case, the trial court did not make any findings directly holding that the FHA was inapplicable. However, it did set out the following conclusion of law:

> 4. Enforcement of the Restrictive Covenant is not discriminatory toward people with handicaps. Nothing in the Covenant prevents a person with a handicap from owning or renting a house in the Subdivision for personal use as a one family residence. The Restrictive Covenant applies equally to people with or without a handicap as defined in the cited statutes. No organization could rent a house for use as is present here to serve as a halfway home in criminal rehabilitation, as a home for recovering alcoholics, as a home for homeless, as a home for unwed mothers, as a home for battered spouses, as a home for delinquent children, as a home for single white males, or as a home for handicap [*sic*] people as defined by . . . federal statutes.

Although the trial court did not discuss its analysis of the applicability of the FHA, reading this conclusion in conjunction with the numerous questions posed to the Community by the trial court at the hearing makes it apparent that the trial court believed that a facially neutral restriction which is equally applicable to both handicapped and nonhandicapped individuals does not implicate the FHA. However, this view of the FHA is incorrect.

Section 3604(f)(1) of the FHA provides in relevant part that it is unlawful "[t]o discriminate in the sale or rental, or to otherwise make unavailable or deny, a dwelling to any buyer or renter because of a handicap of . . . a person residing in or intending to reside in that dwelling after it is sold, rented, or made available." Section 3604(f)(3)(B) states, "For purposes of this subsection, discrimination includes . . . a refusal to make reasonable accommodations in rules, policies, practices, or services, when such accommodations may be necessary to afford such person equal opportunity to use and enjoy a dwelling . . . ."

Courts have interpreted these provisions as creating three distinct claims for violations of §3604(f) of the FHA: discriminatory intent, disparate impact, and reasonable accommodation. *See Stewart B. McKinney Found., Inc. v. Town Plan & Zoning Comm'n,* 790 F.Supp. 1197, 1210-11, 1221 (D.Conn.1992) (discussing each of these theories). The first two are based on §3604(f)(1), whereas the third arises out of §3604(f)(3). The Community has raised each of these claims and we will address each of them in turn.

At the outset, we note that the Neighbors do not contest that persons with AIDS are considered handicapped under the FHA. *See Baxter v. City of Belleville,* 720 F.Supp. 720, 729 (S.D.Ill.1989) (noting that Congress intended to include persons who are HIV-positive under the FHA); *Support Ministries for Persons with AIDS, Inc. v. Village of Waterford,* 808 F.Supp. 120, 129-31 (N.D.N.Y.1992) (same, listing cases). Nor do they challenge the Community's standing to bring suit under the FHA. *See Baxter,* 720 F.Supp. at 730 (discussing standing).

A. Discriminatory Intent

A discriminatory-intent claim focuses on whether a defendant has treated handicapped individuals differently from other similarly situated individuals. *McKinney Foundation,* 790 F.Supp. at 1211. "To prevail on its claim of discriminatory [intent], . . . the plaintiff is not required to show the defendants were motivated by some purposeful, malicious desire to discriminate against HIV-infected persons." *Id.* "[The] 'plaintiff need only show that the handicap of the potential residents [of a group home], a protected group under the FHA, was in some part the basis for' the policy being challenged." *Potomac Group Home Corp. v. Montgomery County,* 823 F.Supp. 1285, 1295 (D.Md.1993) (second alteration in original) (quoting *Baxter,* 720 F.Supp. at 732).

The trial court in this case did not consider whether the residents' handicap served as a basis for enforcing the restrictive covenant. Instead the court focused solely on the neutral language of the covenant itself. The court apparently concluded that the FHA would not be violated by enforcement of a restrictive covenant that was neutral on its face. However, as the *Scott* court noted, "Given its breadth, the [FHA] would reasonably encompass the act of enforcing a neutral restrictive covenant through the judicial system for the purpose of denying equal housing opportunities to disabled individuals." *Scott,* 788 F.Supp. at 1562. In *Scott,* the court concluded that the defendants' efforts to enforce a neutral restrictive covenant with the purpose of keeping handicapped individuals out of the neighborhood violated the discriminatory-intent prong of the FHA. *Id.*

Turning to the present case, the Community argues that the Neighbors were aware of the Community's use of the property as a group home and decided to enforce the covenants, in part, because of antagonism to that use. The Community presented evidence that the Neighbors' traffic complaints began a few days after a newspaper article was published that described the group home and that the Neighbors inquired into the availability of other possible sites for the home outside of their neighborhood. The Community also identified several covenant violations by other landowners in the neighborhood that were not being prosecuted. However, this evidence is equivocal at best. Absent further evidence of an intent to enforce the covenant because of some animus toward the use of the property as a group home because the residents have AIDS, the Community's allegations are insufficient to support a claim for discriminatory enforcement of the covenant.

B. Disparate Impact

To demonstrate a violation of the FHA under the disparate-impact analysis, a plaintiff need only prove that the defendant's conduct actually or predictably results in discrimination or has a discriminatory effect. *Support Ministries,* 808 F.Supp. at 136. "The plaintiff need make no showing whatsoever that the action resulting in . . . discrimination in housing was . . . motivated [by a desire to discriminate against the handicapped]. Effect, and not motivation, is the touchstone." *McKinney Foundation,* 790 F.Supp. at 1216 (quoting *United States v. City of Black Jack,* 508 F.2d 1179, 1184-85 (8th Cir.1974), *cert. denied,* 422 U.S. 1042, 95 S.Ct. 2656, 45 L.Ed.2d 694 (1975)). "This method of proving a violation of the Act relieves the plaintiff of the onerous burden of proving discriminatory intent." *Id.* The court in *Metropolitan Housing Development Corp. v. Village of Arlington Heights,* 558 F.2d 1283, 1290 (7th Cir.1977), *cert. denied,* 434 U.S. 1025, 98 S.Ct. 752, 54 L.Ed.2d 772 (1978), set out four factors to be balanced when evaluating a discriminatory-impact claim: 1) how strong is plaintiff's showing of discriminatory impact; 2) is there any evidence of discriminatory intent; 3) what is the defendant's interest in taking the challenged action; 4) is the plaintiff seeking to compel the defendant to affirmatively provide housing to the handicapped or merely to restrain the defendant from interfering with individual landowners who wish to provide this housing.

In the present case, the trial court failed to analyze any of these factors, again relying solely on the fact that the covenant was equally applicable to all group homes, for both the handicapped and nonhandicapped. However, as the Texas Court of Appeals noted, "It is now well established that the Fair Housing Act prohibits the enforcement of restrictive covenants that discriminate or *have the effect of discriminating* on the basis of handicap." *Kinnear,* 877 S.W.2d at 558 (emphasis added); *see also Martin v. Constance,* 843 F.Supp. 1321, 1326 (E.D.Mo.1994) ("The private defendants' argument that the [FHA] only reaches special restrictive covenants that specifically prohibit the sale or rental of a dwelling to handicapped individuals is . . . without merit.”). Accordingly, enforcement of the Four Hills restrictive covenant is subject to a disparate-impact analysis.

Applying the four-factor balancing test enunciated in *Metropolitan,* we find that the Community has proved that enforcing the covenant as interpreted by the Neighbors would violate the FHA. First, the covenant, which attempts to limit group homes, has the discriminatory effect of denying housing to the handicapped. Individuals with disabling handicaps, such as the one suffered by the Community's residents, frequently require congregate living arrangements for physical assistance and psychological and emotional support in order to live outside of an institution and in a residential community. *See Support Ministries,* 808 F.Supp. at 132 (noting AIDS patients may not be able to live on their own in private residences); *Oxford House, Inc. v. Town of Babylon,* 819 F.Supp. 1179, 1183 (E.D.N.Y.1993) (noting that recovering alcoholics may require group home environment). Without congregate living arrangements many disabled individuals would be unable to reside in traditional neighborhoods or communities and would be forced into hospitals and institutions. *Cf. Fort Stanton,* 757 F.Supp. at 1282-96 (noting that alternative to congregate living arrangements for developmentally disabled individuals is institutionalization and discussing benefits of congregate living arrangements over institutionalization). *See generally Martin,* 843 F.Supp. at 1325-26 (“[The FHA] is intended to prohibit restrictive covenants . . . which have the effect of excluding, for example, congregate living arrangements for persons with handicaps.”). Because the negative effects of covenants that restrict congregate living arrangements are substantially more onerous for the disabled than for others, the first factor weighs heavily in favor of the Community.

The second factor is whether there is any evidence of discriminatory intent that would bolster a disparate-impact claim. As noted in our discussion of the Community's separate discriminatory-intent claim, the evidence the Community has presented with regard to the Neighbors' discriminatory intent is equivocal at best. However, the *Metropolitan* court made clear that this intent factor is the least important of the four factors weighed in a disparate-impact claim, and the lack of significant evidence of intent is by no means detrimental to that claim. *Metropolitan,* 558 F.2d at 1292.

The third factor is the defendant's interest in enforcing the covenant. An important consideration in evaluating this factor is the nature of the interest being enforced, whether it is a private right benefitting individuals or a governmental interest protecting the public welfare. As the *Metropolitan* court explained, “If the defendant is a private individual or a group of individuals seeking to protect private rights, the courts cannot be overly solicitous when the effect is to perpetuate segregated housing.” *Id.* at 1293 (giving more weight to governmental actions in the public interest than to private actions enforcing private rights). Here, the Neighbors' interest is to eliminate the increased traffic that the trial court found had detrimentally altered the residential character of the neighborhood. This is a legitimate interest which weighs in the Neighbors' favor. However, this factor weighs less in our analysis because the interest served by enforcement of the covenant is private rather than public.

Finally, we must consider the nature of the relief that the plaintiff is seeking. The Community is not attempting to force the Neighbors to provide housing for the disabled. It simply seeks to prevent the Neighbors from interfering with its operation of the group home. This factor strongly favors the Community. "[T]he Courts are far more willing to prohibit even nonintentional action . . . which interferes with an individual's plan to use his [or her] own land to provide integrated housing." *Id.*

Accordingly, we must balance the Neighbors' interest in avoiding increased traffic against the Community's interest in providing housing to disabled individuals. We view these interests in light of the fact that the Community is seeking only to prevent the Neighbors from interfering with its ability to provide this housing and is not seeking to require the Neighbors to act affirmatively.

We conclude that the FHA factors weigh in favor of the Community. A covenant that restricts occupancy only to related individuals or that bars group homes has a disparate impact not only on the current residents of the Community's group home who have AIDS but also on all disabled individuals who need congregate living arrangements in order to live in traditional neighborhoods and communities. As we noted above, there is a very strong public policy favoring placement of disabled individuals in congregate living arrangements located in traditional residential community settings such as Four Hills. Of course, one possible consequence of congregate living arrangements is that they have the potential to generate more traffic than a typical nuclear family. In the present case the trial court made a finding that the increased traffic generated by the Community's group home has negatively affected the residential character of the neighborhood. However, we find it significant that the trial court rejected the Neighbors' proposed finding of fact that this additional traffic posed any increased safety hazard to the neighborhood. Failure to adopt a proposed finding of fact is in effect a negative finding with respect to that fact, which binds this Court on appeal. *Kimberly, Inc. v. Hays,* 88 N.M. 140, 143, 537 P.2d 1402, 1405 (1975).

Accordingly, we conclude that the negative effects of increased traffic, without any additional harms, are outweighed by the Community's interest in maintaining its congregate home for individuals with AIDS. Because the Community has proved a "disparate impact" under the FHA, the Neighbors cannot enforce the covenant against the Community. *See Kinnear,* 877 S.W.2d at 556-58 (noting that the FHA prevented enforcement of a "one-family residence" covenant against group home for developmentally disabled); *Scott,* 788 F.Supp. at 1562 (same); *cf. Oxford House,* 819 F.Supp. at 1184 ("Even if the Town's proposed enforcement of its zoning ordinance advances a legitimate governmental interest, the Court nevertheless finds that plaintiffs' showing of discriminatory effect far outweighs the Town's weak justifications."); *Baxter,* 720 F.Supp. at 732 (applying FHA factors and finding likely violation by zoning ordinance that prevented group home for HIV-positive individuals).

C. Reasonable Accommodation

The Community's third claim under the FHA is that the Neighbors failed to make reasonable accommodations under §3604(f)(3)(B). This section provides that "discrimination includes . . . a refusal to make reasonable accommodations in rules, policies, practices or services when such accommodations may be necessary to afford [a handicapped] person equal opportunity to use and enjoy a dwelling." *Id.* " 'Reasonable accommodation' has been defined [to include] 'changing some rule that is generally applicable so as to make its burden less onerous on the handicapped individual.' " *North Shore-Chicago Rehabilitation, Inc. v. Village of Skokie,* 827 F.Supp. 497, 508 (N.D.Ill.1993) (quoting *Oxford House, Inc. v. Township of Cherry Hill,* 799 F.Supp. 450, 462 n. 25 (D.N.J.1992)); *see also United States v. City of Philadelphia,* 838 F.Supp. 223, 228 (E.D.Pa.1993) (noting that cities must waive, change, or make exceptions in restrictive zoning rules to afford handicapped individuals equal opportunity to use and enjoy housing), *aff'd,* 30 F.3d 1488 (3rd Cir.1994). In *City of Philadelphia,* the court explained that "an accommodation is not reasonable (1) if it would require a fundamental alteration in the nature of a program, or (2) if it would impose undue financial or administrative burdens on the defendant." *City of Philadelphia,* 838 F.Supp. at 228. Although §3604(f)(3)(B) is more frequently applied to restrictive zoning ordinances, it is equally applicable to restrictive covenants. *See, e.g., Martin,* 843 F.Supp. at 1326 ("Even if there was a consistent policy and practice of enforcing the restrictive covenant against perceived violations, the Court finds that under the facts of this case the attempt to enforce the covenant constituted a refusal to make a 'reasonable accommodation' necessary to afford plaintiffs an equal opportunity to use and enjoy a dwelling.").

In the present case, the trial court did not consider whether the Neighbors failed to make a reasonable accommodation under the FHA when they enforced the covenant against the Community's group home. Again the trial court apparently was satisfied by the fact that the restrictive covenant was facially neutral, applying equally to all groups, handicapped and nonhandicapped alike. However, as the *City of Philadelphia* court makes clear, there need be no "causal nexus" between the challenged provision and the handicaps of the residents. *City of Philadelphia,* 838 F.Supp. at 229. In other words, the restriction does not need to be directed at the handicapped. It does not even need to have a disparate impact on handicapped groups in general. *Id.* at 230. The restriction need only serve as an impediment to an individual plaintiff who is handicapped and is denied access to housing in order to implicate the "reasonable accommodation" requirement of the FHA. *Id.; see also Horizon House Developmental Servs., Inc. v. Township of Upper Southampton,* 804 F.Supp. 683, 699 (E.D.Pa.1992) ("One of the purposes behind the reasonable accommodation provision is to address *individual* needs and respond to *individual* circumstances." (Emphasis added)), *aff'd,* 995 F.2d 217 (3rd Cir.1993).

In *City of Philadelphia,* a charitable organization wanted to convert a commercially zoned building to a residential use for operation of a group home for the mentally impaired. *City of Philadelphia,* 838 F.Supp. at 226. The local zoning ordinance required that a residential building have a rear yard. *Id.* Although the building lacked a rear yard, it had a large side yard which the organization contended was a reasonable substitution for the rear yard, and the organization requested a variance on that ground. The city declined to issue a variance, which effectively prevented the organization's proposed use of the building for a group home. *Id.* at 226-27. On appeal the city argued that it did not violate the FHA because there was no causal connection between the zoning ordinance and the future residents' handicaps. *Id.* at 229. The court rejected this argument. It noted that requiring a causal connection or discriminatory impact, as with a disparate-impact claim under §3604(f)(1), would render §3604(f)(3)(B) superfluous. *Id.* at 230. Thus, even though the city's rear yard zoning requirement was facially neutral and affected handicapped and nonhandicapped individuals equally, the ordinance prevented those specific handicapped individuals in *City of Philadelphia* from gaining access to the proposed housing, and therefore it implicated the reasonable-accommodation prong of the FHA. *Id.*

In the present case, the proposed interpretation of the Four Hills restrictive covenant also has the effect of denying housing access to the handicapped residents. Accordingly, §3604(f)(3)(B) of the FHA is implicated, and the Neighbors would be required to reasonably accommodate the group home provided it would not require a fundamental alteration in the nature of the restrictions or impose undue financial or administrative burdens on the Neighbors.

The Neighbors do not suggest that allowing the group home to operate would impose any financial or administrative burdens on them. The Neighbors are not responsible for operating or maintaining the group home in any way, nor do they have to pay any additional costs as a result of the group home. Furthermore, nonenforcement of the single-family residence requirement against the Community's group home would not fundamentally alter the nature of the restrictions. As discussed above, the Four Hills restrictive covenants as a whole were designed to regulate the structural appearance of houses and to prevent the use of houses for business purposes. The Community's use of the property for a group home does not affect its structural appearance and is not a business use. The residents use the house like a traditional residential home and act as a second family for one another. Indeed, the Neighbors' stated reason for enforcing the restrictive covenant is not because of the nonresidential nature of the occupancy, but because of the additional traffic generated by the group home. However, traffic regulation is not a fundamental aspect of the Four Hills restrictive covenants.[4]

Accordingly, we conclude that nonenforcement of the Four Hills restrictive covenants against the Community's group home would not impose an undue hardship or burden on the Neighbors and would not interfere with the plain purpose of the covenants. As the *Martin* court noted in a similar case, "A reasonable accommodation would have been not to seek enforcement of the covenant." *Martin,* 843 F.Supp. at 1326. Conversely, the Neighbors' efforts to enforce the covenant as restricting residency to individuals related by blood or by law violated §3604(f)(3)(B) of the FHA because they failed to provide a reasonable accommodation that would afford the current disabled residents continued access to housing. Therefore, the reasonable-accommodation prong of the FHA would also bar enforcement of the restrictive covenant if it prevented the Community's use of the house as a congregate living arrangement for people with AIDS.

The FHA is designed to help provide disabled individuals the opportunity to live in traditional community settings by removing obstacles that hindered their quest for independent living. The FHA's application is clear when disabled individuals are confronted with intentional housing discrimination motivated by bigotry or misunderstanding of their handicaps. However, the FHA is also designed to help the disabled overcome the subtle effects of unintentional, facially neutral, or even well meaning restrictions that have the consequence of denying housing to the handicapped. . . .

IV. . . .

V. CONCLUSION

We conclude that the Community is entitled to continue operating its group home for individuals with AIDS both under the Four Hills restrictive covenants and under the Fair Housing Act. Accordingly, for the reasons discussed above, the trial court's ruling is reversed and the injunction is vacated. The trial court's dismissal of the counterclaim is affirmed.

---

[4] It is important to note again that the trial court found the traffic did not constitute a health or safety hazard to the neighborhood. The FHA expressly prohibits accommodations that would jeopardize the health or safety of others. Section 3604(f)(9) ("Nothing in this subsection requires that a dwelling be made available to an individual whose tenancy would constitute a direct threat to the health or safety of other individuals or whose tenancy would result in substantial physical damage to the property of others.").

NOTES

1. *Single-Family Residential Use Covenant and the FHA.* The court's holding in *Hill* has two alternative bases. First, the court interpreted the single-family residential use covenant to allow the group home. In other words, the court held that use of the house for a group home was a single-family residential use. Second, the court held that the FHA required the house to be permitted as a group home even if it was prohibited by the covenant. In this part of the analysis, the court looked at three different claims related to discrimination based on handicap—discriminatory intent, disparate impact, and reasonable accommodation. Make sure you understand each part.

2. *Group Homes and Zoning.* Covenants imposing single-family residential use are very common. So are zoning regulations requiring single-family residential use. As we will discuss in Chapter 8, the FHA applies to zoning regulations, though with some wrinkles that are not present in the covenants context.

c. Non-Enforcement of Covenants Based on Public Policy

Courts sometimes will refuse to enforce a covenant on public policy grounds. In some circumstances, the public policy reasons will be explicit. In others, the public policy analysis will be implicit in a court's refusal to enforce a covenant on touch and concern or reasonableness grounds. In our next case, the court includes an explicit public policy analysis in its opinion. On the particular procedural posture of the case, the court does not actually reject the covenant on public policy grounds. It does, however, suggest that it might do so in the future.

The particular covenant at issue in the case prohibits the transfer of homes in a common interest community to a certain category of registered sex offender. As you read the case, think about the policy issues discussed by the court. In particular, think about the effect of an enforceable covenant against sex offenders in common interest communities (a) on sex offenders themselves and (b) on other members of the public who do not live in common interest communities.

MULLIGAN V. PANTHER VALLEY PROPERTY OWNERS ASSN.

Superior Court of New Jersey, Appellate Division, 2001
766 A.2d 1186

WEFING, J.A.D.

Plaintiff owns a home in Panther Valley, a private common-interest residential community in Warren County. Defendant Panther Valley Property Owners Association (Association) is a non-profit corporation that was organized in 1968 for the purpose of governing the community. The Association acts through an elected Board of Trustees;

the individual defendants are members of the Association's Board. Plaintiff, as a result of her home ownership, is a member of the Association.

In October 1998, the Association, through a vote of its membership, adopted six amendments to the community's Declaration of Covenants and Restrictions (Declarations) and the Association's bylaws. Plaintiff filed suit challenging five of those amendments. The trial court upheld three of the amendments and struck down two. The parties appeal and cross-appeal from the trial court's judgment. After a careful review of the entire record in light of the arguments advanced on appeal, we affirm in part and reverse in part.

The first of these amendments declared, in substance and effect, that no individual registered as a Tier 3 offender under *N.J.S.A.* 2C:7-8(c)(3) ("Megan's Law") could reside in Panther Valley. Tier 3 is the highest classification within Megan's Law. In order for an individual to be classified as a Tier 3 registrant, that individual must be a sex-offender who has been deemed to pose a high risk of re-offending. Factors that inform the decision whether an individual poses a high risk of re-offending include whether the conduct involved repetitive and compulsive behavior, *N.J.S.A.* 2C:7-8b(3)(a); whether the individual served the maximum term of confinement, *N.J.S.A.* 2C:7-8b(3)(b); and whether the sexual offense was committed against a child, *N.J.S.A.* 2C:7-8b(3)(c). Because such an individual poses a substantial risk to the community, the statute directs that notification of the presence of a Tier 3 offender within the community be more widespread than that provided in the instance of a Tier 1 or Tier 2 offender, who have been deemed to pose low and moderate risks of re-offending. The trial court upheld the amendment precluding such Tier 3 registrants from residing within Panther Valley. . . .

The threshold issue to be determined is the proper standard governing judicial review of these amendments. It is important to note that plaintiff's challenge to the validity of these amendments does not revolve around the manner in which they were adopted, e.g., compliance with procedural requirements. Rather, her challenge is directed to the substance of the amendments themselves. . . .

We pause first to note the unique nature of Panther Valley. It is a gated residential community located within the Township of Allamuchy; it is comprised of more than 2,000 homes, including single-family homes, townhouses and condominium units. *State v. Panther Valley Prop. Owners Ass'n,* 307 *N.J.Super.* 319, 322, 704 *A.2d* 1010 (*App. Div.*1998) (holding that the Association, having asked the Warren County Prosecutor to assume jurisdiction to enforce the provisions of Title 39 over its private roads, lacked the authority to impose independent fines upon its members who committed traffic violations within its borders). The development itself, in light of the mix of ownership types, is not a condominium development but is more properly referred to as a "common interest development." *Id.* at 327, 704 *A.2d* 1010. . . .

One indication that the courts are, indeed, grappling with new concepts is the split that exists in the different approaches of different jurisdictions. California, for instance, has adopted the "reasonableness" test, *Nahrstedt v. Lakeside Village Condominium Ass'n,* 8 Cal.4th 361, 33 Cal.Rptr.2d 63, 878 P.2d 1275 (1994), while New York has adopted the "business judgment" rule. *Levandusky v. One Fifth Avenue Apartment Corp.,* 75 N.Y.2d 530, 554 N.Y.S.2d 807, 553 N.E.2d 1317 (1990). Some courts and commentators recognize a distinction between considering original recorded restrictions, i.e., those extant at the time of purchase, and later-adopted ones. *Ridgely Condo. Ass'n v. Smyrnioudis,* 105 Md.App. 404, 660 A.2d 942, 948 (1995), *aff'd* 343 Md. 357, 681 A.2d 494 (1996); *Sterk, supra,* 77 *B.U. L.Rev.* at 338-39. Other cases turn upon whether the restriction at issue was improperly incorporated in the association's bylaws, rather than the community's underlying declaration. *Shorewood West Condo. Ass'n v. Sadri,* 140 Wash.2d 47, 992 P.2d 1008 (2000) (leasing restriction contained in amendment to bylaws rather than the condominium declaration unenforceable).

The majority of jurisdictions appear to employ the reasonableness standard. *Arabian, supra,* 23 *Pepp. L.Rev.* at 11. We are satisfied that, in the context of this case, the appropriate test to measure the validity of these amendments is that of reasonableness. We reach that conclusion for several reasons. First, we recognize that we are dealing with amendments to the documents governing life at Panther Valley, as opposed to original provisions. None of the terms to which plaintiff objects were contained within the Declaration and bylaws to which she gave her assent by her decision in 1976 to purchase a home at Panther Valley. As amendments, we do not consider them entitled to the "very strong presumption of validity" that some courts have attached to restrictions imposed by a common interest community from the outset of its development. *Ridgely, supra,* 660 A.2d at 947, quoting *Hidden Harbour Estates, Inc. v. Basso,* 393 So.2d 637, 639 (Fla.App. 4 Dist. Ct.1981).

As to the first amendment . . . which precludes residency at Panther Valley by a Tier 3 offender, we decline to pass upon the issue for we are satisfied that the parties did not create a sufficient record in this matter, which was handled as a summary proceeding, to permit a reviewing court to reach a decision that can take into account and reflect the various competing policy considerations.

Plaintiff asserts three reasons why this first amendment is invalid. She contends that it is an unlawful infringement on her right to alienate her property, that it compels her to violate the law by obligating her to seek out and identify such Tier 3 registrants and that it is contrary to public policy. The first two are wholly insubstantial in our view and if plaintiff's argument were confined to them, we would reject her position out of hand.

Defendants have supplied as part of the record in this case statistics that were compiled by the Office of the Attorney General in connection with its overall responsibility for monitoring Megan's Law matters. According to those figures, there were, as of July 30, 1999, only 80 Tier 3 registrants within the entire State of New Jersey. New Jersey has, as of the 2000 census, a population in excess of 8,400,000; that there may be 80 individuals out of a total of 8.4 million to whom plaintiff may not sell her home cannot, in our judgment, seriously be considered an unlawful restriction upon her right to sell or lease her home.

In addition, the restriction, if indeed it can be considered one, does not fall unfairly upon plaintiff; it affects all members of the Association equally. Thus, plaintiff, if she sought to sell or lease her home, would not be relegated to a smaller potential market than another Panther Valley resident. . . . And it cannot escape remarking that the record is entirely barren of any indication that plaintiff has any present plans to sell or lease her home to anyone. To the extent plaintiff is seeking to vindicate the rights of a Tier 3 registrant to reside in Panther Valley, she is not the proper party. . . .

Her second asserted reason flies in the face of the plain language of the amendment. It imposes no such obligation upon her.

The third, however, gives us pause, at least in one regard. Although not contained within the record before us, we are aware that other similar common interest communities within the State have passed similar restrictions upon residency by Tier 3 registrants. 156 N.J.L.J. 361 (May 3, 1999). We do not know from the record how many common interest communities exist within the State and we do not know from the record how many of those communities have seen fit to adopt comparable restrictions and whether they have determined to include a broader group than Tier 3 registrants. We are thus unable to determine whether the result of such provisions is to make a large segment of the housing market unavailable to one category of individual and indeed perhaps to approach "the ogre of vigilantism and harassment," the potential dangers of which the Supreme Court recognized even while upholding the constitutionality of Megan's Law. *Doe v. Poritz*, 142 N.J.1, 110, 662 A. 2d 367 (1995).

The record is deficient in another regard as well for it is entirely unclear if the Association performs quasi-municipal functions, such that its actions perhaps should be viewed as analogous to governmental actions in some regards. As to this issue, see, e.g., *Kennedy, supra*, 105 *Yale L.J.* 761; John B. Owens, *Westec Story: Gated Communities and the Fourth Amendment*, 34 *Am.Crim. L.Rev.* 1127 (1997). We do know, from *State v. Panther Valley, supra*, that the Association has turned over to the township the responsibility for traffic enforcement, for instance, and is precluded from acting independently in that sphere. The record does not disclose whether certain services are provided by the township and others by the Association. It may be somewhat instructive in this regard that we have concluded in another matter involving Panther Valley that the Association's newsletter, "The Panther," could not be compelled to publish an ad submitted by the plaintiff that was apparently critical of the local first-aid squad. *William G. Mulligan Found. for the Control of First Aid Squadders & Roving Paramedics v. Brooks*, 312 N.J.Super. 353, 711 A.2d 961 (App.Div.1998).

We recognize, of course, that Tier 3 registrants (and indeed convicted criminals) are not a protected group within the terms of New Jersey's Law Against Discrimination. *N.J.S.A.*10:5-3. Nor have we been pointed to any authority deeming them handicapped.

In this regard, however see *Arnold Murray Constr., L.L.C. v. Hicks*, 621 N.W.2d 171 (S.D.2001), in which the court upheld the eviction of a handicapped tenant who posed a direct threat to the health and safety of other tenants without the necessity of attempting to provide reasonable accommodations under the federal Fair Housing Act. It does not necessarily follow, however, that large segments of the State could entirely close their doors to such individuals, confining them to a narrow corridor and thus perhaps exposing those within that remaining corridor to a greater risk of harm than they might otherwise have had to confront.

Common interest communities fill a particular need in the housing market but they also pose unique problems for those who remain outside their gates, whether voluntarily or by economic necessity. The understandable desire of individuals to protect themselves and their families from some of the ravages of modern society and thus reside within such communities should not become a vehicle to ensure that those problems remain the burden of those least able to afford a viable solution.

We hasten to add that we recognize that not all gated communities are refuges for the wealthy. They are a spreading phenomenon that can be found among all economic strata. Owens, *supra*, 34 *Am.Crim. L.Rev.* at 1136-37. Their growth has been fueled by the public's fear of crime and need for safety. *Ibid.*; Kennedy, *supra*, 105 *Yale L.J.* at 766.

The Supreme Court has long cautioned against the dangers inherent in courts, presented with a meager record, ruling upon questions having a broad social and legal impact. *Jackson v. Muhlenberg Hosp.*, 53 N.J. 138, 249 A.2d 65 (1969). Although the Supreme Court concluded in *Doe v. Poritz, supra*, that it had no basis to overturn the legislative judgment "that public safety was more important than the potential for [an] unfair . . . impact. . . ." 142 N.J. at 110, 662 A.2d 367, it did so on the basis of a fully-formed record. We decline to write a solution for a problem that has not been fully stated.

Because we have concluded, for the reasons we have set forth, that the record was insufficient to permit determination of the issue, we reverse that portion of the trial court's judgment upholding the validity of the first amendment to the Association's Declaration.

NOTES AND QUESTIONS

1. *Anti-Sex Offender Covenants.* Let's stipulate than no one would want to live next to a Tier 3 sex offender. Should a covenant against sex offenders be enforced? If so, how about a covenant against murders? Or a covenant against felons generally?

2. *Further Reading.* Asmara M. Tekle, *Safe: Restrictive Covenants and the Next Wave of Sex Offender Restrictions*, 62 SMU L. Rev. 1817 (2009); John J. Herman, *Not in My Community: Is it Legal for Private Entities to Ban Sex Offenders From Living in Their Communities?*, 16 Widener L.J. 165 (2006).

THE CONSTITUTION AND COMMON INTEREST COMMUNITIES

With a handful of very narrow exceptions, the U.S. Constitution does not apply to common interest communities because common interest communities are not government entities. As a result, a common interest community may, for example, place prohibitions or restrictions on signs that would violate the First Amendment if imposed by a government actor.

The first possible exception to this rule may be when a common interest community provides services (e.g., policing and garbage pickup) that typically are provided by municipalities. If the common interest community effectively replaces a municipal government, there may by an argument for applying the constitution at least to the common interest community's conduct of quasi-governmental functions. *See* David L. Callies, Paula A. Franzese, & Heidi Kai Guth, Ramapo *Looking Forward: Gated Communities, Covenants, and Concerns*, 35 Urb. Law. 177 (2003); Katherine Rosenberry, *The Application of Federal and State Constitutions to Condominiums, Cooperatives, and Planned Developments*, 19 Real Prop. Prob. & Tr. J. 1 (1984). The *Mulligan* opinion hints at the potentially quasi-governmental nature of common interest communities. This possible exception has some theoretical appeal but to date has not had a major impact in the case law.

The second possible exception comes from the U.S. Supreme Court decision in *Shelley v. Kraemer*, 334 U.S. 1 (1948). In *Shelley*, the Court held that it was a violation of the Fourteenth Amendment's guarantee of equal protection for a court to enforce a racially restrictive covenant. *Shelley* is incredibly important historically and is a landmark civil rights decision. *Shelley* presents some difficulties from a matter of constitutional theory, however, because it treated the lower court's enforcement of the covenant as state action that was subject to the U.S. Constitution. Taken to its logical conclusion, this approach would treat a court's enforcement of any private agreement to be state action, allowing constitutional review of that agreement. The courts have not gone very far in this direction, and it may be best to look at *Shelley* as a case in which the Court took an extraordinary step to address the pernicious effects of racially restrictive covenants. In most housing related contexts, the FHA prevents any need to rely on *Shelley* to address discriminatory conduct. Nonetheless, *Shelley* may still have some relevance to situations not addressed by statute. *See* Shelley Ross Saxer, Shelley v. Kramer's *Fiftieth Anniversary: "A Time for Keeping; A Time For Throwing Away"?*, 47 U. Kan. L. Rev. 61 (1998).

CHAPTER 7

NUISANCE

Recall that use is one of the four classic incidents of property ownership. If you own land, you typically have the right to use it. The owner's right to use land, however, is subject to some limits. In our last chapter, we examined covenants that run with the land. Covenants can serve as a private means of land use control. We saw, for example, that a covenant that runs with the land can be used to restrict lots in a subdivision to single-family residential use. In this chapter, we will examine the law of nuisance. As we will see, nuisance provides some crude private law limits on land use. In the next chapter, we will consider the law of zoning and government-imposed restrictions on land use. The three topics together—covenants, nuisance, and zoning—give us an overview of our legal system's private and public methods of land use control.

Nuisance is a tort that has a strong property component to it. A person commits the tort of nuisance by intentionally and unreasonably interfering with another person's use and enjoyment of her property. The tort has its origins in the common-law maxim *sic utere tuo, ut alienum non laedas*—we should not use our property in a way that injures the property of another. If I use my land in a way that unreasonably interferes with your use of your land, you will be able to bring a claim of nuisance against me. Nuisance thus provides some degree of land use control—my right to use my land is limited by my obligation not to use it in a way that interferes with your rights to your land.

A nuisance is (1) an intentional, (2) unreasonable, (3) substantial interference with the use and enjoyment of another's property. Note the requirement in the third element that the interference be substantial—there will be no nuisance if the interference is only trivial. Other than very minor interferences, the third element is rarely a dispositive issue in nuisance cases. Intent can be an interesting issue in the nuisance context, as we will see momentarily. The most interesting and difficult element, however, is the requirement that the interference be unreasonable. We will spend most of our time focused on the unreasonableness element.

You might think that intent would be a relatively straightforward element, but nuisance is an unusual intentional tort. In most jurisdictions, the intent necessary to commit the tort of nuisance is *intent to do the act*, not intent to interfere with the use and enjoyment of another's property. Imagine, for example, that I am manufacturing concrete on my property, and as a result I am causing huge amounts of dust to fall on your property. For nuisance purposes, we care that I intentionally manufactured the concrete. We do not care whether I intentionally wanted the dust to fall on your property or whether I intended to cause a problem for you. (If I did not act intentionally, I may still be liable under theories of negligence or recklessness. We leave those topics to your torts class.)

By this point in your legal career, you have probably already figured out that the line between reasonable and unreasonable conduct can be hard to pin down. You also may wonder why we are discussing reasonableness in the context of an intentional tort. As we already noted, nuisance is an unusual tort. We will discuss three approaches to unreasonableness in the nuisance context: the *traditional approach*, the *basic Restatement approach*, and the *alternative Restatement approach*:

- *Traditional Approach*: Under the traditional approach, a use is unreasonable if it crosses a poorly defined threshold in its interference with the use of another's property. To be frank, the line between reasonable and unreasonable under this approach is quite blurry and hard to pin down. The requirement that an interference be substantial typically is considered a separate element, but the more substantial the interference, the more likely it is to be considered unreasonable under this approach. Uses that are dirty, smelly, or noisy tend to fare poorly under the traditional approach.

- *Basic Restatement Approach*: The Restatement (Second) of Torts §826(a) takes the approach that a use of property is unreasonable if the "the gravity of the harm outweighs the utility of the actor's conduct." In other words, the basic Restatement approach weighs the benefit of the activity alleged to be a nuisance against the harm caused by that activity. If the benefit outweighs the harm, then the activity is not unreasonable and is not a nuisance. If the harm outweighs the benefit, then the activity is unreasonable and will be nuisance if the other elements of nuisance are met.

- *Alternative Restatement Approach*: The Restatement (Second) of Torts §826(b) states that conduct alleged to be a nuisance is unreasonable if "the harm caused by the conduct is serious and the financial burden of compensating for this and similar harm to others would not make the continuation of the conduct not feasible." Let's return to the concrete manufacturing example. I am manufacturing concrete on my land, causing dust to fall on your land. There is a good chance that the social utility of my conduct outweighs the harm that you are suffering. If so, my conduct would not be a nuisance under the basic Restatement test. The alternative Restatement test gets at this scenario by holding that my action is unreasonable if I can compensate you for the harm you suffered without going out of business myself.

We will consider each of these three approaches in our next two cases. The first case, *Estancias Dallas Corp. v. Schultz*, gives us a good opportunity to think about the distinction between the traditional approach and the basic Restatement approach. The second case, *Boomer v. Atlantic Cement*, gives us a good opportunity to think about the alternative Restatement approach. Indeed, *Boomer* is the source of the alternative Restatement approach. If the alternative Restatement approach is still a bit unclear to you, don't worry about it for now, and reconsider it after we have discussed *Boomer*.

Historically, nuisance was prosecuted criminally. In our chapter on Takings, for example, we will read a case involving a criminal prosecution for nuisance. Gradually, nuisance became a civil rather than criminal matter. The traditional civil remedy for a nuisance was an injunction prohibiting the conduct that caused the nuisance. This type of injunction was often called an *abatement* of the nuisance. Injunctions still are common remedies in nuisance actions. Over time, however, awards of money damages as remedies for nuisance have become more common in certain circumstances. The choice between the equitable remedy of an injunction and the legal remedy of money damages in the nuisance context will be a major theme in this chapter and is a significant issue in all three of our cases.

As you read our first case, think about two things. First, think about whether the conduct at issue would be a nuisance under the traditional approach and under the basic Restatement approach. Second, think about what the court has to say about the choice of remedy between an injunction and an award of money damages. Pay close attention to the court's description of the remedies awarded in prior cases and the court's explanation of why this case is different from those prior cases.

REMEDIES

LAW AND EQUITY

ESTANCIAS DALLAS CORP. V. SCHULTZ

Court of Civil Appeals of Texas, 1973
500 S.W.2d 217

STEPHENSON, Justice.[1]

This is an appeal from an order of the trial court granting a permanent injunction. Trial was by jury and judgment was rendered upon the jury verdict. The parties will be referred to here as they were in the trial court.

Plaintiffs, Thad Schultz and wife, brought this suit asking that defendant, Estancias Dallas Corporation, be permanently enjoined from operating the air conditioning equipment and tower on the property next to plaintiffs' residence. The jury found: that the noise emitted solely from defendant's air conditioning equipment constitutes a nuisance; that the nuisance began May 1, 1969; that it is permanent; that the nuisance has been continuous since it began; that Mrs. Schultz has been damaged $9000 and Thad Schultz $1000, considering material personal discomfort, inconvenience, annoyance and impairment of health as the elements of damages. The jury failed to find that the nuisance proximately caused material personal discomfort, inconvenience, annoyance and impairment of health to either plaintiff. The jury also failed to find that there was any unreasonable delay by plaintiffs in calling the nuisance to the attention of the defendant.

Our record shows that this apartment complex was completed about March or April of 1969 with about 155 rentable apartments in eight buildings. The air conditioning unit

---

[1] [Eds. Note—We have changed the order of parts of this opinion to place the discussion of whether the conduct was a nuisance before the discussion of remedies.]

complained of here served the entire complex. This unit is located at the back side of defendant's property, about five and one-half feet from plaintiffs' property line, about fifty-five feet from plaintiffs' back door, and about seventy feet from plaintiffs' bedroom. According to much of the testimony, the unit sounds like a jet airplane or helicopter. The plaintiffs testified: That this was a quiet neighborhood before these apartments were constructed. That they can no longer do any entertaining in their backyard because of the noise. That they cannot carry on a normal conversation in their home with all their doors and windows closed. That the noise interferes with their sleep at night. Several of the neighbors gave similar testimony.

Plaintiffs testified that the value of their land before was $25,000 and $10,000 after the noise began. One of the neighbors, a real estate broker, placed the value at $25,000 before and $12,500 after. A witness who qualified as an expert metallurgical consultant testified as to the results of tests made at various points as to the sound factors in decibels before and after defendant made changes in an effort to reduce the noise.

A witness testified: That he was the original owner of the apartments. That it cost about $80,000 to construct this air conditioning system and that separate units for the eight buildings would have cost $40,000 more. That it would now cost $150,000 to $200,000 to change to that system. That these apartments could not be rented without air conditioning.

There is no point of error complaining of the definition of the term "nuisance" given by the trial court to the jury. That definition is as follows:

> "You are instructed that by the term 'nuisance' as used in this Charge is meant any condition, brought about by one party in the use of his property, so unusual and excessive that it necessarily causes injury or damage or harm or inconvenience to another party in the use and enjoyment of his property, substantially, materially and unreasonably interfering with the latter's comfort and proper use and enjoyment of his property, taking into consideration the nature and use of the property of both parties and the character of community in which they are situated, and which condition would be substantially offensive, discomforting and annoying to persons of ordinary sensibilities, tastes and habits living in the locality where the premises are situated."

Defendant's first two points of error, briefed together, are that the trial court erred in granting the injunction because plaintiffs failed to secure a jury finding that the nuisance in question was a proximate cause of their alleged discomfort and because the trial court failed to balance the equities in its favor.

We proceed to consider first the matter as to balancing the equities. Even though this matter has arisen many times, we have found little in-depth writing on the subject. The case cited most frequently in this state is *Storey v. Central Hide & Rendering Co.,* 148 Tex. 509, 226 S.W.2d 615 (1950). The rule of law was clearly established in this case that even though a jury finds facts constituting a nuisance, it was held that there should be a balancing of equities in order to determine if an injunction should be granted. The Supreme Court then stated certain guidelines for the trial courts to follow in making such determinations by quoting as follows from 31 Tex.Jur. §35 Nuisances:

> "According to the doctrine of 'comparative injury' or 'balancing of equities' the court will consider the injury which may result to the defendant and the public by granting the injunction as well as the injury to be sustained by the complainant if the writ be denied. If the court finds that the injury to the complainant is slight in comparison to the injury caused the defendant and the public by enjoining the nuisance, relief will ordinarily be refused. It has been pointed out that the cases in which a nuisance is permitted to exist under this doctrine are based on the stern rule of necessity rather than on the right of the author of the nuisance to work a hurt, or injury to his neighbor. The necessity of others may compel the injured party to seek relief by way of an action at law for damages rather than by a suit in equity to abate the nuisance."

> "Some one must suffer these inconveniences rather than that the public interest should suffer. . . . These conflicting interests call for a solution of the question by the application of the broad principles of right and justice, leaving the individual to his remedy by compensation and maintaining the public interests intact; this works hardships on the individual, but they are incident to civilization with its physical developments, demanding more and more the means of rapid transportation of persons and property."

> "On the other hand, an injunction may issue where the injury to the opposing party and the public is slight or disproportionate to the injury suffered by the complainant." (226 S.W.2d at 618-619)

We have found application of the doctrine of balancing the equities in the cases which follow.

Lee v. Bowles, 397 S.W.2d 923, 927 (Tex.Civ.App., San Antonio, 1965, no writ), wherein the jury found the operation of a race track to be a nuisance but the trial judge balanced the equities and denied the injunction. The court of civil appeals affirmed the judgment with this statement:

> "The evidence in this case justified a finding by the trial court that the public generally would benefit from the operation of this track, both from a standpoint of recreational value and as an economic asset. Further, there was no showing that the proposed location was unsuitable."

Schiller v. Raley, 405 S.W.2d 446, 447 (Tex.Civ.App., Waco, 1966, no writ), wherein the trial court enjoined the operation of a cattle feed lot which the jury had found to be a nuisance. The court of civil appeals reversed and remanded the case with this statement:

> "There is evidence that the operation is 'essential to the meat supply of the city,' and 'someone must do it'; this it is a useful and necessary business."

Garland Grain Co. v. D-C Home Owners Improve. Ass'n, 393 S.W.2d 635, 643 (Tex.Civ.App., Tyler, 1965, error ref. n.r.e.), wherein the trial court granted the injunction to abate the operation of cattle feeding pens as a nuisance. The court of civil appeals reversed and rendered the case, balancing the equities in favor of defendants, with this statement:

> "In view of the fact that the question of health is not involved and that defendants' business is located in a rural area where many of the plaintiffs' cattle, to some extent at least, causes obnoxious odor and in view of the fact that there is no other place in this area of the state where such lawful business could be maintained without visiting the same burden on other people and in view of the fact that the cessation of defendants' business would result in harm to the public as well as defendants, we have concluded that the trial court was in error in finding that the equities were balanced in favor of the plaintiffs."

Texas Lime Company v. Hindman, 300 S.W.2d 112, 123 (Tex.Civ.App., Waco, 1957, affirmed 157 Tex. 592, 305 S.W.2d 947 (1957)), wherein the trial court enjoined the operation of a lime plant found to be a nuisance. The court of civil appeals reversed and remanded the case with this statement:

> "We are of the further view that since the lime plant owned by the Limestone Products Company and operated by Texas Lime Company is a lawful, useful and necessary business, and that it does and has contributed to the welfare and prosperity of the community in which it is located, as well as to the health and welfare of the people of the State of Texas, in that useful and necessary products are being produced, that considering the time the plant was located and the conditions surrounding, and all the facts and circumstances surrounding at the time of its location, that the granting of an injunction as requested by the appellees would be unjust, improper, inequitable and would result in an unbalancing of the equities in favor of a few individuals as against the public at large."

Fargason v. Economy Furniture, Inc., 356 S.W.2d 212, 215 (Tex.Civ.App., Austin, 1962, error ref. n.r.e.), wherein the jury found the operation of an incinerator in connection with a furniture plant to be a nuisance, but the trial court refused the injunction. The court of civil appeals affirmed the judgment, holding that the trial court did not abuse its discretion and stating:

> "The abatement of a lawful business is a harsh remedy and there should be a balancing of equities by the Trial Court in order to determine if an injunction should be granted even though the jury found it to be a nuisance."

Lamb v. Kinslow, 256 S.W.2d 903 (Tex.Civ.App., Waco, 1953, error ref. n.r.e.), wherein the trial court granted an injunction against the burning of cotton burrs in connection with defendant's cotton gin. The jury found such burning to be a nuisance. The court of civil appeals affirmed the judgment and held it was proper for the trial court to balance the equities even though that question was raised for the first time on motion for judgment. The appellate court refused to hold that the trial court abused its discretion in not balancing the equities in favor of defendants.

Hill v. Villarreal, 383 S.W.2d 463, 465 (Tex.Civ.App., San Antonio, 1964, error ref. n.r.e.), wherein the trial court refused an injunction against a rendering plant even though the jury found the operation to be a nuisance. The court of civil appeals affirmed, holding the trial court did not abuse its discretion after balancing the equities. Among other factual statements, the following appears in the opinion:

> "The issue presented in this case is thus one involving the conflicting rights of the parties in the respective uses of their properties. In resolving this issue favorably to appellees after balancing the equities, the trial court found: appellees are engaged in an essential and necessary business which promotes the general welfare and good health of the citizens of San Antonio; a rendering plant helps to conserve what would otherwise be wasted and helps to afford an efficient and economical means of disposing of dead animals, scraps and offal. . . ."

Georg v. Animal Defense League, 231 S.W.2d 807, 809-810 (Tex.Civ.App., San Antonio, 1950, error ref. n.r.e.), wherein the trial court denied an injunction sought to close an animal shelter for dogs although the jury found the operation to be a nuisance. The court of civil appeals affirmed, approving the balancing of the equities in favor of defendants, saying:

> "In view of the public interest, it is the general rule that a group of private individuals are not entitled to an injunction restraining the operation of an establishment contributing to the common good, but such parties are relegated to their remedy at law in the form of an action for damages. A suit for injunction will lie only in the unusual case where there is a disproportion of equities, such as where an offensive although necessary undertaking is carried on in an unsuitable place when it could be as easily and economically carried on in some location where it would give no offense."

There is no specific mention in the judgment that the trial court balanced the equities. However, that question was raised by the pleadings, evidence was heard, and there is an implied finding that the trial court balanced the equities in favor of plaintiffs by entering the judgment granting the injunction. We do not find that the trial court abused its discretion in balancing the equities in favor of plaintiffs.

It is significant that the Supreme Court of Texas in the *Storey* case, *supra,* placed great emphasis upon public interest. Also, in all of the other cases cited above, the appellate courts in their opinions refer to the benefit to the public generally in permitting a nuisance to continue through the balancing of equities. We find little or no testimony in the record before us reflecting benefit to the public generally. There is no evidence that there is a shortage of apartments in the City of Houston and that the public would suffer by having no place to live.

Applying the rules of law set forth above in the quotation from the *Storey* case, *supra* (226 S.W.2d at 619), the nuisance in this case will not be permitted to exist "based on the stern rule of necessity rather than on the right of the author of the nuisance to work a hurt, or injury to his neighbor." There is not evidence before us to indicate the "necessity of others . . . compel(s) the injured party to seek relief by way of an action at law for damages rather than by a suit in equity to abate the nuisance." Furthermore, although plaintiffs had a count in their pleading seeking damages, in response to a motion made by defendant, the court forced plaintiffs to elect at the close of their evidence. Thus, defendant's own trial tactics prevented the development of a full record upon which we could predicate the doctrine of balancing the equities.

Plaintiffs were not required to recover damages for a temporary nuisance, that is, for the time when the nuisance began until the date of the trial, in order to secure a permanent injunction. They were entitled to such injunction based upon the affirmative answers given by the jury as set out above. The failure on the part of the jury to give an affirmative answer to the proximate cause issues related to the damage issues or to a temporary nuisance and did not alter the situation. *Columbian Carbon Co. v. Tholen,* 199 S.W.2d 825 (Tex.Civ.App., Galveston, 1947, error ref.), and *King v. Miller,* 280 S.W.2d 331, 333 (Tex.Civ.App., Eastland, 1955, error ref. n.r.e.). . . .

Affirmed.

NOTES AND QUESTIONS

1. *The Traditional Approach vs. the Basic Restatement Approach.* As we noted above, *Estancias* gives us a good opportunity to consider the traditional approach and the basic Restatement approach. Under the traditional approach, a use is unreasonable if it crosses a poorly defined threshold between reasonable and unreasonable. As we noted above, dirty, smelly, and noisy uses tend to fare badly under this approach, and the more substantial the interference the more likely it is to be held unreasonable. *Estancias* doesn't seem to be a close case under this approach, and it doesn't seem to be a stretch to say that it is unreasonable to place an air-conditioning unit that sounds like a jet engine 55 feet from the neighbor's back door.

Under the basic Restatement approach, in contrast, it is far from clear that the air-conditioning unit would even constitute a nuisance. Recall that the basic Restatement approach requires us to weigh the harm of the conduct against the benefit (or utility) of the conduct. In terms of money, the harm to the homeowners was a roughly $12,500 reduction in the value of their property. On the other hand, the owner of the apartment complex saved $40,000 by installing this type of system, and it would cost $150,000 to $200,000 to change the system now that it is installed. The monetary harm to the homeowners therefore was greatly exceeded by the monetary benefit to the owner of the apartment complex. It may be that monetary value is not the only way that we can compare harm and benefit, but the disparity in monetary harm to the homeowner and monetary benefit to the apartment complex suggests that the air-conditioning unit might not be unreasonable, and therefore not a nuisance, under the basic Restatement approach.

Which of the two approaches is better here? If you don't like the apparent outcome under the basic Restatement approach, can you articulate a way of comparing harm and benefit that leads to a different outcome? Put another way, what do we use to measure harm and benefit if we do not use monetary value? Even in monetary terms, can you think of additional facts that might lead us to conclude that the harm of the air-conditioning unit exceeded its benefit?

2. *Remedies and Balancing the Equities.* As we have noted throughout this book, remedies are very important. If a right is not adequately protected by a remedy, it is fair to ask whether that right truly exists at all. Remedies are especially important in the nuisance context. Say that the court in *Estancias* had gone the other way on the balancing of the equities issue and awarded the homeowners damages rather than an injunction. Would the owners have felt that damages were an adequate remedy? (The answer to this question, by the way, may shed some light on some of the questions we asked at the end of the prior note.) All of this said, the harm to the homeowners did not seem to be dispositive on the balancing of the equities issue in *Estancias*. Rather, the court seemed to look at a few factors related to the apartment owner's actions. One of these factors was the public benefit of the action alleged to be a nuisance. How did the air-conditioning unit compare to the actions in prior cases on this factor? How do you think the public benefit should fit into the analysis? Do you think that the remedy awarded to the homeowners in *Estancias* should turn on whether there was public benefit from the air-conditioning units?

REMEDIES

LAW AND EQUITY

The rest of this chapter focuses on the injunction versus damages remedies issue introduced in *Estancias*. Our next case, *Boomer v. Atlantic Cement*, is one of the most important and influential cases in U.S. nuisance law. As we mentioned above, it is the inspiration for the alternative Restatement approach to reasonableness. As you read the case, think about the remedies issues that were just discussing in the context of *Estancias*. How do we measure harm and benefit? How much should the public benefit of the activity factor into the analysis? *Boomer* also gives us an opportunity to think about the respective roles of legislation and the common law of nuisance in regulating polluting activities.

BOOMER V. ATLANTIC CEMENT CO.

Court of Appeals of New York, 1970
26 N.Y.2d 219

Bergan, Judge.

Defendant operates a large cement plant near Albany. These are actions for injunction and damages by neighboring land owners alleging injury to property from dirt, smoke and vibration emanating from the plant. A nuisance has been found after trial, temporary damages have been allowed; but an injunction has been denied.

The public concern with air pollution arising from many sources in industry and in transportation is currently accorded ever wider recognition accompanied by a growing sense of responsibility in State and Federal Governments to control it. Cement plants are obvious sources of air pollution in the neighborhoods where they operate.

But there is now before the court private litigation in which individual property owners have sought specific relief from a single plant operation. The threshold question raised by the division of view on this appeal is whether the court should resolve the litigation between the parties now before it as equitably as seems possible; or whether, seeking promotion of the general public welfare, it should channel private litigation into broad public objectives.

A court performs its essential function when it decides the rights of parties before it. Its decision of private controversies may sometimes greatly affect public issues. Large questions of law are often resolved by the manner in which private litigation is decided. But this is normally an incident to the court's main function to settle controversy. It is a rare exercise of judicial power to use a decision in private litigation as a purposeful mechanism to achieve direct public objectives greatly beyond the rights and interests before the court.

Effective control of air pollution is a problem presently far from solution even with the full public and financial powers of government. In large measure adequate technical procedures are yet to be developed and some that appear possible may be economically impracticable.

It seems apparent that the amelioration of air pollution will depend on technical research in great depth; on a carefully balanced consideration of the economic impact of close regulation; and of the actual effect on public health. It is likely to require massive public expenditure and to demand more than any local community can accomplish and to depend on regional and interstate controls.

A court should not try to do this on its own as a by-product of private litigation and it seems manifest that the judicial establishment is neither equipped in the limited nature of any judgment it can pronounce nor prepared to lay down and implement an effective policy for the elimination of air pollution. This is an area beyond the circumference of one private lawsuit. It is a direct responsibility for government and should not thus be undertaken as an incident to solving a dispute between property owners and a single cement plant—one of many—in the Hudson River valley.

The cement making operations of defendant have been found by the court of Special Term to have damaged the nearby properties of plaintiffs in these two actions. That court, as it has been noted, accordingly found defendant maintained a nuisance and this has been affirmed at the Appellate Division. The total damage to plaintiffs' properties is, however, relatively small in comparison with the value of defendant's operation and with the consequences of the injunction which plaintiffs seek.

The ground for the denial of injunction, notwithstanding the finding both that there is a nuisance and that plaintiffs have been damaged substantially, is the large disparity in economic consequences of the nuisance and of the injunction. This theory cannot, however, be sustained without overruling a doctrine which has been consistently reaffirmed in several leading cases in this court and which has never been disavowed here, namely that where a nuisance has been found and where there has been any substantial damage shown by the party complaining an injunction will be granted.

The rule in New York has been that such a nuisance will be enjoined although marked disparity be shown in economic consequence between the effect of the injunction and the effect of the nuisance.

The problem of disparity in economic consequence was sharply in focus in *Whalen v. Union Bag & Paper Co.,* 208 N.Y. 1, 101 N.E. 805. A pulp mill entailing an investment of more than a million dollars polluted a stream in which plaintiff, who owned a farm, was "a lower riparian owner." The economic loss to plaintiff from this pollution was small. This court, reversing the Appellate Division, reinstated the injunction granted by the Special Term against the argument of the mill owner that in view of "the slight advantage to plaintiff and the great loss that will be inflicted on defendant" an injunction should not be granted (p. 2, 101 N.E. p. 805). "Such a balancing of injuries cannot be justified by the circumstances of this case," Judge Werner noted (p. 4, 101 N.E. p. 805). He continued: "Although the damage to the plaintiff may be slight as compared with the defendant's expense of abating the condition, that is not a good reason for refusing an injunction" (p. 5, 101 N.E. p. 806).

Thus the unconditional injunction granted at Special Term was reinstated. The rule laid down in that case, then, is that whenever the damage resulting from a nuisance is found not "unsubstantial," viz., $100 a year, injunction would follow. This states a rule that had been followed in this court with marked consistency (*McCarty v. Natural Carbonic Gas Co.,* 189 N.Y. 40, 81 N.E. 549; *Strobel v. Kerr Salt Co.,* 164 N.Y. 303, 58 N.E. 142; *Campbell v. Seaman,* 63 N.Y. 568).

There are cases where injunction has been denied. *McCann v. Chasm Power Co.,* 211 N.Y. 301, 105 N.E. 416 is one of them. There, however, the damage shown by plaintiffs was not only unsubstantial, it was non-existent. Plaintiffs owned a rocky bank of the stream in which defendant had raised the level of the water. This had no economic or other adverse consequence to plaintiffs, and thus injunctive relief was denied. Similar is the basis for denial of injunction in *Forstmann v. Joray Holding Co.,* 244 N.Y. 22, 154 N.E. 652 where no benefit to plaintiffs could be seen from the injunction sought (p. 32, 154 N.E. 655). Thus if, within *Whalen v. Union Bag & Paper Co., supra,* which authoritatively states the rule in New York, the damage to plaintiffs in these present cases from defendant's cement plant is "not unsubstantial," an injunction should follow.

Although the court at Special Term and the Appellate Division held that injunction should be denied, it was found that plaintiffs had been damaged in various specific amounts up to the time of the trial and damages to the respective plaintiffs were awarded for those amounts. The effect of this was, injunction having been denied, plaintiffs could maintain successive actions at law for damages thereafter as further damage was incurred.

The court at Special Term also found the amount of permanent damage attributable to each plaintiff, for the guidance of the parties in the event both sides stipulated to the payment and acceptance of such permanent damage as a settlement of all the controversies among the parties. The total of permanent damages to all plaintiffs thus found was $185,000. This basis of adjustment has not resulted in any stipulation by the parties.

This result at Special Term and at the Appellate Division is a departure from a rule that has become settled; but to follow the rule literally in these cases would be to close down the plant at once. This court is fully agreed to avoid that immediately drastic remedy; the difference in view is how best to avoid it.[*]

One alternative is to grant the injunction but postpone its effect to a specified future date to give opportunity for technical advances to permit defendant to eliminate the nuisance; another is to grant the injunction conditioned on the payment of permanent damages to plaintiffs which would compensate them for the total economic loss to their property present and future caused by defendant's operations. For reasons which will be developed the court chooses the latter alternative.

If the injunction were to be granted unless within a short period—e.g., 18 months— the nuisance be abated by improved methods, there would be no assurance that any significant technical improvement would occur.

The parties could settle this private litigation at any time if defendant paid enough money and the imminent threat of closing the plant would build up the pressure on defendant. If there were no improved techniques found, there would inevitably be applications to the court at Special Term for extensions of time to perform on showing of good faith efforts to find such techniques.

Moreover, techniques to eliminate dust and other annoying by-products of cement making are unlikely to be developed by any research the defendant can undertake within any short period, but will depend on the total resources of the cement industry nationwide and throughout the world. The problem is universal wherever cement is made.

For obvious reasons the rate of the research is beyond control of defendant. If at the end of 18 months the whole industry has not found a technical solution a court would be hard put to close down this one cement plant if due regard be given to equitable principles.

On the other hand, to grant the injunction unless defendant pays plaintiffs such permanent damages as may be fixed by the court seems to do justice between the

---

[*] Respondent's investment in the plant is in excess of $45,000,000. There are over 300 people employed there.

contending parties. All of the attributions of economic loss to the properties on which plaintiffs' complaints are based will have been redressed.

The nuisance complained of by these plaintiffs may have other public or private consequences, but these particular parties are the only ones who have sought remedies and the judgment proposed will fully redress them. The limitation of relief granted is a limitation only within the four corners of these actions and does not foreclose public health or other public agencies from seeking proper relief in a proper court.

It seems reasonable to think that the risk of being required to pay permanent damages to injured property owners by cement plant owners would itself be a reasonable effective spur to research for improved techniques to minimize nuisance.

The power of the court to condition on equitable grounds the continuance of an injunction on the payment of permanent damages seems undoubted. (See, e.g., the alternatives considered in *McCarty v. Natural Carbonic Gas Co., supra,* as well as *Strobel v. Kerr Salt Co., supra.*)

The damage base here suggested is consistent with the general rule in those nuisance cases where damages are allowed. "Where a nuisance is of such a permanent and unabatable character that a single recovery can be had, including the whole damage past and future resulting therefrom, there can be but one recovery" (66 C.J.S. Nuisances §140, p. 947). It has been said that permanent damages are allowed where the loss recoverable would obviously be small as compared with the cost of removal of the nuisance (*Kentucky-Ohio Gas Co. v. Bowling,* 264 Ky. 470, 477, 95 S.W.2d 1).

The present cases and the remedy here proposed are in a number of other respects rather similar to *Northern Indiana Public Service Co. v. W. J. & M. S. Vesey,* 210 Ind. 338, 200 N.E. 620 decided by the Supreme Court of Indiana. The gases, odors, ammonia and smoke from the Northern Indiana company's gas plant damaged the nearby Vesey greenhouse operation. An injunction and damages were sought, but an injunction was denied and the relief granted was limited to permanent damages "present, past, and future" (p. 371, 200 N.E. 620).

Denial of injunction was grounded on a public interest in the operation of the gas plant and on the court's conclusion "that less injury would be occasioned by requiring the appellant (Public Service) to pay the appellee (Vesey) all damages suffered by it . . . than by enjoining the operation of the gas plant; and that the maintenance and operation of the gas plant should not be enjoined" (p. 349, 200 N.E. p. 625).

The Indiana Supreme Court opinion continued: "When the trial court refused injunctive relief to the appellee upon the ground of public interest in the continuance of the gas plant, it properly retained jurisdiction of the case and awarded full compensation to the appellee. This is upon the general equitable principle that equity will give full relief in one action and prevent a multiplicity of suits" (pp. 353-354, 200 N.E. p. 627).

It was held that in this type of continuing and recurrent nuisance permanent damages were appropriate. See, also, *City of Amarillo v. Ware,* 120 Tex. 456, 40 S.W.2d 57 where recurring overflows from a system of storm sewers were treated as the kind of nuisance for which permanent depreciation of value of affected property would be recoverable.

There is some parallel to the conditioning of an injunction on the payment of permanent damages in the noted "elevated railway cases" (*Pappenheim v. Metropolitan El. Ry. Co.,* 128 N.Y. 436, 28 N.E. 518 and others which followed). Decisions in these cases were based on the finding that the railways created a nuisance as to adjacent property owners, but in lieu of enjoining their operation, the court allowed permanent damages.

Judge Finch, reviewing these cases in *Ferguson v. Village of Hamburg,* 272 N.Y. 234, 239-240, 5 N.E.2d 801, 803, said: "The courts decided that the plaintiffs had a valuable right which was being impaired, but did not grant an absolute injunction or require the railway companies to resort to separate condemnation proceedings. Instead they held that a court of equity could ascertain the damages and grant an injunction which was not to be effective unless the defendant failed to pay the amount fixed as damages for the past and permanent injury inflicted." (*See, also, Lynch v. Metropolitan El. Ry. Co.,* 129 N.Y. 274, 29 N.E. 315; *Van Allen v. New York El. R.R. Co.,* 144 N.Y. 174, 38 N.E. 997; *Cox v. City of New York,* 265 N.Y. 411, 193 N.E. 251, and similarly, *Westphal v. City of New York,* 177 N.Y. 140, 69 N.E. 369.)

Thus it seems fair to both sides to grant permanent damages to plaintiffs which will terminate this private litigation. The theory of damage is the "servitude on land" of plaintiffs imposed by defendant's nuisance. (*See United States v. Causby,* 328 U.S. 256, 261, 262, 267, 66 S.Ct. 1062, 90 L.Ed. 1206, where the term "servitude" addressed to the land was used by Justice Douglas relating to the effect of airplane noise on property near an airport.)

The judgment, by allowance of permanent damages imposing a servitude on land, which is the basis of the actions, would preclude future recovery by plaintiffs or their grantees (*see Northern Indiana Public Serv. Co. v. W. J. & M. S. Vesey, supra,* p. 351, 200 N.E. 620).

This should be placed beyond debate by a provision of the judgment that the payment by defendant and the acceptance by plaintiffs of permanent damages found by the court shall be in compensation for a servitude on the land.

Although the Trial Term has found permanent damages as a possible basis of settlement of the litigation, on remission the court should be entirely free to re-examine this subject. It may again find the permanent damage already found; or make new findings.

The orders should be reversed, without costs, and the cases remitted to Supreme Court, Albany County to grant an injunction which shall be vacated upon payment by defendant of such amounts of permanent damage to the respective plaintiffs as shall for this purpose be determined by the court.

JASEN, Judge (dissenting).

I agree with the majority that a reversal is required here, but I do not subscribe to the newly enunciated doctrine of assessment of permanent damages, in lieu of an injunction, where substantial property rights have been impaired by the creation of a nuisance.

It has long been the rule in this State, as the majority acknowledges, that a nuisance which results in substantial continuing damage to neighbors must be enjoined. (*Whalen v. Union Bag & Paper Co.,* 208 N.Y. 1, 101 N.E. 805; *Campbell v. Seaman,* 63 N.Y. 568; *see, also, Kennedy v. Moog Servocontrols,* 21 N.Y.2d 966, 290 N.Y.S.2d 193, 237 N.E.2d 356.) To now change the rule to permit the cement company to continue polluting the air indefinitely upon the payment of permanent damages is, in my opinion, compounding the magnitude of a very serious problem in our State and Nation today.

In recognition of this problem, the Legislature of this State has enacted the Air Pollution Control Act (Public Health Law, Consol.Laws, c. 45, §§1264-1299-m) declaring that it is the State policy to require the use of all available and reasonable methods to prevent and control air pollution (Public Health Law §1265).

The harmful nature and widespread occurrence of air pollution have been extensively documented. Congressional hearings have revealed that air pollution causes substantial property damage, as well as being a contributing factor to a rising incidence of lung cancer, emphysema, bronchitis and asthma.

The specific problem faced here is known as particulate contamination because of the fine dust particles emanating from defendant's cement plant. The particular type of nuisance is not new, having appeared in many cases for at least the past 60 years. (*See Hulbert v. California Portland Cement Co.,* 161 Cal. 239, 118 P. 928 (1911)). It is interesting to note that cement production has recently been identified as a significant source of particulate contamination in the Hudson Valley. This type of pollution, wherein very small particles escape and stay in the atmosphere, has been denominated as the type of air pollution which produces the greatest hazard to human health. We have thus a nuisance which not only is damaging to the plaintiffs, but also is decidedly harmful to the general public.

NUISANCE VS. TRESPASS

Judge Jasen notes in his dissent that the fine dust emitted by the cement plant constituted particulate contamination. In *Boomer*, the dust caused by the cement plant was analyzed as a nuisance. Because the dust physically intruded onto the neighbors' land, the dust emissions conceivably could have been analyzed as a trespass. Trespass analysis does not inquire as to the reasonableness of the trespasser's invasion (defenses like necessity aside), so trespass might be more favorable than nuisance for a plaintiff. Perhaps because of tradition, courts tend to analyze pollution cases under nuisance doctrine rather than trespass doctrine.

I see grave dangers in overruling our long-established rule of granting an injunction where a nuisance results in substantial continuing damage. In permitting the injunction to become inoperative upon the payment of permanent damages, the majority is, in effect, licensing a continuing wrong. It is the same as saying to the cement company, you may continue to do harm to your neighbors so long as you pay a fee for it. Furthermore, once such permanent damages are assessed and paid, the incentive to alleviate the wrong would be eliminated, thereby continuing air pollution of an area without abatement. . . .

I would enjoin the defendant cement company from continuing the discharge of dust particles upon its neighbors' properties unless, within 18 months, the cement company abated this nuisance.

It is not my intention to cause the removal of the cement plant from the Albany area, but to recognize the urgency of the problem stemming from this stationary source of air pollution, and to allow the company a specified period of time to develop a means to alleviate this nuisance.

I am aware that the trial court found that the most modern dust control devices available have been installed in defendant's plant, but, I submit, this does not mean that better and more effective dust control devices could not be developed within the time allowed to abate the pollution.

Moreover, I believe it is incumbent upon the defendant to develop such devices, since the cement company, at the time the plant commenced production (1962), was well aware of the plaintiffs' presence in the area, as well as the probable consequences of its contemplated operation. Yet, it still chose to build and operate the plant at this site.

In a day when there is a growing concern for clean air, highly developed industry should not expect acquiescence by the courts, but should, instead, plan its operations to eliminate contamination of our air and damage to its neighbors.

Accordingly, the orders of the Appellate Division, insofar as they denied the injunction, should be reversed, and the actions remitted to Supreme Court, Albany County to grant an injunction to take effect 18 months hence, unless the nuisance is abated by improved techniques prior to said date.

NOTES AND QUESTIONS

1. Boomer *and the Alternative Restatement Approach.* As we noted above, *Boomer* is the inspiration for the alternative Restatement approach. As a reminder, under this approach, conduct alleged to be a nuisance is unreasonable if "the harm caused by the conduct is serious and the financial burden of compensating for this and similar harm to others would not make the continuation of the conduct not feasible." The facts of *Boomer* help flesh out this approach.

As an initial matter, we should be clear about why the facts of *Boomer* would lead to a different result under the basic Restatement test. The utility of the cement plan almost certainly outweighed the harm caused to the neighboring land owners. (Do you see why? Note, in this context, the one footnote in the majority opinion.) If the utility outweighs the harm, then the conduct is not unreasonable under the basic Restatement approach. As a result, under the basic Restatement approach, the cement plant would not be a nuisance at all, and no compensation would be owed to the neighbors.

In *Boomer*, the harm caused by the cement plant was serious, meeting the first prong of the alternative Restatement approach. The cement company was able to compensate the neighbors for their injury without going out of business, meeting the second prong of this approach. The alternative Restatement approach therefore allows for a finding that the conduct is unreasonable and therefore a nuisance, where the basic Restatement approach would not find the conduct to be unreasonable and therefore would find that it was not a nuisance. The alternative Restatement approach also contemplates a remedy that gives monetary compensation rather than an injunction to the complaining neighbors.

What do you think of the alternative Restatement approach? More broadly, what do you think of the outcome of *Boomer*?

2. *Regulation vs. the Common Law of Nuisance*. Both the majority and dissent in *Boomer* discuss legislative regulation of air pollution. Having read *Boomer*, do you think that the ability of the legislature to regulate air pollution should impact the common law of nuisance? Put another way, should the fact that the legislature was considering regulating air pollution have influenced the court's decision in *Boomer* to award damages rather than an injunction?

3. Boomer *and Balancing the Equities*. Prior to *Boomer*, New York did not allow for balancing the equities in deciding whether to enjoin a nuisance. Look back at the discussion in *Estancias* of prior Texas cases that had denied injunctions. Do you think that *Boomer* took a similar approach to those Texas cases, or did *Boomer* do something different?

4. Boomer *and* Estancias *Compared*. In *Boomer*, the winning plaintiffs received damages. In *Estancias*, the winning plaintiffs received an injunction. Do you think that the courts were correct to award different remedies in the two cases? Put another way, are the facts in the two cases sufficiently different to justify different outcomes?

At several points throughout this book, we have talked about rules that take an all-or-nothing approach to legal disputes and have asked whether an award of compensation might be used to reach a better outcome. In the context of adverse possession, for example, we asked whether the best outcome would be for the adverse possessor to get ownership of the land in return for compensation paid to the original owner.

The shift toward awards of damages in the nuisance context reflected in *Boomer* can be seen as a move away from all-or-nothing outcomes. The clearest win for a plaintiff in a nuisance action is the award of an injunction that abates the nuisance. The plaintiffs in *Estancias*, for example, were able to get the court to enjoin the loud air-conditioning unit. An award of damages likely will not be as satisfying for a winning plaintiff. The neighbors in *Boomer*, for example, won the case but did not get their desired remedy. Indeed, the cement company probably was happier with the outcome than the neighbors. Reasonable minds can disagree on whether *Boomer* reached the right result, but the award of damages led to less of an all-or-nothing outcome than the award of an injunction.

Our next case is another landmark. As you will see, the court awards an injunction but takes an innovative approach, avoiding an all-or-nothing outcome.

SPUR INDUSTRIES V. DEL E. WEBB DEVELOPMENT CO.

Supreme Court of Arizona, 1972
494 P.2d 700

CAMERON, Vice Chief Justice.

From a judgment permanently enjoining the defendant, Spur Industries, Inc., from operating a cattle feedlot near the plaintiff Del E. Webb Development Company's Sun City, Spur appeals. Webb cross-appeals. Although numerous issues are raised, we feel that it is necessary to answer only two questions. They are:

1. Where the operation of a business, such as a cattle feedlot is lawful in the first instance, but becomes a nuisance by reason of a nearby residential area, may the feedlot operation be enjoined in an action brought by the developer of the residential area?

2. Assuming that the nuisance may be enjoined, may the developer of a completely new town or urban area in a previously agricultural area be required to indemnify the operator of the feedlot who must move or cease operation because of the presence of the residential area created by the developer?

The facts necessary for a determination of this matter on appeal are as follows. The area in question is located in Maricopa County, Arizona, some 14 to 15 miles west of the urban area of Phoenix, on the Phoenix-Wickenburg Highway, also known as Grand Avenue. About two miles south of Grand Avenue is Olive Avenue which runs east and west. 111th Avenue runs north and south as does the Agua Fria River immediately to the west. See Exhibits A and B below.

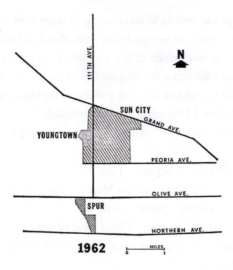

Exhibit A

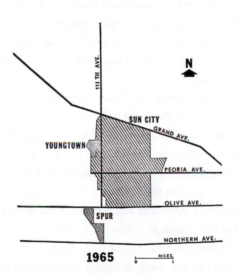

Exhibit B

Farming started in this area about 1911. In 1929, with the completion of the Carl Pleasant Dam, gravity flow water became available to the property located to the west of the Agua Fria River, though land to the east remained dependent upon well water for irrigation. By 1950, the only urban areas in the vicinity were the agriculturally related communities of Peoria, El Mirage, and Surprise located along Grand Avenue. Along 111th Avenue, approximately one mile south of Grand Avenue and 1 1/2 miles north of Olive Avenue, the community of Youngtown was commenced in 1954. Youngtown is a retirement community appealing primarily to senior citizens.

In 1956, Spur's predecessors in interest, H. Marion Welborn and the Northside Hay Mill and Trading Company, developed feed-lots, about 1/2 mile south of Olive Avenue, in an area between the confluence of the usually dry Agua Fria and New Rivers. The area is well suited for cattle feeding and in 1959, there were 25 cattle feeding pens or dairy operations within a 7 mile radius of the location developed by Spur's predecessors. In April and May of 1959, the Northside Hay Mill was feeding between 6,000 and 7,000 head of cattle and Welborn approximately 1,500 head on a combined area of 35 acres.

In May of 1959, Del Webb began to plan the development of an urban area to be known as Sun City. For this purpose, the Marinette and the Santa Fe Ranches, some 20,000 acres of farmland, were purchased for $15,000,000 or $750.00 per acre. This price was considerably less than the price of land located near the urban area of Phoenix, and along with the success of Youngtown was a factor influencing the decision to purchase the property in question.

By September 1959, Del Webb had started construction of a golf course south of Grand Avenue and Spur's predecessors had started to level ground for more feedlot area. In 1960, Spur purchased the property in question and began a rebuilding and expansion program extending both to the north and south of the original facilities. By 1962, Spur's expansion program was completed and had expanded from approximately 35 acres to 114 acres. See Exhibit A above.

Accompanied by an extensive advertising campaign, homes were first offered by Del Webb in January 1960 and the first unit to be completed was south of Grand Avenue and approximately 2 1/2 miles north of Spur. By 2 May 1960, there were 450 to 500 houses completed or under construction. At this time, Del Webb did not consider odors from the Spur feed pens a problem and Del Webb continued to develop in a southerly direction, until sales resistance became so great that the parcels were difficult if not impossible to sell. Thomas E. Breen, Vice President and General Manager of the housing division of Del Webb, testified at deposition as follows:

Q: Did you ever have any discussions with Tony Cole at or about the time the sales office was opened south of Peoria concerning the problem in sales as the development came closer towards the feed lots?

A: Not at the time that that facility was opened. That was subsequent to that.

Q: All right, what is it that you recall about conversations with Cole on that subject?

A: Well, when the feed lot problem became a bigger problem, which, really, to the best of my recollection, commenced to become a serious problem in 1963, and there was some talk about not developing that area because of sales resistance, and to my recollection we shifted—we had planned at that time to the eastern portion of the property, and it was a consideration.

Q: Was any specific suggestion made by Mr. Cole as to the line of demarcation that should be drawn or anything of that type exactly where the development should cease?

A: I don't recall anything specific as far as the definite line would be, other than, you know, that it would be advisable to stay out of the southwestern portion there because of sales resistance.

Q: And to the best of your recollection, this was in about 1963?

A: That would be my recollection, yes.

Q: As you recall it, what was the reason that the suggestion was not adopted to stop developing towards the southwest of the development?

A: Well, as far as I know, that decision was made subsequent to that time.

Q: Right. But I mean at that time?

A: Well, at that time what I am really referring to is more of a long-range planning than immediate planning, and I think it was the case of just trying to figure out how far you could go with it before you really ran into a lot of sales resistance and found a necessity to shift the direction.

Q: So that plan was to go as far as you could until the resistance got to the point where you couldn't go any further?

A: I would say that is reasonable, yes.

By December 1967, Del Webb's property had extended south to Olive Avenue and Spur was within 500 feet of Olive Avenue to the north. See Exhibit B above. Del Webb filed its original complaint alleging that in excess of 1,300 lots in the southwest portion were unfit for development for sale as residential lots because of the operation of the Spur feedlot.

Del Webb's suit complained that the Spur feeding operation was a public nuisance because of the flies and the odor which were drifting or being blown by the prevailing south to north wind over the southern portion of Sun City. At the time of the suit, Spur was feeding between 20,000 and 30,000 head of cattle, and the facts amply support the finding of the trial court that the feed pens had become a nuisance to the people who resided in the southern part of Del Webb's development. The testimony indicated that cattle in a commercial feedlot will produce 35 to 40 pounds of wet manure per day, per head, or over a million pounds of wet manure per day for 30,000 head of cattle, and that despite the admittedly good feedlot management and good housekeeping practices by Spur, the resulting odor and flies produced an annoying if not unhealthy situation as far as the senior citizens of southern Sun City were concerned. There is no doubt that some of the citizens of Sun City were unable to enjoy the outdoor living which Del Webb had advertised and that Del Webb was faced with sales resistance from prospective purchasers as well as strong and persistent complaints from the people who had purchased homes in that area.

Trial was commenced before the court with an advisory jury. The advisory jury was later discharged and the trial was continued before the court alone. Findings of fact and conclusions of law were requested and given. The case was vigorously contested, including special actions in this court on some of the matters. In one of the special actions before this court, Spur agreed to, and did, shut down its operation without prejudice to a determination of the matter on appeal. On appeal the many questions raised were extensively briefed.

It is noted, however, that neither the citizens of Sun City nor Youngtown are represented in this lawsuit and the suit is solely between Del E. Webb Development Company and Spur Industries, Inc.

MAY SPUR BE ENJOINED?

The difference between a private nuisance and a public nuisance is generally one of degree. A private nuisance is one affecting a single individual or a definite small number of persons in the enjoyment of private rights not common to the public, while a public nuisance is one affecting the rights enjoyed by citizens as a part of the public. To constitute a public nuisance, the nuisance must affect a considerable number of people or an entire community or neighborhood. *City of Phoenix v. Johnson,* 51 Ariz. 115, 75 P.2d 30 (1938).

PUBLIC NUISANCE

Section 821B(1) of the Restatement (Second) of Torts defines a public nuisance as "an unreasonable interference with a right common to the general public." Private nuisance and public nuisance have substantial similarities—both are concerned with injuries caused by unreasonable conduct. They are different in that private nuisance is concerned with interference with the use and enjoyment of private property, where public nuisance is concerned with interference with the rights of the public. Public nuisance cases are often brought by public officials seeking to vindicate the rights of the public. For a private party to bring a public nuisance action, that private party must show that they have suffered *special damages* or *special injury*—that is, that they have suffered an injury different in kind from the type of injury suffered by other members of the public. In *Spur,* Del Webb demonstrated special damages because of the loss of sales caused by the feedlot. This injury was different in kind from the general stink suffered by the public as a whole.

Where the injury is slight, the remedy for minor inconveniences lies in an action for damages rather than in one for an injunction. *Kubby v. Hammond,* 68 Ariz. 17, 198 P.2d 134 (1948). Moreover, some courts have held, in the "balancing of conveniences" cases, that damages may be the sole remedy. *See Boomer v. Atlantic Cement Co.,* 26 N.Y.2d 219, 309 N.Y.S.2d 312, 257 N.E.2d 870, 40 A.L.R.3d 590 (1970), and annotation comments, 40 A.L.R.3d 601.

Thus, it would appear from the admittedly incomplete record as developed in the trial court, that, at most, residents of Youngtown would be entitled to damages rather than injunctive relief.

We have no difficulty, however, in agreeing with the conclusion of the trial court that Spur's operation was an enjoinable public nuisance as far as the people in the southern portion of Del Webb's Sun City were concerned.

§36-601, subsec. A reads as follows:

"§36-601. Public nuisances dangerous to public health

"A. The following conditions are specifically declared public nuisances dangerous to the public health:

"1. Any condition or place in populous areas which constitutes a breeding place for flies, rodents, mosquitoes and other insects which are capable of carrying and transmitting disease-causing organisms to any person or persons."

By this statute, before an otherwise lawful (and necessary) business may be declared a public nuisance, there must be a "populous" area in which people are injured:

"... (I)t hardly admits a doubt that, in determining the question as to whether a lawful occupation is so conducted as to constitute a nuisance as a matter of fact, the locality and surroundings are of the first importance. (citations omitted) A business which is not per se a public nuisance may become such by being carried on at a place where the health, comfort, or convenience of a populous neighborhood is affected.... What might amount to a serious nuisance in one locality by reason of the density of the population, or character of the neighborhood affected, may in another place and under different surroundings be deemed proper and unobjectionable...." *MacDonald v. Perry,* 32 Ariz. 39, 49-50, 255 P. 494, 497 (1927).

It is clear that as to the citizens of Sun City, the operation of Spur's feedlot was both a public and a private nuisance. They could have successfully maintained an action to abate the nuisance. Del Webb, having shown a special injury in the loss of sales, had a standing to bring suit to enjoin the nuisance. *Engle v. Clark,* 53 Ariz. 472, 90 P.2d 994 (1939); *City of Phoenix v. Johnson, supra.* The judgment of the trial court permanently enjoining the operation of the feedlot is affirmed.

MUST DEL WEBB INDEMNIFY SPUR?

A suit to enjoin a nuisance sounds in equity and the courts have long recognized a special responsibility to the public when acting as a court of equity:

§104. Where public interest is involved.

"Courts of equity may, and frequently do, go much further both to give and withhold relief in furtherance of the public interest than they are accustomed to go when only private interests are involved. Accordingly, the granting or withholding of relief may properly be dependent upon considerations of public interest. . . ." 27 Am.Jur.2d, Equity, page 626.

In addition to protecting the public interest, however, courts of equity are concerned with protecting the operator of a lawfully, albeit noxious, business from the result of a knowing and willful encroachment by others near his business.

In the so-called "coming to the nuisance" cases, the courts have held that the residential landowner may not have relief if he knowingly came into a neighborhood reserved for industrial or agricultural endeavors and has been damaged thereby:

"Plaintiffs chose to live in an area uncontrolled by zoning laws or restrictive covenants and remote from urban development. In such an area plaintiffs cannot complain that legitimate agricultural pursuits are being carried on in the vicinity, nor can plaintiffs, having chosen to build in an agricultural area, complain that the agricultural pursuits carried on in the area depreciate the value of their homes. The area being primarily agricultural, and opinion reflecting the value of such property must take this factor into account. The standards affecting the value of residence property in an urban setting, subject to zoning controls and controlled planning techniques, cannot be the standards by which agricultural properties are judged.

"People employed in a city who build their homes in suburban areas of the county beyond the limits of a city and zoning regulations do so for a reason. Some do so to avoid the high taxation rate imposed by cities, or to avoid special assessments for street, sewer and water projects. They usually build on improved or hard surface highways, which have been built either at state or county expense and thereby avoid special assessments for these improvements. It may be that they desire to get away from the congestion of traffic, smoke, noise, foul air and the many other annoyances of city life. But with all these advantages in going beyond the area which is zoned and restricted to protect them in their homes, they must be prepared to take the disadvantages." *Dill v. Excel Packing Company*, 183 Kan. 513, 525, 526, 331 P.2d 539, 548, 549 (1958). *See also East St. Johns Shingle Co. v. City of Portland*, 195 Or. 505, 246 P.2d 554, 560-562 (1952).

And:

> ". . . a party cannot justly call upon the law to make that place suitable for his residence which was not so when he selected it. . . . ." *Gilbert v. Showerman,* 23 Mich. 448, 455, 2 Brown 158 (1871).

Were Webb the only party injured, we would feel justified in holding that the doctrine of "coming to the nuisance" would have been a bar to the relief asked by Webb, and, on the other hand, had Spur located the feedlot near the outskirts of a city and had the city grown toward the feedlot, Spur would have to suffer the cost of abating the nuisance as to those people locating within the growth pattern of the expanding city:

> "The case affords, perhaps, an example where a business established at a place remote from population is gradually surrounded and becomes part of a populous center, so that a business which formerly was not an interference with the rights of others has become so by the encroachment of the population . . . ." *City of Ft. Smith v. Western Hide & Fur Co.,* 153 Ark. 99, 103, 239 S.W. 724, 726 (1922).

We agree, however, with the Massachusetts court that:

> "The law of nuisance affords no rigid rule to be applied in all instances. It is elastic. It undertakes to require only that which is fair and reasonable under all the circumstances. In a commonwealth like this, which depends for its material prosperity so largely on the continued growth and enlargement of manufacturing of diverse varieties, 'extreme rights' cannot be enforced. . . ." *Stevens v. Rockport Granite Co.,* 216 Mass. 486, 488, 104 N.E. 371, 373 (1914).

There was no indication in the instant case at the time Spur and its predecessors located in western Maricopa County that a new city would spring up, full-blown, alongside the feeding operation and that the developer of that city would ask the court to order Spur to move because of the new city. Spur is required to move not because of any wrongdoing on the part of Spur, but because of a proper and legitimate regard of the courts for the rights and interests of the public.

Del Webb, on the other hand, is entitled to the relief prayed for (a permanent injunction), not because Webb is blameless, but because of the damage to the people who have been encouraged to purchase homes in Sun City. It does not equitable or legally follow, however, that Webb, being entitled to the injunction, is then free of any liability to Spur if Webb has in fact been the cause of the damage Spur has sustained. It does not seem harsh to require a developer, who has taken advantage of the lesser land values in a rural area as well as the availability of large tracts of land on which to build and develop a new town or city in the area, to indemnify those who are forced to leave as a result.

RIGHT TO FARM STATUTES

Many states have enacted "Right to Farm" statutes that protect agricultural uses from nuisance claims. These statutes are designed to protect pre-existing agricultural uses from encroachment by new development. The statutes would not protect a new agricultural use that moved into an existing residential area from a nuisance claim.

Having brought people to the nuisance to the foreseeable detriment of Spur, Webb must indemnify Spur for a reasonable amount of the cost of moving or shutting down. It should be noted that this relief to Spur is limited to a case wherein a developer has, with foreseeability, brought into a previously agricultural or industrial area the population which makes necessary the granting of an injunction against a lawful business and for which the business has no adequate relief.

It is therefore the decision of this court that the matter be remanded to the trial court for a hearing upon the damages sustained by the defendant Spur as a reasonable and direct result of the granting of the permanent injunction. Since the result of the appeal may appear novel and both sides have obtained a measure of relief, it is ordered that each side will bear its own costs.

Affirmed in part, reversed in part, and remanded for further proceedings consistent with this opinion.

NOTES AND QUESTIONS

1. *Coming to the Nuisance.* Coming to the nuisance is one of those legal doctrines that has a name that aptly describes its function. As the court explains in *Spur*, if the plaintiff came into the area with knowledge of the activity now alleged to be a nuisance, then the defendant can assert coming to the nuisance as a defense. The general view is that coming to the nuisance is not a complete defense to a claim of nuisance and instead is an element that can be factored into the overall nuisance analysis. In *Spur*, the court used the doctrine in its analysis of the remedies issue rather than in its analysis of the preliminary issue of whether there was a nuisance in the first place. You should be aware that there have been many instances where the plaintiffs have come to the nuisance and were able to obtain an injunction abating the nuisance anyway. History is littered with dirty, smelly, and noisy uses that were once located in the middle of nowhere and were later shut down as nuisances when growth led to those uses being surrounded by new development.

2. *The Outcome in* Spur. In *Spur*, the court upheld an injunction but held that the developer had to indemnify the feedlot owner. In other words, the developer was forced to buy out the feedlot owner as the price of obtaining an injunction. Why, exactly, did the court reach this result? Compare the facts of *Spur* to the facts of *Estancias*. Does it make sense that the winning plaintiff in *Spur* was forced to indemnify the losing defendant, where the winning plaintiffs in *Estancias* were not required to indemnify the defendant?

3. *Property Rules, Liability Rules, and Four Possible Outcomes.* The remedies awarded in *Boomer* and *Spur* raise the distinction between *property rules* and *liability rules.* The distinction was introduced in one of the most influential law review articles of all time, Guido Calabresi & A. Douglas Melamed, *Property Rules, Liability Rules and Inalienability: One View of the Cathedral,* 85 Harv. L. Rev. 1089 (1972). If a person has an entitlement that is protected by a property rule, then another person cannot take that entitlement away unless the original owner voluntarily agrees to give it up at a price set by the owner. If, for example, I own a parcel of land, you typically cannot take that land away from me unless I voluntarily agree to transfer it to you at a price that I agree to. If a person has an entitlement that is protected by a liability rule, then another person can take away that entitlement so long as she is willing to pay objectively-determined damages to the original owner. For example, if I own a painting, you could decide to destroy that painting so long as you are willing to pay damages to me that would objectively be determined by a court. (Ignore in this context any potential criminal law problems that might arise if you destroy my painting.) Note that there are two related distinctions between entitlements protected by property rules and those protected by liability rules. First, entitlements protected by property rules can only be taken from the owner as part of a voluntary transaction, where entitlements protected by liability rules can be taken without a voluntary transaction. Second, the price paid to the owner for losing an entitlement protected by a property rule is set by agreement between the parties, where the price paid to the owner for losing an entitlement protected by a liability rule is set objectively by a court or other decision maker.

The holding in *Spur* fills the last square in a box of four potential outcomes that are based on two factors: did the plaintiff or defendant "win," and was the winning party's interest protected by a property rule or a liability rule. We put "win" in scare quotes because the putative winning party in a liability rule case might not be completely happy with the outcome. As we noted above, for example, the neighbors in *Boomer* putatively won their case against the cement company, but the cement company was probably happier with the result than the neighbors were. The four possible outcomes are as follows.

	Plaintiff "wins"	Defendant "wins"
Winning party's interest protected by property rule	① Nuisance enjoined; *Estancias*	③ No nuisance
Winning party's interest protected by liability rule	② Damages awarded for nuisance; *Boomer*	④ Nuisance enjoined but plaintiff must indemnify defendant; *Spur*

In the first square, the plaintiff wins and receives an injunction as a remedy. The plaintiff's interests (i.e., the interests of being free from the conduct alleged to be a nuisance) are protected by a property rule because the defendant is not able to infringe on those interests in return for the payment of damages. *Estancias* is an example of a case that fits in this square. In the second square, the plaintiff "wins" and receives damages as a remedy. The plaintiff's interests are protected by a liability rule because the defendant is able to infringe on those interests in return for the payment of damages. *Boomer* is an example of a case that fits in this square. In the third square, the defendant wins and is able to continue the contested conduct without interference. The defendant's interests (i.e., the interests of being able to engage in the contested conduct) are protected by a property rule because the plaintiff is not able to infringe on those interests in return for the payment of damages. We did not have a case that fit into this box, but you can imagine a case where the plaintiff's nuisance claim loses outright. In the fourth square, the defendant "wins" and is enjoined, but the plaintiff is required to indemnify the defendant. The defendant's interests are protected by a liability rule because the plaintiff is able to infringe on those interests in return for a payment of damages. *Spur* is an example of a case that fits in this square.

4. *Incompatible Land Uses.* Legal academics sometimes say that it is wrong to view nuisance as an issue of whether a person's use of land is reasonable or unreasonable. Instead, these academics say, nuisance is really a problem of incompatible land uses. *Spur* is a good example to use to illustrate this view of nuisance. Under the incompatible land uses view, the case should not be analyzed by looking at whether use of the land as a feedlot was reasonable or unreasonable. Rather, it should be analyzed as a case of incompatible land uses. Feedlots and residential subdivisions are incompatible with each other. Neither use is more or less reasonable than the other. This view of nuisance tends to support outcomes like *Spur*, where the court can be seen as more interested in finding a reasonable solution to the incompatibility than in saying that the use of land as a feedlot is reasonable or unreasonable. How does this view of nuisance cases match up with *Estancias* and *Boomer*? In particular, do you think that it would be helpful to view the facts of *Estancias* as a problem of incompatible land uses? If you think that the answer to this question is "no," what is it about the facts of *Estancias* that make it meaningfully different than *Spur*?

COASIAN BARGAINING AND NUISANCE LAW

The Coase Theorem is an influential concept in law and economics. The theorem is generally attributed to a classic and highly influential essay by the economist Ronald Coase. *The Problem of Social Cost*, 3 J.L. & Econ. 1 (1960). Applied to the nuisance context, the theorem states that absent transaction costs, the economically efficient outcome will occur regardless of whether or not the law holds contested conduct to be a nuisance.

We will explain the concept of transaction costs momentarily. For now, let's start with the main point about economically efficient outcome. Imagine that the present and future operations of the feedlot in *Spur* have an economic value of $1 million, and that it caused $2 million in present and future economic damages to the neighbors. The economically efficient result would be for the feedlot to shut down because it causes more economic harm than economic benefit. A key insight of the Coase Theorem is that absent transaction costs, this result (i.e., the feedlot shutting down) should occur even if the law found that the feedlot was not a nuisance. This result would occur because the feedlot and the neighbors should bargain with each other to reach a mutually beneficial economic outcome. The neighbors and the feedlot owner should be able to agree on a payment from the neighbors to the feedlot owners of some amount between $1 million and $2 million in return for the feedlot owners' agreement to shut the feedlot down. The neighbors would be better off economically because they would no longer be suffering the $2 million in harm. The feedlot would be better off economically because they would receive a payment in excess of the $1 million value of the feedlot. This type of bargaining to reach an economically efficient result is often called *Coasian bargaining*.

Now imagine a scenario that presents the same issue from the opposite angle. The feedlot is now worth $2 million, and the harm to the neighbors is worth $1 million. The neighbors get an injunction against the feedlot. Absent the transaction costs, the feedlot should be able to strike a deal with the neighbors to agree to waive the injunction for some price between $1 million and $2 million. The neighbors would be economically better off because they would receive a payment in excess of the $1 million in economic harm they are suffering. The owner of the feedlot would be economically better off because they would pay the neighbors something less than the $2 million value of the feedlot, which is worthless if the injunction is in place.

People sometimes overstate the impact of the Coase Theorem and say that outcomes under the law of nuisance don't matter because the parties should bargain and reach an economically efficient result. By its terms, however, the Coase Theorem applies only in the absence of transaction costs, and real-world scenarios always involve transaction costs. If the transaction costs are high enough, the parties may not reach an agreement. As the name implies, *transaction costs* are costs incurred in making economic transactions. Transaction costs are broader than just fees incurred in making a transaction and include the costs of reaching an agreement. Certain factors can dramatically increase transaction costs. Imagine, for example, that all of the members of your property class are the neighbors in *Boomer* and are trying to negotiate an agreement with the cement company. It is very hard to reach an agreement among a large group of people. (Indeed, imagine trying to reach an agreement with all the members of your property class about anything.) Because transaction costs exist in the real world, legal rules do matter. The creative remedies approaches in *Boomer* and *Spur* help reach economically efficient outcomes in contexts where transaction costs may impede Coasian bargaining.

PROBLEMS

Explanatory answers to these problems can be found on page 1065.

1. Stauffer Mining, Inc. (SMI) has been operating a marble quarry in the same location for over 50 years. A still-thriving business, it employs 30 people and generates revenue of $10 million per year. SMI uses heavy equipment and explosives in its operations. Large trucks go from the quarry down Old Oak Road to carry the marble to market. Two popular ski areas are also located on Old Oak Road, and as a result a new residential development has sprung up in the area. This development, called Snow Mountain, is located about two miles down Old Oak Road from the SMI quarry. Construction began on homes in Snow Mountain about six years ago. Now there are about 100 single-family homes in the development. The residents have been bothered by the noise created by the quarrying activity, and they recently brought a private nuisance suit against SMI. In their filings, they argue that the noise has caused them to suffer $500,000 damages (in the aggregate, not per person) to the property values to the residents of Snow Mountain. They are seeking a permanent injunction against SMI. Should the court find a nuisance? If so, what remedy should it award?

2. Gerry has been raising pigs on his farm for the last 30 years. He runs the business himself with occasional help from farmhands that he hires on a temporary basis. The farming operation is modestly profitable and is worth around $200,000. As the surrounding area has grown, residential development has started to encroach on traditionally agricultural areas. The ten-home Eagle Creek development went in last year just down the road from Gerry's farm. All ten homes were sold in December and January. The residents of Eagle Creek got a rude surprise in May, when temperatures started to rise, and the smell from the pig farm started to increase. Being typical suburbanites, the Eagle Creek residents were not happy to be living with the stench of pig manure. They therefore have brought a nuisance action against Gerry, alleging that the smells from the pig farm have reduced their property values by $100,000 for each home, or $1,000,000 in the aggregate. Should the court find a nuisance? If so, what remedy should it award? Assume that this jurisdiction does not have a right to farm law.

CHAPTER 8
LAND USE REGULATION

In the last two chapters, we have considered two private sources of land use control—restrictive covenants and nuisance. Nuisance provides a crude form of land use control by placing rough limits on how a property owner can use her property. Restrictive covenants offer a potentially much more sophisticated form of private land use control. Many contemporary common interest communities have elaborate land use controls implemented through their Covenants, Conditions, and Restrictions (CC&Rs). As sophisticated as they may potentially be, private land use controls have their limits. For example, it is impossible, or at least incredibly hard, to use restrictive covenants to implement a land use plan for an entire city.

In this chapter, we provide an introduction to the law of municipal land use regulation. Municipal laws regulating the use of land are typically called zoning laws. Zoning laws get their name from the fact that these laws, as we will see, typically operate by creating a number of zones within a municipality and by limiting the types of land uses permitted in each zone.

A. ZONING FUNDAMENTALS

Most of the issues that we will consider in this chapter involve constitutional or administrative law rules that govern, and often limit, the exercise of municipal zoning laws. Before we get into those issues, we should explain the basic structure of zoning law in the United States. We start on the state level. Land use regulations typically are imposed by states and municipalities, not by the federal government. Each state has the power to enact regulatory laws. This power is called the police power. The word "police" originally was commonly used to refer to the government generally, so you shouldn't think of the police power as being limited by the current common usage of "police" to refer to criminal law enforcement. The police power is an inherent power of sovereignty. Recall in this context that U.S. states are our nation's original sovereigns and are not mere political subdivisions of the United States. The several states transferred some of their sovereign powers to the federal government through the Constitution, but they retain all sovereign power not expressly and exclusively granted to the federal government.

Zoning laws are exercises of state police power. Most zoning laws, however, are enacted at the municipal level rather than the state level. Municipalities (cities, towns, etc.) are legal entities created by state law. As entities created by the state, municipalities have no inherent powers. Instead, they have only those powers granted to them by state law (or, in some contexts, by state constitutions). States delegate the police power authority to regulate land to municipalities through *zoning enabling laws*. Zoning enabling laws give municipalities the power to enact zoning laws. They also set limits on zoning laws—a municipal zoning law may not exceed the scope of the authority granted to the municipality by the state.

Zoning laws originated in the early 1900s as municipalities tried to respond to conflicts between industrial and residential uses. The publication of the Standard State Zoning Enabling Act in 1922 accelerated the spread of zoning. As soon as it developed, the constitutionality of this novel form of government regulation was called into question. The U.S. Supreme Court upheld the constitutionality of zoning in 1926 in our next case, *Euclid v. Ambler Realty*. Before we get to the text of *Euclid*, we want to make three points about the case and its surrounding context.

First, *Euclid* was decided in a very different era of constitutional law than our own. In the era in which the case was decided, the Supreme Court was much more skeptical of economic regulation than it is today. Using the doctrine of economic substantive due process, the Court struck down economic regulations with some frequency. This period of constitutional law is often called the *Lochner* era. The era takes its name from the 1905 case *Lochner v. New York*, in which the Court held that a regulation that limited the number of hours a baker could work in a day was unconstitutional. This era ended in the 1930s, when the Court began to take a much more deferential approach to government economic regulation that continues to be used in the present day. If a novel type of regulation was challenged on economic substantive due process grounds today, the challenge would almost certainly lose. When *Euclid* was decided in 1926, the outcome was far from certain. Indeed, the district court held that the challenged zoning law was unconstitutional, and many informed commentators thought that the Supreme Court might do the same.

Second, in our current era of constitutional law, land use regulations are limited by the doctrine of regulatory takings. If a zoning law is extraordinarily restrictive, it might be viewed as an unconstitutional taking of private property. We will cover regulatory takings law in the next chapter. For now, we will just note that most applications of zoning laws will survive a regulatory takings challenge. We should also note here that *Euclid* is not a regulatory takings case. As we will see in the next chapter in the context of a case called *Lingle v. Chevron*, serious problems can arise when early cases involving economic substantive due process challenges to land use regulations, like *Euclid*, are conflated with cases from the Court's contemporary regulatory takings jurisprudence.

Third, the *Euclid* decision includes a description of the Village of Euclid zoning ordinance at issue in the case. We think that the description of the zoning ordinance is the most important part of the case. *Euclid* is a historically important case, and it is worth considering the Court's reasoning in upholding the zoning law as constitutional. As we noted above, however, the constitutionality of zoning is no longer regarded as a difficult issue. Many zoning ordinances in place today still follow the basic approach of the challenged ordinance in *Euclid*. Indeed, this type of zoning is called *Euclidian zoning*. As you read the description, note how the ordinance is structured. To give you a preview, you will see that the ordinance is designed to segregate different types of land uses into different areas. You will also see that it establishes a hierarchy of types of uses. We will discuss the *Euclidian* approach to zoning further after the case.

VILLAGE OF EUCLID V. AMBLER REALTY CO.

Supreme Court of the United States, 1926
272 U.S. 365

Mr. Justice SUTHERLAND delivered the opinion of the Court.

The village of Euclid is an Ohio municipal corporation. It adjoins and practically is a suburb of the city of Cleveland. Its estimated population is between 5,000 and 10,000, and its area from 12 to 14 square miles, the greater part of which is farm lands or unimproved acreage. It lies, roughly, in the form of a parallelogram measuring approximately 3 1/2 miles each way. East and west it is traversed by three principal highways: Euclid avenue, through the southerly border, St. Clair avenue, through the central portion, and Lake Shore boulevard, through the northerly border, in close proximity to the shore of Lake Erie. The Nickel Plate Railroad lies from 1,500 to 1,800 feet north of Euclid avenue, and the Lake Shore Railroad 1,600 feet farther to the north. The three highways and the two railroads are substantially parallel.

Appellee is the owner of a tract of land containing 68 acres, situated in the westerly end of the village, abutting on Euclid avenue to the south and the Nickel Plate Railroad to the north. Adjoining this tract, both on the east and on the west, there have been laid out restricted residential plats upon which residences have been erected.

On November 13, 1922, an ordinance was adopted by the village council, establishing a comprehensive zoning plan for regulating and restricting the location of trades, industries, apartment houses, two-family houses, single family houses, etc., the lot area to be built upon, the size and height of buildings, etc.

The entire area of the village is divided by the ordinance into six classes of use districts, denominated U-1 to U-6, inclusive; three classes of height districts, denominated H-1 to H-3, inclusive; and four classes of area districts, denominated A-1 to A-4, inclusive. The use districts are classified in respect of the buildings which may be erected within their respective limits, as follows: U-1 is restricted to single family dwellings, public parks, water towers and reservoirs, suburban and interurban electric railway passenger stations and rights of way, and farming, non-commercial greenhouse nurseries, and truck gardening; U-2 is extended to include two-family dwellings; U-3 is further extended to include apartment houses, hotels, churches, schools, public libraries, museums, private clubs, community center buildings, hospitals, sanitariums, public playgrounds, and recreation buildings, and a city hall and courthouse; U-4 is further extended to include banks, offices, studios, telephone exchanges, fire and police stations, restaurants, theaters and moving picture shows, retail stores and shops, sales offices, sample rooms, wholesale stores for hardware, drugs, and groceries, stations for gasoline and oil (not exceeding 1,000 gallons storage) and for ice delivery, skating rinks and dance halls, electric substations, job and newspaper printing, public garages for motor vehicles, stables and wagon sheds (not exceeding five horses, wagons or motor trucks), and distributing stations for central store and commercial enterprises; U-5 is further extended to include billboards and advertising signs (if permitted), warehouses, ice and ice cream manufacturing and cold storage plants, bottling works milk bottling and central distribution stations, laundries, carpet cleaning, dry cleaning, and dyeing establishments, blacksmith, horseshoeing, wagon and motor vehicle repair shops, freight stations, street car barns, stables and wagon sheds (for more than five horses, wagons or motor trucks), and wholesale produce markets and salesroom; U-6 is further extended to include plants for sewage disposal and for producing gas, garbage and refuse incineration, scrap iron, junk, scrap paper, and rag storage, aviation fields, cemeteries, crematories, penal and correctional institutions, insane and feeble-minded institutions, storage of oil and gasoline (not to exceed 25,000 gallons), and manufacturing and industrial operations of any kind other than, and any public utility not included in, a class U-1, U-2, U-3, U-4, or U-5 use. There is a seventh class of uses which is prohibited altogether.

Class U-1 is the only district in which buildings are restricted to those enumerated. In the other classes the uses are cumulative-that is to say, uses in class U-2 include those enumerated in the preceding class U-1; class U-3 includes uses enumerated in the preceding classes, U-2, and U-1; and so on. In addition to the enumerated uses, the ordinance provides for accessory uses; that is, for uses customarily incident to the principal use, such as private garages. Many regulations are provided in respect of such accessory uses.

The height districts are classified as follows: In class H-1, buildings are limited to a height of 2 1/2 stories, or 35 feet; in class H-2, to 4 stories, or 50 feet; in class H-3, to 80 feet. To all of these, certain exceptions are made, as in the case of church spires, water tanks, etc.

The classification of area districts is: In A-1 districts, dwellings or apartment houses to accommodate more than one family must have at least 5,000 square feet for interior lots and at least 4,000 square feet for corner lots; in A-2 districts, the area must be at least 2,500 square feet for interior lots, and 2,000 square feet for corner lots; in A-3 districts, the limits are 1,250 and 1,000 square feet, respectively; in A-4 districts, the limits are 900 and 700 square feet, respectively. The ordinance contains, in great variety and detail, provisions in respect of width of lots, front, side, and rear yards, and other matters, including restrictions and regulations as to the use of billboards, signboards, and advertising signs.

A single family dwelling consists of a basement and not less than three rooms and a bathroom. A two-family dwelling consists of a basement and not less than four living rooms and a bathroom for each family, and is further described as a detached dwelling for the occupation of two families, one having its principal living rooms on the first floor and the other on the second floor.

Appellee's tract of land comes under U-2, U-3 and U-6. The first strip of 620 feet immediately north of Euclid avenue falls in class U-2, the next 130 feet to the north, in U-3, and the remainder in U-6. The uses of the first 620 feet, therefore, do not include apartment houses, hotels, churches, schools, or other public and semi-public buildings, or other uses enumerated in respect of U-3 to U-6, inclusive. The uses of the next 130 feet include all of these, but exclude industries, theaters, banks, shops, and the various other uses set forth in respect of U-4 to U-6, inclusive.

Annexed to the ordinance, and made a part of it, is a zone map, showing the location and limits of the various use, height, and area districts, from which it appears that the three classes overlap one another; that is to say, for example, both U-5 and U-6 use districts are in A-4 area district, but the former is in H-2 and the latter in H-3 height districts. The plan is a complicated one, and can be better understood by an inspection of the map, though it does not seem necessary to reproduce it for present purposes.

The lands lying between the two railroads for the entire length of the village area and extending some distance on either side to the north and south, having an average width of about 1,600 feet, are left open, with slight exceptions, for industrial and all other uses. This includes the larger part of appellee's tract. Approximately one-sixth of the area of the entire village is included in U-5 and U-6 use districts. That part of the village lying south of Euclid avenue is principally in U-1 districts. The lands lying north of Euclid avenue and bordering on the long strip just described are included in U-1, U-2, U-3, and U-4 districts, principally in U-2.

The enforcement of the ordinance is intrusted to the inspector of buildings, under rules and regulations of the board of zoning appeals. Meetings of the board are public, and minutes of its proceedings are kept. It is authorized to adopt rules and regulations to carry into effect provisions of the ordinance. Decisions of the inspector of buildings may be appealed to the board by any person claiming to be adversely affected by any such decision. The board is given power in specific cases of practical difficulty or unnecessary hardship to interpret the ordinance in harmony with its general purpose and intent, so that the public health, safety and general welfare may be secure and substantial justice done. Penalties are prescribed for violations, and it is provided that the various provisions are to be regarded as independent and the holding of any provision to be unconstitutional, void or ineffective shall not affect any of the others.

The ordinance is assailed on the grounds that it is in derogation of section 1 of the Fourteenth Amendment to the federal Constitution in that it deprives appellee of liberty and property without due process of law and denies it the equal protection of the law, and that it offends against certain provisions of the Constitution of the state of Ohio. The prayer of the bill is for an injunction restraining the enforcement of the ordinance and all attempts to impose or maintain as to appellee's property any of the restrictions, limitations or conditions. The court below held the ordinance to be unconstitutional and void, and enjoined its enforcement, 297 F. 307.

Before proceeding to a consideration of the case, it is necessary to determine the scope of the inquiry. The bill alleges that the tract of land in question is vacant and has been held for years for the purpose of selling and developing it for industrial uses, for which it is especially adapted, being immediately in the path or progressive industrial development; that for such uses it has a market value of about $10,000 per acre, but if the use be limited to residential purposes the market value is not in excess of $2,500 per acre; that the first 200 feet of the parcel back from Euclid avenue, if unrestricted in respect of use, has a value of $150 per front foot, but if limited to residential uses, and ordinary mercantile business be excluded therefrom, its value is not in excess of $50 per front foot.

It is specifically averred that the ordinance attempts to restrict and control the lawful uses of appellee's land, so as to confiscate and destroy a great part of its value; that it is being enforced in accordance with its terms; that prospective buyers of land for industrial, commercial, and residential uses in the metropolitan district of Cleveland are deterred from buying any part of this land because of the existence of the ordinance and the necessity thereby entailed of conducting burdensome and expensive litigation in order to vindicate the right to use the land for lawful and legitimate purposes; that the ordinance constitutes a cloud upon the land, reduces and destroys its value, and has the effect of diverting the normal industrial, commercial, and residential development thereof to other and less favorable locations.

The record goes no farther than to show, as the lower court found, that the normal and reasonably to be expected use and development of that part of appellee's land adjoining Euclid avenue is for general trade and commercial purposes, particularly retail stores and like establishments, and that the normal and reasonably to be expected use and development of the residue of the land is for industrial and trade purposes. Whatever injury is inflicted by the mere existence and threatened enforcement of the ordinance is due to restrictions in respect of these and similar uses, to which perhaps should be added—if not included in the foregoing—restrictions in respect of apartment houses. Specifically there is nothing in the record to suggest that any damage results from the presence in the ordinance of those restrictions relating to churches, schools, libraries, and other public and semi-public buildings. It is neither alleged nor proved that there is or may be a demand for any part of appellee's land for any of the last-named uses, and we cannot assume the existence of facts which would justify an injunction upon this record in respect to this class of restrictions. For present purposes the provisions of the ordinance in respect of these uses may therefore be put aside as unnecessary to be considered. It is also unnecessary to consider the effect of the restrictions in respect of U-1 districts, since none of appellee's land falls within that class.

We proceed, then, to a consideration of those provisions of the ordinance to which the case as it is made relates . . . The question is . . . Is the ordinance invalid, in that it violates the constitutional protection "to the right of property in the appellee by attempted regulations under the guise of the police power, which are unreasonable and confiscatory"?

Building zone laws are of modern origin. They began in this country about 25 years ago. Until recent years, urban life was comparatively simple; but, with the great increase and concentration of population, problems have developed, and constantly are developing, which require, and will continue to require, additional restrictions in respect of the use and occupation of private lands in urban communities. Regulations, the wisdom, necessity, and validity of which, as applied to existing conditions, are so apparent that they are now uniformly sustained, a century ago, or even half a century ago, probably would have been rejected as arbitrary and oppressive. Such regulations are sustained, under the complex conditions of our day, for reasons analogous to those which justify traffic regulations, which, before the advent of automobiles and rapid transit street railways, would have been condemned as fatally arbitrary and unreasonable. And in this there is no inconsistency, for, while the meaning of constitutional guaranties never varies, the scope of their application must expand or contract to meet the new and different conditions which are constantly coming within the field of their operation. In a changing world it is impossible that it should be otherwise. But although a degree of elasticity is thus imparted, not to the meaning, but to the application of constitutional principles, statutes and ordinances, which, after giving due weight to the new conditions, are found clearly not to conform to the Constitution, of course, must fall.

The ordinance now under review, and all similar laws and regulations, must find their justification in some aspect of the police power, asserted for the public welfare. The line which in this field separates the legitimate from the illegitimate assumption of power is not capable of precise delimitation. It varies with circumstances and conditions. A regulatory zoning ordinance, which would be clearly valid as applied to the great cities, might be clearly invalid as applied to rural communities. In solving doubts, the maxim *sic utere tuo ut alienum non laedas*, which lies at the foundation of so much of the common low of nuisances, ordinarily will furnish a fairly helpful clew. And the law of nuisances, likewise, may be consulted, not for the purpose of controlling, but for the helpful aid of its analogies in the process of ascertaining the scope of, the power. Thus the question whether the power exists to forbid the erection of a building of a particular kind or for a particular use, like the question whether a particular thing is a nuisance, is to be determined, not by an abstract consideration of the building or of the thing considered apart, but by considering it in connection with the circumstances and the locality. *Sturgis v. Bridgeman,* L. R. 11 Ch. 852, 865. A nuisance may be merely a right thing in the wrong place, like a pig in the parlor instead of the barnyard. If the validity of the legislative classification for zoning purposes be fairly debatable, the legislative judgment must be allowed to control. *Radice v. New York,* 264 U. S. 292, 294, 44 S. Ct. 325, 68 L. Ed. 690.

There is no serious difference of opinion in respect of the validity of laws and regulations fixing the height of buildings within reasonable limits, the character of materials and methods of construction, and the adjoining area which must be left open, in order to minimize the danger of fire or collapse, the evils of overcrowding and the like, and excluding from residential sections offensive trades, industries and structures likely to create nuisances. See *Welch v. Swasey,* 214 U. S. 91, 29 S. Ct. 567, 53 L. Ed. 923; *Hadacheck v. Los Angeles,* 239 U. S. 394, 36 S. Ct. 143, 60 L. Ed. 348, Ann. Cas. 1917B, 927; *Reinman v. Little Rock,* 237 U. S. 171, 35 S. Ct. 511, 59 L. Ed. 900; *Cusack Co. v. City of Chicago,* 242 U. S. 526, 529, 530, 37 S. Ct. 190, 61 L. Ed. 472, L. R. A. 1918A, 136, Am.Ann. Cas. 1917C, 594.

Here, however, the exclusion is in general terms of all industrial establishments, and it may thereby happen that not only offensive or dangerous industries will be excluded, but those which are neither offensive nor dangerous will share the same fate. But this is no more than happens in respect of many practice-forbidding laws which this court has upheld, although drawn in general terms so as to include individual cases that may turn out to be innocuous in themselves. *Hebe Co. v. Shaw,* 248 U. S. 297, 303, 39 S. Ct. 125, 63 L. Ed. 255; *Pierce Oil Corp. v. City of Hope,* 248 U. S. 498, 500, 39 S. Ct. 172, 63 L. Ed. 381. The inclusion of a reasonable margin, to insure effective enforcement, will not put upon a law, otherwise valid, the stamp of invalidity. Such laws may also find their justification in the fact that, in some fields, the bad fades into the good by such insensible degrees that the two are not capable of being readily distinguished and separated in terms of legislation. In the light of these considerations, we are not prepared to say that the end in view was not sufficient to justify the general rule of the ordinance, although some industries of an innocent character might fall within the proscribed class. It cannot be said that the ordinance in this respect "passes the bounds of reason and assumes the character of a merely arbitrary fiat." *Purity Extract Co. v. Lynch,* 226 U. S. 192, 204, 33 S. Ct. 44, 47 (57 L. Ed. 184). Moreover, the restrictive provisions of the ordinance in this particular may be sustained upon the principles applicable to the broader exclusion from residential districts of all business and trade structures, presently to be discussed.

It is said that the village of Euclid is a mere suburb of the city of Cleveland; that the industrial development of that city has now reached and in some degree extended into the village, and in the obvious course of things will soon absorb the entire area for industrial enterprises; that the effect of the ordinance is to divert this natural development elsewhere, with the consequent loss of increased values to the owners of the lands within the village borders. But the village, though physically a suburb of Cleveland, is politically a separate municipality, with powers of its own and authority to govern itself as it sees fit, within the limits of the organic law of its creation and the state and federal Constitutions. Its governing authorities, presumably representing a majority of its inhabitants and voicing their will, have determined, not that industrial development shall cease at its boundaries, but that the course of such development shall proceed within definitely fixed lines. If it be a proper exercise of the police power to relegate industrial establishments to localities separated from residential sections, it is not easy to find a sufficient reason for denying the power because the effect of its exercise is to divert an industrial flow from the course which it would follow, to the injury of the residential public, if left alone, to another course where such injury will be obviated. It is not meant by this, however, to exclude the possibility of cases where the general public interest would so far outweigh the interest of the municipality that the municipality would not be allowed to stand in the way.

We find no difficulty in sustaining restrictions of the kind thus far reviewed. The serious question in the case arises over the provisions of the ordinance excluding from residential districts apartment houses, business houses, retail stores and shops, and other like establishments. This question involves the validity of what is really the crux of the more recent zoning legislation, namely, the creation and maintenance of residential districts, from which business and trade of every sort, including hotels and apartment houses, are excluded. Upon that question this court has not thus far spoken. The decisions of the state courts are numerous and conflicting; but those which broadly sustain the power greatly outnumber those which deny it altogether or narrowly limit it, and it is very apparent that there is a constantly increasing tendency in the direction of the broader view. . . .

The matter of zoning has received much attention at the hands of commissions and experts, and the results of their investigations have been set forth in comprehensive reports. These reports which bear every evidence of painstaking consideration, concur in the view that the segregation of residential, business and industrial buildings will make it easier to provide fire apparatus suitable for the character and intensity of the development in each section; that it will increase the safety and security of home life, greatly tend to prevent street accidents, especially to children, by reducing the traffic and resulting confusion in residential sections, decrease noise and other conditions which produce or intensify nervous disorders, preserve a more favorable environment in which to rear children, etc. With particular reference to apartment houses, it is pointed out that the development of detached house sections is greatly retarded by the coming of apartment houses, which has sometimes resulted in destroying the entire section for private house purposes; that in such sections very often the apartment house is a mere parasite, constructed in order to take advantage of the open spaces and attractive surroundings created by the residential character of the district. Moreover, the coming of one apartment house is followed by others, interfering by their height and bulk with the free circulation of air and monopolizing the rays of the sun which otherwise would fall upon the smaller homes, and bringing, as their necessary accompaniments, the disturbing noises incident to increased traffic and business, and the occupation, by means of moving and parked automobiles, of larger portions of the streets, thus detracting from their safety and depriving children of the privilege of quiet and open spaces for play, enjoyed by those in more favored localities—until, finally, the residential character of the neighborhood and its desirability as a place of detached residences are utterly destroyed. Under these circumstances, apartment houses, which in a different environment would be not only entirely unobjectionable but highly desirable, come very near to being nuisances.

If these reasons, thus summarized, do not demonstrate the wisdom or sound policy in all respects of those restrictions which we have indicated as pertinent to the inquiry, at least, the reasons are sufficiently cogent to preclude us from saying, as it must be said before the ordinance can be declared unconstitutional, that such provisions are clearly arbitrary and unreasonable, having no substantial relation to the public health, safety, morals, or general welfare. *Cusack Co. v. City of Chicago, supra,* pages 530-531 (37 S. Ct. 190); *Jacobson v. Massachusetts,* 197 U. S. 11, 30-31, 25 S. Ct. 358, 49 L. Ed. 643, 3 Ann. Cas. 765. . . .

Decree reversed.

NOTES AND QUESTIONS

1. *A Pig in the Parlor.* Justice Sutherland notes in *Euclid* that "[a] nuisance may be merely a right thing in the wrong place, like a pig in the parlor instead of the barnyard." The parties to our nuisance cases, especially *Spur v. Del Webb*, would likely agree with this observation. Recall that in our materials on nuisance, we discussed the problem of incompatible land uses. One purpose of zoning is to reduce conflicts between land uses by physically separating types of uses into different zones.

2. Euclidian *Zoning.* Note again the overall approach taken by the Village of Euclid zoning law. The law establishes three types of zones—use zones, height zones, and area zones. We will focus here on the use zones. The law created six categories of use zones. U-1 was limited to single-family residential use. The categories then progressed in intensity of use, subsequently allowing multifamily residential uses, commercial uses, and industrial uses. The uses were cumulative. Land within the U-4 zone, for example, could be used not only for U-4 uses but also for U-3, U-2, and U-1 uses. The overall

zoning scheme was designed to segregate uses into different zones. Residential uses, in particular, were separated from commercial and industrial uses, though it was possible to include residential uses in commercial and industrial areas because of the cumulative nature of the zones.

Many municipalities in the United States continue to use this basic approach to zoning. As you are driving around your community, take a look at signs advertising undeveloped parcels of land for sale. These signs will typically list the zoning use category for the land. Residential zones typically begin with R. R1 is typically restricted for single-family residential use. R2, R3, and R4 are typically used for multifamily residential use. Commercial zones begin with C—C1, C2, C3, and so on. Industrial zones might begin with I or another letter.

Despite its widespread use, *Euclidian* zoning has been criticized on various grounds. Three common critiques are that the separation of residential and commercial uses encourages dependency on automobiles, promotes suburban sprawl, and leads to bland uniformity in our communities. Municipalities are increasingly experimenting with New Urbanist and other more flexible approaches to zoning, which encourage the mixture of commercial and residential uses. *See* Michael Lewyn, *New Urbanist Zoning for Dummies*, 58 Ala. L. Rev. 257 (2006).

B. PRE-EXISTING NONCONFORMING USES

Imagine that you own a convenience store. You have been operating the store in its current location for the past 20 years. The store is located in an area that has been zoned for commercial use. Recently, however, your local municipality changed its zoning laws, and your convenience store is now located in an area that is zoned for residential use only. Your convenience store is now a *pre-existing nonconforming use*. It is a nonconforming use because it is a use that is prohibited by the new zoning ordinance. It is pre-existing because the use was in existence at the time the new ordinance was put into place.

Pre-existing nonconforming uses like your convenience store present us with a quandary. On the one hand, it seems unfair to change the rules on you and force you to shut your store down. On the other hand, allowing pre-existing nonconforming uses to continue can seriously undercut the effectiveness of the zoning law.

In some jurisdictions, pre-existing nonconforming uses are allowed to continue in operation as of right. This approach is fair to the property owner but undercuts the effectiveness of zoning laws. In these jurisdictions, destruction of the nonconforming use typically terminates the right to operate it, so if the convenience store burned down, you would lose your right to operate a commercial use in that location. Abandonment will also typically terminate the right to operate a pre-existing nonconforming use.

Remember that abandonment is a question of intent, so your right to continue to operate the store after a period of inactivity will turn on whether you intended to abandon the store or whether you intended to continue operation after a hiatus. The right to operate a pre-existing nonconforming use runs with the land, so in this type of jurisdiction I could continue to operate the convenience store if I bought it from you. In other words, a change in ownership does not terminate the right to operate a pre-existing nonconforming use.

About half of U.S. jurisdictions use an approach called *amortization* to deal with pre-existing nonconforming uses. Amortization strikes a balance between fairness to the property owner and effectiveness of the zoning law by allowing the pre-existing nonconforming use to continue for a set period of time and then requiring it to shut down. The technique gets its name from the fact that it is designed to allow the owner of the pre-existing nonconforming use to amortize, or earn back, all or part of its investment in the nonconforming use. In jurisdictions that follow this approach, the amortization period must be *reasonable*. As you might imagine, there is no consensus on what constitutes a reasonable amortization period. Courts have both upheld and rejected periods ranging from 1 to 30 years.

Our next case is an amortization case. As you read the case, think about where we should strike the balance between the interests of the property owner to continue engaging in a pre-existing nonconforming use and the interests of the public in having zoning laws consistently enforced. Note also the factors used to determine whether a particular amortization period is reasonable. The case includes several references to zoning variances and special use permits. We will cover both of these topics in our next section.

AVR, INC. V. CITY OF ST. LOUIS PARK

Court of Appeals of Minnesota, 1998
585 N.W.2d 411

WILLIS, Judge.

Appellant AVR, Inc., challenges the district court's order granting summary judgment to respondent City of St. Louis Park, claiming that the city's zoning ordinance that establishes a two-year amortization period for appellant's preexisting nonconforming use is unreasonable and violates appellant's right to equal protection of the laws. We affirm.

FACTS

AVR owns and operates a ready-mix concrete plant in the City of St. Louis Park. The plant was constructed in 1954. In 1959, the city passed a zoning ordinance . . . . In 1973, the city amended its zoning code to eliminate ready-mix and concrete block plants as permitted uses in the city. AVR purchased the ready-mix plant in 1974 for $260,000. In May 1980, the city adopted a new comprehensive plan and put AVR on notice that the city intended to phase out the plant and rezone the site for commercial or office use or "as a second choice high density residential use." AVR commenced a declaratory judgment action seeking to invalidate the 1973 zoning ordinance on the ground that it wrongfully eliminated ready-mix plants as permitted uses in industrial zones. The district court declared the ordinance void as applied to AVR, and the city appealed. This court concluded that because the plant was not a public nuisance or a nuisance per se, the city could not legislate it out of existence. *Apple Valley Red-E-Mix v. City of St. Louis Park,* 359 N.W.2d 313, 315 (Minn.App.1984), *review denied* (Minn. Mar. 21, 1985).

In 1990, the city adopted another new comprehensive plan, which provides that, in the area where the AVR plant is located,

> [h]eavy industrial uses including a concrete ready mix plant and outdoor storage of heavy equipment are to be phased out, and the sites are to be used for high density residential use.

St. Louis Park, Minn., Comprehensive Plan 1990-2010 §16, at 16-5 (1990). In 1992, the city rezoned AVR's property from I-4 Industrial to R-4 Multifamily Residential. The ordinance provides that the city council

> shall by ordinance amend the Zoning Ordinance to establish an amortization period for individual land uses not permitted in the City. The amortization period shall commence upon publication of the ordinance establishing the length of amortization period.

St. Louis Park, Minn., Code of Ordinances §14:7-4(D)(4) (1992). The 1992 ordinance required the owners of all properties "that contain a use not permitted in any zoning district [to] register their non-conforming use with the City" within one year of the adoption of the ordinance. *Id.* §14:7-4(B). The ordinance also required the zoning administrator to meet with such property owners, review each registration application, and determine a reasonable amortization period for each nonconforming use. In determining the length of a reasonable amortization period, the zoning administrator was to consider, at a minimum, the following factors:

a. Information relating to the structure located on the property;
b. Nature of the use;
c. Location of the property in relation to surrounding uses;
d. Description of the character of and uses in the surrounding neighborhood;
e. Cost of the property and improvements to the property;
f. Benefit to the public by requiring the termination of the non-conforming use;
g. Burden on the property owner by requiring the termination of the non-conforming use;
h. The length of time the use has been in existence and the length of time the use has been non-conforming.

Id. §14:7-4(D)(2). The city council accepted AVR's registration of the plant property as substantially complete on June 29, 1995.

On July 11, 1995, the city council and planning commission held a joint public hearing for the purpose of adopting an amortization ordinance relating to the AVR plant. City staff presented to the council and planning commission the report and recommendation required by the 1992 ordinance. AVR presented information supporting its position that the plant has an indefinite remaining physical life.

On October 2, 1995, the city amended its zoning ordinance by adopting the following provision:

> The reasonable amortization period applicable to the ready-mix facility owned and operated by [AVR] . . . shall be two (2) years, commencing upon publication of this ordinance. At the conclusion of the two-year amortization period, [AVR's] nonconforming ready-mix use shall terminate and cease to operate.

Id. §14:7-4.1 (1995). In conjunction with the adoption of section 14:7-4.1, the city council adopted a resolution that contained 42 findings of fact supporting the ordinance and that stated:

> The Minnesota Supreme Court has directed, in the *Naegele Outdoor Advertising Co. of Minn. v. Village of Minnetonka* decision, that any amortization period must be "reasonable." Courts in other jurisdictions have identified at least seven (7) factors by which the reasonableness of an amortization period may be evaluated. The St. Louis Park Code of Ordinances incorporates those specific factors in its Amortization Ordinance.

St. Louis Park, Minn., Res. No. 95-131, ¶3 (1995) (citing St. Louis Park, Minn., Code of Ordinances §14:7-4(D)(2)(a-h) (1992)). The city addressed the factors identified in its amortization ordinance in making findings to support its determination of the length of the amortization period for AVR's plant.

The city also considered the useful life of the plant. To assist it in making that determination, the city retained an accounting firm and a real estate appraisal firm. The accounting firm advised the city that, based on generally accepted accounting principles, the plant's "useful life expired no later than 1994" and that AVR had not only recovered its investment but also had earned a return of approximately 560 percent on its investment. *Id.* ¶37. The city council found that

> [b]ased upon the expert opinions of Arthur Andersen and Patchin, the age of [AVR's] St. Louis Park Facility, AVR's proposal to the City nine years ago to replace the existing St. Louis Park structure, AVR's testimony regarding necessary size of potential relocation sites, and the voluntary relocation and/or new construction actions of other ready-mix businesses in the Twin Cities area, AVR's St. Louis Park Facility has passed its useful life and AVR has had a reasonable opportunity to recover its economic investment.

Id. ¶39.

In December 1995, AVR commenced an action seeking a declaration that the city's adoption of the amortization ordinance and the ordinance establishing a two-year amortization period for AVR's plant (1) violate AVR's right to due process of law; (2) violate AVR's right to equal protection of the laws; [and] (3) violate AVR's vested rights by eliminating concrete ready-mix plants as a special or permitted use. AVR and the city made cross-motions for summary judgment. On January 15, 1998, the district court granted summary judgment to the city and dismissed AVR's complaint. This appeal followed.

ISSUES

1. Did the district court err in deferring to the city's broad discretion to adopt an ordinance establishing a two-year amortization period for AVR's plant?

2. Did the district court err in upholding the city's ordinance establishing a two-year amortization period for AVR's plant?

3. Did the district court err in concluding that the city's adoption of an amortization ordinance and an ordinance establishing a two-year amortization period for AVR's plant does not violate AVR's right to equal protection of the laws?

ANALYSIS

On appeal from summary judgment, a reviewing court determines whether any genuine issues of material fact exist and whether the district court erred in applying the law. *Wartnick v. Moss & Barnett,* 490 N.W.2d 108, 112 (Minn.1992). In making its determinations, "the court must view the evidence in the light most favorable to the nonmoving party." *State by Beaulieu v. City of Mounds View,* 518 N.W.2d 567, 571 (Minn.1994).

I.

AVR contends that the city's adoption of an amortization ordinance for AVR's plant is equivalent to a decision to grant or deny a variance or special use permit. Therefore, AVR argues, the city's decision is quasi-judicial and the courts should afford it less deference than they would give a legislative zoning decision. Minnesota courts have distinguished

> between zoning matters which are legislative in nature (rezoning) and those which are quasi-judicial (variances and special use permits). Even so, the standard of review is the same for all zoning matters, namely, whether the zoning authority's action was reasonable. Our cases express this standard in various ways: Is there a "reasonable basis" for the decision? or is the decision "unreasonable, arbitrary or capricious"? or is the decision "reasonably debatable"?

Honn v. City of Coon Rapids, 313 N.W.2d 409, 416-17 (Minn.1981). But application of the reasonableness standard depends on the zoning action at issue:

> [I]n legislative zoning, the municipal body is formulating public policy, so the inquiry focuses on whether the proposed use promotes the public welfare. In quasi-judicial zoning, public policy has already been established and the inquiry focuses on whether the proposed use is contrary to the general welfare as already established in the zoning ordinance. Consequently, the reviewing courts, in determining what is reasonable, should keep in mind that the zoning authority is less circumscribed by judicial oversight when it considers zoning or rezoning than when it considers a special use permit or a variance.

Id. at 417. AVR argues that because the amortization ordinance "does not effect a zoning change to unimproved property" but rather "terminat[es] AVR's use of the property" as a ready-mix plant, it is "equivalent to the grant or denial of a special use permit." We disagree. *See Naegele Outdoor Adver. Co. v. Village of Minnetonka*, 281 Minn. 492, 501, 503, 162 N.W.2d 206, 213, 215 (1968) (identifying ordinance establishing amortization period as legislative device and stating power to enact "this type of zoning requirement" is implied); *DI MA Corp. v. City of St. Cloud*, 562 N.W.2d 312, 319-20 (Minn.App.1997) (analyzing validity of amortization ordinance under statute that establishes requirements for amendments to zoning ordinances).

Because zoning or rezoning classifications are legislative acts, courts must uphold them unless

> [their] opponents prove that the classification is unsupported by any rational basis related to promoting the public health, safety, morals, or general welfare, or that the classification amounts to a taking without compensation. This rule applies regardless of the size of the tract of land involved.

LEGISLATIVE VS. QUASI-JUDICIAL

Zoning laws typically are enacted by the municipal legislature (i.e., the city or town council). These enactments are legislative and typically receive deference from courts so long as they do not exceed the municipality's authority under state law. Courts understand that legislative decision making is different from judicial decision making, and tend to avoid second-guessing legislative decisions. Some actions made in the zoning context, such as the decision of whether or not to grant a variance, are quasi-judicial. We will consider variances in the next section. For now, it is sufficient to know that the decision making process in the variance context resembles a judicial decision more than a legislative decision. Courts are much less deferential to quasi-judicial decisions made by municipalities because the courts are well equipped to review judicial decision making. Courts, after all, specialize in this kind of decision making, and feel comfortable second-guessing quasi-judicial decisions.

State by Rochester Ass'n of Neighborhoods v. City of Rochester, 268 N.W.2d 885, 888 (Minn.1978).

AVR has not shown that the city's adoption of the ordinance establishing an amortization period for AVR's plant is unsupported by any rational basis related to the promotion of the public health, safety, morals, or general welfare. Because the city's establishment of an amortization period for a preexisting nonconforming use was a legislative act, we conclude that the district court did not err in deferring to the city's broad discretion.

II.

AVR contends that the two-year amortization period for its plant is unreasonable. In establishing the length of the amortization period, the city considered the plant's "useful life," a term the Minnesota Supreme Court has used but has not defined. *Naegele,* 281 Minn. at 501, 162 N.W.2d at 213 (stating only "that the useful life of the nonconforming use corresponds roughly to the amortization period"). The city based its determination of useful life on its conclusion that AVR had recouped its original investment and, to a lesser extent, on the fact that the property has been fully depreciated for income tax purposes. In addition, the city considered the other factors it had adopted by ordinance.

AVR argues that the city acted unreasonably in failing to consider "the remaining useful economic or expected life" in determining the length of the amortization period. *See, e.g., City of La Mesa v. Tweed & Gambrell Planing Mill,* 146 Cal.App.2d 762, 304 P.2d 803, 808 (Cal.Dist.Ct.App.1956) (noting estimated 21 years of remaining economic life as one reason for holding five-year amortization period arbitrary and unreasonable). In *Naegele,* the supreme court stated only that the underlying issue in determining the length of an amortization period is whether it is reasonable. 281 Minn. at 501, 162 N.W.2d at 213.

In analyzing the reasonableness of an amortization period, courts in some jurisdictions have considered the property owner's recoupment of its original investment. *See, e.g., Rives v. City of Clarksville,* 618 S.W.2d 502, 510 (Tenn.Ct.App.1981) (considering length of amortization period in relation to property owner's investment); *Town of Islip v. Caviglia,* 73 N.Y.2d 544, 542 N.Y.S.2d 139, 540 N.E.2d 215, 224 (N.Y.1989) (determining reasonableness by examining all facts, including length of amortization period in relation to investment); *City of University Park v. Benners,* 485 S.W.2d 773, 777 (Tex.1972) (noting that termination of nonconforming use after amortization period allowing recoupment of investment is not unconstitutional taking).

Courts also have considered whether the property in question has been fully depreciated for income tax purposes in reviewing the reasonableness of an amortization period, although this factor alone has not been held to be determinative. *See, e.g., Art Neon Co. v. City & County of Denver,* 488 F.2d 118, 122 (10th Cir.1973) (considering depreciation for tax purposes); *National Adver. Co. v. County of Monterey,* 1 Cal.3d 875,

83 Cal.Rptr. 577, 464 P.2d 33, 35-36 (Cal.1970) (holding that where billboards have been fully depreciated for tax purposes, amortization period was not unreasonable); *Village of Skokie v. Walton on Dempster, Inc.,* 119 Ill.App.3d 299, 74 Ill.Dec. 791, 456 N.E.2d 293, 297 (Ill.App.Ct.1983) (concluding that amortization period was reasonable where property was completely depreciated for tax purposes); *Philanz Oldsmobile, Inc. v. Keating,* 51 A.D.2d 437, 381 N.Y.S.2d 916, 920 (N.Y.App.Div.1976) (stating that where signs had been fully depreciated for tax purposes, financial loss is nonexistent).

To the extent AVR's contention that the city should have considered the "remaining useful economic or expected life" of AVR's plant is another way of saying that the amortization period should be based on the plant's fair market value or its replacement cost, the argument leads to illogical and contradictory consequences. As one court has recognized:

> [A]pplication of the market-value standard would result in a vicious circle: market value depends on the period of expected nonconforming use, and the period of nonconforming use allowed depends on market value. . . .
>
> Cost of replacing the nonconforming structure, even with an allowance for depreciation, would also provide an unsatisfactory measure of recoupment. A landowner is not permitted to extend the period of nonconforming use by replacements or improvements because [the owner] would be able to extend the nonconforming use indefinitely . . . To allow replacement cost as a measure of the recoupment allowed would thus allow unjustified extension of the nonconforming use. Moreover, [it] would ignore the factor of obsolescence, which might be substantial . . . .

Murmur Corp. v. Board of Adjustment, 718 S.W.2d 790, 796-97 (Tex.App.1986) (citations omitted).

Here, the city used a combination of recoupment of investment and tax depreciation status as factors in determining the useful life for AVR's plant. The record shows that over the past 23 years the plant provided AVR a return of approximately 560% on its investment and that the plant has been fully depreciated for income tax purposes. These two factors provided the city with a reasonable basis to determine the plant's useful life for purposes of establishing an amortization period.

AVR also argues that the city's findings with respect to the factors it adopted by ordinance are not supported by sufficient evidence, claiming that the city virtually ignored the ordinance factors in favor of other factors and considerations. But the record shows that in establishing the amortization period for AVR's plant, the city considered each of the factors in its amortization ordinance and that the city's findings regarding these factors are supported by record evidence.

AVR further contends that in determining the length of the amortization period, the city gave undue deference to the opinions of area residents instead of applying the factors required by the city's ordinance. In support of its argument, AVR cites *Trisko v. City of Waite Park,* in which this court held that a municipality must base a decision to deny a conditional use permit on "something more concrete than neighborhood opposition and expression of concern for public safety." *Trisko v. City of Waite Park,* 566 N.W.2d 349, 355 (Minn.App.1997) (quoting *Chanhassen Estates Residents Ass'n v. City of Chanhassen,* 342 N.W.2d 335, 340 (Minn.1984)), *review denied* (Minn. Sept. 25, 1997).

This case does not involve denial of a conditional use permit, which is a quasi-judicial determination and therefore subject to closer scrutiny. But even if *Trisko* were applied to the city's adoption of the ordinance establishing a two-year amortization period, the record shows that the city's decision was based on more than neighborhood opposition to AVR's plant and expression of concern for public safety. For example, the city found that the quality of life for surrounding residents will increase by allowing the city to improve the general appearance and image of the city. The city also found that amortization of AVR's plant will create redevelopment opportunities that will help satisfy a demand for certain housing needs and increase property values in the immediate vicinity, which, in turn, will increase real estate taxes and benefit the entire community.

AVR further argues that the two-year period is unreasonable because amortization periods should be lengthened "when the amortization is not consistent with the surrounding area or any solid redevelopment plan," noting that the area surrounding the plant is not exclusively residential. But the record shows that the city's rezoning of AVR's property from I-4 Industrial to R-4 Multifamily Residential is consistent with its plans for the surrounding area. . . .

Finally, AVR argues that the two-year amortization period is unreasonable because the city was motivated by aesthetic rather than health and safety considerations. But "a desire to achieve aesthetic ends should not invalidate an otherwise valid ordinance." *Naegele,* 281 Minn. at 499, 162 N.W.2d at 212. In addition, the city enacted the ordinance establishing the two-year amortization period for several reasons, including improvement of the general welfare by reducing noise, dust, and traffic.

Because the ordinance establishing a two-year amortization period for AVR's plant reflects the city's consideration of the plant's useful life and an analysis of other relevant factors adopted by the city, the district court did not err in upholding the city's two-year amortization period.

III.

AVR contends that the city's amortization ordinance and its ordinance establishing a two-year amortization period for AVR's plant violate its right to equal protection of the laws. "A municipal zoning ordinance is presumed constitutional. The burden of proving the ordinance is unconstitutional rests on the party attacking its validity." *DI MA Corp.,* 562 N.W.2d at 320 (citation omitted).

Under the Equal Protection Clause, "[n]o State shall . . . deny to any person within its jurisdiction the equal protection of the laws." U.S. Const. amend. XIV, §1. The Equal Protection Clause requires that all persons similarly situated be treated alike under the law. *In re Harhut,* 385 N.W.2d 305, 310 (Minn.1986). But where the party complaining of the disparate treatment is not a member of a suspect class and the legislation does not infringe on a fundamental right, this court will uphold a municipality's ordinance where it is rationally related to a legitimate governmental purpose. *Arcadia Dev. Corp. v. City of Bloomington,* 552 N.W.2d 281, 288 (Minn.App.1996), *review denied* (Minn. Oct. 29, 1996).

AVR argues that the city is treating it differently from Al's Liquor Bar, arguing that the two are similarly situated. In the 1992 zoning ordinance, the city identified both properties as preexisting nonconforming uses to be amortized. In 1995, the city excepted all existing bars from amortization. But the district court concluded that the city "has not treated similarly situated entities differently." We agree. There are no other ready-mix plants in the city. AVR's plant is a heavy industrial use that causes "significantly more severe and disruptive" amounts of noise and dust than does Al's Liquor Bar. Because AVR has not shown disparate treatment of similarly situated property owners, the district court did not err in concluding that the city has not violated AVR's equal protection rights.

DECISION

Because the city's action was a legislative decision, the district court did not err in deferring to the city's broad discretion to adopt an ordinance establishing a two-year amortization period for AVR's plant. Additionally, because the ordinance establishing an amortization period for AVR's plant is based on the city's consideration of the plant's useful life and application of other relevant factors, the district court did not err in upholding the city's establishment of a two-year amortization period. Finally, because AVR did not demonstrate disparate treatment of similarly situated property owners resulting from the enactment of the amortization ordinance and the ordinance establishing a two-year amortization period for AVR's plant, the district court did not err in concluding that there is no equal protection violation.

NOTES AND QUESTIONS

1. *The Amortization Factors.* The factors used to determine whether an amortization period is reasonable are quite broad. You can see how courts often reach divergent results in applying these factors. Given the breadth of the factors, it is possible to come up with a good argument both for and against any given amortization period. Which factors seemed most important in *AVR*? Which do you think should be the most important?

2. *Pre-Existing Means Pre-Existing*. Remember that in this section we are discussing the rules for *pre-existing* nonconforming uses. If a property owner begins a nonconforming use *after* the zoning ordinance is enacted, the municipality can shut down the nonconforming use. Period.

3. *Can Pre-Existing Nonconforming Uses Just Be Shut Down?* As we explained in the text before *AVR*, U.S. jurisdictions tend to take one of two approaches to pre-existing nonconforming uses. First, some jurisdictions allow pre-existing nonconforming uses to continue. Second, some jurisdictions allow pre-existing nonconforming uses to be shut down after an amortization period. Could a jurisdiction decide to just shut down pre-existing nonconforming uses without an amortization period? Historically, there has been an assumption that simply shutting down a pre-existing nonconforming use would be unconstitutional. For an analysis of why this assumption might be wrong, see Christopher Serkin, *Existing Uses and the Limits of Land Use Regulations*, 84 N.Y.U. L. Rev. 1222 (2009). We will consider some of the case law relevant to Professor Serkin's analysis in the next chapter.

C. VARIANCES, SPECIAL EXCEPTIONS, AND ZONING AMENDMENTS

There are three methods that a property owner can use to engage in a use that is otherwise not permitted under a zoning law. First, the property owner may receive a variance. Second, the property owner may demonstrate that she meets the requirement of a special exception. Third, the property owner may convince the municipal legislature to amend the zoning laws to permit her desired use of the land. In this section, we consider each of these methods in turn.

A variance involves the grant of a waiver from the requirements of a particular restriction to a particular property owner. A property owner's request for a variance typically is heard by a municipal administrative body, often called the *board of adjustment* or the *zoning board of appeals*. To be entitled to a variance, the property owner typically must show both (a) that she will suffer *undue hardship* if she does not receive a variance and (b) that the grant of a variance will not result in *harm to the public* or seriously undercut the overall zoning plan. As we will see, the undue hardship test is strict and will not be met if the property owner is only able to show that it would be convenient for the variance to be granted. In this context, undue hardship is often contrasted with *mere inconvenience*. Undue hardship will entitle the property owner to a variance if the second factor also is met. Mere inconvenience will not. As we saw above in *AVR*, the grant or denial of a variance is a quasi-judicial decision. Accordingly, courts typically will not be deferential to a decision granting or denying a variance and will take a close look at whether or not the property owner met the requirements of a variance.

COMMONS V. WESTWOOD ZONING BOARD OF ADJUSTMENT

Supreme Court of New Jersey, 1980
410 A.2d 1138

SCHREIBER, J.

We are again called upon to examine the proceedings before and findings of a board of adjustment which denied a zoning variance for construction of a single-family residence on an undersized lot. See *N.J.S.A.* 40:55-39(c). Plaintiffs, Gordon L. Commons, Helen T. Commons and Leo Weingarten, filed a complaint to review the denial of the variance by the Borough of Westwood Zoning Board of Adjustment. The Superior Court, Law Division, and the Appellate Division affirmed the board's action. We granted plaintiffs' petition for certification. 79 *N.J.* 482, 401 *A.2d* 237 (1979).

The facts developed at the hearings before the Board of Adjustment were substantially undisputed. The property in question is a vacant lot, designated as Lot 20 in Block 208 on the tax map of the Borough of Westwood. Located in an established residential area consisting of one and two-family dwellings, this lot is the only undeveloped property in the neighborhood. Plaintiffs Gordon and Helen Commons are the present owners. They and their predecessors in title have owned this plot since 1927. Plaintiff Weingarten, a builder, contracted to purchase the property on the condition that he could construct a one-family residence on the lot.

A variance from the borough's zoning ordinance was necessary for two reasons. The land was located in a District B residential zone requiring a minimum frontage of 75 feet and a minimum area of 7500 square feet. The lot, however, has a frontage on Brickell Avenue of only 30 feet and a total area of 5190 square feet.

When adopted in 1933, the borough's zoning ordinance contained no minimum frontage or area provisions. However, a 1947 amendment required that one-family houses be located on lots with a frontage of at least 75 feet and an area of no less than 7500 square feet. At the time the amendment was adopted there were approximately 32 homes in the immediate area. Only seven satisfied the minimum frontage requirement. The nonconforming lots had frontages varying from 40 to 74 feet. This situation has remained virtually unchanged, only two homes having been constructed thereafter, one in 1948 with a frontage of 70 feet and one in 1970 with a frontage of 113 feet.

Weingarten proposed to construct a single-family, one and one-half story "raised ranch" with four bedrooms, a living room, dining room, kitchen, two baths and a one-car garage. Weingarten had no architectural design of the proposed house, but submitted a plan for a larger home which he claimed could be scaled down. The proposed home would have an approximate width of 19 feet, 18 inches and a depth of 48 feet. It would be centered on the 30-foot lot so as to provide five-foot side yards, the minimum required by the zoning ordinance. The proposed setback would also conform with the zoning plan. Weingarten further explained that the proposed residence would be roughly 18 feet from the house belonging to Robert Dineen located on adjacent land to the north, and 48 feet from the two-family residence owned by David Butler on the property to the south. The Dineen property has a 50-foot frontage, and the Butler frontage measures 74.5 feet.

The proposed home would be offered for sale for about $55,000. That price compared favorably with the market values of other nearby homes which a local realtor, Thomas Reno, estimated at between $45,000 and $60,000. Reno testified that the proposed home would not impair the borough's zoning plan because the house would be new, its value would compare favorably with other homes, its setback from the street would be at least as great as others, and the distances between the adjoining houses on each side would be substantial.

In 1974, plaintiff Gordon Commons had offered to sell the lot to Dineen for $7,500. Negotiations terminated, however, after Dineen countered with a $1,600 proposal, the assessed value of the property. When Weingarten contracted to purchase the land, he sought, albeit unsuccessfully, to purchase from Butler a 10-foot strip, adjacent to the south side of the lot.

Many neighbors opposed the application for a variance. Butler testified that a house on a 30-foot lot would be aesthetically displeasing, would differ in appearance by having a garage in front rather then alongside the dwelling, and would impair property values in the neighborhood. Another property owner, whose home was across the street, expressed her concern about privacy, reasoning that the occupants of a four-bedroom residence on a small lot would cause a spillover effect in terms of noise and trespassing.

The board of adjustment denied the variance, finding "that the applicant failed to demonstrate any evidence to establish hardship" and "that the granting of the variance would substantially impair the intent and purpose of the Zone Plan and Zoning Ordinance of the Borough of Westwood." The trial court, after reviewing the testimony, affirmed because it felt that to permit the variance "would be detrimental to the entire area wherein the property in question is situated." The Appellate Division, holding that the board of adjustment had not acted arbitrarily, affirmed in a brief per curiam opinion. . . .

I.

N.J.S.A. 40:55D-70(c) provides that a board of adjustment shall have power to grant a variance where by reason of the narrowness of the land or other extraordinary and exceptional situation of the property, the strict application of a zoning ordinance would result in exceptional and undue hardship upon the developer of the property. In addition, the statute's negative criteria must be satisfied, that is that the variance can be granted "without substantial detriment to the public good and will not substantially impair the intent and purpose of the zone plan and zoning ordinance." As in *Chirichello v. Monmouth Beach Zoning Bd. of Adjustment,* 78 *N.J.* 544, 397 *A.2d* 646 (1978), where the proposed residence conformed to the use requirement of the zoning ordinance but had insufficient frontage and area, we are called upon to consider and analyze the "undue hardship" concept and the negative criteria.

"Undue hardship" involves the underlying notion that no effective use can be made of the property in the event the variance is denied. Use of the property may of course be subject to reasonable restraint. As Justice Pashman observed in *Taxpayers Association of Weymouth Tp., Inc. v. Weymouth Tp.*, 80 *N.J.* 6, 20, 364 *A.2d* 1016, 1023 (1976), *cert.* den. 430 U.S. 977, 97 S.Ct. 1672, 52 L.Ed.2d 373 (1977), "(z)oning is inherently an exercise of the State's police power" and the property owner's use of the land is subject to regulation "which will promote the public health, safety, morals and general welfare . . . ." *N.J.S.A.* 40:55D-2(a). Put another way an "owner is not entitled to have his property zoned for its most profitable use." *Bow & Arrow Manor v. West Orange*, 63 *N.J.* 335, 350, 307 *A.2d* 563, 571 (1973). See *Shell Oil Co. v. Shrewsbury Zoning Bd. of Adjustment*, 64 *N.J.* 334, 316 *A.2d* 5 (1974). However, when the regulation renders the property unusable for any purpose, the analysis calls for further inquiries which may lead to a conclusion that the property owner would suffer an undue hardship.

It is appropriate to consider first the origin of the existing situation. If the property owner or his predecessors in title created the nonconforming condition, then the hardship may be deemed to be self-imposed. To measure this type of impact it is necessary to know when the zoning ordinance limitations were adopted and the status of the property with respect to those limitations at that time. Thus, if the lot had contained a 75-foot frontage and despite the existence of that requirement, the owner sold a 40-foot strip of the land, he or his successors in title would have little cause to complain. Likewise no undue hardship is suffered by an owner of a lot with a 35-foot frontage who acquired an adjoining 40-foot strip so that the lot complied with the ordinance and then sold a part of the land. These examples serve to illustrate the nature of a self-inflicted hardship which would not satisfy the statutory criteria.

Related to a determination of undue hardship are the efforts which the property owner has made to bring the property into compliance with the ordinance's specifications. Attempts to acquire additional land would be significant if it is feasible to purchase property from the adjoining property owners. Endeavors to sell the property to the adjoining landowners, the negotiations between and among the parties, and the reasonableness of the prices demanded and offered are also relevant considerations. See *Gougeon v. Stone Harbor Bd. of Adjustment*, 52 *N.J.* 212, 224, 245 *A.2d* 7 (1968), where it was held that if an owner of land refused to sell at a "fair and reasonable" price he would not be considered to be suffering an "undue hardship." If on the other hand the owner is willing to sell at a "fair and reasonable" price and the adjoining property owners refuse to make a reasonable offer, then "undue hardship" would exist.

When an undue hardship is found to exist, the board of adjustment must be satisfied that the negative criteria are satisfied before granting a variance. Thus the grant of the variance must not substantially impinge upon the public good and the intent and purpose of the zone plan and ordinance. As we observed in Chirichello, "the variance may be granted only if the spirit of the ordinance and the general welfare are observed." 78 *N.J.* at 552, 397 *A.*2d at 650. In this respect attention must be directed to the manner in and extent to which the variance will impact upon the character of the area. We have frequently observed that the applicant carries the burden of establishing the negative criteria by a fair preponderance of the evidence, but that "(t)he less of an impact, the more likely the restriction is not that vital to valid public interests." *Chirichello v. Monmouth Zoning Bd. of Adjustment,* 78 *N.J.* at 561, 397 *A.*2d at 654. See *Fobe Associates v. Demarest,* 74 *N.J.* 519, 547, 379 *A.*2d 31 (1977).

There lurks in the background of cases of this type the possibility that denial of a variance will zone the property into inutility so that "an exercise of eminent domain (will be) . . . called for and compensation must be paid." *Harrington Glen, Inc. v. Leonia Bd. of Adjustment,* 52 *N.J.* 22, 33, 243 *A.*2d 233, 239 (1968). When that occurs all the taxpayers in the municipality share the economic burden of achieving the intent and purpose of the zoning scheme. Compared to this result is the denial of a variance conditioned upon the sale of the property at a fair market value to the adjoining property owners. They will perhaps receive the more direct benefit of the land remaining undeveloped and it may therefore be fairer for them to bear the cost. In this respect we made the following pertinent comments in Chirichello:

> It would certainly be consonant with the interest of all parties to deny a variance conditioned on the purchase of the land by adjoining property owners at a fair price. The immediate benefit to the adjoining property owners of maintenance of the zoning scheme and aesthetic enjoyment of surrounding vacant land adjacent to their homes is self-evident. The owner of the odd lot would suffer no monetary damage having received the fair value of the land. Of course, if the owner refused to sell, then he would have no cause for complaint. Or if the adjoining owners would not agree to purchase, then perhaps the variance should be granted, less weight being given to their position particularly when the land in question will have been rendered useless. In either event the use of a conditional variance, the condition bearing an overall reasonable relationship to the purposes of the zoning ordinance, may lead to a satisfactory solution. See *Harrington Glen, Inc. v. Leonia Bd. of Adj., supra; Houdaille Const. Materials, Inc. v. Tewksbury Tp. Bd. of Adj.,* 92 *N.J. Super.* 293, 223 *A.*2d 210 (App.Div.1966); *Cohen v. Fair Lawn,* 85 *N.J. Super.* 234, 237-238, 204 *A.*2d 375 (App.Div.1964).

Hearings before the board of adjustment serve as the focal point for resolution of conflicting interests between public restraints on the use of private property and the owner's right to utilize his land as he wishes. A third interest which frequently makes its appearance is represented by other property owners in the immediate vicinity whose major objective is the more limited self-interest of taking whatever position they believe will enhance the value of their property or coincide with their personal preferences. The board of adjustment must settle these disputes by engaging in a "discretionary weighing," a function inherent in the variance process. (78 *N.J.* at 555-556, 397 *A.2d* at 651-52)

We have referred to the fair market value and the fair and reasonable price of the property with respect to considerations of offers to purchase and sell the property as well as the possibility of conditioning the variance. We believe that the preferred method to determine value is on the assumption that a variance had been granted so that a home could be constructed on the lot. See *Gougeon v. Stone Harbor Bd. of Adjustment,* 52 *N.J.* at 224, 245 *A.2d* 7, and *Chirichello v. Monmouth Beach Zoning Bd. of Adjustment,* 78 *N.J.* at 562, 397 *A.2d* 646 (Pashman, J., concurring). It is possible that other methods of valuation may be feasible. However, the parties have not briefed or argued the issue and accordingly we do not foreclose such possibilities.

II.

Here, the board of adjustment concluded that "the applicant failed to demonstrate Any evidence to establish hardship on the part of the applicant." (emphasis supplied) The record does not support that conclusion. Until the 1947 amendment to the zoning ordinance the plaintiffs or their predecessors in title could have constructed a one-family house on the lot. Ownership commenced in 1927 when the Borough of Westwood had no zoning ordinance. Furthermore, an attempt, albeit unsuccessful, had been made to acquire an additional ten-foot strip from Mr. Butler, owner of the property bordering to the south. A 40-foot frontage would have at least brought the property into conformity with one home in the neighborhood and within close proximity of the size of the lots of two other houses. In addition there had been discussions concerning the possible sale of the property to a neighbor, there being a substantial divergence in the offering and asking prices. Lastly, one could reasonably conclude that, if a variance were not granted, the land would be zoned into inutility. In view of all the above, it cannot be said that there was not any evidence to establish hardship.

Passing to the negative criteria, the board of adjustment made only the conclusive statement that the variance would substantially impair the intent and purpose of the zone plan and ordinance. The manner in which the variance would cause that effect is not explained. The board found that the lot was the only 30-foot parcel in the block, that the applicant builder had never constructed a house on a 30-foot lot, and that the proposed house would be 19 feet in width. How these facts relate to the zone plan is not made clear. The proposed use, side yards and setback meet the requirements of the ordinance. The proposed sales price of the home would be within the range of the value of the houses in the neighborhood. The total acreage of the land, exceeding 5,000 square feet, is comparable to 17 other properties in the neighborhood.

Perhaps the proposed house would be smaller in size than others. But in and of itself that would not justify a denial of a variance. Size of the house does not violate any of the traditional zoning purposes of light, air and open space which are reflected in the ordinance. We have recognized that minimum lot size "may be closely related to the goals of public health and safety" but that minimum floor area requirements "are not per se related to public health, safety or morals." *Home Builders League of South Jersey, Inc. v. Berlin Tp.,* 81 *N.J.* 127, 139, 142, 405 *A.2d* 381, 388, 389 (1979).

It is possible that the board of adjustment was concerned with the appearance of the house and its relationship to the neighborhood from an aesthetic and economic viewpoint. These are proper zoning purposes, for the appearance of a house may be related to the character of the district. *N.J.S.A.* 40:55D-62(a). In Home Builders League of South Jersey, Inc. 81 *N.J.* at 145, 405 *A.2d* 381, we recognized that conserving the value of the surrounding properties and aesthetic considerations are appropriate desiderata of zoning. Thus, if the size and layout of the proposed house would have adversely affected the character of the neighborhood, both with respect to a "desirable visual environment," *N.J.S.A.* 40:55D-2(i), and the value of the neighborhood properties, a board may justly conclude that a variance should not be granted.

The board's resolution does not address these problems. They are brought into sharp focus when an articulation of findings and reasoning must be made. We have frequently advised boards of adjustment to make findings predicated upon factual support in the record and directed to the issues involved. We refer again to Justice Francis's statements in *Harrington Glen, Inc.,* 52 *N.J.* at 28, 243 *A.2d* at 236:

> Denial of a variance on a summary finding couched in the conclusionary language of the statute is not adequate. There must be a statement of the specific findings of fact on which the Board reached the conclusion that the statutory criteria for a variance were not satisfied. Unless such findings are recited, a reviewing court cannot determine fairly whether the Board acted properly and within the limits of its authority in refusing a variance. (citations omitted)

In this connection boards should be mindful that they may receive assistance from other municipal employees. The board would not have been amiss here in calling the municipal building inspector to testify to construction requirements. The board or its counsel may also have addressed inquiries with respect to the size and appearance of the other homes, and the aesthetic and economic impact upon those homeowners. We do not mean to imply that the burden of proof is not upon the applicant. It is, but in performing its function as a governmental body, the board may take some action which may be of assistance to it. The difficulty in this case also rests with the applicants. They did not submit a plan of the proposed house, demonstrate compliance with the municipality's building code, and adequately describe the appearance and type of the structure. It is essential in a case of this type that the proponent submit a detailed plan of the proposed house. Under all these circumstances we believe fairness calls for a remand to the board of adjustment so that the record may be supplemented, the matter reconsidered, and adequate findings made.

Reversed and remanded to the Borough of Westwood Zoning Board of adjustment.

NOTES

1. *Undue Hardship.* As the court explains in *Commons*, the undue hardship test is met if the land will be virtually useless unless the variance is granted. This test is a high hurdle for property owners seeking a variance. If the land would still be useful even if the variance were to be denied, the undue hardship test will not have been met because the zoning law imposes mere inconvenience, not undue hardship, on the property owner. If the zoning law makes a parcel of property useless, the property owner will be able to argue that enforcement of the zoning law amounted to a regulatory taking of her property. (We will examine the relevant regulatory takings cases in the next chapter.) As the court noted in *Commons*, the specter of the finding of a regulatory taking "lurks in the background of [variance] cases." The undue hardship test was met in *Commons* because the lot would have been rendered useless if the variance had not been met.

As the court explains in *Commons*, the property owner's conduct can help or hurt an application for a variance. The owner's claim for a variance will be helped if she attempts to mitigate the conditions that lead to noncompliance with the zoning law. In *Commons*, the fact that the owner tried to buy a ten-foot strip of land from a neighbor helped the owner's claim. Conversely, if the property owner's own actions caused the problem, then the owner would not be entitled to a variance. If, for example, an owner of a lot that complies with the zoning law splits it into two lots that are not compliant with the law, the owner's problem will be self-inflicted, and the owner will not be entitled to a variance.

2. *Harm to the Public and Overall Effectiveness of the Zoning Plan.* In *Commons*, the neighbors testified against the application for a variance. Testimony of the neighbors in variance cases often is self-serving. The neighbors' testimony was undercut by the existence of many other houses on noncompliant lots in the neighborhood. The neighbors' testimony was also undercut by the unwillingness of the adjacent property owners to purchase the lot at fair market value. Note, in this context, the court's discussion in *Commons* of the possibility of denying a variance conditioned on the lot being purchased by neighbors for fair market value. Such an outcome forces an objecting neighbor to put her money where her mouth is.

It is possible, of course, to imagine variance applications that fail to satisfy this prong of the variance test. For example, if the lot in *Commons* had been even narrower than it was, then building a house on the lot may indeed have detrimentally changed the character of the neighborhood. This prong would also not be met if the owner proposed a use markedly different from the existing uses in the neighborhood—for example, by seeking a variance to put a convenience store in the middle of an area zoned for residential use. Conversely, applicants will have a very good chance of meeting this test if they propose a use similar to other existing uses of property in the neighborhood.

3. *Variance Practicalities.* The variance at issue in *Commons* was an *area variance*—the property owner was seeking relief from an area-based requirement of the zoning law. A *use variance* is a variance that gives relief from a use-based requirement of the zoning law. An example of a use variance would be one that permitted a commercial use in an area zoned residential. The burden for obtaining a use variance is typically said to be higher for the party seeking a use variance than for a party seeking an area variance.

The general view of land use commentators is that most variances granted by municipal zoning boards would not meet the strict standards set by courts. Many variance requests are not challenged by neighbors or litigated in the courts, and many zoning boards are not as rigorous as they should be. As a result, courts tend to reverse decisions granting a variance more often than they reverse decisions denying a variance.

Special exceptions are our second method by which an owner may obtain permission to engage in a use that is otherwise prohibited by the zoning law. Special exceptions are also called *conditional use permits* or *special use permits*. With a special exception, the use in question is expressly contemplated by the zoning code but is only allowed if certain conditions are met. For example, a zoning ordinance might allow a medical office to be located in a particular area so long as the landowner could provide eight parking spots on the property. Here, the use (a doctor's office) is expressly contemplated by the ordinance so long as a condition (eight available on-lot parking spaces) is met. As you can see, "conditional use permit" and "special use permit" are more descriptive names for this method than the more commonly used term "special exception."

The conditions required in the zoning ordinance for a special exception must be clearly stated and be nondiscretionary. If the conditions fail to meet this requirement, the conditions will not be enforced, and the use will be permitted. Remember in this context that the zoning ordinance expressly contemplates the use but has attempted to set conditions for that use. If the municipality wants the conditions to be enforced, it must make sure that they meet this requirement.

The requirement that the conditions be clear and nondiscretionary has its roots in separation of powers. Zoning laws are enacted by the municipal legislature. Applications for special exceptions are considered by a zoning board of appeals or similar executive administrative agency. A basic principle of administrative law is that a legislature may not delegate legislative authority to an executive administrative agency. Zoning enabling acts grant the power to enact zoning regulations to municipal legislatures. The municipal legislature can delegate enforcement of rules to an administrative agency, but if it does so, it must give clear guidance in how those rules are to be enforced. If the rules are too vague, then the administrative agency will end up making decisions that the state legislature (through the zoning enabling act) required the municipal legislature to make.

VARIANCES VS. SPECIAL EXCEPTIONS

Be sure that you understand the difference between variances and special exceptions. They do very different things and address very different problems. Variances are waivers of zoning requirements that are granted to avoid undue hardship on property owners and to avoid potential constitutional problems that would be caused by rendering a parcel of land useless. Special exceptions address uses that are expressly contemplated by the zoning ordinance but are permitted only if specific conditions are met by the property owner.

Our next case provides a good example of a zoning ordinance that contained special exception conditions that were too vague and discretionary to be enforced. As you read the case, think about why some of the conditions in the ordinance were objectionable and what, if anything, could be done to rewrite those conditions to make them enforceable.

COPE V. TOWN OF BRUNSWICK

Supreme Court of Maine, 1983
464 A.2d 223

WATHEN, Justice.

The plaintiffs, Mitchell and David Cope, appeal from a decision of the Superior Court (Cumberland County) which affirmed a decision of the Brunswick Zoning Board of Appeals (the Board) denying plaintiffs a zoning exception to construct eight multi-unit apartment buildings within the Town of Brunswick. On appeal, the plaintiffs assert *inter alia* that the Brunswick zoning ordinance is facially unconstitutional. Specifically, they argue that the ordinance improperly delegates to the Board the authority to permit the use of land for the construction of an apartment building. We conclude that the ordinance is in part unconstitutional and therefore sustain the appeal.

I.

On March 16, 1982, plaintiffs filed an application with the Brunswick Codes Enforcement Officer requesting that the Board grant them an exception under the Brunswick zoning ordinance permitting them to construct eight six-unit apartment buildings on a twenty-one acre parcel of land located near Jordan Avenue in the Town of Brunswick. The land, an undeveloped and wooded lot, is classified under the Brunswick ordinance for "suburban A residential" use. Under section 402 of the ordinance, multi-unit apartment buildings are permitted in suburban A residential zones, "only as an exception granted by the Board of Appeals."

Section 1107 of the ordinance prescribes the criteria that an applicant must fulfill to qualify for an exception.

Section 1107 Exceptions. The Board of Appeals may grant an exception to the Ordinance and allow the uses in the zones designated as "XA" in Sec. 402. An appellant who seeks a use by exception shall submit to the Board diagrams or photographs, which become part of the record, illustrating the proof required by this section. He must prove the following:

(1) *Certain Requirements Met.* That the use requested meets the requirements of this Ordinance set forth in Chapters 5-8.

(2) *Use Not Adverse.* That the use requested will not adversely affect the health, safety, or general welfare of the public.

(3) *Purpose Upheld.* That the use requested will not tend to defeat the purpose of this Ordinance as set forth in Section 101 or of the Comprehensive Plan for the development of the Town of Brunswick.

(4) *Value Maintained.* That the use requested will not tend to devaluate or alter the essential characteristics of the surrounding property.

Following a public hearing held on March 30 and April 10, 1982, the Board found that plaintiffs' project was in compliance with the ordinance in all respects, with the exception of subsections (2) and (4) of section 1107. The Board found that the proposed use would pose problems that would endanger the safety of the public and that the project would "drastically change the basic characteristics of the existing neighborhood from one of a small quiet not very heavily travelled area to one more dense and heavily travelled."

The Board denied plaintiffs' application for an exception and plaintiffs appealed to Superior Court pursuant to Rule 80B of the Maine Rules of Civil Procedure. On appeal, the Superior Court upheld the constitutionality of the Brunswick ordinance and affirmed the Board's denial of plaintiffs' application for a use exception.

II.

The issue before us arises from the fact that local zoning boards, like municipalities, have no inherent authority to regulate the use of private property. *Town of Windham v. LaPointe,* 308 A.2d 286, 290 (Me.1973). Instead, the power of a town, and therefore that of the local zoning board of appeals, is conferred upon the town by the State. *Id., Mitchell v. City of Rockland,* 45 Me. 496, 504 (1858). *See* 30 M.R.S.A. §2411 (1978 and Supp.1982-1983) (granting municipality authority to establish board of appeals); 30 M.R.S.A. §4962 (1978 and Supp.1982-1983) (governing zoning ordinances). This power may not be delegated from the legislature to the municipality or from the municipality to a local administrative body without a sufficiently detailed statement of policy to:

furnish a guide which will enable those to whom the law is to be applied to reasonably determine their rights thereunder, and so that the determination of those rights will not be left to the purely arbitrary discretion of the administrator.

Stucki v. Plavin, 291 A.2d 508, 510 (Me.1972).

The present case calls into question the constitutionality of two of the standards contained in section 1107 of the ordinance. Under the ordinance, the Board is directed to base its decision upon a determination of whether the proposed use would "adversely affect the health, safety or general welfare of the public," and whether the use would "alter the essential characteristics of the surrounding property."[3] Upon the authority of prior decisions of this Court, we hold that the ordinance improperly delegates legislative authority to the Board and is therefore void.

In *Waterville Hotel Corp. v. Board of Zoning Appeals,* 241 A.2d 50 (Me.1968), this Court struck down a provision of a zoning ordinance which vested absolute power in the Board of Zoning Appeals to approve or disapprove "all major changes of uses of land, buildings or structures . . . ." The land owner in that case sought to construct a service station in a "Commercial C" zone. Although the landowner satisfied all of the specific requirements of the zoning ordinance, the Board of Appeals denied him a building permit on the ground that the proposed use would be inimical of public safety. *Id.* at 51. In striking down that portion of the ordinance making all major changes in the uses of land "subject to the approval of the Board of Zoning Appeals," we stated:

> The legislative body may specify conditions under which certain uses may exist and may delegate to the Board discretion in determining whether or not the conditions have been met. The legislative body cannot, however, delegate to the Board a discretion which is not limited by legislative standards. It cannot give the Board discretionary authority to approve or disapprove applications for permits as the Board thinks best serves the public interest without establishing standards to limit and guide the Board.

Id. at 52.

Although a provision in the Waterville ordinance required the Board to exercise its power "in harmony with the comprehensive plan for municipal development and the purpose and intent of this ordinance, in accordance with the public interest and in support and furtherance of the health, safety and general welfare of the residents of the municipality," this Court held that such general language did not provide sufficient guidance to meet constitutional requirements. *Id.* at 53.

In *Stucki v. Plavin,* 291 A.2d 508 (Me.1972), we held to be facially unconstitutional an ordinance which provided that the less restrictive regulations would apply to a lot split

---

[3] The Board did not find that plaintiffs' proposed use would tend to "devaluate" the surrounding property as is likewise referred to in subsection (4). We do not therefore address the sufficiency of that language as a standard of delegation.

by two zones "provided, however, that such extension of use into the more restricted portion *shall meet the approval* of the Board of Zoning Appeals." *Id.* at 509 (emphasis added).

Similarly, we held a provision of a town zoning ordinance unconstitutional in *Town of Windham v. LaPointe,* 308 A.2d 286 (Me.1973), which vested unguided authority in the selectmen and planning board to approve or disapprove of the location of proposed trailer parks. In striking down that ordinance, the Court noted:

> Such broad delegation of power breeds selectivity in the enforcement of the law. When no standards are provided to guide the discretion of the enforcement authority, the fact that the law might be applied in a discriminatory manner settles its constitutionality.

Id. at 293.

Defendants seek to avoid the implications of the foregoing decisions by relying upon the later decision of *Barnard v. Zoning Board of Appeals of the Town of Yarmouth,* 313 A.2d 741 (Me.1974). The ordinance at issue in that case provided that the Board of Appeals had authority to grant variances, "where necessary to avoid undue hardship, provided there is no substantial departure from the intent of the ordinances." Although acknowledging that the standard was broadly stated, we concluded that it was nonetheless sufficient to guide the Board in granting or denying *variances. Id.* at 748.

Contrary to defendants' assertion, *Barnard* does not represent a departure from our earlier decisions. The standard provided by the ordinance in *Barnard* was sufficient because it related to the granting of a variance and described only the negative findings which were required to be made before the prohibited use could be allowed by variance. In determining absence of a "substantial departure from the intent of the ordinances," it would be the other provisions of the ordinance which would provide substantive guidance for the decision. Moreover, *Barnard* does not have application in judging the sufficiency of standards to permit use by exception as opposed to use by variance. A use by exception, such as the apartment complex proposed in this case, differs substantially from a use by variance:

> A special exception use differs from a variance in that a variance is authority extended to a landowner to use his property in a manner prohibited by the ordinance (absent such variance) while a special exception allows him to put his property to a use which the ordinance expressly permits.

Stucki, 291 A.2d at 511. An exception is a conditional use under a zoning ordinance and results from a legislative determination that such use will not ordinarily be detrimental or injurious to the neighborhood within the zone. *Community School, Inc. v. Zoning Board of Appeals of the Town of Camden,* 369 A.2d 1146, 1149 (Me.1977). Whether the use will generally comply with the health, safety and welfare of the public and the essential character of the area is a legislative question. The delegation is improper if the Board is permitted to decide that same legislative question anew, without specific guidelines which permit the Board to determine what unique or distinctive characteristics of a particular apartment building will render it detrimental or injurious to the neighborhood. *See Phillips Petroleum Company v. Zoning Board of Appeals of the City of Bangor,* 260 A.2d 434, 435 (Me.1970).

We therefore conclude that the relevant portions of subsections (2) and (4) of section 1107 of the Brunswick zoning ordinance upon which the Board relied in denying the permit to plaintiffs are facially unconstitutional. Those standards refer only to the same general considerations which the legislative body was required to address and resolve in enacting the ordinance. As we have previously stated: "[t]here should be no discretion in the Board of Appeals as to whether or not to grant the permit if the conditions stated in the ordinance exist. That determination should be made by the legislators." *Stucki,* 291 A.2d at 511. To permit the broad legislative judgment to be delegated to the Board "would be equivalent to conferring upon the board of appeals the power to rescind the ordinance with respect to such uses." *Phillips Petroleum Company,* 260 A.2d at 435.

Stated simply, by enacting the ordinance, the voters of Brunswick determined that an apartment building was generally suitable for location in a suburban residential zone. The ordinance did not provide the Board with any basis for determining that a particular location was unsuitable because of the existence of certain characteristics which rendered the general legislative determination inapplicable. Since the Board found that plaintiffs were in compliance with all requirements of the ordinance except for those which we now find to be invalid, a permit for the exception should issue.

Judgment reversed. Remanded to the Superior Court for an appropriate order sustaining the appeal and directing issuance of the permit.

NOTES AND QUESTIONS

1. *Clear Conditions.* The conditions for a special exception must be clear. The offending conditions in the Town of Brunswick ordinance required the owner of land to prove that the multifamily residential use would not "adversely affect the health, safety, or general welfare of the public" and would "not tend to devaluate or alter the essential characteristics of the surrounding property." As the court noted, these are very broad and vague conditions. Can you think of specific conditions that a municipality could impose on multifamily residential use that might survive review while getting at the concerns reflected in the broader conditions that the court refused to enforce?

2. *Outcome.* Note the outcome of *Cope*—the court held that the conditions were unenforceable. As a result, the court directed the trial court to issue an order requiring the special exception permit to be granted. With a special exception, the ordinance contemplates the use as permissible but imposes certain conditions on that use. If the conditions are unenforceable, the use will be permitted.

Zoning amendments are our third method by which an owner may obtain permission to engage in a use that is otherwise prohibited by the zoning law. As their name suggests, zoning amendments involve a change to the zoning law by the municipal legislature. The municipal legislature created the zoning law, so the municipal legislature can amend it.

As we discussed above, courts tend to be deferential to legislative decisions but not to quasi-judicial decisions. For a while there was a debate about whether zoning amendments should be treated as legislative or quasi-judicial. The leading case for the proposition that they are quasi-judicial was *Fasano v. Board of County Commrs. of Washington County*, 264 Or. 574, 507 P.2d 23 (1973). The *Fasano* approach never really caught on, and in most jurisdictions today zoning amendments are treated as legislative acts.

Courts will sometimes invalidate zoning amendments on the grounds that they constitute instances of *spot zoning*. Spot zoning is best explained with an example. Imagine that an area is zoned for single-family residential use. A zoning amendment re-zones one parcel of property within this larger area to allow commercial use. After re-zoning, the one parcel is an island of commercial use within an area of residential use. Courts tend to invalidate zoning amendments as illegal spot zoning if the amendment results a parcel being singled out for special treatment that benefits the owner of that parcel and if the re-zoning is inconsistent with the overall zoning plan.

Our next case involves a challenge by neighbors to a zoning amendment that re-zoned a parcel of property from low-density residential use to high-density residential use. As you read the case, think about how the amendment affects the interests of the property owner, the neighbors, and the public as a whole.

STATE V. CITY OF ROCHESTER

Supreme Court of Minnesota, 1978
268 N.W.2d 885

ROGOSHESKE, Justice.

The Rochester Association of Neighborhoods and individual plaintiffs appeal from an order of the trial court denying declaratory judgment and injunctive relief in their action challenging the validity of a zoning ordinance amendment enacted by the Rochester City Council which rezoned a 1.18-acre tract of land from single-family residential use (R-1) and low-density residential use (R-2) to high-density residential use (R-4) to permit the building of a 6-story, 49-unit, condominium apartment building on the land. Plaintiffs contend (1) that this rezoning of a single tract was presumptively invalid as a "quasi-judicial act" by the council not supported with written findings of fact upon substantial evidence; (2) that even if it was a legislative act, the rezoning was arbitrary and capricious because it was inconsistent with the city's land-use plan and without reasonable relation to the health, safety, and welfare of the community; and (3) that the ordinance was invalid "spot zoning." We affirm the decision of the trial court and hold that the promulgation of the Rochester ordinance was a valid exercise of the municipality's delegated legislative power and, upon the record presented, was neither proven to be without reasonable relation to the public health, safety, and welfare, nor to be invalid as "spot zoning."

The 1.18-acre tract rezoned is owned by the A. C. Gooding Trust and is situated three blocks away from the central business district in the city of Rochester. Before the rezoning challenged in this suit, the eastern two-thirds of the subject property was zoned R-2 and the western one-third was zoned R-1. The land is bounded on the west and southwest by an R-1 district of single-family houses known as the Edison Park Neighborhood. On the south is an R-2 district of low-density, multiple-family dwellings. Across the street to the east is an R-4 district with a 24-unit apartment building. Across the street to the north is an R-4 district with a 35-unit condominium. Diagonally across the street to the northeast is a vacant lot zoned "institutional" and owned by the Mayo Clinic. Visible from the rezoned tract are Mayo Clinic Complex buildings located one block north and one block east and another high-rise condominium two blocks away.

Trustees of the A. C. Gooding Trust entered into a purchase agreement to convey the 1.18-acre tract to defendant Rodney Younge contingent upon the rezoning of the property to R-4 by September 1, 1977. On December 23, 1976, the trustees and defendant Younge applied to have the property rezoned to R-4. Younge submitted a "project description" proposing to develop a 60-unit, luxury condominium, later amended to propose a 49-unit condominium building, on the site. The application was referred to the Rochester Planning and Zoning Commission, which held a public hearing on January 12, 1977. The Rochester Consolidated Planning Department recommended to the planning commission that the rezoning be tabled to permit a study to determine whether the city's land-use plan should be amended. The planning commission recommended to the city council that the rezoning application be denied as inconsistent with the city's land-use plan, which called for low-density residential use on the Gooding property. On February 7, 1977, the council rejected the planning commission's recommendation and on March 7, 1977, passed an ordinance rezoning the subject property to R-4. The council gave no written reasons or findings supporting the rezoning. Minutes of the council meetings on February 7 and February 23, 1977, however, show that the council members believed the proposed condominium was needed to serve the city's expanded housing requirements. Council members stated that the Gooding property would be an ideal site since it was located within three blocks of the central business district and since high-density residential uses already across two streets from the property would be compatible with the proposed condominium and made development of the subject property for any other use unlikely. On July 5, 1977, the council amended its land-use plan to conform to the rezoning.

Plaintiffs, individual owners of residences abutting the subject property and their incorporated Association of Neighborhoods, appeared at the January 12, 1977, public hearing and were heard in protest at a February 23, 1977, meeting of the council. On April 8, 1977, plaintiffs filed this suit challenging the validity of the March 7, 1977, rezoning ordinance and seeking declaratory judgment and injunction. The trial court denied the requested relief.

1. On appeal, plaintiffs argue that the council's action in rezoning a single 1.18-acre tract should be subject to close judicial scrutiny as an administrative or quasi-judicial act. This standard of review would place upon the municipality the burden of supporting the ordinance as a valid exercise of the police power by findings of fact based upon substantial evidence. Absent such findings, the ordinance would be presumed invalid. Plaintiffs rely upon *Fasano v. Board of County Commrs. of Washington County*, 264 Or. 574, 507 P.2d 23 (1973), and *Fleming v. City of Tacoma*, 81 Wash.2d 292, 502 P.2d 327 (1972), in which the Oregon and Washington courts characterized the rezoning of a single tract of land as a quasi-judicial act affecting the rights of a few individuals more than the public generally. Those courts placed the burden of justifying the zoning change as reasonable upon the proponents, including the adopting city council.

We decline to follow the rule applied in those jurisdictions, for we have consistently held that "when a municipality adopts or amends a zoning ordinance, it acts in a legislative capacity under its delegated police powers." *Beck v. City of St. Paul*, 304 Minn. 438, 448, 231 N.W.2d 919, 925 (1975). See, also, *Sun Oil Co. v. Village of New Hope*, 300 Minn. 326, 333, 220 N.W.2d 256, 261 (1974); *Alexander v. City of Minneapolis*, 267 Minn. 155, 125 N.W.2d 583 (1963). As a legislative act, a zoning or rezoning classification must be upheld unless opponents prove that the classification is unsupported by any rational basis related to promoting the public health, safety, morals, or general welfare, or that the classification amounts to a taking without compensation. This rule applies regardless of the size of the tract of land involved. See, e. g., *Sun Oil Co. v. Village of New Hope, supra* (1 acre); *Beck v. City of St. Paul, supra* (33 1/2 acres). Our narrow scope of review reflects a policy decision that a legislative body can best determine which zoning classifications best serve the public welfare. In *Beck v. City of St. Paul*, 304 Minn. 438, 448, 231 N.W.2d 919, 925, and *Sun Oil Co. v. Village of New Hope*, 300 Minn. 326, 334, 220 N.W.2d 256, 261, we said:

> "Even where the reasonableness of a zoning ordinance is debatable, or where there are conflicting opinions as to the desirability of the restrictions it imposes . . . , it is not the function of the courts to interfere with the legislative discretion on such issues."

Plaintiffs note that we have not accorded the same presumption of validity to city council action denying special-use permits as we have to adoption or amendment of zoning ordinances. In *Zylka v. City of Crystal*, 283 Minn. 192, 167 N.W.2d 45 (1969), we adopted the rule that where a special use which conforms with the zoning ordinance is requested, a city council's denial of a special-use permit to a single landowner is proved prima facie arbitrary and unreasonable if it is shown that the council failed to support its action by written findings of substantial evidence showing the use impermissible under the permit standards of the ordinance. See, also, *Holasek v. Village of Medina,* 303 Minn. 240, 226 N.W.2d 900 (1975); *Metro 500, Inc. v. City of Brooklyn Park,* 297 Minn. 294, 211 N.W.2d 358 (1973); *Inland Construction Co. v. City of Bloomington,* 292 Minn. 374, 195 N.W.2d 558 (1972). Plaintiffs ask that zoning amendments be reviewed under a like standard and suggest that the only distinction between special-use permits and the rezoning in this case is the label "rezoning" chosen by the council to describe its action. We do not agree. While an amendment of the zoning ordinance can permit particular property to be used in a manner formerly forbidden by the ordinance, "a special use provision permits property, within the discretion of the governing body, to be used in a manner expressly authorized by the ordinance." *Zylka v. City of Crystal,* 283 Minn. 192, 195, 167 N.W.2d 45, 49. In passing a zoning or rezoning ordinance, a city council is required to make a legislative judgment that a certain zoning classification will promote the "public health, safety, morals and general welfare." Minn. St. 462.357, subd. 1. In granting or denying a special-use permit, a city council is not altering the legislative judgment as to the zoning classification. Rather, it has the function, adjudicative in nature, of applying specific use standards set by the zoning ordinance to a particular individual use and must be held strictly to those standards.

The proposed high-density use of the subject land was not in conformity with existing zoning classifications and therefore could not have been accomplished through a special-use permit.[1] The use could be permitted only through amendment of the zoning ordinance. This was not a case where the council was enabled to obtain a lesser standard of judicial scrutiny than would otherwise be applied simply by choosing to label its action "rezoning." An amendment of the zoning ordinance was required and one was passed. No other label could have applied to the council's action. The council's amendment of the ordinance, under our previous holdings, involved a legislative judgment and as such must be reviewed under the narrow scope of judicial review stated.

2. Assuming, as we hold, that the rezoning was a legislative act, plaintiffs ask us to invalidate the ordinance as arbitrary and capricious and without reasonable relation to promoting public health, safety, morals, and general welfare. They emphasize that the ordinance, when adopted against the planning commission's recommendation, was inconsistent with Rochester's land-use plan, which was thereafter amended to conform to the zoning change. Plaintiffs ask that the rezoning be invalidated on this basis.

---

[1] The proposed nonconforming use also could not have been permitted through a variance. Under Minn. St. 462.357, subd. 6, a variance may not be granted to permit any use that is not permitted under the zoning ordinance. Variances are available only with respect to other requirements of the ordinance, such as setback requirements and similar provisions.

Other states have required that a city's zoning ordinances conform exactly to its land-use plan when adopted or have held that the presumption of validity accompanying a legislative act is lifted when a rezoning ordinance is adopted despite city planners' recommendations that it will not be consistent with the comprehensive land-use plan at the time. See, *Baker v. City of Milwaukie,* 271 Or. 500, 533 P.2d 772 (1975); *Udell v. Haas,* 21 N.Y.2d 463, 288 N.Y.S.2d 888, 235 N.E.2d 897 (1968); 1 Anderson, American Law of Zoning (2 ed.) §3.15. We find no such requirement nor any such shifting presumption in our law.

Minn. St. 462.351 to 462.364, Minnesota's municipal planning act, provides for the adoption of a comprehensive land-use plan to guide future developments in a municipality, and §462.357 grants the municipality power to effectuate its land-use plan through zoning. Section 462.357, subd. 2, provides:

> "At any time after the adoption of a land use plan for the municipality, the planning agency, for the purpose of carrying out the policies and goals of the land use plan, may prepare a proposed zoning ordinance and submit it to the governing body with its recommendations for adoption. Subject to the requirements of subdivisions 3, 4 and 5, the governing body may adopt and amend a zoning ordinance by a two-thirds vote of all its members."

Plaintiffs interpret this provision as requiring that the city's land-use plan be amended before a zoning ordinance is amended. We read the statute to require only that a land-use plan be adopted before the initial zoning ordinance is adopted. The statute in fact does not require even that the zoning ordinance conform exactly to the city's land-use plan. While it may seem desirable as a matter of municipal planning to amend the land-use plan before adopting an inconsistent zoning ordinance, such a requirement is properly a matter for the legislature, not for this court, to consider. This court has frequently noted consistency between a city's land-use plan or planning commission's recommendation and the zoning ordinance as a factor supporting the reasonableness of the city's legislative judgment in passing the zoning ordinance. See, e. g., *Olsen v. City of Hopkins,* 276 Minn. 163, 149 N.W.2d 394 (1967); *Beck v. City of St. Paul,* 304 Minn. 438, 231 N.W.2d 919; *Sun Oil Co. v. Village of New Hope,* 300 Minn. 326, 220 N.W.2d 256. But we have never held, nor could we hold under the language of §462.357, that a procedure such as Rochester's of amending the land-use plan after amending the zoning classification could conclusively invalidate the zoning ordinance. The city strictly followed the procedures of §462.357, subds. 3 and 4, requiring that a proposed amendment to the zoning ordinance first be submitted to the planning agency for a recommendation and that a public hearing be held. There is nothing in §462.357 which makes the recommendation of the planning commission binding upon the city council or governing body. Plaintiffs appeared and were heard at a public hearing on January 12, 1977, before adoption of the ordinance, and their attorney was heard in protest proceedings before the February 23, 1977, council meeting after the council had rejected the planning commission's recommendations on February 7, 1977.

Upon the record presented, we hold that the council's legislative decision to rezone the 1.18-acre Gooding property to R-4 high-density was not arbitrary and capricious and was not shown to be without reasonable relation to promotion of the public health, safety, morals, and general welfare. There was evidence of the need for more high-density housing in the city of Rochester. Locating the proposed condominium on the subject property complied with the standards for location of R-4 uses set by the Rochester Code of Ordinances, §66.206, which provides:

> "R-4 HIGH DENSITY DISTRICT: This district is intended to create, preserve, and enhance areas for multi-family use at high densities for both permanent and transient families. It is typically appropriate only in areas of good accessibility to thoroughfares, to public transportation, public community centers, libraries, and major shopping centers and shall be limited to the general area of the central business district."

The evidence established that the Gooding land is within two blocks of two primary thoroughfares; is within two blocks of city bus lines; is near public community centers, a child care center, and a city library; and is within three blocks of the central business district and major shopping area. There was a rational basis for concluding that a six-story condominium would be compatible with existing uses in the neighborhood of the subject property. The property was already surrounded on two sides by high-density R-4 and institutional uses and on one side by R-2 duplexes and smaller apartment buildings; it was bounded only to the west and southwest by plaintiffs' single-family residences. Already across two streets from the property were 24-unit and 35-unit high-rises, and another high-rise and Mayo Clinic buildings were within two blocks and visible from the property. Within these surroundings, it was reasonable for council members to conclude that development of this property for further low-density or single-family use would have been economically unlikely. Further, there was evidence, and the trial court found, that R-4 zoning of the Gooding land would increase tax revenues for the city; would create no traffic problem for the area; and (as stipulated by the parties) could be accommodated by presently adequate fire, police, sewer, water, and electrical services. Based upon all of these facts and circumstances, we cannot find that the rezoning was without rational basis.

Plaintiffs point to other factors such as the apparent stability of the Edison Park single-family neighborhood; the expressed concerns of neighbors that increased noise, traffic, people, and less open space would interfere with the character of that neighborhood; the fact that the Gooding land is also suited for lesser-density R-2 use under the definitions of the Rochester zoning code;[2] and the possibility that high-density

---

[2] Rochester Code of Ordinances, §66.204, provides: "R-2 LOW DENSITY DISTRICT: This district is intended 1) to create low density areas of mixed residential use and 2) To preserve and enhance residential areas undergoing conversion of single-family dwellings to multi-family uses."

use of the Gooding land would decrease values of adjacent property for single-family use. All of these factors may make the reasonableness of the zoning change fairly debatable, but under our standard of review, that is not enough to justify the court's interfering with the council's legislative judgment in passing the ordinance. In particular, plaintiffs' generalized claims that their property may decline in value, absent some evidence of an actual decline sufficient to prove a taking of property without compensation, do not form a basis for invalidating a zoning ordinance or amendment.[3]

3. Finally, plaintiffs urge the court to invalidate the rezoning ordinance as "spot zoning." "Spot zoning" is a label applied to certain zoning amendments invalidated as legislative acts unsupported by any rational basis related to promoting public welfare. 1 Anderson, American Law of Zoning (2 ed.) §5.08. The term applies to zoning changes, typically limited to small plots of land, which establish a use classification inconsistent with surrounding uses and create an island of nonconforming use within a larger zoned district, and which dramatically reduce the value for uses specified in the zoning ordinance of either the rezoned plot or abutting property. See, *Alexander v. City of Minneapolis,* 267 Minn. 155, 125 N.W.2d 583 (1963); *Magnin v. Zoning Comm. of Town of Madison,* 145 Conn. 26, 138 A.2d 522 (1958); *Langer v. Planning & Zoning Comm.,* 163 Conn. 453, 313 A.2d 44 (1972); *Hein v. Daly City,* 165 Cal.App.2d 401, 332 P.2d 120 (1958); *Hermann v. City of Des Moines,* 250 Iowa 1281, 97 N.W.2d 893 (1959). See, generally, Annotation, 51 A.L.R.2d 263; 1 Anderson, American Law of Zoning (2 ed.) §§5.09, 5.12, 5.17; 1 Rathkopf, The Law of Zoning and Planning, c. 26.

In *Hermann v. City of Des Moines, supra,* principally relied upon by plaintiffs, the city of Des Moines rezoned a single city lot located in the middle of an R-2 district to R-3. After rezoning, the spot-zoned lot was surrounded by lots of different classification. In *Alexander v. City of Minneapolis, supra,* we characterized spot-zoning amendments as those which "result in total destruction or substantial diminution of value of property affected thereby." 267 Minn. 155, 160, 125 N.W.2d 583, 586.

The burden of demonstrating that a particular zoning amendment is spot zoning rests with the litigant attacking the ordinance, and the usual presumption of validity attaching to zoning amendments as legislative acts applies. See, *Raffia v. Zoning Board of Appeals of Town of Enfield,* 151 Conn. 484, 199 A.2d 333 (1964); *Crall v. Leominster,* 362 Mass. 95, 284 N.E.2d 610 (1972); 1 Anderson, American Law of Zoning (2 ed.) §5.08, p. 290.

Here, plaintiffs have proved no substantial diminution in their property value due to the rezoning, nor have they shown that the rezoning would create an island of

---

[3] In *Beck v. City of St. Paul,* 304 Minn. 438, 449, 231 N.W.2d 919, 925 (1975), this court said: ". . . The simple fact that certain property values may decline is not of itself a sufficient reason to invalidate a proposed rezoning. Values are not, in and of themselves, the test of validity of a zoning regulation. They are factors for a city council to take into consideration in arriving at its conclusions on the total merits in the interest of the community. The general welfare of the public is paramount in importance to the pecuniary stake of the individual."

nonconforming use as the court found in Hermann. The property to the east and north of the subject tract was already zoned high-density residential. The record presented shows sufficient justification for this rezoning as a proper exercise of legislative power for the public welfare, and we find no basis for invalidation of the ordinance under the "spot zoning" label.

Affirmed.

KELLY, Justice (dissenting).

I respectfully dissent. I would have this court in this case adopt the standard of review placing upon the municipality the burden of supporting the ordinance as a valid exercise of the police power by findings of fact based upon substantial evidence. I am persuaded by the rationale of *Fasano v. Board of County Commrs. of Washington County,* 264 Or. 574, 507 P.2d 23 (1973), and *Fleming v. City of Tacoma,* 81 Wash.2d 292, 502 P.2d 327 (1972), cited in the majority opinion. I would overrule our cases to the contrary.

Furthermore, I think it is illogical to require municipalities to live up to a stricter standard of review in granting or denying a special-use permit than in rezoning a parcel of land. I am not persuaded that characterizing one as legislative and the other as adjudicative in nature is an acceptable answer. Those landowners who buy or improve their lands in reliance on zoning undoubtedly place greater reliance on the zoning of lots as residential than they would on the prospects of getting a special-use permit.

Thus the standard of review should be a higher one for rezoning or at least the same as for securing a special-use permit.

NOTES AND QUESTIONS

1. *The Re-zoning Process.* What do you think of the re-zoning process described in *City of Rochester*? Is there anything that worries you about it? Do you think that the decision to re-zone was justifiable?

2. *Legislative vs. Quasi-Judicial, Again.* Having read the *City of Rochester* case, do you think that zoning amendments are best characterized as legislative or quasi-judicial? The practical impact of this distinction is the degree of deference that a reviewing court will give to the contested decision. We could therefore put the question a different way: do you think that courts should be deferential to a decision to re-zone a parcel? Both the majority and dissent compare zoning amendments to special exceptions (described in the case as special use permits). Does it make sense for courts to be deferential to decisions to re-zone but not to be deferential to decisions to grant (or deny) a special exception?

3. *Spot Zoning.* The court in *City of Rochester* concluded that the contested zoning amendment did not constitute spot zoning. Why? What facts would we need to change to make a stronger case for spot zoning?

CONFLICTS BETWEEN COVENANTS AND ZONING

Often a parcel of land will be subject to both restrictive covenants and zoning regulations. If a zoning law makes compliance with a covenant illegal, the zoning law will prevail. Otherwise, the more restrictive of the two will control. For example, if a covenant restricts a lot to single-family residential use and the local zoning permits multifamily residential use, the covenant will control because it is more restrictive and the land will be limited to single-family residential use. If the covenant permitted multifamily residential use, and the zoning was limited to single-family residential use, then the more restrictive zoning would control.

PROBLEMS

Explanatory answers to these problems can be found on page 1067.

1. Mountain Glade Village is a common interest community, governed by a set of recorded covenants. Mark bought one of the last remaining lots in the development and wants to build his dream getaway home. He wants to build a 5,000 square foot house. The applicable zoning code allows homes to be a maximum of 4,500 square feet. Mountain Glade Village has a covenant that permits homes of up to 5,500 square feet. Mark is upset about the problems he is having. He has sought a variance from the Zoning Board to build his house and in any event doesn't see why he should have to follow the zoning code when the covenants allow bigger houses. Will Mark be entitled to a variance?

2. Tonya is a resident of the town of Anderson. She has owned a convenience store on South Street since before Anderson's zoning code was enacted. The store is in an area zoned R1, but Tonya has been allowed to continue to operate her store. Last month, Tonya sold the convenience store to Alex. The Anderson Zoning Board of Appeals sent Alex a letter telling him that he couldn't run a convenience store on the property because it is zoned R1. Alex disagrees and asserts that he has the right to continue to operate the store. Does Alex have a right to continue to operate the convenience store?

3. Jade owns an undeveloped lot in an area zoned for single-family residential use. Jade was recently able to convince the town council to pass a zoning amendment re-zoning her lot as commercial so that she can open a convenience store. Jade's lot is surrounded by single-family homes on all sides for several blocks. The neighbors have contested the zoning amendment. What is the likely outcome?

4. Susan owns a home located on a major street in Springville. The Springville Zoning Code allows the Zoning Board to grant a permit to allow a building in the area to be used for professional office space so long as (a) the owner provides on-site parking for

four cars, (b) the owner installs a fire-safety system suitable for a commercial building, and (c) "the commercial use not be contrary to the public interest." Susan petitioned the Zoning Board for a permit. In her application, she demonstrated that she had on-site parking for four cars and had installed a commercial-grade fire-safety system. Some neighbors opposed the application on the grounds that it would increase traffic in the area. The Zoning Board denied Susan's application, finding that commercial use of the property would not be in the public interest. Susan has now sued, seeking a court order requiring the Zoning Board to issue the permit. How is the court likely to rule?

D. ZONING AND THE FIRST AMENDMENT

Zoning regulations often regulate the size and location of signs. Signs are a method of speech and expression. The zoning regulation of signs therefore can raise First Amendment concerns. Our next case involves a First Amendment challenge to a zoning ordinance that regulated size and type of signs that could be displayed by homeowners. As you read the case, note the Court's discussion of its prior cases involving the regulation of signs and note how the facts of this case differed from the facts of the prior cases.

CITY OF LADUE V. GILLEO

Supreme Court of the United States, 1994
512 U.S. 43

Justice STEVENS delivered the opinion of the Court.

An ordinance of the City of Ladue prohibits homeowners from displaying any signs on their property except "residence identification" signs, "for sale" signs, and signs warning of safety hazards. The ordinance permits commercial establishments, churches, and nonprofit organizations to erect certain signs that are not allowed at residences. The question presented is whether the ordinance violates a Ladue resident's right to free speech.[1]

---

[1] The First Amendment provides: "Congress shall make no law . . . abridging the freedom of speech, or of the press . . . ." The Fourteenth Amendment makes this limitation applicable to the States, see *Gitlow v. New York*, 268 U.S. 652, 45 S.Ct. 625, 69 L.Ed. 1138 (1925), and to their political subdivisions, see *Lovell v. City of Griffin*, 303 U.S. 444, 58 S.Ct. 666, 82 L.Ed. 949 (1938).

I

Respondent Margaret P. Gilleo owns one of the 57 single-family homes in the Willow Hill subdivision of Ladue.[2] On December 8, 1990, she placed on her front lawn a 24- by 36-inch sign printed with the words, "Say No to War in the Persian Gulf, Call Congress Now." After that sign disappeared, Gilleo put up another but it was knocked to the ground. When Gilleo reported these incidents to the police, they advised her that such signs were prohibited in Ladue. The city council denied her petition for a variance.[3] Gilleo then filed this action under 42 U.S.C. §1983 against the City, the mayor, and members of the city council, alleging that Ladue's sign ordinance violated her First Amendment right of free speech.

The District Court issued a preliminary injunction against enforcement of the ordinance. 774 F.Supp. 1559 (E.D.Mo.1991). Gilleo then placed an 8.5- by 11-inch sign in the second story window of her home stating, "For Peace in the Gulf." The Ladue City Council responded to the injunction by repealing its ordinance and enacting a replacement.[4] Like its predecessor, the new ordinance contains a general prohibition of "signs" and defines that term broadly.[5] The ordinance prohibits all signs except those that fall within 1 of 10 exemptions. Thus, "residential identification signs" no larger than one square foot are allowed, as are signs advertising "that the property is for sale, lease or exchange" and identifying the owner or agent. §35-10, App. to Pet. for Cert. 45a. Also exempted are signs "for churches, religious institutions, and schools," §35-5, *id.*, at 41a, "[c]ommercial signs in commercially zoned or industrial zoned districts,"

---

[2] Ladue is a suburb of St. Louis, Missouri. It has a population of almost 9,000, and an area of about 8.5 square miles, of which only 3% is zoned for commercial or industrial use.

[3] The ordinance then in effect gave the city council the authority to "permit a variation in the strict application of the provisions and requirements of this chapter . . . where the public interest will be best served by permitting such variation." App. 72.

[4] The new ordinance eliminates the provision allowing for variances and contains a grandfather clause exempting signs already lawfully in place.

[5] Section 35-2 of the ordinance declares that "No sign shall be erected [or] maintained" in the City except in conformity with the ordinance; §35-3 authorizes the City to remove nonconforming signs. App. to Pet. for Cert. 40a. Section 35-1 defines "sign" as:

> "A name, word, letter, writing, identification, description, or illustration which is erected, placed upon, affixed to, painted or represented upon a building or structure, or any part thereof, or in any manner upon a parcel of land or lot, and which publicizes an object, product, place, activity, opinion, person, institution, organization or place of business, or which is used to advertise or promote the interests of any person. The word 'sign' shall also include 'banners,' 'pennants,' 'insignia,' 'bulletin boards,' 'ground signs,' 'billboard,' 'poster billboards,' 'illuminated signs,' 'projecting signs,' 'temporary signs,' 'marquees,' 'roof signs,' 'yard signs,' 'electric signs,' 'wall signs,' and 'window signs,' wherever placed out of doors in view of the general public or wherever placed indoors as a window sign." *Id.*, at 39a.

§35-4, *ibid.*, and on-site signs advertising "gasoline filling stations,"[6] §35-6, *id.*, at 42a. Unlike its predecessor, the new ordinance contains a lengthy "Declaration of Findings, Policies, Interests, and Purposes," part of which recites that the

> "proliferation of an unlimited number of signs in private, residential, commercial, industrial, and public areas of the City of Ladue would create ugliness, visual blight and clutter, tarnish the natural beauty of the landscape as well as the residential and commercial architecture, impair property values, substantially impinge upon the privacy and special ambience of the community, and may cause safety and traffic hazards to motorists, pedestrians, and children." *Id.*, at 36a.

Gilleo amended her complaint to challenge the new ordinance, which explicitly prohibits window signs like hers. The District Court held the ordinance unconstitutional, 774 F.Supp. 1559 (ED Mo.1991), and the Court of Appeals affirmed, 986 F.2d 1180 (CA8 1993). Relying on the plurality opinion in *Metromedia, Inc. v. San Diego,* 453 U.S. 490, 101 S.Ct. 2882, 69 L.Ed.2d 800 (1981), the Court of Appeals held the ordinance invalid as a "content based" regulation because the City treated commercial speech more favorably than noncommercial speech and favored some kinds of noncommercial speech over others. 986 F.2d, at 1182. Acknowledging that "Ladue's interests in enacting its ordinance are substantial," the Court of Appeals nevertheless concluded that those interests were "not sufficiently 'compelling' to support a content-based restriction." *Id.*, at 1183-1184 (citing *Simon & Schuster, Inc. v. Members of N.Y. State Crime Victims Bd.,* 502 U.S. 105, 118, 112 S.Ct. 501, 509, 116 L.Ed.2d 476 (1991)).

We granted the City of Ladue's petition for certiorari, 510 U.S. 809, 114 S.Ct. 55, 126 L.Ed.2d 24 (1993), and now affirm.

II

While signs are a form of expression protected by the Free Speech Clause, they pose distinctive problems that are subject to municipalities' police powers. Unlike oral speech, signs take up space and may obstruct views, distract motorists, displace alternative uses for land, and pose other problems that legitimately call for regulation. It is common ground that governments may regulate the physical characteristics of signs—just as they can, within reasonable bounds and absent censorial purpose, regulate audible

---

[6] The full catalog of exceptions, each subject to special size limitations, is as follows: "[M]unicipal signs"; "[s]ubdivision and residence identification" signs; "[r]oad signs and driveway signs for danger, direction, or identification"; "[h]ealth inspection signs"; "[s]igns for churches, religious institutions, and schools" (subject to regulations set forth in §35-5); "identification signs" for other not-for-profit organizations; signs "identifying the location of public transportation stops"; "[g]round signs advertising the sale or rental of real property," subject to the conditions, set forth in §35-10, that such signs may "not be attached to any tree, fence or utility pole" and may contain only the fact of proposed sale or rental and the seller or agent's name and address or telephone number; "[c]ommercial signs in commercially zoned or industrial zoned districts," subject to restrictions set out elsewhere in the ordinance; and signs that "identif[y] safety hazards." §35-4, *id.*, at 41a, 45a.

expression in its capacity as noise. See, *e.g., Ward v. Rock Against Racism,* 491 U.S. 781, 109 S.Ct. 2746, 105 L.Ed.2d 661 (1989); *Kovacs v. Cooper,* 336 U.S. 77, 69 S.Ct. 448, 93 L.Ed. 513 (1949). However, because regulation of a medium inevitably affects communication itself, it is not surprising that we have had occasion to review the constitutionality of municipal ordinances prohibiting the display of certain outdoor signs.

In *Linmark Associates, Inc. v. Willingboro,* 431 U.S. 85, 97 S.Ct. 1614, 52 L.Ed.2d 155 (1977), we addressed an ordinance that sought to maintain stable, integrated neighborhoods by prohibiting homeowners from placing "For Sale" or "Sold" signs on their property. Although we recognized the importance of Willingboro's objective, we held that the First Amendment prevented the township from "achieving its goal by restricting the free flow of truthful information." *Id.,* at 95, 97 S.Ct., at 1619. In some respects *Linmark* is the mirror image of this case. For instead of prohibiting "For Sale" signs without banning any other signs, Ladue has exempted such signs from an otherwise virtually complete ban. Moreover, whereas in *Linmark* we noted that the ordinance was not concerned with the promotion of esthetic values unrelated to the content of the prohibited speech, *id.,* at 93-94, 97 S.Ct., at 1618-1619, here Ladue relies squarely on that content-neutral justification for its ordinance.

In *Metromedia,* we reviewed an ordinance imposing substantial prohibitions on outdoor advertising displays within the city of San Diego in the interest of traffic safety and esthetics. The ordinance generally banned all except those advertising "on-site" activities.[7] The Court concluded that the city's interest in traffic safety and its esthetic interest in preventing "visual clutter" could justify a prohibition of off-site commercial billboards even though similar on-site signs were allowed. 453 U.S., at 511-512, 101 S.Ct., at 2894-2895. Nevertheless, the Court's judgment in *Metromedia,* supported by two different lines of reasoning, invalidated the San Diego ordinance in its entirety. According to Justice White's plurality opinion, the ordinance impermissibly discriminated on the basis of content by permitting on-site commercial speech while broadly prohibiting noncommercial messages. *Id.,* at 514-515, 101 S.Ct., at 2896-2897. On the other hand, Justice Brennan, joined by Justice BLACKMUN, concluded that "the *practical* effect of the San Diego ordinance [was] to eliminate the billboard as an effective medium of communication" for noncommercial messages, and that the city had failed to make the strong showing needed to justify such "content-neutral prohibitions of particular media of communication." *Id.,* at 525-527, 101 S.Ct.,

---

[7] The San Diego ordinance defined "on-site signs" as "those 'designating the name of the owner or occupant of the premises upon which such signs are placed, or identifying such premises; or signs advertising goods manufactured or produced or services rendered on the premises upon which such signs are placed.'" *Metromedia, Inc. v. San Diego,* 453 U.S., at 494, 101 S.Ct., at 2885. The plurality read the "on-site" exemption of the San Diego ordinance as inapplicable to non-commercial messages. See *id.,* at 513, 101 S.Ct., at 2895. Cf. *id.,* at 535-536, 101 S.Ct., at 2906-2907 (Brennan, J., concurring in judgment). The ordinance also exempted 12 categories of displays, including religious signs; for sale signs; signs on public and commercial vehicles; and " '[t]emporary political campaign signs.'" *Id.,* at 495, n. 3, 101 S.Ct., at 2886, n. 3.

at 2902. The three dissenters also viewed San Diego's ordinance as tantamount to a blanket prohibition of billboards, but would have upheld it because they did not perceive "even a hint of bias or censorship in the city's actions" nor "any reason to believe that the overall communications market in San Diego is inadequate." *Id.,* at 552-553, 101 S.Ct., at 2915-2916 (STEVENS, J., dissenting in part). See also *id.,* at 563, 566, 101 S.Ct., at 2921, 2922-2923 (BURGER, C.J., dissenting); *id.,* at 569-570, 101 S.Ct., at 2924-2925 (REHNQUIST, J., dissenting).

In *Members of City Council of Los Angeles v. Taxpayers for Vincent,* 466 U.S. 789, 104 S.Ct. 2118, 80 L.Ed.2d 772 (1984), we upheld a Los Angeles ordinance that prohibited the posting of signs on public property. Noting the conclusion shared by seven Justices in *Metromedia* that San Diego's "interest in avoiding visual clutter" was sufficient to justify a prohibition of commercial billboards, 466 U.S., at 806-807, 104 S.Ct., at 2130 in *Vincent* we upheld the Los Angeles ordinance, which was justified on the same grounds. We rejected the argument that the validity of the city's esthetic interest had been compromised by failing to extend the ban to private property, reasoning that the "private citizen's interest in controlling the use of his own property justifies the disparate treatment." *Id.,* at 811, 104 S.Ct., at 2132. We also rejected as "misplaced" respondents' reliance on public forum principles, for they had "fail[ed] to demonstrate the existence of a traditional right of access respecting such items as utility poles . . . comparable to that recognized for public streets and parks." *Id.,* at 814, 104 S.Ct., at 2133.

These decisions identify two analytically distinct grounds for challenging the constitutionality of a municipal ordinance regulating the display of signs. One is that the measure in effect restricts too little speech because its exemptions discriminate on the basis of the signs' messages. See *Metromedia,* 453 U.S., at 512-517, 101 S.Ct., at 2895-2897 (opinion of WHITE, J.). Alternatively, such provisions are subject to attack on the ground that they simply prohibit too much protected speech. See *id.,* at 525-534, 101 S.Ct., at 2901-2906 (BRENNAN, J., concurring in judgment). The City of Ladue contends, first, that the Court of Appeals' reliance on the former rationale was misplaced because the City's regulatory purposes are content neutral, and, second, that those purposes justify the comprehensiveness of the sign prohibition. A comment on the former contention will help explain why we ultimately base our decision on a rejection of the latter.

III

While surprising at first glance, the notion that a regulation of speech may be impermissibly *underinclusive* is firmly grounded in basic First Amendment principles. Thus, an exemption from an otherwise permissible regulation of speech may represent a governmental "attempt to give one side of a debatable public question an advantage in expressing its views to the people." *First Nat. Bank of Boston v. Bellotti,* 435 U.S. 765, 785-786, 98 S.Ct. 1407, 1420-1421, 55 L.Ed.2d 707 (1978). Alternatively, through the combined operation of a general speech restriction and its exemptions, the government might seek to select the "permissible subjects for public debate" and thereby to "control . . . the search for political truth." *Consolidated Edison Co. of N.Y. v. Public Serv. Comm'n of N.Y.,* 447 U.S. 530, 538, 100 S.Ct. 2326, 2333, 65 L.Ed.2d 319 (1980).

The City argues that its sign ordinance implicates neither of these concerns, and that the Court of Appeals therefore erred in demanding a "compelling" justification for the exemptions. The mix of prohibitions and exemptions in the ordinance, Ladue maintains, reflects legitimate differences among the side effects of various kinds of signs. These differences are only adventitiously connected with content, and supply a sufficient justification, unrelated to the City's approval or disapproval of specific messages, for carving out the specified categories from the general ban. See Brief for Petitioners 18-23. Thus, according to the Declaration of Findings, Policies, Interests, and Purposes supporting the ordinance, the permitted signs, unlike the prohibited signs, are unlikely to contribute to the dangers of "unlimited proliferation" associated with categories of signs that are not inherently limited in number. App. to Pet. for Cert. 37a. Because only a few residents will need to display "for sale" or "for rent" signs at any given time, permitting one such sign per marketed house does not threaten visual clutter. *Ibid.* Because the City has only a few businesses, churches, and schools, the same rationale explains the exemption for on-site commercial and organizational signs. *Ibid.* Moreover, some of the exempted categories (*e.g.*, danger signs) respond to unique public needs to permit certain kinds of speech. *Ibid.* Even if we assume the validity of these arguments, the exemptions in Ladue's ordinance nevertheless shed light on the separate question whether the ordinance prohibits too much speech.

Exemptions from an otherwise legitimate regulation of a medium of speech may be noteworthy for a reason quite apart from the risks of viewpoint and content discrimination: They may diminish the credibility of the government's rationale for restricting speech in the first place. See, *e.g., Cincinnati v. Discovery Network, Inc.,* 507 U.S. 410, 424-426, 113 S.Ct. 1505, 1514-1515, 123 L.Ed.2d 99 (1993). In this case, at the very least, the exemptions from Ladue's ordinance demonstrate that Ladue has concluded that the interest in allowing certain messages to be conveyed by means of residential signs outweighs the City's esthetic interest in eliminating outdoor signs. Ladue has not imposed a flat ban on signs because it has determined that at least some of them are too vital to be banned.

Under the Court of Appeals' content discrimination rationale, the City might theoretically remove the defects in its ordinance by simply repealing all of the exemptions. If, however, the ordinance is also vulnerable because it prohibits too much speech, that solution would not save it. Moreover, if the prohibitions in Ladue's ordinance are impermissible, resting our decision on its exemptions would afford scant relief for respondent Gilleo. She is primarily concerned not with the scope of the exemptions available in other locations, such as commercial areas and on church property; she asserts a constitutional right to display an antiwar sign at her own home.

Therefore, we first ask whether Ladue may properly *prohibit* Gilleo from displaying her sign, and then, only if necessary, consider the separate question whether it was improper for the City simultaneously to *permit* certain other signs. In examining the propriety of Ladue's near-total prohibition of residential signs, we will assume, *arguendo,* the validity of the City's submission that the various exemptions are free of impermissible content or viewpoint discrimination.

IV

In *Linmark* we held that the city's interest in maintaining a stable, racially integrated neighborhood was not sufficient to support a prohibition of residential "For Sale" signs. We recognized that even such a narrow sign prohibition would have a deleterious effect on residents' ability to convey important information because alternatives were "far from satisfactory." 431 U.S., at 93, 97 S.Ct., at 1618. Ladue's sign ordinance is supported principally by the City's interest in minimizing the visual clutter associated with signs, an interest that is concededly valid but certainly no more compelling than the interests at stake in *Linmark.* Moreover, whereas the ordinance in *Linmark* applied only to a form of commercial speech, Ladue's ordinance covers even such absolutely pivotal speech as a sign protesting an imminent governmental decision to go to war.

The impact on free communication of Ladue's broad sign prohibition, moreover, is manifestly greater than in *Linmark.* Gilleo and other residents of Ladue are forbidden to display virtually any "sign" on their property. The ordinance defines that term sweepingly. A prohibition is not always invalid merely because it applies to a sizeable category of speech; the sign ban we upheld in *Vincent,* for example, was quite broad. But in *Vincent* we specifically noted that the category of speech in question-signs placed on public property-was not a "uniquely valuable or important mode of communication," and that there was no evidence that "appellees' ability to communicate effectively is threatened by ever-increasing restrictions on expression." 466 U.S., at 812, 104 S.Ct., at 2133.

Here, in contrast, Ladue has almost completely foreclosed a venerable means of communication that is both unique and important. It has totally foreclosed that medium to political, religious, or personal messages. Signs that react to a local happening or express a view on a controversial issue both reflect and animate change in the life of a community. Often placed on lawns or in windows, residential signs play an important part in political campaigns, during which they are displayed to signal the resident's support for particular candidates, parties, or causes.[12] They may not afford the same opportunities for conveying complex ideas as do other media, but residential signs have long been an important and distinct medium of expression.

---

[12] "[S]mall [political campaign] posters have maximum effect when they go up in the windows of homes, for this demonstrates that citizens of the district are supporting your candidate—an impact that money can't buy." D. Simpson, Winning Elections: A Handbook in Participatory Politics 87 (rev. ed. 1981).

Our prior decisions have voiced particular concern with laws that foreclose an entire medium of expression. Thus, we have held invalid ordinances that completely banned the distribution of pamphlets within the municipality, *Lovell v. City of Griffin,* 303 U.S. 444, 451-452, 58 S.Ct. 666, 669, 82 L.Ed. 949 (1938); handbills on the public streets, *Jamison v. Texas,* 318 U.S. 413, 416, 63 S.Ct. 669, 672, 87 L.Ed. 869 (1943); the door-to-door distribution of literature, *Martin v. City of Struthers,* 319 U.S. 141, 145-149, 63 S.Ct. 862, 864-866, 87 L.Ed. 1313 (1943); *Schneider v. State (Town of Irvington),* 308 U.S. 147, 164-165, 60 S.Ct. 146, 152, 84 L.Ed. 155 (1939), and live entertainment, *Schad v. Mount Ephraim,* 452 U.S. 61, 75-76, 101 S.Ct. 2176, 2186, 68 L.Ed.2d 671 (1981). See also *Frisby v. Schultz,* 487 U.S. 474, 486, 108 S.Ct. 2495, 2503, 101 L.Ed.2d 420 (1988) (picketing focused upon individual residence is "fundamentally different from more generally directed means of communication that may not be completely banned in residential areas"). Although prohibitions foreclosing entire media may be completely free of content or viewpoint discrimination, the danger they pose to the freedom of speech is readily apparent—by eliminating a common means of speaking, such measures can suppress too much speech.

Ladue contends, however, that its ordinance is a mere regulation of the "time, place, or manner" of speech because residents remain free to convey their desired messages by other means, such as *hand-held* signs, "letters, handbills, flyers, telephone calls, newspaper advertisements, bumper stickers, speeches, and neighborhood or community meetings." Brief for Petitioners 41. However, even regulations that do not foreclose an entire medium of expression, but merely shift the time, place, or manner of its use, must "leave open ample alternative channels for communication." *Clark v. Community for Creative Non-Violence,* 468 U.S. 288, 293, 104 S.Ct. 3065, 3069, 82 L.Ed.2d 221 (1984). In this case, we are not persuaded that adequate substitutes exist for the important medium of speech that Ladue has closed off.

Displaying a sign from one's own residence often carries a message quite distinct from placing the same sign someplace else, or conveying the same text or picture by other means. Precisely because of their location, such signs provide information about the identity of the "speaker." As an early and eminent student of rhetoric observed, the identity of the speaker is an important component of many attempts to persuade.[14] A sign advocating "Peace in the Gulf" in the front lawn of a retired general or decorated war veteran may provoke a different reaction than the same sign in a 10-year-old child's bedroom window or the same message on a bumper sticker of a passing automobile. An espousal of socialism may carry different implications when displayed on the grounds of a stately mansion than when pasted on a factory wall or an ambulatory sandwich board.

---

[14] See Aristotle 2, Rhetoric, Book 1, ch. 2, in 8 Great Books of the Western World, Encyclopedia Brittanica 595 (M. Adler ed., 2d ed. 1990) ("We believe good men more fully and more readily than others: this is true generally whatever the question is, and absolutely true where exact certainty is impossible and opinions are divided").

Residential signs are an unusually cheap and convenient form of communication. Especially for persons of modest means or limited mobility, a yard or window sign may have no practical substitute. Cf. *Vincent,* 466 U.S., at 812-813, n. 30, 104 S.Ct., at 2132-2133, n. 30; *Anderson v. Celebrezze,* 460 U.S. 780, 793-794, 103 S.Ct. 1564, 1572-1573, 75 L.Ed.2d 547 (1983); *Martin v. City of Struthers,* 319 U.S., at 146, 63 S.Ct., at 865; *Milk Wagon Drivers v. Meadowmoor Dairies, Inc.,* 312 U.S. 287, 293, 61 S.Ct. 552, 555, 85 L.Ed. 836 (1941). Even for the affluent, the added costs in money or time of taking out a newspaper advertisement, handing out leaflets on the street, or standing in front of one's house with a handheld sign may make the difference between participating and not participating in some public debate.[15] Furthermore, a person who puts up a sign at her residence often intends to reach *neighbors,* an audience that could not be reached nearly as well by other means.

A special respect for individual liberty in the home has long been part of our culture and our law, see, *e.g., Payton v. New York,* 445 U.S. 573, 596-597, and nn. 44-45, 100 S.Ct. 1371, 1385-1386, and nn. 44-45, 63 L.Ed.2d 639 (1980); that principle has special resonance when the government seeks to constrain a person's ability to *speak* there. See *Spence v. Washington,* 418 U.S. 405, 406, 409, 411, 94 S.Ct. 2727, 2728, 2729-2730, 41 L.Ed.2d 842 (1974) (*per curiam*). Most Americans would be understandably dismayed, given that tradition, to learn that it was illegal to display from their window an 8- by 11-inch sign expressing their political views. Whereas the government's need to mediate among various competing uses, including expressive ones, for public streets and facilities is constant and unavoidable, see *Cox v. New Hampshire,* 312 U.S. 569, 574, 576, 61 S.Ct. 762, 765, 765, 85 L.Ed. 1049 (1941); see also *Widmar v. Vincent,* 454 U.S. 263, 278, 102 S.Ct. 269, 278-279, 70 L.Ed.2d 440 (1981) (STEVENS, J., concurring in judgment), its need to regulate temperate speech from the home is surely much less pressing, see *Spence,* 418 U.S., at 409, 94 S.Ct., at 2729-2730.

Our decision that Ladue's ban on almost all residential signs violates the First Amendment by no means leaves the City powerless to address the ills that may be associated with residential signs.[17] It bears mentioning that individual residents themselves have strong incentives to keep their own property values up and to prevent "visual clutter" in their own yards and neighborhoods—incentives markedly different from those of persons who erect signs on others' land, in others' neighborhoods, or

---

[15] The precise location of many other kinds of signs (aside from "on-site" signs) is of lesser communicative importance. For example, assuming the audience is similar, a commercial advertiser or campaign publicist is likely to be relatively indifferent between one sign site and another. The elimination of a cheap and handy medium of expression is especially apt to deter *individuals* from communicating their views to the public, for unlike businesses (and even political organizations) individuals generally realize few tangible benefits from such communication. Cf. *Virginia Bd. of Pharmacy v. Virginia Citizens Consumer Council, Inc.,* 425 U.S. 748, 772, n. 24, 96 S.Ct. 1817, 1831, n. 24, 48 L.Ed.2d 346 (1976) ("Since advertising is the *sine qua non* of commercial profits, there is little likelihood of its being chilled by proper regulation and forgone entirely").

[17] Nor do we hold that every kind of sign must be permitted in residential areas. Different considerations might well apply, for example, in the case of signs (whether political or otherwise) displayed by residents for a fee, or in the case of off-site commercial advertisements on residential property. We also are not confronted here with mere regulations short of a ban.

on public property. Residents' self-interest diminishes the danger of the "unlimited" proliferation of residential signs that concerns the City of Ladue. We are confident that more temperate measures could in large part satisfy Ladue's stated regulatory needs without harm to the First Amendment rights of its citizens. As currently framed, however, the ordinance abridges those rights.

Accordingly, the judgment of the Court of Appeals is

Affirmed.

NOTES AND QUESTIONS

1. *Restricting Too Much Speech and Regulating Too Little Speech.* The Supreme Court held that the City of Ladue ordinance was unconstitutional because it restricted both too much speech and too little speech. Why, exactly, did the ordinance restrict too much and too little speech?

2. *Time, Place, and Manner.* Governments are permitted to impose reasonable time, place, and manner restrictions on speech. Many zoning regulations of signs fall into the category of reasonable time, place, and manner restrictions. Why did the Ladue ordinance not fall into this category?

3. *Common Interest Community Restrictions Compared.* The First Amendment and other provisions of the Bill of Rights only apply to government actors and not to private actors like common interest communities. As a result, a common interest community may impose a restriction on signs that would violate the First Amendment if imposed through a zoning regulation. A court might rule that overly restrictive common interest community restrictions were unreasonable or violated public policy, but as a general matter, common interest communities will be given more latitude than municipalities to restrict signs.

ZONING OF ADULT ENTERTAINMENT

The zoning of adult theaters, stores, and clubs can raise some First Amendment issues. The Supreme Court has permitted two distinct strategies that municipalities can use to zone adult uses. Under the first strategy, the municipality *disperses* the adult uses by requiring a set distance between those uses. The aim of dispersal zoning is to avoid a concentration of adult uses and the creation of a red light district. The dispersal strategy was approved by the Supreme Court in *Young v. American Mini Theaters, Inc.*, 427 U.S. 50 (1976). The second strategy *concentrates* adult uses by limiting them to a specific part of the municipality. The concentration strategy was approved in *City of Renton v. Playtime Theatres, Inc.*, 475 U.S. 41 (1986).

AESTHETIC ZONING

Prior to the 1950s, courts were skeptical of zoning provisions aimed at regulating the aesthetics of the community. Since then, aesthetic zoning regulations have gained widespread acceptance. As a result, municipalities can use zoning laws to impose design standards on development. In the zoning context, these standards need to be clear, and courts will sometimes step in to protect property owners from poorly drafted standards or seemingly arbitrary enforcement of those standards. *See, e.g., Anderson v. City of Issaquah*, 851 P.2d 744 (Wash. Ct. App. 1993).

E. DEFINING "FAMILY" IN THE ZONING CONTEXT

Many municipal zoning ordinances contain definitions of "family." Often, these definitions have two parts. The first part defines family as a group of people related by blood, adoption, or marriage living together. The second part defines family as a limited group of unrelated people living together. Typically, this second part of the definition places a fixed cap on the number of unrelated people living together that may constitute a family. Our next case, for example, involves an ordinance with a definition of family that is limited to two or more unrelated people living together. As a result, three unrelated people living together would not constitute a family within the meaning of the ordinance. Ten people living together but related by blood, adoption, or marriage—for example, a married couple with eight children—would constitute a family.

Our next case involves a constitutional challenge to this type of definition of family. In many contexts, the outcome of a constitutional challenge will turn on the level of scrutiny that a court applies to the statute. If the court applies a low level of scrutiny, the challenge to the statute will likely fail. If the court applies a high level of scrutiny, the challenge to the statute has a better likelihood of success. We leave a detailed discussion of these topics to your Constitutional Law class, and simply point out here that many of our cases turn on the level of scrutiny that the court applies in a given constitutional context to challenges to land use regulations. In *Ladue v. Gilleo*, for example, we saw the Court apply a high level of scrutiny to municipal regulations of political speech.

In our next case, *Belle Terre v. Boraas*, we will see the Court apply a low level of scrutiny and take a deferential approach to the definition of "family." In the following case, *Moore v. East Cleveland*, we will see the Court apply a high level of scrutiny to a definition of "family." As you read the cases, notice not only the Court's stated reasons for applying more or less scrutiny but also how the ordinances fare under the different levels of scrutiny.

VILLAGE OF BELLE TERRE V. BORAAS

Supreme Court of the United States, 1974
416 U.S. 1

Mr. Justice Douglas delivered the opinion of the Court.

Belle Terre is a village on Long Island's north shore of about 220 homes inhabited by 700 people. Its total land area is less than one square mile. It has restricted land use to one-family dwellings excluding lodging houses, boarding houses, fraternity houses, or multiple-dwelling houses. The word "family" as used in the ordinance means, "(o)ne or more persons related by blood, adoption, or marriage, living and cooking together as a single housekeeping unit, exclusive of household servants. A number of persons but not exceeding two (2) living and cooking together as a single housekeeping unit through not related by blood, adoption, or marriage shall be deemed to constitute a family."

Appellees, the Dickmans, are owners of a house in the village and leased it in December 1971 for a term of 18 months to Michael Truman. Later Bruce Boraas became a colessee. Then Anne Parish moved into the house along with three others. These six are students at nearby State University at Stony Brook and none is related to the other by blood, adoption, or marriage. When the village served the Dickmans with an "Order to Remedy Violations" of the ordinance, the owners plus three tenants thereupon brought this action under 42 U.S.C. §1983 for an injunction and a judgment declaring the ordinance unconstitutional. The District Court held the ordinance constitutional, 367 F.Supp. 136, and the Court of Appeals reversed, one judge dissenting. 2 Cir., 476 F.2d 806. The case is here by appeal, 28 U.S.C. §1254(2); and we noted probable jurisdiction, 414 U.S. 907, 94 S.Ct. 234, 38 L.Ed.2d 145. . . .

The present ordinance is challenged on several grounds: that it interferes with a person's right to travel; that it interferes with the right to migrate to and settle within a State; that it bars people who are uncongenial to the present residents; that it expresses the social preferences of the residents for groups that will be congenial to them; that social homogeneity is not a legitimate interest of government; that the restriction of those whom the neighbors do not like trenches on the newcomers' rights of privacy; that it is of no rightful concern to villagers whether the residents are married or unmarried; that the ordinance is antithetical to the Nation's experience, ideology, and self-perception as an open, egalitarian, and integrated society.

We find none of these reasons in the record before us. It is not aimed at transients. Cf. *Shapiro v. Thompson*, 394 U.S. 618, 89 S.Ct. 1322, 22 L.Ed.2d 600. It involves no procedural disparity inflicted on some but not on others such as was presented by *Griffin v. Illinois*, 351 U.S. 12, 76 S.Ct. 585, 100 L.Ed. 891. It involves no "fundamental" right guaranteed by the Constitution, such as voting, *Harper v. Virginia State Board*, 383 U.S. 663, 86 S.Ct. 1079, 16 L.Ed.2d 169; the right of association, *NAACP v. Alabama ex rel. Patterson*, 357 U.S. 449, 78 S.Ct. 1163, 2 L.Ed.2d 1488; the right of access to the courts,

NAACP v. Button, 371 U.S. 415, 83 S.Ct. 328, 9 L.Ed.2d 405; or any rights of privacy, cf. *Griswold v. Connecticut,* 381 U.S. 479, 85 S.Ct. 1678, 14 L.Ed.2d 510; *Eisenstadt v. Baird,* 405 U.S. 438, 453-454, 92 S.Ct. 1029, 1038-1039, 31 L.Ed.2d 349. We deal with economic and social legislation where legislatures have historically drawn lines which we respect against the charge of violation of the Equal Protection Clause if the law be "reasonable, not arbitrary" (quoting *F. S. Royster Guano Co. v. Virginia,* 253 U.S. 412, 415, 40 S.Ct. 560, 561, 64 L.Ed. 989) and bears "a rational relationship to a (permissible) state objective." *Reed v. Reed,* 404 U.S. 71, 76, 92 S.Ct. 251, 254, 30 L.Ed.2d 225.

It is said, however, that if two unmarried people can constitute a "family," there is no reason why three or four may not. But every line drawn by a legislature leaves some out that might well have been included. That exercise of discretion, however, is a legislative, not a judicial, function.

It is said that the Belle Terre ordinance reeks with an animosity to unmarried couples who live together. There is no evidence to support it; and the provision of the ordinance bringing within the definition of a "family" two unmarried people belies the charge.

The ordinance places no ban on other forms of association, for a "family" may, so far as the ordinance is concerned, entertain whomever it likes.

The regimes of boarding houses, fraternity houses, and the like present urban problems. More people occupy a given space; more cars rather continuously pass by; more cars are parked; noise travels with crowds.

A quiet place where yards are wide, people few, and motor vehicles restricted are legitimate guidelines in a land-use project addressed to family needs. This goal is a permissible one within *Berman v. Parker, supra.* The police power is not confined to elimination of filth, stench, and unhealthy places. It is ample to lay out zones where family values, youth values, and the blessings of quiet seclusion and clean air make the area a sanctuary for people. . . .

Reversed.

[The dissenting opinion of Justice Brennan is omitted]

Mr. Justice MARSHALL, dissenting.

This case draws into question the constitutionality of a zoning ordinance of the incorporated village of Belle Terre, New York, which prohibits groups of more than two unrelated persons, as distinguished from groups consisting of any number of persons related by blood, adoption, or marriage, from occupying a residence within the confines of the township. Lessor-appellees, the two owners of a Belle Terre residence, and three unrelated student tenants challenged the ordinance on the ground that it establishes a classification between households of related and unrelated individuals, which deprives them of equal protection of the laws. In my view, the disputed classification burdens the students' fundamental rights of association and privacy guaranteed by the First and Fourteenth Amendments. Because the application of strict equal protection scrutiny is therefore required, I am at odds with my Brethren's conclusion that the ordinance may be sustained on a showing that it bears a rational relationship to the accomplishment of legitimate governmental objectives.

I am in full agreement with the majority that zoning is a complex and important function of the State. It may indeed be the most essential function performed by local government, for it is one of the primary means by which we protect that sometimes difficult to define concept of quality of life. I therefore continue to adhere to the principle of *Village of Euclid v. Ambler Realty Co.,* 272 U.S. 365, 47 S.Ct. 114, 71 L.Ed. 303 (1926), that deference should be given to governmental judgments concerning proper land-use allocation. That deference is a principle which has served this Court well and which is necessary for the continued development of effective zoning and land-use control mechanisms. Had the owners alone brought this suit alleging that the restrictive ordinance deprived them of their property or was an irrational legislative classification, I would agree that the ordinance would have to be sustained. Our role is not and should not be to sit as a zoning board of appeals.

I would also agree with the majority that local zoning authorities may properly act in furtherance of the objectives asserted to be served by the ordinance at issue here: restricting uncontrolled growth, solving traffic problems, keeping rental costs at a reasonable level, and making the community attractive to families. The police power which provides the justification for zoning is not narrowly confined. See *Berman v. Parker,* 348 U.S. 26, 75 S.Ct. 98, 99 L.Ed. 27 (1954). And, it is appropriate that we afford zoning authorities considerable latitude in choosing the means by which to implement such purposes. But deference does not mean abdication. This Court has an obligation to ensure that zoning ordinances, even when adopted in furtherance of such legitimate aims, do not infringe upon fundamental constitutional rights.

When separate but equal was still accepted constitutional dogma, this Court struck down a racially restrictive zoning ordinance. *Buchanan v. Warley,* 245 U.S. 60, 38 S.Ct. 16, 62 L.Ed. 149 (1917). I am sure the Court would not be hesitant to invalidate that ordinance today. The lower federal courts have considered procedural aspects of zoning, and acted to insure that land-use controls are not used as means of confining minorities and the poor to the ghettos of our central cities. These are limited but necessary intrusions on the discretion of zoning authorities. By the same token, I think it clear that the First Amendment provides some limitation on zoning laws. It is inconceivable to me that we would allow the exercise of the zoning power to burden First Amendment freedoms, as by ordinances that restrict occupancy to individuals adhering to particular religious, political, or scientific beliefs. Zoning officials properly concern themselves with the uses of land—with, for example, the number and kind of dwellings to be constructed in a certain neighborhood or the number of persons who can reside in those dwellings. But zoning authorities cannot validly consider who those persons are, what they believe, or how they choose to live, whether they are Negro or white, Catholic or Jew, Republican or Democrat, married or unmarried.

My disagreement with the Court today is based upon my view that the ordinance in this case unnecessarily burdens appellees' First Amendment freedom of association and their constitutionally guaranteed right to privacy. Our decisions establish that the First and Fourteenth Amendments protect the freedom to choose one's associates. *NAACP v. Button,* 371 U.S. 415, 430, 83 S.Ct. 328, 336, 9 L.Ed.2d 405 (1963). Constitutional protection is extended, not only to modes of association that are political in the usual sense, but also to those that pertain to the social and economic benefit of the members. Id., at 430-431, 83 S.Ct., at 336-337 . . . The selection of one's living companions involves similar choices as to the emotional, social, or economic benefits to be derived from alternative living arrangements.

The freedom of association is often inextricably entwined with the constitutionally guaranteed right of privacy. The right to "establish a home" is an essential part of the liberty guaranteed by the Fourteenth Amendment. *Meyer v. Nebraska,* 262 U.S. 390, 399, 43 S.Ct. 625, 626, 67 L.Ed. 1042 (1923); *Griswold v. Connecticut,* 381 U.S. 479, 495, 85 S.Ct. 1678, 1687, 14 L.Ed.2d 510 (1965) (Goldberg, J., concurring). And the Constitution secures to an individual a freedom "to satisfy his intellectual and emotional needs in the privacy of his own home." *Stanley v. Georgia,* 394 U.S. 557, 565, 89 S.Ct. 1243, 1248, 22 L.Ed.2d 542 (1969); see *Paris Adult Theatre I v. Slaton,* 413 U.S. 49, 66-67, 93 S.Ct. 2628, 2640-2641, 37 L.Ed.2d 446 (1973). Constitutionally protected privacy is, in Mr. Justice Brandeis' words, "as against the Government, the right to be let alone . . . the right most valued by civilized man." *Olmstead v. United States,* 277 U.S. 438, 478, 48 S.Ct. 564, 572, 72 L.Ed. 944 (1928) (dissenting opinion). The choice of household companions—of whether a person's "intellectual and emotional needs" are best met by living with family, friends, professional associates, or others— involves deeply personal considerations as to the kind and quality of intimate relationships within the home. That decision surely falls within the ambit of the right to privacy protected by the Constitution. See *Roe v. Wade,* 410 U.S. 113, 153, 93 S.Ct. 705, 727, 35 L.Ed.2d 147 (1973); *Eisenstadt v. Baird,* 405 U.S. 438, 453, 92 S.Ct. 1029, 1038, 31 L.Ed.2d 349 (1972); *Stanley v. Georgia, supra,* 394 U.S., at 564-565, 89 S.Ct., at 1247-1248; *Griswold v. Connecticut, supra,* 381 U.S., at 483, 486, 85 S.Ct., at 1682; *Olmstead v. United States, supra,* 277 U.S., at 478, 48 S.Ct., at 572 (Brandeis, J., dissenting); *Moreno v. Department of Agriculture,* 345 F.Supp. 310, 315 (D.C.1972), aff'd, 413 U.S. 528, 93 S.Ct. 2821, 37 L.Ed.2d 782 (1973).

The instant ordinance discriminates on the basis of just such a personal lifestyle choice as to household companions. It permits any number of persons related by blood or marriage, be it two or twenty, to live in a single household, but it limits to two the number of unrelated persons bound by profession, love, friendship, religious or political affiliation, or mere economics who can occupy a single home. Belle Terre imposes upon those who deviate from the community norm in their choice of living companions significantly greater restrictions than are applied to residential groups who are related by blood or marriage, and compose the established order within the community. The village has, in effect, acted to fence out those individuals whose choice of lifestyle differs from that of its current residents.

This is not a case where the Court is being asked to nullify a township's sincere efforts to maintain its residential character by preventing the operation of rooming houses, fraternity houses, or other commercial or high-density residential uses. Unquestionably, a town is free to restrict such uses. Moreover, as a general proposition, I see no constitutional infirmity in a town's limiting the density of use in residential areas by zoning regulations which do not discriminate on the basis of constitutionally suspect criteria. This ordinance, however, limits the density of occupancy of only those homes occupied by unrelated persons. It thus reaches beyond control of the use of land or the density of population, and undertakes to regulate the way people choose to associate with each other within the privacy of their own homes. . . .

Because I believe that this zoning ordinance creates a classification which impinges upon fundamental personal rights, it can withstand constitutional scrutiny only upon a clear showing that the burden imposed is necessary to protect a compelling and substantial governmental interest, *Shapiro v. Thompson,* 394 U.S. 618, 634, 89 S.Ct. 1322, 1331, 22 L.Ed.2d 600 (1969). And, once it be determined that a burden has been placed upon a constitutional right, the onus of demonstrating that no less intrusive means will adequately protect the compelling state interest and that the challenged statute is sufficiently narrowly drawn, is upon the party seeking to justify the burden. See *Memorial Hospital v. Maricopa County,* 415 U.S. 250, 94 S.Ct. 1076, 39 L.Ed.2d 306 (1974); *Speiser v. Randall,* 357 U.S. 513, 525-526, 78 S.Ct. 1332, 1341-1342, 2 L.Ed.2d 1460 (1958).

A variety of justifications have been proffered in support of the village's ordinance. It is claimed that the ordinance controls population density, prevents noise, traffic and parking problems, and preserves the rent structure of the community and its attractiveness to families. As I noted earlier, these are all legitimate and substantial interests of government. But I think it clear that the means chosen to accomplish these purposes are both overinclusive and underinclusive, and that the asserted goals could be as effectively achieved by means of an ordinance that did not discriminate on the basis of constitutionally protected choices of lifestyle. The ordinance imposes no restriction whatsoever on the number of persons who may live in a house, as long as they are related by marital or sanguinary bonds—presumably no matter how distant their relationship. Nor does the ordinance restrict the number of income earners who may contribute to rent in such a household, or the number of automobiles that may be maintained by its occupants. In that sense the ordinance is underinclusive. On the other hand, the statute restricts the number of unrelated persons who may live in a home to no more than two. It would therefore prevent three unrelated people from occupying a dwelling even if among them they had but one income and no vehicles. While an extended family of a dozen or more might live in a small bungalow, three elderly and retired persons could not occupy the large manor house next door. Thus the statute is also grossly overinclusive to accomplish its intended purposes.

There are some 220 residences in Belle Terre occupied by about 700 persons. The density is therefore just above three per household. The village is justifiably concerned with density of population and the related problems of noise, traffic, and the like. It could deal with those problems by limiting each household to a specified number of adults, two or three perhaps, without limitation on the number of dependent children. The burden of such an ordinance would fall equally upon all segments of the community. It would surely be better tailored to the goals asserted by the village than the ordinance before us today, for it would more realistically restrict population density and growth and their attendant environmental costs. Various other statutory mechanisms also suggest themselves as solutions to Belle Terre's problems—rent control, limits on the number of vehicles per household, and so forth, but, of course, such schemes are matters of legislative judgment and not for this Court. Appellants also refer to the necessity of maintaining the family character of the village. There is not a shred of evidence in the record indicating that if Belle Terre permitted a limited number of unrelated persons to live together, the residential, familial character of the community would be fundamentally affected.

By limiting unrelated households to two persons while placing no limitation on households of related individuals, the village has embarked upon its commendable course in a constitutionally faulty vessel. Cf. *Marshall v. United States*, 414 U.S. 417, 94 S.Ct. 700, 38 L.Ed.2d 618 (1974) (dissenting opinion). I would find the challenged ordinance

EXCLUSIONARY ZONING

Municipalities can use zoning laws to exclude certain types of people from the community as a whole or from certain parts of the community. *Belle Terre* provides an example where the municipality used its zoning law to try to keep out college students. Another example is the strategy taken by Mount Laurel, New Jersey, which dramatically restricted the amount of land in the township that could be used for residential purposes and restricted the development of multifamily housing. This strategy excluded low- and middle-income people from the community. The New Jersey Supreme Court held that this strategy of exclusionary zoning violated the New Jersey Constitution. *Southern Burlington County NAACP v. Township of Mount Laurel*, 336 A.2d 713 (N.J. 1975); *Southern Burlington County NAACP v. Township of Mount Laurel*, 456 A.2d 390 (N.J. 1983). Most states have not followed the New Jersey Supreme Court's lead in policing exclusionary zoning. Even in New Jersey, exclusionary zoning has been hard to eliminate in practice. *See* James E. McGuire, *The Judiciary's Role in Implementing the Mount Laurel Doctrine: Deference or Activism?*, 23 Seton Hall L. Rev. 1276 (1993); Paula A. Franzese, *Mount Laurel III: The New Jersey Supreme Court's Judicious Retreat*, 18 Seton Hall L. Rev. 30 (1988).

unconstitutional. But I would not ask the village to abandon its goal of providing quiet streets, little traffic, and a pleasant and reasonably priced environment in which families might raise their children. Rather, I would commend the village to continue to pursue those purposes but by means of more carefully drawn and even-handed legislation.

I respectfully dissent.

NOTES AND QUESTIONS

1. *Anti-College-Student Ordinances.* Municipalities adopt definitions of family for various reasons. Belle Terre, like many college towns, adopted its definition of family to keep local college students out of areas occupied by traditional families. Having been a college student yourself, what are the arguments for and against these types of ordinances?

2. *Freedom of Association.* In dissent, Justice Marshall argued that the Belle Terre ordinance should be given heightened scrutiny in part because it impinged on the right of free association protected by the First Amendment. The nuances of free association law are beyond the scope of this book, but as a practical matter, do you agree with Justice Marshall that the ordinance negatively impacted the ability of people to freely associate with others? Justice Marshall also references the right to privacy, a complex and fraught area of constitutional law. Again using general principles, do you agree with Justice Marshall that the Belle Terre ordinance negatively impacted the privacy of residents?

The rule in *Belle Terre* is straightforward: Land use ordinances that define family in a way that restricts the number of unrelated people who can live together do not violate the Constitution. Our next case, *Moore v. East Cleveland*, involves a land use ordinance that restricted the number of *related* people who could live together. As we will see, a highly divided Supreme Court held that this statute was unconstitutional. The Court historically has given strong protection to familial choices under the doctrine of substantive due process, and *Moore* can be seen as part of this larger body of case law.

MOORE V. CITY OF EAST CLEVELAND

Supreme Court of the United States, 1977
431 U.S. 494

[The following is a plurality opinion authored by Justice Powell. The justices issued a total of six opinions in this case—Justice Powell's plurality, concurrences by Justice Brennan and Justice Stevens, and dissents by Chief Justice Burger, Justice Stewart, and Justice White.]

East Cleveland's housing ordinance, like many throughout the country, limits occupancy of a dwelling unit to members of a single family. §1351.02. But the ordinance contains an unusual and complicated definitional section that recognizes as a "family" only a few categories of related individuals, §1341.08.[2] Because her family, living together in her home, fits none of those categories, appellant stands convicted of a criminal offense. The question in this case is whether the ordinance violates the Due Process Clause of the Fourteenth Amendment.

I

Appellant, Mrs. Inez Moore, lives in her East Cleveland home together with her son, Dale Moore Sr., and her two grandsons, Dale, Jr., and John Moore, Jr. The two boys are first cousins rather than brothers; we are told that John came to live with his grandmother and with the elder and younger Dale Moores after his mother's death.

In early 1973, Mrs. Moore received a notice of violation from the city, stating that John was an "illegal occupant" and directing her to comply with the ordinance. When she failed to remove him from her home, the city filed a criminal charge. Mrs. Moore moved to dismiss, claiming that the ordinance was constitutionally invalid on its face. Her motion was overruled, and upon conviction she was sentenced to five days in jail and a $25 fine. The Ohio Court of Appeals affirmed after giving full consideration to her constitutional claims, and the Ohio Supreme Court denied review. We noted probable jurisdiction of her appeal, 425 U.S. 949, 96 S.Ct. 1723, 48 L.Ed.2d 193 (1976).

II

The city argues that our decision in *Village of Belle Terre v. Boraas,* 416 U.S. 1, 94 S.Ct. 1536, 39 L.Ed.2d 797 (1974), requires us to sustain the ordinance attacked here. Belle Terre, like East Cleveland, imposed limits on the types of groups that could occupy a single dwelling unit. Applying the constitutional standard announced in this Court's leading land-use case, *Euclid v. Ambler Realty Co.,* 272 U.S. 365, 47 S.Ct. 114, 71 L.Ed. 303 (1926), we sustained the Belle Terre ordinance on the ground that it bore a rational relationship to permissible state objectives.

---

[2] Section 1341.08 (1966) provides:

"'Family' means a number of individuals related to the nominal head of the household or to the spouse of the nominal head of the household living as a single housekeeping unit in a single dwelling unit, but limited to the following:

"(a) Husband or wife of the nominal head of the household.

"(b) Unmarried children of the nominal head of the household or of the spouse of the nominal head of the household, provided, however, that such unmarried children have no children residing with them.

"(c) Father or mother of the nominal head of the household or of the spouse of the nominal head of the household.

"(d) Notwithstanding the provisions of subsection (b) hereof, a family may include not more than one dependent married or unmarried child of the nominal head of the household or of the spouse of the nominal head of the household and the spouse and dependent children of such dependent child. For the purpose of this subsection, a dependent person is one who has more than fifty percent of his total support furnished for him by the nominal head of the household and the spouse of the nominal head of the household.

"(e) A family may consist of one individual."

But one overriding factor sets this case apart from Belle Terre. The ordinance there affected only unrelated individuals. It expressly allowed all who were related by "blood, adoption, or marriage" to live together, and in sustaining the ordinance we were careful to note that it promoted "family needs" and "family values." 416 U.S., at 9, 94 S.Ct., at 1541. East Cleveland, in contrast, has chosen to regulate the occupancy of its housing by slicing deeply into the family itself. This is no mere incidental result of the ordinance. On its face it selects certain categories of relatives who may live together and declares that others may not. In particular, it makes a crime of a grandmother's choice to live with her grandson in circumstances like those presented here.

When a city undertakes such intrusive regulation of the family, neither Belle Terre nor Euclid governs; the usual judicial deference to the legislature is inappropriate. "This Court has long recognized that freedom of personal choice in matters of marriage and family life is one of the liberties protected by the Due Process Clause of the Fourteenth Amendment." *Cleveland Board of Education v. LaFleur,* 414 U.S. 632, 639-640, 94 S.Ct. 791, 796, 39 L.Ed.2d 52 (1974). A host of cases, tracing their lineage to *Meyer v. Nebraska,* 262 U.S. 390, 399-401, 43 S.Ct. 625, 626-627, 67 L.Ed. 1042 (1923), and *Pierce v. Society of Sisters,* 268 U.S. 510, 534-535, 45 S.Ct. 571, 573-574, 69 L.Ed. 1070 (1925), have consistently acknowledged a "private realm of family life which the state cannot enter." *Prince v. Massachusetts,* 321 U.S. 158, 166, 64 S.Ct. 438, 442, 88 L.Ed. 645 (1944). . . . Of course, the family is not beyond regulation. See *Prince v. Massachusetts,* supra, 321 U.S. at 166, 64 S.Ct. at 442. But when the government intrudes on choices concerning family living arrangements, this Court must examine carefully the importance of the governmental interests advanced and the extent to which they are served by the challenged regulation. See *Poe v. Ullman,* supra, 367 U.S., at 554, 81 S.Ct. at 1782 (Harlan, J., dissenting).

When thus examined, this ordinance cannot survive. The city seeks to justify it as a means of preventing overcrowding, minimizing traffic and parking congestion, and avoiding an undue financial burden on East Cleveland's school system. Although these are legitimate goals, the ordinance before us serves them marginally, at best. For example, the ordinance permits any family consisting only of husband, wife, and unmarried children to live together, even if the family contains a half dozen licensed drivers, each with his or her own car. At the same time it forbids an adult brother and sister to share a household, even if both faithfully use public transportation. The ordinance would permit a grandmother to live with a single dependent son and children, even if his school-age children number a dozen, yet it forces Mrs. Moore to find another dwelling for her grandson John, simply because of the presence of his uncle and cousin in the same household. We need not labor the point. Section 1341.08 has but a tenuous relation to alleviation of the conditions mentioned by the city. . . .

Ours is by no means a tradition limited to respect for the bonds uniting the members of the nuclear family. The tradition of uncles, aunts, cousins, and especially grandparents sharing a household along with parents and children has roots equally venerable and equally deserving of constitutional recognition. Over the years millions of our citizens have grown up in just such an environment, and most, surely, have profited from it. Even if conditions of modern society have brought about a decline in extended family households, they have not erased the accumulated wisdom of civilization, gained over the centuries and honored throughout our history, that supports a larger conception of the family. Out of choice, necessity, or a sense of family responsibility, it has been common for close relatives to draw together and participate in the duties and the satisfactions of a common home. Decisions concerning child rearing, which *Yoder, Meyer, Pierce* and other cases have recognized as entitled to constitutional protection, long have been shared with grandparents or other relatives who occupy the same household indeed who may take on major responsibility for the rearing of the children. Especially in times of adversity, such as the death of a spouse or economic need, the broader family has tended to come together for mutual sustenance and to maintain or rebuild a secure home life. This is apparently what happened here.

Whether or not such a household is established because of personal tragedy, the choice of relatives in this degree of kinship to live together may not lightly be denied by the State. *Pierce* struck down an Oregon law requiring all children to attend the State's public schools, holding that the Constitution "excludes any general power of the State to standardize its children by forcing them to accept instruction from public teachers only." 268 U.S., at 535, 45 S.Ct., at 573. By the same token the Constitution prevents East Cleveland from standardizing its children and its adults by forcing all to live in certain narrowly defined family patterns.

Reversed.

NOTES AND QUESTIONS

1. *Drawing the Boundary Between* Moore *and* Belle Terre. *Moore* and *Belle Terre* are easy to reconcile—*Moore* involved people related by blood where *Belle Terre* did not. At some point, however, the boundary between the two cases will blur. *Moore* involved a grandmother living with her grandson. Justice Powell's plurality opinion mentions uncles, aunts, and cousins. Should *Moore* extend to first cousins? Second cousins? Third cousins twice removed? At what point should *Moore*'s protection of family give way to the *Belle Terre* rule?

2. *State Constitutional Protections. Moore* and *Belle Terre* were decided under the U.S. Constitution. Some states have held that restrictive definitions of family in zoning ordinances violate provisions of state law or state constitutions. *See McMinn v. Town of Oyster Bay,* 488 N.E.2d 1240 (N.Y. 1985); *City of Santa Barbara v. Adamson,* 610 P.2d 436 (Cal. 1980).

F. FEDERAL STATUTES LIMITING MUNICIPAL ZONING LAWS

Our last few cases have involved constitutional limits on zoning power. Some federal statutes also place limits on the enforcement of municipal zoning laws. In this section, we will discuss two federal statutes that are important in the land use context.

1. THE FAIR HOUSING ACT

As we saw before in the context of restrictive covenants, the Fair Housing Act (FHA) can limit the enforcement of single-family use restrictions against group homes for people with disabilities. The FHA can do the same thing with single-family use restrictions imposed by zoning laws, as we will see in our next case.

CITY OF EDMONDS V. OXFORD HOUSE, INC.

Supreme Court of the United States, 1995
514 U.S. 725

Justice GINSBURG delivered the opinion of the Court.

The Fair Housing Act (FHA or Act) prohibits discrimination in housing against, *inter alios,* persons with handicaps. Section 807(b)(1) of the Act entirely exempts from the FHA's compass "any reasonable local, State, or Federal restrictions regarding the maximum number of occupants permitted to occupy a dwelling." 42 U.S.C. §3607(b)(1). This case presents the question whether a provision in petitioner City of Edmonds' zoning code qualifies for §3607(b)(1)'s complete exemption from FHA scrutiny. The provision, governing areas zoned for single-family dwelling units, defines "family" as "persons [without regard to number] related by genetics, adoption, or marriage, or a group of five or fewer [unrelated] persons." Edmonds Community Development Code (ECDC) §21.30.010 (1991).

The defining provision at issue describes who may compose a family unit; it does not prescribe "*the* maximum number of occupants" a dwelling unit may house. We hold that §3607(b)(1) does not exempt prescriptions of the family-defining kind, *i.e.,* provisions designed to foster the family character of a neighborhood. Instead, §3607(b)(1)'s absolute exemption removes from the FHA's scope only total occupancy limits, *i.e.,* numerical ceilings that serve to prevent overcrowding in living quarters.

I

In the summer of 1990, respondent Oxford House opened a group home in the City of Edmonds, Washington (City), for 10 to 12 adults recovering from alcoholism and drug addiction. The group home, called Oxford House-Edmonds, is located in a neighborhood zoned for single-family residences. Upon learning that Oxford House had leased and was operating a home in Edmonds, the City issued criminal citations to the owner and a resident of the house. The citations charged violation of the zoning code rule that defines who may live in single-family dwelling units. The occupants of such units must compose a "family," and family, under the City's defining rule, "means an individual or two or more persons related by genetics, adoption, or marriage, or a group of five or fewer persons who are not related by genetics, adoption, or marriage." ECDC §21.30.010. Oxford House-Edmonds houses more than five unrelated persons, and therefore does not conform to the code.

Oxford House asserted reliance on the Fair Housing Act, 102 Stat. 1619, 42 U.S.C. §3601 *et seq.,* which declares it unlawful "[t]o discriminate in the sale or rental, or to otherwise make unavailable or deny, a dwelling to any buyer or renter because of a handicap of . . . that buyer or renter." §3604(f)(1)(A). The parties have stipulated, for purposes of this litigation, that the residents of Oxford House-Edmonds "are recovering alcoholics and drug addicts and are handicapped persons within the meaning" of the Act. App. 106.

Discrimination covered by the FHA includes "a refusal to make reasonable accommodations in rules, policies, practices, or services, when such accommodations may be necessary to afford [handicapped] person[s] equal opportunity to use and enjoy a dwelling." §3604(f)(3)(B). Oxford House asked Edmonds to make a "reasonable accommodation" by allowing it to remain in the single-family dwelling it had leased. Group homes for recovering substance abusers, Oxford urged, need 8 to 12 residents to be financially and therapeutically viable. Edmonds declined to permit Oxford House to stay in a single-family residential zone, but passed an ordinance listing group homes as permitted uses in multifamily and general commercial zones.

Edmonds sued Oxford House in the United States District Court for the Western District of Washington, seeking a declaration that the FHA does not constrain the City's zoning code family definition rule. Oxford House counterclaimed under the FHA, charging the City with failure to make a "reasonable accommodation" permitting maintenance of the group home in a single-family zone. The United States filed a separate action on the same FHA "reasonable accommodation" ground, and the two cases were consolidated. Edmonds suspended its criminal enforcement actions pending resolution of the federal litigation.

On cross-motions for summary judgment, the District Court held that ECDC §21.30.010, defining "family," is exempt from the FHA under §3607(b)(1) as a "reasonable . . . restrictio[n] regarding the maximum number of occupants permitted to occupy a dwelling." App. to Pet. for Cert. B-7. The United States Court of Appeals for the Ninth Circuit reversed; holding §3607(b)(1)'s absolute exemption inapplicable, the Court of Appeals remanded the cases for further consideration of the claims asserted by Oxford

House and the United States. *Edmonds v. Washington State Building Code Council*, 18 F.3d 802 (1994).

The Ninth Circuit's decision conflicts with an Eleventh Circuit decision declaring exempt under §3607(b)(1) a family definition provision similar to the Edmonds prescription. See *Elliott v. Athens,* 960 F.2d 975 (1992). We granted certiorari to resolve the conflict, 513 U.S. 959, 115 S.Ct. 417, 130 L.Ed.2d 332 (1994), and we now affirm the Ninth Circuit's judgment.

II

The sole question before the Court is whether Edmonds' family composition rule qualifies as a "restrictio[n] regarding the maximum number of occupants permitted to occupy a dwelling" within the meaning of the FHA's absolute exemption. 42 U.S.C. §3607(b)(1). In answering this question, we are mindful of the Act's stated policy "to provide, within constitutional limitations, for fair housing throughout the United States." §3601. We also note precedent recognizing the FHA's "broad and inclusive" compass, and therefore according a "generous construction" to the Act's complaint-filing provision. *Trafficante v. Metropolitan Life Ins. Co.,* 409 U.S. 205, 209, 212, 93 S.Ct. 364, 366-367, 368, 34 L.Ed.2d 415 (1972). Accordingly, we regard this case as an instance in which an exception to "a general statement of policy" is sensibly read "narrowly in order to preserve the primary operation of the [policy]." *Commissioner v. Clark,* 489 U.S. 726, 739, 109 S.Ct. 1455, 1463, 103 L.Ed.2d 753 (1989).

A

Congress enacted §3607(b)(1) against the backdrop of an evident distinction between municipal land-use restrictions and maximum occupancy restrictions.

Land-use restrictions designate "districts in which only compatible uses are allowed and incompatible uses are excluded." D. Mandelker, Land Use Law §4.16, pp. 113-114 (3d ed.1993) (hereinafter Mandelker). These restrictions typically categorize uses as single-family residential, multiple-family residential, commercial, or industrial. See, *e.g.,* 1 E. Ziegler, Jr., Rathkopf's The Law of Zoning and Planning §8.01, pp. 8-2 to 8-3 (4th ed.1995); Mandelker §1.03, p. 4; 1 E. Yokley, Zoning Law and Practice §7-2, p. 252 (4th ed.1978).

Land use restrictions aim to prevent problems caused by the "pig in the parlor instead of the barnyard." *Village of Euclid v. Ambler Realty Co.,* 272 U.S. 365, 388, 47 S.Ct. 114, 118, 71 L.Ed. 303 (1926). In particular, reserving land for single-family residences preserves the character of neighborhoods, securing "zones where family values, youth values, and the blessings of quiet seclusion and clean air make the area a sanctuary for people." *Village of Belle Terre v. Boraas,* 416 U.S. 1, 9, 94 S.Ct. 1536, 1541, 39 L.Ed.2d 797 (1974); see also *Moore v. East Cleveland,* 431 U.S. 494, 521, 97 S.Ct. 1932, 1947, 52 L.Ed.2d 531 (1977) (Burger, C.J., dissenting) (purpose of East Cleveland's single-family zoning ordinance "is the traditional one of preserving certain areas as family residential communities"). To limit land use to single-family residences, a municipality must define the term "family"; thus family composition rules are an essential component of single-family residential use restrictions.

Maximum occupancy restrictions, in contradistinction, cap the number of occupants per dwelling, typically in relation to available floor space or the number and type of rooms. See, *e.g.,* International Conference of Building Officials, Uniform Housing Code §503(b) (1988); Building Officials and Code Administrators International, Inc., BOCA National Property Maintenance Code §§PM-405.3, PM-405.5 (1993) (hereinafter BOCA Code); Southern Building Code Congress, International, Inc., Standard Housing Code §§306.1, 306.2 (1991); E. Mood, APHA-CDC Recommended Minimum Housing Standards §9.02, p. 37 (1986) (hereinafter APHA-CDC Standards). These restrictions ordinarily apply uniformly to *all* residents of *all* dwelling units. Their purpose is to protect health and safety by preventing dwelling overcrowding. See, *e.g.,* BOCA Code §§PM-101.3, PM-405.3, PM-405.5 and commentary; Abbott, Housing Policy, Housing Codes and Tenant Remedies, 56 B.U.L.Rev. 1, 41-45 (1976).

We recognized this distinction between maximum occupancy restrictions and land-use restrictions in *Moore v. East Cleveland,* 431 U.S. 494, 97 S.Ct. 1932, 52 L.Ed.2d 531 (1977). In *Moore,* the Court held unconstitutional the constricted definition of "family" contained in East Cleveland's housing ordinance. East Cleveland's ordinance "select[ed] certain categories of relatives who may live together and declare[d] that others may not"; in particular, East Cleveland's definition of "family" made "a crime of a grandmother's choice to live with her grandson." *Id.,* at 498-499, 97 S.Ct., at 1935 (plurality opinion). In response to East Cleveland's argument that its aim was to prevent overcrowded dwellings, streets, and schools, we observed that the municipality's restrictive definition of family served the asserted, and undeniably legitimate, goals "marginally, at best." *Id.,* at 500, 97 S.Ct., at 1936 (footnote omitted). Another East Cleveland ordinance, we noted, "specifically addressed . . . the problem of overcrowding"; that ordinance tied "the maximum permissible occupancy of a dwelling to the habitable floor area." *Id.,* at 500, n. 7, 97 S.Ct., at 1936, n. 7; accord, *id.,* at 520, n. 16, 97 S.Ct., at 1939, n. 16 (STEVENS, J., concurring in judgment). Justice Stewart, in dissent, also distinguished restrictions designed to "preserv[e] the character of a residential area," from prescription of "a minimum habitable floor area per person," *id.,* at 539, n. 9, 97 S.Ct., at 1937, n. 9, in the interest of community health and safety.

Section 3607(b)(1)'s language—"restrictions regarding the maximum number of occupants permitted to occupy a dwelling"—surely encompasses maximum occupancy restrictions. But the formulation does not fit family composition rules typically tied to land-use restrictions. In sum, rules that cap the total number of occupants in order to prevent overcrowding of a dwelling "plainly and unmistakably," see *A.H. Phillips, Inc. v. Walling,* 324 U.S. 490, 493, 65 S.Ct. 807, 808, 89 L.Ed. 1095 (1945), fall within §3607(b)(1)'s absolute exemption from the FHA's governance; rules designed to preserve the family character of a neighborhood, fastening on the composition of households rather than on the total number of occupants living quarters can contain, do not.[9]

B

Turning specifically to the City's Community Development Code, we note that the provisions Edmonds invoked against Oxford House, ECDC §§16.20.010 and 21.30.010, are classic examples of a use restriction and complementing family composition rule. These provisions do not cap the number of people who may live in a dwelling. In plain terms, they direct that dwellings be used only to house families. Captioned "USES," ECDC §16.20.010 provides that the sole "Permitted Primary Us[e]" in a single-family residential zone is "[s]ingle-family dwelling units." Edmonds itself recognizes that this provision simply "defines those uses permitted in a single family residential zone." Pet. for Cert. 3.

A separate provision caps the number of occupants a dwelling may house, based on floor area:

> "Floor Area. Every dwelling unit shall have at least one room which shall have not less than 120 square feet of floor area. Other habitable rooms, except kitchens, shall have an area of not less than 70 square feet. Where more than two persons occupy a room used for sleeping purposes, the required floor area shall be increased at the rate of 50 square feet for each occupant in excess of two." ECDC §19.10.000 (adopting Uniform Housing Code §503(b) (1988)).

This space and occupancy standard is a prototypical maximum occupancy restriction.

Edmonds nevertheless argues that its family composition rule, ECDC §21.30.010, falls within §3607(b)(1), the FHA exemption for maximum occupancy restrictions, because the rule caps at five the number of unrelated persons allowed to occupy a single-family dwelling. But Edmonds' family composition rule surely does not answer the question: "What is the maximum number of occupants permitted to occupy a house?" So long as they are related "by genetics, adoption, or marriage," any number of people can live in a house. Ten siblings, their parents and grandparents, for example, could dwell in a house in Edmonds' single-family residential zone without offending Edmonds' family composition rule.

---

[9] Tellingly, Congress added the §3607(b)(1) exemption for maximum occupancy restrictions at the same time it enlarged the FHA to include a ban on discrimination based on "familial status." See *supra*, at 1778, n. 1. The provision making it illegal to discriminate in housing against families with children under the age of 18 prompted fears that landlords would be forced to allow large families to crowd into small housing units. See, *e.g.*, Fair Housing Amendments Act of 1988: Hearings on H.R. 1158 before the Subcommittee on Civil and Constitutional Rights of the House Committee on the Judiciary, 100th Cong., 1st Sess., 656 (1987) (remarks of Rep. Edwards) (questioning whether a landlord must allow a family with 10 children to live in a two-bedroom apartment). Section 3607(b)(1) makes it plain that, pursuant to local prescriptions on maximum occupancy, landlords legitimately may refuse to stuff large families into small quarters. Congress further assured in §3607(b)(1) that retirement communities would be exempt from the proscription of discrimination against families with minor children. In the sentence immediately following the maximum occupancy provision, §3607(b)(1) states: "Nor does any provision in this subchapter regarding familial status apply with respect to housing for older persons."

Family living, not living space per occupant, is what ECDC §21.30.010 describes. Defining family primarily by biological and legal relationships, the provision also accommodates another group association: Five or fewer unrelated people are allowed to live together as though they were family. This accommodation is the peg on which Edmonds rests its plea for §3607(b)(1) exemption. Had the City defined a family solely by biological and legal links, §3607(b)(1) would not have been the ground on which Edmonds staked its case. See Tr. of Oral Arg. 11-12, 16. It is curious reasoning indeed that converts a family values preserver into a maximum occupancy restriction once a town adds to a related persons prescription "and also two unrelated persons."

Edmonds additionally contends that subjecting single-family zoning to FHA scrutiny will "overturn Euclidian zoning" and "destroy the effectiveness and purpose of single-family zoning." Brief for Petitioner 11, 25. This contention both ignores the limited scope of the issue before us and exaggerates the force of the FHA's antidiscrimination provisions. We address only whether Edmonds' family composition rule qualifies for §3607(b)(1) exemption. Moreover, the FHA antidiscrimination provisions, when applicable, require only "reasonable" accommodations to afford persons with handicaps "equal opportunity to use and enjoy" housing. §§3604(f)(1)(A) and (f)(3)(B).

The parties have presented, and we have decided, only a threshold question: Edmonds' zoning code provision describing who may compose a "family" is not a maximum occupancy restriction exempt from the FHA under §3607(b)(1). It remains for the lower courts to decide whether Edmonds' actions against Oxford House violate the FHA's prohibitions against discrimination set out in §§3604(f)(1)(A) and (f)(3)(B). For the reasons stated, the judgment of the United States Court of Appeals for the Ninth Circuit is

Affirmed.

[The dissenting opinion of Justice Thomas, joined by Justices Scalia and Kennedy, is omitted]

NOTE

1. *The FHA and Group Homes. Edmonds v. Oxford House* held that definitions of family do not fall within the occupancy exception of §3607(b)(1) of the FHA. The Court did not reach the question of whether the application of the zoning law had actually violated the prohibitions on discrimination on the basis of handicap in §3604(f). Consideration of the merits of those discrimination claims would follow the same pattern as those discussed in *Hill v. Community of Damien of Molokai*, which we covered above in our chapter on servitudes.

2. RLUIPA

The Religious Land Use and Institutionalized Persons Act of 2000 (RLUIPA) was intended to protect religious institutions from discrimination in the land use context. Here is the text of the relevant portion of RLUIPA:

Religious Land Use and Institutionalized Persons Act, 42 U.S.C.A. §2000cc

Protection of land use as religious exercise

(a) Substantial burdens

(1) General rule

No government shall impose or implement a land use regulation in a manner that imposes a substantial burden on the religious exercise of a person, including a religious assembly or institution, unless the government demonstrates that imposition of the burden on that person, assembly, or institution—

(A) is in furtherance of a compelling governmental interest; and

(B) is the least restrictive means of furthering that compelling governmental interest.

(2) Scope of application

This subsection applies in any case in which—

(A) the substantial burden is imposed in a program or activity that receives Federal financial assistance, even if the burden results from a rule of general applicability;

(B) the substantial burden affects, or removal of that substantial burden would affect, commerce with foreign nations, among the several States, or with Indian tribes, even if the burden results from a rule of general applicability; or

(C) the substantial burden is imposed in the implementation of a land use regulation or system of land use regulations, under which a government makes, or has in place formal or informal procedures or practices that permit the government to make, individualized assessments of the proposed uses for the property involved.

(b) Discrimination and exclusion

(1) Equal terms

No government shall impose or implement a land use regulation in a manner that treats a religious assembly or institution on less than equal terms with a nonreligious assembly or institution.

(2) Nondiscrimination

No government shall impose or implement a land use regulation that discriminates against any assembly or institution on the basis of religion or religious denomination.

(3) Exclusions and limits

No government shall impose or implement a land use regulation that—

(A) totally excludes religious assemblies from a jurisdiction; or

(B) unreasonably limits religious assemblies, institutions, or structures within a jurisdiction.

Under the general rule stated in §2000cc(a)(1), land use regulations impose a substantial burden on religious institutions will violate the law and be invalidated unless the government can show (A) that the law "is in furtherance of a compelling governmental interest" and (B) that the law "is the least restrictive means of furthering that compelling governmental interest." This language—compelling governmental interest and least restrictive means—mirrors the *strict scrutiny* test that is certain constitutional law contexts. Strict scrutiny is the highest type of scrutiny that is applied to reviewing the constitutionality of the government actions. As we have at several points in this chapter, we will leave a detailed discussion of strict scrutiny to your Constitutional Law class. For our purposes, it is enough for you to know that (a) a person challenging a law under a strict scrutiny standard will have a reasonably good chance of success, and therefore that (b) the imposition of strict scrutiny in RLUIPA is a very big deal.

In addition to this general rule, RLUIPA includes three sets of prohibitions on discrimination in §2000cc(b): (1) a requirement that religious institutions be treated equally to other institutions in the land use context, (2) a prohibition on discrimination on the basis of religion in the land use context, and (3) a prohibition on excluding or unreasonably limiting religious assemblies within a jurisdiction.

The scope of application provisions in §2000cc(a)(2) are quite broad. Subsection (a)(2) potentially is broader than it might initially appear because of the scope of activity that has been held in other contexts to affect interstate commerce. Subsection (a)(3) will capture a wide range of zoning activity, as we will see in our next case.

GURU NANAK SIKH SOCIETY OF YUBA CITY V. COUNTY OF SUTTER

United States Court of Appeals for the Ninth Circuit, 2006
456 F.3d 978

Bea, Circuit Judge:

We must decide whether a local government's denial of a religious group's application for a conditional use permit to construct a temple on a parcel of land zoned "agricultural" constituted a "substantial burden" under the Religious Land Use and Institutionalized Persons Act of 2000 (RLUIPA), 42 U.S.C. §§2000cc, *et seq.*, and if we find that the denial was a substantial burden, whether RLUIPA is constitutional.

We find that the County imposed a substantial burden on Appellee Guru Nanak Sikh Society of Yuba City's ("Guru Nanak's") religious exercise under RLUIPA because the stated reasons and history behind the denial at issue, and a previous denial of Guru Nanak's application to build a temple on a parcel of land zoned "residential," to a significantly great extent lessened the possibility of Guru Nanak constructing a temple in the future. We also decide that the County did not assert, much less prove, compelling interests for its action; last, we find the relevant portion of RLUIPA is a permissible exercise of Congress's remedial power under Section Five of the Fourteenth Amendment.

Accordingly, we affirm the district court's order that granted summary judgment for Guru Nanak, invalidated the County's denial of Guru Nanak's application to build a new temple, and enjoined the County to approve and grant Guru Nanak's conditional use permit immediately, subject only to conditions to which Guru Nanak had previously agreed.

I. FACTS AND BACKGROUND

A. Denial of Guru Nanak's First CUP Application

Guru Nanak is a non-profit organization dedicated to fostering the teachings and practices of the Sikh religion. In 2001, Guru Nanak attempted to obtain a conditional use permit (CUP)[4] for the construction of a Sikh temple—a *gurudwara*—on its 1.89-acre property on Grove Road in Yuba City ("the Grove Road property"). The proposed use included about 5,000 square feet dedicated to an assembly area and related activities. The proposed temple site would have held religious ceremonies for no more than seventy-five people at a time. The Grove Road property was in an area designated for low-density residential use (R-1), intended mainly for large lot single family residences; churches and temples are only conditionally permitted in R-1 districts, through issuance of a CUP.

The Sutter County Planning Division, part of the County Community Services Department, issued a report recommending that the Planning Commission grant a CUP for the Grove Road property. The report stated that while the permit presented potential conflicts with established residences in the area, the conflicts could be minimized by specifically recommended conditions that would be consistent with the General Plan of Sutter County. However, at a public meeting, the Planning Commission voted unanimously to deny the CUP. The denial was based on citizens' voiced fears that the resulting noise and traffic would interfere with the existing neighborhood. Following the Commission's denial, Guru Nanak began searching for a different parcel of property for the proposed temple.

---

[4] The Sutter County Zoning Code describes the purpose of utilizing use permits for certain proposed uses of land:

> The County realizes that certain uses have operational characteristics that, depending on the locations and design, may have the potential to negatively impact adjoining properties and uses. Such uses therefore require a more comprehensive review and approval procedure in order to evaluate and mitigate any potentially detrimental impacts. Use permits, which may be revocable, conditional or valid for a term period, may be issued by the Planning Commission for any of the uses or purposes for which such permits are required or permitted by the terms of this Chapter. Guarantees to ensure compliance with the terms and conditions may be required by the Commission.

Sutter County Zoning Code §1500-8210 (May 2002). *See infra* Part I.C. for further discussion of CUPs.

B. Denial of Guru Nanak's Second CUP Application

In 2002, Guru Nanak acquired the property at issue in this case, a 28.79-acre parcel located on George Washington Boulevard in an unincorporated area of the County, to build a temple there. The site is zoned "AG" (general agricultural district) in the Sutter County Zoning Code. As in R-1 districts, churches and temples are only conditionally permitted in AG districts, through issuance of a CUP. The parcel includes a walnut orchard and an existing 2,300 square foot single family residence, which Guru Nanak proposed to convert into a Sikh temple by increasing the size of the building by approximately 500 square feet. All of the surrounding properties have identical zoning designations and have orchards. The nearest residence to the property is at least 200 feet north of the parcel's northern boundary. The residence to be converted into the temple is located 105 feet south of that northern boundary.

Another Sikh temple already exists on a ten-acre parcel of land zoned "agricultural" located next to Bogue Road, less than a mile southeast from the proposed temple's parcel. Within Yuba City's sphere of influence, the Bogue Road Sikh temple is surrounded by land zoned "agricultural."

Guru Nanak filed an application for a CUP to build a temple limited to approximately 2,850 square feet on the proposed site. The proposed use of the property was for a Sikh temple, assembly hall, worship services, and weddings. As with the Grove Road property, the proposed facility was intended to accommodate religious services of no more than seventy-five people at a time. Various county and state departments reviewed Guru Nanak's application and added a variety of conditions regarding the environmental impact of the proposed use including a twenty-five foot "no development" buffer along the north side of the property, a requirement that ceremonies remain indoors, and required landscaping.

Guru Nanak had to accept these conditions to receive the Planning Division's recommendation to the Planning Commission. The Planning Division issued a "mitigated negative declaration" (*i.e.* that the proposed temple would not create a significant environment impact) because "although the proposed [temple] could have a significant impact on the environment[,] . . . the recommended mitigation measures would reduce the possible impacts to a less-than-significant level." The Planning Division cited the temple's maximum attendance of 75 people, minor building conversion, and stipulated mitigation measures as reasons for finding a less-than-significant impact on the environment.

The Planning Commission held a public meeting to consider Guru Nanak's permit application. A member of Guru Nanak testified that while its previous application was for a 1.9-acre lot in a residential area, the subject application pertained to a 28.8-acre lot that did not border anyone's front or back yard. He also stated that Guru Nanak would accept all the Planning Division's proposed conditions on the land's use. Various potential neighbors spoke against the proposed temple, complaining mainly that the temple would increase traffic and noise, interfere with the agricultural use of their land, and lower property values. The Commission approved the application 4-3, subject to the conditions required by the Planning Division and stipulated to by Guru Nanak, with the commissioners echoing the reasoning voiced by both sides.

Several neighbors filed timely appeals to the Sutter County Board of Supervisors. The Planning Division filed another report in response to the appeals, addressing the specific complaints of the concerned neighbors and continuing to recommend approval of Guru Nanak's CUP application. Subject to revised mitigation conditions including an expanded one-hundred foot setback, the Planning Division found that the proposed temple's effect on neighbors' pesticide spraying, nearby traffic, and noise levels would be minimal.

The Board of Supervisors held a public hearing on the appeals. People attending the hearing reiterated claims regarding effects upon the agricultural use of surrounding land, traffic, and property values. In addition, several people complained that the initial plan for a seventy-five person temple was only a starting point for more ambitious facilities and this piece-meal approval process violated the California Environmental Quality Act (CEQA).

The four-member Board of Supervisors unanimously reversed the Planning Commission's approval and denied Guru Nanak's application. Supervisor Kroon flatly rejected the project based on the "right to farm": the property had been agricultural and should remain so. He argued that long-time farmers should not be affected by someone who wishes to change the use of the property. Supervisor Nelson stated that he was concerned that Guru Nanak's proposed use "was too far away from the city" and would not promote orderly growth. He commented that such development is detrimental to the surrounding agricultural uses and that Guru Nanak should locate its church nearer to his and other existing churches. Supervisors Munger and Silva agreed that the proposed temple site's separation from existing infrastructure, termed "leapfrog development," was a poor idea and denied the 0application on that ground.

C. Local Land Use Law

The Sutter County General Plan is a long-term guide for physical development of land within the County. The Plan empowers the County's Community Services Department to ensure that "new development adjacent to agricultural areas be designed to minimize conflicts with adjacent agricultural uses." Policy Document, at 16. The Plan disfavors development not contiguous to areas currently designated for urban or suburban uses—leapfrog development—because it "has the potential to create land use conflicts and, in most instances, make[s] the provision of services more difficult." *Id.* at 13.

The Sutter County Zoning Code designates twenty-two types of districts. Within each of these districts, the Code categorizes uses as "permitted" as a matter of right, uses that require a "zoning clearance," or uses that require a use permit. Zoning clearance uses need only the review and approval of the Community Services Director. Conditional use permit uses require a more comprehensive review through the Sutter County Planning Commission, and require a public hearing. A church must apply for a CUP to locate within any district available to it. Six of the twenty-two types of districts are made available to churches through the Zoning Code: general agricultural (AG); food processing, agricultural and recreation combining (FPARC); one-family residence (R-1), two-family residence (R-2), neighborhood apartment (R-3), and general apartment (R-4).

D. The Decision Below

The district court granted summary judgment for Guru Nanak because it concluded the County substantially burdened Guru Nanak's religious exercise, and that the County did not proffer evidence of compelling interests to justify such burden. *Guru Nanak Sikh Soc'y of Yuba City,* 326 F.Supp.2d at 1152-54. The district court reasoned that "[t]o meet the 'substantial burden' standard, the governmental conduct being challenged must *actually inhibit* religious activity in a concrete way, and cause more than a mere inconvenience." *Id.* at 1152. Applying its definition of the substantial burden standard to the facts, the district court held that "the denial of the use permit, particularly when coupled with the denial of [Guru Nanak's] previous application, actually inhibits [Guru Nanak's] religious exercise." *Id.* The court also found that Congress did not overstep its constitutional bounds under Section Five of the Fourteenth Amendment when enacting RLUIPA because the statute targets documented religious discrimination. *Id.* at 1156-61. The court rejected the County's CEQA claim because the County's Planning Division had already found that the proposed temple, subject to stipulated mitigation measures, would create "a less-than-significant level" of environmental impacts. *Id.* at 1148-49. Accordingly, the district court invalidated the County's denial of Guru Nanak's CUP application and enjoined the County to approve immediately the CUP. *Id.* at 1161-63.

II. ANALYSIS

. . . We decide that the County made an individualized assessment of Guru Nanak's CUP, thereby making RLUIPA applicable, and that the County's denial of Guru Nanak's CUP application constituted a substantial burden, as that phrase is defined by RLUIPA. Because RLUIPA applies to this case, we address RLUIPA's constitutionality pursuant to Section Five of the Fourteenth Amendment, and decide that RLUIPA is a congruent and proportional exercise of congressional power pursuant to the Fourteenth Amendment.

A. Statutory Claim under RLUIPA

RLUIPA is Congress's latest effort to protect the free exercise of religion guaranteed by the First Amendment from governmental regulation. In *Employment Division, Department of Human Resources of Oregon v. Smith,* 494 U.S. 872, 878-82, 110 S.Ct. 1595,

108 L.Ed.2d 876 (1990), the Supreme Court decided that the Free Exercise Clause of the First Amendment "does not inhibit enforcement of otherwise valid laws of general application that incidentally burden religious conduct." *Cutter v. Wilkinson,* 544 U.S. 709, 125 S.Ct. 2113, 2118, 161 L.Ed.2d 1020 (2005).

In 1993, Congress enacted the Religious Freedom and Restoration Act of (RFRA) in response to the Supreme Court's decision in *Smith.* RFRA "prohibit [ed] '[g]overnment' from 'substantially burden[ing]' a person's exercise of religion even if the burden results from a rule of general applicability unless the government [could] demonstrate the burden '(1) [was] in furtherance of a compelling governmental interest; and (2) [was] the least restrictive means of furthering that compelling governmental interest.'" *City of Boerne v. Flores,* 521 U.S. 507, 515-16, 117 S.Ct. 2157, 138 L.Ed.2d 624 (1997) (second and third alterations in original) (quoting 42 U.S.C. §2000bb-1). In *City of Boerne,* though, the Supreme Court invalidated RFRA, deciding that it was an unconstitutional exercise of congressional power pursuant to Section Five of the Fourteenth Amendment because of a "lack of proportionality or congruence between the means adopted and the legitimate end to be achieved." *Id.* at 533, 117 S.Ct. 2157.

Congress enacted RLUIPA in response to the constitutional flaws with RFRA identified by *City of Boerne.* "RLUIPA 'replaces the void provisions of RFRA[,]' and prohibits the government from imposing 'substantial burdens' on 'religious exercise' unless there exists a compelling governmental interest and the burden is the least restrictive means of satisfying the governmental interest." *San Jose Christian,* 360 F.3d at 1033-34 (quoting *Wyatt v. Terhune,* 315 F.3d 1108, 1112 (9th Cir.2003) (citation omitted)). To avoid RFRA's fate, Congress wrote that RLUIPA would apply only to regulations regarding land use and prison conditions. *See Cutter,* 125 S.Ct. at 2118.

RLUIPA applies only if one of three conditions obtain: (1) If the state "program or activity receives Federal financial assistance," 42 U.S.C. §2000cc(2)(A), implicating congressional authority pursuant to the Spending Clause; (2) if the substantial burden imposed by local law "affects . . . [or] would affect, commerce with foreign nations, among the several States, or with Indian tribes," *id.* §2000cc(2)(B), implicating congressional power pursuant to the Commerce Clause; (3) or, as Guru Nanak argues here, if "the substantial burden is imposed in the *implementation of a land use regulation* or system of land use regulations, under which a government makes, or has in place formal or informal procedures or practices that permit the government to make, *individualized assessments* of the proposed uses for the property involved," 42 U.S.C. §2000cc(2)(C) (emphasis added).

1. Individualized Land Use Assessments

Before we apply the terms of RLUIPA, of course, we first must determine if RLUIPA even applies, by examining whether the actions of the County are "individualized assessments of the proposed uses for the property involved." *Id.* The County argues that its denial of Guru Nanak's second CUP application falls outside the legislative scope of RLUIPA because its use permit process is a neutral law of general applicability. However, the plain meaning of §2000cc(2)(C), quoted above, belies this contention. RLUIPA applies when the government may take into account the particular details of an applicant's proposed use of land when deciding to permit or deny that use.

The Sutter County Zoning Code does not permit churches as a matter of right in any of the six types of zoned areas available for church construction. Rather, an entity intending to build a church must first apply for a CUP and be approved by the County. The Zoning Code states, "The County realizes that certain uses . . . may have the potential to negatively impact adjoining properties and uses. Such uses therefore require a more comprehensive review and approval procedure in order to evaluate and mitigate any potentially detrimental impacts." §1500-8210. The Zoning Code also outlines how the Sutter County Planning Commission, which has original jurisdiction over such use applications, should determine whether to approve or reject an application:

> The Planning Commission may approve or conditionally approve a use permit if it finds that the establishment, maintenance, or operation of the use or building applied for will or will not, *under the circumstances of the particular case,* be detrimental to the health, safety, and general welfare of persons residing or working in the neighborhood of such proposed use, or be detrimental or injurious to property and improvement in the neighborhood or to the general welfare of the County. Additionally, the Commission shall find that the use or activity approved by the use permit is consistent with the General Plan [of Sutter County].

§§1500-8216 (emphasis added). The County Board of Supervisors reviews the Planning Commission's conditional use decisions "de novo and all applications, papers, maps, exhibits and staff recommendations made or presented to the Planning Commission may be considered." *Id.* §1500-312(f). The Sutter County Zoning Code directs the Planning Commission and the Board of Supervisors to "implement [its] system of land use regulations [by making] individualized assessments of the proposed uses of the land involved." 42 U.S.C. §2000cc.

By its own terms, it appears that RLUIPA does not apply directly to land use regulations, such as the Zoning Code here, which typically are written in general and neutral terms. However, when the Zoning Code is applied to grant or deny a certain use to a particular parcel of land, that application is an "implementation" under 42 U.S.C. §2000cc(2)(C). *See Kaahumanu v. County of Maui,* 315 F.3d 1215, 1220-23 (9th Cir.2003) (concluding in a RLUIPA case that a similar permit process resulted in an administrative, rather than legislative, action because it "was based on the circumstances of the particular case and did not effectuate policy"); *Freedom Baptist Church of Delaware County v. Twp. of Middletown,* 204 F.Supp.2d 857, 868-69 (E.D.Pa.2002) ("No one contests that zoning ordinances must by their nature impose individual assessment regimes. That is to say, land use regulations through zoning codes necessarily involve case-by-case evaluations of the propriety of proposed activity against extant land use regulations."). RLUIPA therefore governs the actions of the County in this case.

2. Substantial Burden Under RLUIPA

We next turn to the issue whether the County's denial of Guru Nanak's CUP application substantially burdened its religious exercise within the meaning of RLUIPA.

The statute states, in relevant part:

> (a) Substantial burdens
>
> > (1) General rule
> > No government shall impose or implement a land use regulation in a manner that imposes a *substantial burden on the religious exercise* of a person, including a religious assembly or institution, unless the government demonstrates that imposition of the burden on that person, assembly, or institution—
> > > (A) is in furtherance of a compelling governmental interest; and
> > > (B) is the least restrictive means of furthering that compelling governmental interest.

42 U.S.C. §2000cc (emphasis added). Guru Nanak bears the burden to prove the County's denial of its application imposed a substantial burden on its religious exercise. *Id.* §2000cc-2(b).

The Supreme Court's free exercise jurisprudence is instructive in defining a substantial burden under RLUIPA. The Supreme Court has held that various unemployment compensation regulations imposed a substantial burden on adherents' religious exercise, and thereby were subject to strict scrutiny, because the regulations withheld benefits based on adherents' following their religious tenets. *See Sherbert v. Verner,* 374 U.S. 398, 406, 83 S.Ct. 1790, 10 L.Ed.2d 965 (1963). This choice between unemployment benefits or religious duties imposed a burden because it exerted "substantial pressure on an adherent to modify his behavior and to violate his beliefs." *Thomas v. Review Bd. of the Ind. Employment Sec. Div.,* 450 U.S. 707, 717-18, 101 S.Ct. 1425, 67 L.Ed.2d 624 (1981); *see also Lyng v. Nw. Indian Cemetery Protective Ass'n,* 485 U.S. 439, 450-51, 108 S.Ct. 1319, 99 L.Ed.2d 534 (1988) (explaining that to trigger strict scrutiny under the First Amendment a governmental burden must have a "tendency to coerce individuals into acting contrary to their religious beliefs"). These cases demonstrate "that a 'substantial burden' must place more than an inconvenience on religious exercise." *See Midrash Sephardi, Inc. v. Town of Surfside,* 366 F.3d 1214, 1227 (11th Cir.2004).

Accordingly, interpreting RLUIPA, this court has held: "[F]or a land use regulation to impose a 'substantial burden,' it must be 'oppressive' to a 'significantly great' extent. That is, a 'substantial burden' on 'religious exercise' must impose a significantly great restriction or onus upon such exercise." *San Jose Christian,* 360 F.3d at 1034(quoting Merriam-Webster's Collegiate Dictionary 1170 (10th ed.2002)). Applying *San Jose Christian's* definition of a substantial burden to the particular facts here, we find the district court correctly granted summary judgment for Guru Nanak. Most important to us the history behind Guru Nanak's two CUP application processes, and the reasons given for ultimately denying these applications, to a significantly great extent lessened the possibility that future CUP applications would be successful. *See Saints Constantine & Helen Greek Orthodox Church, Inc. v. City of New Berlin*, 396 F.3d 895, 899-900 (7th Cir.2005) ("*Saint Constantine*") (finding that, to prove a substantial burden under RLUIPA, a religious group need not "show that there was no other parcel of land on which it could build its church"). We need not and do not decide that failing to provide a religious institution with a land use entitlement for a new facility for worship necessarily constitutes a substantial burden pursuant to RLUIPA. At the same time, we do decide the County imposed a substantial burden here based on two considerations: (1) that the County's broad reasons given for its tandem denials could easily apply to all future applications by Guru Nanak; and (2) that Guru Nanak readily agreed to every mitigation measure suggested by the Planning Division, but the County, without explanation, found such cooperation insufficient.

The Zoning Code permits churches in six types of districts. Churches must apply for a CUP within any or all of the six available districts. Each of the district classifications available to churches is intended to provide an area for a distinct form of development. The CUP application process is intended to ensure that a religious group's proposed property use conforms with the type of development that the particular district contemplates.

Guru Nanak initially applied for a CUP to construct a Sikh temple on a 1.89-acre property in an R-1 (One Family Residence) District. The Sutter County Community Services Department had recommended approval of the proposed use because mitigation measures, agreed to by Guru Nanak, would have minimized conflicts with surrounding land. Nevertheless, the County Planning Commission unanimously rejected the application, citing neighbors' complaints regarding increased noise and traffic.

Guru Nanak predictably responded to these voiced complaints by attempting to locate its temple on property far from residents who would be bothered by noise and traffic. The County's stated reasons for denying Guru Nanak's first application implied to Guru Nanak that it should not attempt to locate its temple in higher density districts (two-family residence, neighborhood apartment, general apartment, and the combining district) where nearby neighbors would be similarly bothered.

Accordingly, Guru Nanak proposed a smaller temple, with the same seventy-five person capacity, on a much larger parcel of agricultural land.[16] The agricultural parcel left much more space between the temple and adjacent properties; that space mitigated

---

[16] During the public hearing at which the Sutter County Planning Commission approved Guru Nanak's second application, Commissioner Griffin commented, "We turned . . . down [Guru Nanak's first application] because the noise impact on the neighbors was going to be severe. And more or less told them that they needed to *find more acreage* to set up their facility, and they did that." (Emphasis added.)

the temple's noise and traffic impact on surrounding persons. Both the Community Services Department and the Planning Commission approved this second application because the parcel's size, along with additional setback and use conditions, adequately addressed the noise, traffic, and other complaints related to the temple's possible impact on surrounding agricultural uses.

The County Board of Supervisors' denial of Guru Nanak's second application frustrated Guru Nanak's attempt to comply both with the reasons given for the County's first denial and the Planning Division's various requirements for Guru Nanak to locate a temple on land zoned "agricultural." The Board's primary reason for denying Guru Nanak's second application was that the temple would contribute to "leapfrog development." Although the Zoning Code conditionally permits churches and other non-agricultural activities within agricultural districts, the County could use its concern with leapfrog development effectively to deny churches access to all such land; a great majority of agriculturally zoned land near Yuba City is separated from existing urban development. Moreover, many other churches already exist on agriculturally zoned land,[17] including another Sikh temple located on Bogue Road less than a mile away from the proposed temple. The Bogue Road Sikh temple's parcel of land, like Guru Nanak's land, is surrounded by other agricultural parcels of land, to the extent such parcels are within Yuba City's sphere of influence. Hence, the County inconsistently applied its concern with leapfrog development to Guru Nanak. At the very least, such inconsistent decision-making establishes that any future CUP applications for a temple on land zoned "agricultural" would be fraught with uncertainty. *See id.* at 901(finding a substantial burden where a church's future efforts to locate another parcel of property or file new land use applications would result in "delay, uncertainty, and expense").

In denying the second CUP application, the Board of Supervisors disregarded, without explanation, the Planning Division's finding that Guru Nanak's acceptance of various mitigation conditions would make the proposed temple have a less-than-significant impact on surrounding land uses. We "cannot view [the denial of the second CUP application] 'in isolation'; [rather, it] 'must be viewed in the context of [Guru Nanak's permit process] history.'" *See Westchester Day Sch. v. Vill. of Mamaroneck,* 417 F.Supp.2d 477, 548(S.D.N.Y.2006) (quoting *Living Water Church of God v. Charter Twp. of Meridian,* 384 F.Supp.2d 1123, 1134 (W.D.Mich.2005)). In *Westchester Day School,* the district court found a substantial burden where the zoning board denied the religious day school's land use application despite the day school having "worked for over one-and-a-half years to address the [zoning board's] concerns and offered to make changes to, *inter alia,* parking, the size of [the proposed construction,] landscaping, [the] enrollment cap[, and] a bus

---

[17] At the Planning Commission public hearing, Marie Carney, Guru Nanak's realtor in acquiring the subject property, stated, "[T]here [are] plenty of examples of churches having been built on ag[ricultural] land and they tend to be scattered throughout the community." Although Ms. Carney was not a neutral participant in this land use proceeding, her statement is nowhere disputed in the record.

departure management plan to mitigate the traffic impact." *Id.; see also Living Water,* 384 F.Supp.2d. at 1134 (finding a substantial burden where the Township denied the church's land use proposal after the church had "worked diligently and in good faith with the Township to address its concerns before submitting a revised . . . proposal"). Similarly, during both of its CUP application processes, Guru Nanak agreed to every mitigation condition the Planning Division found necessary to recommend the land entitlements. Regarding the second application in particular, Guru Nanak agreed to a host of conditions proposed specifically to allay the County's concerns with leapfrog development— including a one-hundred foot setback to allow for pesticide spraying, and that all its religious ceremonies be held indoors and limited to seventy-five people. Nevertheless, in denying the second application, the Board of Supervisors neither related why any of such mitigation conditions were inadequate nor suggested additional conditions that would render satisfactory Guru Nanak's application.

While the Zoning Code conditionally permits churches in residential and higher density districts, noise and traffic concerns would likely preclude constructing any other proposed temple on a small parcel of land.[19] Likewise, Guru Nanak would understandably be hesitant to propose a temple on another large, agricultural parcel of land for fear that the County would yet again deny that application because of leapfrog development. Even if Guru Nanak were once again to follow the Planning Division's detailed requirements on mitigating impacts on nearby land, history shows such extensive efforts could very well be in vain. The net effect of the County's two denials—including their underlying rationales and disregard for Guru Nanak's accepted mitigation conditions—is to shrink the large amount of land theoretically available to Guru Nanak under the Zoning Code to several scattered parcels that the County may or may not ultimately approve.[20] Because the County's actions have to a significantly

---

[19] During the Planning Commission public hearing, one complaining neighbor exemplified the perspective of many Sutter County residents that converted Guru Nanak's task of locating suitable property into a predicament: "[N]o family wants to live near a religious temple with all the excessive crowds, traffic, and noise which will increase with a future temple and [Guru Nanak's] proposal."

[20] In denying Guru Nanak's second application, the Board of Supervisors assured Guru Nanak that it would support a future application "if it was in the right location . . . closer towards Yuba City . . . further to the north of this site along with several other churches." The Board of Supervisors also advised that it would informally cooperate with Guru Nanak to locate a suitable site. Admittedly, the availability of other suitable property weighs against a finding of a substantial burden. *See San Jose Christian,* 360 F.3d at 1035. However, RLUIPA does not contemplate that local governments can use broad and discretionary land use rationales as leverage to select the precise parcel of land where a religious group can worship. *See Saint Constantine,* 396 F.3d at 900 (noting that RLUIPA's substantial burden test aims to protect religious groups from "subtle forms of discrimination when, as in the case of the grant or denial of zoning variances, a state delegates essentially standardless discretion to nonprofessionals operating without procedural safeguards"). Moreover, given that Guru Nanak had repeatedly followed the guidance of governmental bodies about how to obtain a land entitlement to no avail, we cannot credit the Board's offer to cooperate as assuring Guru Nanak's future success.

great extent lessened the prospect of Guru Nanak being able to construct a temple in the future, the County has imposed a substantial burden on Guru Nanak's religious exercise.

Our decision contrasts with the facts present in *San Jose Christian,* where we found the plaintiff had not suffered a substantial burden because the city's actions had not lessened the possibility that the college could find a suitable property. In *San Jose Christian,* we considered it centrally important that there was no evidence to suggest that the religious institution desired by San Jose Christian College could not be obtained merely by "submitt[ing] a *complete* application." *San Jose Christian,* 360 F.3d at 1035; *see also id.* ("Should College comply with this request, it is not at all apparent that its re-zoning application will be denied."). Moreover, we noted that even if its complete application were denied, the college had no reason to believe another application would be rejected. *Id.* ("[There is] no evidence in the record demonstrating that College was precluded from using other sites within the city."). *See also Henderson v. Kennedy,* 253 F.3d 12, 17 (D.C.Cir.2001) ("Because the Park Service's ban on sales on the Mall is at most a restriction on one of a *multitude of means,* it is not a substantial burden on their vocation.") (emphasis added).

3. Compelling Interests

The County effectively concedes that it has no compelling interest, much less that the restrictions are narrowly tailored to accomplish such interest. The County presents no such argument in its briefs. Because the County "shall bear the burden of persuasion," 42 U.S.C. §2000cc-2(b), to prove narrowly tailored, compelling interests, we hold that the district court properly invalidated the County's denial of Guru Nanak's CUP application.

B. Constitutionality of RLUIPA's Individual Land Use Assessments Provision

We now turn to the issue of whether RLUIPA as applied to the facts of this case is constitutional. . . .

Unlike RFRA, the predecessor to RLUIPA, RLUIPA applies solely to regulations affecting land use and prison conditions, and therefore does not "displac[e] laws and prohibit[ ] official actions of almost every description and regardless of subject matter. . . . [nor does it] appl[y] to all federal and state law." *See City of Boerne,* 521 U.S. at 532, 117 S.Ct. 2157. RLUIPA has nowhere near the "universal coverage," *id.* at 516, 117 S.Ct. 2157, the Supreme Court found unacceptable in *City of Boerne. See also Cutter,* 125 S.Ct. at 2118 (stating that RLUIPA is "[l]ess sweeping than RFRA"). As with the statutes the Supreme Court has found to be valid as constitutional exercises of Congress's Section Five authority, RLUIPA solely includes "remedies aimed at areas where . . . discrimination has been most flagrant." *See South Carolina v. Katzenbach,*

383 U.S. 301, 315, 86 S.Ct. 803, 15 L.Ed.2d 769 (1966).[21] RLUIPA is a congruent and proportional response to free exercise violations because it targets only regulations that are susceptible, and have been shown, to violate individuals' religious exercise. Therefore, Congress constitutionally enacted RLUIPA pursuant to its enforcement power within Section Five of the Fourteenth Amendment. . . .

III. . . .

IV. CONCLUSION

We AFFIRM the district court's order granting summary judgment for Guru Nanak and enjoining the County immediately to approve and grant Guru Nanak's CUP application.

AFFIRMED.

NOTES AND QUESTIONS

1. *Increased Traffic.* The neighbors objecting to the temple raised concerns about increased traffic. Neighbors opposed to any type of new development often raise traffic concerns, and places of worship do in fact tend to generate a significant amount of traffic when a service or other event is taking place. On the other hand, objections based on increased traffic or other similar concerns can be a pretext for excluding a religious use. How does RLUIPA address the possibility of pretextual objections? On the other hand, how does RLUIPA address legitimate community concerns?

2. *Does RLUIPA Give Religious Groups Too Much Power?* RLUIPA was intended to combat religious discrimination in the land use context. Critics of the law often focus on its application of strict scrutiny to restrictions that burden religious land uses. The application of strict scrutiny places the challenger to a government action in a very strong position. As a result, RLUIPA gives religious organizations tremendous leverage in the land use context. Even if we don't want religious organizations to be subject to

---

[21] We do note two potential concerns regarding the scope of RLUIPA.

First, *City of Boerne* noted a concern with the strict scrutiny test created by RFRA. 521 U.S. at 533-34, 117 S.Ct. 2157 ("The stringent test RFRA demands of state laws reflects a lack of proportionality or congruence between the means adopted and the legitimate end to be achieved . . . . Requiring a State to demonstrate a compelling interest and show that it has adopted the least restrictive means of achieving that interest is the most demanding test known to constitutional law."). While RLUIPA may use the same strict scrutiny standard as did RFRA, it applies the standard only to types of regulations subject to strict scrutiny in the past. *See supra* Part II.B.

Second, RLUIPA defines "religious exercise" to include "any exercise of religion, whether or not compelled by, or central to, a system of religious belief." 42 U.S.C. §2000cc-5(7)(A). This definition of "religious exercise" is broader than the definition in RFRA. *See Civil Liberties*, 342 F.3d at 760. However, RLUIPA's expanded meaning of "religious exercise" applies, as is relevant here, only to individualized assessments pursuant to land use regulations. As noted above, Congress sufficiently documented how local governments stifle religious groups' religious exercise by denying such groups the ability to use property for religious purposes.

land use discrimination, we might not want them to be given special treatment in the land use context either. The fear of facing a RLUIPA suit might lead a municipality to give a religious institution more favorable treatment than it might give to a non-religious organization. Considering the issues discussed in this note and the prior note, do you think that RLUIPA strikes the right balance between the interests of religious groups and legitimate community land use concerns?

3. *Further Reading.* For further discussion of RLUIPA, *see* Alan C. Weinstein, *The Effects of RLUIPA's Land Use Provisions on Local Governments*, 39 Fordham Urb. L.J. 1221 (2012); Bram Alden, *Reconsidering RLUIPA: Do Religious Land Use Protections Really Benefit Religious Land Users?*, 57 UCLA L. Rev. 1779 (2010); Patricia E. Salkin & Amy Lavine, *The Genesis of RLUIPA and Federalism: Evaluating the Creation of a Federal Statutory Right and its Impact on Local Government*, 40 Urb. Law. 195 (2008).

CHAPTER 9

TAKINGS

In this chapter, we will explore the constitutional limits on the government's power to take private property. For the most part, we will focus on the Just Compensation Clause of the Fifth Amendment:

> [N]or shall private property be taken for public use, without just compensation.

Looking at the text, you will see four distinct concepts: "private property," "taken," "public use," and "just compensation." As is the case with most areas of constitutional law, each of these concepts has a contestable meaning.

We will use the four concepts in the Just Compensation Clause to organize this chapter. We will begin with the power of eminent domain and the issues of just compensation and public use. Although there is abundant room for controversy in these areas, the U.S. Supreme Court has provided relatively clear answers to the meaning of both "just compensation" and "public use." The state of the law on public use and just compensation therefore is relatively clear.

We will then move to the regulatory takings question: when, if ever, will a government regulation of private property constitute a taking of private property within the meaning of the Just Compensation Clause? This question implicates the meaning of "private property" and "taken." Unlike the public use and just compensation issues, the U.S. Supreme Court has not provided clear answers to the regulatory takings question. Indeed, regulatory takings is widely considered to be one of the most conceptually and doctrinally confused areas of constitutional law. The regulatory takings problem is also fascinating and raises profound questions about the power of the government over private property.

Before we proceed, we should briefly address the two other clauses in the Constitution that protect against the deprivation of private property. These are the Due Process Clauses of the Fifth and Fourteenth Amendments. The Fifth Amendment's Due Process Clause states:

> No person shall . . . be deprived of life, liberty, or property, without due process of law. . . .

The Fourteenth Amendment's Due Process Clause states:

> [N]or shall any state deprive any person of life, liberty, or property, without due process of law. . . .

We will leave in-depth coverage of the Due Process Clauses to your Constitutional Law class. The Due Process Clauses, however, play an important role in some of the takings issues we will consider in this chapter, so we need to say a couple of things about them now.

First, there are two categories of due process issues that come up in U.S. constitutional law. The first category is *procedural due process*. As its name implies, procedural due process is concerned with the procedural protections given to people before they are deprived of life, liberty, or property. We saw procedural due process concerns reflected in our discussion of the need to join junior parties to a foreclosure action. If junior interest holders are joined as parties, they are given the procedural protections of the legal process. The second category is *substantive due process*. The boundaries and legitimacy of the doctrine of substantive due process are both hotly contested. In contemporary cases, substantive due process often features in cases involving fundamental individual rights. If a government action infringes on a fundamental right, then that action may be unconstitutional under the doctrine of substantive due process. In our last chapter, we saw an example of this type of due process analysis in *Moore v. East Cleveland*, where the Court held that enforcement of the municipal ordinance violated the plaintiff's fundamental right to live with members of her immediate family. In this chapter, we will talk about substantive due process in terms of government power. If the government acts in a way that (a) deprives a person of life, liberty, or property and (b) exceeds the government's power, then that government action is unconstitutional on substantive due process grounds. *Euclid v. Ambler Realty* is an example of this type of analysis from the prior chapter. Although *Euclid* held that the zoning law was constitutional, the Court analyzed the question before it in terms of whether zoning exceeded the scope of the state's police power. Today, substantive due process is in disfavor in most property contexts. We will need to be aware of the doctrine, however, to be able to fully understand aspects of both older cases and contemporary cases. We will explicitly highlight these substantive due process issues when they come up.

Second, it is important to understand that the Just Compensation Clause, like other provisions of the Bill of Rights, initially applied only to the federal government and did not apply to the states. These provisions now apply to the states because they were *incorporated* into the Due Process Clause of the Fourteenth Amendment, which, as you can see above, expressly applies to the states. Again, we will leave an in-depth analysis of incorporation to your Constitutional Law class. For our purposes, it is important to know that the Just Compensation Clause was expressly incorporated and thus extended to the states, in the 1897 case *Chicago, Burlington, & Quincy Railroad Co. v. City of Chicago*, 166 U.S. 226. In other words, until the ratification of the Fourteenth Amendment in 1868, the Just Compensation Clause did not apply to the states, and the Clause's applicability to the states did not become clear until it was expressly incorporated by the Supreme Court in 1897.

A. EMINENT DOMAIN, "JUST COMPENSATION," AND "PUBLIC USE"

Sovereign governments have the power of eminent domain. This power allows the government to take private property. When the government exercises eminent domain, we often say that it has *condemned* the property. You may associate the word "condemnation" with the taking and destruction of dilapidated buildings. In this context, "condemnation" is often used more broadly to refer to the taking by eminent domain of any property interest, regardless of its physical condition.

Eminent domain is an incredibly potent power and places a fundamental limit on the extent of private property. It is potentially subject to abuse, and Justice Patterson famously called the power of eminent domain the "despotic power."[1] On the other hand, it is a necessary power. Consider, for example, the problem of building a road. Without the power of eminent domain, the government would have to negotiate with each and every property owner who owned land along the road's route. Holdout problems very well could make the expense of land acquisition prohibitive. With the power of eminent domain, the government can take the needed property. This power, used properly, should benefit the public as a whole. With eminent domain, however, there is a tremendous potential for a conflict between the interests of the public and the interests of the property owners who are having their property taken.

The Just Compensation Clause addresses this potential for conflict between the public interest and private property owners. As a preliminary matter, it is important to understand that the Just Compensation Clause does not create the eminent domain power. *Eminent domain is an inherent power of sovereignty.* The Just Compensation Clause *implicitly recognizes the government's eminent domain power and places limits on the exercise of that power.* In the United States, both the state and federal governments are sovereigns, and each has the power of eminent domain. Local governments (cities, towns, counties, etc.) may exercise the power of eminent domain if it is delegated to them by the state.

The Just Compensation Clause creates two potential limits on the exercise of eminent domain. First, the government must pay just compensation for taken property. Second, the government arguably must take the property for public use. We will look at these two limits in turn. As we will see, the just compensation requirement is well established and creates a clear limit on government exercises of eminent domain. In contrast, the public use limitation, as interpreted by the Supreme Court, does not place a meaningful restriction on governmental use of eminent domain.

---

[1] *Van Horne's Lessee v. Dorrance*, 2 U.S. (2 Dall.) 304 (1795).

1. JUST COMPENSATION

The text of the Just Compensation Clause clearly establishes a compensation requirement: "nor shall private property be taken for public use, without just compensation." The government may take private property by eminent domain, but must pay just compensation if it does so. Note again that the Clause does not prohibit takings of private property. Rather, it prohibits *uncompensated* takings of private property. The compensation requirement reduces the conflict between the public interest and the interest of the property owner by compensating the property owner for her loss and by requiring the government to take the obligation to pay compensation into account in deciding to take the property.

The U.S. Supreme Court has consistently held that the just compensation requirement is met by the payment of the fair market value of the property to the owner. For example, the Court held in *United States v. 564.54 Acres of Land*, 441 U.S. 506, 511 (1979), that:

> In giving content to the just compensation requirement of the Fifth Amendment, this Court has sought to put the owner of condemned property "in as good a position pecuniarily as if his property had not been taken." *Olson v. United States*, 292 U.S. 246, 255, 54 S.Ct. 704, 708 (1934). However, this principle of indemnity has not been given its full and literal force. Because of serious practical difficulties in assessing the worth an individual places on particular property at a given time, we have recognized the need for a relatively objective working rule. *See United States v. Miller*, 317 U.S. 369, 374, 63 S.Ct. 276, 280, 87 L.Ed. 336 (1943); *United States v. Cors*, 337 U.S. 325, 332, 69 S.Ct. 1086, 1090, 93 L.Ed. 1392 (1949). The Court therefore has employed the concept of fair market value to determine the condemnee's loss. Under this standard, the owner is entitled to receive "what a willing buyer would pay in cash to a willing seller" at the time of the taking. *United States v. Miller, supra*, 317 U.S. at 374, 63 S.Ct., at 280. . . .

The concept of fair market value is something of an artifice, because we cannot know for certain what a willing buyer would pay to a willing seller without a consensual market transaction. When a government exercises eminent domain, we have a forced, rather than consensual, sale. This said, the concept of fair market value is a familiar one to most real estate professionals, and it is a relatively straightforward process for an appraiser to come up with an estimate of the fair market value of a given parcel of property. Real estate appraisal falls short of being an exact science, and it should come as no surprise that appraisal experts hired by the government and by the private property owner often come to significantly different values in eminent domain proceedings. Even with these difficulties, fact finders in eminent domain proceedings typically are able to come up with a reasonably accurate fair market value for the taken property.

Although it is easy to administer, fair market value compensation can be criticized because it often falls far short of full compensation for the owner. If the owner was truly willing to sell for fair market value, then the owner would sell the property to the government voluntarily, and the use of eminent domain would not have been necessary. An owner unwilling to sell for fair market value likely places some additional personal value on the property. This personal value may have many sources and might be based, for example, on sentimental attachment to a home, the hassle of moving, or proximity to family or work. As Judge Posner explained,

> "[J]ust compensation" has been held to be satisfied by payment of market value, *see*, e.g., *United States v. Reynolds*, 397 U.S. 14, 16, 90 S.Ct. 803, 805, 25 L.Ed.2d 12 (1970). Compensation in the constitutional sense is therefore not full compensation, for market value is not the value that every owner of property attaches to his property but merely the value that the marginal owner attaches to his property. Many owners are "intramarginal," meaning that because of relocation costs, sentimental attachments, or the special suitability of the property for their particular (perhaps idiosyncratic) needs, they value their property at more than its market value (i.e., it is not "for sale"). Such owners are hurt when the government takes their property and gives them just its market value in return. The taking in effect confiscates the additional (call it "personal") value that they obtain from the property, but this limited confiscation is permitted provided the taking is for a public use.

Coniston Corp. v. Village of Hoffman Estates, 844 F.2d 461, 464 (7th Cir. 1988). As Judge Posner states, there is no requirement that the owner be compensated for personal value under the Supreme Court's case law. The just compensation requirement is met when the owner is paid the fair market value of the taken property.

2. PUBLIC USE

Let's take another look at the text of the Just Compensation Clause:

> [N]or shall private property be taken for public use, without just compensation.

We will spend the rest of this section considering the meaning of the words "public use." Before we get to that issue, we should focus for a moment on a related question: what is the role (as opposed to the meaning) of the words "public use" in the Just Compensation Clause? There are at least three options:

> First, we could see "public use" as an explicit prohibition on the use of eminent domain to take property for something other than public use (whatever meaning we end up giving to "public use"). On this view, a government taking of property for something other than public use would violate the Just Compensation Clause.

Second, we could see "public use" as an implicit limitation, suggesting that the eminent domain power is inherently limited to the taking of private property for public use. In other words, on this interpretation, the eminent domain power itself is limited to taking property for public use. Under this view, a government taking of property for something other than public use would exceed the power of eminent domain. Because it exceeded the government's power to act, it would be unconstitutional on the grounds that it violated substantive due process, rather than on the grounds that it violated the Just Compensation Clause.

Third, we could see "public use" as not being a limitation on government power at all. Under this view, the words merely describe the most common reason why the government might exercise eminent domain. Takings for public or non-public use would be permitted, so long as just compensation is paid.

Presuming that they constitute either an explicit or implicit limit on the power of eminent domain, we need to return to the meaning of the words "public use." The meaning of these words has been the subject of controversy almost since the ratification of the Constitution. You might intuitively think that permissible public use would be limited to classic exercises of eminent domain where the government takes land for a road or a school and that a use of eminent domain to transfer property from one private owner to another would constitute the use of eminent domain for an improper private purpose. As we will see, however, the line between permissible public use and prohibited private use has never been particularly clear.

Our end point in this section will be the Supreme Court's 2005 decision in *Kelo v. New London*. *Kelo* articulated a very broad conception of "public use" and permitted the use of eminent domain to take private property and transfer it to a private developer to promote economic development. *Kelo* may very well be the most unpopular Supreme Court decision of all time—polls showed that 90 percent of respondents disagreed with the outcome of the case. (Many of the Court's decisions are controversial, but they tend to have their supporters and detractors. Pretty much everyone disliked *Kelo*.) The fact that *Kelo* is unpopular, however, does not mean that it was wrong. To be able to fully evaluate *Kelo*, we need to provide some historical context. We therefore lead up to *Kelo* by taking a look at how courts have applied the concept of public use over time.

We begin with an excerpt from an article surveying the history of "public use" from pre-founding America to the mid-twentieth century. In reading this excerpt, remember well that the Just Compensation Clause was not clearly understood to apply to the states until it was incorporated into the Due Process Clause of the Fourteenth Amendment by the U.S. Supreme Court in 1897. The Just Compensation Clause would therefore be at most a source of persuasive authority for state courts grappling with the scope of the power of eminent domain in earlier cases.

CHARLES E. COHEN, *EMINENT DOMAIN AFTER* KELO V. CITY OF NEW LONDON: *AN ARGUMENT FOR BANNING ECONOMIC DEVELOPMENT TAKINGS*

29 Harv. J.L. & Pub. Pol'y 491 (2006)[2]

[C]onceptions of public use can be generally divided into two categories: the "narrow" view and the "broad" view. Under the narrow view, the term "public use" means "use by the public." Under this approach, property is taken for "public use" only if the public has the right to use the property, or the property is owned by the government, after it is taken. Under the broad view, property is taken for "public use" if the taking results in some public advantage or benefit. Under this view, anything that enhances public welfare constitutes a "public use." The broad view is almost universally accepted; indeed, throughout most of American history, it has been the dominant view. . . .

A. PUBLIC-PRIVATE TAKINGS IN THE COLONIAL AND REVOLUTIONARY ERAS

Although the principle that private property could only be taken for public use did not become firmly entrenched in American law until after the Revolution, actual practices prior to the ratification of the U.S. Constitution are highly relevant to the later debates over the scope of the "public use" requirement. Based on colonial land use practices, at least initially, there were virtually no limits on nonconsensual property transfers between private individuals. The taking of land to build dams and private roads and to drain private land was commonplace. Today, many of these takings would be considered public-private takings, in that private individuals or entities, rather than the government, were permitted (literally or in effect) to condemn the property of others. Eminent domain transfers to the government were common as well: There were, for example, formal statutes authorizing local governments to take land to build roads as early as 1639. But of greater interest to the study of the public use requirement are legislative schemes that, by limiting the traditional legal remedies available for trespass and other common-law actions, had the effect of facilitating nonconsensual transfers to private individuals or entities. The most commonly cited examples of these schemes are the so-called "Mill Acts" and various other legislative schemes permitting landlocked property owners to condemn ways of access over their neighbors' land.

Under the Mill Acts, colonial governments dramatically limited the remedies available to upper riparian landowners for flooding caused by the construction of lower riparian mill dams. One constructing a mill under the Mill Acts was liable only

---

[2] [Ed. note: Most of the footnotes have been omitted from this excerpt. The numbering and formatting of the footnotes that have been included have been modified.]

for annual or permanent damages and enjoyed a privileged status compared with his common-law forebears, whose aggrieved upper riparian neighbors could resort to the remedies of self-help, punitive damages, and injunctive relief. The effect of this regime was that "the lower riparian had a right to condemn the lands of his upper neighbor by flooding."[3] In virtually all Mill Act states, the mills were heavily regulated and required to serve any paying customer. Thus, although the Mill Acts permitted forced property transfers to private individuals, the mills constructed on property so transferred were, in Nathan Sales's words, "public utilities." These takings would be considered to comport with the narrow view of public use. One important exception, however, was Maryland's Mill Act, enacted in 1719, which extended Mill Act protections to builders of private mills used for iron production, and which did not require that these mills be available for use by the public. But even in states whose Mill Acts did require access to the mills by the public, some courts spoke of the mills in terms of the general benefits they would produce for the public at large, rather than the benefits provided to those who actually used the mills. At the same time, many colonial legislatures authorized property owners lacking access to public roads to condemn, upon payment of compensation, rights of way over surrounding lands. Thus, by the colonial era, "[a]lready eminent domain's exercise was split between governmental bodies and private parties."[4]

Other colonial land use practices would raise eyebrows among today's advocates of a strict public use requirement. John F. Hart, in his study of colonial land use practices,[5] catalogued numerous colonial statutes authorizing transfers from one private party to another if the original owner failed to make productive use of the land. In the Plymouth colony, for example, one who failed to begin productive operations within a year of discovering a mine would forfeit the mine and the government could appoint another person to operate that mine for his own profit. Similar statutes in other colonies allowed private individuals to condemn sites suitable for mill construction if the present owner failed to build a mill or to take property of owners who allowed sites amenable to forges and foundries to lay idle. Several colonial acts threatened owners of undeveloped urban lots with forfeiture if they failed to develop the land within prescribed time periods or in a manner determined by law. Thus, "antient proprietors" of land in James City, Virginia who failed to build on their holdings could lose their property interest if another person built a "decent house" on the undeveloped land. None of these takings resulted in actual use by the public. Instead, they were intended to advance communities' needs for economic development and population growth. . . .

[A] public use requirement of any kind did not begin to emerge until later, under circumstances that remain to some extent unclear. Pennsylvania and Virginia were the first colonies to insert the phrase "public use" into their constitutions in 1776.

---

[3] Lawrence Berger, *The Public Use Requirement in Eminent Domain*, 57 Or. L. Rev. 203, 206 (1978).

[4] Errol E. Meidinger, *The "Public Uses" of Eminent Domain: History and Policy*, 11 Envtl. L. 1, 16 (1980)

[5] John F. Hart, *Colonial Land Use Law and Its Significance for Modern Takings Doctrine*, 109 Harv. L. Rev. 1252 (1996).

Pennsylvania's constitution provided that "no part of a man's property can be justly taken from him, or applied to public uses, without his own consent, or that of his legal representatives. . . ." Virginia's "public use" clause stated that citizens "cannot be taxed or deprived of their property for public uses, without their own consent, or that of their representatives so elected. . . ." However, the language of neither provision clearly states that eminent domain may only be exercised for public uses, and history does not reveal the drafters' exact intentions. . . . [O]nly after the outbreak of the Revolution did most of the other original thirteen states add public use language to their constitutions, beginning with Vermont in 1777 and concluding with South Carolina in 1868. These latter provisions, like the ones in Virginia and Pennsylvania, often did not specify the actual permitted uses and limitations of the eminent domain power.

B. PUBLIC-PRIVATE TAKINGS IN THE NINETEENTH CENTURY

As a result of the vagueness of limitations on the takings power, eminent domain doctrine developed piecemeal, decision by decision, in the state courts. Lacking explicit direction from their respective state or colonial takings provisions, the courts turned to civil law, natural law, and common law for guidance. Among the key principles developed by the courts during this period was that eminent domain was a power inherent in government and that it "could be legitimately exercised by the state only for a 'public use' or 'public purpose.'"[6] William B. Stoebuck, in his classic *A General Theory of Eminent Domain*, noted that the early civil law theorists Grotius, Vattel, Pufendorf, and Bynkershoek all argued for limitations on the power of eminent domain, insisting, respectively, that the power should be used only for "public advantage," "public welfare," "necessity of the state," or "public utility." Stoebuck further noted that these theorists, often quoted in American judicial opinions, "apparently influenced" the American development of the "public use" requirement.[7] Alternatively, Philip Nichols, Jr. concluded that

> American courts seem to have evolved [the public use requirement] by reference to the "higher law," with some assistance from an implication by negative inference from the phrase in the Fifth Amendment to the Federal Constitution, and in many state constitutions, "nor shall private property be taken for public use without just compensation."[8]

In any case, even absent explicit legislative or constitutional provisions, many early decisions held that governments lacked the power to permit the nonconsensual taking of private property for private use. Some such holdings were based on natural law theories,

---

[6] Harry N. Scheiber, *The Road to Munn: Eminent Domain and the Concept of Public Purpose in the State Courts*, in *Law in American History* 327, 335 (Donald Fleming & Bernard Bailyn eds., 1971).

[7] William B. Stoebuck, *A General Theory of Eminent Domain*, 47 Wash. L. Rev. 553, 586 (1972).

[8] Philip Nichols, Jr., *The Meaning of Public Use in the Law of Eminent Domain*, 20 B.U. L. Rev. 615, 616 (1940) (citations omitted).

while other courts reached the same result by concluding that state constitutional language implied that property could only be taken for a public use.

Initially, the principle that private property could not be taken for a private use had little impact on the actual uses of the takings power. Eminent domain practices changed little during the first decades following independence, focusing primarily on roads and dams. In fact, even general exploitation of natural resources was widely seen by early nineteenth-century courts as a "public use."

As the Nineteenth Century progressed, however, the use of eminent domain expanded dramatically. In an effort to foster investment and speed economic development, legislatures in every state granted the power of eminent domain to private corporations building or operating railroads, turnpikes, bridges, and canals. Courts generally upheld these takings on the theory that the companies were what would today be called common carriers, obligated to provide service to any member of the public, or on the theory that the ultimate uses of the taken property would produce a public benefit. In addition, the number and scope of Mill Acts grew dramatically. No longer limited to "public" grist mills for use by neighboring farmers, mills constructed under these later acts were increasingly devoted to processing lumber, cotton, and pulp, or to fueling foundries. Despite the obvious lack of any "public use" of such mills, courts repeatedly upheld the private takings to foster their construction. In most cases, the courts echoed the reasoning applied to railroads, turnpikes, bridges, and canals: that the ultimate uses of the taken property would provide a "public benefit."

In the 1840s and 1850s, however, a different view began to emerge: In some jurisdictions, actual use by members of the public became an essential element of "public use." The impetus for this development was increasing concern among courts that the explosive growth in the use of eminent domain, made possible by wide judicial adoption of the broad view of public use, threatened the institution of private property, and that legislatures had been co-opted into favoring powerful private interests over the public good. Other judges feared that excessive support for private enterprise might bring additional government regulation. There is some scholarly disagreement over how widespread this use-by-the-public view ever became. Philip Nichols, Jr. concluded that this "narrow view" eventually became the majority position.[9] Lawrence Berger, however, contended that

> [w]hile the narrow view of public use held considerable sway, especially in the latter half of the nineteenth century, it never completely took over the field. The two doctrines competed, leaving the commentators in hopeless confusion as to what the "true rule" (for in those days they believed in such things) was.[10]

Meidinger agreed with Berger, arguing that "two separate positions, the 'broad' public benefit view and the 'narrow' use-by-the-public view, began to grow up beside each other."[11]

---

[9] Nichols, *supra*, at 619.

[10] Berger, *supra*, at 209.

[11] Meidinger, *supra*, at 24.

Nonetheless, adherence to a use-by-the-public standard, even where it existed, was often more rhetorical than actual, although some legislative acts were struck down under the rule. Stoebuck described the use-by-the-public rule as "mostly fabeled [sic]."[12] Part of the problem was that the test was difficult to apply, requiring a court to determine the extent of, or conditions on, public access necessary to meet the use-by-the-public standard. Philip Nichols, Jr. noted that

> [m]ore important [than the stated doctrines in jurisdictions adopting the use-by-the-public test] were the loopholes, the limitations, and the evasions which courts giving lip service to the majority view were forced to sanction, in order to avoid bringing that view into irreconcilable conflict with the expanding industrialism of the times, and the quick exploitation of natural resources which was felt to be necessary.[13]

The tendency to permit liberal use of the eminent domain power reached its peak toward the end of the Nineteenth Century. By the 1870s, it became routine for governments to delegate eminent domain powers to private interests. The western states, in their eagerness to foster development, "followed Colorado's lead in handing out eminent domain to practically any source of capital that could use it."[14]

C. PUBLIC-PRIVATE TAKINGS IN THE EARLY TWENTIETH CENTURY

By the Twentieth Century it appeared that the narrow doctrine, where it still ostensibly existed, constituted at best a minor hindrance to liberal use of the eminent domain power. On those rare occasions in the Nineteenth Century when the U.S. Supreme Court addressed public use cases, it did so under the Fourteenth Amendment's Due Process Clause on the theory that a taking for private use violated fundamental principles of justice. The Court's limited case law tended to favor the "broad public benefit" view of public use: In 1897, the Court incorporated the Fifth Amendment's public use requirement against the States through the Fourteenth Amendment in *Chicago, Burlington & Quincy Railroad Co. v. Chicago*.[15] In 1905, the Court upheld a Utah law empowering an individual to condemn a neighbor's land in order to convey water.[16] Thereafter, in *Hairston v. Danville & Western Railway Co.*, the Court emphasized "[t]he propriety of keeping in view by this court, while enforcing the Fourteenth Amendment, the diversity of local conditions and of regarding with great respect the judgments of the state courts upon what should be

---

[12] Stoebuck, *supra*, at 590.

[13] Nichols, *supra*, at 619.

[14] Meidinger, *supra*, at 28.

[15] 166 U.S. 226, 228 (1897).

[16] Clark v. Nash, 198 U.S. 361 (1905).

deemed public uses in that State."[17] In 1916, the Court, in upholding a power company's authority to condemn land and water rights in order to produce and sell hydroelectric power, formally rejected the use-by-the-public test, with Justice Holmes declaring, "The inadequacy of the use by the general public as a universal test is established."[18] A few years later in *Rindge Co. v. Los Angeles County*, the Court elaborated that it was "not essential that the entire community, nor even any considerable portion, should directly enjoy or participate in an improvement in order to constitute a public use."[19]

The next major development in the application of eminent domain law came in the first half of the Twentieth Century, with an increase in urban redevelopment programs. The 1920s brought an upsurge in urban projects, aided by the newly prominent profession of "urban planner." These programs, generally designed to eliminate slums and blight or to foster commercial development, began in earnest during the Great Depression. Some courts initially struck down attempts to use the eminent domain power to carry out some of these programs, because the projects as constructed would be either owned or occupied by private individuals. But the majority trend was for courts to uphold these takings under the "public advantage" approach to the public use rule. The United States Housing Act of 1937 made funds available to local governments for slum removal and the development of affordable public housing, and the Housing Act of 1949 provided a massive influx of funds for use by local agencies for urban redevelopment. These acts led to a generation of additional public use litigation, with the courts again generally upholding takings under the public advantage test.

Professor Cohen's historical summary brings us up to a crucial period in the development of the U.S. Supreme Court's public use jurisprudence. As he notes, the use of eminent domain for urban renewal grew dramatically from the 1920s through the 1940s. Urban renewal programs were designed, at least nominally, to clear blighted slums and replace them with new development. Many programs, however, went beyond blight clearance and were aimed at general improvement of the urban environment. Regardless of their specific aims, urban renewal programs typically used eminent domain to take private property, clear it, and transfer it to a private developer. In a very real sense, then, urban renewal programs took private property from one private person and transferred it to another private person (the developer).

The constitutionality of urban renewal came before the Supreme Court in the 1954 case *Berman v. Parker*. Berman and his co-appellants owned a department store that was not itself blighted but that was slated to be taken by eminent domain as part of the clearance of a larger

---

[17] 208 U.S. 598, 607 (1908).

[18] Mt. Vernon-Woodberry Cotton Duck Co. v. Ala. Interstate Power Co., 240 U.S. 30, 32 (1916).

[19] 262 U.S. 700, 707 (1923).

blighted area. Berman challenged the constitutionality of this taking on public use grounds. We will excerpt *Berman v. Parker* below. Before we get to the Supreme Court's analysis, however, we will excerpt portions of the lower court opinion that was appealed to the Supreme Court. This opinion was written by E. Barrett Prettyman, a respected D.C. Circuit judge who was sitting by designation as part of a special three-member district court panel convened to hear Berman's constitutional challenge. While Judge Prettyman's opinion was technically affirmed, the Supreme Court rejected his analysis. We present it here because Judge Prettyman's approach offers a strong contrast to the approach taken by the Supreme Court in *Berman* and later cases. We move directly from the District Court's opinion to the Supreme Court's opinion. As you read them, compare how the two courts approached the public use issues.

SCHNEIDER V. DISTRICT OF COLUMBIA

United States District Court for the District of Columbia, 1953
117 F. Supp. 705, aff'd with modification sub nom Berman v. Parker, *348 U.S. 26 (1954).*

PRETTYMAN, Circuit Judge. These are two civil actions, consolidated, in which the constitutionality of the District of Columbia Redevelopment Act of 1945 is challenged. The defendant Government bodies and officials filed motions to dismiss or, in the alternative, for summary judgment. Affidavits, with exhibits attached, were annexed to the motions. The plaintiffs filed cross-motions for summary judgment.

The plaintiffs are the owners of properties, one at 712 and the other at 716 Fourth Street, Southwest, both in the District of Columbia. One property is a department store owned and operated by the plaintiff Morris, and the other property is a retail hardware store owned and operated by the plaintiff Schneider. The defendants are the members of the District of Columbia Redevelopment Land Agency, that Agency itself (a corporation), the members of the National Capital Park and Planning Commission (called in this statute the "Planning Commission"), the members of the Board of Commissioners of the District of Columbia, and the District of Columbia, a municipal corporation. . . .

The plaintiffs say that the Redevelopment Act itself is unconstitutional on two grounds, (1) that it authorizes the taking by eminent domain of the fee title to private property and the sale or lease of that title to other private persons for private uses; and (2) that the statute authorizes the taking of property in "blighted areas" without defining that term and thus fails to establish any standard sufficiently definite to sustain the delegation of power. They also say that the statute is unconstitutional in its application to the properties of the plaintiffs, which are commercial properties; that the statute should be construed strictly and, as thus construed, does not apply to commercial property or to any property upon which slum conditions do not exist. The respondent Government agencies and officials say that the Act is constitutional, that the constitutionality of statutes similar in all substantial respects to the local statute has been sustained by the highest courts of many states and by the Supreme Court of the United States; that the elimination of slum areas, injurious to the public health, safety, morals and welfare, is a public purpose; that the condemnation of title to the property in the entire project Area B is incidental and essential to the elimination of the slum area; that, since Congress has declared the condemnation of fee title to this property, the courts are without power to disturb that declaration; that Congress has validly delegated to the administrative agencies the power to determine the boundaries of a redevelopment area project.

We can quickly dispose of the case in so far as it relates to certain parts of the property in the project area. The power to acquire by eminent domain property to be devoted to streets (including the "expressway"), schools, recreation centers, parks (including the "greenway"), and other "public uses" is established beyond question. Likewise the power to acquire by eminent domain real estate to be used for the construction of low-cost housing is established in this jurisdiction by *Keyes v. United States*. Our problem concerns the remainder of the property in the area, which is to be acquired by eminent domain and sold or leased to private persons for private uses, with the provision that not less than one-third of the housing accommodations to be built on the property are to be for low-rent housing. . . .

We come, then, to the problem presented in the cases at bar. It lies in three parts.

1. First, there is the slum. A slum is made up of houses (or substitutes for houses), the appurtenances thereto, and people. The houses and appurtenances are such that the people live in filth and breed disease and crime. A slum can be eliminated by tearing down the houses, destroying the appurtenances, and either building new housing on the spot for the people or moving the people away.

2. Second, there is the land upon which a slum exist. The land itself neither contributes to nor detracts from a slum. It is the same whether a slum or a model building exists upon it. The land cannot be destroyed or moved. Only its ownership and its use can be changed. If cleared, the land upon which a slum presently exists would have no harmful effects upon the public. Neither does naked ownership of land, apart from use, have any harmful public effects. A slum and the legal title to the naked land upon which it exists are separate things.

3. Third, there are sections of cities which are not at the present time used to their fullest economic possibility, or are not arranged to fit current ideas of city development. An outstanding example is Trinity Church and its surrounding cemetery at the corner of Wall Street and Broadway in New York City. Old streets are not so wide as new ones would be. Apartment houses would be more economically efficient than are single dwellings. Phrases used to describe this situation are "inadequate planning of the area," "excessive land coverage by the buildings thereon," "defective design and arrangement of the buildings thereon," "faulty street or lot layout," "economically or socially undesirable land uses." The statutes dealing with these areas are usually called "urban

redevelopment" laws. The areas are frequently called "blighted." They are in no sense slums, or similar to slums; they are out-of-date. They do not breed disease or crime; they fail to measure up to their maximum potential use in terms of economic, social, architectural, or civic desirability.

These three distinct factual situations present three distinct sets of legal questions.

I.

First, we have the problem of the slum. There is no doubt concerning the power of Congress to delegate to the District Government the power to clear slums. The power lies within the well-established concepts of police power, which is the protection of the public health, safety, morals and welfare. . . . Moreover, the clearance of a slum is a public purpose, and the condemnation of improvements upon land—buildings and appurtenances—which create the hazards to health, safety, etc., is within the power of eminent domain. Since the Government can condemn such property without compensation under the police power, a fortiori it can condemn any pay reasonable compensation. Since there is power to condemn without compensation there is power to condemn with compensation. . . .

The problem of the slum includes not only the elimination of presently existing slums but also the prevention of future slums. That objective involves questions different from and more difficult than the elimination of present conditions. Prevention deals with developments which may occur in the future, not merely with conditions which exist in the present. So the problem of prevention is: What should be done with property to prevent future developments which will eventuate in slums? Regulations affecting the use of property, designed to prevent the breeding and spread of disease and crime, are within the police power and, when reasonable, are clearly valid. And it seems to us that the prevention of such conditions is a public purpose which would sustain the validity of seizure by eminent domain where the seizure is necessary for the purpose. But that conclusion poses problems. Among these problems are: Is the seizure necessary to the prevention of slums? Does the proposed disposition of the property after seizure reasonably serve the purpose of prevention? Perhaps the problem is more vividly phrased this way: If no slum exists, either because none has ever existed at that place or because an existing slum has been cleared, may the Government seize property in order to prevent the future development of a slum? Practical questions are immediately obvious. Why is such a drastic step by the Government necessary or appropriate to prevent a future slum on a certain parcel of land? Will the proposed disposition of the property prevent slum conditions from occurring on it? The buildings, appurtenances, etc., which constitute the slum itself are usually simply destroyed. The puzzling questions relating to slum prevention, therefore, relate more directly to the title to the land than they do to the ownership of the improvements. We therefore discuss the matter in more detail in the next section of this opinion.

II.

Second, we have the problem of the title to the land upon which a slum now exists. Can the Government seize title to land from which a slum has been or could be cleared, and sell it to a private person for private uses? If the land is to be devoted to schools, roads, parks and such, or to public housing, or to needed low-cost housing, it is to be devoted to a public use, and so its seizure under the power of eminent domain is clearly authorized. But, if the sale subsequent to the seizure is to a private person for a purely private use—such, for example, as apartment houses, stores or theaters—the validity of the seizure of the title is a different problem.

The traditional definition of the power of eminent domain is in terms of public use. It contemplates the use to which the property is to be put after it has been taken. Illustrations are those we have just mentioned, the taking of property for schools, streets, parks, etc. But the term "public use" has progressed as economic facts have progressed, and so projects such as railroads, public power plants, the operation of mines under some conditions, and, more recently, low-cost housing have been held to be public uses for which private property may be seized. Moreover, the traditional concept of use as the keystone of eminent domain has been enlarged in modern thought and cases. We find it described as public purpose. The variation in the term from "use" to "purpose" indicates a progression in thought. The idea is that the taking itself, as distinguished from the subsequent use of the property, may be required in the public interest. The Supreme Court has not gone far in that direction, but we think we see it indicated in the Brown and T.V.A. cases, which we have discussed. We so hold. We hold that the taking of title to real estate for the public purpose of eliminating or of preventing slums is within the power of eminent domain, even though the use to which the property is put after seizure is not a public use; provided (1) that the seizure of the title if necessary to the elimination of the slum or (2) that the proposed disposition of the title may reasonably be expected to prevent the otherwise probable development of a slum. . . .

We are of opinion that title to real estate cannot be seized by the Government merely because a slum presently exists upon the land. Some further necessitous circumstance must exist to validate such a seizure. It must be either that the clearance of the slum is impracticable without taking the title to the land or that proposed restrictions which can be imposed only through the medium of a resale are fairly calculated to prevent recurrence of slum conditions. Ordinarily the seizure of the fee title to land would seem to be neither necessary nor reasonably incidental to the clearance of a slum. But we readily see that there could be circumstances—such, for example, as an obdurate landlord or an impoverished homeowner—in which the seizure of the title, with compensation therefor, ought in reason accompany the condemnation of the buildings. Valid seizure for prevention purposes frequently occurs when the changing of a neighborhood from residential to manufacturing, maritime, or major commercial leaves a remnant of housing accommodations which nurture slum conditions and which ought to be removed to permit other uses.

Whether the taking of a certain piece of property is necessary for a certain public use or purpose is initially and almost wholly a legislative question. But like every other legislative determination it is subject to the Constitution. Congress itself could not deprive a person of his property without due process of law. It is the duty of the courts, when a legislative act is challenged as violative of the Constitution, to determine that issue. . . .

With these principles in mind we hold that the seizure of title to real estate upon which slums exist or upon which a slum may be foreseen would be valid under the Constitution only to the extent that the taking is reasonably necessary to the accomplishment of the asserted public purpose. We hold that the Redevelopment Act goes no further than that, that it confers upon the administrative officials power to seize property, under the limitations we have described, only for the purpose of eliminating or preventing conditions injurious to the public health, safety, morals or welfare. Thus construed, we hold the statute to be valid. We hold that the necessity for the seizure of the title to a parcel of real estate involves facts and judgment, that these are essentially for the administrators, and that the function of the courts is limited to determining whether the conclusions of the administrators are within reason upon the record and within the congressional delegation of authority.

III.

Third, we have the problem of the area which is not a slum but which is out-of-date, called by the Government "blighted" or "deteriorated." The Government says the statute is not limited to slum clearance but extends to what is called "urban redevelopment"; and that as thus construed the statute is valid. The word in the statute upon which the Government rests its view is "blighted," which is not defined in the statute. A hint of a meaning such as that urged by the Government is found in the phrase "backward and stagnant and therefore blighted," which appears near the end of Section 3(n) of the Act. But we have already indicated our conclusion that the more direct provisions of the statute control its scope, that it is the clearly expressed intent of the Congress to authorize in this statute the seizure of property only for the purpose of eliminating and preventing thereafter conditions injurious to the public health, safety, morals and welfare. If we did not find this meaning clear upon the face of the statute, we would be impelled to construe it with that meaning, because otherwise the statute would be unconstitutional.

The contention as to "blight" and "urban redevelopment" would cover two possible factual situations: one where the plan is to redevelop an area in which no slums exist, and the other where the plan is to redevelop an area which the Government deems "appropriate" for redevelopment but upon only a part of which slums exist. We first discuss the two possibilities separately.

The hypothesis in the first phase of this consideration is an urban area which does not breed disease or crime, is not a slum. Its fault is that it fails to meet what are called modern standards. Let us suppose that it is backward, stagnant, not properly laid out, economically Eighteenth Century—anything except detrimental to health, safety or morals. Suppose its owners and occupants like it that way. Suppose they are old-fashioned, prefer single-family dwellings, like small flower gardens, believe that a plot of ground is the place to rear children, prefer fresh to conditioned air, sun to fluorescent light. In many circles all such views are considered "backward and stagnant." Are those who hold them "therefore blighted"? Can they not, nevertheless, own property? Choice of antiques is a right of property. Or suppose these people own these homes and can afford none more modern. The poor are entitled to own what they can afford. The slow, the old, the small in ambition, the devotee of the outmoded have no less right to property than have the quick, the young, the aggressive, and the modernistic or futuristic.

Is a modern apartment house a better breeder of men than is the detached or row house? Is the local corner grocer a less desirable community asset than the absentee stockholder in the national chain or the wage-paid manager? Are such questions as these to be decided by the Government? And, if the decisions be adverse to the erstwhile owners and occupants, is their entire right to own the property thereby destroyed? Even if the line between regulation and seizure, between the power to regulate and the power to seize, is not always etched deeply, it is there. And, even if we progress in our concepts of the "general welfare," we are not at liberty to obliterate the boundary of governmental power fixed by the Constitution.

The terms "public use" and "public purpose" have never been defined with precision, and cannot be. Localities, customs and times change, and with them the needs of the public may change. But even the most liberal courts have put boundaries upon the meanings. One eminent authority [2 Nichols, Eminent Domain §7.2 et seq. (3d ed. 1950)] sums up the matter by saying that the courts which go furthest in sustaining the power of eminent domain hold that "anything which tends to enlarge the resources, increase the industrial energies, and promote the productive power of any considerable number of the inhabitants of a section of the state, or which leads to the growth of towns and the creation of new resources for the employment of capital and labor" constitutes a public use. We think so unqualified a definition cannot be sustained, because every factory or mercantile house of any size meets that definition to some degree, and most certainly the Government has not an unrestricted power to seize one man's property and sell it to another for the building of a factory or a store. The decisions of the courts which used such sweeping language and which are cited to us fall far short of supporting the contention made to us in the present case. We shall discuss them in a moment. . . .

We are of opinion that the Congress, in legislating for the District of Columbia, has no power to authorize the seizure by eminent domain of property for the sole purpose of redeveloping the area according to its, or its agents,' judgment of what a well-developed, well-balanced neighborhood would be; lest this sentence be misconstrued out of context, we repeat our hypothetical assumption for the purposes of this first phase of Section III of our opinion that no slum exists on the hypothetical property or in the area and that the seizure is not for a public use.

But the Government rests the present case upon a narrower basis. And this brings us to the second phase of the problem posed in this section of the opinion. This concerns a situation where the plan is to redevelop an area upon only a part of which slums exist. The state cases hold, the Government says, that "where from a comprehensive standpoint there is a public benefit, such as slum clearance, flowing from the project, the taking is for a public use regardless of the ultimate disposition of the particular piece of property." The Government says that it has determined that Project Area B in the case at bar is an appropriate area for "redevelopment," that slums exist in that area, and that therefore it may seize the title to all the land in the area and, having replanned it, sell it to private persons for the building of row houses, apartment houses, commercial establishments, etc. In essence the claim is that if slums exist the Government may seize, redevelop and sell all the property in any area it may select as appropriate, so long as the area includes the slum area. This amounts to a claim on the part of the authorities for unreviewable power to seize and sell whole sections of the city. . . .

This brings us to consider the redevelopment plan before us. It covers about fifteen square city blocks. . . . The key to the plan, apart from slum clearance, is the opinion of the Government authorities that residential neighborhoods should be "well-balanced" and that the area should contain housing for all income groups. The plan points out that "redevelopment" will inevitably raise the average income level and make it possible to introduce housing for higher-income families at a later stage in the program. It says that generally the Southwest area "should be predominantly a moderate to lower-income area." The recommendations as to the percentages of the types of accommodations to be built in the area are said to be "based upon a conservative analysis of the present local real estate market." The plan says: "The purpose of redevelopment is to clear the slums and replace them with that pattern of land use most appropriate to the overall development of the community." . . .

In sum the purpose of the plan, in addition to the elimination of slum conditions, is to create a pleasant neighborhood, in which people in well-balanced proportions as to income may live. The Government is to determine what conditions are pleasant, what constitutes the "most appropriate" pattern of land use, what is a good balance of income groups for a neighborhood, how many poor people, how many moderately well-to-do people, how many families of two, how many of four, etc., should be provided for in this neighborhood, and what the proper development of a community should be.

Of course the plan as pictured in the prospectus is attractive. In all probability it would enhance the beauty and the livability of the area. If undertaken by private persons the project would be most laudable. It would be difficult to think of a village, town or city in the United States which a group of artists, architects and builders could not improve vastly if they could tear down the whole community and rebuild the whole of it. But as yet the courts have not come to call such pleasant accomplishments a public purpose which validates Government seizure of private property. The claim of Government power for such purposes runs squarely into the right of the individual to own property and to use it as he pleases. Absent impingement upon rights of others, and absent public use or compelling public necessity for the property, the individual's right is superior to all rights of the Government and is impregnable to the efforts of government to seize it. That the individual is in a low-income group or in a high-income group or falls in the middle of the groups is wholly immaterial. One man's land cannot be seized by the Government and sold to another man merely in order that the purchaser may build upon it a better house or a house which better meets the Government's idea of what is appropriate or well-designed.

We hold that Congress did not in the Redevelopment Act confer power to seize property beyond the reasonable necessities of slum clearance and prevention, the word "slum" meaning conditions injurious to the public health, safety, morals and welfare.

If property is seized for the purpose of eliminating or preventing slums within the limitations and in accordance with the rules we have described, the fact that it may be sold subsequently to private persons does not vitiate the validity of the seizure.

The complaints in the two actions at bar are pitched entirely upon a challenge of the constitutionality of the Redevelopment Act, and, except the issue as to commercial property, no other issue as to the application of the statute to the property of plaintiffs, is raised by the pleadings. Therefore, since the statute, as we construe it, is constitutional, we must grant the motion to dismiss.

BERMAN V. PARKER

United States Supreme Court, 1954
348 U.S. 26

Mr. Justice DOUGLAS delivered the opinion of the Court. This is an appeal, 28 U.S.C. §1253, 28 U.S.C.A. §1253, from the judgment of a three-judge District Court which dismissed a complaint seeking to enjoin the condemnation of appellants' property under the District of Columbia Redevelopment Act of 1945, 60 Stat. 790, D.C.Code 1951, §§5-701 to 5-719. The challenge was to the constitutionality of the Act, particularly as applied to the taking of appellants' property. The District Court sustained the constitutionality of the Act. 117 F.Supp. 705. . . .

Appellants own property in Area B at 712 Fourth Street, S.W. It is not used as a dwelling or place of habitation. A department store is located on it. Appellants object to the appropriation of this property for the purposes of the project. They claim that their property may not to taken constitutionally for this project. It is commercial, not residential property; it is not slum housing; it will be put into the project under the management of a private, not a public, agency and redeveloped for private, not public, use. That is the argument; and the contention is that appellants' private property is being taken contrary to two mandates of the Fifth Amendment—(1) "No person shall . . . be deprived of . . . property, without due process of law"; (2) "nor shall private property be taken for public use, without just compensation." To take for the purpose of ridding the area of slums is one thing; it is quite another, the argument goes, to take a man's property merely to develop a better balanced, more attractive community. The District Court, while agreeing in general with that argument, saved the Act by construing it to mean that the Agency could condemn property only for the reasonable necessities of slum clearance and prevention, its concept of "slum" being the existence of conditions "injurious to the public health, safety, morals and welfare." 117 F.Supp. 705, 724-725.

The power of Congress over the District of Columbia includes all the legislative powers which a state may exercise over its affairs. *See District of Columbia v. John R. Thompson Co.,* 346 U.S. 100, 108, 73 S.Ct. 1007, 1011, 97 L.Ed. 1480. We deal, in other words, with what traditionally has been known as the police power. An attempt to define its reach or trace its outer limits is fruitless, for each case must turn on its own facts. The definition is essentially the product of legislative determinations addressed to the purposes of government, purposes neither abstractly nor historically capable of complete definition. Subject to specific constitutional limitations, when the legislature has spoken, the public interest has been declared in terms well-nigh conclusive. In such cases the legislature, not the judiciary, is the main guardian of the public needs to be served by social legislation, whether it be Congress legislating concerning the District of Columbia, see *Block v. Hirsh,* 256 U.S. 135, 41 S.Ct. 458, 65 L.Ed. 865, or the States legislating concerning local affairs. *See Olsen v. State of Nebraska,* 313 U.S. 236, 61 S.Ct. 862, 85 L.Ed. 1305; *Lincoln Federal Labor Union No. 19129, A.F. of L. v. Northwestern Co.,* 335 U.S. 525, 69 S.Ct. 251, 93 L.Ed. 212; *California State Ass'n Inter-Ins. Bureau v. Maloney,* 341 U.S. 105, 71 S.Ct. 601, 95 L.Ed. 788. This principle admits of no exception merely because the power of eminent domain is involved. The role of the judiciary in determining whether that power is being exercised for a public purpose is an extremely narrow one. *See Old Dominion Land Co. v. United States,* 269 U.S. 55, 66, 46 S.Ct. 39, 40, 70 L.Ed. 162; *United States ex rel. Tennessee Valley Authority v. Welch,* 327 U.S. 546, 552, 66 S.Ct. 715, 718, 90 L.Ed. 843.

Public safety, public health, morality, peace and quiet, law and order—these are some of the more conspicuous examples of the traditional application of the police power to municipal affairs. Yet they merely illustrate the scope of the power and do not delimit it. *See Noble State Bank v. Haskell,* 219 U.S. 104, 111, 31 S.Ct. 186, 188, 55 L.Ed. 112. Miserable and disreputable housing conditions may do more than spread disease and crime and immorality. They may also suffocate the spirit by reducing the people who live there to the status of cattle. They may indeed make living an almost insufferable burden. They may also be an ugly sore, a blight on the community which robs it of charm, which makes it a place from which men turn. The misery of housing may despoil a community as an open sewer may ruin a river.

We do not sit to determine whether a particular housing project is or is not desirable. The concept of the public welfare is broad and inclusive. *See Day-Brite Lighting, Inc. v. State of Missouri*, 342 U.S. 421, 424, 72 S.Ct. 405, 407, 96 L.Ed. 469. The values it represents are spiritual as well as physical, aesthetic as well as monetary. It is within the power of the legislature to determine that the community should be beautiful as well as healthy, spacious as well as clean, well-balanced as well as carefully patrolled. In the present case, the Congress and its authorized agencies have made determinations that take into account a wide variety of values. It is not for us to reappraise them. If those who govern the District of Columbia decide that the Nation's Capital should be beautiful as well as sanitary, there is nothing in the Fifth Amendment that stands in the way.

Once the object is within the authority of Congress, the right to realize it through the exercise of eminent domain is clear. For the power of eminent domain is merely the means to the end. *See Luxton v. North River Bridge Co.*, 153 U.S. 525, 529-530, 14 S.Ct. 891, 892, 38 L.Ed. 808; *United States v. Gettysburg Electric R. Co.*, 160 U.S. 668, 679, 16 S.Ct. 427, 429, 40 L.Ed. 576. Once the object is within the authority of Congress, the means by which it will be attained is also for Congress to determine. Here one of the means chosen is the use of private enterprise for redevelopment of the area. Appellants argue that this makes the project a taking from one businessman for the benefit of another businessman. But the means of executing the project are for Congress and Congress alone to determine, once the public purpose has been established. *See Luxton v. North River Bridge Co., supra; cf. Highland v. Russell Car Co.*, 279 U.S. 253, 49 S.Ct. 314, 73 L.Ed. 688. The public end may be as well or better served through an agency of private enterprise than through a department of government—or so the Congress might conclude. We cannot say that public ownership is the sole method of promoting the public purposes of community redevelopment projects. What we have said also disposes of any contention concerning the fact that certain property owners in the area may be permitted to repurchase their properties for redevelopment in harmony with the overall plan. That, too, is a legitimate means which Congress and its agencies may adopt, if they choose.

In the present case, Congress and its authorized agencies attack the problem of the blighted parts of the community on an area rather than on a structure-by-structure basis. That, too, is opposed by appellants. They maintain that since their building does not imperil health or safety nor contribute to the making of a slum or a blighted area, it cannot be swept into a redevelopment plan by the mere dictum of the Planning Commission or the Commissioners. The particular uses to be made of the land in the project were determined with regard to the needs of the particular community. The experts concluded that if the community were to be healthy, if it were not to revert again to a blighted or slum area, as though possessed of a congenital disease, the area must be planned as a whole. It was not enough, they believed, to remove existing buildings that were insanitary or unsightly. It was important to redesign the whole area so as to eliminate the conditions that cause slums—the overcrowding of dwellings, the lack of parks, the lack of adequate streets and alleys, the absence of recreational areas, the lack of light and air, the presence of outmoded street patterns. It was believed that the piecemeal approach, the removal of individual structures that were offensive, would be only a palliative. The entire area needed redesigning so that a balanced, integrated plan could be developed for the region, including not only new homes but also schools, churches, parks, streets, and shopping centers. In this way it was hoped that the cycle of decay of the area could be controlled and the birth of future slums prevented. *Cf. Gohld Realty Co. v. City of Hartford*, 141 Conn. 135, 141-144, 104 A.2d 365, 368-370; *Hunter v. Norfolk Redevelopment Authority*, 195 Va. 326, 338-339, 78 S.E.2d 893, 900-901. Such diversification in future use is plainly relevant to the maintenance of the desired housing standards and therefore within congressional power.

The District Court below suggested that, if such a broad scope were intended for the statute, the standards contained in the Act would not be sufficiently definite to sustain the delegation of authority. 117 F.Supp. 705, 721. We do not agree. We think the standards prescribed were adequate for executing the plan to eliminate not only slums as narrowly defined by the District Court but also the blighted areas that tend to produce slums. Property may of course be taken for this redevelopment which, standing by itself, is innocuous and unoffending. But we have said enough to indicate that it is the need of the area as a whole which Congress and its agencies are evaluating. If owner after owner were permitted to resist these redevelopment programs on the ground that his particular property was not being used against the public interest, integrated plans for redevelopment would suffer greatly. The argument pressed on us is, indeed, a plea to substitute the landowner's standard of the public need for the standard prescribed by Congress. But as we have already stated, community redevelopment programs need not, by force of the Constitution, be on a piecemeal basis—lot by lot, building by building.

It is not for the courts to oversee the choice of the boundary line nor to sit in review on the size of a particular project area. Once the question of the public purpose has been decided, the amount and character of land to be taken for the project and the need for a particular tract to complete the integrated plan rests in the discretion of the legislative branch. *See Shoemaker v. United States*, 147 U.S. 282, 298, 13 S.Ct. 361, 390, 37 L.Ed. 170; *United States ex rel. Tennessee Valley Authority v. Welch, supra*, 327 U.S. at page 554, 66 S.Ct. at page 718; *United States v. Carmack*, 329 U.S. 230, 247, 67 S.Ct. 252, 260, 91 L.Ed. 209.

The District Court indicated grave doubts concerning the Agency's right to take full title to the land as distinguished from the objectionable buildings located on it. 117 F.Supp. 705, 715-719. We do not share those doubts. If the Agency considers it necessary in carrying out the redevelopment project to take full title to the real property involved, it may do so. It is not for the courts to determine whether it is necessary for successful consummation of the project that unsafe, unsightly, or insanitary buildings alone be taken or whether title to the land be included, any more than it is the function of the courts to sort and choose among the various parcels selected for condemnation.

The rights of these property owners are satisfied when they receive that just compensation which the Fifth Amendment exacts as the price of the taking.

The judgment of the District Court, as modified by this opinion, is affirmed.

As you can see, the Supreme Court wanted nothing to do with the hard questions that Judge Prettyman asked about public use and the government's power of eminent domain.[20] The Court's opinion in *Berman* is highly deferential to the legislature and takes a very broad view of the permissible constitutional uses of eminent domain. The Court took a similar approach in its next canonical public use case, which follows.

HAWAII HOUSING AUTHORITY V. MIDKIFF

United States Supreme Court, 1984
467 U.S. 229

Justice O'CONNOR delivered the opinion of the Court. The Fifth Amendment of the United States Constitution provides, in pertinent part, that "private property [shall not] be taken for public use, without just compensation." These cases present the question whether the Public Use Clause of that Amendment, made applicable to the States through the Fourteenth Amendment, prohibits the State of Hawaii from taking, with just compensation, title in real property from lessors and transferring it to lessees in order to reduce the concentration of ownership of fees simple in the State. We conclude that it does not.

---

[20] For further analysis of the *Berman* opinion, including discussion of personal notes from some of the Justices that highlight their rejection of Judge Prettyman's approach, *see* D. Benjamin Barros, *Nothing "Errant" About It: The* Berman *and* Midkiff *Conference Notes and How the Supreme Court Got to* Kelo *with Its Eyes Wide Open*, in *Private Property, Community Development, and Eminent Domain*, 57 (Robin Paul Malloy ed., (2008)).

I.

[The Court explained that because of ownership patterns that emerged from early settlement of the Hawaiian Islands, land ownership in Hawaii was remarkably concentrated. The Hawaii Legislature found that almost 49 percent of the land in Hawaii was owned by the state or federal government, and that 47 percent was owned by 72 private landowners. Many people lived in homes leased from these large landowners. The landowners claimed that the main reason they preferred to lease rather than sell was the significant federal tax liability that would accompany a voluntary sale.

The Legislature enacted the Land Reform Act of 1967 (the "Act") to address this high concentration of land ownership. The Act allowed groups of tenants living in leased homes to ask the Hawaii Housing Authority ("HHA") to use eminent domain to condemn the fee simple ownership of the homes and accompanying land. The HHA would pay compensation to the landowner and then convey fee simple ownership to the tenants. Because the takings by eminent domain were involuntary, the tax consequences would be less severe for the owners than consensual sales.

Some landowners filed suit challenging the constitutionality of the Act on public use grounds. The landowners lost in the district court.]

The Court of Appeals for the Ninth Circuit reversed. 702 F.2d 788 (CA9 1983). First, the Court of Appeals decided that the District Court had permissibly chosen not to abstain from the exercise of its jurisdiction. Then, the Court of Appeals determined that the Act could not pass the requisite judicial scrutiny of the Public Use Clause. It found that the transfers contemplated by the Act were unlike those of takings previously held to constitute "public uses" by this Court. The court further determined that the public purposes offered by the Hawaii Legislature were not deserving of judicial deference. The court concluded that the Act was simply "a naked attempt on the part of the state of Hawaii to take the private property of A and transfer it to B solely for B's private use and benefit." *Id.*, at 798. One judge dissented.

On applications of HHA and certain private appellants who had intervened below, this Court noted probable jurisdiction. 464 U.S. 932, 104 S.Ct. 334, 78 L.Ed.2d 304 (1983). We now reverse. . . .

III.

The majority of the Court of Appeals next determined that the Act violates the "public use" requirement of the Fifth and Fourteenth Amendments. On this argument, however, we find ourselves in agreement with the dissenting judge in the Court of Appeals.

A.

The starting point for our analysis of the Act's constitutionality is the Court's decision in *Berman v. Parker*, 348 U.S. 26, 75 S.Ct. 98, 99 L.Ed. 27 (1954). In *Berman*, the

Court held constitutional the District of Columbia Redevelopment Act of 1945. That Act provided both for the comprehensive use of the eminent domain power to redevelop slum areas and for the possible sale or lease of the condemned lands to private interests. In discussing whether the takings authorized by that Act were for a "public use," *id.*, at 31, 75 S.Ct., at 101, the Court stated:

> "We deal, in other words, with what traditionally has been known as the police power. An attempt to define its reach or trace its outer limits is fruitless, for each case must turn on its own facts. The definition is essentially the product of legislative determinations addressed to the purposes of government, purposes neither abstractly nor historically capable of complete definition. Subject to specific constitutional limitations, when the legislature has spoken, the public interest has been declared in terms well-nigh conclusive. In such cases the legislature, not the judiciary, is the main guardian of the public needs to be served by social legislation, whether it be Congress legislating concerning the District of Columbia . . . or the States legislating concerning local affairs. . . . This principle admits of no exception merely because the power of eminent domain is involved. . . ." *Id.*, at 32, 75 S.Ct., at 102 (citations omitted).

The Court explicitly recognized the breadth of the principle it was announcing, noting:

> "Once the object is within the authority of Congress, the right to realize it through the exercise of eminent domain is clear. For the power of eminent domain is merely the means to the end. . . . Once the object is within the authority of Congress, the means by which it will be attained is also for Congress to determine. Here one of the means chosen is the use of private enterprise for redevelopment of the area. Appellants argue that this makes the project a taking from one businessman for the benefit of another businessman. But the means of executing the project are for Congress and Congress alone to determine, once the public purpose has been established." *Id.*, at 33, 75 S.Ct., at 102.

The "public use" requirement is thus coterminous with the scope of a sovereign's police powers.

There is, of course, a role for courts to play in reviewing a legislature's judgment of what constitutes a public use, even when the eminent domain power is equated with the police power. But the Court in *Berman* made clear that it is "an extremely narrow" one. *Id.*, at 32, 75 S.Ct., at 102. The Court in *Berman* cited with approval the Court's decision in *Old Dominion Co. v. United States*, 269 U.S. 55, 66, 46 S.Ct. 39, 40, 70 L.Ed. 162 (1925), which held that deference to the legislature's "public use" determination is required "until it is shown to involve an impossibility." The *Berman* Court also cited to *United States ex rel. TVA v. Welch*, 327 U.S. 546, 552, 66 S.Ct. 715, 718, 90 L.Ed. 843 (1946), which emphasized that "[a]ny departure from this judicial restraint would result in courts deciding on what is and is not a governmental function and in their invalidating legislation on the basis of their view on that question at the moment of decision, a practice which has proved impracticable in other fields." In short, the Court has made clear that it will not substitute its judgment for a legislature's judgment as to what constitutes a public use "unless the use be palpably without reasonable foundation." *United States v. Gettysburg Electric R. Co.*, 160 U.S. 668, 680, 16 S.Ct. 427, 429, 40 L.Ed. 576 (1896).

To be sure, the Court's cases have repeatedly stated that "one person's property may not be taken for the benefit of another private person without a justifying public purpose, even though compensation be paid." *Thompson v. Consolidated Gas Corp.*, 300 U.S. 55, 80, 57 S.Ct. 364, 376, 81 L.Ed. 510 (1937). *See, e.g., Cincinnati v. Vester*, 281 U.S. 439, 447, 50 S.Ct. 360, 362, 74 L.Ed. 950 (1930); *Madisonville Traction Co. v. St. Bernard Mining Co.*, 196 U.S. 239, 251-252, 25 S.Ct. 251, 255-256, 49 L.Ed. 462 (1905); *Fallbrook Irrigation District v. Bradley*, 164 U.S. 112, 159, 17 S.Ct. 56, 63, 41 L.Ed. 369 (1896). Thus, in *Missouri Pacific R. Co. v. Nebraska*, 164 U.S. 403, 17 S.Ct. 130, 41 L.Ed. 489 (1896), where the "order in question was not, and was not claimed to be, . . . a taking of private property for a public use under the right of eminent domain," *id.*, at 416, at 135 (emphasis added), the Court invalidated a compensated taking of property for lack of a justifying public purpose. But where the exercise of the eminent domain power is rationally related to a conceivable public purpose, the Court has never held a compensated taking to be proscribed by the Public Use Clause. *See Berman v. Parker, supra; Rindge Co. v. Los Angeles*, 262 U.S. 700, 43 S.Ct. 689, 67 L.Ed. 1186 (1923); *Block v. Hirsh*, 256 U.S. 135, 41 S.Ct. 458, 65 L.Ed. 865 (1921); *cf. Thompson v. Consolidated Gas Corp., supra* (invalidating an uncompensated taking).

On this basis, we have no trouble concluding that the Hawaii Act is constitutional. The people of Hawaii have attempted, much as the settlers of the original 13 Colonies did, to reduce the perceived social and economic evils of a land oligopoly traceable to their monarchs. The land oligopoly has, according to the Hawaii Legislature, created artificial deterrents to the normal functioning of the State's residential land market and forced thousands of individual homeowners to lease, rather than buy, the land underneath their homes. Regulating oligopoly and the evils associated with it is a classic exercise of a State's police powers. *See Exxon Corp. v. Governor of Maryland*, 437 U.S. 117, 98 S.Ct. 2207, 57 L.Ed.2d 91 (1978); *Block v. Hirsh, supra; see also People of Puerto Rico v. Eastern Sugar Associates*, 156 F.2d 316 (CA1), *cert. denied*, 329 U.S. 772, 67 S.Ct. 190, 91 L.Ed. 664 (1946). We cannot disapprove of Hawaii's exercise of this power.

Nor can we condemn as irrational the Act's approach to correcting the land oligopoly problem.. . . . Of course, this Act, like any other, may not be successful in achieving its intended goals. But "whether in fact the provision will accomplish its objectives is not the question: the [constitutional requirement] is satisfied if . . . the . . . [state] Legislature rationally could have believed that the [Act] would promote its objective." *Western & Southern Life Ins. Co. v. State Bd. of Equalization*, 451 U.S. 648, 671-672, 101 S.Ct. 2070,

2084-2085, 68 L.Ed.2d 514 (1981); *see also Minnesota v. Clover Leaf Creamery Co.*, 449 U.S. 456, 466, 101 S.Ct. 715, 725, 66 L.Ed.2d 659 (1981); *Vance v. Bradley*, 440 U.S. 93, 112, 99 S.Ct. 939, 950, 59 L.Ed.2d 171 (1979). When the legislature's purpose is legitimate and its means are not irrational, our cases make clear that empirical debates over the wisdom of takings—no less than debates over the wisdom of other kinds of socioeconomic legislation—are not to be carried out in the federal courts. Redistribution of fees simple to correct deficiencies in the market determined by the state legislature to be attributable to land oligopoly is a rational exercise of the eminent domain power. Therefore, the Hawaii statute must pass the scrutiny of the Public Use Clause.

B.

The Court of Appeals read our cases to stand for a much narrower proposition. First, it read our "public use" cases, especially *Berman*, as requiring that government possess and use property at some point during a taking. Since Hawaiian lessees retain possession of the property for private use throughout the condemnation process, the court found that the Act exacted takings for private use. 702 F.2d, at 796-797. Second, it determined that these cases involved only "the review of . . . congressional determination[s] that there was a public use, not the review of . . . state legislative determination[s]." *Id.*, at 798 (emphasis in original). Because state legislative determinations are involved in the instant cases, the Court of Appeals decided that more rigorous judicial scrutiny of the public use determinations was appropriate. The court concluded that the Hawaii Legislature's professed purposes were mere "statutory rationalizations." *Ibid.* We disagree with the Court of Appeals' analysis.

The mere fact that property taken outright by eminent domain is transferred in the first instance to private beneficiaries does not condemn that taking as having only a private purpose. The Court long ago rejected any literal requirement that condemned property be put into use for the general public. "It is not essential that the entire community, nor even any considerable portion, . . . directly enjoy or participate in any improvement in order [for it] to constitute a public use." *Rindge Co. v. Los Angeles*, 262 U.S., at 707, 43 S.Ct., at 692. "[W]hat in its immediate aspect [is] only a private transaction may . . . be raised by its class or character to a public affair." *Block v. Hirsh*, 256 U.S., at 155, 41 S.Ct., at 459. As the unique way titles were held in Hawaii skewed the land market, exercise of the power of eminent domain was justified. The Act advances its purposes without the State's taking actual possession of the land. In such cases, government does not itself have to use property to legitimate the taking; it is only the taking's purpose, and not its mechanics, that must pass scrutiny under the Public Use Clause.

Similarly, the fact that a state legislature, and not the Congress, made the public use determination does not mean that judicial deference is less appropriate. Judicial deference is required because, in our system of government, legislatures are better able to assess what public purposes should be advanced by an exercise of the taking power.

State legislatures are as capable as Congress of making such determinations within their respective spheres of authority. *See Berman v. Parker*, 348 U.S., at 32, 75 S.Ct., at 102. Thus, if a legislature, state or federal, determines there are substantial reasons for an exercise of the taking power, courts must defer to its determination that the taking will serve a public use.

IV.

The State of Hawaii has never denied that the Constitution forbids even a compensated taking of property when executed for no reason other than to confer a private benefit on a particular private party. A purely private taking could not withstand the scrutiny of the public use requirement; it would serve no legitimate purpose of government and would thus be void. But no purely private taking is involved in these cases. The Hawaii Legislature enacted its Land Reform Act not to benefit a particular class of identifiable individuals but to attack certain perceived evils of concentrated property ownership in Hawaii—a legitimate public purpose. Use of the condemnation power to achieve this purpose is not irrational. Since we assume for purposes of these appeals that the weighty demand of just compensation has been met, the requirements of the Fifth and Fourteenth Amendments have been satisfied. Accordingly, we reverse the judgment of the Court of Appeals, and remand these cases for further proceedings in conformity with this opinion.

When Justice O'Connor circulated her draft opinion in *Midkiff* to the other Justices, Justice Powell sent her the following memorandum:

> Dear Sandra:
>
> This refers to our brief conversation yesterday. I should have been in touch with you sooner. My suggested changes, set forth below, do not affect your basic analysis. I have been concerned by the sweep of language that can be read as saying that any "social" purpose may justify the taking of private property. The language to this effect is primarily on page 14.
>
> I suggest the following as a substitute for the next to the last sentence in the paragraph on p. 14 that carries over from p. 13:
>
> > "As the unique way titles were held in Hawaii skewed the land market, exercise of the power of eminent domain was justified. The Act advances its purposes without the state taking actual possession of the land. In such cases,"
>
> . . .

The paragraph that begins on p. 14 also can be read broadly to the effect that "social problems" may be addressed by taking private property pursuant to "social legislation." I suggest revisions of some of the language of this paragraph, beginning with the second sentence, along the following lines:

> "Judicial deference is required here because, in our system of government, legislatures are better able to assess what public purposes should be advanced by an exercise of the taking power. State legislatures are as capable as Congress of making such determinations within their respective spheres of authority. *See Berman v Parker*, 348 U.S., at 32. Thus, if there are substantial reasons for an exercise of the taking power, courts must . . ."

The first full sentence on page 13 states that "redistribution of fees simply to reduce the economic and social evils . . . is a rational exercise of the power of eminent domain." Again, I am troubled by the emphasis without limits on "economic and social evils." In this case we are concerned only with a very specific and unique evil. I would suggest omission of the phrase "reduce the economic evils," replacing it with "correct deficiencies in the market." . . .

This *is* a unique case, and I think we may regret language that could encourage Congress and state legislatures to justify taking private property for any perceived social evil.

I am not sending this letter to the Conference, in the hope that changes along these lines will be acceptable to you. If not, I probably will write briefly.

I do appreciate your willingness to consider these.

Sincerely,

[LFP][21]

As you can see from our excerpt above, Justice O'Connor included Justice Powell's proposed language in the *Midkiff* opinion. Do you think that Justice Powell's proposed changes addressed his concerns about the broad language in *Midkiff*? Keep this issue in mind when you read the various opinions in *Kelo*, including Justice O'Connor's dissent.

---

[21] *See* D. Benjamin Barros, *Nothing "Errant" About It: The* Berman *and* Midkiff *Conference Notes and How the Supreme Court Got to* Kelo *with Its Eyes Wide Open*, in *Private Property, Community Development, and Eminent Domain*, 71-72 (Robin Paul Malloy ed., (2008)).

KELO V. CITY OF NEW LONDON

United States Supreme Court (2005)

545 U.S. 469

Justice Stevens delivered the opinion of the Court. In 2000, the city of New London approved a development plan that, in the words of the Supreme Court of Connecticut, was "projected to create in excess of 1,000 jobs, to increase tax and other revenues, and to revitalize an economically distressed city, including its downtown and waterfront areas." 268 Conn. 1, 5, 843 A.2d 500, 507 (2004). In assembling the land needed for this project, the city's development agent has purchased property from willing sellers and proposes to use the power of eminent domain to acquire the remainder of the property from unwilling owners in exchange for just compensation. The question presented is whether the city's proposed disposition of this property qualifies as a "public use" within the meaning of the Takings Clause of the Fifth Amendment to the Constitution.

I.

The city of New London (hereinafter City) sits at the junction of the Thames River and the Long Island Sound in southeastern Connecticut. Decades of economic decline led a state agency in 1990 to designate the City a "distressed municipality." In 1996, the Federal Government closed the Naval Undersea Warfare Center, which had been located in the Fort Trumbull area of the City and had employed over 1,500 people. In 1998, the City's unemployment rate was nearly double that of the State, and its population of just under 24,000 residents was at its lowest since 1920.

These conditions prompted state and local officials to target New London, and particularly its Fort Trumbull area, for economic revitalization. To this end, respondent New London Development Corporation (NLDC), a private nonprofit entity established some years earlier to assist the City in planning economic development, was reactivated. In January 1998, the State authorized a $5.35 million bond issue to support the NLDC's planning activities and a $10 million bond issue toward the creation of a Fort Trumbull State Park. In February, the pharmaceutical company Pfizer Inc. announced that it would build a $300 million research facility on a site immediately adjacent to Fort Trumbull; local planners hoped that Pfizer would draw new business to the area, thereby serving as a catalyst to the area's rejuvenation. After receiving initial approval from the city council, the NLDC continued its planning activities and held a series of neighborhood meetings to educate the public about the process. In May, the city council authorized the NLDC to formally submit its plans to the relevant state agencies for review. Upon obtaining state-level approval, the NLDC finalized an integrated development plan focused on 90 acres of the Fort Trumbull area.

The Fort Trumbull area is situated on a peninsula that juts into the Thames River. The area comprises approximately 115 privately owned properties, as well as the 32 acres of land formerly occupied by the naval facility (Trumbull State Park now occupies 18 of those 32 acres). The development plan encompasses seven parcels. Parcel 1 is designated for a waterfront conference hotel at the center of a "small urban village" that will include restaurants and shopping. This parcel will also have marinas for both recreational and commercial uses. A pedestrian "riverwalk" will originate here and continue down the coast, connecting the waterfront areas of the development. Parcel 2 will be the site of approximately 80 new residences organized into an urban neighborhood and linked by public walkway to the remainder of the development, including the state park. This parcel also includes space reserved for a new U.S. Coast Guard Museum. Parcel 3, which is located immediately north of the Pfizer facility, will contain at least 90,000 square feet of research and development office space. Parcel 4A is a 2.4-acre site that will be used either to support the adjacent state park, by providing parking or retail services for visitors, or to support the nearby marina. Parcel 4B will include a renovated marina, as well as the final stretch of the riverwalk. Parcels 5, 6, and 7 will provide land for office and retail space, parking, and water-dependent commercial uses. App. 109-113.

The NLDC intended the development plan to capitalize on the arrival of the Pfizer facility and the new commerce it was expected to attract. In addition to creating jobs, generating tax revenue, and helping to "build momentum for the revitalization of downtown New London," *id.*, at 92, the plan was also designed to make the City more attractive and to create leisure and recreational opportunities on the waterfront and in the park.

The city council approved the plan in January 2000, and designated the NLDC as its development agent in charge of implementation. *See* Conn. Gen.Stat. §8-188 (2005). The city council also authorized the NLDC to purchase property or to acquire property by exercising eminent domain in the City's name. §8-193. The NLDC successfully negotiated the purchase of most of the real estate in the 90-acre area, but its negotiations with petitioners failed. As a consequence, in November 2000, the NLDC initiated the condemnation proceedings that gave rise to this case.

II.

Petitioner Susette Kelo has lived in the Fort Trumbull area since 1997. She has made extensive improvements to her house, which she prizes for its water view. Petitioner Wilhelmina Dery was born in her Fort Trumbull house in 1918 and has lived there her entire life. Her husband Charles (also a petitioner) has lived in the house since they married some 60 years ago. In all, the nine petitioners own 15 properties in Fort Trumbull—4 in parcel 3 of the development plan and 11 in parcel 4A. Ten of the parcels are occupied by the owner or a family member; the other five are held as investment properties. There is no allegation that any of these properties is blighted or otherwise in poor condition; rather, they were condemned only because they happen to be located in the development area.

In December 2000, petitioners brought this action in the New London Superior Court. They claimed, among other things, that the taking of their properties would violate the "public use" restriction in the Fifth Amendment. After a 7-day bench trial, the Superior Court granted a permanent restraining order prohibiting the taking of the properties located in parcel 4A (park or marina support). It, however, denied petitioners relief as to the properties located in parcel 3 (office space). App. to Pet. for Cert. 343-350.

After the Superior Court ruled, both sides took appeals to the Supreme Court of Connecticut. That court held, over a dissent, that all of the City's proposed takings were valid. It began by upholding the lower court's determination that the takings were authorized by chapter 132, the State's municipal development statute. *See* Conn. Gen.Stat. §8-186 et seq. (2005). That statute expresses a legislative determination that the taking of land, even developed land, as part of an economic development project is a "public use" and in the "public interest." 268 Conn., at 18-28, 843 A.2d, at 515-521. Next, relying on cases such as *Hawaii Housing Authority v. Midkiff*, 467 U.S. 229, 104 S.Ct. 2321, 81 L.Ed.2d 186 (1984), and *Berman v. Parker*, 348 U.S. 26, 75 S.Ct. 98, 99 L.Ed. 27 (1954), the court held that such economic development qualified as a valid public use under both the Federal and State Constitutions. 268 Conn., at 40, 843 A.2d, at 527.

Finally, adhering to its precedents, the court went on to determine, first, whether the takings of the particular properties at issue were "reasonably necessary" to achieving the City's intended public use, *id.*, at 82-84, 843 A.2d, at 552-553, and, second, whether the takings were for "reasonably foreseeable needs," *id.*, at 93-94, 843 A.2d, at 558-559. The court upheld the trial court's factual findings as to parcel 3, but reversed the trial court as to parcel 4A, agreeing with the City that the intended use of this land was sufficiently definite and had been given "reasonable attention" during the planning process. *Id.*, at 120-121, 843 A.2d, at 574.

The three dissenting justices would have imposed a "heightened" standard of judicial review for takings justified by economic development. Although they agreed that the plan was intended to serve a valid public use, they would have found all the takings unconstitutional because the City had failed to adduce "clear and convincing evidence" that the economic benefits of the plan would in fact come to pass. *Id.*, at 144, 146, 843 A.2d, at 587, 588 (Zarella, J., joined by Sullivan, C. J., and Katz, J., concurring in part and dissenting in part).

We granted certiorari to determine whether a city's decision to take property for the purpose of economic development satisfies the "public use" requirement of the Fifth Amendment. 542 U.S. 965, 125 S.Ct. 27, 159 L.Ed.2d 857 (2004).

III.

Two polar propositions are perfectly clear. On the one hand, it has long been accepted that the sovereign may not take the property of A for the sole purpose of transferring it to another private party B, even though A is paid just compensation. On the other hand, it is equally clear that a State may transfer property from one private party to another if future "use by the public" is the purpose of the taking; the condemnation of land for a railroad with common-carrier duties is a familiar example. Neither of these propositions, however, determines the disposition of this case.

As for the first proposition, the City would no doubt be forbidden from taking petitioners' land for the purpose of conferring a private benefit on a particular private party. *See Midkiff*, 467 U.S., at 245, 104 S.Ct. 2321 ("A purely private taking could not withstand the scrutiny of the public use requirement; it would serve no legitimate purpose of government and would thus be void"); *Missouri Pacific R. Co. v. Nebraska*, 164 U.S. 403, 17 S.Ct. 130, 41 L.Ed. 489 (1896).[22] Nor would the City be allowed to take property under the mere pretext of a public purpose, when its actual purpose was to bestow a private benefit. The takings before us, however, would be executed pursuant to a "carefully considered" development plan. 268 Conn., at 54, 843 A.2d, at 536. The trial judge and all the members of the Supreme Court of Connecticut agreed that there was no evidence of an illegitimate purpose in this case.[23] Therefore, as was true of the statute challenged in *Midkiff*, 467 U.S., at 245, 104 S.Ct. 2321, the City's development plan was not adopted "to benefit a particular class of identifiable individuals."

On the other hand, this is not a case in which the City is planning to open the condemned land—at least not in its entirety—to use by the general public. Nor will the private lessees of the land in any sense be required to operate like common carriers, making their services available to all comers. But although such a projected use would be sufficient to satisfy the public use requirement, this "Court long ago rejected any literal requirement that condemned property be put into use for the general public." *Id.*,

---

[22] *See also Calder v. Bull*, 3 Dall. 386, 388, 1 L.Ed. 648 (1798) ("An act of the Legislature (for I cannot call it a law) contrary to the great first principles of the social compact, cannot be considered a rightful exercise of legislative authority . . . . A few instances will suffice to explain what I mean . . . . [A] law that takes property from A. and gives it to B: It is against all reason and justice, for a people to entrust a Legislature with such powers; and, therefore, it cannot be presumed that they have done it. The genius, the nature, and the spirit, of our State Governments, amount to a prohibition of such acts of legislation; and the general principles of law and reason forbid them" (emphasis deleted)).

[23] *See* 268 Conn., at 159, 843 A.2d, at 595 (Zarella, J., concurring in part and dissenting in part) ("The record clearly demonstrates that the development plan was not intended to serve the interests of Pfizer, Inc., or any other private entity, but rather, to revitalize the local economy by creating temporary and permanent jobs, generating a significant increase in tax revenue, encouraging spin-off economic activities and maximizing public access to the waterfront"). And while the City intends to transfer certain of the parcels to a private developer in a long-term lease—which developer, in turn, is expected to lease the office space and so forth to other private tenants—the identities of those private parties were not known when the plan was adopted. It is, of course, difficult to accuse the government of having taken A's property to benefit the private interests of B when the identity of B was unknown.

at 244, 104 S.Ct. 2321. Indeed, while many state courts in the mid-19th century endorsed "use by the public" as the proper definition of public use, that narrow view steadily eroded over time. Not only was the "use by the public" test difficult to administer (e.g., what proportion of the public need have access to the property? at what price?), but it proved to be impractical given the diverse and always evolving needs of society. Accordingly, when this Court began applying the Fifth Amendment to the States at the close of the 19th century, it embraced the broader and more natural interpretation of public use as "public purpose." *See, e.g., Fallbrook Irrigation Dist. v. Bradley*, 164 U.S. 112, 158-164, 17 S.Ct. 56, 41 L.Ed. 369 (1896). Thus, in a case upholding a mining company's use of an aerial bucket line to transport ore over property it did not own, Justice Holmes' opinion for the Court stressed "the inadequacy of use by the general public as a universal test." *Strickley v. Highland Boy Gold Mining Co.*, 200 U.S. 527, 531, 26 S.Ct. 301, 50 L.Ed. 581 (1906). We have repeatedly and consistently rejected that narrow test ever since.

The disposition of this case therefore turns on the question whether the City's development plan serves a "public purpose." Without exception, our cases have defined that concept broadly, reflecting our longstanding policy of deference to legislative judgments in this field.

In *Berman v. Parker*, 348 U.S. 26, 75 S.Ct. 98, 99 L.Ed. 27 (1954), this Court upheld a redevelopment plan targeting a blighted area of Washington, D. C., in which most of the housing for the area's 5,000 inhabitants was beyond repair. Under the plan, the area would be condemned and part of it utilized for the construction of streets, schools, and other public facilities. The remainder of the land would be leased or sold to private parties for the purpose of redevelopment, including the construction of low-cost housing.

The owner of a department store located in the area challenged the condemnation, pointing out that his store was not itself blighted and arguing that the creation of a "better balanced, more attractive community" was not a valid public use. *Id.*, at 31, 75 S.Ct. 98. Writing for a unanimous Court, Justice Douglas refused to evaluate this claim in isolation, deferring instead to the legislative and agency judgment that the area "must be planned as a whole" for the plan to be successful. *Id.*, at 34, 75 S.Ct. 98. The Court explained that "community redevelopment programs need not, by force of the Constitution, be on a piecemeal basis—lot by lot, building by building." *Id.*, at 35, 75 S.Ct. 98. The public use underlying the taking was unequivocally affirmed:

> "We do not sit to determine whether a particular housing project is or is not desirable. The concept of the public welfare is broad and inclusive. . . . The values it represents are spiritual as well as physical, aesthetic as well as monetary. It is within the power of the legislature to determine that the community should be beautiful as well as healthy, spacious as well as clean, well-balanced as well as carefully patrolled. In the present case, the Congress and its authorized agencies have made

determinations that take into account a wide variety of values. It is not for us to reappraise them. If those who govern the District of Columbia decide that the Nation's Capital should be beautiful as well as sanitary, there is nothing in the Fifth Amendment that stands in the way." *Id.*, at 33, 75 S.Ct. 98.

In *Hawaii Housing Authority v. Midkiff*, 467 U.S. 229, 104 S.Ct. 2321, 81 L.Ed.2d 186 (1984), the Court considered a Hawaii statute whereby fee title was taken from lessors and transferred to lessees (for just compensation) in order to reduce the concentration of land ownership. We unanimously upheld the statute and rejected the Ninth Circuit's view that it was "a naked attempt on the part of the state of Hawaii to take the property of A and transfer it to B solely for B's private use and benefit." *Id.*, at 235, 104 S.Ct. 2321 (internal quotation marks omitted). Reaffirming *Berman*'s deferential approach to legislative judgments in this field, we concluded that the State's purpose of eliminating the "social and economic evils of a land oligopoly" qualified as a valid public use. 467 U.S., at 241-242, 104 S.Ct. 2321. Our opinion also rejected the contention that the mere fact that the State immediately transferred the properties to private individuals upon condemnation somehow diminished the public character of the taking. "[I]t is only the taking's purpose, and not its mechanics," we explained, that matters in determining public use. *Id.*, at 244, 104 S.Ct. 2321. . . .

Viewed as a whole, our jurisprudence has recognized that the needs of society have varied between different parts of the Nation, just as they have evolved over time in response to changed circumstances. Our earliest cases in particular embodied a strong theme of federalism, emphasizing the "great respect" that we owe to state legislatures and state courts in discerning local public needs. *See Hairston v. Danville & Western R. Co.*, 208 U.S. 598, 606-607, 28 S.Ct. 331, 52 L.Ed. 637 (1908) noting that these needs were likely to vary depending on a State's "resources, the capacity of the soil, the relative importance of industries to the general public welfare, and the long-established methods and habits of the people"). For more than a century, our public use jurisprudence has wisely eschewed rigid formulas and intrusive scrutiny in favor of affording legislatures broad latitude in determining what public needs justify the use of the takings power.

IV.

Those who govern the City were not confronted with the need to remove blight in the Fort Trumbull area, but their determination that the area was sufficiently distressed to justify a program of economic rejuvenation is entitled to our deference. The City has carefully formulated an economic development plan that it believes will provide appreciable benefits to the community, including—but by no means limited to—new jobs and increased tax revenue. As with other exercises in urban planning and development, the City is endeavoring to coordinate a variety of commercial, residential, and recreational uses of land, with the hope that they will form a whole greater than the sum of its parts. To effectuate this plan, the City has invoked a state statute that specifically authorizes the use of eminent domain to promote economic development. Given the comprehensive character of the plan, the thorough deliberation that preceded its adoption, and the limited scope of our review, it is appropriate for us, as it was in *Berman*, to resolve the challenges of the individual owners, not on a piecemeal basis, but rather in light of the entire plan. Because that plan unquestionably serves a public purpose, the takings challenged here satisfy the public use requirement of the Fifth Amendment.

To avoid this result, petitioners urge us to adopt a new bright-line rule that economic development does not qualify as a public use. Putting aside the unpersuasive suggestion that the City's plan will provide only purely economic benefits, neither precedent nor logic supports petitioners' proposal. Promoting economic development is a traditional and long-accepted function of government. There is, moreover, no principled way of distinguishing economic development from the other public purposes that we have recognized. In our cases upholding takings that facilitated agriculture and mining, for example, we emphasized the importance of those industries to the welfare of the States in question, see, e.g., *Strickley*, 200 U.S. 527, 26 S.Ct. 301; in *Berman*, we endorsed the purpose of transforming a blighted area into a "well-balanced" community through redevelopment, 348 U.S., at 33, 75 S.Ct. 98;[24] in *Midkiff*, we upheld the interest in breaking up a land oligopoly that "created artificial deterrents to the normal functioning of the State's residential land market," 467 U.S., at 242, 104 S.Ct. 2321; and in Monsanto, we accepted Congress' purpose of eliminating a "significant barrier to entry in the pesticide market," 467 U.S., at 1014-1015, 104 S.Ct. 2862. It would be incongruous to hold that the City's interest in the economic benefits to be derived from the development of the Fort Trumbull area has less of a public character than any of those other interests. Clearly, there is no basis for exempting economic development from our traditionally broad understanding of public purpose. . . .

Just as we decline to second-guess the City's considered judgments about the efficacy of its development plan, we also decline to second-guess the City's determinations as to what lands it needs to acquire in order to effectuate the project. "It is not for the courts to oversee the choice of the boundary line nor to sit in review on the size of a particular project area. Once the question of the public purpose has been

---

[24] It is a misreading of *Berman* to suggest that the only public use upheld in that case was the initial removal of blight. *See* Reply Brief for Petitioners 8. The public use described in *Berman* extended beyond that to encompass the purpose of developing that area to create conditions that would prevent a reversion to blight in the future. *See* 348 U.S., at 34-35, 75 S.Ct. 98 ("It was not enough, [the experts] believed, to remove existing buildings that were insanitary or unsightly. It was important to redesign the whole area so as to eliminate the conditions that cause slums . . . . The entire area needed redesigning so that a balanced, integrated plan could be developed for the region, including not only new homes, but also schools, churches, parks, streets, and shopping centers. In this way it was hoped that the cycle of decay of the area could be controlled and the birth of future slums prevented"). Had the public use in *Berman* been defined more narrowly, it would have been difficult to justify the taking of the plaintiff's nonblighted department store.

decided, the amount and character of land to be taken for the project and the need for a particular tract to complete the integrated plan rests in the discretion of the legislative branch." *Berman*, 348 U.S., at 35-36, 75 S.Ct. 98.

In affirming the City's authority to take petitioners' properties, we do not minimize the hardship that condemnations may entail, notwithstanding the payment of just compensation. We emphasize that nothing in our opinion precludes any State from placing further restrictions on its exercise of the takings power. Indeed, many States already impose "public use" requirements that are stricter than the federal baseline. Some of these requirements have been established as a matter of state constitutional law, while others are expressed in state eminent domain statutes that carefully limit the grounds upon which takings may be exercised. As the submissions of the parties and their amici make clear, the necessity and wisdom of using eminent domain to promote economic development are certainly matters of legitimate public debate. This Court's authority, however, extends only to determining whether the City's proposed condemnations are for a "public use" within the meaning of the Fifth Amendment to the Federal Constitution. Because over a century of our case law interpreting that provision dictates an affirmative answer to that question, we may not grant petitioners the relief that they seek.

The judgment of the Supreme Court of Connecticut is affirmed.

Justice KENNEDY, concurring.

I join the opinion for the Court and add these further observations.

This Court has declared that a taking should be upheld as consistent with the Public Use Clause, U.S. Const., Amdt. 5, as long as it is "rationally related to a conceivable public purpose.". . . . The determination that a rational-basis standard of review is appropriate does not, however, alter the fact that transfers intended to confer benefits on particular, favored private entities, and with only incidental or pretextual public benefits, are forbidden by the Public Use Clause.

A court applying rational-basis review under the Public Use Clause should strike down a taking that, by a clear showing, is intended to favor a particular private party, with only incidental or pretextual public benefits, just as a court applying rational-basis review under the Equal Protection Clause must strike down a government classification that is clearly intended to injure a particular class of private parties, with only incidental or pretextual public justifications. . . .

A court confronted with a plausible accusation of impermissible favoritism to private parties should treat the objection as a serious one and review the record to see if it has merit, though with the presumption that the government's actions were reasonable and intended to serve a public purpose. Here, the trial court conducted a careful and extensive inquiry into "whether, in fact, the development plan is of primary benefit to . . . the developer [i.e., Corcoran Jennison], and private businesses which may eventually locate in the plan area [e.g., Pfizer], and in that regard, only of incidental benefit to the city." App. to Pet. for Cert. 261. The trial court considered testimony from government officials and corporate officers, *id.*, at 266-271; documentary evidence of communications between these parties, *ibid.*; respondents' awareness of New London's depressed economic condition and evidence corroborating the validity of this concern, *id.*, at 272-273, 278-279; the substantial commitment of public funds by the State to the development project before most of the private beneficiaries were known, *id.*, at 276; evidence that respondents reviewed a variety of development plans and chose a private developer from a group of applicants rather than picking out a particular transferee beforehand, *id.*, at 273, 278; and the fact that the other private beneficiaries of the project are still unknown because the office space proposed to be built has not yet been rented, *id.*, at 278.

The trial court concluded, based on these findings, that benefiting Pfizer was not "the primary motivation or effect of this development plan"; instead, "the primary motivation for [respondents] was to take advantage of Pfizer's presence." *Id.*, at 276. Likewise, the trial court concluded that "[t]here is nothing in the record to indicate that . . . [respondents] were motivated by a desire to aid [other] particular private entities." *Id.*, at 278. *See also* ante, at 2661-2662. Even the dissenting justices on the Connecticut Supreme Court agreed that respondents' development plan was intended to revitalize the local economy, not to serve the interests of Pfizer, Corcoran Jennison, or any other private party. 268 Conn. 1, 159, 843 A.2d 500, 595 (2004) (Zarella, J., concurring in part and dissenting in part). This case, then, survives the meaningful rational-basis review that in my view is required under the Public Use Clause. . . .

My agreement with the Court that a presumption of invalidity is not warranted for economic development takings in general, or for the particular takings at issue in this case, does not foreclose the possibility that a more stringent standard of review than that announced in *Berman* and *Midkiff* might be appropriate for a more narrowly drawn category of takings. There may be private transfers in which the risk of undetected impermissible favoritism of private parties is so acute that a presumption (rebuttable or otherwise) of invalidity is warranted under the Public Use Clause. *Cf. Eastern Enterprises v. Apfel*, 524 U.S. 498, 549-550, 118 S.Ct. 2131, 141 L.Ed.2d 451 (1998) (KENNEDY, J., concurring in judgment and dissenting in part) (heightened scrutiny for retroactive legislation under the Due Process Clause). This demanding level of scrutiny, however, is not required simply because the purpose of the taking is economic development.

This is not the occasion for conjecture as to what sort of cases might justify a more demanding standard, but it is appropriate to underscore aspects of the instant case that convince me no departure from *Berman* and *Midkiff* is appropriate here. This taking occurred in the context of a comprehensive development plan meant to address a serious citywide depression, and the projected economic benefits of the project cannot be characterized as de minimis. The identities of most of the private beneficiaries were unknown at the time the city formulated its plans. The city complied with elaborate procedural requirements that facilitate review of the record and inquiry into the city's purposes. In sum, while there may be categories of cases in which the transfers are so suspicious, or the procedures employed so prone to abuse, or the purported benefits are so trivial or implausible, that courts should presume an impermissible private purpose, no such circumstances are present in this case.

For the foregoing reasons, I join in the Court's opinion.

Justice O'CONNOR, with whom The Chief Justice, Justice SCALIA, and Justice THOMAS join, dissenting.

> Over two centuries ago, just after the Bill of Rights was ratified, Justice Chase wrote: "An act of the Legislature (for I cannot call it a law) contrary to the great first principles of the social compact, cannot be considered a rightful exercise of legislative authority. . . . A few instances will suffice to explain what I mean. . . . [A] law that takes property from A. and gives it to B: It is against all reason and justice, for a people to entrust a Legislature with such powers; and, therefore, it cannot be presumed that they have done it." *Calder v. Bull*, 3 Dall. 386, 388, 1 L.Ed. 648 (1798) (emphasis deleted).

Today the Court abandons this long-held, basic limitation on government power. Under the banner of economic development, all private property is now vulnerable to being taken and transferred to another private owner, so long as it might be upgraded—i.e., given to an owner who will use it in a way that the legislature deems more beneficial to the public—in the process. To reason, as the Court does, that the incidental public benefits resulting from the subsequent ordinary use of private property render economic development takings "for public use" is to wash out any distinction between private and public use of property—and thereby effectively to delete the words "for public use" from the Takings Clause of the Fifth Amendment. Accordingly I respectfully dissent. . . .

The Fifth Amendment to the Constitution, made applicable to the States by the Fourteenth Amendment, provides that "private property [shall not] be taken for public use, without just compensation." When interpreting the Constitution, we begin with the unremarkable presumption that every word in the document has independent meaning, "that no word was unnecessarily used, or needlessly added." *Wright v. United States*, 302 U.S. 583, 588, 58 S.Ct. 395, 82 L.Ed. 439 (1938). In keeping with that presumption, we have read the Fifth Amendment's language to impose two distinct conditions on the exercise of eminent domain: "[T]he taking must be for a 'public use' and 'just compensation' must be paid to the owner." *Brown v. Legal Foundation of Wash.*, 538 U.S. 216, 231-232, 123 S.Ct. 1406, 155 L.Ed.2d 376 (2003).

These two limitations serve to protect "the security of Property," which Alexander Hamilton described to the Philadelphia Convention as one of the "great obj[ects] of Gov[ernment]." 1 *Records of the Federal Convention of 1787*, p. 302 (M. Farrand ed.1911). Together they ensure stable property ownership by providing safeguards against excessive, unpredictable, or unfair use of the government's eminent domain power—particularly against those owners who, for whatever reasons, may be unable to protect themselves in the political process against the majority's will.

While the Takings Clause presupposes that government can take private property without the owner's consent, the just compensation requirement spreads the cost of condemnations and thus "prevents the public from loading upon one individual more than his just share of the burdens of government." *Monongahela Nav. Co. v. United States*, 148 U.S. 312, 325, 13 S.Ct. 622, 37 L.Ed. 463 (1893); *see also Armstrong v. United States*, 364 U.S. 40, 49, 80 S.Ct. 1563, 4 L.Ed.2d 1554 (1960). The public use requirement, in turn, imposes a more basic limitation, circumscribing the very scope of the eminent domain power: Government may compel an individual to forfeit her property for the public's use, but not for the benefit of another private person. This requirement promotes fairness as well as security. *Cf. Tahoe-Sierra Preservation Council, Inc. v. Tahoe Regional Planning Agency*, 535 U.S. 302, 336, 122 S.Ct. 1465, 152 L.Ed.2d 517 (2002) ("The concepts of 'fairness and justice' . . . underlie the Takings Clause").

Where is the line between "public" and "private" property use? We give considerable deference to legislatures' determinations about what governmental activities will advantage the public. But were the political branches the sole arbiters of the public-private distinction, the Public Use Clause would amount to little more than hortatory fluff. An external, judicial check on how the public use requirement is interpreted, however limited, is necessary if this constraint on government power is to retain any meaning. *See Cincinnati v. Vester*, 281 U.S. 439, 446, 50 S.Ct. 360, 74 L.Ed. 950 (1930) ("It is well established that . . . the question [of] what is a public use is a judicial one"). . . .

This case returns us for the first time in over 20 years to the hard question of when a purportedly "public purpose" taking meets the public use requirement. It presents an issue of first impression: Are economic development takings constitutional? I would hold that they are not. We are guided by two precedents about the taking of real property by eminent domain. In *Berman*, we upheld takings within a blighted neighborhood of Washington, D.C. The neighborhood had so deteriorated that, for example, 64.3% of its dwellings were beyond repair. . . .

In *Midkiff*, we upheld a land condemnation scheme in Hawaii whereby title in real property was taken from lessors and transferred to lessees. At that time, the State and Federal Governments owned nearly 49% of the State's land, and another 47% was in the hands of only 72 private landowners. Concentration of land ownership was so dramatic that on the State's most urbanized island, Oahu, 22 landowners owned 72.5% of the fee simple titles. *Id.*, at 232, 104 S.Ct. 2321. The Hawaii Legislature had concluded that the oligopoly in land ownership was "skewing the State's residential fee simple market, inflating land prices, and injuring the public tranquility and welfare," and therefore enacted a condemnation scheme for redistributing title. *Ibid.*

In those decisions, we emphasized the importance of deferring to legislative judgments about public purpose. Because courts are ill equipped to evaluate the efficacy of proposed legislative initiatives, we rejected as unworkable the idea of courts' "'deciding on what is and is not a governmental function and . . . invalidating legislation on the basis of their view on that question at the moment of decision, a practice which has proved impracticable in other fields.'" *Id.*, at 240-241, 104 S.Ct. 2321 (quoting *United States ex rel. TVA v. Welch*, 327 U.S. 546, 552, 66 S.Ct. 715, 90 L.Ed. 843 (1946)). . . .

Yet for all the emphasis on deference, *Berman* and *Midkiff* hewed to a bedrock principle without which our public use jurisprudence would collapse: "A purely private taking could not withstand the scrutiny of the public use requirement; it would serve no legitimate purpose of government and would thus be void." *Midkiff*, 467 U.S., at 245, 104 S.Ct. 2321 . . . To protect that principle, those decisions reserved "a role for courts to play in reviewing a legislature's judgment of what constitutes a public use . . . [though] the Court in *Berman* made clear that it is 'an extremely narrow' one." *Midkiff, supra*, at 240, 104 S.Ct. 2321 (quoting *Berman, supra*, at 32, 75 S.Ct. 98).

The Court's holdings in *Berman* and *Midkiff* were true to the principle underlying the Public Use Clause. In both those cases, the extraordinary, precondemnation use of the targeted property inflicted affirmative harm on society—in *Berman* through blight resulting from extreme poverty and in *Midkiff* through oligopoly resulting from extreme wealth. And in both cases, the relevant legislative body had found that eliminating the existing property use was necessary to remedy the harm. *Berman, supra*, at 28-29, 75 S.Ct. 98; *Midkiff, supra*, at 232, 104 S.Ct. 2321. Thus a public purpose was realized when the harmful use was eliminated. Because each taking directly achieved a public benefit, it did not matter that the property was turned over to private use. Here, in contrast, New London does not claim that Susette Kelo's and Wilhelmina Dery's well-maintained homes are the source of any social harm. . . .

In moving away from our decisions sanctioning the condemnation of harmful property use, the Court today significantly expands the meaning of public use. It holds that the sovereign may take private property currently put to ordinary private use, and give it over for new, ordinary private use, so long as the new use is predicted to generate some secondary benefit for the public—such as increased tax revenue, more jobs, maybe even esthetic pleasure. But nearly any lawful use of real private property can be said to generate some incidental benefit to the public. Thus, if predicted (or even guaranteed) positive side effects are enough to render transfer from one private party to another constitutional, then the words "for public use" do not realistically exclude any takings, and thus do not exert any constraint on the eminent domain power.

There is a sense in which this troubling result follows from errant language in *Berman* and *Midkiff*. In discussing whether takings within a blighted neighborhood were for a public use, *Berman* began by observing: "We deal, in other words, with what traditionally has been known as the police power." 348 U.S., at 32, 75 S.Ct. 98. From there it declared that "[o]nce the object is within the authority of Congress, the right to realize it through the exercise of eminent domain is clear." *Id.*, at 33, 75 S.Ct. 98.

Following up, we said in *Midkiff* that "[t]he 'public use' requirement is coterminous with the scope of a sovereign's police powers." 467 U.S., at 240, 104 S.Ct. 2321. This language was unnecessary to the specific holdings of those decisions. *Berman* and *Midkiff* simply did not put such language to the constitutional test, because the takings in those cases were within the police power but also for "public use" for the reasons I have described. The case before us now demonstrates why, when deciding if a taking's purpose is constitutional, the police power and "public use" cannot always be equated. . . .

It was possible after *Berman* and *Midkiff* to imagine unconstitutional transfers from A to B. Those decisions endorsed government intervention when private property use had veered to such an extreme that the public was suffering as a consequence. Today nearly all real property is susceptible to condemnation on the Court's theory. . . .

Any property may now be taken for the benefit of another private party, but the fallout from this decision will not be random. The beneficiaries are likely to be those citizens with disproportionate influence and power in the political process, including large corporations and development firms. As for the victims, the government now has license to transfer property from those with fewer resources to those with more. The Founders cannot have intended this perverse result. "[T]hat alone is a just government," wrote James Madison, "which impartially secures to every man, whatever is his own." For the National Gazette, Property (Mar. 27, 1792), reprinted in 14 Papers of James Madison 266 (R. Rutland et al. eds.1983).

I would hold that the takings in both Parcel 3 and Parcel 4A are unconstitutional, reverse the judgment of the Supreme Court of Connecticut, and remand for further proceedings.

Justice THOMAS, dissenting.

Long ago, William Blackstone wrote that "the law of the land . . . postpone[s] even public necessity to the sacred and inviolable rights of private property." 1 *Commentaries on the Laws of England* 134-135 (1765) (hereinafter Blackstone). The Framers embodied that principle in the Constitution, allowing the government to take property not for "public necessity," but instead for "public use." Amdt. 5. Defying this understanding, the Court replaces the Public Use Clause with a " '[P]ublic [P]urpose' " Clause, ante, at 2662-2663 (or perhaps the "Diverse and Always Evolving Needs of Society" Clause, ante, at 2662 (capitalization added)), a restriction that is satisfied, the Court instructs, so long as the purpose is "legitimate" and the means "not irrational," ante, at 2667 (internal quotation marks omitted). This deferential shift in phraseology enables the Court to hold, against all common sense, that a costly urban-renewal project whose stated purpose is a vague promise of new jobs and increased tax revenue, but which is also suspiciously agreeable to the Pfizer Corporation, is for a "public use."

I cannot agree. If such "economic development" takings are for a "public use," any taking is, and the Court has erased the Public Use Clause from our Constitution, as Justice O'CONNOR powerfully argues in dissent. Ante, at 2671, 2675-2677. I do not believe that this Court can eliminate liberties expressly enumerated in the Constitution and therefore join her dissenting opinion. Regrettably, however, the Court's error runs deeper than this. Today's decision is simply the latest in a string of our cases construing the Public Use Clause to be a virtual nullity, without the slightest nod to its original meaning. In my view, the Public Use Clause, originally understood, is a meaningful limit on the government's eminent domain power. Our cases have strayed from the Clause's original meaning, and I would reconsider them. . . .

The most natural reading of the Clause is that it allows the government to take property only if the government owns, or the public has a legal right to use, the property, as opposed to taking it for any public purpose or necessity whatsoever. At the time of the founding, dictionaries primarily defined the noun "use" as "[t]he act of employing any thing to any purpose." 2 S. Johnson, *A Dictionary of the English Language* 2194 (4th ed. 1773) (hereinafter Johnson). The term "use," moreover, "is from the Latin utor, which means 'to use, make use of, avail one's self of, employ, apply, enjoy, etc." J. Lewis, *Law of Eminent Domain* §165, p. 224, n. 4 (1888) (hereinafter Lewis). When the government takes property and gives it to a private individual, and the public has no right to use the property, it strains language to say that the public is "employing" the property, regardless of the incidental benefits that might accrue to the public from the private use. The term "public use," then, means that either the government or its citizens as a whole must actually "employ" the taken property. *See* id., at 223 (reviewing founding-era dictionaries). . . .

Early American eminent domain practice largely bears out this understanding of the Public Use Clause. . . .

Our current Public Use Clause jurisprudence, as the Court notes, has rejected this natural reading of the Clause. Ante, at 2662-2664. The Court adopted its modern reading blindly, with little discussion of the Clause's history and original meaning, in two distinct lines of cases: first, in cases adopting the "public purpose" interpretation of the Clause, and second, in cases deferring to legislatures' judgments regarding what constitutes a valid public purpose. Those questionable cases converged in the boundlessly broad and deferential conception of "public use" adopted by this Court in *Berman v. Parker*, 348 U.S. 26, 75 S.Ct. 98, 99 L.Ed. 27 (1954), and *Hawaii Housing Authority v. Midkiff*, 467 U.S. 229, 104 S.Ct. 2321, 81 L.Ed.2d 186 (1984), cases that take center stage in the Court's opinion. *See* ante, 2663-2664. The weakness of those two lines of cases, and consequently *Berman* and *Midkiff*, fatally undermines the doctrinal foundations of the Court's decision. Today's questionable application of these cases is further proof that the "public purpose" standard is not susceptible of principled application. This Court's reliance by rote on this standard is ill advised and should be reconsidered. . . .

For all these reasons, I would revisit our Public Use Clause cases and consider returning to the original meaning of the Public Use Clause: that the government may take property only if it actually uses or gives the public a legal right to use the property.

The consequences of today's decision are not difficult to predict, and promise to be harmful. So-called "urban renewal" programs provide some compensation for the properties they take, but no compensation is possible for the subjective value of these lands to the individuals displaced and the indignity inflicted by uprooting them from their homes. Allowing the government to take property solely for public purposes is bad enough, but extending the concept of public purpose to encompass any economically beneficial goal guarantees that these losses will fall disproportionately on poor communities. Those communities are not only systematically less likely to put their lands to the highest and best social use, but are also the least politically powerful. If ever there were justification for intrusive judicial review of constitutional provisions that protect "discrete and insular minorities," *United States v. Carolene Products Co.*, 304 U.S. 144, 152, n. 4, 58 S.Ct. 778, 82 L.Ed. 1234 (1938), surely that principle would apply with great force to the powerless groups and individuals the Public Use Clause protects. The deferential standard this Court has adopted for the Public Use Clause is therefore deeply perverse. It encourages "those citizens with disproportionate influence and power in the political process, including large corporations and development firms," to victimize the weak. Ante, at 2677 (O'Connor, J., dissenting).

Those incentives have made the legacy of this Court's "public purpose" test an unhappy one. In the 1950's, no doubt emboldened in part by the expansive understanding of "public use" this Court adopted in *Berman*, cities "rushed to draw plans" for downtown development. B. Frieden & L. Sagalyn, *Downtown, Inc. How America Rebuilds Cities* 17 (1989). "Of all the families displaced by urban renewal from 1949 through 1963, 63 percent of those whose race was known were nonwhite, and of these families, 56 percent of nonwhites and 38 percent of whites had incomes low enough to qualify for public housing, which, however, was seldom available to them." *Id.*, at 28, 75 S.Ct. 98. Public works projects in the 1950's and 1960's destroyed predominantly minority communities in St. Paul, Minnesota, and Baltimore, Maryland. *Id.*, at 28-29, 75 S.Ct. 98. In 1981, urban planners in Detroit, Michigan, uprooted the largely "lower-income and elderly" Poletown neighborhood for the benefit of the General Motors Corporation. J. Wylie, *Poletown: Community Betrayed* 58 (1989). Urban renewal projects have long been associated with the displacement of blacks; "[i]n cities across the country, urban renewal came to be known as 'Negro removal.'" Pritchett, *The "Public Menace" of Blight: Urban Renewal and the Private Uses of Eminent Domain*, 21 Yale L. & Pol'y Rev. 1, 47 (2003). Over 97 percent of the individuals forcibly removed from their homes by the "slum-clearance" project upheld by this Court in *Berman* were black. 348 U.S., at 30, 75 S.Ct. 98. Regrettably, the predictable consequence of the Court's decision will be to exacerbate these effects.

The Court relies almost exclusively on this Court's prior cases to derive today's far-reaching, and dangerous, result. *See* ante, at 2662-2664. But the principles this Court should employ to dispose of this case are found in the Public Use Clause itself, not in Justice Peckham's high opinion of reclamation laws, see *supra*, at 2683. When faced with a clash of constitutional principle and a line of unreasoned cases wholly divorced from the text, history, and structure of our founding document, we should not hesitate to resolve the tension in favor of the Constitution's original meaning. For the reasons I have given, and for the reasons given in Justice O'CONNOR's dissent, the conflict of principle raised by this boundless use of the eminent domain power should be resolved in petitioners' favor. I would reverse the judgment of the Connecticut Supreme Court.

NOTES AND QUESTIONS

1. *Considering* Kelo. Do you think that the Supreme Court reached the right result in *Kelo*? You might want to break this larger question into two parts. First, does *Kelo* correctly follow the Supreme Court's public use precedents? Second, imagining that there was no prior "public use" precedent, does *Kelo* correctly interpret the Just Compensation Clause?

2. *The* Kelo *Dissents.* If you disagree with the outcome of *Kelo*, do you agree with either of the dissents? If so, why? Which of the two dissents is more persuasive to you?

3. *What Is Left of "Public Use"?* The Supreme Court has consistently asserted that the "public use" requirement places a meaningful limit on the exercise of eminent domain. Having read *Berman*, *Midkiff*, and *Kelo*, can you come up with a hypothetical exercise of eminent domain that would violate the "public use" requirement?

4. *Judge Prettyman's Alternative Approach.* Go back and look at Judge Prettyman's approach in *Schneider*. Is it preferable to the Supreme Court's approach in *Berman*, *Midkiff*, and *Kelo*? In thinking about this question, take seriously the Supreme Court's stated reasons in *Berman* (later echoed in *Midkiff* and *Kelo*) for not following this approach.

5. *From Unanimous to Highly Divided.* *Berman* and *Midkiff* were both unanimous decisions. In *Kelo*, the Supreme Court split 5-4. Why do you think that *Kelo* proved to be more divisive to the Court?

6. *Justice Stevens on* Kelo. Consider these remarks made by Justice Stevens about *Kelo*:

> Whereas *Lingle* [*v. Chevron*, a regulatory takings case we will discuss below] corrected a past misunderstanding, the second case, *Kelo v. City of New London*, which upheld an integrated development plan designed to revitalize a city's economy, adhered to precedent while noting that different plans may well pose questions for the future.
>
> Though much criticized, the *Kelo* opinion was surely not an example of "judicial activism" because it rejected arguments that federal judges should review the feasibility of redevelopment plans, that they should evaluate the justification for the taking of each individual parcel rather than the entire plan, and that they should craft a constitutional distinction between blighted areas and depressed areas targeted for redevelopment. Indeed, the dissent criticized the opinion for being unduly deferential to the decisions of state legislative and administrative bodies.

A second criticism, however, brings me back to the thought that I expressed at the outset of these remarks. It is the criticism that the opinion was not faithful to—indeed, that it was "wholly divorced from"—the text of the Constitution. The relevant constitutional text provides that private property shall not "be taken for public use, without just compensation." As Justice O'Connor explained in her *Lingle* opinion, that text does not prohibit any taking of private property, but instead merely places a condition on the exercise of the takings power. Thus, just as a purely literal reading of the text of the Due Process Clause would confine its coverage to procedural safeguards and entirely eliminate its substantive protections, including those that have made provisions of the first ten Amendments applicable to the states, a purely literal reading of the Takings Clause would limit its coverage to a guarantee of just compensation.

We have nevertheless assumed that the reference to "public use" does describe an implicit limit on the power to condemn private property, but over the years we have frequently and consistently read those words broadly to refer to a "public purpose." Because one of the opinions rejecting "use by the public" as the proper interpretation of those words was authored by Justice Holmes, and because the debate between Holmes and Brandeis in the Pennsylvania Coal case [another regulatory takings case we will discuss below] demonstrates that Brandeis's views with respect to takings were even more deferential than Holmes's, I am confident that both of them would have endorsed our holding in *Kelo*, just as both of them ultimately endorsed the doctrine of substantive due process.

John Paul Stevens, *Learning on the Job*, 74 Fordham L. Rev. 1561, 1566-1567 (2006). In thinking about these remarks, recall our initial comment on the role of the words "public use" in the Just Compensation Clause, where we noted that "public use" could be seen as an explicit limitation, an implicit limitation, or no limitation at all on government exercises of eminent domain. Which view does Justice Stevens appear to hold?

7. *Aftermath*. At oral arguments before the Supreme Court in *Kelo*, the attorneys representing New London took the unusual step of displaying an exhibit that showed the plans for the proposed redevelopment of the property taken under the redevelopment program. (Recall in this context Judge Prettyman's remark in *Schneider* that "Of course the plan as pictured in the prospectus is attractive."). The redevelopment project, however, never lived up to the plans. Indeed, the project largely failed, and the land taken remains undeveloped. Pfizer left New London in 2010, relocating all of its existing facilities to another town. For a discussion of the background of the *Kelo* litigation and its aftermath, *see* Jeff Benedict, *Little Pink House: A True Story of Defiance and Courage* (2009).

8. *Legislative Response*. Responding to the strong public outcry against the *Kelo* decision, many states passed laws restricting the use of eminent domain. Some did in fact reduce the permissible scope of eminent domain, but many were ineffective in

achieving their stated goals. *See* Ilya Somin, *The Limits of Backlash: Assessing the Political Response to* Kelo, 93 Minn. L. Rev. 2100 (2009).

9. *Where Would You Draw the Line?* As the Supreme Court noted in *Kelo*, states are free to restrict the use of eminent domain. Imagine that you could get an eminent domain law passed in your state. How would you draw the line between permissible and impermissible uses of eminent domain? As you think about these issues, consider whether the following examples would be permissible under your law. In each case, a municipality would take the property by eminent domain and transfer it to a new owner for the stated use:

- The new owner would be a private developer. The use would be a new stadium for the local NFL team. After construction, the stadium would be privately owned by the NFL team.
- The new owner would be a public agency. The use would be a new stadium for the local NFL team. After construction, the stadium would be owned by the public in fee simple and leased to the football team.
- The new owner would be a public university. The use would be for new classroom buildings and student housing on the university's campus.
- The new owner would be a private university. The use would be for new classroom buildings and student housing on the university's campus.
- The new owner would be a private health care corporation. The use would be for a new hospital.
- The new owner would be a private developer. The use would be for a new shopping mall.
- The new owner would be a private developer. The use would be for an office building for an insurance company.
- The new owner would be a municipality. The use would be for a public park.
- The new owner would be a private land conservation entity. The use would be for a park open to the public.
- The new owner would be a private land conservation entity. The use would be to preserve the land in an undisturbed state, and the land would be closed to the public.
- The new owner would be the state. The use would be for a public highway.
- The new owner would be a private developer. The use would be for a privately owned toll road. The public could use the road but would have to pay a toll to do so.

Try to find a consistent and coherent explanation for why you drew the line where you did between permissible and impermissible uses of eminent domain. Are there other things you would include in your law? Should the nature of the property being taken matter? For example, should it make a difference if the property being taken is residential or commercial? Blighted or not blighted? Economically depressed or not economically depressed? Does your experience in line drawing affect your views on how closely courts should scrutinize public use determinations?

B. "PRIVATE PROPERTY," "TAKEN," AND THE REGULATORY TAKINGS PROBLEM

In the last section, we focused on issues related to explicit government exercises of eminent domain. There, the government's intent to take the property was clear, and the effect of the exercise of eminent domain was to take ownership of the property from the owner. In this section, we consider a different issue: when, if ever, might a government regulation amount to a taking under the Just Compensation Clause? This is the regulatory takings problem. As we will see, the answer to our question will depend in part on how we interpret the words "private property" and "taken."

When a state government expressly takes property, it exercises the power of eminent domain. When the state regulates property, it exercises the *police power*. The exact contours of the scope of the police power may be the subject to some debate, but today it is clear that the police power gives states broad regulatory authority. As we noted in the previous chapter, the word "police" may be misleading to modern readers. Today, we most often use the word in the context of law enforcement, but in earlier times it was frequently used more broadly to refer to civilization or civil organization. William Blackstone, for example, described the public police as "the due regulation and domestic order of the kingdom."[25] The federal government, of course, has regulatory power, and federal regulations present many of the same issues as state regulations. We will focus our discussion, however, on state regulation.

WHY DO WE HAVE A JUST COMPENSATION CLAUSE?

Like the other provisions of the Bill of Rights, the Just Compensation Clause was written by James Madison. Unlike the other provisions of the Bill of Rights, however, the Just Compensation Clause was not requested at any of the state conventions held to ratify the Constitution. The historical background of the Clause therefore is a bit sparse. Treatise writer St. George Tucker, who was well positioned to comment on the ratification of the Clause, suggested that it "was probably intended to restrain the arbitrary and oppressive mode of obtaining supplies for the army, and other public uses, by impressments, as was too frequently practiced during the revolutionary war."[26] For more on the historical context of the Just Compensation Clause, see William Michael Treanor, *The Original Understanding of the Takings Clause and the Political Process*, 95 Colum. L. Rev. 782 (1995).

---

[25] 4 William Blackstone, *Commentaries on the Laws of England* 162 (1769).

[26] 1 William Blackstone, *Commentaries with Notes of References to the Constitution and Laws of the Federal Government of the United States, and of the Commonwealth of Virginia* (St. George Tucker ed., Rothman Reprints 1969 (1803)).

As we did with our materials on "public use," we will again take a historical approach to the regulatory takings issue. Early courts held that an exercise of the police power could never be an impermissible taking. As we will see, modern courts do not follow this view. Reading the early cases, however, provides some important context that will help us understand the more contemporary cases.

1. EARLY REGULATORY TAKINGS CASES

Our first case, *Commonwealth v. Alger*, was written by Chief Justice Lemuel Shaw of the Massachusetts Supreme Court. Shaw was one of the great judges in U.S. history, and the *Alger* opinion was tremendously important. Leonard Levy, who wrote a biography of Shaw, called *Alger* "one of the most influential and frequently cited [opinions] in constitutional law."[27] In the opinion, Shaw offers a sophisticated and thoughtful analysis of the regulation of private property and the difference between the police power and the power of eminent domain.

Alger owned waterfront property on Boston Harbor. Boston had enacted a regulation that limited how far out a wharf could be built into the water. Alger built a wharf that went past the permissible line established by these regulations. The parties agreed that the wharf did not actually impede navigation. Alger argued that under these circumstances the regulation exceeded the scope of the police power and was therefore unconstitutional. By focusing on the legitimate scope of the police power, Shaw was engaged in what we might now label a substantive due process analysis. Recall that the Just Compensation Clause was not clearly incorporated and applied to the states until 1897, and that the Due Process Clause of the Fourteenth Amendment was not enacted until well after *Alger* was decided. Shaw's analysis therefore will differ from contemporary regulatory takings analysis in some subtle ways. Nonetheless, *Alger* presents an excellent introduction to issues that still concern us today.

COMMONWEALTH V. ALGER

Supreme Court of Massachusetts, 1851
61 Mass. (7 Cush.) 53

SHAW, C. J. In proceeding to give judgment in the present case, the court are deeply impressed with the importance of the principles which it involves, and the magnitude and extent of the great public interests, and the importance and value of the private rights, directly or indirectly to be affected by it. It affects the relative rights of the public and of individual proprietors, in the soil lying on tide waters, between high and low water mark, over which the sea ebbs and flows, in the ordinary action of the tides.

---

[27] Leonard W. Levy, *The Law of the Commonwealth and Chief Justice Shaw* 247-248 (1957).

The defendant has been indicted for having erected and built a wharf over and beyond certain lines, described as the commissioners' lines, into the harbor of Boston. The case comes before this court, upon a report of the judge of the municipal court, who, deeming the questions of law involved in the case doubtful and important, with the consent of the defendant, pursuant to the statute, reported the same for the consideration of this court. Probably the opinion was given pro forma, and a verdict taken by consent, with a view to present the whole question to this court.

The case thus presented, must depend on the construction, validity, and effect of the laws in question, establishing the lines of the harbor, as they affect public and private rights; regarding, as they do, the rights of the public in tide waters and the arms of the sea, and the nature, extent, and limits of the rights of private proprietors in flats and sea-shores. The uncontested facts in the present case are, that the defendant was owner of land, bounded on a cove or arm of the sea, in which the tide ebbed and flowed, that he built the wharf complained of, on the flats before his said land, between high and low water mark, and within one hundred rods of his upland, but below the commissioners' line as fixed by one of these statutes; although it was so built as not to obstruct or impede navigation. This certainly presents the case most favorably for the defendant. . . .

Assuming . . . that the defendant was owner in fee of the soil and flats upon which the wharf in question was built, it becomes necessary to inquire whether it was competent for the legislature to pass the acts establishing the harbor lines, and what is the legal validity and effect of those acts. . . .

We think it is a settled principle, growing out of the nature of well ordered civil society, that every holder of property, however absolute and unqualified may be his title, holds it under the implied liability that his use of it may be so regulated, that it shall not be injurious to the equal enjoyment of others having an equal right to the enjoyment of their property, nor injurious to the rights of the community. All property in this commonwealth, as well that in the interior as that bordering on tide waters, is derived directly or indirectly from the government, and held subject to those general regulations, which are necessary to the common good and general welfare. Rights of property, like all other social and conventional rights, are subject to such reasonable limitations in their enjoyment, as shall prevent them from being injurious, and to such reasonable restraints and regulations established by law, as the legislature, under the governing and controlling power vested in them by the constitution, may think necessary and expedient.

This is very different from the right of eminent domain, the right of a government to take and appropriate private property to public use, whenever the public exigency requires it; which can be done only on condition of providing a reasonable compensation therefor. The power we allude to is rather the police power, the power vested in the legislature by the constitution, to make, ordain and establish all manner of wholesome and reasonable laws, statutes and ordinances, either with penalties or without, not repugnant to the constitution, as they shall judge to be for the good and welfare of the commonwealth, and of the subjects of the same.

It is much easier to perceive and realize the existence and sources of this power, than to mark its boundaries, or prescribe limits to its exercise. There are many cases in which such a power is exercised by all well ordered governments, and where its fitness is so obvious, that all well regulated minds will regard it as reasonable. Such are the laws to prohibit the use of warehouses for the storage of gunpowder near habitations or highways; to restrain the height to which wooden buildings may be erected in populous neighborhoods, and require them to be covered with slate or other incombustible material; to prohibit buildings from being used for hospitals for contagious diseases, or for the carrying on of noxious or offensive trades; to prohibit the raising of a dam, and causing stagnant water to spread over meadows, near inhabited villages, thereby raising noxious exhalations, injurious to health and dangerous to life.

Nor does the prohibition of such noxious use of property, a prohibition imposed because such use would be injurious to the public, although it may diminish the profits of the owner, make it an appropriation to a public use, so as to entitle the owner to compensation. If the owner of a vacant lot in the midst of a city could erect thereon a great wooden building, and cover it with shingles, he might obtain a larger profit of his land, than if obliged to build of stone or brick, with a slated roof. If the owner of a warehouse in a cluster of other buildings could store quantities of gunpowder in it for himself and others, he might be saved the great expense of transportation. If a landlord could let his building for a smallpox hospital, or a slaughter-house, he might obtain an increased rent. But he is restrained; not because the public have occasion to make the like use, or to make any use of the property, or to take any benefit or profit to themselves from it; but because it would be a noxious use, contrary to the maxim, sic utere tuo, ut alienum non laedas. It is not an appropriation of the property to a public use, but the restraint of an injurious private use by the owner, and is therefore not within the principle of property taken under the right of eminent domain. The distinction, we think, is manifest in principle, although the facts and circumstances of different cases are so various, that it is often difficult to decide whether a particular exercise of legislation is properly attributable to the one or the other of these two acknowledged powers. . . .

Things done may or may not be wrong in themselves, or necessarily injurious and punishable as such at common law; but laws are passed declaring them offences, and making them punishable, because they tend to injurious consequences; but more especially for the sake of having a definite, known and authoritative rule which all can understand and obey. In the case already put, of erecting a powder magazine or slaughterhouse, it would be indictable at common law, and punishable as a nuisance, if in fact erected so near an inhabited village as to be actually dangerous or noxious to life or health. Without a positive law, every body might agree that two hundred feet would be too near, and that two thousand feet would not be too near; but within this wide margin, who shall say, who can know, what distance shall be too near or otherwise? An authoritative rule, carrying with it the character of certainty and precision, is needed. The tradesman needs to know, before incurring expense, how near he may build his works without violating the law or committing a nuisance; builders of houses need to know, to what distance they must keep from the obnoxious works already erected, in order to be sure of the protection of the law for their habitations. This requisite certainty and precision can only be obtained by a positive enactment, fixing the distance, within which the use shall be prohibited as noxious, and beyond which it will be allowed, and enforcing the rule thus fixed, by penalties. . . .

The reason why it is necessary to have a certain and authoritative law, is shown by the difficulty, not to say impracticability, of inquiring and deciding as a fact, in each particular case, whether a certain erection in tide water is a nuisance at common law or not; and when ascertained and adjudged, it affords no rule for any other case, and can have little effect in maintaining and protecting the acknowledged public right. It is this consideration, (the expediency and necessity of defining and securing the rights of the public,) which creates the exigency, and furnishes the legislature with the authority to make a general and precise law; but when made, because it was just and expedient, and because it is law, it becomes the duty of every person to obey it and comply with it. The question under the statute therefore is, not whether any wharf, built after the statute was made and promulgated, was an actual obstruction to navigation, but whether it was within the prohibited limit.

On the whole, the court are of opinion that the act fixing a line within the harbor of Boston, beyond which no riparian proprietor should erect a wharf or other permanent structure, although to some extent it prohibited him from building such structure on flats of which he owned the fee, was a constitutional law, and one which it was competent for the legislature to make; that it was binding on the defendant, and rendered him obnoxious to its penalties, if he violated its provisions.

NOTES AND QUESTIONS

1. *Legislative Line Drawing*. *Alger* has often been read to stand for the proposition that states can regulate land under the police power because property ownership is inherently limited by the *sic utere* doctrine's admonition that an owner should not use property in a manner that will harm another. Another way of putting this point is that property owners do not have a right to engage in a nuisance. If a regulation prohibits an owner from engaging in a nuisance, then that regulation is simply prohibiting the owner from doing something that she had no right to do in the first place. In these

circumstances, the owner cannot legitimately complain that the regulation deprived her of the right to engage in a particular use of the property.

Although there is some truth to this interpretation of *Alger*, the case does far more than equate the police power with the regulation of common-law nuisances. The parties conceded that Alger's wharf did not impede navigation. The crux of Alger's argument was that because his wharf was not harming anyone, the regulation that prohibited his wharf exceeded the scope of the police power. It is important to understand why Chief Justice Shaw rejected this argument. Make sure that you understand what Shaw had to say about the importance of legislative line drawing. Shaw uses the evocative example of a powder magazine or slaughterhouse located near an inhabited area. Everyone might agree that it would be a nuisance to build a powder magazine too close to an inhabited area. But how can you tell how close is too close unless there is a regulation that draws the line?

2. *Diminution in Value.* Shaw's opinion in *Alger* gives us a subtle introduction to another concept that is very important in contemporary regulatory takings cases. By restricting an owner's use of land, a regulation will often reduce the value of the property. We often call this reduction the *diminution in value* caused by regulation. Diminution in value will be a recurring theme in this chapter. Shaw acknowledges the financial impact of regulation on owners, noting at one point that "[i]f the owner of a vacant lot in the midst of a city could erect thereon a great wooden building, and cover it with shingles, he might obtain a larger profit of his land, than if obliged to build of stone or brick, with a slated roof." Shaw goes on to note that the same could be said for other types of uses, but that the government regulates those uses not because it wants to capture that value but because the use is harmful. For this reason, Shaw explained, eminent domain and the police power are different, and there is no constitutional problem just because a regulation of a potentially harmful use reduces the value of property. Do not, by the way, underestimate the danger that wooden buildings presented to communities during this time period. Fire was an ever-present danger, and many municipalities regulated the construction of buildings in cities and towns with fire prevention in mind. For a thorough analysis of U.S. land use regulation in the 1700s and 1800s, *see* William J. Novak, *The People's Welfare* (1996).

DIMINUTION IN VALUE

3. *Courts, Legislatures, and Nuisance.* Returning to our point about legislative line drawing, the court's discussion in *Alger* sets up an issue that will be relevant to our contemporary regulatory takings cases: Who gets to define a nuisance or to label a use as potentially harmful? The courts or the legislature? In our next case, the U.S. Supreme Court addresses that very issue.

DEFINING "NUISANCE"

MUGLER V. KANSAS

United States Supreme Court (1887)
123 U.S. 623

[Peter Mugler had opened a brewery in Salina, Kansas, in 1877. By state constitutional amendment and statute, Kansas prohibited the manufacture of "intoxicating beverages." The prohibition law became effective in 1881. Mugler continued to brew beer after the prohibition law became effective, and he was criminally prosecuted for violation of the statute.]

The trial was had in this case before the court, without a jury, upon an agreed statement of facts, which statement of facts is as follows: "It is hereby stipulated and agreed that the facts in the above-entitled case are, and that the evidence would prove them to be, as follows:

That the defendant, Peter Mugler, . . . erected and furnished a brewery on lots Nos. 152 and 154, on Third street, in the city of Salina, . . . Kansas, for use in the manufacture of an intoxicating malt liquor, commonly known as beer;

that such building was specially constructed and adapted for the manufacture of such malt liquor, at an actual cost and expense to said defendant of ten thousand dollars, and was used by him for the purpose for which it was designed and intended after its completion in 1877, and up to May 1, 1881;

that said brewery was at all times after its completion, and on May 1, 1881, worth the sum of ten thousand dollars for use in the manufacture of said beer, and is not worth to exceed the sum of twenty-five hundred dollars for any other purpose;

DIMINUTION IN VALUE

that said defendant, since October 1, 1881, has used said brewery in the manner and for the purpose for which it was constructed and adapted, by the manufacture therein of such intoxicating malt liquors, and at the time of the manufacture of said malt liquor said defendant had no permit to manufacture the same for medical, scientific, or mechanical purposes, as provided by chapter 128 of the Laws of 1881.

And the foregoing was all the evidence introduced in this case, and upon which a finding of guilty was made." The defendant was found guilty, and fined $100, and appealed to the supreme court of the state of Kansas, where the court below was affirmed. [Mugler appealed to the U.S. Supreme Court, arguing that the prohibition law was unconstitutional.]

Plaintiff in error invoked in the argument before the supreme court of the state of Kansas a portion of the first section of the fourteenth amendment to the constitution of the United States, which provides: "Nor shall any state deprive any person of life, liberty, or property without due process of law." The amendment to the constitution of the state of Kansas which is complained of is as follows: "The manufacture and sale of intoxicating liquors shall be forever prohibited in this state, except for medical, scientific, and mechanical purposes." Const. Kan. art. 15, §10. This amendment was adopted by the people November 2, 1880. The statute complained of is chapter 128 of the Laws of Kansas, passed in 1881. That statute became operative May 1, 1881. Section 8 of that statute is as follows: "Any person, without taking out and having a permit to manufacture intoxicating liquors as provided in this act, who shall manufacture, or aid, assist, or abet in the manufacture, of any of the liquors mentioned in section 1 of this act, shall be deemed guilty of a misdemeanor, and, upon conviction thereof, shall suffer the same punishment as provided in the last preceding section of this act for unlawfully selling such liquors." . . .

[In the trial court, Mugler] filed an answer, containing a general denial, and also an averment to the effect that the defendant's brewery, which is alleged to be of the value of $60,000, was erected prior to the adoption of the prohibitory amendment to the constitution of this state, and the passage of the prohibitory law, for the purpose of manufacturing beer, and that it is adapted to no other purpose, and that if the defendants are prevented from the operation thereof for the purpose for which it was erected, the same will be wholly lost to the defendants, and that said prohibitory act is unconstitutional and void. . . .

DIMINUTION IN VALUE

Mr. Justice HARLAN, . . . delivered the opinion of the court. The general question in each case is whether the foregoing statutes of Kansas are in conflict with that clause of the fourteenth amendment, which provides that "no state shall make or enforce any law which shall abridge the privileges or immunities of citizens of the United States; nor shall any state deprive any person of life, liberty, or property without due process of law." That legislation by a state prohibiting the manufacture within her limits of intoxicating liquors, to be there sold or bartered for general use as a beverage, does not necessarily infringe any right, privilege, or immunity secured by the constitution of the United States, is made clear by the decisions of this court, rendered before and since the adoption of the fourteenth amendment; to some of which, in view of questions to be presently considered, it will be well to refer. . . .

The principle that no person shall be deprived of life, liberty, or property without due process of law, was embodied, in substance, in the constitutions of nearly all, if not all, of the states at the time of the adoption of the fourteenth amendment; and it has never been regarded as incompatible with the principle, equally vital, because essential to the peace and safety of society, that all property in this country is held under the implied obligation that the owner's use of it shall not be injurious to the community. *Beer Co. v. Massachusetts*, 97 U. S. 32; *Com. v. Alger*, 7 Cush. 53. . . .

Another decision very much in point upon this branch of the case, is *Fertilizing Co. v. Hyde Park*, 97 U. S. 659, 667, also decided after the adoption of the fourteenth amendment. The court there sustained the validity of an ordinance of the village of Hyde Park, in Cook county, Illinois, passed under legislative authority, forbidding any person from transporting through that village offal or other offensive or unwholesome matter, or from maintaining or carrying on an offensive or unwholesome business or establishment within its limits. The fertilizing company, had, at large expense, and under authority expressly conferred by its charter, located its works at a particular point in the county. Besides, the charter of the village, at that time, provided that it should not interfere with parties engaged in transporting animal matter from Chicago, or from manufacturing it into a fertilizer or other chemical product. The enforcement of the ordinance in question operated to destroy the business of the company, and seriously to impair the value of its property. As, however, its business had become a nuisance to the community in which it was conducted, producing discomfort, and often sickness, among large masses of people, the court maintained the authority of the village, acting under legislative sanction, to protect the public health against such nuisance. It said: "We cannot doubt that the police power of the state was applicable and adequate to give an effectual remedy. That power belonged to the states when the federal constitution was adopted. They did not surrender it, and they all have it now. It extends to the entire property and business within their local jurisdiction. Both are subject to it in all proper cases. It rests upon the fundamental principle that every one shall so use his own as not to wrong and injure another. To regulate and abate nuisances is one of its ordinary functions."

It is supposed by the defendants that the doctrine for which they contend is sustained by *Pumpelly v. Green Bay Co.*, 13 Wall. 168. But in that view we do not concur. [*Pumpelly* involved the flooding of the owner's property by a government dam project. As a result of the flooding, the property was rendered useless.]. This court said it would be a very curious and unsatisfactory result, were it held that, "if the government refrains from the absolute conversion of real property to the uses of the public, it can destroy its value entirely, can inflict irreparable and permanent injury to any extent, can, in effect, subject it to total destruction, without making any compensation, because, in the narrowest sense of that word, it is not taken for the public use. Such a construction would pervert the constitutional provision into a restriction upon the rights of the citizen, as those rights stood at the common law, instead of the government, and make it an authority for the invasion of private rights under the pretext of the public good, which had no warrant in the laws or practices of our ancestors."

These principles have no application to the case under consideration. The question in *Pumpelly v. Green Bay Co.*, arose under the state's power of eminent domain; while the question now before us arises under what are, strictly, the police powers of the state, exerted for the protection of the health, morals, and safety of the people. That case, as this court said in *Transportation Co. v. Chicago*, 99 U. S. 642, was an extreme qualification of the doctrine, universally held, that "acts done in the proper exercise of governmental powers, and not directly encroaching upon private property, though these consequences may impair its use," do not constitute a taking within the meaning of the constitutional provision, or entitle the owner of such property to compensation from the state or its agents, or give him any right of action. It was a case in which there was a "permanent flooding of private property," a "physical invasion of the real estate of the private owner, and a practical ouster of his possession." His property was, in effect, required to be devoted to the use of the public, and, consequently, he was entitled to compensation.

As already stated, the present case must be governed by principles that do not involve the power of eminent domain, in the exercise of which property may not be taken for public use without compensation. A prohibition simply upon the use of property for purposes that are declared, by valid legislation, to be injurious to the health, morals, or safety of the community, cannot, in any just sense, be deemed a taking or an appropriation of property for the public benefit. Such legislation does not disturb the owner in the control or use of his property for lawful purposes, nor restrict his right to dispose of it, but is only a declaration by the state that its use by any one, for certain forbidden purposes, is prejudicial to the public interests. Nor can legislation of that character come within the fourteenth amendment, in any case, unless it is apparent that its real object is not to protect the community, or to promote the general well-being, but, under the guise of police regulation, to deprive the owner of his liberty and property, without due process of law. The power which the states have of prohibiting such use by individuals of their property, as will be prejudicial to the health, the morals, or the safety of the public, is not, and, consistently with the existence and safety of organized society, cannot be, burdened with the condition that the state must compensate such individual owners for pecuniary losses they may sustain, by reason of their not being permitted, by a noxious use of their property, to inflict injury upon the community. The exercise of the police power by the destruction of property which is itself a public nuisance, or the prohibition of its use in a particular way, whereby its value becomes depreciated, is very different from taking property for public use, or from depriving a person of his property without due process of law. In the one case, a nuisance only is abated; in the other, unoffending property is taken away from an innocent owner. It is true, when the defendants in these cases purchased or erected their breweries, the laws of the state did not forbid the manufacture of intoxicating liquors. But the state did not thereby give any assurance, or come under an obligation, that its legislation upon that subject would remain unchanged. Indeed, as was said in *Stone v. Mississippi*, 101 U. S. 814, the supervision of the public health and the public morals is a governmental power, "continuing in its nature," and "to be dealt with as the special exigencies of the moment may require;" and that, "for this purpose, the largest legislative discretion is allowed, and the discretion cannot be parted with any more than the power itself." So in *Beer Co. v. Massachusetts*, 97 U. S. 32: "If the public safety or the public morals require the discontinuance of any manufacture or traffic, the hand of the legislature cannot be stayed from providing for its discontinuance by any incidental inconvenience which individuals or corporations may suffer."

DEFINING "NUISANCE"

NOTES AND QUESTIONS

1. *Courts, Legislatures, and Nuisance, Again.* The last paragraph of our excerpt from *Mugler* is crucially important. *Alger* introduced the concept that a regulation of a nuisance is not an unconstitutional taking, and *Mugler* follows this basic approach. But this raises the question that we noted above—who gets to define a nuisance? The courts or the legislature? The facts of *Mugler* clearly present this issue, because there is no suggestion that the manufacture of beer was a common-law nuisance. One day, Mugler was engaged in the lawful brewing of beer. The next day, when the prohibition law took effect, he was acting illegally. Mugler therefore was not engaged in a common-law nuisance. Rather, he was engaged in an activity that had been "declared, by valid legislation, to be injurious to the health, morals, or safety of the community." This quote, and other language from the opinion, suggests that the legislature has the power to define an activity as a nuisance and that the regulation of an activity labeled as a nuisance cannot be an unconstitutional taking.

DEFINING "NUISANCE"

2. *Regulations vs. Eminent Domain.* Together, *Alger* and *Mugler* stand for the proposition that exercises of the police power can never be a taking. The opinions suggest that this rule is based on two concepts. First, this rule appears to be based on the concept of nuisance that we discussed in the previous note. Second, this rule appears to be based on a formalist distinction between the police power and the power of eminent domain. Both *Alger* and *Mugler* suggest that these two powers are fundamentally different. Where the government uses eminent domain to take property for public use, the government uses the police power to enact regulations to protect the public welfare. As we will see, this formal distinction between eminent domain and the police power will begin to break down in our subsequent cases.

3. *Bearing the Cost of Legal Change.* *Mugler* raises a conceptual issue that is important to keep in mind as we think about the regulatory takings issue. When Mugler built his brewery, the manufacture of beer was legal. A few years later, the law changed. Should he have to bear the cost of this legal change? Or should the public bear the cost? Does our answer to this question depend on whether the prohibited activity (here, the brewing of beer) can be deemed to be harmful in some way?

4. *Diminution in Value.* As we mentioned after the *Alger* case, diminution in value is an important factor in contemporary regulatory takings cases. Diminution in value can be measured by comparing the value of the property before the regulation with the value of the property after the regulation. Diminution in value did not play a major role in the Court's analysis in *Mugler*, but the parties' stipulated facts addressed it: the property was worth $10,000 as a brewery, but no more than $2,500 if used for another purpose. In other words, the regulation led to a 75 percent diminution in the value of the property. Looking back at the case from a contemporary perspective, judges and scholars sometimes misstate the diminution in value that was involved in *Mugler*. As stated in our excerpt from the case, Mugler submitted an answer in the trial court claiming

that the property was worth $60,000 before the regulation, but was worth nothing afterwards. Contemporary readers sometimes read this claim as suggesting that the regulation rendered Mugler's property valueless, resulting in a 100 percent diminution in value. This reading is wrong, however, because it confuses the allegation in Mugler's pleading (that the property was rendered valueless) with the stipulated facts that were

DIMINUTION IN VALUE

actually used by the trial and appellate courts (that the property was reduced in value from $10,000 to $2,500). As we will soon see, the distinction between a 100 percent diminution in value and a 75 percent diminution in value is crucially important in contemporary regulatory takings law.

5. Pumpelly *and Contemporary Takings Rules.* The Court's analysis in *Mugler* discussed an earlier case, *Pumpelly v. Green Bay Co.*, 80 U.S. 166 (1872). *Pumpelly* involved a takings claim based on flooding of the owner's property. The portions of the *Pumpelly* opinion quoted in *Mugler* raise three important concepts that are reflected in the more contemporary cases that we will study below. First, *Pumpelly* rejected the argument that the government could only take property by an express exercise of eminent domain. Second, in the same quote, the Court expressed its concern about a government action that "can destroy [property's] value entirely," raising the diminution in value issue again. Third, the Court discussed how the flooding was "permanent" and constituted a "physical invasion" of the property. We will see each of these ideas again soon.

2. THE BEGINNINGS OF THE MODERN ERA

As we have seen, courts in the 1800s consistently held that regulations enacted under the police power were never unconstitutional takings. This changed in our next case, *Pennsylvania Coal Co. v. Mahon.* Justice Rehnquist later called *Mahon* the "foundation of our 'regulatory takings' jurisprudence." Although we derive our contemporary rules for regulatory takings from other cases, *Mahon* introduces a number of concepts that are still relevant today.

As we will see, *Mahon* involved legislation addressing the problem of subsidence. Coal mining created underground voids as the coal was removed. These voids could cause the surface to subside, especially in areas where the coal was located near the surface. The Pennsylvania Legislature enacted a law, the Kohler Act, to address the problem of subsidence. The Kohler Act prohibited mining coal in a way that would cause subsidence underneath people's homes.

The litigation was complicated by a quirk in Pennsylvania's law of mineral rights. Most states recognize two types of interests relevant to coal mining: the surface rights and the mineral rights. Pennsylvania recognized a third interest: the support right. The support right was the right to mine coal that was supporting a structure. In other words, the support right was the right to mine coal that, if removed, might cause the surface to subside. Subsidence could damage or destroy buildings on the surface.

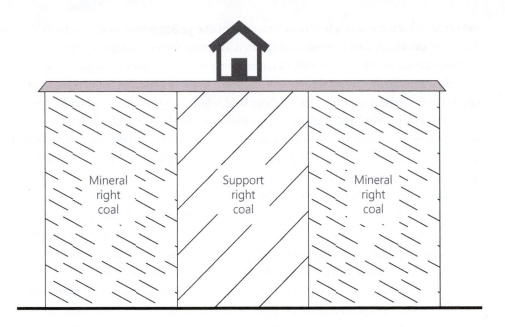

In *Mahon*, the Pennsylvania Coal Company owned the support right and had expressly reserved the right to mine the coal under the home. The homeowner sued to enjoin mining of the support-right coal, relying on the Kohler Act.

PENNSYLVANIA COAL CO. V. MAHON

United States Supreme Court, 1922
260 U.S. 393

Mr. Justice HOLMES delivered the opinion of the Court. This is a bill in equity brought by the defendants in error to prevent the Pennsylvania Coal Company from mining under their property in such way as to remove the supports and cause a subsidence of the surface and of their house. The bill sets out a deed executed by the Coal Company in 1878, under which the plaintiffs claim. The deed conveys the surface but in express terms reserves the right to remove all the coal under the same and the grantee takes the premises with the risk and waives all claim for damages that may arise from mining out the coal. But the plaintiffs say that whatever may have been the Coal Company's rights, they were taken away by an Act of Pennsylvania, approved May 27, 1921 (P. L. 1198), commonly known there as the Kohler Act. The Court of Common Pleas found that if not restrained the defendant would cause the damage to prevent which the bill was brought but denied an injunction, holding that the statute if applied to this case would be unconstitutional. On appeal the Supreme Court of the State agreed that the defendant had contract and property rights protected by the Constitution of the United States, but held that the statute was a legitimate exercise of the police power and directed a decree for the plaintiffs. A writ of error was granted bringing the case to this Court.

The statute forbids the mining of anthracite coal in such way as to cause the subsidence of, among other things, any structure used as a human habitation, with certain exceptions, including among them land where the surface is owned by the owner of the underlying coal and is distant more than one hundred and fifty feet from any improved property belonging to any other person. As applied to this case the statute is admitted to destroy previously existing rights of property and contract. The question is whether the police power can be stretched so far.

Government hardly could go on if to some extent values incident to property could not be diminished without paying for every such change in the general law. As long recognized some values are enjoyed under an implied limitation and must yield to the police power. But obviously the implied limitation must have its limits or the contract and due process clauses are gone. One fact for consideration in determining such limits is the extent of the diminution. When it reaches a certain magnitude, in most if not in all cases there must be an exercise of eminent domain and compensation to sustain the act. So the question depends upon the particular facts. The greatest weight is given to the judgment of the legislature but it always is open to interested parties to contend that the legislature has gone beyond its constitutional power.

DIMINUTION IN VALUE

This is the case of a single private house. No doubt there is a public interest even in this, as there is in every purchase and sale and in all that happens within the commonwealth. Some existing rights may be modified even in such a case. *Rideout v. Knox*, 148 Mass. 368, 19 N. E. 390, 2 L. R. A. 81, 12 Am. St. Rep. 560. But usually in ordinary private affairs the public interest does not warrant much of this kind of interference. A source of damage to such a house is not a public nuisance even if similar damage is inflicted on others in different places. The damage is not common or public. *Wesson v. Washburn Iron Co.*, 13 Allen (Mass.) 95, 103, 90 Am. Dec. 181. The extent of the public interest is shown by the statute to be limited, since the statute ordinarily does not apply to land when the surface is owned by the owner of the coal. Furthermore, it is not justified as a protection of personal safety. That could be provided for by notice. Indeed the very foundation of this bill is that the defendant gave timely notice of its intent to mine under the house. On the other hand the extent of the taking is great. It purports to abolish what is recognized in Pennsylvania as an estate in land—a very valuable estate— and what is declared by the Court below to be a contract hitherto binding the plaintiffs. If we were called upon to deal with the plaintiffs' position alone we should think it clear that the statute does not disclose a public interest sufficient to warrant so extensive a destruction of the defendant's constitutionally protected rights.

But the case has been treated as one in which the general validity of the act should be discussed. The Attorney General of the State, the City of Scranton and the representatives of other extensive interests were allowed to take part in the argument below and have submitted their contentions here. It seems, therefore, to be our duty to go farther in the statement of our opinion, in order that it may be known at once, and that further suits should not be brought in vain.

It is our opinion that the act cannot be sustained as an exercise of the police power, so far as it affects the mining of coal under streets or cities in places where the right to mine such coal has been reserved. As said in a Pennsylvania case, "For practical purposes, the right to coal consists in the right to mine it." *Commonwealth v. Clearview Coal Co.*, 256 Pa. 328, 331, 100 Atl. 820, L. R. A. 1917E, 672. What makes the right to mine coal valuable is that it can be exercised with profit. To make it commercially impracticable to mine certain coal has very nearly the same effect for constitutional purposes as appropriating or destroying it. This we think that we are warranted in assuming that the statute does.

It is true that in *Plymouth Coal Co. v. Pennsylvania*, 232 U. S. 531, 34 Sup. Ct. 359, 58 L. Ed. 713, it was held competent for the legislature to require a pillar of coal to the left along the line of adjoining property, that with the pillar on the other side of the line would be a barrier sufficient for the safety of the employees of either mine in case the other should be abandoned and allowed to fill with water. But that was a requirement for the safety of employees invited into the mine, and secured an average reciprocity of advantage that has been recognized as a justification of various laws.

The rights of the public in a street purchased or laid out by eminent domain are those that it has paid for. If in any case its representatives have been so short sighted as to acquire only surface rights without the right of support we see no more authority for supplying the latter without compensation than there was for taking the right of way in the first place and refusing to pay for it because the public wanted it very much. The protection of private property in the Fifth Amendment presupposes that it is wanted for public use, but provides that it shall not be taken for such use without compensation. A similar assumption is made in the decisions upon the Fourteenth Amendment. *Hairston v. Danville & Western Ry. Co.*, 208 U. S. 598, 605, 28 Sup. Ct. 331, 52 L. Ed. 637, 13 Ann. Cas. 1008. When this seemingly absolute protection is found to be qualified by the police power, the natural tendency of human nature is to extend the qualification more and more until at last private property disappears. But that cannot be accomplished in this way under the Constitution of the United States.

The general rule at least is that while property may be regulated to a certain extent, if regulation goes too far it will be recognized as a taking. It may be doubted how far exceptional cases, like the blowing up of a house to stop a conflagration, go—and if they go beyond the general rule, whether they do not stand as much upon tradition as upon principle. *Bowditch v. Boston*, 101 U. S. 16, 25 L. Ed. 980. In general it is not plain that a man's misfortunes or necessities will justify his shifting the damages to his neighbor's shoulders. *Spade v. Lynn & Boston Ry. Co.*, 172 Mass. 488, 489, 52 N. E. 747, 43 L. R. A.

832, 70 Am. St. Rep. 298. We are in danger of forgetting that a strong public desire to improve the public condition is not enough to warrant achieving the desire by a shorter cut than the constitutional way of paying for the change. As we already have said this is a question of degree—and therefore cannot be disposed of by general propositions. But we regard this as going beyond any of the cases decided by this Court. The late decisions upon laws dealing with the congestion of Washington and New York, caused by the war, dealt with laws intended to meet a temporary emergency and providing for compensation determined to be reasonable by an impartial board. They were to the verge of the law but fell far short of the present act. *Block & Hirsh*, 256 U. S. 135, 41 Sup. Ct. 458, 65 L. Ed. 865, 16 A. L. R. 165; *Marcus Brown Holding Co. v. Feldman*, 256 U. S. 170, 41 Sup. Ct. 465, 65 L. Ed. 877; *Levy Leasing Co. v. Siegel*, 258 U. S. 242, 42 Sup. Ct. 289, 66 L. Ed. 595, March 20, 1922.

We assume, of course, that the statute was passed upon the conviction that an exigency existed that would warrant it, and we assume that an exigency exists that would warrant the exercise of eminent domain. But the question at bottom is upon whom the loss of the changes desired should fall. So far as private persons or communities have seen fit to take the risk of acquiring only surface rights, we cannot see that the fact that their risk has become a danger warrants the giving to them greater rights than they bought.

Decree reversed.

Mr. Justice BRANDEIS dissenting. The Kohler Act prohibits, under certain conditions, the mining of anthracite coal within the limits of a city in such a manner or to such an extent "as to cause the . . . subsidence of . . . any dwelling or other structure used as a human habitation, or any factory, store, or other industrial or mercantile establishment in which human labor is employed." Act Pa. May 27, 1921, §1 (P. L. 1198). Coal in place is land, and the right of the owner to use his land is not absolute. He may not so use it as to create a public nuisance, and uses, once harmless, may, owing to changed conditions, seriously threaten the public welfare. Whenever they do, the Legislature has power to prohibit such uses without paying compensation; and the power to prohibit extends alike to the manner, the character and the purpose of the use. Are we justified in declaring that the Legislature of Pennsylvania has, in restricting the right to mine anthracite, exercised this power so arbitrarily as to violate the Fourteenth Amendment?

Every restriction upon the use of property imposed in the exercise of the police power deprives the owner of some right theretofore enjoyed, and is, in that sense, an abridgment by the state of rights in property without making compensation. But restriction imposed to protect the public health, safety or morals from dangers threatened is not a taking. The restriction here in question is merely the prohibition of a noxious use. The property so restricted remains in the possession of its owner. The state does not appropriate it or make any use of it. The state merely prevents the owner from making a use which interferes with

DEFINING
"NUISANCE"

paramount rights of the public. Whenever the use prohibited ceases to be noxious—as it may because of further change in local or social conditions—the restriction will have to be removed and the owner will again be free to enjoy his property as heretofore.

The restriction upon the use of this property cannot, of course, be lawfully imposed, unless its purpose is to protect the public. But the purpose of a restriction does not cease to be public, because incidentally some private persons may thereby receive gratuitously valuable special benefits. Thus, owners of low buildings may obtain, through statutory restrictions upon the height of neighboring structures, benefits equivalent to an easement of light and air. *Welch v. Swasey*, 214 U. S. 91, 29 Sup. Ct. 567, 53 L. Ed. 923. *Compare Lindsley v. Natural Carbonic Gas Co.*, 220 U. S. 61, 31 Sup. Ct. 337, 55 L. Ed. 369, Ann. Cas. 1912C, 160; *Walls v. Midland Carbon Co.*, 254 U. S. 300, 41 Sup. Ct. 118, 65 L. Ed. 276. Furthermore, a restriction, though imposed for a public purpose, will not be lawful, unless the restriction is an appropriate means to the public end. But to keep coal in place is surely an appropriate means of preventing subsidence of the surface; and ordinarily it is the only available means. Restriction upon use does not become inappropriate as a means, merely because it deprives the owner of the only use to which the property can then be profitably put. The liquor and the oleomargine cases settled that. *Mugler v. Kansas*, 123 U. S. 623, 668, 669, 8 Sup. Ct. 273, 31 L. Ed. 205; *Powell v. Pennsylvania*, 127 U. S. 678, 682, 8 Sup. Ct. 992, 1257, 32 L. Ed. 253. *See also Hadacheck v. Los Angeles*, 239 U. S. 394, 36 Sup. Ct. 143, 60 L. Ed. 348, Ann. Cas. 1917B, 927; *Pierce Oil Corporation v. City of Hope*, 248 U. S. 498, 39 Sup. Ct. 172, 63 L. Ed. 381. Nor is a restriction imposed through exercise of the police power inappropriate as a means, merely because the same end might be effected through exercise of the power of eminent domain, or otherwise at public expense. Every restriction upon the height of buildings might be secured through acquiring by eminent domain the right of each owner to build above the limiting height; but it is settled that the state need not resort to that power. *Compare Laurel Hill Cemetery v. San Francisco*, 216 U. S. 358, 30 Sup. Ct. 301, 54 L. Ed. 515; *Missouri Pacific Railway Co. v. Omaha*, 235 U. S. 121, 35 Sup. Ct. 82, 59 L. Ed. 157. If by mining anthracite coal the owner would necessarily unloose poisonous gases, I suppose no one would doubt the power of the state to prevent the mining, without buying his coal fields. And why may not the state, likewise, without paying compensation, prohibit one from digging so deep or excavating so near the surface, as to expose the community to like dangers? In the latter case, as in the former, carrying on the business would be a public nuisance.

It is said that one fact for consideration in determining whether the limits of the police power have been exceeded is the extent of the resulting diminution in value, and that here the restriction destroys existing rights of property and contract. But values are relative. If we are to consider the value of the coal kept in place by the restriction, we should compare it with the value of all other parts of the land. That is, with the value not of the coal alone,

DIMINUTION IN VALUE

but with the value of the whole property. The rights of an owner as against the public are not increased by dividing the interests in his property into surface and subsoil. The sum of the rights in the parts can not be greater than the rights in the whole. The estate of an owner in land is grandiloquently described as extending ab orco usque ad coelum. But I suppose no one would contend that by selling his interest above 100 feet from the surface he could prevent the state from limiting, by the police power, the height of structures in a city. And why should a sale of underground rights bar the state's power? For aught that appears the value of the coal kept in place by the restriction may be negligible as compared with the value of the whole property, or even as compared with that part of it which is represented by the coal remaining in place and which may be extracted despite the statute. Ordinarily a police regulation, general in operation, will not be held void as to a particular property, although proof is offered that owing to conditions peculiar to it the restriction could not reasonably be applied. *See Powell v. Pennsylvania*, 127 U. S. 678, 681, 684, 8 Sup. Ct. 992, 1257, 32 L. Ed. 253; *Murphy v. California*, 225 U. S. 623, 629, 32 Sup. Ct. 697, 56 L. Ed. 1229, 41 L. R. A. (N. S.) 153. But even if the particular facts are to govern, the statute should, in my opinion be upheld in this case. For the defendant has failed to adduce any evidence from which it appears that to restrict its mining operations was an unreasonable exercise of the police power. *Compare Reinman v. Little Rock*, 237 U. S. 171, 177, 180, 35 Sup. Ct. 511, 59 L. Ed. 900; *Pierce Oil Corporation v. City of Hope*, 248 U. S. 498, 500, 39 Sup. Ct. 172, 63 L. Ed. 381. Where the surface and the coal belong to the same person, self-interest would ordinarily prevent mining to such an extent as to cause a subsidence. It was, doubtless, for this reason that the Legislature, estimating the degrees of danger, deemed statutory restriction unnecessary for the public safety under such conditions. . . .

NOTES AND QUESTIONS

1. *Going "Too Far."* Before *Mahon*, courts had taken the position that a regulatory exercise of the police power could never be a taking. After *Mahon*, "if regulation goes too far it will be recognized as a taking." Justice Holmes's opinion gives us very little help in determining when a regulation might go "too far." Beginning with *Mahon*, however, the answer to our core question—when, if ever, a regulation might be an unconstitutional taking?—shifted from "never" to "sometimes."

2. *A Bit More on Subsidence.* In his book, *Regulatory Takings: Law, Economics, and Politics* (1995), William Fischel provided a fascinating historical account of the problem of subsidence, the Kohler Act, and the impact of the *Mahon* decision. In his research, he found that:

> The damage [from subsidence] was often dramatic. Pictures show whole houses swallowed up, and reports indicated that lives were sometimes lost, which seemed to belie Holmes's suggestion that notice alone was enough to provide for personal safety. Surface damage, nonetheless, seems to have been episodic and limited; cities were not literally falling into the earth.

Id. at 26. Professor Fischel found that most coal companies voluntarily paid compensation for surface damage, both before and after *Mahon* was decided. The Kohler Act was inspired in part by uncompensated damages caused by one rogue coal mining company. *See id.* at 26-42.

3. *Diminution in Value and the Denominator Problem.* Justice Holmes's short and somewhat cryptic opinion does very little to establish a regulatory takings test. It does, however, raise some issues and concepts that will be important as we consider the cases that give us our contemporary regulatory takings rules. The first, and perhaps most important, issue is the denominator problem. To fully explain this issue, we need to say a bit more on the concept of *diminution in value*—that is, the reduction in value to the property caused by the regulation. Both Justice Holmes and Justice Brandeis discuss this concept in their opinions in *Mahon*.

DIMINUTION IN VALUE

We can calculate the diminution in value by dividing the reduction in value caused by the regulation by the value of the property pre-regulation. Let's start by defining some terms. *Value Before Regulation* is the value of the property before the regulation was enacted. *Value After Regulation* is the value of the property after the regulation was enacted. *Reduction in Value* is the dollar value of the difference between Value After Regulation and Value Before Regulation. If the regulation in fact reduces the value of the property, then this will be a negative number. *Diminution in Value* is the ratio between the Reduction in Value and the Value Before Regulation. It is often expressed as a percentage.

Before we get to an example, here are two things to note for those of you who haven't thought about this kind of thing since elementary school math. First, we will indicate negative numbers with parentheses. So −5 will be (5), −$50,000 will be ($50,000), and −50 percent will be (50%). Second, the numerator is the number that goes on the top of a division equation, and the denominator is the number that goes on the bottom.

In our first example, let's assume that the property's Value Before Regulation was $100,000 and the Value After Regulation was $30,000. In this example, the Reduction in Value would be ($70,000), calculated as follows:

Reduction in Value = Value After Regulation − Value Before Regulation
= $30,000 − $100,000
= ($70,000)

Our diminution in value would be (7/10) or (70%), calculated as follows:

Diminution in Value = Reduction in Value/Value Before Regulation
= ($70,000)/$100,000
= (7/10), or (70%)

If all these equations bother you, just put yourself in the position of the property owner. Before the regulation, your property was worth $100,000. After the regulation, your property was worth $30,000. As a result, you suffered a 70 percent diminution in the value of your property.

This relatively straightforward calculation masks a complicated issue: what value should we use as the denominator in the equation? This is the *denominator problem*. We have two likely options.

First, we could use the *affected portion* approach. The affected portion approach uses only the value of the portion of the property affected by the regulation as the denominator.

Second, we could use the *entire parcel* approach. The entire parcel approach uses the value of the entire parcel of property as the denominator.

If the regulation affects the entire parcel of property, these two approaches will lead to the same result. If, however, the regulation only affects part of the parcel of property, these two approaches will lead to different results.

The *Mahon* fact pattern presents a good opportunity to illustrate these approaches. We will need to make a few assumptions not in the case. First, let's assume that the coal that constitutes the support right was worth $10,000. Let's also assume that the Pennsylvania Coal Company also owned the coal surrounding the support right and that this coal was worth $90,000. The support right and the surrounding coal constitute the entire parcel. The value of the entire parcel (the support right and the surrounding coal) was $100,000 before the regulation.

The Kohler Act prevented the mining of the coal that constituted the support right but did not impact the Pennsylvania Coal Company's ability to mine the surrounding coal. The support right, therefore, is the affected portion of the Pennsylvania Coal Company's property—that is, it is the portion of the property owned by the Company that is affected by the regulation.

The Kohler Act rendered the coal in the support right valueless. Before the regulation, the coal was worth $10,000; after it was worth $0. The Reduction in Value, therefore, is ($10,000). You can get the same result by subtracting the value of the entire parcel before the regulation, $100,000, from the value of the entire parcel after the regulation, $90,000. No matter how you look at it, on our facts the Kohler Act led to a $10,000 reduction in value of the Pennsylvania Coal Company's property.

Using the affected portion approach, our Diminution in Value calculation would be:

Diminution in Value = Reduction in Value/Value of Affected Portion
Before Regulation
= ($10,000)/$10,000
= (1), or (100%)

In other words, using the affected portion approach, we would have a total Diminution in Value—the Kohler Act rendered the support right, previously worth $10,000, valueless.

Using the parcel as a whole approach, our Diminution in Value calculation would be:

Diminution in Value = Reduction in Value/Value of Whole Parcel
Before Regulation
= ($10,000)/$100,000
= (1/10), or (10%)

In other words, using the parcel as a whole approach, the Diminution in Value would be far lower than it would be using the affected portion approach: (10%) as compared to (100%).

The larger point here is that the Diminution in Value can vary dramatically depending on which approach a court chooses to take in solving the denominator problem. Using the affected portion approach will magnify the percentage loss to the property owner, while the parcel as a whole approach will minimize the percentage loss.

In *Mahon*, Justice Holmes implicitly took the affected portion approach. He speaks of the support right as being a distinct property interest under Pennsylvania law and of that right being rendered valueless. In this context, do you think that the fact that Pennsylvania law recognized the support right as a distinct interest in property was important to Holmes's approach to the denominator problem? Justice Brandeis, in contrast, explicitly advocated for the parcel as a whole approach and suggested that the Court had erred in focusing only on the coal affected by the Kohler Act. Be sure that you read this portion of Justice Brandeis's dissenting opinion carefully.

We will return to the denominator problem below in the context of our contemporary regulatory takings cases. You might also see the denominator problem referred to as the *conceptual severance* issue. Conceptual severance refers to the strategy behind the affected portion approach—the affected portion is "conceptually severed" from the rest of the parcel. The term comes from an influential article, Margaret Jane Radin, *The Liberal Conception of Property: Cross Currents in the Jurisprudence of Takings*, 88 Colum. L. Rev. 1667 (1988).

At the outset of this unit, we noted that the regulatory takings issue revolved around the interpretation of words "private property" and "taken" in the Just Compensation Clause. Many regulatory takings issues fit broadly within the category of "taken." The denominator problem fits within the category of "private property." Put another way, we can frame the denominator problem in terms of constitutional interpretation. What does "private property" in the Just Compensation Clause mean? The affected portion or the entire parcel?

4. *Average Reciprocity of Advantage.* Justice Holmes's opinion referred to the *average reciprocity of advantage*, a concept that remains important in contemporary regulatory takings jurisprudence. The basic idea of average reciprocity of advantage is that the property owner might benefit from the regulation's restrictions on other property owners, and this benefit might outweigh any harm the owner suffers from the regulation. Average reciprocity of advantage is relevant in the regulatory takings context because it weighs against a finding that a regulation was an unconstitutional taking—if there is high average reciprocity, then the property owner benefits as much or more than she is harmed by the regulation.

Justice Holmes uses a particularly evocative example to illustrate this point. Imagine that you and I own the mineral rights to adjoining parcels of property. A regulation prohibits both of us from mining right up to the property boundary. Instead, we each have to leave a pillar of coal at the boundary. On one level, each of us is harmed by the regulation—we cannot mine the coal in the pillar. On another, however, we both benefit from the regulation, because the pillar prevents water from one of our mines from flooding into the other mine. For example, say that I extracted the coal on my property first and then abandoned the mine. Over time, the mine filled with water. If you later mined your coal up to the boundary, you might break through the wall and confront a dangerous flood of water into your mine.

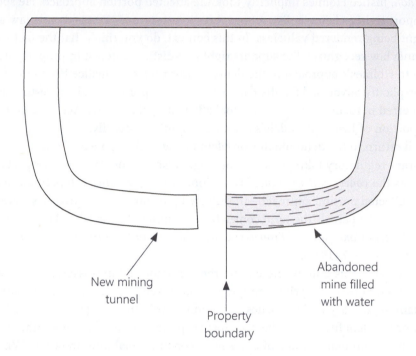

New mining
tunnel

Property
boundary

Abandoned
mine filled
with water

Zoning provides another example of average reciprocity of advantage. Say that you and I are neighbors. The local zoning law prohibits each of us from using our property for commercial purposes. On one level, the zoning law harms you—you could make a great deal of money if you could build a convenience store on your property. On another level, you benefit greatly by the restriction that prevents me from building a convenience store on my property. We both benefit from the same restriction being placed on everyone else in the neighborhood.

5. *Bearing the Cost of Legal Change, Again.* After our excerpt from *Mugler*, we raised the question of who should bear the cost of regulatory change—the property owner or the public at large. What did Justice Holmes have to say about this issue in his *Mahon* opinion?

6. *Justice Holmes and the Police Power.* Justice Holmes's opinion is short and somewhat cryptic. The holding of *Mahon* seems to contradict the well-established rule,

reflected in *Alger* and *Mugler*, that a police power regulation can never be a taking. Justice Brandeis cited *Mugler* in dissent, but Holmes did not even address it. Justice Holmes had written about the police power in other contexts. Although they have no direct bearing on the *Mahon* opinion, the following quotes might provide some helpful context.

First, in a book review written early in his career, Holmes "suggested that the term police power was 'invented to cover certain acts of the legislature which are seen to be unconstitutional, but which are believed to be necessary.'"[28]

Second, as a Justice of the Massachusetts Supreme Court, Holmes wrote in the 1889 case *Rideout v. Knox* that "Some small limitations of previously existing rights incident to property may be imposed for the sake of preventing a manifest evil; large ones could not be, except by the exercise of eminent domain."[29] Holmes cited *Rideout* in his *Mahon* opinion.

Third, in another Massachusetts case, Holmes wrote:

> It would be open to argument at least that an owner might be stripped of his rights so far as to amount to a taking without any physical interference with his land. On the other hand, we assume that even the carrying away or bodily destruction of property might be of such small importance that it would be justified under the police power, without compensation. We assume that one of the uses of the convenient phrase, "police power" is to justify those small diminutions of property rights which, although within the letter of the constitutional protection, are necessarily incident to the free play of the machinery of government. It may be that the extent to which such diminutions are lawful without compensation is larger when the harm is inflicted only as an incident to some general requirement of public welfare. But, whether the last-mentioned element enters into the problem or not, the question is one of degree, and sooner or later we reach a point at which the Constitution applies and forbids physical appropriation and legal restrictions alike, unless they are paid for.[30]

Fourth, in a 1908 U.S. Supreme Court case, Holmes wrote:

> [T]he police power may limit the height of buildings in a city, without compensation. To that extent it cuts down what otherwise would be the rights of property. But if it should attempt to limit the height so far as to make an ordinary building lot wholly useless, the rights of property would prevail over the other public interest, and the police power would fail.

---

[28] William Michael Treanor, *The Original Understanding of the Takings Clause and the Political Process*, 95 Colum. L. Rev. 782, 798-799 (1995) (quoting *Book Review*, 6 Am. L. Rev. 140, 141-142 (1871-1872)).

[29] *Rideout v. Knox*, 148 Mass. 368, 372-373 (1889).

[30] *Bent v. Emery*, 173 Mass. 495, 496 (1899).

To set such a limit would need compensation and the power of eminent domain.[31]

Fifth, in a letter to a friend written shortly after *Mahon* was decided, Holmes wrote:

> But nevertheless when the premises [of *Mahon*] are a little more emphasized as they should have been by me, I confess to feeling as much confidence as I often do. I always have thought that old Harlan's decision in *Mugler v. Kansas* was pretty fishy.[32]

3. CONTEMPORARY REGULATORY TAKINGS LAW

By holding that police power regulations could sometimes go "too far" and be unconstitutional takings, *Mahon* represented a break from the approach taken by prior cases like *Alger* and *Mugler*. Justice Holmes's opinion, however, did not give much guidance on how to determine when a regulation has gone "too far." To answer that question, we turn to the Supreme Court's more recent regulatory takings cases.

As we will see, the Supreme Court has adopted two types of regulatory takings rules. First, the Court has adopted an ad hoc multifactor analysis that provides our general regulatory takings test. This multifactor analysis is easy to articulate but very hard to apply with any certainty. Second, the Court has adopted three per se rules, providing relatively clear answers to certain types of takings questions.

In this section, we first cover the basic takings tests, beginning with the general rule taken from *Penn Central Transportation Co. v. New York City* and then proceeding to the three per se tests. We then discuss the gloss that some recent cases have placed on the regulatory takings inquiry. Finally, we consider two regulatory takings problems that raise issues separate and apart from the general regulatory takings question: exactions and judicial takings.

a. The General Rule: *Penn Central*

Our next case is the source of our contemporary general rule for regulatory takings. As such, it is an incredibly important decision. The case involves the designation of Grand Central Terminal in New York City as an historic landmark. Penn Central Transportation Co., the owners of Grand Central Terminal, wanted to build a large skyscraper on the site. The landmark designation prevented them from building the new tower as they planned, and they brought a regulatory takings challenge to the New York Landmarks Preservation Law.

Both the majority and dissenting opinions cover a lot of ground. Here are three things to focus on in the opinion. First, what, exactly, did the Landmarks Preservation Law do to Penn Central's ability to build in the airspace above Grand Central Terminal? Second, how does the Landmarks Preservation Law compare with zoning regulations

---

[31] *Hudson County Water Co. v. McCarter*, 209 U.S. 349, 355 (1908).

[32] Mark DeWolfe Howe, *Holmes-Laski Letters* 473 (1953) (letter of Jan. 13, 1923).

on the issue of average reciprocity of advantage? Put another way, does the owner of a property designated as an historic landmark benefit from restrictions on other property owners in the same way that the owner of zoned property benefits from restrictions on other property owners? Third, we have already told you that this case provides our contemporary general rule for regulatory takings. What factors does the Court identify as being relevant to the regulatory takings analysis?

PENN CENTRAL TRANSPORTATION CO. V. CITY OF NEW YORK

United States Supreme Court, 1978
438 U.S. 104

Mr. Justice BRENNAN delivered the opinion of the Court. The question presented is whether a city may, as part of a comprehensive program to preserve historic landmarks and historic districts, place restrictions on the development of individual historic landmarks—in addition to those imposed by applicable zoning ordinances—without effecting a "taking" requiring the payment of "just compensation." Specifically, we must decide whether the application of New York City's Landmarks Preservation Law to the parcel of land occupied by Grand Central Terminal has "taken" its owners' property in violation of the Fifth and Fourteenth Amendments.

I.

A.

Over the past 50 years, all 50 States and over 500 municipalities have enacted laws to encourage or require the preservation of buildings and areas with historic or aesthetic importance. These nationwide legislative efforts have been precipitated by two concerns. The first is recognition that, in recent years, large numbers of historic structures, landmarks, and areas have been destroyed without adequate consideration of either the values represented therein or the possibility of preserving the destroyed properties for use in economically productive ways. The second is a widely shared belief that structures with special historic, cultural, or architectural significance enhance the quality of life for all. Not only do these buildings and their workmanship represent the lessons of the past and embody precious features of our heritage, they serve as examples of quality for today. "[H]istoric conservation is but one aspect of the much larger problem, basically an environmental one, of enhancing— or perhaps developing for the first time—the quality of life for people."[4]

New York City, responding to similar concerns and acting pursuant to a New York State enabling Act, adopted its Landmarks Preservation Law in 1965. *See* N.Y.C. Admin.

---

[4] Gilbert, Introduction, Precedents for the Future, 36 Law & Contemp. Prob. 311, 312 (1971), quoting address by Robert Stipe, 1971 Conference on Preservation Law, Washington, D. C., May 1, 1971 (unpublished text, pp. 6-7).

Code, ch. 8-A, §205-1.0 et seq. (1976). The city acted from the conviction that "the standing of [New York City] as a world-wide tourist center and world capital of business, culture and government" would be threatened if legislation were not enacted to protect historic landmarks and neighborhoods from precipitate decisions to destroy or fundamentally alter their character. §205-1.0(a). The city believed that comprehensive measures to safeguard desirable features of the existing urban fabric would benefit its citizens in a variety of ways: e. g., fostering "civic pride in the beauty and noble accomplishments of the past"; protecting and enhancing "the city's attractions to tourists and visitors"; "support[ing] and stimul[ating] business and industry"; "strengthen[ing] the economy of the city"; and promoting "the use of historic districts, landmarks, interior landmarks and scenic landmarks for the education, pleasure and welfare of the people of the city." §205-1.0(b).

The New York City law is typical of many urban landmark laws in that its primary method of achieving its goals is not by acquisitions of historic properties,[6] but rather by involving public entities in land-use decisions affecting these properties and providing services, standards, controls, and incentives that will encourage preservation by private owners and users. While the law does place special restrictions on landmark properties as a necessary feature to the attainment of its larger objectives, the major theme of the law is to ensure the owners of any such properties both a "reasonable return" on their investments and maximum latitude to use their parcels for purposes not inconsistent with the preservation goals.

The operation of the law can be briefly summarized. The primary responsibility for administering the law is vested in the Landmarks Preservation Commission (Commission), a broad based, 11-member agency assisted by a technical staff. The Commission first performs the function, critical to any landmark preservation effort, of identifying properties and areas that have "a special character or special historical or aesthetic interest or value as part of the development, heritage or cultural characteristics of the city, state or nation." §207-1.0(n); see §207-1.0(h). If the Commission determines, after giving all interested parties an opportunity to be heard, that a building or area satisfies the ordinance's criteria, it will designate a building to be a "landmark," §207-1.0(n),[9] situated on a particular "landmark site," §207-1.0(o),[10] or will designate an

---

[6] The consensus is that widespread public ownership of historic properties in urban settings is neither feasible nor wise. Public ownership reduces the tax base, burdens the public budget with costs of acquisitions and maintenance, and results in the preservation of public buildings as museums and similar facilities, rather than as economically productive features of the urban scene. See Wilson & Winkler, The Response of State Legislation to Historic Preservation, 36 Law & Contemp. Prob. 329, 330-331, 339-340 (1971).

[9] "'Landmark.' Any improvement, any part of which is thirty years old or older, which has a special character or special historical or aesthetic interest or value as part of the development, heritage or cultural characteristics of the city, state or nation and which has been designated as a landmark pursuant to the provisions of this chapter." §207-1.0(n).

[10] "'Landmark site.' An improvement parcel or part thereof on which is situated a landmark and any abutting improvement parcel or part thereof used as and constituting part of the premises on which the landmark is situated, and which has been designated as a landmark site pursuant to the provisions of this chapter." §207-1.0(o).

area to be a "historic district," §207-1.0(h).[11] After the Commission makes a designation, New York City's Board of Estimate, after considering the relationship of the designated property "to the master plan, the zoning resolution, projected public improvements and any plans for the renewal of the area involved," §207-2.0(g)(1), may modify or disapprove the designation, and the owner may seek judicial review of the final designation decision. Thus far, 31 historic districts and over 400 individual landmarks have been finally designated, and the process is a continuing one.

Final designation as a landmark results in restrictions upon the property owner's options concerning use of the landmark site. First, the law imposes a duty upon the owner to keep the exterior features of the building "in good repair" to assure that the law's objectives not be defeated by the landmark's falling into a state of irremediable disrepair. *See* §207-10.0(a). Second, the Commission must approve in advance any proposal to alter the exterior architectural features of the landmark or to construct any exterior improvement on the landmark site, thus ensuring that decisions concerning construction on the landmark site are made with due consideration of both the public interest in the maintenance of the structure and the landowner's interest in use of the property. *See* §§207-4.0 to 207-9.0.

In the event an owner wishes to alter a landmark site, three separate procedures are available through which administrative approval may be obtained. First, the owner may apply to the Commission for a "certificate of no effect on protected architectural features": that is, for an order approving the improvement or alteration on the ground that it will not change or affect any architectural feature of the landmark and will be in harmony therewith. *See* §207-5.0. Denial of the certificate is subject to judicial review.

Second, the owner may apply to the Commission for a certificate of "appropriateness." *See* §207-6.0. Such certificates will be granted if the Commission concludes—focusing upon aesthetic, historical, and architectural values—that the proposed construction on the landmark site would not unduly hinder the protection, enhancement, perpetuation, and use of the landmark. Again, denial of the certificate is subject to judicial review. Moreover, the owner who is denied either a certificate of no exterior effect or a certificate of appropriateness may submit an alternative or modified plan for approval. The final procedure—seeking a certificate of appropriateness on the ground of "insufficient return," see §207-8.0—provides special mechanisms, which vary depending on whether or not the landmark enjoys a tax exemption, to ensure that designation does not cause economic hardship.

---

[11] "'Historic district.' Any area which: (1) contains improvements which: (a) have a special character or special historical or aesthetic interest or value; and (b) represent one or more periods or styles of architecture typical of one or more eras in the history of the city; and (c) cause such area, by reason of such factors, to constitute a distinct section of the city; and (2) has been designated as a historic district pursuant to the provisions of this chapter." §207-1.0(h). The Act also provides for the designation of a "scenic landmark," *see* §207-1.0(w), and an "interior landmark." *See* §207-1.0(m).

Although the designation of a landmark and landmark site restricts the owner's control over the parcel, designation also enhances the economic position of the landmark owner in one significant respect. Under New York City's zoning laws, owners of real property who have not developed their property to the full extent permitted by the applicable zoning laws are allowed to transfer development rights to contiguous parcels on the same city block. *See* New York City, Zoning Resolution Art. I, ch. 2, §12-10 (1978) (definition of "zoning lot"). A 1968 ordinance gave the owners of landmark sites additional opportunities to transfer development rights to other parcels. Subject to a restriction that the floor area of the transferee lot may not be increased by more than 20% above its authorized level, the ordinance permitted transfers from a landmark parcel to property across the street or across a street intersection. In 1969, the law governing the conditions under which transfers from landmark parcels could occur was liberalized, see New York City Zoning Resolutions 74-79 to 74-793, apparently to ensure that the Landmarks Law would not unduly restrict the development options of the owners of Grand Central Terminal. *See* Marcus, Air Rights Transfers in New York City, 36 Law & Contemp. Prob. 372, 375 (1971). The class of recipient lots was expanded to include lots "across a street and opposite to another lot or lots which except for the intervention of streets or street intersections f [or]m a series extending to the lot occupied by the landmark building [, provided that] all lots [are] in the same ownership." New York City Zoning Resolution 74-79 (emphasis deleted). In addition, the 1969 amendment permits, in highly commercialized areas like midtown Manhattan, the transfer of all unused development rights to a single parcel. *Ibid.*

B.

This case involves the application of New York City's Landmarks Preservation Law to Grand Central Terminal (Terminal). The Terminal, which is owned by the Penn Central Transportation Co. and its affiliates (Penn Central), is one of New York City's most famous buildings. Opened in 1913, it is regarded not only as providing an ingenious engineering solution to the problems presented by urban railroad stations, but also as a magnificent example of the French beaux-arts style.

The Terminal is located in midtown Manhattan. Its south facade faces 42d Street and that street's intersection with Park Avenue. At street level, the Terminal is bounded on the west by Vanderbilt Avenue, on the east by the Commodore Hotel, and on the north by the Pan-American Building. Although a 20-story office tower, to have been located above the Terminal, was part of the original design, the planned tower was never constructed.[15]

The Terminal itself is an eight-story structure which Penn Central uses as a railroad station and in which it rents space not needed for railroad purposes to a variety of commercial interests. The Terminal is one of a number of properties owned by appellant

---

[15] The Terminal's present foundation includes columns, which were built into it for the express purpose of supporting the proposed 20-story tower.

Penn Central in this area of midtown Manhattan. The others include the Barclay, Biltmore, Commodore, Roosevelt, and Waldorf-Astoria Hotels, the Pan-American Building and other office buildings along Park Avenue, and the Yale Club. At least eight of these are eligible to be recipients of development rights afforded the Terminal by virtue of landmark designation.

On August 2, 1967, following a public hearing, the Commission designated the Terminal a "landmark" and designated the "city tax block" it occupies a "landmark site." The Board of Estimate confirmed this action on September 21, 1967. Although appellant Penn Central had opposed the designation before the Commission, it did not seek judicial review of the final designation decision.

On January 22, 1968, appellant Penn Central, to increase its income, entered into a renewable 50-year lease and sublease agreement with appellant UGP Properties, Inc. (UGP), a wholly owned subsidiary of Union General Properties, Ltd., a United Kingdom corporation. Under the terms of the agreement, UGP was to construct a multistory office building above the Terminal. UGP promised to pay Penn Central $1 million annually during construction and at least $3 million annually thereafter. The rentals would be offset in part by a loss of some $700,000 to $1 million in net rentals presently received from concessionaires displaced by the new building.

Appellants UGP and Penn Central then applied to the Commission for permission to construct an office building atop the Terminal. Two separate plans, both designed by architect Marcel Breuer and both apparently satisfying the terms of the applicable zoning ordinance, were submitted to the Commission for approval. The first, Breuer I, provided for the construction of a 55-story office building, to be cantilevered above the existing facade and to rest on the roof of the Terminal. The second, Breuer II Revised, called for tearing down a portion of the Terminal that included the 42d Street facade, stripping off some of the remaining features of the Terminal's facade, and constructing a 53-story office building. The Commission denied a certificate of no exterior effect on September 20, 1968. Appellants then applied for a certificate of "appropriateness" as to both proposals. After four days of hearings at which over 80 witnesses testified, the Commission denied this application as to both proposals.

The Commission's reasons for rejecting certificates respecting Breuer II Revised are summarized in the following statement: "To protect a Landmark, one does not tear it down. To perpetuate its architectural features, one does not strip them off." Record 2255. Breuer I, which would have preserved the existing vertical facades of the present structure, received more sympathetic consideration. The Commission first focused on the effect that the proposed tower would have on one desirable feature created by the present structure and its surroundings: the dramatic view of the Terminal from Park Avenue South. Although appellants had contended that the Pan-American Building had already destroyed the silhouette of the south facade and that one additional tower could do no further damage and might even provide a better background for the facade, the

Commission disagreed, stating that it found the majestic approach from the south to be still unique in the city and that a 55-story tower atop the Terminal would be far more detrimental to its south facade than the Pan-American Building 375 feet away. Moreover, the Commission found that from closer vantage points the Pan Am Building and the other towers were largely cut off from view, which would not be the case of the mass on top of the Terminal planned under Breuer I. In conclusion, the Commission stated:

> "[We have] no fixed rule against making additions to designated buildings—it all depends on how they are done. . . . But to balance a 55-story office tower above a flamboyant Beaux-Arts facade seems nothing more than an aesthetic joke. Quite simply, the tower would overwhelm the Terminal by its sheer mass. The 'addition' would be four times as high as the existing structure and would reduce the Landmark itself to the status of a curiosity.
>
> "Landmarks cannot be divorced from their settings—particularly when the setting is a dramatic and integral part of the original concept. The Terminal, in its setting, is a great example of urban design. Such examples are not so plentiful in New York City that we can afford to lose any of the few we have. And we must preserve them in a meaningful way—with alterations and additions of such character, scale, materials and mass as will protect, enhance and perpetuate the original design rather than overwhelm it." *Id.*, at 2251.

Appellants did not seek judicial review of the denial of either certificate. Because the Terminal site enjoyed a tax exemption, remained suitable for its present and future uses, and was not the subject of a contract of sale, there were no further administrative remedies available to appellants as to the Breuer I and Breuer II Revised plans. *See* n. 13, *supra.* Further, appellants did not avail themselves of the opportunity to develop and submit other plans for the Commission's consideration and approval. Instead, appellants filed suit in New York Supreme Court, Trial Term, claiming, inter alia, that the application of the Landmarks Preservation Law had "taken" their property without just compensation in violation of the Fifth and Fourteenth Amendments and arbitrarily deprived them of their property without due process of law in violation of the Fourteenth Amendment. Appellants sought a declaratory judgment, injunctive relief barring the city from using the Landmarks Law to impede the construction of any structure that might otherwise lawfully be constructed on the Terminal site, and damages for the "temporary taking" that occurred between August 2, 1967, the designation date, and the date when the restrictions arising from the Landmarks Law would be lifted. The trial court granted the injunctive and declaratory relief, but severed the question of damages for a "temporary taking."[20]

---

[20] Although that court suggested that any regulation of private property to protect landmark values was unconstitutional if "just compensation" were not afforded, it also appeared to rely upon its findings: first, that the cost to Penn Central of operating the Terminal building itself, exclusive of purely railroad operations, exceeded the revenues received from concessionaires and tenants in the Terminal; and second, that the special transferable development rights afforded Penn Central as an owner of a landmark site did not "provide compensation to plaintiffs or minimize the harm suffered by plaintiffs due to the designation of the Terminal as a landmark."

TAKINGS REMEDIES AND TEMPORARY TAKINGS

There are two major categories of remedies for regulatory takings. The first is *invalidation*—the offending regulation is rendered invalid. The second is *inverse condemnation*—the offending regulation remains in force, but the government is required to pay just compensation to the property owner for the taking. The availability of the inverse condemnation remedy was questionable for some time, but was eventually established by the U.S. Supreme Court in *First English Evangelical Lutheran Church of Glendale v. Los Angeles*, 482 U.S. 304 (1987).

A *temporary taking* occurs when a government act that takes property is later withdrawn or invalidated. *First English* established that the property owner may make a claim for compensation for the deprivation of the use of the property during the time the offending government act was in force. In doing so, the Court analogized a temporary taking to the taking of a leasehold interest:

> In the present case the interim ordinance was adopted by the County of Los Angeles in January 1979, and became effective immediately. Appellant filed suit within a month after the effective date of the ordinance and yet when the California Supreme Court denied a hearing in the case on October 17, 1985, the merits of appellant's claim had yet to be determined. The United States has been required to pay compensation for leasehold interests of shorter duration than this. The value of a leasehold interest in property for a period of years may be substantial, and the burden on the property owner in extinguishing such an interest for a period of years may be great indeed. . . . Where this burden results from governmental action that amounted to a taking, the Just Compensation Clause of the Fifth Amendment requires that the government pay the landowner for the value of the use of the land during this period.

Note well that the temporary takings rule only applies if the government act in fact is determined to be a taking. As we will see below when we briefly discuss the *Tahoe Sierra* case, not every temporary restriction on land use is a taking.

Appellees appealed, and the New York Supreme Court, Appellate Division, reversed. 50 A.D.2d 265, 377 N.Y.S.2d 20 (1975). The Appellate Division held that the restrictions on the development of the Terminal site were necessary to promote the legitimate public purpose of protecting landmarks and therefore that appellants could sustain their constitutional claims only by proof that the regulation deprived them of all reasonable beneficial use of the property. The Appellate Division held that the evidence appellants introduced at trial—"Statements of Revenues and Costs," purporting to show a net operating loss for the years 1969 and 1971, which were prepared for the instant litigation—had not satisfied their burden. First, the court rejected the claim that these statements showed that the Terminal was operating at a loss, for in the court's view, appellants had improperly attributed some railroad operating expenses and taxes to their real estate operations and compounded that error by failing to impute any rental value to the vast space in the Terminal devoted to railroad purposes. Further, the Appellate Division concluded that appellants had failed to establish either that they were unable to increase the Terminal's commercial income by transforming vacant or underutilized space to revenue-producing use, or that the unused development rights over the Terminal could not have been profitably transferred to one or more nearby sites. The Appellate Division concluded that all appellants had succeeded in showing was that they had been deprived of the property's most profitable use, and that this showing did not establish that appellants had been unconstitutionally deprived of their property.

The New York Court of Appeals affirmed. 42 N.Y.2d 324, 397 N.Y.S.2d 914, 366 N.E.2d 1271 (1977). That court summarily rejected any claim that the Landmarks Law had "taken" property without "just compensation," *id.*, at 329, 397 N.Y.S.2d, at 917, 366 N.E.2d, at 1274, indicating that there could be no "taking" since the law had not transferred control of the property to the city, but only restricted appellants' exploitation of it. In that circumstance, the Court of Appeals held that appellants' attack on the law could prevail only if the law deprived appellants of their property in violation of the Due Process Clause of the Fourteenth Amendment. Whether or not there was a denial of substantive due process turned on whether the restrictions deprived Penn Central of a "reasonable return" on the "privately created and privately managed ingredient" of the Terminal. *Id.*, at 328, 397 N.Y.S.2d, at 916, 366 N.E.2d, at 1273. The Court of Appeals concluded that the Landmarks Law had not effected a denial of due process because: (1) the landmark regulation permitted the same use as had been made of the Terminal for more than half a century; (2) the appellants had failed to show that they could not earn a reasonable return on their investment in the Terminal itself; (3) even if the Terminal proper could never operate at a reasonable profit some of the income from Penn Central's extensive real estate holdings in the area, which include hotels and office buildings, must realistically be imputed to the Terminal; and (4) the development rights above the Terminal, which had been made transferable to numerous sites in the vicinity of the Terminal, one or two of which were suitable for the construction of office buildings, were valuable to appellants and provided "significant, perhaps 'fair,' compensation for the loss of rights above the terminal itself." *Id.*, at 333-336, 397 N.Y.S.2d, at 922, 366 N.E.2d, at 1276-1278.

Observing that its affirmance was "[o]n the present record," and that its analysis had not been fully developed by counsel at any level of the New York judicial system, the Court of Appeals directed that counsel "should be entitled to present . . . any additional submissions which, in the light of [the court's] opinion, may usefully develop further the factors discussed." *Id.*, at 337, 397 N.Y.S.2d, at 922, 366 N.E.2d, at 1279. Appellants chose not to avail themselves of this opportunity and filed a notice of appeal in this Court. We noted probable jurisdiction. 434 U.S. 983 (1977). We affirm.

II

The issues presented by appellants are (1) whether the restrictions imposed by New York City's law upon appellants' exploitation of the Terminal site effect a "taking" of appellants' property for a public use within the meaning of the Fifth Amendment, which of course is made applicable to the States through the Fourteenth Amendment, see *Chicago, B. & Q. R. Co. v. Chicago*, 166 U.S. 226, 239, 17 S.Ct. 581, 585, 41 L.Ed. 979 (1897), and, (2), if so, whether the transferable development rights afforded appellants constitute "just compensation" within the meaning of the Fifth Amendment. We need only address the question whether a "taking" has occurred.[25]

A

Before considering appellants' specific contentions, it will be useful to review the factors that have shaped the jurisprudence of the Fifth Amendment injunction "nor shall private property be taken for public use, without just compensation." The question of what constitutes a "taking" for purposes of the Fifth Amendment has proved to be a problem of considerable difficulty. While this Court has recognized that the "Fifth Amendment's guarantee . . . [is] designed to bar Government from forcing some people alone to bear public burdens which, in all fairness and justice, should be borne by the public as a whole," *Armstrong v. United States*, 364 U.S. 40, 49, 80 S.Ct. 1563, 1569, 4 L.Ed.2d 1554 (1960), this Court, quite simply, has been unable to develop any "set formula" for determining when "justice and fairness" require that economic injuries caused by public action be compensated by the government, rather than remain disproportionately concentrated on a few persons. *See Goldblatt v. Hempstead*, 369 U.S. 590, 594, 82 S.Ct. 987, 990, 8 L.Ed.2d 130 (1962). Indeed, we have frequently observed that whether a particular restriction will be rendered invalid by the government's failure to pay for any losses proximately caused by it depends largely "upon the particular circumstances [in that] case." *United States v. Central Eureka Mining Co.*, 357 U.S. 155, 168, 78 S.Ct. 1097, 1104, 2 L.Ed.2d 1228 (1958); *see United States v. Caltex, Inc.*, 344 U.S. 149, 156, 73 S.Ct. 200, 203, 97 L.Ed. 157 (1952).

In engaging in these essentially ad hoc, factual inquiries, the Court's decisions have identified several factors that have particular significance. The economic impact of the regulation on the claimant and, particularly, the extent to which the regulation has interfered with distinct investment-backed expectations are, of course, relevant considerations. *See Goldblatt v. Hempstead, supra*, 369 U.S., at 594, 82 S.Ct., at 990. So, too, is the character of the governmental action. A "taking" may more readily be found when the interference with property can be characterized as a physical invasion by government, *see, e. g., United States v. Causby*,

DIMINUTION IN VALUE

---

[25] As is implicit in our opinion, we do not embrace the proposition that a "taking" can never occur unless government has transferred physical control over a portion of a parcel.

328 U.S. 256, 66 S.Ct. 1062, 90 L.Ed. 1206 (1946), than when interference arises from some public program adjusting the benefits and burdens of economic life to promote the common good.

"Government hardly could go on if to some extent values incident to property could not be diminished without paying for every such change in the general law," *Pennsylvania Coal Co. v. Mahon*, 260 U.S. 393, 413, 43 S.Ct. 158, 159, 67 L.Ed. 322 (1922), and this Court has accordingly recognized, in a wide variety of contexts, that government may execute laws or programs that adversely affect recognized economic values. Exercises of the taxing power are one obvious example.

A second are the decisions in which this Court has dismissed "taking" challenges on the ground that, while the challenged government action caused economic harm, it did not interfere with interests that were sufficiently bound up with the reasonable expectations of the claimant to constitute "property" for Fifth Amendment purposes. *See*, e. g., *United States v. Willow River Power Co.*, 324 U.S. 499, 65 S.Ct. 761, 89 L.Ed. 1101 (1945) (interest in high-water level of river for runoff for tailwaters to maintain power head is not property); *United States v. Chandler-Dunbar Water Power Co.*, 229 U.S. 53, 33 S.Ct. 667, 57 L.Ed. 1063 (1913) (no property interest can exist in navigable waters); *see also Demorest v. City Bank Co.*, 321 U.S. 36, 64 S.Ct. 384, 88 L.Ed. 526 (1944); *Muhlker v. Harlem R. Co.*, 197 U.S. 544, 25 S.Ct. 522, 49 L.Ed. 872 (1905); Sax, *Takings and the Police Power*, 74 Yale L.J. 36, 61-62 (1964).

More importantly for the present case, in instances in which a state tribunal reasonably concluded that "the health, safety, morals, or general welfare" would be promoted by prohibiting particular contemplated uses of land, this Court has upheld land-use regulations that destroyed or adversely affected recognized real property interests. *See Nectow v. Cambridge*, 277 U.S. 183, 188, 48 S.Ct. 447, 448, 72 L.Ed. 842 (1928). Zoning laws are, of course, the classic example, see *Euclid v. Ambler Realty Co.*, 272 U.S. 365, 47 S.Ct. 114, 71 L.Ed. 303 (1926) (prohibition of industrial use); *Gorieb v. Fox*, 274 U.S. 603, 608, 47 S.Ct. 675, 677, 71 L.Ed. 1228 (1927) (requirement that portions of parcels be left unbuilt); *Welch v. Swasey*, 214 U.S. 91, 29 S.Ct. 567, 53 L.Ed. 923 (1909) (height restriction), which have been viewed as permissible governmental action even when prohibiting the most beneficial use of the property. *See Goldblatt v. Hempstead, supra*, 369 U.S., at 592-593, 82 S.Ct., at 988-989, and cases cited; *see also Eastlake v. Forest City Enterprises, Inc.*, 426 U.S. 668, 674, n. 8, 96 S.Ct. 2358, 2362 n. 8, 49 L.Ed.2d 132 (1976).

Zoning laws generally do not affect existing uses of real property, but "taking" challenges have also been held to be without merit in a wide variety of situations when the challenged governmental actions prohibited a beneficial use to which individual parcels had previously been devoted and thus caused substantial individualized harm. *Miller v. Schoene*, 276 U.S. 272, 48 S.Ct. 246, 72 L.Ed. 568 (1928), is illustrative. In that case, a state entomologist, acting pursuant to a state statute, ordered the claimants to cut down a large number of ornamental red cedar trees because they produced cedar rust fatal to apple trees cultivated nearby. Although the statute provided for recovery of any expense incurred in removing the cedars, and permitted claimants to use the felled trees, it did not provide compensation for the value of the standing trees or for the resulting decrease in market value of the properties as a whole. A unanimous Court held that this latter omission did not render the statute invalid. The Court held that the State might properly make "a choice between the preservation of one class of property and that of the other" and since the apple industry was important in the State involved, concluded that the State had not exceeded "its constitutional powers by deciding upon the destruction of one class of property [without compensation] in order to save another which, in the judgment of the legislature, is of greater value to the public." *Id.*, at 279, 48 S.Ct., at 247.

Again, *Hadacheck v. Sebastian*, 239 U.S. 394, 36 S.Ct. 143, 60 L.Ed. 348 (1915), upheld a law prohibiting the claimant from continuing his otherwise lawful business of operating a brickyard in a particular physical community on the ground that the legislature had reasonably concluded that the presence of the brickyard was inconsistent with neighboring uses. *See also United States v. Central Eureka Mining Co., supra* (Government order closing gold mines so that skilled miners would be available for other mining work held not a taking); *Atchison, T. & S. F. R. Co. v. Public Utilities Comm'n*, 346 U.S. 346, 74 S.Ct. 92, 98 L.Ed. 51 (1953) (railroad may be required to share cost of constructing railroad grade improvement); *Walls v. Midland Carbon Co.*, 254 U.S. 300, 41 S.Ct. 118, 65 L.Ed. 276 (1920) (law prohibiting manufacture of carbon black upheld); *Reinman v. Little Rock*, 237 U.S. 171, 35 S.Ct. 511, 59 L.Ed. 900 (1915) (law prohibiting livery stable upheld); *Mugler v. Kansas*, 123 U.S. 623, 8 S.Ct. 273, 31 L.Ed. 205 (1887) (law prohibiting liquor business upheld).

Goldblatt v. Hempstead, supra, is a recent example. There, a 1958 city safety ordinance banned any excavations below the water table and effectively prohibited the claimant from continuing a sand and gravel mining business that had been operated on the particular parcel since 1927. The Court upheld the ordinance against a "taking" challenge, although the ordinance prohibited the present and presumably most beneficial use of the property and had, like the regulations in *Miller* and *Hadacheck*, severely affected a particular owner. The Court assumed that the ordinance did not prevent the owner's reasonable use of the property since the owner made no showing of an adverse effect on the value of the land. Because the restriction served a substantial public purpose, the Court thus held no taking had occurred. It is, of course, implicit in *Goldblatt* that a use restriction on real property may constitute a "taking" if not reasonably necessary to the effectuation of a substantial public purpose, see *Nectow v. Cambridge, supra; cf. Moore v. East Cleveland*, 431 U.S. 494, 513-514, 97 S.Ct. 1932, 1943, 52 L.Ed.2d 531 (1977) (STEVENS, J., concurring), or perhaps if it has an unduly harsh impact upon the owner's use of the property.

Pennsylvania Coal Co. v. Mahon, 260 U.S. 393, 43 S.Ct. 158, 67 L.Ed. 322 (1922), is the leading case for the proposition that a state statute that substantially furthers important public policies may so frustrate distinct investment-backed expectations as to amount to a "taking." There the claimant had sold the surface rights to particular parcels of property, but expressly reserved the right to remove the coal thereunder. A Pennsylvania statute, enacted after the transactions, forbade any mining of coal that caused the subsidence of any house, unless the house was the property of the owner of the underlying coal and was more than 150 feet from the improved property of another. Because the statute made it commercially impracticable to mine the coal, *id.*, at 414, 43 S.Ct., at 159, and thus had nearly the same effect as the complete destruction of rights claimant had reserved from the owners of the surface land, see *id.*, at 414-415, 43 S.Ct., at 159-160, the Court held that the statute was invalid as effecting a "taking" without just compensation. *See also Armstrong v. United States*, 364 U.S. 40, 80 S.Ct. 1563, 4 L.Ed.2d 1554 (1960) (Government's complete destruction of a materialman's lien in certain property held a "taking"); *Hudson Water Co. v. McCarter*, 209 U.S. 349, 355, 28 S.Ct. 529, 531, 52 L.Ed. 828 (1908) (if height restriction makes property wholly useless "the rights of property . . . prevail over the other public interest" and compensation is required). *See generally Michelman, Property, Utility, and Fairness: Comments on the Ethical Foundations of "Just Compensation" Law*, 80 Harv.L.Rev. 1165, 1229-1234 (1967).

Finally, government actions that may be characterized as acquisitions of resources to permit or facilitate uniquely public functions have often been held to constitute "takings." *United States v. Causby*, 328 U.S. 256, 66 S.Ct. 1062, 90 L.Ed. 1206 (1946), is illustrative. In holding that direct overflights above the claimant's land, that destroyed the present use of the land as a chicken farm, constituted a "taking," Causby emphasized that Government had not "merely destroyed property [but was] using a part of it for the flight of its planes." *Id.*, 328 U.S., at 262-263, n. 7, 66 S.Ct., at 1066. *See also Griggs v. Allegheny County*, 369 U.S. 84, 82 S.Ct. 531, 7 L.Ed.2d 585 (1962) (overflights held a taking); *Portsmouth Co. v. United States*, 260 U.S. 327, 43 S.Ct. 135, 67 L.Ed. 287 (1922) (United States military installations' repeated firing of guns over claimant's land is a taking); *United States v. Cress*, 243 U.S. 316, 37 S.Ct. 380, 61 L.Ed. 746 (1917) (repeated floodings of land caused by water project is taking); *but see YMCA v. United States*, 395 U.S. 85, 89 S.Ct. 1511, 23 L.Ed.2d 117 (1969) (damage caused to building when federal officers who were seeking to protect building were attacked by rioters held not a taking). *See generally Michelman, supra,* at 1226-1229; Sax, *Takings and the Police Power*, 74 Yale L.J. 36 (1964).

B

In contending that the New York City law has "taken" their property in violation of the Fifth and Fourteenth Amendments, appellants make a series of arguments, which, while tailored to the facts of this case, essentially urge that any substantial restriction imposed pursuant to a landmark law must be accompanied by just compensation if it is to be constitutional. Before considering these, we emphasize what is not in dispute.

Because this Court has recognized, in a number of settings, that States and cities may enact land-use restrictions or controls to enhance the quality of life by preserving the character and desirable aesthetic features of a city, see *New Orleans v. Dukes*, 427 U.S. 297, 96 S.Ct. 2513, 49 L.Ed.2d 511 (1976); *Young v. American Mini Theatres, Inc.*, 427 U.S. 50, 96 S.Ct. 2440, 49 L.Ed.2d 310 (1976); *Village of Belle Terre v. Boraas*, 416 U.S. 1, 9-10, 94 S.Ct. 1536, 39 L.Ed.2d 797 (1974); *Berman v. Parker*, 348 U.S. 26, 33, 75 S.Ct. 98, 102, 99 L.Ed. 27 (1954); *Welch v. Swasey*, 214 U.S., at 108, 29 S.Ct., at 571, appellants do not contest that New York City's objective of preserving structures and areas with special historic, architectural, or cultural significance is an entirely permissible governmental goal. They also do not dispute that the restrictions imposed on its parcel are appropriate means of securing the purposes of the New York City law. Finally, appellants do not challenge any of the specific factual premises of the decision below. They accept for present purposes both that the parcel of land occupied by Grand Central Terminal must, in its present state, be regarded as capable of earning a reasonable return,[26] and that the transferable development rights afforded appellants by virtue of the Terminal's designation as a landmark are valuable, even if not as valuable as the rights to construct above the Terminal. In appellants' view none of these factors derogate from their claim that New York City's law has effected a "taking."

They first observe that the airspace above the Terminal is a valuable property interest, citing *United States v. Causby, supra*. They urge that the Landmarks Law has deprived them of any gainful use of their "air rights" above the Terminal and that, irrespective of the value of the remainder of their parcel, the city has "taken" their right to this superadjacent airspace, thus entitling them to "just compensation" measured by the fair market value of these air rights.

Apart from our own disagreement with appellants' characterization of the effect of the New York City law, see *infra*, at 2665, the submission that appellants may establish a "taking" simply by showing that they have been denied the ability to exploit a property interest that they heretofore had believed was available for development is quite simply untenable. Were this the rule, this Court would have erred not only in upholding laws restricting the development of air rights, see *Welch v. Swasey, supra*, but also in approving those prohibiting both the subjacent, see *Goldblatt v. Hempstead*, 369 U.S. 590, 82 S.Ct. 987, 8 L.Ed.2d 130 (1962), and the lateral, see *Gorieb v. Fox*, 274 U.S. 603, 47 S.Ct.

---

[26] Both the Jurisdictional Statement 7-8, n. 7, and Brief for Appellants 8 n. 7 state that appellants are not seeking review of the New York courts' determination that Penn Central could earn a "reasonable return" on its investment in the Terminal. Although appellants suggest in their reply brief that the factual conclusions of the New York courts cannot be sustained unless we accept the rationale of the New York Court of Appeals, *see* Reply Brief for Appellants 12 n. 15, it is apparent that the findings concerning Penn Central's ability to profit from the Terminal depend in no way on the Court of Appeals' rationale.

675, 71 L.Ed. 1228 (1927), development of particular parcels.[27] "Taking" jurisprudence does not divide a single parcel into discrete segments and attempt to determine whether rights in a particular segment have been entirely abrogated. In deciding whether a particular governmental action has effected a taking, this Court focuses rather both on the character of the action and on the nature and extent of the interference with rights in the parcel as a whole—here, the city tax block designated as the "landmark site."

Secondly, appellants, focusing on the character and impact of the New York City law, argue that it effects a "taking" because its operation has significantly diminished the value of the Terminal site. Appellants concede that the decisions sustaining other land-use regulations, which, like the New York City law, are reasonably related to the promotion of the general welfare, uniformly reject the proposition that diminution in property value, standing alone, can establish a "taking," see *Euclid v. Ambler Realty Co.*, 272 U.S. 365, 47 S.Ct. 114, 71 L.Ed. 303 (1926) (75% diminution in value caused by zoning law); *Hadacheck v. Sebastian*, 239 U.S. 394, 36 S.Ct. 143, 60 L.Ed. 348 (1915) (87 1/2 % diminution in value); *cf. Eastlake v. Forest City Enterprises, Inc.*, 426 U.S., at 674 n. 8, 96 S.Ct., at 2362 n.8, and that the "taking" issue in these contexts is resolved by focusing on the uses the regulations permit. *See also Goldblatt v. Hempstead, supra.* Appellants, moreover, also do not dispute that a showing of diminution in property value would not establish a taking if the restriction had been imposed as a result of historic-district legislation, see generally *Maher v. New Orleans*, 516 F.2d 1051 (CA5 1975), but appellants argue that New York City's regulation of individual landmarks is fundamentally different from zoning or from historic-district legislation because the controls imposed by New York City's law apply only to individuals who own selected properties.

Stated baldly, appellants' position appears to be that the only means of ensuring that selected owners are not singled out to endure financial hardship for no reason is to hold that any restriction imposed on individual landmarks pursuant to the New York City scheme is a "taking" requiring the payment of "just compensation." Agreement with this argument would, of course, invalidate not just New York City's law, but all comparable landmark legislation in the Nation. We find no merit in it.

It is true, as appellants emphasize, that both historic-district legislation and zoning laws regulate all properties within given physical communities whereas landmark laws apply only to selected parcels. But, contrary to appellants' suggestions, landmark laws

DIMINUTION IN VALUE

---

[27] These cases dispose of any contention that might be based on *Pennsylvania Coal Co. v. Mahon*, 260 U.S. 393, 43 S.Ct. 158, 67 L.Ed. 322 (1922), that full use of air rights is so bound up with the investment-backed expectations of appellants that governmental deprivation of these rights invariably—i. e., irrespective of the impact of the restriction on the value of the parcel as a whole—constitutes a "taking." Similarly, Welch, Goldblatt, and Gorieb illustrate the fallacy of appellants' related contention that a "taking" must be found to have occurred whenever the land-use restriction may be characterized as imposing a "servitude" on the claimant's parcel.

are not like discriminatory, or "reverse spot," zoning: that is, a land-use decision which arbitrarily singles out a particular parcel for different, less favorable treatment than the neighboring ones. *See* 2 A. Rathkopf, The Law of Zoning and Planning 26-4, and n. 6 (4th ed. 1978). In contrast to discriminatory zoning, which is the antithesis of land-use control as part of some comprehensive plan, the New York City law embodies a comprehensive plan to preserve structures of historic or aesthetic interest wherever they might be found in the city,[28] and as noted, over 400 landmarks and 31 historic districts have been designated pursuant to this plan.

Equally without merit is the related argument that the decision to designate a structure as a landmark "is inevitably arbitrary or at least subjective, because it is basically a matter of taste," Reply Brief for Appellants 22, thus unavoidably singling out individual landowners for disparate and unfair treatment. The argument has a particularly hollow ring in this case. For appellants not only did not seek judicial review of either the designation or of the denials of the certificates of appropriateness and of no exterior effect, but do not even now suggest that the Commission's decisions concerning the Terminal were in any sense arbitrary or unprincipled. But, in any event, a landmark owner has a right to judicial review of any Commission decision, and, quite simply, there is no basis whatsoever for a conclusion that courts will have any greater difficulty identifying arbitrary or discriminatory action in the context of landmark regulation than in the context of classic zoning or indeed in any other context.

Next, appellants observe that New York City's law differs from zoning laws and historic-district ordinances in that the Landmarks Law does not impose identical or similar restrictions on all structures located in particular physical communities. It follows, they argue, that New York City's law is inherently incapable of producing the fair and equitable distribution of benefits and burdens of governmental action which is characteristic of zoning laws and historic-district legislation and which they maintain is a constitutional requirement if "just compensation" is not to be afforded. It is, of course, true that the Landmarks Law has a more severe impact on some landowners than on others, but that in itself does not mean that the law effects a "taking." Legislation designed to promote the general welfare commonly burdens some more than others. The owners of the brickyard in *Hadacheck*, of the cedar trees in *Miller v. Schoene*, and of the gravel and sand mine in *Goldblatt v. Hempstead*, were uniquely burdened by the

---

[28] Although the New York Court of Appeals contrasted the New York City Landmarks Law with both zoning and historic-district legislation and stated at one point that landmark laws do not "further a general community plan," 42 N.Y.2d 324, 330, 397 N.Y.S.2d 914, 918, 366 N.E.2d 1271, 1274 (1977), it also emphasized that the implementation of the objectives of the Landmarks Law constitutes an "acceptable reason for singling out one particular parcel for different and less favorable treatment." *Ibid.*, 397 N.Y.S.2d, at 918, 366 N.E.2d, at 1275. Therefore, we do not understand the New York Court of Appeals to disagree with our characterization of the law.

legislation sustained in those cases.[30] Similarly, zoning laws often affect some property owners more severely than others but have not been held to be invalid on that account. For example, the property owner in *Euclid* who wished to use its property for industrial purposes was affected far more severely by the ordinance than its neighbors who wished to use their land for residences.

In any event, appellants' repeated suggestions that they are solely burdened and unbenefited is factually inaccurate. This contention overlooks the fact that the New York City law applies to vast numbers of structures in the city in addition to the Terminal—all the structures contained in the 31 historic districts and over 400 individual landmarks, many of which are close to the Terminal.[31] Unless we are to reject the judgment of the New York City Council that the preservation of landmarks benefits all New York citizens and all structures, both economically and by improving the quality of life in the city as a whole—which we are unwilling to do—we cannot conclude that the owners of the Terminal have in no sense been benefited by the Landmarks Law. Doubtless appellants believe they are more burdened than benefited by the law, but that must have been true, too, of the property owners in *Miller, Hadacheck, Euclid*, and *Goldblatt*.[32]

Appellants' final broad-based attack would have us treat the law as an instance, like that in *United States v. Causby*, in which government, acting in an enterprise capacity, has appropriated part of their property for some strictly governmental purpose. Apart from the fact that Causby was a case of invasion of airspace that destroyed the use of the farm beneath and this New York City law has in nowise impaired the present use of the Terminal, the Landmarks Law neither exploits appellants' parcel for city purposes nor facilitates nor arises from any entrepreneurial operations of the city. The situation is not remotely like that in *Causby* where the airspace above the property was in the

---

[30] Appellants attempt to distinguish these cases on the ground that, in each, government was prohibiting a "noxious" use of land and that in the present case, in contrast, appellants' proposed construction above the Terminal would be beneficial. We observe that the uses in issue in *Hadacheck, Miller*, and *Goldblatt* were perfectly lawful in themselves. They involved no "blameworthiness, . . . moral wrongdoing or conscious act of dangerous risk-taking which induce[d society] to shift the cost to a pa[rt]icular individual." Sax, *Takings and the Police Power*, 74 Yale L.J. 36, 50 (1964). These cases are better understood as resting not on any supposed "noxious" quality of the prohibited uses but rather on the ground that the restrictions were reasonably related to the implementation of a policy—not unlike historic preservation—expected to produce a widespread public benefit and applicable to all similarly situated property. Nor, correlatively, can it be asserted that the destruction or fundamental alteration of a historic landmark is not harmful. The suggestion that the beneficial quality of appellants' proposed construction is established by the fact that the construction would have been consistent with applicable zoning laws ignores the development in sensibilities and ideals reflected in landmark legislation like New York City's. *Cf. West Bros. Brick Co. v. Alexandria*, 169 Va. 271, 282-283, 192 S.E. 881, 885-886, appeal dismissed for want of a substantial federal question, 302 U.S. 658, 58 S.Ct. 369, 82 L.Ed. 508 (1937).

[31] There are some 53 designated landmarks and 5 historic districts or scenic landmarks in Manhattan between 14th and 59th Streets. *See* Landmarks Preservation Commission, *Landmarks and Historic Districts* (1977).

[32] It is, of course, true that the fact the duties imposed by zoning and historic-district legislation apply throughout particular physical communities provides assurances against arbitrariness, but the applicability of the Landmarks Law to a large number of parcels in the city, in our view, provides comparable, if not identical, assurances.

flight pattern for military aircraft. The Landmarks Law's effect is simply to prohibit appellants or anyone else from occupying portions of the airspace above the Terminal, while permitting appellants to use the remainder of the parcel in a gainful fashion. This is no more an appropriation of property by government for its own uses than is a zoning law prohibiting, for "aesthetic" reasons, two or more adult theaters within a specified area, see *Young v. American Mini Theatres, Inc.*, 427 U.S. 50, 96 S.Ct. 2440, 49 L.Ed.2d 310 (1976), or a safety regulation prohibiting excavations below a certain level. *See Goldblatt v. Hempstead.*

C

Rejection of appellants' broad arguments is not, however, the end of our inquiry, for all we thus far have established is that the New York City law is not rendered invalid by its failure to provide "just compensation" whenever a landmark owner is restricted in the exploitation of property interests, such as air rights, to a greater extent than provided for under applicable zoning laws. We now must consider whether the interference with appellants' property is of such a magnitude that "there must be an exercise of eminent domain and compensation to sustain [it]." *Pennsylvania Coal Co. v. Mahon*, 260 U.S., at 413, 43 S.Ct., at 159. That inquiry may be narrowed to the question of the severity of the impact of the law on appellants' parcel, and its resolution in turn requires a careful assessment of the impact of the regulation on the Terminal site.

Unlike the governmental acts in *Goldblatt, Miller, Causby, Griggs*, and *Hadacheck*, the New York City law does not interfere in any way with the present uses of the Terminal. Its designation as a landmark not only permits but contemplates that appellants may continue to use the property precisely as it has been used for the past 65 years: as a railroad terminal containing office space and concessions. So the law does not interfere with what must be regarded as Penn Central's primary expectation concerning the use of the parcel. More importantly, on this record, we must regard the New York City law as permitting Penn Central not only to profit from the Terminal but also to obtain a "reasonable return" on its investment.

Appellants, moreover, exaggerate the effect of the law on their ability to make use of the air rights above the Terminal in two respects.[33] First, it simply cannot be maintained, on this record, that appellants have been prohibited from occupying any portion of the airspace above the Terminal. While the Commission's actions in denying applications to construct an office building in excess of 50 stories above the Terminal may indicate that it will refuse to issue a certificate of appropriateness for any comparably sized structure, nothing the Commission has said or done suggests an intention to prohibit any construction above the Terminal. The Commission's report emphasized that whether

---

[33] Appellants, of course, argue at length that the transferable development rights, while valuable, do not constitute "just compensation." Brief for Appellants 36-43.

any construction would be allowed depended upon whether the proposed addition "would harmonize in scale, material and character with [the Terminal]." Record 2251. Since appellants have not sought approval for the construction of a smaller structure, we do not know that appellants will be denied any use of any portion of the airspace above the Terminal.[34]

Second, to the extent appellants have been denied the right to build above the Terminal, it is not literally accurate to say that they have been denied all use of even those pre-existing air rights. Their ability to use these rights has not been abrogated; they are made transferable to at least eight parcels in the vicinity of the Terminal, one or two of which have been found suitable for the construction of new office buildings. Although appellants and others have argued that New York City's transferable development-rights program is far from ideal, the New York courts here supportably found that, at least in the case of the Terminal, the rights afforded are valuable. While these rights may well not have constituted "just compensation" if a "taking" had occurred, the rights nevertheless undoubtedly mitigate whatever financial burdens the law has imposed on appellants and, for that reason, are to be taken into account in considering the impact of regulation. *Cf. Goldblatt v. Hempstead*, 369 U.S., at 594 n. 3, 82 S.Ct., at 990 n. 3.

On this record, we conclude that the application of New York City's Landmarks Law has not effected a "taking" of appellants' property. The restrictions imposed are substantially related to the promotion of the general welfare and not only permit reasonable beneficial use of the landmark site but also afford appellants opportunities further to enhance not only the Terminal site proper but also other properties.[36]

Affirmed.

Mr. Justice REHNQUIST, with whom The Chief Justice and MR. Justice STEVENS join, dissenting.

Of the over one million buildings and structures in the city of New York, appellees have singled out 400 for designation as official landmarks. The owner of a building might initially be pleased that his property has been chosen by a distinguished committee of architects, historians, and city planners for such a singular distinction. But he may well discover, as appellant Penn Central Transportation Co. did here, that the landmark designation imposes upon him a substantial cost, with little or no offsetting

---

[34] Counsel for appellants admitted at oral argument that the Commission has not suggested that it would not, for example, approve a 20-story office tower along the lines of that which was part of the original plan for the Terminal. *See* Tr. of Oral Arg. 19.

[36] We emphasize that our holding today is on the present record, which in turn is based on Penn Central's present ability to use the Terminal for its intended purposes and in a gainful fashion. The city conceded at oral argument that if appellants can demonstrate at some point in the future that circumstances have so changed that the Terminal ceases to be "economically viable," appellants may obtain relief. *See* Tr. of Oral Arg. 42-43.

benefit except for the honor of the designation. The question in this case is whether the cost associated with the city of New York's desire to preserve a limited number of "landmarks" within its borders must be borne by all of its taxpayers or whether it can instead be imposed entirely on the owners of the individual properties.

Only in the most superficial sense of the word can this case be said to involve "zoning." Typical zoning restrictions may, it is true, so limit the prospective uses of a piece of property as to diminish the value of that property in the abstract because it may not be used for the forbidden purposes. But any such abstract decrease in value will more than likely be at least partially offset by an increase in value which flows from similar restrictions as to use on neighboring properties. All property owners in a designated area are placed under the same restrictions, not only for the benefit of the municipality as a whole but also for the common benefit of one another. In the words of Mr. Justice Holmes, speaking for the Court in *Pennsylvania Coal Co. v. Mahon*, 260 U.S. 393, 415, 43 S.Ct. 158, 160, 67 L.Ed. 322 (1922), there is "an average reciprocity of advantage."

Where a relatively few individual buildings, all separated from one another, are singled out and treated differently from surrounding buildings, no such reciprocity exists. The cost to the property owner which results from the imposition of restrictions applicable only to his property and not that of his neighbors may be substantial—in this case, several million dollars—with no comparable reciprocal benefits. And the cost associated with landmark legislation is likely to be of a completely different order of magnitude than that which results from the imposition of normal zoning restrictions. Unlike the regime affected by the latter, the landowner is not simply prohibited from using his property for certain purposes, while allowed to use it for all other purposes. Under the historic-landmark preservation scheme adopted by New York, the property owner is under an affirmative duty to preserve his property as a landmark at his own expense. To suggest that because traditional zoning results in some limitation of use of the property zoned, the New York City landmark preservation scheme should likewise be upheld, represents the ultimate in treating as alike things which are different. The rubric of "zoning" has not yet sufficed to avoid the well-established proposition that the Fifth Amendment bars the "Government from forcing some people alone to bear public burdens which, in all fairness and justice, should be borne by the public as a whole." *Armstrong v. United States*, 364 U.S. 40, 49, 80 S.Ct. 1563, 1569, 4 L.Ed.2d 1554 (1960). *See* discussion *infra*, at pp. 2671-2672.

In August 1967, Grand Central Terminal was designated a landmark over the objections of its owner Penn Central. Immediately upon this designation, Penn Central, like all owners of a landmark site, was placed under an affirmative duty, backed by criminal fines and penalties, to keep "exterior portions" of the landmark "in good repair." Even more burdensome, however, were the strict limitations that were thereupon imposed on Penn Central's use of its property. At the time Grand Central was designated a landmark, Penn Central was in a precarious financial condition. In an effort to increase its sources of revenue, Penn Central had entered into a lease agreement with appellant UGP Properties, Inc., under which UGP would construct and operate a multistory office building cantilevered above the Terminal building. During the period of construction, UGP would pay Penn Central $1 million per year. Upon completion, UGP would rent the building for 50 years, with an option for another 25 years, at a guaranteed minimum rental of $3 million per year. The record is clear that the proposed office building was in full compliance with all New York zoning laws and height limitations. Under the Landmarks Preservation Law, however, appellants could not construct the proposed office building unless appellee Landmarks Preservation Commission issued either a "Certificate of No Exterior Effect" or a "Certificate of Appropriateness." Although appellants' architectural plan would have preserved the facade of the Terminal, the Landmarks Preservation Commission has refused to approve the construction.

I

The Fifth Amendment provides in part: "nor shall private property be taken for public use, without just compensation." In a very literal sense, the actions of appellees violated this constitutional prohibition. Before the city of New York declared Grand Central Terminal to be a landmark, Penn Central could have used its "air rights" over the Terminal to build a multistory office building, at an apparent value of several million dollars per year. Today, the Terminal cannot be modified in any form, including the erection of additional stories, without the permission of the Landmark Preservation Commission, a permission which appellants, despite good-faith attempts, have so far been unable to obtain. Because the Taking Clause of the Fifth Amendment has not always been read literally, however, the constitutionality of appellees' actions requires a closer scrutiny of this Court's interpretation of the three key words in the Taking Clause—"property," "taken," and "just compensation."[4]

A

Appellees do not dispute that valuable property rights have been destroyed. And the Court has frequently emphasized that the term "property" as used in the Taking Clause includes the entire "group of rights inhering in the citizen's [ownership]." *United States v. General Motors Corp.*, 323 U.S. 373, 65 S.Ct. 357, 89 L.Ed. 311 (1945). The term is not used in the

---

[4] The Court's opinion touches base with, or at least attempts to touch base with, most of the major eminent domain cases decided by this Court. Its use of them, however, is anything but meticulous. In citing to *United States v. Caltex, Inc.*, 344 U.S. 149, 156, 73 S.Ct. 200, 97 L.Ed. 157 (1952), for example, ante, at 2659, the only language remotely applicable to eminent domain is stated in terms of "the destruction of respondents' terminals by a trained team of engineers in the face of their impending seizure by the enemy." 344 U.S., at 156, 73 S.Ct., at 203.

"vulgar and untechnical sense of the physical thing with respect to which the citizen exercises rights recognized by law. [Instead, it] . . . denote [s] the group of rights inhering in the citizen's relation to the physical THING, AS THE RIGHT TO POSSESS, USE AND DISPOSE OF IT. . . . the constitutional provision is addressed to every sort of interest the citizen may possess." *Id.*, at 377-378, 65 S.Ct., at 359 (emphasis added).

While neighboring landowners are free to use their land and "air rights" in any way consistent with the broad boundaries of New York zoning, Penn Central, absent the permission of appellees, must forever maintain its property in its present state.[5] The property has been thus subjected to a nonconsensual servitude not borne by any neighboring or similar properties.[6]

B

Appellees have thus destroyed—in a literal sense, "taken"—substantial property rights of Penn Central. While the term "taken" might have been narrowly interpreted to include only physical seizures of property rights, "the construction of the phrase has not been so narrow. The courts have held that the deprivation of the former owner rather than the accretion of a right or interest to the sovereign constitutes the taking." *Id.*, at 378, 65 S.Ct., at 359. *See also United States v. Lynah*, 188 U.S. 445, 469, 23 S.Ct. 349, 47 L.Ed. 539 1903); *Dugan v. Rank*, 372 U.S. 609, 625, 83 S.Ct. 999, 1009, 10 L.Ed.2d 15 (1963). Because "not every destruction or injury to property by governmental action has been held to be a 'taking' in the constitutional sense," *Armstrong v. United States*, 364 U.S., at 48, 80 S.Ct., at 1568, however, this does not end our inquiry. But an examination of the two exceptions where the destruction of property does not constitute a taking demonstrates that a compensable taking has occurred here.

1

As early as 1887, the Court recognized that the government can prevent a property owner from using his property to injure others without having to compensate the owner for the value of the forbidden use.

---

[5] In particular, Penn Central cannot increase the height of the Terminal. This Court has previously held that the "air rights" over an area of land are "property" for purposes of the Fifth Amendment. *See United States v. Causby*, 328 U.S. 256, 66 S.Ct. 1062, 90 L.Ed. 1206 (1946) ("air rights" taken by low-flying airplanes); *Griggs v. Allegheny County*, 369 U.S. 84, 82 S.Ct. 531, 7 L.Ed.2d 585 (1962) (same); *Portsmouth Harbor Land & Hotel Co. v. United States*, 260 U.S. 327, 43 S.Ct. 135, 67 L.Ed. 287 (1922) (firing of projectiles over summer resort can constitute taking). *See also Butler v. Frontier Telephone Co.*, 186 N.Y. 486, 79 N.E. 716 (1906) (stringing of telephone wire across property constitutes a taking).

[6] It is, of course, irrelevant that appellees interfered with or destroyed property rights that Penn Central had not yet physically used. The Fifth Amendment must be applied with "reference to the uses for which the property is suitable, having regard to the existing business or wants of the community, or such as may be reasonably expected in the immediate future." *Boom Co. v. Patterson*, 98 U.S. 403, 408, 25 L.Ed. 206 (1879) (emphasis added).

"A prohibition simply upon the use of property for purposes that are declared, by valid legislation, to be injurious to the health, morals, or safety of the community, cannot, in any just sense, be deemed a taking or an appropriation of property for the public benefit. Such legislation does not disturb the owner in the control or use of his property for lawful purposes, nor restrict his right to dispose of it, but is only a declaration by the State that its use by any one, for certain forbidden purposes, is prejudicial to the public interests. . . . The power which the States have of prohibiting such use by individuals of their property as will be prejudicial to the health, the morals, or the safety of the public, is not—and, consistently with the existence and safety of organized society, cannot be—burdened with the condition that the State must compensate such individual owners for pecuniary losses they may sustain, by reason of their not being permitted, by a noxious use of their property, to inflict injury upon the community." *Mugler v. Kansas*, 123 U.S. 623, 668-669, 8 S.Ct. 273, 301, 31 L.Ed. 205.

Thus, there is no "taking" where a city prohibits the operation of a brickyard within a residential area, see *Hadacheck v. Sebastian*, 239 U.S. 394, 36 S.Ct. 143, 60 L.Ed. 348 (1915), or forbids excavation for sand and gravel below the water line, see *Goldblatt v. Hempstead*, 369 U.S. 590, 82 S.Ct. 987, 8 L.Ed.2d 130 (1962). Nor is it relevant, where the government is merely prohibiting a noxious use of property, that the government would seem to be singling out a particular property owner. *Hadacheck, supra*, at 413, 36 S.Ct., at 146.[8]

The nuisance exception to the taking guarantee is not coterminous with the police power itself. The question is whether the forbidden use is dangerous to the safety, health, or welfare of others. Thus, in *Curtin v. Benson*, 222 U.S. 78, 32 S.Ct. 31, 56 L.Ed. 102 (1911), the Court held that the Government, in prohibiting the owner of property within the boundaries of Yosemite National Park from grazing cattle on his property, had taken the owner's property. The Court assumed that the Government could constitutionally require the owner to fence his land or take other action to prevent his cattle from straying onto others' land without compensating him.

"Such laws might be considered as strictly regulations of the use of property, of so using it that no injury could result to others. They would have the effect of making the owner of land herd his cattle on his own land and of making him responsible for a neglect of it." *Id.*, at 86, 32 S.Ct., at 33.

The prohibition in question, however, was "not a prevention of a misuse or illegal use but the prevention of a legal and essential use, an attribute of its ownership." *Ibid*.

Appellees are not prohibiting a nuisance. The record is clear that the proposed addition to the Grand Central Terminal would be in full compliance with zoning,

---

[8] Each of the cases cited by the Court for the proposition that legislation which severely affects some landowners but not others does not effect a "taking" involved noxious uses of property. *See Hadacheck; Miller v. Schoene*, 276 U.S. 272, 48 S.Ct. 246, 72 L.Ed. 568 (1928); *Goldblatt. See ante*, at 2660-2661, 2664.

height limitations, and other health and safety requirements. Instead, appellees are seeking to preserve what they believe to be an outstanding example of beaux-arts architecture. Penn Central is prevented from further developing its property basically because too good a job was done in designing and building it. The city of New York, because of its unadorned admiration for the design, has decided that the owners of the building must preserve it unchanged for the benefit of sightseeing New Yorkers and tourists.

Unlike land-use regulations, appellees' actions do not merely prohibit Penn Central from using its property in a narrow set of noxious ways. Instead, appellees have placed an affirmative duty on Penn Central to maintain the Terminal in its present state and in "good repair." Appellants are not free to use their property as they see fit within broad outer boundaries but must strictly adhere to their past use except where appellees conclude that alternative uses would not detract from the landmark. While Penn Central may continue to use the Terminal as it is presently designed, appellees otherwise "exercise complete dominion and control over the surface of the land," *United States v. Causby*, 328 U.S. 256, 262, 66 S.Ct. 1062, 1066, 90 L.Ed. 1206 (1946), and must compensate the owner for his loss. *Ibid.* "Property is taken in the constitutional sense when inroads are made upon an owner's use of it to an extent that, as between private parties, a servitude has been acquired." *United States v. Dickinson*, 331 U.S. 745, 748, 67 S.Ct. 1382, 1385, 91 L.Ed. 1789 (1947). *See also Dugan v. Rank, supra*, 372 U.S., at 625, 83 S.Ct., at 1009.

2

Even where the government prohibits a noninjurious use, the Court has ruled that a taking does not take place if the prohibition applies over a broad cross section of land and thereby "secure[s] an average reciprocity of advantage." *Pennsylvania Coal Co. v. Mahon*, 260 U.S., at 415, 43 S.Ct., at 160. It is for this reason that zoning does not constitute a "taking." While zoning at times reduces individual property values, the burden is shared relatively evenly and it is reasonable to conclude that on the whole an individual who is harmed by one aspect of the zoning will be benefited by another.

Here, however, a multimillion dollar loss has been imposed on appellants; it is uniquely felt and is not offset by any benefits flowing from the preservation of some 400 other "landmarks" in New York City. Appellees have imposed a substantial cost on less than one one-tenth of one percent of the buildings in New York City for the general benefit of all its people. It is exactly this imposition of general costs on a few individuals at which the "taking" protection is directed. The Fifth Amendment

"prevents the public from loading upon one individual more than his just share of the burdens of government, and says that when he surrenders to the public something more and different from that which is exacted from other members of the public, a full and just equivalent shall be returned to him." *Monongahela Navigation Co. v. United States*, 148 U.S. 312, 325, 13 S.Ct. 622, 626, 37 L.Ed. 463 (1893).

Less than 20 years ago, this Court reiterated that the

"Fifth Amendment's guarantee that private property shall not be taken for a public use without just compensation was designed to bar Government from forcing some people alone to bear public burdens which, in all fairness and justice, should be borne by the public as a whole." *Armstrong v. United States*, 364 U.S., at 49, 80 S.Ct., at 1569.

Cf. Nashville, C. & St. L. R. Co. v. Walters, 294 U.S. 405, 428-430, 55 S.Ct. 486, 494-495, 79 L.Ed. 949 (1935).[11]

As Mr. Justice Holmes pointed out in *Pennsylvania Coal Co. v. Mahon*, "the question at bottom" in an eminent domain case "is upon whom the loss of the changes desired should fall." 260 U.S., at 416, 43 S.Ct., at 160. The benefits that appellees believe will flow from preservation of the Grand Central Terminal will accrue to all the citizens of New York City. There is no reason to believe that appellants will enjoy a substantially greater share of these benefits. If the cost of preserving Grand Central Terminal were spread evenly across the entire population of the city of New York, the burden per person would be in cents per year—a minor cost appellees would surely concede for the benefit accrued. Instead, however, appellees would impose the entire cost of several million dollars per year on Penn Central. But it is precisely this sort of discrimination that the Fifth Amendment prohibits.

Appellees in response would argue that a taking only occurs where a property owner is denied all reasonable value of his property.[13] The Court has frequently held that, even where a destruction of property rights would not otherwise constitute a taking, the inability of the owner to make a reasonable return on his property requires compensation under the Fifth Amendment. *See*, e. g., *United States v. Lynah*, 188 U.S., at 470, 23 S.Ct., at 357. But the converse is not true. A taking does not become a

---

[11] "It is true that the police power embraces regulations designed to promote public convenience or the general welfare, and not merely those in the interest of public health, safety and morals. . . . But when particular individuals are singled out to bear the cost of advancing the public convenience, that imposition must bear some reasonable relation to the evils to be eradicated or the advantages to be secured. . . . While moneys raised by general taxation may constitutionally be applied to purposes from which the individual taxed may receive no benefit, and indeed, suffer serious detriment, . . . so-called assessments for public improvements laid upon particular property owners are ordinarily constitutional only if based on benefits received by them." 294 U.S., at 429-430, 55 S.Ct., at 494-495.

[13] Difficult conceptual and legal problems are posed by a rule that a taking only occurs where the property owner is denied all reasonable return on his property. Not only must the Court define "reasonable return" for a variety of types of property (farmlands, residential properties, commercial and industrial areas), but the Court must define the particular property unit that should be examined. For example, in this case, if appellees are viewed as having restricted Penn Central's use of its "air rights," all return has been denied. *See Pennsylvania Coal Co. v. Mahon*, 260 U.S. 393, 43 S.Ct. 158, 67 L.Ed. 322 (1922). The Court does little to resolve these questions in its opinion. Thus, at one point, the Court implies that the question is whether the restrictions have "an unduly harsh impact upon the owner's use of the property," ante, at 2661; at another point, the question is phrased as whether Penn Central can obtain "a 'reasonable return' on its investment," ante, at 2666; and, at yet another point, the question becomes whether the landmark is "economically viable," ante, at 2666 n. 36.

noncompensable exercise of police power simply because the government in its grace allows the owner to make some "reasonable" use of his property. "[I]t is the character of the invasion, not the amount of damage resulting from it, so long as the damage is substantial, that determines the question whether it is a taking." *United States v. Cress*, 243 U.S. 316, 328, 37 S.Ct. 380, 385, 61 L.Ed. 746 (1917); *United States v. Causby*, 328 U.S., at 266, 66 S.Ct., at 1068. *See also Goldblatt v. Hempstead*, 369 U.S., at 594, 82 S.Ct., at 990.

C

Appellees, apparently recognizing that the constraints imposed on a landmark site constitute a taking for Fifth Amendment purposes, do not leave the property owner empty-handed. As the Court notes, ante, at 2654-2655, the property owner may theoretically "transfer" his previous right to develop the landmark property to adjacent properties if they are under his control. Appellees have coined this system "Transfer Development Rights," or TDR's.

Of all the terms used in the Taking Clause, "just compensation" has the strictest meaning. The Fifth Amendment does not allow simply an approximate compensation but requires "a full and perfect equivalent for the property taken." *Monongahela Navigation Co. v. United States*, 148 U.S., at 326, 13 S.Ct., at 626.

> "[I]f the adjective 'just' had been omitted, and the provision was simply that property should not be taken without compensation, the natural import of the language would be that the compensation should be the equivalent of the property. And this is made emphatic by the adjective 'just.' There can, in view of the combination of those two words, be no doubt that the compensation must be a full and perfect equivalent for the property taken." *Ibid.*

See also United States v. Lynah, supra, 188 U.S., at 465, 23 S.Ct., at 355; *United States v. Pewee Coal Co.*, 341 U.S. 114, 117, 71 S.Ct. 670, 671, 95 L.Ed. 809 (1951). And the determination of whether a "full and perfect equivalent" has been awarded is a "judicial function." *United States v. New River Collieries Co.*, 262 U.S. 341, 343-344, 43 S.Ct. 565, 566-567, 67 L.Ed. 1014 (1923). The fact that appellees may believe that TDR's provide full compensation is irrelevant.

> "The legislature may determine what private property is needed for public purposes—that is a question of a political and legislative character; but when the taking has been ordered, then the question of compensation is judicial. It does not rest with the public, taking the property, through Congress or the legislature, its representative, to say what compensation shall be paid, or even what shall be the rule of compensation. The Constitution has declared that just compensation shall be paid, and the ascertainment of that is a judicial inquiry." *Monongahela Navigation Co. v. United States, supra*, 148 U.S., at 327, 13 S.Ct., at 626.

Appellees contend that, even if they have "taken" appellants' property, TDR's constitute "just compensation." Appellants, of course, argue that TDR's are highly imperfect compensation. Because the lower courts held that there was no "taking," they did not have to reach the question of whether or not just compensation has already been awarded. The New York Court of Appeals' discussion of TDR's gives some support to appellants:

> "The many defects in New York City's program for development rights transfers have been detailed elsewhere. . . . The area to which transfer is permitted is severely limited [and] complex procedures are required to obtain a transfer permit." 42 N.Y.2d 324, 334-335, 397 N.Y.S.2d 914, 920, 366 N.E.2d 1271, 1277 (1977).

And in other cases the Court of Appeals has noted that TDR's have an "uncertain and contingent market value" and do "not adequately preserve" the value lost when a building is declared to be a landmark. *French Investing Co. v. City of New York*, 39 N.Y.2d 587, 591, 385 N.Y.S.2d 5, 7, 350 N.E.2d 381, 383, appeal dismissed 429 U.S. 990, 97 S.Ct. 515, 50 L.Ed.2d 602 (1976). On the other hand, there is evidence in the record that Penn Central has been offered substantial amounts for its TDR's. Because the record on appeal is relatively slim, I would remand to the Court of Appeals for a determination of whether TDR's constitute a "full and perfect equivalent for the property taken."[14]

II

Over 50 years ago, Mr. Justice Holmes, speaking for the Court, warned that the courts were "in danger of forgetting that a strong public desire to improve the public condition is not enough to warrant achieving the desire by a shorter cut than the constitutional way of paying for the change." *Pennsylvania Coal Co. v. Mahon*, 260 U.S., at 416, 43 S.Ct., at 160. The Court's opinion in this case demonstrates that the danger thus foreseen has not abated. The city of New York is in a precarious financial state, and some may believe that the costs of landmark preservation will be more easily borne by corporations such as Penn Central than the overburdened individual taxpayers of New York. But these concerns do not allow us to ignore past precedents construing the Eminent Domain Clause to the end that the desire to improve the public condition is, indeed, achieved by a shorter cut than the constitutional way of paying for the change.

---

[14] The Court suggests, ante, at 2663, that if appellees are held to have "taken" property sights of landmark owners, not only the New York City Landmarks Preservation Law, but "all comparable landmark legislation in the Nation" must fall. This assumes, of course, that TDR's are not "just compensation" for the property rights destroyed. It also ignores the fact that many States and cities in the Nation have chosen to preserve landmarks by purchasing or condemning restrictive easements over the facades of the landmarks and are apparently quite satisfied with the results. *See*, e. g., Ore.Rev.Stat. §§271.710, 271.720 (1977); Md.Ann.Code, Art. 41, §181A (1978); Va.Code §§10-145.1 and 10-138(e) (1978); Richmond, Va., City Code §§21-23 et seq. (1975). The British National Trust has effectively used restrictive easements to preserve landmarks since 1937. *See* National Trust Act, 1937, 1 Edw. 8 and 1 Geo. 6 ch. lvii, §§4 and 8. Other States and cities have found that tax incentives are also an effective means of encouraging the private preservation of landmark sites. *See*, e. g., Conn.Gen.Stat. §12-127a (1977); Ill.Rev.Stat., ch. 24, §11-48.2-6 (1976); Va.Code §10-139 (1978). The New York City Landmarks Preservation Law departs drastically from these traditional, and constitutional, means of preserving landmarks.

NOTES AND QUESTIONS

1. *Ad Hoc, Factual Inquiries, and the* Penn Central *Factors.* Drawing on earlier cases, including *Mahon*, Justice Brennan's opinion of the Court noted that the Court approached regulatory takings cases using "ad hoc, factual inquiries." Justice Brennan identified three factors relevant to the regulatory takings inquiry: (a) the economic impact of the regulation on the property owner, (b) the degree to which the economic impact interferes with investment-backed expectations, and (c) the character of the government action. We will take a look at each of these factors in the following notes. Before looking at the individual factors, though, we should note that it is far from clear that Justice Brennan's opinion was intended to set up a multifactor balancing test that would apply to all regulatory takings claims. Regardless of the original purpose of the factors, subsequent courts have applied the *Penn Central* factors as a multifactor balancing test.

2. *Economic Impact: Diminution in Value, the Denominator Problem, and Transferred Development Rights.* The first *Penn Central* factor is *economic impact.* We can treat this factor as being equivalent to diminution in value in the property caused by the regulation. (Economic impact might be a broader concept than diminution in value, but most, if not all, economic impacts on the property owner caused by a regulation should be reflected in the value of the property.)

DIMINUTION IN VALUE

As we have seen before, diminution in value raises the denominator problem. *Penn Central* supports the "parcel as a whole" approach. Indeed, the "parcel as a whole" approach takes its name from this passage from Justice Brennan's opinion: "In deciding whether a particular governmental action has effected a taking, this Court focuses rather both on the character of the action and on the nature and extent of the interference with rights in the parcel as a whole—here, the city tax block designated as the 'landmark site.'" Note well that even if the Court had looked at the air rights above Grand Central Terminal alone, it would not have found a total reduction in value. Although this point about *Penn Central* is often misunderstood, we think it is clear that the majority of the Court thought that the owners likely could build a tower over the Terminal, even if it was smaller in scope than the one that they wanted to build. Do you see why?

The diminution in value in *Penn Central* was complicated by the use of *transferred development rights* (TDRs). As their name implies, TDRs involve the transfer of development rights from a parcel affected by a regulation ("parcel A") to a property or properties located elsewhere ("parcel B"). The transfer of the development rights to parcel B would allow parcel B to be developed more than would be permitted under existing regulations. If, for example, the applicable zoning regulations restricted parcel B to ten-story buildings, the transfer of development rights to parcel B might allow the owner to build a 15-story building on the property. TDRs therefore are valuable to the owner of the regulated property.

The value of TDRs presents an interesting issue that divided the Court in *Penn Central*: how should the value of TDRs factor into the regulatory takings analysis? Justice Brennan's majority opinion suggested that TDRs should be considered in measuring the economic impact of the property and therefore should be relevant to the question of whether an unconstitutional taking had occurred. Justice Rehnquist's dissent, in contrast, suggested that TDRs should not be relevant to the question of whether there had been a taking and instead should be relevant to whether compensation was sufficient for a taking that had occurred. Which approach do you think is the correct one?

3. *Interference with Investment-Backed Expectations.* While the exact contours of this factor are a bit fuzzy, it generally looks at the reasonable expectations of the property owner at the time of purchase. If the property owner purchased property in reasonable reliance on one set of land use regulations, and those regulations later changed in a manner contrary to those expectations, then this factor would weigh toward the finding of a taking. Justice Brennan's majority opinion referred to *Mahon* as an example of a regulatory change that was profoundly contrary to investment-backed expectations. In contrast, the majority opinion repeatedly noted that Penn Central could earn a reasonable rate of return on Grand Central Terminal even after it was designated as a landmark, suggesting that the regulation was not contrary to Penn Central's investment-backed expectations. What do you think this factor adds to the regulatory takings analysis? Does the diminution in value factor already capture interference with investment-backed expectations? If we care about property owner expectations, should we care more about the expectations of purchasers for value than for donees (whose expectations presumably are not investment backed)?

4. *Character of the Government Action.* This is the vaguest of the *Penn Central* factors. In Justice Brennan's opinion, the factor is introduced with a contrast between a government action that physically invades the property and a "public program adjusting the benefits and burdens of economic life to promote the common good." As we will see in the next section, the Court later held that government actions or regulations that physically invade private property are per se takings. One narrow reading of this factor, then, is that it simply anticipated this per se rule and recognized the differences between physical invasions and other types of government regulations.

Another interpretation of the character of the government action factor is that it should weigh against the finding of a taking if the government regulation is enacted to promote an important public interest. Put another way, this factor can be interpreted to balance the impact on the property owner (measured by diminution in value and interference with investment-backed expectations), on the one hand, and the perceived importance of the government regulation (reflected in the character of the government action), on the other. This interpretation would allow a court to avoid a finding of a taking even if the regulation caused a severe negative impact on the property owner.

5. *Singling Out, Average Reciprocity of Advantage, and the* Armstrong *Principle.* Where a zoning law typically applies to all property owners in a given area, the Landmarks Preservation Law at issue in *Penn Central* only applied to the relatively small number of property owners who owned historic landmarks. The property owners affected by the Landmarks Preservation Law could therefore claim that they were being *singled out* to bear the burdens of the law. The public at large benefited from the preservation of the landmarked buildings, while the property owners bore the entire cost. Because the landmarked buildings were dispersed throughout the city, the owners were unlikely to benefit from the restrictions on similarly situated neighboring property owners. Put another way, the Landmarks Preservation Law had low average reciprocity of advantage, especially when compared to the typical zoning law. It also had low average reciprocity of advantage as compared to an historical preservation law that applied to all buildings in a designated historic district. (Do you see why?)

It is not obvious how the singling-out issue should fit into our regulatory takings test. Of the factors that we have identified so far, singling out might best fit into the vague character of the government-action prong of the *Penn Central* analysis. Or, it could be that singling out should be considered its own factor. Both the majority and dissenting opinions quote what is often referred to as the "*Armstrong* principle." According to this principle, the Just Compensation Clause is intended to prevent the "Government from forcing some people alone to bear public burdens which, in all fairness and justice, should be borne by the public as a whole." *Armstrong v. United States*, 364 U.S. 40, 49 (1960). The *Armstrong* principle is vague, making it hard to translate into an applicable legal test. It does, however, provide room to fit the singling-out issue into the regulatory takings analysis. It seems plausible to argue that if a regulation singles out an individual or small group of property owners, it might be placing a burden on those property owners that should be more fairly placed on the public as a whole. Note, however, that the majority and dissent in *Penn Central* both quoted the *Armstrong* principle but disagreed on their reaction to Penn Central's argument that it was being unfairly singled out by the Landmarks Preservation Law.

6. *The Nuisance Exception.* In his dissent, Justice Rehnquist refers to "[t]he nuisance exception to the takings guarantee." The nuisance exception is the rule that the regulation of a nuisance is never a taking. You are already familiar with this general idea from *Alger* and *Mugler*. We noted above that the *Alger* and *Mugler* approach was broader than the regulation of common-law nuisance. We also raised, in our discussion of those cases and of *Mahon*, the important issue of whether the legislature could avoid a takings claim by defining the regulated activity as a nuisance. We return to these issues shortly in our discussion of *Lucas v. South Carolina Coastal Council*.

7. *The Typical* Penn Central *Outcome.* In applying the *Penn Central* factors to a hypothetical set of facts, you might think that the property owner should have a strong

ARMSTRONG V. UNITED STATES

Armstrong's most significant impact on contemporary regulatory takings jurisprudence comes from ritual quotation of the *Armstrong* principle. The case is interesting for at least two other reasons. First, it is unusual in that it involved application of the Just Compensation Clause to an exercise of sovereign immunity. The complaining property owners were contractors who had held mechanics' liens in ships being built for the U.S. Navy. When the shipbuilder defaulted on its obligations to build the ships and went bankrupt, the United States exercised a contractual right to take ownership of the ships. Once the United States took ownership, the liens became unenforceable because of sovereign immunity. The Court held that the destruction of the liens was a taking of property and that the contractors were entitled to just compensation. Second, it is unusual in that the members of the Court initially voted in conference to rule against the contractors. Justice Harlan circulated a draft opinion that rejected the takings claim on the formalistic basis that an exercise of sovereign immunity is not an exercise of eminent domain. Justices Black and Brennan circulated dissents. Justice Black's dissent included the appeal to fairness that came to be known as the *Armstrong* principle. When it became clear that the majority view had shifted, Justice Black was assigned the task of writing the opinion of the Court. The rhetorical force of the *Armstrong* principle likely played a role in convincing some of the Justices to change their votes.[33]

regulatory takings claim. The factors are relatively vague, and it often is easy to come up with good arguments for each side. You should know, however, that property owners almost always lose *Penn Central* takings claims. Why do you think that this would be the case?

b. Our First Per Se Rule: Physical Invasions

A government regulation that causes a permanent physical invasion of private property is a per se taking. Over time, a number of Supreme Court cases had found government actions that resulted in physical invasions of property to be takings. This trend crystallized into a per se rule in the 1982 case, *Loretto v. Teleprompter Manhattan CATV Corp.* A brief excerpt from *Loretto* follows. The excerpt describes a number of earlier cases that provide useful examples of the broad range of physical invasions that have been found to be takings.

---

[33] *See* Justice Hugo Black Papers, Manuscript Division, Library of Congress, Washington D.C., Box 340; Justice William Brennan Papers, Manuscript Division, Library of Congress, Washington D.C., Box I:28, Folder 20; Box I:40, Folder; and Box II:6, Folder 2; Justice William O. Douglas Papers, Manuscript Division, Library of Congress, Washington, D.C., Box 1215; Justice Earl Warren Papers, Manuscript Division, Library of Congress, Washington D.C., Box 458, Folder 270.

LORETTO V. TELEPROMPTER MANHATTAN CATV CORP.

Supreme Court of the United States, 1982
458 U.S. 419

Justice MARSHALL delivered the opinion of the Court. This case presents the question whether a minor but permanent physical occupation of an owner's property authorized by government constitutes a "taking" of property for which just compensation is due under the Fifth and Fourteenth Amendments of the Constitution. New York law provides that a landlord must permit a cable television company to install its cable facilities upon his property. N.Y.Exec.Law §828(1) (McKinney Supp. 1981-1982). In this case, the cable installation occupied portions of appellant's roof and the side of her building. The New York Court of Appeals ruled that this appropriation does not amount to a taking. 53 N.Y.2d 124, 440 N.Y.S.2d 843, 423 N.E.2d 320 (1981). Because we conclude that such a physical occupation of property is a taking, we reverse.

Appellant Jean Loretto purchased a five-story apartment building located at 303 West 105th Street, New York City, in 1971. The previous owner had granted appellees Teleprompter Corp. and Teleprompter Manhattan CATV (collectively Teleprompter) permission to install a cable on the building and the exclusive privilege of furnishing cable television (CATV) services to the tenants. The New York Court of Appeals described the installation as follows:

"On June 1, 1970 TelePrompter installed a cable slightly less than one-half inch in diameter and of approximately 30 feet in length along the length of the building about 18 inches above the roof top, and directional taps, approximately 4 inches by 4 inches by 4 inches, on the front and rear of the roof. By June 8, 1970 the cable had been extended another 4 to 6 feet and cable had been run from the directional taps to the adjoining building at 305 West 105th Street." *Id.*, at 135, 440 N.Y.S.2d, at 847, 423 N.E.2d, at 324.

Teleprompter also installed two large silver boxes along the roof cables. The cables are attached by screws or nails penetrating the masonry at approximately two-foot intervals, and other equipment is installed by bolts. . . .

Prior to 1973, Teleprompter routinely obtained authorization for its installations from property owners along the cable's route, compensating the owners at the standard rate of 5% of the gross revenues that Teleprompter realized from the particular property. To facilitate tenant access to CATV, the State of New York enacted §828 of the Executive Law, effective January 1, 1973. Section 828 provides that a landlord may not "interfere with the installation of cable television facilities upon his property or premises," and may not demand payment from any tenant for permitting CATV, or demand payment from any CATV company "in excess of any amount which the [State Commission on Cable Television] shall, by regulation, determine to be reasonable." The landlord may, however, require the CATV company or the tenant to bear the cost of installation and to indemnify for any damage caused by the installation. Pursuant to §828(1)(b), the State Commission has ruled that a one-time $1 payment is the normal fee to which a landlord is entitled. . . . The Commission ruled that this nominal fee, which the Commission concluded was equivalent to what the landlord would receive if the property were condemned pursuant to New York's Transportation Corporations Law, satisfied constitutional requirements "in the absence of a special showing of greater damages attributable to the taking." Statement of General Policy, App. 52.

Appellant did not discover the existence of the cable until after she had purchased the building. She brought a class action against Teleprompter in 1976 on behalf of all owners of real property in the State on which Teleprompter has placed CATV components, alleging that Teleprompter's installation was a trespass and, insofar as it relied on §828, a taking without just compensation. She requested damages and injunctive relief. . . .

In *Penn Central Transportation Co. v. New York City, supra*, the Court surveyed some of the general principles governing the Takings Clause. The Court noted that no "set formula" existed to determine, in all cases, whether compensation is constitutionally due for a government restriction of property. Ordinarily, the Court must engage in "essentially ad hoc, factual inquiries." *Id.*, at 124, 98 S.Ct., at 2659. But the inquiry is not standardless. The economic impact of the regulation, especially the degree of interference with investment-backed expectations, is of particular significance. "So, too, is the character of the governmental action. A 'taking' may more readily be found when the interference with property can be characterized as a physical invasion by government, than when interference arises from some public program adjusting the benefits and burdens of economic life to promote the common good." *Ibid.* (citation omitted).

As *Penn Central* affirms, the Court has often upheld substantial regulation of an owner's use of his own property where deemed necessary to promote the public interest. At the same time, we have long considered a physical intrusion by government to be a property restriction of an unusually serious character for purposes of the Takings Clause. Our cases further establish that when the physical intrusion reaches the extreme form of a permanent physical occupation, a taking has occurred. In such a case, "the character of the government action" not only is an important factor in resolving whether the action works a taking but also is determinative.

When faced with a constitutional challenge to a permanent physical occupation of real property, this Court has invariably found a taking. As early as 1872, in *Pumpelly v. Green Bay Co.*, 13 Wall. (80 U.S.) 166, 20 L.Ed. 557, this Court held that the defendant's construction, pursuant to state authority, of a dam which permanently flooded plaintiff's property constituted a taking. A unanimous Court stated, without qualification, that "where real estate is actually invaded by superinduced additions of water, earth, sand, or other material, or by having any artificial structure placed on it, so as to effectually destroy or impair its usefulness, it is a taking, within the meaning of the Constitution." *Id.*, 13 Wall. (80 U.S.) at 181. . . .

More recent cases confirm the distinction between a permanent physical occupation, a physical invasion short of an occupation, and a regulation that merely restricts the use of property. In *United States v. Causby*, 328 U.S. 256, 66 S.Ct. 1062, 90 L.Ed. 1206 (1946), the Court ruled that frequent flights immediately above a landowner's property constituted a taking, comparing such overflights to the quintessential form of a taking:

> "If, by reason of the frequency and altitude of the flights, respondents could not use this land for any purpose, their loss would be complete. It would be as complete as if the United States had entered upon the surface of the land and taken exclusive possession of it." *Id.*, at 261, 66 S.Ct., at 1065 (footnote omitted).

As the Court further explained,

> "We would not doubt that, if the United States erected an elevated railway over respondents' land at the precise altitude where its planes now fly, there would be a partial taking, even though none of the supports of the structure rested on the land. The reason is that there would be an intrusion so immediate and direct as to subtract from the owner's full enjoyment of the property and to limit his exploitation of it." *Id.*, at 264-265, 66 S.Ct., at 1067.

The Court concluded that the damages to the respondents "were not merely consequential. They were the product of a direct invasion of respondents' domain." *Id.*, at 265-266, 66 S. Ct., at 1067-1068. . . . [See sidebar for more on *Causby*.]

Although this Court's most recent cases have not addressed the precise issue before us, they have emphasized that physical invasion cases are special and have not repudiated the rule that any permanent physical occupation is a taking. The cases state or imply that a physical invasion is subject to a balancing process, but they do not suggest that a permanent physical occupation would ever be exempt from the Takings Clause.

Penn Central Transportation Co. v. New York City, as noted above, contains one of the most complete discussions of the Takings Clause. The Court explained that resolving whether public action works a taking is ordinarily an ad hoc inquiry in which several factors are particularly significant—the economic impact of the regulation, the extent to which it interferes with investment-backed expectations, and the character of the governmental action. 438 U.S., at 124, 98 S.Ct., at 2659. The opinion does not repudiate the rule that a permanent physical occupation is a government action of such a unique character that it is a taking without regard to other factors that a court might ordinarily examine.

In *Kaiser Aetna v. United States*, 444 U.S. 164, 100 S.Ct. 383, 62 L.Ed.2d 332 (1979), the Court held that the Government's imposition of a navigational servitude requiring public access to a pond was a taking where the landowner had reasonably relied on

UNITED STATES V. CAUSBY

Causby is an interesting case. The property at issue was near the runway for an airport that was used for frequent military flights. The owners lived on the property and operated a chicken farm there. On their approach to the runway, planes could come within 100 feet of the surface of the property. As described by the Court:

> [The planes] come close enough at times to appear barely to miss the tops of the trees and at times so close to the tops of the trees as to blow the old leaves off. The noise is startling. And at night the glare from the planes brightly lights up the place. As a result of the noise, respondents had to give up their chicken business. As many as six to ten of their chickens were killed in one day by flying into the walls from fright. The total chickens lost in that manner was about 150. Production also fell off. The result was the destruction of the use of the property as a commercial chicken farm. Respondents are frequently deprived of their sleep and the family has become nervous and frightened.

The Court noted that the ancient *ad coleum* doctrine, under which the surface property owner owned from the sky to the center of the earth, "has no place in the modern world." Nonetheless, the surface property owner "must have exclusive control of the immediate reaches of the enveloping atmosphere" if the owner was "to have full enjoyment of the land." The owner "owns at owns at least as much of the space above the ground as he can occupy or use in connection with the land." Because the airplane overflights intruded into this space, the government was held to have appropriated an easement over the property.

Government consent in connecting the pond to navigable water. The Court emphasized that the servitude took the landowner's right to exclude, "one of the most essential sticks in the bundle of rights that are commonly characterized as property." *Id.*, at 176, 100 S.Ct., at 391. The Court explained:

> "This is not a case in which the Government is exercising its regulatory power in a manner that will cause an insubstantial devaluation of petitioner's private property; rather, the imposition of the navigational servitude in this context will result in an actual physical invasion of the privately owned marina. . . . And even if the Government physically invades only an easement in property, it must nonetheless pay compensation. *See United States v. Causby*, 328 U.S. 256, 265 [66 S.Ct. 1062, 1067, 90 L.Ed. 1206] (1946); *Portsmouth Co. v. United States*, 260 U.S. 327 [43 S.Ct. 135, 67 L.Ed. 287] (1922)." *Id.*, at 180, 100 S.Ct., at 393 (emphasis added).

Although the easement of passage, not being a permanent occupation of land, was not considered a taking per se, Kaiser Aetna reemphasizes that a physical invasion is a government intrusion of an unusually serious character. . . .

In short, when the "character of the governmental action," *Penn Central*, 438 U.S., at 124, 98 S.Ct., at 2659, is a permanent physical occupation of property, our cases uniformly have found a taking to the extent of the occupation, without regard to whether the action achieves an important public benefit or has only minimal economic impact on the owner. . . .

Our holding today is very narrow. We affirm the traditional rule that a permanent physical occupation of property is a taking. In such a case, the property owner entertains a historically rooted expectation of compensation, and the character of the invasion is qualitatively more intrusive than perhaps any other category of property regulation. We do not, however, question the equally substantial authority upholding a State's broad power to impose appropriate restrictions upon an owner's *use* of his property.

[The dissenting opinion of Justice Blackmun, joined by Justices Brennan and White, is omitted.]

NOTE

Under the *Loretto* rule, any government action that results in a permanent physical invasion is a per se taking. This is true even if, as in *Loretto*, the invasion is trivial. (The complaining property owner in *Loretto* ultimately was awarded $1 in compensation.) Physical invasions include flooding (*Pumpelly*) and airplane overflights (*Causby*). They also include requirements that the public be allowed to physically access the property (*Kaiser Aetna*). A later case made it even clearer that a regulation requiring that the property owner permit public access to the property, in effect acquiring a public easement across the property, would be a taking under the *Loretto* rule. *See Nollan v. California Coastal Commn.*, 483 U.S. 825 (1987). We will discuss *Nollan* further below when we get to the topic of exactions.

c. Two More Per Se Rules: Total Diminutions and the Nuisance/Background Principles Exception

Our next case, *Lucas v. South Carolina Coastal Council*, establishes a rule that regulations that cause total diminutions in value are per se takings. It also provides us with our best statement of the current status of the "nuisance exception"—that is, the rule that the regulation of a nuisance is never a taking. At several points in our prior discussion, we highlighted the issue of whether the legislature can avoid takings liability by labeling the regulated use a nuisance. Pay close attention to what the Justices have to say about this issue, both in the opinion of the Court and in dissents.

DIMINUTION IN VALUE

DEFINING "NUISANCE"

LUCAS V. SOUTH CAROLINA COASTAL COUNCIL

United States Supreme Court, 1992
505 U.S. 1003

Justice SCALIA delivered the opinion of the Court. In 1986, petitioner David H. Lucas paid $975,000 for two residential lots on the Isle of Palms in Charleston County, South Carolina, on which he intended to build single-family homes. In 1988, however, the South Carolina Legislature enacted the Beachfront Management Act, S.C.Code Ann. §48-39-250 et seq. (Supp.1990), which had the direct effect of barring petitioner from erecting any permanent habitable structures on his two parcels. *See* §48-39-290(A). A state trial court found that this prohibition rendered Lucas's parcels "valueless." App. to Pet. for Cert. 37. This case requires us to decide whether the Act's dramatic effect on the economic value of Lucas's lots accomplished a taking of private property under the Fifth and Fourteenth Amendments requiring the payment of "just compensation." U.S. Const., Amdt. 5.

I

A

South Carolina's expressed interest in intensively managing development activities in the so-called "coastal zone" dates from 1977 when, in the aftermath of Congress's passage of the federal Coastal Zone Management Act of 1972, 86 Stat. 1280, as amended, 16 U.S.C. §1451 et seq., the legislature enacted a Coastal Zone Management Act of its own. *See* S.C.Code Ann. §48-39-10 et seq. (1987). In its original form, the South Carolina Act required owners of coastal zone land that qualified as a "critical area" (defined in the legislation to include beaches and immediately adjacent sand dunes, §48-39-10(J)) to obtain a permit from the newly created South Carolina Coastal Council (Council) (respondent here) prior to committing the land to a "use other than the use the critical area was devoted to on [September 28, 1977]." §48-39-130(A).

In the late 1970's, Lucas and others began extensive residential development of the Isle of Palms, a barrier island situated eastward of the city of Charleston. Toward the close of the development cycle for one residential subdivision known as "Beachwood East," Lucas in 1986 purchased the two lots at issue in this litigation for his own account. No portion of the lots, which were located approximately 300 feet from the beach, qualified as a "critical area" under the 1977 Act; accordingly, at the time Lucas acquired these parcels, he was not legally obliged to obtain a permit from the Council in advance of any development activity. His intention with respect to the lots was to do what the owners of the immediately adjacent parcels had already done: erect single-family residences. He commissioned architectural drawings for this purpose.

The Beachfront Management Act brought Lucas's plans to an abrupt end. Under that 1988 legislation, the Council was directed to establish a "baseline" connecting the landward-most "point[s] of erosion . . . during the past forty years" in the region of the Isle of Palms that includes Lucas's lots. S.C.Code Ann. §48-39-280(A)(2) (Supp.1988). In action not challenged here, the Council fixed this baseline landward of Lucas's parcels. That was significant, for under the Act construction of occupiable improvements[2] was flatly prohibited seaward of a line drawn 20 feet landward of, and parallel to, the baseline. §48-39-290(A). The Act provided no exceptions.

B

Lucas promptly filed suit in the South Carolina Court of Common Pleas, contending that the Beachfront Management Act's construction bar effected a taking of his property without just compensation. Lucas did not take issue with the validity of the Act as a lawful exercise of South Carolina's police power, but contended that the Act's complete extinguishment of his property's value entitled him to compensation regardless of whether the legislature had acted in furtherance of legitimate police power objectives. Following a bench trial, the court agreed. Among its factual determinations was the finding that "at the time Lucas purchased the two lots, both were zoned for single-family residential construction and . . . there were no restrictions imposed upon such use of the property by either the State of South Carolina, the County of Charleston, or the Town of the Isle of Palms." App. to Pet. for Cert. 36. The trial court further found that the Beachfront Management Act decreed a permanent ban on construction insofar as Lucas's lots were concerned, and that this prohibition "deprive[d] Lucas of any reasonable economic use of the lots, . . . eliminated the unrestricted right of use, and render[ed] them valueless." Id., at 37. The court thus concluded that Lucas's properties had been "taken" by operation of the Act, and it ordered respondent to pay "just compensation" in the amount of $1,232,387.50. Id., at 40.

DIMINUTION IN VALUE

The Supreme Court of South Carolina reversed. It found dispositive what it described as Lucas's concession "that the Beachfront Management Act [was] properly and validly designed to preserve . . . South Carolina's beaches." 304 S.C. 376, 379, 404 S.E.2d 895, 896 (1991). Failing an attack on the validity of the statute as such, the court believed itself bound to accept the "uncontested . . . findings" of the South Carolina Legislature that new construction in the coastal zone—such as petitioner intended—threatened this public resource. Id., at 383, 404 S.E.2d, at 898. The court ruled that when a regulation respecting the use of property is designed "to prevent serious public harm," id., at 383,

---

[2] The Act did allow the construction of certain nonhabitable improvements, e.g., "wooden walkways no larger in width than six feet," and "small wooden decks no larger than one hundred forty-four square feet." §§48-39-290(A)(1) and (2).

404 S.E.2d, at 899 (citing, *inter alia*, *Mugler v. Kansas*, 123 U.S. 623, 8 S.Ct. 273, 31 L.Ed. 205 (1887)), no compensation is owing under the Takings Clause regardless of the regulation's effect on the property's value.

DEFINING "NUISANCE"

Two justices dissented. They acknowledged that our *Mugler* line of cases recognizes governmental power to prohibit "noxious" uses of property—i.e., uses of property akin to "public nuisances"—without having to pay compensation. But they would not have characterized the Beachfront Management Act's "primary purpose [as] the prevention of a nuisance." 304 S.C., at 395, 404 S.E.2d, at 906 (Harwell, J., dissenting). To the dissenters, the chief purposes of the legislation, among them the promotion of tourism and the creation of a "habitat for indigenous flora and fauna," could not fairly be compared to nuisance abatement. *Id.*, at 396, 404 S.E.2d, at 906. As a consequence, they would have affirmed the trial court's conclusion that the Act's obliteration of the value of petitioner's lots accomplished a taking.

We granted certiorari.

II

As a threshold matter, we must briefly address the Council's suggestion that this case is inappropriate for plenary review. After briefing and argument before the South Carolina Supreme Court, but prior to issuance of that court's opinion, the Beachfront Management Act was amended to authorize the Council, in certain circumstances, to issue "special permits" for the construction or reconstruction of habitable structures seaward of the baseline. *See* S.C.Code Ann. §48-39-290(D)(1) (Supp.1991). According to the Council, this amendment renders Lucas's claim of a permanent deprivation unripe, as Lucas may yet be able to secure permission to build on his property. "[The Court's] cases," we are reminded, "uniformly reflect an insistence on knowing the nature and extent of permitted development before adjudicating the constitutionality of the regulations that purport to limit it." *MacDonald, Sommer & Frates v. Yolo County*, 477 U.S. 340, 351, 106 S.Ct. 2561, 2567, 91 L.Ed.2d 285 (1986). *See also Agins v. City of Tiburon*, 447 U.S. 255, 260, 100 S.Ct. 2138, 2141, 65 L.Ed.2d 106 (1980). Because petitioner "has not yet obtained a final decision regarding how [he] will be allowed to develop [his] property," *Williamson County Regional Planning Comm'n v. Hamilton Bank of Johnson City*, 473 U.S. 172, 190, 105 S.Ct. 3108, 3118, 87 L.Ed.2d 126 (1985), the Council argues that he is not yet entitled to definitive adjudication of his takings claim in this Court.

We think these considerations would preclude review had the South Carolina Supreme Court rested its judgment on ripeness grounds, as it was (essentially) invited to do by the Council. *See* Brief for Respondent 9, n. 3. The South Carolina Supreme Court shrugged off the possibility of further administrative and trial proceedings, however, preferring to dispose of Lucas's takings claim on the merits. *Cf.*, e.g., *San Diego Gas & Electric Co. v. San Diego*, 450 U.S. 621, 631-632, 101 S.Ct. 1287, 1293-1294, 67 L.Ed.2d 551 (1981). . . . In these circumstances, we think it would not accord with sound process to insist that Lucas pursue the late-created "special permit" procedure before his takings claim can be considered ripe. . . .

III

A

Prior to Justice Holmes's exposition in *Pennsylvania Coal Co. v. Mahon*, 260 U.S. 393, 43 S.Ct. 158, 67 L.Ed. 322 (1922), it was generally thought that the Takings Clause reached only a "direct appropriation" of property, *Legal Tender Cases*, 12 Wall. 457, 551, 20 L.Ed. 287 (1871), or the functional equivalent of a "practical ouster of [the owner's] possession," *Transportation Co. v. Chicago*, 99 U.S. 635, 642, 25 L.Ed. 336 (1879). *See also Gibson v. United States*, 166 U.S. 269, 275-276, 17 S.Ct. 578, 580, 41 L.Ed. 996 (1897). Justice Holmes recognized in *Mahon*, however, that if the protection against physical appropriations of private property was to be meaningfully enforced, the government's power to redefine the range of interests included in the ownership of property was necessarily constrained by constitutional limits. 260 U.S., at 414-415, 43 S.Ct., at 160. If, instead, the uses of private property were subject to unbridled, uncompensated qualification under the police power, "the natural tendency of human nature [would be] to extend the qualification more and more until at last private property disappear[ed]." *Id.*, at 415, 43 S.Ct., at 160. These considerations gave birth in that case to the oft-cited maxim that, "while property may be regulated to a certain extent, if regulation goes too far it will be recognized as a taking." *Ibid.*

Nevertheless, our decision in *Mahon* offered little insight into when, and under what circumstances, a given regulation would be seen as going "too far" for purposes of the Fifth Amendment. In 70-odd years of succeeding "regulatory takings" jurisprudence, we have generally eschewed any "'set formula'" for determining how far is too far, preferring to "engag[e] in . . . essentially ad hoc, factual inquiries." *Penn Central Transportation Co. v. New York City*, 438 U.S. 104, 124, 98 S.Ct. 2646, 2659, 57 L.Ed.2d 631 (1978) (quoting *Goldblatt v. Hempstead*, 369 U.S. 590, 594, 82 S.Ct. 987, 990, 8 L.Ed.2d 130 (1962)). *See* Epstein, *Takings: Descent and Resurrection*, 1987 S.Ct. Rev. 1, 4. We have, however, described at least two discrete categories of regulatory action as compensable without case-specific inquiry into the public interest advanced in support of the restraint. The first encompasses regulations that compel the property owner to suffer a physical "invasion" of his property. In general (at least with regard to permanent invasions), no matter how minute the intrusion, and no matter how weighty the public purpose behind it, we have required compensation. For example, in *Loretto v. Teleprompter Manhattan CATV Corp.*, 458 U.S. 419, 102 S.Ct. 3164, 73 L.Ed.2d 868 (1982), we determined that New York's law requiring landlords to allow television cable companies to emplace cable facilities in their apartment buildings constituted a taking, *id.*, at 435-440, 102 S.Ct., at 3175-3178, even though the facilities occupied at most only 1

1/2 cubic feet of the landlords' property, see *id.*, at 438, n. 16, 102 S.Ct., at 3177. *See also United States v. Causby*, 328 U.S. 256, 265, and n. 10, 66 S.Ct. 1062, 1067, and n. 10, 90 L.Ed. 1206 (1946) (physical invasions of airspace); *cf. Kaiser Aetna v. United States*, 444 U.S. 164, 100 S.Ct. 383, 62 L.Ed.2d 332 (1979) (imposition of navigational servitude upon private marina).

DIMINUTION IN VALUE

The second situation in which we have found categorical treatment appropriate is where regulation denies all economically beneficial or productive use of land. *See Agins*, 447 U.S., at 260, 100 S.Ct., at 2141; *see also Nollan v. California Coastal Comm'n*, 483 U.S. 825, 834, 107 S.Ct. 3141, 3147, 97 L.Ed.2d 677 (1987); *Keystone Bituminous Coal Assn. v. DeBenedictis*, 480 U.S. 470, 495, 107 S.Ct. 1232, 1247, 94 L.Ed.2d 472 (1987); *Hodel v. Virginia Surface Mining & Reclamation Assn., Inc.*, 452 U.S. 264, 295-296, 101 S.Ct. 2352, 2370, 69 L.Ed.2d 1 (1981).[6] As we have said on numerous occasions, the Fifth Amendment is violated when land-use regulation "does not substantially advance legitimate state interests or denies an owner economically viable use of his land." *Agins*, *supra*, 447 U.S., at 260, 100 S.Ct., at 2141 (citations omitted) (emphasis added).[7]

---

[6] We will not attempt to respond to all of Justice Blackmun's mistaken citation of case precedent. Characteristic of its nature is his assertion that the cases we discuss here stand merely for the proposition "that proof that a regulation does not deny an owner economic use of his property is sufficient to defeat a facial takings challenge" and not for the point that "denial of such use is sufficient to establish a takings claim regardless of any other consideration." Post, at 2911, n. 11. The cases say, repeatedly and unmistakably, that "'[t]he test to be applied in considering [a] facial [takings] challenge is fairly straightforward. A statute regulating the uses that can be made of property effects a taking if it "denies an owner economically viable use of his land."'" Keystone, 480 U.S., at 495, 107 S.Ct., at 1247 (quoting Hodel, 452 U.S., at 295-296, 101 S.Ct., at 2370 (quoting Agins, 447 U.S., at 260, 100 S.Ct., at 2141)) (emphasis added).

Justice BLACKMUN describes that rule (which we do not invent but merely apply today) as "alter[ing] the long-settled rules of review" by foisting on the State "the burden of showing [its] regulation is not a taking." Post, at 2909. This is of course wrong. Lucas had to do more than simply file a lawsuit to establish his constitutional entitlement; he had to show that the Beachfront Management Act denied him economically beneficial use of his land. Our analysis presumes the unconstitutionality of state land-use regulation only in the sense that any rule with exceptions presumes the invalidity of a law that violates it—for example, the rule generally prohibiting content-based restrictions on speech. See, e.g., Simon & Schuster, Inc. v. N.Y. Members of State Crime Victims Bd., 502 U.S. 105, 115, 112 S.Ct. 501, 508, 116 L.Ed.2d 476 (1991) ("A statute is presumptively inconsistent with the First Amendment if it imposes a financial burden on speakers because of the content of their speech"). Justice BLACKMUN's real quarrel is with the substantive standard of liability we apply in this case, a long-established standard we see no need to repudiate.

[7] Regrettably, the rhetorical force of our "deprivation of all economically feasible use" rule is greater than its precision, since the rule does not make clear the "property interest" against which the loss of value is to be measured. When, for example, a regulation requires a developer to leave 90% of a rural tract in its natural state, it is unclear whether we would analyze the situation as one in which the owner has been deprived of all economically beneficial use of the burdened portion of the tract, or as one in which the owner has suffered a mere diminution in value of the tract as a whole. (For an extreme—and, we think, unsupportable—view of the relevant calculus, see *Penn Central Transportation Co. v. New York City*, 42 N.Y.2d 324, 333-334, 397 N.Y.S.2d 914, 920, 366 N.E.2d 1271, 1276-1277 (1977), *aff'd*, 438 U.S. 104, 98 S.Ct. 2646, 57 L.Ed.2d 631 (1978), where the state court examined

We have never set forth the justification for this rule. Perhaps it is simply, as Justice Brennan suggested, that total deprivation of beneficial use is, from the landowner's point of view, the equivalent of a physical appropriation. *See San Diego Gas & Electric Co. v. San Diego*, 450 U.S., at 652, 101 S.Ct., at 1304 (dissenting opinion). "[F]or what is the land but the profits thereof[?]" 1 E. Coke, *Institutes*, ch. 1, §1 (1st Am. ed. 1812). Surely, at least, in the extraordinary circumstance when no productive or economically beneficial use of land is permitted, it is less realistic to indulge our usual assumption that the legislature is simply "adjusting the benefits and burdens of economic life," *Penn Central Transportation Co.*, 438 U.S., at 124, 98 S.Ct., at 2659, in a manner that secures an "average reciprocity of advantage" to everyone concerned, *Pennsylvania Coal Co. v. Mahon*, 260 U.S., at 415, 43 S.Ct., at 160. And the functional basis for permitting the government, by regulation, to affect property values without compensation—that "Government hardly could go on if to some extent values incident to property could not be diminished without paying for every such change in the general law," *id.*, at 413, 43 S.Ct., at 159—does not apply to the relatively rare situations where the government has deprived a landowner of all economically beneficial uses.

On the other side of the balance, affirmatively supporting a compensation requirement, is the fact that regulations that leave the owner of land without economically beneficial or productive options for its use—typically, as here, by requiring land to be left substantially in its natural state—carry with them a heightened risk that private property is being pressed into some form of public service under the guise of mitigating serious public harm. *See, e.g., Annicelli v. South Kingstown*, 463 A.2d 133, 140-141 (R.I.1983) (prohibition on construction adjacent to beach justified on twin grounds of safety and "conservation of open space"); *Morris County Land Improvement Co. v. Parsippany-Troy Hills Township*, 40 N.J. 539, 552-553, 193 A.2d 232, 240 (1963) (prohibition on filling marshlands imposed in order to preserve region as water detention basin and create wildlife refuge). As Justice Brennan explained: "From the government's point of view, the benefits flowing to the public from preservation of open space through regulation may be equally great as from creating a wildlife refuge through

---

the diminution in a particular parcel's value produced by a municipal ordinance in light of total value of the takings claimant's other holdings in the vicinity.) Unsurprisingly, this uncertainty regarding the composition of the denominator in our "deprivation" fraction has produced inconsistent pronouncements by the Court. *Compare Pennsylvania Coal Co. v. Mahon*, 260 U.S. 393, 414, 43 S.Ct. 158, 160, 67 L.Ed. 322 (1922) (law restricting subsurface extraction of coal held to effect a taking), *with Keystone Bituminous Coal Assn. v. DeBenedictis*, 480 U.S. 470, 497-502, 107 S.Ct. 1232, 1248-1251, 94 L.Ed.2d 472 (1987) (nearly identical law held not to effect a taking); *see also id.*, at 515-520, 107 S.Ct., at 1257-1260 (REHNQUIST, C.J., dissenting); Rose, *Mahon Reconstructed: Why the Takings Issue is Still a Muddle*, 57 S.Cal.L.Rev. 561, 566-569 (1984). The answer to this difficult question may lie in how the owner's reasonable expectations have been shaped by the State's law of property—i.e., whether and to what degree the State's law has accorded legal recognition and protection to the particular interest in land with respect to which the takings claimant alleges a diminution in (or elimination of) value. In any event, we avoid this difficulty in the present case, since the "interest in land" that Lucas has pleaded (a fee simple interest) is an estate with a rich tradition of protection at common law, and since the South Carolina Court of Common Pleas found that the Beachfront Management Act left each of Lucas's beachfront lots without economic value.

formal condemnation or increasing electricity production through a dam project that floods private property." *San Diego Gas & Elec. Co., supra*, 450 U.S., at 652, 101 S.Ct., at 1304 (dissenting opinion). The many statutes on the books, both state and federal, that provide for the use of eminent domain to impose servitudes on private scenic lands preventing developmental uses, or to acquire such lands altogether, suggest the practical equivalence in this setting of negative regulation and appropriation. *See*, e.g., 16 U.S.C. §410ff-1(a) (authorizing acquisition of "lands, waters, or interests [within Channel Islands National Park] (including but not limited to scenic easements)"); §460aa-2(a) (authorizing acquisition of "any lands, or lesser interests therein, including mineral interests and scenic easements" within Sawtooth National Recreation Area); §§3921-3923 (authorizing acquisition of wetlands); N.C. Gen.Stat. §113A-38 (1990) (authorizing acquisition of, inter alia, " 'scenic easements' " within the North Carolina natural and scenic rivers system); Tenn.Code Ann. §§11-15-101 to 11-15-108 (1987) (authorizing acquisition of "protective easements" and other rights in real property adjacent to State's historic, architectural, archaeological, or cultural resources).

DIMINUTION IN
VALUE

We think, in short, that there are good reasons for our frequently expressed belief that when the owner of real property has been called upon to sacrifice all economically beneficial uses in the name of the common good, that is, to leave his property economically idle, he has suffered a taking.[8]

---

[8] Justice STEVENS criticizes the "deprivation of all economically beneficial use" rule as "wholly arbitrary," in that "[the] landowner whose property is diminished in value 95% recovers nothing," while the landowner who suffers a complete elimination of value "recovers the land's full value." Post, at 2919. This analysis errs in its assumption that the landowner whose deprivation is one step short of complete is not entitled to compensation. Such an owner might not be able to claim the benefit of our categorical formulation, but, as we have acknowledged time and again, "[t]he economic impact of the regulation on the claimant and . . . the extent to which the regulation has interfered with distinct investment-backed expectations" are keenly relevant to takings analysis generally. *Penn Central Transportation Co. v. New York City*, 438 U.S. 104, 124, 98 S.Ct. 2646, 2659, 57 L.Ed.2d 631 (1978). It is true that in at least some cases the landowner with 95% loss will get nothing, while the landowner with total loss will recover in full. But that occasional result is no more strange than the gross disparity between the landowner whose premises are taken for a highway (who recovers in full) and the landowner whose property is reduced to 5% of its former value by the highway (who recovers nothing). Takings law is full of these "all-or-nothing" situations.

Justice STEVENS similarly misinterprets our focus on "developmental" uses of property (the uses proscribed by the Beachfront Management Act) as betraying an "assumption that the only uses of property cognizable under the Constitution are developmental uses." Post, at 2919, n. 3. We make no such assumption. Though our prior takings cases evince an abiding concern for the productive use of, and economic investment in, land, there are plainly a number of noneconomic interests in land whose impairment will invite exceedingly close scrutiny under the Takings Clause. *See*, e.g., *Loretto v. Teleprompter Manhattan CATV Corp.*, 458 U.S. 419, 436, 102 S.Ct. 3164, 3176, 73 L.Ed.2d 868 (1982) (interest in excluding strangers from one's land).

B

The trial court found Lucas's two beachfront lots to have been rendered valueless by respondent's enforcement of the coastal-zone construction ban.[9] Under Lucas's theory of the case, which rested upon our "no economically viable use" statements, that finding entitled him to compensation. Lucas believed it unnecessary to take issue with either the purposes behind the Beachfront Management Act, or the means chosen by the South Carolina Legislature to effectuate those purposes. The South Carolina Supreme Court, however, thought otherwise. In its view, the Beachfront Management Act was no ordinary enactment, but involved an exercise of South Carolina's "police powers" to mitigate the harm to the public interest that petitioner's use of his land might occasion. 304 S.C., at 384, 404 S.E.2d, at 899. By neglecting to dispute the findings enumerated in the Act or otherwise to challenge the legislature's purposes, petitioner "concede [d] that the beach/dune area of South Carolina's shores is an extremely valuable public resource; that the erection of new construction, inter alia, contributes to the erosion and destruction of this public resource; and that discouraging new construction in close proximity to the beach/dune area is necessary to prevent a great public harm." *Id.*, at 382-383, 404 S.E.2d, at 898. In the court's view, these concessions brought petitioner's challenge within a long line of this Court's cases sustaining against Due Process and Takings Clause challenges the State's use of its "police powers" to enjoin a property owner from activities akin to public nuisances. *See Mugler v. Kansas*, 123 U.S. 623, 8 S.Ct. 273, 31 L.Ed. 205 (1887) (law prohibiting manufacture of alcoholic beverages); *Hadacheck v. Sebastian*, 239 U.S. 394, 36 S.Ct. 143, 60 L.Ed. 348 (1915) (law barring operation of brick mill in residential area); *Miller v. Schoene*, 276 U.S. 272, 48 S.Ct. 246, 72 L.Ed. 568 (1928) (order to destroy diseased cedar trees to prevent infection of nearby orchards); *Goldblatt v. Hempstead*, 369 U.S. 590, 82 S.Ct. 987, 8 L.Ed.2d 130 (1962) (law effectively preventing continued operation of quarry in residential area).

It is correct that many of our prior opinions have suggested that "harmful or noxious uses" of property may be proscribed by government regulation without the requirement of compensation. For a number of reasons, however, we think the South Carolina Supreme Court was too quick to conclude that that principle decides the present case. The "harmful or noxious uses" principle was the Court's early attempt to describe in theoretical terms why government may, consistent with the Takings Clause, affect property values by regulation without incurring an obligation to compensate—a reality we nowadays acknowledge explicitly with respect to the full scope of the State's police

---

[9] This finding was the premise of the petition for certiorari, and since it was not challenged in the brief in opposition we decline to entertain the argument in respondent's brief on the merits, see Brief for Respondent 45-50, that the finding was erroneous. Instead, we decide the question presented under the same factual assumptions as did the Supreme Court of South Carolina. *See Oklahoma City v. Tuttle*, 471 U.S. 808, 816, 105 S.Ct. 2427, 2432, 85 L.Ed.2d 791 (1985).

power. *See, e.g.*, Penn Central Transportation Co., 438 U.S., at 125, 98 S.Ct., at 2659 (where State "reasonably conclude[s] that 'the health, safety, morals, or general welfare' would be promoted by prohibiting particular contemplated uses of land," compensation need not accompany prohibition); *see also Nollan v. California Coastal Comm'n*, 483 U.S., at 834-835, 107 S.Ct., at 3147 ("Our cases have not elaborated on the standards for determining what constitutes a 'legitimate state interest[,]' [but] [t]hey have made clear . . . that a broad range of governmental purposes and regulations satisfy these requirements"). We made this very point in Penn Central Transportation Co., where, in the course of sustaining New York City's landmarks preservation program against a takings challenge, we rejected the petitioner's suggestion that *Mugler* and the cases following it were premised on, and thus limited by, some objective conception of "noxiousness" . . . "Harmful or noxious use" analysis was, in other words, simply the progenitor of our more contemporary statements that "land-use regulation does not effect a taking if it 'substantially advance[s] legitimate state interests'. . . ." *Nollan, supra*, 483 U.S., at 834, 107 S.Ct., at 3147 (quoting *Agins v. Tiburon*, 447 U.S., at 260, 100 S.Ct., at 2141); *see also Penn Central Transportation Co., supra*, 438 U.S., at 127, 98 S.Ct., at 2660; *Euclid v. Ambler Realty Co.*, 272 U.S. 365, 387-388, 47 S.Ct. 114, 118, 71 L.Ed. 303 (1926).

The transition from our early focus on control of "noxious" uses to our contemporary understanding of the broad realm within which government may regulate without compensation was an easy one, since the distinction between "harm-preventing" and "benefit-conferring" regulation is often in the eye of the beholder. It is quite possible, for example, to describe in either fashion the ecological, economic, and esthetic concerns that inspired the South Carolina Legislature in the present case. One could say that imposing a servitude on Lucas's land is necessary in order to prevent his use of it from "harming" South Carolina's ecological resources; or, instead, in order to achieve the "benefits" of an ecological preserve.[11] Compare, e.g., 5 *Claridge v. New Hampshire Wetlands Board*, 125 N.H. 745, 752, 485 A.2d 287, 292 (1984) (owner may, without compensation, be barred from filling wetlands because landfilling would deprive adjacent coastal habitats and marine fisheries of ecological

---

[11] In the present case, in fact, some of the "[South Carolina] legislature's 'findings'" to which the South Carolina Supreme Court purported to defer in characterizing the purpose of the Act as "harm-preventing," 304 S.C. 376, 385, 404 S.E.2d 895, 900 (1991), seem to us phrased in "benefit-conferring" language instead. For example, they describe the importance of a construction ban in enhancing "South Carolina's annual tourism industry revenue," S.C. Code Ann. §48-39-250(1)(b) (Supp.1991), in "provid[ing] habitat for numerous species of plants and animals, several of which are threatened or endangered," §48-39-250(1)(c), and in "provid[ing] a natural healthy environment for the citizens of South Carolina to spend leisure time which serves their physical and mental well-being," §48-39-250(1)(d). It would be pointless to make the outcome of this case hang upon this terminology, since the same interests could readily be described in "harm-preventing" fashion.

Justice BLACKMUN, however, apparently insists that we must make the outcome hinge (exclusively) upon the South Carolina Legislature's other, "harm-preventing" characterizations, focusing on the declaration that

support), *with*, e.g., *Bartlett v. Zoning Comm'n of Old Lyme*, 161 Conn. 24, 30, 282 A.2d 907, 910 (1971) (owner barred from filling tidal marshland must be compensated, despite municipality's "laudable" goal of "preserv[ing] marshlands from encroachment or destruction"). Whether one or the other of the competing characterizations will come to one's lips in a particular case depends primarily upon one's evaluation of the worth of competing uses of real estate. *See* Restatement (Second) of Torts §822, Comment g, p. 112 (1979) ("Practically all human activities unless carried on in a wilderness interfere to some extent with others or involve some risk of interference"). A given restraint will be seen as mitigating "harm" to the adjacent parcels or securing a "benefit" for them, depending upon the observer's evaluation of the relative importance of the use that the restraint favors. *See* Sax, *Takings and the Police Power*, 74 Yale L.J. 36, 49 (1964) ("[T]he problem [in this area] is not one of noxiousness or harm-creating activity at all; rather it is a problem of inconsistency between perfectly innocent and independently desirable uses"). Whether Lucas's construction of single-family residences on his parcels should be described as bringing "harm" to South Carolina's adjacent ecological resources thus depends principally upon whether the describer believes that the State's use interest in nurturing those resources is so important that any competing adjacent use must yield.[12]

When it is understood that "prevention of harmful use" was merely our early formulation of the police power justification necessary to sustain (without compensation) any regulatory diminution in value; and that the distinction between regulation that "prevents harmful use" and that which "confers benefits" is difficult, if not impossible, to discern on an objective, value-free basis; it becomes self-evident that noxious-use logic cannot serve as a touchstone to distinguish regulatory "takings"—which require compensation—from regulatory deprivations that do not require compensation. A fortiori the legislature's recitation of a noxious-use justification cannot be the basis for departing from our categorical rule that total regulatory takings must be compensated. If it were, departure would virtually always be allowed. The South Carolina Supreme Court's

DEFINING "NUISANCE"

"prohibitions on building in front of the setback line are necessary to protect people and property from storms, high tides, and beach erosion." Post, at 2906. He says "[n]othing in the record undermines [this] assessment," *ibid.*, apparently seeing no significance in the fact that the statute permits owners of existing structures to remain (and even to rebuild if their structures are not "destroyed beyond repair," S.C. Code Ann. §48-39-290(B) (Supp.1988)), and in the fact that the 1990 amendment authorizes the Council to issue permits for new construction in violation of the uniform prohibition, *see* S.C. Code Ann. §48-39-290(D)(1) (Supp.1991).

[12] In Justice Blackmun's view, even with respect to regulations that deprive an owner of all developmental or economically beneficial land uses, the test for required compensation is whether the legislature has recited a harm-preventing justification for its action. *See* post, at 2906, 2910-2912. Since such a justification can be formulated in practically every case, this amounts to a test of whether the legislature has a stupid staff. We think the Takings Clause requires courts to do more than insist upon artful harm-preventing characterizations.

DEFINING "NUISANCE"

approach would essentially nullify *Mahon*'s affirmation of limits to the noncompensable exercise of the police power. Our cases provide no support for this: None of them that employed the logic of "harmful use" prevention to sustain a regulation involved an allegation that the regulation wholly eliminated the value of the claimant's land. *See Keystone Bituminous Coal Assn.*, 480 U.S., at 513-514, 107 S.Ct., at 1257 (Rehnquist, C.J., dissenting).

Where the State seeks to sustain regulation that deprives land of all economically beneficial use, we think it may resist compensation only if the logically antecedent inquiry into the nature of the owner's estate shows that the proscribed use interests were not part of his title to begin with. This accords, we think, with our "takings" jurisprudence, which has traditionally been guided by the understandings of our citizens regarding the content of, and the State's power over, the "bundle of rights" that they acquire when they obtain title to property. It seems to us that the property owner necessarily expects the uses of his property to be restricted, from time to time, by various measures newly enacted by the State in legitimate exercise of its police powers; "[a]s long recognized, some values are enjoyed under an implied limitation and must yield to the police power." *Pennsylvania Coal Co. v. Mahon*, 260 U.S., at 413, 43 S.Ct., at 159. And in the case of personal property, by reason of the State's traditionally high degree of control over commercial dealings, he ought to be aware of the possibility that new regulation might even render his property economically worthless (at least if the property's only economically productive use is sale or manufacture for sale). *See Andrus v. Allard*, 444 U.S. 51, 66-67, 100 S.Ct. 318, 327, 62 L.Ed.2d 210 (1979) (prohibition on sale of eagle feathers). In the case of land, however, we think the notion pressed by the Council that title is somehow held subject to the "implied limitation" that the State may subsequently eliminate all economically valuable use is inconsistent with the historical compact recorded in the Takings Clause that has become part of our constitutional culture.[15]

Where "permanent physical occupation" of land is concerned, we have refused to allow the government to decree it anew (without compensation), no matter how weighty

---

[15] After accusing us of "launch[ing] a missile to kill a mouse," post, at 2904, Justice Blackmun expends a good deal of throw-weight of his own upon a noncombatant, arguing that our description of the "understanding" of land ownership that informs the Takings Clause is not supported by early American experience. That is largely true, but entirely irrelevant. The practices of the States prior to incorporation of the Takings and Just Compensation Clauses, see *Chicago, B. & Q.R. Co. v. Chicago*, 166 U.S. 226, 17 S.Ct. 581, 41 L.Ed. 979 (1897)—which, as Justice Blackmun acknowledges, occasionally included outright physical appropriation of land without compensation, see post, at 2915—were out of accord with any plausible interpretation of those provisions. Justice Blackmun is correct that early constitutional theorists did not believe the Takings Clause embraced regulations of property at all, see post, at 2915, and n. 23, but even he does not suggest (explicitly, at least) that we renounce the Court's contrary conclusion in *Mahon*. Since the text of the Clause can be read to encompass regulatory as well as physical deprivations (in contrast to the text originally proposed by Madison, see *Speech Proposing Bill of Rights (June 8, 1789)*, in 12 J. Madison, *The Papers of James Madison* 201 (C. Hobson, R. Rutland, W. Rachal, & J. Sisson ed. 1979) ("No person shall be . . . obliged to relinquish his property, where it may be necessary for public use, without a just compensation")), we decline to do so as well.

the asserted "public interests" involved, *Loretto v. Teleprompter Manhattan CATV Corp.*, 458 U.S., at 426, 102 S.Ct., at 3171—though we assuredly would permit the government to assert a permanent easement that was a pre-existing limitation upon the land owner's title. *Compare Scranton v. Wheeler*, 179 U.S. 141, 163, 21 S.Ct. 48, 57, 45 L.Ed. 126 (1900) (interests of "riparian owner in the submerged lands . . . bordering on a public navigable water" held subject to Government's navigational servitude), *with Kaiser Aetna v. United States*, 444 U.S., at 178-180, 100 S.Ct., at 392-393 (imposition of navigational servitude on marina created and rendered navigable at private expense held to constitute a taking). We believe similar treatment must be accorded confiscatory regulations, i.e., regulations that prohibit all economically beneficial use of land: Any limitation so severe cannot be newly legislated or decreed (without compensation), but must inhere in the title itself, in the restrictions that background principles of the State's law of property and nuisance already place upon land ownership. A law or decree with such an effect must, in other words, do no more than duplicate the result that could have been achieved in the courts—by adjacent landowners (or other uniquely affected persons) under the State's law of private nuisance, or by the State under its complementary power to abate nuisances that affect the public generally, or otherwise.[16]

On this analysis, the owner of a lake-bed, for example, would not be entitled to compensation when he is denied the requisite permit to engage in a landfilling operation that would have the effect of flooding others' land. Nor the corporate owner of a nuclear generating plant, when it is directed to remove all improvements from its land upon discovery that the plant sits astride an earthquake fault. Such regulatory action may well have the effect of eliminating the land's only economically productive use, but it does not proscribe a productive use that was previously permissible under relevant property and nuisance principles. The use of these properties for what are now expressly prohibited purposes was always unlawful, and (subject to other constitutional limitations) it was open to the State at any point to make the implication of those background principles of nuisance and property law explicit. *See* Michelman, *Property, Utility, and Fairness, Comments on the Ethical Foundations of "Just Compensation" Law*, 80 Harv.L.Rev. 1165, 1239-1241 (1967). In light of our traditional resort to "existing rules or understandings that stem from an independent source such as state law" to define the range of interests that qualify for protection as "property" under the Fifth and Fourteenth Amendments, *Board of Regents of State Colleges v. Roth*, 408 U.S. 564, 577, 92 S.Ct. 2701, 2709, 33 L.Ed.2d 548 (1972); *see, e.g., Ruckelshaus v. Monsanto Co.*, 467 U.S. 986, 1011-1012, 104 S.Ct. 2862, 2877, 81 L.Ed.2d 815 (1984); *Hughes v. Washington*, 389 U.S.

---

[16] The principal "otherwise" that we have in mind is litigation absolving the State (or private parties) of liability for the destruction of "real and personal property, in cases of actual necessity, to prevent the spreading of a fire" or to forestall other grave threats to the lives and property of others. *Bowditch v. Boston*, 101 U.S. 16, 18-19, 25 L.Ed. 980 (1880); *see United States v. Pacific R., Co.*, 120 U.S. 227, 238-239, 7 S.Ct. 490, 495-496, 30 L.Ed. 634 (1887).

290, 295, 88 S.Ct. 438, 441, 19 L.Ed.2d 530 (1967) (Stewart, J., concurring), this recognition that the Takings Clause does not require compensation when an owner is barred from putting land to a use that is proscribed by those "existing rules or understandings" is surely unexceptional. When, however, a regulation that declares "off-limits" all economically productive or beneficial uses of land goes beyond what the relevant background principles would dictate, compensation must be paid to sustain it.

The "total taking" inquiry we require today will ordinarily entail (as the application of state nuisance law ordinarily entails) analysis of, among other things, the degree of harm to public lands and resources, or adjacent private property, posed by the claimant's proposed activities, see, e.g., Restatement (Second) of Torts §§826, 827, the social value of the claimant's activities and their suitability to the locality in question, see, e.g., *id.*, §§828(a) and (b), 831, and the relative ease with which the alleged harm can be avoided through measures taken by the claimant and the government (or adjacent private landowners) alike, see, e.g., *id.*, §§827(e), 828(c), 830. The fact that a particular use has long been engaged in by similarly situated owners ordinarily imports a lack of any common-law prohibition (though changed circumstances or new knowledge may make what was previously permissible no longer so, see *id.*, §827, Comment g. So also does the fact that other landowners, similarly situated, are permitted to continue the use denied to the claimant.

It seems unlikely that common-law principles would have prevented the erection of any habitable or productive improvements on petitioner's land; they rarely support prohibition of the "essential use" of land, *Curtin v. Benson*, 222 U.S. 78, 86, 32 S.Ct. 31, 33, 56 L.Ed. 102 (1911). The question, however, is one of state law to be dealt with on remand. We emphasize that to win its case South Carolina must do more than proffer the legislature's declaration that the uses Lucas desires are inconsistent with the public interest, or the conclusory assertion that they violate a common-law maxim such as sic utere tuo ut alienum non laedas. As we have said, a "State, by ipse dixit, may not transform private property into public property without compensation. . . ." *Webb's Fabulous Pharmacies, Inc. v. Beckwith*, 449 U.S. 155, 164, 101 S.Ct. 446, 452, 66 L.Ed.2d 358 (1980). Instead, as it would be required to do if it sought to restrain Lucas in a common-law action for public nuisance, South Carolina must identify background principles of nuisance and property law that prohibit the uses he now intends in the circumstances in which the property is presently found. Only on this showing can the State fairly claim that, in proscribing all such beneficial uses, the Beachfront Management Act is taking nothing.

The judgment is reversed, and the case is remanded for proceedings not inconsistent with this opinion.

Justice KENNEDY, concurring in the judgment. . . . The finding of no value must be considered under the Takings Clause by reference to the owner's reasonable, investment-backed expectations. *Kaiser Aetna v. United States*, 444 U.S. 164, 175, 100

S.Ct. 383, 390, 62 L.Ed.2d 332 (1979); *Penn Central Transportation Co. v. New York City*, 438 U.S. 104, 124, 98 S.Ct. 2646, 2659, 57 L.Ed.2d 631 (1978); *see also W.B. Worthen Co. v. Kavanaugh*, 295 U.S. 56, 55 S.Ct. 555, 79 L.Ed. 1298 (1935). The Takings Clause, while conferring substantial protection on property owners, does not eliminate the police power of the State to enact limitations on the use of their property. *Mugler v. Kansas*, 123 U.S. 623, 669, 8 S.Ct. 273, 301, 31 L.Ed. 205 (1887). The rights conferred by the Takings Clause and the police power of the State may coexist without conflict. Property is bought and sold, investments are made, subject to the State's power to regulate. Where a taking is alleged from regulations which deprive the property of all value, the test must be whether the deprivation is contrary to reasonable, investment-backed expectations.

There is an inherent tendency towards circularity in this synthesis, of course; for if the owner's reasonable expectations are shaped by what courts allow as a proper exercise of governmental authority, property tends to become what courts say it is. Some circularity must be tolerated in these matters, however, as it is in other spheres. E.g., *Katz v. United States*, 389 U.S. 347, 88 S.Ct. 507, 19 L.Ed.2d 576 (1967) (Fourth Amendment protections defined by reasonable expectations of privacy). The definition, moreover, is not circular in its entirety. The expectations protected by the Constitution are based on objective rules and customs that can be understood as reasonable by all parties involved.

In my view, reasonable expectations must be understood in light of the whole of our legal tradition. The common law of nuisance is too narrow a confine for the exercise of regulatory power in a complex and interdependent society. *Goldblatt v. Hempstead*, 369 U.S. 590, 593, 82 S.Ct. 987, 989, 8 L.Ed.2d 130 (1962). The State should not be prevented from enacting new regulatory initiatives in response to changing conditions, and courts must consider all reasonable expectations whatever their source. The Takings Clause does not require a static body of state property law; it protects private expectations to ensure private investment. I agree with the Court that nuisance prevention accords with the most common expectations of property owners who face regulation, but I do not believe this can be the sole source of state authority to impose severe restrictions. Coastal property may present such unique concerns for a fragile land system that the State can go further in regulating its development and use than the common law of nuisance might otherwise permit.

The Supreme Court of South Carolina erred, in my view, by reciting the general purposes for which the state regulations were enacted without a determination that they were in accord with the owner's reasonable expectations and therefore sufficient to support a severe restriction on specific parcels of property. *See* 304 S.C. 376, 383, 404 S.E.2d 895, 899 (1991). The promotion of tourism, for instance, ought not to suffice to deprive specific property of all value without a corresponding duty to compensate. Furthermore, the means, as well as the ends, of regulation must accord with the owner's reasonable expectations. Here, the State did not act until after the property had been zoned for individual lot development and most other parcels had been improved, throwing the whole burden of the regulation on the remaining lots. This too must be measured in the balance. *See Pennsylvania Coal Co. v. Mahon*, 260 U.S. 393, 416, 43 S.Ct. 158, 160, 67 L.Ed. 322 (1922).

With these observations, I concur in the judgment of the Court.

Justice BLACKMUN, dissenting.

Today the Court launches a missile to kill a mouse.

The State of South Carolina prohibited petitioner Lucas from building a permanent structure on his property from 1988 to 1990. Relying on an unreviewed (and implausible) state trial court finding that this restriction left Lucas' property valueless, this Court granted review to determine whether compensation must be paid in cases where the State prohibits all economic use of real estate. According to the Court, such an occasion never has arisen in any of our prior cases, and the Court imagines that it will arise "relatively rarely" or only in "extraordinary circumstances." Almost certainly it did not happen in this case.

Nonetheless, the Court presses on to decide the issue, and as it does, it ignores its jurisdictional limits, remakes its traditional rules of review, and creates simultaneously a new categorical rule and an exception (neither of which is rooted in our prior case law, common law, or common sense). I protest not only the Court's decision, but each step taken to reach it. More fundamentally, I question the Court's wisdom in issuing sweeping new rules to decide such a narrow case. Surely, as Justice KENNEDY demonstrates, the Court could have reached the result it wanted without inflicting this damage upon our Takings Clause jurisprudence.

My fear is that the Court's new policies will spread beyond the narrow confines of the present case. For that reason, I, like the Court, will give far greater attention to this case than its narrow scope suggests—not because I can intercept the Court's missile, or save the targeted mouse, but because I hope perhaps to limit the collateral damage. . . .

The Court creates its new takings jurisprudence based on the trial court's finding that the property had lost all economic value. This finding is almost certainly erroneous. Petitioner still can enjoy other attributes of ownership, such as the right to exclude others, "one of the most essential sticks in the bundle of rights that are commonly characterized as property." *Kaiser Aetna v. United States*, 444 U.S. 164, 176, 100 S.Ct. 383, 391, 62 L.Ed.2d 332 (1979). Petitioner can picnic, swim, camp in a tent, or live on the property in a movable trailer. State courts frequently have recognized that land has economic value where the only residual economic uses are recreation or camping. *See*, e.g., *Turnpike Realty Co. v. Dedham*, 362 Mass. 221, 284 N.E.2d 891 (1972) *cert. denied*, 409 U.S. 1108, 93 S.Ct. 908, 34 L.Ed.2d 689 (1973); *Turner v. County of Del Norte*, 24 Cal.App.3d 311, 101 Cal.Rptr. 93 (1972); *Hall v. Board of Environmental Protection*, 528 A.2d 453 (Me.1987). Petitioner also retains the right to alienate the land, which would have value for neighbors and for those prepared to enjoy proximity to the ocean without a house.

Yet the trial court, apparently believing that "less value" and "valueless" could be used interchangeably, found the property "valueless." The court accepted no evidence from the State on the property's value without a home, and petitioner's appraiser testified that he never had considered what the value would be absent a residence. Tr. 54-55. The appraiser's value was based on the fact that the "highest and best use of these lots . . . [is] luxury single family detached dwellings." *Id.*, at 48. The trial court appeared to believe that the property could be considered "valueless" if it was not available for its most profitable use. Absent that erroneous assumption, see *Goldblatt*, 369 U.S., at 592, 82 S.Ct., at 989, I find no evidence in the record supporting the trial court's conclusion that the damage to the lots by virtue of the restrictions was "total." Record 128 (findings of fact). I agree with the Court, ante, at 2896, n. 9, that it has the power to decide a case that turns on an erroneous finding, but I question the wisdom of deciding an issue based on a factual premise that does not exist in this case, and in the judgment of the Court will exist in the future only in "extraordinary circumstance[s]," ante, at 2894.

DIMINUTION OF VALUE

Clearly, the Court was eager to decide this case. But eagerness, in the absence of proper jurisdiction, must—and in this case should have been—met with restraint.

The Court does not reject the South Carolina Supreme Court's decision simply on the basis of its disbelief and distrust of the legislature's findings. It also takes the opportunity to create a new scheme for regulations that eliminate all economic value. From now on, there is a categorical rule finding these regulations to be a taking unless the use they prohibit is a background common-law nuisance or property principle. *See* ante, at 2899-2901.

I first question the Court's rationale in creating a category that obviates a "case-specific inquiry into the public interest advanced," ante, at 2893, if all economic value has been lost. If one fact about the Court's takings jurisprudence can be stated without contradiction, it is that "the particular circumstances of each case" determine whether a specific restriction will be rendered invalid by the government's failure to pay compensation. *United States v. Central Eureka Mining Co.*, 357 U.S. 155, 168, 78 S.Ct. 1097, 1104, 2 L.Ed.2d 1228 (1958). This is so because although we have articulated certain factors to be considered, including the economic impact on the property owner, the ultimate conclusion "necessarily requires a weighing of private and public interests." *Agins*, 447 U.S., at 261, 100 S.Ct., at 2141. When the government regulation prevents the owner from any economically valuable use of his property, the private interest is unquestionably substantial, but we have never before held that no public interest can outweigh it. Instead the Court's prior decisions "uniformly reject the proposition that diminution in property value, standing alone, can establish a 'taking.'" *Penn Central Transp. Co. v. New York City*, 438 U.S. 104, 131, 98 S.Ct. 2646, 2663, 57 L.Ed.2d 631 (1978).

This Court repeatedly has recognized the ability of government, in certain circumstances, to regulate property without compensation no matter how adverse the financial effect on the owner may be. More than a century ago, the Court explicitly upheld the right of States to prohibit uses of property injurious to public health, safety, or welfare without paying compensation: "A prohibition simply upon the use of property for purposes that are declared, by valid legislation, to be injurious to the health, morals, or safety of the community, cannot, in any just sense, be deemed a taking or an appropriation of property." *Mugler v. Kansas*, 123 U.S., at 668-669, 8 S.Ct., at 301. On this basis, the Court upheld an ordinance effectively prohibiting operation of a previously lawful brewery, although the "establishments will become of no value as property." *Id.*, at 664, 8 S.Ct., at 298; *see also id.*, at 668, 8 S.Ct., at 300. *Mugler* was only the beginning in a long line of cases. . . .

The Court recognizes that "our prior opinions have suggested that 'harmful or noxious uses' of property may be proscribed by government regulation without the requirement of compensation," ante, at 2897, but seeks to reconcile them with its categorical rule by claiming that the Court never has upheld a regulation when the owner alleged the loss of all economic value. Even if the Court's factual premise were correct, its understanding of the Court's cases is distorted. In none of the cases did the Court suggest that the right of a State to prohibit certain activities without paying compensation turned on the availability of some residual valuable use. Instead, the cases depended on whether the government interest was sufficient to prohibit the activity, given the significant private cost.

These cases rest on the principle that the State has full power to prohibit an owner's use of property if it is harmful to the public. "[S]ince no individual has a right to use his property so as to create a nuisance or otherwise harm others, the State has not 'taken' anything when it asserts its power to enjoin the nuisance-like activity." *Keystone Bituminous Coal*, 480 U.S., at 491, n. 20, 107 S.Ct., at 1245, n. 20. It would make no sense under this theory to suggest that an owner has a constitutionally protected right to harm others, if only he makes the proper showing of economic loss. *See Pennsylvania Coal Co. v. Mahon*, 260 U.S. 393, 418, 43 S.Ct. 158, 161, 67 L.Ed. 322 (1922) (Brandeis, J., dissenting) ("Restriction upon [harmful] use does not become inappropriate as a means, merely because it deprives the owner of the only use to which the property can then be profitably put").

Ultimately even the Court cannot embrace the full implications of its per se rule: It eventually agrees that there cannot be a categorical rule for a taking based on economic value that wholly disregards the public need asserted. Instead, the Court decides that it will permit a State to regulate all economic value only if the State prohibits uses that would not be permitted under "background principles of nuisance and property law."[15] Ante, at 2901.

---

[15] Although it refers to state nuisance and property law, the Court apparently does not mean just any state nuisance and property law. Public nuisance was first a common-law creation, see Newark, *The Boundaries of Nuisance*, 65

Until today, the Court explicitly had rejected the contention that the government's power to act without paying compensation turns on whether the prohibited activity is a common-law nuisance.[16] The brewery closed in *Mugler* itself was not a common-law nuisance, and the Court specifically stated that it was the role of the legislature to determine what measures would be appropriate for the protection of public health and safety. *See* 123 U.S., at 661, 8 S.Ct., at 297. In upholding the state action in *Miller*, the Court found it unnecessary to "weigh with nicety the question whether the infected cedars constitute a nuisance according to common law; or whether they may be so declared by statute." 276 U.S., at 280, 48 S.Ct., at 248. *See also Goldblatt*, 369 U.S., at 593, 82 S.Ct., at 989; *Hadacheck*, 239 U.S., at 411, 36 S.Ct., at 146. Instead the Court has relied in the past, as the South Carolina court has done here, on legislative judgments of what constitutes a harm. . . .

DEFINING "NUISANCE"

The threshold inquiry for imposition of the Court's new rule, "deprivation of all economically valuable use," itself cannot be determined objectively. As the Court admits, whether the owner has been deprived of all economic value of his property will depend on how "property" is defined. The "composition of the denominator in our 'deprivation' fraction," ante, at 2894, n. 7, is the dispositive inquiry. Yet there is no "objective" way to define what that denominator should be. "We have long understood that any land-use regulation can be characterized as the 'total' deprivation of an aptly defined entitlement. . . . Alternatively, the same regulation can always be characterized as a mere 'partial' withdrawal from full, unencumbered ownership of the landholding affected by the regulation. . . ." Michelman, *Takings*, 1987, 88 Colum.L.Rev. 1600, 1614 (1988). . . .

Even more perplexing, however, is the Court's reliance on common-law principles of nuisance in its quest for a value-free takings jurisprudence. In determining what is a nuisance at common law, state courts make exactly the decision that the Court finds so troubling when made by the South Carolina General Assembly today: They determine

---

L.Q.Rev. 480, 482 (1949) (attributing development of nuisance to 1535), but by the 1800's in both the United States and England, legislatures had the power to define what is a public nuisance, and particular uses often have been selectively targeted. *See* Prosser, *Private Action for Public Nuisance*, 52 Va.L.Rev. 997, 999-1000 (1966); J. Stephen, *A General View of the Criminal Law of England* 105-107 (2d ed. 1890). The Court's references to "common-law" background principles, however, indicate that legislative determinations do not constitute "state nuisance and property law" for the Court.

[16] Also, until today the fact that the regulation prohibited uses that were lawful at the time the owner purchased did not determine the constitutional question. The brewery, the brickyard, the cedar trees, and the gravel pit were all perfectly legitimate uses prior to the passage of the regulation. *See Mugler v. Kansas*, 123 U.S., at 654, 8 S.Ct., at 293; *Hadacheck v. Sebastian*, 239 U.S. 394, 36 S.Ct. 143, 60 L.Ed. 348 (1915); *Miller*, 276 U.S., at 272, 48 S.Ct., at 246; *Goldblatt v. Hempstead*, 369 U.S. 590, 82 S.Ct. 987, 8 L.Ed.2d 130 (1962). This Court explicitly acknowledged in *Hadacheck* that "[a] vested interest cannot be asserted against [the police power] because of conditions once obtaining. To so hold would preclude development and fix a city forever in its primitive conditions." 239 U.S., at 410, 36 S.Ct., at 145 (citation omitted).

whether the use is harmful. Common-law public and private nuisance law is simply a determination whether a particular use causes harm. *See* Prosser, *Private Action for Public Nuisance*, 52 Va.L.Rev. 997 (1966) ("Nuisance is a French word which means nothing more than harm"). There is nothing magical in the reasoning of judges long dead. They determined a harm in the same way as state judges and legislatures do today. If judges in the 18th and 19th centuries can distinguish a harm from a benefit, why not judges in the 20th century, and if judges can, why not legislators? There simply is no reason to believe that new interpretations of the hoary common-law nuisance doctrine will be particularly "objective" or "value free."[19] Once one abandons the level of generality of sic utere tuo ut alienum non laedas, ante, at 2901, one searches in vain, I think, for anything resembling a principle in the common law of nuisance.

Finally, the Court justifies its new rule that the legislature may not deprive a property owner of the only economically valuable use of his land, even if the legislature finds it to be a harmful use, because such action is not part of the "'long recognized'" "understandings of our citizens." Ante, at 2899. These "understandings" permit such regulation only if the use is a nuisance under the common law. Any other course is "inconsistent with the historical compact recorded in the Takings Clause." Ante, at 2900. It is not clear from the Court's opinion where our "historical compact" or "citizens' understanding" comes from, but it does not appear to be history.

The principle that the State should compensate individuals for property taken for public use was not widely established in America at the time of the Revolution. . . .

Although, prior to the adoption of the Bill of Rights, America was replete with land-use regulations describing which activities were considered noxious and forbidden, see Bender, The Takings Clause: Principles or Politics?, 34 Buffalo L.Rev. 735, 751 (1985); L. Friedman, A History of American Law 66-68 (1973), the Fifth Amendment's Takings Clause originally did not extend to regulations of property, whatever the effect.[23] *See* ante, at 2892. Most state courts agreed with this narrow interpretation of a taking. "Until the end of the nineteenth century . . . jurists held that the constitution protected

---

[19] "There is perhaps no more impenetrable jungle in the entire law than that which surrounds the word 'nuisance.' It has meant all things to all people, and has been applied indiscriminately to everything from an alarming advertisement to a cockroach baked in a pie." W. Keeton, D. Dobbs, R. Keeton & D. Owen, *Prosser and Keeton on The Law of Torts* 616 (5th ed. 1984) (footnotes omitted). It is an area of law that "straddles the legal universe, virtually defies synthesis, and generates case law to suit every taste." W. Rodgers, *Environmental Law* §2.4, p. 48 (1986) (footnotes omitted). The Court itself has noted that "nuisance concepts" are "often vague and indeterminate." *Milwaukee v. Illinois*, 451 U.S. 304, 317, 101 S.Ct. 1784, 1792, 68 L.Ed.2d 114 (1981).

[23] James Madison, author of the Takings Clause, apparently intended it to apply only to direct, physical takings of property by the Federal Government. *See* Treanor, *The Origins and Original Significance of the Just Compensation Clause of the Fifth Amendment*, 94 Yale L.J. 694, 711 (1985). Professor Sax argues that although "contemporaneous commentary upon the meaning of the compensation clause is in very short supply," 74 Yale L.J., at 58, the "few authorities that are available" indicate that the Clause was "designed to prevent arbitrary government action," not to protect economic value. *Id.*, at 58-60.

---

possession only, and not value." Siegel, *Understanding the Nineteenth Century Contract Clause: The Role of the Property-Privilege Distinction and "Takings" Clause Jurisprudence,* 60 S.Cal.L.Rev. 1, 76 (1986); Bosselman 106. Even indirect and consequential injuries to property resulting from regulations were excluded from the definition of a taking. *See ibid.; Callender v. Marsh,* 1 Pick. 418, 430 (Mass.1823). . . .

Nor does history indicate any common-law limit on the State's power to regulate harmful uses even to the point of destroying all economic value. Nothing in the discussions in Congress concerning the Takings Clause indicates that the Clause was limited by the common-law nuisance doctrine. Common-law courts themselves rejected such an understanding. They regularly recognized that it is "for the legislature to interpose, and by positive enactment to prohibit a use of property which would be injurious to the public." *Tewksbury,* 11 Metc., at 57. Chief Justice Shaw explained in upholding a regulation prohibiting construction of wharves, the existence of a taking did not depend on "whether a certain erection in tide water is a nuisance at common law or not." *Alger,* 7 Cush., at 104; *see also State v. Paul,* 5 R.I. 185, 193 (1858); *Commonwealth v. Parks,* 155 Mass. 531, 532, 30 N.E. 174 (1892) (Holmes, J.) ("[T]he legislature may change the common law as to nuisances, and may move the line either way, so as to make things nuisances which were not so, or to make things lawful which were nuisances").

In short, I find no clear and accepted "historical compact" or "understanding of our citizens" justifying the Court's new takings doctrine. Instead, the Court seems to treat history as a grab bag of principles, to be adopted where they support the Court's theory, and ignored where they do not. If the Court decided that the early common law provides the background principles for interpreting the Takings Clause, then regulation, as opposed to physical confiscation, would not be compensable. If the Court decided that the law of a later period provides the background principles, then regulation might be compensable, but the Court would have to confront the fact that legislatures regularly determined which uses were prohibited, independent of the common law, and independent of whether the uses were lawful when the owner purchased. What makes the Court's analysis unworkable is its attempt to package the law of two incompatible eras and peddle it as historical fact.[26]

The Court makes sweeping and, in my view, misguided and unsupported changes in our takings doctrine. While it limits these changes to the most narrow subset of government regulation—those that eliminate all economic value from land—these

---

[26] The Court asserts that all early American experience, prior to and after passage of the Bill of Rights, and any case law prior to 1897 are "entirely irrelevant" in determining what is "the historical compact recorded in the Takings Clause." *Ante,* at 2900 and n. 15. Nor apparently are we to find this compact in the early federal takings cases, which clearly permitted prohibition of harmful uses despite the alleged loss of all value, whether or not the prohibition was a common-law nuisance, and whether or not the prohibition occurred subsequent to the purchase. *See supra,* at 2910, 2912-2913, and n. 16. I cannot imagine where the Court finds its "historical compact," if not in history.

changes go far beyond what is necessary to secure petitioner Lucas' private benefit. One hopes they do not go beyond the narrow confines the Court assigns them to today.

I dissent.

Justice STEVENS, dissenting.

Today the Court restricts one judge-made rule and expands another. In my opinion it errs on both counts. Proper application of the doctrine of judicial restraint would avoid the premature adjudication of an important constitutional question. Proper respect for our precedents would avoid an illogical expansion of the concept of "regulatory takings." . . .

In its analysis of the merits, the Court starts from the premise that this Court has adopted a "categorical rule that total regulatory takings must be compensated," ante, at 2899, and then sets itself to the task of identifying the exceptional cases in which a State may be relieved of this categorical obligation, ante, at 2899-2900. The test the Court announces is that the regulation must do no more than duplicate the result that could have been achieved under a State's nuisance law. Ante, at 2900. Under this test the categorical rule will apply unless the regulation merely makes explicit what was otherwise an implicit limitation on the owner's property rights.

In my opinion, the Court is doubly in error. The categorical rule the Court establishes is an unsound and unwise addition to the law and the Court's formulation of the exception to that rule is too rigid and too narrow.

As the Court recognizes, ante, at 2892-2893, *Pennsylvania Coal Co. v. Mahon*, 260 U.S. 393, 43 S.Ct. 158, 67 L.Ed. 322 (1922), provides no support for its—or, indeed, any—categorical rule. . . . Nor does the Court's new categorical rule find support in decisions following *Mahon*. . . Although in dicta we have sometimes recited that a law "effects a taking if [it] . . . denies an owner economically viable use of his land," *Agins v. City of Tiburon*, 447 U.S. 255, 260, 100 S.Ct. 2138, 2141, 65 L.Ed.2d 106 (1980), our rulings have rejected such an absolute position. We have frequently—and recently—held that, in some circumstances, a law that renders property valueless may nonetheless not constitute a taking. . . .

DIMINUTION IN VALUE

In addition to lacking support in past decisions, the Court's new rule is wholly arbitrary. A landowner whose property is diminished in value 95% recovers nothing, while an owner whose property is diminished 100% recovers the land's full value. The case at hand illustrates this arbitrariness well. The Beachfront Management Act not only prohibited the building of new dwellings in certain areas, it also prohibited the rebuilding of houses that were "destroyed beyond repair by natural causes or by fire." 1988 S.C. Acts 634, §3; *see also Esposito v. South Carolina Coastal Council*, 939 F.2d 165, 167 (CA4 1991). Thus, if the homes adjacent to Lucas' lot were destroyed by a hurricane one day after the Act took effect, the owners would not be able to rebuild, nor would they be assured recovery. Under the Court's categorical approach, Lucas (who has lost the opportunity to build) recovers, while his neighbors (who have lost both the opportunity to build and their homes) do not recover. The arbitrariness of such a rule is palpable.

Moreover, because of the elastic nature of property rights, the Court's new rule will also prove unsound in practice. In response to the rule, courts may define "property" broadly and only rarely find regulations to effect total takings. This is the approach the Court itself adopts in its revisionist reading of venerable precedents. We are told that—notwithstanding the Court's findings to the contrary in each case—the brewery in *Mugler*, the brickyard in *Hadacheck*, and the gravel pit in *Goldblatt* all could be put to "other uses" and that, therefore, those cases did not involve total regulatory takings.[3] Ante, at 2899, n. 13.

This highlights a fundamental weakness in the Court's analysis: its failure to explain why only the impairment of "economically beneficial or productive use," ante, at 2893 (emphasis added), of property is relevant in takings analysis. I should think that a regulation arbitrarily prohibiting an owner from continuing to use her property for bird watching or sunbathing might constitute a taking under some circumstances; and, conversely, that such uses are of value to the owner. Yet the Court offers no basis for its assumption that the only uses of property cognizable under the Constitution are developmental uses.

On the other hand, developers and investors may market specialized estates to take advantage of the Court's new rule. The smaller the estate, the more likely that a regulatory change will effect a total taking. Thus, an investor may, for example, purchase the right to build a multifamily home on a specific lot, with the result that a zoning regulation that allows only single-family homes would render the investor's property interest "valueless." In short, the categorical rule will likely have one of two effects: Either courts will alter the definition of the "denominator" in the takings "fraction," rendering the Court's categorical rule meaningless, or investors will manipulate the relevant property interests, giving the Court's rule sweeping effect. To my mind, neither of these results is desirable or appropriate, and both are distortions of our takings jurisprudence.

Finally, the Court's justification for its new categorical rule is remarkably thin. The Court mentions in passing three arguments in support of its rule; none is convincing. First, the Court suggests that "total deprivation of feasible use is, from the landowner's point of view, the equivalent of a physical appropriation." Ante, at 2894. This argument proves too much. From the "landowner's point of view," a regulation that diminishes a lot's value by 50% is as well "the equivalent" of the condemnation of half of the lot. Yet, it is well established that a 50% diminution in value does not by itself constitute a taking.

---

[3] Of course, the same could easily be said in this case: Lucas may put his land to "other uses"—fishing or camping, for example—or may sell his land to his neighbors as a buffer. In either event, his land is far from "valueless."

See Euclid v. Ambler Realty Co., 272 U.S. 365, 384, 47 S.Ct. 114, 117, 71 L.Ed. 303 (1926) (75% diminution in value). Thus, the landowner's perception of the regulation cannot justify the Court's new rule.

Second, the Court emphasizes that because total takings are "relatively rare" its new rule will not adversely affect the government's ability to "go on." Ante, at 2894. This argument proves too little. Certainly it is true that defining a small class of regulations that are per se takings will not greatly hinder important governmental functions—but this is true of any small class of regulations. The Court's suggestion only begs the question of why regulations of this particular class should always be found to effect takings.

Finally, the Court suggests that "regulations that leave the owner . . . without economically beneficial . . . use . . . carry with them a heightened risk that private property is being pressed into some form of public service." *Ibid.* As discussed more fully below, I agree that the risks of such singling out are of central concern in takings law. However, such risks do not justify a per se rule for total regulatory takings. There is no necessary correlation between "singling out" and total takings. . . . What matters in such cases is not the degree of diminution of value, but rather the specificity of the expropriating act. For this reason, the Court's third justification for its new rule also fails.

In short, the Court's new rule is unsupported by prior decisions, arbitrary and unsound in practice, and theoretically unjustified. In my opinion, a categorical rule as important as the one established by the Court today should be supported by more history or more reason than has yet been provided.

Like many bright-line rules, the categorical rule established in this case is only "categorical" for a page or two in the U.S. Reports. No sooner does the Court state that "total regulatory takings must be compensated," ante, at 2899, than it quickly establishes an exception to that rule.

The exception provides that a regulation that renders property valueless is not a taking if it prohibits uses of property that were not "previously permissible under relevant property and nuisance principles." Ante, at 2901. The Court thus rejects the basic holding in *Mugler v. Kansas*, 123 U.S. 623, 8 S.Ct. 273, 31 L.Ed. 205 (1887). There we held that a state-wide statute that prohibited the owner of a brewery from making alcoholic beverages did not effect a taking, even though the use of the property had been perfectly lawful and caused no public harm before the statute was enacted. We squarely rejected the rule the Court adopts today:

> "It is true, that, when the defendants . . . erected their breweries, the laws of the State did not forbid the manufacture of intoxicating liquors. But the State did not thereby give any assurance, or come under an obligation, that its legislation upon that subject would remain unchanged. [T]he supervision of the public health and the public morals is a governmental power, 'continuing in its nature,' and 'to be

dealt with as the special exigencies of the moment may require;' . . .
'for this purpose, the largest legislative discretion is allowed, and the
discretion cannot be parted with any more than the power itself.'" *Id.*, at
669, 8 S.Ct., at 301.

Under our reasoning in *Mugler*, a State's decision to prohibit or to regulate certain uses of property is not a compensable taking just because the particular uses were previously lawful. Under the Court's opinion today, however, if a State should decide to prohibit the manufacture of asbestos, cigarettes, or concealable firearms, for example, it must be prepared to pay for the adverse economic consequences of its decision. One must wonder if government will be able to "go on" effectively if it must risk compensation "for every such change in the general law." *Mahon*, 260 U.S., at 413, 43 S.Ct., at 159.

The Court's holding today effectively freezes the State's common law, denying the legislature much of its traditional power to revise the law governing the rights and uses of property. Until today, I had thought that we had long abandoned this approach to constitutional law. . . .

Arresting the development of the common law is not only a departure from our prior decisions; it is also profoundly unwise. The human condition is one of constant learning and evolution—both moral and practical. Legislatures implement that new learning; in doing so they must often revise the definition of property and the rights of property owners. Thus, when the Nation came to understand that slavery was morally wrong and mandated the emancipation of all slaves, it, in effect, redefined "property." . . .

The Court's categorical approach rule will, I fear, greatly hamper the efforts of local officials and planners who must deal with increasingly complex problems in land-use and environmental regulation. As this case—in which the claims of an individual property owner exceed $1 million—well demonstrates, these officials face both substantial uncertainty because of the ad hoc nature of takings law and unacceptable penalties if they guess incorrectly about that law. . . .

Viewed more broadly, the Court's new rule and exception conflict with the very character of our takings jurisprudence. We have frequently and consistently recognized that the definition of a taking cannot be reduced to a "set formula" and that determining whether a regulation is a taking is "essentially [an] ad hoc, factual inquir[y]." *Penn Central Transportation Co. v. New York City*, 438 U.S. 104, 124, 98 S.Ct. 2646, 2659, 57 L.Ed.2d 631 (1978) (quoting *Goldblatt v. Hempstead*, 369 U.S., at 594, 82 S.Ct., at 990. This is unavoidable, for the determination whether a law effects a taking is ultimately a matter of "fairness and justice," *Armstrong v. United States*, 364 U.S. 40, 49, 80 S.Ct. 1563, 1569, 4 L.Ed.2d 1554 (1960), and "necessarily requires a weighing of private and public interests," *Agins*, 447 U.S., at 261, 100 S.Ct., at 2141. The rigid rules fixed by the Court today clash with this enterprise: "fairness and justice" are often disserved by categorical rules. . . .

It is well established that a takings case "entails inquiry into [several factors:] the character of the governmental action, its economic impact, and its interference with reasonable investment-backed expectations." *PruneYard*, 447 U.S., at 83, 100 S.Ct., at 2042. The Court's analysis today focuses on the last two of these three factors: The categorical rule addresses a regulation's "economic impact," while the nuisance exception recognizes that ownership brings with it only certain "expectations." Neglected by the Court today is the first and, in some ways, the most important factor in takings analysis: the character of the regulatory action.

The Just Compensation Clause "was designed to bar Government from forcing some people alone to bear public burdens which, in all fairness and justice, should be borne by the public as a whole." *Armstrong*, 364 U.S., at 49, 80 S.Ct., at 1569. Accordingly, one of the central concerns of our takings jurisprudence is "prevent[ing] the public from loading upon one individual more than his just share of the burdens of government." *Monongahela Navigation Co. v. United States*, 148 U.S. 312, 325, 13 S.Ct. 622, 626, 37 L.Ed. 463 (1893). We have, therefore, in our takings law frequently looked to the generality of a regulation of property. . . .

In analyzing takings claims, courts have long recognized the difference between a regulation that targets one or two parcels of land and a regulation that enforces a statewide policy. . . . In considering Lucas' claim, the generality of the Beachfront Management Act is significant. The Act does not target particular landowners, but rather regulates the use of the coastline of the entire State. . . . This generality indicates that the Act is not an effort to expropriate owners of undeveloped land.

Admittedly, the economic impact of this regulation is dramatic and petitioner's investment-backed expectations are substantial. Yet, if anything, the costs to and expectations of the owners of developed land are even greater: I doubt, however, that the cost to owners of developed land of renourishing the beach and allowing their seawalls to deteriorate effects a taking. The costs imposed on the owners of undeveloped land, such as petitioner, differ from these costs only in degree, not in kind.

The impact of the ban on developmental uses must also be viewed in light of the purposes of the Act. The legislature stated the purposes of the Act as "protect[ing], preserv[ing], restor[ing] and enhanc[ing] the beach/dune system" of the State not only for recreational and ecological purposes, but also to "protec[t] life and property." S.C. Code Ann. §48-39-260(1)(a) (Supp.1990). The State, with much science on its side, believes that the "beach/dune system [acts] as a buffer from high tides, storm surge, [and] hurricanes." *Ibid.* This is a traditional and important exercise of the State's police power, as demonstrated by Hurricane Hugo, which in 1989, caused 29 deaths and more than $6 billion in property damage in South Carolina alone.

In view of all of these factors, even assuming that petitioner's property was rendered valueless, the risk inherent in investments of the sort made by petitioner, the generality of the Act, and the compelling purpose motivating the South Carolina Legislature persuade me that the Act did not effect a taking of petitioner's property.

Accordingly, I respectfully dissent.

Statement of Justice Souter.

I would dismiss the writ of certiorari in this case as having been granted improvidently. After briefing and argument it is abundantly clear that an unreviewable assumption on which this case comes to us is both questionable as a conclusion of Fifth Amendment law and sufficient to frustrate the Court's ability to render certain the legal premises on which its holding rests.

The petition for review was granted on the assumption that the State by regulation had deprived the owner of his entire economic interest in the subject property. Such was the state trial court's conclusion, which the State Supreme Court did not review. It is apparent now that in light of our prior cases, . . . the trial court's conclusion is highly questionable. . . .

NOTES AND QUESTIONS

1. *The Total Diminutions Rule.* The *Lucas* rule is often stated in terms of diminution in value: if a regulation renders a properly valueless, the regulation constitutes a per se taking. Put another way, if the regulation results in a 100 percent reduction in value, then it is a per se taking. This statement of the rule is based, at least in part, on the trial court's holding that the Beachfront Management Act rendered Lucas's lots "valueless." In discussing the rule, however, Justice Scalia's opinion of the Court speaks in terms of economically beneficial use, rather than value: "[W]hen the owner of real property has been called upon to sacrifice all economically beneficial uses in the name of the common good, that is, to leave his property economically idle, he has suffered a taking." It makes intuitive sense that a property will be valueless if it cannot be used for economically beneficial use. It is worth considering, however, whether the total diminution in value and deprivation of all economically beneficial use formulations of the rule are precisely the same.

DIMINUTION IN VALUE

2. *Was Lucas's Property Rendered Valueless?* A number of the Justices questioned the trial court's determination that Lucas's property was rendered truly valueless by the Beachfront Management Act. Justice Blackmun suggested that the lots had some value because Lucas could "picnic, swim, camp in a tent or live on the property in a moveable trailer." William Fischel looked into the facts of the case and described his findings in his book, *Regulatory Takings: Law, Economics, and Politics*, 59-60 (1995). As a preliminary matter, he noted that Lucas's two lots were surrounded by existing buildings. As a result, the two lots appeared at the time "like two missing pickets in a long fence of development that included condominiums as well as five-thousand-square-foot houses." *Id.* at 59. Of Justice Blackmun's suggested alternative uses, Professor Fischel wrote:

My November 1994 visit to Wild Dunes revealed that such options were either impossible or valueless to Lucas. The director of the Wild Dunes Architectural Review Board informed me that covenants explicitly forbade trailers and tents. She said that picknicking would be permitted . . . as would swimming. But such activities would be valueless to Lucas, given that his lots fronted on a wide public beach, on which picnicking and swimming are permitted to anyone without charge. (Automobile access to the lots is restricted, but one can easily walk to them along the beach, which is open to the public.) The trial court's conclusion seems correct.

Id. at 60.

3. *The Aftermath, and More on Value.* After subsequent proceedings in the South Carolina courts, the State of South Carolina bought the two lots from Lucas. The state then turned around and sold the property to a developer. What does this suggest about the willingness of the state to bear the costs that were imposed on Lucas by the Beachfront Management Act?

Professor Fischel notes that after the state had purchased the lots, "the owner of a house next to one of Lucas's parcels offered the state $315,000 for one of them, promising to keep it undeveloped to protect his view." *Id.* at 61. The state refused this offer, deciding instead to sell to a developer at a higher price. Note, by the way, that the neighbor was willing to pay $315,000 after the litigation was complete and at a time when the state was in the process of selling the lots to a developer. Do you see why the neighbor would have been unlikely to pay $315,000, or perhaps anything, for the lot if Lucas had lost his takings challenge and the Beachfront Management Act was still in force?

4. *The Nuisance and Background Principles Exception.* We presume that you have carefully read the discussion of the nuisance exception in Justice Scalia's opinion of the Court. Read it again. There is a lot going on in the discussion. You should have a good handle by now on the law of nuisance and on the treatment of this issue in *Alger*, *Mugler*, and *Mahon*. You therefore should be able to follow and critically evaluate the steps in Justice Scalia's analysis. You should also be able to critically evaluate the discussion of this issue in the dissents by Justices Blackmun and Stevens. Who do you think has the better of the argument? Why?

Justice Scalia's opinion does at least three things to the nuisance exception. First, it suggests that the theory of the nuisance exception is that the property owner did not have a property right to engage in a nuisance in the first place: "Where the State seeks to sustain regulation that deprives land of all economically beneficial use, we think it may resist compensation only if the logically antecedent inquiry into the nature of the owner's estate shows that the proscribed use interests were not part of his title to begin with." Second, it holds that the legislature cannot avoid takings liability by labeling a prohibited use a nuisance. (Note, in this context, Justice Scalia's remarks in footnote 12 of his opinion.) The word "nuisance" in this exception

DEFINING "NUISANCE"

therefore refers to the court-made common law of nuisance. Third, it broadens the applicability of this exception beyond the law of nuisance: "Any limitation so severe cannot be newly legislated or decreed (without compensation), but must inhere in the title itself, in the restrictions that background principles of the State's law of property and nuisance already place upon land ownership."

In light of this last point, we think that it is incomplete to refer to this exception as the "nuisance exception." It is better to refer to it as the "nuisance and background principles exception." If a property owner did not have the right to engage in a use under the state's existing law, then a regulation prohibiting that use does not take anything from the property owner. The law of nuisance is only a subset (though an important one) of the background principles that define the scope of the property owner's interests.

5. *The Denominator Problem and the Total Diminutions Rule.* As Justice Scalia noted in footnote 7 of his opinion, the facts of *Lucas* did not raise the denominator problem because the Beachfront Management Act affected the entirety of Lucas's lots. To tee up the denominator issue, let's imagine another circumstance, where only a portion of Lucas's lots were affected by the Beachfront Management Act. Let's say that the value of one lot before the regulation was $1 million. After the regulation was put in place, the owner of the lot could only build in the back half of the lot. The owner couldn't do anything at all with the front half of the lot, other than cross the sand to get to the public beach. Because of the reduced amount of usable space on the lot, the size of the house that could be built on the lot would be reduced. As a result, the value of the whole parcel would be reduced from $1 million to $500,000—a 50 percent reduction in value.

DIMINUTION IN VALUE

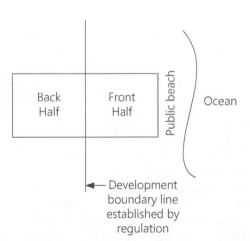

A plausible case can be made on these facts that the owner has been deprived all economically valuable use of the front half of the lot. The total diminution per se rule announced in *Lucas* therefore would have a much broader impact if we followed the affected portion approach to the denominator problem than if we followed the parcel as a whole approach. Subsequent case law, however, has strongly supported the parcel as a whole approach to the denominator problem (see Sidebar), limiting the practical significance of the total deprivations rule.

TAHOE SIERRA AND THE CURRENT STATE OF THE DENOMINATOR PROBLEM

The Supreme Court's most recent case involving the denominator problem was *Tahoe-Sierra Preservation Council, Inc. v. Tahoe Regional Planning Agency*, 535 U.S. 302 (2002). The case involved a challenge to development moratoria in the region around Lake Tahoe. These moratoria temporarily prevented landowners from developing their land. As we noted above, the Supreme Court permitted claims for temporary takings in the *First English* case. The complaining property owners tried to combine this rule from *First English* with the total deprivations rule from *Lucas* to argue that the development moratoria were compensable per se takings. The Supreme Court, in an opinion by Justice Stevens, rejected the takings complaint. As part of his analysis, Justice Stevens strongly asserted that the parcel as a whole approach is the correct solution to the denominator problem:

> Justice Brennan's opinion for the Court in Penn Central did, however, make it clear that even though multiple factors are relevant in the analysis of regulatory takings claims, in such cases we must focus on "the parcel as a whole": " 'Taking' jurisprudence does not divide a single parcel into discrete segments and attempt to determine whether rights in a particular segment have been entirely abrogated. In deciding whether a particular governmental action has effected a taking, this Court focuses rather both on the character of the action and on the nature and extent of the interference with rights in the parcel as a whole. . . .
>
> Certainly, our holding that the permanent "obliteration of the value" of a fee simple estate constitutes a categorical taking does not answer the question whether a regulation prohibiting any economic use of land for a 32-month period has the same legal effect. Petitioners seek to bring this case under the rule announced in *Lucas* by arguing that we can effectively sever a 32-month segment from the remainder of each landowner's fee simple estate, and then ask whether that segment has been taken in its entirety by the moratoria. Of course, defining the property interest taken in terms of the very regulation being challenged is circular. With property so divided, every delay would become a total ban; the moratorium and the normal permit process alike would constitute categorical takings. Petitioners' "conceptual severance" argument is unavailing because it ignores Penn Central's admonition that in regulatory takings cases we must focus on "the parcel as a whole." . . . We have consistently rejected such an approach to the "denominator" question.

In dissent, Justice Thomas, joined by Justice Scalia, noted that "The majority's decision to embrace the 'parcel as a whole' doctrine as *settled* is puzzling," because the Court had treated the issue as open in *Lucas* and in *Palazzolo v. Rhode Island*, 533 U.S. 606 (2001).

One plausible reading of *Tahoe Sierra* is that it resolves the denominator problem once and for all, in favor of the parcel as a whole approach. Another plausible reading is that the denominator problem is still an open issue, although the broad language in *Tahoe Sierra* gives strong rhetorical support to advocates of the parcel as a whole approach. *Tahoe Sierra* involved a facial challenge to the development moratoria. As a result, Justice Stevens noted that the property owners " 'face an uphill battle' that is made especially steep by their desire for a categorical rule requiring compensation whenever government imposes such a moratorium on development" (citation omitted). The Court's holding was also limited to its rejection of the argument that development moratoria are per se takings. Justice Stevens' opinion ends with the following two sentences:

> There may be moratoria that last longer than one year which interfere with reasonable investment-backed expectations, but as the District Court's opinion illustrates, petitioners' proposed rule is simply "too blunt an instrument" for identifying those cases. We conclude, therefore, that the interest in "fairness and justice" will be best served by relying on the familiar *Penn Central* approach when deciding cases like this, rather than by attempting to craft a new categorical rule.

In other words, the Court left open the possibility that a development moratorium might be a taking under *Penn Central*. In this context, the broad language supporting the parcel as a whole approach arguably is unnecessary to the holding of the case and is therefore dicta.

Our own view is that *Tahoe Sierra* provides strong support for the parcel as a whole approach, but it is best to treat the denominator problem as potentially open. There is clear skepticism of the parcel as a whole approach among some members of the Court. We can imagine the Court accepting the affected portion approach in certain circumstances, especially if the property owner could show strong investment-backed expectations that center on the affected portion of the property.

d. *Lingle*: Equivalence and Substantive Due Process

We have already seen references to the idea that a government regulation is a taking if it is the equivalent of a physical appropriation of the property. Justice Scalia, for example, addressed justification of the total deprivation rule in *Lucas* in these terms: "Perhaps it is simply, as Justice Brennan suggested, that total deprivation of beneficial use is, from the landowner's point of view, the equivalent of a physical appropriation." We can refer to this idea as the concept of *equivalence*.

The following excerpt from the Supreme Court's decision in *Lingle v. Chevron U.S.A., Inc.*, 544 U.S. 528 (2005) provides a useful overview of the takings rules that we discussed in the previous sections. It also highlights the role that the concept of equivalence plays in the Supreme Court's regulatory takings jurisprudence.

Our precedents stake out two categories of regulatory action that generally will be deemed per se takings for Fifth Amendment purposes. First, where government requires an owner to suffer a permanent physical invasion of her property—however minor—it must provide just compensation. *See Loretto v. Teleprompter Manhattan CATV Corp.*, 458 U.S. 419, 102 S.Ct. 3164, 73 L.Ed.2d 868 (1982) (state law requiring landlords to permit cable companies to install cable facilities in apartment buildings effected a taking). A second categorical rule applies to regulations that completely deprive an owner of "*all* economically beneficial us[e]" of her property. *Lucas*, 505 U.S., at 1019, 112 S.Ct. 2886 (emphasis in original). We held in *Lucas* that the government must pay just compensation for such "total regulatory takings," except to the extent that "background principles of nuisance and property law" independently restrict the owner's intended use of the property. *Id.*, at 1026-1032, 112 S.Ct. 2886.

Outside these two relatively narrow categories . . . , regulatory takings challenges are governed by the standards set forth in *Penn Central Transp. Co. v. New York City*, 438 U.S. 104, 98 S.Ct. 2646, 57 L.Ed.2d 631 (1978). The Court in *Penn Central* acknowledged that it had hitherto been "unable to develop any 'set formula'" for evaluating regulatory takings claims, but identified "several factors that have particular significance." *Id.*, at 124, 98 S.Ct. 2646. Primary among those factors are "[t]he economic impact of the regulation on the claimant and, particularly, the extent to which the regulation has interfered with distinct investment-backed expectations." *Ibid.* In addition, the "character of the governmental action"—for instance whether it amounts to a physical invasion or instead merely affects property interests through "some public program adjusting the benefits and burdens of economic life to promote the common good"—may be relevant in discerning whether a taking has occurred. *Ibid.* The *Penn Central* factors—though each has given rise to vexing subsidiary questions—have served as the principal guidelines for resolving regulatory takings claims that do not fall within the physical takings or *Lucas* rules. . . .

DIMINUTION IN VALUE

Although our regulatory takings jurisprudence cannot be characterized as unified, these three inquiries (reflected in *Loretto*, *Lucas*, and *Penn Central*) share a common touchstone. Each aims to identify regulatory actions that are functionally equivalent to the classic taking in which government directly appropriates private property or ousts the owner from his domain. Accordingly, each of these tests focuses directly upon the severity of the burden that government imposes upon private property rights. . . .

As this excerpt suggests, the concept of equivalence is not an express part of the Court's regulatory takings rules. Rather, it is a principle that can be used to understand the

Court's regulatory takings jurisprudence and perhaps to offer an organizing idea to unify a fairly confused area of law.

Lingle is also notable in that it recognized how the Court's regulatory takings analysis had been contaminated with substantive due process analysis from early cases. As the preceding excerpt indicates, the Court described the regulatory takings question as focusing on the regulation's impact on the property owner. The substantive due process analysis, in contrast, focuses on whether the regulation was a legitimate exercise of government power.

You may have noticed in our prior case references to a putative rule that a regulation is an unconstitutional taking if it fails to substantially advance a legitimate state interest. This "rule" was introduced in a passing reference in *Agins v. City of Tiburon*, 477 U.S. 255 (1980), and subsequent cases repeated the *Agins* language in summaries of takings law. *Lingle* was the first case to actually examine the "substantially advances" rule. The Court held the rule was a substantive due process rule, not a regulatory takings rule, and rejected the challenge based on it:

> In stark contrast to the three regulatory takings tests discussed above, the "substantially advances" inquiry reveals nothing about the magnitude or character of the burden a particular regulation imposes upon private property rights. Nor does it provide any information about how any regulatory burden is distributed among property owners. In consequence, this test does not help to identify those regulations whose effects are functionally comparable to government appropriation or invasion of private property; it is tethered neither to the text of the Takings Clause nor to the basic justification for allowing regulatory actions to be challenged under the Clause.
>
> Chevron appeals to the general principle that the Takings Clause is meant "'to bar Government from forcing some people alone to bear public burdens which, in all fairness and justice, should be borne by the public as a whole.'" *Brief for Respondent* 17-21 (quoting *Armstrong*, 364 U.S., at 49, 80 S.Ct. 1563). But that appeal is clearly misplaced, for the reasons just indicated. A test that tells us nothing about the actual burden imposed on property rights, or how that burden is allocated, cannot tell us when justice might require that the burden be spread among taxpayers through the payment of compensation. . . .
>
> Instead of addressing a challenged regulation's effect on private property, the "substantially advances" inquiry probes the regulation's underlying validity. But such an inquiry is logically prior to and distinct from the question whether a regulation effects a taking, for the Takings Clause presupposes that the government has acted in pursuit of a valid public purpose. The Clause expressly requires compensation where government takes private property "for public use." It does not bar

government from interfering with property rights, but rather requires compensation "in the event of *otherwise proper interference* amounting to a taking." *First English Evangelical Lutheran Church*, 482 U.S., at 315, 107 S.Ct. 2378 (emphasis added). Conversely, if a government action is found to be impermissible—for instance because it fails to meet the "public use" requirement or is so arbitrary as to violate due process—that is the end of the inquiry. No amount of compensation can authorize such action.

There are two important lessons to take from this aspect of *Lingle*. First, it is important to use care in reading early cases that present issues that resemble contemporary regulatory takings issues. The *Euclid* case, for example, superficially resembles a regulatory takings challenge because it involves a constitutional challenge to a land use regulation. The dissents in *Lucas* treated *Euclid* as a regulatory takings case. The Court recognized in *Lingle*, however, that *Euclid* was a substantive due process case, not a regulatory takings case. Second, it is always important to remember that courts make mistakes. The substantially advances test was introduced in what effectively was a citation error and then was repeated without examination in subsequent cases. When squarely confronted with the test in *Lingle*, the Court recognized its prior error and corrected it.

REGULATORY TAKINGS ANALYSIS SUMMARY

- Does regulation require a physical invasion of property?
  - Per se taking (*Loretto*)
  - Example: government requires public access to what had been private property.
- Does the regulation prevent owner from engaging in a common-law nuisance or other activity that the property holder does not have a right to engage in under the state's background principles of property law?
  - Per se *not* a taking.
  - *Lucas*—legislature cannot define nuisance. Nuisance exception applies only if the use would have been a *common-law* nuisance. Rejects the *Alger/Mugler* approach that the legislature can avoid takings claims by labeling the prohibited activity a nuisance.
- What is the diminution in value?
  - Denominator problem—do we use the affected portion or the parcel as a whole?
    - Supreme Court cases tend to support parcel as a whole, but it safest to treat this as an open issue.

- If 100 percent diminution in value (or deprivation of all economic use), per se taking under *Lucas*.
- If less than 100 percent diminution in value, apply *Penn Central* analysis.
- *Penn Central* analysis.
  - Ad hoc, factual inquiries
  - Three major factors:
    - Diminution in value is important.
    - Interference with investment backed expectations
      - Similar to diminution in value. But look for some expenditure of money in reliance on the pre-regulatory state of affairs.
    - Character of the government action
      - Very vague factor. Courts often use this factor to emphasize the importance of the government's purpose in acting and use this factor to weigh against a taking. On the other hand, courts sometimes use this factor to emphasize the impact on the property owner and use this factor to weigh in favor of a taking.
  - Other relevant factors:
    - Singling out
      - Does the regulation single out a relatively small percentage of landowners for regulation? If so, it is more likely to be found to be a taking.
    - Average reciprocity of advantage
      - Can be related to singling out. If a regulation takes away some of the property owner's rights, does the property owner benefit from those same rights being taken from her neighbors?
    - *Armstrong* principle. Does the regulation force property owners to bear costs that in all fairness and justice should be borne by the public as a whole?
      - So vague as to be kind of useless, but can often be used for pro-property owner rhetoric.
    - Equivalence principle. Not from *Penn Central*, but can be seen as part of the overall analysis. Discussed in *Lucas*, reinforced in *Lingle*. From the property owner's perspective, is the regulation the functional equivalent to an exercise of eminent domain? The closer the answer is to "yes," the better the property owner's takings claim.

e. The Exactions Issue

Imagine that you are the owner of a beach house. You want to renovate the house. To do so, you need a permit from the local government. The local government tells you that it will grant you the permit, but only if you allow the public access to the private areas of your beach. In other words, the government is telling you that it will give you what you want (the permit) in return for something it wants (public access to the beach). This is an example of an *exaction*. The government is attempting to get, or exact, something from you in return for the permit approval.

The ability of the government to demand an exaction from you is limited by the unconstitutional conditions doctrine. This doctrine protects individual constitutional rights by limiting the government's ability to coerce people into giving up those rights. Generally speaking, the government cannot deny a person a benefit because that person has exercised a constitutional right. For example, the government cannot deny a benefit to someone because that person has exercised her right to free speech.

The Supreme Court has crafted rules on exactions that translate the unconstitutional conditions doctrine into the property context. The core of these rules come from two cases, *Nollan v. California Coastal Commn.*, 483 U.S. 825 (1987) and *Dolan v. City of Tigard*, 512 U.S. 374 (1994).

Before we get to the details of the *Nollan* and *Dolan* rules, we need to underscore one crucial point. *An exaction only raises a constitutional problem if the concession demanded by the government would have been a taking if the government had tried to impose it on the property owner.* In our introductory example, the government was demanding public access to the beach. We know that a government action that requires public access to private property would be a per se taking under *Loretto*. Because the access demanded as an exaction would be a taking if imposed directly by the government, our *Nollan* and *Dolan* rules for exactions would apply.

If, in contrast, the exaction demanded by the government would not have been a taking if imposed by the government, then the exaction would be permissible, and the specialized *Nollan* and *Dolan* rules would not apply. Let's modify our original example. You still need a government permit to renovate you beach house, but we will modify the condition set by the government. Rather than requiring you to grant public access to the beach, the government now requires you to make repairs to the sidewalk in front of your house as a condition for granting the permit. This requirement would not trigger the *Nollan* and *Dolan* rules because the government could impose it directly on you without violating the Takings Clause—the government, for example, could constitutionally impose a regulation that required property owners to maintain their sidewalks.

Nollan and *Dolan*, then, establish rules that govern when an exaction will be permitted even though it would be an unconstitutional taking if imposed directly by the government. *Nollan* involved facts similar to our basic example. The Nollans wanted to buy a beachfront bungalow, demolish it, and replace it with a new, larger, house. The demolition and new construction required a permit from the California Coastal Commission. The Commission granted the permit on the condition that the Nollans grant a public easement for access across private portions of the beach. In his opinion of the Court, Justice Scalia described the Commission's factual findings in support of the condition as follows:

> It found that the new house would increase blockage of the view of the ocean, thus contributing to the development of "a 'wall' of residential structures" that would prevent the public "psychologically . . . from realizing a stretch of coastline exists nearby that they have every right

to visit." *Id.,* at 58. The new house would also increase private use of the shorefront. *Id.,* at 59. These effects of construction of the house, along with other area development, would cumulatively "burden the public's ability to traverse to and along the shorefront." *Id.,* at 65-66. Therefore the Commission could properly require the Nollans to offset that burden by providing additional lateral access to the public beaches in the form of an easement across their property.

483 U.S. at 819-820. The California Coastal Commission justified the public-easement exaction by focusing on the negative impact that the construction of the house would have on the public's view of the beach and on the resulting impairment of public access to the beach. You might wonder about the connection between the problem (the impairment of the view of the beach) and the exacted solution (a public easement across the beach). This connection, or lack thereof, was a problem for the Supreme Court:

> The Commission argues that a permit condition that serves the same legitimate police-power purpose as a refusal to issue the permit should not be found to be a taking if the refusal to issue the permit would not constitute a taking. We agree. Thus, if the Commission attached to the permit some condition that would have protected the public's ability to see the beach notwithstanding construction of the new house—for example, a height limitation, a width restriction, or a ban on fences—so long as the Commission could have exercised its police power (as we have assumed it could) to forbid construction of the house altogether, imposition of the condition would also be constitutional. Moreover (and here we come closer to the facts of the present case), the condition would be constitutional even if it consisted of the requirement that the Nollans provide a viewing spot on their property for passersby with whose sighting of the ocean their new house would interfere. Although such a requirement, constituting a permanent grant of continuous access to the property, would have to be considered a taking if it were not attached to a development permit, the Commission's assumed power to forbid construction of the house in order to protect the public's view of the beach must surely include the power to condition construction upon some concession by the owner, even a concession of property rights, that serves the same end. If a prohibition designed to accomplish that purpose would be a legitimate exercise of the police power rather than a taking, it would be strange to conclude that providing the owner an alternative to that prohibition which accomplishes the same purpose is not.
>
> The evident constitutional propriety disappears, however, if the condition substituted for the prohibition utterly fails to further the end advanced as the justification for the prohibition. When that essential nexus is eliminated, the situation becomes the same as if California law forbade

shouting fire in a crowded theater, but granted dispensations to those willing to contribute $100 to the state treasury. While a ban on shouting fire can be a core exercise of the State's police power to protect the public safety, and can thus meet even our stringent standards for regulation of speech, adding the unrelated condition alters the purpose to one which, while it may be legitimate, is inadequate to sustain the ban. Therefore, even though, in a sense, requiring a $100 tax contribution in order to shout fire is a lesser restriction on speech than an outright ban, it would not pass constitutional muster. Similarly here, the lack of nexus between the condition and the original purpose of the building restriction converts that purpose to something other than what it was. The purpose then becomes, quite simply, the obtaining of an easement to serve some valid governmental purpose, but without payment of compensation. Whatever may be the outer limits of "legitimate state interests" in the takings and land-use context, this is not one of them. In short, unless the permit condition serves the same governmental purpose as the development ban, the building restriction is not a valid regulation of land use but "an out-and-out plan of extortion." . . .

The Commission claims that it concedes as much, and that we may sustain the condition at issue here by finding that it is reasonably related to the public need or burden that the Nollans' new house creates or to which it contributes. We can accept, for purposes of discussion, the Commission's proposed test as to how close a "fit" between the condition and the burden is required, because we find that this case does not meet even the most untailored standards. The Commission's principal contention to the contrary essentially turns on a play on the word "access." The Nollans' new house, the Commission found, will interfere with "visual access" to the beach. That in turn (along with other shorefront development) will interfere with the desire of people who drive past the Nollans' house to use the beach, thus creating a "psychological barrier" to "access." The Nollans' new house will also, by a process not altogether clear from the Commission's opinion but presumably potent enough to more than offset the effects of the psychological barrier, increase the use of the public beaches, thus creating the need for more "access." These burdens on "access" would be alleviated by a requirement that the Nollans provide "lateral access" to the beach.

Rewriting the argument to eliminate the play on words makes clear that there is nothing to it. It is quite impossible to understand how a requirement that people already on the public beaches be able to walk across the Nollans' property reduces any obstacles to viewing the beach created by the new house. It is also impossible to understand how it lowers any "psychological barrier" to using the public beaches, or how it helps to remedy any additional congestion on them caused by construction of the Nollans' new house. We therefore find that the Commission's imposition of the permit condition cannot be treated as an exercise of its land-use power for any of these purposes.

483 U.S. 837-839. *Nollan*, then, created a requirement that there is a "nexus" between the problem that provides a justification for the exaction and the exaction itself. Because the California Coastal Commission had failed to meet this nexus, the exaction was invalid.

Dolan added an extra layer to the *Nollan* nexus requirement. Florence Dolan owned a hardware store in Tigard, Oregon. The property was located next to a creek and was therefore adjacent to a floodplain. She applied for a permit to expand her store, doubling its size and paving a 39-space parking lot. The City approved the permit on the condition that Dolan (a) dedicate approximately 10 percent of the lot to improving storm drainage and (b) dedicate a 15-foot strip for a public pathway to be used by pedestrians and bicyclists. As part of a variance proceeding brought by Dolan, the City Planning Commission made a number of findings about the relationship between the impacts of Dolan's proposed project and the exactions required for approval:

> First, the Commission noted that "[i]t is reasonable to assume that customers and employees of the future uses of this site could utilize a pedestrian/bicycle pathway adjacent to this development for their transportation and recreational needs." City of Tigard Planning Commission Final Order No. 91-09 PC, App. to Pet. for Cert. G-24. The Commission noted that the site plan has provided for bicycle parking in a rack in front of the proposed building and "[i]t is reasonable to expect that some of the users of the bicycle parking provided for by the site plan will use the pathway adjacent to Fanno Creek if it is constructed." *Ibid.* In addition, the Commission found that creation of a convenient, safe pedestrian/bicycle pathway system as an alternative means of transportation "could offset some of the traffic demand on [nearby] streets and lessen the increase in traffic congestion." *Ibid.*
>
> The Commission went on to note that the required floodplain dedication would be reasonably related to petitioner's request to intensify the use of the site given the increase in the impervious surface [by paving the previously unpaved parking lot]. The Commission stated that the "anticipated increased storm water flow from the subject property to an already strained creek and drainage basin can only add to the public need to manage the stream channel and floodplain for drainage purposes." *Id.,* at G-37. Based on this anticipated increased storm water flow, the Commission concluded that "the requirement of dedication of the floodplain area on the site is related to the applicant's plan to intensify development on the site." *Ibid.*

512 U.S. at 381-382. The Supreme Court, in an opinion by Chief Justice Rehnquist, held that the exactions met the nexus test announced in *Nollan*:

> Undoubtedly, the prevention of flooding along Fanno Creek and the reduction of traffic congestion in the Central Business District qualify as the type of legitimate public purposes we have upheld. . . . It seems equally obvious that a nexus exists between preventing flooding along Fanno Creek and limiting development within the creek's 100-year floodplain. Petitioner proposes to double the size of her retail store and to pave her now-gravel parking lot, thereby expanding the impervious surface on the property and increasing the amount of storm water runoff into Fanno Creek.
>
> The same may be said for the city's attempt to reduce traffic congestion by providing for alternative means of transportation. In theory, a pedestrian/bicycle pathway provides a useful alternative means of transportation for workers and shoppers: "Pedestrians and bicyclists occupying dedicated spaces for walking and/or bicycling . . . remove potential vehicles from streets, resulting in an overall improvement in total transportation system flow." A. Nelson, Public Provision of Pedestrian and Bicycle Access Ways: Public Policy Rationale and the Nature of Private Benefits 11, Center for Planning Development, Georgia Institute of Technology, Working Paper Series (Jan. 1994).

512 U.S. at 387-388. The Court, however, imposed an additional requirement on exactions:

> The second part of our analysis requires us to determine whether the degree of the exactions demanded by the city's permit conditions bears the required relationship to the projected impact of petitioner's proposed development. . . .
>
> The city required that petitioner dedicate "to the City as Greenway all portions of the site that fall within the existing 100-year floodplain [of Fanno Creek] . . . and all property 15 feet above [the floodplain] boundary." *Id.,* at 113, n. 3, 854 P.2d, at 439, n. 3. In addition, the city demanded that the retail store be designed so as not to intrude into the greenway area. The city relies on the Commission's rather tentative findings that increased storm water flow from petitioner's property "can only add to the public need to manage the [floodplain] for drainage purposes" to support its conclusion that the "requirement of dedication of the floodplain area on the site is related to the applicant's plan to intensify development on the site." City of Tigard Planning Commission Final Order No. 91-09 PC, App. to Pet. for Cert. G-37.
>
> The city made the following specific findings relevant to the pedestrian/ bicycle pathway:

"In addition, the proposed expanded use of this site is anticipated to generate additional vehicular traffic thereby increasing congestion on nearby collector and arterial streets. Creation of a convenient, safe pedestrian/bicycle pathway system as an alternative means of transportation could offset some of the traffic demand on these nearby streets and lessen the increase in traffic congestion." *Id.,* at G-24.

The question for us is whether these findings are constitutionally sufficient to justify the conditions imposed by the city on petitioner's building permit. Since state courts have been dealing with this question a good deal longer than we have, we turn to representative decisions made by them.

In some States, very generalized statements as to the necessary connection between the required dedication and the proposed development seem to suffice. We think this standard is too lax to adequately protect petitioner's right to just compensation if her property is taken for a public purpose.

Other state courts require a very exacting correspondence, described as the "specifi[c] and uniquely attributable" test. . . . The Supreme Court of Illinois first developed this test in *Pioneer Trust & Savings Bank v. Mount Prospect,* 22 Ill.2d 375, 380, 176 N.E.2d 799, 802 (1961). Under this standard, if the local government cannot demonstrate that its exaction is directly proportional to the specifically created need, the exaction becomes "a veiled exercise of the power of eminent domain and a confiscation of private property behind the defense of police regulations." *Id.,* at 381, 176 N.E.2d, at 802. We do not think the Federal Constitution requires such exacting scrutiny, given the nature of the interests involved.

A number of state courts have taken an intermediate position, requiring the municipality to show a "reasonable relationship" between the required dedication and the impact of the proposed development. . . .

We think the "reasonable relationship" test adopted by a majority of the state courts is closer to the federal constitutional norm than either of those previously discussed. But we do not adopt it as such, partly because the term "reasonable relationship" seems confusingly similar to the term "rational basis" which describes the minimal level of scrutiny under the Equal Protection Clause of the Fourteenth Amendment. We think a term such as "rough proportionality" best encapsulates what we hold to be the requirement of the Fifth Amendment. No precise mathematical calculation is required, but the city must make some sort of individualized determination that the required dedication is related both in nature and extent to the impact of the proposed development.

512 U.S. 388-391. The Supreme Court held that the findings developed by the city did not demonstrate compliance with this "rough proportionality" standard and remanded the case for further proceedings.

Combined, *Nollan* and *Dolan* create a two-part test for the validity of an exaction that, if directly imposed by the government, would be a taking. First, there must be a *nexus* between the problem asserted as justification and the demanded exaction. In *Nollan*, this required nexus was absent; in *Dolan*, it was present. Second, the government must make "some sort of individualized determination" that establishes a *rough proportionality* between the exaction and "the impact of the proposed development." *Note well* that the nexus/rough proportionality test applies only to exaction cases, and does not apply to regulatory takings more broadly.

f. The Judicial Takings Issue

When we introduced the regulatory takings issue, we framed it in this way: when, if ever, might a government regulation amount to a taking under the Just Compensation Clause? The judicial takings issue can be stated in a similar way: when, if ever, might an action by the judiciary amount to a taking under the Just Compensation Clause? One way of bringing this issue into focus is to think about a government action that would clearly be a taking if it was performed by the legislature and ask whether it would be a taking if it was performed by the judiciary. For example, if a legislature required public access to beachfront property when the owner previously had been able to exclude the public, the legislative action would almost certainly be a per se taking under the physical invasions rule. What would happen if the judiciary effectively did the same thing by redefining the state's property law to hold that the private property owner did not, in fact, have the right to exclude the public?

In *Stop the Beach Renourishment, Inc. v. Florida Department of Environmental Protection*, 560 U.S. 702 (2010), the U.S. Supreme Court granted *certiorari* to address the judicial takings question. The facts of the case are somewhat complex, but the issue involved public access to beachfront property in Florida. The Court unanimously held that there was no unconstitutional taking because the contested judicial action was consistent with prior Florida law. Beyond that holding, however, the Court was deeply fragmented. Justice Scalia's plurality opinion, joined by Chief Justice Roberts and Justices Thomas and Alito, expressed strong support for the idea that judicial actions could violate the Just Compensation Clause. Justice Kennedy's concurrence, joined by Justice Sotomayor, focused on procedural and substantive due process. Justice Breyer's concurrence, joined by Justice Ginsburg, was noncommittal on the judicial takings issue. (Justice Stevens recused himself because he owns Florida beachfront property.)

In other words, the Supreme Court raised the profile of the judicial takings issue by granting *certiorari* in *Stop the Beach*, but failed to resolve the core question of whether or not judicial actions could ever qualify as takings. For now, you should be aware that the issue exists. Time will tell if the Court will eventually recognize or reject a judicial takings doctrine.

CHAPTER 10

INTANGIBLE PROPERTY, INTELLECTUAL PROPERTY, AND PROPERTY IN THE HUMAN BODY

So far, we have focused on property rights in relatively routine tangible objects—land, houses, rings, foxes, baseballs, and so on. In this chapter, we introduce some issues relating to ownership of intangible things. As more and more of our economy moves online, intangible property is becoming increasingly important. We also introduce some issues relating to ownership of human body parts. As we will see, the question of whether we should have property rights in our bodies is anything but routine.

We begin with a question that couldn't have been asked too long ago—is it possible to commit the tort of conversion by misappropriating an Internet domain name? As you know, domain names can be very valuable. They are intangible and represent a type of asset that is relatively new to both our economy and our legal system. We then provide a brief overview of intellectual property law and introduce some of the fundamental policy issues that underlie our protection of patents, trademarks, copyrights, and other types of intellectual property. Finally, we consider whether we should have property rights in our organs and other body parts.

A. INTANGIBLE PROPERTY

Our next case involves the misappropriation of a very valuable domain name and raises the question of whether intangible property is subject to the tort of conversion. Recall that real property is ownership of land and things attached to land, and personal property is ownership of everything else. Intangible things therefore are owned as personal property. A person who destroys or refuses to return another's personal property may be liable to the owner under the tort of conversion.

How, if at all, can someone convert intangible property? Some types of intangible property are incorporated into a document. For example, a share of stock in a corporation might be incorporated into a physical share certificate. Similarly, a right to receive a payment of money might be incorporated into a physical bond certificate. In each of these examples, the intangible asset—the share of stock and the right to receive a payment of money—is far more valuable than the piece of paper into which the intangible asset is incorporated. In some circumstances, the destruction of the physical certificate may destroy the intangible asset that is incorporated into the certificate.

In cases like this, the law of torts has long held that the conversion of the document also gives rise to liability for conversion of the intangible asset that is merged into the document. The Restatement (Second) of Torts suggested that intangible assets that are not merged into a document could not be converted. Unlike share certificates, domain names are not merged into documents. Does that mean that domain names are not subject to the tort of conversion? In our next case, Judge Alex Kozinski of the United States Court of Appeals for the Ninth Circuit considers this issue. We include another opinion by Judge Kozinski a bit later in this chapter. You will soon see why—whether you agree with him or disagree with him on the merits, we think that you will agree that he writes a great opinion.

KREMEN V. COHEN

United States Court of Appeals for the Ninth Circuit, 2003
337 F.3d 1024

KOZINSKI, Circuit Judge:

We decide whether Network Solutions may be liable for giving away a registrant's domain name on the basis of a forged letter.

BACKGROUND

"Sex on the Internet?," they all said. "*That'll* never make any money." But computer-geek-turned-entrepreneur Gary Kremen knew an opportunity when he saw it. The year was 1994; domain names were free for the asking, and it would be several years yet before Henry Blodget and hordes of eager NASDAQ day traders would turn the Internet into the Dutch tulip craze of our times. With a quick e-mail to the domain name registrar Network Solutions, Kremen became the proud owner of sex.com. He registered the name to his business, Online Classifieds, and listed himself as the contact.

Con man Stephen Cohen, meanwhile, was doing time for impersonating a bankruptcy lawyer. He, too, saw the potential of the domain name. Kremen had gotten it first, but that was only a minor impediment for a man of Cohen's boundless resource and bounded integrity. Once out of prison, he sent Network Solutions what purported to be a letter he had received from Online Classifieds. It claimed the company had been "forced to dismiss Mr. Kremen," but "never got around to changing our administrative contact with the internet registration [*sic*] and now our Board of directors has decided to *abandon* the domain name sex.com." Why was this unusual letter being sent via Cohen rather than to Network Solutions directly? It explained:

> Because we do not have a direct connection to the internet, we request that you notify the internet registration on our behalf, to delete our domain name sex.com. Further, we have no objections to your use of the domain name sex.com and this letter shall serve as our authorization to the internet registration to transfer sex.com to your corporation.

Despite the letter's transparent claim that a company called "*Online* Classifieds" had no Internet connection, Network Solutions made no effort to contact Kremen. Instead, it accepted the letter at face value and transferred the domain name to Cohen. When Kremen contacted Network Solutions some time later, he was told it was too late to undo the transfer. Cohen went on to turn sex.com into a lucrative online porn empire.

And so began Kremen's quest to recover the domain name that was rightfully his. He sued Cohen and several affiliated companies in federal court, seeking return of the domain name and disgorgement of Cohen's profits. The district court found that the letter was indeed a forgery and ordered the domain name returned to Kremen . . . It awarded $ 40 million in compensatory damages and another $ 25 million in punitive damages.

Kremen, unfortunately, has not had much luck collecting his judgment. The district court froze Cohen's assets, but Cohen ignored the order and wired large sums of money to offshore accounts. His real estate property, under the protection of a federal receiver, was stripped of all its fixtures—even cabinet doors and toilets—in violation of another order. The court commanded Cohen to appear and show cause why he shouldn't be held in contempt, but he ignored that order, too. The district judge finally took off the gloves—he declared Cohen a fugitive from justice, signed an arrest warrant and sent the U.S. Marshals after him.

Then things started getting *really* bizarre. Kremen put up a "wanted" poster on the sex.com site with a mug shot of Cohen, offering a $ 50,000 reward to anyone who brought him to justice. Cohen's lawyers responded with a motion to vacate the arrest warrant. They reported that Cohen was under house arrest in Mexico and that gunfights between Mexican authorities and would-be bounty hunters seeking Kremen's reward money posed a threat to human life. The district court rejected this story as "implausible" and denied the motion. Cohen, so far as the record shows, remains at large.

Given his limited success with the bounty hunter approach, it should come as no surprise that Kremen seeks to hold someone else responsible for his losses. That someone is Network Solutions, the exclusive domain name registrar at the time of Cohen's antics. Kremen sued it for mishandling his domain name, invoking four theories at issue here . . . His third theory is that he has a property right in the domain name sex.com, and Network Solutions committed the tort of conversion by giving it away to Cohen.

The district court granted summary judgment in favor of Network Solutions on all claims. *Kremen v. Cohen*, 99 F. Supp. 2d 1168 (N.D. Cal. 2000). [the court discusses the first two claims] . . . The conversion claim fared no better. The court agreed that sex.com was Kremen's property. It concluded, though, that it was intangible property to which the tort of conversion does not apply. *Id.* at 1173.

Kremen appeals, and we consider each of his four theories in turn.

CONVERSION

Kremen's conversion claim is another matter. To establish that tort, a plaintiff must show "ownership or right to possession of property, wrongful disposition of the property right and damages." *G.S. Rasmussen & Assoc., Inc. v. Kalitta Flying Service, Inc.*, 958 F.2d 896, 906 (9th Cir. 1992). The preliminary question, then, is whether registrants have property rights in their domain names. Network Solutions all but concedes that they do. This is no surprise, given its positions in prior litigation. *See Network Solutions, Inc. v. Umbro Int'l, Inc.*, 259 Va. 759, 529 S.E.2d 80, 86 (Va. 2000) ("[Network Solutions] acknowledged during oral argument before this Court that the right to use a domain name is a form of intangible personal property."); *Network Solutions, Inc. v. Clue Computing, Inc.*, 946 F. Supp. 858, 860 (D. Colo. 1996) (same). The district court agreed with the parties on this issue, as do we.

Property is a broad concept that includes "every intangible benefit and prerogative susceptible of possession or disposition." *Downing v. Mun. Court*, 88 Cal. App. 2d 345, 350, 198 P.2d 923 (1948) (internal quotation marks omitted). We apply a three-part test to determine whether a property right exists: "First, there must be an interest capable of precise definition; second, it must be capable of exclusive possession or control; and third, the putative owner must have established a legitimate claim to exclusivity." *G.S. Rasmussen*, 958 F.2d at 903 (footnote omitted). Domain names satisfy each criterion. Like a share of corporate stock or a plot of land, a domain name is a well-defined interest. Someone who registers a domain name decides where on the Internet those who invoke that particular name—whether by typing it into their web browsers, by following a hyperlink, or by other means—are sent. Ownership is exclusive in that the registrant alone makes that decision. Moreover, like other forms of property, domain names are valued, bought and sold, often for millions of dollars, *see* Greg Johnson, *The Costly Game for Net Names*, L.A. Times, Apr. 10, 2000, at A1, and they are now even subject to in rem jurisdiction, *see* 15 U.S.C. §1125(d)(2).

Finally, registrants have a legitimate claim to exclusivity. Registering a domain name is like staking a claim to a plot of land at the title office. It informs others that the domain name is the registrant's and no one else's. Many registrants also invest substantial time and money to develop and promote websites that depend on their domain names. Ensuring that they reap the benefits of their investments reduces uncertainty and thus encourages investment in the first place, promoting the growth of the Internet overall. *See G.S. Rasmussen*, 958 F.2d at 900.

Kremen therefore had an intangible property right in his domain name, and a jury could find that Network Solutions "wrongfully disposed of" that right to his detriment by handing the domain name over to Cohen. *Id.* at 906. The district court nevertheless rejected Kremen's conversion claim. It held that domain names, although a form of property, are intangibles not subject to conversion. This rationale derives from a distinction tort law once drew between tangible and intangible property: Conversion was originally a remedy for the wrongful taking of another's lost goods, so it applied only to tangible property. *See Prosser and Keeton on the Law of Torts* §15, at 89, 91 (W. Page Keeton ed., 5th ed. 1984). Virtually every jurisdiction, however, has discarded this rigid limitation to some degree. *See id.* at 91. Many courts ignore or expressly reject it. *See Kremen*, 325 F.3d at 1045-46 n.5 (Kozinski, J., dissenting) (citing cases); *Astroworks, Inc. v. Astroexhibit, Inc.*, 257 F. Supp. 2d 609, 618 (S.D.N.Y. 2003) (holding that the plaintiff could maintain a claim for conversion of his website); Val D. Ricks, *The Conversion of Intangible Property: Bursting the Ancient Trover Bottle with New Wine*, 1991 B.Y.U. L. Rev. 1681, 1682. Others reject it for some intangibles but not others. The *Restatement*, for example, recommends the following test:

(1) Where there is conversion of a document in which intangible rights are merged, the damages include the value of such rights.

(2) One who effectively prevents the exercise of intangible rights of the kind customarily *merged in a document* is subject to a liability similar to that for conversion, even though the document is not itself converted.

Restatement (Second) of Torts §242 (1965) (emphasis added). An intangible is "merged" in a document when, "by the appropriate rule of law, the right to the immediate possession of a chattel and the power to acquire such possession is *represented by* [the] document," or when "an intangible obligation [is] *represented by* [the] document, which is regarded as equivalent to the obligation." *Id.* cmt. a (emphasis added). The district court applied this test and found no evidence that Kremen's domain name was merged in a document.

The court assumed that California follows the *Restatement* on this issue. Our review, however, revealed that "there do not appear to be any California cases squarely addressing whether the 'merged with' requirement is a part of California law." *Kremen*, 325 F.3d at 1042. We invoked the California Supreme Court's certification procedure to offer it the opportunity to address the issue. *Id.* at 1043; Cal. Rules of Court 29.8. The Court declined, *Kremen v. Cohen*, 2003 Cal. LEXIS 1342, No. S112591 (Cal. Feb. 25, 2003), and the question now falls to us.

We conclude that California does not follow the *Restatement*'s strict merger requirement. Indeed, the leading California Supreme Court case rejects the tangibility requirement altogether. In *Payne v. Elliot*, 54 Cal. 339 (1880), the Court considered whether shares in a corporation (as opposed to the share certificates themselves) could be converted. It held that they could, reasoning: "The action no longer exists as it did at common law, but has been developed into a remedy for the conversion of *every species of personal property."* *Id.* at 341 (emphasis added). While *Payne*'s outcome might be reconcilable with the *Restatement*, its rationale certainly is not: It recognized conversion of shares, not because they are customarily represented by share certificates, but because they are a species of personal property and, perforce, protected. *Id.* at 342.

Notwithstanding *Payne*'s seemingly clear holding, the California Court of Appeal held in *Olschewski v. Hudson*, 87 Cal. App. 282, 262 P. 43 (1927), that a laundry route was not subject to conversion. It explained that *Payne*'s rationale was "too broad a statement as to the application of the doctrine of conversion." *Id.* at 288. Rather than follow binding California Supreme Court precedent, the court retheorized *Payne* and held that corporate stock could be converted only because it was "represented by" a tangible document. *Id.*; *see also Adkins v. Model Laundry Co.*, 92 Cal. App. 575, 583, 268 P. 939 (1928) (relying on *Olschewski* and holding that no property right inhered in "the intangible interest of an exclusive privilege to collect laundry").

Were *Olschewski* the only relevant case on the books, there might be a plausible argument that California follows the *Restatement*. But in *Palm Springs-La Quinta Development Co. v. Kieberk Corp.*, 46 Cal. App. 2d 234, 115 P.2d 548 (1941), the court of appeal allowed a conversion claim for intangible information in a customer list when some of the index cards on which the information was recorded were destroyed. The court allowed damages not just for the value of the cards, but for the value of the intangible information lost. *See id.* at 239. Section 242(1) of the *Restatement*, however, allows recovery for intangibles only if they are merged in the converted document. Customer information is not merged in a document in any meaningful sense. A Rolodex is not like a stock certificate that actually *represents* a property interest; it is only a means of recording information.

Palm Springs and *Olschewski* are reconcilable on their facts—the former involved conversion of the document itself while the latter did not. But this distinction can't be squared with the *Restatement*. The plaintiff in *Palm Springs* recovered damages for the value of his intangibles. But if those intangibles were merged in the index cards for purposes of section 242(1), the plaintiffs in *Olschewski* and *Adkins* should have recovered under section 242(2)—laundry routes surely are customarily written down *somewhere*. "Merged" can't mean one thing in one section and something else in the other.

California courts ignored the *Restatement* again in *A & M Records, Inc. v. Heilman*, 75 Cal. App. 3d 554, 142 Cal. Rptr. 390 (1977), which applied the tort to a defendant who sold bootlegged copies of musical recordings. The court held broadly that "such misappropriation and sale of the intangible property of another without authority from the owner is conversion." *Id.* at 570. It gave no hint that its holding depended on whether the owner's intellectual property rights were merged in some document. One might imagine physical things with which the intangible was associated—for example, the medium on which the song was recorded. But an intangible intellectual property right in a song is not merged in a phonograph record in the sense that the record *represents* the composer's intellectual property right. The record is not like a certificate of ownership; it is only a medium for one instantiation of the artistic work.

Federal cases applying California law take an equally broad view. We have applied *A & M Records* to intellectual property rights in an audio broadcast, *see Lone Ranger Television, Inc. v. Program Radio Corp.*, 740 F.2d 718, 725 (9th Cir. 1984), and to a regulatory filing, *see G.S. Rasmussen*, 958 F.2d at 906-07. Like *A & M Records*, both decisions defy the *Restatement*'s "merged in a document" test. An audio broadcast may be recorded on a tape and a regulatory submission may be typed on a piece of paper, but neither document *represents* the owner's intangible interest.

The Seventh Circuit interpreted California law in *FMC Corp. v. Capital Cities/ABC, Inc.*, 915 F.2d 300 (7th Cir. 1990). Observing that "'there is perhaps no very valid and essential reason why there might not be conversion' of intangible property," *id.* at 305 (quoting *Prosser & Keeton, supra*, §15, at 92), it held that a defendant could be liable merely for depriving the plaintiff of the use of his confidential information, *id.* at 304. In rejecting the tangibility requirement, *FMC* echoes *Payne*'s holding that personal property of any species may be converted. And it flouts the *Restatement* because the intangible property right in confidential information is not represented by the documents on which the information happens to be recorded.

Our own recent decision in *Bancroft & Masters, Inc. v. Augusta National Inc.*, 223 F.3d 1082 (9th Cir. 2000), is especially relevant. That case involved a domain name—precisely the type of property at issue here. The primary question was personal jurisdiction, but a majority of the panel joined the judgment only on the understanding that the defendant had committed conversion of a domain name, which it characterized as "tortious conduct." *Id.* at 1089 (Sneed & Trott, JJ., concurring); *cf. Astroworks, Inc.*, 257 F. Supp. 2d at 618 (holding that the plaintiff could maintain a claim for conversion of his website).

In short, California does not follow the *Restatement*'s strict requirement that some document must actually represent the owner's intangible property right. On the contrary, courts routinely apply the tort to intangibles without inquiring whether they are merged in a document and, while it's often possible to dream up *some* document the intangible is connected to in some fashion, it's seldom one that represents the owner's property interest. To the extent *Olschewski* endorses the strict merger rule, it is against the weight of authority. That rule cannot be squared with a jurisprudence that recognizes conversion of music recordings, radio shows, customer lists, regulatory filings, confidential information and even domain names.

Kremen's domain name is protected by California conversion law . . . Exposing Network Solutions to liability when it gives away a registrant's domain name on the basis of a forged letter is no different from holding a corporation liable when it gives away someone's shares under the same circumstances. *See Schneider v. Union Oil Co.*, 6 Cal. App. 3d 987, 992, 86 Cal. Rptr. 315 (1970); *Ralston v. Bank of Cal.*, 112 Cal. 208, 213, 44 P. 476 (1896). We have not "created new tort duties" in reaching this result. *Cf. Moore v. Regents of the Univ. of Cal.*, 51 Cal.3d 120, 146, 271 Cal. Rptr. 146, 793 P.2d 479 (1990). We have only applied settled principles of conversion law to what the parties and the district court all agree is a species of property.

The district court supported its contrary holding with several policy rationales, but none is sufficient grounds to depart from the common law rule. The court was reluctant to apply the tort of conversion because of its strict liability nature. This concern rings somewhat hollow in this case because the district court effectively exempted Network Solutions from liability to Kremen altogether, whether or not it was negligent. Network Solutions made no effort to contact Kremen before giving away his domain name, despite receiving a facially suspect letter from a third party. A jury would be justified in finding it was unreasonably careless.

We must, of course, take the broader view, but there is nothing unfair about holding a company responsible for giving away someone else's property even if it was not at fault. Cohen is obviously the guilty party here, and the one who should in all fairness pay for his theft. But he's skipped the country, and his money is stashed in some offshore bank account. Unless Kremen's luck with his bounty hunters improves. Cohen is out of the picture. The question becomes whether Network Solutions should be open to liability for its decision to hand over Kremen's domain name. Negligent or not, it was Network Solutions that gave away Kremen's property. Kremen never did anything. It would not be unfair to hold Network Solutions responsible and force *it* to try to recoup its losses by chasing down Cohen. This, at any rate, is the logic of the common law, and we do not lightly discard it.

The district court was worried that "the threat of litigation threatens to stifle the registration system by requiring further regulations by [Network Solutions] and potential increases in fees." *Kremen*, 99 F. Supp. 2d at 1174. Given that Network Solutions's "regulations" evidently allowed it to hand over a registrant's domain name on the basis of a facially suspect letter without even contacting him, "further regulations" don't seem like such a bad idea. And the prospect of higher fees presents no issue here that it doesn't in any other context. A bank could lower its ATM fees if it didn't have to pay security guards, but we doubt most depositors would think that was a good idea.

The district court thought there were "methods better suited to regulate the vagaries of domain names" and left it "to the legislature to fashion an appropriate statutory scheme." *Id.* The legislature, of course, is always free (within constitutional bounds) to refashion the system that courts come up with. But that doesn't mean we should throw up our hands and let private relations degenerate into a free-for-all in the meantime. We apply the common law until the legislature tells us other-wise. And the common law does not stand idle while people give away the property of others.

The evidence supported a claim for conversion, and the district court should not have rejected it.

Kremen had a viable claim for conversion. The judgment of the district court is reversed on this count, and the case is remanded for further proceedings.

NOTE

1. *Rivalrous vs. Non-Rivalrous Goods.* Judge Kozinski rejected the argument that intangible assets need to be merged into a document to be subject to conversion. Even under the holding in *Kremen*, however, not all intangible assets are subject to conversion because some types of intangible assets by their nature simply cannot be converted. To help explain why this is so, we want to introduce the distinction between *rivalrous* and *non-rivalrous* goods. If my consumption of a good prevents you from consuming that good, then that good is rivalrous. For example, my consumption of a cookie prevents you from consuming that cookie. A cookie therefore is rivalrous. If my consumption of a good does not prevent you from consuming that good, then that good is non-rivalrous. For example, if I watch a video on YouTube, my consumption of that good (by watching the video) does not prevent you from consuming the same good (by watching the video yourself). Domain names are rivalrous—if I am using one domain name, you cannot use the same one. Hence domain names can be converted. Videos on YouTube are non-rivalrous. The videos are subject to copyright laws (which we will discuss below). If a video is posted onto YouTube in violation of copyright laws, then the owner of the video's copyright may be *infringed*. The common-law tort of conversion would not apply because the use of the video by the infringer does not destroy the video or prevent its use by the owner.

VIRTUAL PROPERTY

People increasingly are spending their time and money in virtual worlds. Massively multiplayer online role-playing games (MMORPGs), for example, are a multi-billion-dollar industry. Virtual assets in these games have substantial real world-value. Players, for example, exchange weapons or equipment in these games for real-world money. Some virtual objects trade for thousands of dollars. (Google "Incredibly valuable game loot" for a sample). Virtual real estate in worlds like Entropia and Second Life can sell for thousands of dollars. Ownership of these assets presents a host on unanswered legal issues. The contractual terms of service for a virtual world are likely to govern many ownership issues but may not be dispositive in all circumstances.

For discussion of these and other related issues, *see* Greg Lastowka, *Virtual Justice: The New Laws of Online Worlds* (2010); Christopher J. Cifrino, *Virtual Property, Virtual Rights: Why Contract Law, Not Property Law, Must Be the Governing Paradigm in the Law of Virtual Worlds*, 55 B.C. L. Rev. 235 (2014); John William Nelson, *The Virtual Property Problem: What Property Rights in Virtual Resources Might Look Like, How They Might Work, and Why They Are a Bad Idea*, 41 McGeorge L. Rev. 281 (2010); Juliet M. Moringiello, *What Virtual Worlds Can Do For Property Law*, 62 Fla. L. Rev. 159 (2010); Joshua A.T. Fairfield, *Virtual Property*, 85 B.U. L. Rev. 1047 (2005). If you are interested in virtual worlds, you should read Neal Stephenson's novel *Snow Crash*. The novel popularized terms like "avatar" and has been influential on the development of virtual worlds like Second Life.

B. A BRIEF INTRODUCTION TO INTELLECTUAL PROPERTY

Every year, intellectual property becomes an increasingly important part of our economy. In this section, we provide a very brief overview of the law of intellectual property and of some of the fundamental theoretical issues that underlie our intellectual property rules. Most law schools offer several upper-level classes on intellectual property, and we encourage you to explore them as your legal education progresses.

Our legal system has three major types of intellectual property: copyrights, patents, and trademarks. Article I, Section 8 of the Constitution expressly gives Congress the power to enact laws "[t]o promote the progress of science and useful arts, by securing for limited times to authors and investors the exclusive right to their respective writings and discoveries." The common law gave some protection to intellectual property, and common-law rights can still be important in some contexts. For the most part, however, our modern law of copyright, trademark, and patent is governed by federal statute.

Perhaps the most important policy issue in intellectual property law involves striking a balance between the creation and consumption of intellection property. As we will see, each type of intellectual property gives certain rights to the creators of intellectual property. These rights incentivize the production of intellectual property. While we want to promote the creation of intellectual property, we also want the public to be able to consume the intellectual property. If we give creators too little protection, they may not produce new intellectual property. If we give creators too much protection, then the public consumption of intellectual property will be overly constrained. A related policy issue involves striking the balance between the interests of present and future creators of intellectual property. As we will see, new intellectual property tends to build on older intellectual property. We therefore need to make sure that we do not unduly stifle future creators by giving present creators too much protection.

Each type of intellectual property strikes the balance between creation and consumption in different ways. *Patents* give protection to the inventors of new products and processes. To qualify for protection, the invention must be useful, novel, and non-obvious. Patents incentivize production of intellectual property by giving the patent holder an effective monopoly on the use of the invention for the duration of the patent term. Patents typically last for 20 years from the time that the original application was submitted to the Patent Office. The relatively short duration of patents incentivizes consumption. For example, once a drug patent expires, that drug typically is available to consumers at greatly reduced cost from generic drug manufacturers.

Copyrights protect the expression of ideas. Books, songs, and videos, for example, are copyrightable. Ideas themselves are not copyrightable. Compared to other intellectual property rights, copyrights last for a relatively long time. The duration of copyrights has changed over the years, but today the typical copyright will last for the life of the creator plus 70 years. The interests of consumers and subsequent creators are served by the fair use doctrine, which allows for the limited use of copyrighted work without permission from or payment to the copyright holder. Subsequent creators are protected by a subcategory of fair use called transformative use. As its name suggests, transformative use protects a new creator who uses previously copyrighted material in a completely new or unexpected way. Parodies are good examples of transformative use.

A *trademark* is a "word, name, symbol, or device, or any combination thereof" used by a person "to identify and distinguish his or her goods, including a unique product, from those manufactured or sold by others. . . ." 15 U.S.C.A. §1127. The interests of creators and consumers are balanced in a slightly different way in the trademark context than in the patent and copyright context. Consumers do not actually consume trademarks. Rather, they consume goods identified and distinguished by trademarks. Trademarks incentivize production by rewarding trademark holders who create brands and products that consumers value. Trademarks help consumers who want a specific product identify that product. Trademark law protection is typically limited by the degree to which a consumer might be confused by an allegedly infringing product. This is why, for example, you will see generic products on store shelves that have a somewhat similar look and feel to a trademarked product. A generic product typically will not infringe on the trademark so long as it is unlikely that a consumer will be confused between the genuine trademarked product and a generic imitation.

We provide excerpts from only two of the hundreds of fascinating cases in the intellectual property cannon. The first case, *International News Service v. Associated Press* is a classic early case involving the collection and dissemination of news. Often referred to by the abbreviation *INS v. AP*, the case gives us an opportunity to think about issues that continue to be relevant in the Internet age. Say that you run a website devoted to covering news on a particular topic. I run a competing website devoted to the same topic. I read news on your website and then post reports on those topics on my website. Can you bring a claim against me for appropriating the news that you gathered?

INTERNATIONAL NEWS SERVICE V. ASSOCIATED PRESS

Supreme Court of the United States, 1918
248 U.S. 215

Mr. Justice PITNEY delivered the opinion of the Court.

The parties are competitors in the gathering and distribution of news and its publication for profit in newspapers throughout the United States. The Associated Press, which was complainant in the District Court, is a co-operative organization, incorporated under the Membership Corporations Law of the state of New York, its members being individuals who are either proprietors or representatives of about 950 daily newspapers published in all parts of the United States. . . . Complainant gathers in all parts of the world, by means of various instrumentalities of its own, by exchange with its members, and by other appropriate means, news and intelligence of current and recent events of interest to newspaper readers and distributes it daily to its members for publication in their newspapers. The cost of the service, amounting approximately to $3,500,000 per annum, is assessed upon the members and becomes a part of their costs of operation, to be recouped, presumably with profit, through the publication of their several newspapers. Under complainant's by-laws each member agrees upon assuming membership that news received through complainant's service is received exclusively for publication in a particular newspaper, language, and place specified in the certificate of membership, that no other use of it shall be permitted, and that no member shall furnish or permit any one in his employ or connected with his newspaper to furnish any of complainant's news in advance of publication to any person not a member. And each member is required to gather the local news of his district and supply it to the Associated Press and to no one else.

Defendant is a corporation organized under the laws of the state of New Jersey, whose business is the gathering and selling of news to its customers and clients, consisting of newspapers published throughout the United States, under contracts by which they pay certain amounts at stated times for defendant's service. It has widespread news-gathering agencies; the cost of its operations amounts, it is said, to more than $2,000,000 per annum; and it serves about 400 newspapers located in the various cities of the United States and abroad, a few of which are represented, also, in the membership of the Associated Press.

The parties are in the keenest competition between themselves in the distribution of news throughout the United States; and so, as a rule, are the newspapers that they serve, in their several districts.

Complainant in its bill, defendant in its answer, have set forth in almost identical terms the rather obvious circumstances and conditions under which their business is conducted. The value of the service, and of the news furnished, depends upon the promptness of transmission, as well as upon the accuracy and impartiality of the news; it being essential that the news be transmitted to members or subscribers as early or earlier than similar information can be furnished to competing newspapers by other news services, and that the news furnished by each agency shall not be furnished to newspapers which do not contribute to the expense of gathering it. And further, to quote from the answer:

> "Prompt knowledge and publication of worldwide news is essential to the conduct of a modern newspaper, and by reason of the enormous expense incident to the gathering and distribution of such news, the only practical way in which a proprietor of a newspaper can obtain the same is, either through co-operation with a considerable number of other newspaper proprietors in the work of collecting and distributing such news, and the equitable division with them of the expenses thereof, or by the purchase of such news from some existing agency engaged in that business."

The bill was filed to restrain the pirating of complainant's news by defendant in three ways: First, by bribing employees of newspapers published by complainant's members to furnish Associated Press news to defendant before publication, for transmission by telegraph and telephone to defendant's clients for publication by them; second, by inducing Associated Press members to violate its by-laws and permit defendant to obtain news before publication; and, third, by copying news from bulletin boards and from early editions of complainant's newspapers and selling this, either bodily or after rewriting it, to defendant's customers.

The District Court, upon consideration of the bill and answer, with voluminous affidavits on both sides, granted a preliminary injunction under the first and second heads, but refused at that stage to restrain the systematic practice admittedly pursued by defendant, of taking news bodily from the bulletin boards and early editions of complainant's newspapers and selling it as its own. The court expressed itself as satisfied that this practice amounted to unfair trade, but as the legal question was one of first impression it considered that the allowance of an injunction should await the outcome of an appeal. 240 Fed. 983, 996. Both parties having appealed, the Circuit Court of Appeals sustained the injunction order so far as it went, and upon complainant's appeal modified it and remanded the cause, with directions to issue an injunction also against any bodily taking of the words or substance of complainant's news until its commercial value as news had passed away. 245 Fed. 244, 253, 157 C. C. A. 436. The present writ of certiorari was then allowed. 245 U. S. 644, 38 Sup. Ct. 10, 62 L. Ed. 528.

The only matter that has been argued before us is whether defendant may lawfully be restrained from appropriating news taken from bulletins issued by complainant or any of its members, or from newspapers published by them, for the purpose of selling it to defendant's clients. Complainant asserts that defendant's admitted course of conduct in this regard both violates complainant's property right in the news and constitutes unfair competition in business. And notwithstanding the case has proceeded only to the stage of a preliminary injunction, we have deemed it proper to consider the underlying questions, since they go to the very merits of the action and are presented upon facts that are not in dispute. As presented in argument, these questions are: (1) Whether there is any property in news; (2) Whether, if there be property in news collected for the purpose of being published, it survives the instant of its publication in the first newspaper to which it is communicated by the news-gatherer; and (3) whether defendant's admitted course of conduct in appropriating for commercial use matter taken from bulletins or early editions of Associated Press publications constitutes unfair competition in trade. . . .

Complainant's news matter is not copyrighted. It is said that it could not, in practice, be copyrighted, because of the large number of dispatches that are sent daily; and, according to complainant's contention, news is not within the operation of the copyright act. Defendant, while apparently conceding this, nevertheless invokes the analogies of the law of literary property and copyright, insisting as its principal contention that, assuming complainant has a right of property in its news, it can be maintained (unless the copyright act by complied with) only by being kept secret and confidential, and that upon the publication with complainant's consent of uncopyrighted news of any of complainant's members in a newspaper or upon a bulletin board, the right of property is lost, and the subsequent use of the news by the public or by defendant for any purpose whatever becomes lawful. . . .

No doubt news articles often possess a literary quality, and are the subject of literary property at the common law; nor do we question that such an article, as a literary production, is the subject of copyright by the terms of the act as it now stands. In an early case at the circuit Mr. Justice Thompson held in effect that a newspaper was not within the protection of the copyright acts of 1790 (1 Stat. 124) and 1802 (2 Stat. 171). *Clayton v. Stone*, 2 Paine, 382, Fed. Cas. No. 2,872. But the present act is broader; it provides that the works for which copyright may be secured shall include "all the writings of an author," and specifically mentions "periodicals, including newspapers." Act of March 4, 1909, c. 320, §§4 and 5, 35 Stat. 1075, 1076 (Comp. St. 1916, §§9520, 9521). Evidently this admits to copyright a contribution to a newspaper, notwithstanding it also may convey news; and such is the practice of the copyright office, as the newspapers of the day bear witness. *See* Copyright Office Bulletin No. 15 (1917) pp. 7, 14, 16, 17.

But the news element—the information respecting current events contained in the literary production—is not the creation of the writer, but is a report of matters that ordinarily are publici juris; it is the history of the day. It is not to be supposed that the framers of the Constitution, when they empowered Congress "to promote the progress of science and useful arts, by securing for limited times to authors and inventors the exclusive right to their respective writings and discoveries" (Const. art. 1, §8, par. 8), intended to confer upon one who might happen to be the first to report a historic event the exclusive right for any period to spread the knowledge of it.

We need spend no time, however, upon the general question of property in news matter at common law, or the application of the copyright act, since it seems to us the case must turn upon the question of unfair competition in business. And, in our opinion, this does not depend upon any general right of property analogous to the common-law right of the proprietor of an unpublished work to prevent its publication without his consent; nor is it foreclosed by showing that the benefits of the copyright act have been waived. We are dealing here not with restrictions upon publication but with the very facilities and processes of publication. The peculiar value of news is in the spreading of it while it is fresh; and it is evident that a valuable property interest in the news, as news, cannot be maintained by keeping it secret. Besides, except for matters improperly disclosed, or published in breach of trust or confidence, or in violation of law, none of which is involved in this branch of the case, the news of current events may be regarded as common property. What we are concerned with is the business of making it known to the world, in which both parties to the present suit are engaged. That business consists in maintaining a prompt, sure, steady, and reliable service designed to place the daily events of the world at the breakfast table of the millions at a price that, while of trifling moment to each reader, is sufficient in the aggregate to afford compensation for the cost of gathering and distributing it, with the added profit so necessary as an incentive to effective action in the commercial world. The service thus performed for newspaper readers is not only innocent but extremely useful in itself, and indubitably constitutes a legitimate business. The parties are competitors in this field; and, on fundamental principles, applicable here as elsewhere, when the rights or privileges of the one are liable to conflict with those of the other, each party is under a duty so to conduct its own business as not unnecessarily or unfairly to injure that of the other. *Hitchman Coal & Coke Co. v. Mitchell,* 245 U. S. 229, 254, 38 Sup. Ct. 65, 62 L. Ed. 260, L. R. A. 1918C, 497, Ann. Cas. 1918B, 461.

Obviously, the question of what is unfair competition in business must be determined with particular reference to the character and circumstances of the business. The question here is not so much the rights of either party as against the public but their rights as between themselves. *See Morison v. Moat,* 9 Hare, 241, 258. And, although we may and do assume that neither party has any remaining property interest as against the public in uncopyrighted news matter after the moment of its first publication, it by no means follows that there is no remaining property interest in it as between themselves. For, to both of them alike, news matter, however little susceptible of ownership or dominion in the absolute sense, is stock in trade, to be gathered at the cost of enterprise, organization, skill, labor, and money, and to be distributed and sold to those who will pay money for it, as for any other merchandise. Regarding the news, therefore, as but the material out of which both parties are seeking to make profits at the same time and in the same field, we hardly can fail to recognize that for this purpose, and as between them, it must be regarded as quasi property, irrespective of the rights of either as against the public.

In order to sustain the jurisdiction of equity over the controversy, we need not affirm any general and absolute property in the news as such. The rule that a court of equity concerns itself only in the protection of property rights treats any civil right of a pecuniary nature as a property right (*In re Sawyer,* 124 U. S. 200, 210, 8 Sup. Ct. 482, 31 L. Ed. 402; *In re Debs,* 158 U. S. 564, 593, 15 Sup. Ct. 900, 39 L. Ed. 1092); and the right to acquire property by honest labor or the conduct of a lawful business is as much entitled to protection as the right to guard property already acquired (*Truax v. Raich,* 239 U. S. 33, 37-38, 36 Sup. Ct. 7, 60 L. Ed. 131, L. R. A. 1916D, 545, Ann. Cas. 1917B, 283; *Brennan v. United Hatters,* 73 N. J. Law, 729, 742, 65 Atl. 165, 9 L. R. A. [N. S.] 254, 118 Am. St. Rep. 727, 9 Ann. Cas. 698; *Barr v. Essex Trades Council,* 53 N. J. Eq. 101, 30 Atl. 881). It is this right that furnishes the basis of the jurisdiction in the ordinary case of unfair competition.

The question, whether one who has gathered general information or news at pains and expense for the purpose of subsequent publication through the press has such an interest in its publication as may be protected from interference, has been raised many times, although never, perhaps, in the precise form in which it is now presented.

Board of Trade v. Christie Grain & Stock Co., 198 U. S. 236, 250, 25 Sup. Ct. 637, 49 L. Ed. 1031, related to the distribution of quotations of prices on dealings upon a board of trade, which were collected by plaintiff and communicated on confidential terms to numerous persons under a contract not to make them public. This court held that, apart from certain special objections that were overruled, plaintiff's collection of quotations was entitled to the protection of the law; that, like a trade secret, plaintiff might keep to itself the work done at its expense, and did not lose its right by communicating the result to persons, even if many, in confidential relations to itself, under a contract not to make it public; and that strangers should be restrained from getting at the knowledge by inducing a breach of trust.

In *National Tel. News Co. v. Western Union Tel. Co.,* 119 Fed. 294, 56 C. C. A. 198, 60 L. R. A. 805, the Circuit Court of Appeals for the Seventh Circuit dealt with news matter gathered and transmitted by a telegraph company, and consisting merely of a notation of current events having but a transient value due to quick transmission and distribution; and, while declaring that this was not copyrightable although printed on a tape by tickers in the offices of the recipients, and that it was a commercial not a literary product, nevertheless held that the business of gathering and communicating the news— the service of purveying it—was a legitimate business, meeting a distinctive commercial want and adding to the facilities of the business world, and partaking of the nature of property in a sense that entitled it to the protection of a court of equity against piracy.

Other cases are cited, but none that we deem it necessary to mention.

Not only do the acquisition and transmission of news require elaborate organization and a large expenditure of money, skill, and effort; not only has it an exchange value to the gatherer, dependent chiefly upon its novelty and freshness, the regularity of the service, its reputed reliability and thoroughness, and its adaptability to the public needs; but also, as is evident, the news has an exchange value to one who can misappropriate it.

The peculiar features of the case arise from the fact that, while novelty and freshness form so important an element in the success of the business, the very processes of distribution and publication necessarily occupy a good deal of time. Complainant's service, as well as defendant's, is a daily service to daily newspapers; most of the foreign news reaches this country at the Atlantic seaboard, principally at the city of New York, and because of this, and of time differentials due to the earth's rotation, the distribution of news matter throughout the country is principally from east to west; and, since in speed the telegraph and telephone easily outstrip the rotation of the earth, it is a simple matter for defendant to take complainant's news from bulletins or early editions of complainant's members in the eastern cities and at the mere cost of telegraphic transmission cause it to be published in western papers issued at least as early as those served by complainant. Besides this, and irrespective of time differentials, irregularities in telegraphic transmission on different lines, and the normal consumption of time in printing and distributing the newspaper, result in permitting pirated news to be placed in the hands of defendant's readers sometimes simultaneously with the service of competing Associated Press papers, occasionally even earlier.

Defendant insists that when, with the sanction and approval of complainant, and as the result of the use of its news for the very purpose for which it is distributed, a portion of complainant's members communicate it to the general public by posting it upon bulletin boards so that all may read, or by issuing it to newspapers and distributing it indiscriminately, complainant no longer has the right to control the use to be made of it; that when it thus reaches the light of day it becomes the common possession of all to whom it is accessible; and that any purchaser of a newspaper has the right to communicate the intelligence which it contains to anybody and for any purpose, even for the purpose of selling it for profit to newspapers published for profit in competition with complainant's members.

The fault in the reasoning lies in applying as a test the right of the complainant as against the public, instead of considering the rights of complainant and defendant, competitors in business, as between themselves. The right of the purchaser of a single newspaper to spread knowledge of its contents gratuitously, for any legitimate purpose not unreasonably interfering with complainant's right to make merchandise of it, may be admitted; but to transmit that news for commercial use, in competition with complainant—which is what defendant has done and seeks to justify—is a very different matter. In doing this defendant, by its very act, admits that it is taking material that has been acquired by complainant as the result of organization and the expenditure of labor, skill, and money, and which is salable by complainant for money, and that defendant in appropriating it and selling it as its own is endeavoring to reap where it has not sown, and by disposing of it to newspapers that are competitors of complainant's members is appropriating to itself the harvest of those who have sown. Stripped of all disguises, the process amounts to an unauthorized interference with the normal operation of complainant's legitimate business precisely at the point where the profit is to be reaped, in order to divert a material portion of the profit from those who have earned it to those who have not; with special advantage to defendant in the competition because of the fact that it is not burdened with any part of the expense of gathering the news. The transaction speaks for itself and a court of equity ought not to hesitate long in characterizing it as unfair competition in business.

The underlying principle is much the same as that which lies at the base of the equitable theory of consideration in the law of trusts—that he who has fairly paid the price should have the beneficial use of the property. Pom. Eq. Jur. §981. It is no answer to say that complainant spends its money for that which is too fugitive or evanescent to be the subject of property. That might, and for the purposes of the discussion we are assuming that it would furnish an answer in a common-law controversy. But in a court of equity, where the question is one of unfair competition, if that which complainant has acquired fairly at substantial cost may be sold fairly at substantial profit, a competitor who is misappropriating it for the purpose of disposing of it to his own profit and to the disadvantage of complainant cannot be heard to say that it is too fugitive or evanescent to be regarded as property. It has all the attributes of property necessary for determining that a misappropriation of it by a competitor is unfair competition because contrary to good conscience.

The contention that the news is abandoned to the public for all purposes when published in the first newspaper is untenable. Abandonment is a question of intent, and the entire organization of the Associated Press negatives such a purpose. The cost of the service would be prohibited if the reward were to be so limited. No single newspaper, no small group of newspapers, could sustain the expenditure. Indeed, it is one of the most obvious results of defendant's theory that, by permitting indiscriminate publication by anybody and everybody for purposes of profit in competition with the news-gatherer, it would render publication profitless, or so little profitable as in effect to cut off the service by rendering the cost prohibitive in comparison with the return. The practical needs and requirements of the business are reflected in complainant's by-laws which have been referred to. Their effect is that publication by each member must be deemed not by any means an abandonment of the news to the world for any and all purposes, but a publication for limited purposes; for the benefit of the readers of the bulletin or the newspaper as such; not for the purpose of making merchandise of it as news, with the result of depriving complainant's other members of their reasonable opportunity to obtain just returns for their expenditures.

It is to be observed that the view we adopt does not result in giving to complainant the right to monopolize either the gathering or the distribution of the news, or, without complying with the copyright act, to prevent the reproduction of its news articles, but only postpones participation by complainant's competitor in the processes of distribution and reproduction of news that it has not gathered, and only to the extent necessary to prevent that competitor from reaping the fruits of complainant's efforts and expenditure, to the partial exclusion of complainant. and in violation of the principle that underlies the maxim "sic utere tuo," etc.

It is said that the elements of unfair competition are lacking because there is no attempt by defendant to palm off its goods as those of the complainant, characteristic of the most familiar, if not the most typical, cases of unfair competition. *Howe Scale Co. v. Wyckoff, Seamans & Benedict,* 198 U. S. 118, 140, 25 Sup. Ct. 609, 49 L. Ed. 972. But

LAW AND EQUITY

we cannot concede that the right to equitable relief is confined to that class of cases. In the present case the fraud upon complainant's rights is more direct and obvious. Regarding news matter as the mere material from which these two competing parties are endeavoring to make money, and treating it, therefore, as quasi property for the purposes of their business because they are both selling it as such, defendant's conduct differs from the ordinary case of unfair competition in trade principally in this that, instead of selling its own goods as those of complainant, it substitutes misappropriation in the place of misrepresentation, and sells complainant's goods as its own.

Besides the misappropriation, there are elements of imitation, of false pretense, in defendant's practices. The device of rewriting complainant's news articles, frequently resorted to, carries its own comment. The habitual failure to give credit to complainant for that which is taken is significant. Indeed, the entire system of appropriating complainant's news and transmitting it as a commercial product to defendant's clients and patrons amounts to a false representation to them and to their newspaper readers that the news transmitted is the result of defendant's own investigation in the field. But these elements, although accentuating the wrong, are not the essence of it. It is something more than the advantage of celebrity of which complainant is being deprived.

. . .

In the case before us, in the present state of the pleadings and proofs, we need go no further than to hold, as we do, that the admitted pursuit by complainant of the practice of taking news items published by defendant's subscribers as tips to be investigated, and, if verified, the result of the investigation to be sold—the practice having been followed by defendant also, and by news agencies generally—is not shown to be such as to constitute an unconscientious or inequitable attitude towards its adversary so as to fix upon complainant the taint of unclean hands, and debar it on this ground from the relief to which it is otherwise entitled.

There is some criticism of the injunction that was directed by the District Court upon the going down of the mandate from the Circuit Court of Appeals. In brief, it restrains any taking or gainfully using of the complainant's news, either bodily or in substance from bulletins issued by the complainant or any of its members, or from editions of their newspapers, *"until its commercial value as news to the complainant and all of its members has passed away."* The part complained of is the clause we have italicized; but if this be indefinite, it is no more so than the criticism. Perhaps it would be better that the terms of the injunction be made specific, and so framed as to confine the restraint to an extent consistent with the reasonable protection of complainant's newspapers, each in its own area and for a specified time after its publication, against the competitive use of pirated news by defendant's customers. But the case presents practical difficulties; and we have not the materials, either in the way of a definite suggestion of amendment, or in the way of proofs, upon which to frame a specific injunction; hence, while not expressing approval of the form adopted by the District Court, we decline to modify it at this preliminary stage of the case, and will leave that court to deal with the matter upon appropriate application made to it for the purpose.

The decree of the Circuit court of Appeals will be

Affirmed.

[The concurring opinion of Justice Holmes and the dissenting opinion of Justice Brandeis are omitted.]

NOTES AND QUESTIONS

1. *Misappropriation of News.* Copyright law has changed since *INS v. AP* was decided, but the basic legal landscape remains the same in some important respects. It is possible to copyright a news story, but it is not possible to copyright the underlying facts in the report. If I copy articles verbatim from your website and post them on my website, you will likely have a copyright claim against me. If I write my own stories based on the facts on your website, you will likely not have a copyright claim against me. The misappropriation of news theory from *INS v. AP* has been raised in some recent Internet-era copying cases. *See* Elaine Stoll, *Hot News Misappropriation: More Than Nine Decades After* INS v. AP*, Still and Important Remedy for News Piracy*, 79 U. Cin. L. Rev. 1239 (2011). Do you think that the Supreme Court reached the right result in *INS v. AP*? Recall that one of the fundamental policy issues in intellectual property law is the balance between incentivizing production and incentivizing consumption. Does the case strike the right balance? When thinking about incentivizing production, recall Justice Livingston's dissent in *Pierson v. Post*. Who would bother getting out of bed in the morning to hunt foxes, he asked, if someone could just come in at the end of the chase and grab the fox? A possible answer to Justice Livingston's objection is that requiring people to obtain physical control of the fox would incentivize them to try harder and invest in better hunting resources and technology. Can a similar argument be made in the news context? That is, if we allow copying of news, would we incentivize companies like AP to improve their product to remain profitable?

2. *Is Imitation the Highest Form of Flattery?* When a high-end designer comes out with a new product, imitators often come out with knockoffs shortly thereafter. Exact copies will typically violate trademark or copyright laws. Companies that make the copies, however, are good at making imitations that resemble the original product but that are different enough to skirt the edge of violating the original designer's intellectual property. Are knockoffs a good thing or a bad thing? Put another way, should intellectual property laws be strengthened to do more to prevent knockoffs?

Our next case involves the *right of publicity.* This right allows a person to control the commercial use of her name, image, likeness, voice, and other aspects of personal identity. The right of publicity has common-law origins but has been codified by statute in some states. The opinion, our second from Judge Kozinski, criticizes an extension of the right of publicity in a highly questionable context. Judge Kozinski's opinion also contains an impassioned defense of the importance of the public domain to the creative process.

Before we get to Judge Kozinski's opinion, we should explain the unusual procedural posture in which it arose. Appellate courts often hear cases in three-judge panels. The losing party may make a motion to have the dispute heard by a larger group of judges. This larger group is often composed of all of the judges on that particular court. For courts with especially large numbers of judges, the larger group might be only a subset of the entire group. In any event, when the larger group hears a case, it is said to be sitting *en banc*, and the losing party's motion to have the case heard by the larger group is typically called a motion or a petition for a rehearing *en banc*. In this case, a losing party petitioned for rehearing *en banc*. The petition was rejected by the judges of the Ninth Circuit. Judge Kozinski's opinion is his dissent, joined by two other judges, from the decision not to grant the petition for a rehearing *en banc*. This type of dissent is very unusual and only occurs when a judge has a strong desire to publish an opinion on the topic at issue.

This case involved a suit by Vanna White against Samsung Electronics. Vanna White's claim to fame was turning the letters on the game show Wheel of Fortune. Samsung ran a series of ads that were intended to show that its products would be used in the future. One of these ads showed a robot standing in front of a game board similar to that used on Wheel of Fortune. The robot and the set were clearly intended to evoke Vanna White and the Wheel of Fortune set. The ad, however, did not actually use Vanna White's name or likeness. The trial court granted summary judgment for Samsung. A panel of the Ninth Circuit reversed in part, holding that disputed issues of material fact precluded a grant of summary judgment. The Ninth Circuit as a whole rejected Samsung's petition for rehearing *en banc*. Judge Kozinski's opinion is his dissent from that decision.

WHITE V. SAMSUNG ELECTRONICS AMERICA

United States Court of Appeals for the Ninth Circuit, 1993
989 F.2d 1512

KOZINSKI, Circuit Judge, with whom Circuit Judges O'SCANNLAIN and KLEINFELD join, dissenting from the order rejecting the suggestion for rehearing en banc.

Saddam Hussein wants to keep advertisers from using his picture in unflattering contexts. Clint Eastwood doesn't want tabloids to write about him. Rudolf Valentino's heirs want to control his film biography. The Girl Scouts don't want their image soiled by association with certain activities. George Lucas wants to keep Strategic Defense Initiative fans from calling it "Star Wars." Pepsico doesn't want singers to use the word "Pepsi" in their songs. Guy Lombardo wants an exclusive property right to ads that show big bands playing on New Year's Eve. Uri Geller thinks he should be paid for ads showing psychics bending metal through telekinesis. Paul Prudhomme, that household name, thinks the same about ads featuring corpulent bearded chefs. And scads of copyright holders see purple when their creations are made fun of.

Trademarks are often reflected in the mirror of our popular culture. *See* Truman Capote, *Breakfast at Tiffany's* (1958); Kurt Vonnegut, Jr., *Breakfast of Champions* (1973); Tom Wolfe, *The Electric Kool-Aid Acid Test* (1968) (which, incidentally, includes a chapter on the Hell's Angels); Larry Niven, *Man of Steel, Woman of Kleenex*, in *All the Myriad*

Ways (1971); *Looking for Mr. Goodbar* (1977); *The Coca-Cola Kid* (1985) (using Coca-Cola as a metaphor for American commercialism); *The Kentucky Fried Movie* (1977); *Harley Davidson and the Marlboro Man* (1991); *The Wonder Years* (ABC 1988-present) ("Wonder Years" was a slogan of Wonder Bread); Tim Rice & Andrew Lloyd Webber, *Joseph and the Amazing Technicolor Dream Coat* (musical).

Hear Janis Joplin, *Mercedes Benz*, on *Pearl* (CBS 1971); Paul Simon, *Kodachrome*, on *There Goes Rhymin' Simon* (Warner 1973); Leonard Cohen, *Chelsea Hotel,* on *The Best of Leonard Cohen* (CBS 1975); Bruce Springsteen, *Cadillac Ranch,* on *The River* (CBS 1980); Prince, *Little Red Corvette, on 1999* (Warner 1982); dada, *Dizz Knee Land*, on *Puzzle* (IRS 1992) ("I just robbed a grocery store—I'm going to Disneyland / I just flipped off President George—I'm going to Disneyland"); Monty Python, *Spam,* on *The Final Rip Off* (Virgin 1988); Roy Clark, *Thank God and Greyhound [You're Gone]*, on *Roy Clark's Greatest Hits Volume I* (MCA 1979); Mel Tillis, *Coca-Cola Cowboy,* on *The Very Best of* (MCA 1981) ("You're just a Coca-Cola cowboy / You've got an Eastwood smile and Robert Redford hair . . .").

Dance to Talking Heads, *Popular Favorites 1976-92: Sand in the Vaseline* (Sire 1992); Talking Heads, *Popsicle,* on *id. Admire* Andy Warhol, *Campbell's Soup Can. Cf.* REO Speedwagon, 38 Special, and Jello Biafra of the Dead Kennedys.

The creators of some of these works might have gotten permission from the trademark owners, though it's unlikely Kool-Aid relished being connected with LSD, Hershey with homicidal maniacs, Disney with armed robbers, or Coca-Cola with cultural imperialism. Certainly no free society can *demand* that artists get such permission.

Something very dangerous is going on here. Private property, including intellectual property, is essential to our way of life. It provides an incentive for investment and innovation; it stimulates the flourishing of our culture; it protects the moral entitlements of people to the fruits of their labors. But reducing too much to private property can be bad medicine. Private land, for instance, is far more useful if separated from other private land by public streets, roads and highways. Public parks, utility rights-of-way and sewers reduce the amount of land in private hands, but vastly enhance the value of the property that remains.

So too it is with intellectual property. Overprotecting intellectual property is as harmful as underprotecting it. Creativity is impossible without a rich public domain. Nothing today, likely nothing since we tamed fire, is genuinely new: Culture, like science and technology, grows by accretion, each new creator building on the works of those who came before. Overprotection stifles the very creative forces it's supposed to nurture.

The panel's opinion is a classic case of overprotection. Concerned about what it sees as a wrong done to Vanna White, the panel majority erects a property right of remarkable and dangerous breadth: Under the majority's opinion, it's now a tort for advertisers to *remind* the public of a celebrity. Not to use a celebrity's name, voice, signature or likeness; not to imply the celebrity endorses a product; but simply to evoke the celebrity's image in the public's mind. This Orwellian notion withdraws far more from the public domain than prudence and common sense allow. It conflicts with the Copyright Act and the Copyright Clause. It raises serious First Amendment problems. It's bad law, and it deserves a long, hard second look.

Samsung ran an ad campaign promoting its consumer electronics. Each ad depicted a Samsung product and a humorous prediction: One showed a raw steak with the caption "Revealed to be health food. 2010 A.D." Another showed Morton Downey, Jr. in front of an American flag with the caption "Presidential candidate. 2008 A.D."[12] The ads were meant to convey—humorously—that Samsung products would still be in use twenty years from now.

The ad that spawned this litigation starred a robot dressed in a wig, gown and jewelry reminiscent of Vanna White's hair and dress; the robot was posed next to a Wheel-of-Fortune-like game board. *See* Appendix. The caption read "Longest-running game show. 2012 A.D." The gag here, I take it, was that Samsung would still be around when White had been replaced by a robot.

Perhaps failing to see the humor, White sued, alleging Samsung infringed her right of publicity by "appropriating" her "identity." Under California law, White has the exclusive right to use her name, likeness, signature and voice for commercial purposes. Cal.Civ.Code §3344(a); *Eastwood v. Superior Court,* 149 Cal.App.3d 409, 417, 198 Cal.Rptr. 342, 347 (1983). But Samsung didn't use her name, voice or signature, and it certainly didn't use her likeness. The ad just wouldn't have been funny had it depicted White or someone who resembled her—the whole joke was that the game show host(ess) was a robot, not a real person. No one seeing the ad could have thought this was supposed to be White in 2012.

The district judge quite reasonably held that, because Samsung didn't use White's name, likeness, voice or signature, it didn't violate her right of publicity. 971 F.2d at 1396-97. Not so, says the panel majority: The California right of publicity can't possibly be limited to name and likeness. If it were, the majority reasons, a "clever advertising strategist" could avoid using White's name or likeness but nevertheless remind people of her with impunity, "effectively eviscerat[ing]" her rights. To prevent this "evisceration," the panel majority holds that the right of publicity must extend beyond name and likeness, to any "appropriation" of White's "identity"—anything that "evoke[s]" her personality. *Id.* at 1398-99.

But what does "evisceration" mean in intellectual property law? Intellectual property rights aren't like some constitutional rights, absolute guarantees protected against all kinds of interference, subtle as well as blatant. They cast no penumbras, emit no emanations: The very point of intellectual property laws is that they protect only against certain specific kinds of appropriation. I can't publish unauthorized copies of, say,

---

[12] I had never heard of Morton Downey, Jr., but I'm told he's sort of like Rush Limbaugh, but not as shy.

Presumed Innocent; I can't make a movie out of it. But I'm perfectly free to write a book about an idealistic young prosecutor on trial for a crime he didn't commit. So what if I got the idea from *Presumed Innocent?* So what if it reminds readers of the original? Have I "eviscerated" Scott Turow's intellectual property rights? Certainly not. All creators draw in part on the work of those who came before, referring to it, building on it, poking fun at it; we call this creativity, not piracy.

The majority isn't, in fact, preventing the "evisceration" of Vanna White's existing rights; it's creating a new and much broader property right, a right unknown in California law. It's replacing the existing balance between the interests of the celebrity and those of the public by a different balance, one substantially more favorable to the celebrity. Instead of having an exclusive right in her name, likeness, signature or voice, every famous person now has an exclusive right to *anything that reminds the viewer of her.* After all, that's all Samsung did: It used an inanimate object to remind people of White, to "evoke [her identity]." 971 F.2d at 1399.

Consider how sweeping this new right is. What is it about the ad that makes people think of White? It's not the robot's wig, clothes or jewelry; there must be ten million blond women (many of them quasi-famous) who wear dresses and jewelry like White's. It's that the robot is posed near the "Wheel of Fortune" game board. Remove the game board from the ad, and no one would think of Vanna White. *See* Appendix. But once you include the game board, anybody standing beside it—a brunette woman, a man wearing women's clothes, a monkey in a wig and gown—would evoke White's image, precisely the way the robot did. It's the "Wheel of Fortune" set, not the robot's face or dress or jewelry that evokes White's image. The panel is giving White an exclusive right not in what she looks like or who she is, but in what she does for a living.

Once the right of publicity is extended beyond specific physical characteristics, this will become a recurring problem: Outside name, likeness and voice, the things that most reliably remind the public of celebrities are the actions or roles they're famous for. A commercial with an astronaut setting foot on the moon would evoke the image of Neil Armstrong. Any masked man on horseback would remind people (over a certain age) of Clayton Moore. And any number of songs—"My Way," "Yellow Submarine," "Like a Virgin," "Beat It," "Michael, Row the Boat Ashore," to name only a few—instantly evoke an image of the person or group who made them famous, regardless of who is singing. *See also* Carlos V. Lozano, *West Loses Lawsuit over Batman TV Commercial,* L.A. Times, Jan. 18, 1990, at B3 (Adam West sues over Batman-like character in commercial); *Nurmi v. Peterson,* 10 U.S.P.Q.2d 1775, 1989 WL 407484 (C.D.Cal.1989) (1950s TV movie hostess "Vampira" sues 1980s TV hostess "Elvira"); text accompanying notes 7-8 (lawsuits brought by Guy Lombardo, claiming big bands playing at New Year's Eve parties remind people of him, and by Uri Geller, claiming psychics who can bend metal remind people of him). *Cf. Motschenbacher,* where the claim was that viewers would think plaintiff was actually in the commercial, and not merely that the commercial reminded people of him.

This is entirely the wrong place to strike the balance. Intellectual property rights aren't free: They're imposed at the expense of future creators and of the public at large. Where would we be if Charles Lindbergh had an exclusive right in the concept of a heroic solo aviator? If Arthur Conan Doyle had gotten a copyright in the idea of the detective story, or Albert Einstein had patented the theory of relativity? If every author and celebrity had been given the right to keep people from mocking them or their work? Surely this would have made the world poorer, not richer, culturally as well as economically.

This is why intellectual property law is full of careful balances between what's set aside for the owner and what's left in the public domain for the rest of us: The relatively short life of patents; the longer, but finite, life of copyrights; copyright's idea-expression dichotomy; the fair use doctrine; the prohibition on copyrighting facts; the compulsory license of television broadcasts and musical compositions; federal preemption of overbroad state intellectual property laws; the nominative use doctrine in trademark law; the right to make soundalike recordings. All of these diminish an intellectual property owner's rights. All let the public use something created by someone else. But all are necessary to maintain a free environment in which creative genius can flourish.

The intellectual property right created by the panel here has none of these essential limitations: No fair use exception; no right to parody; no idea-expression dichotomy. It impoverishes the public domain, to the detriment of future creators and the public at large. Instead of well-defined, limited characteristics such as name, likeness or voice, advertisers will now have to cope with vague claims of "appropriation of identity," claims often made by people with a wholly exaggerated sense of their own fame and significance. *See* pp. 1512-13 & notes 1-10 *supra*. Future Vanna Whites might not get the chance to create their personae, because their employers may fear some celebrity will claim the persona is too similar to her own. The public will be robbed of parodies of celebrities, and our culture will be deprived of the valuable safety valve that parody and mockery create.

Moreover, consider the moral dimension, about which the panel majority seems to have gotten so exercised. Saying Samsung "appropriated" something of White's begs the question: *Should* White have the exclusive right to something as broad and amorphous as her "identity"? Samsung's ad didn't simply copy White's schtick—like all parody, it created something new. True, Samsung did it to make money, but White does whatever she does to make money, too; the majority talks of "the difference between fun and profit," 971 F.2d at 1401, but in the entertainment industry fun *is* profit. Why is Vanna White's right to exclusive for-profit use of her persona—a persona that might not even be her own creation, but that of a writer, director or producer—superior to Samsung's right to profit by creating its own inventions? Why should she have such absolute rights to control the conduct of others, unlimited by the idea-expression dichotomy or by the fair use doctrine?

To paraphrase only slightly *Feist Publications, Inc. v. Rural Telephone Service Co.*, 499 U.S. 340, ___-___, 111 S.Ct. 1282, 1289-90, 113 L.Ed.2d 358 (1991), it may seem unfair that much of the fruit of a creator's labor may be used by others without compensation. But this is not some unforeseen byproduct of our intellectual property system; it is the system's very essence. Intellectual property law assures authors the right to their original expression, but encourages others to build freely on the ideas that underlie it. This result is neither unfair nor unfortunate: It is the means by which intellectual property law advances the progress of science and art. We give authors certain exclusive rights, but in exchange we get a richer public domain. The majority ignores this wise teaching, and all of us are the poorer for it. . . .

For better or worse, we *are* the Court of Appeals for the Hollywood Circuit. Millions of people toil in the shadow of the law we make, and much of their livelihood is made possible by the existence of intellectual property rights. But much of their livelihood—and much of the vibrancy of our culture—also depends on the existence of other intangible rights: The right to draw ideas from a rich and varied public domain, and the right to mock, for profit as well as fun, the cultural icons of our time.

In the name of avoiding the "evisceration" of a celebrity's rights in her image, the majority diminishes the rights of copyright holders and the public at large. In the name of fostering creativity, the majority suppresses it. Vanna White and those like her have been given something they never had before, and they've been given it at our expense. I cannot agree.

NOTES AND QUESTIONS

1. *The Right Plaintiff?* Was Vanna White the right plaintiff to bring this suit? Or should it have been brought by the creators of Wheel of Fortune? Put another way, whose rights were really infringed (if at all) here?

2. *The Public Domain.* Judge Kozinski's opinion in *White v. Samsung* justifiably is famous for its defense of the importance of the public domain. Creators are influenced and inspired by what has come before. If we give too much protection to current creators of intellectual property, we might stifle the efforts of future creators. We don't, however, want to give current creators too little protection. The issue is where to strike the balance. Where do you think the balance should have been struck in *White v. Samsung?*

C. PROPERTY IN THE HUMAN BODY

Should we have property rights in our bodies? Political philosophers often refer to self-ownership, but they often do so as a way of talking about personal autonomy. Should we actually be able to own our bodies to the degree that we could, say, sell our body parts to the highest bidder? Should we be able to sue medical researchers who use our body tissues for profitable medical research without our consent for conversion? Our next case involves the second question. As we will see, however, concerns about the first question were in at least some of the justices' minds as they considered the second question.

MOORE V. REGENTS OF THE UNIVERSITY OF CALIFORNIA

Supreme Court of California, 1991
793 P.2d 479

PANELLI, Justice.

We granted review in this case to determine whether plaintiff has stated a cause of action against his physician and other defendants for using his cells in potentially lucrative medical research without his permission. Plaintiff alleges that his physician failed to disclose preexisting research and economic interests in the cells before obtaining consent to the medical procedures by which they were extracted. The superior court sustained all defendants' demurrers to the third amended complaint, and the Court of Appeal reversed. We hold that the complaint states a cause of action for breach of the physician's disclosure obligations, but not for conversion.

FACTS

[The facts as described by the court are as alleged in Moore's complaint]. The plaintiff is John Moore (Moore), who underwent treatment for hairy-cell leukemia at the Medical Center of the University of California at Los Angeles (UCLA Medical Center). The five defendants are: (1) Dr. David W. Golde (Golde), a physician who attended Moore at UCLA Medical Center; (2) the Regents of the University of California (Regents), who own and operate the university; (3) Shirley G. Quan, a researcher employed by the Regents; (4) Genetics Institute, Inc. (Genetics Institute); and (5) Sandoz Pharmaceuticals Corporation and related entities (collectively Sandoz).

Moore first visited UCLA Medical Center on October 5, 1976, shortly after he learned that he had hairy-cell leukemia. After hospitalizing Moore and "withdr[awing] extensive amounts of blood, bone marrow aspirate, and other bodily substances," Golde confirmed that diagnosis. At this time all defendants, including Golde, were aware that "certain blood products and blood components were of great value in a number of commercial and scientific efforts" and that access to a patient whose blood contained these substances would provide "competitive, commercial, and scientific advantages."

On October 8, 1976, Golde recommended that Moore's spleen be removed. Golde informed Moore "that he had reason to fear for his life, and that the proposed splenectomy operation . . . was necessary to slow down the progress of his disease." Based upon Golde's representations, Moore signed a written consent form authorizing the splenectomy.

Before the operation, Golde and Quan "formed the intent and made arrangements to obtain portions of [Moore's] spleen following its removal" and to take them to a separate research unit. Golde gave written instructions to this effect on October 18 and 19, 1976. These research activities "were not intended to have . . . any relation to [Moore's] medical . . . care." However, neither Golde nor Quan informed Moore of their plans to conduct this research or requested his permission. Surgeons at UCLA Medical Center, whom the complaint does not name as defendants, removed Moore's spleen on October 20, 1976.

Moore returned to the UCLA Medical Center several times between November 1976 and September 1983. He did so at Golde's direction and based upon representations "that such visits were necessary and required for his health and well-being, and based upon the trust inherent in and by virtue of the physician-patient relationship. . . ." On each of these visits Golde withdrew additional samples of "blood, blood serum, skin, bone marrow aspirate, and sperm." On each occasion Moore travelled to the UCLA Medical Center from his home in Seattle because he had been told that the procedures were to be performed only there and only under Golde's direction.

"In fact, [however,] throughout the period of time that [Moore] was under [Golde's] care and treatment, . . . the defendants were actively involved in a number of activities which they concealed from [Moore]. . . ." Specifically, defendants were conducting research on Moore's cells and planned to "benefit financially and competitively . . . [by exploiting the cells] and [their] exclusive access to [the cells] by virtue of [Golde's] ongoing physician-patient relationship. . . ."

Sometime before August 1979, Golde established a cell line from Moore's T-lymphocytes. [A T-lymphocyte is a type of white blood cell. T-lymphocytes produce lymphokines, or proteins that regulate the immune system. Some lymphokines have potential therapeutic value. If the genetic material responsible for producing a particular lymphokine can be identified, it can sometimes be used to manufacture large quantities of the lymphokine through the techniques of recombinant DNA.] On January 30, 1981, the Regents applied for a patent on the cell line, listing Golde and Quan as inventors. "[B]y virtue of an established policy . . . , [the] Regents, Golde, and Quan would share in any royalties or profits . . . arising out of [the] patent." The patent issued on March 20, 1984, naming Golde and Quan as the inventors of the cell line and the Regents as the assignee of the patent.

While the genetic code for lymphokines does not vary from individual to individual, it can nevertheless be quite difficult to locate the gene responsible for a particular lymphokine. Because T-lymphocytes produce many different lymphokines, the relevant gene is often like a needle in a haystack. Moore's T-lymphocytes were interesting to the defendants because they overproduced certain lymphokines, thus making the corresponding genetic material easier to identify. (In published research papers, defendants and other researchers have shown that the overproduction was caused by a virus, and that normal T-lymphocytes infected by the virus will also overproduce.)

Cells taken directly from the body (primary cells) are not very useful for these purposes. Primary cells typically reproduce a few times and then die. One can, however, sometimes continue to use cells for an extended period of time by developing them into a "cell line," a culture capable of reproducing indefinitely. This is not, however, always an easy task. "Long-term growth of human cells and tissues is difficult, often an art," and the probability of succeeding with any given cell sample is low, except for a few types of cells not involved in this case.

The Regent's patent also covers various methods for using the cell line to produce lymphokines. Moore admits in his complaint that "the true clinical potential of each of the lymphokines . . . [is] difficult to predict, [but] . . . competing commercial firms in these relevant fields have published reports in biotechnology industry periodicals predicting a potential market of approximately $3.01 Billion Dollars by the year 1990 for a whole range of [such lymphokines]. . . ."

With the Regents' assistance, Golde negotiated agreements for commercial development of the cell line and products to be derived from it. Under an agreement with Genetics Institute, Golde "became a paid consultant" and "acquired the rights to 75,000 shares of common stock." Genetics Institute also agreed to pay Golde and the Regents "at least $330,000 over three years, including a pro-rata share of [Golde's] salary and fringe benefits, in exchange for . . . exclusive access to the materials and research performed" on the cell line and products derived from it. On June 4, 1982, Sandoz "was added to the agreement," and compensation payable to Golde and the Regents was increased by $110,000. "[T]hroughout this period, . . . Quan spent as much as 70 [percent] of her time working for [the] Regents on research" related to the cell line.

Based upon these allegations, Moore attempted to state 13 causes of action. Each defendant demurred to each purported cause of action. The superior court, however, expressly considered the validity of only the first cause of action, conversion. Reasoning that the remaining causes of action incorporated the earlier, defective allegations, the superior court sustained a general demurrer to the entire complaint. . . .

With one justice dissenting, the Court of Appeal reversed, holding that the complaint did state a cause of action for conversion. The Court of Appeal agreed with the superior court that the allegations against Genetics Institute and Sandoz were insufficient, but directed the superior court to give Moore leave to amend. The Court of Appeal also directed the superior court to decide "the remaining causes of action, which [had] never been expressly ruled upon."

DISCUSSION

A. Breach of Fiduciary Duty and Lack of Informed Consent

Moore repeatedly alleges that Golde failed to disclose the extent of his research and economic interests in Moore's cells before obtaining consent to the medical procedures by which the cells were extracted. These allegations, in our view, state a cause of action against Golde for invading a legally protected interest of his patient. This cause of action can properly be characterized either as the breach of a fiduciary duty to disclose facts material to the patient's consent or, alternatively, as the performance of medical procedures without first having obtained the patient's informed consent. . . .

B. Conversion

Moore also attempts to characterize the invasion of his rights as a conversion—a tort that protects against interference with possessory and ownership interests in personal property. He theorizes that he continued to own his cells following their removal from his body, at least for the purpose of directing their use, and that he never consented to their use in potentially lucrative medical research. Thus, to complete Moore's argument, defendants' unauthorized use of his cells constitutes a conversion. As a result of the alleged conversion, Moore claims a proprietary interest in each of the products that any of the defendants might ever create from his cells or the patented cell line.

No court, however, has ever in a reported decision imposed conversion liability for the use of human cells in medical research. While that fact does not end our inquiry, it raises a flag of caution. In effect, what Moore is asking us to do is to impose a tort duty on scientists to investigate the consensual pedigree of each human cell sample used in research. To impose such a duty, which would affect medical research of importance to all of society, implicates policy concerns far removed from the traditional, two-party ownership disputes in which the law of conversion arose. Invoking a tort theory originally used to determine whether the loser or the finder of a horse had the better title, Moore claims ownership of the results of socially important medical research, including the genetic code for chemicals that regulate the functions of every human being's immune system.

We have recognized that, when the proposed application of a very general theory of liability in a new context raises important policy concerns, it is especially important to face those concerns and address them openly. Moreover, we should be hesitant to "impose [new tort duties] when to do so would involve complex policy decisions" especially when such decisions are more appropriately the subject of legislative deliberation and resolution. This certainly is not to say that the applicability of common law torts is limited to the historical or factual contexts of existing cases. But on occasions when we have opened or sanctioned new areas of tort liability, we "have noted that the 'wrongs and injuries involved were both comprehensible and assessable within the existing judicial framework.'"

Accordingly, we first consider whether the tort of conversion clearly gives Moore a cause of action under existing law. We do not believe it does. Because of the novelty of Moore's claim to own the biological materials at issue, to apply the theory of conversion in this context would frankly have to be recognized as an extension of the theory. Therefore, we consider next whether it is advisable to extend the tort to this context.

1. Moore's Claim Under Existing Law

"To establish a conversion, plaintiff must establish an actual interference with his *ownership* or *right of possession*. . . . Where plaintiff neither has title to the property alleged to have been converted, nor possession thereof, he cannot maintain an action for conversion."

Since Moore clearly did not expect to retain possession of his cells following their removal, to sue for their conversion he must have retained an ownership interest in them. But there are several reasons to doubt that he did retain any such interest. First, no reported judicial decision supports Moore's claim, either directly or by close analogy. Second, California statutory law drastically limits any continuing interest of a patient in excised cells. Third, the subject matters of the Regents' patent—the patented cell line and the products derived from it—cannot be Moore's property.

Neither the Court of Appeal's opinion, the parties' briefs, nor our research discloses a case holding that a person retains a sufficient interest in excised cells to support a cause of action for conversion. We do not find this surprising, since the laws governing such things as human tissues, transplantable organs, blood, fetuses, pituitary glands, corneal tissue, and dead bodies deal with human biological materials as objects sui generis, regulating their disposition to achieve policy goals rather than abandoning them to the general law of personal property. It is these specialized statutes, not the law of conversion, to which courts ordinarily should and do look for guidance on the disposition of human biological materials.

Lacking direct authority for importing the law of conversion into this context, Moore relies, as did the Court of Appeal, primarily on decisions addressing privacy rights. One line of cases involves unwanted publicity. These opinions hold that every person has a proprietary interest in his own likeness and that unauthorized, business use of a likeness is redressible as a tort. But in neither opinion did the authoring court expressly base its holding on property law. Each court stated, following Prosser, that it was "pointless" to debate the proper characterization of the proprietary interest in a likeness. For purposes of determining whether the tort of conversion lies, however, the characterization of the right in question is far from pointless. Only property can be converted. . . .

Not only are the wrongful-publicity cases irrelevant to the issue of conversion, but the analogy to them seriously misconceives the nature of the genetic materials and research involved in this case. Moore, adopting the analogy originally advanced by the Court of Appeal, argues that "[i]f the courts have found a sufficient proprietary interest in one's persona, how could one not have a right in one's own genetic material, something far more profoundly the essence of one's human uniqueness than a name or a face?" However, as the defendants' patent makes clear—and the complaint, too, if read with an understanding of the scientific terms which it has borrowed from the patent—the goal and result of defendants' efforts has been to manufacture lymphokines.

Lymphokines, unlike a name or a face, have the same molecular structure in every human being and the same, important functions in every human being's immune system. Moreover, the particular genetic material which is responsible for the natural production of lymphokines, and which defendants use to manufacture lymphokines in the laboratory, is also the same in every person; it is no more unique to Moore than the number of vertebrae in the spine or the chemical formula of hemoglobin. . . .

The next consideration that makes Moore's claim of ownership problematic is California statutory law, which drastically limits a patient's control over excised cells. Pursuant to Health and Safety Code section 7054.4, "[n]otwithstanding any other provision of law, recognizable anatomical parts, human tissues, anatomical human remains, or infectious waste following conclusion of scientific use shall be disposed of by interment, incineration, or any other method determined by the state department [of health services] to protect the public health and safety." Clearly the Legislature did not specifically intend this statute to resolve the question of whether a patient is entitled to compensation for the nonconsensual use of excised cells. A primary object of the statute is to ensure the safe handling of potentially hazardous biological waste materials. Yet one cannot escape the conclusion that the statute's practical effect is to limit, drastically, a patient's control over excised cells. By restricting how excised cells may be used and requiring their eventual destruction, the statute eliminates so many of the rights ordinarily attached to property that one cannot simply assume that what is left amounts to "property" or "ownership" for purposes of conversion law. . . .

Finally, the subject matter of the Regents' patent—the patented cell line and the products derived from it—cannot be Moore's property. This is because the patented cell line is both factually and legally distinct from the cells taken from Moore's body. Federal law permits the patenting of organisms that represent the product of "human ingenuity," but not naturally occurring organisms. Human cell lines are patentable because "[l]ong-term adaptation and growth of human tissues and cells in culture is difficult—often considered an art . . . ," and the probability of success is low. (OTA Rep., supra, at p. 33; see fn. 2, ante.) It is this *inventive effort* that patent law rewards, not the discovery of naturally occurring raw materials. Thus, Moore's allegations that he owns the cell line and the products derived from it are inconsistent with the patent, which constitutes an authoritative determination that the cell line is the product of invention. Since such allegations are nothing more than arguments or conclusions of law, they of course do not bind us.

2. Should Conversion Liability Be Extended?

There are three reasons why it is inappropriate to impose liability for conversion based upon the allegations of Moore's complaint. First, a fair balancing of the relevant policy considerations counsels against extending the tort. Second, problems in this area are better suited to legislative resolution. Third, the tort of conversion is not necessary to protect patients' rights. For these reasons, we conclude that the use of excised human cells in medical research does not amount to a conversion.

Of the relevant policy considerations, two are of overriding importance. The first is protection of a competent patient's right to make autonomous medical decisions. That right, as already discussed, is grounded in well-recognized and long-standing principles of fiduciary duty and informed consent. This policy weighs in favor of providing a remedy to patients when physicians act with undisclosed motives that may affect their professional judgment. The second important policy consideration is that we not threaten with disabling civil liability innocent parties who are engaged in socially useful activities, such as researchers who have no reason to believe that their use of a particular cell sample is, or may be, against a donor's wishes.

To reach an appropriate balance of these policy considerations is extremely important. In its report to Congress, the Office of Technology Assessment emphasized that "[u]ncertainty about how courts will resolve disputes between specimen sources and specimen users could be detrimental to both academic researchers and the infant biotechnology industry, particularly when the rights are asserted long after the specimen was obtained. The assertion of rights by sources would affect not only the researcher who obtained the original specimen, but perhaps other researchers as well.

"Biological materials are routinely distributed to other researchers for experimental purposes, and scientists who obtain cell lines or other specimen-derived products, such as gene clones, from the original researcher could also be sued under certain legal theories [such as conversion]. Furthermore, the uncertainty could affect product developments as well as research. Since inventions containing human tissues and cells may be patented and licensed for commercial use, companies are unlikely to invest heavily in developing, manufacturing, or marketing a product when uncertainty about clear title exists."

Indeed, so significant is the potential obstacle to research stemming from uncertainty about legal title to biological materials that the Office of Technology Assessment reached this striking conclusion: "[R]egardless of the merit of claims by the different interested parties, resolving the current uncertainty may be more important to the future of biotechnology than resolving it in any particular way."

We need not, however, make an arbitrary choice between liability and nonliability. Instead, an examination of the relevant policy considerations suggests an appropriate balance: Liability based upon existing disclosure obligations, rather than an unprecedented extension of the conversion theory, protects patients' rights of privacy and autonomy without unnecessarily hindering research.

To be sure, the threat of liability for conversion might help to enforce patients' rights indirectly. This is because physicians might be able to avoid liability by obtaining patients' consent, in the broadest possible terms, to any conceivable subsequent research use of excised cells. Unfortunately, to extend the conversion theory would utterly sacrifice the other goal of protecting innocent parties. Since conversion is a strict liability tort, it would impose liability on all those into whose hands the cells come, whether or not the particular defendant participated in, or knew of, the inadequate disclosures that violated the patient's right to make an informed decision. In contrast to the conversion theory, the fiduciary-duty and informed-consent theories protect the patient directly, without punishing innocent parties or creating disincentives to the conduct of socially beneficial research.

Research on human cells plays a critical role in medical research. This is so because researchers are increasingly able to isolate naturally occurring, medically useful biological substances and to produce useful quantities of such substances through genetic engineering. These efforts are beginning to bear fruit. Products developed through biotechnology that have already been approved for marketing in this country include treatments and tests for leukemia, cancer, diabetes, dwarfism, hepatitis-B, kidney transplant rejection, emphysema, osteoporosis, ulcers, anemia, infertility, and gynecological tumors, to name but a few.

The extension of conversion law into this area will hinder research by restricting access to the necessary raw materials. Thousands of human cell lines already exist in tissue repositories, such as the American Type Culture Collection and those operated by the National Institutes of Health and the American Cancer Society. These repositories respond to tens of thousands of requests for samples annually. Since the patent office requires the holders of patents on cell lines to make samples available to anyone, many patent holders place their cell lines in repositories to avoid the administrative burden of responding to requests. At present, human cell lines are routinely copied and distributed to other researchers for experimental purposes, usually free of charge. This exchange of scientific materials, which still is relatively free and efficient, will surely be compromised if each cell sample becomes the potential subject matter of a lawsuit.

Finally, there is no pressing need to impose a judicially created rule of strict liability, since enforcement of physicians' disclosure obligations will protect patients against the very type of harm with which Moore was threatened. So long as a physician discloses research and economic interests that may affect his judgment, the patient is protected from conflicts of interest. Aware of any conflicts, the patient can make an informed decision to consent to treatment, or to withhold consent and look elsewhere for medical assistance. As already discussed, enforcement of physicians' disclosure obligations protects patients directly, without hindering the socially useful activities of innocent researchers.

For these reasons, we hold that the allegations of Moore's third amended complaint state a cause of action for breach of fiduciary duty or lack of informed consent, but not conversion.

ARABIAN, Justice, concurring.

I join in the views cogently expounded by the majority. I write separately to give voice to a concern that I believe informs much of that opinion but finds little or no expression therein. I speak of the moral issue.

Plaintiff has asked us to recognize and enforce a right to sell one's own body tissue *for profit*. He entreats us to regard the human vessel—the single most venerated and protected subject in any civilized society—as equal with the basest commercial commodity. He urges us to commingle the sacred with the profane. He asks much.

My learned colleague, Justice Mosk, in an impressive if ultimately unpersuasive dissent, recognizes the moral dimension of the matter. "Our society," he writes, "acknowledges a profound ethical imperative to respect the human body as the physical and temporal expression of the unique human persona." He concludes, however, that morality militates in favor of recognizing plaintiff's claim for conversion of his body tissue. Why? Essentially, he answers, because of these defendants' moral shortcomings, duplicity and greed. Let them be compelled, he argues, to disgorge a portion of their ill-gotten gains to the uninformed individual whose body was invaded and exploited and without whom such profits would not have been possible.

I share Justice Mosk's sense of outrage, but I cannot follow its path. His eloquent paean to the human spirit illuminates the problem, not the solution. Does it uplift or degrade the "unique human persona" to treat human tissue as a fungible article of commerce? Would it advance or impede the human condition, spiritually or scientifically, by delivering the majestic force of the law behind plaintiff's claim? I do not know the answers to these troubling questions, nor am I willing—like Justice Mosk—to treat them simply as issues of "tort" law, susceptible of *judicial* resolution.

It is true, that this court has not often been deterred from deciding difficult legal issues simply because they require a choice between competing social or economic policies. The difference here, however, lies in the nature of the conflicting moral, philosophical and even religious values at stake, and in the profound implications of the position urged. The ramifications of recognizing and enforcing a property interest in body tissues are not known, but are greatly feared—the effect on human dignity of a marketplace in human body parts, the impact on research and development of competitive bidding for such materials, and the exposure of researchers to potentially limitless and uncharted tort liability.

Whether, as plaintiff urges, his cells should be treated as property susceptible to conversion is not, in my view, ours to decide. The question implicates choices which not only reflect, but which ultimately define our essence. A mark of wisdom for us as expositors of the law is the recognition that we cannot cure every ill, mediate every dispute, resolve every conundrum. Sometimes, as Justice Brandeis said, "the most important thing we do, is not doing."

Where then shall a complete resolution be found? Clearly the Legislature, as the majority opinion suggests, is the proper deliberative forum. Indeed, a legislative response creating a licensing scheme, which establishes a fixed rate of profit sharing between researcher and subject, has already been suggested. Such an arrangement would not only avoid the moral and philosophical objections to a free market operation in body tissue, but would also address stated concerns by eliminating the inherently coercive effect of a waiver system and by compensating donors regardless of temporal circumstances.

The majority view is not unmindful of the seeming injustice in a result that denies plaintiff a claim for conversion of his body tissue, yet permits defendants to retain the fruits thereof. As we have explained, the reason for our holding is essentially two fold: First, plaintiff in this matter is not without a remedy; he remains free to pursue defendants on a breach-of-fiduciary-duty theory, as well as, perhaps, other tort claims not before us. Second, a judicial pronouncement, while supple, is not without its limitations. Courts cannot and should not seek to fashion a remedy for every "heartache and the thousand natural shocks that flesh is heir to." Sometimes, the discretion of forbearance *is* the better part of responsive valor. This is such an occasion.

BROUSSARD, Justice, concurring and dissenting.

. . . I dissent from the majority's conclusion that the facts alleged in this case do not state a cause of action for conversion.

If this were a typical case in which a patient consented to the use of his removed organ for general research purposes and the patient's doctor had no prior knowledge of the scientific or commercial value of the patient's organ or cells, I would agree that the patient could not maintain a conversion action. In that common scenario, the patient has abandoned any interest in the removed organ and is not entitled to demand compensation if it should later be discovered that the organ or cells have some unanticipated value. I cannot agree, however, with the majority that a patient may *never* maintain a conversion action for the unauthorized use of his excised organ or cells, even against a party who knew of the value of the organ or cells before they were removed and breached a duty to disclose that value to the patient. Because plaintiff alleges that defendants wrongfully interfered with his right to determine, prior to the removal of his body parts, how those parts would be used after removal, I conclude that the complaint states a cause of action under traditional, common law conversion principles.

In analyzing the conversion issue, the majority properly begins with the established requirements of a common law conversion action, explaining that a plaintiff is required to demonstrate an actual interference with his "ownership or right of possession" in the property in question. Although the majority opinion, at several points, appears to suggest that a removed body part, by its nature, may never constitute "property" for purposes of a conversion action, there is no reason to think that the majority opinion actually intends to embrace such a broad or dubious proposition. If, for example, another medical center or drug company had stolen all of the cells in question from the UCLA Medical Center laboratory and had used them for its own benefit, there would be no question but that a cause of action for conversion would properly lie against the thief, and the majority opinion does not suggest otherwise. Thus, the majority's analysis cannot rest on the broad proposition that a removed body part is not property, but rather rests on the proposition that *a patient* retains no ownership interest in a body part once the body part has been removed from his or her body.

The majority opinion fails to recognize, however, that, in light of the allegations of the present complaint, the pertinent inquiry is not whether a patient generally retains an ownership interest in a body part after its removal from his body, but rather whether a patient has a right to determine, before a body part is removed, the use to which the part will be put after removal. Although the majority opinion suggests that there are "reasons to doubt" that a patient retains "any" ownership interest in his organs or cells after removal, the opinion fails to identify any statutory provision or common law authority that indicates that a patient does not generally have the right, before a body part is removed, to choose among the permissible uses to which the part may be put after removal. . . .

Although the majority opinion does not acknowledge that plaintiff's conversion action is supported by existing common law principles, its reasoning suggests that the majority would, in any event, conclude that considerations of public policy support a judicially crafted limitation on a patient's right to sue anyone involved in medical research activities for conversion of a patient's excised organs or cells. For a number of reasons, I cannot agree that this court should carve out such a broad immunity from general conversion principles.

One of the majority's principal policy concerns is that "[t]he extension of conversion law into this area will hinder research by restricting access to the necessary raw materials"—the thousands of cell lines and tissues already in cell and tissue repositories. The majority suggests that the "exchange of scientific materials, which still is relatively free and efficient, will surely be compromised if each cell sample becomes the potential subject matter of a lawsuit."

This policy argument is flawed in a number of respects. First, the majority's stated concern does not provide any justification for barring plaintiff from bringing a conversion action against a party who does not obtain organs or cells from a cell bank but who directly interferes with or misappropriates a patient's right to control the use of his organs or cells. . . .

Second, even with respect to those persons who are not involved in the initial conversion, the majority's policy arguments are less than compelling. To begin with, the majority's fear that the availability of a conversion remedy will restrict access to existing cell lines is unrealistic. In the vast majority of instances the tissues and cells in existing repositories will *not* represent a potential source of liability because they will have come from patients who consented to their organ's use for scientific purposes under circumstances in which such consent was not tainted by a failure to disclose the known valuable nature of the cells. Because potential liability under a conversion theory will exist in only the exceedingly rare instance in which a doctor knowingly concealed from the patient the value of his body part or the patient's specific directive with regard to the use of the body part was disregarded, there is no reason to think that application of settled conversion law will have any negative effect on the primary conduct of medical researchers who use tissue and cell banks. . . .

Finally, the majority's analysis of the relevant policy considerations tellingly omits a most pertinent consideration. In identifying the interests of the patient that are implicated by the decision whether to recognize a conversion cause of action, the opinion speaks only of the "patient's right to make autonomous medical decisions" and fails even to mention the patient's interest in obtaining the economic value, if any, that may adhere in the subsequent use of his own body parts. . . .

Mosk, Justice, dissenting.

I dissent.

Contrary to the principal holding of the Court of Appeal, the majority conclude that the complaint does not—in fact cannot—state a cause of action for conversion. I disagree with this conclusion for all the reasons stated by the Court of Appeal, and for additional reasons that I shall explain.

The majority first take the position that Moore has no cause of action for conversion under existing law because he retained no "ownership interest" in his cells after they were removed from his body. . . . The majority . . . [found] three "reasons to doubt" that Moore retained a sufficient ownership interest in his cells, after their excision, to support a conversion cause of action. In my view the majority's three reasons, taken singly or together, are inadequate to the task.

The majority's first reason is that "no reported judicial decision supports Moore's claim, either directly or by close analogy." Neither, however, is there any reported decision rejecting such a claim. The issue is as new as its source—the recent explosive growth in the commercialization of biotechnology.

The majority next cite several statutes regulating aspects of the commerce in or disposition of certain parts of the human body, and conclude in effect that in the present case we should also "look for guidance" to the Legislature rather than to the law of conversion. Surely this argument is out of place in an opinion of the highest court of this state. As the majority acknowledge, the law of conversion is a creature of the common law. "The inherent capacity of the common law for growth and change is its most significant feature. Its development has been determined by the social needs of the community which it serves. It is constantly expanding and developing in keeping with advancing civilization and the new conditions and progress of society, and adapting itself to the gradual change of trade, commerce, arts, inventions, and the needs of the country." . . .

The majority's second reason for doubting that Moore retained an ownership interest in his cells after their excision is that "California statutory law . . . drastically limits a patient's control over excised cells." For this proposition the majority rely on Health and Safety Code section 7054.4. The majority concede that the statute was not meant to directly resolve the question whether a person in Moore's position has a cause of action for conversion, but reason that it indirectly resolves the question by limiting the patient's control over the fate of his excised cells: "By restricting how excised cells may be used and requiring their eventual destruction, the statute eliminates so many of the rights ordinarily attached to property that one cannot simply assume that what is left amounts to 'property' or 'ownership' for purposes of conversion law." As will appear, I do not believe section 7054.4 supports the just quoted conclusion of the majority.

First, in my view the statute does not authorize the principal use that defendants claim the right to make of Moore's tissue, i.e., its commercial exploitation. . . . By its terms, section 7054.4 permits only "scientific use" of excised body parts and tissue before they must be destroyed. We must therefore determine the usual and ordinary meaning of that phrase. I would agree that "scientific use" at least includes routine postoperative examination of excised tissue conducted by a pathologist for diagnostic or prognostic reasons (e.g., to verify preoperative diagnosis or to assist in determining postoperative treatment). I might further agree that "scientific use" could be extended to include purely scientific study of the tissue by a disinterested researcher for the purpose of advancing medical knowledge—provided of course that the patient gave timely and informed consent to that use. It would stretch the English language beyond recognition, however, to say that commercial exploitation of the kind and degree alleged here is also a usual and ordinary meaning of the phrase "scientific use."

The majority dismiss this difficulty by asserting that I read the statute to define "scientific use" as "not-for-profit scientific use," and by finding "no reason to believe that the Legislature intended to make such a distinction." The objection misses my point. I do not stress the concept of profit, but the concept of *science:* the distinction I draw is not between nonprofit scientific use and scientific use that happens to lead to a marketable by-product; it is between a truly *scientific* use and the blatant commercial exploitation of Moore's tissue that the present complaint alleges.

Secondly, even if section 7054.4 does permit defendants' commercial exploitation of Moore's tissue under the guise of "scientific use," it does not follow that—as the majority conclude—the statute "eliminates so many of the rights ordinarily attached to property" that what remains does not amount to "property" or "ownership" for purposes of the law of conversion. The concepts of property and ownership in our law are extremely broad. A leading decision of this court approved the following definition: " 'The term "property" is sufficiently comprehensive to include every species of estate, real and personal, and everything which one person can own and transfer to another. It extends to every species of right and interest capable of being enjoyed as such upon which it is practicable to place a money value.'" Being broad, the concept of property is also abstract: rather than referring directly to a material object such as a parcel of land or the tractor that cultivates it, the concept of property is often said to refer to a "bundle of rights" that may be exercised with respect to that object—principally the rights to possess the property, to use the property, to exclude others from the property, and to dispose of the property by sale or by gift. "Ownership is not a single concrete entity but a bundle of rights and privileges as well as of obligations." But the same bundle of rights does not attach to all forms of property. For a variety of policy reasons, the law limits or even forbids the exercise of certain rights over certain forms of property. For example, both law and contract may limit the right of an owner of real property to use his parcel as he sees fit.[6] Owners of various forms of personal property may likewise be subject to restrictions on the time, place, and manner of their use.[7] Limitations on the disposition of real property, while less common, may also be imposed.[8] Finally, some types of personal property may be sold but not given away,[9] while others may be given away but not sold,[10] and still others may neither be given away nor sold.[11]

In each of the foregoing instances, the limitation or prohibition diminishes the bundle of rights that would otherwise attach to the property, yet what remains is still deemed in law to be a protectible property interest. "Since property or title is a complex bundle of rights, duties, powers and immunities, the pruning away of some or a great many of these elements does not entirely destroy the title. . . ." (*People v. Walker* (1939) 33 Cal.App.2d 18, 20, 90 P.2d 854 [even the possessor of contraband has certain property rights in it against anyone other than the state].) The same rule applies to Moore's interest in his own body tissue: even if we assume that section 7054.4 limited the use and disposition of his excised tissue in the manner claimed by the majority, Moore nevertheless retained valuable rights in that tissue. Above all, at the time of its excision

---

[6] Zoning or nuisance laws, or covenants running with the land or equitable servitudes, or condominium declarations, may prohibit certain uses of the parcel or regulate the number, size, location, etc., of buildings an owner may erect on it. Even if rental of the property is a permitted use, rent control laws may limit the benefits of that use. Other uses may, on the contrary, be compelled: e.g., if the property is a lease to extract minerals, the lease may be forfeited by law or contract if the lessee does not exploit the resource. Historic preservation laws may prohibit an owner from demolishing a building on the property, or even from altering its appearance. And endangered species laws may limit an owner's right to develop the land from its natural state.

[7] Public health and safety laws restrict in various ways the manufacture, distribution, purchase, sale, and use of such property as food, drugs, cosmetics, tobacco, alcoholic beverages, firearms, flammable or explosive materials, and waste products. Other laws regulate the operation of private and commercial motor vehicles, aircraft, and vessels.

[8] Provisions in a condominium declaration may give the homeowners association a right of first refusal over a proposed sale by a member. Provisions in a commercial lease may require the lessor's consent to an assignment of the lease.

[9] A person contemplating bankruptcy may sell his property at its "reasonably equivalent value," but he may not make a gift of the same property. (See 11 U.S.C. §548(a).)

[10] A sportsman may give away wild fish or game that he has caught or killed pursuant to his license, but he may not sell it. (Fish & Game Code, §§3039, 7121.)

[11] E.g., a license to practice a profession, or a prescription drug in the hands of the person for whom it is prescribed.

---

he at least had *the right to do with his own tissue whatever the defendants did with it*: i.e., he could have contracted with researchers and pharmaceutical companies to develop and exploit the vast commercial potential of his tissue and its products. Defendants certainly believe that *their* right to do the foregoing is not barred by section 7054.4 and is a significant property right, as they have demonstrated by their deliberate concealment from Moore of the true value of his tissue, their efforts to obtain a patent on the Mo cell line, their contractual agreements to exploit this material, their exclusion of Moore from any participation in the profits, and their vigorous defense of this lawsuit. The Court of Appeal summed up the point by observing that "Defendants' position that plaintiff cannot own his tissue, but that they can, is fraught with irony." It is also legally untenable. As noted above, the majority cite no case holding that an individual's right to develop and exploit the commercial potential of his own tissue is *not* a right of sufficient worth or dignity to be deemed a protectible property interest. In the absence of such authority—or of legislation to the same effect—the right falls within the traditionally broad concept of property in our law.

The majority's third and last reason for their conclusion that Moore has no cause of action for conversion under existing law is that "the subject matter of the Regents' patent—the patented cell line and the products derived from it—cannot be Moore's property." The majority then offer a dual explanation: "This is because the patented cell line is *factually* and *legally* distinct from the cells taken from Moore's body." (*Ibid.,* italics added.) Neither branch of the explanation withstands analysis.

First, in support of their statement that the Mo cell line is "factually distinct" from Moore's cells, the majority assert that "Cells change while being developed into a cell line and continue to change over time," and in particular may acquire an abnormal number of chromosomes. No one disputes these assertions, but they are nonetheless irrelevant. For present purposes no distinction can be drawn between Moore's cells and the Mo cell line. It appears that the principal reason for establishing a cell line is not to "improve" the quality of the parent cells but simply to extend their life indefinitely, in order to permit long-term study and/or exploitation of the qualities already present in such cells. The complaint alleges that Moore's cells naturally produced certain valuable proteins in larger than normal quantities; indeed, that was why defendants were eager to culture them in the first place. Defendants do not claim that the cells of the Mo cell line are in any degree more productive of such proteins than were Moore's own cells. Even if the cells of the Mo cell line in fact have an abnormal number of chromosomes, at the present stage of this case we do not know if that fact has any bearing whatever on their capacity to produce proteins; yet it is in the commercial exploitation of that capacity— not simply in their number of chromosomes—that Moore seeks to assert an interest. For all that appears, therefore, the emphasized fact is a distinction without a difference.

Second, the majority assert in effect that Moore cannot have an ownership interest in the Mo cell line because defendants patented it. The majority's point wholly fails to meet Moore's claim that he is entitled to compensation for defendants' unauthorized use of his bodily tissues *before* defendants patented the Mo cell line: defendants undertook such use immediately after the splenectomy on October 20, 1976, and continued to extract and use Moore's cells and tissue at least until September 20, 1983; the patent, however, did not issue until March 20, 1984, more than seven years after the unauthorized use began. Whatever the legal consequences of that event, it did not operate retroactively to immunize defendants from accountability for conduct occurring long before the patent was granted.

Nor did the issuance of the patent in 1984 necessarily have the drastic effect that the majority contend. To be sure, the patent granted defendants the exclusive right to make, use, or sell the invention for a period of 17 years. But Moore does not assert any such right for himself. Rather, he seeks to show that he is entitled, in fairness and equity, to some share in the profits that defendants have made and will make from their commercial exploitation of the Mo cell line. I do not question that the cell line is primarily the product of defendants' inventive effort. Yet likewise no one can question Moore's crucial contribution to the invention—an invention named, ironically, after him: but for the cells of Moore's body taken by defendants, *there would have been no Mo cell line.* Thus the complaint alleges that Moore's "Blood and Bodily Substances were absolutely essential to defendants' research and commercial activities with regard to his cells, cell lines, [and] the Mo cell-line, . . . and that defendants could not have applied for and had issued to them the Mo cell-line patent and other patents described herein without obtaining and culturing specimens of plaintiff's Blood and Bodily Substances." Defendants admit this allegation by their demurrers, as well they should: for all their expertise, defendants do not claim they could have extracted the Mo cell line out of thin air.

Nevertheless the majority conclude that the patent somehow cut off all Moore's rights—past, present, and future—to share in the proceeds of defendants' commercial exploitation of the cell line derived from his own body tissue. The majority cite no authority for this unfair result, and I cannot believe it is compelled by the general law of patents: a patent is not a license to defraud. . . .

Having concluded—mistakenly, in my view—that Moore has no cause of action for conversion under existing law, the majority next consider whether to "extend" the conversion cause of action to this context. . . . The majority [focuses on a] policy consideration, i.e., their concern "that we not threaten with disabling civil liability innocent parties who are engaged in socially useful activities, such as researchers who have no reason to believe that their use of a particular cell sample is, or may be, against a donor's wishes." As will appear, in my view this concern is both overstated and outweighed by contrary considerations. . . .

The majority begin their analysis by stressing the obvious facts that research on human cells plays an increasingly important role in the progress of medicine, and that the manipulation of those cells by the methods of biotechnology has resulted in numerous beneficial products and treatments. Yet it does not necessarily follow that, as the majority claim, application of the law of conversion to this area "will hinder research by restricting access to the necessary raw materials," i.e., to cells, cell cultures, and cell lines. The majority observe that many researchers obtain their tissue samples, routinely and at little or no cost, from cell-culture repositories. The majority then speculate that "This exchange of scientific materials, which still is relatively free and efficient, will surely be compromised if each cell sample becomes the potential subject matter of a lawsuit." There are two grounds to doubt that this prophecy will be fulfilled.

To begin with, if the relevant exchange of scientific materials was ever "free and efficient," it is much less so today. Since biological products of genetic engineering became patentable in 1980 human cell lines have been amenable to patent protection and, as the Court of Appeal observed in its opinion below, "The rush to patent for exclusive use has been rampant." Among those who have taken advantage of this development, of course, are the defendants herein: as we have seen, defendants Golde and Quan obtained a patent on the Mo cell line in 1984 and assigned it to defendant Regents. With such patentability has come a drastic reduction in the formerly free access of researchers to new cell lines and their products: the "novelty" requirement for patentability prohibits public disclosure of the invention at all times up to one year before the filing of the patent application. Thus defendants herein recited in their patent specification, "At no time has the Mo cell line been available to other than the investigators involved with its initial discovery and only the conditioned medium from the cell line has been made available to a limited number of investigators for collaborative work with the original discoverers of the Mo cell line."

An even greater force for restricting the free exchange of new cell lines and their products has been the rise of the biotechnology industry and the increasing involvement of academic researchers in that industry. When scientists became entrepreneurs and negotiated with biotechnological and pharmaceutical companies to develop and exploit the commercial potential of their discoveries—as did defendants in the case at bar—layers of contractual restrictions were added to the protections of the patent law.

In their turn, the biotechnological and pharmaceutical companies demanded and received exclusive rights in the scientists' discoveries, and frequently placed those discoveries under trade secret protection. Trade secret protection is popular among biotechnology companies because, among other reasons, the invention need not meet the strict standards of patentability and the protection is both quickly acquired and unlimited in duration. Secrecy as a normal business practice is also taking hold in university research laboratories, often because of industry pressure "One of the most serious fears associated with university-industry cooperative research concerns keeping work private and not disclosing it to the researcher's peers. . . . Economic arrangements between industry and universities inhibit open communication between researchers, especially for those who are financially tied to smaller biotechnology firms."

Secondly, to the extent that cell cultures and cell lines may still be "freely exchanged," e.g., for purely research purposes, it does not follow that the researcher who obtains such material must necessarily remain ignorant of any limitations on its use: by means of appropriate recordkeeping, the researcher can be assured that the source of the material has consented to his proposed use of it, and hence that such use is not a conversion. To achieve this end the originator of the tissue sample first determines the extent of the source's informed consent to its use—e.g., for research only, or for public but academic use, or for specific or general commercial purposes; he then enters this information in the record of the tissue sample, and the record accompanies the sample into the hands of any researcher who thereafter undertakes to work with it. "Record keeping would not be overly burdensome because researchers generally keep accurate records of tissue sources for other reasons: to trace anomalies to the medical history of the patient, to maintain title for other researchers and for themselves, and to insure reproducibility of the experiment." (Note, *Toward the Right of Commerciality,* 34 UCLA L. Rev. at p. 241.) As the Court of Appeal correctly observed, any claim to the contrary "is dubious in light of the meticulous care and planning necessary in serious modern medical research." . . .

In any event, in my view whatever merit the majority's single policy consideration may have is outweighed by two contrary considerations, i.e., policies that are promoted by recognizing that every individual has a legally protectible property interest in his own body and its products. First, our society acknowledges a profound ethical imperative to respect the human body as the physical and temporal expression of the unique human persona. One manifestation of that respect is our prohibition against direct abuse of the body by torture or other forms of cruel or unusual punishment. Another is our prohibition against indirect abuse of the body by its economic exploitation for the sole benefit of another person. The most abhorrent form of such exploitation, of course, was the institution of slavery. Lesser forms, such as indentured servitude or even debtor's prison, have also disappeared. Yet their specter haunts the laboratories and boardrooms of today's biotechnological research-industrial complex. It arises wherever scientists or industrialists claim, as defendants claim here, the right to appropriate and exploit a patient's tissue for their sole economic benefit—the right, in other words, to freely mine or harvest valuable physical properties of the patient's body: "Research with human cells that results in significant economic gain for the researcher and no gain for the patient offends the traditional mores of our society in a manner impossible to quantify. Such research tends to treat the human body as a commodity—a means to a profitable end. The dignity and sanctity with which we regard the human whole, body as well as mind and soul, are absent when we allow researchers to further their own interests without the patient's participation by using a patient's cells as the basis for a marketable product."

A second policy consideration adds notions of equity to those of ethics. Our society values fundamental fairness in dealings between its members, and condemns the unjust enrichment of any member at the expense of another. This is particularly true when, as here, the parties are not in equal bargaining positions. . . . We are repeatedly told that the commercial products of the biotechnological revolution "hold the promise of tremendous profit." (Note, *Toward the Right of Commerciality*, 34 UCLA L. Rev. at p. 211.) In the case at bar, for example, the complaint alleges that the market for the kinds of proteins produced by the Mo cell line was predicted to exceed $3 billion by 1990. These profits are currently shared exclusively between the biotechnology industry and the universities that support that industry. The profits are shared in a wide variety of ways, including "direct entrepreneurial ties to genetic-engineering firms" and "an equity interest in fledgling biotechnology firms." Thus the complaint alleges that because of his development of the Mo cell line defendant Golde became a paid consultant of defendant Genetics Institute and acquired the rights to 75,000 shares of that firm's stock at a cost of 1 cent each; that Genetics Institute further contracted to pay Golde and the Regents at least $330,000 over 3 years, including a pro rata share of Golde's salary and fringe benefits; and that defendant Sandoz Pharmaceuticals Corporation subsequently contracted to increase that compensation by a further $110,000.

There is, however, a third party to the biotechnology enterprise—the patient who is the source of the blood or tissue from which all these profits are derived. While he may be a silent partner, his contribution to the venture is absolutely crucial: as pointed out above, but for the cells of Moore's body taken by defendants there would have been no Mo cell line at all. Yet defendants deny that Moore is entitled to any share whatever in the proceeds of this cell line. This is both inequitable and immoral. As Dr. Thomas H. Murray, a respected professor of ethics and public policy, testified before Congress, "the person [who furnishes the tissue] should be justly compensated. . . . If biotechnologists fail to make provision for a just sharing of profits with the person whose gift made it possible, the public's sense of justice will be offended and no one will be the winner." . . .

The majority's second reason for declining to extend the conversion cause of action to the present context is that "the Legislature should make that decision." I do not doubt that the Legislature is competent to act on this topic. The fact that the Legislature may intervene if and when it chooses, however, does not in the meanwhile relieve the courts of their duty of enforcing—or if need be, fashioning—an effective judicial remedy for the wrong here alleged. . . .

The inference I draw from the current statutory regulation of human biological materials, moreover, is the opposite of that drawn by the majority. By selective quotation of the statutes the majority seem to suggest that human organs and blood cannot legally be sold on the open market—thereby implying that if the Legislature were to act here it would impose a similar ban on monetary compensation for the use of human tissue in biotechnological research and development. But if that is the argument, the premise is unsound: contrary to popular misconception, it is not true that human organs and blood cannot legally be sold.

As to organs, the majority rely on the Uniform Anatomical Gift Act for the proposition that a competent adult may make a post mortem gift of any part of his body but may not receive "valuable consideration" for the transfer. But the prohibition of the UAGA against the sale of a body part is much more limited than the majority recognize: by its terms the prohibition applies only to sales for "transplantation" or "therapy." Yet a different section of the UAGA authorizes the transfer and receipt of body parts for such additional purposes as "medical or dental education, research, or advancement of medical or dental science." No section of the UAGA prohibits anyone from selling body parts for any of those additional purposes; by clear implication, therefore, such sales are legal. Indeed, the fact that the UAGA prohibits *no* sales of organs other than sales for "transportation" or "therapy" raises a further implication that it is also legal for anyone to sell human tissue to a biotechnology company for research and development purposes.

With respect to the sale of human blood the matter is much simpler: there is in fact no prohibition against such sales. The majority rely on Health and Safety Code section 1606, which provides in relevant part that the procurement and use of blood for transfusion "shall be construed to be, and is declared to be . . . the rendition of a service . . . and shall not be construed to be, and is declared not to be, a sale. . . ." There is less here, however, than meets the eye: the statute does *not* mean that a person cannot sell his blood or, by implication, that his blood is not his property. "While many jurisdictions have classified the transfer of blood or other human tissue as a service rather than a sale, this position does not conflict with the notion that human tissue is property." The reason is plain: "No State or Federal statute prohibits the sale of blood, plasma, semen, or other replenishing tissues if taken in nonvital amounts. Nevertheless, State laws usually characterize these paid transfers as the provision of services rather than the sale of a commodity. . . . The primary legal reason for characterizing these transactions as involving services rather than goods is to avoid liability for contaminated blood products under either general product liability principles or the [Uniform Commercial Code's] implied warranty provisions." The courts have repeatedly recognized that the foregoing is the real purpose of this harmless legal fiction. Thus despite the statute relied on by the majority, it is perfectly legal in this state for a person to sell his blood for transfusion or for any other purpose indeed, such sales are commonplace, particularly in the market for plasma.

It follows that the statutes regulating the transfers of human organs and blood do not support the majority's refusal to recognize a conversion cause of action for commercial exploitation of human blood cells without consent. On the contrary, because such statutes treat both organs and blood as property that can legally be sold in a variety of circumstances, they impliedly support Moore's contention that his blood cells are likewise property for which he can and should receive compensation, and hence are protected by the law of conversion.

The majority's final reason for refusing to recognize a conversion cause of action on these facts is that "there is no pressing need" to do so because the complaint also states another cause of action that is assertedly adequate to the task; that cause of action is "the breach of a fiduciary duty to disclose facts material to the patient's consent or, alternatively, . . . the performance of medical procedures without first having obtained the patient's informed consent" Although last, this reason is not the majority's least; in fact, it underlies much of the opinion's discussion of the conversion cause of action, recurring like a leitmotiv throughout that discussion.

The majority hold that a physician who intends to treat a patient in whom he has either a research interest or an economic interest is under a fiduciary duty to disclose such interest to the patient before treatment; that his failure to do so may give rise to a nondisclosure cause of action; and that the complaint herein states such a cause of action at least against defendant Golde. I agree with that holding as far as it goes.

I disagree, however, with the majority's further conclusion that in the present context a nondisclosure cause of action is an adequate—in fact, a superior—substitute for a conversion cause of action. In my view the nondisclosure cause of action falls short on at least three grounds.

First, the majority reason that "enforcement of physicians' disclosure obligations" will ensure patients' freedom of choice. The majority do not spell out how those obligations will be "enforced"; but because they arise from judicial decision (the majority opinion herein) rather than from legislative or administrative enactment, we may infer that the obligations will primarily be enforced by the traditional judicial remedy of an action for damages for their breach. Thus the majority's theory apparently is that the threat of such an action will have a prophylactic effect: it will give physician-researchers incentive to disclose any conflicts of interest before treatment, and will thereby protect their patients' right to make an informed decision about what may be done with their body parts.

The remedy is largely illusory. "[A]n action based on the physician's failure to disclose material information sounds in negligence. As a practical matter, however, it may be difficult to recover on this kind of negligence theory because the patient must prove a *causal connection* between his or her injury and the physician's failure to inform." There are two barriers to recovery. First, "the patient must show that if he or she had been informed of all pertinent information, he or she would have declined to consent to the procedure in question." . . . The second barrier to recovery is still higher, and is erected on the first: it is not even enough for the plaintiff to prove that he personally would have refused consent to the proposed treatment if he had been fully informed; he must also prove that in the same circumstances *no reasonably prudent person* would have given such consent. . . .

[T]he nondisclosure cause of action fails to reach a major class of potential defendants: all those who are outside the strict physician-patient relationship with the plaintiff. Thus the majority concede that here only defendant Golde, the treating physician, can be directly liable to Moore on a nondisclosure cause of action: "The Regents, Quan, Genetics Institute, and Sandoz are not physicians. In contrast to Golde, none of these defendants stood in a fiduciary relationship with Moore or had the duty to obtain Moore's informed consent to medical procedures." . . .

My respect for this court as an institution compels me to make one last point: I dissociate myself completely from the amateur biology lecture that the majority impose on us throughout their opinion. For several reasons, the inclusion of most of that material in an opinion of this court is improper.

First, with the exception of defendants' patent none of the material in question is part of the record on appeal as defined by the California Rules of Court. Because this appeal is taken from a judgment of dismissal entered after the sustaining of general and special demurrers, there is virtually no record other than the pleadings. The case has never been tried, and hence there is no evidence whatever on the obscure medical topics on which the majority presume to instruct us. Instead, all the documents that the majority rely on for their medical explanations appear in an appendix to defendant Golde's opening brief on the merits. Such an appendix, however, is no more a part of the *record* than the brief itself, because the record comprises only the materials before the trial court when it made its ruling. . . .

Second, most of these documents bear solely or primarily on the majority's discussion of whether Moore's "genetic material" was or was not "unique," but that entire discussion is legally irrelevant to the present appeal. As Justice Broussard correctly observes in his separate opinion, "the question of uniqueness has no proper bearing on plaintiff's basic right to maintain a conversion action; ordinary property, as well as unique property, is, of course, protected against conversion."

Third, this nonissue is also a noncontention. The majority claim that "Moore relies . . . primarily" on an analogy to certain right-of-privacy decisions, but this is not accurate. Under our rules, as in appellate practice generally, the parties to an appeal are confined to the contentions raised in their briefs. In his brief on the merits in this court Moore does not even cite, less still "rely primarily," on the right-of-privacy decisions discussed by the majority, nor does he draw any analogy to the rule of those decisions. It is true that in the course of oral argument before this court, counsel for Moore briefly paraphrased the analogy argument that the majority now attribute to him; but a party may not, of course, raise a new contention for the first time in oral argument.

Fourth, much of the material that the majority rely on in this regard is written in highly technical scientific jargon by and for specialists in the field of contemporary molecular biology. As far as I know, no member of this court is trained as a molecular biologist, or even as a physician; without expert testimony in the record, therefore, the majority are not competent to explain these arcane points of medical science any more than a doctor would be competent to explain esoteric questions of the law of negotiable instruments or federal income taxation, or the rule against perpetuities. In attempting to expound this science the majority run two serious risks. First, because they have no background in molecular biology the majority may simply misunderstand what they are reading, much as a layman might misunderstand a highly technical article in a professional legal journal. Indeed, I suggest the majority have already fallen into this very trap, since some of their explanations appear either mistaken, confused, or incomplete. . . .

The second risk is that of omission. The majority have access to most of the legal literature published in this country; but even if the majority could understand the medical literature, as a practical matter they have access to virtually none of it. This is demonstrated by the fact that every one of the medical articles now relied on by the majority came into their possession as reprints furnished to this court by one of the parties to this lawsuit—obviously not an unbiased source. Because the majority are thus not equipped to independently research the medical points they seek to make, they risk presenting only one side of the story; it may well be that other researchers have reached different or even contrary results, reported in publications that defendants, acting in self-interest, have not furnished to the court. I leave it to professionals in molecular biology to say whether the majority's explanations on this topic are both correct and balanced. Because I fear they may be neither, I cannot subscribe to any of them.

I would affirm the decision of the Court of Appeal to direct the trial court to overrule the demurrers to the cause of action for conversion.

NOTES AND QUESTIONS

1. *The Immortal Life of Henrietta Lacks.* Rebecca Skloot's book *The Immortal Life of Henrietta Lacks* examines a story similar to that involved in *Moore.* Henrietta Lacks was a poor black tobacco farmer. Her cells were taken without her knowledge in 1951 and were used to create a cell line that was widely used in medical research. If you are interested in the issues in *Moore,* we highly recommend that you read the book.

2. *Medical Research.* Let's leave aside for a moment the issue of whether we should be able to sell our body parts. Did the court reach the right result on Moore's conversion claim? Should Moore have a right to share in the profits from the products made from his cells without his knowledge?

3. *Selling Body Parts and Other Contested Commodities.* The question of whether we should be able to sell body parts has and continues to be the subject of great debate. We can only scratch the surface of the issues here. Here are some things to consider as you think about the question. People typically are allowed to donate body parts during their lives, at least to the degree that the removal of those body parts does not threaten their health. People are also typically allowed to donate their organs and tissues at death. Certain types of body parts (e.g., blood) may be sold. People, however, are typically not allowed to sell their organs. Why should this be the case? Why should we have

a problem with selling body parts when we allow the donation of body parts? Why shouldn't a person be able to sell their kidney? Or why should we prevent someone from receiving payment for an agreement to allow for the medical use of their body after their death? One potential answer to these questions is the problem of *economic coercion*—we might worry that people would be coerced by their financial situation into selling body parts. Another potential answer is the problem of *commodification*—we might worry about turning our bodies into commodities that are subject to market exchange. On the other hand, a robust market for body parts already exists—the original donor typically can't be paid, but after donation body parts are bought and sold by medical providers. We also have chronic shortages of organs for transplantation. Shouldn't we rely on market incentives to increase the supply of needed organs?

The literature on these topics is rich. Here are some suggestions for further reading: James Stacey Taylor, *Stakes and Kidneys: Why Markets in Human Body Parts Are Morally Imperative* (2005); Martha Ertman & Joan C. Williams, *Rethinking Commodification: Cases and Readings in Law and Culture* (2005); Margaret Jane Radin, *Contested Commodities: The Trouble With Trade in Sex, Children, Body Parts, and Other Things* (1996); Imogen Goold et al., *The Human Body as Property? Possession, Control, and Commodification*, 40 J. Med. Ethics 1 (2014) (the first article in a special issue on the topic); Robin Feldman, *Whose Body is it Anyway? Human Cells and the Strange Effects of Property and Intellectual Property Law*, 63 Stan. L. Rev. 1377 (2011); Julia D. Mahoney, *The Market for Human Tissue*, 86 Va. L. Rev. 163 (2000); Stephen R. Munzer, *An Uneasy Case Against Property Rights in Body Parts*, 11 Soc. Phil. & Pol'y 259 (1994).

EXPLANATORY ANSWERS

CHAPTER 1

BAILMENTS PROBLEMS

1. This bailment was created in a commercial context, so under the common-law classification system, it is a mutual benefit bailment. The bailee is held to an ordinary standard of care under the traditional common-law approach and is held to the similar standard of ordinary care under the circumstances under the modern approach.

2. Again, this is a mutual benefit bailment, but because this is a case of misdelivery, the bailee will be held strictly liable.

3. This bailment is created solely for the benefit of April, the bailee. As a result, under the traditional common-law approach, she would be held to a standard of great care. Under the modern approach, she would be held to the standard of ordinary care under the circumstances.

4. There is no bailment created here because Lashuan maintained control of the car. This is the park-and-lock scenario that we mentioned in the text. There may or may not be some sort of liability created in some person for the damage to the car, but it does not arise out of the law of bailments.

FINDING PROBLEMS

1. From the two cases, we have five categories of found property: lost, mislaid, abandoned, treasure trove, and embedded. We can eliminate two relatively quickly. Treasure trove is defined as coins or currency that are concealed by the owner. Treasure trove also has an element of antiquity. The backpack was not concealed (it was on the floor by the door), and facts say that the currency is new, so the element of antiquity is not met. The backpack was not attached to the property or embedded to the ground, so the embedded category does not apply here. We mentioned a sixth category, contraband, in the notes after *Benjamin*. There are no facts given here that would allow the government to prove that the property was contraband, so that category likely does not apply.

That leaves lost, mislaid, or abandoned. It is possible to make arguments in support of each of them, but we think that mislaid probably fits this fact pattern best. Mislaid property is intentionally placed by the owner in a particular location and then later forgotten by the owner. Lost property is not intentionally placed—the owner accidentally drops the object or otherwise unintentionally parts with possession. It seems hard (though not impossible) to imagine a scenario where a person unintentionally parts with possession of a backpack, so it seems likely that the property was mislaid and not lost. Our last category, abandoned, turns on the owner's intent. We typically would presume that someone would not intend to abandon money or anything else of value. We might imagine, however, that it was abandoned if we thought the money was stolen or otherwise obtained illegally. See, in this context, the dissent in *Benjamin*. Because mislaid property goes to the owner of the locus, Cindy seems to have the best claim on these facts. Lost and abandoned property goes to the finder. On these facts, Paul might be able to make a decent claim by arguing that the backpack was abandoned.

What if the money was found in an envelope rather than a backpack? It is easier to imagine a person accidentally losing an envelope than a backpack. Perhaps it was in the owner's bag or coat pocket and fell out when the owner reached in to get something else. This strengthens the argument that the money was lost rather than mislaid, giving Paul a stronger claim. If the envelope was found on the counter rather than on the floor, we would be back to having a good argument that it was mislaid—it is easy to imagine someone placing the envelope on the counter, then forgetting it. On the other hand, we could also imagine the envelope falling out of someone's bag or coat pocket onto the counter. The envelope on the counter strikes us and the scenario that best supports arguments for both lost and mislaid.

We should emphasize here that the lines between the categories of lost, mislaid, and abandoned are blurry and that reasonable minds can disagree about how they apply to a particular set of facts. We discussed the vagueness of these rules in the notes after *Benjamin*. When dealing with vague rules, you should focus on making the best arguments that you can because it is often impossible to identify an answer that is exactly correct.

2. This scenario is even blurrier than the last. We think the most plausible categories are embedded or lost. Mislaid doesn't seem to work well here—it is hard to imagine a person intentionally placing a ring in a gully. Even here, though, it is possible to come up with a scenario—imagine a marriage proposal gone wrong when the person making the proposal hides the ring in the park but then forgets exactly where it is. Abandoned also seems unlikely—who would abandon a valuable ring? Treasure trove might be plausible; the ring is old, satisfying the antiquity element, but treasure trove is typically defined in terms of coin or bullion, not jewelry.

The ring was found in a small gully caused by a recent rainstorm. It may have been embedded and exposed when the rain washed away the soil. The ring was very dirty, suggesting that it may have been buried. If it was embedded, Theresa would get the ring as owner of the locus. We can also imagine, however, the ring falling off of someone's finger while they were walking through the park. The age of the ring would be consistent with this story—it is not unusual for a person today to wear an antique ring. So is the fact that the ring was dirty—rings that sit in the dirt for a while get dirty. If it was lost, then Ryan would get it as the finder.

GIFT PROBLEMS

1. Maurice made a valid *inter vivos* gift to Sally, but it is revocable. Maurice's words indicate that he intended to make a present gift, not a gift that was to occur on his death. He delivered the ring to Sally, and she accepted it. Because the gift was made by Maurice in view of his impending death, it is a gift *causa mortis*, allowing Maurice to revoke the gift after he recovered.

2. Theresa did not make a valid *inter vivos* gift under the traditional common-law rules. She intended to make an *inter vivos* gift, and we can presume acceptance by Holly. The element of delivery, however, was not met under the traditional standard. A court strictly construing the delivery requirement of "if it can be handed over, it must be handed over" would require the car to be physically delivered to Holly's possession. At a minimum, a traditional court would require delivery of the keys. A court taking a more modern approach might find that symbolic delivery was made through the card. Note that *Gruen* does not lend direct support to Holly because unlike *Gruen*, the problem does not involve the gift of a future interest.

3. Nick did not make a valid *inter vivos* gift to Katie. The delivery and acceptance elements are met here—Nick handed the lamp over to Katie, and Katie took it. The problem here is intent. Nick's words indicate that he intended to transfer ownership at death. Because there was no intent to make a present transfer of ownership during life, and instead a transfer of ownership at death, the attempted gift is invalid. Nick owns the lamp.

ADVERSE POSSESSION PROBLEMS

1. 1998. C's minority doesn't matter on this hypothetical. The statute gives the person under a disability the longer of (a) ten years from when the disability is lifted (here, C turned 18 in 1983, so an extra 10 years would be 1993) or (b) the 21-year period (which expires here in 1998). As we pointed out in Example 1, we only apply the disability period if it benefits the owner.

2. (a) B wins in 1994. As of 1993, A has been in possession for 21 years, but the statute has been tolled because of O's imprisonment. O's disability of imprisonment was removed by death in 1985. B, who is "claiming from, by, or under" O, gets the benefit of the ten-year disabilities period. Adding ten years to 1985, we find that the statute will expire in A's favor in 1995. So B will win in 1994. "But wait," you might say—B is a minor, but this disability wasn't in place at the time A entered. True, but B isn't relying here on being a minor here. Rather, B wins based on O's disability alone.

(b) A wins. As we just explained, the extra ten years from O's disability expires in 1995. B cannot claim more time based on being a minor because B was not a disabled owner of Blackacre when A entered. This specific fact pattern, which we illustrated in Example 5, involves a disabled heir, but it is illustrative of the larger point illustrated by Example 4—disabilities do not matter unless they were in place at the time the adverse possessor enters. (c) A wins for same reasons as (b).

3. O wins. The 21-year statute of limitations would have run in A's favor in 1996, but A died before the limitations period expired. B had only been on the property for seven years by the time O sued. So for B to win, B would have to *tack* A's 15 years of possession onto her 7 years of possession. But B can't tack because there was no voluntary transfer of possession, and therefore no *privity*, between A and B.

4. B wins with a caveat. Here, there is a voluntary transfer of *possession* between A and B. A and B therefore are in privity, so B can tack A's 15 years onto her 7 years of possession, satisfying the 21-year statute of limitations. The caveat is that if the court applied the rule used by the *trial court* in *Howard v. Kunto*, that privity requires a transfer of an *estate,* and that transfer of possession alone doesn't qualify, then O would win because without privity B can't tack.

5. It depends. O's disability occurred after A took possession and therefore is irrelevant. A has possessed part of Blackacre for the statutory period and in an open and notorious manner (the fence). If the court follows the Maine rule/bad faith standard, though, A's mistaken possession won't qualify as adverse and under a claim of right, and O would win. If the court follows the majority rule that mistaken possession qualifies as adverse, A would win.

6. C would win in 1997. A entered after ownership had been split into present and future interests. The statute of limitations doesn't run against a future interest holder until that person's interest becomes possessory. In other words, the clock does not run against C until B dies. When B dies, B's life estate ends, and C's future interest becomes possessory. So A loses in 1997 even though A has possessed Blackacre for more than 21 years. The statute started to run against C in 1979 and expires against C in 2000. So A would win if the action for ejectment was brought in 2002.

CHAPTER 2

ESTATES AND FUTURE INTERESTS PROBLEM SET—PART 1

1. A has a life estate. O has a reversion in fee simple absolute.

2. The School Board has a fee simple determinable. O has a possibility of reverter in fee simple absolute.

3. A has a life estate. O has a vested remainder in fee simple absolute. The conveyance created a vested remainder in fee simple absolute in B. B then conveyed that interest to O. The remainder keeps its name even though it is now held by the grantor.

4. A has a term of years. O has a reversion in fee simple absolute.

5. A has a life estate. B has a contingent remainder in fee simple absolute. O has a reversion in fee simple absolute.

6. A owns Blackacre in fee simple absolute.

7. Under the most common modern approach, A would own Blackacre in fee simple absolute. At traditional common law, A would own Blackacre in fee tail, and O would have a reversion.

8. The School Board has a fee simple subject to executory limitation. The State University has an executory interest in fee simple absolute.

9. A has a life estate. A's children have a contingent remainder in fee simple absolute. O has a reversion in fee simple absolute. The remainder is contingent because it is in an unascertained person.

10. A has a life estate. B has a vested remainder in an open class in fee simple.

11. A has a life estate. B has a vested remainder subject to divestment in fee simple absolute. C has an executory interest that may divest B's vested remainder in fee simple absolute.

12. The School Board has a fee simple subject to condition subsequent. O has a right of entry in fee simple absolute.

13. A has a life estate. B has an alternative contingent remainder in fee simple absolute. C has an alternative contingent remainder in fee simple absolute.

14. A has a life estate. B has a vested remainder in life estate. A's children have a contingent remainder in fee simple absolute. O has a reversion in fee simple absolute. As in problem 9, the remainder is contingent because it is in an unascertained person.

15. A has a life estate. B has a vested remainder in life estate. C has a vested remainder in an open class.

ESTATES AND FUTURE INTERESTS PROBLEM SET—PART 2

16. A has a life estate. The School Board has a vested remainder in fee simple determinable. O has a possibility of reverter in fee simple absolute.

17. The School Board has a fee simple determinable. O has a possibility of reverter in fee simple absolute.

18. O owns Blackacre in fee simple absolute.

19. A has a life estate. A's children have an alternative contingent remainder in fee simple absolute. C has an alternative contingent remainder in fee simple absolute. The remainder in A's children is contingent both because it is in an unascertained person and because it is subject to a condition precedent.

20. Basically the same answer as 19. A has a life estate. D has an alternative contingent remainder in fee simple. C has an alternative contingent remainder in fee simple. Even though we now have an ascertained person for the remainder in A's children, it is still subject to a condition precedent.

21. D owns Blackacre in fee simple absolute.

22. A has a life estate. B has a vested remainder in life estate. C has a contingent remainder in fee simple absolute. O has a reversion in fee simple absolute.

23. A has a life estate. C has a contingent remainder in fee simple absolute. O has a reversion in fee simple absolute. Because B died before A, B's life estate has disappeared.

24. A has a life estate. O has a reversion in fee simple absolute.

25. A has a life estate. C has a contingent remainder in fee simple absolute. B has a contingent remainder in fee simple, though not one that is alternative to C's—the contingencies are different. O has a reversion in fee simple absolute.

26. A has a life estate. B has a vested remainder in an open class subject to divestment in fee simple absolute. C has an executory interest in fee simple absolute.

27. B and D have a fee simple subject to executory limitation in common. C has an executory interest in fee simple absolute.

28. B and D own Blackacre in common in fee simple absolute.

29. A has a life estate. B has a contingent remainder in life estate. O has a reversion in fee simple absolute.

30. C has a life estate measured by A's life (also known as a life estate *per autre vie*). B has a contingent remainder in life estate. O has a reversion in fee simple absolute.

31. A has a defeasible life estate. B has a vested remainder in fee simple absolute. O has a possibility of reverter in life estate. If A leaves the church, then O's possibility of reverter will automatically transfer the life estate back to O; on A's death, the life estate will expire (regardless of whether A still has it or whether it has reverted back to O), and B will own Blackacre in fee simple absolute.

32. A has a life estate. B has a vested remainder in an open class subject to divestment in fee simple absolute. C has an executory interest in fee simple absolute.

33. A has a life estate. D has a vested remainder in an open class subject to divestment in fee simple absolute. C has an executory interest in fee simple absolute. D has just stepped into B's shoes. If A dies without having more children, C's executory interest will divest D's interest. If A has another child and that child survives A, then D's interest will become possessory.

34. A has a life estate. B has an alternative contingent remainder in fee simple absolute. (If you said that B's contingent remainder was also in an open class, you would be conceptually correct, but by convention we do not use "in an open class" to describe a contingent remainder). C has an alternative contingent remainder in fee simple absolute.

35. A has a life estate. B has a contingent remainder in fee simple absolute. C has a contingent remainder in fee simple absolute. O has a reversion in fee simple absolute. Note that the contingent remainders are not alternative—children and issue are different categories. A could die with no surviving children but a surviving grandchild. In this case, the property would revert back to O.

RULE AGAINST PERPETUITIES PROBLEM SET

1. *Without RAP*: A has a life estate, A's oldest child has a contingent remainder in life estate, A's grandchildren have a contingent remainder in fee simple absolute, and O has a reversion in fee simple absolute. The reversion is exempt from the RAP, so we only need to worry about the two contingent remainders.

Common Law: The correct answer is: A has a life estate, A's oldest child has a contingent remainder in life estate, and O has a reversion in fee simple absolute. The first contingent remainder is fine—it will vest (or fail if no child is living) at A's death, and A is a life in being. The second contingent remainder violates the RAP—(a) A could have a child, B, after the conveyance; (b) B could be the oldest living child on A's death, and any children born before the conveyance could die; (c) B could die more than 21 years after A's death, in which case the contingent remainder would vest or fail more than 21 years after lives in being. So, under the common law, you strike out the invalid conveyance.

Wait and See: The correct answer is: A has a life estate, A's oldest child has a contingent remainder in life estate, A's grandchildren have a contingent remainder in fee simple absolute that may become invalid based on actual events, and O has a reversion in fee simple. Under the wait-and-see approach, you don't invalidate the interest until you find out what actually happens. If A doesn't have a child after the conveyance, then the contingent remainder will be valid (it will vest or fail at the death of A's oldest child, who in this scenario is a life in being). If A has an afterborn child, and if the contingent remainder does not vest within 21 years of a life-in-being who affects vesting (A or A's children), then the contingent remainder will be void.

2. *Without RAP*: A has a life estate, B has a vested remainder in life estate, B's children have a contingent remainder in fee simple absolute (contingent because we don't know whether B has any kids, so "B's children" is unascertained), O has a reversion in fee simple absolute. Our RAP analysis would not change if B had a living child, making the remainder a vested remainder in an open class because the RAP requires vested remainders in an open class to close during the perpetuities period.

Common Law: The contingent remainder does not violate the RAP, so the answer is as stated above. The contingent remainder will vest or fail at B's death (or at A's death if B predeceases A); because it will vest or fail at the death of a life in being, it is fine.

Wait and See: Same as above.

3. *Without RAP*: A has a life estate, A's children have a contingent remainder in fee simple absolute (because we don't know if A has any children), the Widener City School Board has a contingent remainder in fee simple absolute, O has a reversion in fee simple absolute. (Why does O have a reversion? If A dies without having children neither of the contingent remainders would be satisfied. If A had a child, then A's child would have a vested remainder in an open class subject to divestment, WCSB would have an executory interest, O's reversion would disappear).

Common Law: The correct answer is: A has a life estate, A's children have a contingent remainder in fee simple absolute, O has a reversion in fee simple absolute. The children's contingent remainder is fine because it will vest or fail on A's death. The WCSB's contingent remainder is void under the rule against perpetuities—one of A's great-great grandchildren could be convicted of a felony 200 years from now. The charity-charity exception only applies if both the interests are in charities, which is not the case here.

Wait and See: The correct answer is: A has a life estate, A's children have a contingent remainder in fee simple absolute, the WCSB has a contingent remainder in fee simple absolute that will only be valid for lives in being plus 21 years, O has a reversion in fee simple absolute. Under the wait-and-see approach, WCSB could get the property if the contingency (A's issue convicted of a felony) happens within lives in being plus 21 years. The relevant lives in being would be A and any of A's issue alive at the time of the conveyance. Twenty-one years after the last one of these people dies, the contingent remainder disappears if it hasn't done so already (as it would if A dies without having children).

4. *Without RAP*: A has a life estate; B and C have vested remainders in life estate in an open class; B1, B2, C1 and C2 have vested remainders in life estate in an open class; A's great-grandchildren have a contingent remainder in fee simple absolute; T's estate has a reversion in fee simple absolute.

Common Law: The correct answer is: A has a life estate; B and C have vested remainders in life estate in an open class; T's estate has a reversion in fee simple absolute. B and C's vested remainders are fine because the class (A's children) will close at A's death. The grandchildren's vested remainder in an open class fails because A could have an afterborn child who could die more than 21 years after lives in being. See the discussion of Example 47 in the text for a detailed explanation of why a conveyance in a living person's grandchildren is problematic under the RAP. The contingent remainder in A's great-grandchildren is even more remote.

Wait and See: The correct answer is: A has a life estate; B and C have vested remainders in life estate in an open class; B1, B2, C1, and C2 have vested remainders in life estate in an open class that may become invalid on actual events, A's great-grandchildren have a contingent remainder in fee simple absolute that may become invalid on actual events, T's estate has a reversion in fee simple absolute.

5. *Common Law*: The correct answer is: T's estate owns Blackacre in fee simple. This follows from the result above.

Wait and See: The correct answer is: B1, B2, C1, and C2 [the grandchildren] have a life estate in Blackacre as tenants in common; B3, C3, and C4 [the great-grandchildren] have vested remainders in an open class in fee simple absolute. As things have turned out, there haven't been any afterborn children to screw up the grandchildren's interest, and there haven't been any afterborn grandchildren to screw up the great-grandchildren's interest. The grandchildren's vested remainder closed on the death of B and C (who couldn't have any more children). The great-grandchildren's vested remainder in an open class is fine because it will close at the deaths of the grandchildren, B1, B2, C1, and C2, who all were alive at the time of the conveyance.

A

A's children: B and C

A's grandchildren: B1, B2, C1, and C2

A's great-grandchildren: B2, C3, C4

6. *Without RAP*: T's widow has a life estate, T's issue have a contingent remainder in fee simple absolute, T's estate has a reversion absolute.

Common Law: All of the interests are valid, so the answer is the same as above. But what about the unborn widow problem? At T's death, we know who T's widow is. Put another way, T isn't going to be marrying anyone else. So the contingent remainder is fine; it will vest or fail on T's widow's death.

Wait and See: Same as above.

7. *Without RAP*: O owns Blackacre in fee simple absolute; A has an option to purchase Blackacre from O.

Common Law: The correct answer is: O owns Blackacre in fee simple absolute; the option is invalid. O and A could die tomorrow; A's estate could exercise its option more than 21 years after the death of these lives in being.

Wait and See: The correct answer is: O owns Blackacre in fee simple absolute; A has an option to purchase Blackacre that will either 30 years from the date of execution of the option or 21 years after the deaths of O and A, whichever is first.

8. *Without RAP*: A has a life estate; A1 and A2 have vested remainders in an open class in life estate; B1, B2, and B3 have vested remainders in fee simple absolute. The last interest is not in an open class because at the time of the conveyance B has already died.

Common Law: All of the interests are valid, so the answer is the same as above. The only interest subject to the RAP is the vested remainder in an open class, and that vests or fails on A's death.

Wait and See: Same as above.

9. *Without RAP*: O's children have a life estate in common, O's first grandchild has a contingent remainder in fee simple absolute, O has a reversion in fee simple absolute.

Common Law: The correct answer is: O's children have a life estate in common, O has a reversion in fee simple absolute. This one is fairly easy—O's first grandchild to reach 25 could be born after the conveyance and could outlive all lives in being.

Wait and See: The correct answer is: O's children have a life estate in common, O's first grandchild has a continent remainder in fee simple absolute that may become void on actual events, O has a reversion in fee simple absolute. If any of O's grandchildren reach 25 within 21 years of lives in being, the contingent remainder will become vested and will be valid.

10. *Without RAP*: O's children have a life estate in common, O's grandchildren have a contingent remainder in fee simple absolute, O has a reversion in fee simple absolute.

Common Law: The correct answer is: O's children have a life estate in common, O has a reversion in fee simple absolute. O could have an afterborn child, who in turn could have a child (O's grandchild) who reaches 21 more than 21 years after lives in being.

Wait and See: The correct answer is: O's children have a life estate in common, O's grandchildren have a contingent remainder in fee simple absolute that may become void on actual events, O has a reversion in fee simple absolute. If O's grandchildren reach 21 (or die before doing so) within 21 years of lives in being, the grandchildren's interest is good.

11. *Without RAP*: A and B have a life estate in common, T's grandchildren have a contingent remainder in life estate, T's issue have a contingent remainder in fee simple absolute, T's estate has a reversion in fee simple absolute.

Common Law: The correct answer is: A and B have a life estate in common, T's grandchildren have a contingent remainder in life estate, T's estate has a reversion in fee simple absolute. T's grandchildren's interest is fine—T's children provide the measuring lives, and because this is a testamentary gift, we know that there won't be any afterborn children. T's issue's contingent remainder is invalid because one of T's children could have an afterborn child [T's grandchild] who could die more than 21 years after lives in being, causing T's issue's contingent remainder to vest or fail outside of the perpetuities period.

Wait and See: The correct answer is: A and B have a life estate in common, T's grandchildren have a contingent remainder in life estate, T's issue have a contingent remainder in fee simple absolute that may become invalid on actual events, T's estate has a reversion in fee simple absolute.

12. *Without RAP*: T's estate owns the NWC estate in fee simple, T's issue have an executory interest in the proceeds of sale.

Common Law: The correct answer is: T's estate owns the NWC estate in fee simple. This is the slothful executor problem—it is possible that the estate won't be sold for more than 21 years after the death of T and other lives in being.

Wait and See: The correct answer is: T's estate owns the NWC estate in fee simple absolute, T's issue have an executory interest in the proceeds of sale that may become invalid on actual events. Presuming that the executor of T's estate is vaguely competent, T's issue's interest will be fine. Something to think about: what does "my surviving issue" mean? Surviving at T's death or surviving when the estate is finally sold? We would argue that the Testator's intent was probably surviving at T's death because T probably imagined that the sale would happen quickly. When you are drafting, you should try to avoid this kind of ambiguity.

13. *Without RAP*: A has a life estate, B has a vested remainder in an open class in fee simple absolute, C has a vested remainder in an open class and subject to divestment in fee simple absolute, B has an executory interest in fee simple absolute.

Common Law: The correct answer is: A has a life estate, B and C have vested remainders in an open class in fee simple absolute. The vested remainders in an open class are fine because the class will become closed on A's death. The executory interest fails because A could have an afterborn child who graduates from college (or fails to do so by age 30) more than 21 years after lives in being.

Wait and See: The correct answer is: A has a life estate, B has a vested remainder in an open class in fee simple absolute, C has a vested remainder in an open class and subject to divestment in fee simple absolute, B has an executory interest in fee simple absolute that may become invalid on actual events.

14. *Without RAP*: A and B have a life estate in common. C has a contingent remainder in fee simple absolute. T's estate has a reversion in fee simple absolute.

Common Law: The correct answer is: A and B have a life estate in common. T's estate has a reversion in fee simple absolute. The contingent remainder is void. A could have an afterborn child, D, who would be one of T's grandchildren. If A, B, and C die the next year, then D would reach the age of 25 (or not), more than 21 years after lives in being.

Wait and See: The correct answer is: A and B have a life estate in common; C has a contingent remainder in fee simple absolute that may become invalid on actual events; T's estate has a reversion in fee simple absolute. So long as all of the grandchildren reach the age of 25 within the perpetuities period, the interest in the grandchildren will be valid.

15. *Without RAP*: A has a life estate, A's children have a contingent remainder in life estate, A's issue have a contingent remainder in fee simple absolute, O has a reversion in fee simple absolute.

Common Law: All of the interests are valid, so same as above. The contingent remainder in A's children is fine because it vests at A's death. The contingent remainder in A's issue is fine because it will vest (i.e., the class will close) on the death of the last Kennedy issue alive at the time of the conveyance. This is a fairly common way around the RAP—the Kennedy issue qualify as lives in being because by the terms of the conveyance they both (a) were alive when the conveyance was made and (b) affect the vesting.

Wait and See: Same as above.

16. *Without RAP*: A has a fee simple subject to executory limitation; B's children have an executory interest in fee simple absolute.

Common Law: All of the interests are valid, so same as above. The executory interest will vest or fail in a closed class of people on A's death.

Wait and See: Same as above.

17. *Without RAP*: Maura has a life estate, Max has a contingent remainder in life estate, their children have a contingent remainder in fee simple absolute, T's estate has a reversion in fee simple absolute.

Common Law: All of the interests are valid, so same as above. Max's contingent remainder will vest or fail on Maura's death. The unborn widow(er) problem is avoided by naming a specific person, Max, so the children's contingent remainder is fine—it will vest or fail in a closed class on either Max's or Maura's death. (It would work even if the "then living" was omitted because the class of their children would be closed on their death.)

Wait and See: Same as above.

18. *Without RAP*: A has a fee simple subject to executory limitation, A's grandchild has an executory interest in fee simple absolute.

Common Law: The correct answer is: A has a fee simple determinable, O has a possibility of reverter in fee simple absolute. The executory interest in the grandchild fails because O could have an afterborn child, who could then have a child who turns out to be the first grandchild to reach 21 more than 21 years after lives in being. Note that the possibility of reverter would expire, and A would have Blackacre in fee simple absolute, if it turns out that none of O's grandchildren reach the age of 21.

Wait and See: The correct answer is: A has a fee simple subject to executory limitation, A's grandchild has an executory interest that will be valid only if the first grandchild reaches 21 within 21 years of lives in being.

19. *Without RAP*: David has a life estate, Katie and Laura have vested remainders in an open class in life estate, David's grandchildren have contingent remainders in fee simple absolute, T's estate has a reversion in fee simple absolute.

Common Law: The correct answer is: David has a life estate, Katie and Laura have vested remainders in an open class in life estate, T's estate has a reversion in fee simple absolute. The grandchildren's interest fails because David could have another child, who in turn could have a child more than 21 years after lives in being.

Wait and See: The correct answer is: David has a life estate, Katie and Laura have vested remainders in an open class in life estate, the grandchildren have contingent remainders in absolute ownership that will be valid if the class closes within 21 years of lives in being, T's estate has a reversion.

20. *Without RAP*: Essentially the same answer as 19, but the classifications have changed. Katie and Laura have life estates, their children have contingent remainders in fee simple absolute and T's estate has a reversion in fee simple absolute.

Common Law: Essentially the same answer as 19, but the classifications have changed. Katie and Laura have life estates, and T's estate has a reversion in fee simple absolute.

Wait and See: Katie and Laura have life estates; the grandchildren have contingent remainders in fee simple absolute that are valid under the RAP, T's estate has a reversion in fee simple absolute. The grandchildren's contingent remainder will now never be invalidated under the RAP because it will vest in a complete class or fail on the deaths of Katie and Laura, both of whom were lives in being.

CHAPTER 3

PARTITION PROBLEM

As illustrated in *Ark Land*, the law has a strong presumption in favor of partition in kind. In many contexts, dividing a 12-acre parcel in kind among three tenants in common would be straightforward—each of the three co-tenants would get a four-acre parcel. The local zoning law, however, presents a problem here because it imposes a five-acre minimum lot size. Under these circumstances, dividing the property into three four-acre parcels would greatly diminish the value of the property because none of the lots would be buildable under the zoning law. John therefore would have a strong argument that partition in kind would be severely economically harmful—the value of the unbuildable four-acre lots together would be *much* less than the value of the whole 12-acre parcel. On the other hand, *Ark Land* held that negative economic impact is not dispositive, especially when there is a long-standing emotional attachment to the property. The court would almost certainly order a partition in kind if Zach and Cathy agreed to take a seven-acre parcel together and give John a five-acre parcel. This would preserve the value of the parcels and would avoid the economic hardship problem caused by the minimum lot size requirement imposed by the zoning law. If Zach and Cathy insisted on dividing the 12 acres into three equal four-acre plots, the court would be forced to decide whether the negative economic consequences would outweigh Zach and Cathy's emotional attachment to the property and the presumption in favor of partition in kind. Note in this context that John is a family member. Unlike Ark Land, he did not buy into the property taking a risk about the outcome in the partition process. Also note that Ark Land was still able to mine coal with the land partitioned in kind, albeit more expensively than if the land was partitioned by sale. *Ark Land* held that economic impact was not dispositive, but it did not hold that it is irrelevant. We set the problem up so that it is a close case, and we could see a court going either way.

The best result here would probably be for Zach and Cathy to buy out John. A buyout would give both parties what they want. Zach and Cathy would keep the property, and John would get the money he needs to start his business. Parties sometimes have a hard time negotiating for the best result, though, especially when they are members of the same family. The buyout procedure set up by the Uniform Partition of Heirs Property Act would help by establishing the fair market value of the property and providing a procedure for the parties opposing partition by sale (here, Zach and Cathy) to buy out the party proposing partition by sale (here, John).

ACCOUNTING FOR COSTS AND RENT PROBLEM

In the accounting proceeding, Angela will be entitled to contribution from Maya for half of the costs of the mortgage and the upkeep. Angela paid $15,000 per year for two years, for a total of $30,000. Maya's share of these costs is $15,000.

Angela occupied the warehouse for one year. Generally speaking, absent ouster, a co-tenant in possession (here, Angela) is not liable to the other co-tenant (here, Maya) for the rental value of the property. In *Esteves*, however, the court noted that if the co-tenant in possession is seeking contribution for operating and maintenance costs, the tenant out of possession should be able to set off her proportional share of the fair rental value against the costs. Here, Angela is seeking contribution for costs, so Maya should be able to claim the fair rental value against Angela for the year Angela was in sole possession. The fair rental value for that year was $12,000. Maya's proportional share of the fair rental value is $6,000. So far, Maya owes Angela $9,000 (the $15,000 in costs, less the $6,000 in fair rental value).

Angela also needs to account to Maya for Maya's share of the rent actually collected from Sidney. Sidney paid $6,000 for the year ($500 per month for one year). Maya's share is $3,000. At the end of the day, Maya owes Angela $6,000 (the $9,000 owed in the last step, less Maya's $3,000 share of the rent collected from Sidney).

If there had been an ouster, Maya's entitlement to her share of fair rental value from Angela for the year that Angela was in sole possession would be even clearer. It does not matter a great deal in this particular context because Maya already has a good claim to the rental value as a set off against the mortgage and upkeep costs paid by Angela. In a different context, Maya's entitlement for her share of fair rental value could be very important.

Also, with an ouster, Maya would be entitled to half of the fair rental value for the year that Sidney rented the property rather than just half of the rent that Angela actually collected from Sidney. The fair rental value for that year was $12,000. Maya would be entitled to half of that, or $6,000. Recall that Maya owed Angela $9,000 before we accounted for the rent from Sidney. If there had been an ouster, we would credit Maya with $6,000 (half of the fair rental value) rather than $3,000 (half of the rent actually collected). So if there had been an ouster, Maya would owe Angela $3,000 ($9,000 less the $6,000 share of the fair rental value).

JOINT TENANCY PROBLEM

At the beginning of the fact pattern, Cathy, John, and Louise are joint tenants:

In 1985, Louise sold her share to Ralph. This severed the joint tenancy relationship for Louise's share. Cathy and John remain joint tenants, and they are tenants in common with Ralph:

Cathy then mortgages her share to Bill. This leaves us with two possibilities. In a jurisdiction where the unilateral mortgage by one joint tenant severs the joint tenancy,

Cathy, John and Ralph are all tenants in common. In a jurisdiction where the mortgage does not sever, Cathy and John are still joint tenants with each other and tenants in common with Ralph. At this point, Bill has a valid mortgage on Cathy's interest in both scenarios:

Cathy now dies, leaving all of her property to Jeremy. In a jurisdiction where the mortgage severs the joint tenancy, Jeremy inherits Cathy's share, and Bill's mortgage survives. Jeremy, John, and Ralph are tenants in common, each with a 1/3 share. Jeremy's share is subject to Bill's mortgage. In a jurisdiction where the mortgage did not sever the joint tenancy, Cathy's interest disappears, leaving John as the sole owner of the 2/3 that they owned as joint tenants. When Cathy's interest disappears, Bill's mortgage disappears. John and Ralph are tenants in common, with John having a 2/3 share and Ralph having a 1/3 share:

The outcomes between the parties therefore depend on the jurisdiction's approach to whether a mortgage severs a joint tenancy. If yes, then Bill's mortgage survives, and Jeremy, John, and Ralph are tenants in common with 1/3 shares. If no, then Bill's mortgage does not survive, and John (2/3 share) and Ralph (1/3 share) are tenants in common.

TENANCY BY THE ENTIRETY PROBLEM

The answer depends on the jurisdiction's approach to whether the creditor of one spouse can reach the property held by the entirety to satisfy the debt. In a Group II jurisdiction, Perry will be successful in attaching Julia's share. Perry will have equal rights to possess and use the property with Larry. Perry will also step into Julia's shoes for the right of survivorship. If Julia dies first, Larry will own the property under the right of survivorship free and clear of Perry's interest. If Larry dies first, Perry will own the property outright. In a Group III jurisdiction, Perry would not be successful because Group III does not allow the creditor of one spouse to attach the property held by the entirety. Perry's mortgage on Julia's share would be ineffective. Julia and Larry would own the property as tenants by the entirety, and the property held by the entirety would be immune from claims by Perry based on the debt Julia owes to him. (Note that this result arguably is fairer here than in *Sawada* because Perry was a contract creditor who voluntarily entered into the transaction with Julia and who could have taken steps to protect himself from this risk in advance.) In a Group IV jurisdiction, Perry will not be able to get access to the property while Julia and Larry were still alive, but Perry will be able to get Julia's right of survivorship. As in Group II, if Julia dies first, Larry will own the property under the right of survivorship free and clear of Perry's interest. If Larry dies first, Perry will own the property outright.

SEPARATE PROPERTY PROBLEMS

1. No. New Jersey does not recognize a professional degree as marital property subject to equitable distribution. A New Jersey court, however, will consider compensating James with reimbursement alimony, if he can show that he "has suffered a loss or reduction of support, or has incurred a lower standard of living, or has been deprived of a better standard of living in the future." *Mahoney*, 452 A.2d at 534.

2. Yes. New York recognizes a professional degree as marital property. The court in *O'Brien* disagreed with the majority of jurisdictions that reimbursement in the form of alimony equitably reimburses the supporting spouse. *O'Brien*, 489 N.E.2d at 718.

COMMUNITY PROPERTY PROBLEMS

1. James and Jillian would both own the $100,000 because the earnings are community property.

2. James and Jillian would both own the lake house because it is community property. They would each hold an equal, undivided share in the lake house, but neither one could transfer their share to a third party, and neither Jillian nor James would have a right of survivorship.

3. Jillian would own the $50,000 as her separate property because it came to her as an inheritance. It would not belong to James.

4. No. Separately owned property cannot be used in Arizona to satisfy the debt. In California, the bank account could be used to satisfy James's gambling debt because the bank account would be considered community property.

COMMUNITY PROPERTY—WHEN ONE SPOUSE DIES PROBLEM

James can leave his half of the community property to his favorite charity or anyone he chooses because he owns one-half of the community property, and Jillian does not have an automatic right to his half upon her death.

MIGRATING COUPLES PROBLEM

The court would consider the definitions of community property, separate property, and quasi-community property and determine the domicile of James at the time of death and the domicile of James at the time of acquisition of each piece of personal and real property. For example, all personal and real property situated in California and purchased while residing in California would be considered community property. James's personal property acquired in New Jersey would be classified as quasi-community property if it would have been community property when James had been domiciled in California at the time he acquired the personal property.

CHAPTER 4

TYPES OF LEASEHOLD INTERESTS PROBLEMS

1. (a) This is a term of years leasehold. Its duration is for a fixed period of time. (b) The student would be liable for rent because the term of years has not yet expired. Notice has nothing to do with it—if you are a tenant in a term of years lease, you are liable for rent for the entire period. Put another way, neither the landlord nor the tenant can unilaterally terminate a term of years tenancy before its expiration date. (c) No, the student would not be liable for rent because the term of years had expired by its terms.

2. (a) This is a year-to-year periodic tenancy. (b) The student would be liable for rent. If the student gave no notice, then the student would be liable for rent for successive year-long periods until proper notice was given. If the student gave one month's notice, the periodic tenancy would not be terminated for the following year because six months' notice is required to terminate a year-to-year periodic tenancy. Recall that there are two approaches on how to treat untimely notice of termination. Under the first (and better) approach, the notice would be effective to terminate the tenancy at the end of the next period. Under the second approach, the notice would be treated as a nullity, and the periodic tenancy would continue to renew until the student provided good notice. (c) Yes, the student would be liable for rent if the student moved out on August 14 without providing notice. The periodic tenancy will continue to renew until notice is given.

3. (a) This is a tenancy at will. It is not a term of years because we can't translate "for as long as you are a law student" to a definite period of time or fixed calendar dates. Maybe the student will drop out of law school tomorrow. Maybe the student will take six years to graduate. (b) The student would not be liable for rent, regardless of notice. A tenancy at will may be terminated at any time. The problems presume there are no applicable statutes, so there is no statutory minimum notice period. (c) No. Again, because this is a tenancy at will, it can be ended at any time.

4. (a) The family have the right to stay in the home for the full year. (b) The professor can terminate the month-to-month periodic tenancy by giving a month's notice and can move back in after it terminates. (c) The professor can immediately terminate the

lease and move back in immediately. Of course, there will be some practical difficulties in giving the family time to physically move out. Presuming no applicable statute, the tenancy at will is terminable by either party at any time without notice.

5. This is a periodic tenancy. In some jurisdictions, it would create a year-to-year periodic tenancy. In others, it would create a month-to-month periodic tenancy.

6. This is a term of years tenancy. The duration is for one year, beginning August 1. The language establishing monthly payments simply established the frequency of payments.

DELIVERY OF POSSESSION PROBLEMS

The answer will depend on whether our jurisdiction uses the American rule or the English rule. Under the American rule, Fiona will prevail because she delivered the right of possession to Martha and has no obligation to deliver actual possession. Put another way, getting Edith out of the apartment is Martha's problem under the American rule. Under the English rule, Martha will prevail because Fiona has the obligation to deliver actual possession. Put another way, getting Edith out of the apartment is Fiona's problem under the English rule. *Reminder*—don't be confused by the labels of the rules. Both the American and English rules are rules used in the U.S. courts. The English rule is the better rule and is the majority rule in the United States.

FHA PROBLEMS

1. a. The advertisement violates 3604(c) of the FHA which prohibits advertisements that state a discriminatory preference. Even though the owner is living in the home and the unit has four or fewer families living in it, the Mrs. Murphy exception (§3603(b)(2)) does not extend to advertisements.

b. This conduct does not violate the FHA. The conduct, standing alone, would come within the prohibition of §3604(a). The landlord, however, is protected by the Mrs. Murphy exception (§3603(b)(2)) because (a) the landlord lives there and (b) there are four or fewer units in the building. Arguing that this is racial discrimination that falls within the CRA would be a stretch, even if you could find an 1866 reference to someone talking about "the Muslim race," because the context suggests that this is discrimination based on religion.

c. This conduct does not violate the FHA. As with the previous problem, the Mrs. Murphy exception would protect the landlord. The landlord's conduct, however, does violate the CRA because the landlord was discriminating based on race. The CRA does not have an equivalent to the Mrs. Murphy exception.

d. This conduct does not violate the FHA. Marital status is not one of the protected categories in the FHA. Family status in the FHA means the presence or absence of minor children, not marital status. §3602(k)

e. This conduct would violate §3604(a) of the FHA, which prohibits discrimination based on family status. Note that it is the presence of children, not the fact that the mother is unmarried, that makes this scenario fall within the purview of the FHA. §3602(k).

f. This conduct probably does not violate the FHA. Asking for a larger security deposit falls within the prohibition in §3604(b) against discriminating in the terms and conditions of a rental, and the focus on kids brings this within the scope of "family circumstances" as defined by the FHA. §3602(k). Here, however, the landlord likely can show a reasonable non-discriminatory reason for asking for a higher security deposit. Kids really do tend to cause a good amount of wear and tear, and it is not unreasonable in this context to ask for a higher security deposit.

g. This conduct probably does not violate the FHA. Lawyers and law students are not a protected class under the FHA. The law student might be able to make a prima facie case of discrimination but will only be able to win at the end of the day if he can show that the landlord's stated desire to not rent to law students is a pretext for racial discrimination.

h. This conduct likely violates the FHA. It sure looks like the landlord is acting out of racial animus. Unless the landlord can show some other explanation for the statement (e.g., the parents in the family are lawyers, and the landlord has had trouble renting to lawyers before), then the landlord's conduct likely is impermissible racial discrimination. Asking for a higher security deposit violates §3604(b) because it constitutes discrimination in the terms and conditions of the rental of a dwelling.

i. This conduct probably violates the FHA because the landlord is not making a reasonable accommodation for a person with a handicap. §3604(f)(3)(B). The landlord would only be able to prevail by showing that there was there was no reasonable way to accommodate the type of pet in the rental or that the dog presented a real risk to the safety or property of other residents.

2. Mary's ad violates the FHA. As an initial matter, the Mrs. Murphy exception (§3603(b)(2)) does not apply. Mary lives in the home, and she might have been protected by the Mrs. Murphy exception if she had discriminated in the actual rental of the apartment. Her ad, however, falls within §3604(c), and §3604(c) is an exception to the Mrs. Murphy exception. The ad itself violates §3604(c) for at least two reasons. First, the preference for "white" renters violates the prohibition on discrimination based on race. Second, the statement "no kids" violates the prohibition on discrimination based on family circumstances. Mary might be able to come up with a reasonable, non-discriminatory explanation for the prohibition on kids. The statement "no pets" would only violate the FHA only if she refused to make a reasonable accommodation to a person with a handicap. The preference for a "married . . . couple" does not violate the FHA because marital status is not protected by the FHA.

IMPLIED WARRANTY OF HABITABILITY AND COVENANT OF QUIET ENJOYMENT PROBLEM

Nancy has a good claim against Kurt for a violation of the implied warranty of habitability (IWH). The IWH is violated by conditions that threaten the tenant's health or safety. Here, the odors made Nancy ill. Municipal code violations also are relevant to an IWH claim. Here, an inspection revealed a building code violation in the ventilation system. Nancy gave Kurt the required opportunity to fix the problem. Kurt is still liable for the breach even though he tried to fix the problem. The IWH permits Nancy to stay in the apartment while withholding rent. Nancy may also have a claim against Kurt for a breach of the covenant of quiet enjoyment (CQE) because the smell arguably interferes with her use of the property. Nancy hasn't moved out, so she can't claim constructive eviction and stop paying rent under the CQE (though, as noted above, she can withhold rent under the IWH). If she can establish a violation of the CQE, Nancy can still sue for damages for breach of the CQE—moving out and claiming constructive eviction is only essential if she wants to withhold rent.

LANDLORD/TENANT PRIVITY PROBLEMS

1. L is in privity of contract and privity of estate with T. T's transfer to T_1 is a sublease (it is for less than the entire term). T is in privity of contract and privity of estate with T_1.

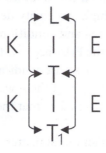

2. L can sue T under privity of contract (from the original lease) and T_1 under privity of estate (because of the assignment from T to T_1). The privity relationships at the time of the breach are: L is in privity of K with T and privity of estate with T_1; T is in privity of K with T_1; T_1 is in privity of contract and privity of estate with T_2.

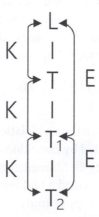

3. L can sue T under privity of contract and privity of estate. The privity relationships at the time of the breach are: L is in privity of contract and privity of estate with T; T is in privity of contract with T_1 and privity of estate with T_2; T_1 is in privity of contract with T_2.

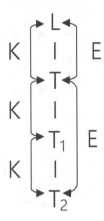

4. L can sue T and T_3 under privity of contract and T_2 under privity of estate. The privity relationships at the time of the breach are: L is in privity of contract with T and T_3 and privity of estate with T_2; T is in privity of contract with T_1; T_1 is in privity of contract with T_2; T_2 is in privity of contract and privity of estate with T_3.

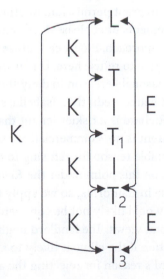

5. L can sue T under privity of contract and privity of estate and T_1 under privity of contract. The privity relationships at the time of the breach are: L is in privity of contract and privity of estate with T and privity of contract with T_1; T is in privity of contract with T_1 and privity of estate with T_2; T_1 is in privity of contract with T_2.

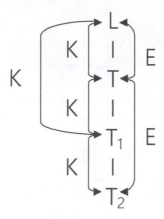

RESTRICTING THE TENANT'S RIGHT TO TRANSFER PROBLEMS

1. Stuart, the landlord, is likely to be able to refuse permission in a jurisdiction that follows the traditional approach but is likely to not be able to refuse permission in a jurisdiction that follows the *Kendall* approach. In a traditional jurisdiction, the landlord may arbitrarily refuse to grant permission. In other words, under the traditional approach, the clause "No assignments or subleases without landlord's permission" is enforced as written. Under this approach, Stuart can refuse permission without giving a good reason, so he should be able to refuse here. Under the *Kendall* approach, Stuart needs to give a commercially reasonable reason to deny the assignment. Richard has a good business track record and better credit than Isabella, so on these facts Stuart isn't going to be able to assert that Richard is a riskier tenant than Isabella. *Kendall* also held that demanding an increase in rent is not commercially reasonable. Stuart therefore does not have a commercially reasonable reason for refusing to consent to the assignment and would lose against Isabella on this point under the *Kendall* approach.

2. These problems take place in California, so we apply the rules from *Kendall*.

a. The landlord's objection would likely not be commercially reasonable because it is based on the landlord's moral views. The landlord might be able to construct a commercially reasonable objection if the clinic is likely to attract protestors. On the facts given, though, the landlord's reason for rejecting the assignment is moral, not commercial.

b. The landlord's reason would likely be commercially reasonable. As much as we hate to say it because we are bibliophiles, bookstores have been closing all over the country. Under the circumstances, the landlord probably is commercially reasonable in refusing to assign to a bookstore.

c. L's objection would likely be reasonable because of the conflict between tenants. A landlord has good commercial reasons to want tenants to succeed in business and in avoiding competition between tenants.

DUTY TO MITIGATE PROBLEMS

1. Whether or not Cylie is liable to Gordon for the rent will depend on the jurisdiction. In a jurisdiction that follows the *Sommer* rule and imposes a duty to mitigate, Cylie would not owe rent to Gordon. Gordon failed to do anything to re-rent the apartment and turned away a potential tenant for the apartment. Gordon therefore did not meet his duty to mitigate damages. In a jurisdiction that does not impose a duty to mitigate, Cylie would owe the back rent to Gordon.

2. Mary will owe rent to Steve in all jurisdictions. Steve made a good faith effort to mitigate damages by advertising the apartment and by showing the apartment to prospective tenants. To satisfy the duty to mitigate, the landlord only has to make a good faith effort to try to mitigate. The landlord does not have to be successful. Because Steve satisfied his obligation to try to mitigate, Mary will owe him rent even in a jurisdiction that follows *Sommer*. Of course, Mary will also owe him rent in a jurisdiction that does not impose a duty to mitigate.

HOLDOVERS AND TENANCY AT SUFFERANCE PROBLEMS

As a landlord facing a holdover tenant, Linda has two options. First, she could treat Margo like a trespasser and bring an action to evict her from the premises. Second, she could hold Margo over to a new term. The key lesson from *Creshale* is that Margo needs to make a choice and go one way or the other. If, for example, she accepts monthly rent checks from Margo, she may be held to have entered a month-to-month periodic tenancy from Margo. If Linda wants to have Margo as a tenant for another year, she should elect to hold Margo over to another year term. If not, she should bring an action to evict Margo.

SELF-HELP EVICTION PROBLEMS

Courts in most jurisdictions would hold that Keith wrongfully evicted Trisha. The majority rule is that the landlord cannot resort to self-help and must use legal process to evict the tenant. Even in a jurisdiction that allowed self-help, there may be a problem of whether Keith's lock out of Tricia was peaceable. In a state that allows self-help, it probably would be deemed peaceable, but it is worth considering the *Berg* court's skeptical view of whether a lockout could ever be peaceable in this context. If this lockout is not peaceable, then it is hard to see how a landlord could ever peaceably use self-help to evict a tenant.

CHAPTER 5

BASIC RECORDING PROBLEMS

1. Here is the timeline for problem 1:

2000: O conveys to A. A does not record.

2001: O conveys to B. B has no notice of A's deed.

B records.

2002: A records.

a. Under a race statute, B would win because B recorded first.

b. Under a notice statute, B would win because B has no notice of A's deed.

c. Under a race-notice statute, B would win because B both recorded first and had no notice of A's deed.

2. Here is the timeline for problem 2:

2000: O conveys to A. A does not record.

2001: O conveys to B. B has notice of A's deed.

B records.

2002: A records.

a. Under a race statute, B would win because B recorded first.

b. Under a notice statute, A would win because B had notice of A's deed.

c. Under a race-notice statute, A would win because B had notice of A's deed. Remember that under a race-notice statute, the subsequent purchaser must both record first and have no notice.

3. Here is the timeline for problem 3:

2000: O conveys to A. A does not record.

Jan. 2001: O conveys to B. B has no notice of A's deed.

Feb. 2001: A records.

Mar. 2001: B records

a. Under a race statute, A would win because A recorded first.

b. Under a notice statute, B would win because B had no notice of A's deed.

c. Under a race-notice statute, A would win because A recorded first. Again, Remember that under a race-notice statute, the subsequent purchaser must both record first and have no notice.

4. Here is the timeline for problem 4, which starts the same way as problem 1:

2000: O conveys to A. A does not record.

2001: O conveys to B. B has no notice of A's deed.

B records.

2002: A records.

2003: B conveys to C. C has notice of A's deed.

C records.

a. Because B would win against A in a race jurisdiction for the reasons stated in problem 1 and because B conveyed to C, C would win under the Shelter Rule.

b. Because B would win against A in a notice jurisdiction for the reasons stated in problem 1 and because B conveyed to C, C would win under the Shelter Rule.

c. Because B would win against A in a race-notice jurisdiction for the reasons stated in problem 1 and because B conveyed to C, C would win under the Shelter Rule.

ADVANCED RECORDING PROBLEMS

1. This problem raises the two classic inquiry notice fact patterns that we discussed in *Harper* and *Clare House*, though there are some twists in the facts of the problem. We placed the property in a race-notice jurisdiction so that notice would matter to the outcome. We could have achieved the same result by using a notice jurisdiction. In a race jurisdiction, however, Yvette would win on both issues because she recorded first and because notice is not relevant in pure race jurisdictions.

Yvette is facing two issues. The first involves Rosie's claim to own the property. This fact pattern closely resembles that in *Harper*. The recorded 1970 deed references the unrecorded 1930 deed. It turns out that the 1930 deed only conveyed a life estate. Based on these facts alone, Yvette was probably on inquiry notice of the 1930 deed. Yvette, however, inquired of Tom about the 1930 deed. Remember, inquiry notice will be defeated if a person makes a reasonable inquiry. We can't know for sure whether Yvette's inquiry would be deemed reasonably diligent by a court. On the one hand, all she did is ask the grantor about the deed. On the other hand, as a practical matter, what more was she supposed to do? The fact that the property had been in Tom's family for generations may make it more reasonable for Yvette to rely on his representation. We think that Yvette would have a good argument that she made a reasonable inquiry under the circumstances. Again, however, we can't be sure she would win.

The second issue involves Gail's use of the unrecorded driveway easement. There is a good argument that Yvette was on inquiry notice of the easement. Although it was unpaved, a driveway across the property would put a potential buyer on notice that someone might be using the driveway pursuant to an unrecorded interest. Following the logic of *Clare House*, Yvette should at least have inquired about the driveway.

2. This problem is an example of the common grantor problem. We have a group of properties subdivided by a common grantor. All of the lots are governed by a set of recorded covenants. Because of a clerical error, the covenants are not recorded for one lot. As we noted in the text, U.S. jurisdictions are split on what to do about this problem. About half of jurisdictions will hold that the covenants are enforceable for the lot despite

the lack of recording. In these jurisdictions, Brian will not be able to build a gas station. About half of jurisdictions will hold that the covenants are not enforceable for the lot. In these jurisdictions, Brian will be able to build the gas station (at least as a matter of recording and the covenants—local zoning ordinances, which we will study in a later chapter, will likely have something to say on this subject as well). The fact that 30 of the 42 lots already had single-family lots on them might weigh toward the covenant being enforced—if you buy a vacant lot in a neighborhood where all of the existing structures are single-family homes, you might be on inquiry notice that some sort of restriction exists.

3. This is a wild deed problem. Here are the Blackacre conveyances in chronological order:

> 2000: Owen grants to Nate, Nate records deed.
>
> 2004: Nate grants to Talia, Talia does not record deed.
>
> 2009: Talia grants to Camille. Camille records deed.
>
> 2013: Nate grants to Rick. Rick records deed. Rick has no actual notice of prior interests.

The Talia-Camille deed is a wild deed. This deed was recorded, but it is outside of the chain of title because the Nate-Talia deed was not recorded. As a result, Rick would not have been able to find the Talia-Camille deed even though he did a thorough title search. Rick therefore should win the quiet title action.

MARKETABLE TITLE PROBLEM

a. The facts state that the contract disclosed the existence of the covenants and that the buyer waived any objection to them. The mere existence of the covenants therefore does not render title unmarketable. There is no current violation of the covenants. Linda therefore will not be able to refuse to close on marketable title grounds. Linda's plan to build an addition that would violate the covenants in the *future* also does not make title unmarketable *now*. The seller's obligation is to deliver title that it marketable at the time of closing. (If Maurice had represented to Linda that she could build her addition under the covenants, then there might have been a misrepresentation issue. There is nothing in these facts, however, about such a representation. If there had been facts about misrepresentation, those facts still would not be relevant to the marketability of title issue. On these facts, title will be marketable at the time of closing.)

b. Mere existence of a covenant renders title unmarketable. When the facts are changed so that there was no disclosure and waiver of the existence of the covenant, title is unmarketable, and Linda can refuse to close.

c. When the facts are changed so that the house is only 12 feet from a boundary, the covenant is violated. This violation of the covenant would make title unmarketable. There is nothing in the facts to suggest that Linda waived this violation. Linda therefore can refuse to close on marketable title grounds.

d. The mere existence of zoning or other land use regulations does not make title unmarketable. The existence of the zoning regulations therefore does not present marketability problems whether or not they are addressed in the contract. Linda therefore cannot refuse to close on marketable title grounds.

e. Although the mere existence of zoning regulations does not make title unmarketable, a violation of such a regulation does make title unmarketable. When the facts are changed so that the zoning regulation is violated, then title is unmarketable, and Linda can refuse to close on marketable title grounds.

GENERAL WARRANTY DEED PROBLEM

Before we get to the substance of the issues raised by this exercise, we want to make a few exam-taking points. The questions on your final may or may not resemble this exercise, but the exercise raises some exam-taking issues that are applicable to a wide-range of questions. First, we changed the statute of limitations from 10 years in the examples to 15 years in the exercise. Read questions carefully! Second, the *call of the question* asks you whether Dorothy can sue Beatrice. Dorothy's ability (or lack thereof) to sue Angela or Cathy is not directly relevant to the answer. If this was an exam question, you might want to address Angela or Cathy in a sentence or two, but you should not spend a lot of time on them because the call is limited to Beatrice. Third, exam answers should address both majority and minority rules unless the question or your professor clearly tell you otherwise. *Many law students lose points on exams every year by just discussing the majority rule.* Fourth, you should briefly outline or chart out your answer before you write. Opinions differ on how long you should spend outlining an answer. This exercise illustrates the need to do at least some thinking before you get into the answer. There are a lot of things going on in the exercise, and if you don't do some outlining, you are likely to miss one or more of the components to the answer.

The question asks whether Dorothy can sue Beatrice. The answer will depend on (a) whether the deed covenants were violated, (b) whether the statute of limitations has run on any claims against Dorothy, and (c) whether the deed covenants run with the land (or whether claims under them are implicitly assigned) to Dorothy. Because present and future covenants operate differently in some important respects, it is useful to answer these three questions separately for each type of covenant.

Present Covenants

a. Were the present covenants violated? Yes—all three of them were. The covenants of seisin and of right to covey were violated because Beatrice did not own two of the ten acres she sold to Cathy. The covenant against encumbrances was violated because of the mortgage.

b. Did the statute of limitations run on the present covenants? No. The present covenants are breached, if at all, at the time the deed is transferred from the buyer to the seller. For Beatrice's deed, this happened in 1996. The 15-year statute of limitations had not run out when Dorothy brought her action in 2009.

c. Were the claims under the present covenants implicitly assigned to Dorothy? Maybe. Under the majority rule, claims under the present covenants are not implicitly assigned. Under the minority rule, the claims on the present covenants held by the prior owner (here, Cathy), are implicitly assigned to the subsequent owner (here, Dorothy).

Dorothy should win against Beatrice for breach of all three of the present covenants in a jurisdiction that follows the minority rule on present covenants running with the land but will lose against Beatrice for the present covenants in a majority rule jurisdiction.

Future Covenants

a. Were the future covenants violated? Yes. The covenant of general warranty and the covenant of quiet enjoyment were violated when Eleanor sued Dorothy and asserted superior title to the two acres. The facts state that Dorothy would lose against Eleanor on an adverse possession claim to make it clear that Eleanor's claim is lawful. Note that these two covenants similarly would have been violated if the holder of the mortgage brought an action or otherwise asserted a claim regarding the property. But the holder of the mortgage hasn't done anything yet. So, if the claim for breach of the present covenant against encumbrances is not implicitly assigned to Dorothy (majority view, above), Dorothy can't assert any claim right now against Beatrice for the mortgage.

b. Did the statute of limitations run on the future covenants? No. The future covenants are not breached until someone asserts superior title and the grantor refuses to fix the problem. The clock did not start running until Eleanor showed up and claimed the two acres. As a practical matter, it would be a rare case where the statute of limitations is an issue for the future covenants.

c. Do the future covenants run with the land? Yes, in all jurisdictions.

Dorothy will win against Beatrice for breach of the covenants of general warranty and quiet enjoyment in all jurisdictions for Eleanor's lawful claim to the two acres. Dorothy cannot raise a claim against Beatrice under the future covenants for the mortgage problem because the holder of the mortgage has not yet foreclosed on the property.

STATUTE OF FRAUDS PROBLEM

The initial issue in this problem is whether the check constitutes a memorandum that will satisfy the Statute of Frauds. There are three elements that a putative memorandum must meet in the real estate context. First, it must be signed by the party to be bound. The party to be bound is the party trying to back out of the deal. Here, Linda is trying to back out and is the party to be bound. Linda did not sign the check (a person endorses a check by signing it; the facts say that Linda had not endorsed the check). Therefore, the check is not signed by the party to be bound. (We could stop here, but it is important to get into the habit of completing the legal analysis of a fact pattern—stopping too soon can cause you to lose points on an exam.) Second, it must describe the real estate. Here, the memo line of the check listed the street address of the property. The street address is probably enough to uniquely identify the property to be conveyed, probably satisfying this element. A court taking a strict approach to the Statute of Frauds, however, might insist on a full legal description, which is not met here. Third, it must state the price. This element is met here because the check stated that the purchase price was $250,000. Although the second and third elements are probably met, the check does not constitute a memorandum that would satisfy the Statute of Frauds because it is not signed by the party to be bound.

In the initial version of the facts, there is nothing to suggest that one of the exceptions to the Statute of Frauds might apply. This changes if Celia had entered into a binding contract to sell her condominium in reliance on Linda's promise to sell the house to her. As modified, these facts resemble *Hickey v. Green*. The estoppel exception to the Statute of Frauds applies where a purchaser or seller of real estate reasonably and detrimentally relied on an oral promise by the other party. By entering into a binding contract to sell her condominium, Celia detrimentally relied on Linda's promise. Following *Hickey v. Green*, her reliance was probably reasonable. Therefore, under the modified facts, Celia can probably get specific performance from Linda because the estoppel exception to the Statute of Frauds would apply.

CHAPTER 6

RESERVATIONS IN THIRD PERSONS PROBLEMS

1. Amy may not have the right to use the easement because it was created by a reservation in a third person. The easement was reserved for Steve in a deed granting Whiteacre from Eduardo to Ashley. Therefore the easement was created by a reservation in a third party. In a jurisdiction that follows the traditional rule against reservations in a third party (reflected in *Tripp v. Huff*), then the attempted reservation would be invalid. Amy does not have an easement over Whiteacre. Depending on the approach taken by the jurisdiction, the attempted reservation may be treated as a nullity (meaning that no easement was created), or it may be treated as reserving an easement in the grantor, Eduardo. In a jurisdiction that follows the approach that permits reservation in a third person (reflected in *Willard*), then the reservation would be valid, and Amy has a valid easement.

2. This problem is similar to the last one. Stella attempted to reserve an easement in a Hillside College in a deed conveying the lot from Stella to Jake. This attempted reservation in a third person may or may not be valid for the reasons state in the answer to the prior problem. Note that in this problem, the reserved easement was in gross, where in the last example it was appurtenant. The in gross/appurtenant distinction does not matter in this context—if the rule against reservations in a third person applies in a jurisdiction, it applies against both appurtenant and in gross easements.

NON-EXPRESS EASEMENTS PROBLEMS

1. Hal neglected to reserve an express easement in himself when he transferred the 20-acre parcel to Shirley. There are four types of non-express easements. It is best to get in the habit of mentioning all four, so that you do not miss some easy points on an exam. This problem primarily involves easements implied by existing use and easements by necessity. It is best to also mention easements by prescription and easements by estoppel. Let's get those two out of the way first. There is no easement by prescription here because the transaction only happened four years ago, and this jurisdiction's statute for prescription is ten years. There is no easement by estoppel because there is no detrimental change in position by Hal in reasonable reliance Shirley's conduct.

There likely is an easement implied by existing use on these fact. There are four elements to an easement implied by existing use: (1) unity of ownership, (2) visible or apparent existing use/quasi easement, (3) continuous use, and (4) reasonable necessity (with a minority applying strict necessity, especially to an implied reservation). The first element is met because Hal owned the whole parcel. The second element is met by Hal's use of the driveway before the division of the parcels. The third element is met because Hal had "always used an unpaved driveway to get from his home to Route 74." The fourth element may or may not be met. Hal can construct a new driveway for $200,000, making Hal's use of the driveway reasonably necessary but not strictly necessary. Under the majority reasonable necessity standard, Hal would meet this requirement. Under the minority strict necessity standard, Hal would not meet this requirement. The fact that this is an implied reservation (because Hal would impliedly be reserving the driveway easement in himself) makes it more likely that a court would apply the strict necessity standard. Hal therefore is likely to have an easement implied by existing use, but he won't have one if the court applies a strict necessity standard rather than a reasonable necessity standard.

There likely is not an easement implied by necessity on these facts. There are three elements to an easement by necessity: (1) unity of ownership, (2) a parcel must be landlocked after division of the parcels, and (3) strict necessity. The first element is met because Hal originally owned both parcels. The second element is met because the division created a landlocked parcel. (You might be inclined to say that the parcel is not landlocked because of the possibility that Hal could build a driveway to reach Slate Hill Road. That would be fine, but we think that this issue is best covered in the discussion of strict necessity.) The third element, however, probably is not met because a court is likely to find that the driveway is not strictly necessary. As we saw from our cases, strict necessity is strict. A court might hold that the $200,000 expense meets this standard. A court taking the *Schwab* approach, however, would hold that it is not strictly necessary. Hal therefore is likely not to have an easement by necessity, and his only chance of winning on this issue is if the court is lenient on the strict necessity standard.

Overall, Hal is likely to win on easement implied by existing use unless the court applied a strict necessity standard. He is likely to lose on easement by necessity and certain to lose on these facts on easement by prescription and easement by estoppel.

2. Nestor likely has an easement by estoppel and an easement by necessity. We don't have enough facts to know whether he has an easement implied by existing use or prescription.

Let's start with the least likely. This particular problem doesn't give you enough facts to be certain about prescription, but it isn't likely. Nestor has only owned the parcel for three years, so he hasn't met the ten-year statute of limitations. If a prior owner had used the driveway for seven years prior, Nestor may be able to meet the statutory period by tacking. It might be unlikely that a prior owner had used the driveway because the lot was vacant. On the other hand, the driveway had "always been there," so presumably someone used it for something.

Nestor has a strong claim for an easement by estoppel. Easements by estoppel have two elements—(1) conduct by the owner of the serviette estate and (2) a detrimental change in position by the owner of the dominant estate in reasonable reliance on that conduct. This problem presents prototypical easement by estoppel facts. Greg orally gave Nestor permission to use the driveway, and Nestor relied on that permission to expend money and build a house. Greg therefore will be likely to be estopped from preventing Nestor from using the driveway. This fact pattern highlights the idea that easements by estoppel are irrevocable licenses. Greg gave permission for Nestor to use the driveway. This license would typically be revocable but becomes irrevocable because of Nestor's reasonable detrimental reliance.

The facts state that the two parcels were at one time owned by Chuck. This meets the unity of ownership requirement for both easement implied by existing use and easement by necessity. The facts also say there is no other way for Nestor to reach the road. Nestor's parcel therefore is landlocked, and the driveway is strictly necessary for Nestor to reach the road. The three elements of an easement by necessity (unity of ownership, landlocked parcel, and strict necessity therefore are met). As with prescription, we don't really have enough facts—we aren't told whether the driveway was used as a quasi-easement at the time the parcels were divided.

Nestor therefore should win on easement by estoppel and easement by necessity. We don't know enough to come to a conclusion one way or the other on prescription and easement implied by existing use.

3. On these facts, Jim has colorable claims for easements by prescription, easement implied by existing use, and easement by necessity. He does not have a claim for an easement by estoppel because there are no estoppel facts—he built his home before he divided the property, and there was no conduct by Marc for Jim to rely on.

Jim will probably win on a claim for easement by necessity. We listed the elements above in the answer to problem 1. The land was initially owned by one person, and the division of the parcels created a landlocked parcels. Because of the geography of the lot, there is no other way for Jim to reach his land. He can't even get there by boat. The strict necessity element therefore is met. Jim therefore meets all three elements of an easement by necessity.

Jim will probably also win on a claim for easement implied by existing use. Again, we listed the elements above in the answer to problem 1. We have unity of ownership, an existing use/quasi-easement for the driveway, the driveway was continuously used, and the need for the driveway satisfies both the strict and reasonable necessity standards. Jim therefore will likely win even if the court imposes a strict necessity standard because this is an implied reservation.

Jim also has a good claim for an easement by prescription. Easements by prescription have three elements—prescriptive use that is (a) visible, (b) non-permissive, and (c) continuous for the statutory period. Jim's use of the driveway was visible—it was the only way he could get to his house, and it would not be credible for Marc to claim he didn't know about it. The non-permissive element is probably met under the objective approach discussed in *McDonald*—Jim acted as if he had the right to use the driveway at all times. Also, there are no facts that state that Marc affirmatively granted permission to Jim to use the driveway. The property was divided in 1999, and the facts state that Jim used the driveway continuously, so Jim met the requirement that he use the driveway continuously for the ten-year statutory period. Jim therefore likely meets the requirements of an easement by prescription.

Jim therefore has good claims for an easement by necessity, easement implied by existing use, and easement by prescription. There are no facts in this problem to support an easement by estoppel.

MISUSE OF EASEMENTS PROBLEMS

1. This problem is similar to *Brown v. Voss*. Mario wants to use the easement over Will's property to access the new five-acre parcel where he wants to build his house. Mario can use the driveway to reach Hilton Ranch (the dominant parcel), but it would be a misuse of the easement to use it to access the new parcel. Under the traditional approach, Will will be able to get an injunction against Mario using the driveway to reach the new parcel. Under the approach to remedies taken in *Brown v. Voss*, Will may only be able to get money damages for Mario's misuse of the easement.

2. For the most part, this problem is similar to the first one. Sarah is misusing the express driveway easement to benefit the new parcel. Looking at the misuse issue alone, Eric may be able to get an injunction or damages, depending on the court's approach to remedies. These facts differ, however, from both the first problem and *Brown v. Voss* because Sarah's house was completed at the time of the falling out. In the first problem, Mario had not yet started construction, and in *Brown v. Voss*, the Browns had spent only $11,000 preparing the site for construction. This raises the question of whether Eric might be estopped from preventing Sarah from using the driveway. Recall that conduct in the estoppel context can be either action or inaction. Sarah might be able to argue that she reasonably relied on Eric's inaction to build the house. If so, we might conclude that Sarah acquired an easement by estoppel to reach the new house. Alternatively, a court might consider these facts in choosing whether to allow Eric to get the equitable remedy

of an injunction. Finally, the fact that Sarah's new parcel borders Queen's Church Road might have a role in this equitable analysis, though that fact is in the problem largely to make it clear that Sarah would not be entitled to an easement by necessity to reach the new parcel.

TERMINATION OF EASEMENTS PROBLEMS

1. This problem involves termination of an easement by merger. When Rick bought Whiteacre, he owned both the dominant and servient parcels. When both the dominant and servient parcels are owned by one person, the easement is terminated by merger. Rick failed to re-create the easement by reservation when he later conveyed Whiteacre to Marshall. Therefore, there is no express easement that gives Rick the right to use the driveway. Rick may or may not have an easement implied by existing use or an easement implied by necessity on these facts. We won't do the full implied easements analysis here, but you can think it through on your own. We mentioned the fact that Rick could reach a road on another side of his property to cue you to think about these issues. If Rick's land was truly landlocked, then he would have a strong easement by necessity claim. Because he can get out the other side, he would have trouble meeting the elements of an easement by necessity. Because this would be an implied reservation, he might also have a problem meeting the requirements of an easement implied by existing use because a court might apply a strict, rather than reasonable, necessity standard.

2. Blackacre has the benefit of an easement by necessity across Whiteacre. By building the new road, the county has ended the necessity that justified the easement by necessity in the first place. Sure, it would be expensive for Max to build the new driveway, but the easement across Whiteacre is no longer strictly necessary. Therefore the easement by necessity has terminated because easements by necessity end when the necessity ends.

3. The Great Eastern easement has not terminated on these facts. Easements may terminate by abandonment. Mere non-use, however, does not constitute abandonment. The problem does not give any facts beyond non-use to lead to the conclusion that Great Eastern abandoned the easement. If we had more facts that could be used to show that Great Eastern intended to abandon the easement, Starla would have a better argument.

COVENANTS THAT RUN WITH THE LAND PROBLEMS

1. Before we get to the facts of this problem, we want to make two points about answering questions about covenants that run with the land. First, the remedy requested by the party asserting the violation tells you a lot about what you need to discuss in your answer. If the party is seeking money damages, then you need to talk about the requirements for a promise to run with the land at law as a real covenant. If the party is seeking an injunction, then you need to talk about the requirements for a promise to run with the land in equity as an equitable servitude. If the party is seeking both money

damages and an injunction, you need to talk about both. Unsurprisingly, in each of our three problems, the aggrieved party is seeking both money damages and an injunction, so you need to talk about both.

Second, the elements of real covenants and equitable servitudes overlap. If a promise meets all of the elements of a real covenant, it will also meet all of the elements of an equitable servitude. You can approach a question that raises both in one of three ways. First, you could talk about whether the promise runs with the land as a real covenant, then briefly address how the analysis would play out in the equitable servitude context. Second, you could talk about equitable servitudes, then address the additional elements of real covenants. Third, you could try to address both real covenants and equitable servitudes together. In our experience, the first two approaches work well. The third can be hard to pull off, especially under exam pressure.

We will take the first approach and start with the question of whether the promise runs with the land at law as a real covenant. Rose bought the house from Alex and then violated the covenant, so we are concerned with whether the burden runs with the land. A real covenant has six elements for the burden to run: (1) writing, (2) intent to run with the land, (3) notice, (4) touch and concern, (5) horizontal privity (only required in some jurisdictions), and (6) vertical privity. Here, most of these elements are easy. The facts say that the covenant was written, intended to run with the land, and recorded. Recording provides notice to subsequent purchasers, so the first three elements are met. (Note, by the way, that a covenant has to be written to be recorded, so if a problem says that something is recorded but doesn't say anything about writing, you can infer the writing.) The restriction on satellite dishes has to do with the use of the land, so the touch and concern element is met. The sixth element, vertical privity, is also met. Vertical privity requires a consensual transfer of title or possession, and Alex voluntarily sold the property to Rose. The fifth element, however, is not met in jurisdictions that require it. Horizontal privity requires that the promise be made in the context of a land transaction. Here, the promise was not made in the context of a land transaction. Therefore, in a jurisdiction that requires horizontal privity for the burden to run, the promise would not meet the requirements of a real covenant, and Larry would not be able to seek money damages from Rose. In a jurisdiction that does not require horizontal privity for the burden to run, all of the elements of a real covenant would be met, and Larry could seek money damages.

Regardless of the jurisdiction, Larry will be able to seek an injunction against Rose. There are four elements for a promise to run with the land in equity as an equitable servitude: (1) writing, (2) intent to run with the land, (3) touch and concern, and (4) notice. As we explained above in the context of the promise running with the land in law as a real covenant, these four elements are met here. Neither horizontal nor vertical privity are required for a promise to run with the land as an equitable servitude. Larry therefore will be able to obtain an injunction against Rose.

2. As with the prior problem, we will start with real covenants and then go to equitable servitudes. The answer is similar to the prior problem, but in this example

the horizontal privity requirement is met. There are six elements that need to be met for a promise to run with the land at law: (1) writing, (2) intent to run with the land, (3) notice, (4) touch and concern, (5) horizontal privity (only required in some jurisdictions), and (6) vertical privity. The writing and notice requirements are met because the covenant was recorded. The intent to run with the land element is met because the facts say that the covenants were intended to run with the land. The touch and concern element is met because the covenant restricts the use of land by restricting the color of the houses in the development. The horizontal privity requirement is met because the covenants were put into place in the context of a land transaction—here, the subdivision of the land. Recall that we mentioned in the text that horizontal privity tends not to be a problem in the subdivision/common interest community context because the covenants are put into place in subdivision transaction. Vertical privity is met because Daphna bought the house from the original owner, which constitutes a voluntary transfer of title and possession. The four elements of equitable servitudes overlap with the six elements of real covenants. Because all of the real covenant elements are met, all of the equitable servitude elements are met. Therefore, the homeowners' association should be able to get both money damages and an injunction from Daphna.

3. This problem asks about two different covenants. We will talk about the house building covenant first, then talk about the pink house covenant. The house building covenant is similar to the one at issue in the *Caullett* case. It might be tempting to skip right to the benefit in gross/vagueness issues mentioned in that case. It is better, however, to do a full analysis of whether the covenant runs with the land in law and/or equity. In an exam, you are likely to miss points if you don't do the full analysis.

There are six elements that need to be met for a promise to run with the land at law: (1) writing, (2) intent to run with the land, (3) notice, (4) touch and concern, (5) horizontal privity (only required in some jurisdictions), and (6) vertical privity. The writing and notice elements are met because the covenant was written and recorded. The text of the covenant states that it is intended to run with the land, so that element is met. Horizontal privity is met because the covenant was imposed as part of the transaction where Max conveyed the land to Lee Anne. The vertical privity requirement is met because Lee Anne voluntarily transferred the property to Peggy. The touch and concern element, however, is not met here. The benefit of this covenant is held in gross by MW Homes LLC. The concerns about benefit in gross reflected in *Caullett* are typically categorized under touch and concern. The covenant also might fail on vagueness grounds discussed in *Caullett*. The home building promise therefore is likely not to be enforced as a real covenant. The home building promise also is likely not to be enforced as an equitable servitude. Three of the four elements of an equitable servitude—writing, intent to run, and notice—are met here, for the reasons discussed in the real covenant context. The touch and concern element, however, is not met, again for the reasons stated in the real covenant context.

The pink houses covenant is similar to the covenant in problem one—all of the elements other than horizontal privity are met. We have a written covenant intended to run with the land that was recorded, so the first three elements are met. House painting concerns the use of land, and so the touch and concern requirement is met. Ownership was voluntarily transferred from Lee Anne to Peggy, so the vertical privity requirement is met. The promise, however, was not made in the context of a land transaction, so the horizontal privity requirement is not met. In jurisdictions that require horizontal privity, the promise would not run with the land at law. In jurisdictions that do not require horizontal privity, the promise would run with the land at law. The covenant would run with the land in equity in all jurisdictions. Horizontal privity is not a requirement for a covenant to run with the land in equity. All four of the equitable servitudes elements are met for the reasons discussed in the real covenant context. Therefore, Max will be able to get an injunction for violation of the equitable servitude in all jurisdictions. He will be able to get money damages in jurisdictions that do not require horizontal privity but will not be able to get money damages in jurisdictions that do require horizontal privity.

CHANGED CIRCUMSTANCES PROBLEM

The court should rule against Sarah. This is not a close call. The changed circumstances standard is strict, and a court will only terminate a covenant based on changed circumstances if it is no longer possible to achieve the original purpose of the covenant. The purpose of the covenant was to maintain the single family residential nature of the community. Restricting Sarah's lot is consistent with that purpose. To be sure, Sarah has commercial uses on one side of her. As we saw in *Western Land*, however, someone has to own the lots on the edge of the community. If Sarah's lot converts to commercial use, the lots with houses bordering hers will lose their buffer from the commercial use. The fact that Sarah's lot would be more valuable without the restriction is irrelevant, as the court explained in *Western Land*.

REASONABLENESS PROBLEMS

Jane raises two objections to the enforcement of the covenant against her. Her first objection is that she wasn't a party to the original covenant. Jane is still bound, however, because the covenant runs with the land. This covenant satisfies both the requirements of a real covenant and an equitable servitude for similar reasons to the covenant in the second problem in the first problem set about covenants that run with the land. It is written, intended to run with the land, recorded (providing notice), and touches and concerns the land (because it controls land use). Horizontal privity is likely met because it is a common interest community. Vertical privity is met because Jane bought the house in a voluntary transaction from Will, who in turn bought it in a voluntary transaction from the original owner. The covenant therefore runs with the land in both law and equity and binds Jane.

Her second objection is that the enforcement of the covenant is unreasonable as applied to her. Covenants will not be enforced if they are unreasonable. As we discussed in the context of *Nahrstedt*, there are two ways of looking at reasonableness. First, there is the approach taken by the California Supreme Court in *Nahrstedt*, where we ask whether the covenant is reasonable in the context of the entire community. Under this approach, Jane would almost certainly lose—it is at least as reasonable for a community to bar commercial uses as it is for it to bar pets. Concerns about traffic and the character of the neighborhood provide a reasonable justification for the covenant. Second, there is the approach taken by the intermediate appellate court in *Nahrstedt*, where we ask whether the covenant is reasonable as applied to each individual homeowner. Jane would have a better argument under this standard, but even here she might lose. In *Nahrstedt*, the homeowner argued that her cats caused no harm to anyone. Here, Jane would argue that her yoga classes would cause no harm. The yoga classes, however, would increase traffic in the neighborhood and so would cause more of a problem outside of Jane's home than the cats from *Nahrstedt*. Jane would have a colorable claim under this standard but still might lose.

CHAPTER 7

NUISANCE PROBLEMS

1. The first issue is whether SMI's operations constitute a nuisance. Private nuisance has three elements: intent, unreasonableness, and substantial interference with another's property. In the nuisance context, intent is intent to do the act, not intent to cause harm. SMI intentionally engages in its operations, so the first element is met. The mining operations cause $500,000 in harm to the neighbors, so the third element of substantial interference with another's property is met.

The second element, unreasonableness, is more complex. There are three approaches to this element. Under the traditional approach, conduct is unreasonable if it crosses a poorly defined threshold of causing a substantial negative impact on the neighbors. Dirty, smelly, and noisy uses often fare badly under this approach. Here, SMI's operations are noisy and cause a substantial negative impact on the neighbors. SMI's operations therefore have a good chance of being deemed unreasonable under the traditional approach. Because the other two elements are met, SMI's operations likely would be a nuisance under the traditional approach.

Under the basic Restatement approach, conduct is unreasonable if the harm of the conduct outweighs the benefit of the conduct. Here, the harm is $500,000 in damages to the neighbors. The benefit is employment of 30 people and profits of $10 million per year. Even though economic value might not be a perfect measure of harm and benefit, on these facts the benefit almost certainly outweighs the harm. Therefore it is likely that SMI's operations would be found to be reasonable, and not to be a nuisance, under the basic Restatement approach.

Under the alternative Restatement approach, conduct is unreasonable if the person engaging in the conduct can compensate the affected parties for the negative impacts of the conduct without going out of business. The classic example of the application of this approach is *Boomer*. Here, the harm and benefit facts are similar to those in *Boomer*. SMI could compensate the neighbors for the harm caused by SMI's operations without going out of business. It therefore is likely that SMI's operations would be found to be unreasonable, and therefore a nuisance, under the alternative Restatement approach.

The complaining neighbors came to the nuisance—SMI had been in business for 50 years, and the residential development began only six years ago. SMI therefore can assert coming to the nuisance as a defense. In most circumstances, coming to the nuisance is not a complete defense and instead is a factor that may factor into the initial issue of whether there was a nuisance at all. Under the traditional approach and the alternative Restatement approach, the court might find that the fact that the neighbors came to the nuisance should lead to a conclusion that there was no actionable nuisance here. Even if a nuisance is found, coming to the nuisance also might factor into the next issue involving the appropriate remedy.

The second issue is the appropriate remedy if a nuisance is found. Under the balancing of the equities approach discussed in *Estancias* and under the similar approach taken in *Boomer*, the appropriate remedy on these facts is likely to be an award of damages to the neighbors. SMI's plant serves an important public purpose, is highly profitable, and employs 30 people. The neighbors also came to the nuisance. Under these circumstances, a court is unlikely to award an injunction that would shut the plant down. The court could follow the *Spur* approach and award an injunction on the condition that the neighbors indemnify SMI. That approach would not make a lot of sense in this context, however, because the value of the plant is so high compared to the harm to the property owners. It therefore is unlikely that the neighbors would want to, or be able to, indemnify SMI for shutting the plant down. It therefore likely would be better for the landowners to get an award of damages than an injunction conditioned on indemnification.

2. As discussed in the prior answer, nuisance has three elements. The intent element is met here because Gerry is intentionally raising pigs. The substantial interference element is met because a $1 million impact on the neighbors is substantial. The unreasonableness element is likely to be met. Under the traditional approach, Gerry's use is likely to be deemed unreasonable because it is smelly and because it has a substantial negative impact on the neighbors. Under the basic Restatement approach, Gerry's use is likely to be unreasonable because the harm outweighs the benefit—using dollar values as a measure of harm and benefit, the value of the farm is $200,000, while the harm is $1 million. The alternative Restatement approach would not apply here because that approach contemplates a scenario where the benefit exceeds the harm.

The residents came to the nuisance. As discussed in the prior answer, this might be a factor into whether there is a nuisance or factor into the remedy. In light of the fact that the harm appears to substantially outweigh the benefit, it seems unlikely that a court would allow coming to the nuisance to be a complete defense. These facts also resemble the facts in *Spur*, so there is a good case to be made to use the *Spur* approach and factor coming to the nuisance into the remedies analysis. There is a wrinkle in the coming to the nuisance facts in the problem, in that the residents didn't know about the nuisance before they moved in because they bought their houses in the winter. We don't think that this should have too much of an impact because the residents should have known that they were moving into an agricultural area. But this might give the residents a way of arguing against coming to the nuisance.

The most appropriate remedy on these facts is probably an injunction accompanied by an obligation on the neighbors to indemnify Gerry. A straight damages award doesn't make much sense because the damages exceed the value of the farming operation—Gerry would be better off consenting to an injunction. Because the harm exceeds the benefit and because the pig farm probably has only a modest public benefit, an injunction would also be appropriate under the balancing the equities approach. The facts strongly resemble *Spur* in both the relationship between harm and benefit and in the fact that the neighbors came to the nuisance (with the wrinkle noted above). So an injunction shutting down Gerry's operation accompanied by an obligation for the neighbors to compensate Gerry is probably the most appropriate remedy.

CHAPTER 8

NONCONFORMING USES, VARIANCES, SPECIAL EXCEPTIONS, AND ZONING AMENDMENTS PROBLEMS

1. Mark will likely be out of luck. To be entitled to a variance, a property owner must demonstrate undue hardship. Undue hardship is met if the property is useless or near useless without the variance. The desire to build a 5,000 square foot home rather than a 4,500 square foot home is not undue hardship and instead is mere inconvenience. As a result, Mark will not be entitled to a variance. He is bound by the zoning because in the case of a conflict between zoning and covenants, the more restrictive will prevail.

2. Alex will likely be able to continue to operate the convenience store. The convenience store is a pre-existing nonconforming use because it existed before the zoning law was enacted. The right to engage in a pre-existing nonconforming use typically runs with the land. In other words, the change in ownership does not terminate the right to continue the pre-existing nonconforming use. Depending on the jurisdiction, the town may be able to shut down the convenience store after an amortization period.

3. The neighbors will have a good argument that the zoning amendment was illegal spot zoning. A zoning amendment constitutes spot zoning if it creates an island of use different from the surrounding area in circumstances where the re-zoning uniquely benefits the property owner and the re-zoning is inconsistent with the overall zoning plan. Here, the zoning amendment creates an island of commercial use surrounded by residential use. The re-zoning benefits Jade. It also appears to be inconsistent with the

overall zoning plan and would undercut the residential character of the neighborhood. Thus, there is a good chance that a court would invalidate the zoning amendment as illegal spot zoning.

4. Susan is seeking a special exception. The zoning code specifically contemplates commercial use of her property but has imposed conditions that need to be met before a permit to engage in the use is granted. As we saw in Cope, these conditions must be clear and non-discretionary. Otherwise, they are likely to be invalidated as unconstitutional delegations of legislative power to the administrative agency charged with issuing the permit. Here, the first two conditions seem sufficiently specific. Susan has shown that she has complied with each of these conditions. The third condition is very broad and discretionary and likely would be invalidated. It is for the municipal legislature, not the administrative Zoning Board, to decide what is in the public interest. With that condition removed, Susan is entitled to the special exception permit. A court therefore would likely order that the permit be granted.

TABLE OF CASES

Principal cases are indicated by *italics*.

INDEX

landlord-tenant law, contract law vs. property law, 272, 327, 356

leases, hybrid property-contract nature of, 272

physical condition risk, contract law vs. tort law, 469

purchase and sale contract, 383

tenancies by entirety, contract creditors vs. tort creditors, 241

Contractual allocation of risk, 407

Contribution, liability in tenancies in common, 218

Cooperating agents, 388

Cooperatives, 661

Copyrights, 988–989

Counterparty risk, 407

Covenants

encumbrances, against, 451

of further assurances, 452

of general warranty, 452

physical condition risk, 478

of quiet enjoyment, 303–308. *See also* Quiet enjoyment, covenant of

real covenants. *See* Real covenants

restrictive covenants. *See* Restrictive covenants

of right to convey, 451

running with land. *See* Covenants running with land

of seisin, 451

single-family residential use covenants, 706

of special warranty, 452

statutes of limitations for, 452

Covenants, conditions, and restrictions (CC&Rs), 660–661, 678–679

Covenants running with land, 631–711

abandonment of covenant, 680–689

benefits held in gross, 642–648

changed circumstances, 650–660

common interest communities, 660–711. *See also* Common interest communities

contract law vs. property law, 648

defined, 541

elements of, 633–635

as encumbrances, 409

environmental cleanup and, 638–641

as equitable servitudes, 632–635, 637, 642

FHA and, 689–706

horizontal privity, 634–636

intent requirement, 634

law vs. equity, 632

notice, 634

overview, 631–650

problems and explanatory answers, 648–649, 660, 1061–1065

public policy, non-enforcement based on, 706–710

as real covenants, 632–635, 637

remedies for breach, 632

restrictive covenants. *See* Restrictive covenants

"touch and concern" requirement, 634, 642, 648

vertical privity, 634–636

writing requirement, 633–634

Coverture, 243

Creditors

separate property and, 246

tenancies by entirety and, 241

Credit risk, 407

Criminal activity

landlord liability for, 308

tenancies by entirety and, 241

Curtesy, 243–244

Damages

constructive eviction vs., 308

implied warranty of habitability, 328–329

nuisances, 715–730

real estate transactions, 500

trespass, 123–126

Death, effect on separate property, 257–258

Debt, community property and, 260

Deeds, 502–513

conditional delivery, 511

deed poll, 512

delivery of, 506–512

donative intent, 511

essential terms, 503

estoppel by, 506

forgery of, 513

fraud, procured by, 513

sample language, 504–505

signature requirement, 503

Statute of Frauds and, 503, 506

third party, delivery to, 511–512

"time is of the essence" clauses, 502

of trust, 516–518. *See also* Deeds of trust

validity of, 503

writing requirement, 503

Deeds of trust, 516–518

defined, 516

granting clause, 517

overview, 517

Deed warranties, 447–457, 461

Default allocation of risk, 407

Defeasible interests, 141–143

Deficiency judgments, foreclosure and, 520–522